AUTOMATIC TRANSAXLES AND TRANSMISSIONS

J. Gary Campbell

PRENTICE HALL
Upper Saddle River, NJ 07458 Columbus, Ohio

Library of Congress Cataloging-in-Publication Data

Campbell, J. Gary
Automatic transaxles and transmissions/J. Gary Campbell.
p. cm.
Includes index.
ISBN 0-13-291147-7
1. Automobiles—Transmission devices, Automatic—Maintenance and repair. I. Title.
TL263.C36 1995
629.24'46'0288—dc20 94-36828
CIP

Cover art/photo: Printed with permission of General Motors Corp
Editor: Ed Francis
Production Coordination: WordCrafters Editorial Services, Inc.
Cover Designer: Brian Deep
Production Buyer: Pamela D. Bennett
Illustrations: Freehold Studio
Interior Photography: J. Gary Campbell

This book was set in Century by Progressive Information Technologies and was printed and bound by Semline, Inc., a Quebecor American Book Group Company. The cover was printed by Phoenix Color Corp.

Printed in the United States of America

10 9 8 7 6 5 4 3 2 1

ISBN 0-13-291147-7

Prentice-Hall International (UK) Limited,London
Prentice-Hall of Australia Pty. Limited, Sydney
Prentice-Hall Canada Inc., Toronto
Prentice-Hall Hispanoamericana, S.A., Mexico
Prentice-Hall of India Private Limited, New Delhi
Prentice-Hall of Japan, Inc., Tokyo
Pearson Education Asia Pte. Ltd., Singapore
Editora Prentice-Hall do Brasil, Ltda., Rio de Janeiro

This book is dedicated to my family,
without whose support this effort would have been impossible.
To Susan, for your hard work in word processing the text and
filling in for me in family matters,
I will always be indebted.
To Joseph, the light of our lives,
for his unselfish attitude in giving us the time to do this project,
thank you for being the person you are.

◀ CONTENTS ▶

◀ PREFACE ▶

This book is designed to provide a basic explanation of the operation of an automatic transmission/ transaxle, providing the fundamental knowledge that an automotive student needs to become an entry-level automatic transmission/transaxle technician.

The book is divided into three parts. Part 1, Transmission Theory, covers the general theory of how components and systems function and how they are constructed. In the second part, Shop Procedures, we study the diagnostic and repair procedures used in servicing automatic transmissions. The third part, Specific Applications, provides specific descriptions of a broad range of current automatic transmissions/transaxles.

In Chapter 1 we describe the use and operation of a transmission and then study gear function, starting with how a mechanical advantage is created by use of a lever. The principles of the lever used in a pulley to create rotary motion are studied next. This information provides the basic physics for understanding how gears produce a mechanical advantage. Different types of gears used in an automatic transmission are described, along with an explanation of gear ratios. This fundamental information provides the foundation for understanding how gears work.

The next three chapters are arranged according to how engine power flows through an automatic transmission/transaxle. Engine torque first travels through the torque converter, then through the gear train, which is controlled by the hydraulic system. The book is arranged in this manner to provide a logical progression through transmission systems following the power flow. By providing the information in the context of its function, the concepts are more easily understood.

In Chapter 2 we explain how modern torque converters have been developed from the earlier fluid coupling models. The constuction and function of the fluid coupling, an early hydrodynamic device, is described to provide a foundation for understanding how the torque converter works. Construction of the torque converter and how it functions are described with a full explanation of fluid movement in the converter. The principles of torque increase in a hydrodynamic device are also explained. Converter clutch devices that allow the torque converter to make a mechanical connection between the engine and the transmission are included in this chapter.

In Chapter 3 planetary gear sets are covered so that the new technician will understand how various gear ratios are achieved. The two main types of compound planetary gear sets, Simpson and Ravigneaux, are described in detail. The power flow of two-, three-, and four-speed automatic transmissions are used to describe how each type of planetary gear set can be used. The coupling and holding devices that connect or hold the planetary gear set components are described in full and their functions are explained. The final drive section of a transaxle is the subject of the final section of this chapter.

Chapter 4 begins with a detailed explanation of the principles of hydraulics and how they apply to automatic transmissions/transaxles. The next section deals with the hydraulic system components used in automatic transmissions/transaxles. These components are described from the basis of their construction and how each component is designed to operate.

An expanation of how the individual components work together to form the hydraulic circuits of a transmission is next, with each section of the hydraulic system, pressure source, torque converter, gear train, and shift control explained in detail. The area of most recent growth in automatic transmission design, computer control of shifting, is also covered in this chapter.

In Chapter 5, special-interest items are covered that are not included in earlier chapters. Described are seals, thrust washers, bushings, snap rings, gaskets, filters, and fluids. Each section covers the subject matter as it applies to automatic transmissions, giving explanations of both their construction and method of operation.

Part 2, Shop Procedures, deals with general maintenance, diagnosis of failures, and repair and rebuilding procedures. In learning the subject matter the theory should not become secondary to the repair procedures. It is essential that the student understand the theory before trying to master the repair skills.

Chapter 6 covers normal filter and fluid service with an in-depth look at ATF. Chapter 7 presents a systematic procedure for finding the exact problem in a malfunctioning transmission. Chapter 8 deals with all the service procedures that can be done with the transmission still in the car. In Chapter 9 we describe the technical procedures used to overhaul the components of an automatic transmission.

In Part 3, Specific Applications, we describe 16 different automatic transmissions/transaxles that are representative of the transmissions currently in use in passenger vehicles. Five of the transmissions are designed for rear-wheel-drive (RWD) applications, and the remaining 11 are transaxles for front-wheel-drive (FWD) applications. Both domestic and import transmissions/transaxles are described, with seven of the transaxles having computer shift control.

There are five chapters in the third part, in which the transmissions/transaxles are grouped together by manufacturer. Two of the chapters deal with Asian and European imports, and the remaining chapters cover domestic manufacturers, including their import vehicles.

In Chapter 10 we describe four automatic transmissions/transaxles in use in both Chrysler and American Motors vehicles. Each transmission/transaxle is described in a separate section that has eight subsections: transmission description, power flow, clutch and band chart, identification, components, pressure tests, air tests, and special attention items. The same eight subsection categories are used to describe each transmission/transaxle discussed in the book.

Chapter 11 covers four transmissions/transaxles used in Ford products. The chapter sections and subsections are in the same format as that used for Chapter 10. In Chapter 12 we describe four transmissions/transaxles used in General Motors products. In Chapter 13, two of the more popular automatic transmissions/transaxles used in Japanese import vehicles are described. Chapter 14 covers two widely used European transaxles, one of which is electronically controlled.

The information included in Part 3 is not intended to be an in-depth study of the various transmissions/transaxles. The text provides the information to give the new automotive service technician a basic knowledge of transmission operation without information overload. By presenting the specific information in a uniform format, it is easier for the student to generalize the theory into specific applications and see the similarities among different transmissions. Further information regarding operation and service may be obtained from service manuals specific to each transmission.

The ability to understand the basic theory first and then how it applies to transmission systems is the foundation for becoming a successful transmission technician. The purpose of this book is to provide that foundation.

We are indebted to the following colleagues for their critiques of the manuscript: Roger Donovan, Illinois Central College; Brian Bakota, Gloucester County Institute of Technology; and Matt Seehorn, Skagt Valley College.

◀ Part 1 ▶

TRANSMISSION THEORY

Chapter 1

FUNDAMENTALS OF GEARS

INTRODUCTION

The purpose of this chapter is, first, to demonstrate the need for a transmission in a motor vehicle. Then we explain how gears can create a mechanical advantage and increase engine torque. Since a gear is a rotary lever, the explanation of how a gear functions starts with the simple lever. The same principles are then put to work in rotary motion in the pulley. This foundation information is essential to understanding gear function fully. Descriptions of various types of gears that are commonly found in automatic transmissions are next. In the final sections we explain gear ratios and how they affect engine speed and torque.

1.1 PERFORMANCE OBJECTIVES

After studying this chapter, you should have fulfilled the following performance objectives by being able to:

1. Discuss why an automobile needs a transmission.
2. Fully explain the action of a lever.
3. Describe how pulleys and levers are similar.
4. Explain what mechanical advantage means.
5. Describe the types of gears used in an automatic transmission/transaxle.
6. Explain how gear ratios are expressed.
7. Discuss what the term *overdrive* means.
8. Complete all the competency objectives listed for this chapter.
9. Complete the self-test with at least the minimum score required by your instructor.

1.2 COMPETENCY OBJECTIVES

The competency objectives are different from the performance objectives in being more job related. The automotive terms must be well understood so that the theory will be clear. The terms are used to describe the service procedures outlined in Part II. The competency tasks are related to job skills needed to perform service and repair procedures and should be understood thoroughly.

1.2.1 Automotive Terms

The following list may include terms that are unfamiliar to you. Read the terms, then note their definitions as you study the chapter.

drivetrain	lever
dynamometer	mechanical advantage
external gear	output gear
fulcrum	overdrive
gear ratio	planetary gear set
gear reduction	pulley
gear train	ring-and-pinion gear
helical gear	speed increase
hypoid drive	spur gear
input gear	torque
internal gear	torque increase

1.2.2 Competency Tasks

The competency tasks listed here are related directly to knowledge or skills needed to become a successful automatic transmission/transaxle technician. Be sure to complete all the tasks before going on to Chapter 2.

1. Explain why a vehicle needs a transmission.
2. Explain how a first-class *lever* works.
3. List six major types of gears.

4. Describe four different types of gear combinations.

5. Explain how gears can change speed.

6. Explain how gears can increase or decrease engine *torque.*

7. Explain what is meant by the term *4:1 gear ratio.*

8. Explain what is meant by the term *0.7:1 gear ratio.*

1.3 NEED FOR A TRANSMISSION

Before you start learning about the various automatic transmission/transaxle systems, review the basic reasons why a transmission is needed in a vehicle. Those reasons are:

1. To be able to disengage the engine from the *drivetrain*

2. To be able to change the direction of vehicle movement

3. To increase engine torque to the drivetrain

1.3.1 Disengage Engine

To drive any vehicle safely, the operator must be able to disengage the engine from the drivetrain. In a vehicle with a standard transmission, this job is done by the manual clutch, which the operator has to disengage with the clutch pedal. In a vehicle with an automatic transmission, the job of disengaging the engine from the drivetrain is performed by the torque converter (Figure 1–1). The torque converter is a fluid coupling that uses hydraulic fluid to transfer engine torque into the transmission. Below a certain engine rpm value the fluid will not transfer engine torque, leaving the engine and drivetrain disengaged.

1.3.2 Change Direction

It is rather obvious how awkward it would be if automobiles could move only in a forward direction. To make them easier to drive a reverse gear is incorporated in the transmission that allows the operator to back up.

To design a transmission with a reverse gear is simple. In a vehicle with a standard transmission, the direction of rotation of the output shaft of the transmission can be changed by adding another gear, the reverse idler, to the *gear train* (Figure 1–2). In vehicles with automatic transmissions, another means is used to achieve a reverse gear.

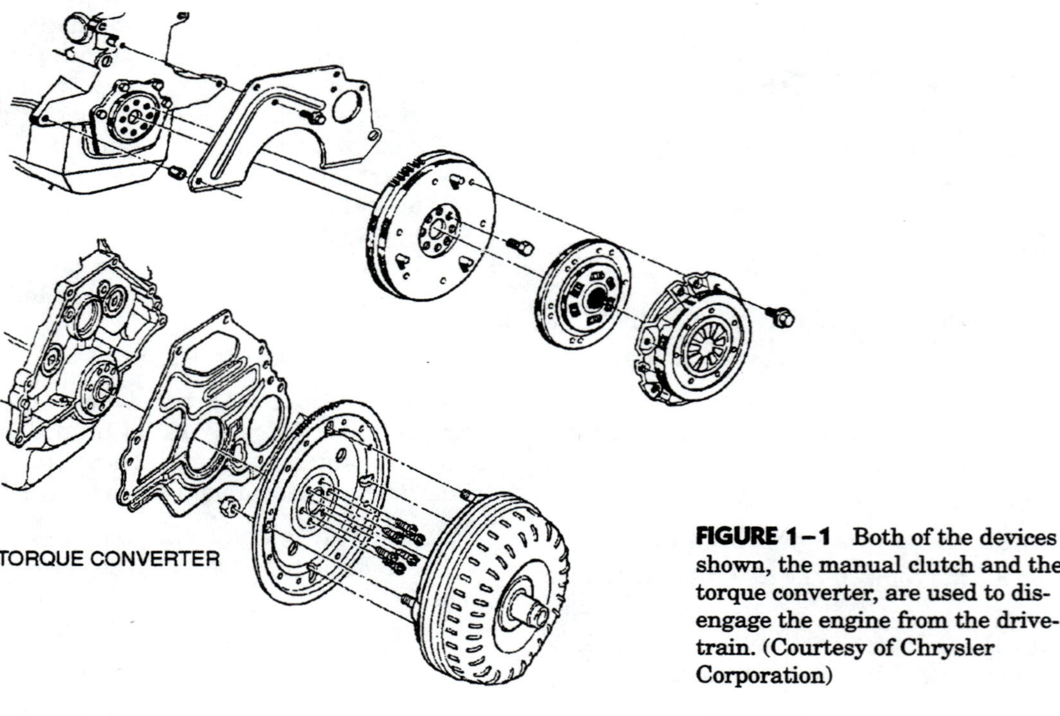

FIGURE 1–1 Both of the devices shown, the manual clutch and the torque converter, are used to disengage the engine from the drivetrain. (Courtesy of Chrysler Corporation)

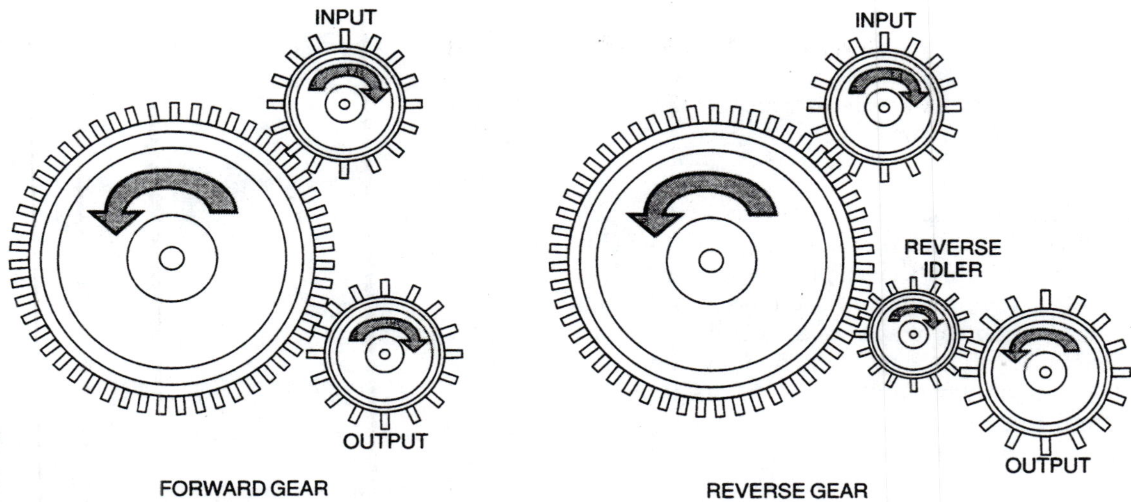

FIGURE 1–2 To produce a reverse gear in a standard transmission, a reverse gear idler is added to the gear train to reverse the direction of rotation of the transmission output shaft.

Almost all automatic transmissions use planetary gear sets as part of the gear train. The planetary gear set will produce a reverse gear when the sun gear is the input member, the planet carrier is being held as the reaction member, and the ring gear is the output member (Figure 1–3). A full explanation of the function of planetary gear sets is given in Chapter 3. Both designs of transmissions provide the reverse gear needed by the vehicle, but they are achieved in very different ways.

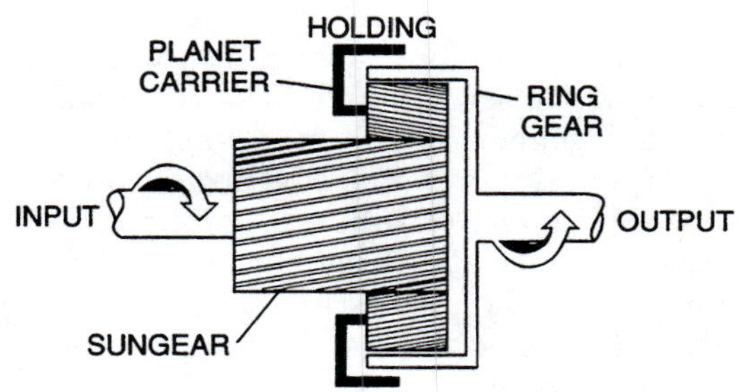

FIGURE 1–3 In an automatic transmission using a planetary gear set to achieve reverse gear, the sun gear is the input source, the planet carrier is held, acting as the reaction member, and the ring gear is the output member.

1.3.3 Increase Torque

The definition of *torque* as the term is used in this book is the twisting or turning force that is produced by the crankshaft of the engine. This twisting force, torque, is measured in pound-feet (lb-ft) when using the English measurement system or in newton-meters (N-m) when using the metric system (Figure 1–4). Torque is also used to describe how much turning force should be applied to a bolt to tighten it properly in place. The torque produced by the engine itself is not adequate for acceptable performance, for reasons explained in the following section.

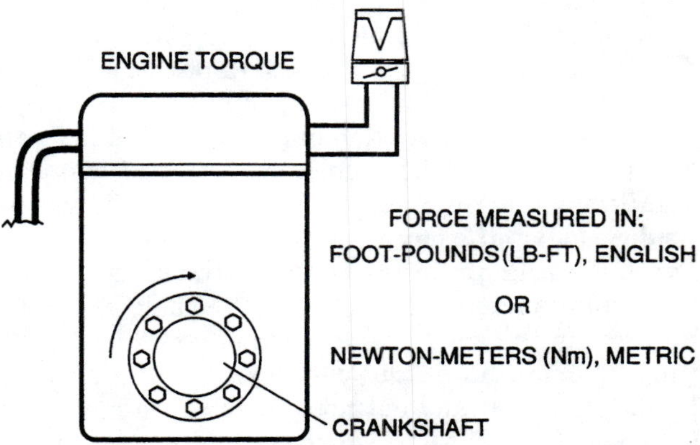

FIGURE 1–4 The twisting or turning force that is produced by the engine's crankshaft is known as engine torque. Engine torque is measured in pound-feet (lb-ft) or newton-meters (N-m).

1. Low-Torque Engines

At slow engine speeds (low rpm levels) most internal combustion engines produce a small amount of torque. As the rpm level increases, the torque output will also increase. Maximum engine torque is usually produced in the engine's middle-speed range of approximately 1600 to 3800 rpm. This means that the engine is not producing sufficient torque at idle speed to accelerate the vehicle properly from a standing start.

2. Torque versus Mass
When a vehicle is stopped at an intersection waiting for a green light, the weight or mass of the vehicle is at rest. To start the vehicle moving requires the greatest amount of torque of almost any driving condition. The inertia of a mass at rest, plus the internal friction and rolling friction, must be overcome to start the vehicle moving. This takes more torque than the engine can produce at low speeds, so what torque is available must be increased through the use of gear reduction in the transmission.

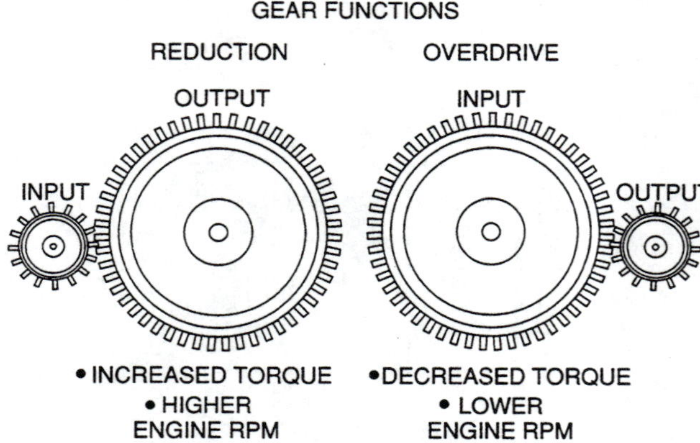

FIGURE 1–5 There are two different types of gear functions, reduction and overdrive. Both types of gear functions affect engine torque and speed but in different ways. Reduction increases torque and engine speed, whereas overdrive reduces torque and engine speed.

1.4 GEAR FUNCTION

The function of gears used in *gear reduction* is twofold. The first job is to multiply the engine's torque, and the second is to allow the engine to operate at a higher rpm level, which will produce more torque. Gears can also be designed to produce *overdrive,* in which case the torque is reduced and the engine operating rpm value is decreased (Figure 1–5). To understand how gears can increase or decrease torque, you must first understand the operation of basic levers.

1.4.1 Basic Levers

The lever is probably one of the oldest simple machines used by human beings. It can be as simple as a long stick and a rock, or more complicated, like a clutch throw-out bearing fork and linkage. All levers share the same basic components. These components are the shaft or bar, a pivot point called the *fulcrum,* an input force, and an output force (Figure 1–6). The portion of the shaft that is on the input side of the fulcrum is called the input arm, while the remaining part of the shaft on the output side is called the output arm (Figure 1–7). Starting with the fulcrum in the center of the shaft, there is an equal amount of shaft on either side of the fulcrum and the lever is said to be in equilibrium. The input force and output force will be the same: to state the input and output force as a ratio, it is 1:1 (Figure 1–8). Now move the fulcrum closer to the output end until one-third of the lever is on the output side and two-thirds is on the input side (Figure 1–9). The ratio of this lever is 2:1. This means two things: the output force is twice the input force,

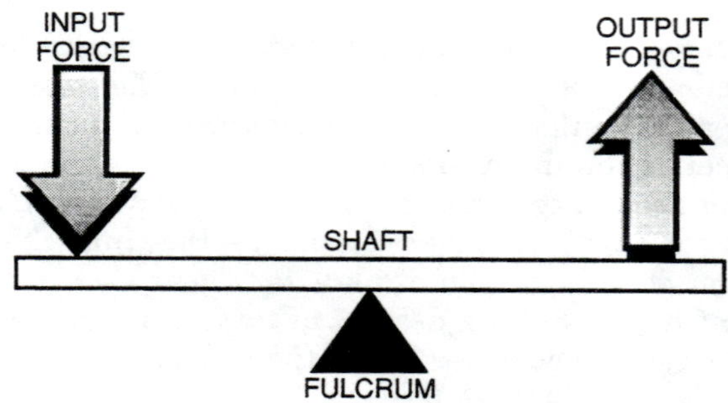

FIGURE 1–6 The basic parts of a lever are the shaft, or bar, the fulcrum, and the input and output force.

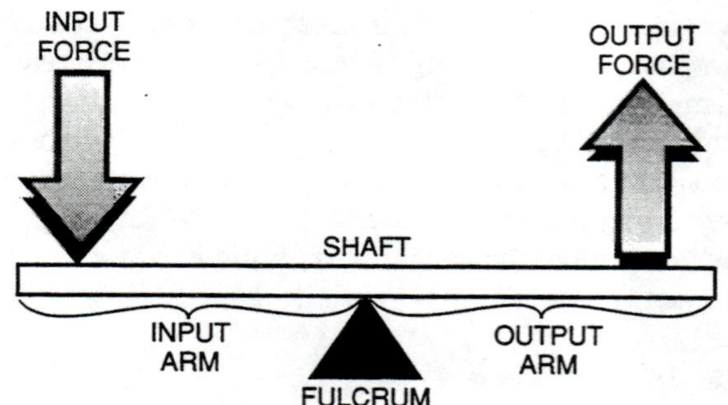

FIGURE 1–7 The portion of the shaft on the input side of the fulcrum is known as the input arm, and the portion on the output side is the output arm.

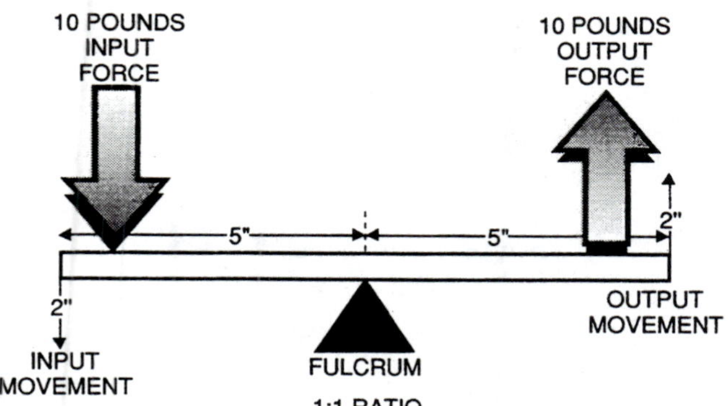

FIGURE 1–8 Lever that is in equilibrium, or balanced. Both arms of the lever are of the same length, which keeps the input and output forces equal and the lever movement at each end the same.

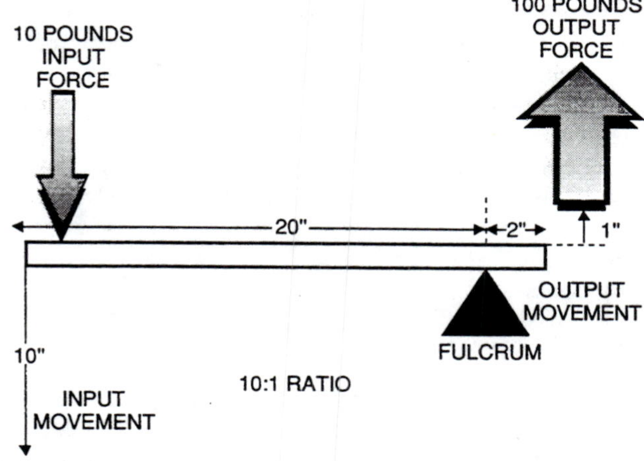

FIGURE 1–10 With a 10:1 ratio lever, the output force is 10 times greater than the input force, but the output movement is only one-tenth of the input movement.

which means that we have gained a mechanical advantage. At the same time, we have also lost something. We lost distance of movement at the output end of the lever, as compared to the distance traveled at the input end of the lever. As you see in Figure 1–9, the lever with a 2:1 ratio has doubled input force but moves only one-half the input distance. Now move the fulcrum closer to the output end until the input arm is 10 times longer than the output arm. This will give a 10:1 ratio (Figure 1–10): the output force will be 10 times greater than the input force with the output arm movement being only one-tenth the input distance. As the *mechanical advantage* increases, the distance traveled will decrease. So you are not getting something for nothing; instead, you are making a trade-off: more force for less distance. In stating the ratio of the lever, we compare the length of the input arm to the output arm, which in Figure 1–10 was 10:1. The first portion of the ratio will always refer to the input amount, while the second portion refers to the output amount. Although all our examples of levers to this point have gained mechanical advantage, it is also possible to lose it. If we start again at the point of equilibrium but this time move the fulcrum toward the input end, we will cause the lever to lose force but increase distance traveled. If we place the fulcrum so that the input arm is one-third of the lever and the output is two-thirds, the lever ratio would be 1:2, which could be reduced to 0.5:1 (Figure 1–11). With this ratio, output force

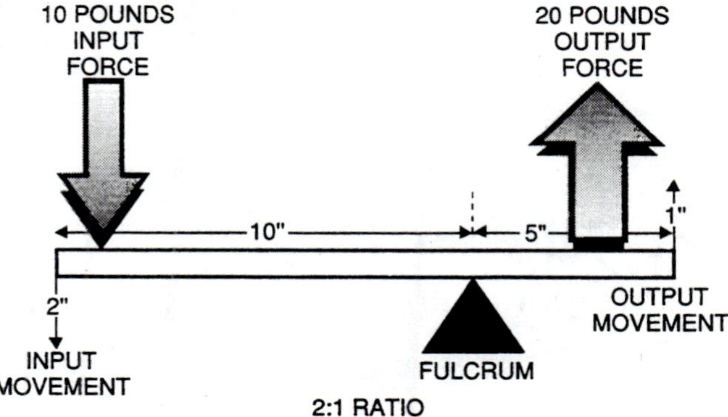

FIGURE 1–9 With a 2:1 ratio lever, the input arm is twice as long as the output arm. The 10-lb input force is doubled to 20 lb of output force because of the mechanical advantage created by the lever and fulcrum. But notice that as force is gained, the lever movement is lost.

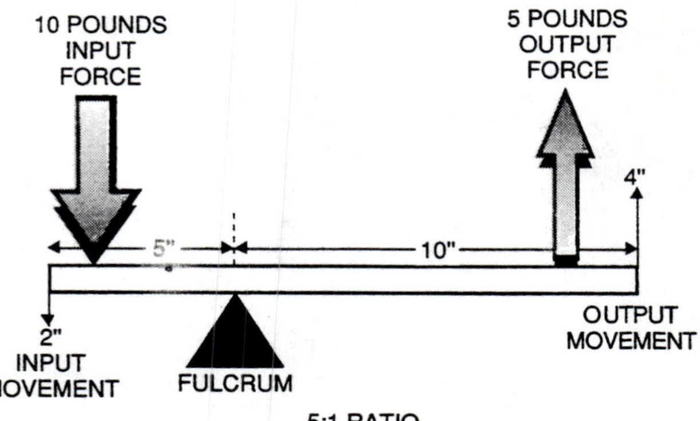

FIGURE 1–11 With a 0.5:1 ratio lever, mechanical advantage is lost and output force is less than input force, but the distance of movement of the output arm is increased.

will be less than input force, but the output distance will be more than the input distance, which is the exact reverse of the other levers.

To sum up, the amount of mechanical advantage gained is in proportion to the ratio of the lever. The higher the ratio, the greater the force increase and the greater the movement loss. When the input side of the ratio becomes a decimal, the mechanical advantage is lost but the output distance traveled is increased.

1.4.2 Pulleys

The pulley is the next step in the progression from a lever to a gear. Like the lever, the pulley can increase force through gaining a mechanical advantage. The main difference is that with a pulley we are working with rotary force, turning a shaft or axle, rather than with the linear force of a lever.

Shown in Figure 1–12 are the parts of a pulley: the mounting hub, with a keyway and pinch bolt, the pulley wheel, a belt groove, and a V-belt to transfer power from one pulley to another. The pulley can perform three basic jobs: transfer power from one shaft to another, increase or decrease the output torque, and increase or decrease the output speed. The speed at which the pulleys turn is measured in revolutions per minute (rpm) and the twisting force of the torque is measured in pound-feet (lb-ft).

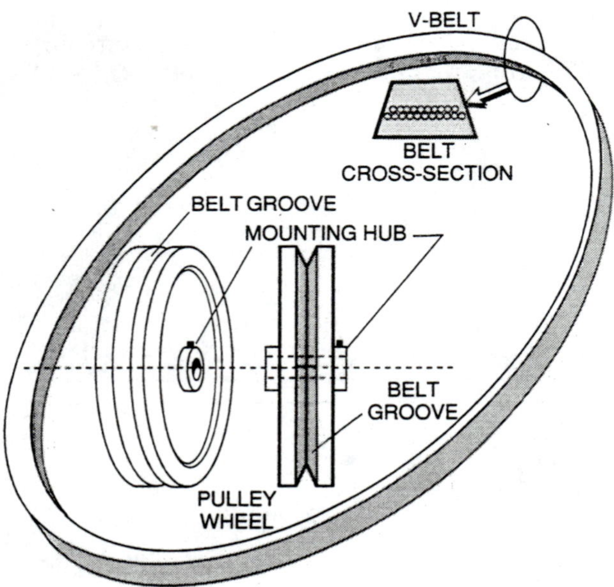

FIGURE 1–12 The parts of a pulley are the pulley wheel, belt groove, mounting hub, and V-belt.

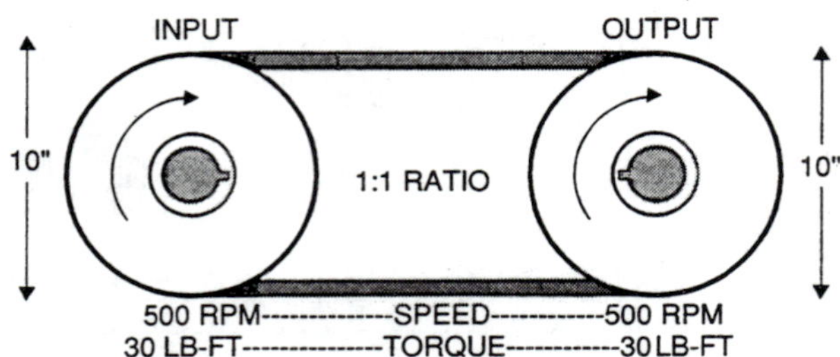

FIGURE 1–13 Since both pulleys are the same size, the ratio is 1:1, which will neither increase nor decrease the torque or speed.

Pulleys are always used in pairs, with the size of the pulley's diameter determining how much torque or speed change there will be. If we start with two pulleys with the same diameter, or a 1:1 ratio (Figure 1–13), the input and output speed and torque will remain the same; no change will occur. This is the same condition as a lever that is in equilibrium. Next we change the size of the input pulley to 5 in., which gives us a pulley ratio of 2:1. As you can see in Figure 1–14, the output torque has doubled while the output speed is only one-half the input speed. The larger the difference in size between the input pulley and the output pulley, or the higher the ratio, the greater the *torque increase* and the greater the speed reduction.

If the position of the pulleys is changed so that the 10-in. pulley is the input and the 5-in. pulley is the output, we lose the mechanical advantage that increased the torque. With this pulley setup, the output speed is increased while the torque is reduced (Figure 1–15). Understanding the basic operating principles of the lever and pulley will give you a better foundation for studying how gears work.

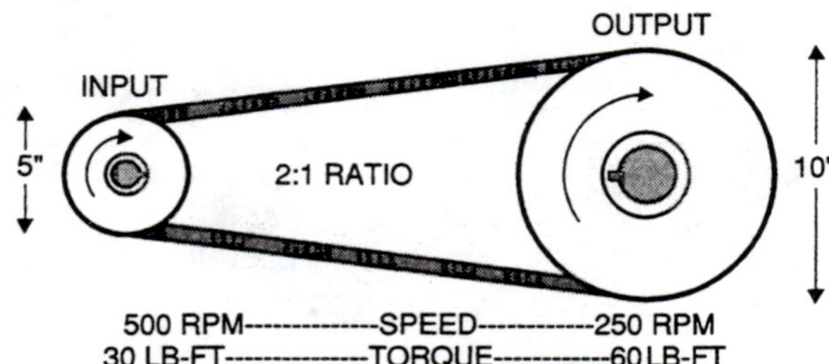

FIGURE 1–14 With the input pulley one-half the size of the output pulley, the set ratio is 2:1. The output torque will be two times greater and the speed will be one-half as fast as the input.

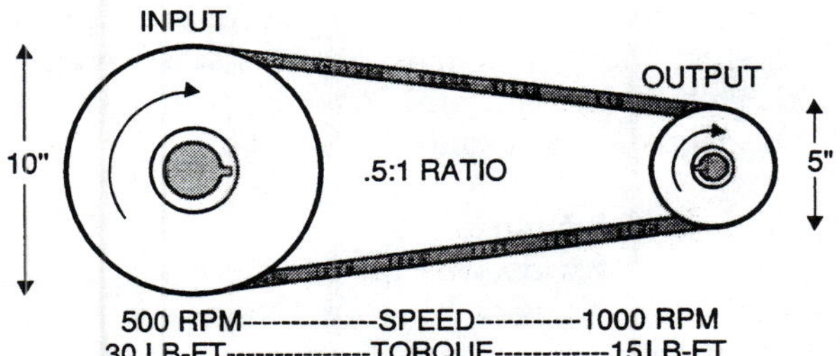

FIGURE 1–15 A pulley set that will increase output speed and decrease the torque because of its 0.5:1 ratio.

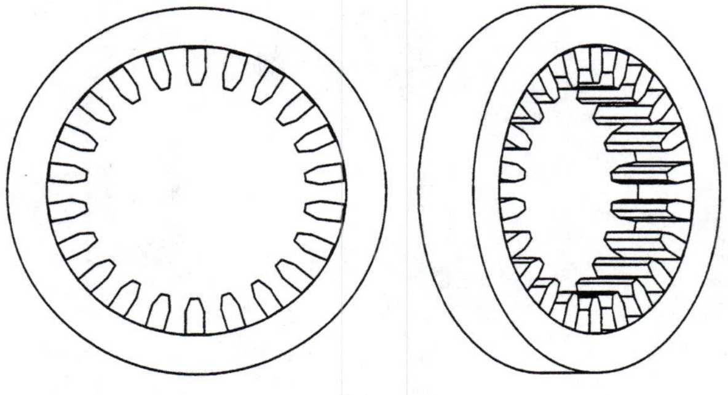

FIGURE 1–17 The internal gear has teeth around its inside diameter.

1.4.3 Gear Types

A gear is a wheel, which rotates on its own axis, with teeth cut into its outer diameter. These teeth mesh with the teeth of another gear so that power can be transferred from one gear to another as they rotate (Figure 1–16). The gear described above is called an *external gear* because its teeth are located around the outside diameter of the gear. In an *internal gear,* also called an internal gear ring gear or annulus gear, the teeth are located around the inside diameter (Figure 1–17).

1. Types of Gear Teeth
The gear teeth are cut at various angles. In a *spur gear,* or straight-cut gear, the teeth are cut parallel to the axis of the gear (Figure 1–18). The name *helical cut* is given to gear teeth that are cut at a slight angle to the gear axis rather than parallel to it. This angle or helical cut allows the gears to run together very quietly. Straight-cut or spur gears are slightly stronger than *helical gears* and run with less internal friction, but they produce a loud gear whine that is unacceptable in a passenger vehicle. For this reason, helical cut gears are used almost exclusively in automotive transmissions.

2. Changing Direction of Power Flow
The gears just described all have a parallel axis of rotation, which means that the direction of the power flow will remain the same. A number of different types of gear sets are used in automatic transmissions to change the direction of power flow. These gear sets include:

1. Worm gears
2. Ring-and-pinion gears
3. Hypoid drive gears

The worm gear arrangement can be used to change the direction of power flow as well as to provide gear reduction (Figure 1–19). The worm gear drive is used in many automatic transmissions to drive the speedometer. In most turbo Hydra-Matic transmissions it is used to drive the governors. The driven gear, which is attached to the speedometer cable or governor body, is meshed with the driving gear on the transmission output shaft. As the out-

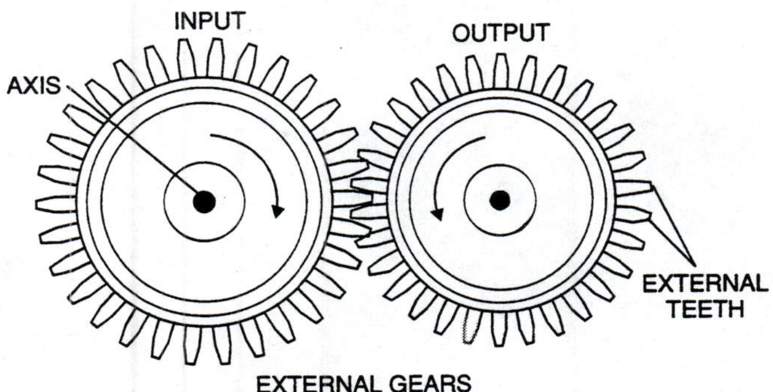

FIGURE 1–16 The external gear has teeth around its outer diameter and rotates on its own axis.

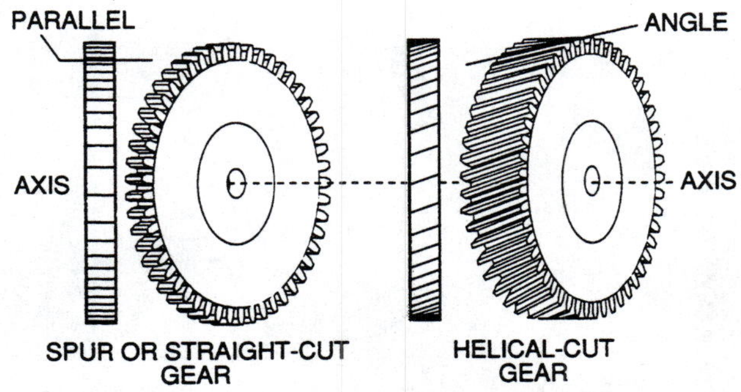

FIGURE 1–18 Spur or straight-cut gear teeth are machined parallel to the gear's axis, whereas helical teeth are cut at an angle to the gear's axis.

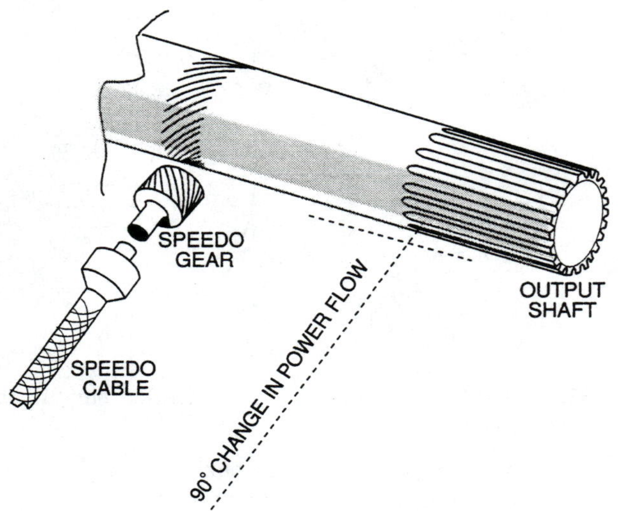

FIGURE 1–19 A worm gear is used to drive the speedometer cable to change the direction of power flow.

put shaft gear turns, the worm gear turns at a 90° angle to the transmission output shaft.

The ring-and-pinion gear set and hypoid drive gear set, shown in Figure 1–20, are commonly used in drive axles and in some transaxles. The ring-and-pinion design was used in most early vehicles, but as cars were designed closer and closer to the ground, more driveshaft tunnel clearance was needed, so the hypoid drive gear set was developed. Both ring-and-pinion and hypoid designs are used in the final drives of some transaxles.

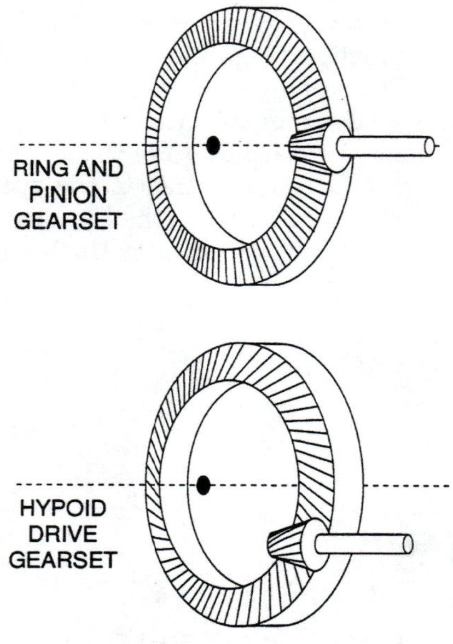

FIGURE 1–20 The ring-and-pinion and hypoid drive gear set are used to change the direction of power flow in transaxles whose drive axles are perpendicular to the engine's crankshaft.

3. Gear Combinations

The variety of ways in which gears could be combined is limited only by your imagination. Many complex gear trains have been designed and produced to meet the specific requirements of industry.

An automotive transmission is an excellent example of complex gear combinations. The transmission's gear ratios are designed to meet the individual vehicle's needs according to its size, weight, engine torque output, and rpm range.

There are many mechanical principles that apply to gears, a few of which will help you understand gear combinations better. If an external gear set has an even number of gears, the direction of rotation of the *output gear* will be opposite that of the input gear. In an external gear set with an odd number of gears, the direction of rotation of the output will be the same as that of the input. In a simple gear set with more than two gears, the idler gears (those in between the input and output gears) do not necessarily change the gear ratio of the set.

The most important gear combination in an automatic transmission is the planetary gear set. The basic parts, or members, of the planetary gear set are the sun gear, the planet pinions and planet carrier, and the ring gear (Figure 1–21). The planetary gear set is capable of producing the following gear actions: neutral, low-ratio reduction, high-ratio reduction, low-ratio overdrive, high-ratio overdrive, reverse reduction, reverse overdrive, and

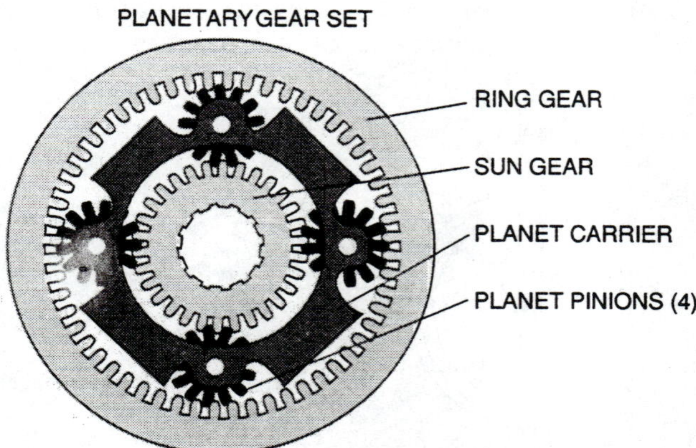

FIGURE 1–21 The parts, members of a simple planetary gear set, are the sun gear, planet pinions and planet carrier, and ring gear.

direct drive. All parts of the planetary gear set stay meshed at all times, with gear changes being caused by coupling different parts of the planetary gear set to input or by holding one part as a reaction member. In Chapter 3 we provide a detailed explanation of how a planetary gear set works.

1.4.4 Torque Increase

We have seen how levers and pulleys can increase force, and the same basic principles apply to how a gear works. Whenever the output gear is larger than the input gear or has more teeth than the input gear, the torque will be increased. Just as with the levers and pulleys, we cannot get something for nothing. To gain the torque increase, we must reduce the output speed of rotation or rpm level. The amounts of torque increase and speed reduction are inversely proportional: as one gets larger, the other gets smaller.

If we have two gears with the same number of teeth, the output will be the same as the input (Figure 1–22). But if we change the gear combination so that the output gear has twice as many teeth as the *input gear,* we get twice the torque from the output gear but only one-half the speed of the input (Figure 1–23). Let's change the gear combination again so that the output gear has 10 times more teeth than the input gear. This will increase the output torque 10 times over the input torque but at only one-tenth of the input speed (Figure 1–24).

Any time an engine's speed is geared down, the torque output will be increased. The greater the gear reduction, the larger the torque increase. Next we will look at the reverse of this.

1.4.5 Speed Increase

We have just talked about how an engine can be geared down to increase the torque by reducing the output speed, but what if you want to increase the speed and don't really care how much torque you have? In this case the input gear in the gear train will be larger or will have more teeth than the output gear (Figure 1–25). When an engine is geared up, the output speed will be greater than the engine speed. By gearing the engine up, or using *overdrive* as it is called, the vehicle is able to maintain a set speed with the engine turning at a lower rpm level. By lowering the engine speed, the fuel economy is increased and since the overdrive gear is used only at highway speeds, the corresponding loss of torque is not a problem. The amount of

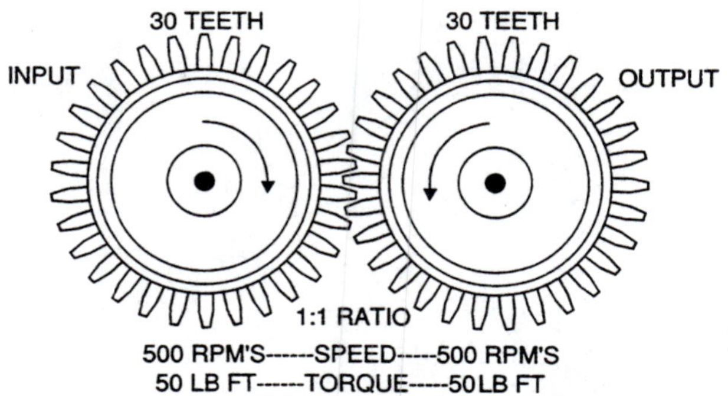

FIGURE 1–22 In a 1:1 ratio gear set, the output torque and speed will be the same as the input.

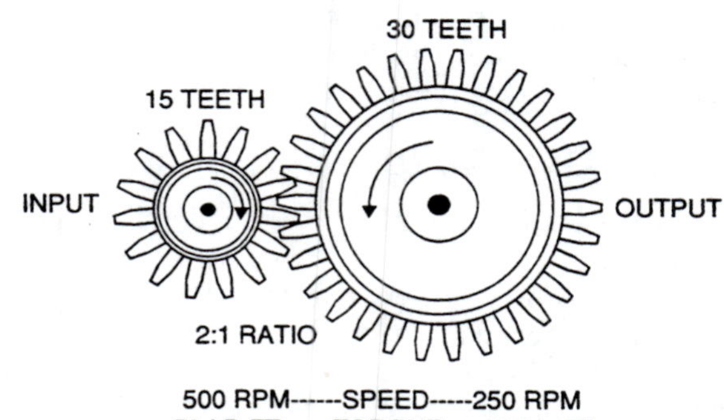

FIGURE 1–23 In a 2:1 ratio gear set, the output torque is doubled while the speed is only one-half the input speed.

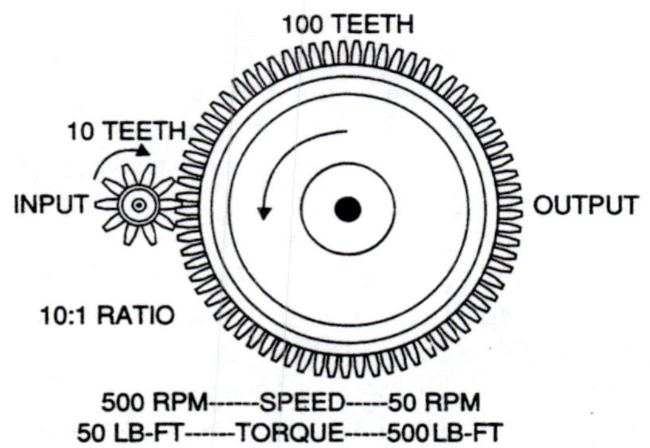

FIGURE 1–24 In a 10:1 ratio gear set, the output torque went to 500 lb-ft at 50 rpm.

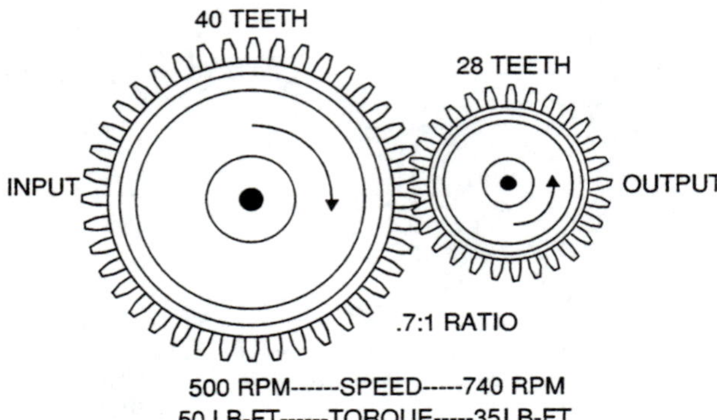

FIGURE 1–25 In a 0.7:1 ratio gear set, the output speed is increased to 740 rpm while the torque dropped to 35 lb-ft.

speed increase and torque reduction are again inversely proportional; if we double the speed, we will have only one-half the torque. It is the same rule that applied to torque increase.

1.4.6 Gear Ratios

When an engine is either geared down or geared up, the amount of gearing used is expressed in a gear ratio. The ratio compares the input speed to the output speed as shown in Figure 1–26. The first number in the ratio represents the input gear speed, and the second number represents the output gear speed. To simplify and better understand what the ratio means, the output portion of a ratio, the second number, is always stated as 1, which represents one revolution of the output gear. The first number in the ratio indicates how many revolutions the input gear must turn to make the output gear turn one full revolution. As the amount of gear reduction increases, the first number in the ratio gets larger. As the reduction decreases, the ratio number becomes smaller—until it reaches a ratio of 1:1, which is direct drive. As we go from gear reduction to overdrive, the first number becomes a decimal since now it takes only a fraction of a turn on the input gear to rotate the output gear one full revolution (Figure 1–27).

To find the gear ratio of a gear set, simply divide the number of teeth on the output gear by the number of teeth on the input gear, as shown in Figure 1–28, and compare that number to 1. If a gear set has a third gear added to change the direction of the output gear, the gear ratio will remain the same. The extra gear acts as an idler gear and does not affect the gear ratio; it simply transmits power from the input gear to the output gear.

GEAR RATIO

3.5 : 1

INPUT SPEED : OUTPUT SPEED

FIGURE 1–26 A gear ratio is a simple comparison that shows how many times the input shaft must turn to rotate the output one revolution.

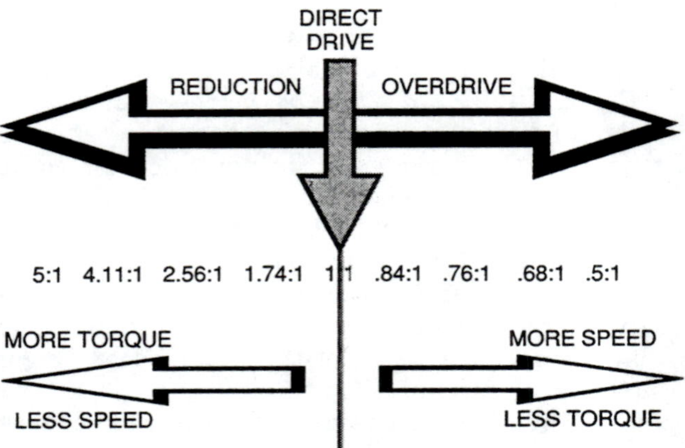

FIGURE 1–27 Any gear set that provides reduction will increase the torque and lose speed, whereas any overdrive gear set will gain speed and lose torque.

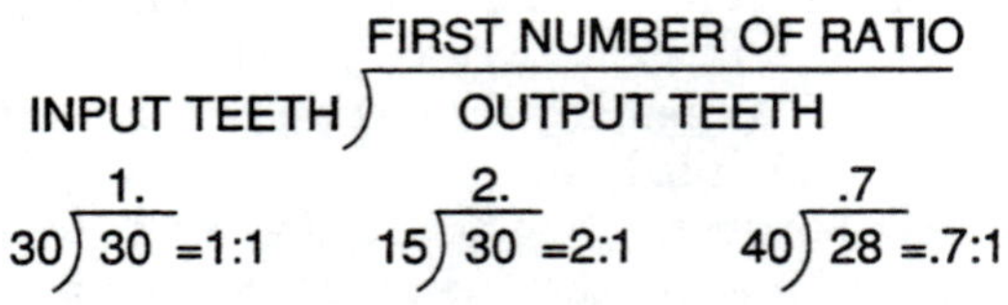

FIRST NUMBER OF RATIO

INPUT TEETH) OUTPUT TEETH

30) 30 = 1. =1:1 15) 30 = 2. =2:1 40) 28 = .7 =.7:1

FIGURE 1–28 The first number of a gear ratio is obtained by dividing the number of output teeth by the number of input teeth.

SUMMARY

Need for Transmissions

- The manual clutch with standard transmission is used to disengage the engine from the drivetrain.
- The torque converter is used to disengage the engine from the drivetrain on vehicles with automatic transmission.
- The transmission is used to change the direction of travel of a vehicle.
- Most engines produce low amounts of torque at slow engine speeds.
- Engine torque must be increased to provide better acceleration.

Gear Functions

- Gears are used to increase engine torque.
- The lever is a good example of how mechanical advantage can be gained.
- Pulleys are a form of rotary lever.
- When an engine is geared down, the output speed is reduced but the torque is increased.
- When an engine is geared up, the output speed is increased but the torque is reduced.
- In a gear ratio the first number indicates the number of turns the input gear must make to turn the output gear one revolution.
- There are many different gear designs.
- A gear combination used in almost all automatic transmissions is the planetary gear set.

SELF-TEST

Before going on to the next chapter, complete the self-test according to your instructor's directions. Read carefully and choose the best answer.

1. The ________________ disengages the engine from the drivetrain on vehicles with manual transmissions.

a. Manual clutch
b. Torque converter
c. Flywheel
d. Crankshaft

2. The ________________ disengages the engine from the drivetrain on vehicles with automatic transmissions.

a. Manual clutch
b. Torque converter
c. Flywheel
d. Crankshaft

3. A vehicle needs a transmission to ________________.

a. Be able to back up
b. Be able to stop without killing the engine
c. Increase engine torque for better performance
d. All of the above

4. Technician A says that a lever can be used to increase force. Technician B says that a lever will give you a mechanical advantage. Who is right?

a. A
b. B
c. Both A and B
d. Neither A nor B

5. Pulleys can be used to ________________.

a. Increase force
b. Increase speed
c. Decrease speed
d. All of the above

6. As engine speed is reduced through a gear set, the output gear will have ________________.

a. More torque
b. More speed
c. Less torque
d. All of the above

7. When torque is increased through a gear set, speed is ________________.

a. Increased
b. Decreased
c. Maintained
d. Modulated

8. In a gear ratio such as 3.6:1, the first number represents the number of revolutions the ________________ gear is turning.

a. Output
b. Idler
c. Input
d. None of the above

9. A widely used type of gear that is noted for its quiet operation is the ________________ gear.

a. Spur
b. Worm
c. Bevel
d. Helical

10. The most common type of gear combinations used in automatic transmissions today are ________________.

a. Rack and pinions
b. Hypoid drives
c. Planetary gear sets
d. Solar sets

GLOSSARY

drivetrain components that transmit power between the engine and drive wheels.

dynamometer device used to measure the torque output of an engine.

external gear gear whose teeth are located on the outside surface.

fulcrum pivot point of a lever.

gear reduction the input driving gear rotates more revolutions than the output driven gear in a transmission; *or* torque is multiplied and speed decreased by the factor of the gear ratio.

gear train intermeshing gears that provide torque changes as power input is transmitted to power output.

helical gear wheel with teeth cut at an angle across the external or internal face.

hypoid drive (hypoid gears) pinion-and-ring gear design in which the centerline of the pinion is offset from the centerline of the ring gear; *or* design in which a gear is mounted lower than center or lower than normal.

input gear gear that provides power to the output gear of the differential in an automatic transmission.

internal gear gear with teeth pointing inward toward the center of the gear; *or* the circular gear meshing with the planetary pinions in a planetary gear set.

lever rigid piece that transmits and modifies force or motion when force is applied at one point, resistance to the force at another point, and a pivot is used at a third point.

mechanical advantage increase in torque gained by using reduction gears.

output gear gear that drives the differential case on an automatic transaxle and corresponds to the differential ring gear in a rear-wheel-drive application.

overdrive gear ratio that produces the opposite effect of gear reduction.

ring-and-pinion gear gear set used in the final drive to provide reduction and change the direction of power flow 90°.

spur gear straight-toothed gear with the teeth parallel to the shaft.

torque twisting, turning effort.

torque increase result of meshing a small driving gear and a large driven gear to reduce speed and increase output torque.

Chapter 2

TORQUE CONVERTERS

INTRODUCTION

The first component of the automatic transmission to receive engine torque is the torque converter. This device serves a number of functions: to disengage the engine from the drivetrain at engine idle, to transfer torque from the engine to the transmission input shaft, and to multiply the engine torque under certain operating conditions. The function and design of a torque converter are based on a simpler device, the fluid coupling. To fully understand the operation of a torque converter, it is best to start with fluid coupling. The vortex and rotary fluid flow in a fluid coupling operate the same as those in torque converters but are easier to understand because of the simplicity of the coupling.

The basic function and construction of a torque converter is explained in detail together with descriptions of the fluid movement. The purpose of the stator and its operation are fully described, as is the way in which engine torque is increased by the torque converter.

Many types of converter clutch devices have been developed to provide a positive mechanical power path through the torque converter to improve high-speed efficiency. The various types of converter clutch devices are explained and studied individually to provide a clear understanding of their operation.

An automatic transmission uses both hydraulic and mechanical devices to transmit engine torque. The torque converter is a hydrodynamic unit, which means fluid in motion. Hydraulics, the study of fluids under pressure, is an important subject area that is covered in Chapter 4. The mechanical devices are the gear sets used for gear reduction and direction change.

2.1 PERFORMANCE OBJECTIVES

After studying this chapter, you should have fulfilled the following performance objectives by being able to:

1. Describe the construction and operation of a fluid coupling.
2. Describe the construction and operation of a torque converter.
3. Describe the fluid movement inside a torque converter.
4. Explain how engine torque is increased by a torque converter.
5. Describe four types of converter clutch devices.
6. Complete all the competency objectives listed for this chapter.
7. Complete the self-test with at least the minimum score required by your instructor.

2.2 COMPETENCY OBJECTIVES

The competency objectives are different from the performance objectives in being more job related. The automotive terms must be well understood so that the theory will be clear. The terms are used to describe the service procedures outlined in Part 2. The competency tasks are related to job skills needed to perform service and repair procedures and should be understood thoroughly.

2.2.1 Automotive Terms

The following list may include terms that are unfamiliar to you. Read the terms, then note their definitions as you study the chapter.

centrifugal force	rotary flow
centrifugal lockup clutch	stall speed
converter lockup clutch	stator
dual-output converters	thrust washer
fluid coupling	turbine
hydraulic lockup clutch	turbine shaft
impeller	variable-pitch stator
90% speed ratio	vibration damper
one-way clutch	viscous converter clutch
resultant force	vortex flow
rolling inertia	zero speed ratio

2.2.2 Competency Tasks

The competency tasks listed here are related directly to knowledge or skills needed to become a successful automatic transmission/transaxle technician. Be sure to complete all the tasks before going on to Chapter 3.

1. Explain the operation of a fluid coupling.
2. Describe the construction of a fluid coupling.
3. Describe the parts and construction of a torque converter.
4. Explain the operation of a torque converter.
5. Explain vortex flow in a torque converter.
6. Explain rotary flow in a torque converter.
7. Explain how the stator can increase the torque output of a torque converter.
8. Describe the hydraulic lockup clutch.
9. Describe the centrifugal lockup clutch.
10. Describe the viscous converter clutch.
11. Describe the dual-output converters.

2.3 FLUID COUPLINGS

The fluid coupling is a hydrodynamic power transfer device that is widely used in industry. The fluid coupling consists of three major parts: the fluid *housing,* which is driven by the crankshaft; the *impeller* or pump, which is attached to the fluid housing; and the *turbine,* which is splined to the transmission input shaft (Figure 2–1). The automotive fluid coupling serves four major functions:

1. To provide mass to replace the flywheel
2. To dampen out crankshaft vibrations
3. To provide an automatic clutch to disengage the engine from the drivetrain
4. To transfer engine torque to the transmission

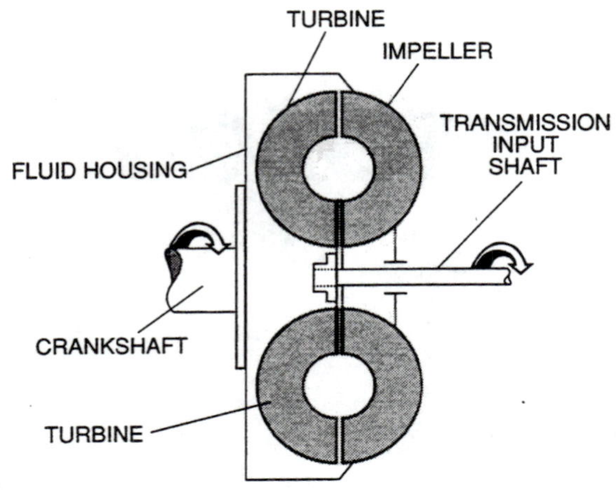

FIGURE 2–1 The major parts of a fluid coupling are the fluid housing, the impeller or pump, and the turbine.

Because of its heavy weight, the fluid coupling and the fluid that fills it can replace the cast iron flywheel. The weight of the fluid coupling and fluid provides the inertia to keep the engine rotating through the exhaust, intake, and compression cycles.

The fluid in the fluid coupling works to dampen torsional vibrations. The sudden increase in torque after the power stroke, followed by a decrease in torque while the engine rotates through the other three strokes, causes torsional vibrations to occur in the crankshaft. The fluid in the fluid coupling will not transfer these vibrations, so they are dampened out.

The fluid coupling is designed to transfer torque above a certain rpm value. As long as the impeller is driven at a speed above the minimum rpm level, it will pump fluid to the turbine, thereby transferring torque to the turbine. Once the speed of the impeller drops below the minimum rpm level, it can no longer pump enough fluid to the turbine to keep it rotating. At this point, torque transfer will stop. In this way fluid coupling provides an automatic clutch.

The transfer of torque can occur through a fluid coupling any time that the impeller is being driven above its minimum rpm level. At that speed, fluid is pumped from the impeller toward the turbine at a high enough rate of flow that the torque from the engine is transmitted through the hydraulic fluid to the turbine, thereby driving the turbine and the rest of the power train. In the following sections we examine the construction, operations, and fluid movement of a fluid coupling at greater length.

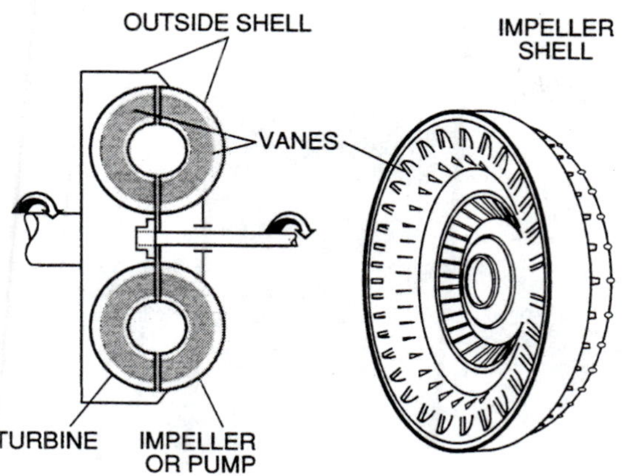

FIGURE 2–2 The impeller and turbine have an outer shell shaped like a donut that has been cut in half. Inside this shell are mounted vanes that radiate from its center.

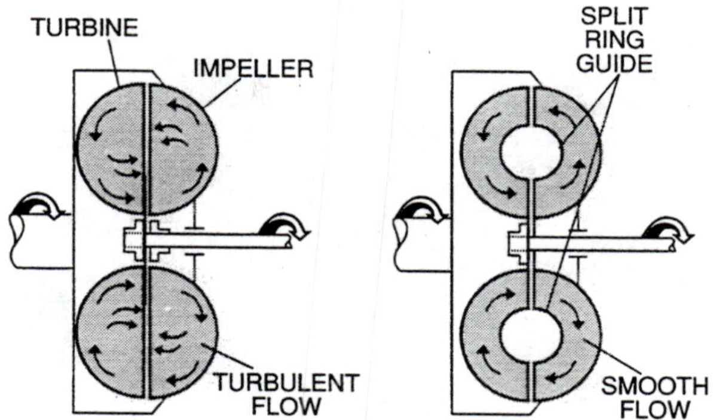

FIGURE 2–3 Turbulence in the flow of fluid going from the impeller to the turbine can reduce torque transfer. By adding a split guide ring to both the impeller and the turbine, the turbulence is greatly reduced.

2.3.1 Construction

As stated earlier, the fluid coupling has three basic parts: the impeller, turbine, and fluid housing, as shown in Figure 2–1. The impeller and turbine have a circular shape very similar to a donut that has been cut in half through the middle. Vanes radiate from the center of this circular shape to its outer diameter and attach to the inside surface (Figure 2–2). The impeller and turbine are enclosed in the fluid housing, which surrounds these units completely, providing a liquidtight enclosure. This fluid housing also provides a means of attaching the fluid coupling to the crankshaft of the engine through a flywheel or flex plate and also provides a location for mounting the starter ring gear. The fluid housing and impeller are joined together to form one unit so that whenever the engine is running the impeller is rotating. The turbine, which has an internally splined hub for connecting to the transmission input shaft, is mounted inside the fluid housing on *thrust washers* so that it may turn freely. A split guide ring (Figure 2–3) is added to the center section of both the impeller and the turbine to minimize turbulence in the hydraulic fluid as it is pumped from the impeller to the turbine and returns to the impeller.

2.3.2 Function

The basic operation of the fluid coupling is as follows: As the impeller rotates with the engine, the fluid is pumped by centrifugal action toward the turbine. As the fluid strikes the turbine vanes, the force is transferred to the turbine, causing it to rotate. The speed at which the impeller and turbine turn in comparison to each other is called the speed ratio. At *zero speed ratio* the impeller is rotating but the turbine is not; at a high speed ratio the impeller and the turbine are both rotating at nearly the same speed. For a turbine speed below the impeller speed, a percentage is used to describe the ratio. For example, if the turbine is turning 9 revolutions to every 10 revolutions of the impeller, we speak of a *90% speed ratio,* (Figure 2–4).

Stall speed, another term used in describing the function of a fluid coupling, is the maximum engine speed that can be obtained at full throttle with the turbine held stationary. Stall speed is designed into a fluid coupling and is relative to coupling size:

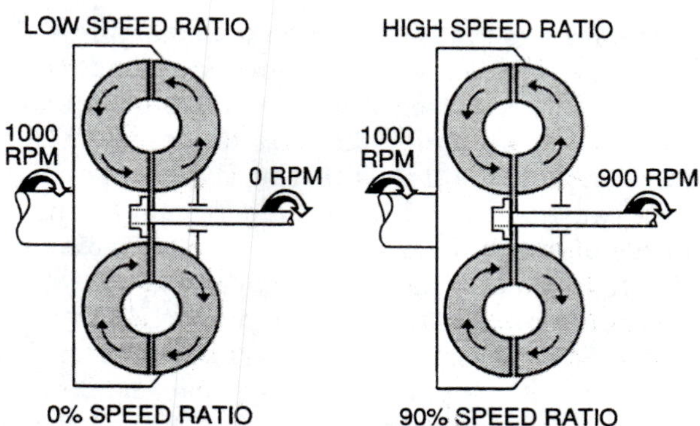

FIGURE 2–4 In this example both impellers are being driven at 1000 rpm. In the left coupling the turbine is stationary, giving a 0% speed ratio (the turbine is turning 0% of the impeller rpm value), while in the right coupling the turbine is turning 90% of the impeller speed, giving a 90% speed ratio.

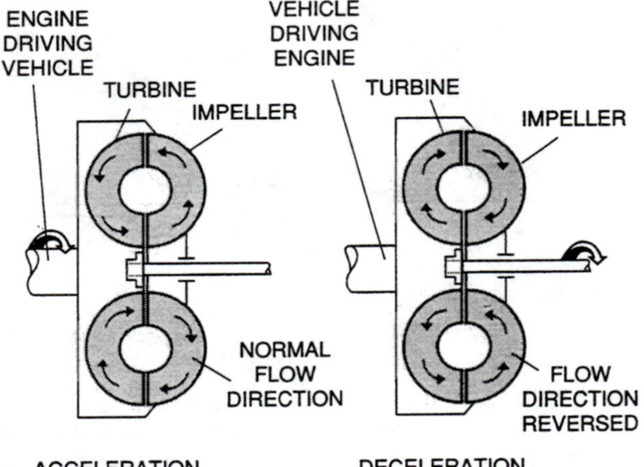

FIGURE 2–5 On deceleration, the impeller and turbine change jobs. The turbine, being driven by the vehicle's mass, pumps fluid.

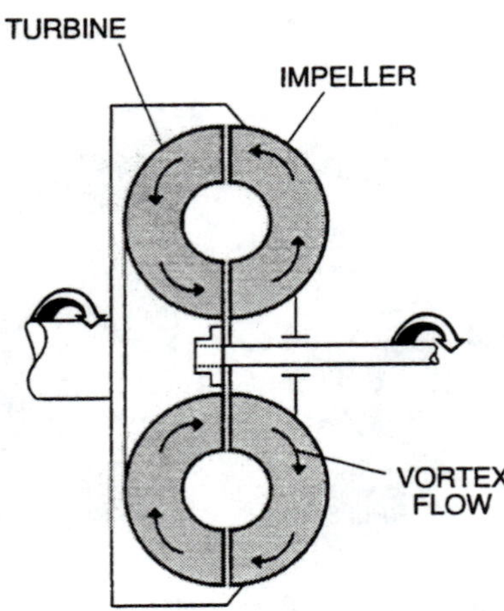

FIGURE 2–6 The vortex flow is created by centrifugal force pushing the fluid toward the outside diameter of the impeller as it rotates. The maximum vortex flow occurs at low speed ratios.

the larger the diameter, the lower the stall speed, and the smaller the diameter, the higher the stall speed.

Torque transfer also occurs in a fluid coupling during deceleration of a vehicle (Figure 2–5). As the throttle is closed, the engine stops producing power and the inertia of the vehicle's mass takes over. *Rolling inertia* forces the power train to turn the turbine, which then pumps fluid in the direction opposite to normal flow into the impeller. The impeller then turns the engine, which provides engine braking for the vehicle, causing it to slow down.

2.3.3 Fluid Movement

There are two types of fluid flow patterns in a fluid coupling, vortex flow and rotary flow. Understanding these flow patterns will make the torque converter easier to understand. As the impeller in the fluid coupling rotates with the engine, *centrifugal force* causes the hydraulic fluid to move from the center of the fluid coupling to its outer diameter. This force causes the fluid to leave the outer edge of the impeller at a rate of flow in proportion to engine speed. The higher the engine rpm, the greater the fluid flow. As the fluid leaves the impeller and moves toward the turbine, it is flowing in a circular path. Called *vortex flow* (Figure 2–6), this flow of fluid from the impeller to the turbine is what transfers the engine torque.

Vortex flow is greatest at zero speed ratio, when the impeller is turning but the turbine is not. As the turbine starts to turn and picks up speed, the same centrifugal action that causes fluid to flow from the impeller begins to build in the turbine (Figure 2–7). This turbine pumping action works against the vortex flow and increases as the turbine speed increases, causing a reduction in vortex flow. As the vortex flow is reduced, *rotary flow* begins to appear. The rotary flow travels around the inside of the fluid housing in the same direction as the impeller rotation (Figure 2–8). As the speed of the

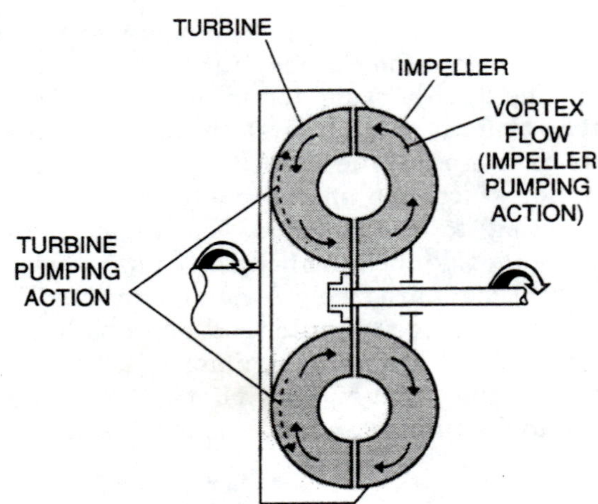

FIGURE 2–7 As turbine speed increases, the centrifugal pumping action that caused the vortex flow starts to build in the turbine. This resistance to vortex flow helps start the rotary flow in motion.

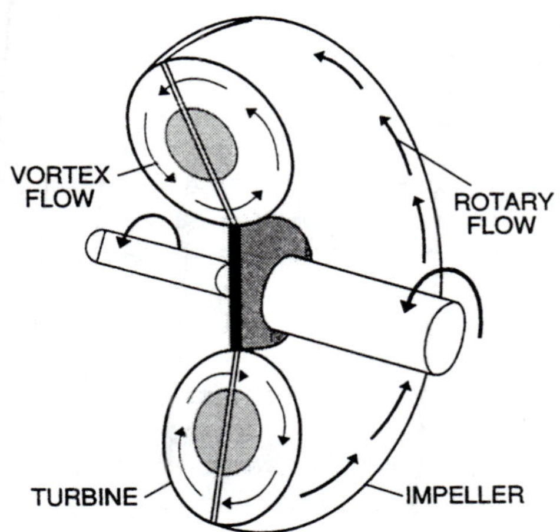

FIGURE 2–8 As the speed ratio increases, rotary flow begins to appear. The higher the speed ratio, the greater the rotary flow, until at maximum speed ratio there is only a slight vortex flow left.

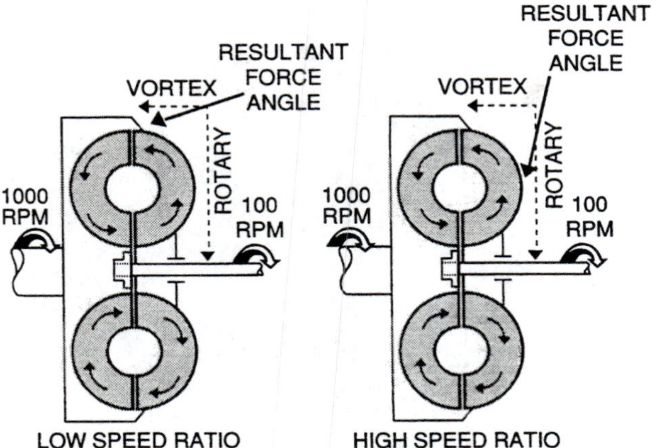

FIGURE 2–9 In the left coupling, which is operating at a low speed ratio, the resultant force angle is close to that of the vortex flow. In the right coupling, which has a high speed ratio, the resultant force angle has changed and is closer to the rotary flow.

turbine increases, the rotary flow increases until at the maximum speed ratio, very little vortex flow remains. If vortex flow were to stop completely, torque transfer would be lost. Thus there will always be a small vortex flow.

The combination of rotary and vortex flow form what is referred to as *resultant force*. The direction, or angle, of this force depends on which flow is strongest (Figure 2–9). With a high vortex flow, the resultant force path is close to that of the vortex flow, while with a high rotary flow, the resultant force path changes to follow the rotary flow. The resultant force angle is the angle at which the fluid leaving the impeller contacts the turbine vanes.

2.4 TORQUE CONVERTERS

Through the addition of devices called the *stator* and the stator *one-way clutch,* the fluid coupling is changed into a torque converter. The stator is used to redirect the fluid flow as it leaves the turbine so that it can reenter the impeller at a better angle. It also provides a reaction surface for the fluid to push against. The stator one-way clutch holds the stator stationary when force is applied to it from one direction but will allow it to turn freely when force is applied from the opposite direction. The stator and stator one-way clutch operation are examined in detail in later sections.

All the functions and characteristics of the fluid coupling apply to the torque converter. The improvement over the fluid coupling is reflected in its name, *torque converter,* because of its ability to increase the engine's torque. This torque increase, which is fully explained later, is not the same as that gained through mechanical advantage.

2.4.1 Construction

The torque converter has the same parts as a fluid coupling: an impeller, a turbine, and a fluid housing plus the additional stator and one-way clutch as shown in Figure 2–10. As you can see in the illustration, the shape of the impeller and turbine is slightly different, with part of the inner portion being removed to make room for the stator. The stator mounts on a one-way clutch that is splined to the reaction shaft, which is an extension of the oil pump housing. The vanes in the impeller and turbine are curved to improve fluid flow. The curved vanes cause an acceleration of fluid flow in the impeller and improve torque transfer in the turbine. The vanes of the stator are curved in the opposite direction to redirect flow back into the impeller (Figure 2–11).

A device called a guide ring has also been added to improve the vortex flow. The guide ring looks like a donut sliced in half.

A hub is attached to the back of the fluid housing, which engages with and drives the transmission oil pump. In this way, whenever the engine is

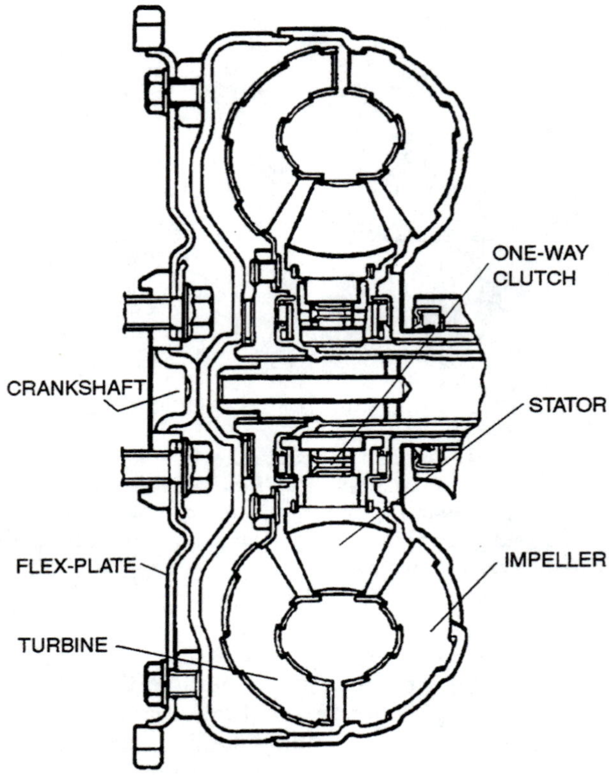

FIGURE 2–10 The components of the torque converter are the impeller, turbine, fluid housing, stator, and one-way clutch. (Reprinted with permission of General Motors Corporation)

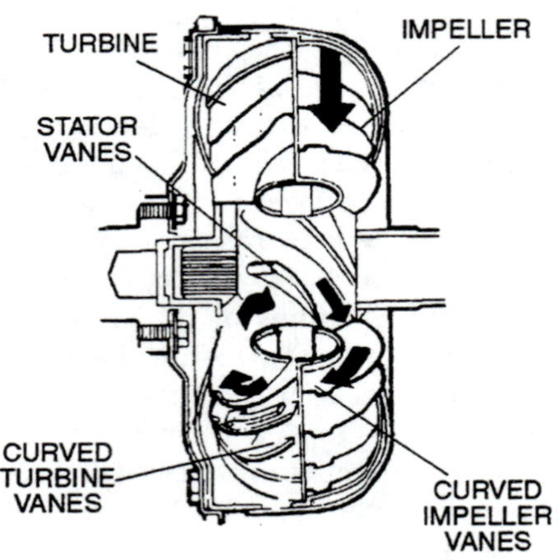

FIGURE 2–11 In a torque converter the impeller and turbine vanes are curved to increase flow rate from the impeller and to create more reaction surface on the turbine vanes. The stator provides a new reaction surface and redirects the vortex flow to allow easy reentry into the impeller.

running the transmission will have flow and pressure in the hydraulic system.

2.4.2 Function

The torque converter has two basic functions in addition to the functions listed for the fluid couplings. Those are to increase the engine torque at slow vehicle speeds and to provide high-efficiency fluid coupling at higher speeds. Later-model torque converters also have a converter clutch device that creates a mechanical direct drive through the converter at vehicle cruising speeds to improve fuel mileage. Each type of converter clutch device is covered in detail later in this chapter.

2.4.3 Fluid Movement

The movement of hydraulic fluid in a torque converter is basically the same as the movement in fluid coupling. At a low speed ratio there is high vortex flow and low rotary flow. As the speed ratio increases, the vortex decreases and the rotary flow increases until at a high speed ratio there is maximum rotary flow with only a small amount of vortex flow remaining. During high vortex flow, heat is generated in the fluid because of the speed difference between the impeller and turbine. If not controlled, this heat will cause fluid deterioration. This process is explained in Chapter 4.

The path of the fluid flow has changed somewhat from that of the fluid coupling. The curved vanes in the impeller improve the pumping action to provide greater velocity to the fluid as it leaves the impeller. The curve in the vanes of the turbine cause the fluid to change direction of travel drastically through the turbine (Figure 2–12).

A basic principle of hydraulics states that the more the direction of fluid flow is changed, the greater the force transferred to the surface that changed the flow direction. So by curving the vanes, more torque is transferred. After the fluid leaves the turbine, it flows into the stator, which during torque increase is stationary. The vanes of the stator change the direction of fluid flow again so that as the fluid leaves the stator it can reenter the impeller to start the process once more.

2.4.4 Stator Action

The stator is mounted on a one-way clutch that allows the stator to rotate freely in one direction while preventing rotation, or "locking up," in the opposite direction (Figure 2–13). The center race of the one-way clutch is splined to the stator support,

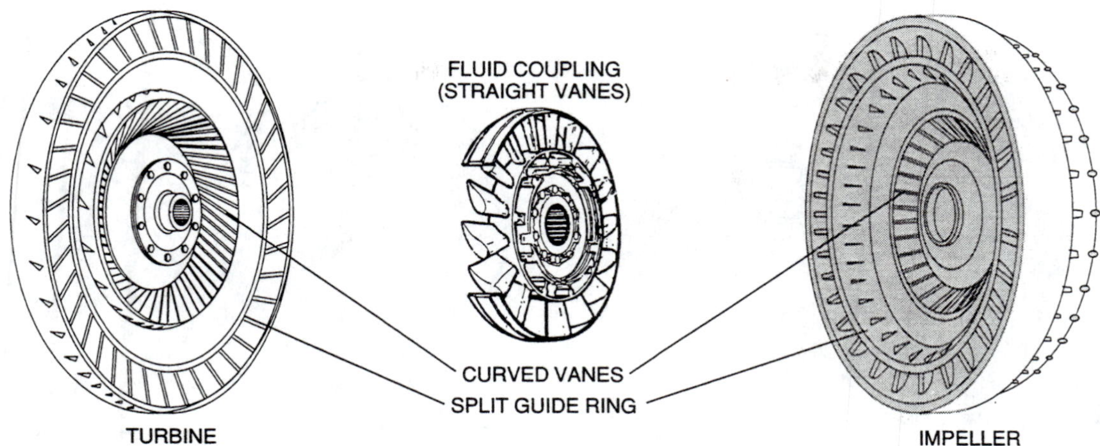

FIGURE 2–12 The curved vanes in the torque converter turbine absorb more hydraulic force than could be absorbed by the straight vanes in the fluid coupling.

which extends from the transmission oil pump. The outer race of the one-way clutch is attached to the stator by a press fit.

2.4.5 Torque Increase

The vanes of the stator are curved similar to those of the turbine but in the opposite direction. As the vortex oil flow leaves the turbine it strikes the face of the stator vanes, which changes the direction of flow by approximately 90° (Figure 2–14). The force applied to the stator tries to push the vanes back, but the one-way clutch prevents rotation in that direction. In effect, this gives the vortex flow a stationary surface to push against which in turn increases the amount of force transferred into the turbine. This is how, simply by adding a stator to a fluid coupling, it becomes a torque converter which will increase the torque output.

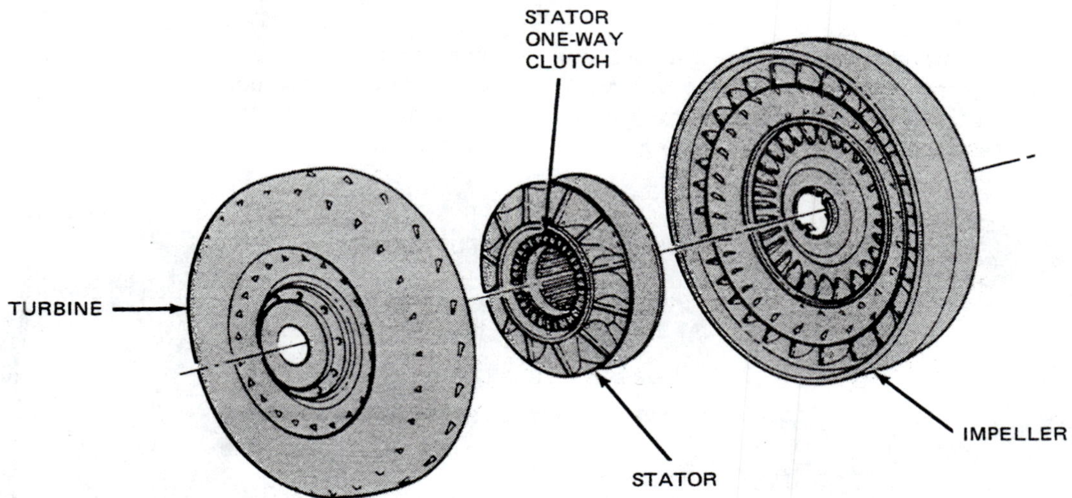

FIGURE 2–13 The stator and its one-way clutch are located between the impeller and the turbine. The stationary inner race of the one-way clutch is splined to the stator support. (Courtesy of Ford)

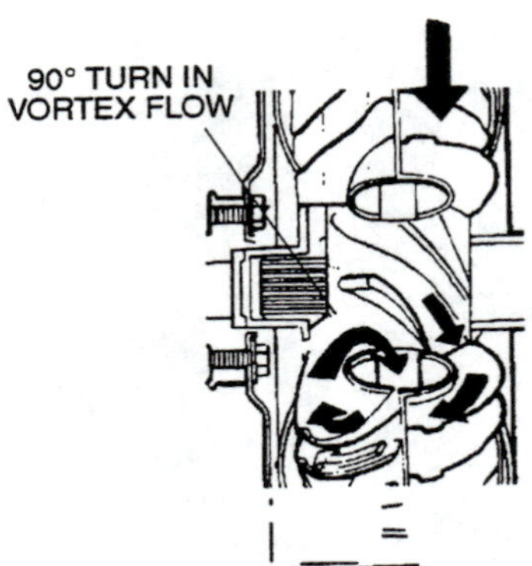

FIGURE 2–14 As the vortex flow leaves the turbine, it is forced to make a 90° turn by the stator vanes. (Courtesy of Ford)

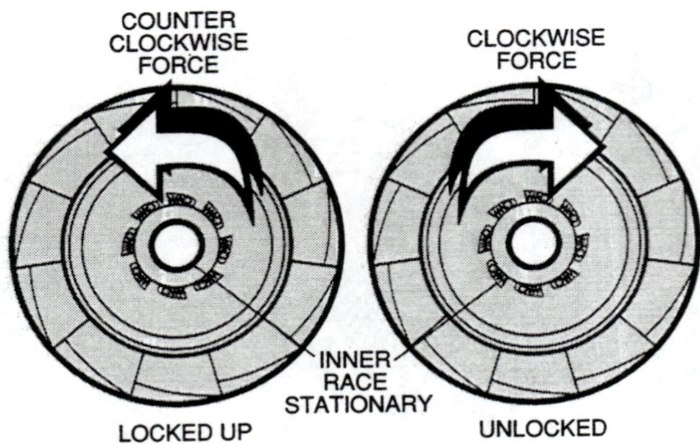

FIGURE 2–16 In the stator shown at the left, force is being applied to the stator in a counterclockwise direction, which causes the one-way clutch to lock up. On the right, the force is reversed and the stator rotates freely. (Courtesy of Ford)

2.4.6 One-Way Clutch

Because of its design, the one-way clutch will turn freely in one direction and lock up in the other direction (Figure 2–15). The preceding description of how torque is increased has dealt only with what is happening during vortex flow when there is a low speed ratio. As the speed of the turbine increases, so does the rotary flow. When the torque converter reaches a speed ratio of 85 to 90%, the rotary flow is now pushing on the back of the stator vanes (Figure 2–16).

This force is being applied in the direction that will cause the one-way clutch to turn freely. The stator will now rotate with the impeller and turbine to reduce the resistance to rotary flow. As long as the speed ratio of the torque converter remains high, the stator will continue to rotate with the rotary flow. But as soon as the speed ratio drops and the vortex flow increases, the stator is forced to move in the opposite direction, causing the one-way clutch to lock up.

2.4.7 Variable-Pitch Stators

The torque converter stators that have been discussed up to now have had a fixed blade angle, with the stator cast as one piece. To increase the performance of some earlier transmissions, movable stator vanes were developed (Figure 2–17). By increasing the angle of the stator blades, a greater torque increase was achieved, providing faster acceleration. But while this improved the acceleration performance, the increased stator blade angle reduced the engine fuel economy. So to preserve good economy the stator blade angle is decreased during part throttle cruising (Figure 2–18).

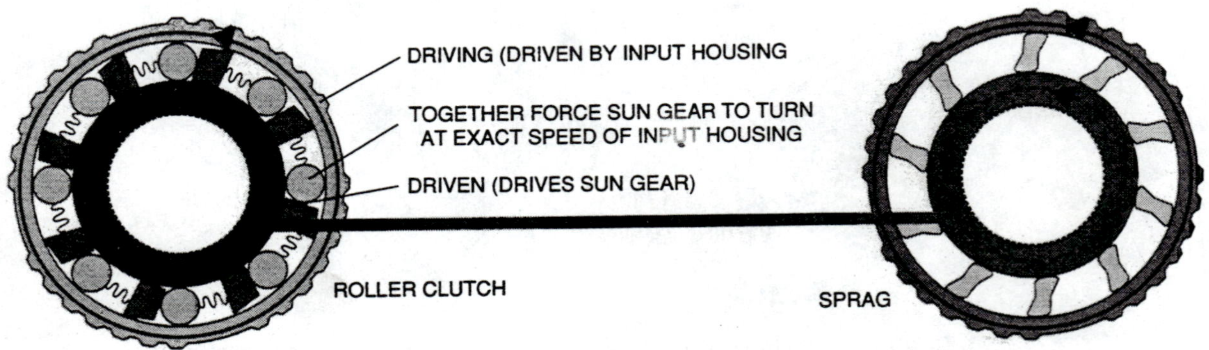

FIGURE 2–15 The one-way clutch, both roller and sprag types, allows rotation when turned in one direction, but locks up when turned the other direction.

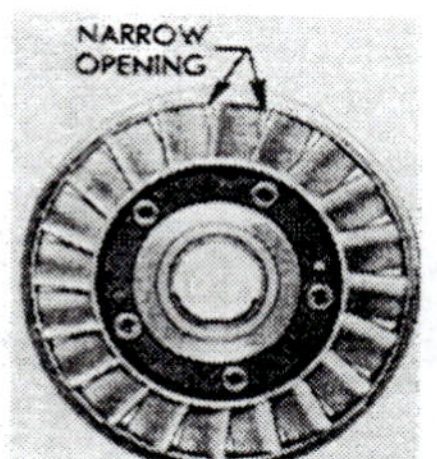

FIGURE 2–17 This variable-pitch stator's vanes are set for maximum torque increase. (Reprinted with permission of General Motors Corporation)

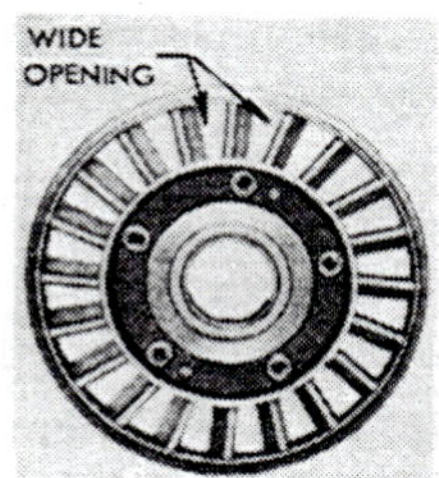

FIGURE 2–18 The stator vanes are now set for maximum economy, causing less change of vortex flow. (Reprinted with permission of General Motors Corporation)

To build a stator that could change the angle of the blades, or have variable pitch, requires a movable blade that pivots at its leading edge and the necessary linkage to change the blade angle (Figure 2–19). Different types of control systems are used to move the blade settings, including hydraulic, mechanical, and electrical. Variable-pitch stators have been used in the past, but at this time no manufacturers use this device in their automatic transmissions.

2.5 CONVERTER CLUTCH DEVICES

Due to the basic principles of fluid power transfer, a 100% speed ratio cannot be achieved. The turbine will always be turning slower than the impeller, which means that there is a slight loss of power through the torque converter. To avoid this loss of power and to increase fuel economy, automotive engineers developed a variety of devices known as lockup clutches that provide a mechanical connection between the input and output sections of the torque converter. These lockup devices allow the torque converter to do its job of torque multiplication at lower speed ratios, but once higher speed ratios are reached, the lockup devices are activated and provide a mechanical path for power flow. This mechanical power flow eliminates the loss of power that takes place in the hydraulic power transfer and provides a much more efficient transfer of power. Several types of converter clutch devices are currently in use. They are:

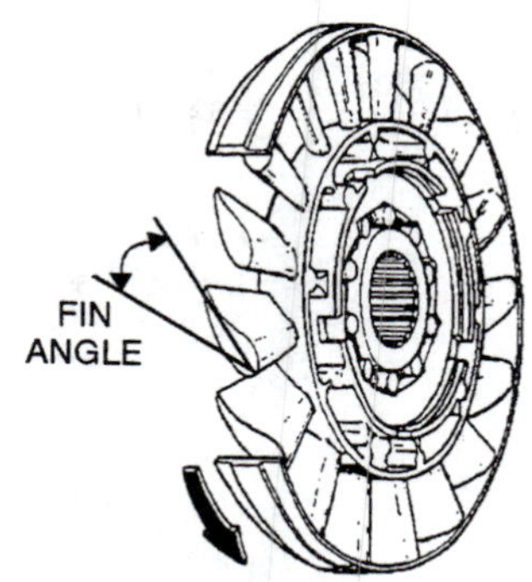

FIGURE 2–19 The variable-pitch stator has movable stator vanes that pivot at their leading edge and are controlled by mechanical linkage. (Reprinted with permission of General Motors Corporation)

1. Hydraulic lockup clutch
2. Centrifugal lockup clutch
3. Viscous converter clutch
4. Dual-output converter

2.5.1 Hydraulic Lockup Clutch

The hydraulically operated clutch is the most widely used torque converter lockup device. This converter clutch is a large pressure plate which is about the same diameter as the torque converter (Figure 2–20). A hub at the center of the pressure plate is splined to the turbine and is free to move forward and backward. The hub is connected to the pressure plate through a set of torsional springs whose job is to smooth out the engine's torsional vibrations. A friction material much like that used on the clutch discs in the automatic transmission is bonded to the front surface of the plate in two areas, around the splined hub and in the outer inch of the face. The outer friction surface provides the path for the mechanical power flow, while the center friction area adds support to the plate to prevent flexing during clutch application. Some manufacturers use friction material only around the outer portion of the plate, while one manufacturer has used a free-floating friction disc which is

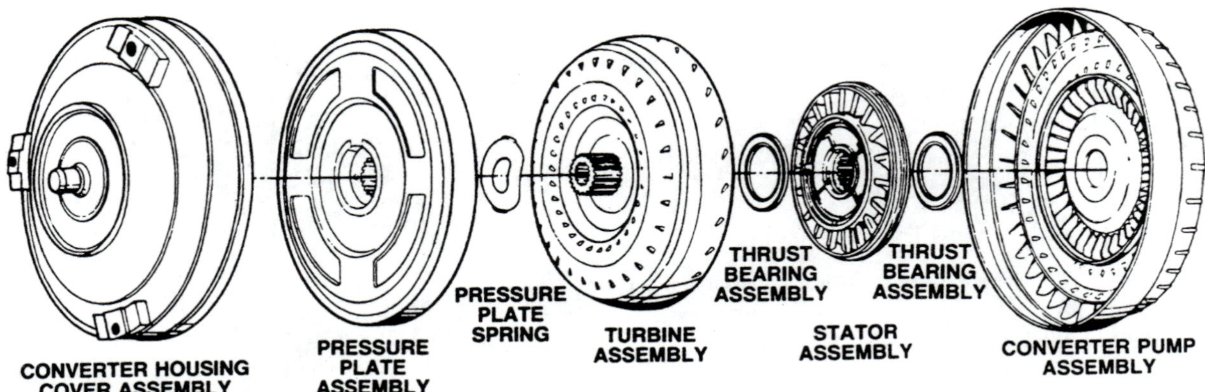

FIGURE 2–20 Components of a typical hydraulic lockup clutch. The pressure plate assembly provides the ability to "lock up" the converter. (Reprinted with permission of General Motors Corporation)

held in place by the pressure plate. The friction surfaces of the converter clutch are forced against the inside surface of the torque converter housing cover by hydraulic pressure when the clutch is applied (Figure 2–21). When the oil that is used to fill the torque converter is directed to flow through a passage that empties into the converter behind the converter clutch plate, the oil pressure, which is approximately 130 psi, forces the plate to slip forward

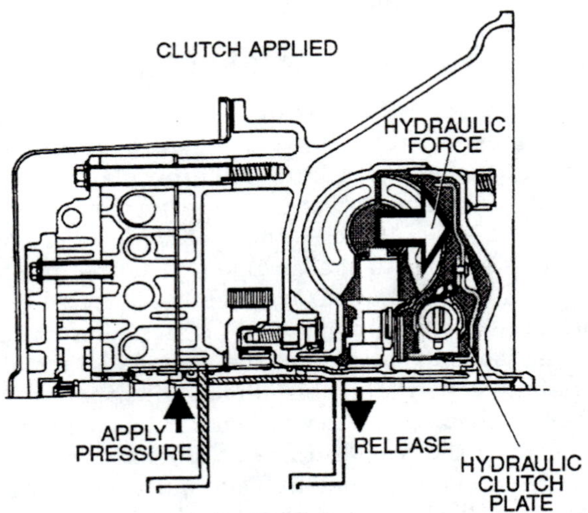

FIGURE 2–21 To apply the clutch, fluid enters the torque converter behind the pressure plate. The hydraulic pressure pushes the plate forward until it contacts the housing cover, providing a mechanical path for the power flow. Any fluid trapped in front of the plate is exhausted through a passageway in the turbine shaft.

on its splines and be pressed against the converter cover, engaging the lockup clutch. By multiplying the hydraulic pressure times the surface area of the pressure plate, you find that the total force being applied to the lockup clutch is over 10,000 lb.

To release the converter clutch, the same oil pressure is redirected to flow through passages that will empty in front of the converter clutch. The oil pressure then forces the plate to slide backward on its splines, moving it out of contact with the converter cover (Figure 2–22). Some designs also use a return spring to assist the release pressure in disengaging the plate.

The apply and release oil is controlled by a system of hydraulic valves located in the valve body and on later-model vehicles is aided by the computer, which operates clutch control solenoids. The control systems are explained further in Chapter 4.

2.5.2 Centrifugal Lockup Clutch

The centrifugal converter clutch assembly is constructed in the following manner. A one-way clutch called the coasting one-way clutch is attached to the turbine hub on its front surface between the turbine and the converter cover. The damper assembly is attached to the outer race of the coasting one-way clutch. The clutch plate is different from the hydraulic converter clutch in that it does not move backward or forward to apply or release the clutch. Instead, the clutch plate has a series of centrifugal clutch shoes attached to its outer diameter. The outermost surface of these shoes is covered with a friction pad.

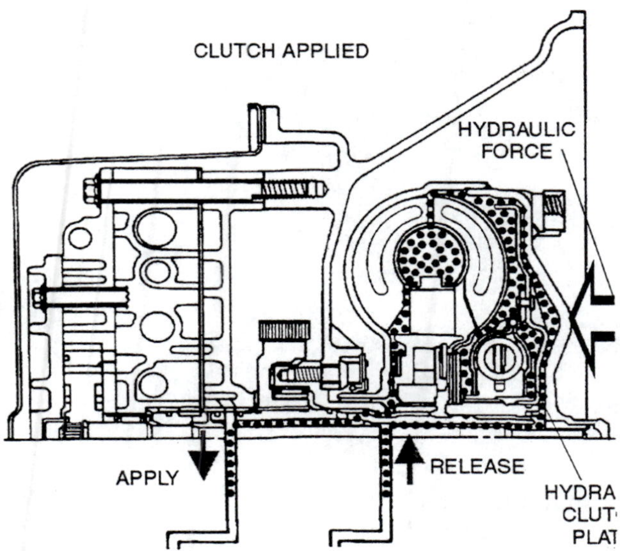

FIGURE 2–22 To release the clutch, hydraulic pressure is routed to the front side of the plate through the turbine shaft passage, which pushes the plate away from the cover. The fluid then fills the converter and exits through the same passage used for application pressure. (Reprinted with permission of General Motors Corporation)

The centrifugal converter clutch operates in the following way. As the engine speed increases, the impeller pumps more fluid, increasing the vortex flow within the converter. The fluid movement causes the centrifugal clutch plate to rotate along with the turbine. As the speed approaches 900 rpm, centrifugal force causes the clutch shoes to move out and come in contact with the converter housing cover, providing a mechanical path for power transfer.

The power is transmitted through the shoes, clutch plate damper springs, coasting one-way clutch (which is locked up), turbine, and into the *turbine shaft.* As long as the vehicle is under power, the coasting one-way clutch will remain locked up, but as soon as the engine's rpm level drops, the clutch will freewheel. If the load on the vehicle is increased greatly, the centrifugal shoes will slip, allowing the torque converter to increase the torque output through its hydraulic drive. The centrifugal converter clutch does not have a separate control system but relies on its basic design to determine under which conditions it will lock up. The two conditions affecting the clutch are converter rotation, or speed, and vehicle load. The centrifugal clutch is engaged under the following conditions: high turbine rpm value and a light vehicle load, which then provides a mechanical path for the power flow.

2.5.3 Viscous Converter Clutch

The viscous converter clutch serves the same function as that of the other lockup clutches and operates basically the same as the hydraulic lockup clutch, except for one major difference. Instead of the spring-mounted hub used in the hydraulic clutches to dampen vibration and cushion the apply of the clutch, the viscous converter clutch uses a viscous silicone fluid to transfer the power from the disc to the hub. The fluid provides a smooth application of the clutch and prevents the hard shift feel that some converter lockup clutches have. The silicone fluid used to transfer the power cannot provide a total lockup, slipping at about a 2% rate.

The apply and release of the viscous clutch are controlled by the vehicle's electronic control module, which regulates hydraulic pressures that provide the application or release force. The viscous clutch can apply at 25 mph in second gear if the transmission oil temperature is below 200°F. With the oil temperature between 200 and 315°F the clutch will apply at around 38 mph. At temperatures above 315°F, the viscous clutch will not apply, to protect the transmission from overheating. The viscous converter clutch is shown in Figure 2–23.

2.5.4 Dual-Output Converter

One thing common to most torque converters, with or without converter lockup clutches, is the fact that they have one power output connection. This is usually called the turbine shaft or transmission input shaft. In an effort to develop a different means of mechanical power flow through the torque converter, Ford Motor Company has designed dual-output converters for the ATX and AOD transmissions. The ATX uses both the turbine shaft and the intermediate shaft as power input into the transmission, while the AOD uses the turbine shaft and the direct-drive shaft as input.

1. ATX Converter

The converter used in the ATX front-wheel-drive transaxle uses a planetary gear set to provide the mechanical power flow path. The gear that the transmission is in determines the power path in the converter. In first gear and reverse the output of the converter is 100% hydraulic, in second gear it is 38% hydraulic and 62% mechanical, and in third gear it is 7% hydraulic and 93% mechanical. The choice of hydraulic or mechanical paths is controlled by clutch and band applications in the transmission, which also controls the gear selection. The parts of the ATX dual-output converter

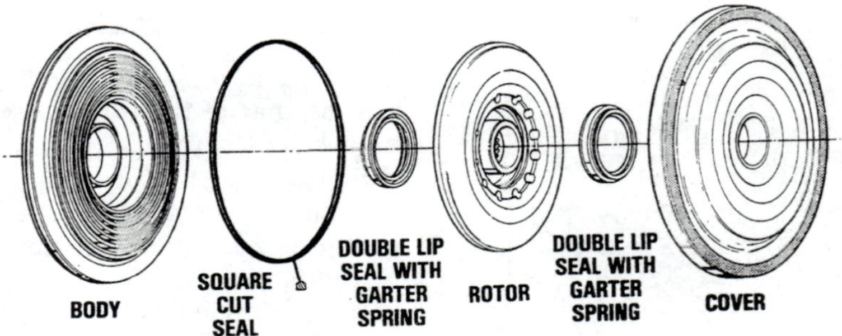

FIGURE 2–23 Components of a viscous converter clutch, together with a cross-sectional drawing of the clutch. The engine torque is transmitted through a viscous silicone fluid to provide the smoothest transfer possible. (Reprinted with permission of General Motors Corporation)

are shown in Figure 2–24. The dual power inputs of the ATX transmission are described in Section 11.8.

2. AOD Converter

The AOD transmission that was designed for large-engine rear-wheel-drive vehicles also uses a dual-output converter. The two output drives are the turbine shaft and the direct-drive shaft, shown in Figure 2–25. In reverse gear, first gear, and second gear, the transmission receives all the power input from the hydraulic path through the turbine shaft. When the transmission shifts into third gear, 40% of the power input is hydraulic and 60% is mechan-

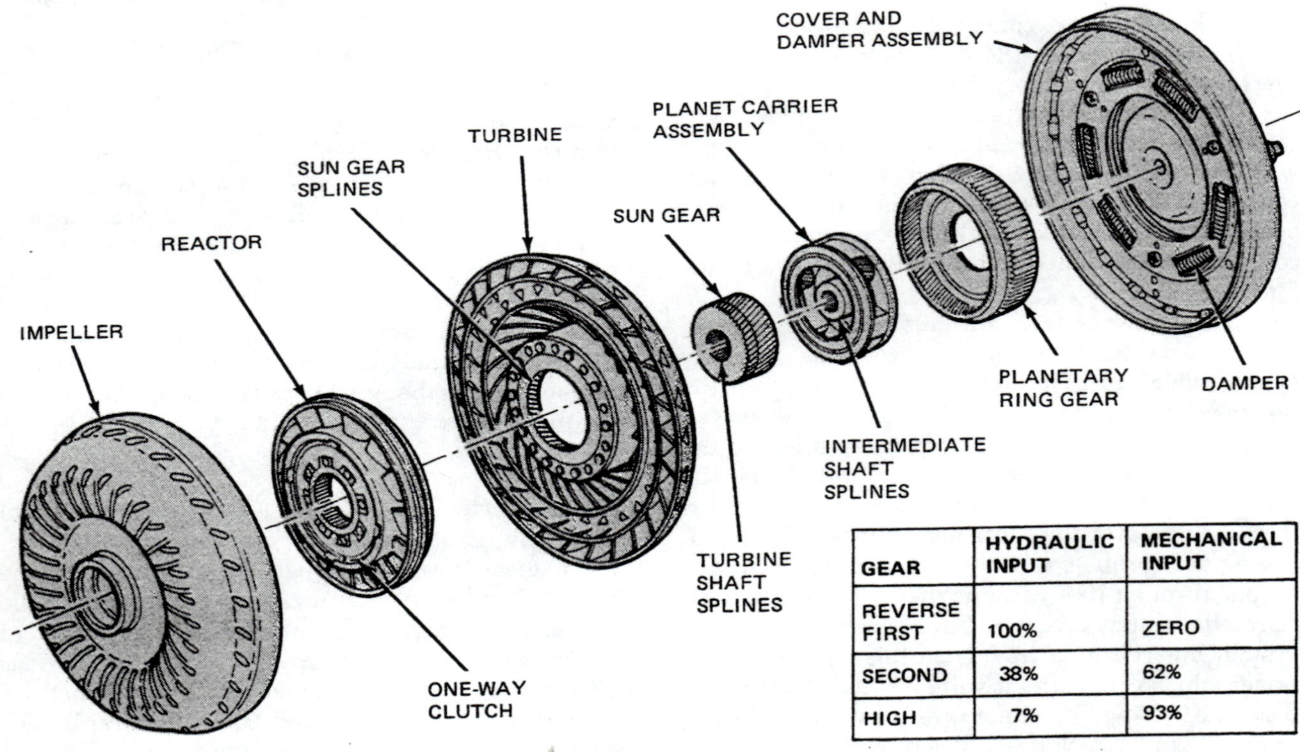

GEAR	HYDRAULIC INPUT	MECHANICAL INPUT
REVERSE FIRST	100%	ZERO
SECOND	38%	62%
HIGH	7%	93%

FIGURE 2–24 Parts of the Ford ATX dual-output torque converter. This converter drives both the turbine shaft and the intermediate shaft as power input to the transmission. (Courtesy of Ford)

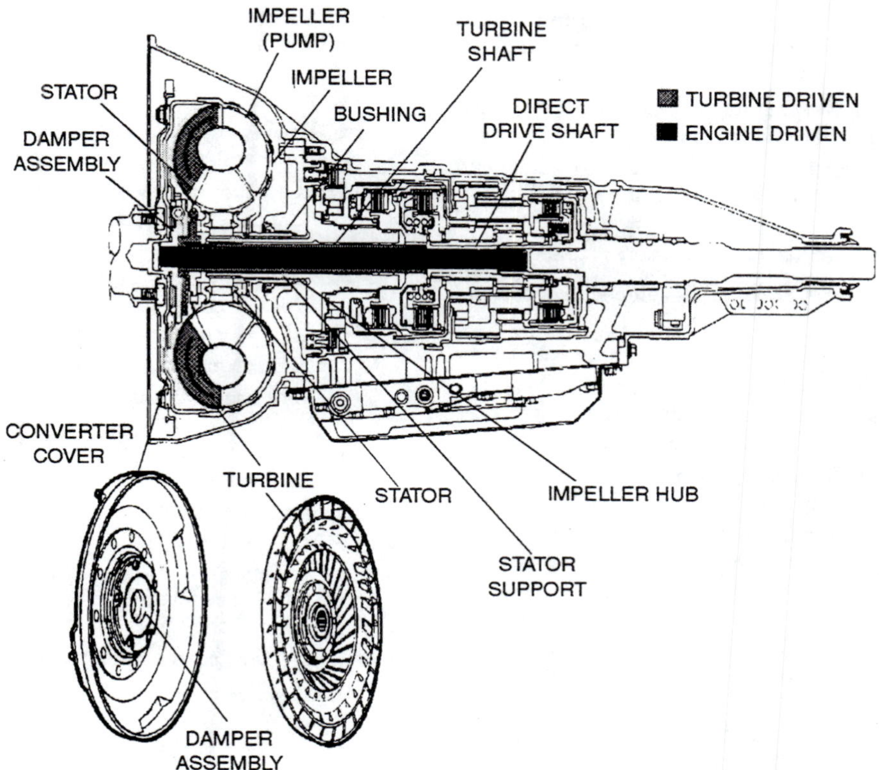

FIGURE 2–25 The Ford AOD torque converter is a dual-output converter that drives the turbine shaft with the turbine hydraulically and drives the direct-drive shaft through a damper assembly mounted to the converter clutch mechanically. (Courtesy of Ford)

ical through the direct-drive shaft. Once the transmission shifts into fourth gear, which is overdrive, all the power input is delivered through the mechanical power path. To learn more about these unique torque converters, refer to the Ford service manual covering these transmissions.

SUMMARY

Fluid Couplings

- A fluid coupling will act as a flywheel or an automatic clutch, dampen vibrations, and transfer torque.
- A fluid coupling has three main parts: the turbine, the impeller, and the fluid housing.
- A split guide ring is used to minimize turbulence in the fluid.
- As the impeller rotates, centrifugal action forces fluid toward the turbine.
- The force of the fluid striking the vanes of the turbine causes it to turn.
- The relationship of the speeds of the impeller and turbine is called the speed ratio.
- The two types of fluid flow are vortex and rotary.
- A fluid coupling can only transfer torque; it cannot increase it.

Torque Converters

- By adding a stator and one-way clutch to a fluid coupling, it becomes a torque converter.
- The torque converter performs the same job as the fluid coupling and it increases the engine's torque.
- The impeller and turbine vanes are curved to improve flow.
- The curved vanes of the turbine allow more force to be transferred from the impeller to the turbine.
- The vanes of the stator provide a stationary surface for the vortex flow to push against.

- The stator is mounted on a one-way clutch that can turn one direction but locks up the other direction.
- As rotary flow takes over, the stator will turn with the impeller and turbine.
- Variable-pitch stators have been used which can change the angle of the stator vanes.

Converter Clutch Devices

- Converter clutches were developed to improve fuel economy.
- Converter clutches provide a mechanical power flow path through the torque converter.
- The hydraulic lockup clutch utilizes hydraulic pressure to apply and release the clutch.
- The centrifugal lockup clutch utilizes centrifugal force to apply the clutch.
- The viscous converter clutch is similar to the hydraulic lockup clutch but utilizes a viscous fluid drive to smooth its application.
- The dual-output converters are not true *converter lockup clutches,* but they do the same job in providing a mechanical flow path through the converter.
- Converter lockup clutches are engaged only in mid- to high-speed ranges.
- Most converter lockup clutches are controlled by the vehicle computer system.

SELF-TEST

Before going on to the next chapter, complete the self-test according to your instructor's directions. Read carefully and choose the best answer.

1. The main parts of a fluid coupling are ________.
   a. A stator and a turbine
   b. A turbine and an impeller
   c. A stator and an impeller
   d. A stator and a one-way clutch
2. The two types of fluid flow are ________.
   a. Rotary and directional
   b. Rotary and turbulent
   c. Vortex and directional
   d. Vortex and rotary
3. Speed ratio refers to the difference in speed between the engine and ________.
   a. Impeller
   b. Stator
   c. Turbine
   d. None of the above
4. Technician A says that a one-way clutch will lock up when turned one direction. Technician B says that a one-way clutch will freewheel when turned one direction. Who is right?
   a. A
   b. B
   c. Both A and B
   d. Neither A nor B
5. The stator is used to redirect fluid back into the ________.
   a. Impeller
   b. Turbine
   c. Fluid housing
   d. All of the above
6. During torque increase the stator is ________.
   a. Rotating with turbine
   b. Not in use
   c. Turning very slowly
   d. Held stationary
7. The most vortex flow occurs at ________.
   a. Zero speed ratio
   b. 50% speed ratio
   c. 100% speed ratio
   d. None of the above
8. Converter lockup clutches are designed to improve ________.
   a. Acceleration
   b. Thermal efficiency
   c. Fuel economy
   d. All of the above
9. Converter lockup clutches provide an ________ power flow path through the torque converter.
   a. Hydraulic
   b. Mechanical
   c. Electrical
   d. Simple
10. The viscous converter clutch operates basically the same as the ________.
    a. Hydraulic clutch
    b. Centrifugal clutch
    c. Dual-output converter
    d. None of the above
11. Converter lockup clutches are controlled and applied by ________.
    a. Hydraulic pressure
    b. Mechanical action
    c. Computer control
    d. All of the above

GLOSSARY

centrifugal force force generated by a rotating mass outward from a center of rotation.

centrifugal lockup clutch converter clutch that uses centrifugal force to apply the clutch. This type of clutch is used in some Ford transaxles.

converter lockup clutch device that will provide a mechanical power flow path through a torque converter when applied.

dual-output converter torque converter that has two power output connections.

fluid coupling assembly in which power is transmitted from one turbine wheel to another through a liquid medium.

hydraulic lockup clutch (hydraulic clutch) manual transmission clutch design in which fluid transmits force to operate the clutch.

impeller pumping member of a fluid coupling or torque converter. It is rotated to pump fluid toward the turbine.

90% speed ratio reflects the efficiency of a fluid drive: impeller speed versus turbine speed.

one-way clutch device that permits rotation in one direction only. The one-way clutch is composed of a set of rollers that roll on an inner and outer race. The rollers permit rotation in one direction, but jam the races and prevent rotation in the other direction.

resultant force combined effect of vortex and rotor flow in the torque converter. The term is used to describe the angle of force acting on the turbine.

rolling inertia (rolling resistance) resistance against which the engine must drive a vehicle over a road surface.

rotary flow flow of fluid inside a torque converter that follows the same direction as the impeller and turbine movement. Rotary flow is present at high speed ratios.

stall speed in automatic transmission applications, stall speed is the maximum engine rpm level with the transmission engaged, the vehicle stationary, and the carburetor throttle valve wide open.

stator small hub to which vanes are attached in a radial position. It is placed so that oil leaving the torque converter turbine strikes the stator vanes and is redirected into the impeller at the most effective angle for efficient operation. The stator makes torque multiplication possible.

thrust washer washer designed to take up end thrust and prevent excessive end play.

turbine designates the output or driven member of a fluid coupling or fluid torque converter.

turbine shaft shaft that is splined to the turbine and serves as the power input to the gear train.

variable-pitch stator stator with movable vanes. The angle of the stator vanes can be changed to provide more power flow or more efficiency.

vibration damper device mounted on the front end of the crankshaft to dampen out harmonic vibrations. Also called a harmonic balancer.

viscous converter clutch converter clutch that utilizes a silicone fluid to transmit the power to provide a smooth operation.

vortex flow fluid force generated by the centrifugal pumping action of an impeller or pump, cycling the fluid between the impeller and turbine members. Vortex flow is present at low speed ratios.

zero speed ratio refers to the speed at which the impeller and turbine are turning in relation to each other. Zero speed ratio means that one is stationary while the other is turning.

◀ Chapter 3 ▶

GEAR TRAINS

INTRODUCTION

In Chapter 2 you learned how engine torque is transferred from the engine to the transmission and how it is increased. You also learned that the torque converter delivers the torque to the transmission input shaft or shafts—but that was as far as we went. In this chapter we begin where we left off and explain the gear train totally. All the individual components of a gear train are fully described from the standpoint of construction and function. The components fall into major groups, which include planetary gear sets, coupling and holding devices, and transaxle final drives.

After an explanation of planetary gear sets and coupling and holding devices, we proceed to study how the parts work together to form a gear train. Examples of two-, three-, and four-speed gear trains, using both Simpson and Ravigneaux planetary designs, are described in detail to illustrate how different gear trains can be achieved using the same basic components. Understanding the power flow of these examples will provide a foundation for comprehending the gear train operation of any automatic transmission/transaxle.

To explain the entire gear train of the transaxle, the final drive components must be included; therefore, in this chapter we also study the major types of transaxle final drive systems.

3.1 PERFORMANCE OBJECTIVES

After studying this chapter, you should have fulfilled the following performance objectives by being able to:

1. Discuss the simple planetary gear set, naming its parts and describing how it is constructed.
2. Explain the five modes of operation possible with a simple planetary gear set and how they are achieved.
3. Describe the difference between a Simpson gear set and a Ravigneaux gear set.
4. Explain the purpose of coupling and holding devices in an automatic transmission.
5. Discuss the power flow in all gears through a two-speed Powerglide transmission.
6. Discuss the power flow in all gears through a three-speed Torque Flite transmission.
7. Discuss the power flow in all gears through a four-speed Ford AOD transmission.
8. Complete all the competency objectives listed for this chapter.
9. Complete the self-test with at least the minimum score required by your instructor.

3.2 COMPETENCY OBJECTIVES

The competency objectives are different from the performance objectives in being more job related. The automotive terms must be well understood so that the theory will be clear. The terms are used to describe the service procedures outlined in Part 2. The competency tasks are related to job skills needed to perform service and repair procedures and should be understood thoroughly.

3.2.1 Automotive Terms

The following list may include terms that are unfamiliar to you. Read the terms, then note their definitions as you study the chapter.

cantilever linkage	driven member
clutch and band chart	driving member
clutch discs	flexible band
clutch drum	friction material
clutch piston	gear reduction
coupling device	graduated rod linkage
direct drive	holding device
double-acting servo	input member

multidisc clutch
neutral
one-way clutch
output member
overdrive
pawl
planetary carrier
planetary gear set
pressure plate
Ravigneaux gear set
reaction member
reverse
rigid band
ring gear
roller clutch
selective fit
servo
Simpson gear set
sprag clutch
sun gear
transaxle final drive
wave spring

3.2.2 Competency Tasks

The competency tasks listed here are related directly to knowledge or skills needed to become a successful automatic transmission/transaxle technician. Be sure to complete all the tasks before going to Chapter 4.

1. Name the parts of a simple planetary gear set.
2. Describe how a simple planetary gear set is constructed.
3. Explain from memory how neutral is achieved in a simple planetary gear set, listing the function of each member.
4. Explain from memory how gear reduction is achieved in a simple planetary gear set, listing the function of each member.
5. Explain from memory how direct drive is achieved in a simple planetary gear set, listing the function of each member.
6. Explain from memory how reverse is achieved in a simple planetary gear set, listing the function of each member.
7. Explain from memory how overdrive is achieved in a simple planetary gear set, listing the function of each member.
8. Describe the construction of a Simpson gear set.
9. Describe the construction of a Ravigneaux gear set.
10. Describe four types of coupling and holding devices used in an automatic transmission.
11. Describe the power flow in each gear of a two-speed Powerglide transmission using a Ravigneaux gear set. Include a clutch and band chart in your description.
12. Describe the power flow in each gear of a three-speed Torque Flite transmission using a Simpson gear set. Include a clutch and band chart in your description.
13. Describe the power flow in each gear of a four-speed Ford AOD transmission using a Ravigneaux gear set. Include a clutch and band chart in your description.
14. Describe three types of final drive gear sets used in transaxles.

3.3 PLANETARY GEARS

To be able to understand and diagnose an automatic transmission fully, you must first understand how a simple planetary gear set works. You must learn the five basic gear functions of a simple planetary gear set and how they are achieved. What a driving, driven, or *reaction member* is and how the Simpson and Ravigneaux gear sets function are knowledge you must have to understand how an automatic transmission works.

In Chapter 1 you were introduced to a *planetary gear set,* shown in Figure 3–1. The three parts, or members of the set—the *ring gear,* the planet pinion gears and carrier, and the *sun gear*—can all serve different functions. Any part could be the *driving member,* the *driven member,* or the *reaction member.* The driving member is the power input, the driven member is the power output, and the reaction member is held stationary while the other members rotate and react against it (Figure 3–2). The rules that cover planetary gear operation are important—remember them.

Rule 1: One planetary member must be coupled to the input shaft.

Rule 2: One planetary member must be coupled to the output shaft.

Rule 3: The remaining member must be coupled to the input shaft or held stationary.

The five gear functions of planetary gear set that you will study are *neutral, gear reduction, direct drive, reverse,* and *overdrive.* How each of these functions is achieved is discussed in the following sections.

3.3.1 Neutral

As we mentioned above, the parts of the planetary gear set can serve as either input, output, or reaction members to provide different gear functions. To interrupt the power flow and create a neutral condition in a planetary gear set, the reaction member is released and allowed to rotate freely (Figure

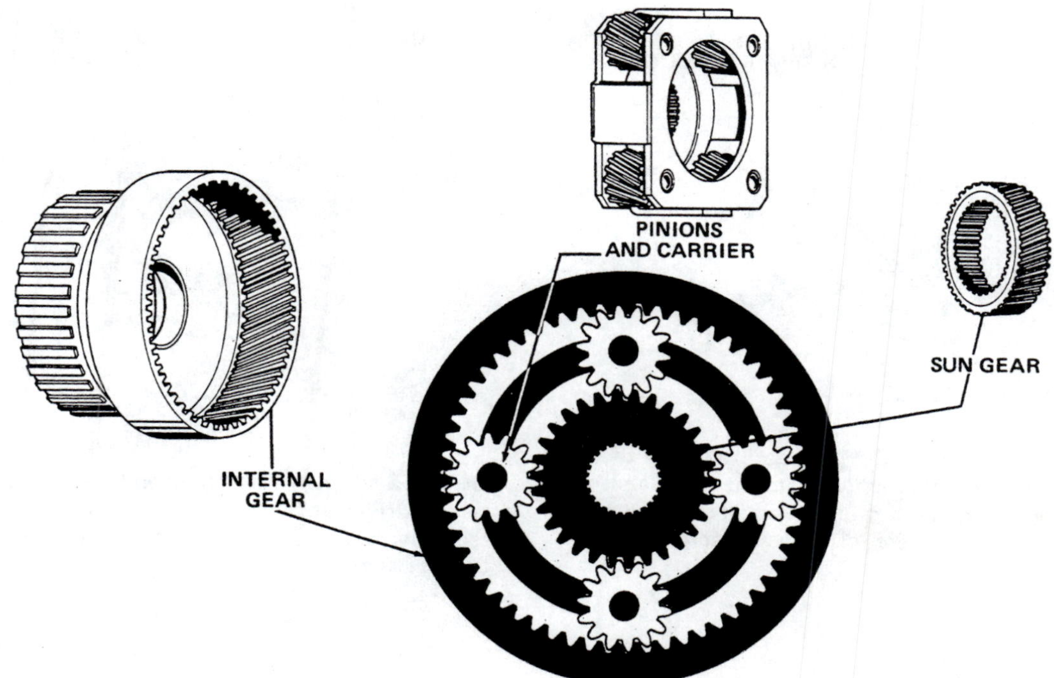

FIGURE 3–1 The simple planetary gear set consists of the ring gear, the planet pinions and carrier, and the sun gear. (Reprinted with permission of General Motors Corporation)

3–3). The input is turning but without the reaction member to rotate against power will not transfer to the *output member*. The only action that will occur is the rotation of the reaction member.

3.3.2 Gear Reduction

Any combination of planetary gear members that uses the planet carrier as the output will cause a gear reduction. Two combinations of members are possible, but only one is used because it provides a desirable gear ratio. With the ring gear as the *input member* and the planet carrier as the output member, the sun gear is held to become the reaction member. As the input ring gear rotates, it causes

POWER INPUT MEMBER	=	DRIVING MEMBER
POWER OUTPUT MEMBER	=	DRIVEN MEMBER
REACTION MEMBER	=	STATIONARY MEMBER

FIGURE 3–2 As shown, the power input and driving members are the same, the power output and the driven member are the same, and the reaction member is held stationary.

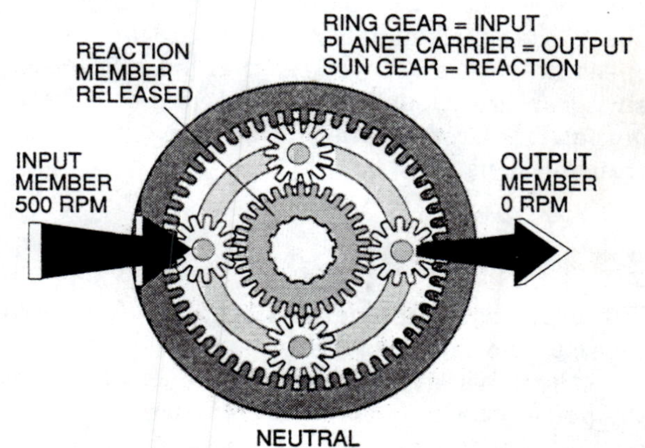

FIGURE 3–3 When the reaction member is not held stationary but is free to rotate, the gear set is in neutral. (Reprinted with permission of General Motors Corporation)

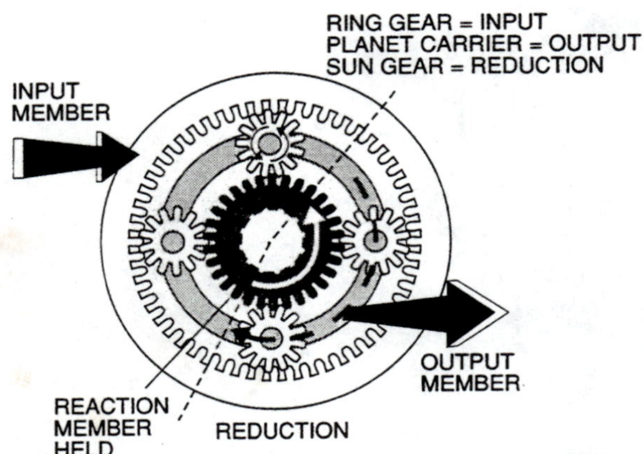

FIGURE 3–4 With the ring gear as input and the sun gear as the stationary reaction member, the planet carrier is driven at a reduced rate, causing a gear reduction. (Reprinted with permission of General Motors Corporation)

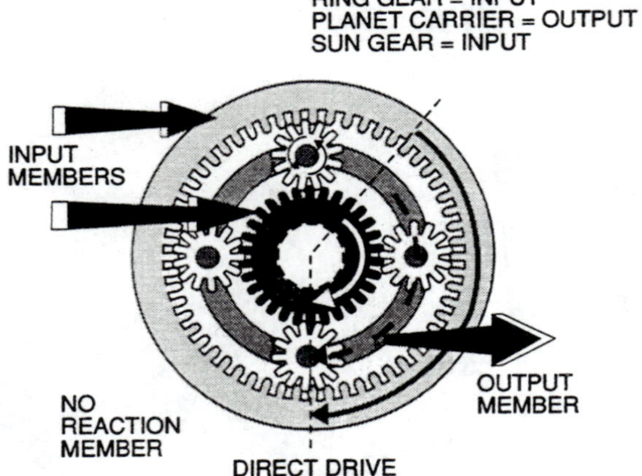

FIGURE 3–5 Any time two members of a planetary gear set are driven at the same speed, the unit will provide direct drive. (Reprinted with permission of General Motors Corporation)

the planet gears to rotate on their shafts and walk around the stationary sun gear. This forces the planet carrier to rotate in the same direction as the input ring gear, but at a slower speed, causing gear reduction (Figure 3–4).

3.3.3 Direct Drive

Direct drive is easy to achieve. Whenever any two members of a planetary gear set are driven at the same speed or are connected to the same input shaft, the third member will rotate at the same speed. In Figure 3–5 you see that the ring gear and sun gear are input, leaving the planet carrier as output. This combination is used in all automatic transmissions.

3.3.4 Reverse

There are two combinations of gears that provide reverse, one giving overdrive (speed increase) and the other giving gear reduction. To obtain reverse, the planet carrier must be the reaction member and be held stationary. For reduction mode, the sun gear is the input member, with the ring gear being the output member. As the input sun gear is turned in a clockwise direction, the planet gears are driven in a counterclockwise direction because the planet carrier is being held stationary. As the planets revolve counterclockwise, they drive the ring gear in the same direction. Since the sun gear has fewer teeth than the ring gear, this mode will provide a gear reduction as well as changing the direction of rotation (Figure 3–6).

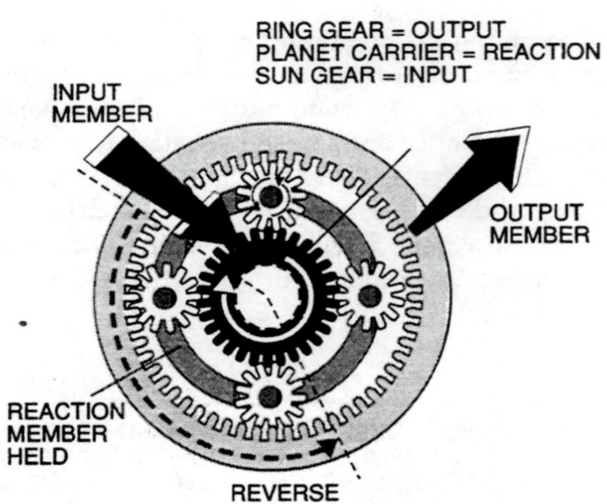

FIGURE 3–6 To achieve reverse, the sun gear is input, the ring gear is output, and the planet carrier is held stationary as the reaction member. (Reprinted with permission of General Motors Corporation)

3.3.5 Overdrive

A gear train is said to be in overdrive when the output shaft is turning faster, or at a higher rpm level, than the input shaft. The planetary gear set can provide two overdrive ratios. The most widely used ratio is achieved by using the planet carrier as the input member, the ring gear as the output, with the sun gear held as the reaction member (Figure 3–7).

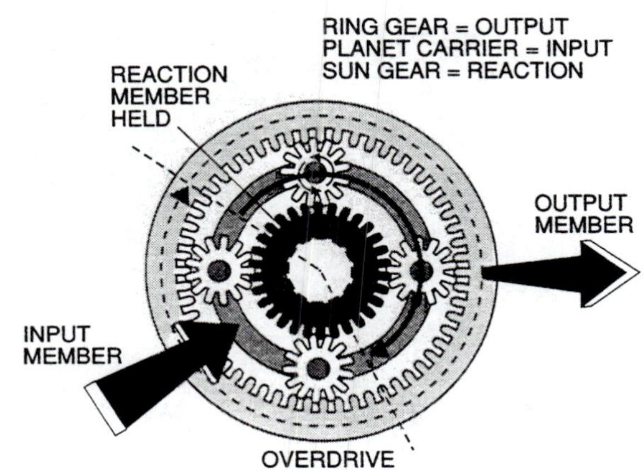

FIGURE 3–7 The most widely used overdrive ratio is achieved by having the planet carrier as input, the ring gear as output, and the sun gear held as the reaction member. (Reprinted with permission of General Motors Corporation)

3.3.6 Function Review

Figure 3–8 shows all the possible combinations of a simple planetary gear set and what drive gearing can be achieved with them. If you spend some time studying the chart, you should find the following to be true:

- The gear set is in neutral when there is no reaction member, no member being held, or no power input.
- The gear set is in reduction when the planet carrier is the output member.
- The gear set is in direct drive when any two members are coupled together or when they are driven at the same speed.
- The gear set is in reverse when the planet carrier is held stationary. The idler gear action of the planet gears causes the direction of rotation to change between the input and output members.
- The gear set is in overdrive when the planet carrier is the input member.

Study this section until you know the workings of the planetary gear set by memory. This information is the foundation for understanding power flow and gear reductions in all automatic transmissions.

3.4 SIMPSON GEAR SET

The Simpson gear set is a popular compound gear set used in automatic transmissions today. The term *compound gear set* refers to a gear set that has more members than a simple planetary gear set. In the case of the Simpson gear set, shown in Figure 3–9, we have two ring gears, two planet carriers, and one sun gear, which is shared by both planet carriers. To transmit power through the Simpson gear set, we must be able to connect and disconnect various members of the gear set to the input shaft. We also need to hold and release other

GEAR ACTION	INPUT MEMBER	OUTPUT MEMBER	REACTION
NEUTRAL	ANY	ANY	RELEASED
GEAR REDUCTION			
HIGH RATIO	RING	CARRIER	SUN (HELD)
LOW RATIO	SUN	CARRIER	RING (HELD)
DIRECT DRIVE			
1:1 RATIO	SUN/RING	CARRIER	
1:1 RATIO	SUN/CARRIER	RING	
1:1 RATIO	CARRIER/RING	SUN	
REVERSE			
OVERDRIVE RATIO	RING	SUN	CARRIER (HELD)
REDUCTION RATIO	SUN	RING	CARRIER (HELD)
OVERDRIVE			
HIGH RATIO	CARRIER	SUN	RING (HELD)
LOW RATIO	CARRIER	RING	SUN (HELD)

FIGURE 3–8 Chart that shows all the combinations of planetary members and what gear action is produced by each combination.

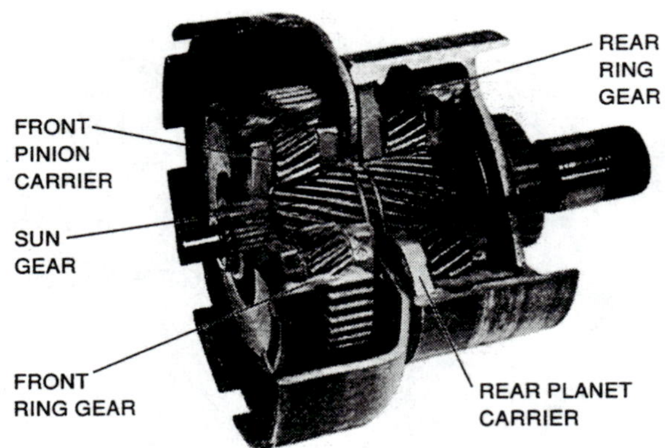

FIGURE 3–9 The Simpson gear set has one sun gear, which is shared by two planet carriers and two ring gears.

members so that they can function as reaction members of the gear set. The job of connecting and holding members of the gear set is performed by *coupling devices,* which are described in a later section. In most applications of the Simpson gear set, the members serve the following functions: the front ring gear and sun gear are input members, the front planet carrier and rear ring gear are output members, with the sun gear and rear planet carrier working as reaction members (Figure 3–10). We will study the power flow in each individual gear in a later section.

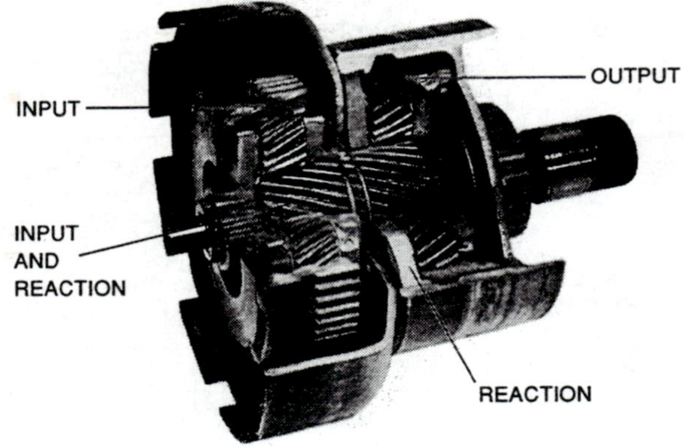

FIGURE 3–10 In the more common applications of Simpson gear sets, the front ring gear and sun gear act as input members, the front planet carrier and rear ring gear are output members, and the rear planet carrier and sun gear act as reaction members.

3.5 RAVIGNEAUX GEAR SET

The Ravigneaux gear set is different in many ways from the Simpson gear just covered. As you can see in Figure 3–11, this compound gear set has two sun gears: front and rear; two sets of planetary pinion gears: short and long, which mesh together and are contained in a single planet carrier; and one ring gear.

The Ravigneaux gear set is used in two-, three-, and four-speed automatic transmissions and was used widely before the Simpson gear set was developed. The function of the various members of the gear set change, depending on the number of forward speeds the transmission is designed to have. In a two-speed transmission, the front sun gear is the main power input member, with the planet carrier serving as the output member. The rear sun gear serves as both reaction member and input member in different gears, while the ring gear is used only as a reaction member (Figure 3–12). To achieve a three-speed transmission, the members of the Ravigneaux gear set must serve different functions. The front sun gear is still the main power input member, but the ring gear is now serving as the output member. The planet carrier serves as reaction member, while the rear sun gear serves as both input and reaction member in different gears (Figure 3–13). Later, in Section 3.7, we discuss the power flow through the two-, three-, and four-speed Ravigneaux gear sets, showing the flow in all gear speeds as well as introducing you to clutch and band application charts.

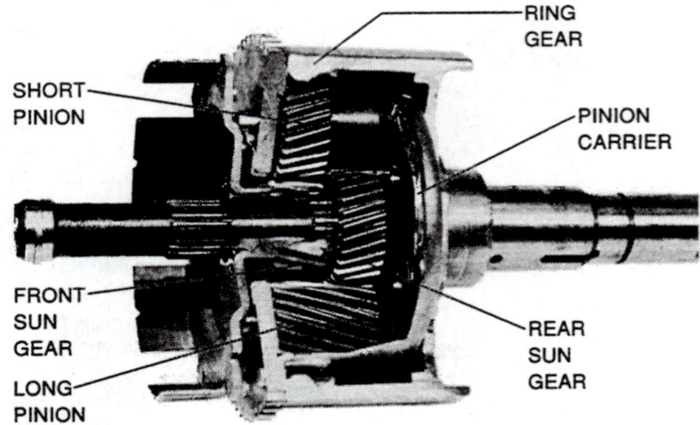

FIGURE 3–11 The Ravigneaux gear set has two sun gears, front and rear. It also has two sets of planetary pinion gears, one short and one long, which are meshed together and have a common planet carrier, and one ring gear.

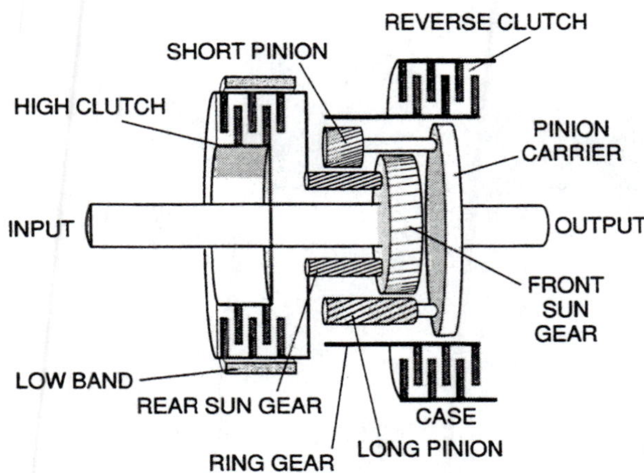

FIGURE 3–12 In this two-speed application, the Ravigneaux gear set uses the front sun gear as the power input member, the planet carrier as the output member, with the ring gear as the reaction member and the rear sun as both reaction and input in different gears.

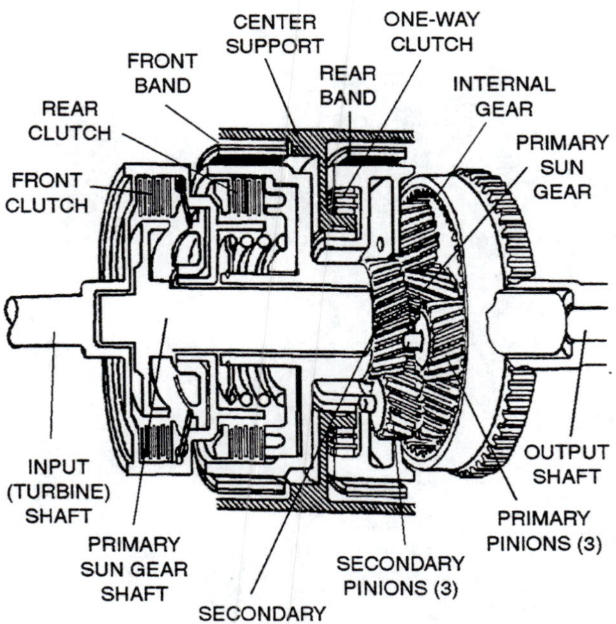

FIGURE 3–13 In this three-speed application, the front sun gear is input, the ring gear is output, with the planet carrier serving as reaction member, and the rear sun gear serves as both input and reaction in different gears

3.6 COUPLING AND HOLDING DEVICES

What we will be referring to as coupling devices are mechanical connectors that are used in the automatic transmission to join members of the compound planetary gear sets temporarily to the power input source. In most transmissions this coupling job is performed by a hydraulically activated *multidisc clutch* (Figure 3–14). *One-way clutches* are also used in some transmissions to couple the input source to gear train components.

The job of holding devices is different in that they are used to hold various members of the compound planetary gear sets stationary so that they will work as reaction members in the gear sets, or to lock the gear train to the case to prevent rotation of the output shaft. There are four basic types of

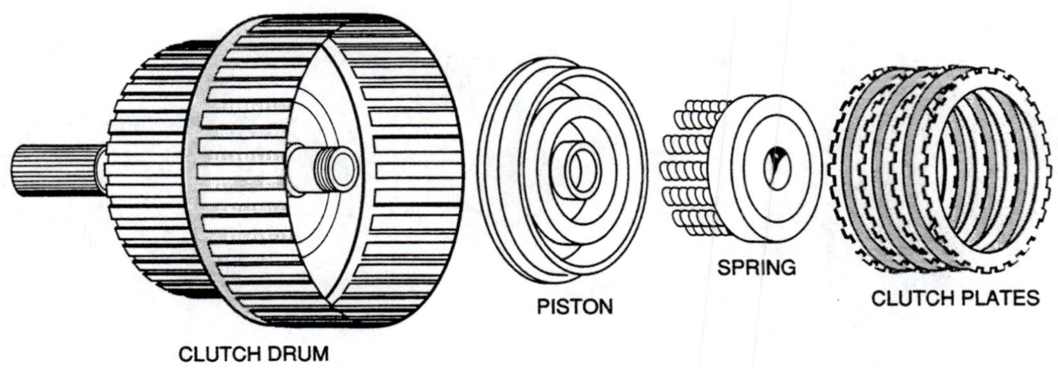

FIGURE 3–14 The purpose of the multidisc clutch is to connect the input shaft temporarily to the input member of the gear set, or to hold the reaction member. This device is both a coupling and a holding device. (Reprinted with permission of General Motors Corporation)

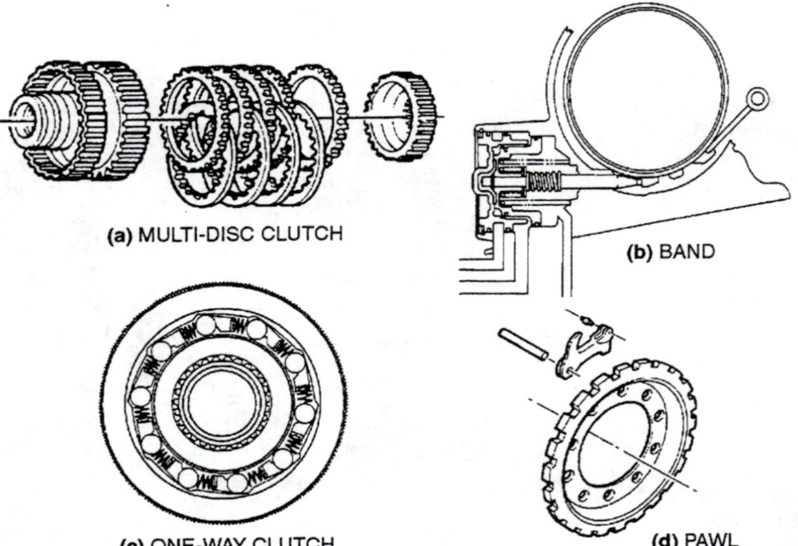

FIGURE 3–15 The four types of coupling and holding devices are the multidisc clutch, band, one-way clutch, and pawl.

holding devices: multidisc clutch, band, one-way clutch, and *pawl* (Figure 3–15). The first three devices are used in holding planetary members, and the last item, the pawl, is used to lock the output shaft to the case. In the following sections, each of the coupling and holding devices is described and discussed in detail.

3.6.1 Multidisc Clutches

The multidisc clutch is comprised of the following parts: a hydraulic piston with seals, a return spring or springs for the piston, a *clutch drum* in which the piston and clutch discs are housed, one set of clutch plates called "steels" which have no friction

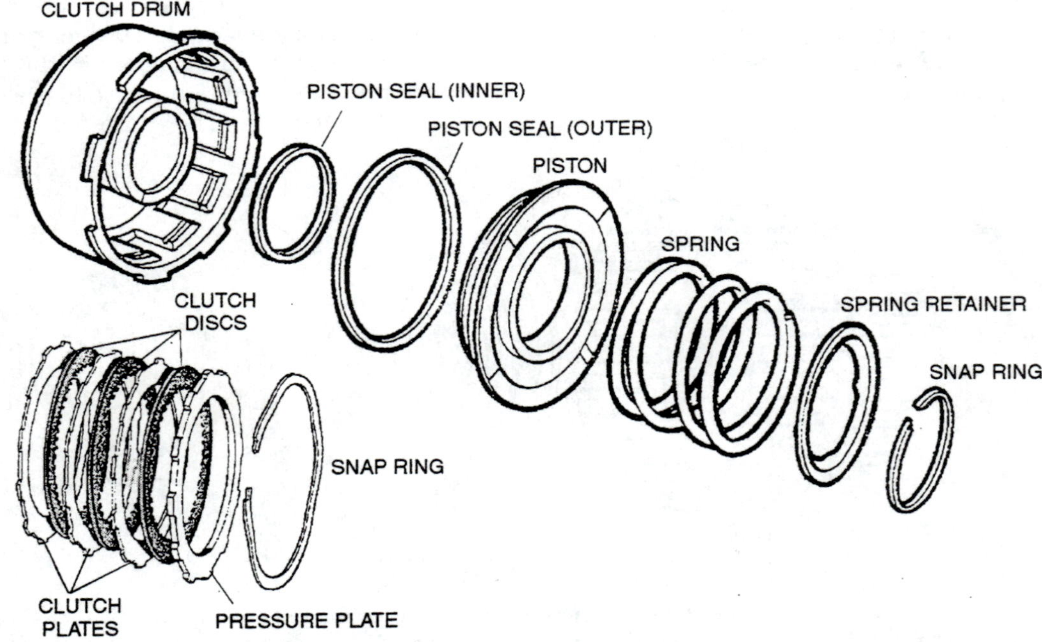

FIGURE 3–16 The parts of a multidisc clutch are the clutch drum, piston and seals, return spring and retainer, clutch plates, clutch discs, pressure plate, and snap ring.

FIGURE 3–17 The smooth area at the inner end of the clutch drum is where the piston seals ride.

FIGURE 3–18 The grooves running the length of the clutch drums provide a means for driving the steel plates of the clutch pack when the clutch drum is rotating.

material, one set of clutch discs partially covered with a friction material, a pressure plate, and a retaining snap ring (Figure 3–16).

1. Clutch Drums

The operation of the coupling clutch is quite simple. The clutch drum, which is cylindrical in shape, is made from machined cast iron or from stamped steel. The innermost portion of the inside surface is smooth, to provide a surface for the piston seal to ride against (Figure 3–17). The inner end of the clutch drum also has a hub to support the inner surface of the piston. Closer to the opening of the drum, still on the inside surface, splines or grooves are machined or stamped into the drum (Figure 3–18). These grooves provide a place for the tangs on the outer diameter of the steel plate to ride, thus causing the "steels" to rotate with the drum whenever it is turned. The outside surface of the drum is smooth and is sometimes used as the application surface for a band.

2. Clutch Pistons

The clutch piston is used to convert hydraulic pressure into mechanical force to squeeze the clutch disc together (Figure 3–19). The piston is usually the shape of a flat disc with grooves cut in the inner and outer diameters to house piston seals. The seals are usually a square-cut O-ring or a lip-type seal made of neoprene, a synthetic rubber. The

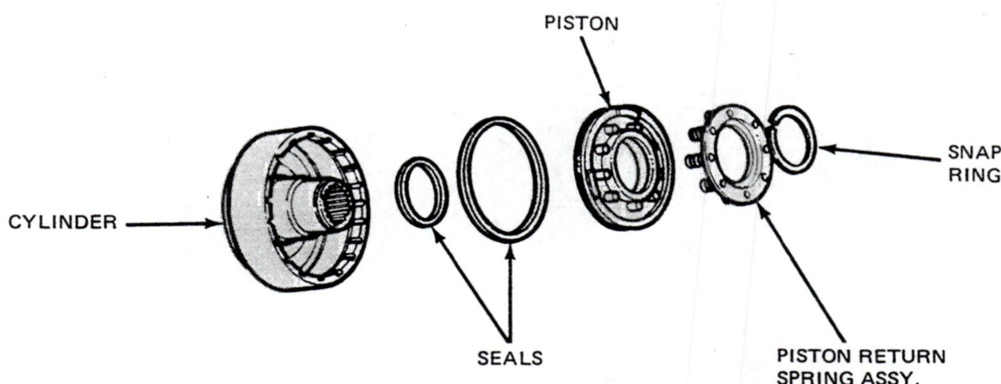

FIGURE 3–19 The clutch piston has seals on its inner and outer diameters and rides inside the clutch drum.

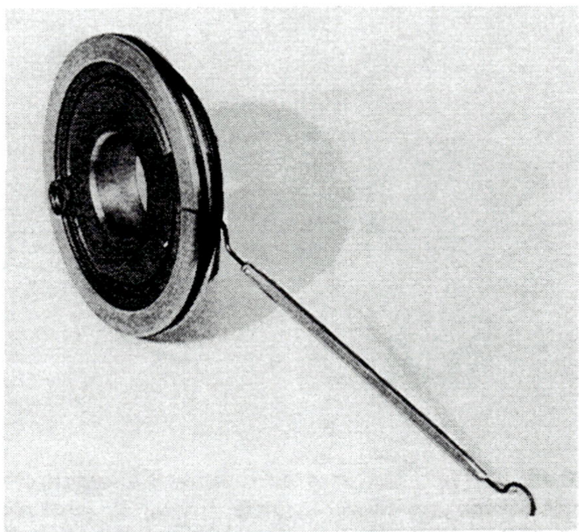

FIGURE 3–20 The clutch piston has grooves on its inside and outside diameters to accept seals. The most common types of seals are square-cut O-rings or lip seals.

seal's job is to prevent loss of hydraulic pressure past the piston (Figure 3–20).

Each clutch piston must have help in returning to its at-rest position after the hydraulic pressure has been released. This job is performed by the clutch piston return springs (Figure 3–21). These springs mount between the back surface of the piston and a retainer that is held in the clutch drum by a snap ring. As the hydraulic pressure is applied to the clutch piston, the piston moves out, compressing the return springs and forcing the clutch discs together (Figure 3–22). As the pressure is released, the return springs push the piston back to its at-rest position (Figure 3–23).

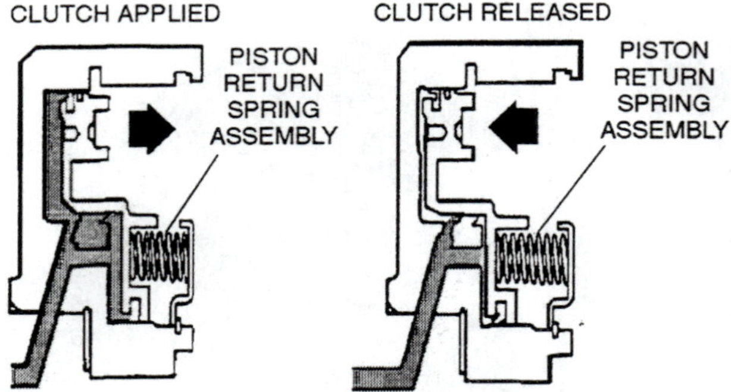

FIGURE 3–21 The return springs force the piston to return to its at-rest position after the application pressure is removed.

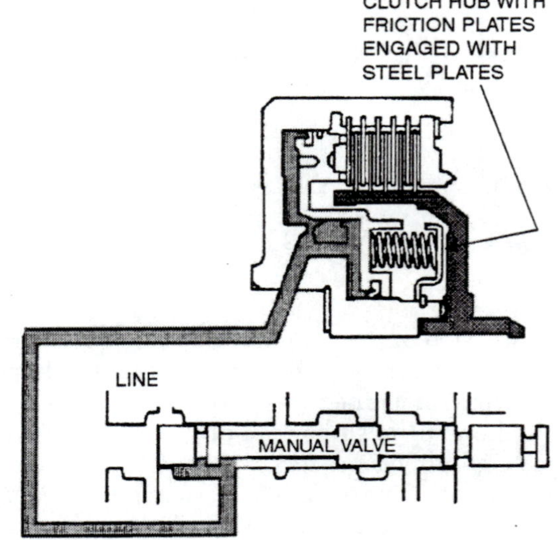

FIGURE 3–22 With the application pressure on, the piston engages the clutch pack.

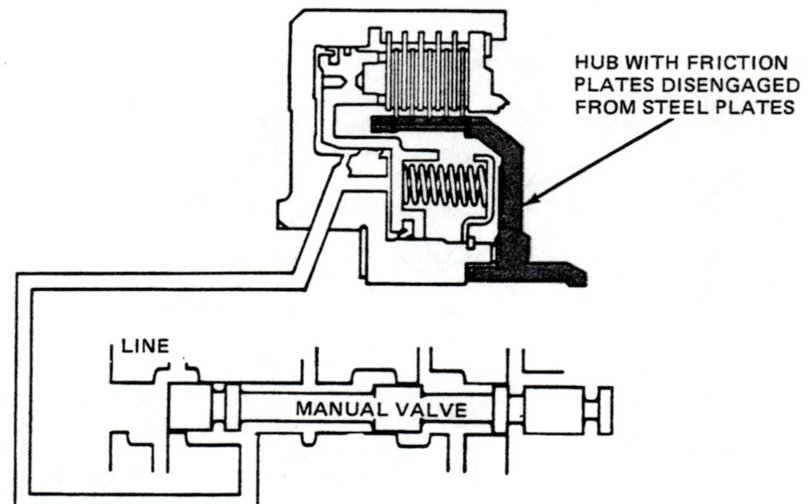

FIGURE 3–23 With the application pressure off, the return springs disengage the clutches.

3. Clutch Discs

The clutch discs are designed to transfer input torque from the input shaft to one or more members of the compound planetary gear set. The clutch is applied when hydraulic pressure is applied to the clutch piston forcing the clutch discs together.

There are two different types of clutch discs: the clutch plates or "steels," which have attaching tangs around their outer diameter and have no friction material added, and the friction discs, which have their attaching tangs around their inside diameter and have friction material bonded to both sides (Figure 3–24). The friction material used on the discs will vary depending on the transmission application. In transmissions for large, heavy vehicles designed for heavy-duty use, the friction material is usually powdered copper and graphite forming a metallic lining for the discs. Organic materials are also used, including paper and some asbestos, along with the adhesives used to bond the friction material to the disc. The various friction materials have different friction characteristics, which makes each type of material especially suited to a special application.

The clutch discs are alternated, first a steel disc next to the piston, then a friction disc, then steel, then friction, and so on. This group of clutch discs is called a clutch pack. The number of clutch discs in a pack is determined by the torque load they will have to carry; the higher the torque, the more clutch discs will be needed. By adding more clutch discs the surface area is increased so that it can handle the extra torque. An average-sized clutch pack has three or four pairs of clutch discs.

4. Pressure Plates

At the opposite end of the clutch pack from the piston is the pressure plate, which is the stationary part of the clutch pack. The pressure plate has attaching tabs around its outer diameter. The tabs slide into the same grooves that the steels attach to inside the clutch drum. A large snap ring fits into an internal groove in the drum behind the pressure plate to keep it from being pushed out when the piston is applied (Figure 3–25). This stationary pressure plate and snap ring serve as the backstop against which the steel and friction discs are pushed by the clutch piston.

5. Wave Springs

To aid in smooth application of the clutch, a wave spring is added to some clutch packs. The wave spring looks like a large washer, about the size of the discs, which has waves in it (Figure 3–26). This wave spring is always placed between the clutch piston and the first clutch disc. As the clutch piston moves toward the clutch pack, it must compress the wave spring before it can apply full pressure to the clutch pack. As the wave spring is being compressed, it transmits an increasing amount of force to the clutch pack until, when fully compressed, the full piston force is applied.

6. Clutch Pack Clearance

For the clutch pack to operate properly when it is released, there must be a minimum amount of

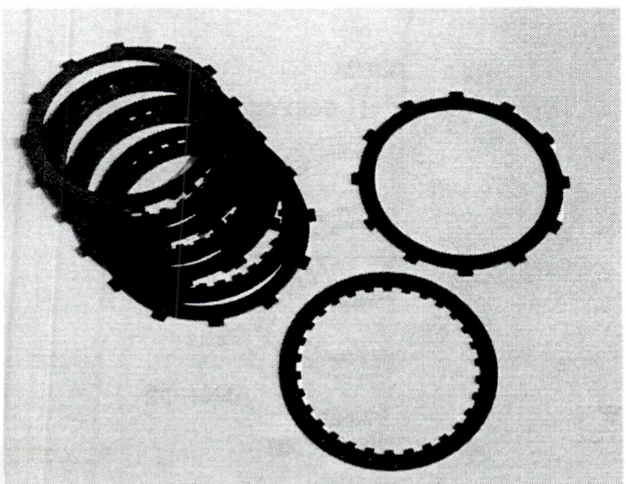

FIGURE 3–24 The clutch plates or "steels" are made only of steel, whereas clutch discs or "friction discs" have a coating of friction material on both sides.

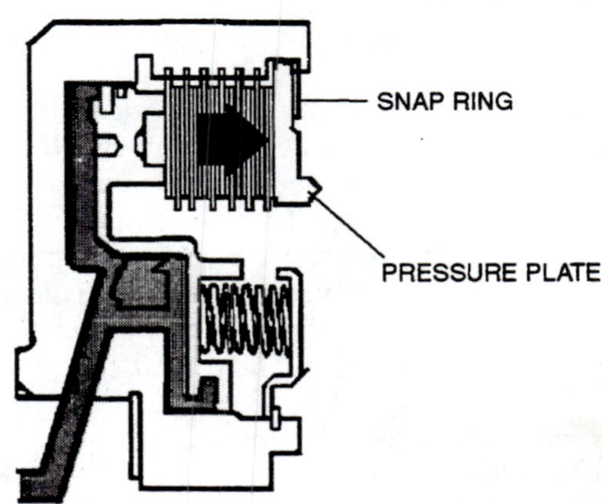

FIGURE 3–25 The pressure plate is held in place in the clutch drum by a snap ring.

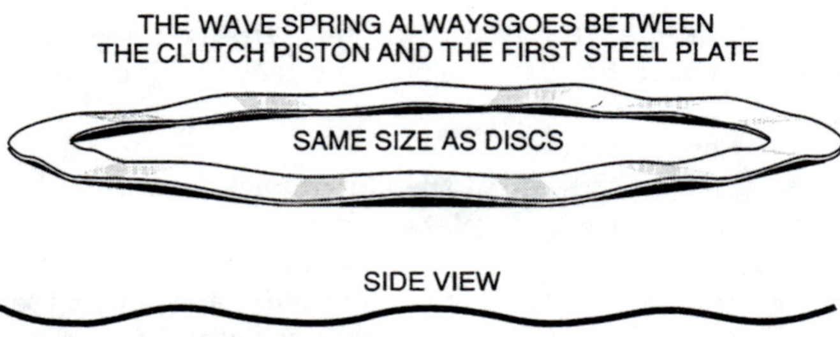

FIGURE 3–26 The wave spring is about the same size as the clutch discs but has no mounting tangs on the inside or outside.

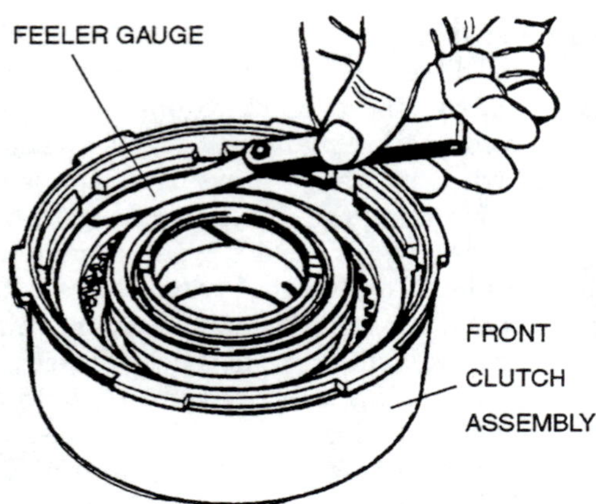

FIGURE 3–27 If clutch pack clearance is not properly adjusted to provide the necessary free play when disengaged, clutch pack failure will occur. (Courtesy of Chrysler)

clearance between the clutch discs to prevent unwanted friction. The clearance is measured with a feeler gauge between the last clutch disc and the *pressure plate,* or the pressure plate and the snap ring (Figure 3–27). Various means are used by the different manufacturers to adjust the clutch pack clearance. The two most popular methods are the *selective-fit* pressure plate and the selective-fit snap ring. When a part is referred to as being selective fit, that means it is produced in a number of different thicknesses, usually four or five basic sizes, so by changing the pressure plate or snap ring to one of the proper size, the clutch pack clearances can be adjusted. A more complete description of adjusting clutch pack clearance is given in Part II.

3.6.2 Bands

The multidisc clutch we just studied can be used to couple parts together—input source to a planetary member—as well as to hold a member of a planetary gear set stationary. The only job a band performs is to hold members of a planetary gear set stationary (Figure 3–28). Being held stationary causes that member of the planetary gear set to act as the reaction member. By changing the input members and reaction members, we cause the gear ratios to change and the transmission shifts gears. The band, like the multidisc clutch, is applied with hydraulic pressure. A piston is used to convert the hydraulic pressure in linear force which tightens the band around the drum, holding it stationary.

1. Rigid and Flexible Bands

There are two types of bands, rigid and flexible (Figure 3–29). The rigid type is cast steel, which retains its round shape and can be either double- or single-wrap design. The double-wrap band is used to hold the low-reverse drum because of its greater holding power and self-energizing ability. The rigid, single-wrap, and flexible bands are used to hold other drums, which transfer less torque. The *friction materials* used to line the bands can range from soft, organic material to hard, metallic material, depending on the design requirements of the band. A balance of band design, lining material drum material, and surface finish, as well as applied force, must be maintained to assure proper shift quality.

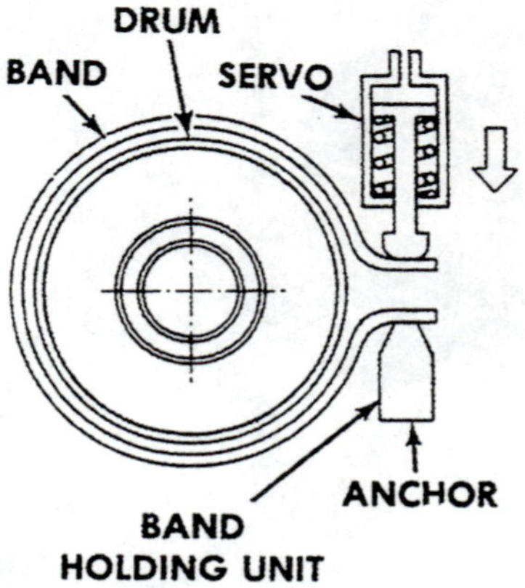

FIGURE 3–28 The only purpose of the band is to hold the drum that it encircles stationary when it is applied. (Reprinted with permission of General Motors Corporation)

FIGURE 3–29 There are two types of rigid bands, single wrap and double wrap. Both rigid design bands will retain their shape when removed from the transmission. A flexible design band will not retain its shape when released.

2. Servos

The servo is a hydraulic piston that converts hydraulic pressure into applied force to tighten and hold the band around its drum. The servo piston is usually large, with piston seals around the outer diameter and a piston rod extending from one side (Figure 3–30). The servo piston operates in a bore in the transmission case and has a return spring to release the band. There are two types of servo action: single acting and double acting. The single-acting servo uses hydraulic pressure on only one side of the piston. When the servo is applied, a shift valve directs line pressure to the servo bore, which pushes against the piston, compressing the return spring and putting applied force on the band (Figure 3–31). When the line pressure is cut off, the fluid is exhausted from the servo bore as the return spring pushes the piston back. The *double-acting servo* works in the same manner as the single-acting servo as it is being applied, but the release is entirely different (Figure 3–32). To release the servo and band, another hydraulic pressure is applied on the other side of the servo piston. This release force, plus the return spring force, overcome the apply pressure and push the piston back. The reason for releasing the servo and band this way is so that hydraulic pressure will be applied to the servo at all times, which would allow instant application of the band when needed. Simply cut off the release oil and the band will engage and hold in a fraction of a second.

3. Servo Linkages

There are two main types of servo linkage that are used to transfer the force of the servo to the band, the rod and strut, the lever, and the cantilever designs. As shown in Figure 3–33, the rod and strut design uses a push rod directly from the servo piston to the band, while at the other end of the band a strut is used to connect the band to the adjustment screw, which serves as the anchor for the band. Another type of rod linkage is the graduated rod. These rods are available from the manufacturer in different lengths, which are used to adjust the band for proper clearance. With this type of linkage, the anchor end of the band mounts directly to the case, not to an adjusting screw.

The next type of servo linkage is the lever type. With this design, a lever is used to increase the force of the servo and change the direction of the force (Figure 3–34). As the servo pushes on the lever, the force is transferred to the band through a strut. Some levers carry the band adjustment screw used in setting band clearance.

A *cantilever linkage* is used in some transmissions (Figure 3–35). This type of linkage acts on both ends of the band at once and uses the pivot pin of the linkage as the anchor point for the band.

4. Adjustments

For a band to work properly, it must be able to hold its drum stationary when applied and allow the drum to turn freely when the band is released. To do the job, the band must be adjusted to its proper clearance, and this is done with adjusting screws or graduated rods. The adjustment screws can be inside or outside the transmission case, depending on how the transmission was designed, as shown in Figure 3–36. The procedure for adjusting band clearance is different for each transmission model but most include variations of two similar steps. The first step is to loosen the locking nut, tighten the adjusting screw to a specified torque setting, then back the band adjustment screw out a given number of turns to provide proper clearance. If band adjustment is set improperly, the shift timing of the transmission is altered, meaning that the band could be released too soon or too late in respect to a clutch that is being applied. For a smooth shift, the band must be released just as the clutch is being applied and an incorrect band adjustment will change the timing. Band adjustment procedures for specific transmissions will be covered in depth in Part 2.

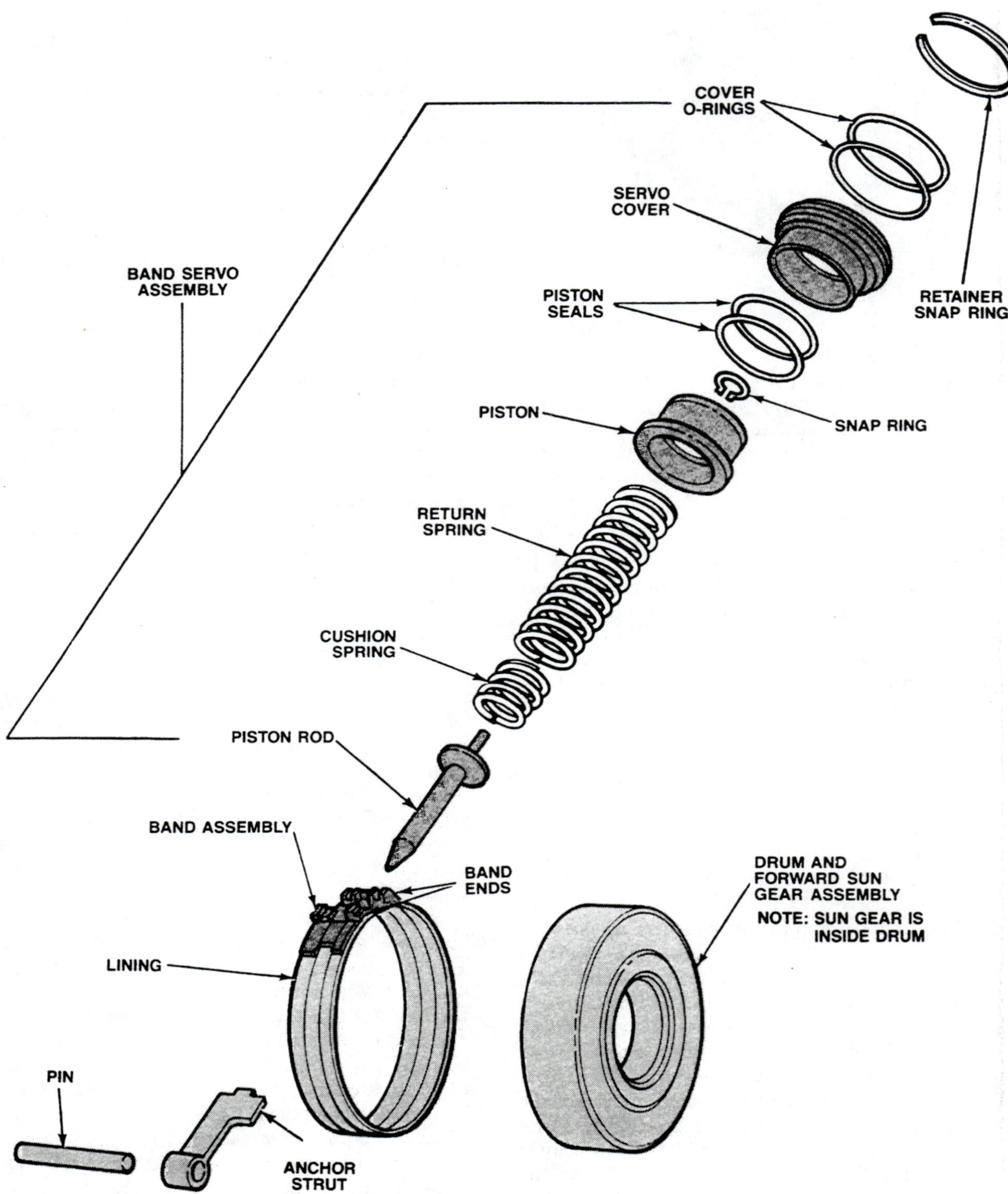

FIGURE 3–30 The components of a typical band and servo assembly. (Courtesy of Ford)

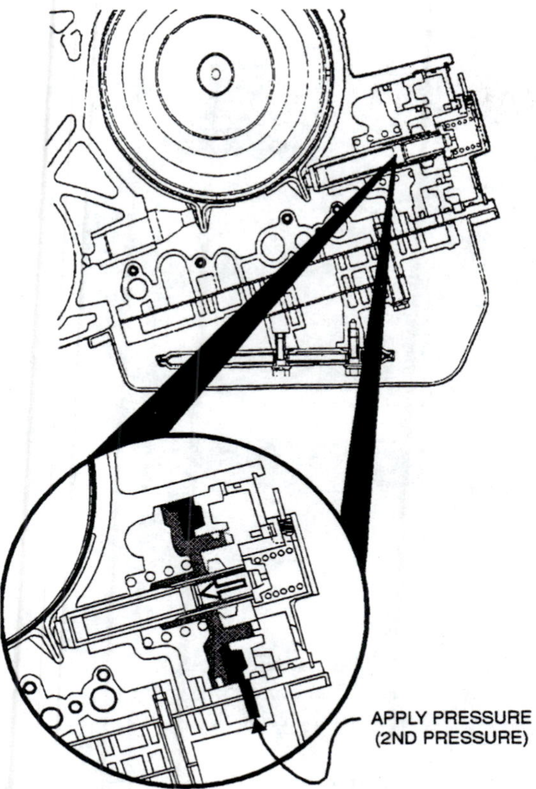

FIGURE 3–31 Hydraulic pressure acting on the servo piston is applying the band. (Courtesy of Chrysler)

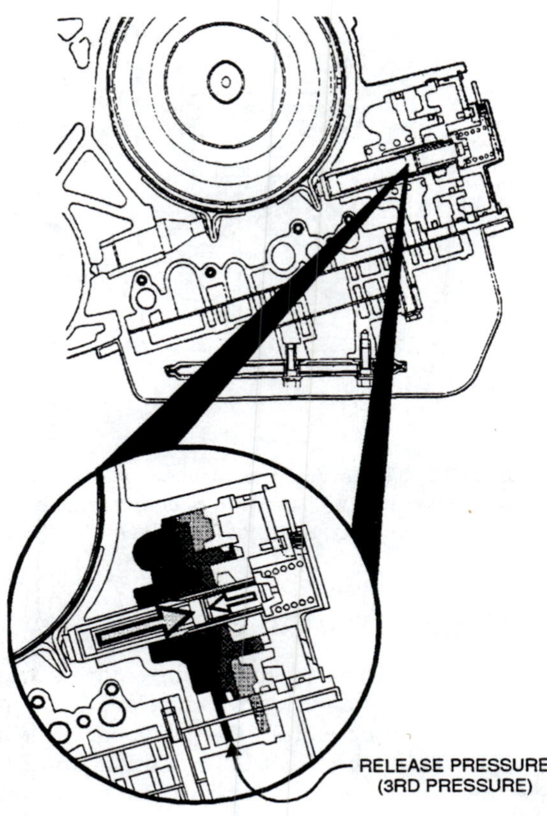

FIGURE 3–32 While the servo application pressure is still being applied, servo release pressure is applied to the bottom side of the piston. This release pressure, along with the return spring, forces the piston back, disengaging the band. (Courtesy of Chrysler)

FIGURE 3–33 The rod and strut linkage uses a straight push rod to connect the servo piston to the band. The other end of the band is anchored to the case through the anchor strut. (Courtesy of Ford)

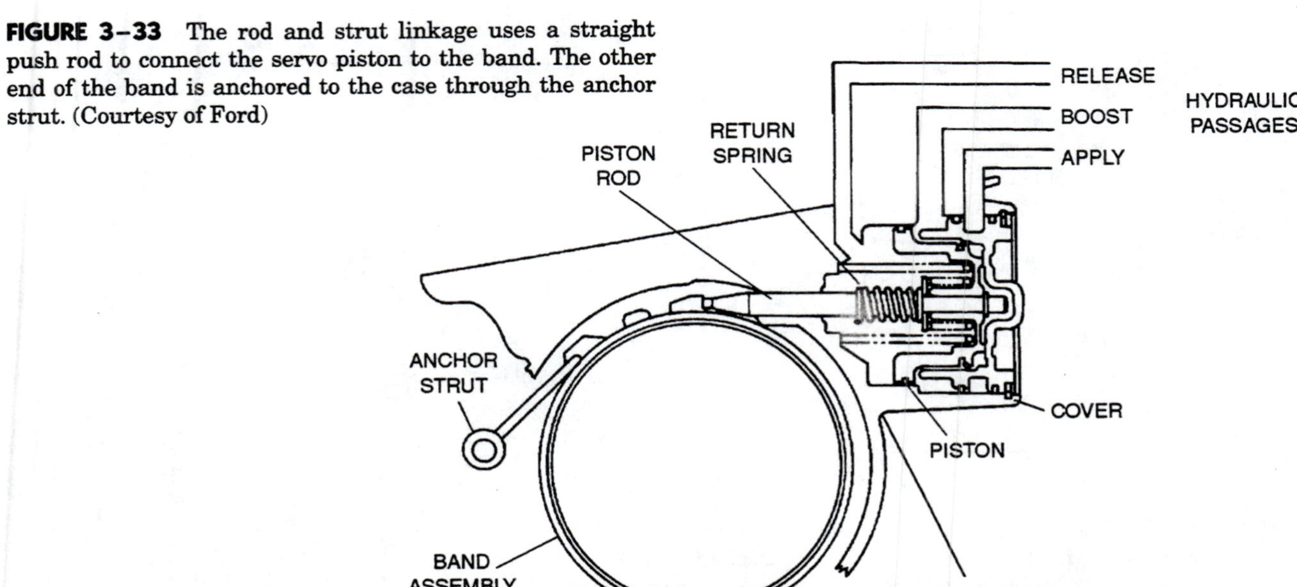

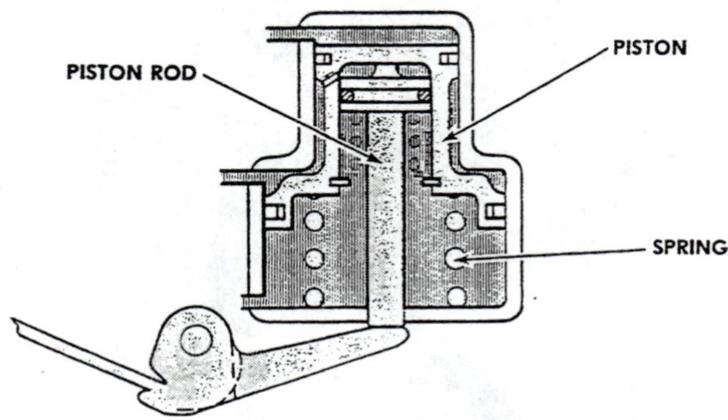

FIGURE 3–34 The lever linkage shown uses the lever to increase the force to the band and to change the direction of force of the servo. (Courtesy of Chrysler)

FIGURE 3–35 The cantilever linkage design applies force to both ends of the band and uses the lever pivot pin to anchor the band to the case.

3.6.3 One-Way Clutches

Another type of holding or coupling device widely used in today's automatic transmissions is the one-way or overrunning clutch. The job it performs as a holding device is simple; it holds a drum stationary when the turning force tries to turn the drum in one direction and release the drum to turn freely in the other direction. The one-way clutch can be designed to lock up or release in either direction, depending on the needs of the transmission. As a coupling device, the one-way clutch is used to connect input shafts to planetary members in many late-model four-speed automatic transmissions. Its operation is fully automatic, requiring no control devices to apply or release.

1. Sprag-Type Clutch

The sprag-type one-way clutch is shown in Figure 3–37. Its basic design and function are as follows: the sprag has an inner and an outer race, with the outer surface of the outer race being splined for at-

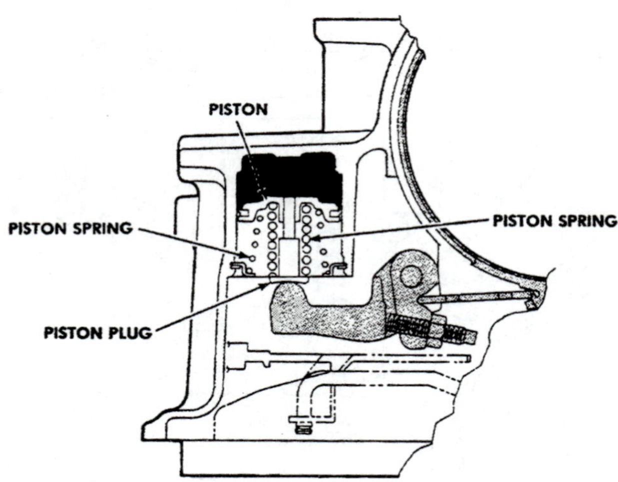

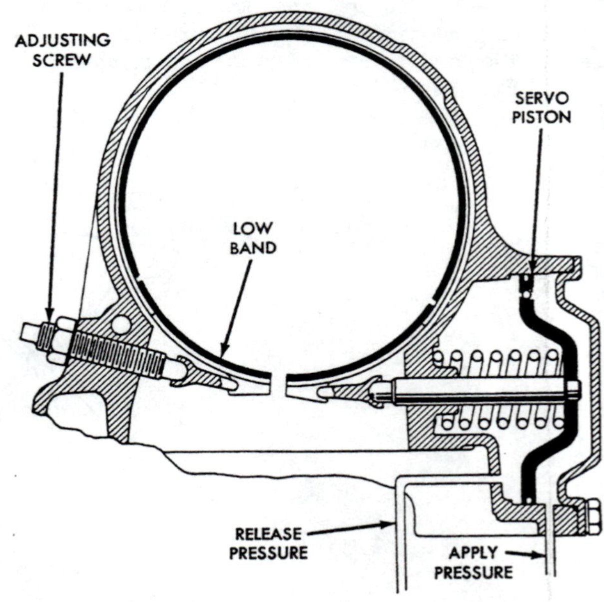

FIGURE 3–36 The adjustment on the left is made inside the transmission with the pan removed. The adjustment at the right is made from outside the transmission. (Courtesy of Chrysler)

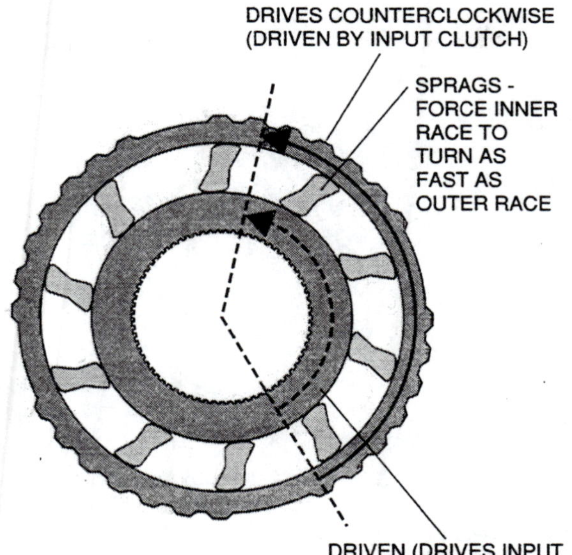

FIGURE 3–37 The sprag one-way clutch has an inner race, an outer race, and sprags in a retaining case. (Reprinted with permission of General Motors Corporation)

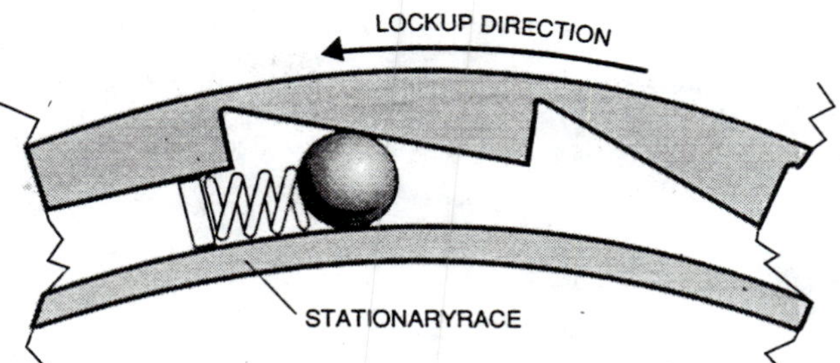

FIGURE 3–38 As the movable race moves in the lockup direction, the sprags are wedged in between the two races, locking up the one-way clutch.

tachment to other parts of the transmission. The inner surfaces of the races are smooth and round. Mounted in between the races are the sprags and their retaining case. The shape of the sprags is similar to an hourglass with their end-to-end dimension being slightly larger than the inner-to-outer race dimension. The sprigs lie at an angle between the inner and outer races, being supported by their retainer. One race is attached to the case and does not move. The other is attached to a reaction member of the planetary gear set. As the movable race begins to move in the lockup direction, the force of rotation tries to stand the sprigs up straight, wedging them between the races (Figure 3–38). This action occurs almost instantly, with no slippage. When the direction of rotation is changed, the force on the sprigs is reversed and they become unlocked and the movable race is free to rotate. Care must be taken when servicing a *sprag clutch* because it can be reassembled backward, which will change the direction of lockup, with disastrous effects on the transmission.

2. Roller-Type Clutch

The operating principles of the *roller clutch* are similar to the sprag clutch, but the parts are different. The inner race remains the same, while the outer race is divided into sections that have an angled surface to provide a cam effect (Figure 3–39). Each section has a roller and spring positioned between the races. The spring pushes the roller into the narrow end of its section, and as the movable race turns in the lockup direction, the rollers are wedged in between the races and lockup is achieved, as shown in Figure 3–40. When the direction of rotation is changed, the movable race pushes the rollers away from the narrow end and is allowed to turn freely. The roller, being held in place by a spring, is always ready for lockup if the

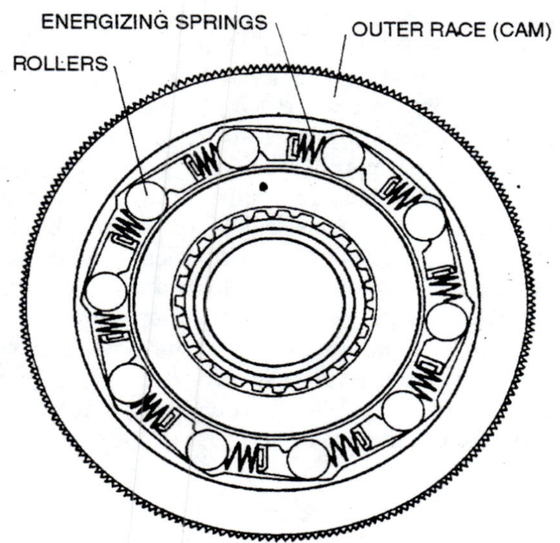

FIGURE 3–39 The roller one-way clutch has a smooth inner race and an outer race surface with cam-shaped sections. Each section has a roller and spring and some type of retainer. (Reprinted with permission of General Motors Corporation)

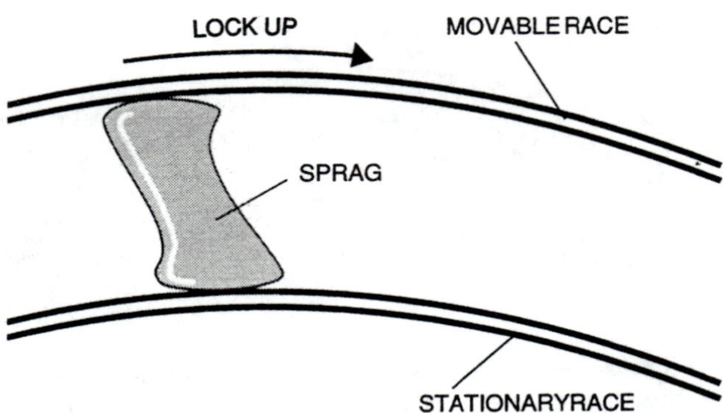

FIGURE 3–40 As the movable race starts to rotate in the lockup direction, the roller is forced into the wedge-shaped area between the inner and outer race, locking the two races together.

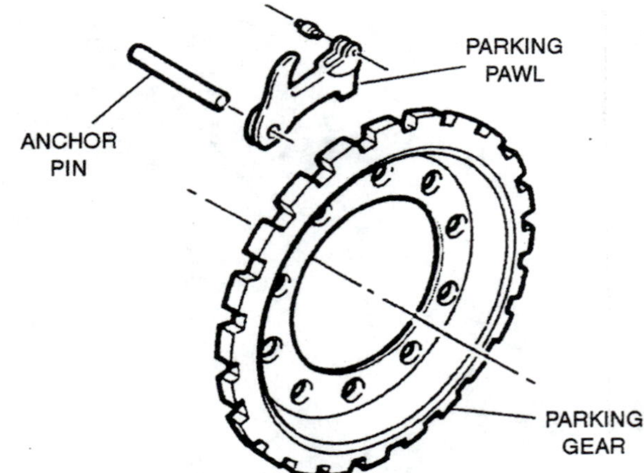

FIGURE 3–41 The pawl is used to provide a mechanical lock for the output shaft of the transmission, which occurs when the gear selector is moved into park position. (Courtesy of Ford)

direction of rotation should change. As with the sprag, the roller clutch is fully automatic and self-activating, so its operation is smooth and does not need to be timed with the hydraulic devices.

3.6.4 Pawls

The last type of holding device used in automatic transmissions is the pawl, which is a simple mechanical device. As you can see in Figure 3–41, the pawl is a metal stamping that is anchored to the case at one end and is free to pivot on its anchor bolt. The pawl can be moved by linkage attached to the gear selector linkage so that the pawl is engaged in a cog gear, or parking gear, which is attached to the output shaft. Once the pawl is engaged, the transmission output shaft is held stationary. This provides a mechanical lockup of the drivetrain known as *park*. Because the pivot end of the pawl mounts in the cast aluminum transmission case, the amount of force the pawl can withstand is limited. It is easy to see the damage that would occur if the transmission was placed in park position while moving.

3.7 POWER FLOW

Up until now we have been talking about individual components and how they work and what their job is in the automatic transmission. You have learned what a simple planetary gear set can do and what a compound planetary gear set is. You have also learned what coupling and holding devices are and how they function. It is time now to combine the action of the individual parts and learn how the various gears of the automatic transmission are achieved.

As we describe the power flow through the five different transmissions we have chosen as examples, we will be talking about power input and output. Power input is coming from the turbine, or converter clutch, in the torque converter through the turbine shaft to the planetary gear set. Multidisc or one-way clutches are used to couple the turbine shaft to the input members of the planetary gear set (Figure 3–42). The bands, one-way clutches, and holding multidisc clutches are holding the reaction members of the gear set. The output members of the gear set are splined to the transmission output shaft.

As we look at the various transmissions, we will use a *clutch and band chart* to show which coupling or holding devices are used in each gear. The chart is organized as follows: across the top of the chart are the coupling and holding devices used in that particular transmission. The first group of clutches will be coupling devices, followed by hold-

MULTIDISC CLUTCH ONE-WAY CLUTCH	} INPUT DEVICES

FIGURE 3–42 The coupling devices used to provide power input to the planetary gear set are multidisc clutches and one-way clutches.

ing clutches and then holding bands. These devices are applied hydraulically, giving them the common control source of the hydraulic system. The next group of holding devices are the one-way clutches, which operate automatically, not requiring a control device. The next column is for torque converter clutch application, showing in which gears the clutch is applied. The last column is for the last holding device, the parking pawl. The order in which the clutches and bands are listed across the chart is the order in which they would be found from the front of the transmission to the rear, and then separated into like groups. Figure 3–43 shows how the separation works.

The various gears of the transmission are shown down the left side of the chart, starting with park (P), then neutral (N), drive first gear (D1), drive second gear (D2), drive third gear (D3), drive fourth gear (D4), manual first gear (1), manual second gear (2), manual third gear (3), and reverse (R). The term *drive first gear* refers to the gear selector lever in drive position, while *manual first gear* indicates that the selector would be in first or low position. Only the gears used in transmissions being described are listed on the chart. The clutch and band chart for the first transmission is shown in Figure 3–43. By using this format for all the clutch and band charts, the similarities of one transmission to another will be more easily seen. Now let's look at the transmissions.

3.7.1 Two-Speed RWD Powerglide (Ravigneaux Gear Set)

The first transmission power flow we will look at is that of the two-speed Powerglide designed for rear wheel drive. The Powerglide uses a Ravigneaux gear set and has one coupling (high clutch) and two holding (low band and reverse clutch) devices. The input sun gear, which is the rear or larger sun gear, is splined to the turbine shaft. The low sun gear, the front or smaller sun gear, is attached to the high clutch drum and serves as both reaction and input member. The planet carrier is the output member, with the ring gear serving as a reaction member, as shown in Figure 3–44. With the selector in park (P), the park pawl is engaged to lock the output shaft to the case, with the rest of the transmission in neutral. In neutral (N) all the clutches and bands are released, so no reaction members are being held. The gear set freewheels with no power being transmitted, as shown in Figure 3–45. When the gear selector is placed in drive, as shown in Figure 3–46, the transmission goes into D1 and the low band is applied. The low band holds the high clutch drum stationary, which also holds the low sun gear as the reaction member. The torque input from the input sun gear is transferred to the pinions, which are forced to walk around the stationary low sun gear, causing a gear reduction to the *planetary carrier*, which is the output member.

	1ST COUPLING CLUTCH	2ND COUPLING CLUTCH	1ST HOLDING CLUTCH	2ND HOLDING CLUTCH	1ST BAND	2ND BAND	1ST ONE-WAY CLUTCH	2ND ONE-WAY CLUTCH	PARK PAWL	CONVERTER CLUTCH
P										
N										
D1										
D2										
D3										
D4										
1										
2										
3										
R										

FIGURE 3–43 Standard format used for all clutch and band charts included in this book. As you compare them to the manufacturers' charts, you should notice some differences.

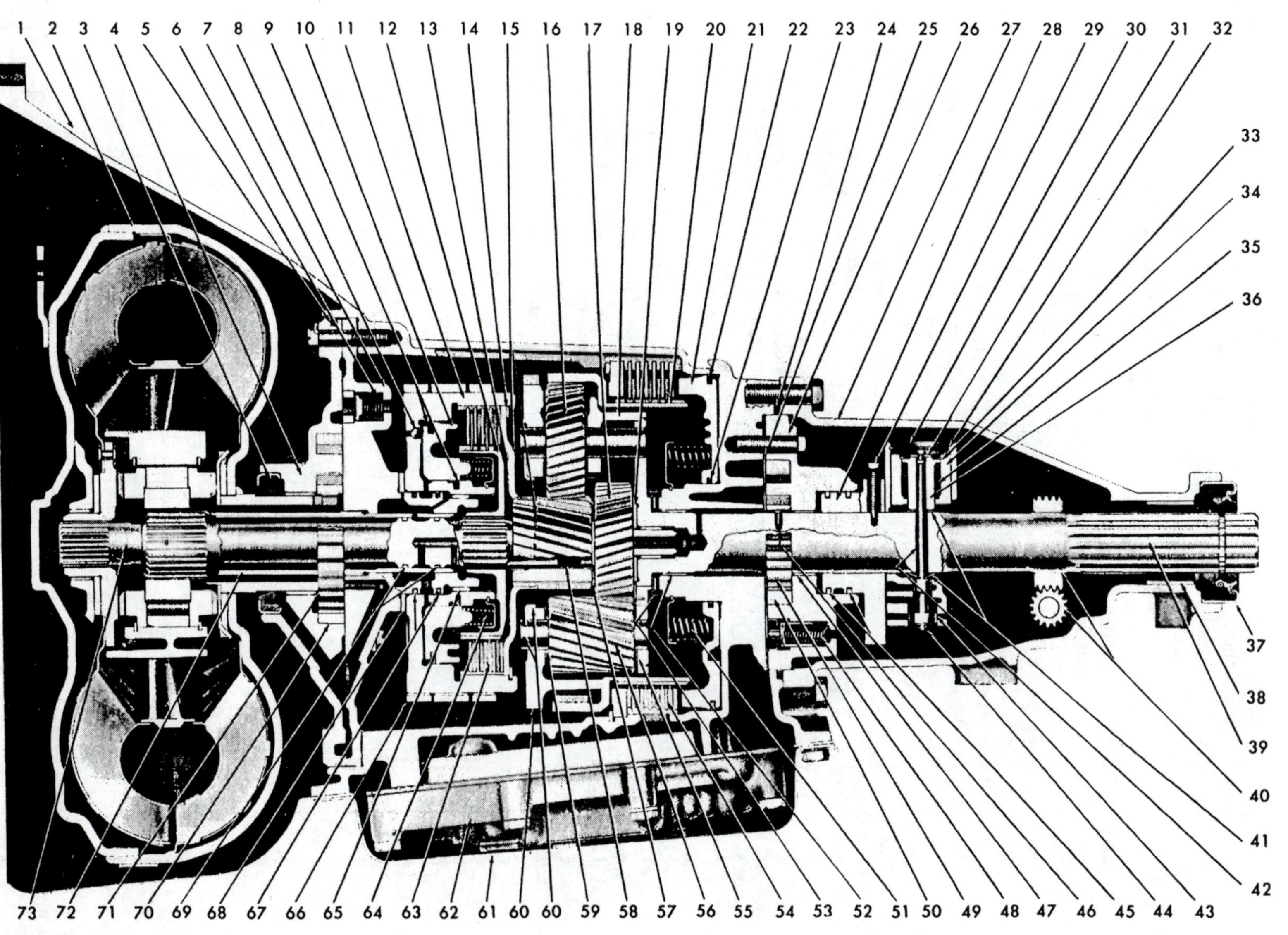
1
2
3
4
5
6
7
8
9
10
11
12
13
14
15
16
17
18
19
20
21
22
23
24
25
26
27
28
29
30
31
32
33
34
35
36
37
38
39
40
41
42
43
44
45
46
47
48
49
50
51
52
53
54
55
56
57
58
59
60
60
61
62
63
64
65
66
67
68
69
70
71
72
73

1. Transmission Case
2. Welded Converter
3. Front Oil Pump Seal Assembly
4. Front Oil Pump Body
5. Front Oil Pump Body Square Ring Seal
6. Lube Relief Valve
7. Front Oil Pump Cover
8. Clutch Relief Valve Ball
9. Clutch Piston Inner and Outer Seal
10. Clutch Piston
11. Clutch Drum
12. Clutch Hub
13. Clutch Hub Thrust Washer
14. Clutch Flange Retainer Ring
15. Low Sun Gear and Clutch Flange Assembly
16. Planet Short Pinion
17. Planet Input Sun Gear
18. Planet Carrier
19. Planet Input Sun Gear Thrust Washer
20. Ring Gear
21. Reverse Piston
22. Reverse Piston Outer Seal
23. Reverse Piston Inner Seal
24. Extension Seal Ring
25. Rear Pump Wear Plate
26. Rear Pump
27. Extension
28. Governor Hub
29. Governor Hub Drive Screw
30. Governor Body
31. Governor Shaft Retainer Clip
32. Governor Outer Weight Retainer Ring
33. Governor Inner Weight Retainer Ring
34. Governor Outer Weight
35. Governor Spring
36. Governor Inner Weight
37. Extension Rear Oil Seal
38. Extension Rear Bushing
39. Output Shaft
40. Speedometer Drive and Driven Gear
41. Governor Shaft Belleville Springs
42. Governor Shaft
43. Governor Valve
44. Governor Valve Retaining Clip
45. Governor Hub Seal Rings
46. Rear Pump Drive Pin
47. Rear Pump Bushing
48. Rear Pump Priming Valve
49. Rear Pump Drive Gear
50. Rear Pump Driven Gear
51. Reverse Piston Return Springs, Retainer and Retainer Ring
52. Transmission Rear Case Bushing
53. Output Shaft Thrust Bearing
54. Reverse Clutch Pack
55. Pinion Thrust Washer
56. Planet Long Pinion
57. Low Sun Gear Thrust Washer
58. Low Sun Gear Bushing (Splined)
59. Pinion Thrust Washer
60. Parking Lock Gear
61. Transmission Oil Pan
62. Valve Body
63. High Clutch Pack
64. Clutch Piston Return Springs, Retainer and Retainer Ring
65. Clutch Drum Bushing
66. Low Brake Band
67. High Clutch Seal Rings
68. Clutch Drum Thrust Washer (Selective)
69. Turbine Shaft Seal Rings
70. Front Pump Driven Gear
71. Front Pump Drive Gear
72. Stator Shaft
73. Input Shaft

FIGURE 3–44 Powerglide cross-sectional view. (Reprinted with permission of General Motors Corporation)

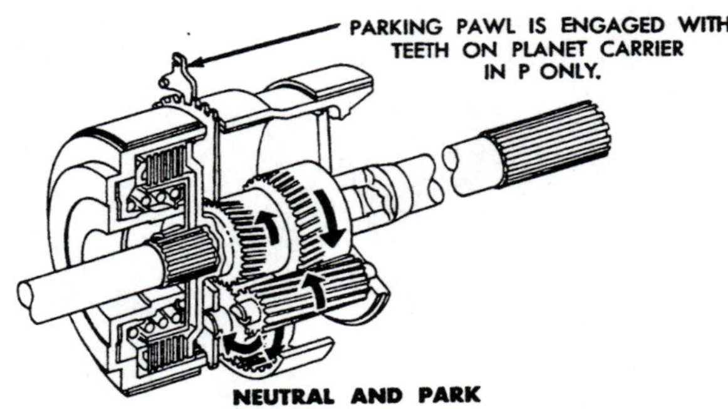

FIGURE 3–45 Powerglide in neutral gear. (Reprinted with permission of General Motors Corporation)

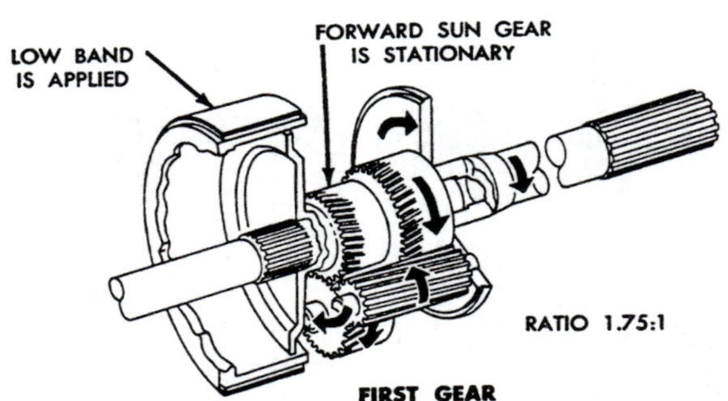

FIGURE 3–46 Powerglide in first gear. (Reprinted with permission of General Motors Corporation)

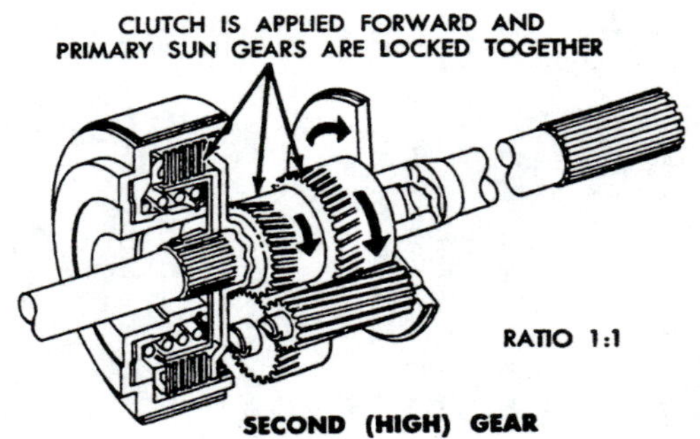

FIGURE 3–47 Powerglide in second gear. (Reprinted with permission of General Motors Corporation)

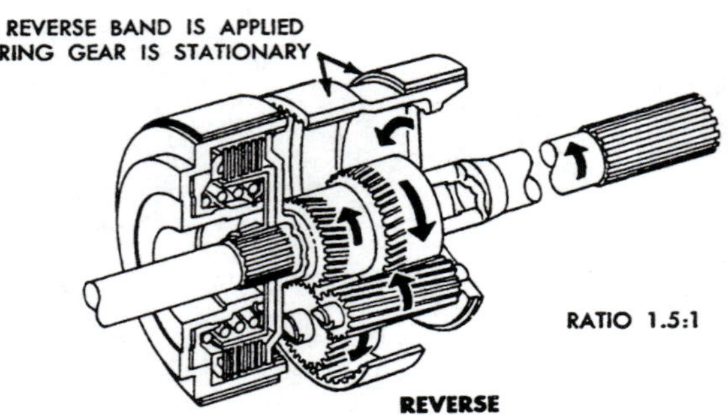

FIGURE 3–48 Powerglide in reverse gear. (Reprinted with permission of General Motors Corporation)

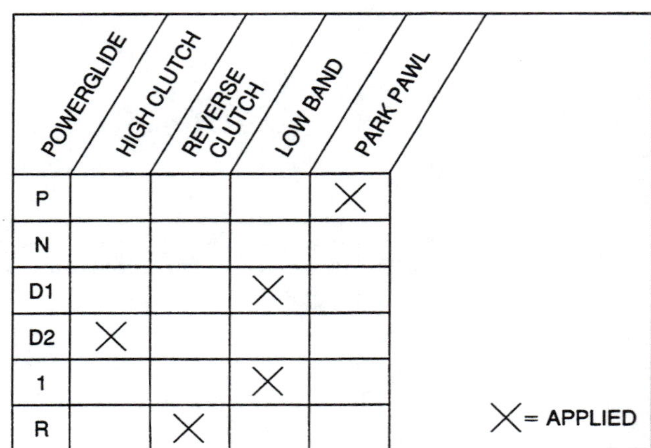

POWERGLIDE	HIGH CLUTCH	REVERSE CLUTCH	LOW BAND	PARK PAWL
P				X
N				
D1			X	
D2	X			
1			X	
R		X		

X = APPLIED

FIGURE 3–49 The clutch and band chart for the Powerglide shows which coupling or holding devices are used to achieve each gear.

When the transmission shifts from D1 to D2, the low band is released and the high clutch is applied as shown in Figure 3–47. The center hub of the high clutch is splined to the input shaft, so when the clutch is applied the low sun gear, which is attached to the high clutch drum, becomes an input member. With both the input sun gear and low sun gear serving as input members, the planetary gear set will be in direct drive. When the gear selector is placed in reverse (R), the reverse clutch is applied, which causes the ring gear to become the reaction member. The input sun gear drives the planet pinions, which must walk around the inside of the stationary ring gear, driving the planet carrier in the opposite direction, as shown in Figure 3–48.

A quick, easy-to-understand summary of which coupling or holding device is applied in each gear is shown in the clutch and band chart in Figure 3–49. This type of transmission is the simplest automatic transmission made, with only two forward speeds and using only three coupling and holding devices.

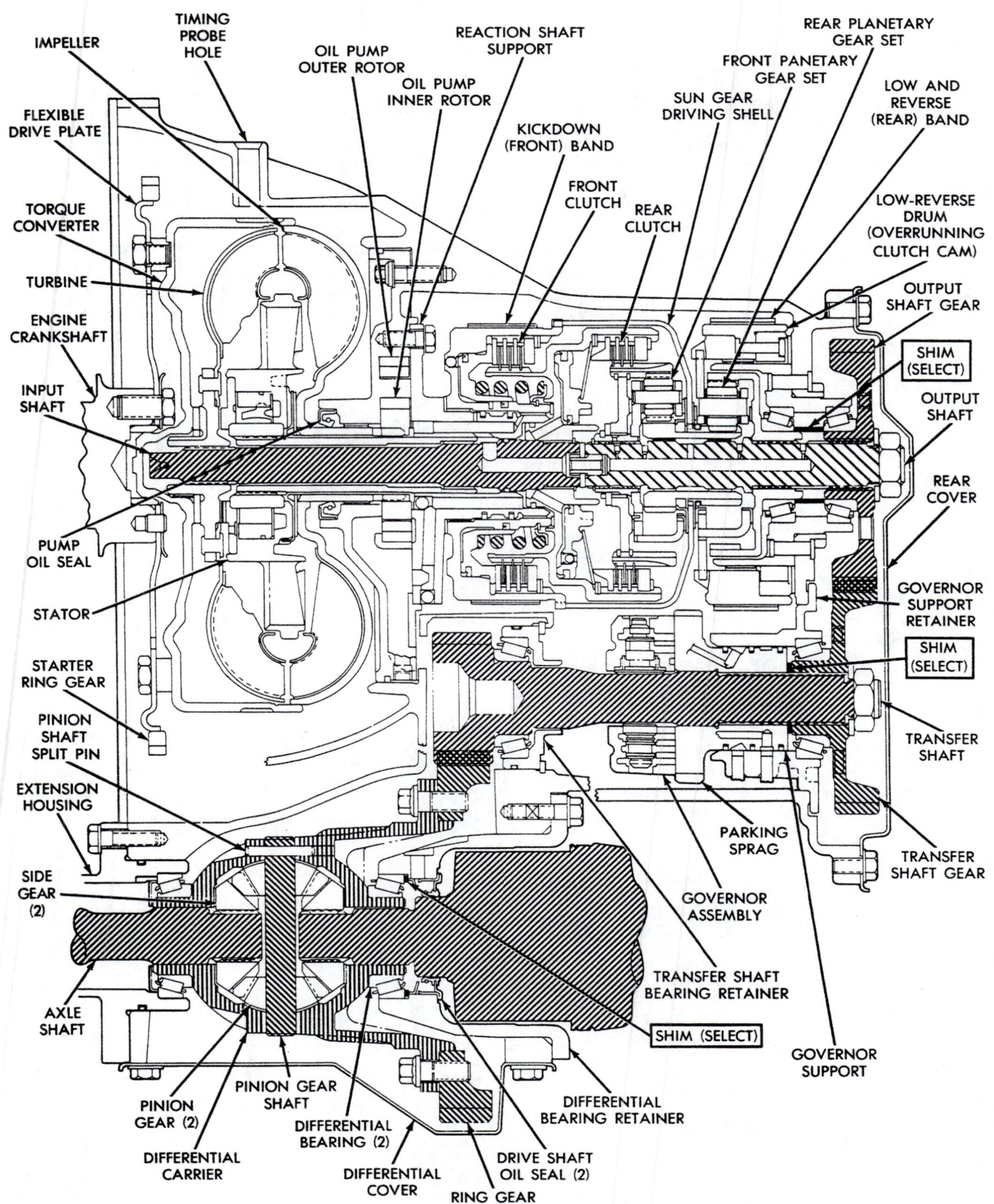

FIGURE 3–50 This cross-sectional drawing of a Torque Flite A-404 transaxle identifies the components of the gear train necessary to study the power flow. (Courtesy of Chrysler)

3.7.2 Three-Speed FWD Torque Flite (Simpson Gear Set)

Next we study a three-speed transmission designed for front wheel drive, the Chrysler Torque Flite A-404 (Figure 3–50), which uses the Simpson gear set with two coupling devices, front and rear clutch, and three holding devices, the front (kickdown) and rear (low–reverse) bands and a one-way or overrunning clutch. In park (P) and neutral (N), none of the coupling or holding devices are applied, except for the park pawl, so there is no input or reaction members and no power flow. When the transmission is placed in drive range on the selector, it goes into D1. In D1 the rear clutch, which is splined to the input shaft, is applied, causing the front ring gear to become the input member. The ring gear drives the pinions, which rotate, driving the sun gear in the opposite direction. The front planet carrier acts as a reaction member since the output shaft is stationary. The sun gear then rotates the rear pinions, which drive the output ring gear. The rear planet carrier is the reaction member, being held by the one-way or overrunning clutch (Figure 3–51). In manual first gear, the rear (low–reverse) band is also applied for better holding power and engine braking. The front planetary carrier and the rear ring gear are splined to the output shaft and are the output members. As the transmission shifts to D2, the front (kickdown) band is applied. The band holds the front clutch drum, which is connected to the sun gear by the sun gear driving shell. This holds the sun gear, making it the reaction member. The rear planetary carrier, which was the reaction member in D1, now rotates freely (Figure 3–52). In both D2 and manual 2 the cou-

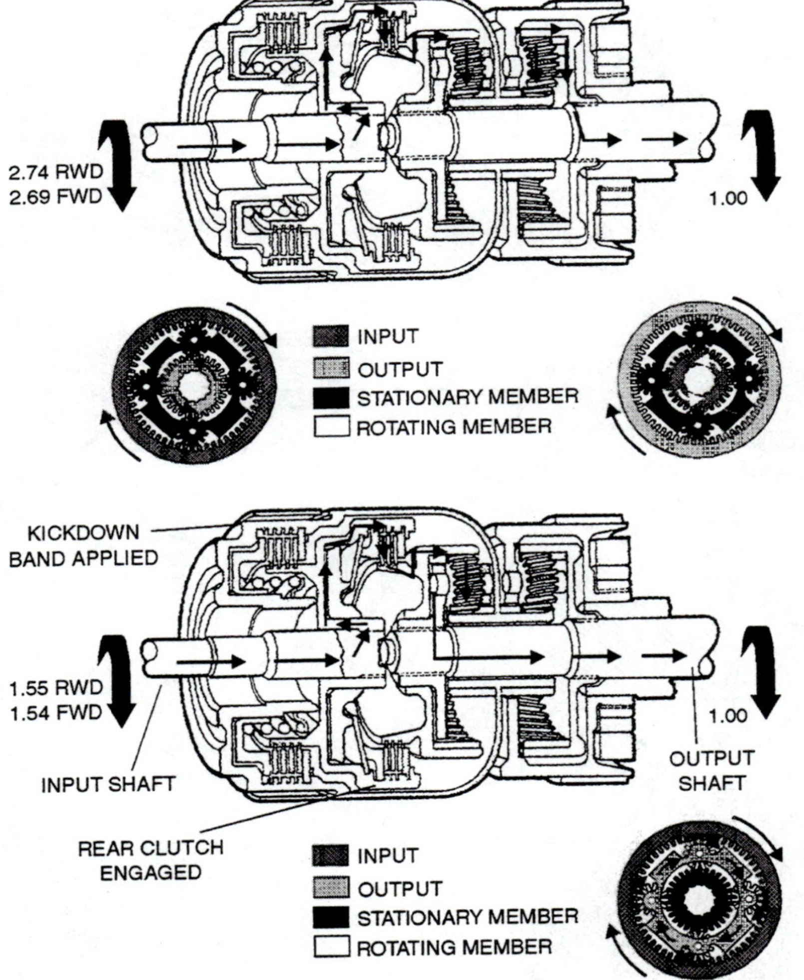

FIGURE 3–51 In D1 the rear clutch is applied, making the front ring gear the input member. The one-way clutch holds the rear planet carrier as reaction member. This combination causes first gear. (Courtesy of Chrysler)

FIGURE 3–52 In second gear the rear clutch is still applied, providing input, and the front or kickdown band is also engaged. (Courtesy of Chrysler)

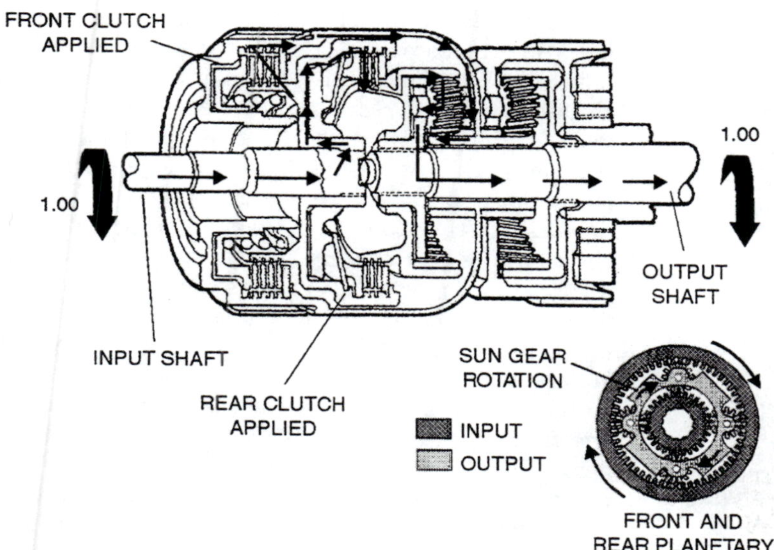

FIGURE 3–53 For third gear the front (kickdown) band is released and the front clutch is applied. With both the front and rear clutches applied, the gear set is in direct drive. (Courtesy of Chrysler)

pling and holding devices are the same. The rear clutch remains applied in D2, and as the transmission shifts into D3 it is still applied. For third speed (D3) the front (kickdown) band is released and the front clutch is applied. The front clutch hub is splined to the input shaft, with the clutch drum being connected to the sun gear through the sun gear driving shell, which now drives the sun gear as an input member. With both the sun gear and front ring gear as input, the gear set will be in direct drive (Figure 3–53). Moving the selector to reverse (R), the rear clutch is released while the front clutch and rear (low and reverse) band are applied. With the front clutch applied, the sun gear is the input member and the rear planet carrier is the reaction member, being held by the band (Figure 3–54). As you can see in the clutch and band chart (Figure 3–55), the rear clutch is applied in all forward gears and the coupling and holding devices applied in D2 and 2 are the same.

3.7.3 Three-Speed RWD Ford FMX (Ravigneaux Gear Set)

Our next transmission is the Ford FMX, which is a three-speed rear-wheel-drive design (Figure 3–56). The FMX uses a Ravigneaux gear set and has two coupling devices: the front (forward) and rear (high–reverse) clutches and three holding devices: the front (intermediate) and rear (low–reverse) band, and a one-way or overrunning clutch. The

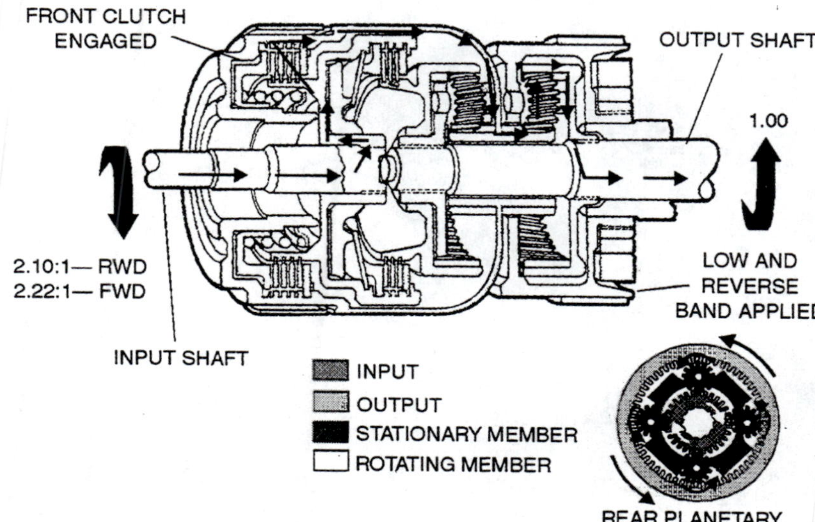

FIGURE 3–54 In reverse gear the front clutch is applied, providing input through the sun gear. The rear (low–reverse) band is also applied, holding the rear planet carrier, which causes a reverse gear. (Courtesy of Chrysler)

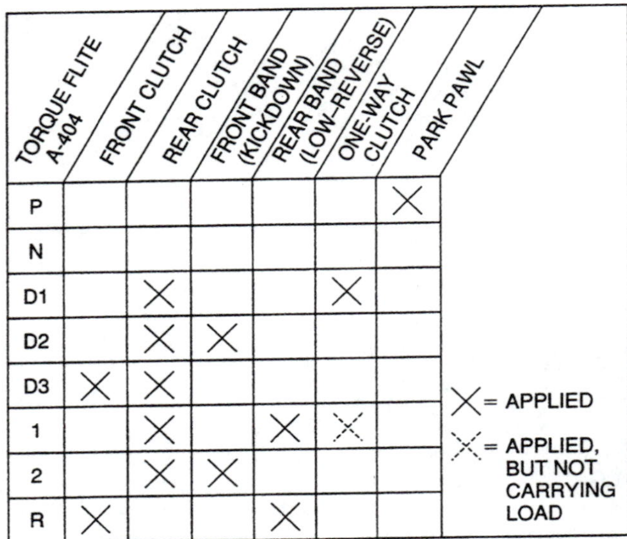

TORQUE FLITE A-404	FRONT CLUTCH	REAR CLUTCH	FRONT BAND (KICKDOWN)	REAR BAND (LOW-REVERSE)	ONE-WAY CLUTCH	PARK PAWL
P						X
N						
D1		X			X	
D2		X	X			
D3	X	X				
1		X		X	X (dashed)	
2		X	X			
R	X			X		

FIGURE 3–55 The Torque Flite A-404 clutch and band chart is typical of many three-speed automatic transmissions. (Courtesy of Chrysler)

primary (rear) sun gear serves as the input member with the secondary (front) sun gear serving as both reaction and input member. The planetary carrier acts as a reaction member, while the ring gear is the output. With the gear selector in park (P), the park pawl is mechanically engaged to lock the output shaft and all the coupling and holding devices are released. In neutral (N) (Figure 3–57) the coupling and holding devices are still released and the park pawl is also released, so the vehicle is free to roll. Putting the selector in drive, the transmission goes into D1, applying the front (forward) clutch, which causes the one-way or overrunning clutch to lock up, holding the planetary carrier as shown in Figure 3–58. With the shift to second gear (D2), the front (forward) clutch remains applied and the front (intermediate) band is applied. The band holds the secondary (front) sun gear stationary so that it becomes the reaction member and the planetary carrier is free to rotate, as shown in Figure 3–59. As the transmission shifts into third (D3), the front (intermediate) band is released and the rear (high–reverse) clutch is applied. With the

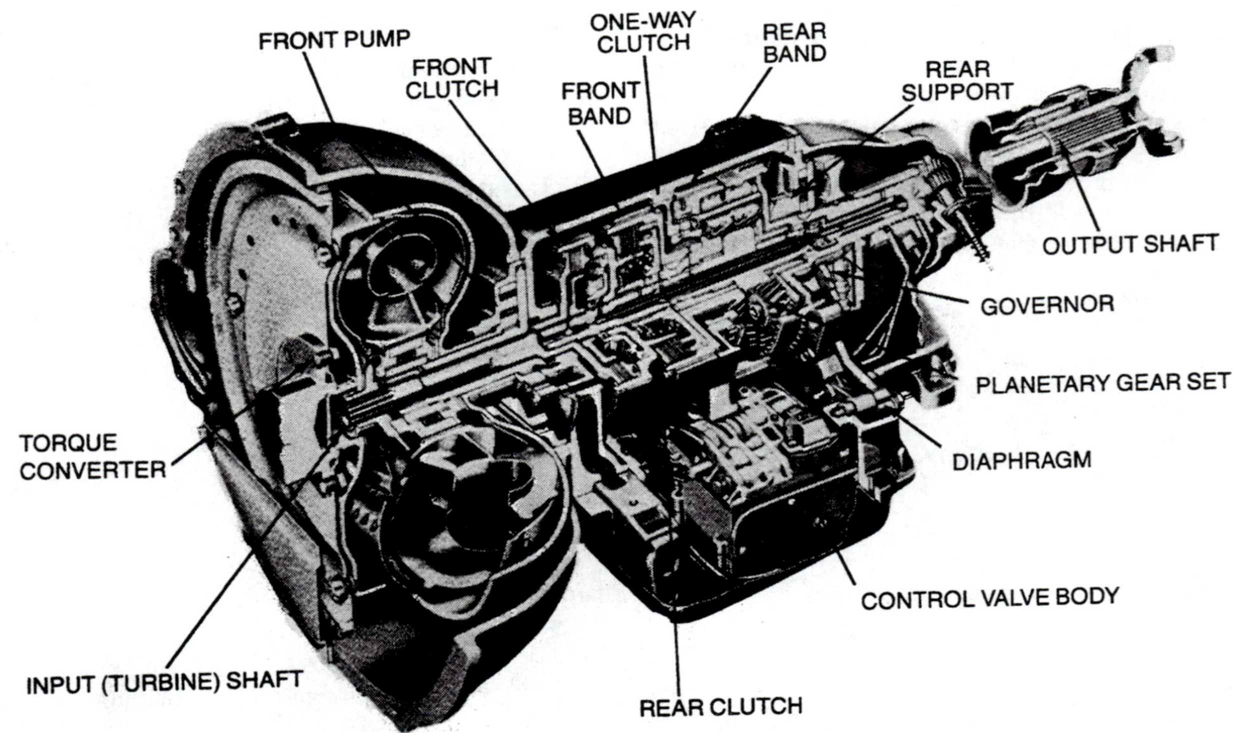

FIGURE 3–56 This cutaway drawing of the Ford FMX transmission identifies the major components of the transmission. (Courtesy of Ford)

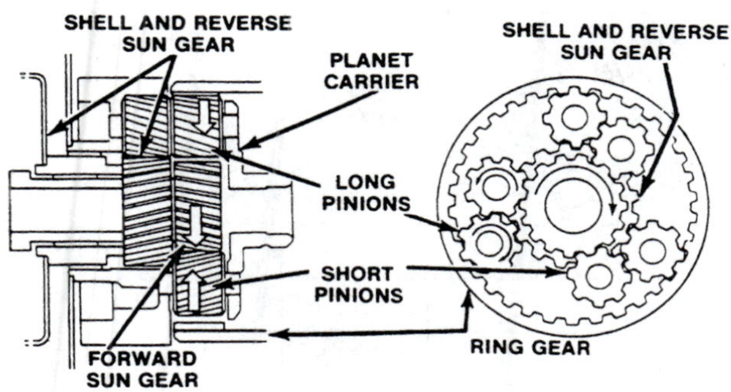

FIGURE 3–57 In neutral, all bands and clutches are released, so no power can flow. (Courtesy of Ford)

rear clutch applied, the secondary (front) sun gear becomes an input member, which along with the input of the primary (rear) sun gear causes a direct drive, as shown in Figure 3–60. In manual first gear, the rear (low–reverse) band is applied to increase holding power and to provide engine braking, which does not occur in D1. Manual second (2) and drive second (D2) gears use the same coupling and holding devices. For the transmission to be in reverse (R), the rear (high–reverse) clutch is applied, which makes the secondary (front) sun gear the input member. The rear (low–reverse) band is applied holding the planetary carrier as the reaction member, as shown in Figure 3–61. Take time to compare this clutch and band chart (Figure 3–62) with the previous transmissions (Figure 3–55). You will find the charts very similar except for the first two vertical columns, which seem to have exchanged places.

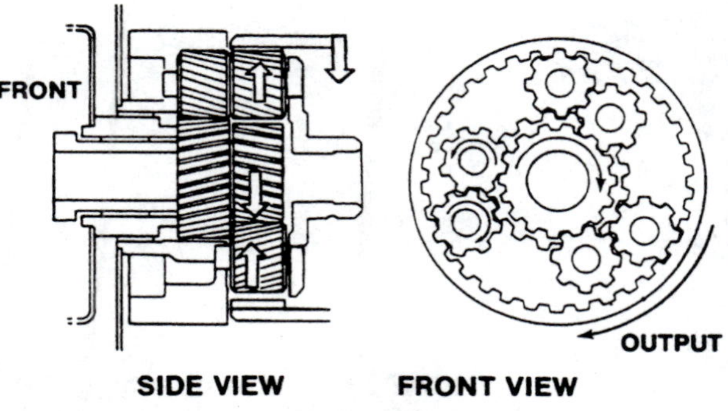

FIGURE 3–58 In first gear the front (forward) clutch is applied, driving the primary (rear) sun gear as input. The one-way clutch holds the planet carrier as the reaction member. (Courtesy of Ford)

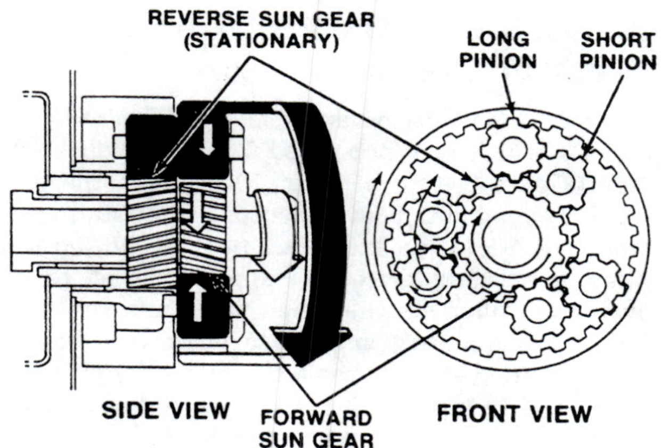

FIGURE 3–59 For second gear, the front (forward) clutch remains applied and the front (intermediate) band is applied, which holds the front (secondary) sun gear. (Courtesy of Ford)

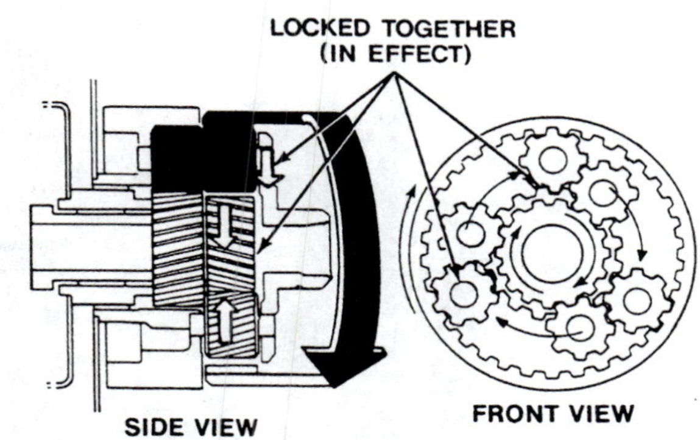

FIGURE 3–60 In third gear the band is released, and both the front (forward) and rear (high–reverse) clutches are applied. (Courtesy of Ford)

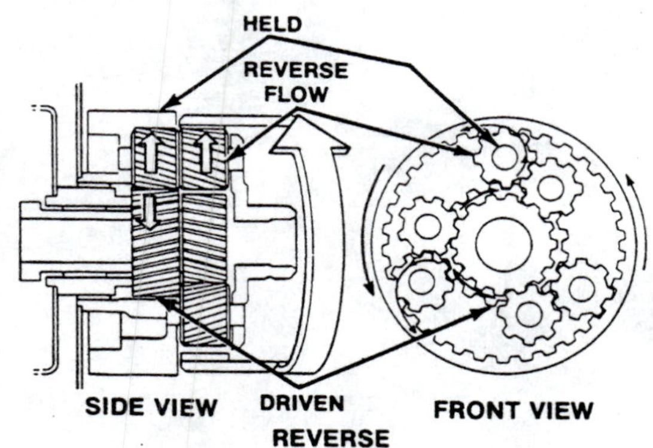

FIGURE 3–61 Reverse gear is obtained by applying the rear (high–reverse) clutch and the rear (low–reverse) band. (Courtesy of Ford)

3.7.4 Four-Speed FWD-THM 325-4L (Simpson Gear Set)

The next transmission is the General Motors THM 325-4L, which is a four-speed front-wheel-drive design (Figure 3–63). In park (P) position, the park pawl is engaged to hold the output shaft stationary, whereas in both park (P) and neutral (N), no coupling or holding devices are applied except for the overdrive roller clutch, which transmits converter torque to the main gear train through the overdrive unit (Figure 3–64). As the transmission is placed in drive (D1) (Figure 3–65) the forward clutch is applied and the low and reverse roller clutch is holding. Throughout all gears, except overdrive (D4), the overdrive roller clutch is holding and in all forward gears the forward clutch will be applied as you can see in the clutch and band chart (Figure 3–70). To shift second gear (D2) (Figure 3–66), the

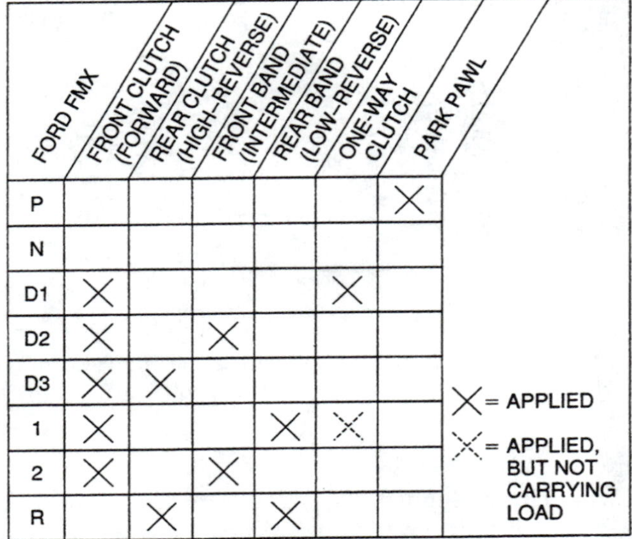

FORD FMX	FRONT CLUTCH (FORWARD)	REAR CLUTCH (HIGH-REVERSE)	FRONT BAND (INTERMEDIATE)	REAR BAND (LOW-REVERSE)	ONE-WAY CLUTCH	PARK PAWL
P						X
N						
D1	X				X	
D2	X		X			
D3	X	X				
1	X			X	X (applied, but not carrying load)	
2	X		X			
R		X		X		

X = APPLIED
X (dotted) = APPLIED, BUT NOT CARRYING LOAD

FIGURE 3–62 The clutch and band chart for the Ford FMX transmission is similar to the Torque Flite chart except for one major difference. Can you identify the difference?

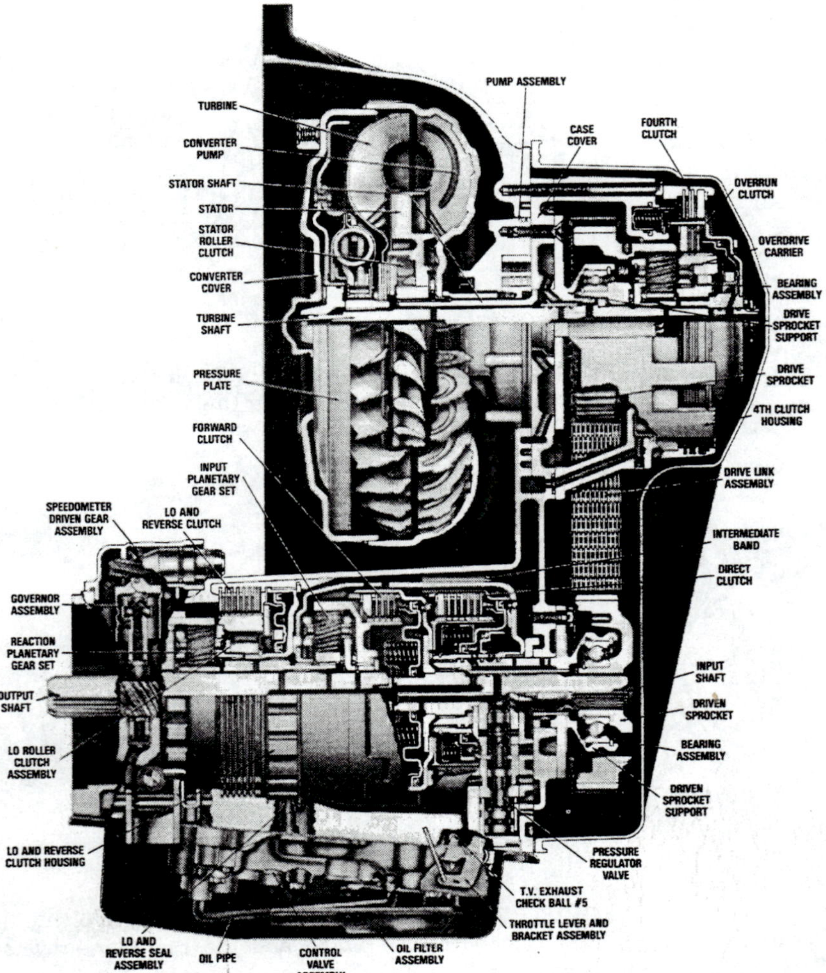

FIGURE 3–63 This cutaway drawing identifies all the components of the THM 325-4L transaxle. (Reprinted with permission of General Motors Corporation)

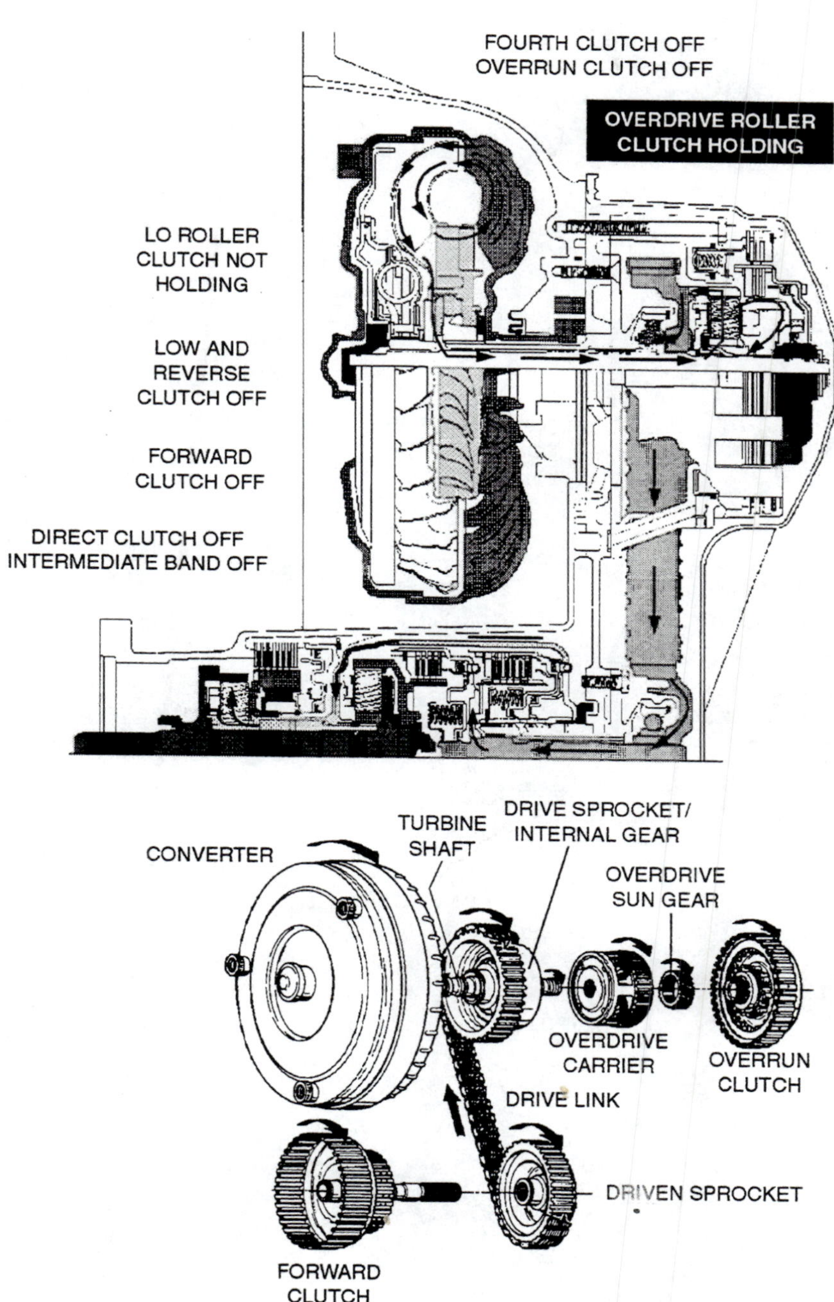

FIGURE 3–64 THM 325-4L in neutral gear. (Reprinted with permission of General Motors Corporation)

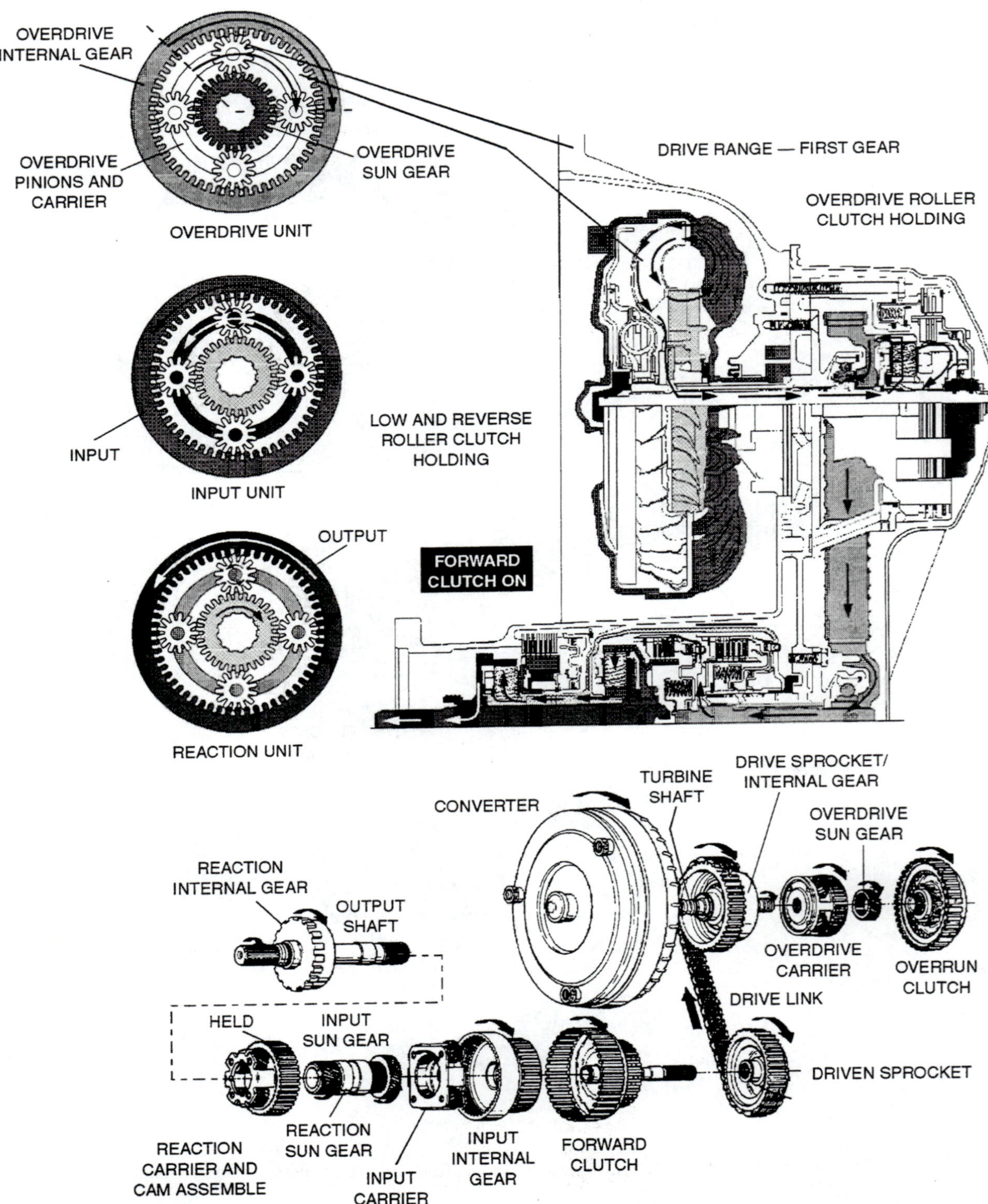

FIGURE 3–65 THM 325-4L in first gear. (Reprinted with permission of General Motors Corporation)

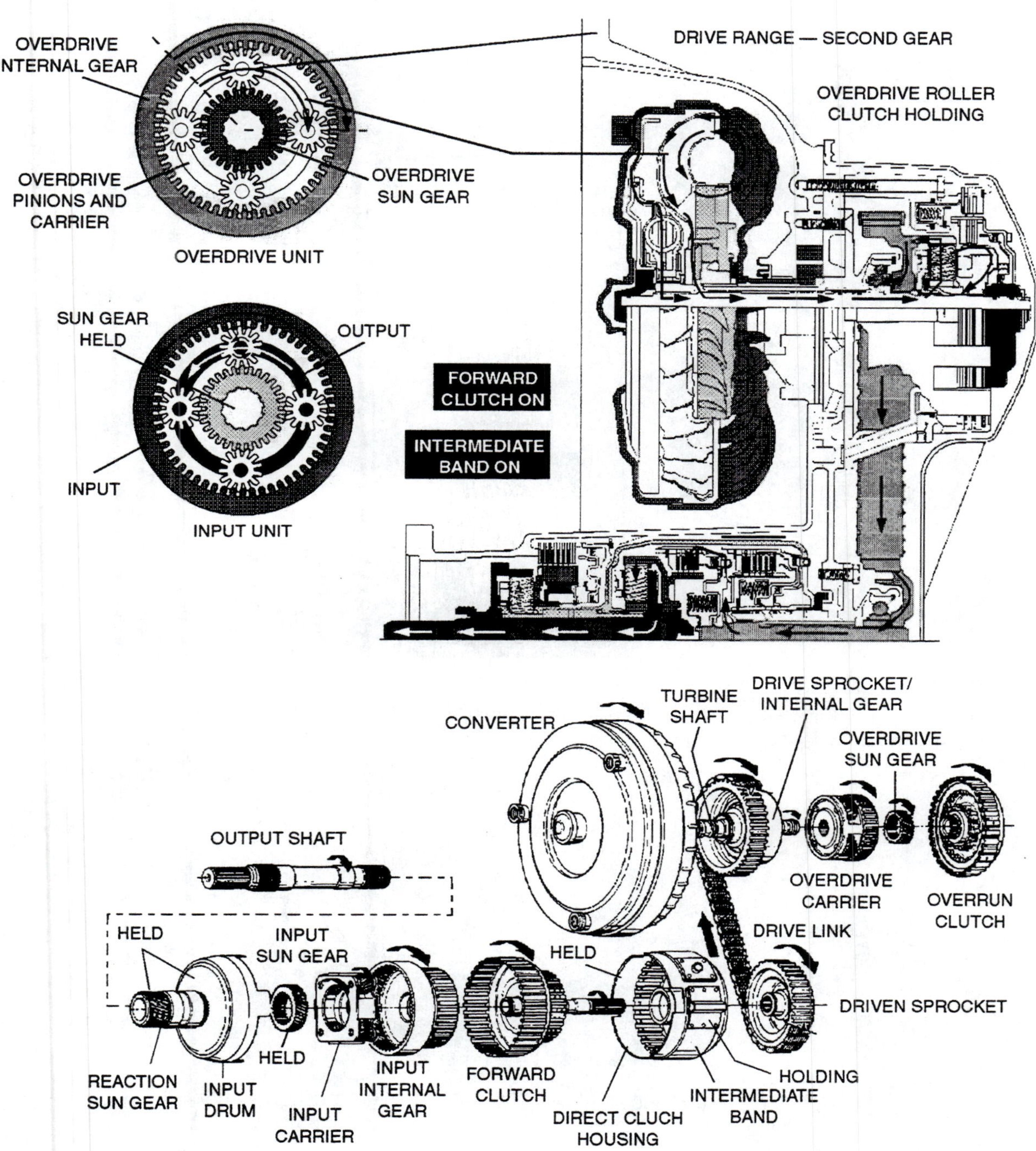

FIGURE 3–66 THM 325-4L in second gear. (Reprinted with permission of General Motors Corporation)

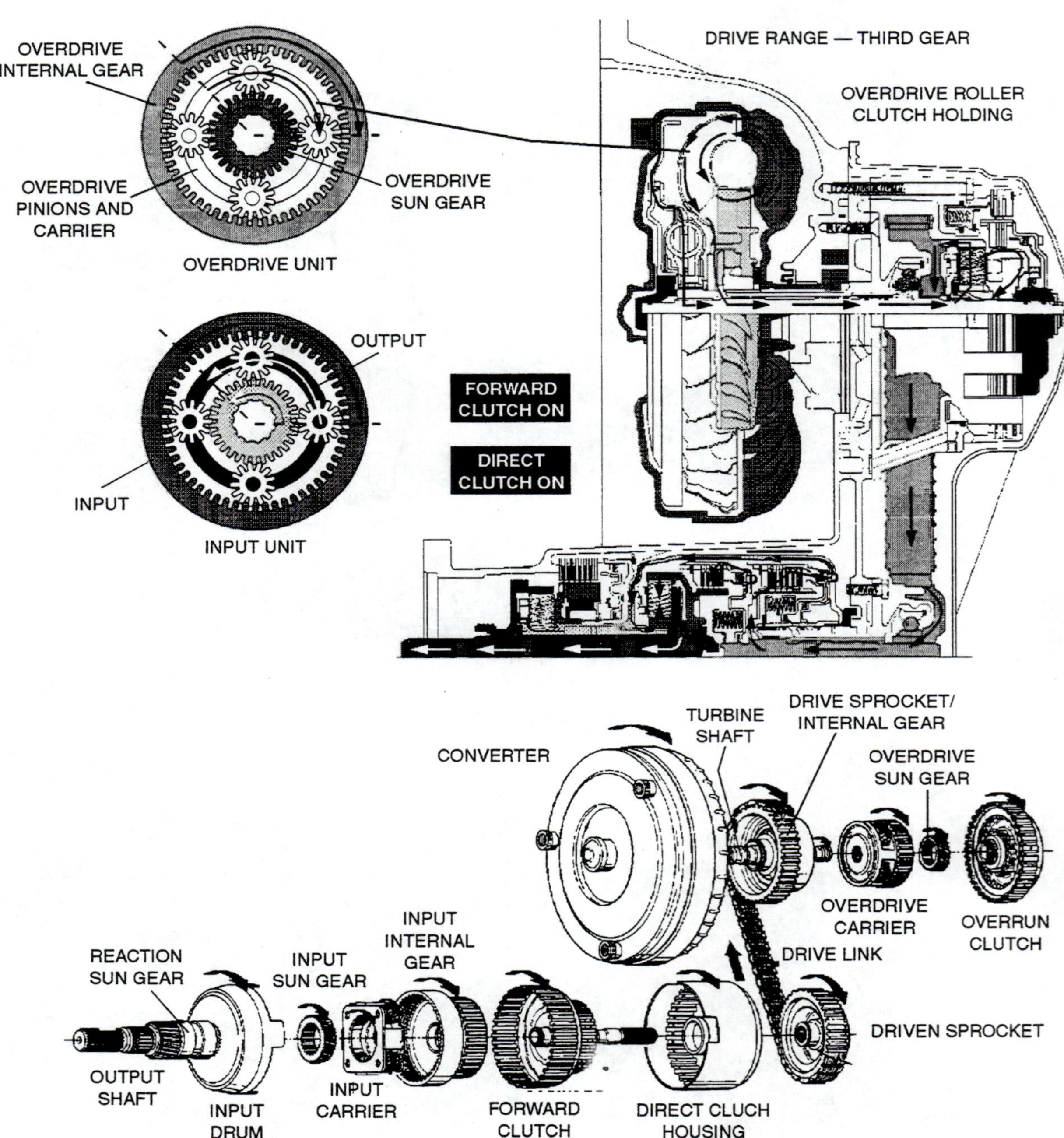

FIGURE 3–67 THM 325-4L in third gear. (Reprinted with permission of General Motors Corporation)

forward clutch and overdrive roller are still applied and the intermediate band is also applied. For manual second (2) the overrun clutch is also applied. As it shifts to third speed (D3) (Figure 3–67), the intermediate band is released, and the direct clutch is applied, the forward clutch is still applied. If you look closely at the main gear train, you will see that it is the same Simpson gear set we learned about with regard to the Torque Flite transmission, and even though the names of the clutches have changed, their function is still the same: they connect to the same members of the gear set and do the same jobs. The one major difference in this transmission is the overdrive unit, which provides fourth gear. As the shift to overdrive (D4) occurs, the fourth clutch is applied along with the forward and direct clutch (Figure 3–68). With the fourth clutch applied the overdrive sun gear is held as the reaction member and the input carrier drives the output ring gear at an overdrive gear ratio. The rest of the main gear train remains in direct drive. For reverse (R) (Figure 3–69) the overdrive roller clutch is holding and the overdrive unit is in direct drive. In the main gear train the direct clutch and low–reverse clutch are applied. By studying the clutch and band chart (Figure 3–70) you can see that the main gear train in this transmission operates the same as any other Simpson gear set; the only thing different is the overdrive unit.

3.7.5 Four-Speed RWD Ford AOD (Ravigneaux Gear Set)

The last power flow we will study is that of the Ford AOD four-speed rear-wheel-drive transmission. This transmission uses a Ravigneaux gear set similar to the Ford FMX and has three coupling clutches, one holding clutch and two bands, and two one-way clutches, shown in Figure 3–71. The torque converter used in the AOD is a dual-output type which has a turbine shaft for normal hydraulic power output plus a direct drive shaft for mechanical power output. Study how this feature works as we go on.

In park (P), the park pawl is engaged to prevent rotation of the output shaft. In neutral (N), the park pawl is released and the low–reverse band is applied but does not cause a drive condition (Figure 3–72). Placing the selector in drive (D1), the forward clutch is applied, coupling the turbine shaft to the forward sun gear making it the input member. The low one-way clutch is holding the planetary carrier as the reaction member, leaving the ring gear as the output member, as shown in Figure 3–73. In manual low gear the low–reverse band is applied to provide better holding power on the reaction member and to also give engine braking.

In second gear (D2), the forward clutch remains applied with the forward sun gear as input, and the intermediate clutch is applied, causing the intermediate one-way clutch to hold the reverse sun gear as the reaction member. The forward sun gear drives the planetary pinions, which walk around the stationary reverse sun gear and drive the ring gear, as shown in Figure 3–74.

With the shift to third gear (D3), the direct clutch is applied, which couples the direct drive shaft to the planetary carrier to make it an input member. The forward clutch is still applied, coupling the turbine shaft to the forward sun gear. With two inputs the gear set is in direct drive. The torque delivery to the gear set is about 60% mechanical through the direct drive shaft and 40% hydraulic through the turbine shaft (Figure 3–75). In manual third gear, the same devices are used but the transmission will not upshift automatically into fourth. This transmission does not have a manual second-gear selection.

With the shift to fourth gear (D4), the forward clutch is released and the overdrive band is applied to hold the reverse sun gear as the reaction member. The direct clutch is still applied, driving the planetary carrier with 100% mechanical power flow. With the planetary carrier as input and the reverse sun gear as the reaction member, the ring gear is driven in overdrive, as shown in Figure 3–76. For reverse (R), the reverse clutch is applied, coupling the turbine shaft to the reverse sun gear as input. The low–reverse band is applied, holding the planetary carrier as the reaction member, which puts the gear set in reverse mode, as shown in Figure 3–77. This clutch and band chart (Figure 3–78) should be compared to the other charts to determine what is similar or different among the transmission power flows you just studied.

3.7.6 Transaxle Final Drives

To fully understand the power flow through an automatic transmission, you need to follow the flow after it leaves the transmission. This is easy to do on RWD vehicles with the engine in the front and rear wheel drive. The output planetary member is connected to the output shaft, which extends to the rear of the transmission tail housing. At that point a splined yoke slides over the splined end of the output shaft and connects the transmission to the drive shaft, and the power flow leaves the transmission as shown in Figure 3–79.

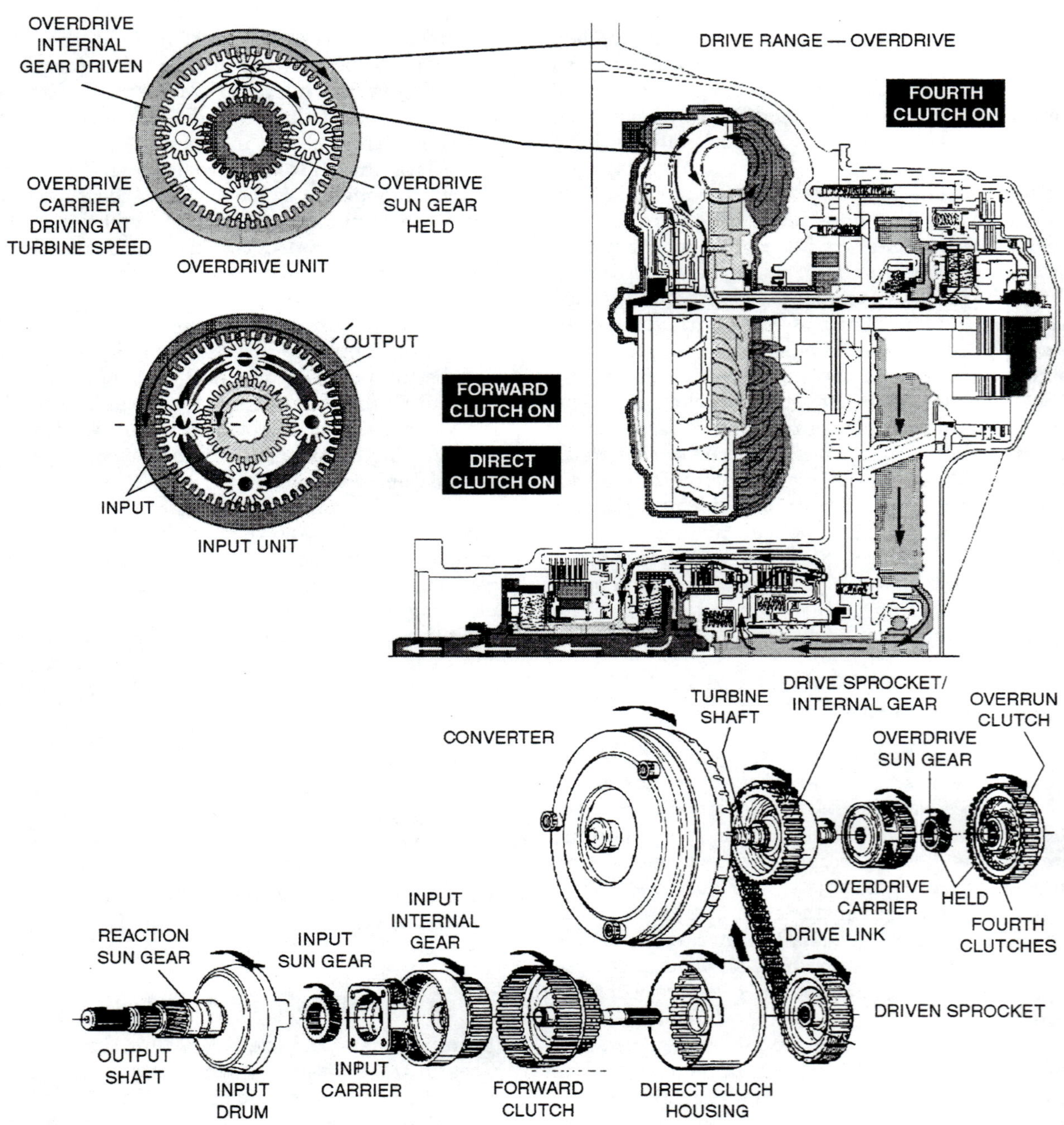

FIGURE 3–68 THM 325-4L in fourth gear. (Reprinted with permission of General Motors Corporation)

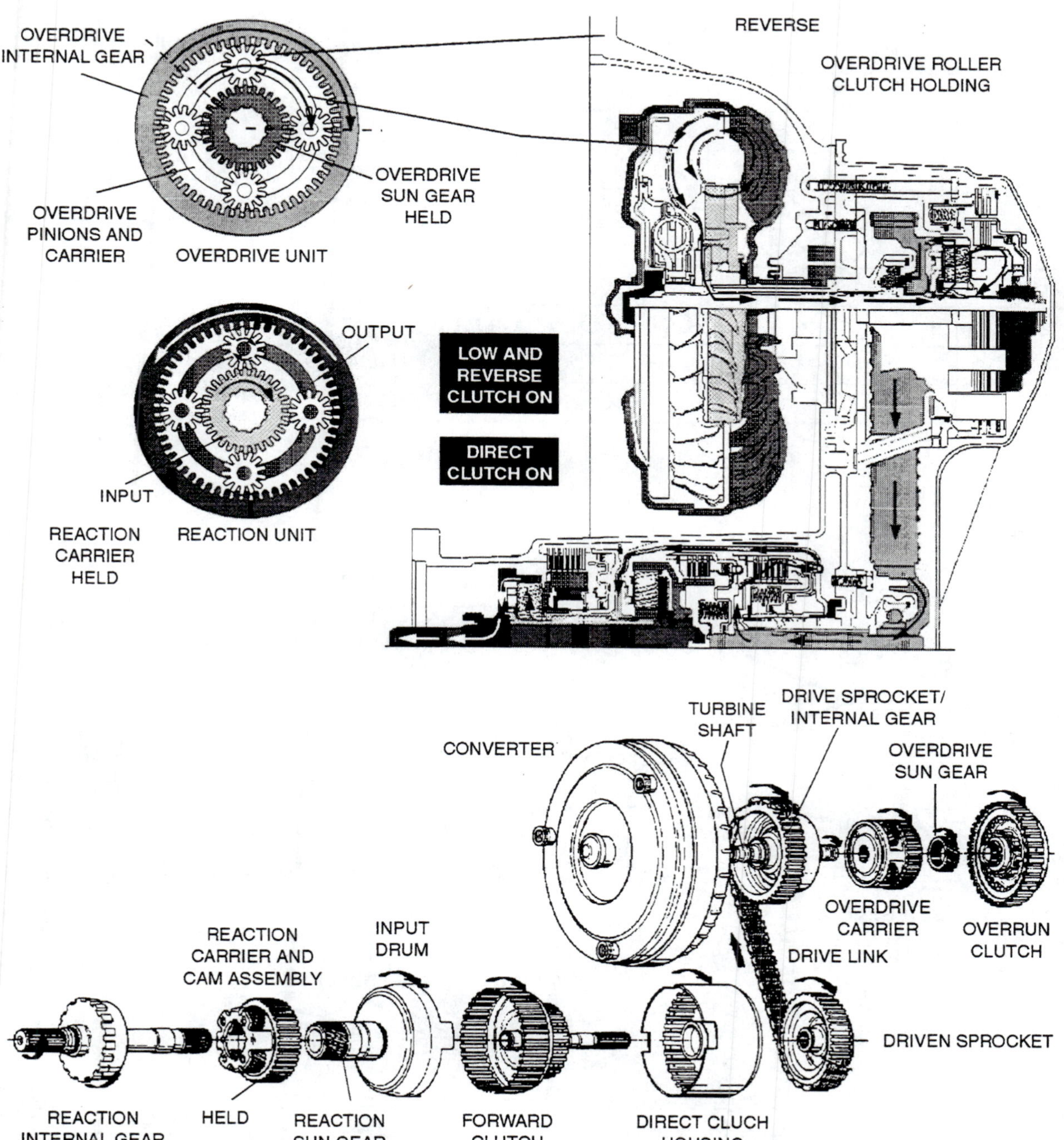

FIGURE 3–69 THM 325-4L in reverse gear. (Reprinted with permission of General Motors Corporation)

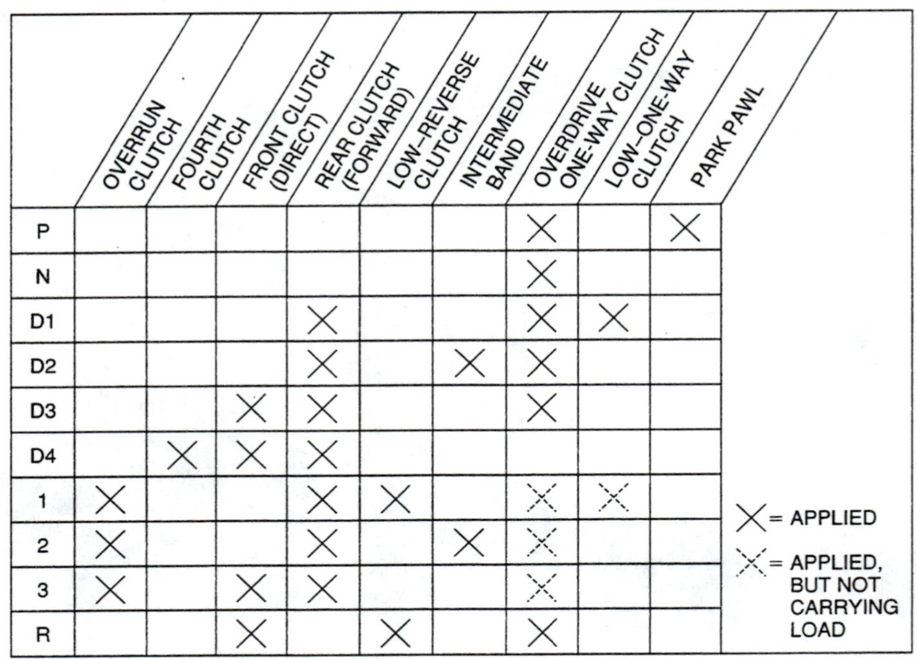

	OVERRUN CLUTCH	FOURTH CLUTCH	FRONT CLUTCH (DIRECT)	REAR CLUTCH (FORWARD)	LOW–REVERSE CLUTCH	INTERMEDIATE BAND	OVERDRIVE ONE-WAY CLUTCH	LOW–ONE-WAY CLUTCH	PARK PAWL
P							X		X
N							X		
D1				X			X	X	
D2				X		X	X		
D3			X	X			X		
D4		X	X	X					
1	X			X	X		(X)	(X)	
2	X			X		X	(X)		
3	X		X	X			(X)		
R			X		X		X		

X = APPLIED

(X) = APPLIED, BUT NOT CARRYING LOAD

FIGURE 3–70 THM 325-4L clutch and band chart, standardized version.

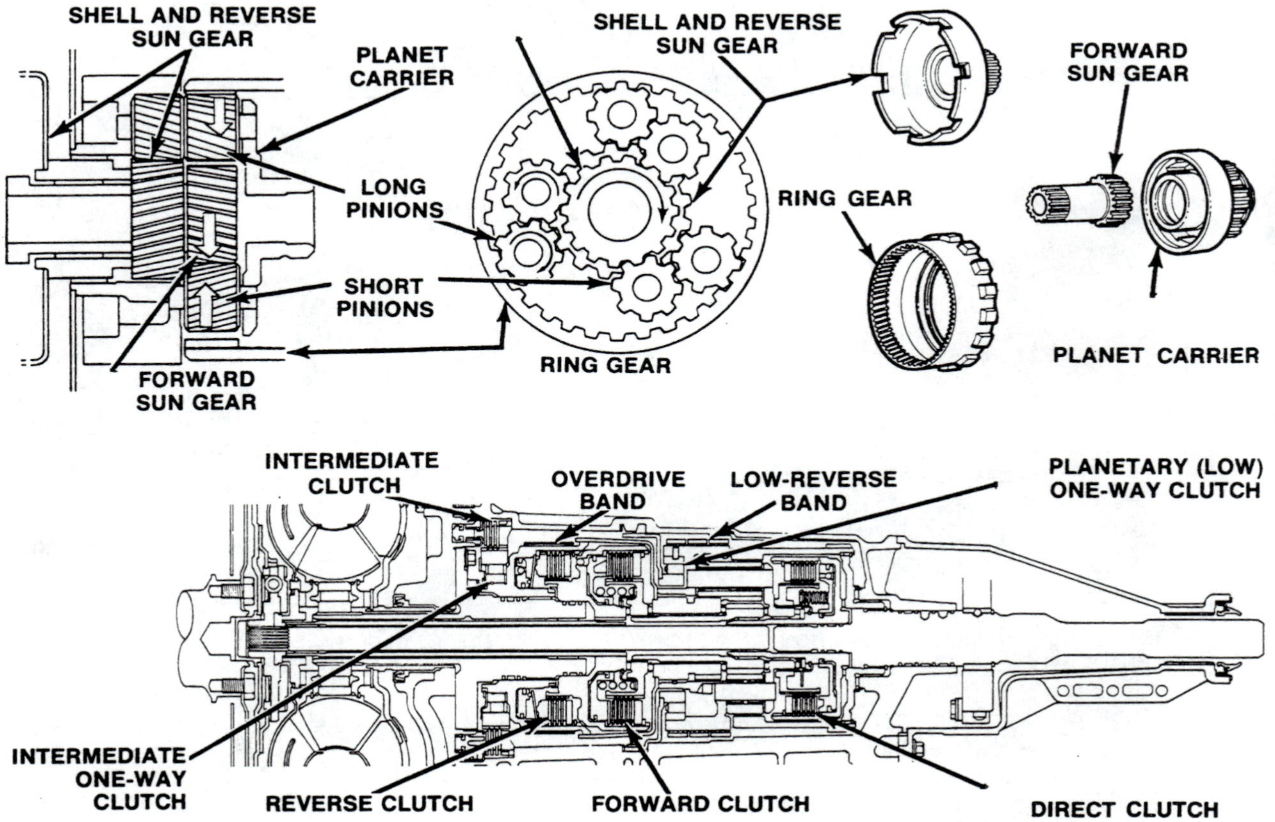

FIGURE 3–71 AOD cutaway view. (Courtesy of Ford)

APPLIED IN P
MECHANICAL INPUT
TURBINE INPUT

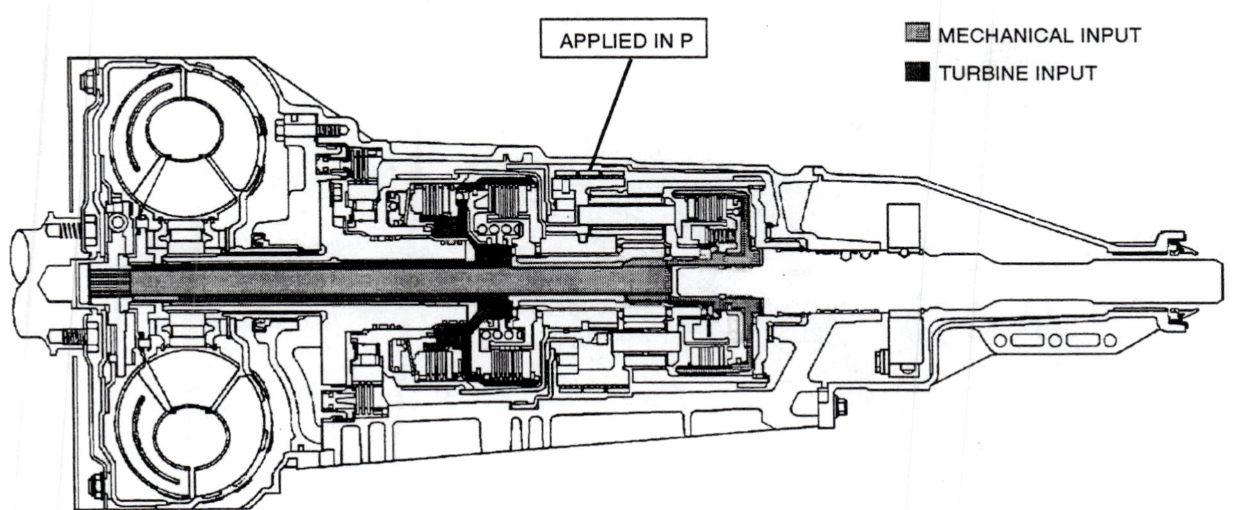

FIGURE 3–72 AOD in neutral gear. (Courtesy of Ford)

APPLIED
HOLDING
INPUT
HELD
OUTPUT
POWER FLOW
TURBINE
FORWARD CLUTCH
FORWARD SUN GEAR
RING GEAR
OUTPUT SHAFT

FIGURE 3–73 AOD in first gear. (Courtesy of Ford)

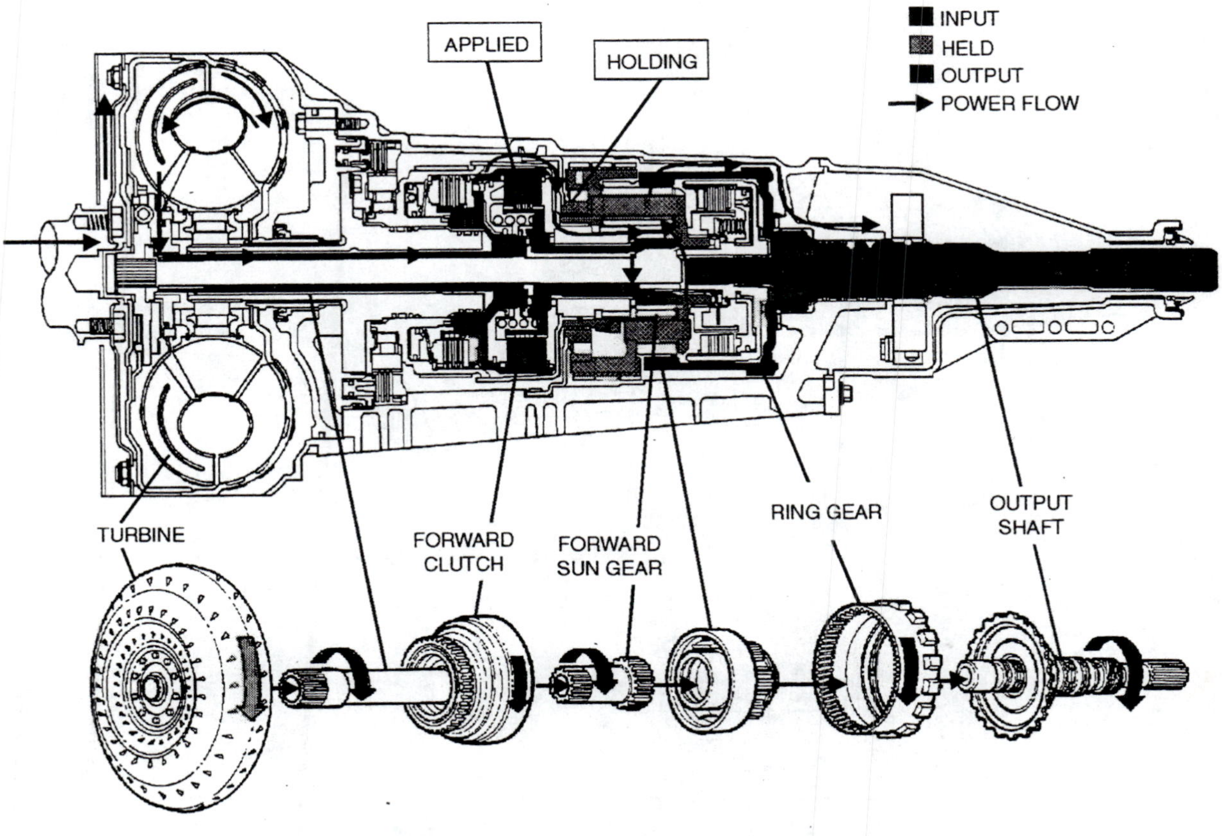

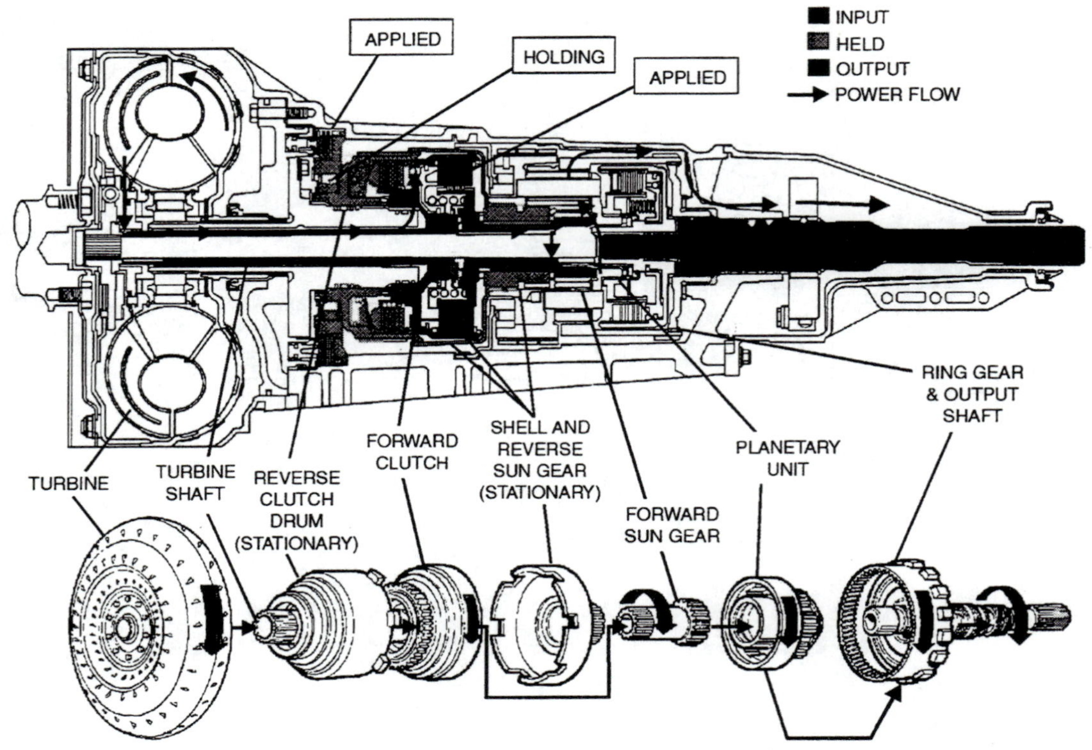

FIGURE 3–74 AOD in second gear. (Courtesy of Ford)

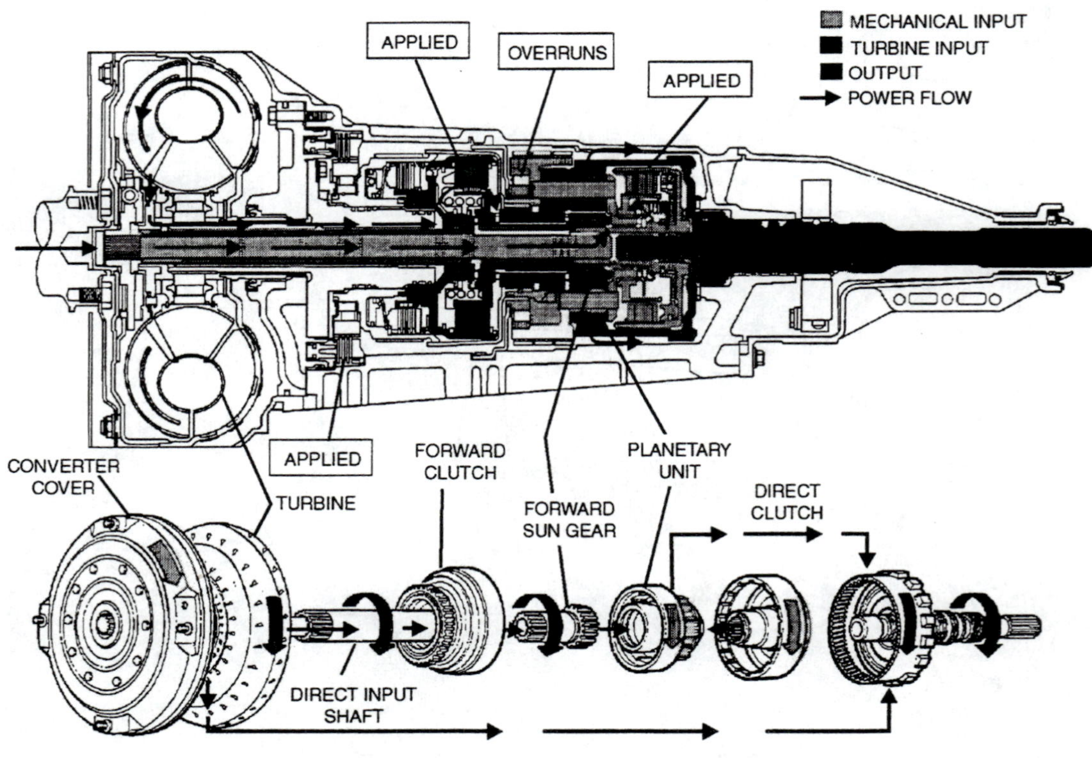

FIGURE 3–75 AOD in third gear. (Courtesy of Ford)

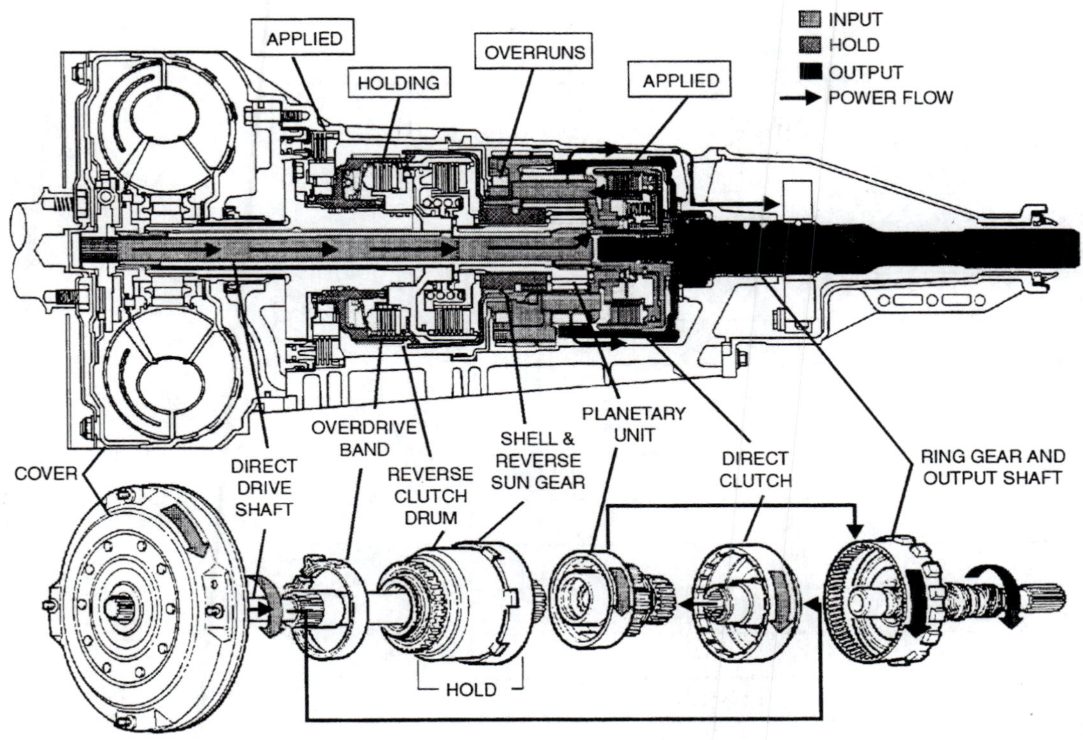

FIGURE 3–76 AOD in fourth gear. (Courtesy of Ford)

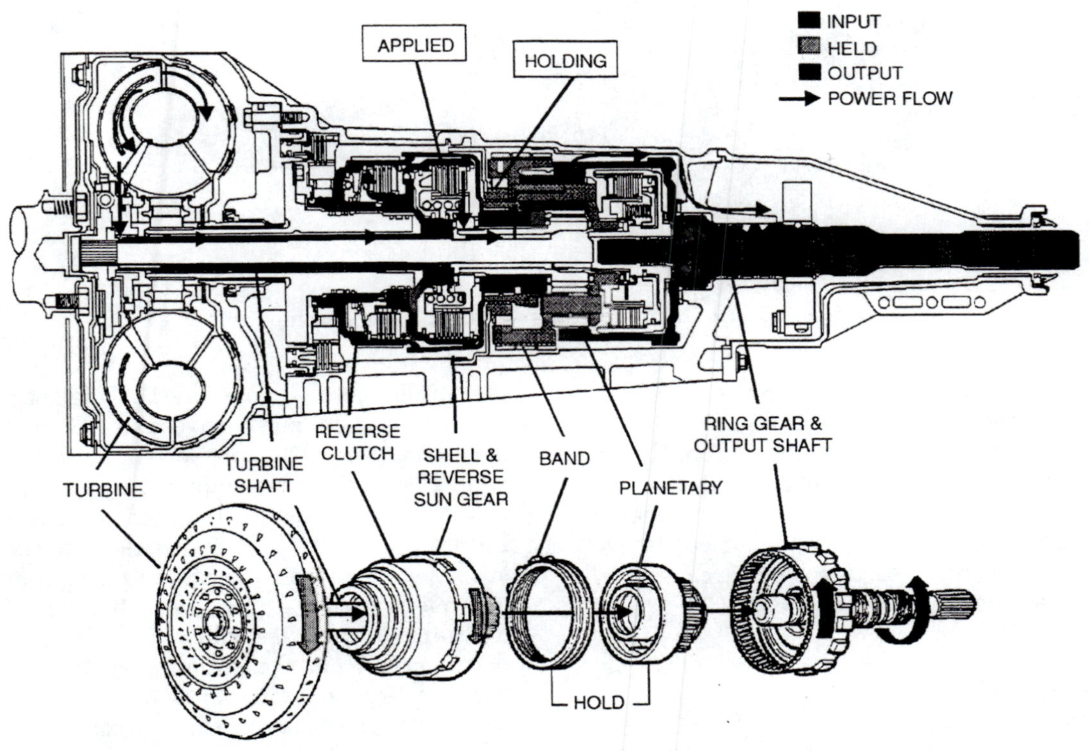

FIGURE 3–77 AOD in reverse gear. (Courtesy of Ford)

FORD AOD	INTERMEDIATE CLUTCH	REVERSE CLUTCH	FORWARD CLUTCH	DIRECT CLUTCH	FRONT BAND (OVERDRIVE)	LOW-REVERSE BAND	INTERMEDIATE ONE-WAY CLUTCH	LOW-ONE-WAY CLUTCH	PARK PAWL
P						X			X
N									
D1			X					X	
D2	X		X				X		
D3	(X)		X	X					
D4	(X)			X	X				
1			X					(X)	
2	X		X				X		
3	(X)		X	X					
R		X				X			

X = APPLIED

(X) (dotted) = APPLIED, BUT NOT CARRYING LOAD

FIGURE 3–78 AOD clutch and band chart, standardized version.

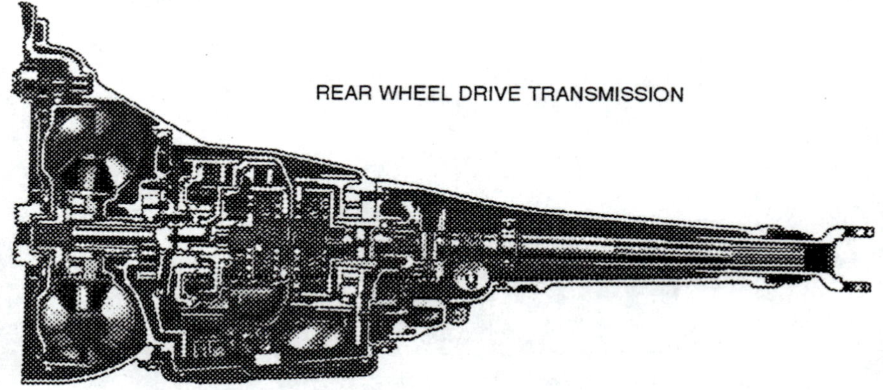

FIGURE 3–79 Rear-wheel-drive transmission power output.

The transaxle designed for front-wheel-drive vehicles is another story. The transaxle combines all the parts of an automatic transmission, the final gear reduction unit, and the differential unit all in one case. This means that the power flow does not end with the transmission output shaft but must go through the final drive section before reaching the axle shafts, as shown in Figure 3–80.

1. Ring-and-Pinion Gears

On vehicles with the crankshaft of the engine-mounted perpendicular to the axles, the direction of power flow must be changed through use of a ring-and-pinion gear (Figure 3–81). This gear is similar to that used in most drive axles, with the necessary changes made to allow it to function in the transaxle. A good example of this type of transaxle is the earlier-model Volkswagen transaxle shown in Figure 3–82. In this transaxle the transmission output shaft is connected to the pinion gear, which is in mesh with the ring gear, which is bolted to the differential case assembly. As the power flow is transferred from the pinion gear to the ring gear, the direction of the power flow is changed 90°. The power flow then leaves the transaxle through the axle shafts, which connect to the differential side gears.

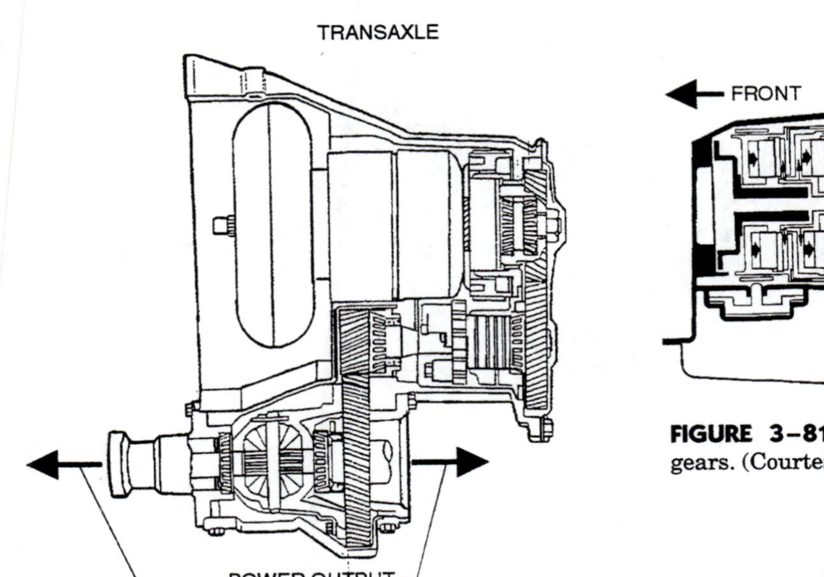

FIGURE 3–80 Front-wheel-drive transaxle power output.

RING GEAR
PINION GEAR
FRONT

FIGURE 3–81 Volkswagen transaxle ring-and-pinion gears. (Courtesy of Volkswagen)

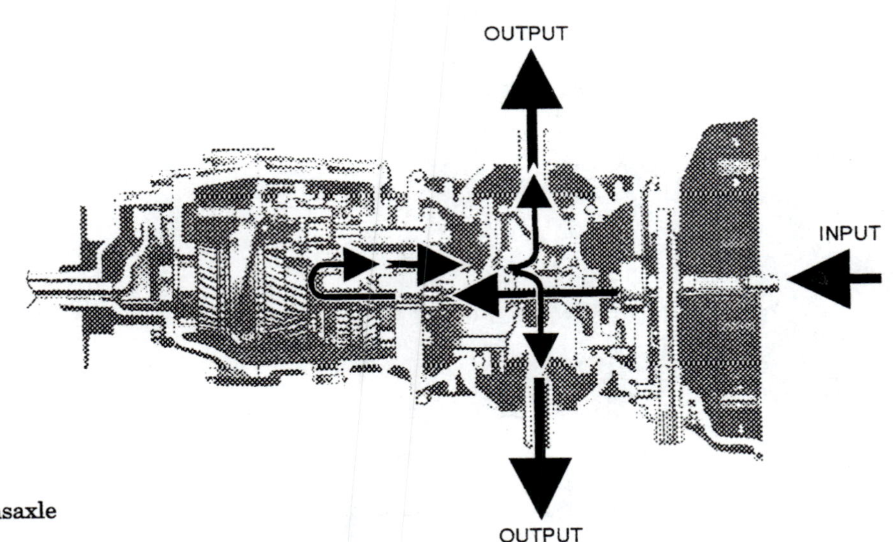

FIGURE 3–82 Volkswagen transaxle power flow. (Courtesy of Volkswagen)

2. *Helical Spur Gears*
On vehicles whose engine crankshaft is mounted parallel to the axles, such as the front-wheel-drive traverse engine design (Figure 3–83), the direction of power flow does not have to be changed. This means that the power flow from the transmission output can move through a series of helical gears and shafts to the final drive section of the transaxle. A helical spur gear set is used to provide the final drive gear reduction and then the power flows through the differential unit to the axle shafts as shown in Figure 3–84. An example of a helical spur gear final drive is the Chrysler Torque Flite transaxle shown in Figure 3–85. The output shaft gear is located at the back end of the transmission output shaft. Running parallel to the output shaft is the transfer shaft and at the back end of it is the transfer shaft gear, which is meshed with the output shaft gear. At the other end of the transfer shaft is the transfer shaft gear, which is meshed

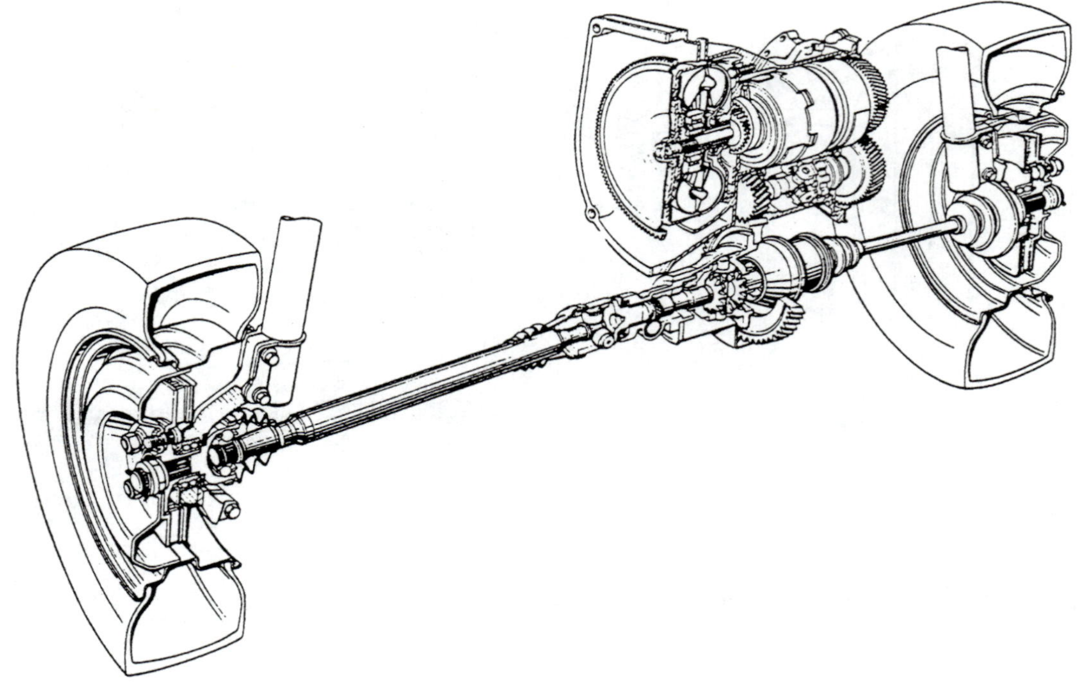

FIGURE 3–83 Traverse-mounted engine with front wheel drive.

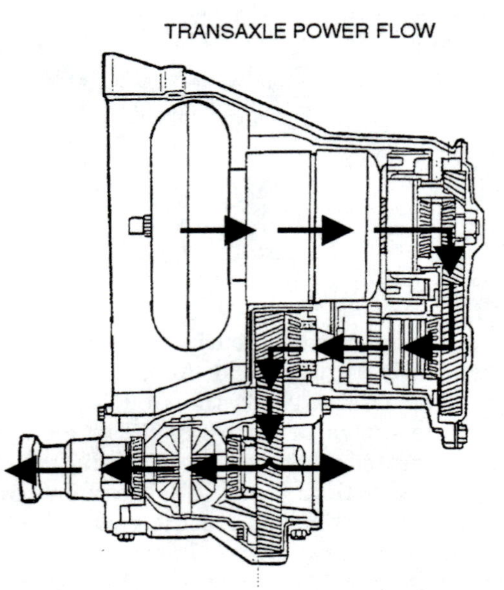

FIGURE 3–84 Front-wheel-drive transaxle power flow.

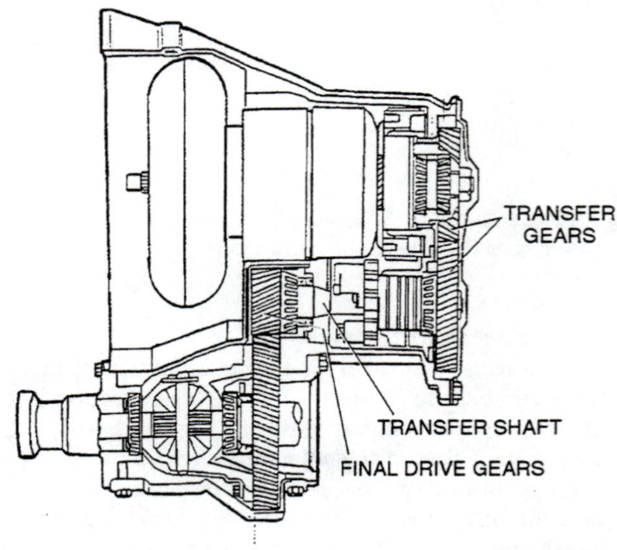

FIGURE 3–85 A-404 Torque Flite transfer shaft and gears. (Courtesy of Chrysler)

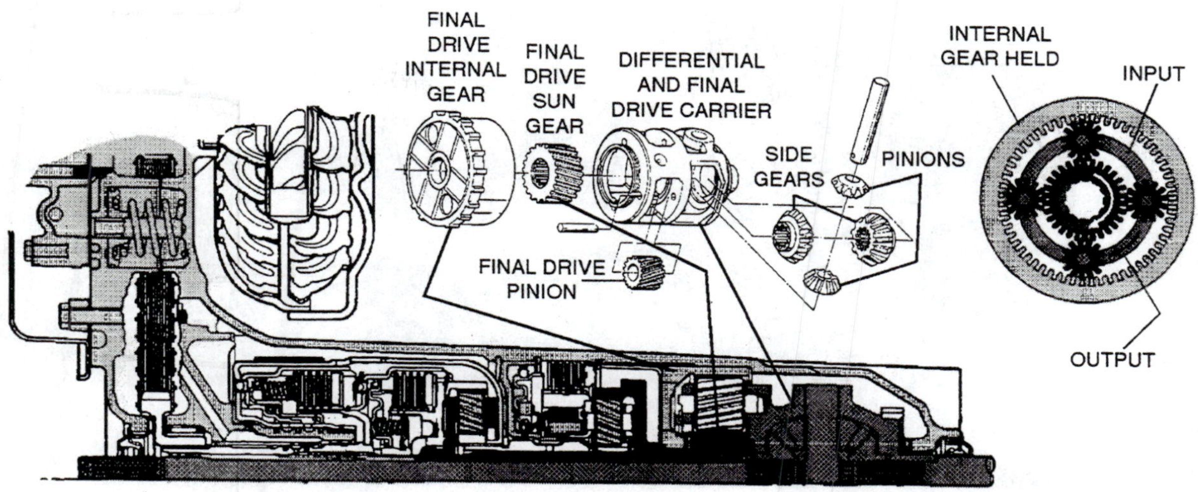

FIGURE 3–86 THM 125 final drive parts. (Reprinted with permission of General Motors Corporation)

with the final drive gear. The power flow moves from the output shaft through the transfer gears to the transfer shaft, then through the final drive gears into the differential carrier, then through the differential side gears to the axle shafts.

3. Planetary Gears

The last type of transaxle final drive we will look at uses planetary gears for the final gear reduction. Our example is the General Motors THM 125 transaxle. The final drive planetary gear set is a simple gear set with one sun gear as the input member, one planetary carrier with four pinions as the output member, and one ring gear that is splined to the case as the reaction member (Figure 3–86). The power flows from the transmission output shaft to the final drive sun gear, which drives the pinion, causing them to walk around the inside of the stationary ring gear. This action drives the planetary carrier, which is also part of the differential case, in the gear reduction mode, providing the final drive reduction. The power flows from the transmission output shaft through the final drive sun gear into the differential and final drive carrier through final drive pinions (Figure 3–87). The power then flows through the differential and final drive carrier to the differential side gears and out to the axle shafts.

SUMMARY

This was a large chapter covering a lot of information, so review it carefully. Reread any area you did not fully understand the first time through.

Planetary Gears

- The main parts of a planetary gear set are: the sun gear, planet pinions and planetary carrier, and ring gear.
- Each part can perform any of the following functions: input member, output member, or reaction member.
- By changing the function of the parts, a planetary gear set can provide the following gear modes: neutral, low and high gear reduction, low and high overdrive reduction and overdrive reverse, and direct drive.
- The Simpson gear set is very widely used and has two ring gears, two planetary carriers, and one sun gear.
- The Ravigneaux gear set is also widely used and has two sun gears, one planetary carrier with three long and three short pinions, and one ring gear.

Coupling and Holding Devices

- Hydraulic pressure is converted into force by the clutch pistons and servos.

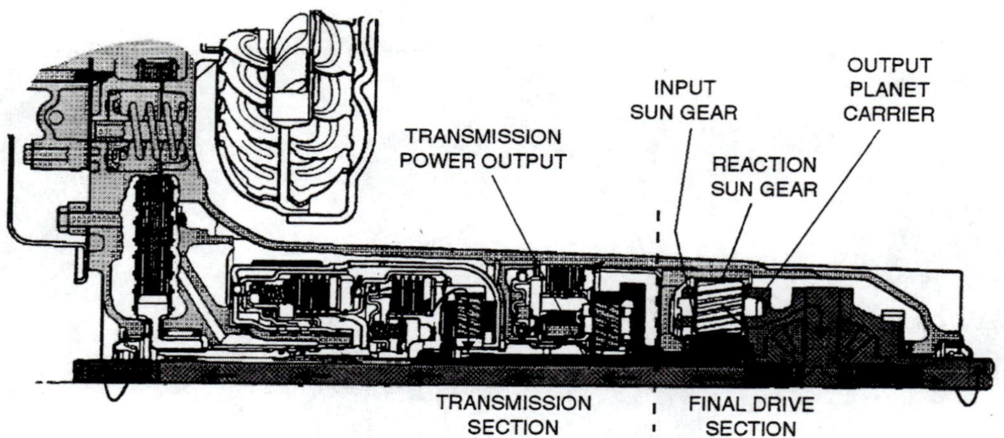

FIGURE 3–87 THM 125 final drive power flow. (Reprinted with permission of General Motors Corporation)

- The one-way or overrunning clutches (sometimes called a sprag clutch or roller clutch) are fully automatic devices, locking when turned one direction and turning freely in the other direction.
- The pawl is mechanically engaged to lock the output shaft to the case in park.

Power Flow

- Refer to the sections dealing with power flow for full descriptions.
- The coupling and holding devices used to achieve each gear speed are shown clearly in the clutch and band chart.
- Transaxles contain all the parts of the normal automatic transmission plus the final drive reduction gears and differential.
- Transaxles use three different types of final drive gearing: ring and pinion, helical spur gears, and planetary gears.

SELF-TEST

Before going on to the next chapter, complete the self-test according to your instructor's directions. Read carefully and choose the best answer.

1. The part of a planetary gear set that is connected to the engine's torque is the ____________ member.
   a. Input
   b. Reaction
   c. Output
   d. None of the above
2. The part of a planetary gear set that is connected to the drive shaft is the ____________ member.
   a. Input
   b. Reaction
   c. Output
   d. None of the above
3. The part of a planetary gear set that is connected to the transmission case is the ____________ member.
   a. Input
   b. Reaction
   c. Output
   d. None of the above
4. A planetary gear set is capable of providing the ____________ mode.
   a. Gear reduction
   b. Direct drive
   c. Overdrive
   d. All of the above
5. A compound planetary gear set that contains two ring gears, two planet carriers, and one sun gear is a(n) ____________.
   a. Simpson gear set
   b. Samson gear set
   c. Ravigneaux gear set
   d. Overdrive gear set
6. The ____________ gear set has two sun gears, one ring gear, and one carrier with three long and three short pinions.
   a. Simpson
   b. Samson
   c. Ravigneaux
   d. Overdrive

7. A multidisc clutch can be a ________________.
   a. Coupling device
   b. Holding device
   c. Both a and b
   d. Neither a nor b

8. A ________________ connects the transmission input shaft to the planetary input member.
   a. Coupling device
   b. Holding device
   c. Spline
   d. Gear

9. The reaction members in the planetary gear set are made stationary by the ________________.
   a. Clutch brake
   b. Coupling device
   c. Holding device
   d. All of the above

10. The ________________ is applied to activate a transmission band.
   a. Clutch piston
   b. Servo
   c. Servee
   d. None of the above

11. A multidisc clutch has ________________ types of clutch discs.
   a. One
   b. Two
   c. Three
   d. Four

12. The ________________ clutch disc is free to turn inside the clutch drum when the clutch is released.
   a. Friction
   b. Steel
   c. Wave
   d. Worn

13. The ________________ disc is splined to the inside of the clutch drum.
   a. Friction
   b. Steel
   c. Wave
   d. All of the above

14. The pressure plate is held in the clutch drum by a ________________.
   a. Bolt
   b. Pin
   c. Snap ring
   d. Slip ring

15. Selective snap rings or pressure plates are used to adjust clutch pack ________________.
   a. Clearance
   b. Side load
   c. End load
   d. Skim

16. A double-acting servo:
   a. Works twice as hard
   b. Can push in two directions
   c. Is twice as big
   d. Is both applied and released with hydraulic pressure

17. An overrunning clutch is ________________.
   a. Hydraulic
   b. Mechanical
   c. Computer controlled
   d. None of the above

18. A roller overrunning clutch is used to hold ________________.
   a. The output shaft in park
   b. The input member to the case
   c. The output member to the shaft
   d. None of the above

19. The device used to lock the output shaft to the case in park is a ________________.
   a. Block
   b. Nub
   c. Pawl
   d. Stop

20. The automatic transaxle uses a ________________ type of final drive.
   a. Ring-and-pinion gear
   b. Helical spur gear
   c. Planetary gear
   d. All of the above.

GLOSSARY

cantilever linkage band linkage that uses a cantilever design to increase the servo force.

clutch and band chart chart used to show which coupling or holding devices are applied in each gear.

clutch disc a friction disc that is used in multidisc clutches.

clutch drum cylindrical part that houses the clutch piston and discs and plates.

clutch piston part used to convert hydraulic pressure into force to hold clutch discs and plates together.

coupling device any multidisc clutch or one-way clutch that connects the torque input source to the planetary input.

direct drive direct engagement between the engine and the driveshaft where the engine crankshaft and driveshaft turn at the same rpm level.

double-acting servo servo that uses hydraulic pressure on both sides of the piston at times.

driven member (driven gear) gear meshed directly with the driving gear to provide torque multiplication, reduction, or a change of direction.

driving member all gear sets use one of their gears as the input gear. This gear is also called the driving gear.

flexible band type of band made from a strip of flexible steel that will lay flat when released.

friction material material bonded to the surface of clutch discs and bands to provide the needed amount of friction.

gear reduction the input driving gear rotates more revolutions than the output driven gear in a transmission.

graduated rod linkage uses a selective-fit rod to adjust the clearance of a band.

holding device any multidisc clutch, one-way clutch, band, or pawl, which holds a planetary reaction member stationary.

input member any member of a planetary gear set that is coupled to the torque input source.

multidisc clutch clutch using a number of discs and plates to lock and unlock a planetary member. Multidisc clutches use hydraulic pressure applied to a set of clutch discs to hold a planetary member. They provide a great deal of friction area in a small package.

neutral condition in a transmission when there is no connection between input and output shafts.

one-way clutch device used in automatic transmissions that permits rotation in one direction only. The one-way clutch can be composed of a set of rollers that roll on an inner and outer race. The rollers permit rotation in one direction but jam the races and prevent rotation in the other.

output member any member of a planetary gear set that is connected to the transmission output shaft.

overdrive gear ratio that produces the opposite effect of that of a gear reduction. Torque is reduced and speed is increased by the factor of the gear ratio.

pawl metal rod or arm that can be moved into a hole or slot to lock something in place.

planetary carrier (planet carrier) rigid member of a planetary gear set that houses the planet pinion gears. In addition, the carrier can act independently and serve as an output member, an input member, or a reaction member.

planetary gear set gear set that includes a ring gear, a planetary carrier with planet pinion gears, and a sun gear.

pressure plate pressure plate is mounted in the clutch drum at the opposite end from the clutch piston and is held in position with a snap ring. The piston pushes the discs against the pressure plate to apply the clutch.

Ravigneaux gear set gear system named for its designer, with small and large sun gears, long and short planetary pinions, planetary carrier, and ring carrier.

reaction member any one of the planetary members that may be held stationary during operation. This is accomplished through the use of friction and wedging devices, called holding devices, such as bands, disc clutches, and one-way clutches.

reverse (reverse gear) arrangement that reverses the direction of rotation of the output shaft.

rigid band type of band cast from cast iron or steel that holds its circular shape at all times.

ring gear ringlike outer gear of a planetary gear set with the gear teeth cut on the inside of the ring to provide a mesh with the planet pinions.

roller clutch same as a one-way clutch; a type of one-way clutch design using cams and rollers.

selective fit part (a thrust washer, snap ring, pressure plate, etc.) that is available in different thicknesses or lengths for the purpose of adjusting clearances.

servo piston and cylinder assembly that converts hydraulic pressure into mechanical force and movement in an automatic transmission. Used in the control and application of brake or friction bands.

Simpson gear set gear set that combines two planetary gear sets using one shared sun gear. Its parts include two ring gears, two planet pinion carriers, and one sun gear shared by both pinion carriers.

sprag clutch same as a one-way clutch, but uses flat plates of metal instead of rollers.

sun gear in a planetary gear set, the center gear that meshes with a cluster of planet pinions.

transaxle final drive (final drive gears) main driving gears located in the axle area of the transaxle housing.

wave spring curved flat spring placed between the piston and first steel plate to cushion the clutch engagement.

the driver's foot moves the master cylinder piston, which causes fluid movement pressure buildup to other brake parts, until all the clearance is removed. Once all the movement of parts stops, the force being applied to the pedal by the driver becomes a static force.

In this case the type of force used is physical force, because the driver was physically pushing the pedal. The other types of force used to control and operate the automatic transmission are spring, pressure differential between atmospheric pressure and engine vacuum, and hydraulic.

Spring force is used with valves in the valve body to provide a predetermined amount of push against the valve when the spring is compressed (Figure 4–3). Spring force can also pull if the spring is stretched, but in most automotive application the springs will be compressed.

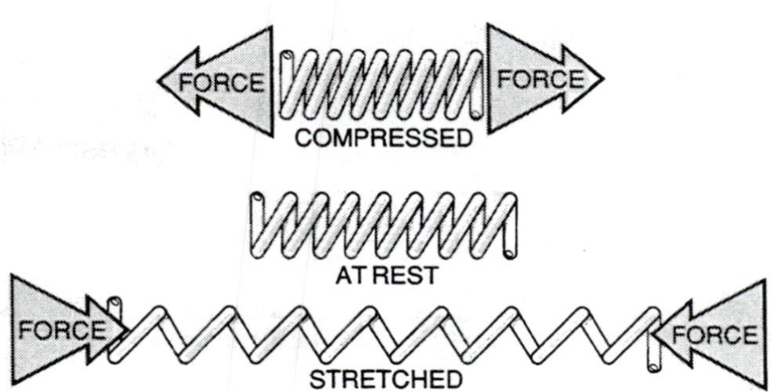

FIGURE 4–3 Spring force.

Atmospheric force is measured as atmospheric pressure and is referred to in pounds per square inch (psi). What is being measured is the actual weight of a column of air 1 inch square starting at ground level and going straight up until there is no atmosphere left (Figure 4–4). Because our atmosphere has some of the same properties as a fluid, it covers the surface of the earth, leaving a smooth outer surface. The surface of earth is not smooth, and as the elevation increases, the amount of air above any given point decreases, causing the atmospheric pressure to be less. Figure 4–5 shows how starting from sea level with an atmospheric pressure of 14.7 psi, the pressure steadily decreases as the elevation increases. Also remember that air, like a fluid, will exert its pressure evenly over the entire surface of all objects, no matter what their shape.

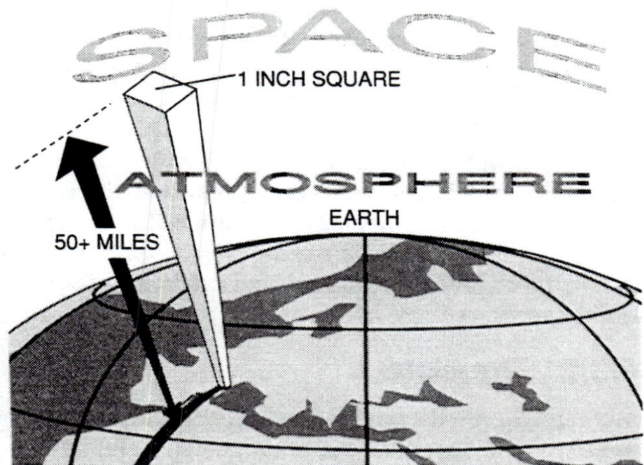

FIGURE 4–4 Atmospheric pressure is equal to the weight of a column of air 1 inch square reaching up through the atmosphere.

Vacuum is a condition that can be described as any pressure less than atmospheric pressure. A good example of how a vacuum is formed and used in an automobile is the internal combustion (IC) engine. As the four-cycle engine begins its intake stroke, the intake valve is opened by the camshaft while the piston is at top dead center (TDC). As the piston moves downward, the volume inside the enclosed cylinder increases, and as the enclosed volume increases, the pressure inside the cylinder decreases. This low-pressure area inside the cylinder is connected to the outside atmospheric pressure by the fuel induction system, as seen in Figure 4–6. The difference in pressure between the inside of the cylinder and atmospheric pressure, referred to as *pressure differential,* is what causes air to flow through the fuel induction system into the cylinder. The low pressure inside the cylinder and intake

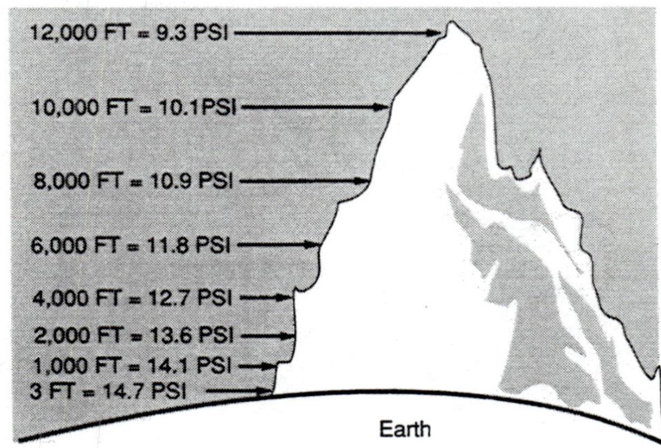

FIGURE 4–5 Atmospheric pressure drops as altitude increases.

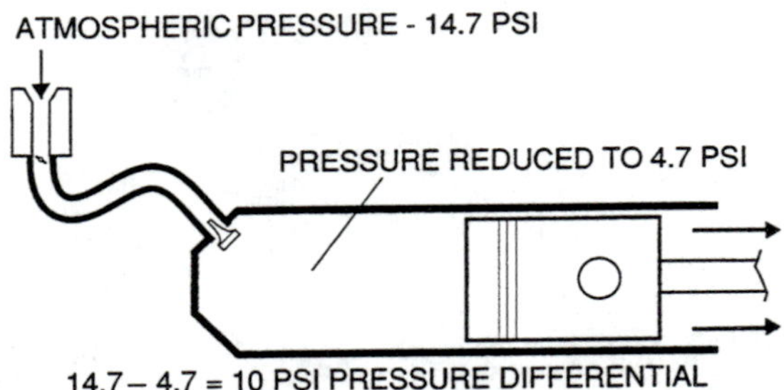

FIGURE 4–6 It is pressure differential that causes air to flow into the cylinder of an engine.

manifold is commonl called *intake vacuum.* This vacuum level can be used to measure the load on the engine. Any time there is a pressure differential the higher pressure will move toward the lower pressure until they have equalized. In the example we just studied this flow brought fuel and air into the cylinder. The principle of pressure differential is used in many ways in an automatic transmission. Hydraulic force or pressure is the subject of this chapter and is explained and studied in the following sections.

4.3.2 Pressure

Any force applied to a fluid in an enclosed system is equally distributed throughout the system. If the force applied to the piston in Figure 4–7 is 200 lb and the piston has a surface area of 1 in^2, the pressure in the system will be 200 psi. The definition of pressure, force per unit area, can be found by multiplying the force times the surface area of the piston to find the amount of pressure, in this case

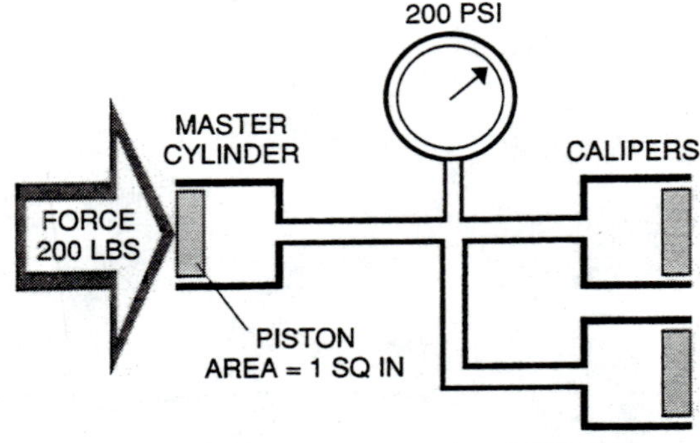

FIGURE 4–7 This is how hydraulic force is calculated.

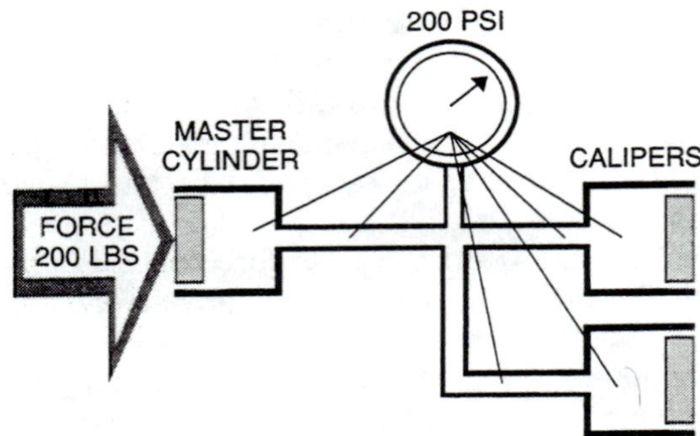

FIGURE 4–8 Hydraulic pressure is the same at any point in the system.

stated in pounds per square inch (psi). To state pressure in the metric system, the unit of measure is a kilopascal (kPa). A kilopascal is 1000 pascal, a pascal being equal to 1 newton per square meter (N/m^2). The newton represents the amount of force times the surface area stated in square meters.

4.3.3 Confined Liquids

An automotive hydraulic brake system is used to illustrate hydraulic principles, since an automotive student should be familiar with this system. The medium used to transfer the force and pressure from the master cylinder to the caliper piston is brake fluid, a type of *hydraulic fluid.* The brake fluid works in a sealed or confined system that includes the master cylinder, lines, calipers, and wheel cylinders. The brake fluid takes the shape of its containers, filling all the interior space. The brake fluid or any other liquids cannot be compressed. When force or pressure is applied to a liquid, its volume will stay the same; it will not decrease. The pressure being applied will also be distributed equally throughout the liquid in the system (Figure 4–8). That means that every square inch of surface inside the system will have the same amount of pressure applied to it. But if the container or pistons do not contain the liquid completely, there will be no pressure developed in the system. The force on the master cylinder piston will only cause fluid flow through the leak, as shown in Figure 4–9. For a hydraulic system to build up pressure, there must be resistance to flow—the liquid must be confined in the system.

4.3.4 Pascal's Law

The foundation for hydraulics and the study of liquids under pressure is based on the work of the French scientist Blaise Pascal. By experimenting

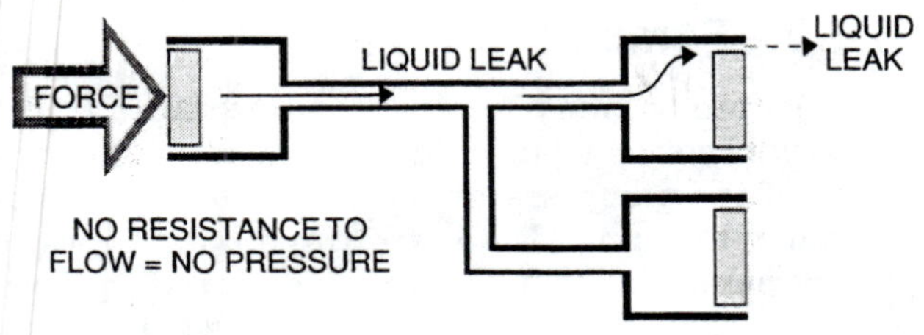

FIGURE 4–9 If a hydraulic system has a leak, there will be no resistance to fluid flow and no pressure will develop.

with confined liquids, Pascal discovered that motion and force could be transferred through a liquid. Based on the data from his experiments, Pascal said, "Pressure on a confined fluid is transmitted equally in all directions and acts with equal force on equal areas." This statement, known as *Pascal's law,* is the basis of hydraulics.

4.3.5 Liquid Lever

During his experiments with confined liquids, Pascal discovered that a mechanical advantage or force multiplication could be gained through a hydraulic system. The hydraulic force multiplication shown in his experiments was exactly the same as the mechanical advantage produced by the use of a simple lever. Output force is increased at the cost of distance traveled, as shown in Figure 4–10. The 100-lb input force being applied to the 1 in^2 of input piston area creates a *hydraulic pressure* of 100 psi. The 100-psi pressure pushing against the 3-in^2 surface area of the output piston causes a 300-lb output force or three times the input force, but with only one-third the movement of the input. With his discoveries, Pascal founded the science of hydraulics on which the operation of all automatic transmissions is based.

4.4 HYDRAULIC SYSTEM COMPONENTS

In this section we study the basic hydraulic system components used in an automatic transmission. The components we study are fluid, *reservoir, pump, spool valve, pressure regulator, pressure modulators, flow control valves, force output devices,* and *accumulators.*

4.4.1 Fluid

The liquid used as the hydraulic fluid in an automatic transmission is commonly called automatic transmission fluid (ATF). ATF has many jobs to perform in the transmission: transfer engine torque through the torque converter, deliver hydraulic pressure to the system components, provide lubrication, clean internal parts, cool the transmission, and many other jobs. The various types of ATF are explained fully in Chapter 5.

4.4.2 Reservoir

Every hydraulic system has a place where the fluid is stored during the time it is not being used. This place, called a *reservoir* or *sump,* is usually located in the bottom of the transmission, so that gravity can return the ATF to the sump. The sump must be large enough to hold all the ATF needed to fill and operate all the hydraulic circuits plus a reserve amount of ATF to guarantee that the sump will not run dry. If the sump ever runs dry during operation, the hydraulic system pressure would drop instantly and torque transfer through the transmis-

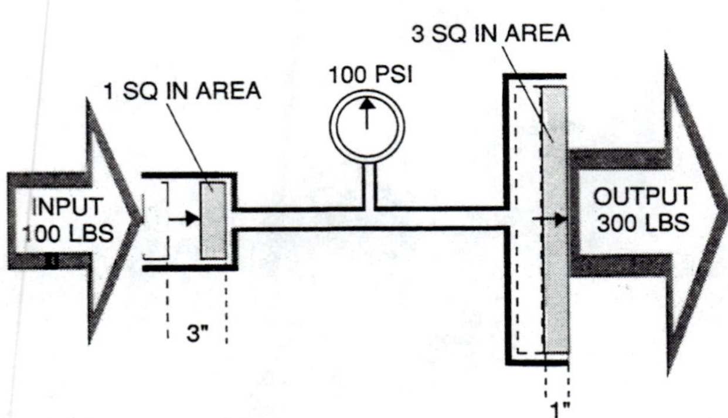

FIGURE 4–10 Whenever the force output is increased, the distance the output travels is decreased.

FIGURE 4–11 The level of ATF in the oil pan is very important and should be closely maintained.

sion would stop. Figure 4–11 shows the fluid levels in an automatic transmission. The sump must always be vented to atmospheric pressure to allow the pump to function. In the next section, you will learn how the pumps work.

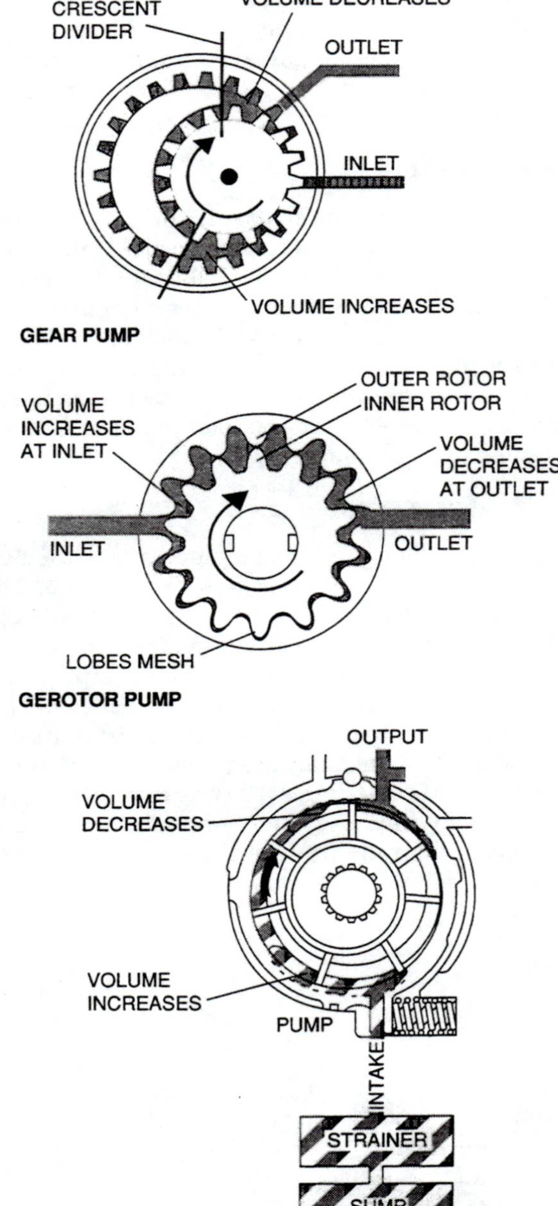

FIGURE 4–12 The three types of oil pumps used in automatic transmissions.

4.4.3 Pumps

The hydraulic pump used in the automatic transmission is a rotary pump design. The moving rotary parts of the pump are driven by the engine whenever it is running. There are three basic types of rotary pump design that are widely used in automatic transmissions today: the gear type, the gerotor type, and the vane type, shown in Figure 4–12. The job of the pump is to provide a continuous flow of ATF to the hydraulic circuits with enough volume to meet all the transmission requirements. A pump's size is rated by the volume of fluid it can pump at a given rpm value. This volume is determined by the physical size of the pumping components and is measured in gallons per minute of flow. Gear and gerotor pumps have a fixed capacity and will deliver the same amount of fluid for each revolution of the pump. The *vane pump* is designed with a variable capacity to be able to provide high volume when it is needed, or low volume to save power. These pumps are described in detail later. It is important to remember that pumps do not pump pressure; they pump volume of fluid, or flow. Pressure is created in a hydraulic system when there is a resistance to flow; the greater the resistance, the higher the pressure for a given flow.

1. Gear Type

The gear-type pump, shown in Figure 4–13, consists of two circular gears, one large with internal teeth and a smaller gear with external teeth. The gears fit into the pump body so that at one point they mesh, in this case at the bottom. The small gear is driven by the torque converter hub, so it will turn whenever the engine is running. The larger gear is driven by the small gear but rotates on a

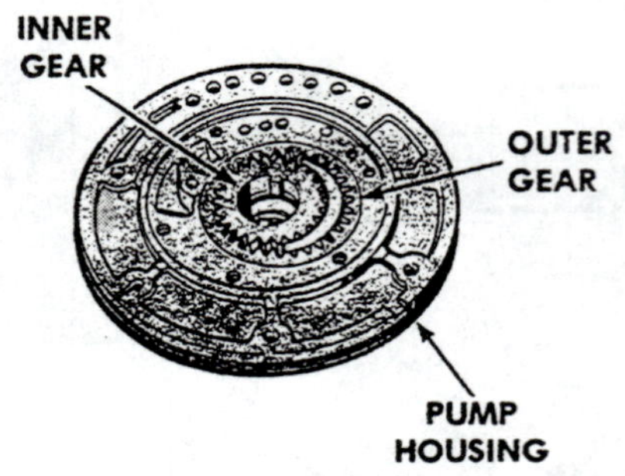

FIGURE 4–13 Parts of a gear pump.

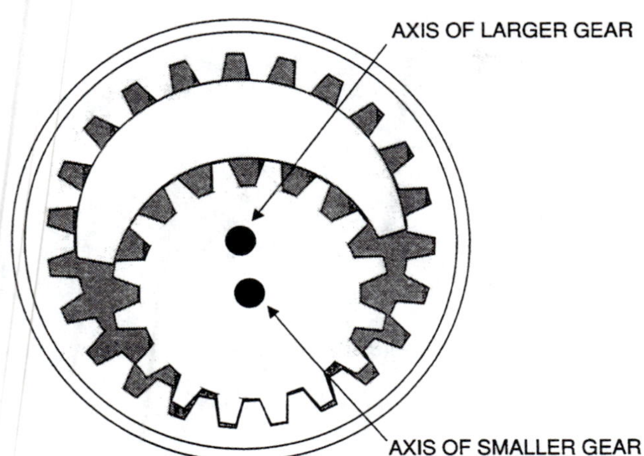

FIGURE 4–14 The axis of the driving and driven gears are different, which allows them to mesh.

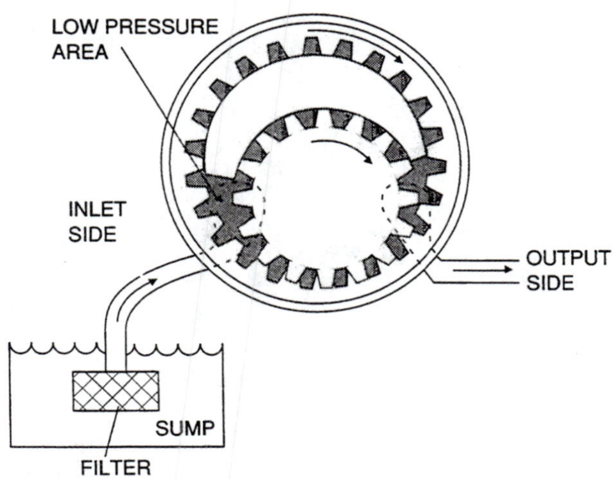

FIGURE 4–15 A low-pressure area is created on the pump's inlet side as the gear teeth unmesh.

different axis because of its larger diameter, as shown in Figure 4–14. The space between the gears is filled by a crescent-shaped divider; its job is explained later. The gears are sealed in by the pump cover. Internal passageways in the pump lead from the inlet side of the gears to the fluid sump. Another passage leads from the outlet side to the hydraulic system circuits. Due to the tight fit between the gear teeth, the gears and the pump body, and the gears and the crescent, a sealed compartment is formed at both the inlet and outlet areas in the pump. As the gears rotate clockwise in Figure 4–15, the gear teeth in the inlet side become unmeshed and separate as they turn. As they move away from each other, the volume of the inlet section increases, lowering the pressure inside the section. The pressure differential caused by the low pressure in the inlet section and the atmospheric pressure pushing on the sump causes the fluid to flow through the filter and into the inlet section of the pump, as shown in Figure 4–16. The fluid is then trapped between the teeth of the gears and the crescent and is carried by the movement of the gears to the outlet section of the pump. Once the fluid reaches the outlet section of the pump (Figure 4–17) it is sealed off from the inlet section and cannot return in that direction. The movement of the gears brings the teeth back into mesh again, and as this happens the volume of the output chamber is decreased. Since the fluid cannot be compressed, it is forced out of the output *port* of the pump into the hydraulic system. The *gear pump* is a fixed-capacity, positive-displacement type of pump, which means that for every revolution of the pump gears a fixed quantity of fluid is moved from the inlet section to the outlet section of the pump. If the speed of the pump is doubled, its output of fluid is also doubled. After we look at the other types of pumps, you will learn how the volume of flow and pressure are regulated.

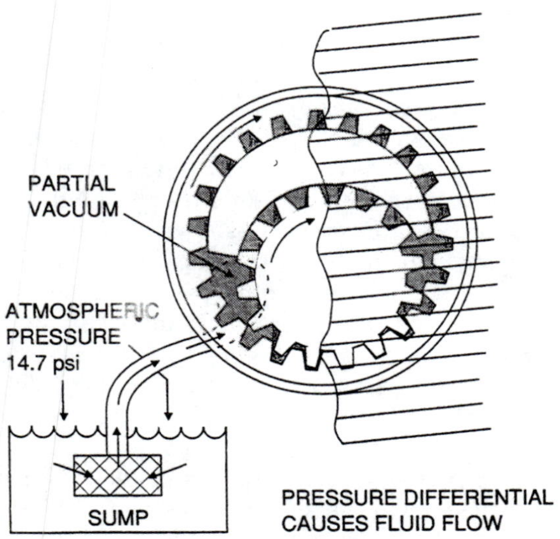

FIGURE 4–16 Atmospheric pressure forces the fluid to flow into the inlet side of the pump.

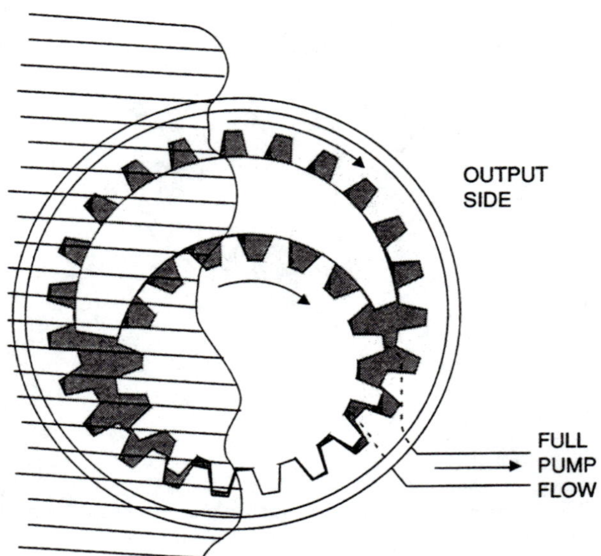

FIGURE 4–17 In the outlet section of the fluid the gear teeth mesh again and force oil out of the pump.

2. Rotor Type

The rotor-type pump, called a *gerotor pump* by some manufacturers, works on the same principles as those described for the gear pump. Its only basic difference can easily be seen in Figure 4–18, as the shape of its rotors is different from the gears in a gear pump. The gears form a V shape, with sharp points at the tip and root of each tooth, while the rotor's teeth have a smooth, flowing, rounded form with a large radius at both the tip and root of each tooth. The inner rotor is the drive member being turned by the torque converter hub, and the outer rotor is the driven member. The inner rotor will always have one tooth less than the outer rotor. Unlike the gear pump, which needs a crescent divider to seal the inlet and output sections, the rotor design can provide its own seal—and here is how it is done. With the teeth of the inner and outer rotors engaged at the bottom, as shown in Figure 4–19, the tips of the teeth at the top have just enough clearance to pass each other as the inner rotor's teeth slide past the outer rotor's teeth. As the inner rotor turns, driving the outer rotor, the teeth begin to unmesh, causing low pressure in the inlet section. As the teeth continue to unmesh, the tips of the teeth become aligned, holding fluid in the chamber that is formed. At this point the chamber has moved past the end of the inlet port and is sealed. As the rotors continue to move, the teeth begin to mesh again, forcing the fluid out through the output port of the pump. The separation of the

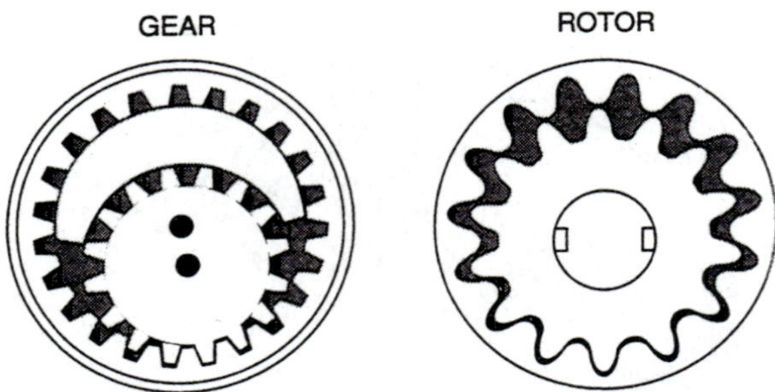

FIGURE 4–18 Comparison of a gear crescent pump and a gerotor pump.

ports is shown clearly in Figure 4–20 with these types of ports being used in most automatic transmission pumps.

3. Vane Type

The vane-type pump is a variable-displacement pump, which means that it can change the amount of flow it produces to adjust for different hydraulic system needs. During upshifts, the hydraulic system requires more flow than during highway cruise. The parts of a vane pump are very different from those of a gear or rotor pump, with the pump housing and cover being the only similar parts. The pumping components are the rotor, which is driven by the torque converter hub; the vanes, which ride

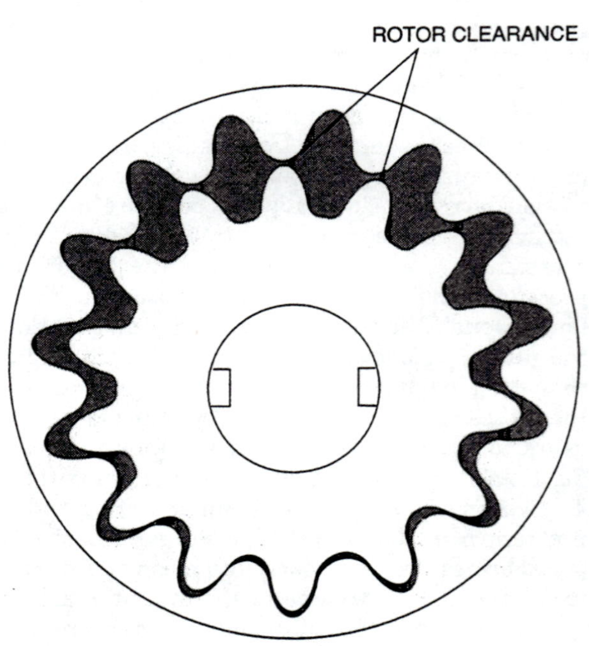

FIGURE 4–19 Gerotor type pump.

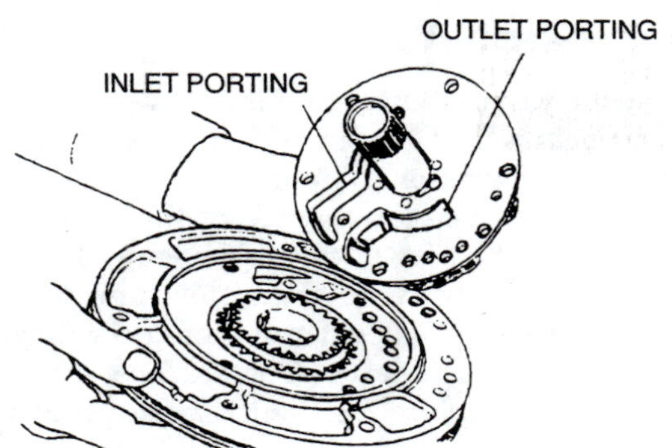

FIGURE 4–20 The inlet and output ports in an oil pump are clearly separated.

in radial slots in the rotor; a vane ring, which rides behind the inner end of the vanes to keep the vanes held in place; the slide; priming springs; and pivot pin (Figure 4–21). The part of this pump that allows it to change displacement is the slide, which is mounted on a pivot pin. The slide is free to move back and forth as it pivots on the pivot pin inside the slide housing area in the pump body. The rotor and vanes that run inside the slide are not free to move back and forth but rotate on a fixed-axis centerline. Because the slide can pivot, the amount of axis offset between the rotor and slide can be changed. With the slide at maximum offset, the largest possible pump chamber is formed between the rotor and slide, producing the maximum flow shown in Figure 4–22. When the slide moves to a point of less offset, the pump chamber size will decrease, cutting the flow rate. If the axis centerlines of the rotor and slide became the same, pumping action would stop because the volume of each pumping chamber would remain the same during full rotation of the pump. Two opposing forces are used to control the movement of the slide: hydraulic pressure and spring pressure. The priming spring forces the slide to the maximum flow position, shown in Figure 4–23. As soon as the flow requirements of the hydraulic system are met and the pressure increases, the pressure regulator valve directs a flow of fluid into the decrease circuit which will apply pressure to one side of the slide, pushing it toward the priming spring. As the pressure becomes greater than the spring force, the slide is moved and the flow rate decreases. This balance of hydraulic and spring pressure will respond to the needs of the hydraulic system but at the same time will save wasted energy.

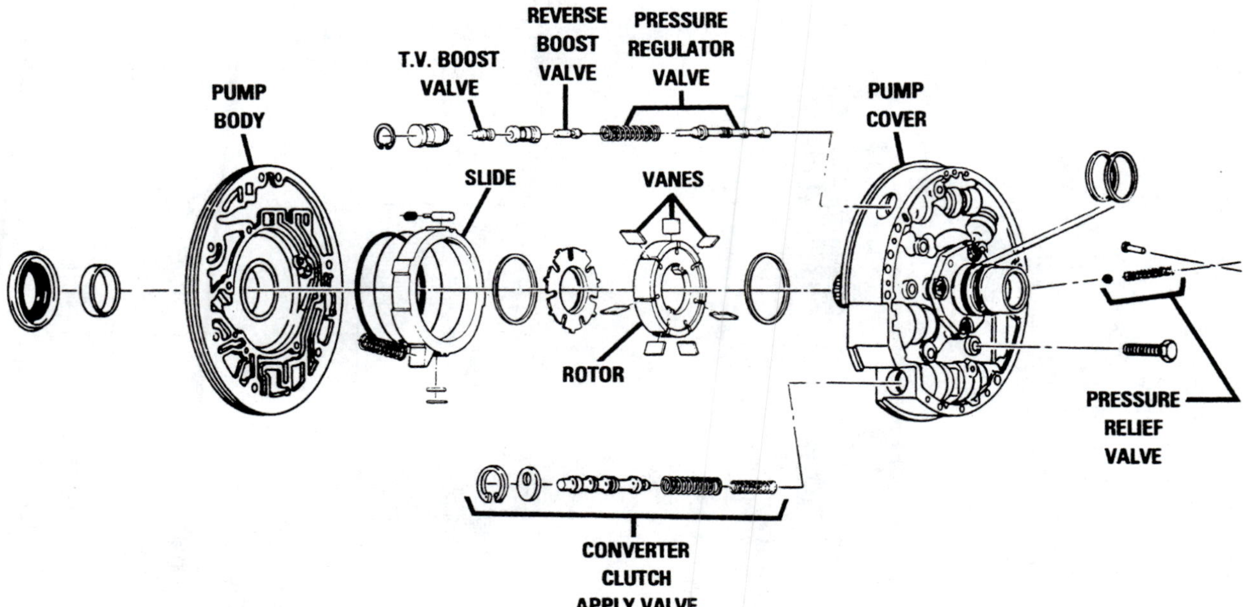

FIGURE 4–21 Study the parts of this vane pump closely. (Reprinted with permission of General Motors Corporation)

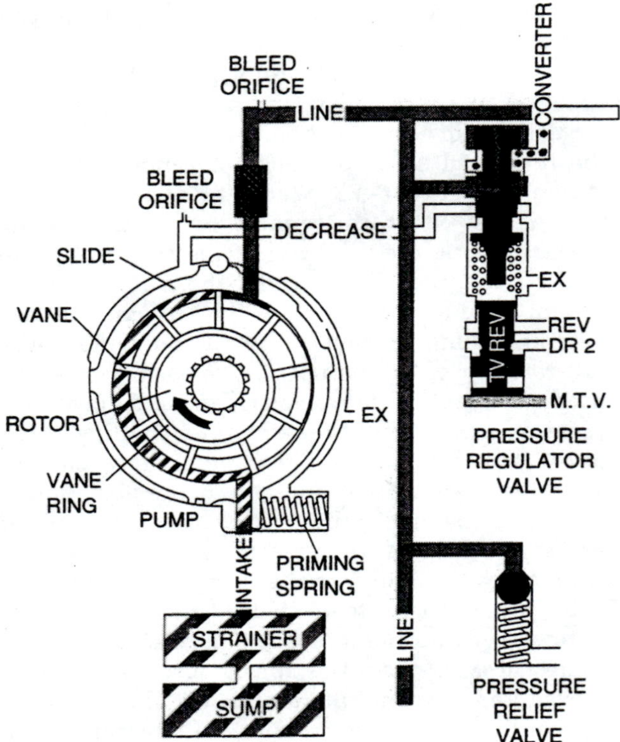

FIGURE 4–22 Variable-displacement vane pump in maximum-flow position. (Reprinted with permission of General Motors Corporation)

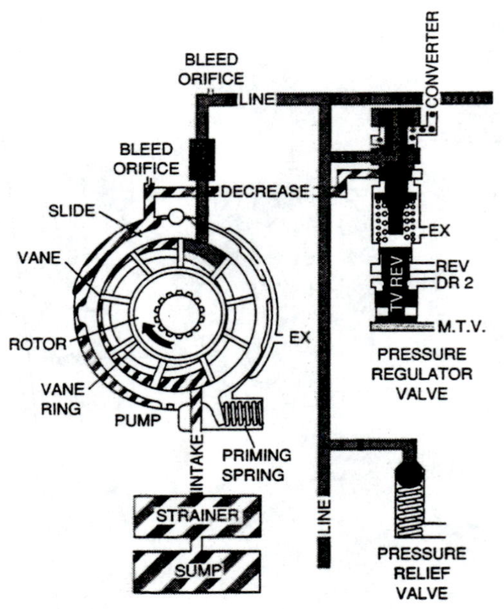

FIGURE 4–23 Variable-displacement vane pump in minimum-flow position. (Reprinted with permission of General Motors Corporation)

4.4.4 Spool Valve

The spool valve shown in Figure 4–24 is one of the basic building blocks of a complex hydraulic system. The parts of a simple spool valve are the *lands,* the outer circumference of the valve, which rides against the bore of the valve body; the *valleys,* the cutout area between the lands; and the *faces,* the vertical surface at each end of the valleys and at both ends of the valve. The surface area of the faces provides surface for the hydraulic pressure to act against. If one land of a spool valve has a larger diameter than another, its faces will have a greater surface area than the other land. If the same hydraulic pressure is applied to the ends of this valve, the land with the most face surface area would create the most force, causing the valve to move, as shown in Figure 4–25. If the same pressure is applied between the lands (Figure 4–26), the land with the most face area would again produce the greater force, causing the valve to move in that direction. The automatic transmission uses many multiland spool valves in the valve body to perform a number of different jobs. Each type of spool valve application will be studied later.

4.4.5 Pressure Regulator Valves

Without some sort of protective device in the hydraulic circuits, the hydraulic pressure in automatic transmission can build to the point that the seals would fail and internal damage would result. To prevent this problem, pressure regulators are used to control the maximum pressure the hy-

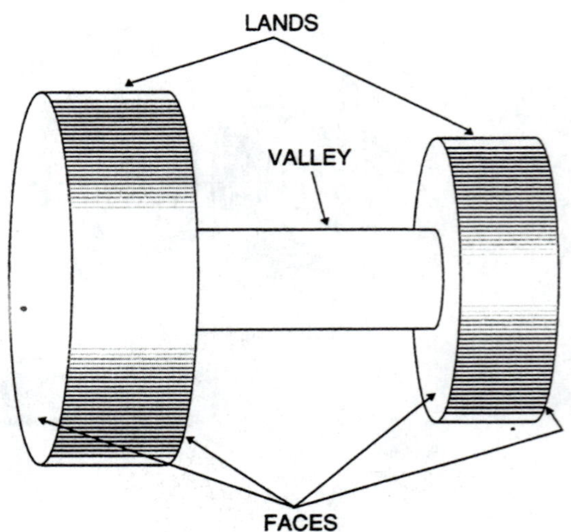

FIGURE 4–24 The spool valve is the most widely used type of hydraulic valve.

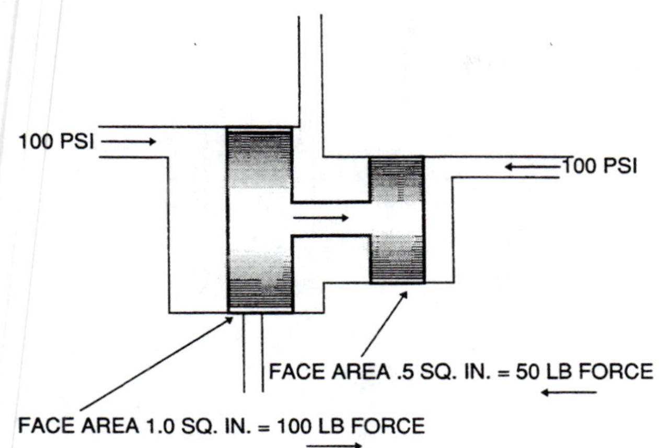

FIGURE 4–25 The valve face with the most surface area will produce the most force when exposed to the same pressure.

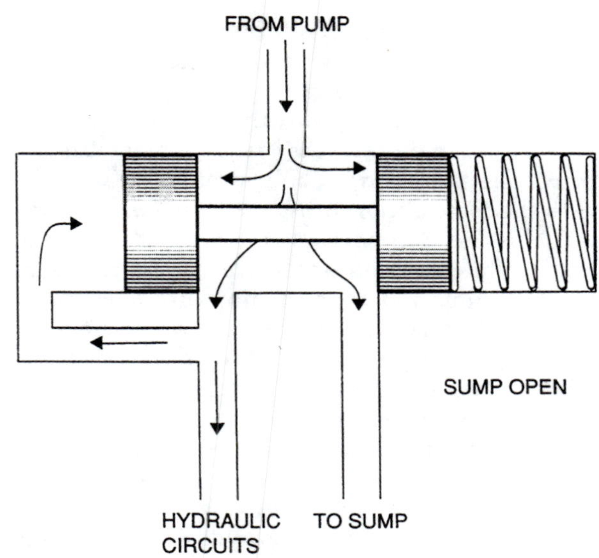

FIGURE 4–27 The balance valve uses spring and hydraulic pressure working against each other to provide a pressure regulator.

draulic system can produce. In the following sections we study three different types of pressure regulator valves.

1. Spool Valve

The spool valve is used in a balance type of pressure regulator. The theory behind this type of regulator is to balance the hydraulic pressure with a spring force. In Figure 4–27 you see a spool valve in a balance-type pressure regulator. Fluid flow and pressure coming from the pump are exposed to three faces of the valve; the two center faces cancel each other out, leaving the force created on the left face to push the valve to the right. As the valve moves right, the spring resists the movement as it is compressed. When the hydraulic force and spring force are equal, the valve is in balance. At this balance point the port leading to the sump is covered by the right spool land. As the pressure starts to rise above the balance point, the valve will move farther to the right, uncovering the sump port, as shown in Figure 4–28. With this port open, some fluid flow is returned to the sump and the pressure

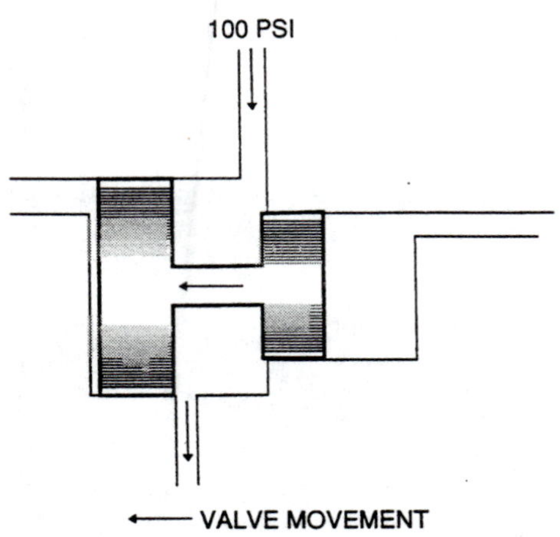

FIGURE 4–26 With the same pressure applied to the valley area, the valve will move in the other direction.

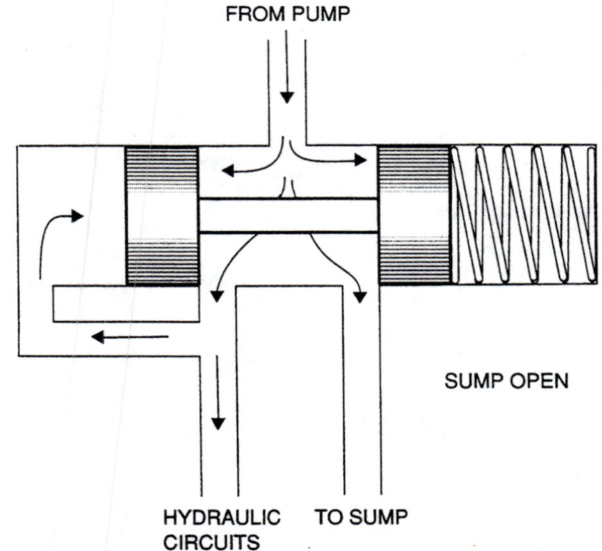

FIGURE 4–28 When the hydraulic pressure becomes greater than the spring pressure, the valve moves toward the spring and opens the port to the sump.

is reduced. When the pressure drops to the balance point, the spring forces the valve to the left, closing the sump port, and the pressure begins to rise again. In this way, the spool valve moves back and forth trying to maintain the balance point and a uniform system pressure. The hydraulic pressure is equal to the force of the spring in the *balance valve,* so by changing the spring, the pressure can be changed. While it is not practical to change the spring every time you want the pressure to change, it is practical to add an additional force, called an *auxiliary force,* which can be either mechanical or hydraulic. Mechanical auxiliary force is added to the balance spring through the uses of a lever or linkage which works to compress the balance spring partially from its other end, raising the spring force applied to the spool valve, as shown in Figure 4–29. In this case the hydraulic pressure would be equal to the combined forces of the lever and spring.

Hydraulic auxiliary force is widely used to increase the hydraulic circuit pressure in automatic transmissions by placing a spool valve, with different-size faces, at the right end of the balance spring (Figure 4–30). Hydraulic force can be added to spring force to raise the hydraulic pressure. The amount of auxiliary hydraulic force is controlled by the auxiliary valve size and the amount of pressure applied to it. You will learn more about this later in this chapter when you study the pressure boost valves.

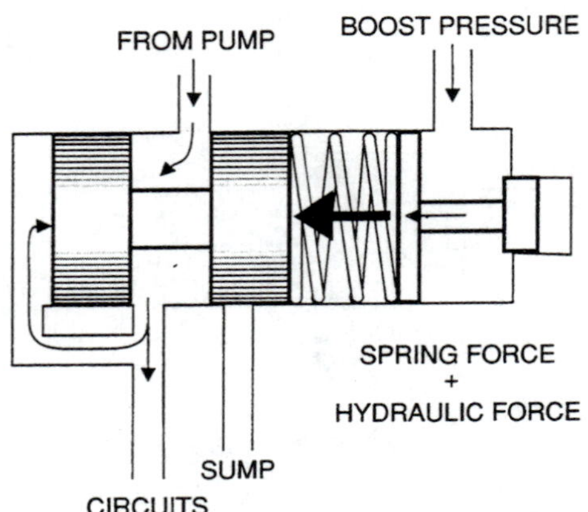

FIGURE 4–30 Hydraulic force can also be used as the auxiliary force.

2. *Pressure Relief Valve*

A pressure *relief valve* is a simple type of pressure regulator using a valve and spring force to control maximum pressure. Three types of valve designs are used in relief valves: the piston, the ball, and the cone. In Figure 4–31 you see a piston-type relief valve shown in closed and open positions. The operation of the valve is very simple. The hydraulic pressure pushes on the piston, compressing the spring and moving the piston back until the sump port is uncovered, at which point the excess flow and pressure are bled off. The ball and cone types work in the same manner, as shown in Figure 4–32. These valves can serve another function beside controlling maximum pressure in a circuit;

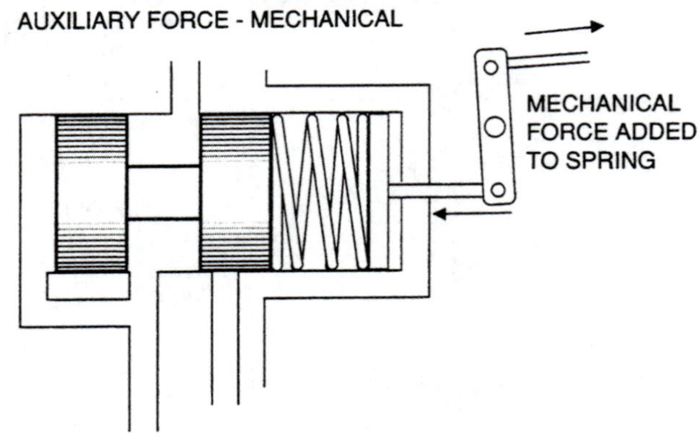

FIGURE 4–29 Mechanical auxiliary force can be added to increase spring force and raise the overall pressure.

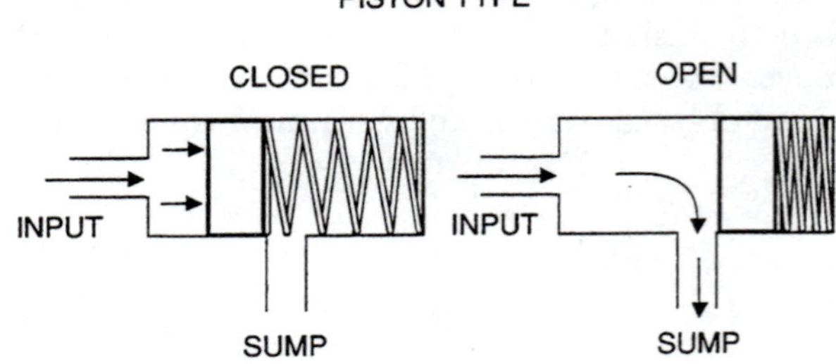

FIGURE 4–31 This drawing shows a piston pressure relief valve in open and closed positions.

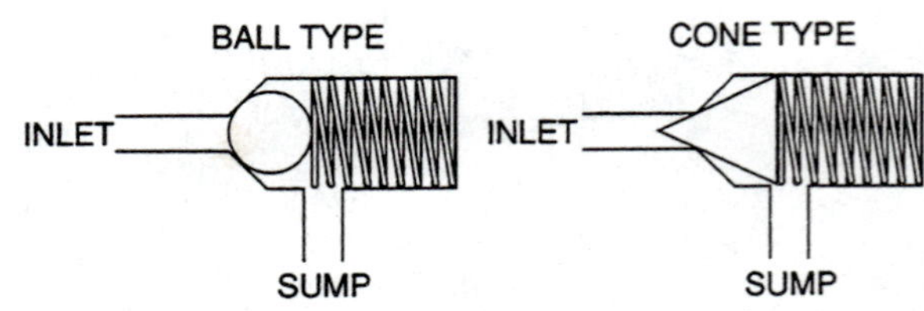

FIGURE 4–32 Two other types of relief valves are the ball type and the cone type.

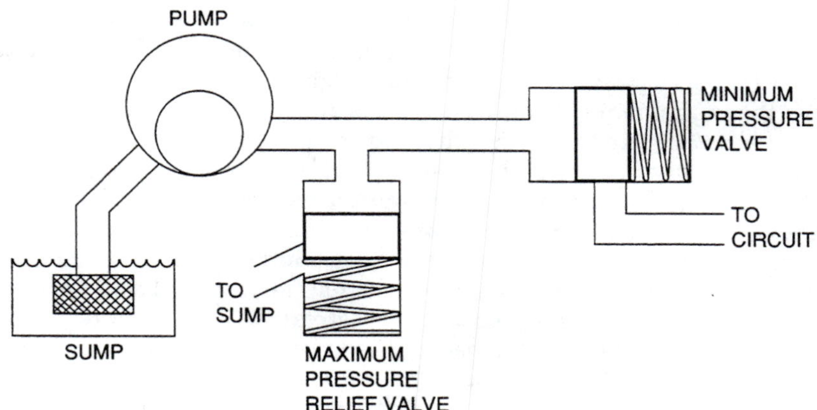

FIGURE 4–33 Pressure relief valves can be used to control both the maximum and minimum pressure in a circuit.

they can also be designed to control the minimum pressure at which a circuit can operate. By placing a pressure relief valve in a circuit and changing the routing of the fluid leaving the valve, it can regulate the amount of pressure entering a given circuit, as shown in Figure 4–33.

3. Orifice
The orifice is the simplest pressure reducer used in an automatic transmission. An orifice is a restriction in a hydraulic circuit, a small hole in the valve body, or a small inlet port into a piston or servo. As fluid flows from the pump through the hydraulic circuits, as it meets resistance, the pressure will increase. As part of the flow goes through the restriction, the pressure is reduced and will remain so as long as the flow is constant, as shown in Figure 4–34. As the circuit and hydraulic devices fill with fluid, the pressure beyond the restriction will rise in proportion with the percentage of the system that is filled, as shown in Figure 4–35. By using an orifice in a circuit, the device being applied will engage in a smooth, gentle manner and not a hard, sudden application.

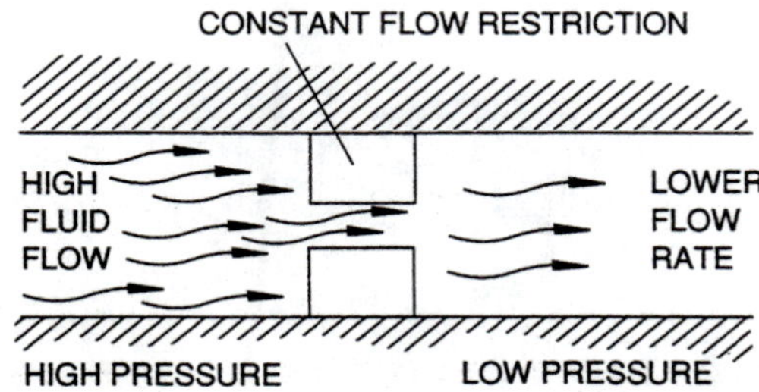

FIGURE 4–34 The orifice is the simplest type of pressure regulator.

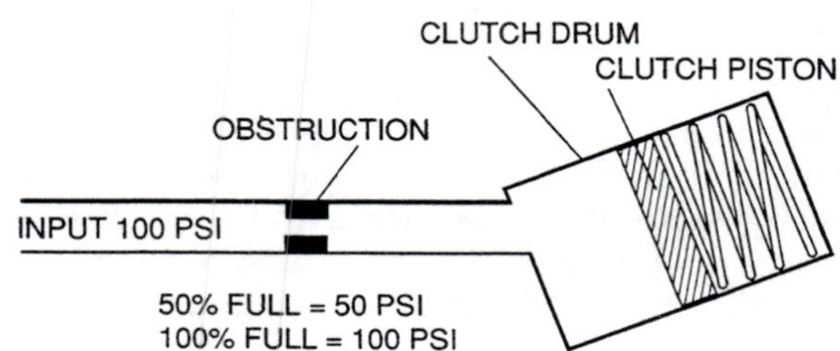

FIGURE 4–35 When pressure is first applied to a circuit that has an orifice, the pressure beyond the restriction will increase in proportion to the amount of the circuit that is filled with fluid.

4.4.6 Pressure Boost Valves

Under certain driving conditions, the mainline pressure must be raised to assure that clutches or bands will not slip under increased torque loads. The *pressure boost valve* is used to increase the mainline pressure by providing an auxiliary force on the pressure regulator spool valve. The typical boost valve shown in Figure 4–36 is a spool valve with two different-sized lands. There are two differ-

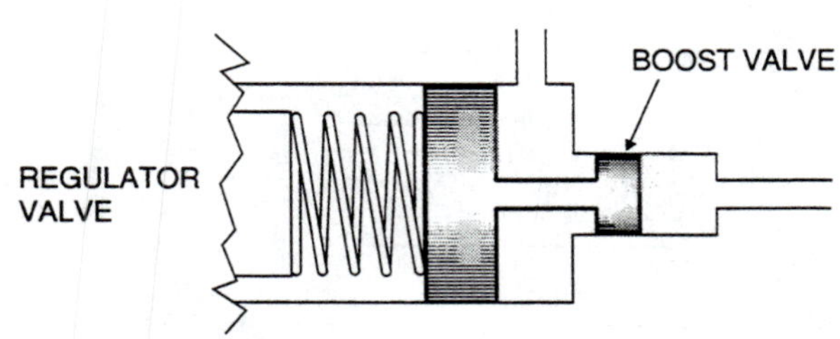

FIGURE 4–36 The pressure boost valve is used to add auxiliary force to a pressure regulator valve.

ent pressure-applied areas on this valve: one area between the two lands and the other on the outer end of the right land. In most automatic transmissions the mainline pressure, which is the regulated *pressure source* that provides hydraulic force to all transmission devices, is raised as the engine load increases. The greater the engine torque, the higher the mainline pressure needed to prevent clutch or band slippage. When the transmission is in reverse, there are high-torque loads, so reverse circuit pressure is routed to the boost valve to raise the overall mainline pressure (Figure 4–37). Another condition that calls for increased mainline pressure is hard acceleration in any forward gear.

The engine's torque load is monitored and converted into a hydraulic pressure that is used by the transmission as a control pressure. This pressure, called throttle pressure, will be studied in detail in a later unit. Throttle pressure is routed to the far-right end of the boost valve (Figure 4–38) to act as an auxiliary force to raise the mainline pressure. As the engine load increases, the throttle pressure also increases, which applies more pressure to the boost valve, thereby raising the mainline pressure.

4.4.7 Pressure Modulator Valves

A *modulator* is a device that regulates or adjusts something. In this case the mainline pressure is being readjusted to a lower valve. You just learned how the mainline pressure can be increased by a boost valve to match the torque loads on the clutches and bands, but this readjustment on mainline pressure is for a different purpose. The pressure modulator valves are used to readjust mainline pressure into a pressure that represents a vehicle operating condition. These new pressures, called *control pressures,* are used to represent the vehicle speed and the engine load. These pressures are used to determine the proper shift speed under varying vehicle operating conditions. The two types of pressure modulator valves used in most automatic transmissions are the governor, which represents vehicle road speed, and the *throttle valve,* which gives engine load information to the transmission.

1. Governor Valve

The *governor valve* modulates, or reduces, mainline pressure to a lower pressure that is proportional to the road speed of the vehicle. With the vehicle stopped and the gear selector in drive range, mainline pressure is routed to the governor but the valve is closed so that little or no governor pressure is being produced. The governor valves are always mounted on, or driven by, the output shaft of the transmission. The valves are moved by centrifugal force as the output shaft starts to rotate. As the valve opens, it provides a small opening or orifice which allows a flow of mainline fluid through the valve at reduced pressure. The amount the valve opens is proportional to the amount of centrifugal force applied to the valve. The faster the output shaft rotates, the greater the centrifugal force will be, opening the governor valve wider and producing more governor pressure. As the vehicle slows down, springs in the governor assembly return the valve to its closed position. The range of governor pressure that can be produced goes from a minimum of 0 psi up to a maximum of whatever the mainline pressure is. The governor cannot produce pressure higher than the mainline pressure.

Two basic designs of governor are popular in today's transmissions. The type 1 governor shown in Figure 4–39 is mounted directly on the output shaft and rotates with it as one. As it spins, centrifugal force moves the weight out, opening the valve and producing a governor pressure. This type

REVERSE CIRCUIT PRESSURE

AUXILIARY FORCE TO INCREASE REGULATED FORCE

FIGURE 4–37 The auxiliary force applied to the regulator valve will cause the regulated pressure to rise.

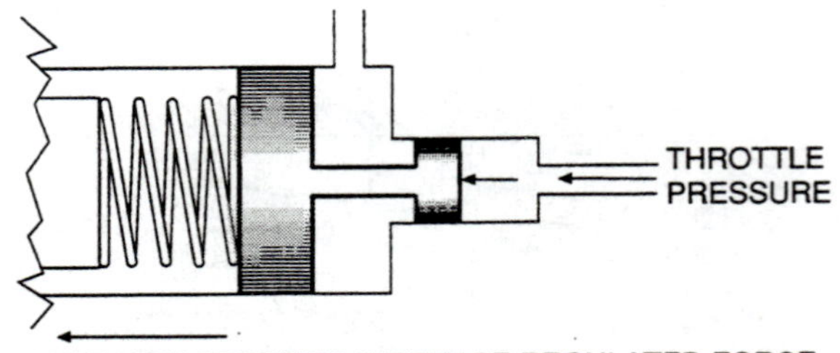

FIGURE 4–38 Other areas of the boost valve can be used to provide a different amount of pressure increase.

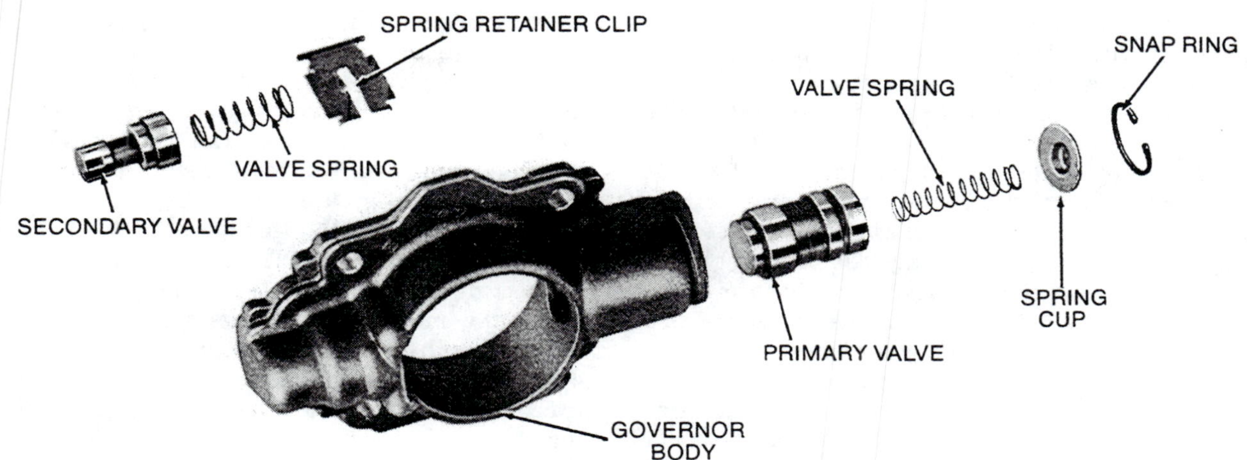

FIGURE 4–39 This is a type 1 or shaft-mounted governor. (Courtesy of Ford)

of governor turns inside a governor support that is bolted to the case and provides the hydraulic passages for mainline and governor pressures. The governor uses sealing rings to seal the fluid passages between the governor and the support, as shown in Figure 4–40.

The type 2 governor, shown in Figure 4–41, is mounted in the case perpendicular to the output shaft. A gear at the end of the governor assembly meshes with a drive gear on the output shaft and spins the entire governor. Primary and secondary centrifugal weights are mounted on pivot pins at the top end of the governor body. As the body spins, the centrifugal force moves the weights outward, and as they pivot on their pins, they push on the

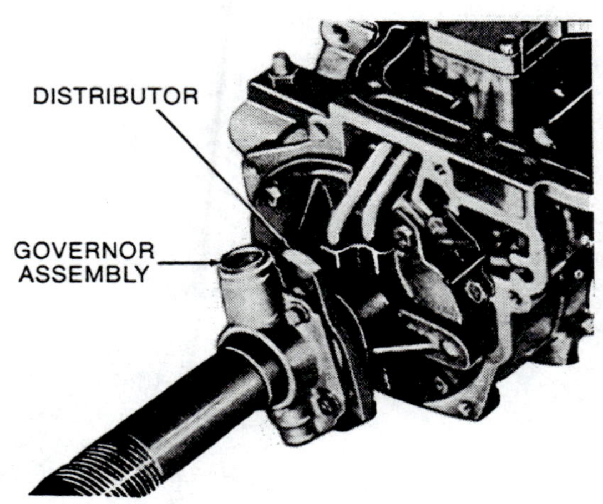

FIGURE 4–40 The sealing rings control mainline pressure going into the governor and governor pressure coming out.

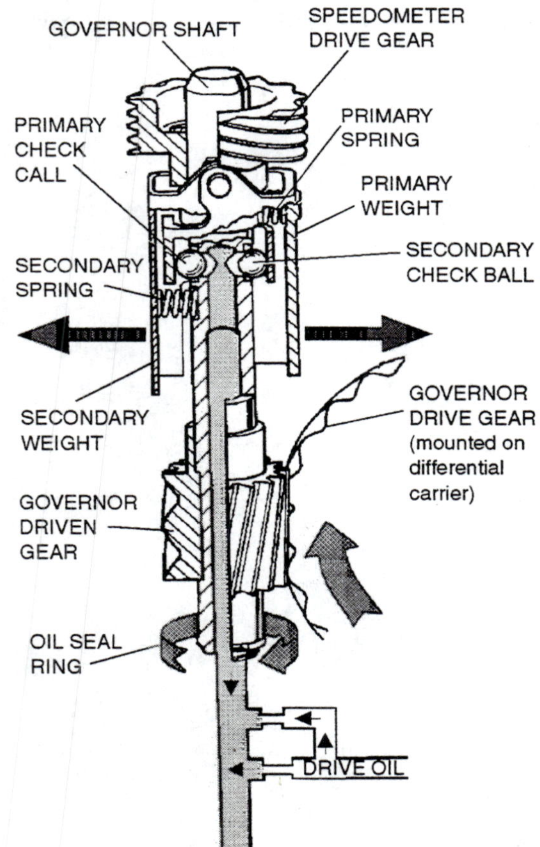

FIGURE 4–41 A type 2 or drop-in governor can easily be removed and installed when service is needed. (Reprinted with permission of General Motors Corporation)

end of the spool valve. As the valve moves, first the exhaust port is closed and then the mainline port begins to open, creating a governor pressure. Two different sets of centrifugal weights are used to give better governor response at slow vehicle speeds. The primary weights, which are heavier, work at slow speeds, with the lighter secondary weights taking over during the medium- and high-speed ranges. No sealing rings are needed on this type of governor because the governor body-to-case clearance is very small. A pair of small springs are also used to assist the secondary weights. There are different adaptations of the type 2 design in uses today, so check a shop manual for an exact description of the governor used in the transmission you are studying.

2. *Throttle Valve*

The throttle valve is another type of pressure modulator valve, which changes mainline pressure into a control pressure that reflects the engine's load. On some transmissions the throttle valve is connected by a linkage rod or cable to the carburetor linkage, so that when the driver steps on the throttle, the linkage will open the throttle valve as shown in Figure 4–42. As the throttle valve moves in its bore, the mainline pressure port is uncovered, creating throttle pressure. The farther down the throttle is pushed, the more the throttle valve is opened and the greater the throttle pressure will be. At no point can the throttle pressure be higher than mainline pressure. There is another method of connecting the throttle valve to the engine without using the mechanical linkage we just discussed, and that is the *vacuum modulator,* shown in Figure 4–43. Engine intake manifold vacuum provides an excellent measure of how hard the engine is working. A vacuum modulator is a vacuum diaphragm assembly which is spring loaded so that the throttle valve is pushed wide open. The vacuum modulator mounts to the transmission case so that it can push directly, or through a push rod, on the end of the throttle valve. Intake manifold vacuum is routed to the modulator housing on the side of the diaphragm with the spring. The other side of the diaphragm is open to atmospheric pressure. High manifold vac-

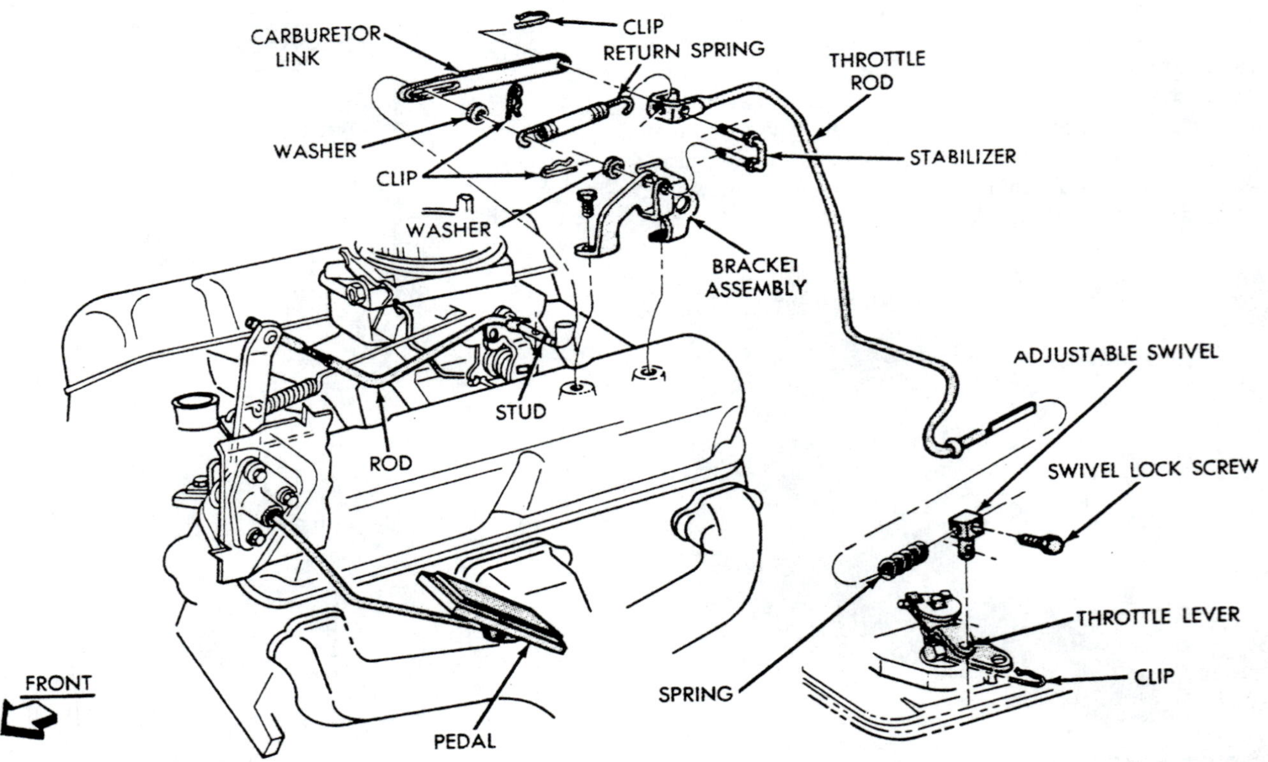

FIGURE 4–42 This linkage on a Torque Flite transmission actuates the throttle valve. (Courtesy of Chrysler)

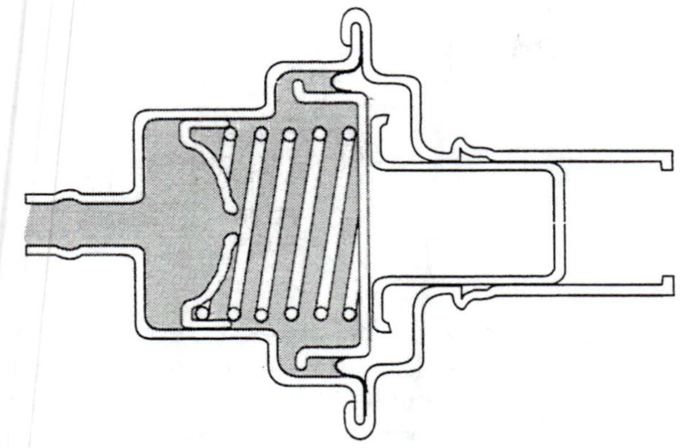

FIGURE 4–43 A vacuum modulator is used to convert intake manifold vacuum into throttle pressure (Reprinted with permission of General Motors Corporation)

uum from the engine at idle lowers the pressure on the spring side of the diaphragm while atmospheric pressure pushes on the other side, compressing the spring. As the spring is compressed, the throttle valve returns to the closed position. At idle there is little or no throttle pressure; then as the driver steps on the accelerator, the manifold vacuum will drop according to how wide the throttle has been opened, which causes the throttle valve to open, increasing the throttle pressure. The balance of force between the vacuum working on the diaphragm and the spring pressure make the vacuum modulator extremely sensitive to changes in engine load. In Figure 4–44 you see the vacuum modulator under two different conditions: first with high vacuum, which will give a low throttle pressure, then with low vacuum, which produces a high throttle pressure. Just how the throttle valve pressure is used by the transmission is explained in detail later in this chapter.

4.4.8 Flow Control Valves

This next group of valves are used to direct hydraulic fluid from one circuit to another, to prevent backflow in a circuit, or to switch entire circuits on or off. The types of valves that are used to control fluid flow are *ball check valves,* poppet check valves, *manual valves, shift valves,* and *shift solenoids.* In this section we discuss how these valves operate and why they are needed in an automatic transmission.

1. Ball Check Valves

The ball check valves are an extremely simple device. A round ball of steel, rubber, or plastic is placed in a specially shaped chamber in the hydraulic passageway. The one-way ball check valve shown in Figure 4–45 will allow fluid to flow in only one direction. As the fluid flows through the

MODULATOR SYSTEM EVALUATION CHART

Vacuum @ MOD in /Hg	LINE PRESSURES @ SEA LEVEL Barometric pressure assumed to be 28 in. Hg							
	Models AN, AP, AS, AT, and AY		Models AA, AB, AD, AF, AM, AR, CF, CM, CN, HB, and HJ		Models AC, BA, BB BC, BD, BH, BL, BM, BS, BT, BY, and BZ		Model AW	
	PSI	KPa	PSI	KPa	PSI	KPa	PSI	KPa
0	161-171	1110-1179	161-171	1110-1179	179-189	1234-1303	179-189	1234-1303
2	143-153	986-1055	143-153	986-1055	160-170	1103-1172	160-170	1103-1172
4	125-135	862-931	125-135	862-931	140-150	965-1034	140-150	965-1034
6	107-117	738-807	107-117	738-807	120-130	827-896	120-130	827-896
8	88-98	607-676	88-98	607-676	101-111	696-765	101-111	696-765
10	70-80	483-552	70-80	483-552	81-91	558-627	81-91	558-627
12	60-70	414-483	60-70	414-483	65-75	448-517	65-75	448-517
14	60-70	414-483	60-70	414-483	60-70	414-483	60-70	414-483
Models AN, AP, AS, AT, AW, and AY have an aneroid modulator. For these models, line pressures will drop by 44.8 KPa or 6.5 PSI for every thousand feet of altitude when engine manifold vacuum is less than 10 inches Hg.								

FIGURE 4–44 When the vacuum is high, the throttle pressure is low, and as the vacuum drops, the throttle pressure increases. (Reprinted with permission of General Motors Corporation)

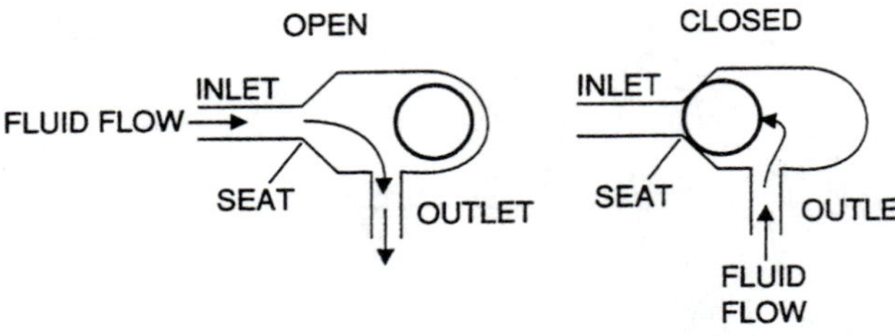

FIGURE 4–45 A one-way check ball valve is used to control the direction of fluid flow in a circuit.

ball check valve chamber in the correct direction, according to the circuit design, the check ball is carried away from its seat and the fluid is free to flow through the outlet port. As soon as the fluid flow in the circuit tries to reverse its direction of flow, the check ball is moved against its seat and the hydraulic force will hold the ball in place, cutting off the reverse flow.

Two-way ball check valves are also used to allow fluid flow to enter a circuit from two different sources, one at a time. The two-way chamber shown in Figure 4–46 has two seats, one at each inlet port, and a single outlet port. As fluid flow enters through the right inlet, the ball is forced against the left seat, sealing off that passage. The fluid continues on through the outlet port while holding the ball in place. As the fluid flow in the circuits changes, fluid could now enter the chamber from the left end, which would force the ball against the right seat, sealing off that passage. The fluid will still flow through the outlet port in the same direction. In this way a circuit can use two different sources of fluid flow without having to use a more complex valve system.

2. *Poppet Check Valves*

The poppet-type check valve (shuttle valve) shown in Figure 4–47 is a one-way check valve, which allows fluid to flow in only one direction. The valve has a poppet disc that is held against its seat by a spring. As fluid flows through the inlet passage, the disc is forced back, compressing the spring and allowing the fluid to flow through the check valve. If fluid tries to flow in the opposite direction, the spring pushes the disc to its seat and the port is closed, stopping the flow. This type of valve is very similar to the minimum pressure valve studied earlier, the main difference being the strength of the springs.

3. *Manual Valve*

The manual valve is connected by linkage to the gear selector inside the vehicle. When the driver moves the selector, the manual valve moves in its bore in the valve body. As it moves its lands cover or uncover ports in the valve body, which switches various hydraulic circuits on or off, as shown in Figure 4–48. The number of gear selections on the indicator in the vehicle is the same as the number of the manual valve positions in the valve body. The manual valve is held firmly in each position by a detent device, which prevents the valve from slipping from one gear to another. A typical detent device is shown in Figure 4–49.

In each gear position, the manual valve switches on the hydraulic circuits needed to make that gear operate. The circuits are designed so that only the hydraulic units needed for that single gear

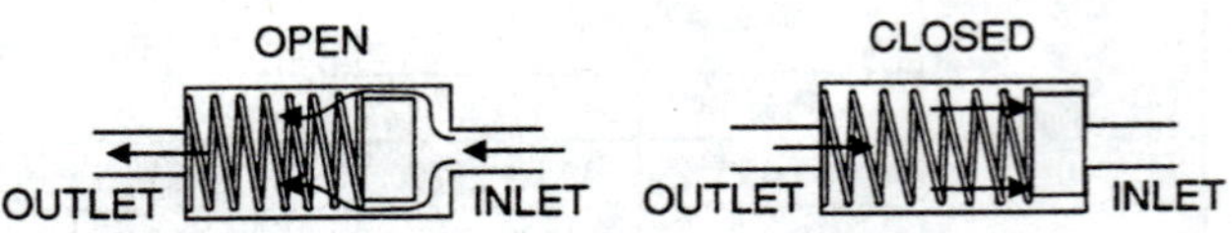

FIGURE 4–47 Operation of a poppet-type check valve.

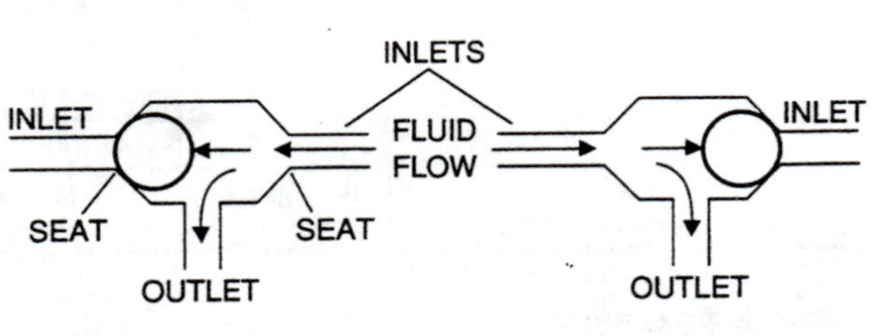

FIGURE 4–46 A two-way check ball valve has two inlet sources with only one outlet.

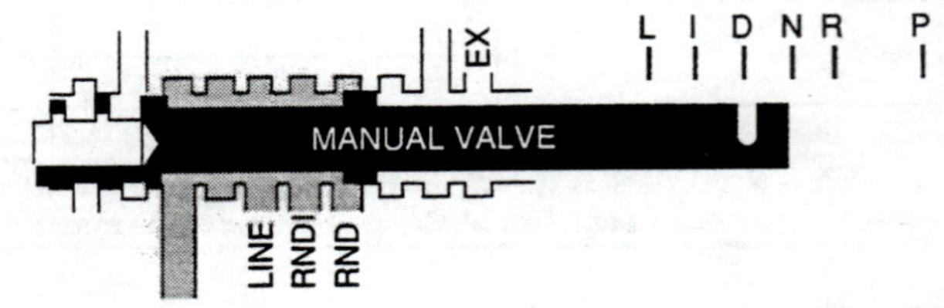

FIGURE 4–48 A manual valve is used to select the gear range the transmission will operate in. (Courtesy of Ford)

FIGURE 4–49 A detent holds the manual valve in place. (Courtesy of Ford)

will receive fluid. In reverse gear that would mean that the coupling and holding devices necessary to produce reverse gear in the planetary gear set would be turned on but that no fluid would go to the other devices or shift valves. In drive position, many more circuits are switched on to provide automatic shift control in all speed ranges and to provide the control pressures needed to make the transmission respond to different driving conditions. The different manual valve positions and the circuits open in each position are shown in Figure 4–50.

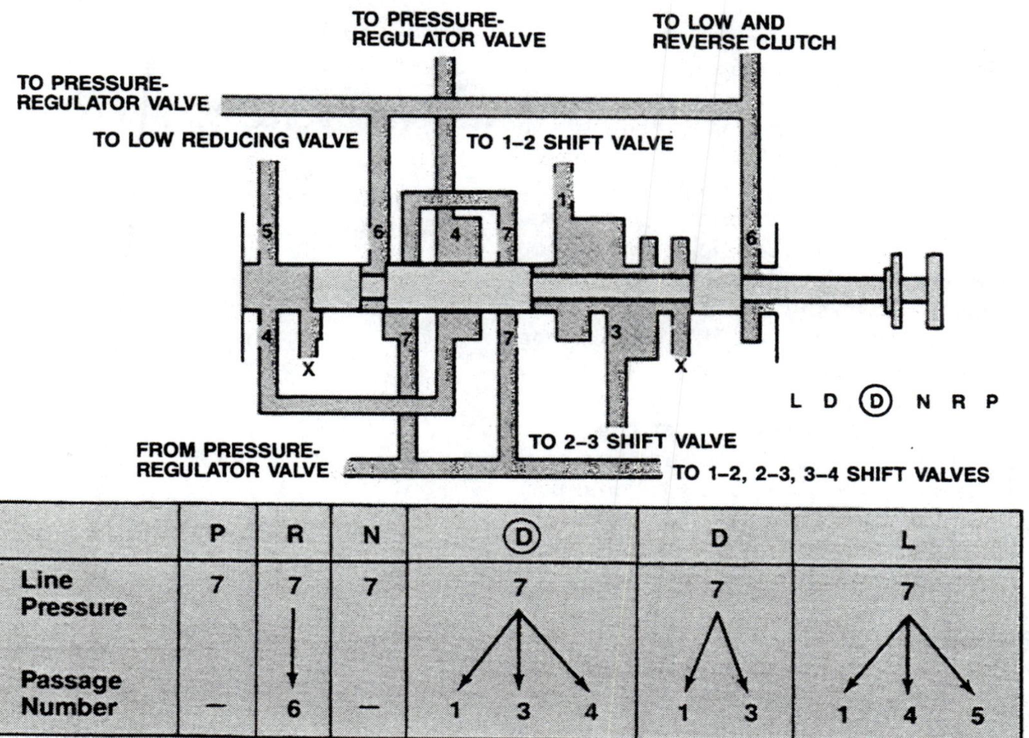

	P	R	N	(D)	D	L
Line Pressure	7	7	7	7	7	7
Passage Number	—	6	—	1 3 4	1 3	1 4 5

FIGURE 4–50 The possible passage connections made by the manual valve are shown above.

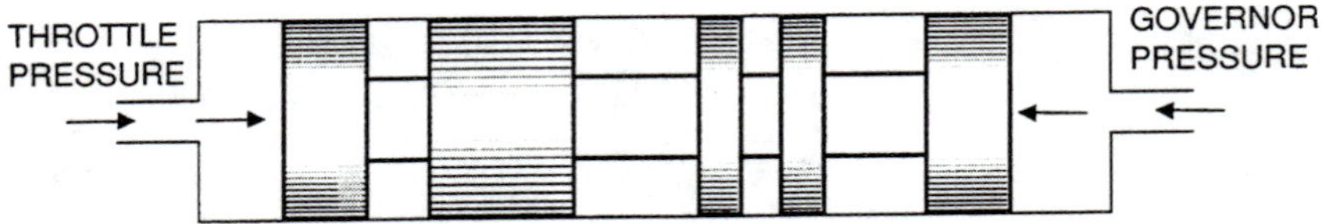

FIGURE 4–51 Movement of the shift valve is caused by the control pressures working against each other.

4. Shift Valve

The shift valve is a spool-type flow control valve that is used to turn on or off specific coupling or holding devices to achieve an upshift or downshift in the gear train. Unlike the manual valve, which is moved mechanically by the driver, the shift valves are moved by the control pressures, which come from the throttle and governor valves (Figure 4–51). Governor pressure is applied to one end of the shift valve and pushes the valve in the direction that will cause an upshift. Throttle pressure is routed to the other end of the shift valve and pushes against the valve, trying to keep it from moving. The throttle pressure works against governor pressure to resist movement of the valve. The harder the engine is working, the higher the throttle pressure, so more governor pressure will be needed to overcome the higher throttle pressure and move the shift valve to the upshift position. By balancing the shift valves with the control pressures, the transmission can respond to how the vehicle is being driven. During hard acceleration the upshifts will come at the highest possible speed, letting the engine provide maximum power and rpm in each gear. While under light acceleration, the transmission will shift at much lower speeds, providing smooth, easy shifts and maximum fuel economy, as shown in Figure 4–52. To upshift from one gear to the next, the governor pressure must overcome the throttle pressure and move the shift valve. To downshift, the opposite must happen, in that throttle pressure overcomes governor pressure and forces the shift valve back to its original position, causing a downshift. In most transmissions there are additional valves involved with downshifts, and those valves will be explained later.

5. Shift Solenoids

As our vehicles use computers to control more and more functions, the job of controlling shifts, both upshifts and downshifts, is being taken over by the computer. The job that has been done by the hydraulic control pressures for so long is being turned over to computers. In transmissions using computer-controlled shifts, the governor and throttle pressure functions are replaced with a shift solenoid, which is electrically controlled by the computer as shown in Figure 4–53. The shift solenoid is most commonly used as a bleed-off valve, meaning that when the solenoid is energized by the computer, it opens an exhaust port and dumps the hydraulic flow and pressure from that circuit (Figure 4–54). The circuit controlled by the solenoid provides pressure that will move the shift valve to provide an upshift or downshift. The computer has information about vehicle speed and engine load sent to it by the sensors used in controlling engine fuel delivery and spark timing. Most vehicles using a hydraulic lockup-type torque converter have its function controlled by the computer through the use of a lockup solenoid similar to the shift solenoids. This approach to shift control is explained further in later sections.

4.4.9 Force Output Devices

A force output device is any component that converts hydraulic pressure into mechanical force. The two most common force output devices found in au-

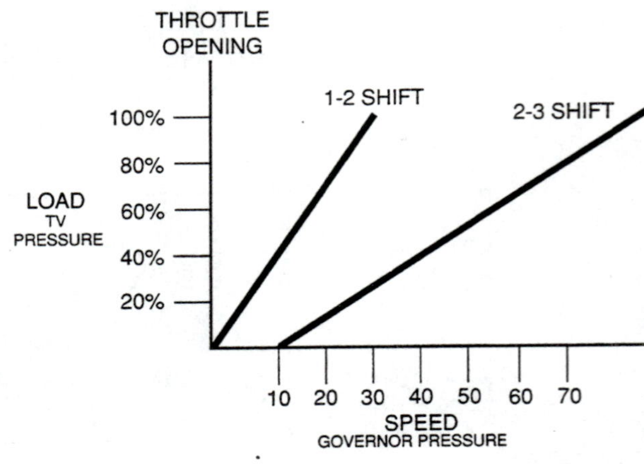

FIGURE 4–52 Control pressures needed to move the shift valve at different speeds and loads are shown above.

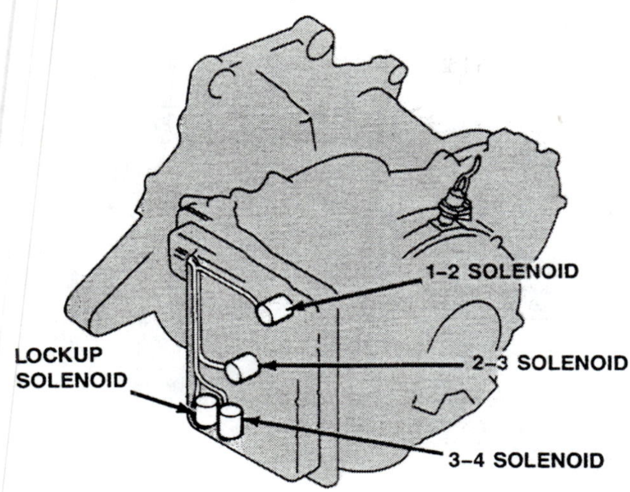

FIGURE 4–53 Shift solenoids are controlled by the on-board computer. (Courtesy of Ford)

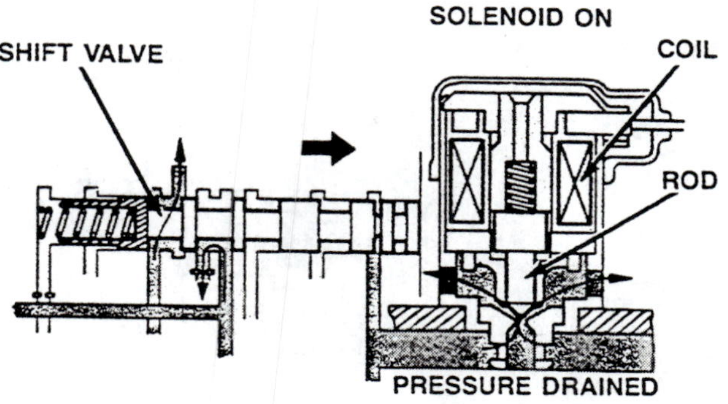

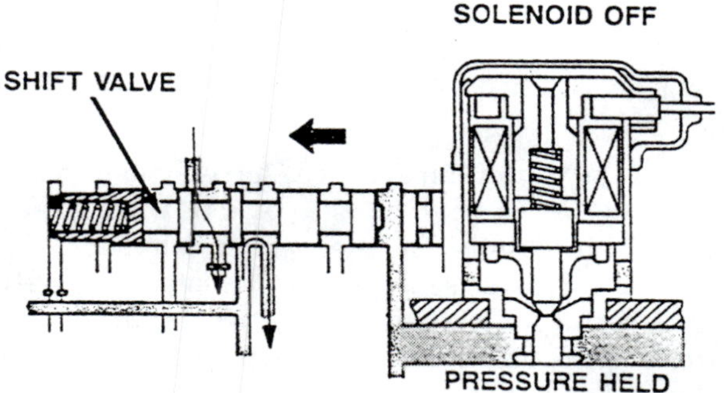

FIGURE 4–54 Operation of the shift solenoid. (Courtesy of Ford)

tomatic transmissions are clutch pistons and band apply servos. Although both devices were mentioned in earlier chapters, they are described fully in the following sections.

1. Clutch Pistons

The clutch piston is a movable metal disc that can be located inside the clutch drum, in the transmission case, or in the pump housing. Clutch pistons are a variety of shapes and sizes and almost always have a large hole in the center (Figure 4–55). This hole and the outside edge of the piston have grooves cut in them to accept seals. The seals used are replaceable and are one of the following design types: lip seal, lathe-cut seal, or O-ring seal. Each manufacturer prefers a certain type of seal for a given application, and a wide variety is seen throughout the industry. The clutch piston is held in place by a return spring and retainer. This component also has a number of different designs: the single coil return spring, multicoil spring units, and the Belleville spring type. Each type of return spring is described in detail in Part II during the clutch piston seal replacement unit.

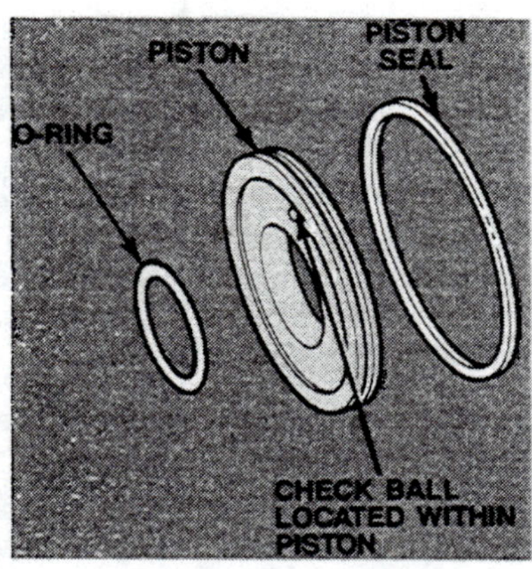

FIGURE 4–55 Basic clutch piston. (Courtesy of Ford)

Some clutch pistons contain a small ball check valve. This check valve is used to improve clutch release as the hydraulic pressure is cut off. When the clutch is applied, hydraulic fluid flowing through the check valve forces the ball to seat, closing the valve. As long as pressure is applied, the ball will remain seated (Figure 4–56), but as soon as the pressure is released, centrifugal action forces the ball away from its seat and the check valve is open to let the fluid escape from the piston chamber (Figure 4–57). This allows a much faster piston release, which means less clutch disc wear.

2. Servos

A servo is another type of piston that is used to apply a band. A servo is usually smaller than a clutch piston in diameter and does not have the large hole

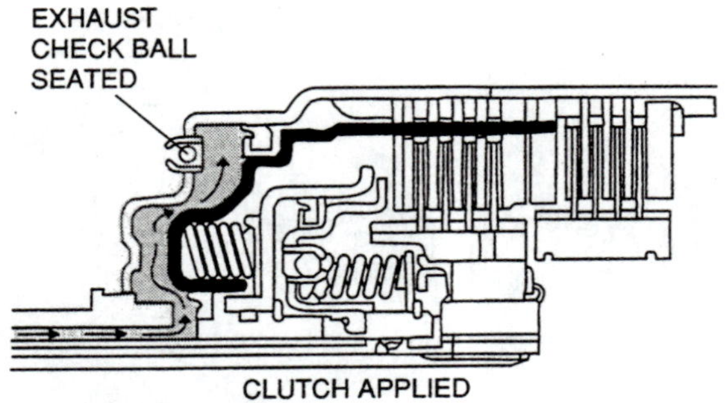

FIGURE 4–56 Clutch check valve in closed position. (Reprinted with permission of General Motors Corporation)

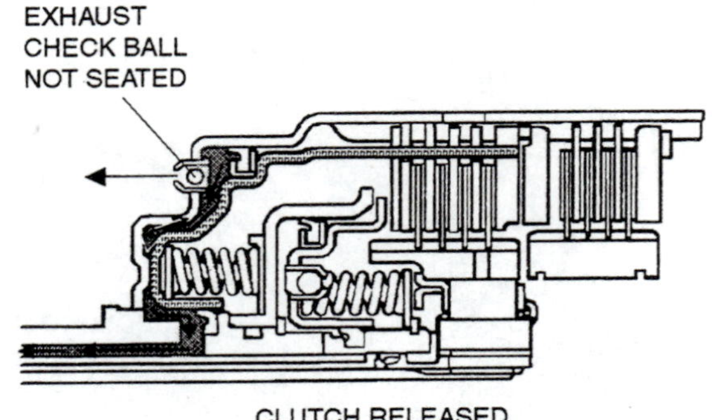

FIGURE 4–57 Clutch check valve in open position. (Reprinted with permission of General Motors Corporation)

through the center. Most servos have a push rod attached to the center of the piston with a seal around the outside of the piston, as shown in Figure 4–58. The seal can be a metal or plastic ring, a lathe-cut or O-ring seal, or in some servo pistons, a lip seal bonded to the piston. The piston and seal move inside a cylinder in the case. As the hydraulic pressure is applied to the servo, the piston moves and applies force on the band to hold the drum. As the piston applies force to the band, it compresses, a return spring that will release the band when the apply pressure is cut off. The servo just described is a one-way servo. The two-way servo is similar to the one-way servo with this addition: a release pressure is used on the opposite side of the piston to release the band while the pressure is still being applied. The reason for keeping the pressure on is so that when a downshift occurs, the servo will be ready to apply the band instantly. The two-way servo is shown in both the applied and released positions in Figure 4–59.

4.4.10 Accumulators

The accumulator serves a simple function. Its job is to soften the apply of clutches so that there will be no sudden jerk from harsh engagement. Most vehicle owners want a shift so smooth they cannot feel it happen. The accumulator makes a shift smooth by allowing the pressure in a force output device to rise evenly from a low pressure to a high pressure over a short period of time. The accumulator is a free piston moving in a cylinder with a spring mounted between the piston and the case (Figure 4–60). The open end of the accumulator is attached by a passageway to the circuit it is to work with, let's say the high reverse clutch. As the 2–3 shift valve sends apply pressure to the high reverse clutch, the fluid also fills the 2–3 accumulator. As the pressure builds, the accumulator spring compresses, allowing the pressure to rise evenly as the spring is compressed. This applies the clutch discs with a smooth, steady increase of pressure, not a sudden pressure spike. This action is shown in Figure 4–61. The action an accumulator provides could be compared to that of a shock absorber on a wheel—it smooths out the bumps in the clutch application.

4.5 HYDRAULIC SYSTEM FUNCTION

In this section we study how the various hydraulic components work together to complete the many tasks performed by the hydraulic system. To simplify the systems as much as possible, hydraulic circuit diagrams are used. In our diagrams, the various devices are represented by the symbols shown in Figure 4–62. We begin by looking at the pressure source; then the torque converter is covered, followed by the power train with clutch and band application charts, and then the shift control, including computer shift control.

4.5.1 Pressure Source

To provide a pressure source for the hydraulic needs of the transmission, there must first be an adequate supply of automatic transmission fluid to fill all the systems and components and have an ample reserve in the sump or reservoir to allow for drain-back time. All rear-wheel-drive transmissions

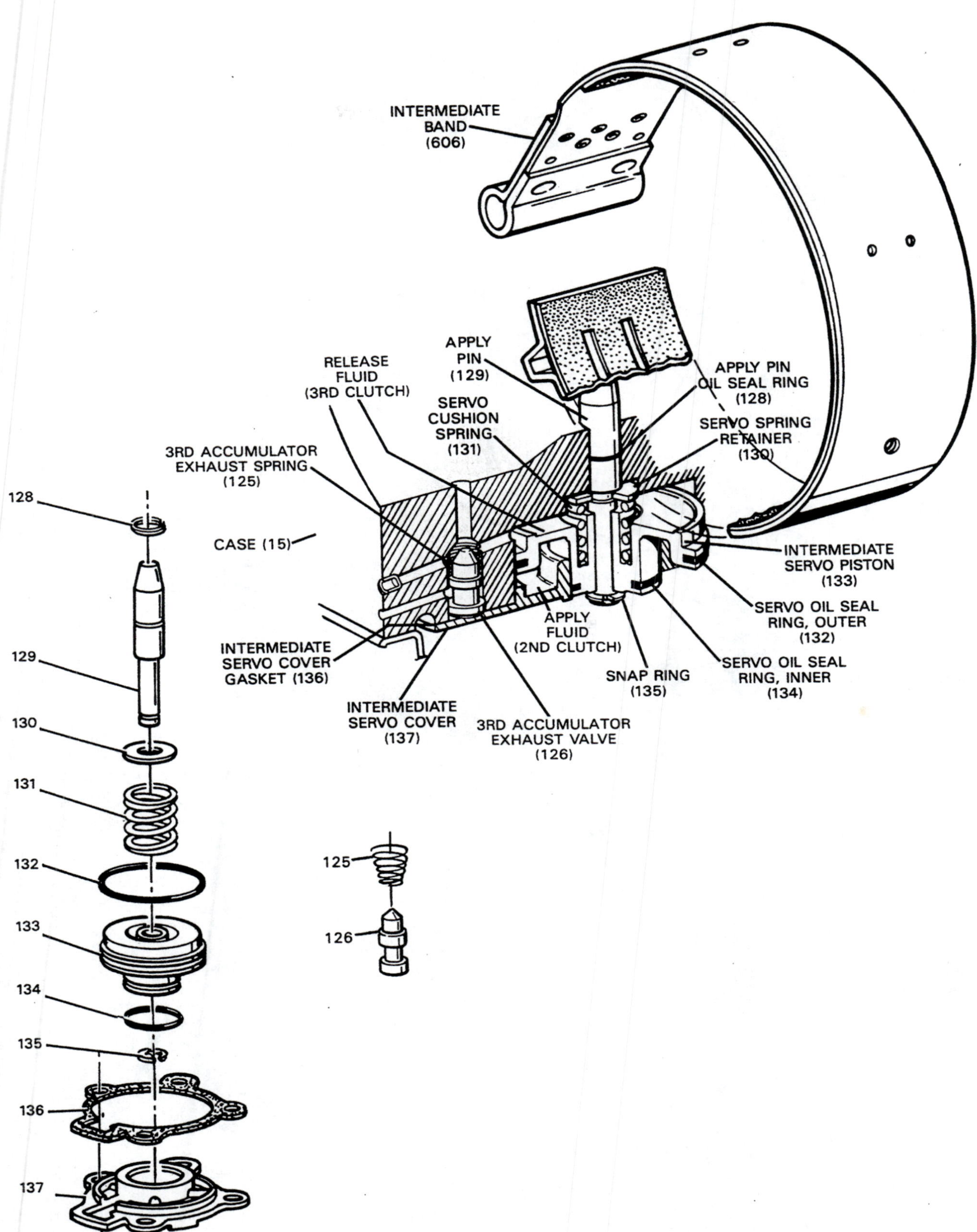

FIGURE 4–58 Basic servo piston. (Courtesy of Ford)

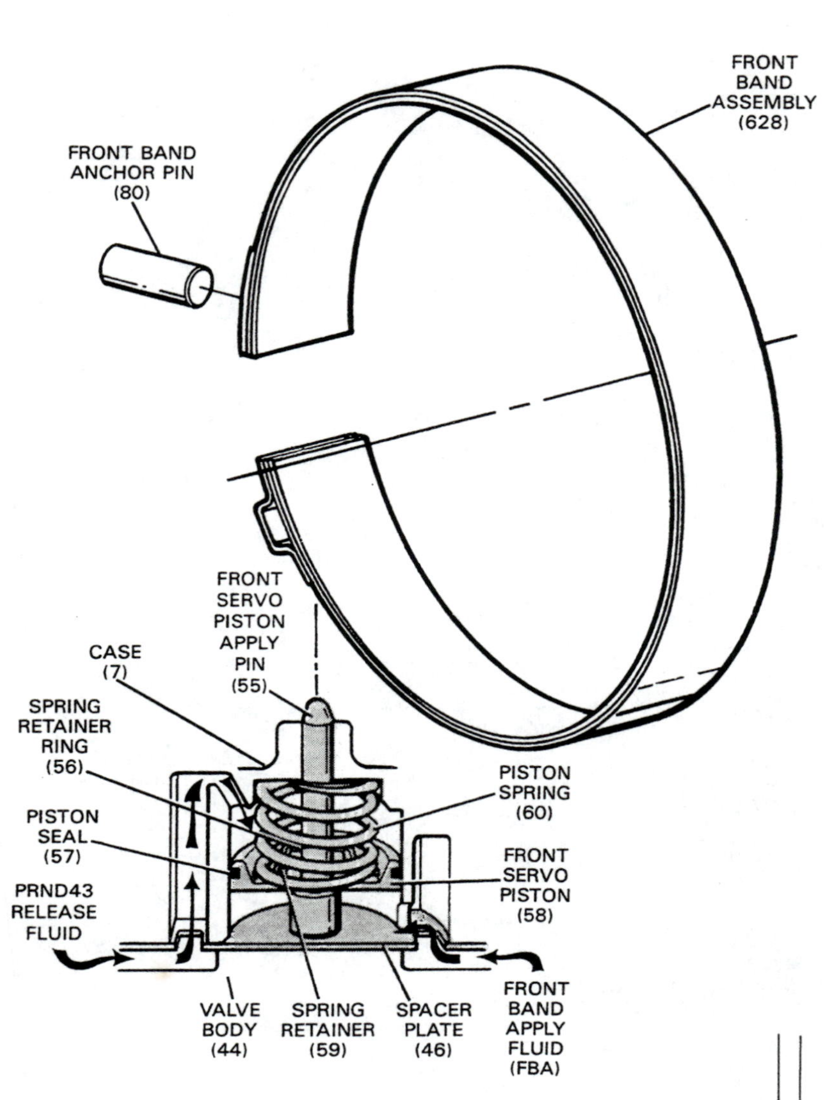

FIGURE 4–59 The two-way servo is applied and released by hydraulic pressure. (Courtesy of Ford)

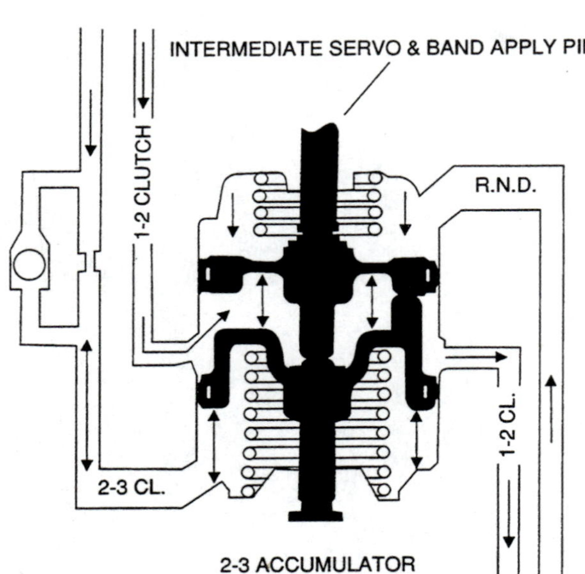

FIGURE 4–60 Basic accumulator. (Courtesy of Ford)

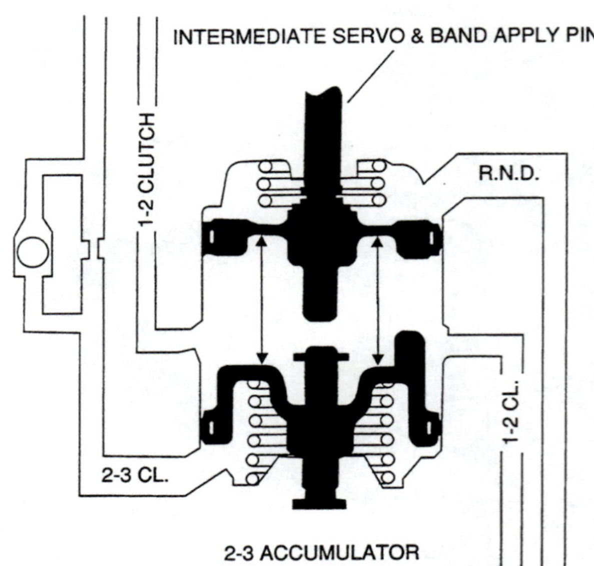

FIGURE 4–61 As pressure is applied to a circuit that includes an accumulator, the pressure forces the piston to compress the spring, which provides a shock absorber effect. (Courtesy of Ford)

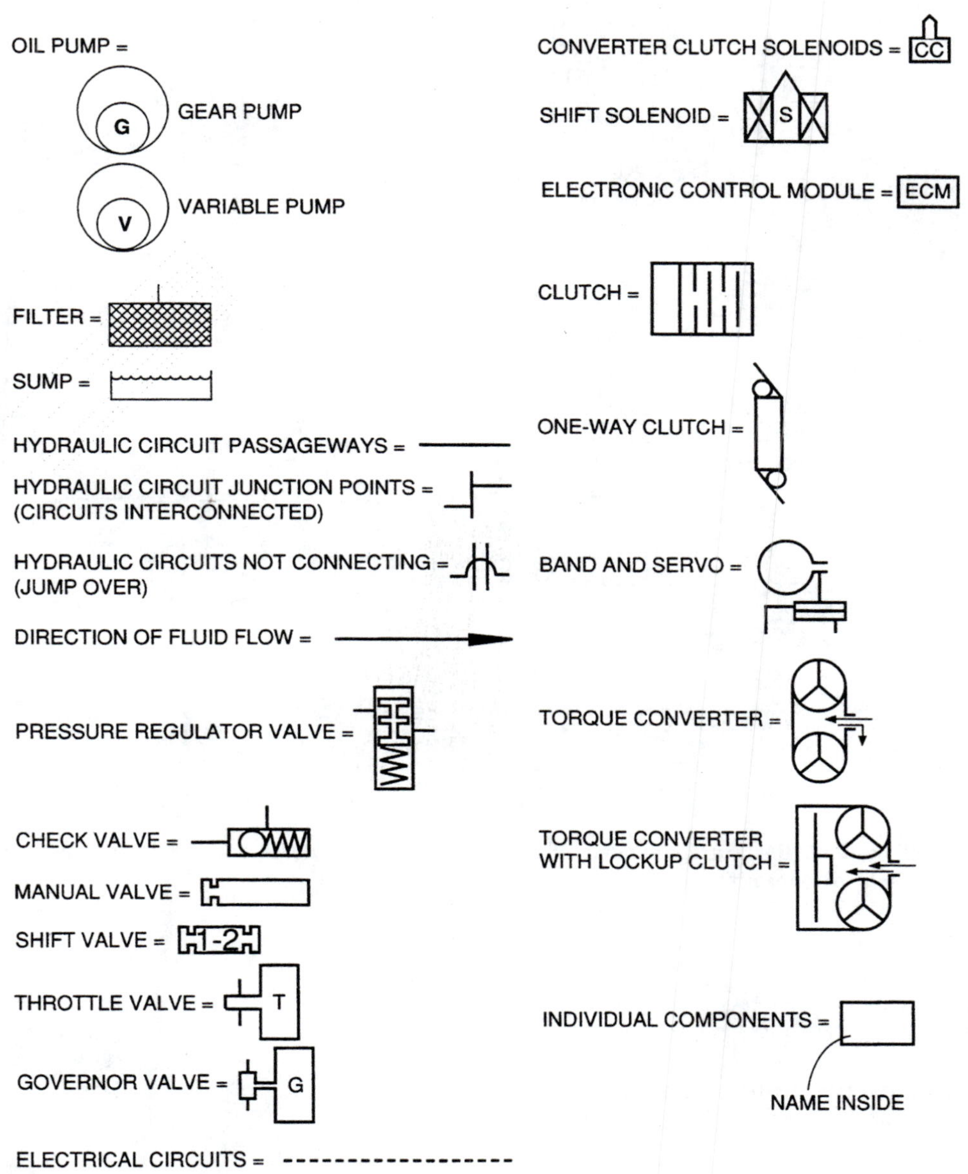

FIGURE 4–62 Hydraulic circuit symbols.

store the supply of ATF in the oil pan at the bottom of the transmission. Some automatic transaxles store the ATF in two locations, part in the oil pan and part in the side cover pan. When the transmission is cold, most of the ATF is stored in the oil pan. But as the ATF warms up and reaches operating temperature, a thermal valve is closed near the bottom of the side cover pan and the ATF is then stored in the side cover. The location and layout of these two sump systems are shown in Figure 4–63.

Before the ATF arrives at the pump it must be filtered. The main function of the filter is to filter out the small particles of material which is carried in the ATF and prevent them from damaging transmission components or sticking valves in the valve body.

The ATF is pushed through the filter and up into the inlet side of the pump by atmospheric pressure, as described in earlier sections. Then, as the fluid is pushed out the outlet side of the pump, the flow of fluid encounters the resistance of the circuits and pressure is created. To prevent excessive

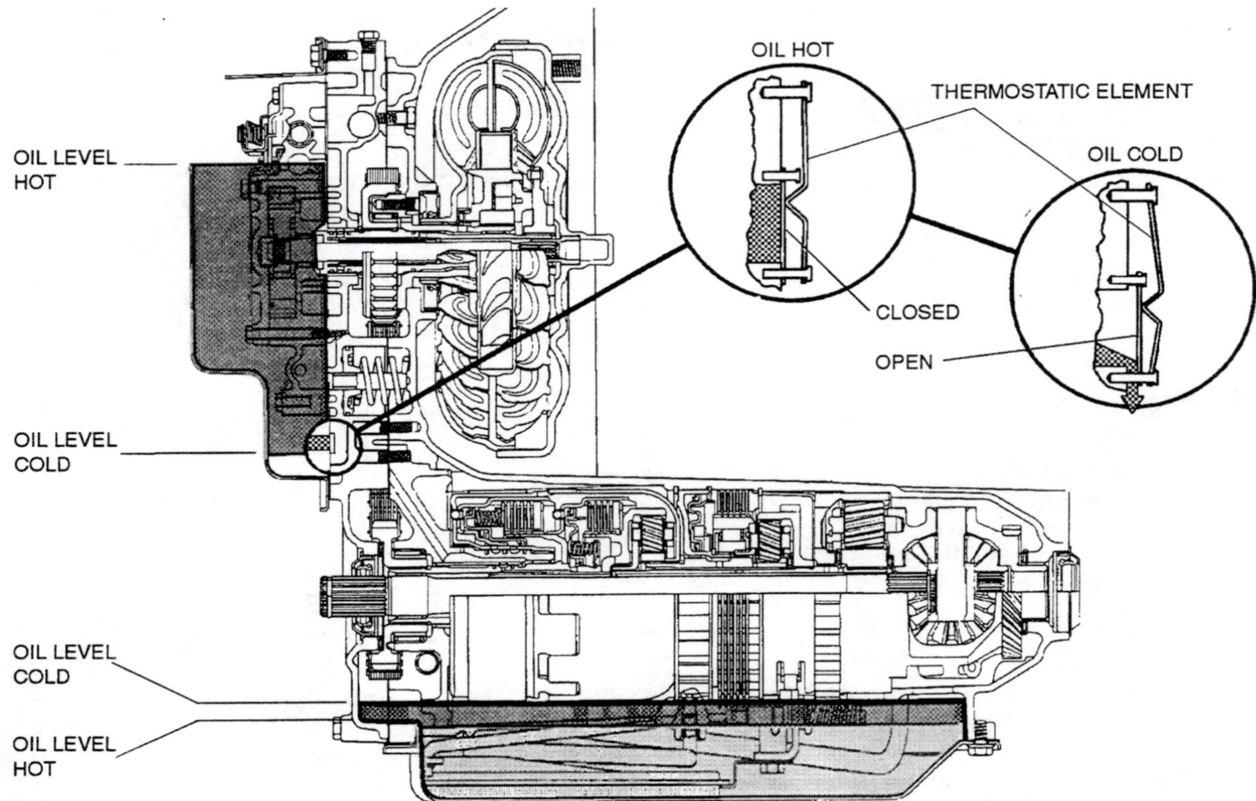

FIGURE 4–63 Basic arrangement of the ATF sump for RWD and FWD system. (Reprinted with permission of General Motors Corporation)

pressure from damaging the transmission components, the pressure must be controlled, and that is the job of the pressure regulator valve.

The pressure regulator valve is designed to control the pump output flow, and therefore the pressure, by bleeding off any flow and pressure above the amount needed to operate the transmission. As mentioned earlier, the pressure regulator uses a balance valve design which has an auxiliary boost valve that can raise the mainline pressure regulated by the pressure regulator to meet the changing needs of the transmission. The components discussed so far are shown in Figure 4–64, which is a close-up of the hydraulic system diagram showing less than one-fifth of the total system. As new components are described, the diagram will grow until the entire system is shown.

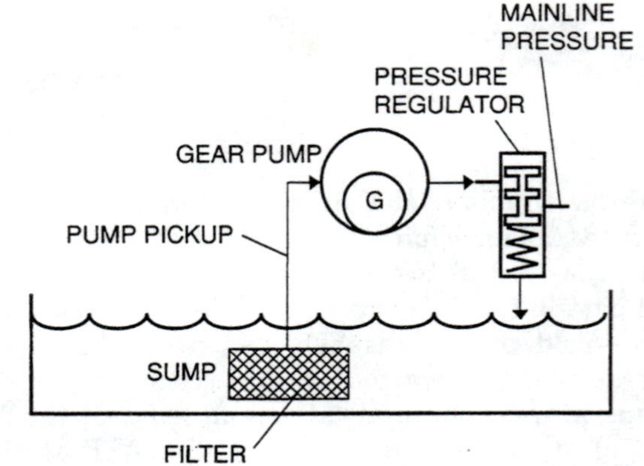

FIGURE 4–64 Hydraulic system pressure source.

4.5.2 Torque Converter

Once the fluid flow leaves the pressure regulator, it is referred to as mainline pressure and is available for all of the transmission's hydraulic needs. Mainline fluid feeds the torque converter fill circuit with a constant supply of cool ATF direct from the pressure regulator. The converter fill circuit has a pressure relief valve to control the maximum pressure to the torque converter. The mainline fluid fills the torque converter through the inlet passage until the converter is full. Because of the action of the torque converter, the fluid is heated to a high temperature. The hot fluid leaves the converter through the outlet passage and a drain-back check valve. This check valve is to prevent fluid drain back from the converter into the sump when the engine is not running. From there, the fluid leaves the transmission case and flows through a steel line to the cooler in the radiator. As it passes through the cooler engine, coolant in the radiator removes heat from the ATF. The cool fluid returns to the transmission through another steel line and goes back into the transmission to lubricate the gear train and then return to the sump. This portion of the diagram is shown in Figure 4–65. What was just described is the system used with a standard torque converter not having a converter lockup clutch. As explained earlier, application and release of the converter lockup clutch is achieved by using two separate passages for the converter fill fluid and special control valves, both hydraulic and electrical, to direct flow to the proper passageway. In Figure 4–66 the application and release circuits show where the fill fluid is routed. When the release circuit is activated by the control valves, the fill fluid enters the converter in front of the converter clutch plate, forcing the plate away from the converter. In release position the converter clutch control valve connects the application passage to the sump so that the application passage becomes the outlet route. The higher pressure of the fill fluid in front of the disc holds the clutch plate back until the control valves change. When the control valves change to apply the converter clutch, the fill fluid is rerouted by the valve to enter through the application passage, behind the clutch plate, while the release passage is connected to the sump, becoming the outlet route. The higher pressure behind the clutch plate now pushes it against the converter cover, making the mechanical contact.

There are many driving conditions that are not suited for converter clutch lockup. The combination of hydraulic and electrical control of the circuit gives maximum control of the system. The hydraulic control valves (some systems use two and others only one) react to the vehicle's driving conditions through the use of control pressures in the same way that shift valves are positioned. But more control is needed to ensure smooth operation of the converter clutch. This extra control is provided by the electronic control module (ECM) or onboard computer. The ECM has many sensors sending it information constantly, so it can determine the perfect conditions for applying the converter clutch. The ECM controls converter clutch application through the use of a solenoid in the control valve system. This solenoid acts as a bleed-off

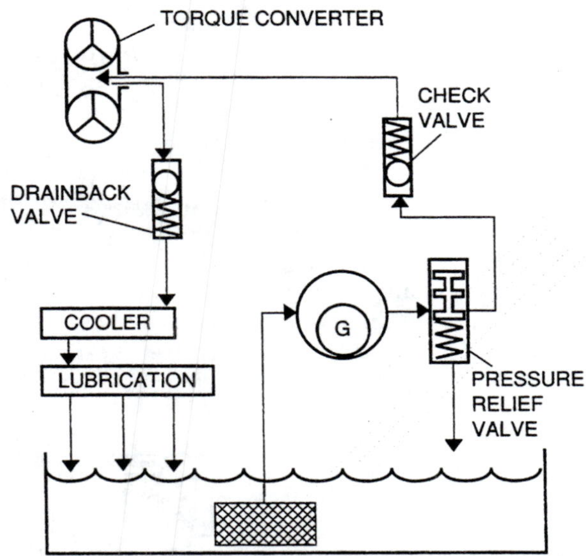

FIGURE 4–65 Hydraulic system that includes a torque converter.

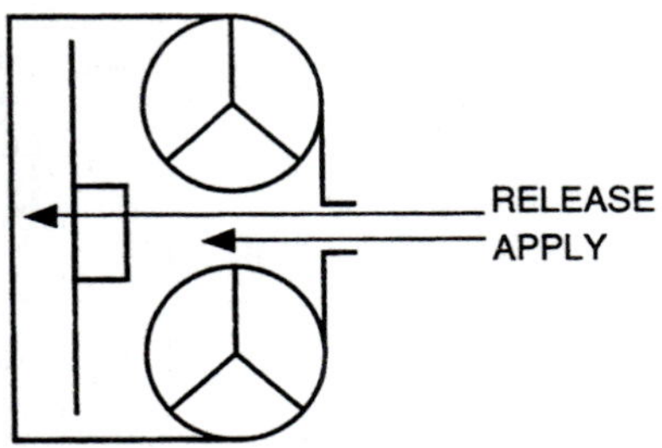

FIGURE 4–66 Hydraulic converter clutch.

device, which means that when the solenoid is not energized or turned off, a port is open which bleeds off pressure from the circuit being controlled. In Figure 4–67 the same solenoid is shown in both open and closed positions. With the solenoid open, the circuit will not work, so the computer has ultimate control over the system. The circuit will function only when the solenoid is energized, or turned on. A diagram of the torque converter fill circuit for a converter lockup clutch system is shown in Figure 4–68. The remainder of the circuit is basically the same as for the standard converter system, with the fluid going to the cooler, then returning to lubricate the gear train.

4.5.3 Gear Train

The fluid flow to the gear train is simple to understand with the help of the clutch and band application chart. You know that to engage each different gear ratio, a different combination of clutches, bands, and one-way clutches is used. The quickest way to know which coupling and holding devices are applied in a given gear is to refer to the clutch and band application chart.

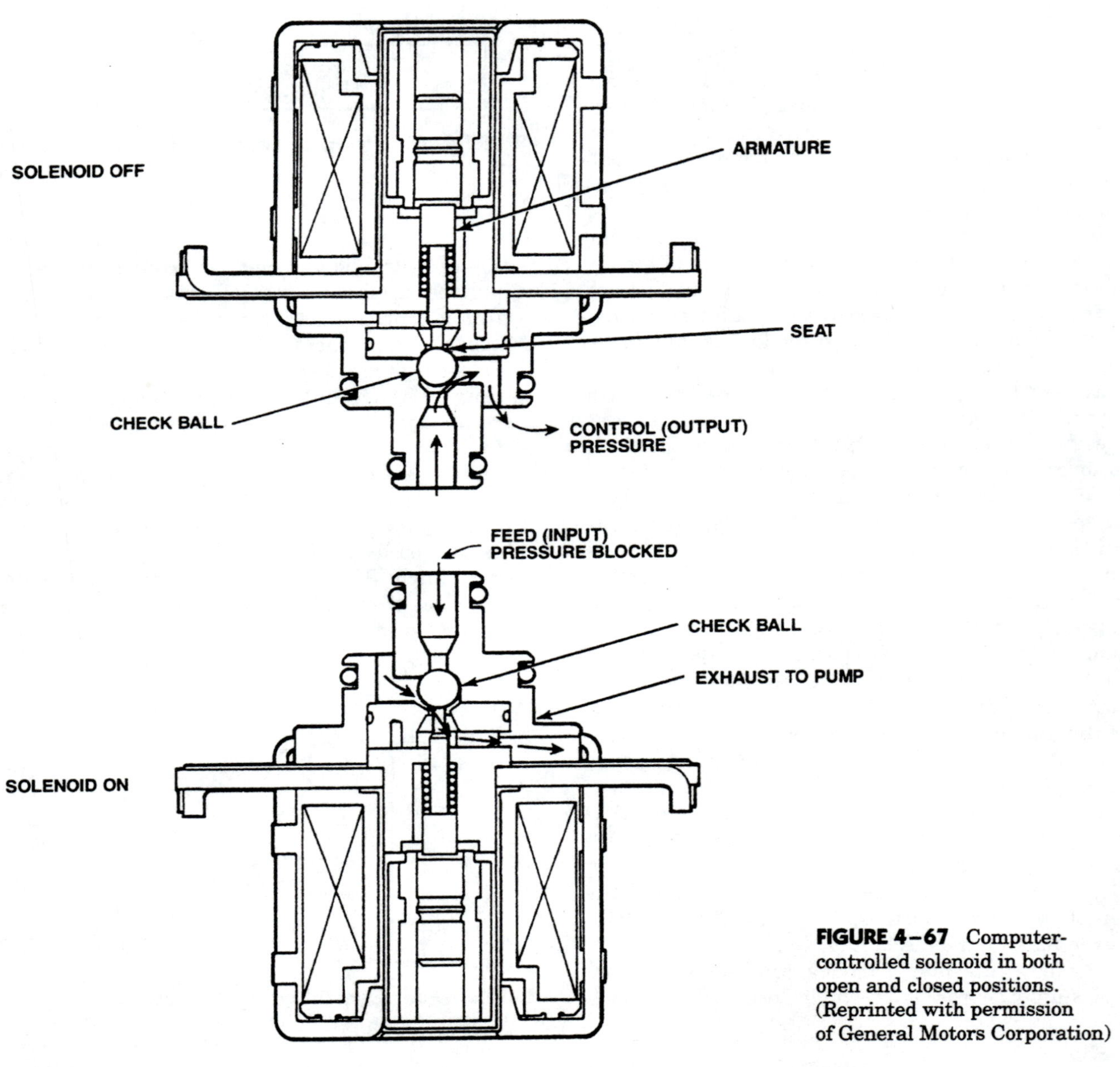

FIGURE 4–67 Computer-controlled solenoid in both open and closed positions. (Reprinted with permission of General Motors Corporation)

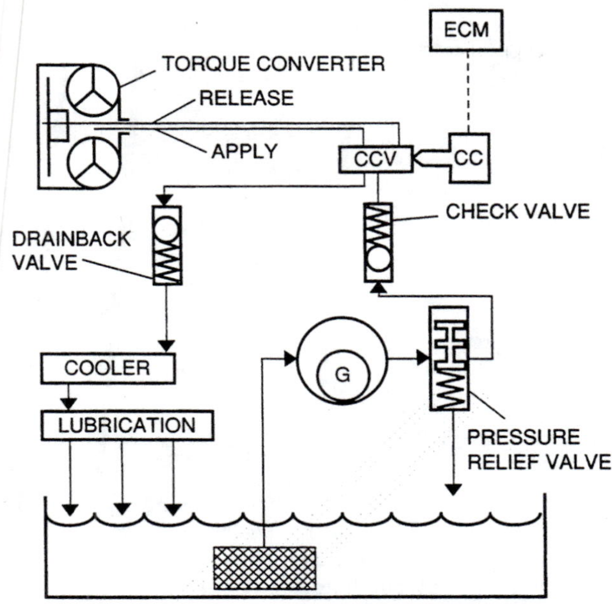

FIGURE 4–68 Converter clutch computer control system.

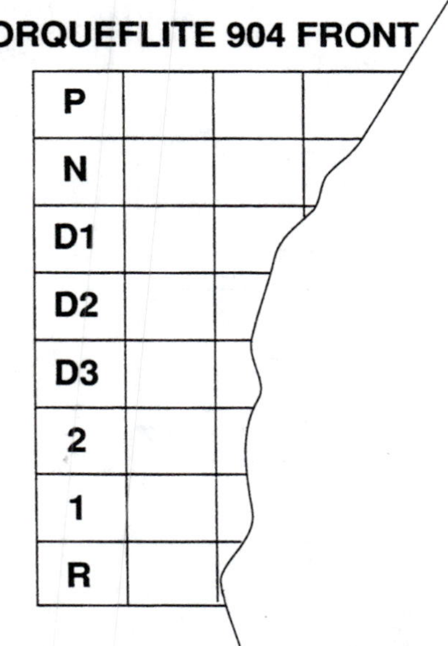

FIGURE 4–70 The gear selections on each clutch and band chart are arranged in this order.

1. Clutch and Band Charts

The clutch and band charts that appear in this book are not the same as those used by manufacturers in their service manuals. Each manufacturer has its own layout of coupling and holding devices, gear selection, and names for the major components, so each chart is different and must be studied closely to be fully understood. To simplify the charts as much as possible, we will use one format for all the charts. Across the top of the chart, starting from the left, will be the multidisc clutches as they are arranged in the transmission according to power flow. Each clutch will use the manufacturer's name and in parentheses the functional name. Following all the clutches will be the bands, with the first band listed being nearest the front of the gear train. Last will be the one-way clutches, again listing the closest to the front first. An example of how the layout for a Chrysler Torque Flite transmission would look is shown in Figure 4–69. The gear selection will be shown vertically on the left side starting at the top with park (P), neutral (N), then the various speeds in drive (D1, D2, D3, etc.), then manual second (2) and manual first (1), with reverse (R) at the bottom of the list. This arrangement is shown in Figure 4–70 with the transmission name and model shown above the gear positions. This format will be used with all the transmissions discussed in this book.

2. Coupling and Holding Devices

The coupling and holding devices of the power train are shown in the diagrams using the symbols listed earlier. The function of each device is described during the power flow description of each transmission in Part III of the book. By using the same format on the clutch and band charts for all the

	←CLUTCHES→ FRONT TO REAR		←BANDS→ FRONT TO REAR		←1-WAY CLUTCHES FRONT TO REAR
TORQUE FLITE 904	(HI–REV)	(FORWARD)	KICKDOWN (2ND SPEED)	LOW–REVERSE	LOW 1-WAY ROLLER
P					
N					

FIGURE 4–69 The coupling and holding devices shown in each clutch and band chart are arranged in this order.

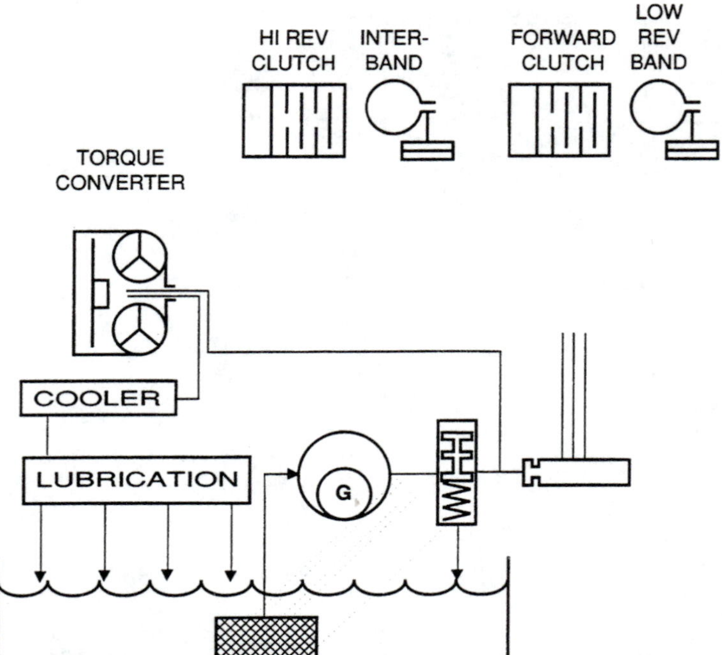

FIGURE 4–71 The coupling and holding devices are labeled using the same names that appear on the clutch and band charts.

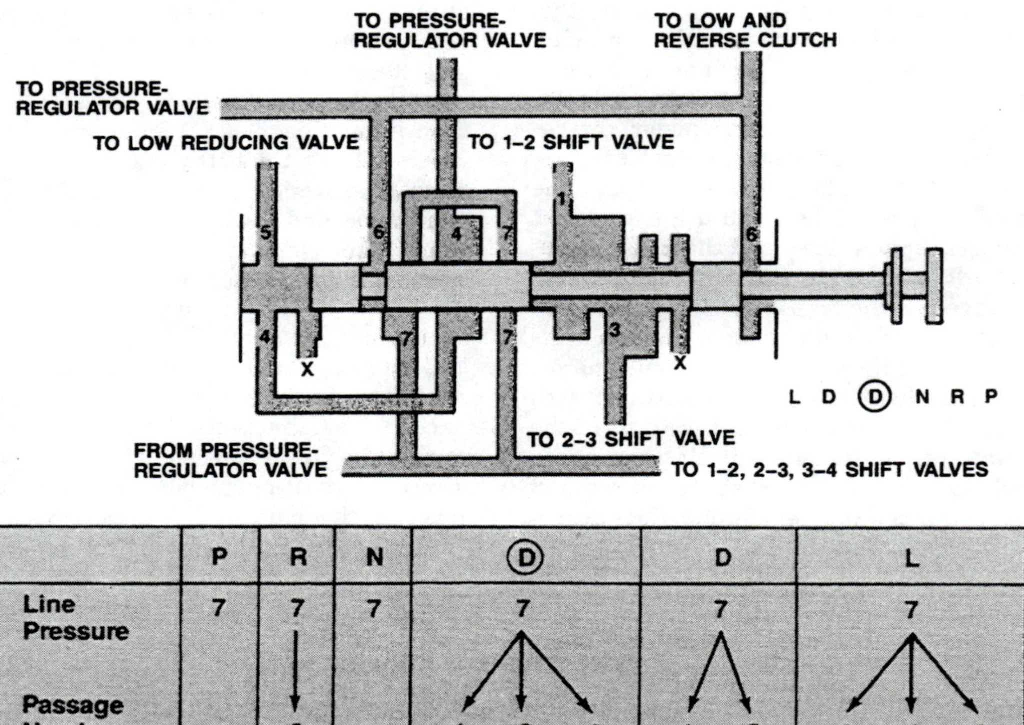

	P	R	N	Ⓓ	D	L
Line Pressure	7	7	7	7	7	7
Passage Number	—	6	—	1 3 4	1 3	1 4 5

FIGURE 4–72 A manual valve provides a means of connecting the passageway shown here.

transmissions studied, you should be able to find many similarities between the various transmissions and also easily see the differences. In showing the coupling and holding devices for transmissions in the diagrams, each device is labeled with the same names as those used in the clutch and band charts, as shown in Figure 4–71.

4.5.4 Shift Control

The last and probably most important part of the hydraulic system function is shift control. The ability to upshift or downshift to meet varying operating conditions of the vehicle, as well as to sense engine load and vehicle speed, allows the transmissions to be truly automatic in their operations. In this section the components of the valve bodies are added to the circuits to complete the hydraulic system.

1. Manual Valve

After the mainline fluid leaves the pressure regulator, it goes to the manual valve, which is the main directional control valve. The manual valve's position is controlled by the driver of the vehicle as he or she moves the gear selector lever. The number of gear selections possible is determined by the transmission design and the number of forward gears in the transmission. The manual valve routes mainline fluid to the appropriate coupling or holding devices, to the throttle and governor valves, and to the shift valves according to which gear has been selected. In Figure 4–72 the different combinations of passage connections are shown for a four-speed overdrive transmission. This illustration is part of a manufacturer's hydraulic system schematic, which goes into great detail. During our study of specific transmissions, the manufacturer's schematics will be used, but for now the general hydraulic system diagrams will be used to show basic system operation. In Figure 4–73 a manual valve has been added to the diagram.

2. Governor Pressure

As explained earlier, the transmission must have a speed reference of some type to provide the proper shift timing for the vehicle's operating conditions. On the latest computer-controlled transmission, this reference is supplied to the computer by its sensors, but on the earlier hydraulic controlled transmissions, the governor valve provides a hydraulic pressure that is proportional to the vehicle road speed (Figure 4–74). With the vehicle stopped, there is no governor pressure and as the vehicle starts moving, the governor pressure slowly starts to rise. The faster the vehicle goes, the higher the governor pressure builds until maximum pressure is reached. If the vehicle is maintaining a steady

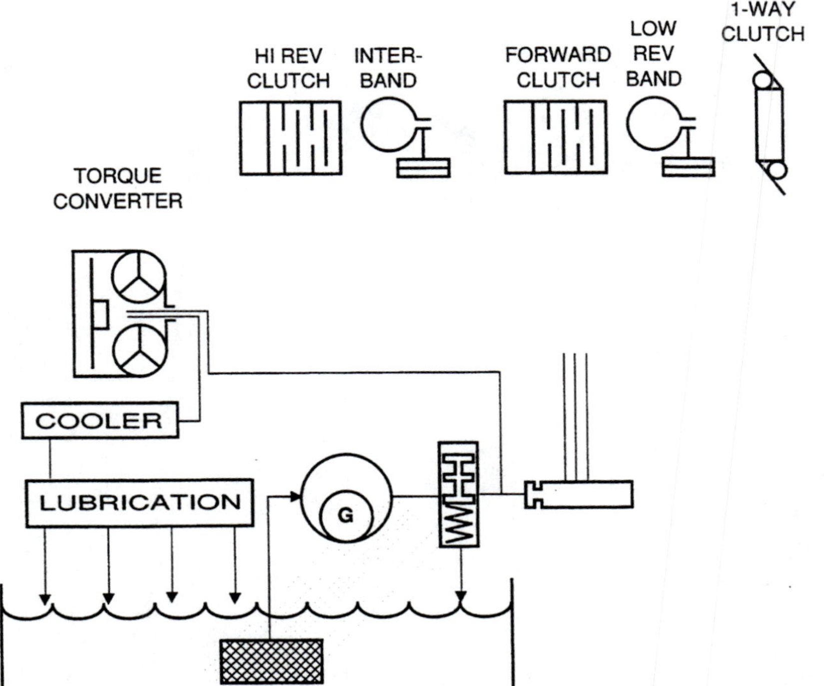

FIGURE 4–73 A manual valve is added to the basic hydraulic system diagram.

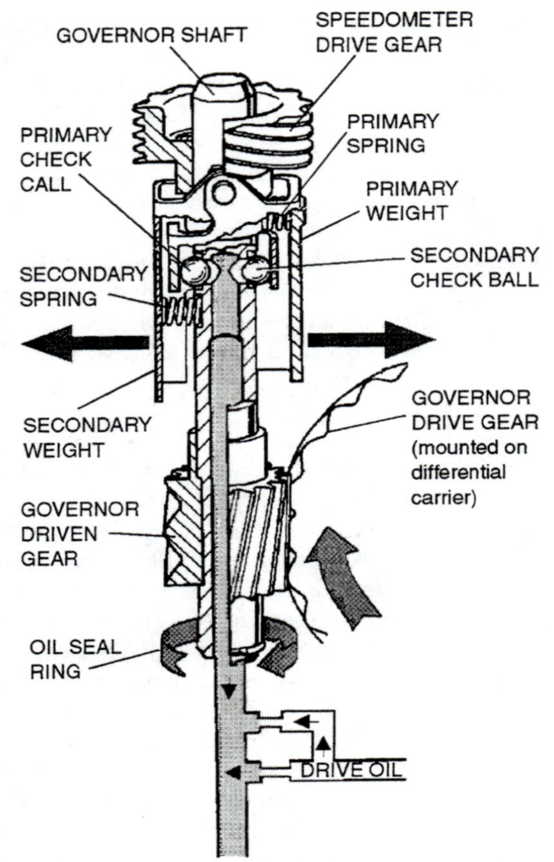

FIGURE 4–74 A governor valve modulates the mainline pressure to represent the speed of the vehicle.

cruising speed, the governor pressure will remain the same in proportion to the speed, and as the vehicle slows down, the governor pressure drops. Governor pressure is routed to one end of the shift valves, where it tries to push the valve into the upshift position. The movement of the shift valve is resisted by spring pressure and by the other control pressure, throttle pressure. In Figure 4–75 a governor valve has been added to the diagram.

3. *Throttle Pressure*

Throttle pressure is the second control pressure, governor pressure being the first, which is used to control transmission shifting. Throttle pressure is a proportional pressure representing engine load. At idle there is very little or no throttle pressure, but as the throttle is opened and engine load increases, so does the throttle pressure. The throttle pressure is routed to the opposite end of the shift valves from the governor pressure and works to keep the valve from moving and upshifting until the governor pressure is greater than the throttle pressure (Figure 4–76). This balance of control pressures is what allows the transmission to upshift at lower speeds at part throttle or at higher speeds at full throttle. The harder the engine is working, the higher the throttle pressure, so the governor must produce more pressure to overcome the throttle pressure and force the upshift. To force an upshift, governor pressure must become greater than throttle pressure. But once the upshift has happened, if

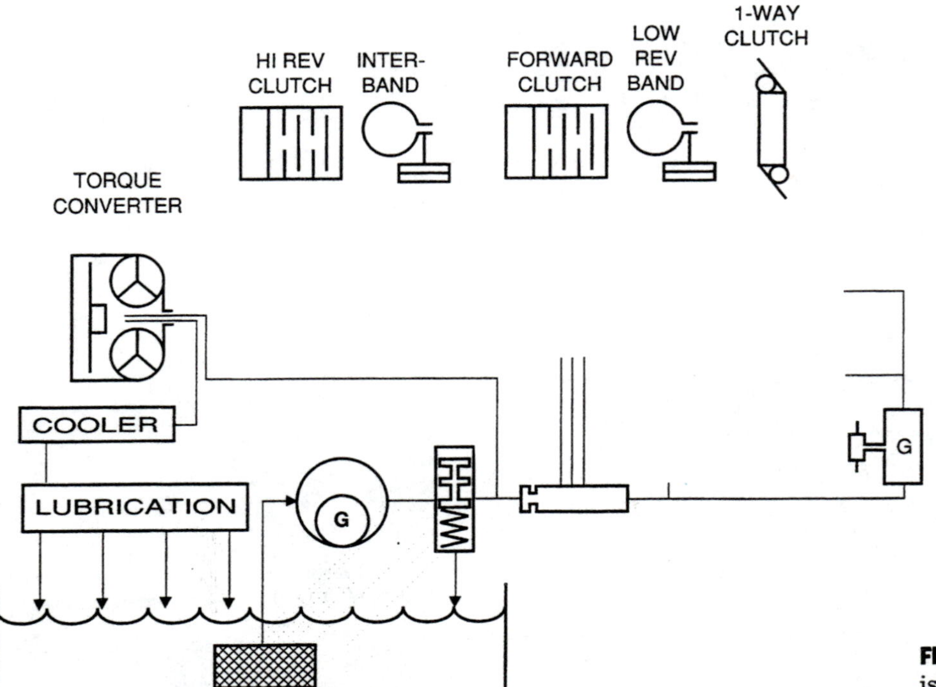

FIGURE 4–75 A governor valve is added to the diagram.

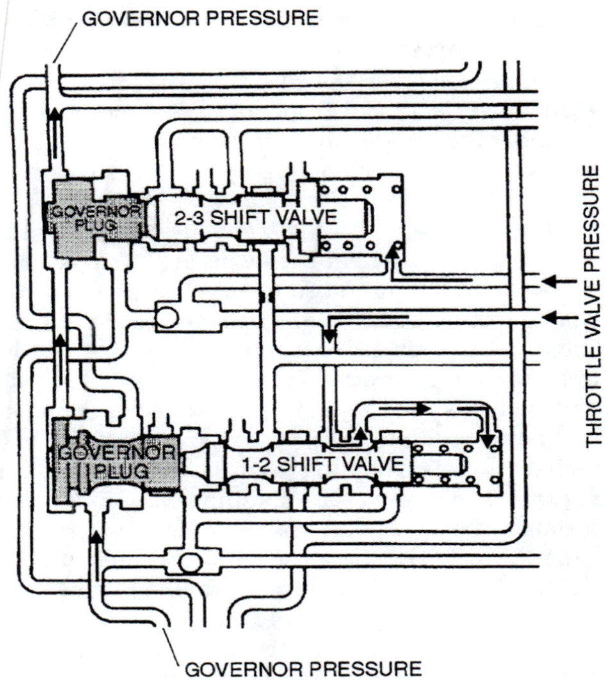

FIGURE 4–76 Throttle valve pressure is applied to one end of the shift valve while governor pressure is applied to the other end.

throttle pressure becomes greater, the shift valve is forced back and a downshift occurs.

Throttle pressure is also routed to the pressure regulator boost valve so that when the engine is under heavy load, the mainline pressure will increase to handle the extra stress on the coupling and holding devices. This new route is shown in Figure 4–77.

4. Shift Valves

The shift valves are directional control valves, which are used to change the routing of mainline pressure to different coupling or holding devices to achieve a gear change. A shift valve is able to control only one upshift, so there must be a separate shift valve for each possible upshift of the transmission. They are usually named by the shift they control: the 1–2, 2–3, or 3–4 shift valve. These valves are located in the valve body and are spring loaded to return to their base position. In Figure 4–78 you see a typical valve body and the shift valves. To see how the shift valves work, let's follow them through their upshifts. The complete hydraulic system diagram is shown in Figure 4–79. As we go through the upshifts, the circuits in use will be highlighted.

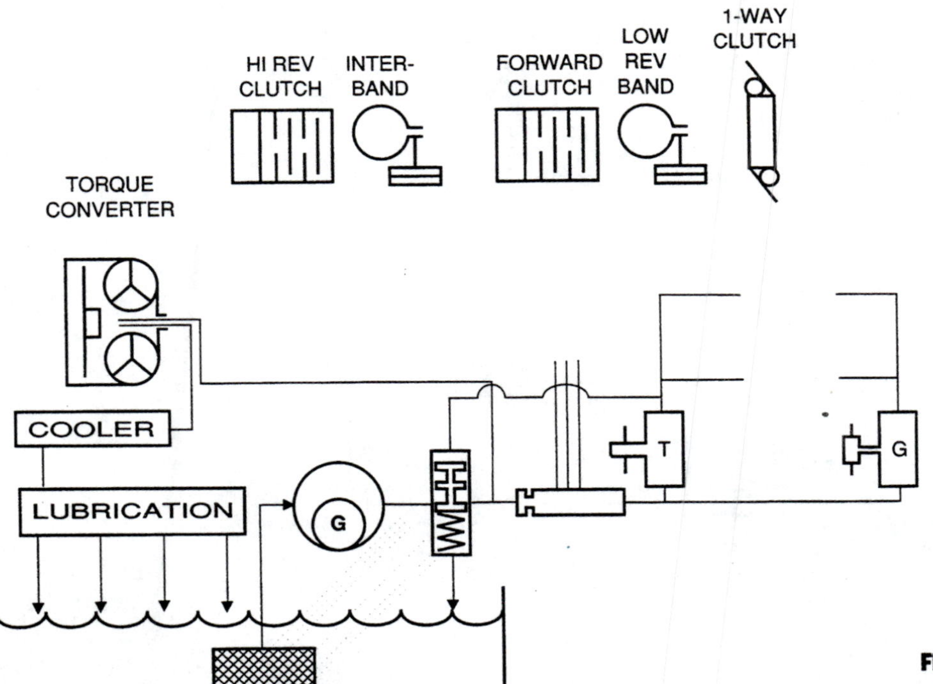

FIGURE 4–77 A throttle valve is added to the diagram.

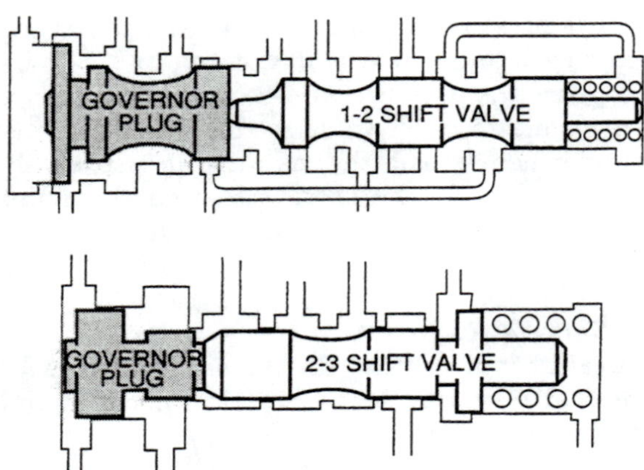

FIGURE 4–78 Shift valves are located in the valve body.

The vehicle is started and the driver places the gear selector in drive. The manual valve sends mainline pressure to the forward clutch, the 1–2 shift valve, the governor, and the throttle valve, as shown in Figure 4–80, which engages D1. As the driver steps on the accelerator, the vehicle starts moving forward, and as it does, governor and throttle valve pressures are being produced and routed to opposite ends of the shift valves (Figure 4–81). When the governor pressure builds to the point at which it overcomes the throttle valve pressure, the shift valve is moved from its base position to the upshift position and mainline pressure is routed to another coupling or holding device, in this case the intermediate band (Figure 4–82). With the intermediate band applied, the transmission is in second gear. With the 1–2 shift valve in upshift position, it routes mainline pressure to the 2–3 shift valve so that it can function. As the vehicle speed increases, the governor pressure continues to rise until it overcomes the throttle valve pressure on the 2–3 shift valve. As the 2–3 shift valve moves from base to upshift position, mainline pressure is again redirected to new coupling and holding devices. In Figure 4–83 you see mainline pressure going through the 2–3 shift valve to the intermediate band servo for band release and the high–reverse clutch. This has both clutches applied, which provides third speed in this transmission. Part- or full-throttle downshifts can occur when the throttle valve pressure becomes greater than the governor pressure as the driver applies more pressure on the accelerator. As the vehicle slows to a stop, the springs on the shift valves return them to their base positions.

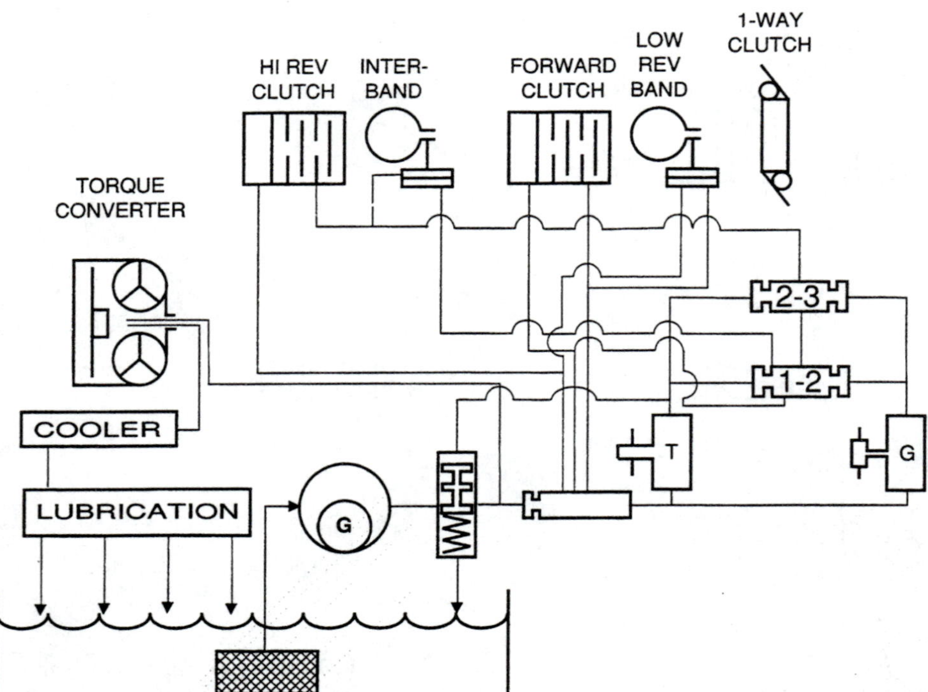

FIGURE 4–79 Complete basic hydraulic system diagram.

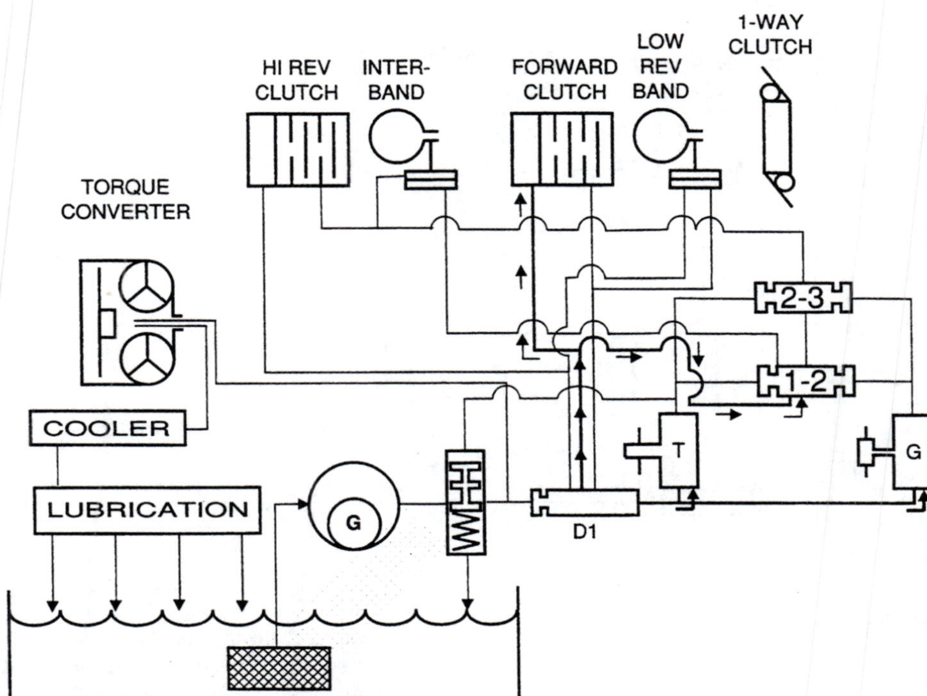

FIGURE 4–80 As the driver places the transmission in gear (D1), the manual valve directs fluid to the forward clutch, 1–2 shift valve, governor, and throttle valve.

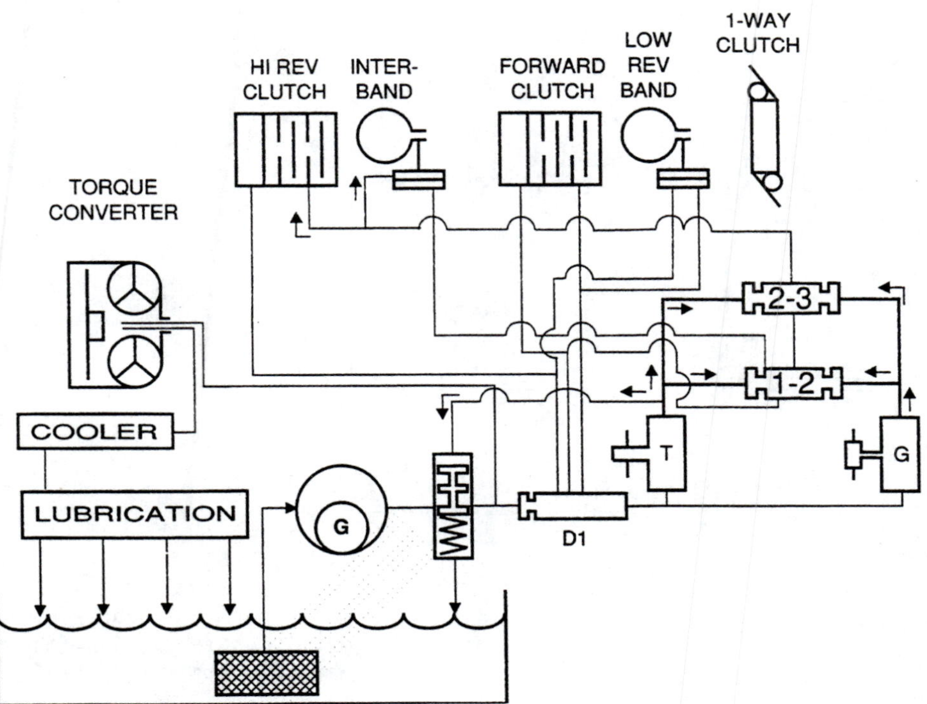

FIGURE 4–81 As the vehicle starts moving, control pressures (governor and throttle) are produced and are sent to the shift valves.

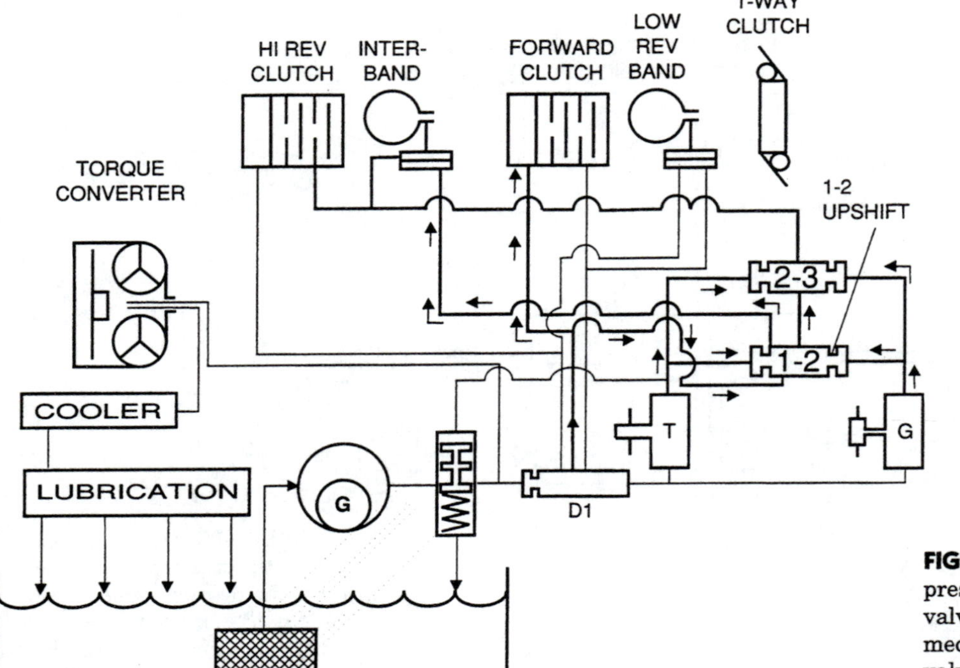

FIGURE 4–82 Once governor pressure moves the 1–2 shift valve, fluid is directed to the intermediate band and to the 2–3 shift valve.

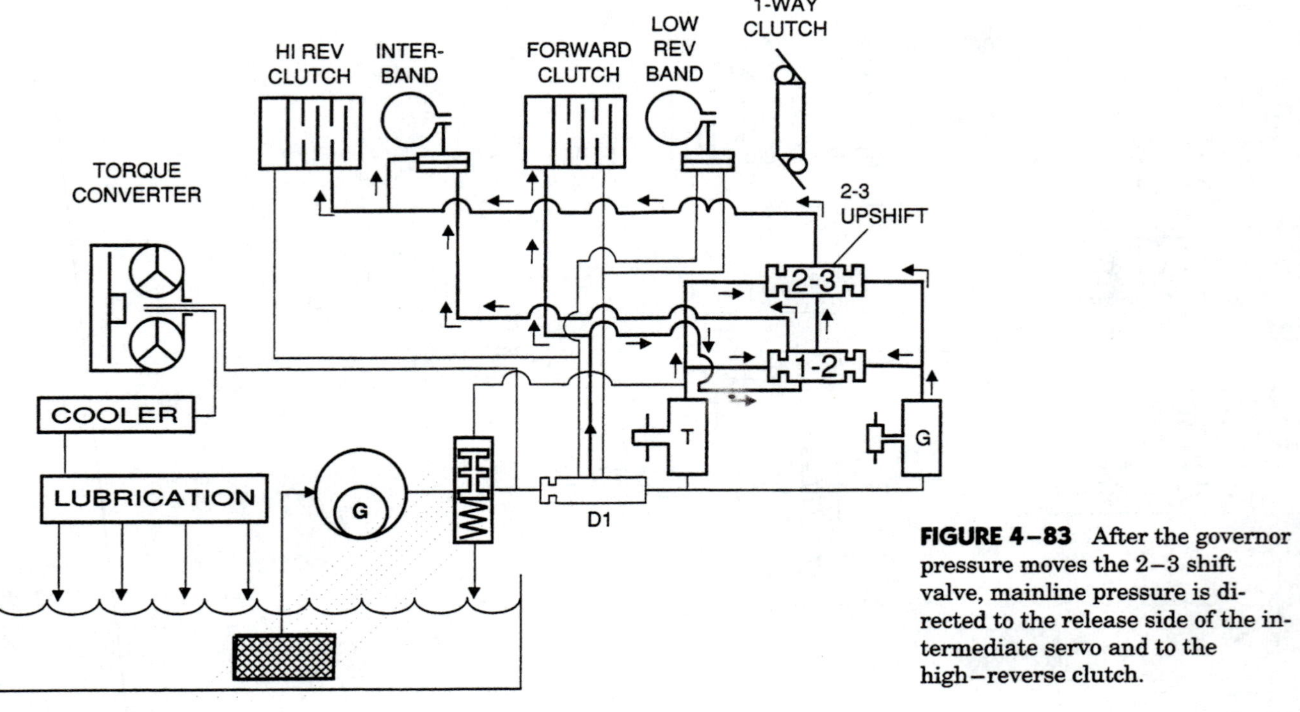

FIGURE 4–83 After the governor pressure moves the 2–3 shift valve, mainline pressure is directed to the release side of the intermediate servo and to the high–reverse clutch.

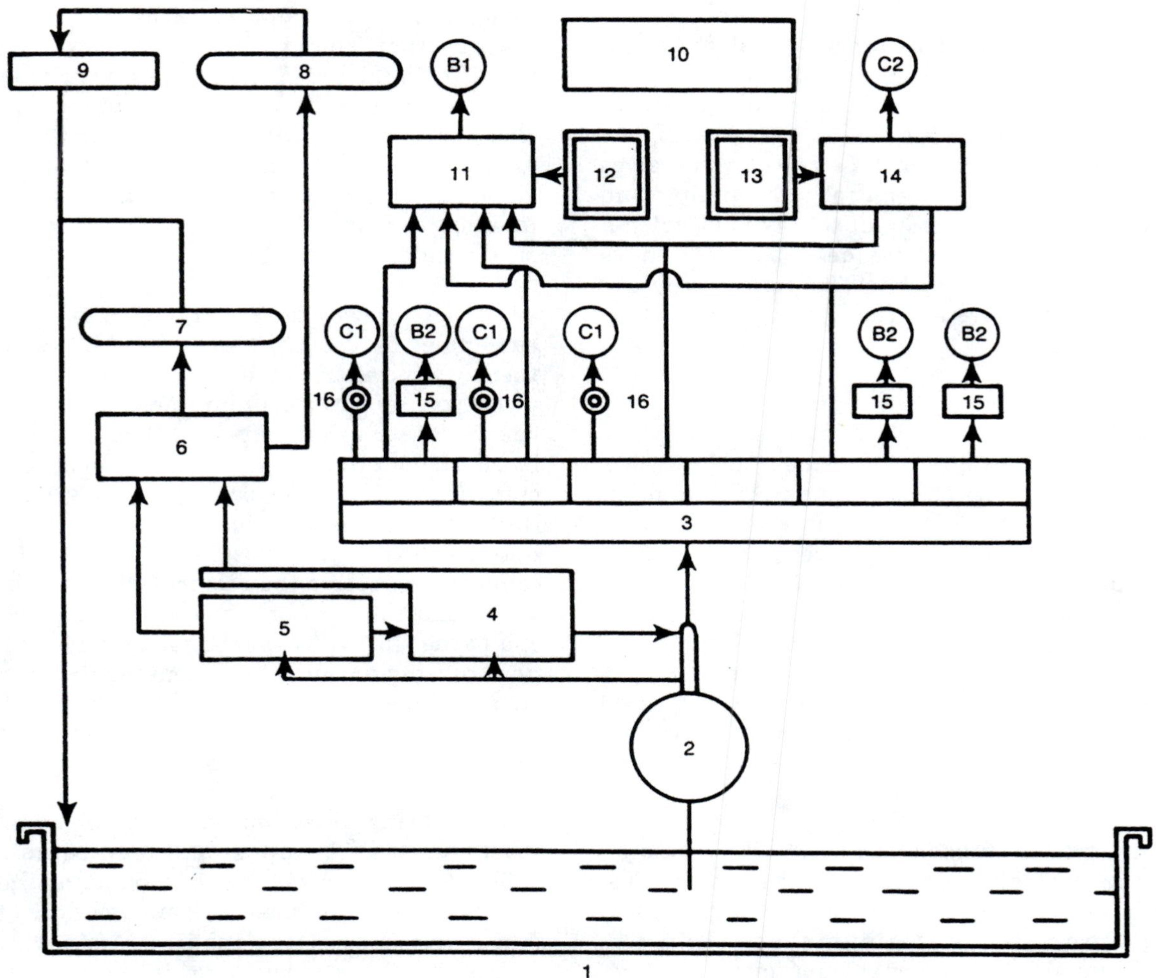

1. OIL PAN
2. OIL PUMP
3. MANUAL VALVE
4. PRIMARY REGULATOR VALVE
5. THROTTLE VALVE
6. SECONDARY REGULATOR VALVE
7. LUBRICATION
8. TORQUE CONVERTER
9. OIL COOLER
10. CONTROLLER (COMPUTER)
11. 1-2 SHIFT VALVE
12. SECOND (2ND) BRAKE SOLENOID
13. DIRECT CLUTCH SOLENOID
14. 2-3 SHIFT VALVE
15. B2 CONTROL VALVE
16. ACCUMULATOR

C1. FORWARD CLUTCH
C2. DIRECT CLUTCH
B1. SECOND (2ND) BRAKE
B2. 1ST-REVERSE BRAKE

FIGURE 4–84 In a computer-controlled transmission, a governor is not used.

5. *Shift Quality Valves*

Throughout the history of automatic transmissions, manufacturers have concentrated on developing and producing transmissions that would provide a smooth, soft shift from one gear to the next. To help improve shift quality, many special-purpose valves have been developed to control shift timing and pressure buildup. We will call this type of valve a *shift quality valve* when we describe the various specific transmissions in later chapters. Many different names are given to the various shift quality valves:

cutback	limit
shuttle	kickdown
converter control	backout
servo modulator	capacity modulator
orifice control	throttle valve limit
relay	sequence
accumulator	line bias
3–2 control	4–3 torque demand
detent	throttle downshift
torque demand control	coast control
overdrive servo regulator	inhibit
low-range coasting boost	throttle pressure booster

The specific function of each shift quality valve is best explained in reference to the transmission from which it comes. The specific explanation of each valve is best stated in the manufacturers' service manuals. This advance information is more easily understood when dealing with one specific transmission at a time.

6. *Computer Shift Controls*

On some vehicles the on-board computers used to control engine operation have now been given control of the transmission shift functions. The control pressures from the throttle valve and the governor are being replaced by a computer-controlled solenoid. In the hydraulically controlled transmission the governor and throttle valve created pressures that represented vehicle speed and engine load. These control pressures worked against each other at opposite ends of the shift valve to control shift timing. In the new electronic control system the computer has much more input data available through the engine sensor system. These extra data can mean better shift control and improved operation because more operating conditions are being monitored. In a computer-controlled transmission the governor and governor pressure system are entirely eliminated (Figure 4–84). Vehicle speed information is supplied to the computer by the vehicle speed sensor (VSS), which replaces the governor system on some electronic transaxles. Throttle valve (TV) pressure is still used to raise and lower mainline pressure through its action on the pressure regulator valve, but it is no longer routed to the shift valves. Since governor and TV pressure are no longer used to control the shifts, a new pressure must be used to move the shift valves from their base position to the upshift position. In Figure 4–85 you see that mainline pressure is routed to one end of each shift valve and that each shift valve has a computer-controlled shift solenoid on that circuit. The shift solenoid (Figure 4–86) is spring loaded in the open position, which allows the mainline pressure to exhaust to the sump. When the computer energizes the solenoid, the exhaust valve closes and the mainline pressure is applied to the end of the shift valve, moving it to the upshift position, causing an upshift. As long as the solenoid is on, mainline pressure will hold the shift valve in an upshift position. When the solenoid is turned off by the computer, mainline pressure is exhausted to the sump, the shift valve is returned to base position by spring force, and a downshift occurs. The spool type of shift valve is still used because of its ability to switch a number of circuits at the same time. This is a job a solenoid could not do, so the designers chose to retain the spool shift valve and control it with a solenoid through the computer.

As you study specific individual transmissions, you will find that there are many electronically controlled transmissions in use today. In the future most transmissions will probably be controlled by electronics, so now is the time to learn how they function.

SUMMARY

Although this has been an extremely long chapter, the material covered is essential to understanding how an automatic transmission functions. The hydraulic system is the heart and brains of the automatic transmission and must be studied carefully to fully grasp its operation.

Due to the importance of the material covered in this chapter, we will not try to capsulate the information in a summary but encourage you to go back through the chapter and review any subject you do not understand thoroughly.

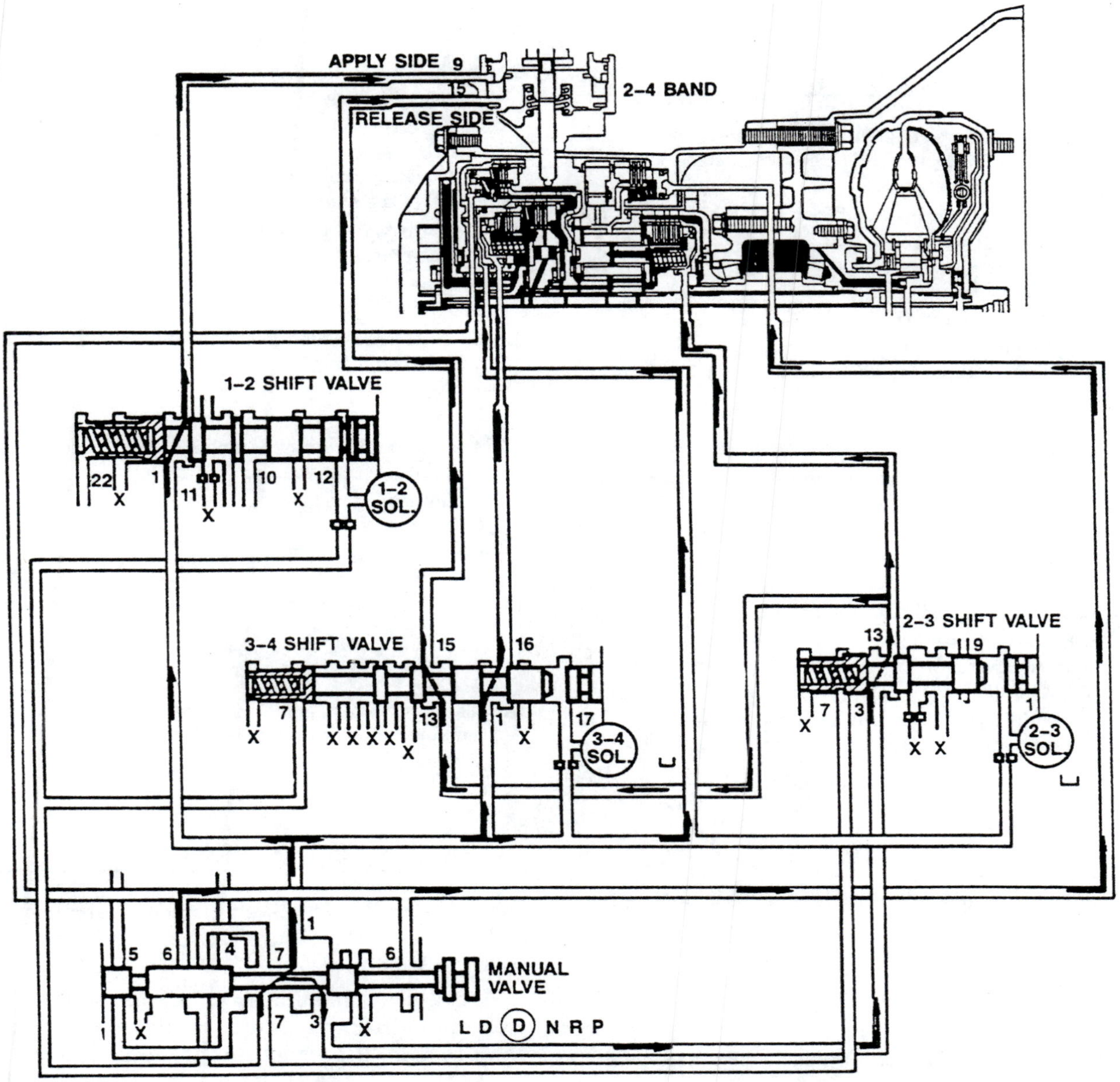

FIGURE 4–85 Mainline pressure controlled by shift solenoids replaces the control pressures.

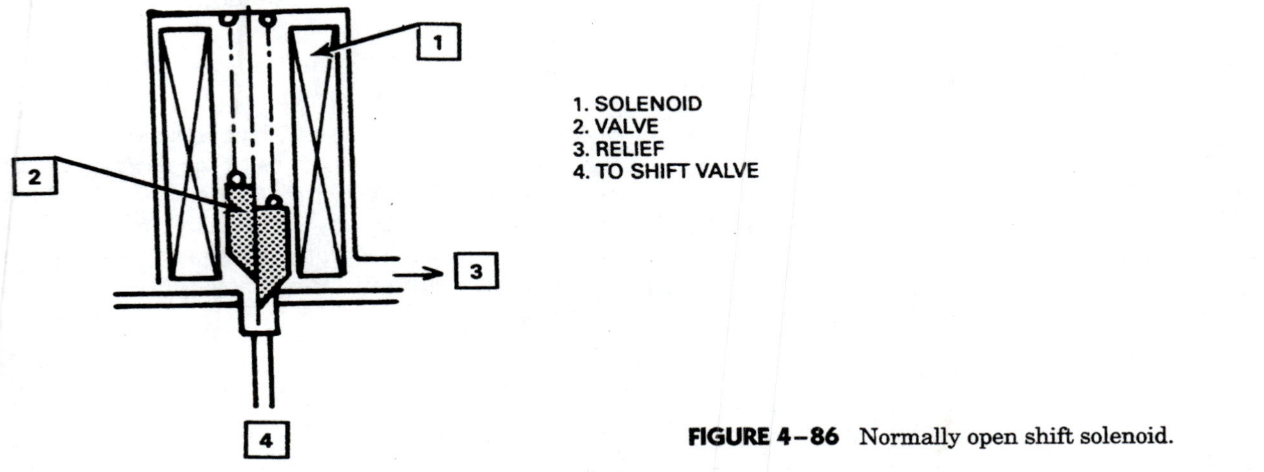

FIGURE 4–86 Normally open shift solenoid.

SELF-TEST

Before going on to the next chapter, complete the self-test according to your instructor's directions. Read carefully and choose the best answer.

1. The force that moves the ATF into the inlet section of the oil pump is ______.
   a. Mainline pressure
   b. Throttle pressure
   c. Governor pressure
   d. Atmospheric pressure
2. An oil pump is measured by its ______.
   a. Pressure
   b. Flow
   c. Torque output
3. For a hydraulic circuit to build pressure there must be ______ to flow.
   a. Assistance
   b. Need
   c. Resistance
4. A hydraulic system can provide a ______.
   a. Force increase
   b. Transfer of power
   c. Both of the above
5. If you multiply the hydraulic pressure times the area of a hydraulic piston, the answer will give you the ______.
   a. Input force
   b. Side pressure
   c. Back pressure
   d. Output force
6. The name of one of the parts of a spool valve is the ______.
   a. Land
   b. Valley
   c. Face
   d. All of the above
7. A balance valve balances hydraulic pressure against ______.
   a. A lever
   b. Spring pressure
   c. Atmospheric pressure
   d. Throttle pressure
8. After the ATF has left the pump and gone through the pressure regulator, it is called ______.
   a. Governor pressure
   b. Mainline pressure
   c. Throttle pressure
   d. None of the above
9. The ______ valve is used in selecting which gear a vehicle is in.
   a. Shift
   b. Throttle
   c. Manual
   d. Reverse
10. A shift valve is controlled by ______ pressures.
    a. Throttle and upshift
    b. Throttle and governor
    c. Governor and converter
    d. All of the above
11. Throttle valve pressure tells the transmission how fast a vehicle is moving.
    a. True
    b. False
12. Governor pressure tells the transmission how fast a vehicle is moving.
    a. True
    b. False
13. A vacuum modulator is another way of producing a ______.
    a. Governor pressure
    b. Throttle valve pressure
    c. Mainline pressure
    d. All of the above
14. Most valves are found in many different places in the transmission case.
    a. True
    b. False
15. Electronic shift control has replaced both hydraulic control pressures used for shift control.
    a. True
    b. False

GLOSSARY

accumulators piston-and-cylinder arrangement used to control pressure during application of a clutch or band.

auxiliary force (auxiliary pressure) added fluid pressure introduced into a regulator or balanced valve system. It functions either to increase or decrease the response of the regulator valve to input or supply pressure.

balance valve regulating valve that controls pressure on the right valve to balance other forces acting on the valve.

ball check valve valve that allows fluid to flow in only one direction in a circuit.

boost valve (booster valve) transmission pressure regulator valve system. It is incorporated in the pressure regulator valve system so that auxiliary fluid pressures may be introduced to vary the spring load on the regulator valve and increase the transmission hydraulic pressure to higher values as needed.

circuit (hydraulic circuit) any number of hydraulic devices connected together by a common passage.

confined liquids liquids enclosed in a hydraulic circuit. A confined liquid has no way to escape from its container.

dynamic of or relating to a physical force or energy in motion.

face front surface of an object.

flow control valve device used to control the direction or amount of flow in a hydraulic circuit.

force push or pull effort on an object mass, measured in units of weight.

force output device hydraulic device that converts hydraulic pressure into mechanical force. The clutch-piston and servo are examples.

gear pump pump using two gears in mesh to carry fluid from an inlet to an outlet. A gear pump consists of two gears with external teeth meshed together in a housing, with a crescent-shaped divider in between the unmeshed portions of the gears.

gerotor pump oil pump that uses an inner and an outer rotor which intermesh. The inner rotor is driven by the torque converter hub and rotates the outer rotor. The movement of the lobes on the rotors produces a pumping action.

governor valve device used to sense vehicle speed. The governor valve is attached to the transmission output shaft. Since the output shaft is connected to the drive shaft, the governor is able to sense vehicle speed for automatic upshifts and downshifts.

hydraulic fluid liquid that meets or exceeds the specific needs of a hydraulic system.

hydraulic pressure pressure transmitted through a liquid in an enclosed container.

kPa (kilopascal) unit of measurement in the metric system used to describe the pressure on liquids or gases.

land large-diameter part of a sliding valve that is fitted to the valve bore.

manual valve valve used to manually select the operating gear of the transmission. The manual control valve is moved by linkage connected to the shifting quadrant inside the vehicle. The driver selects drive, low, park, reverse, and so on, by moving the quadrant lever into position.

N/m^2 (newtons/square meter) metric system measurement used to describe the amount of torque or turning force.

orifice calibrated restriction in a hydraulic circuit line that controls fluid flow and pressure.

Pascal's law law formulated by the French scientist Pascal which states that pressure on a confined fluid is transmitted equally in all directions and acts with equal force on equal areas.

port opening in the side of a valve bore that is opened and closed by the movement of the valve.

pressure differential in a hydraulic circuit, when one area has high pressure and another area has low pressure, there is a pressure differential between the two areas. This differential will cause fluid to move from the high-pressure area to the low-pressure area.

pressure modulator pressure regulator that reduces a source (or mainline) pressure to reflect a certain type of information input needed by the transmission. The throttle valve and governor are both types of pressure modulators.

pressure regulator (pressure regulator valve) valve used to maintain a specific amount of hydraulic pressure. This valve acts to bleed off pressure in excess of that required for transmission operation.

pressure source any oil pump that produces a fluid flow.

psi (pounds per square inch) unit for measuring pressure of liquids or gases. Used in the English measurement system.

pump engine-driven mechanical device of rotary design that creates fluid flow.

relief valve valve used to protect against excessive pressure. Valve body circuits are often protected against excessive pressure which might result if the normal pressure regulator should malfunction.

reservoir storehouse for fluid until it is needed in the system.

shift solenoid electrical solenoid valve controlled by the on-board computer used to control upshifts and downshifts and to apply the converter clutch.

shift valve valve that directs automatic upshift or downshift. The shift valve responds to engine load and vehicle speed to cause an upshift or downshift.

spool valve cylindrically shaped valve with two or more valleys between the lands. Spool valves are used to direct flow. Fluid passages are opened or closed depending on the valve land position.

spring force tension in a spring when it is compressed or stretched.

static exerting force alone without motion.

throttle valve valve used to modulate pressure to reflect how hard the engine is working. The throttle valve is connected to the accelerator pedal by linkage or cable. This pressure reflects how hard the engine is working and sends this pressure to the shift valve to regulate the shift points.

vacuum absence of air, or pressures below atmospheric pressure levels.

vacuum modulator device used to sense engine load by monitoring engine vacuum.

valleys annular groove; the smaller-diameter horizontal surface of a spool valve, the stem part. When an annular groove is aligned with an oil passage, fluid flows into and through that groove.

vane pump pump using a series of spring-loaded vanes that sweep an eccentric cavity. Some automatic transmissions utilize this pump, but it is expensive because of the large number of parts.

Chapter 5

SMALL PARTS

INTRODUCTION

In this chapter, small parts, all of the small items that were not covered in earlier chapter, are explained. Seals are the first items described, including dynamic and static seals and how a lip seal functions. Thrust washers are examined next: both the simple thrust washer and the roller thrust bearing. Bushings and snap rings follow, with an explanation of the construction and function of these items. Gaskets are the next subject, with a section on filters following. The last section describes the makeup of automatic transmission fluid and what affects its service life.

This chapter completes the general theory section of the book, completing the explanations of how an automatic transmission works in theory. The remaining chapters deal with specific transmission/transaxles so that you can see how the theory works in practical application.

5.1 PERFORMANCE OBJECTIVES

After studying this chapter, you should have fulfilled the following performance objectives by being able to:

1. Describe the types of seals used in the automatic transmission.
2. Explain the difference between a dynamic seal and a static seal.
3. Describe the use of a selective-fit thrust washer.
4. List four types of snap rings.
5. List seven types of automatic transmission fluid.
6. Complete all the competency objectives listed for this chapter.
7. Complete the self-test with at least the minimum score required by your instructor.

5.2 COMPETENCY OBJECTIVES

The competency objectives are different from the performance objectives in being more job related. The automotive terms must be well understood so that the theory will be clear. The terms are used to describe the service procedures outlined in Part II. The competency tasks are related to job skills needed to perform service and repair procedures and should be understood thoroughly.

5.2.1 Automotive Terms

The following list may include terms that are unfamiliar to you. Read the terms, then note their definitions as you study the chapter.

alignment pens
bushing
diagonal-cut snap ring
lathe-cut seal
lip seal
metal body sip seal
micron rating
O-ring seal
roller thrust bearing
sealing rings
selective-fit snap ring
selective-fit thrust washer
Teflon
throwaway snap ring
thrust washer
Tru-Arc retainer

5.2.2 Competency Tasks

The competency tasks listed here are related directly to knowledge or skills needed to become a successful automatic transmission/transaxle technician. Be sure to complete all the tasks before going on to Chapter 6.

1. Describe how a lip seal should be installed.
2. Explain what *dynamic* means.
3. Explain what *static* means.
4. Describe the use of selective-fit thrust washer.
5. Describe a roller thrust bearing.

6. Explain the purpose of a bushing.

7. Describe at least four types of snap rings.

8. What steps should be observed in replacing a gasket in an automatic transmission?

9. Discuss the micron rating of a filter.

10. List seven different types of automatic transmission fluid.

5.3 SEALS

Because of the hydraulic system used in the automatic transmissions, there are needs for many different types of fluid seals (Figure 5–1). Being able to seal the hydraulic fluid into its circuits is essential for proper operation of individual systems. The materials used to make seals in the past varied, but the material of choice for flexible seals currently is neoprene and other types of synthetic rubber. Synthetic rubbers are more heat and chemical resistant than natural rubber, thereby having a much longer service life as a seal. To fulfill certain design requirements, some seals are made of *Teflon plastic,* while others are made of cast iron. In this section we study the various types of seals used in a modern automatic transmission.

5.3.1 Lip Seals

The lip seals used in automatic transmissions fall into two groups: plain lip seals and lip seals with metal bodies, sometimes called metal clad. Lip seals are circular in shape with a lip extending from one side of the main body, either toward the outside or inside, depending on where it will be placed on the piston. Shown in Figure 5–2 are cross sections of a lip seal with internal and external lips. Lip seals are always installed with the lip pointing toward the fluid that it is trying to retain. With the lip in this position, the hydraulic pressure pushes the lip against the bore for a better seal. If the seal is installed backward, the fluid will easily push past, as shown in Figure 5–3. This plain type of lip seal is used to seal the pistons in the coupling and holding clutches and is effective with parts that have axial movement.

The lip seal with a metal body is more familiar to most people. This type of seal is often used around a rotating shaft and is known as a dynamic seal because the parts that it seals are in motion. In addition to the metal body and lip seal, there is usually a garter spring, which encircles the seal to keep it tightly engaged with the shaft (Figure 5–4). The outside surface of the metal body usually has a coating of boretite, which acts as a sealer to prevent leaks between the seal and the case. This type of seal is used as the torque converter seal and output shaft seal, and also on linkage shafts that extend through the transmission case.

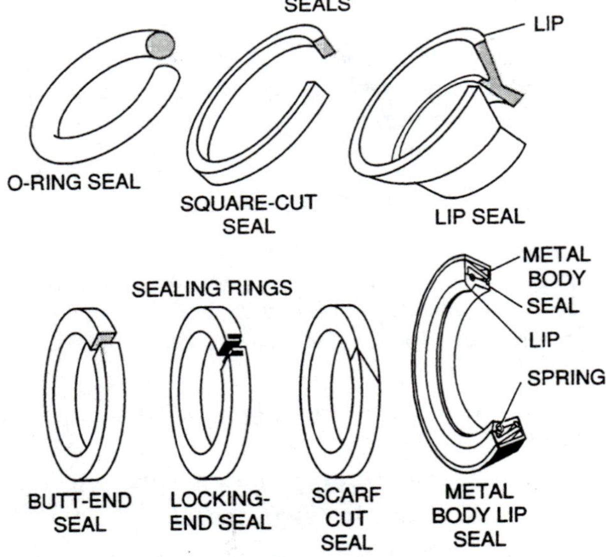

FIGURE 5–1 All of the various types of seals shown are used in automatic transmissions. (Courtesy of Ford)

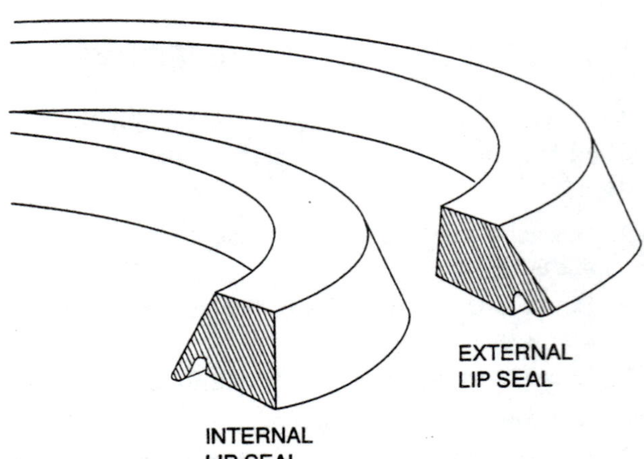

FIGURE 5–2 The internal lip seal is designed to seal the inner diameter of a clutch piston to the clutch drum hub. The external lip seal is used around the outside of the piston.

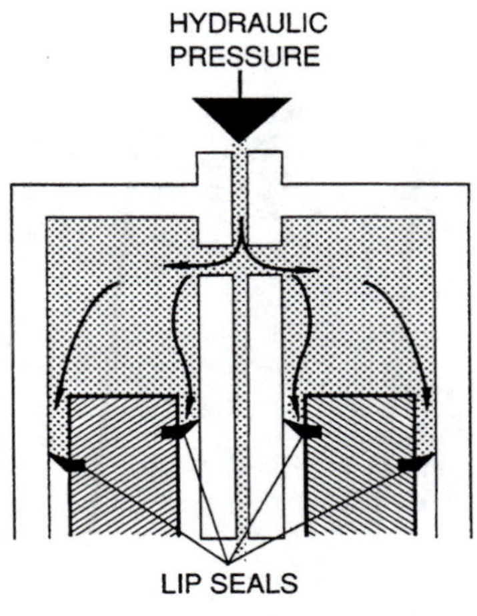

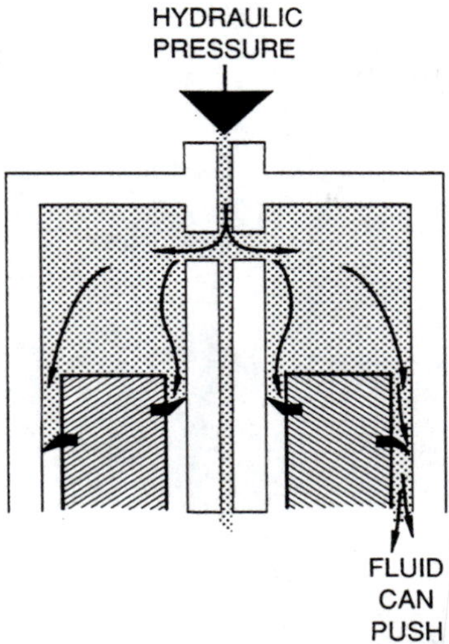

FIGURE 5–3 In the drawing at the left, lip seals are installed in the proper direction and are sealing the fluid. At the right, with the seal upside down, the pressure easily pushes past the seal and leaks out. (Courtesy of Ford)

5.3.2 Square-cut Seals

The square-cut or lathe-cut seal is circular in shape, with a square cross section (Figure 5–5). The square-cut seal is often used as a clutch piston seal. This type of seal works well with the axial movement of a piston but cannot stand up to rotary movements. As pressure is applied to the piston and it moves, the square shape of the seal is distorted as the outer surface moves along the clutch drum bore (Figure 5–6). When the pressure is removed, the seal returns to its normal shape and helps retract the piston.

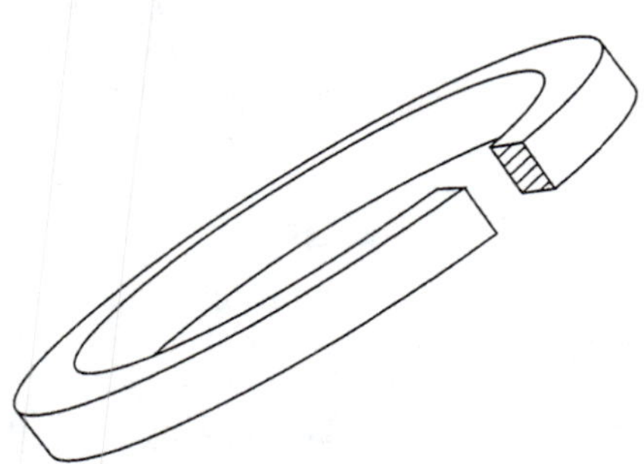

FIGURE 5–5 A square-cut seal is also referred to as a lathe-cut seal. (Courtesy of Ford)

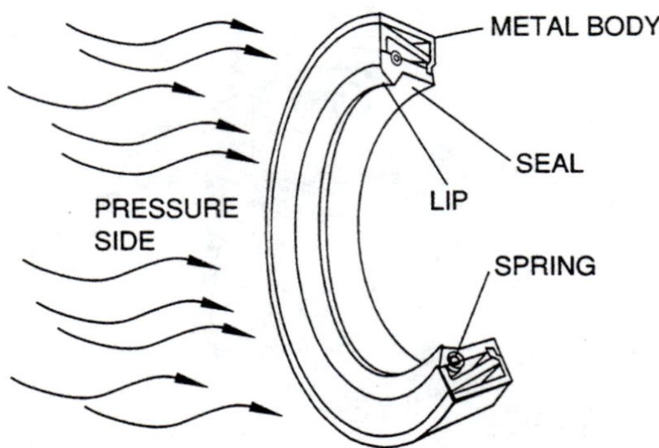

FIGURE 5–4 This type of lip seal with a metal body is commonly used as the torque converter-to-pump seal and also as an output shaft seal. (Courtesy of Ford)

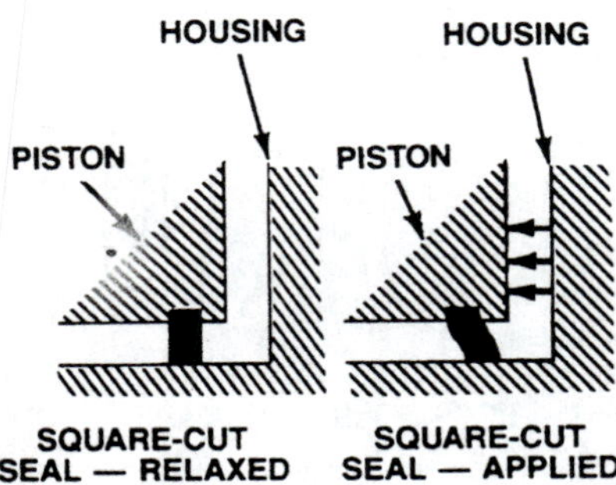

FIGURE 5–6 Movement of the piston as it is applied distorts the shape of a square-cut seal. When pressure is cut off to the piston, the seal returns to its normal shape, retracting the piston. (Courtesy of Ford)

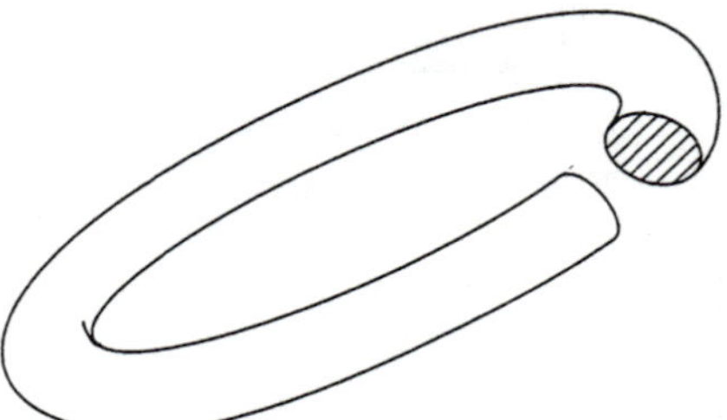

FIGURE 5–7 A circular O-ring seal is usually made of neoprene, a synthetic rubber. (Courtesy of Ford)

5.3.3 O-ring Seals

The O-ring seal is circular in shape with a round cross section (Figure 5–7). The O-ring seal is an effective static seal when used between parts that do not move. The seal is usually slightly larger than the groove in which it fits, so that when the parts are assembled, the O-ring is compressed, providing sealing force on all surfaces (Figure 5–8). In a few transmissions, O-rings are used as dynamic piston seals.

5.3.4. Sealing Rings

Sealing rings, which are similar to piston compression rings, are also used to seal hydraulic circuits. The rings currently used have four basic designs: the end-butting type, the locking-end type, the overlapping taper or scarf cut, and the one-piece Teflon seal (Figure 5–9). The material used in some of the seals is cast iron, with the seals being produced in the same way that engine piston rings are made. Some manufacturers use Teflon sealing rings in their transmissions. There are two types of Teflon seals: one is scarf cut and the other is one piece with no cuts. Special tools and procedures are used to install and size the Teflon seals. If the seals are installed improperly, they will leak, causing a malfunction and a comeback. Sealing rings, shown in Figure 5–10, are used to control hydraulic flow from a stationary source to a moving component. This type of dynamic seal permits the delivery of hydraulic flow and pressure to rotating components such as clutch drums.

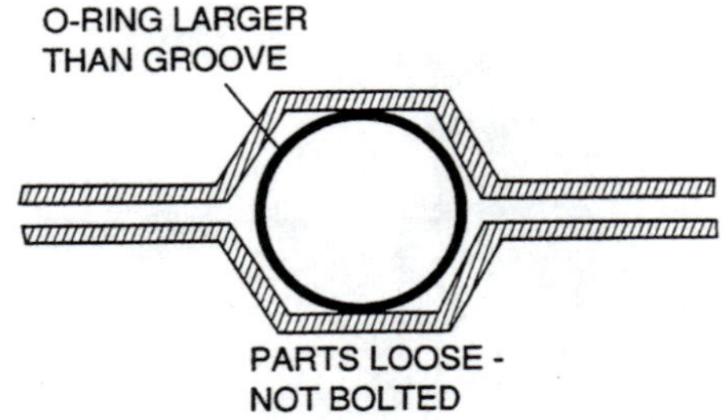

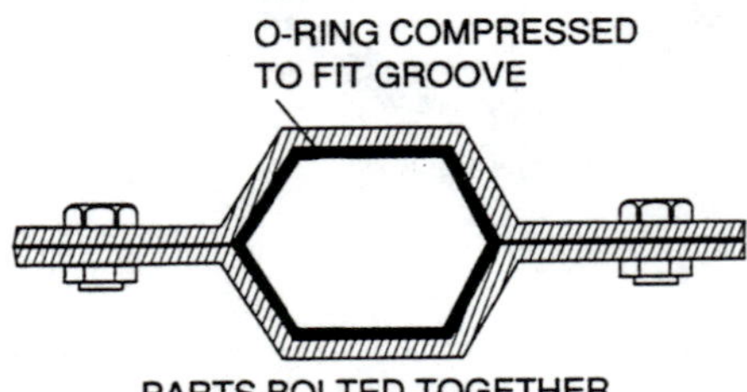

FIGURE 5–8 An O-ring is normally larger than the grooves in which it is designed to fit (see the figure at top), so that when the parts are assembled, the O-ring is compressed to provide maximum sealing ability.

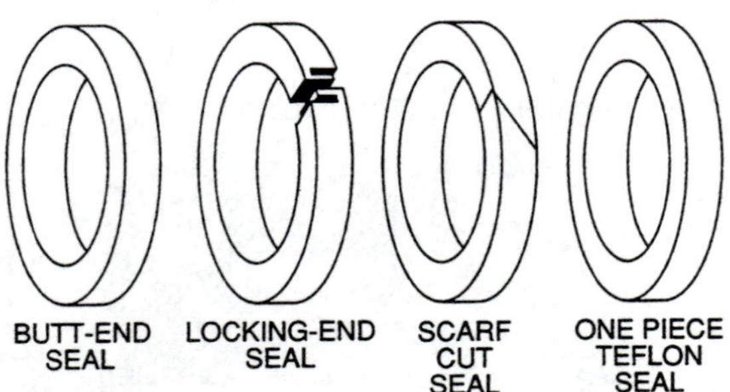

FIGURE 5–9 The four basic types of sealing rings used in automatic transmissions are the butt-end seal, locking-end seal, scarf-cut (overlapping taper) seal, and one-piece Teflon seal. (Courtesy of Ford)

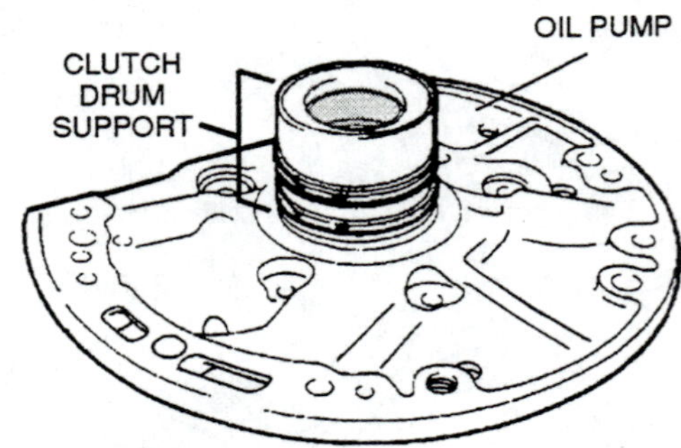

FIGURE 5–10 The sealing rings shown are mounted on the clutch drum support portion of the oil pump. These rings seal the hydraulic circuits that apply the clutch packs. (Courtesy of Chrysler)

5.4 THRUST WASHERS

For any mechanical device to operate properly, its individual parts must be free to move as they were designed to do. Too much free movement will cause parts to misalign and bind, leading to abnormal wear.

5.4.1 Simple Thrust Washers

The simple thrust washer is a spacer, which maintains a minimum clearance between two parts. It is usually found between components that are mounted on a shaft. By controlling the end play, they keep the parts aligned and reduce wear. Figure 5–11 shows the placement of thrust washers in the automatic transmission of a Chrysler import.

The material used in thrust washers varies according to the engineering needs of the transmission. Plastic, brass, copper, and steel with layers of bearing material coating the friction surface are used as thrust washers. Some thrust washers have a selective fit, which means that they come in different thicknesses, so the overall end play can be adjusted (Figure 5–12). Some transmissions use more than one *selective-fit thrust washer,* so check the manuals carefully.

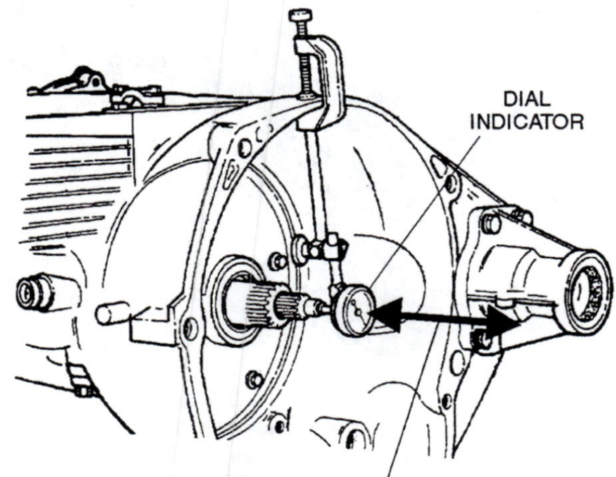

FIGURE 5–12 Input shaft end play is measured to determine the selective thrust washer thickness that should be used. (Courtesy of Chrysler)

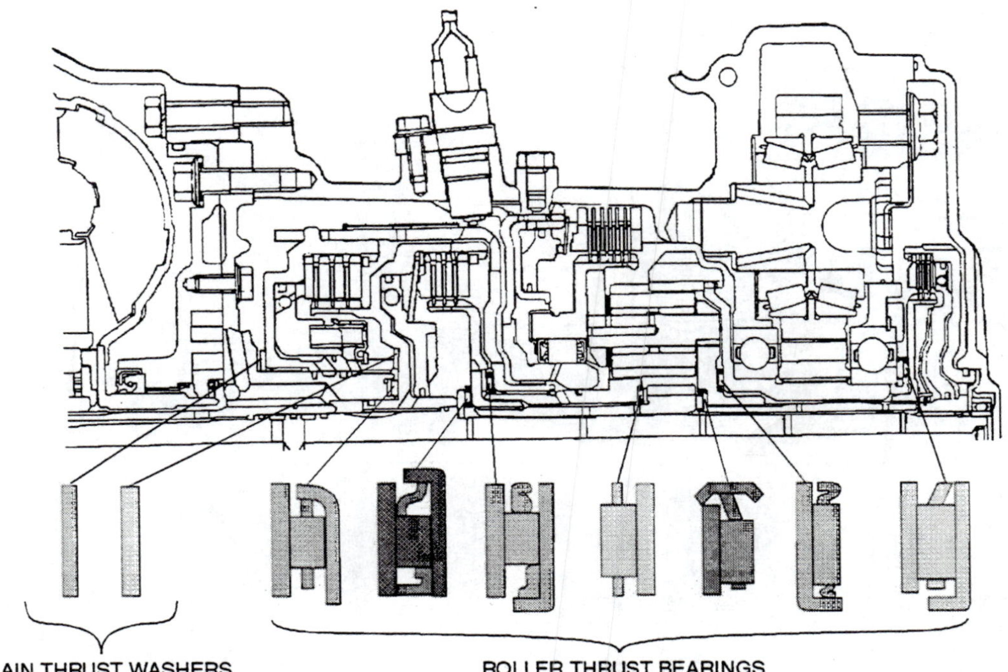

FIGURE 5–11 Cross-sectional drawing of a transaxle, showing the location of the 13 plain and roller thrust washers used in the transaxle. Note that some of the thrust washers are connected. (Courtesy of Chrysler)

FIGURE 5–13 The parts of a roller thrust bearing are the cage and roller assembly and the races. When removing a roller thrust bearing, note carefully how it was installed, to assure proper reinstallation.

FIGURE 5–14 The bushings used throughout automatic transmissions come in a variety of sizes.

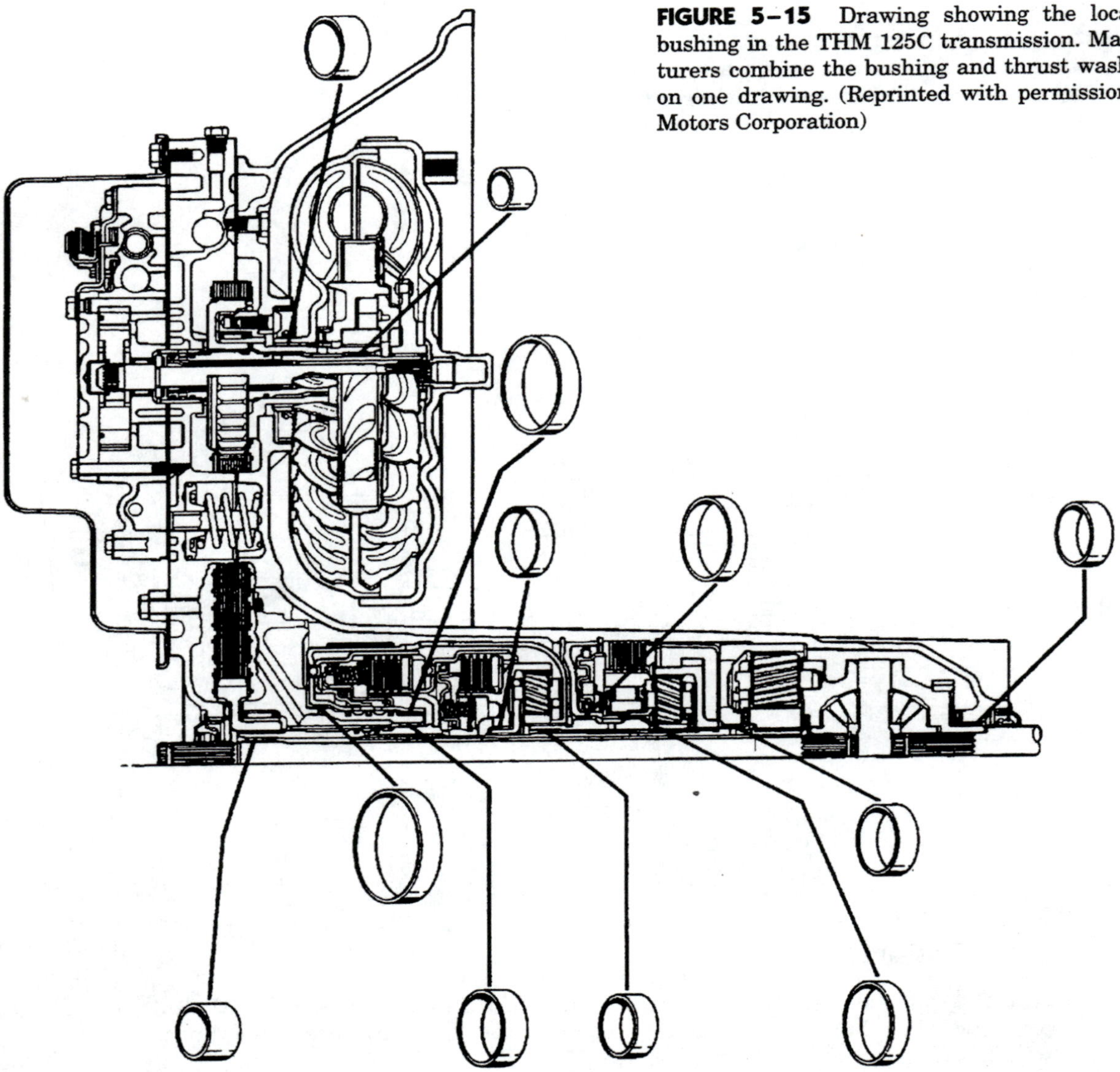

FIGURE 5–15 Drawing showing the location of the bushing in the THM 125C transmission. Many manufacturers combine the bushing and thrust washer locations on one drawing. (Reprinted with permission of General Motors Corporation)

5.4.2 Roller Thrust Bearings

On components with heavy axial, or end-to-end loads, a roller thrust bearing is used. The roller thrust bearing has two races with rollers mounted in a cage in between the races (Figure 5–13). Care must be taken to note where the roller thrust bearings are located and how their parts are assembled, because improper assembly will cause bearing failure. The measurement and setting of overall transmission end play are covered in Part 2.

5.5 BUSHINGS

Bushings are friction-type bearings designed to control the radial play of a drum or gear on a shaft. The radial load on any one bushing is light because the precision maching of the gear train parts causes the total load to be shared by all the bushings. The bushing is a hard metal sleeve with a bearing alloy lining on its inner surface (Figure 5–14). Rapid wear of the bushing in most transmissions is unusual, but if wear is found, the bushing can be easily replaced. The replacement of bushings will be explained in Part 2. In Figure 5–15 you can see the location of the bushings, thrust bearings, and thrust washer in the THM 125C automatic transaxle.

5.6 SNAP RINGS

Snap rings are retaining devices used throughout automatic transmissions. There are different designs to meet specific needs, but they all fall into two basic groups: internal and external (Figure 5–16). The internal snap ring seats in a groove cut on the inside diameter of a drum or cylinder and must be compressed to remove. The external snap ring seats in a groove around the outside of a shaft and must be expanded to be removed.

One design of snap ring, called a *Tru-Arc retainer,* has a hole located at each end of the ring so that special pliers can be used to install and remove them (Figure 5–17). The Tru-Arc retainer is made in both an internal and an external design. Due to the stamping operation used in manufacturing the retainers, one side of the retainer has a sharp edge while the other side is rounded off (Figure 5–18). To obtain the best holding power from the retainer, it should always be installed with the sharp edge up.

One design for external snap rings uses a diagonal cut on the ends of the ring as shown in Figure 5–19. The diagonal angle is cut on both

FIGURE 5–16 A large variety of internal and external snap rings are used in an automatic transmission.

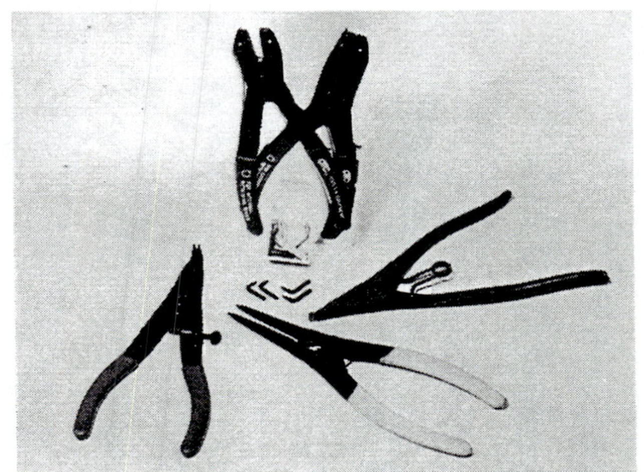

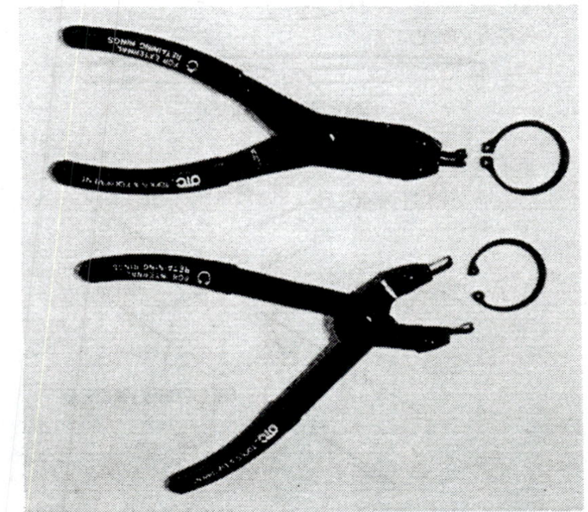

FIGURE 5–17 Tru-Arc pliers come with an assortment of different-size tips to fit all sizes of Tru-Arc retainers.

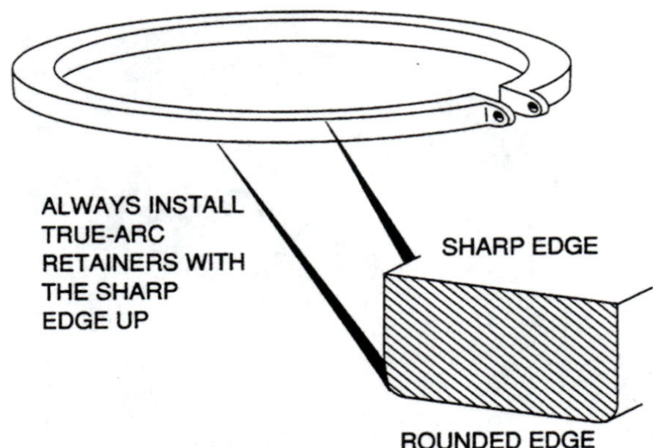

FIGURE 5–18 When the Tru-Arc retainer is installed with the sharp edge up, it allows the retainer to dig into the groove, providing a better grip.

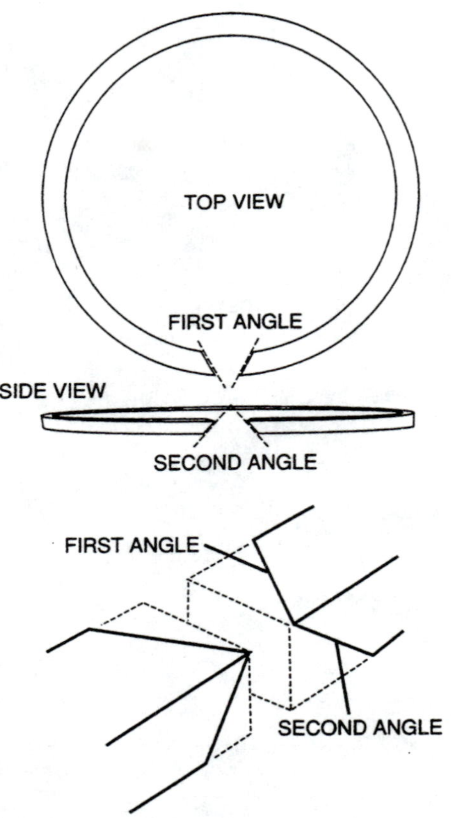

FIGURE 5–19 The diagonal cuts on the snap ring form a sharp point. The side of the snap ring that has the sharp point should always be installed up.

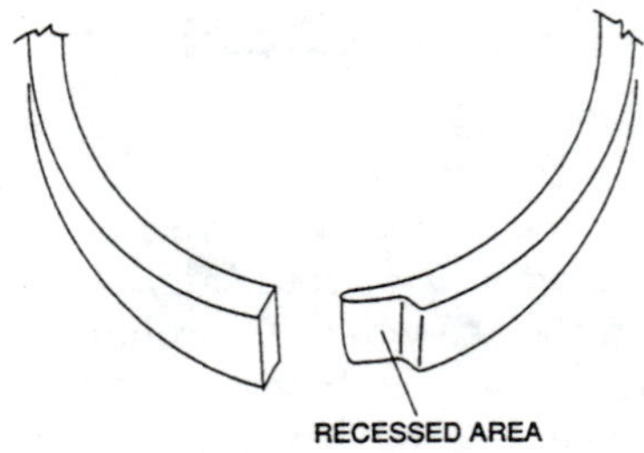

FIGURE 5–20 Providing a recessed area at one end of this snap ring makes it easy to remove with a screwdriver.

planes of the snap ring so that the cuts produce a sharp point on one side of the ring. This point is designed to help grip the surface of the snap ring pliers used for installation. The pointed side should always be placed up to aid in installing and removing. Other internal snap rings have a recessed cut in the outside edge near the end of the ring to allow a screwdriver to be used to pry the end of the ring out of the groove, as shown in Figure 5–20. Another type of external snap ring looks like it is made of wire, having a round cross section. This type of snap ring is called a throwaway because it is not to be reused. The manufacturer recommends that the old snap ring be discarded and a new one used for reassembly. Some retainers are called *selective-fit snap rings* because they are available in different thicknesses to be able to adjust clutch pack clearance. The manufacturer's service manual is the best source of information about what types of snap rings are used in a specific automatic transmission.

5.7 GASKETS

Gaskets are used to assure a fluid-tight seal between various components in the automatic transmission. Some gaskets also control the flow of fluid between passages. Most transmission gaskets are made of paper or composition materials, but other materials are also used.

5.7.1 Gasket Sealers

Replacing gaskets during transmission repair work is different than with engine work. With engine work, you should use gasket sealers to guarantee a good seal, but not so with transmissions. No gasket sealer should be used in transmission work. The risk of getting sealer in the hydraulic system is too great, so gasket sealer should not be used unless instructed otherwise by the manufacturer's manual.

FIGURE 5–21 By having several bolt holes small enough to fit snugly around the bolt threads, a pan gasket can easily be held in place for installation.

5.7.2 Pan Gaskets

The pan gasket is usually made of composition materials or pressed cork particles. Some gasket manufacturers produce a pan gasket which has some of the bolt holes just the size of the bolt's threads so that bolts can be pushed through the pan and gasket to hold the gasket in place on the pan while it is being installed (Figure 5–21). For the conventional type of gaskets, *alignment pins* will help in replacing the pan. Aligning pins can be made by taking a 2-inch bolt of the same thread size as the pan bolts and sawing off the bolt head and then cutting a screwdriver slot in the end for easy removal.

One gasket manufacturer has a cork particle gasket made in three layers. The outside layers are cork particles bonded to the center layer, which is metal (Figure 5–22). The metal gives the gasket the ability to retain its shape and not shrink, while the cork provides an excellent seal.

5.7.3 Paper Gaskets

The oil pump, extension housing, and valve body use a paper gasket. This type of gasket does its job as long as all of the old gasket is removed and the sealing surfaces are free of nicks or bumps. Great care must be used when working with the soft aluminum transmission parts. If the gasket surfaces are damaged, they will leak.

5.8 FILTERS

For an automatic transmission to operate properly, it must have an adequate supply of clean hydraulic fluid. The filter cleans the fluid of any foreign matter as the fluid is drawn into the inlet side of the oil pump. Two main types of filters are widely used: screen and paper (Figure 5–23).

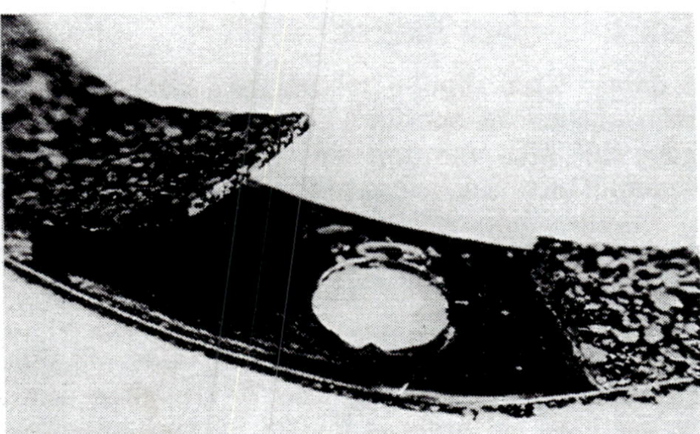

FIGURE 5–22 This new approach to gasket manufacturing provides the excellent sealing quality of cork without the shrinking problems normally found with cork gaskets.

5.8.1 Screen Filters

In the screen filter a very fine mesh metal or plastic screen is used. As long as there are no cuts, tears, or holes in the screen when it is inspected during service, it can be washed in solvent and reused. If the screen is badly clogged, it should be replaced. The screen filter was used on many older automatic transmissions before the need for better filtration was so important.

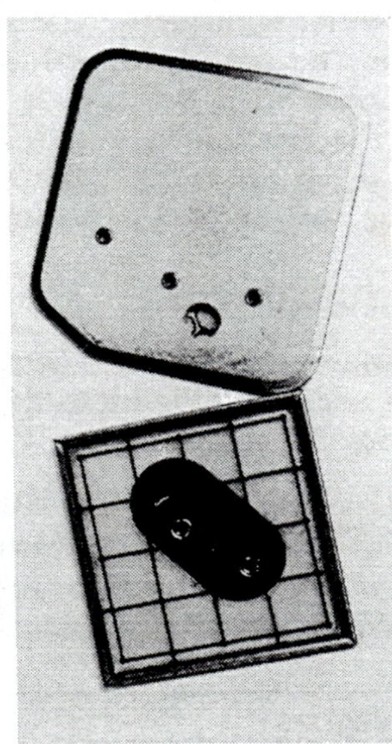

FIGURE 5–23 The two principal types of transmission filters utilize screen and paper elements.

5.8.2 Paper Filters

A paper filter should be replaced each time the transmission is serviced. The new filter should meet the *micron rating* set by the manufacturer. The micron rating refers to the size of the openings in the filter material, which in turn determines the size of the particles which will pass through the filter or be caught. One manufacturer recently reduced the micron rating of their filters from 70 μm to 40 μm after a problem of sticking valves in their transmissions was found. The 70-μm filter would let particles as large as 0.0028 in. through while the largest particles the 40-μm filter could pass are 0.0016 in. The new filter solved the valve sticking problem; however, the smaller holes in the filter means that the filter must be changed more often. In this case the recommended service interval was shortened to once a year or every 15,000 miles. The newer transmissions need to be serviced more often than the older transmissions did, so check the manufacturer's service requirements closely.

5.9 FLUIDS

The performance of the automatic transmission fluid (ATF) is critical to the life and smooth operation of an automatic transmission. The ATF performs many jobs; it must transmit the engine power through the torque converter and provide a hydraulic power medium to apply the clutches and bands. It must also clean, cool, and lubricate the transmission while maintaining the proper coefficient of friction (degree of slipperiness). It must also be compatible with the metals used in the transmission, the friction material and bonding agents, the seal materials, and the electrical devices and wiring used in today's transmissions.

5.9.1 Fluid Additives

Automatic transmission fluid is a petroleum-based oil with special additives (Figure 5–24). The major additives used in ATF are:

1. *Oxidation inhibitors:* an additive to reduce the oxidation of ATF at high temperatures.

2. *Foam inhibitors:* an additive to release air trapped in the ATF, preventing aeration of the fluid.

3. *Viscosity index improvers:* an additive that causes an oil to become thicker, or have a higher viscosity rating, as its temperature increases; used to make multiweight oils.

4. *Corrosion and rust inhibitors:* additives designed to neutralize acids and prevent rust from forming. These are sacrificial additives that are used up as they do their jobs.

5. *Detergents–Dispersants:* the detergent breaks down and dissolves sludge and varnish deposits while the dispersent holds the material in suspension in the fluid until it can be filtered out.

6. *Pour-point depressant:* an additive to improve the ability of the fluid to flow at low temperatures.

7. *Extreme pressure agents:* an additive that provides a tough surface film of lubricant which will resist extremely high pressure and prevent metal-to-metal contact.

8. *Friction modifiers:* additives used to raise or lower the coefficient of friction of the fluid.

5.9.2 Fluid Oxidation

The most important additive is the oxidation inhibitors which work to retard oxidation of the oil. If an operating temperature of 175°F was never exceeded, it would take 100,000 miles of service for the fluid to oxidize to the point at which it should be replaced. But as the operating temperature of the ATF goes up, the oxidation occurs much faster. If the ATF temperature runs at 275°F, the life of the oil before oxidation causes it to break down is only 3000 miles. For every 20°F of temperature rise above the normal temperature of 175°F, the useful life of the ATF is cut in half, as shown in Figure 5–25. At temperatures above 300°F, the internal parts of the transmission start to warp and distort, causing extensive damage. An ATF temperature of over 300°F can be reached in a matter of 2 to 3 minutes while trying to rock a vehicle out of snow or mud. The effect that oxidation has on the ATF is to degrade the fluid until it can no longer perform the jobs for which it is designed. Oxidation affects the ATF in a number of ways. The friction characteristics (coefficient of friction) of the fluid is changed, causing clutch and band slippage. The viscosity rating (weight) of the fluid is increased,

OXIDATION INHIBITORS	DETERGENTS–DISPERSANTS
FOAM INHIBITORS	POUR-POINT DEPRESSANT
VISCOSITY INDEX IMPROVERS	EXTREME PRESSURE AGENTS
CORROSION AND RUST INHIBITORS	FRICTION MODIFIERS

FIGURE 5–24 The additives listed are essential ingredients of automatic transmission fluid.

AVERAGE OPERATING TEMPERATURE	SERVICE LIFE OF AUTOMATIC TRANSMISSION FLUID
175°F	100,000 miles
195°F	50,000 "
212°F	25,000 "
235°F	12,000 "
255°F	6,250 "
275°F	3,000 "
295°F	1,500 "
315°F	750 "
335°F	325 "
355°F	160 "
375°F	80 "
390°F	40 "
415°F	Less than 30 minutes

FIGURE 5–25 This chart shows the effects of high temperature on automatic transmission fluid.

which slows the flow rate. The effectiveness of the foam inhibitors is greatly decreased, allowing aeration of the fluid, which also adds more slippage. Undesirable compounds formed during oxidation include acids or peroxides, which attack all transmission components; varnish, which forms a brown film on components and causes valves to stick; and sludge, which can plug the filter and block passageways. All of these problems are caused by oxidation of the fluid, which in turn is caused by excessive fluid temperatures; the higher the operating temperatures, the shorter the fluid life.

5.9.3 Fluid Types

At the present time, seven types of ATF are used by automotive manufacturers; some types are used very widely, whereas others have a limited application. Most of the different fluids need the same additives as those described earlier in this chapter, so they are similar in this respect. The primary difference between the major types of ATF is the fluid's coefficient of friction (slipperiness). The two fluids farthest apart on the coefficient of friction scale are Dexron II and Type F. Dexron II fluid is the slipperier of the two, which allows it to provide smoother shifts with less grab. The Type F fluid, which is less slippery, causes a more positive shift with less slippage. The friction material used on the clutches and bands are designed to work properly with only one type of ATF. If another fluid with the wrong coefficient of friction is used, the clutches and bands will either slip or grab. These conditions will greatly shorten the service life of the transmission. The seven major types of ATF are Dexron II, Type F, Type CJ, Type H, Type MV, Mercon, and Type 7176. Further information about these fluids is provided in Chapter 6.

SUMMARY

Seals

- There are two types of lip seals: plain lip seal and lip seal with metal body.
- A lip seal is a dynamic seal.
- *Metal body lip seals* are used at the torque converter and output shaft.
- The lip points toward the fluid to be retained.
- Square-cut or *lathe-cut seals* are both static and dynamic seals.
- O-rings make good static seals.
- Sealing rings are made of cast iron or Teflon.

Thrust Washers

- Thrust washers are used to control end play of parts on a shaft.
- Thrust washers are made of metal or plastic.
- Thrust washers can be selective-fit to adjust end-play clearance.
- Roller thrust bearings have a roller cage and two races.

Bushings

- A bushing controls radial play of parts on a shaft.
- Bushings can be replaced.

Snap Rings

- There are internal and external types.
- Tru-Arc retainers have holes at the ends of the ring.
- Tru-Arc retainers are installed with the sharp edge up.
- *Diagonal-cut snap rings* are installed with the point side up.
- *Throwaway snap rings* should not be reused.
- Some snap rings are selective-fit to adjust clutch pack clearance.

Gaskets

- Match new gaskets to old used gaskets.
- A gasket sealer should not be used unless recommended by the manufacturer.
- All old gaskets must be removed.
- Do not damage the gasket surface.

Filters

- Screens can be washed and reused if not worn or clogged.
- Always replace paper filters with transmission service.
- Use a filter with the correct micron rating.

Fluids

- Types of ATF: Dexron II, Type F, Type CJ, Type H, Type MV, Mercon, and Type 7176.
- The high ATF operating temperature cuts fluid life.
- Change fluid according to the manufacturer's recommendations.

SELF-TEST

Before going on to the next chapter, complete the self-test according to your instructor's directions. Read carefully and choose the best answer.

1. Technician A says, "When installing a lip seal, the lip should point toward the fluid." Technician B says, "If the seal is a garter spring, it should go in next to the fluid." Who is right?
   a. A only
   b. B only
   c. Both A and B
   d. Neither A nor B
2. Technician A says, "A dynamic seal works between parts that do not move." Technician B says, "A static seal works between moving parts." Who is right?
   a. A only
   b. B only
   c. Both A and B
   d. Neither A nor B
3. Technician A says, "Sealing rings are made like piston rings." Technician B says, "Sealing rings wear so little, you don't need to check them during an overhaul." Who is right?
   a. A only
   b. B only
   c. Both A and B
   d. Neither A nor B
4. Technician A says, "A thrust washer is used to reduce end play of parts on a shaft." Technician B says, "A thrust washer is used to reduce radial play parts on a shaft." Who is right?
   a. A only
   b. B only
   c. Both A and B
   d. Neither A nor B
5. A selective-fit thrust washer is used to adjust the ________ ________ clearance.
   a. Side play
   b. End play
   c. Radial play
   d. None of the above
6. A roller thrust bearing:
   a. Has a cage and rollers
   b. Has two races
   c. Controls axial load
   d. All of the above
7. Technician A says, "A bushing is used to reduce end play of parts on a shaft." Technician B says, "A bushing is used to reduce radial play of parts on a shaft." Who is right?
   a. A only
   b. B only
   c. Both A and B
   d. Neither A nor B
8. Snap rings are used to:
   a. Hold parts on shafts
   b. Hold clutch packs in place
   c. Adjust clutch pack clearance
   d. All of the above
9. Technician A says, "All snap rings are easy to install with no special tools." Technician B says, "Each different design of snap ring needs a special snap ring pliers." Who is right?
   a. A only
   b. B only
   c. Both A and B
   d. Neither A nor B
10. Technician A says, "If some of the old gasket remains on the case, the new gasket might not seal." Technician B says, "Using a gasket sealer to assure a good seal is important." Who is right?
    a. A only
    b. B only
    c. Both A and B
    d. Neither A nor B

11. Any paper filter can be used on an automatic transmission as long as it fits properly.
    a. True
    b. False

GLOSSARY

alignment pins resemble a bolt without a head but with a screwdriver slot cut in the end. They are used to align parts and gaskets during assembly.

bushing cylindrical lining used as a bearing assembly. Made of steel, brass, bronze, nylon, or plastic, it is used to carry radial loads.

diagonal-cut snap ring split spring-type ring located in an external groove to retain a part. The ends of the ring are cut on a diagonal with the pointed end on its outside diameter.

dynamic refers to a physical force or energy in motion.

end play amount of free play between parts mounted on a shaft, measured while moving the parts in the direction of the axis of the shaft.

lathe-cut seal (square-cut seal) this type of seal, which has a smooth outer side (no lip) and a rectangular cross section, provides a good static seal.

lip seal molded seal that works on the deflection principle, used extensively for dynamic applications.

metal body lip seal combines a lip seal and metal body so that the body can be driven into a case to position and hold the seal.

micron rating referring to the size of the holes in a filter, which regulate the size of the particles that are trapped by the filter. The hole size is measured in microns, which are equal to one thousandth of a millimeter, or 0.000039 in.

O-ring seal with a round cross section that is used as a static seal.

radial load force acting at right angles to the axis of a shaft.

roller thrust bearing roller bearing designed to handle axial loads between gear train components.

sealing rings sealing devices used around shafts or hubs to seal hydraulic circuits, which must go from the stationary case to a rotating part. They may be of cast iron or Teflon plastic.

selective-fit snap ring snap ring with varying thicknesses used to adjust clutch pack clearances.

selective-fit thrust washer thrust washer available in various thicknesses to adjust the end play of gear train components.

static exerting force alone without motion.

Teflon material used for making seals that has a nonbinding quality at both relatively high and very low temperatures.

throwaway snap ring this type of snap ring should be replaced with a new snap ring whenever it is removed. It is designed to be used only one time, then replaced.

thrust washer washer designed to provide bearing material between rotating parts and control excessive end play.

Tru-Arc retainer spring type of retainer used in both internal and external grooves to retain parts. They feature a small hole in each end of the ring for the installing tool.

◀ Part 2 ▶

SHOP PROCEDURES

Chapter 6

GENERAL MAINTENANCE

INTRODUCTION

In this chapter the most basic skills of the transmission technician are studied. The procedure for checking fluid level is explained along with diagnosis of the fluid on the dipstick. Because the correct fluid change interval varies for different vehicles, determination of the proper interval is explained in detail. The major types of ATF are described along with which vehicles use them. The filter and fluid change procedure is described step by step. The process for flushing a torque converter and cooler is also covered. Job procedures and skills are introduced. The procedures are outlined in detail and should be followed precisely. It is critical for the beginning technician to have a sound knowledge of service procedures before judgment is used to make shortcuts.

6.1 PERFORMANCE OBJECTIVES

After studying this chapter, you should have fulfilled the following performance objectives by being able to:

1. Explain the ATF change interval.
2. Describe how the ATF is diagnosed.
3. Check the ATF level in any transmission.
4. List the major types of ATF and which vehicles use them.
5. Perform a fluid change job on an automatic transmission following the proper procedure.
6. Perform a converter and cooler flush job following the proper procedure.
7. Complete all the competency objectives listed for this chapter.
8. Complete the self-test with at least the minimum score required by your instructor.

6.2 COMPETENCY OBJECTIVES

The competency objectives differ from the performance objectives in being more job related. The automotive terms must be well understood so that the theory will be clear. The terms are used to describe the service procedures outlined in Part II. The competency tasks are related to job skills needed to perform service and repair procedures and should be understood thoroughly.

6.2.1 Automotive Terms

The following list may include terms that are unfamiliar to you. Read the terms, then note their definitions as you study the chapter.

change interval
Dexron II
fluid diagnosis
fluid level
Mercon
normal usage
oxidation
severe usage
Type CJ
Type F
Type H
Type MV
Type 7176

6.2.2 Competency Tasks

The competency tasks listed here are related directly to knowledge or skills needed to become a successful automatic transmission/transaxle technician. Be sure to complete all of the tasks before going on to Chapter 7.

1. Determine the automatic transmission fluid change interval for any vehicle according to how it is used.

2. Diagnose the automatic transmission fluid to determine what service is needed.

3. Be able to check accurately the fluid level of any automatic transmission.

4. Know the different types of automatic transmission fluid (ATF) and which vehicles they are used in.

5. Prepare a vehicle safely for transmission service.
6. Use a reference manual to identify the vehicle and transmission and find the service procedure.
7. Draw fluid with a minimum of spill.
8. Identify particles in the bottom of the pan.
9. Replace the filter correctly.
10. Straighten the pan lip to prevent oil leaks.
11. Install the pan with a new gasket.
12. Refill the transmission properly and look for leaks.
13. Test-drive the vehicle.
14. Flush the converter and cooler.

6.3 FLUID CHANGE INTERVAL

A major focus of automotive manufacturers is the testing and evaluation of products to determine the appropriate maintenance intervals for their products. More and more drivers prefer a vehicle that will require a minimum amount of maintenance, and manufacturers design vehicles to be as maintenance free as possible. However, we know that any machine must have periodic maintenance to perform at its best and fulfill its expected service life. The most important part of any maintenance program is the lubrication service; the cleaner the oil, the longer the machine will last. Manufacturers' recommendations for transmission fluid change intervals vary greatly but are usually based on the type of driving conditions under which the vehicle is operated.

6.3.1 Normal Use

For most domestic vehicles driven in a normal manner there is no recommended transmission fluid change interval. Manufacturers feel that under normal use the fluid should last the lifetime of the vehicle. What is normal use, and how do you determine a customer's driving habits? Information regarding the use of the vehicle should be obtained from the customer. In most cases the vehicle will probably fall within the normal use category (Figure 6–1). Under normal driving conditions, American Motors, Chrysler, and Ford all feel that a change of ATF is not necessary and that the original fluid will last the life of the vehicle. General Motors recommends a change of ATF every 24,000 miles, or in some cases less than that, for its vehicles driven under normal conditions. The definition of normal use is if the vehicle is not operated under severe operating conditions. In the next section we define severe conditions.

NORMAL DRIVING =

NO LONG IDLES
NO HEAVY LOADS
NO STOP-AND-GO TRAFFIC
NO TEMPERATURE EXTREMES

FIGURE 6–1 Normal use of a vehicle would include these types of driving conditions.

6.3.2 Severe Usage

The manufacturers' definition of severe operating conditions is any driving situation that will cause higher-than-normal operating temperatures (Figure 6–2). Many things can cause higher fluid temperature, such as driving in heavy traffic in hot weather; commercial use, such as a taxi or limousine; use as a police car; or when towing a trailer. Anything that raises the operating temperature of the fluid causes it to oxidize faster, thus shortening its service life. Ask the customer about any type of operation that might put a severe load on the transmission, causing it to overheat.

For vehicles operated under severe conditions, manufacturers recommend service on a shorter interval. American Motors, Chrysler, and Ford recommend a change of ATF at 24,000 miles, and in some cases 12,000 miles, for vehicles in severe use. General Motors requires an ATF change at 12,000 miles for severe use. The manufacturer's recommendations for a specific vehicle should always be checked in the shop manual. These recommendations, combined with evaluating the fluid, will allow you to service the automatic transmission in a way that will assure the maximum life of the unit.

SEVERE OPERATING CONDITIONS =

HEAVY STOP-AND-GO TRAFFIC
HOT WEATHER
PULLING TRAILER
CARRYING HEAVY LOADS
PROLONGED IDLING
COMMERCIAL USE

FIGURE 6–2 Severe operating conditions include these types of driving conditions.

6.3.3 Effects of Heat

As we mentioned in Part I, heat is the enemy of automatic transmission fluid. The fluid is designed to have a service life of over 100,000 miles if it is operated at a temperature of 175°F or less.

But due to the chemical makeup of the fluid, at increased temperature the service life of the fluid is reduced by one-half.

To control heat buildup in vehicles that receive severe usage, aftermarket parts manufacturers have developed auxiliary transmission fluid coolers. These extra fluid radiators are usually mounted in front of the engine coolant radiator in the cool airstream. They are connected in series with the factory fluid cooler located in the engine's radiator. They provide the extra cooling ability needed to reduce the operating temperatures of the ATF in most severe-duty vehicles.

6.4 FLUID DIAGNOSIS

The transmission fluid from an automatic transmission can tell the trained technician much about the condition of the transmission. In this section you will learn what to look for when checking the level of the fluid in the transmission. You will learn how to tell if the clutches are wearing, if the transmission is overheating, or if the fluid cooler is leaking. A careful examination of the transmission fluid while remembering a few basic facts about the fluid will provide this information.

6.4.1 Check Fluid Level

To operate properly, an automatic transmission must have the correct amount of fluid. If the fluid level is too low, the oil pump pickup can draw in air, causing the mainline pressure to drop drastically and allowing the coupling and holding devices to slip. If this slipping were to continue for very long, the clutches and bands could be burned and the transmission would need to be overhauled. Such extensive damage can occur because of a low ATF level. Most manufacturers recommend that the fluid level be checked when the engine oil is changed. If the driver of the vehicle notices oil leaking from the transmission, the level must be checked frequently to prevent running low on fluid and severely damaging the transmission.

A fluid level that is too high can also damage the transmission. When too much fluid is added to the transmission, the oil lever raises until it comes in contact with the gear train components, which are rotating. This churns the fluid, causing tiny air bubbles to be trapped in the fluid. As this aerated fluid enters the hydraulic circuits of the transmission, the air is compressed and the system pressure drops, leading to transmission failure if the condition continues. For these reasons it is critical to keep the fluid level within the manufacturer's specification.

The steps for properly checking the fluid level of an automatic transmission are:

1. Make sure that the vehicle is level.
2. Pull the dipstick and wipe it clean.
3. Hold the tip of the dipstick between the fingers. If it is too hot to hold, the transmission is at operating temperature.
4. Read the dipstick for instructions; most transmissions are checked when hot, but some are checked cold. If instructions are not stated on the dipstick, read the shop manual.
5. Start the engine, and with your foot on the brake, place the transmission in each gear for 4 to 5 seconds, then return the transmission to park position.
6. With the engine running, insert the dip stick until fully seated, then remove it.
7. Read the fluid level on the dipstick. If the reading is unclear, wipe the dipstick clean and repeat the procedure (Figure 6–3).

If the transmission is not to full operating temperature, the reading will be a little low because the fluid has not expanded as much as it will at full temperature. If you can hold the end of the dipstick in your fingers after removing it from the transmission, the fluid is only warm. A quick way to heat the fluid if the vehicle is being started cold is to place the transmission in drive, then while holding the brakes applied, bring the engine level up to 1000 to 1200 for a few minutes. This causes a great amount of heat to be generated in the torque converter, heating the fluid quickly. Some manufacturers recommend that the vehicle be driven for 15 to 20 miles to reach full operating temperature. When adding fluid to a transmission, pour a pint or less at a time, then check the level. It is better to be a little below the level than to overfill.

6.4.2 Fluid Evaluation

Reading the fluid level is a simple procedure. It is now necessary to do more than check the level of the fluid on the dipstick. Look at the color of the

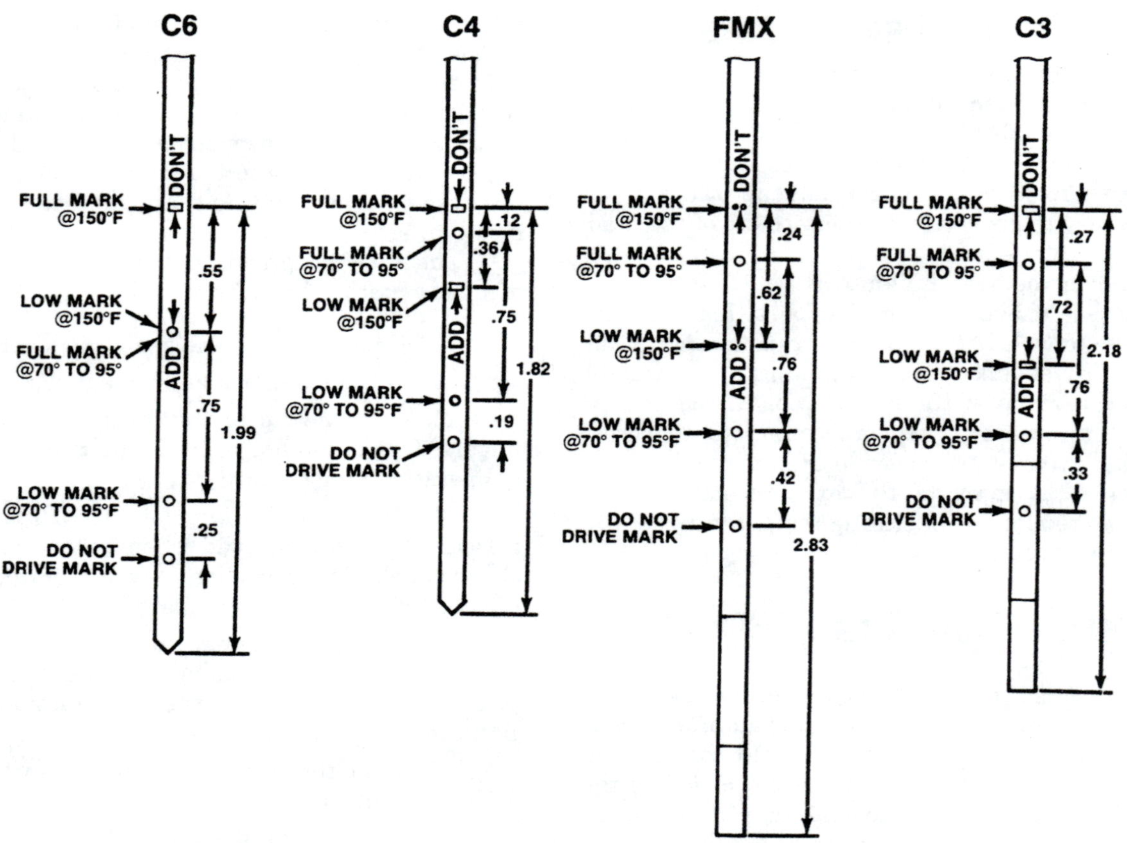

FIGURE 6–3 Check the manual if you do not understand how the dipstick is marked.

fluid, smell it, and put some on your fingers and feel it. In the next section we explain what to look for in the fluid and what it means.

1. Color

The normal color of ATF is clear red, with some slight differences between different types of fluid. As you learned earlier, heat causes *oxidation* of the fluid, which makes its color change from red to brown. The greater the oxidation of the fluid,the darker the fluid becomes, until it is a dark brown. Through most of this color change, the fluid remains clear or transparent. Only when it becomes very dark brown will it lose this quality.

If the fluid cooler springs a leak and allows engine coolant to enter and mix with the transmission fluid, the fluid will turn a milky pink color. Whenever this condition occurs, immediate action must be taken to repair the transmission. Once a transmission has had engine coolant in it, the transmission must be over-hauled. The coolant causes the adhesives that bond the friction material to the clutches and bands to disintegrate and the friction material is lost. A fluid change is not enough to save the transmission, and it would not be wise to recommend only the fluid service.

The transmission must be thoroughly cleaned and overhauled, with new seals and friction parts. The radiator must be removed and the fluid cooler replaced, along with flushing the cooler lines and torque converter. The color of the fluid can vary from the milky pink color if the fluid has oxidized. This would create a milky brown color and would necessitate the same immediate repairs as outlined in the preceding case.

A quick reference list of various fluid colors follows:

1. *Clear red:* good, clean ATF; safe to use.
2. *Milky pink:* coolant in ATF; transmission repair necessary.
3. *Light brown:* ATF oxidized; fluid should be changed soon.
4. *Brown:* ATF oxidized; change fluid immediately.

5. *Dark brown:* heavy oxidation; check transmission for damage.

6. *Milky brown:* coolant in oxidized ATF; repair transmission.

Water can collect in the transmission because of condensation if the vehicle is used in a short-trip, stop-and-go manner. This moisture can be purged by driving at highway speeds for 25 to 30 miles. The high temperatures will boil off the water, leaving the oil free of contamination.

2. Odor
As automatic transmission fluid is oxidized, it forms a type of varnish. This odor can be detected in the fluid and in extreme cases can be found on the dipstick. This varnish odor will become stronger as the fluid becomes darker. This varnish buildup can cause the valves to stick in the valve body and prevent proper operation of the transmission.

Another odor that can indicate problems is a scorched smell. This scorched smell will almost always indicate a slipping clutch. The fluid will be very dark in color with a strong burned odor. When a transmission is found with fluid like this, immediate overhaul is recommended.

3. Particles
The last thing to look for in the fluid is small particles of friction material. The best way to detect these small particles is to use a small piece of smooth white notepaper. As soon as you remove the dipstick from the transmission, place the tip of the dipstick on the paper and allow the oil to run down the stick onto the paper. Now you can carefully examine the oil for friction material particles. If particles are found, the clutches or bands are disintegrating and an overhaul is called for right away.

Much can be learned about the condition of a transmission simply by examining the ATF closely. The color, odor, and texture of the fluid can tell a story if you know how to read it.

6.5 TYPES OF AUTOMATIC TRANSMISSION FLUID

As automatic transmissions become more highly developed, the manufacturers are requiring more from the automatic transmission fluid they use in their products. To provide smooth, trouble-free performance only the fluid recommended by the manufacturer should be used in any transmission. Following are the major types of automatic transmission fluids and the vehicles that use them.

6.5.1 Dexron II

Dexron II is used in all General Motors transmissions and in Chrysler transmissions through 1984 models. It is also used in many imports, such as Nissan, Volkswagen, Toyota, Renault, and Ford ZF.

6.5.2 Type F ATF

Type F is used in Ford transmissions of the following models:

C-3: 1980 and earlier
C-4: 1979 and earlier
C-6: 1976 and earlier
FMX: all years
FX: all years
MX: all years
CW: all years
JATCO: Courier models
Datsun: 1971 and earlier
Mazda: some models; check manual
Saab: some models; check manual
Toyota: some models; check manual
Volvo: some models; check manual

6.5.3 Type CJ ATF

Type CJ ATF is used in the following Ford transmissions:

C3: 1981 and after
C4: 1979 and after
C6: 1977 and after
AOD: all models
ATX: all models
A4LD: all models
AXOD: all models

Type CJ and Dexron II are considered interchangeable by manufacturers.

6.5.4 Type H ATF

Type H ATF is used only in the Ford C5 transmission with a centrifugal converter clutch.

6.5.5 Type MV ATF

Type MV ATF is used only in the Ford ATX transmission in cold climates.

6.5.6 Type 7176 ATF

Type 7176 is used in all Chrysler and American Motors transmissions since 1985.

6.5.7 Mercon

Mercon ATF is used in the Ford 4EAT transmission and other Ford applications as well as in the American Motors ZF and AR4 transmissions. Always check the manufacturer's service manual for the specific requirements of the vehicle on which you are working.

6.6 FILTER AND OIL CHANGE PROCEDURE

The following steps will provide you with the logical procedure for performing this common service operation.

6.6.1 Safety

Always approach any automotive service or repair job with a safety awareness. All major shop manuals, either aftermarket or from the manufacturers, have lists of safety procedures that should always be followed. It is unwise to try to save time on a job by cutting corners on safety. The price you may end up paying is too high. If your knowledge of general shop safety rules is lacking, please review that material with your instructor. It is your body and your life—take care of them.

6.6.2 Check Manual

Before starting any automotive service procedure, you should always refer to a good-quality shop manual for proper instructions on how the job should be performed. Once you become familiar with the procedure and the vehicle on which you are working, it is less important to check the manual every time. But whenever you are performing a procedure new to you or are working on an unfamiliar vehicle, you should always read the manual first. The information on how to do the job correctly is there—all you have to do is use it.

6.6.3 Prepare Vehicle

Following the recommended jacking procedures from the manual, (Figure 6–4), raise the vehicle and place it on jack stands. It should be high enough off the ground to give you adequate working space. Make sure that the vehicle is solid on the stands before starting work. If you are using a hoist to raise the vehicle, use a manual to identify the lifting point, then carefully raise the car to the proper working height. It is a good idea to lower the hoist slightly to engage the mechanical safety stop so if there is a hoist failure, the safety stop would already be in place and working. For best results on a fluid change the fluid should be at operating temperature so that it will hold contaminants in suspension while draining.

6.6.4 Drain Fluid

After placing a large drain pan under the transmission and selecting the needed tools, you are ready to drain the fluid. To drain most transmissions the pan must be removed, as few transmissions currently use drain plugs in their pans. The trick is to release the pan without covering yourself and the shop with ATF.

Using a socket and a speed handle, remove all but three bolts from the pan. The remaining bolts should be in the following pattern. One bolt in the middle of one side of the pan, with the other two bolts on the other side of the pan at each end (Figure 6–5). With the other bolts removed, turn the last three bolts halfway out; now loosen the pan by striking it with a hammer, in a sideways motion to break the gasket loose. With the pan loose remove the single bolt and let the pan tilt, draining most of the fluid. Carefully remove the remaining bolts and remove the pan.

6.6.5 Examine Pan Contents

After draining any remaining fluid, examine the inside of the pan closely. In most transmissions you will find deposits in the pan. Identifying the deposits will help you determine the condition of the transmission. It is normal to find a small quantity of fine black powder in the pan. If small fibers are found in the pan, they are from the friction material on the clutches and bands. A large amount of this fiber material indicates that the friction components are failing and should be replaced.

Copper or brass shavings in the pan would indicate excess thrust washer wear; friction thrust washers are usually make from a copper alloy on older transmissions. If there is a large amount of shavings, the transmission should be overhauled.

Aluminum shavings will sometimes be found in the oil pan. The aluminum will probably be from the transmission case. Transmission components such as a center support or clutch steel discs that are anchored to the case can become loose and

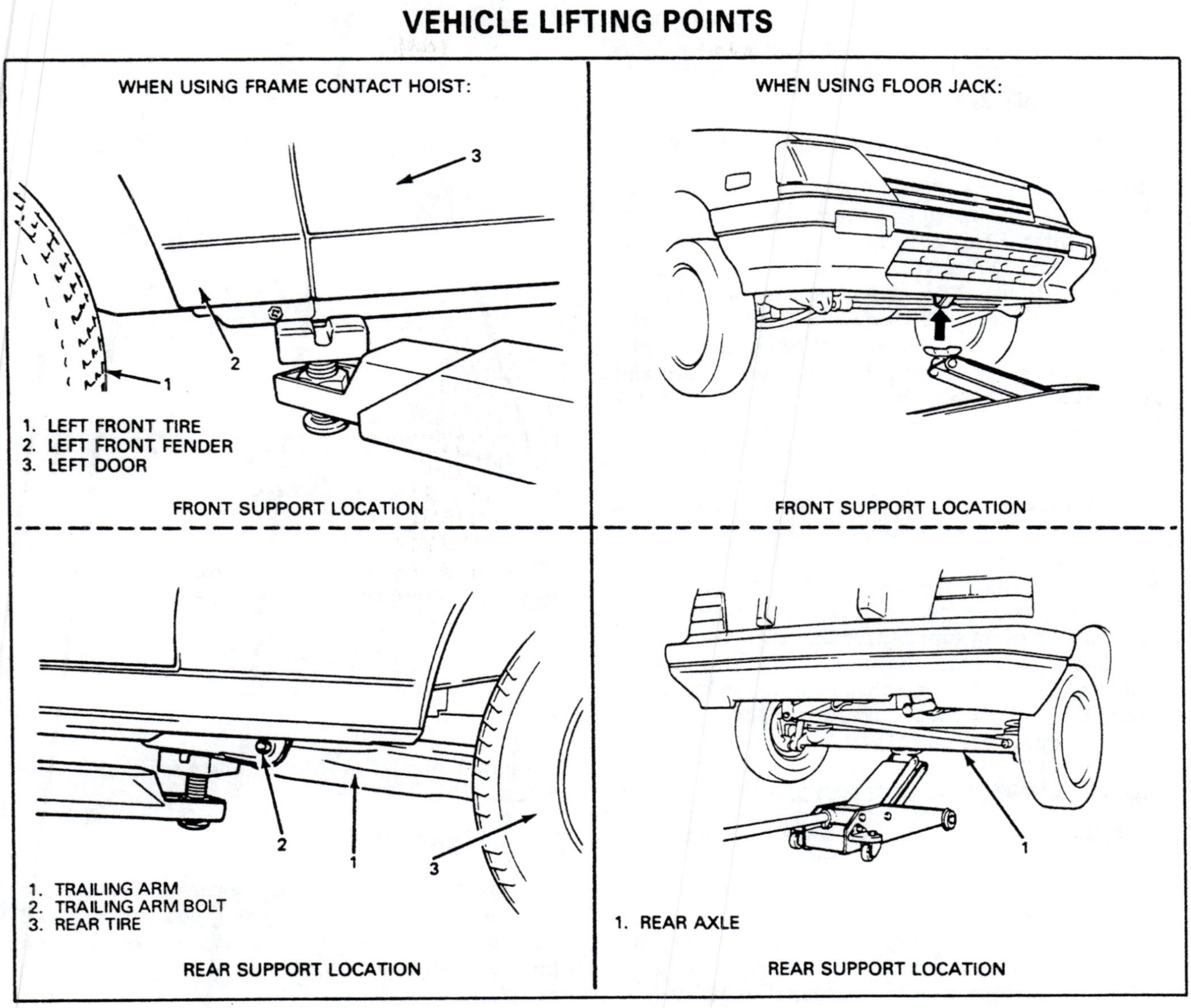

VEHICLE LIFTING POINTS
WHEN USING FRAME CONTACT HOIST:
3
2
1
1. LEFT FRONT TIRE
2. LEFT FRONT FENDER
3. LEFT DOOR
FRONT SUPPORT LOCATION
WHEN USING FLOOR JACK:
FRONT SUPPORT LOCATION
2
1
3
1. TRAILING ARM
2. TRAILING ARM BOLT
3. REAR TIRE
REAR SUPPORT LOCATION
1
1. REAR AXLE
REAR SUPPORT LOCATION

FIGURE 6–4 The lifting procedure for each vehicle should be checked in the manual, or damage may occur.

UNSCREW HALFWAY
UNSCREW HALFWAY
OILPAN

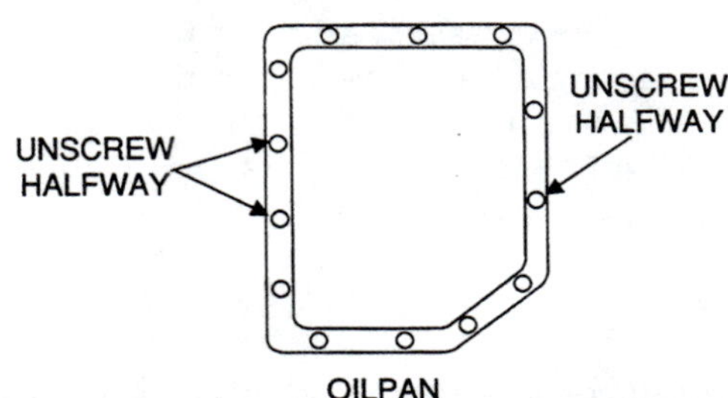

FIGURE 6–5 By leaving three bolts in the pan partly unscrewed, the pan will not fall off when the gasket seal is broken.

cause wear on the case. If aluminum is found in the pan, disassemble the transmission and inspect the case and any other aluminum parts for damage. Replace worn parts.

If steel (magnetic) particles are found in the oil pan, this is an indication of gear train or bearing wear. If the planet carrier or planet pinions are starting to fail, steel particles that are ground off will end up in the oil pan. Roller or ball bearings that are starting to flake will also produce steel particles. If large deposits of steel particles are found, the transmission should be disassembled and closely inspected to find the worn or failed part. All bearings must be closely inspected in this case because steel particles can quickly ruin any antifriction bearing.

6.6.6 Replace Filter

The transmission filter is removed next. Check the manual for special instructions about removing the filter. Some transmissions use the filter to hold valves in the valve body, and these small parts can be easily lost if you are not aware of them. Remove any gasket or O-ring used to seal the filter. Remember how the filter was attached: some screw to the valve body, others simply push into place and are held by an O-ring. Most filters are mounted in a rigid manner so they cannot move, but some filters are free to move. Check the manual to answer any questions. Compare the old and new filters to make sure that the new filter is the correct part. Small design changes are normal, so the new filter may not look exactly the same as the old. Check to see how the new filter mounts and seals to make sure that it will work properly. If it is not a proper fit, check with a parts supplier for the proper filter.

Carefully install the new filter, using a new gasket or O-ring to assure that no air leaks to the pump inlet. Tighten all screws or bolts to the proper torque specifications.

6.6.7 Clean and Straighten Pan

Wash the pan in an approved solvent to clean the inside and outside. Remove the old gasket completely by using a rotary wire brush or scraper. Scrape and wipe clean the gasket surface on the transmission, being careful not to damage the surface. It must be smooth and flat so that the gasket can seal properly. Then, using a straightedge, check the gasket surface of the pan for smoothness. Place the straightedge directly over the bolt holes along the edge of the pan and look for clearance between the straightedge and the pan. If the pan has had the bolts overtightened (too much torque applied), the holes will be pulled out of shape as shown in Figure 6–6.

A pan in this condition must be straightened so that the gasket will not leak. To straighten the pan, support the lip of the pan on the edge of a work bench and tap the bolt hole area with the round end of a medium weight biplane hammer. When the surface looks smooth, feel the area with your finger since it is easier to feel a small surface defect than to see one. Tap all the bolt holes around the pan, then check with a straightedge. The pan

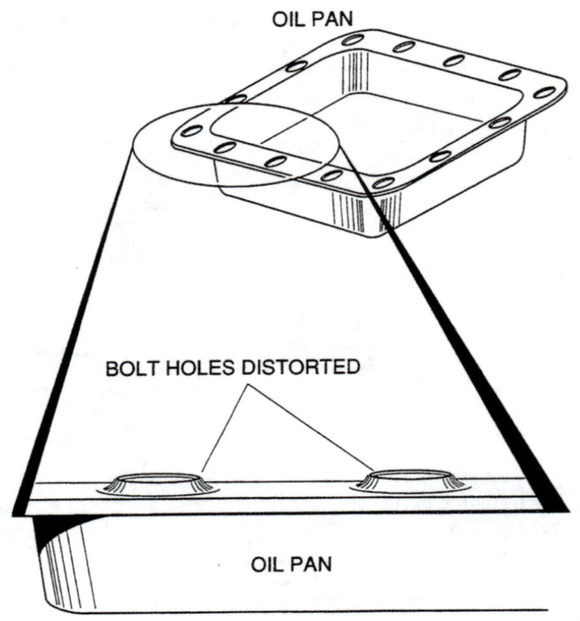

FIGURE 6–6 Overtightening the pan bolts will distort the gasket surface and allow the pan to leak.

will now be leak free when reinstalled with a new gasket.

6.6.8 Install Pan

With the new filter in place, the case gasket surface clean, and the pan straightened, you can reinstall the pan. Although some manufacturers recommend the use of silicone RTV instead of a regular gasket, many transmission rebuilders recommend using a regular gasket. Most rebuilders recommend not using gasket sealers during transmission repair except in special cases as outlined in the service manuals. Aligning pins can be used to aid in installation of the new gasket. Aligning pins are easy to make by buying a 3-in.-long bolt of the same thread size as the pan bolts and cutting the bolt head. Grind a slight chamfer on the cut end, then, using a hacksaw, cut a screwdriver slot in the end of the pin. It is a good idea to make four at a time, so that if you lose one or two you will still have enough to do the job.

Install two or three aligning pins equally spaced in the pan holes. Slip the gasket over the pins and up against the case. Small amounts of transmission assembly grease can be used to hold the gasket to the case if it is falling off. Slide the pan over the pins and start the pan bolts. Then remove the aligning pins and start those bolts. Tighten the bolts using a socket and a speed handle until they are snug, not fully tightened. Then use a torque wrench to set the factory recommended torque on the bolts. This will prevent overtightening, which distorts the gasket, causing oil leaks.

6.6.9 Refill Transmission

Remember that the transmission should not be overfilled, so start the refill with less fluid than you know it will take to fill the transmission. This information will be in the shop manual, so look it up first. If the refill is going to take approximately 6 quarts, start by putting in 4 quarts. Start the engine, leaving the gear selector in park (P), then check the fluid level on the dipstick. If there is no fluid on the stick, add another quart of fluid, then check again with the dipstick. Keep adding this way until you see fluid on the dipstick, then add fluid at the amount of ½ quart or 1 pint at a time, then check the level again. Once you see fluid on the dipstick, you need to run the transmission through the gear selections to fill all the hydraulic circuits. To do this, sit behind the wheel and apply the brakes; then, with the engine still running, place the transmission in each gear for 10 to 15 seconds, then go to the next gear. After engaging each gear, return to park (P). Now check the level again and add more fluid. It is best to stop filling when you reach the add mark on the dipstick. The fluid is still below operating temperature, so if you would fill the transmission to the full mark, it would be overfull when the fluid is heated to operating temperature.

6.6.10 Check for Leaks

It is impossible to overstate how important this step is in performing a good-quality service job. When a customer finds an oil leak after having service work performed, it indicates that the quality of the service job was poor. Always protect yourself from a comeback by checking for leaks after all the work has been completed. Do not forget this step; the comeback could cost you the price of a transmission overhaul if the transmission has run out of fluid. Always check for leaks.

6.6.11 Test Drive

The last step for any service or repair procedure should be to test the vehicle and see if it performs properly after the work is finished. In this case, drive the vehicle around the block to make sure that the transmission is shifting properly and does not slip. This does not have to be a full road test but simply enough to confirm that the transmission is working before the customer receives the vehicle. Needless to say, any problem found during the test drive should be fixed at this time.

6.6.12 Final Fluid-Level Check

As soon as you return from test driving the vehicle, leave the engine running and check the fluid level again now that the fluid is hot. You can safely bring the fluid level up to the full mark at this time. Make sure that the dipstick is fully seated to prevent dirt from entering.

6.6.13 Flushing the Converter and Cooler

During a normal fluid change, only the fluid in the pan is drained. The fluid in the torque converter and cooler is not replaced. If the fluid being replaced was in normal condition, this will not be a problem, but if the fluid is highly oxidized, dark brown to almost black in color with a varnish smell, all the fluid should be changed. Most manufacturers do not put a drain plug on the torque converter, so a flushing procedure must be used. After you have replaced the filter and pan, loosen the fitting and remove the cooler return line from the transmission case. On many transmissions the return line attaches in the middle of the transmission case to provide lubrication for the gear train. If both lines attach in the same area, check the service manual to identify the output and input lines properly. Slip a short piece of small hose over the end of the line and run it to an empty drain pan, placed so that you can see the fluid coming out of the hose.

If the manual indicated that the refill should take 6 quarts of fluid, put 3 quarts in at this time. Then have a helper start the vehicle and stay in it while you watch the fluid leaving the hose. When the fluid shows bubbles or comes out in spurts, this means that the transmission is running out of fluid. Stop the engine as soon as those signs appear and add 2 more quarts of fluid. Restart the engine and watch for clear new fluid coming from the hose. As soon as fresh fluid is seen, stop the engine and connect the cooler line to the case, making sure that it is properly tightened and has no leaks. When tightening or loosening cooler lines, always use a flair wrench on the line fitting while using an open-end wrench to hold the fitting in the case. This will prevent damage to the lines. Once the cooler line is attached, continue the refill procedure as outlined in Section 6.6.9.

The decision to flush the torque converter and cooler should be made when you evaluate the fluid with the customer present. That way you can explain before the job is started why more labor and fluid will be needed.

SUMMARY

The following are the major points covered in this chapter:

- To determine the proper ATF change interval, you must know how the vehicle is used.
- Vehicles operated under normal conditions require few ATF changes.
- Vehicles operated under severe conditions require ATF changes more often.
- Heat destroys automatic transmission fluid through oxidation.
- The color, smell, and texture of the oil are used to evaluate its condition.
- The various types of ATF are Dexron II, Type F, Type CJ, Type H, Type MV, Mercon, and Type 7176.
- Flush torque converter and cooler if necessary.
- Follow the ATF change procedure as discussed in this chapter to guarantee a good-quality job the first time with no comebacks.

SELF-TEST

Before going on to the next chapter, complete the self-test according to your instructor's directions. Read carefully and choose the best answer.

1. The fluid change interval for any automatic transmission is controlled by ______.
   a. Factory recommendations
   b. How the vehicle is used
   c. Evaluation of the ATF
   d. All of the above
2. ATF that is clear red in color is ______.
   a. Oxidized
   b. Contaminated with coolant
   c. Usable
   d. None of the above
3. ATF that is milky pink in color is ______.
   a. Oxidized
   b. Contaminated with coolant
   c. Usable
   d. None of the above
4. ATF that is dark brown in color is ______.
   a. Oxidized
   b. Contaminated with coolant
   c. Usable
   d. None of the above
5. The odor of varnish means that the ATF is ______.
   a. Oxidized
   b. Contaminated with coolant
   c. Usable
   d. None of the above
6. Small particles of friction material are normally found in the ATF.
   a. True
   b. False
7. Particles of metal found in the transmission oil pan have no importance.
   a. True
   b. False
8. To prevent oil leaks in the oil pan, you should always ______.
   a. Clean all gasket surfaces
   b. Straighten oil pan lip
   c. Use new gaskets
   d. All of the above
9. It is impossible to change the fluid in a torque converter that does not have a drain plug.
   a. True
   b. False
10. It is better to have the fluid level a little overfull than a little underfull.
    a. True
    b. False

GLOSSARY

change interval acceptable space of time between one ATF change to the next.

Dexron II automatic transmission fluid that has passed a given qualification requirement. Dexron is a fluid formulated to General Motors specifications for their late-model transmissions.

fluid diagnosis analysis of an existing condition in the automatic transmission by examination of the ATF.

fluid level level of ATF in a transmission as indicated by the dipstick. To get a correct reading of the fluid level, the manufacturer's procedures must be followed.

Mercon ATF developed by Ford and used in some of its latest-model transaxles, such as the 4EAT.

normal usage vehicle that is driven under normal conditions as outlined in the manufacturer's service manual.

oxidation deterioration of a substance by chemical combination with oxygen.

severe usage using a vehicle in any way other than normal use. Any operation that increases the vehicle load or operating temperature.

Type CJ automatic transmission fluid developed by Ford for its transmissions. Type CJ and Dexron II are considered compatible, so Dexron II can be substituted for Type CJ.

Type F automatic transmission fluid specification. Type F fluid specifications were developed by Ford as an improvement over Type A, Suffix A fluids.

Type H automatic transmission fluid developed by Ford for use in the C-5 transmission equipped with a converter clutch.

Type MV ATF developed by Ford for use in the ATX transaxle for cold-climate operation. "MV" stands for "multiple viscosity."

Type 7176 ATF developed by Chrysler for its transmissions/transaxles. Type 7176 is compatible with Dexron II, which can be substituted if Type 7176 is unavailable.

Chapter 7

DIAGNOSTIC PROCEDURES

INTRODUCTION

The purpose of this chapter is to provide a systematic approach to the task of diagnosing automatic transmission/transaxle failures. The most common types of failures are described first, together with their possible causes, to provide the necessary background knowledge. Each type of failure requires a different diagnostic procedure to determine the exact cause of the failure.

All diagnostic procedures begin with collecting information about the problem. This should start with the customer's description of the problem. The technician or service writer needs to ask the customer specific questions about the operating conditions of the vehicle to isolate the problem area. Checking the ATF is the next step. Diagnosis of the fluid provides valuable information about the condition of the transmission, and in some cases, tells the whole story. If the fluid shows no problems, the general condition of the engine and linkages is checked next. If the engine is not performing properly, the transmission will be affected. All linkage and cable adjustments to the transmission must be checked and readjusted if found to be incorrect. The road test is the next step in the procedure. The overall performance of the transmission is checked closely, with the technician noting the shift quality, upshift speeds, downshift speeds, and any unusual conditions.

In many cases the fluid diagnosis and the road test will provide sufficient information to allow the technician to make service recommendations without further testing. If that is the case, the technician reports the findings to the service manager or customer and the repair is scheduled. But if there was not enough information on which to base a diagnosis, more tests must be made to identify the problem clearly. All the optional tests used to gather additional information are explained in full.

7.1 PERFORMANCE OBJECTIVES

Upon studying this chapter, you should have fulfilled the following performance objectives by being able to:

1. Describe and discuss the common types of transmission failures.
2. Describe how information is collected in diagnosing a transmission problem.
3. Describe what optional tests are used to gather additional information about transmission performance.
4. Complete all the competency objectives listed for this chapter.
5. Complete the self-test with at least the minimum score required by your instructor.

7.2 COMPETENCY OBJECTIVES

The competency objectives differ from the performance objectives in being more job related. The automotive terms must be well understood so that the theory will be clear. The terms are used to describe the service procedures outlined in Part II. The competency tasks are related to job skills needed to perform service and repair procedures and should be understood thoroughly.

7.2.1 Automotive Terms

The following list may include terms that are unfamiliar to you. Read the terms, then note their definitions as you study the chapter.

air test
converter clutch test
diagnostic chart
diagnostic check sheet
diagnostic guide
governor test
jumper wires
leakage
low-pressure gauge
no drive

no shift
pressure gauge
pressure test
road test
scan tool
slippage
stall test
tee
test plate
throttle valve test
transmission
vacuum gauge
vaccuum hand pump

7.2.2 Competency Tasks

The competency tasks listed here are related directly to knowledge or skills needed to become a successful automotive transmission/transaxle technician. Be sure to complete all the tasks before going on to Chapter 8.

1. Explain in detail five common types of transmission failures.
2. Know what questions you should ask a customer about a no-shift problem.
3. Know what questions you should ask a customer about a slippage problem.
4. Know what questions you should ask a customer about a no-drive problem.
5. Know what questions you should ask a customer about a leakage problem.
6. Know what questions you should ask a customer about a noise problem.
7. Describe in full the four steps of collecting information to diagnose an automatic transmission.
8. List 10 optional transmission tests and describe their purpose.
9. Perform a leak diagnosis.
10. Perform a noise diagnosis.
11. Perform a pressure test.
12. Perform a stall test.
13. Perform throttle valve tests.
14 Perform a governor test.
15. Perform a cooler flow test.
16. Perform a converter clutch test.
17. Perform electronic control tests.
18. Perform air tests.

7.3 COMMON FAILURE CATEGORIES

Before you can learn to diagnose a specific problem in a transmission, you must learn what types of failures commonly occur in automatic transmissions. The most common failures fall into five major categories, which are named after the primary symptom: no shift, slippage, no drive, leakage, and noise.

7.3.1 No Shift

With this type of failure the vehicle can still operate in a limited manner. The no-shift condition could affect all forward speeds or only one particular speed. The problem can also include delayed shifts, which would be a shift that would occur later or at a higher speed than normal. Early-shifting problems, or shifting at a slower speed than normal, will also fall into this category of complaints (Figure 7–1). Any type of shifting problem, such as early or delayed shifting, no upshift or downshift, and shifting back and forth between two gears, falls into this group of failures. At this point in the chapter, only the different types of failures will be described.

7.3.2 Slippage

Slippage can refer to the condition in which a coupling clutch pack is unable to "lock up" when it is applied. Instead of the components turning as one unit, the clutch discs slip when under load, allowing the engine to race. This type of problem is very self-destructive, in that once a clutch pack starts slipping, it destroys the clutch disc in a short length of time (Figure 7–2).

Slippage can also occur with a holding clutch or band. If the clutch or band is unable to lock up the reaction member that it is holding, it will be able to turn. If it was the front band of a three-speed transmission slipping, there would be a problem with the slipping 1–2 shift. Slippage is an

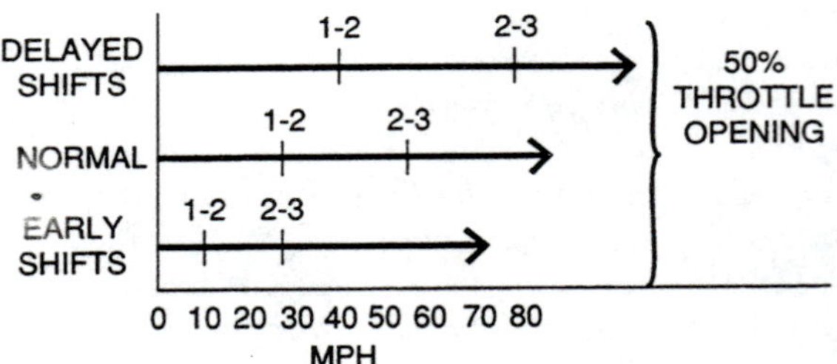

FIGURE 7–1 In the graph, the throttle setting on the vehicle is the same at 50%. The early shifts occur before they should normally, and delayed shifts happen much later than normal. An imbalance in the shift control pressures usually is the cause of this type of problem.

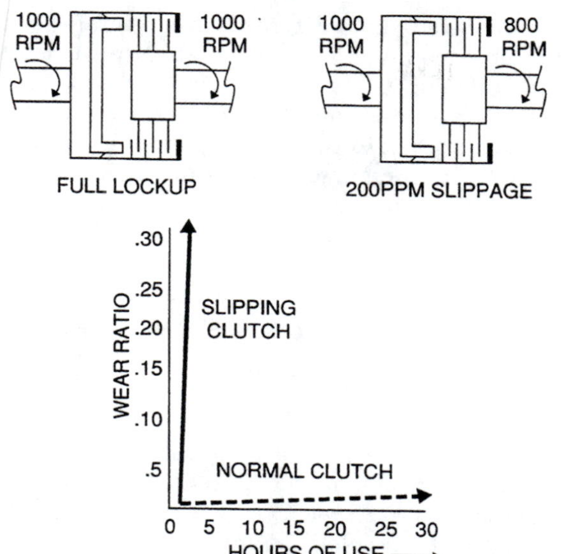

FIGURE 7–2 A clutch pack that achieves full lockup will have a very slow wear rate on its discs, but a clutch pack that is slipping will destroy the discs in a very short period of time.

important symptom indicating that a major failure is about to occur. If the vehicle operator does not pay attention to this early warning sign, he or she could be stranded by a major breakdown.

7.3.3 No Drive

The no-drive type of failure can be as simple as its name, with the transmission having no drive in any gear range. It can also be more complex, with the condition affecting only one gear. The condition of delayed engagement is also included in this grouping of failures. Delayed engagement is when there is a long delay between the time the transmission is placed in gear and when it actually engages (Figure 7–3). In some extreme cases, the delay can be as much as 10 minutes or longer. In most cases the delay is much shorter, ranging in length from a few seconds to a few minutes.

Delayed engagement is another symptom that should not be ignored. If the problem causing the delayed engagement is not repaired, it can cause a major transmission failure.

NO DRIVE IN ALL GEARS
NO DRIVE IN ONLY ONE GEAR
DELAYED ENGAGEMENT WHEN HOT
DELAYED ENGAGEMENT WHEN COLD

FIGURE 7–3 These four transmission problems are grouped together as "no-drive" failures.

FIGURE 7–4 Every fluid leak should be repaired as soon as it is noticed to prevent possible major transmission damage.

7.3.4 Leakage

Leakage is the type of problem that may seem unimportant if the leak is small. Even a small leak is significant because if the ATF level in the transmission gets low enough to cause a drop in hydraulic pressure, damage will occur. As soon as pressure drops, clutch packs and bands will start to slip and the damage is done. All leaks, no matter how small, should be repaired as soon as they are observed, to prevent the possibility of major transmission failure (Figure 7–4). The procedure for leak diagnosis is explained at length later in the chapter.

7.3.5 Noise

Unusual noises coming from any mechanical device are always a symptom of a failure in progress. As parts wear beyond their acceptable wear limits, they become loose enough to cause noise. In some cases the noise is closely followed by the parts failure, but in other cases the parts can be noisy and never fail. Learning to identify the various types of noises and locate them is the key to noise diagnosis (Figure 7–5). Procedures for locating the source of the noise and how to identify different noises are explained later.

7.4 COLLECTION OF INFORMATION

To diagnose transmission problems accurately requires a complete profile of the transmission. The information required to create the profile is col-

WHAT NOISE IS IT MAKING?

• RATTLE	• WHINE
• THUMP	• BUZZ
• KNOCK	• DRONE
• CLUNK	• HUM
• GROWL	• RUMBLE
• SQUEAL	• GRIND
• SCRAPE	• CHATTER

FIGURE 7–5 The noises listed above are all symptoms of various problems. Some of the words have very similar meanings, so communication with the customer should be clear and specific.

SOURCES OF INFORMATION

- CUSTOMER DESCRIPTION
- FLUID DIAGNOSIS
- VEHICLE CONDITION
- SIMPLE ROAD TEST

FIGURE 7–6 All four sources of information about the transmission are used when collecting information, to provide the best possible service recommendations.

lected from four different sources. The first source is the customer's description of the problem. The next source of information is the transmission fluid itself, provided by diagnosing the fluid. The condition of the vehicle is considered next, evaluating engine performance and adjustment of linkage and cables. A simple *road test* is used last to provide accurate performance information about the transmission (Figure 7–6). Most manufacturers recommend the use of a *diagnostic checksheet* while collecting information about a transmission problem. Using the checksheet provides a systematic approach to obtaining information, which in turn leads to accurate service recommendations (Figures 7–7 through 7–10).

In some cases the information gained from only one or two sources is enough to base a decision on. The ability to make these judgments is based on years of experience working with automatic transmissions. Trying to make those kinds of decisions without the experience is a mistake. It is more profitable to make a correct diagnosis and repair the transmission properly than to guess wrong and have a comeback.

7.4.1 Customer Description

The first information you will receive comes from the customer when he or she brings the vehicle in to be repaired. In most cases the average owner does not have much knowledge about automobiles. Some will find it hard to describe the problem, so the service writer must ask questions about the problem in order to collect the proper information. The technical language used by automotive technicians can be a problem at this point, so avoid the use of technical terms in questions. The service writer needs to communicate with the customer on the customer's level. The questions to be asked fall into two groups: general questions and specific questions.

1. General Questions
The purpose of the general questions is to start eliminating possible problem areas. By asking what the symptoms are, you can determine the failure category of the problem (Figure 7–11). The general questions should include:

1. What is the vehicle doing?
2. When does it happen?
3. Is the engine cold or hot?
4. At what speed does it happen?
5. Does it happen all the time?
6. What gear selector position does it happen in?
7. What gear is the transmission in when it happens?
8. Have you had the vehicle repaired or serviced lately?

Once the customer has answered these questions you will be able to choose the failure category in which the problem fits.

2. Specific Questions
Next you ask specific questions about the particular type of failure that seems to be the problem. Each group of questions is designed to provide more information about the specific problem so that the search can be narrowed even further. Ask only the questions that apply to the failure category involved.

If "no shift," ask:

1. Does it shift early, before it normally should?
2. Does it shift late, after it normally should?
3. Does it shift at all?
4. At what speed does it shift?
5. Does it downshift?

AUTOMATIC TRANSMISSION	**CUSTOMER QUESTIONNAIRE**

1. How long have you had the condition? R. O. ____________

☐ Since car was new
☐ Recently (when?) ____________
☐ Came on gradually ☐ Suddenly

2. Describe the condition?
____
____

	P-R-N-D-2-1 SELECTOR POSITION(S)	CHECK AS APPROPRIATE WHICH GEAR? HIGH	INTERMEDIATE	LOW
☐ Slow Engagement	____	____	____	____
☐ Rough Engagement	____	____	____	____
☐ Slip	____	____	____	____
☐ No Drive	____	____	____	____
☐ No Upshift	____	____	____	____
☐ No Downshift	____	____	____	____
☐ Slip During Shift	____	____	____	____
☐ Wrong Shift Speed(s)	____	____	____	____
☐ Rough Shift	____	____	____	____
☐ Mushy Shift	____	____	____	____
☐ Erratic Shift	____	____	____	____
☐ Engine "runaway or "buzzy"	____	____	____	____
☐ No Kickdown	____	____	____	____

☐ Starts in high gear in D
☐ Starts in intermediate gear in D
☐ Oil leak (where?) ____________

3. Which of the following cause or affect the condition?

☐ Transmission cold
☐ After warm-up
☐ High speed
☐ Cruising speed
☐ Low Speed
☐ Accelerating
☐ Engine at fast (cold) idle
☐ Normal idle
☐ Wet road
☐ Dry road
☐ Braking
☐ Coasting down

4. Does the engine need a tune-up?

☐ Yes ☐ No ☐ When was last tune-up? ____________

5. Describe any strange noises

☐ Rumble
☐ Knock
☐ Chatter
☐ Snap or pop
☐ Buzz
☐ Whine
☐ Squeak
☐ Grind
☐ Hiss
☐ Scrape
☐ Other (describe)____________
____

FIGURE 7–7 Diagnostic checksheet used by Ford service departments to gather customer information. (Courtesy of Ford)

AUTOMATIC TRANSMISSIONS DIAGNOSIS CHECK SHEET

R.O. ________ Trans. ________

Engine ________

Code on Diagnosis Wheel	Check/Test	Remarks

☐ B — TRANSMISSION FLUID
1. Level ________ ________
2. Condition ________ ________

☐ C — ENGINE
Idle ________ ________
Power ________ ________

☐ D — EGR SYSTEM

☐ E — LINKAGE
Downshift ________ ________
Manual ________ ________

☐ F — SHIFT TESTS

Throttle Opening	Range	Shift	Shift Points (MPH)	
			Record Actual	Record Spec.
Minimum (Above 12" Vacuum)	D	1-2		
	D	2-3		
	D	3-1		
	1	2-1		
To Detent (Torque Demand)	D	1-2		
	D	2-3		
		3-2		
Thru Detent (wide open Throttle)	D	1-2		
	D	2-3		
	D	3-2		
	D	2-1 or 3-1		

☐ G — PRESSURE TEST

Engine RPM	Manifold Vacuum In-Hg	Throttle	Range	PSI	
				Record Actual	Record Spec.
Idle	Above 12	Closed	P		
			N		
			D		
			2		
			1		
			R		
As Required	10	As Required	D, 2, 1		
As Required	Below 3	Wide Open	D		
			2		
			1		
			R		

☐ H — STALL TEST

Range	Specified Engine RPM	Record Actual Engine RPM
D		
2		
1		
R		

Results ________

☐ I — GOVERNOR TEST
Cutback Speed (C3, C4, C6)
10" Vacuum ______ MPH ________
0-2" Vacuum ______ MPH ________
Pressure at MPH (FMX)
10 ______ PSI ________
20 ______ PSI ________
30______ PSI ________

☐ J — LEAK TEST

CHECK THESE	OK	OIL/FLUID *(COLOR)
CONVERTER AREA		
OIL PAN GASKET		
FILLER TUBE/SEAL		
COOLER/CONNECTIONS		
LEVER SHAFT SEALS		
PRESSURE PORT PLUGS		
EXTENSION/CASE GASKET		
EXTENSION SEAL/BUSHING		
SPEEDOMETER ADAPTER		
SERVO COVERS		
AIR VENT		

*Color Codes		
	Auto. Trans.	Red
	Power Steering	Yellow-Green
	Engine Oil	Golden Brown

☐ K — VACUUM HOSE ROUTING

☐ L — BAND AND SERVO
1. Intermediate Band Adj.
2. Reverse Band Adj.
3. Polished, Glazed Band, Drum

☐ M — DRIVESHAFT, U-JOINTS, ENGINE MOUNTS

☐ N — TRANSMISSION END PLAY

☐ O — CLUTCH PACK FREE PLAY

☐ P — VALVE BODY DIRTY, STICKING

☐ Q — INTERNAL LINKAGE

☐ R — VALVE BODY BOLT TORQUE

☐ S — AIR PRESSURE TEST

☐ T — MECHANICAL PARTS

☐ U — VERIFY PROBLEM

☐ V — VALVE BODY MOUNTING FACES

☐ W — SPEEDO DRIVEN GEAR

☐ X — VACUUM TO DIAPHRAGM

☐ Y — CHECK DIAPHRAGM FOR LEAKAGE

REFER TO DIAGNOSIS WHEEL OR TO CAR DIAGNOSIS MANUAL FOR ACTION TO TAKE ON ANY "NOT OK" CONDITION.

FIGURE 7–8 Diagnostic checksheet used by Ford service technicians for the systematic collection of information about a transmission problem. (Courtesy of Ford)

DATE ____ / ____ / ____

TRANSMISSION/TRANSAXLE CONCERN CHECK SHEET

(★ — INFORMATION REQUIRED FOR TECHNICAL ASSISTANCE)

SERVICE ADVISOR

★VIN ____________ ★MILEAGE ________ R.O.# ________

★MODEL YEAR ______ ★VEHICLE MODEL ____________ ★ENGINE ________

★TRANS. MODEL ________ ★TRANS. SERIAL # ____________

★CUSTOMER'S CONCERN

____

____

____

____

CHECK THE ITEMS THAT DESCRIBE THE CONCERN —

WHAT:	WHEN:	OCCURS:	USUALLY NOTICED:
__NO POWER	__VEHICLE WARM	__ALWAYS	__IDLING
__SHIFTING	__VEHICLE COLD	__INTERMITTENT	__ACCELERATING
__SLIPS	__ALWAYS	__SELDOM	__COASTING
__NOISE	__NOT SURE	__FIRST TIME	__BRAKING
__SHUDDER			AT ______ MPH

TECHNICIAN

PRELIMINARY CHECK PROCEDURES

INSPECT

- FLUID LEVEL & CONDITION
- ENGINE PERFORMANCE — VACUUM & ECM CODES
- TV CABLE AND/OR MODULATOR VACUUM
- MANUAL LINKAGE ADJUSTMENT
- ROAD TEST TO VERIFY CONCERN★

NOTE FINDINGS

____

____

____

NOTE: DUPLICATE THE CONDITIONS UNDER WHICH CUSTOMER'S CONCERN WAS OBSERVED

★PROPOSED OR COMPLETED REPAIRS

ON-CAR	BENCH

(OVER)

FIGURE 7–9 Diagnostic checksheet used by General Motors technicians. (Reprinted with permission of General Motors Corporation)

★TRANS. TEMPERATURE _______ HOT _______ COLD

★VACUUM READINGS AT MODULATOR
(180C, 250C, 350C, 400, 440-T4)

READING AT MODULATOR ________________ IN. HG. (ENGINE AT HOT IDLE, TRANS. IN DRIVE)

CHECK FOR VACUUM RESPONSE DURING ACCELERATOR MOVEMENT

PRESSURE TEST

★TRANS. LINE PRESSURES

	MINIMUM SPEC. (FROM MANUAL)	MINIMUM ACTUAL	MAXIMUM SPEC. (FROM MANUAL)	MAXIMUM ACTUAL
P	______	______	______	______
R	______	______	______	______
N	______	______	______	______
[D]	______	______	______	______
D	______	______	______	______
2	______	______	______	______
1	______	______	______	______

ROAD TEST

★FINDINGS BASED ON ROAD TEST

CHECK ITEMS FOUND ON ROAD TEST THAT DESCRIBE THE CUSTOMER'S COMMENTS ABOUT:

GARAGE SHIFT FEEL
- __ENGINE STOPS
- __HARSH
- __DELAYED
- __NO DRIVE

UPSHIFTS
- __EARLY
- __HARSH
- __DELAYED
- __SLIPS
- __NO UPSHIFT

DOWNSHIFTS
- __BUSYNESS
- __HARSH
- __DELAYED
- __SLIPS
- __NO DOWNSHIFT

TORQUE CONVERTER CLUTCH
- __BUSYNESS
- __HARSH
- __NO RELEASE
- __SHUDDER
- __EARLY APPLY
- __NO APPLY
- __LATE APPLY

CONCERNS OCCUR WHEN/DURING:

✓	GEAR	RANGE
		P - N
	1st	[D]
	2nd	
	3rd	
	4th	
	1st	D
	2nd	
	3rd	
	1st	2
	2nd	
	1st	1
	REVERSE	R

DURING
- __1-2 UPSHIFT
- __2-3 UPSHIFT
- __3-4 UPSHIFT
- __4-3 DOWNSHIFT
- __3-2 DOWNSHIFT
- __2-1 DOWNSHIFT

THROTTLE POSITION
- __LIGHT
- __MEDIUM
- __HEAVY
- __W.O.T.

NOISE

TYPE
- __BUZZ
- __WHINE
- __CLUNK

WHEN NOTICED
- __ALWAYS
- __LOAD SENSITIVE
- __STEERING SENSITIVE
  AT _______ MPH
  IN _______ GEAR

PITCH
- __LOW
- __MEDIUM
- __HIGH

LEVEL
- __LIGHT
- __MEDIUM
- __HEAVY

FIGURE 7–10 Back of the checksheet shown in Figure 7–9. (Reprinted with permission of General Motors Corporation)

FIGURE 7–11 To track down the exact problem, the service writer or technician must ask the right questions about a transmission complaint.

6. Is the engine running smoothly?
7. Do you have to add ATF to the transmission occasionally?

In most cases no-shift problems will involve the valve body and/or the control pressure devices. Problems can sometimes be caused by a failed clutch pack or hydraulic circuit leak, but further testing will be necessary to locate the exact problem.

If slippage, ask:

1. In which gear does it happen?
2. Is the vehicle hot or cold?
3. When did it start?

With all slippage problems, damage has already occurred to the transmission and it will need to be rebuilt. The purpose of the questions at this point is to identify which clutches or bands have failed so that you can look for the cause of the failure as the transmission is disassembled.

If "no drive," ask:

1. Will it engage in gear at all?
2. How long is the delay?
3. Will revving the engine help?
4. In which selector position does it happen?
5. Is the vehicle hot or cold?
6. When it engages, is it smooth or harsh?
7. Do you have to add ATF to the transmission occasionally?

With no-drive or late-engagement problems the cause is usually in the hydraulic system. Low pump output, hardened seals, torn seals, sealing ring leaks, and plugged filters can all cause this type of problem. More tests are needed to find the exact problem.

If leakage, ask:

1. How often do you add ATF?
2. Can you see ATF dripping off the car?
3. Where does it collect when the car is parked?
4. How much will leak overnight?
5. Have you noticed any new, unusual noises?

Once you have identified that leakage is the main problem, you must locate the source of the leak. Procedures for doing that will be explained in later units. Whenever leakage has been a problem, you must fully evaluate the transmission to determine if other damage has occurred because of a low fluid level. Never assume that the transmission is undamaged; test to be sure.

If noise, ask:

1. In what selector position do you hear the noise?
2. In what gears do you hear it?
3. What driving conditions make it happen?
4. What driving conditions make it stop?
5. Can you tell where it is coming from?
6. What type of noise is it? Choose one of the following.

rattle	thump
whine	buzz
knock	drone
clunk	hum
growl	rumble
squeal	grind
scrape	chatter

The answers to these questions will help direct you to a specific part of the transmission. Diagnostic procedures for finding the noise are discussed later in the chapter.

7.4.2 Fluid Diagnosis

Once all the questions have been asked and answered it is time for the next step in collecting information. You should check the fluid condition and level next (Figure 7–12). As you examine the fluid on the dipstick, you should be asking yourself:

- Is the fluid level correct?
- Is the ATF color good? If not, what is wrong with it?

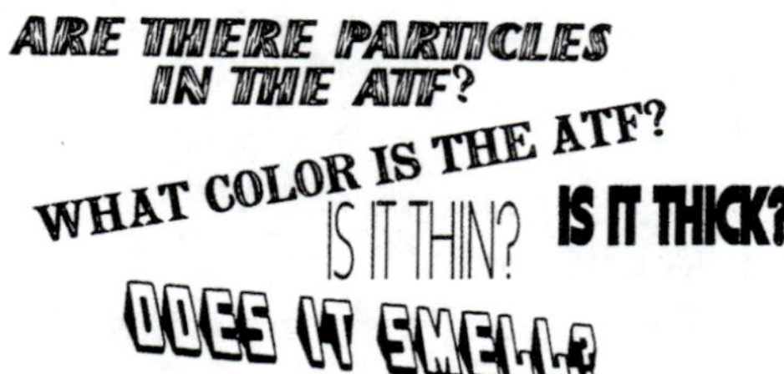

FIGURE 7–12 Important information about the condition of a transmission can be collected by diagnosing the fluid.

- Are there bubbles in the ATF?
- How does the ATF smell?
- Is there varnish on the dipstick?
- Can you see particles in the ATF?
- Can you feel particles in the ATF?

If you are not sure of your evaluation of the fluid, review the section on fluid diagnosis. Ask the opinion of an experienced technician; don't be afraid to ask questions.

Now evaluate the information you collected about the fluid and see what conclusions can be made. It can be helpful to rank the quality of the fluid as:

1. Fresh, like new, no signs of oxidation or contamination.

2. Used, shows signs of oxidation through its darker color and varnish smell; should be replaced.

3. Damaged; fluid has burned smell, very dark color, particles of clutch material in the fluid—all of which indicate internal damage.

Other conditions that may be found during fluid diagnosis are listed in the flowchart in Figure 7–13.

7.4.3 Vehicle Condition

The operating condition of the vehicle must also be evaluated to determine if poor engine performance or improperly adjusted linkage are part of the transmission problem.

1. Engine Performance
Any engine malfunctions will affect transmission performance in some way. In many cases an engine that is not performing properly will cause the transmission to shift erratically (Figure 7–14).

By placing the engine under load, some performance problems will become more apparent. A quick method for checking rough engine performance begins with the engine at operating temperature.

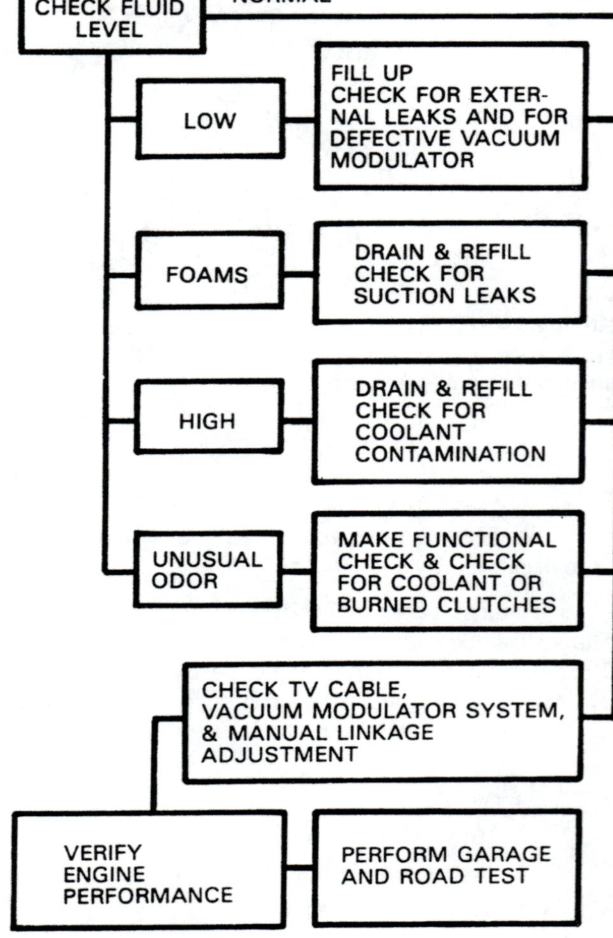

FIGURE 7–13 Flowchart listing different fluid conditions and what actions should be taken to correct problems. (Reprinted with permission of General Motors Corporation)

1. Start the engine.
2. Apply the parking brake.
3. Apply the service brakes fully.

FIX ALL ENGINE PROBLEMS BEFORE TESTING THE TRANSMISSION

FIGURE 7–14 Engine malfunctions must be diagnosed and corrected before a transmission can be tested accurately.

4. Place the gear selector in drive (D) position.

5. Steadily raise the engine rpm's until stall speed is reached.

6. Listen for engine miss.

7. Do not hold the engine at stall speed for over a few seconds.

8. Release the accelerator.

9. With the engine at idle, move the selector to neutral (N).

10. Raise the engine speed to 1000 to 1200 rpm for a few minutes to cool the ATF.

If the engine has a weak or dead cylinder, the load test will make the symptoms easier to detect. This type of engine problem is easier to notice than other types of malfunctions.

2. Possible Engine Problems
Some of the other types of engine problems to look for are:

- Hard starting, hot or cold
- Cuts out
- Missing
- Dieseling
- Poor mileage
- Hesitates
- Stalls, hot or cold
- Surges
- Popping sound from intake or exhaust
- Rough idle, cold or hot
- Detonation
- Sluggish

This list includes most of the engine performance problems that occur regularly. The procedures for diagnosing and repairing these conditions are fully explained in the manufacturer's service manual or in any good-quality shop manual. Any engine problem found should be corrected before continuing with the transmission diagnosis.

3. Linkage and Cable Adjustment
Proper adjustment of the manual linkage and throttle valve cable is essential for proper transmission operation. The linkage connecting the gear selector inside the vehicle to the manual valve in the transmission should be inspected to verify proper operation and adjustment (Figure 7–15). If the transmission uses a throttle valve (TV) cable, its operation and adjustment must be checked (Figure 7–16). On transmissions that use a vacuum modulator, the vacuum lines should be inspected and vacuum at the modulator should be verified by removing the vacuum line from the modulator with the engine operating at approximately 1000 rpm. You should be able to feel a vacuum at the end of the hose. Reconnect all lines before continuing the tests. Correct all malfunctions before continuing.

Once you have established that the engine is performing properly and that the linkage and vacuum systems are functioning and adjusted correctly, you can proceed to the last test.

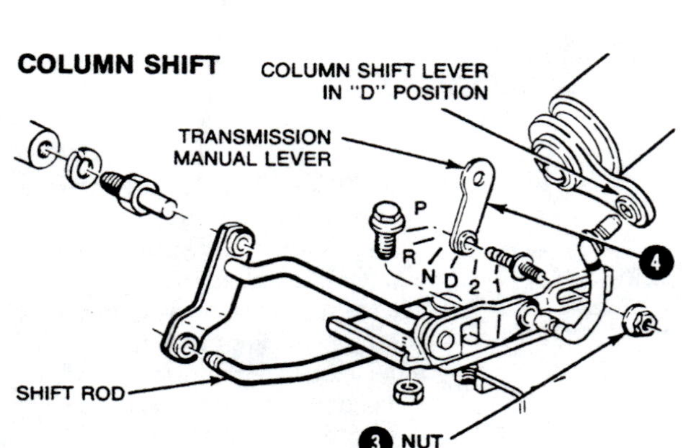

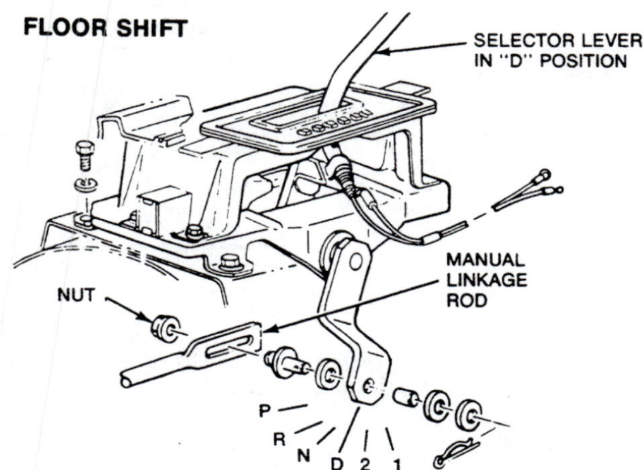

FIGURE 7–15 The manual shift linkage adjustment should be checked to eliminate that potential problem area. (Courtesy of Ford)

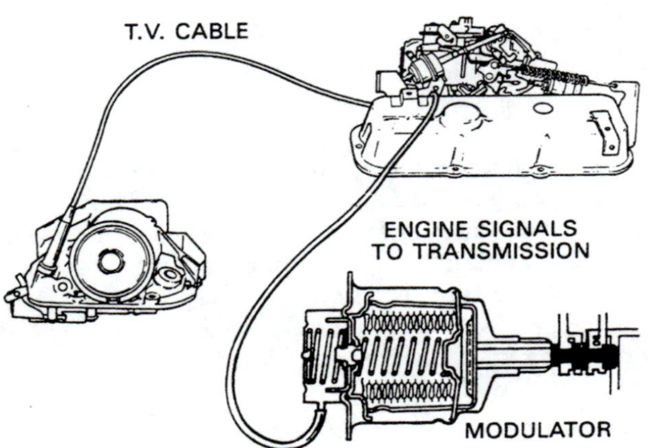

FIGURE 7–16 The throttle valve (TV) cable and vacuum modulator systems should be checked for proper operation and adjustment. (Reprinted with permission of General Motors Corporation)

7.4.4 Simple Road Test

The reason this test is named the simple road test is because no diagnostic equipment is used for this procedure. The main purpose of this test is to gather information about how the transmission performs. At this point you are trying to form an overall picture of how the transmission is performing and what its malfunction could be. This test is to check the speeds at which shifts occur. The service manual will provide the specific shift speeds for the vehicle you are testing. Write these speeds on the check sheet and refer to them during the road test. The road test should duplicate the condition described by the customer as much as possible.

The vehicle should be driven so all modes of operation are included in the road test. The various driving modes are:

- Full throttle acceleration from stop
- Light throttle acceleration from stop
- Full throttle acceleration from 25 mph
- Full throttle acceleration from 45 mph
- Closed throttle coast down (checking downshifts)

It is best to follow the road test sequence listed on your checksheet so that nothing will be forgotten. By using a systematic test procedure and always following it step by step, you eliminate the possibility of tests being different or not standardized. If the test is not run the same way each time, the test results may vary. To become a good diagnostician you must be able to take information gathered from tests on many different vehicles and generalize it into failure patterns. Without standardized test procedures, this is impossible.

7.5 SERVICE RECOMMENDATIONS

Once the transmission performance information has been gathered, the next step is to review the information. As you review the information from each of the four sources, parts of the puzzle will start falling in place (Figure 7–17). In some cases the puzzle is solved quickly, while in other cases it is much more difficult.

Most factory service manuals include automatic transmission *diagnostic charts,* which can be very helpful in the decision-making process. The diagnostic charts are usually made up of three

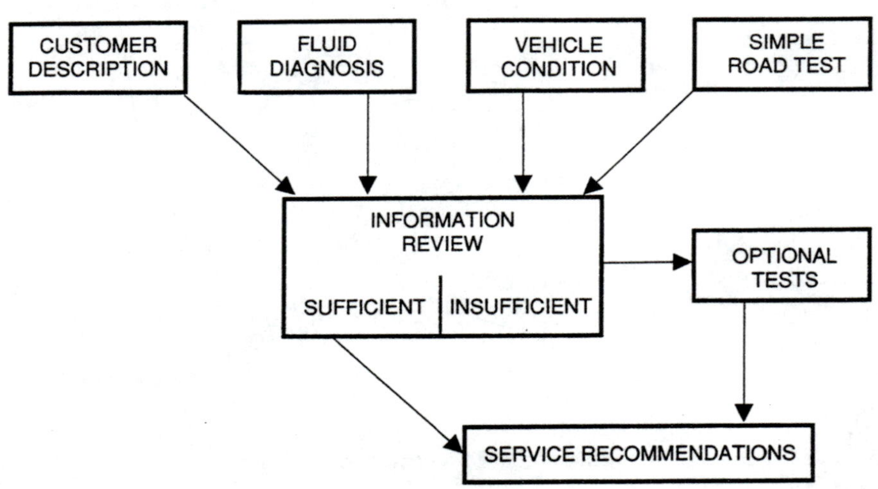

FIGURE 7–17 After the information is gathered from the customer's description, fluid diagnosis, vehicle condition, and simple road test, it is reviewed, and if there is sufficient information for a decision, service recommendations are made. If the information is insufficient, optional tests are performed to provide additional information so that the diagnosis can be completed.

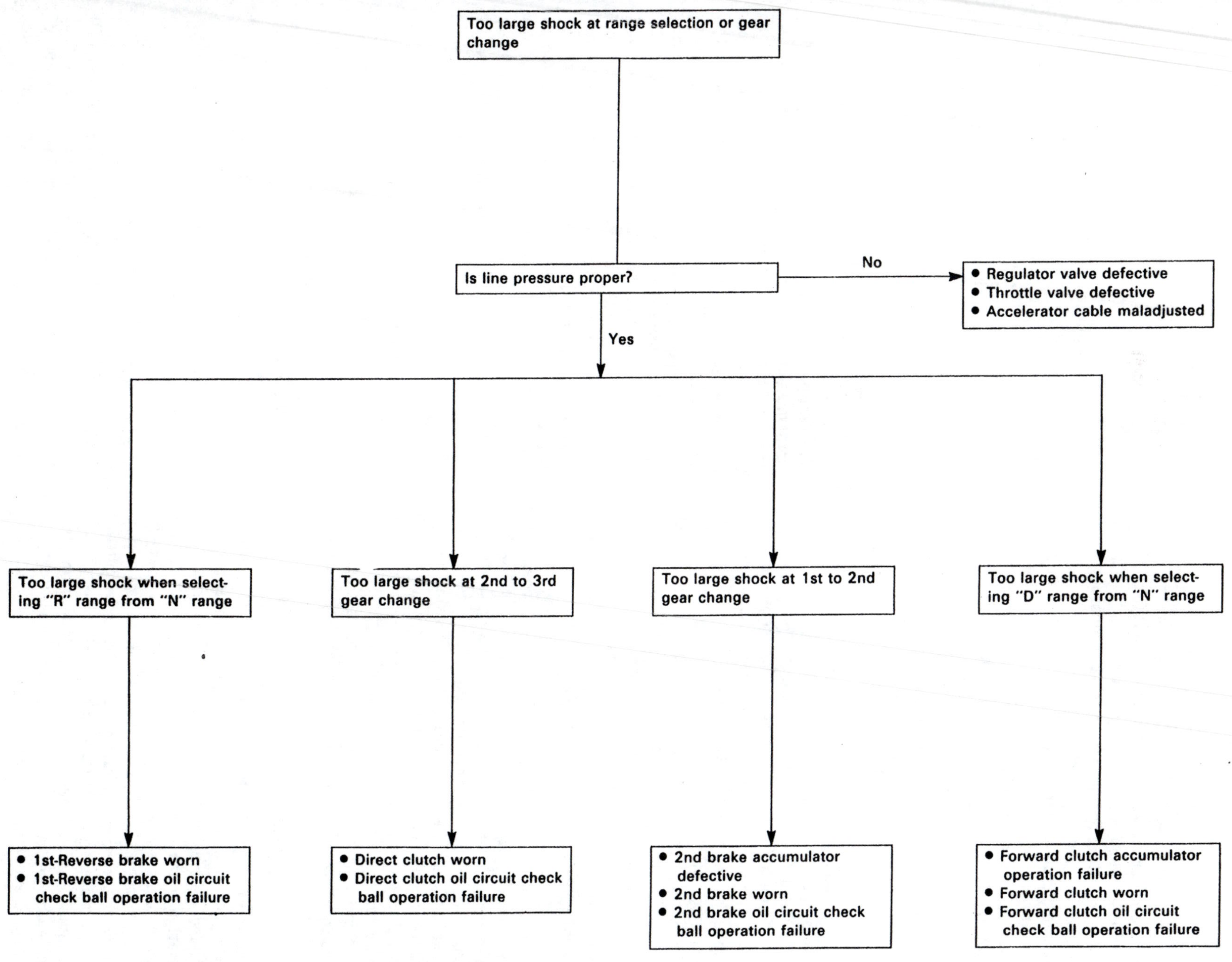

FIGURE 7–18 Diagnostic chart used by Ford. (Courtesy of Ford)

columns. The first column shows the problem condition, the second column names the possible causes of the problem, and the third column lists the repair procedures that will resolve the problem. A sample diagnostic chart is shown in Figure 7–18. This example is short and shows only five problem conditions. The complete diagnostic charts for most transmissions are usually from 10 to 15 pages in length and cover all phases of operation.

The Torque Flite diagnosis chart, shown in Figure 7–19, presents the information in a different format, which lists only the problem condition and the possible cause. This type of diagnostic chart is good for quick reference but will not suggest repair corrections.

To simplify the use of the diagnostic charts, two manufacturers, Ford and General Motors, have condensed the information into *diagnostic guides.* The General Motors diagnosis guide, shown in Figure 7–20, is designed like a slide rule. You use the guide by moving the slide until the indicator is lined up with the transmission problem. Then read the letters shown in the circuit/system window at the right side of the guide. These letters refer to possible problem areas listed on the guide.

The Ford diagnostic guide uses a wheel design. Two circular charts are overlaid with a pivot in the center. The top wheel is slightly smaller than the bottom one and has lists of transmission conditions, test results, checks and tests, and repair corrections (Figure 7–21). There is also a window slot and the indicator arrow to use the guide. Turn the top wheel until the arrow lines up with the number representing the condition on the bottom wheel. Letters can then be seen through the window slot which refer to items on the check-and-test and repair correction lists. This type of diagnostic guide has much more information on it than the other type and can be a great help in reaching a decision.

7.5.1 Sufficient Information

If the information collected from the four sources is sufficient to lead to a decision, the diagnosis is completed. In most cases there should be enough information by this point to make accurate service recommendations. A technician with experience in transmission diagnosis is usually able to arrive at a correct service recommendation by shortcutting some of the information gathering. The technician is able to make the proper recommendations because of his or her experience, and the only way to get that experience is to do the job.

7.5.2 Insufficient Information

If the information gathered so far does not provide a clear picture of what the problem is, additional tests must be performed. In Section 7.6 we will describe 10 additional tests that should be able to supply the more detailed information needed. If there is any question about needing more information, assume that you do need more and perform the necessary tests. It is always better to have more information than you need rather than not enough. As you become more knowledgeable and experienced, diagnosis will become much easier.

7.6 OPTIONAL TESTS

The simple tests used to collect data about the transmission malfunction can provide enough information for diagnosis if the problem is simple and straightforward. But if the problem is more complex, the optional tests must be used to locate the problem clearly. The optional tests are designed to check the specific function of an individual system in the transmission. In this section we examine 10 optional tests that are representative of special transmission tests. Each manufacturer develops special tests for its transmissions to be able to service them properly. The best source for finding out which special tests are used for a particular transmission is the manufacturer's service manual. Aftermarket manuals are not able to cover the subject in the same depth as are factory manuals. The 10 optional tests that will be explained are:

1. Leak diagnosis
2. Noise diagnosis
3. Pressure tests
4. Stall tests
5. Vacuum modulator tests
6. *Governor tests*
7. Cooler flow tests
8. *Converter clutch tests*
9. Electronic control tests
10. *Air tests*

7.6.1 Leak Diagnosis

A visual inspection of a leaking transmission will usually locate the leak. If the leak has been present for a long time, it will be harder to locate because of the fluid covering the surface. Start by looking un-

POSSIBLE CAUSE		CONDITION: HARSH ENGAGEMENT FROM NEUTRAL TO D	R	DELAYED ENGAGEMENT FROM NEUTRAL TO D	R	RUNAWAY UPSHIFT	NO UPSHIFT	3-2 KICKDOWN RUNAWAY	NO KICKDOWN OR NORMAL DOWNSHIFT	SHIFTS ERRATIC	SLIPS IN FORWARD DRIVE POSITIONS	SLIPS IN REVERSE ONLY	SLIPS IN ALL POSITIONS	NO DRIVE IN ANY POSITION	NO DRIVE IN FORWARD DRIVE POSITIONS	NO DRIVE IN REVERSE	DRIVES IN NEUTRAL	DRAGS OR LOCKS	GRATING, SCRAPING GROWLING NOISE	BUZZING NOISE	HARD TO FILL, OIL BLOWS OUT FILLER HOLE	TRANSAXLE OVERHEATS	HARSH UPSHIFT	DELAYED UPSHIFT
Overrunning clutch inner race damaged.	33																			X				
Overrunning clutch worn, broken or seized.	32										X				X			X	X					
Planetary gear sets broken or seized.	31													X	X	X		X	X					
Rear Clutch dragging.	30																X							
Worn or faulty rear clutch.	29	X	X	X	X						X				X	X	X							
Insufficient clutch plate clearance.	28																X					X		
Faulty cooling system.	27																					X		
Kickdown band adjustment too tight.	26																	X				X		
Hydraulic pressure too high.	25	X	X																				X	
High fluid level.	24																				X			
Worn or faulty front clutch.	23				X	X	X	X		X		X				X								X
Kickdown servo band or linkage malfunction.	22					X	X	X	X	X														X
Governor malfunction.	21						X		X	X														X
Worn or broken reaction shaft support seal rings.	20				X	X	X			X		X				X								X
Governor support seal rings broken or worn.	19						X	X		X														X
Drive shaft(s) bushing(s) damaged.	18																		X					
Overrunning clutch not holding.	17										X				X									
Kickdown band out of adjustment.	16							X											X				X	X
Incorrect throttle linkage adjustment.	15					X	X	X	X	X	X												X	X
Engine idle speed too low.	14			X	X																			
Aerated fluid.	13			X	X	X		X		X	X	X	X							X	X			
Worn or broken input shaft seal rings.	12			X	X						X		X		X									
Faulty oil pump.	11			X	X					X	X	X	X	X								X		
Oil filter clogged.	10			X	X	X				X	X		X	X							X			
Incorrect gearshift control linkage adjustment.	9			X	X		X			X	X	X				X	X					X		
Low fluid level.	8			X	X	X	X	X		X	X	X	X	X	X					X		X		
Low-reverse servo, band or linkage malfunction.	7		X		X							X				X								
Valve body malfunction or leakage.	6	X		X	X	X	X	X	X	X	X	X	X	X	X	X	X			X				
Low-reverse band worn out.	5		X		X							X				X		X	X					
Hydraulic pressures too low.	4			X	X	X	X	X		X	X	X	X	X	X	X						X	X	
Engine idle speed too high.	3	X	X																			X		
Stuck switch valve.	2																					X		
Low-reverse band mis-adjusted (A-413 & A-470).	1		X		X							X												

FIGURE 7–19 Chrysler Torque Flite diagnostic chart. (Courtesy of Chrysler)

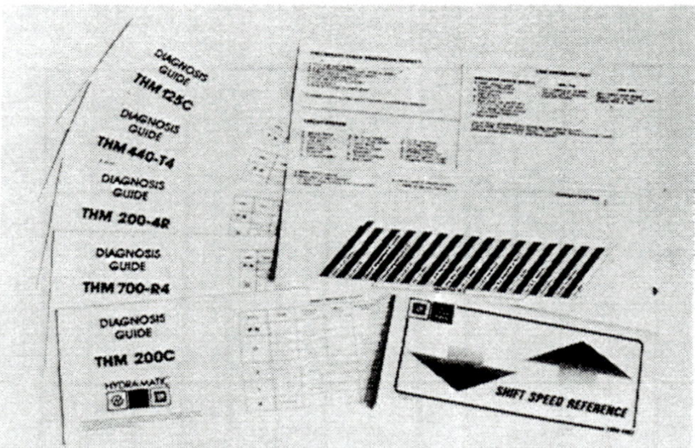

FIGURE 7–20 General Motors diagnostic guide. (Reprinted with permission of General Motors Corporation)

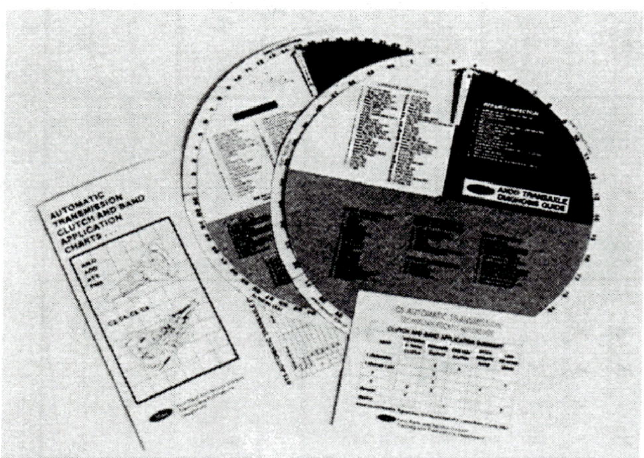

FIGURE 7–21 Ford diagnostic wheel and charts. (Courtesy of Ford)

der the vehicle to see where the fluid is dripping. If you find no drips, drive the vehicle until its operating temperature is reached; then after parking the vehicle, place a large piece of paper or cardboard under the transmission (Figure 7–22). The drips on the paper will give you the general location of the leak. Raise the vehicle and inspect the transmission and cooler lines for the leak. If you find the leak, make repairs and test to verify the repair. If you could not find the leak, continue looking.

1. Clean and Look Method

Next examine the transmission, using a drop light, to find areas that are wetter with fluid. After identifying these "suspected areas," clean the areas with solvent or degreaser and blow dry with shop air. Now drive the vehicle again until the operating temperature is reached, and then raise the vehicle and inspect for fresh fluid. If you still cannot locate the leak, the powder method should be tried.

2. Powder Method

Reclean the suspected areas with solvent and blow dry with shop air. Apply an even coating of aerosol foot powder to the suspected areas, then drive the vehicle (Figure 7–23). The leak will leave a trail on the powder that will lead to the source of the leak.

3. Fluorescent Dye Method

For problem leaks that seem impossible to find, the fluorescent dye and black light method is the last resort (Figure 7–24). The manufacturer's instructions for using the equipment will provide the best results in finding the leak. Its operation is basically as follows:

1. Dye is added to the ATF.
2. The vehicle is operated under normal conditions.

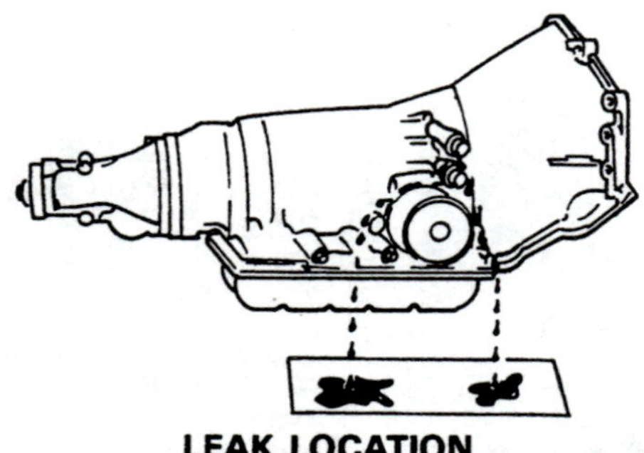

FIGURE 7–22 Placing clean paper or cardboard under a vehicle will help find a leak.

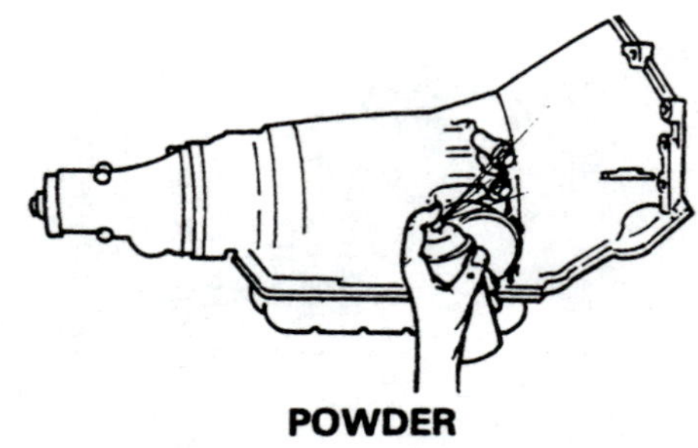

FIGURE 7–23 Use aerosol spray powder to coat a suspected area. (Reprinted with permission of General Motors Corporation)

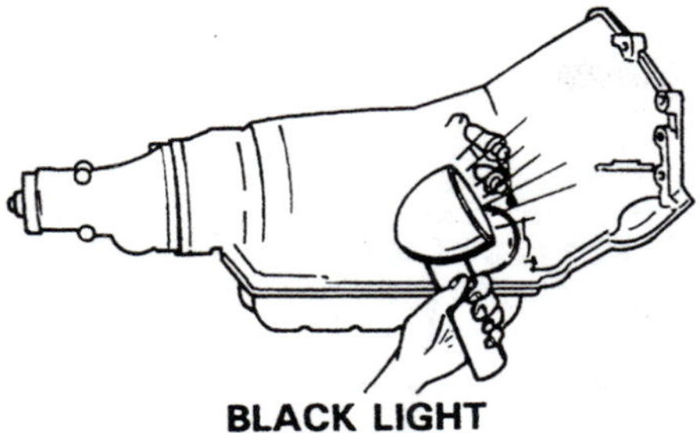

FIGURE 7–24 A "black light" can be used with fluorescent dye to find a leak. (Reprinted with permission of General Motors Corporation)

3. Black light is used to examine for leak.
4. Black light causes fluorescent dye to glow.

4. Torque Converter Leaks
Leaks around the torque converter area can be hard to pinpoint if you do not have a plan. In this case the plan is simple: Don't disturb the evidence.

To repair any leak in the torque converter area, the transmission must be removed. Once the transmission is out, carefully remove the torque converter and look for the fluid trails on the oil pump and transmission case. Examine the converter itself for fluid trails. Also examine the flywheel and the back of the engine block for fluid trails. Figure 7–25 provides a description of what type of trail is left by a particular leak. Special test equipment is available that can be used to pressurize a torque converter to find cracked welds or other leaks (Figure 7–26).

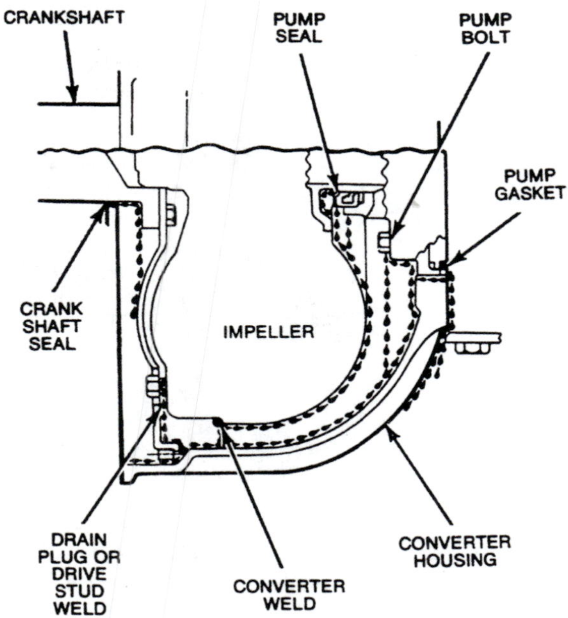

FIGURE 7–25 Basic types of torque converter leaks. (Courtesy of Ford)

Finding and repairing fluid leaks is not hard if you will follow a few simple rules.

1. Examine all parts of the transmission.
2. Thoroughly clean the suspected areas.
3. Use the powder method.
4. Retest repairs when finished.

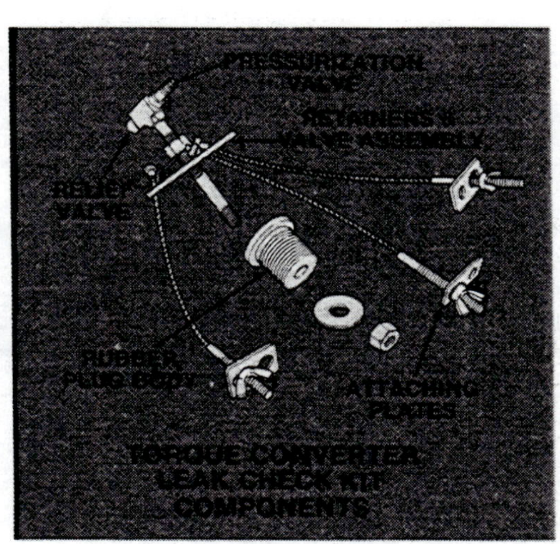

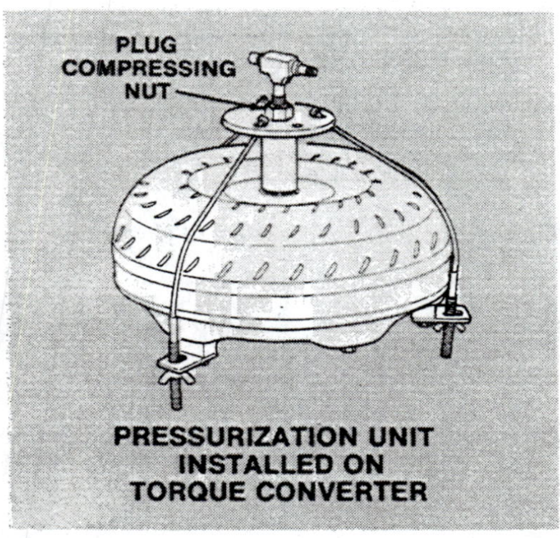

FIGURE 7–26 Torque converter pressure testing equipment. (Courtesy of Ford)

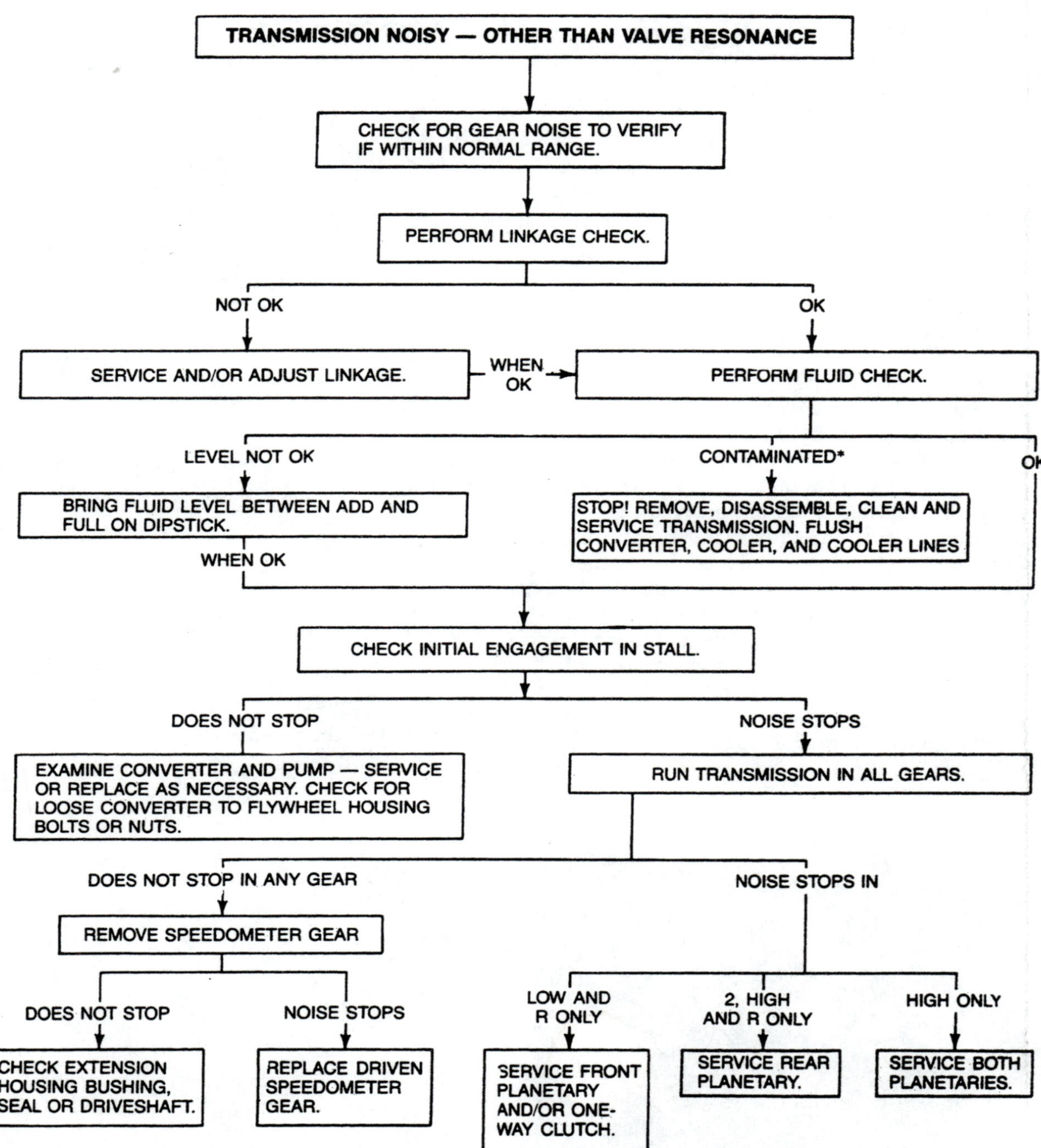

FIGURE 7–27 Noise diagnostic flowchart. (Courtesy of Ford)

7.6.2 Noise Diagnosis

In rear-wheel-drive transmissions most of the noise problems are located in the torque converter and planetary gear sets. Transaxles share those areas as well as the sprocket-and-chain assemblies and the final drive.

To identify what is making the noise, test drive the vehicle and listen to the pitch of the noise, what gear it is present in, if it is load sensitive, and during what driving conditions it occurs. Many factory service manuals use a diagnostic flowchart to guide the technician through the procedure. It is extremely important that you understand how to use a flowchart, because most diagnostic procedures are presented in this form in the manufacturer's service manuals. A flowchart dealing with noise diagnosis is shown in Figure 7–27. Study it closely by following the flow from one test or procedure to the next. Using the factory manual and the data gathered during the test drive, you should be able to identify the source of the noise. If the noise is hard to identify, you can try to operate the vehicle on a hoist so that listening devices can be used on the transmission to locate the source of the noise. Three simple listening devices are a piece of steel rod, a piece of heater hose, and a stethoscope. By placing a 3-foot piece of steel rod against the transmission case, then touching the other end of the rod to your mastoid bone (just behind your ear), the sound is transferred directly to your inner ear. Then, by moving the contact point of the rod around on the transmission, you can listen to different areas of the transmission. Extreme care must be used when working near the revolving drive shaft. A 3- to 4-foot piece of heater hose can be used as a listening device by placing one open end of the hose directly over your ear and then moving the other end of the hose around near the transmission. The hose shields out all of the noise except what is exactly in front of the open end. The stethoscope is simple to use: put the headset end in your ears and touch the probe end to the transmission case.

With proper use of the shop manual and listening devices, you should be able to diagnosis most noise problems.

7.6.3 Pressure Tests

Since hydraulic pressure is the power source used to apply the transmissions's clutches and bands, much information can be gained about transmission condition and operation by measuring different circuit pressures. The usual circuits that are measured are:

- Mainline pressure
- Governor pressure
- Throttle valve pressure
- Cooler line pressure
- Individual clutch or band applied pressure

The normal pressures that should be found in each circuit are listed in a pressure chart found in the shop service manual (Figure 7–28).

All automatic transmissions have pressure test points, or taps, located on the case of the transmission. These test points are normally plugged with a small pipe plug which can be removed so that a *pressure gauge* can be attached. Each test point has an internal passageway connecting to a specific hydraulic circuit inside the transmission. In Figure 7–29 you see the seven test points used for pressure testing this Chrysler automatic transaxle.

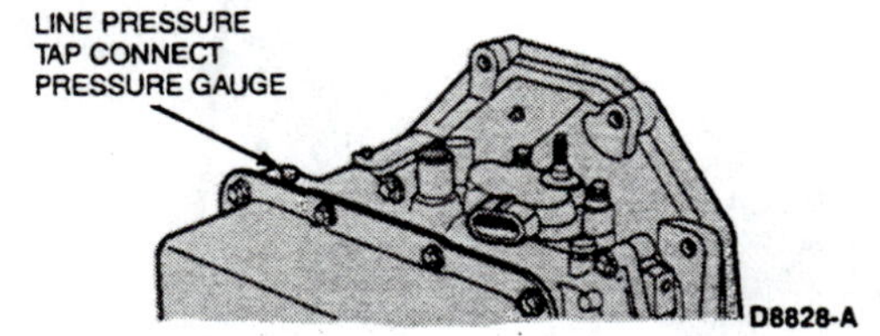

Range	Idle		WOT Stall	
	kPa	psi	kPa	psi
P, N	331-531	48-77	—	—
R	421-683	61-99	1827-2089	265-303
Ⓓ, D	331-531	48-77	1226-1393	177-202
L	331-531	48-77	1443-1641	208-238

FIGURE 7–28 Line pressure test chart. (Courtesy of Ford)

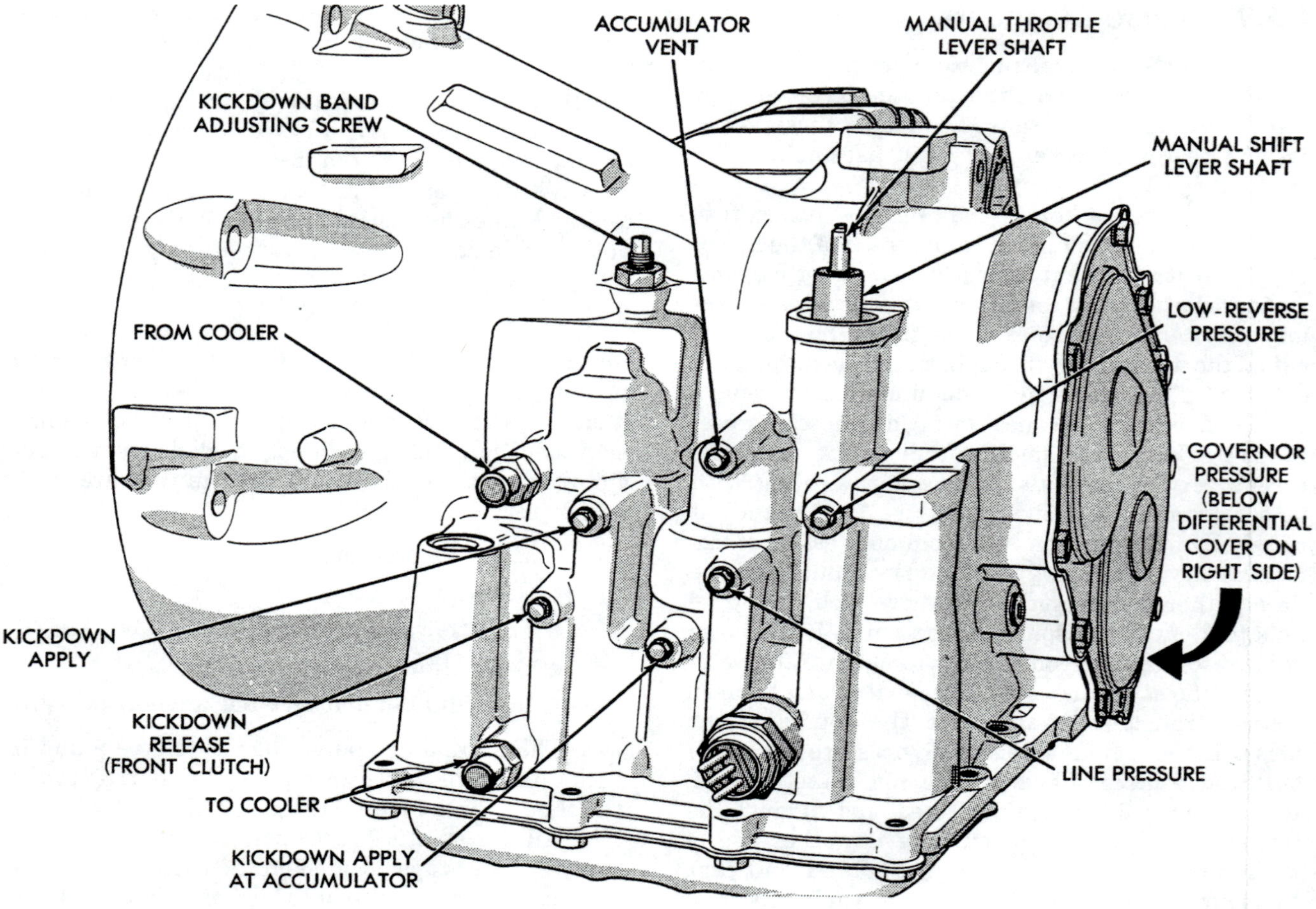

FIGURE 7–29 Chrysler transaxle pressure test points. (Courtesy of Chrysler)

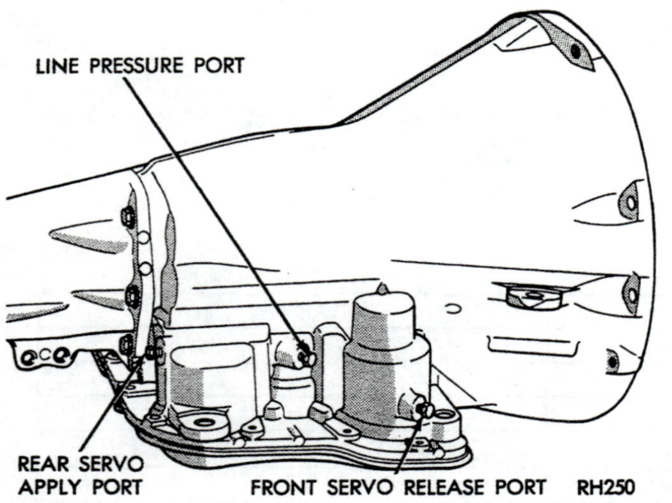

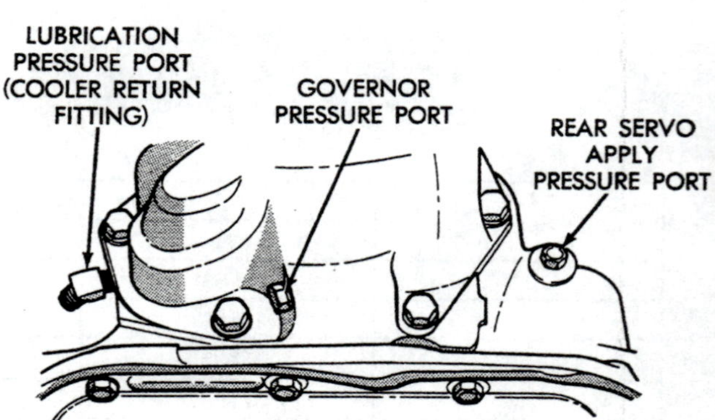

FIGURE 7–30 Chrysler Torque Flite RWD transmission pressure test points. (Courtesy of Chrysler)

The number of test points on Chrysler transmissions can vary from three to seven. The pressures checked are:

1. front servo release pressure
2. line pressure
3. low reverse pressure
4. governor pressure
5. lubrication pressure
6. kickdown apply at accumulator
7. kickdown apply at servo

In most cases you do not need to take pressure readings at all the test points, but only at the circuits that are involved in the problem. The main line pressure should be checked first since it is the hydraulic power source. If the main line pressure is low, then all the other pressures will be low also. Remember that low pressure reduces the holding force on the clutches and bands which will allow them to slip. The pressure test points for a Torque Flite RWD transmission are shown in Figure 7–30.

1. Test Equipment
The equipment that is needed to pressure test a transmission will vary according to transmission design. The basic test equipment that is used is a 0 to 50-psi pressure gauge, a 0 to 100-psi pressure gauge, a 0 to 350-psi pressure gauge, a hand-held engine tachometer, a *vacuum gauge,* and a vacuum hand pump (Figure 7–31). The various gauges need the proper-length hoses and proper adapter to connect to the transmission.

To simplify the job of transmission pressure testing, special test equipment is available. The testers include the same individual gauges mentioned earlier, mounted in a case (Figure 7–32). Instructions for using testers are found in the factory service manual. Connecting the gauges to the proper test points is critical, so follow the factory instructions to the letter. A typical installation of a *transmission tester* on a THM 700-R4 transmission is shown in Figure 7–33. Another type of tester is shown in Figure 7–34 connected to a Ford Jatco transmission.

2. Test Procedures
Because the exact test procedures for all transmissions are not the same, you must always refer to the manual for the specific procedure that applies to the transmission being tested.

This general *pressure test* procedure should be followed for testing all transmissions:

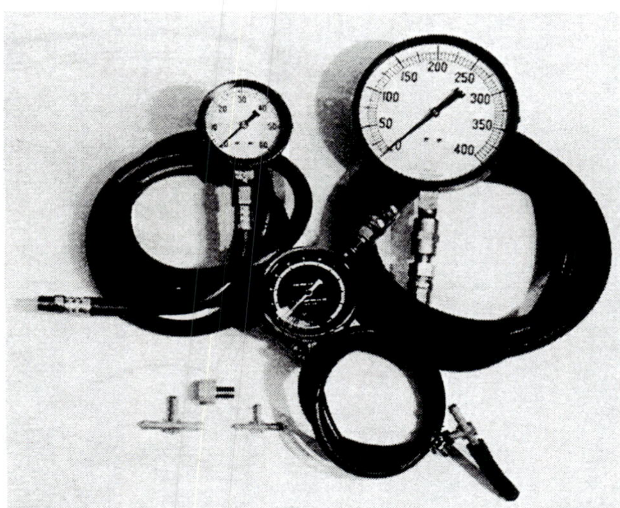

FIGURE 7–31 Test equipment used to pressure test a transmission.

1. Refer to the manual for the specific test procedure.

2. Copy the pressure specification onto the diagnostic checksheets.

3. Install the test equipment according to manual instructions.

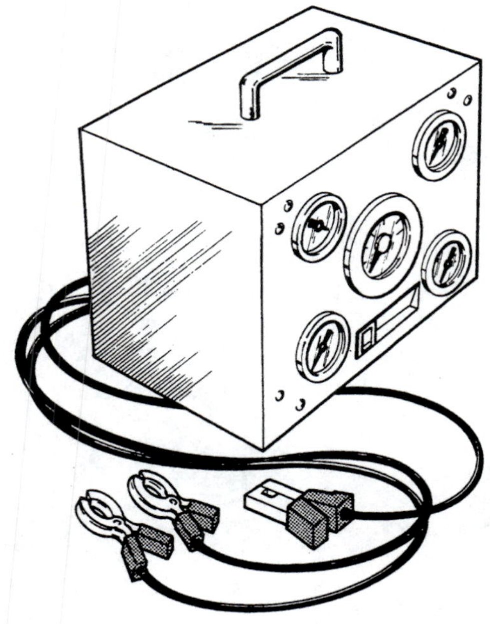

FIGURE 7–32 Drawing of a General Motors transmission tester. (Reprinted with permission of General Motors Corporation)

FIGURE 7–33 Transmission tester hooked up to a THM 700-R4 transmission.

700-R4 ILLUSTRATED
CAUTION
WHEN USING THE INDUCTION PICKUP CONNECT TO A PLUG WIRE THAT IS A SAFE DISTANCE FROM A HEAT SOURCE, SUCH AS THE EXHAUST MANIFOLD.
CAUTION
BEWARE OF EXTREME ENGINE HEAT. SOME ADAPTERS ARE MADE OUT OF PLASTIC AND RUBBER TUBING.

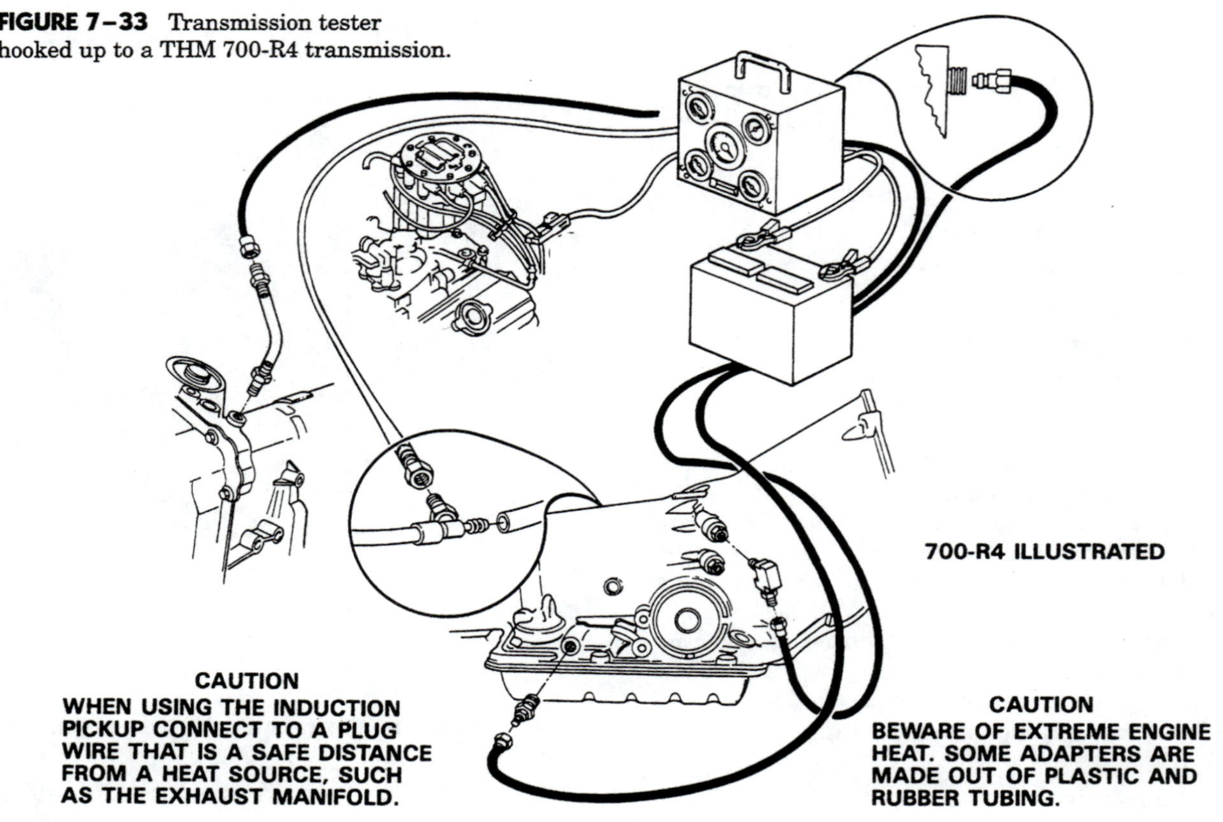

FIGURE 7–34 Ford tester hooked up to a Jatco transmission. (Courtesy of Ford)

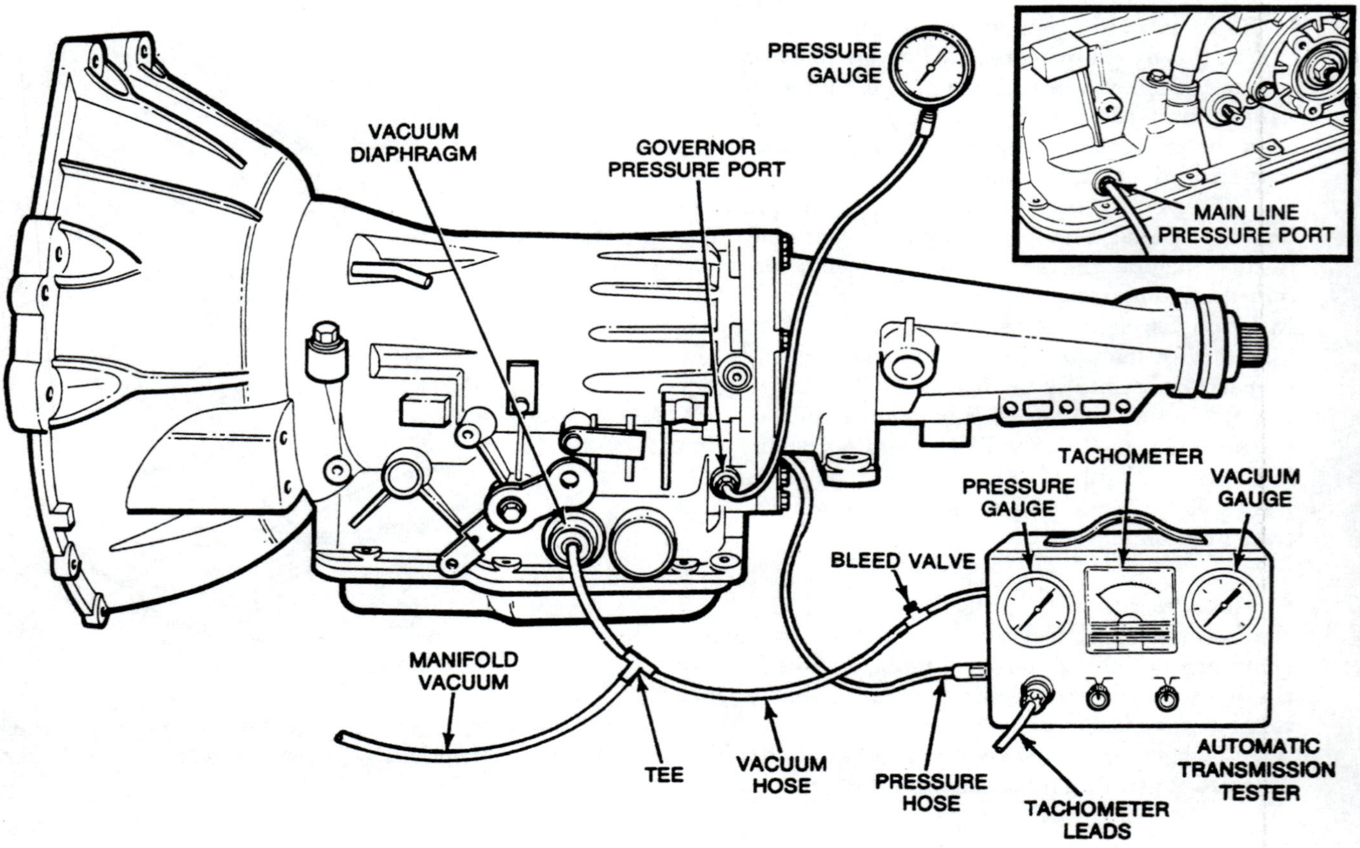

PRESSURE GAUGE
VACUUM DIAPHRAGM
GOVERNOR PRESSURE PORT
MAIN LINE PRESSURE PORT
TACHOMETER
PRESSURE GAUGE
VACUUM GAUGE
BLEED VALVE
MANIFOLD VACUUM
TEE
VACUUM HOSE
PRESSURE HOSE
TACHOMETER LEADS
AUTOMATIC TRANSMISSION TESTER

4. Check the test equipment for leaks.

5. Check the ATF level and warm the vehicle to operating temperature.

6. Operate the vehicle, either by road testing or in the shop on jack stands.

7. Follow the test procedure steps listed in the manual.

8. Record the test data on a diagnostic check sheet.

9. Compare the test results with the diagnostic charts in the manual to pinpoint the problem.

10. Make a decision as to service recommendations.

3. Test Results

The diagnostic charts found in the factory service manuals are very useful in interpreting the test results and should always be used when available. If the main line pressure is below specification, a pump or pressure regulator problem is indicated. The throttle valve operation could also be at fault. The full list of possible problem areas listed in the diagnostic charts must be checked out. A low-pressure reading in only one hydraulic circuit usually indicates an internal leak in that circuit from a torn piston seal or worn sealing ring. During disassembly special attention should be paid to that circuit to find the failed part.

7.6.4 Stall Tests

The stall test is used to evaluate the holding power of clutch packs, bands, and torque converter operation. With the parking and service brakes fully applied and the wheels blocked, the transmission is tested in each gear range by opening the throttle momentarily and noting the rpm level to which the engine rises. **Warning:** Some manufacturers do not recommend this test for their vehicles because it puts extremely heavy loads on all transmission components and can easily cause damage if performed incorrectly. Always check the manual for the manufacturer's recommendations about using the stall test.

1. Test Equipment

The only test equipment needed to perform a stall test is a shop service manual to provide the proper rpm specifications and a tachometer. The tachometer should be installed according to instructions and placed where it can be seen from the driver's seat. The specifications for the stall test are usually stated as an rpm range with minimum and maximum amounts. After finding the specification in the manual, the maximum rpm value should be marked on the face of the tachometer with a grease pencil for easy reference. If a minimum rpm level is given, mark it also (Figure 7–35).

2. Test Procedures

The following steps for a stall test may differ for various vehicles. Always read the procedures described in the factory service manual. Most stall tests will include these steps:

1. Check the engine coolant and ATF levels and correct if low.

2. Warm the engine coolant and ATF to the operating temperature.

3. Block both sides of the drive wheels with wheel chocks.

4. Hook up the engine tachometer.

5. Look up the stall specification in the manual.

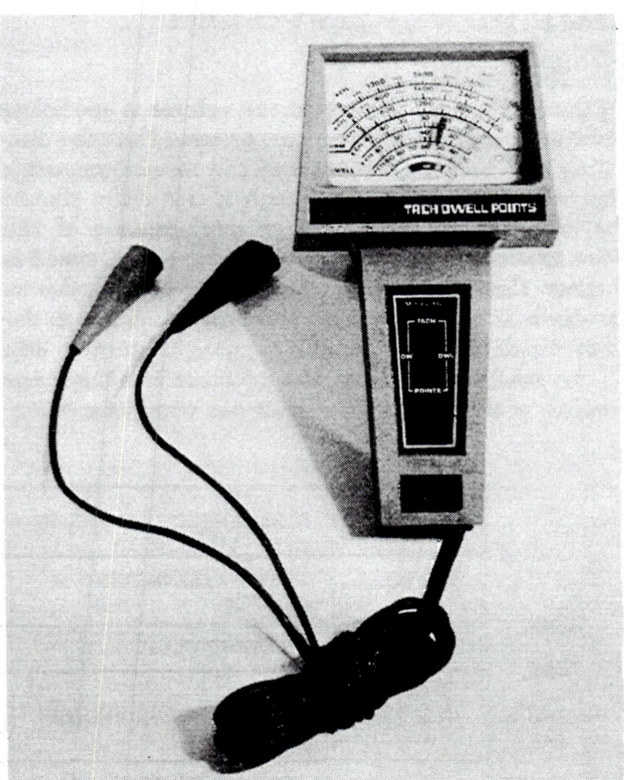

FIGURE 7–35 Marking the maximum rpm value on the face of the tachometer will make stall testing easier.

6. Mark the test rpm value on the face of the tachometer with a grease pencil.

7. Start the engine.

8. Place the selector in the first gear range to be tested.

9. Apply the parking and service brakes fully.

10. Open the throttle momentarily to the wide-open position while watching the tachometer.

11. As soon as the tachometer needle stops moving, note the rpm level and release the throttle immediately.

12. If the needle moves past the maximum rpm mark on the tachometer, release the throttle.

13. In no case should the throttle be held open for more than 5 seconds.

14. Record the test results on the diagnostic sheet.

15. Place the transmission in neutral and run the engine at approximately 1000 rpm for a few minutes to cool the fluid.

16. Go back to step 8 and place the gear selector in the next range and repeat steps 9 through 15 until all gear ranges have been tested.

3. Test Results

If the test results show that the vehicle is operating within specifications, you can assume that the coupling and holding devices and the torque converter are working properly, although a test drive should be included to verify proper performance of the transmission in all gear ranges. If the stall speed is higher than normal, a coupling or holding-device problem is indicated. Use a diagnostic chart to decide which clutch or band is slipping (Figure 7–36). If the stall speed is low, the problem is either poor engine performance or the torque converter stator one-way clutch is malfunctioning. In this case a test drive will also help analyze the decision. If the acceleration is poor at all speeds, engine performance is the problem. If the acceleration is poor up to about 30 mph, then normal above that speed, the problem is a slipping stator one-way clutch. If the acceleration is normal at low speed but the vehicle cannot go faster than 50 to 60 mph with the engine overheating, the problem is a locked-up stator one-way clutch which will not allow the stator to rotate.

7.6.5 Throttle Valve Tests

As you remember, the throttle valve circuit provides the control pressure that represents engine load. Throttle valve pressure is low at engine idle or under light load. As the throttle is opened and engine load increases, the throttle valve pressure rises. If the throttle valve pressure is not correct, the transmission will not shift properly and the mainline pressure could be either high or low. There are two types of throttle valve actuating systems in current use. One design uses a cable that connects the carburetor or injector throttle plate linkage to the throttle valve in the transmission. The other system uses engine vacuum to power a vacuum modulator which moves the throttle valve. On some transmissions both systems are used (Figure 7–37).

1. Test Equipment

To perform throttle valve pressure tests you attach a 0 to 300-psi gauge to the mainline pressure test point. If the transmission has a vacuum modulator, a *vacuum hand pump* will be needed along with a vacuum gauge. Since most transmissions do not have a test point for testing throttle valve pressure, mainline pressure is read to see if the pressure boost that is caused by throttle pressure is working properly.

	SELECTOR POSITION	STALL SPEEDS HIGH (SLIP)	STALL SPEEDS LOW
STALL TEST RESULTS	D ONLY	TRANSMISSION ONE-WAY CLUTCH	
	D, 2 & 1	FORWARD CLUTCH	
	D, 2, 1 & R	CONTROL PRESSURE TEST	CONVERTER STATOR ONE-WAY CLUTCH OR ENGINE PERFORMANCE
	R ONLY	HIGH AND REVERSE CLUTCH OR LOW-REVERSE CLUTCH	

FIGURE 7–36 Stall test diagnostic chart. (Courtesy of Ford)

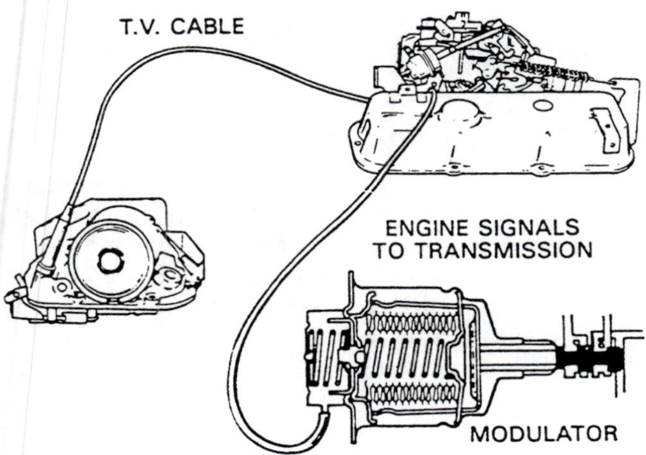

FIGURE 7–37 The THM 4T60 transaxle uses a throttle valve cable and vacuum modulator. (Reprinted with permission of General Motors Corporation)

2. Test Procedures

If the vehicle is equipped with a vacuum modulator, the first thing to check is the vacuum at the modulator. Raise the vehicle and place it on a jack stand so that a creeper can be used to reach the underside of the transmission. Avoid going under the vehicle when the engine is running but if you must, use extreme caution and be aware of all moving parts. *Tee* a vacuum gauge into the vacuum line at the modulator (Figure 7–38) and take a reading. The vacuum reading should be the same as a reading taken directly from the intake manifold. The standard vacuum readings should read between 14 and 22 in.Hg if taken at sea level; for every 1000 ft of elevation above sea level, subtract 1 in. of vacuum from the standard amount. If the vacuum is low, correct the problem and proceed with the test. Disconnect the regular vacuum line from the modulator and plug the vacuum line. Attach the vacuum hand pump to the modulator. Pump the vacuum pump until the gauge reads the same amount of vacuum as was indicated during the first part of the test. Block the wheels and set the parking brake, then start the engine and place the transmission in drive range and raise the engine speed to 1000 rpm. While watching the mainline pressure gauge, slowly release the vacuum from the hand pump (Figure 7–39). The mainline should raise as the vacuum is released and then should lower as the vacuum is pumped up again. Check service manuals for the proper specifications (Figure 7–40).

If the vehicle is equipped with a throttle valve cable, the same basic test can be performed by running the engine at around 1000 rpm and pulling on the throttle valve cable such that the valve is forced

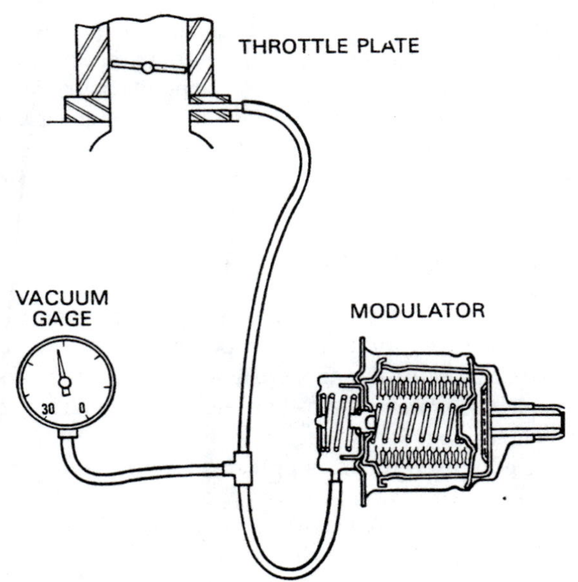

FIGURE 7–38 Vacuum gauge installed in the vacuum modulator line. (Reprinted with permission of General Motors Corporation)

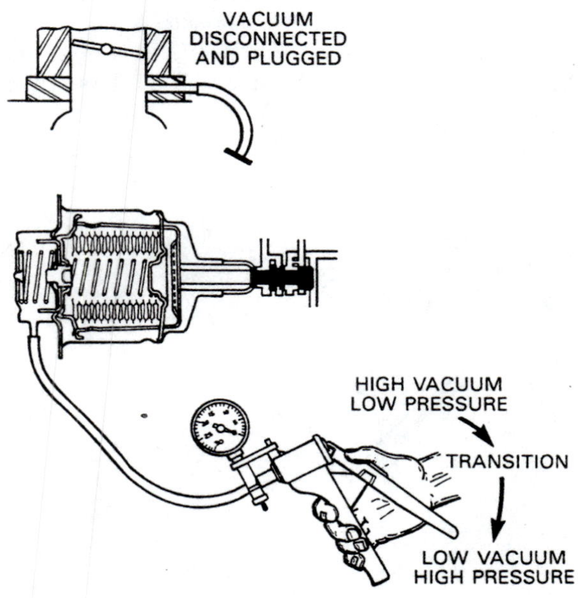

FIGURE 7–39 A hand vacuum pump can be used to check the pressure boost function. (Reprinted with permission of General Motors Corporation)

MODULATOR SYSTEM EVALUATION CHART (Consult H.D.S. For Specific Models)		
VACUUM @ MOD (IN/Hg)	LINE PRESSURES	
	*KPA	*PSI
0	1145	166
2	1020	148
4	895	130
6	770	112
8	645	94
10	520	75
12	450	65
14	450	65
*(+ or − 35 KPA)/(+ or − 5 PSI)		

FIGURE 7–40 Mainline pressure chart. (Reprinted with permission of General Motors Corporation)

open. This rise in TV pressure should cause the mainline pressure to rise also.

3. Test Results
If the mainline pressure increase goes according to the manual specifications, the system is working properly. If, while testing the vacuum modulator with the vacuum pump, you found that the modulator would not hold a vacuum, the unit has a vacuum leak and must be replaced (Figure 7–41). If the inside of the vacuum hose and its connection on the vacuum modulator are wet with ATF, the modulator must be replaced. On vehicles using cables, the free operation of the cable should be checked

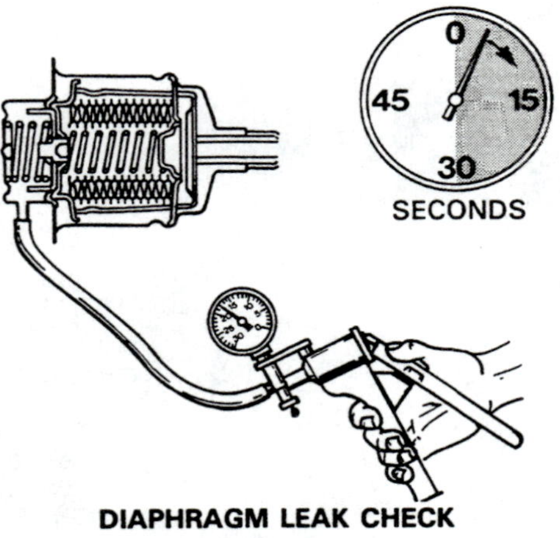

FIGURE 7–41 A vacuum hand pump is used to test for a leaking diaphragm. (Reprinted with permission of General Motors Corporation)

and any problems corrected before adjusting the cable. The adjustment procedure is covered in Chapter 8.

7.6.6 Governor Tests

Since the governor circuit provides the control pressure that reflects the speed of the vehicle, this test must be performed either during a road test or with the vehicle raised on jack stands. **Warning:** Some manufacturers do not recommend testing their FWD transaxles on jack stands because of the extreme U-joint angles present under this condition.

1. Test Equipment
The only gauge necessary is a pressure gauge with enough capacity to handle the maximum pressure shown in the manual specifications. This gauge is connected to the governor test point on the transmission case. Position the gauge so that it is easily visible from the driver's seat, then proceed with the test.

2. Test Results
Slowly increase the vehicle speed while watching the pressure gauge. Look for a smooth increase in pressure as the speed increases and also a smooth decrease as the speed is reduced. The manufacturer's service manual should be checked for specifications and procedure recommendations.

3. Test Procedures
If the governor pressure readings are in specifications with a smooth rise and fall in pressure, the system is operating properly. If the pressure is high or low or has a rough increase or decrease, the governor must be examined and repaired so that it can move freely. The repair procedures are discussed in Chapter 8.

7.6.7 Cooler Flow Tests

There are two basic tests used to determine if the ATF cooler is functioning properly. A flow test and a pressure test are used to provide information about cooler and transmission operation. If the ATF cooler becomes clogged for any reason, the result will be reduced flow and less pressure in the lubrication circuit of the transmission. The reduced flow will also raise the operating temperature of the fluid and decrease fluid service life.

1. Test Equipment
To measure the cooler flow rate, you will need a quart container, a stopwatch, and a short piece of

$\frac{3}{8}$-inch hose. To perform the pressure test, a *low-pressure gauge* and the necessary fitting to tee into the cooler lines will be needed. Check the manual to help select the proper gauge.

2. *Test Procedures*
The flow test is performed by disconnecting the cooler return line fitting at the transmission. The short piece of hose is slipped over the end of the tubing so that the flow can be directed into the container. First add 2 quarts of ATF to the transmission, let the engine run for 30 seconds, and then stop the engine. Next, check the amount of fluid in the container. The normal amount for General Motors transmissions is approximately 3 quarts, with Chrysler and Ford transmissions flowing about 2 quarts. The minimum acceptable flow is one-half the normal flow rate. As always, check the service manual for specific information about the vehicle that is being tested. Once the flow test is completed, the adapter fitting for the low-pressure (0 to 50) gauge is installed between the transmission and return cooler line. With the gauge in place, you can read the cooler return line pressure.

3. *Test Results*
If the flow test shows insufficient flow, the cooler is partially blocked and must be back flushed and blown out with low-pressure (30 psi) compressed air. After cleaning the cooler, another flow test should be performed to verify the repair. If the cooler remains blocked, it should be repaired at a radiator shop.

The pressure test can have a wide range of results, but as a general rule if the pressure is below 10 psi, the cooler could be restricted. The service manual must be used to provide the normal pressure range.

Any restriction of flow through the cooler will increase the operating temperature of the fluid and shorten the service life of the transmission. All cooler flow problems must be corrected as soon as they are diagnosed.

7.6.8 Converter Clutch Tests

Diagnosing converter clutch problem can be a big task. Some of the common complaints that customers have are total lack of converter clutch application, converter clutch will not disengage and stalls the engine when stopping, early or late application of the converter clutch, early or late release of the converter clutch, converter clutch shutter during application, or underacceleration. Because the hydraulic converter clutch systems are so complex, there are many different areas that must be tested (Figure 7–42). The areas fall into the following groups:

DIAGNOSTIC TEST AREAS FOR TORQUE CONVERTER CLUTCH PROBLEMS
1. COMPUTERIZED ENGINE CONTROLS
2. ENGINE MECHANICAL CONDITION
3. TRANSMISSION ELECTRICAL SYSTEM
4. CONVERTER CLUTCH HYDRAULIC SYSTEM

FIGURE 7–42 Torque converter clutch tests fall into four areas.

1. Computerized engine controls
2. Engine mechanical condition
3. Transmission electrical system
4. Converter clutch hydraulic system

1. *Test Equipment*
To perform most of the computerized engine control tests, the following test equipment is used:

1. *Scan tool*
2. Digital volt-ohmmeter (high impedance)
3. Tachometer
4. *Test light*
5. *Jumper wires*
6. Vacuum gauge
7. Vacuum pump

Basic engine evaluation test equipment is needed for the mechanical condition tests, which includes the following:

1. Electronic engine analyzer
2. Compression gauge
3. Cylinder leakage gauge
4. Vacuum gauge

The transmission electrical system tests use the following test equipment:

1. Analog volt-ohmmeter (low impedance)
2. Test light
3. Jumper wires
4. Special electrical test equipment

The converter clutch hydraulic system tests use the following test equipment:

1. A 0 to 50-psi gauge
2. Adapter fittings

The sheer amount and type of test equipment listed above should indicate the complexity of diagnosing the torque converter clutch system.

2. Test Procedures
Because of the many different types and designs of converter clutch systems, it is best to rely on the manufacturer's service manual for the exact tests and procedures recommended for each type of transmission. A thorough knowledge of the operation of the particular converter clutch system being tested is also essential.

3. Test Results
The test data collected from the four test areas are used with the diagnostic charts found in the factory service manuals to pinpoint the malfunction.

Because of the design differences between systems, only the recommended test procedures and diagnostic charts should be used for diagnosis. By following the factory recommendations closely, the difficult job of diagnosing converter clutch problems accurately is simplified.

7.6.9 Electronic Control Tests

Use of the on-board computer to control the shifting of the transmission has added an entirely new area of diagnosis. Before computer control, only the hydraulic and mechanical systems needed to be diagnosed, but now the electronic system must also be checked.

The electronic control system uses shift solenoids to control the pressure in the circuit, which moves the shift valves. Most electronic transmissions (as they are called) have two shift solenoids, which are turned on and off by the computer in the proper sequence to provide the next gear in the upshift or downshift. The design and operation of the computer control systems varies between manufacturers, so consequently their test procedures are also different.

Some of the most advanced electronic transmissions include a self-diagnosis program in the control computer. Whenever one of the transmission sensors is producing a signal that is out of the normal operational range, the computer will store a fault code. This fault code can be retrieved in the same manner as engine trouble codes. The fault code diagnostic chart shown in Figure 7–43 is used after the code is retrieved to find the problem area. One electronic transmission also includes a fail-safe system that will lock the transmission in second or third gear after the computer has counted certain fault codes occurring for the fourth time. This will alert the vehicle owner to have service performed before extensive damage is done to the transmission. The fail-safe code descriptions are shown in Figure 7–44.

1. Electronic Troubleshooting Procedures
This type of procedure is designed for each individual transmission, so always find the proper procedure in a service manual for the transmission being tested. Two different basic approaches are used to isolate the problem. With some electronic transmissions the computer wiring to the transmission can be disconnected and the vehicle road tested while shifting the transmission manually. A systematic testing of upshifts and downshifts using the gear selector is used to verify operation of the mechanical and hydraulic systems. If those systems prove to be working, the problem is in the electronics.

The other method of troubleshooting involves testing operation of the shift solenoid valves by disconnecting them from the computer and using jumper wires to activate the solenoids. The vehicle is raised on jack stands and with the engine running, the solenoids are "hot wired" in the proper sequence to provide each gear. Factory service manual procedures must be followed closely to avoid damage to the electronic components. If the transmission performs properly during the hot-wire tests, the problem is located in the electronics and that system must be diagnosed.

The use of a computer to control the automatic transmission has improved its performance just as computer engine controls have improved engine performance and fuel economy. The drawback comes when the computer control system has a malfunction because it requires a totally different diagnostic procedure.

7.6.10 Air Tests

Air tests provide the technician with a means of checking the operation of hydraulic system components while the transmission is not operating. Compressed air that is regulated to the recommended pressure is applied to selected points of the hydraulic circuits once the valve body has been removed (Figure 7–45). The force of the compressed air will apply the piston or servo that is being tested. If the seals of the piston are good, a "thud" will be heard as the piston is applied. After piston application, very little air should be heard leaking from the circuit. There is usually a small amount of air leakage, but a large leak indicates a failed seal, which will also prevent the piston from applying.

Output code		Diagnosis item	Remarks
No.	Display pattern		
25		Open circuit or poor contact in kickdown servo switch	
26		Short circuit in kickdown servo switch	
27		Open circuit in ignition pulse pickup cable	
28	 12A0107	Short circuit in accelerator switch or poor adjustment	
31		Computer fault	Fail-safe item
32	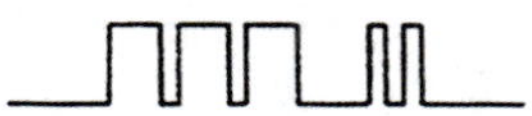	1st gear commanded when driving at high speed	Fail-safe item
33	 12R0468	Open circuit in pulse generator B	Fail-safe item
41		Open circuit in shift control solenoid valve A	Fail-safe item
42	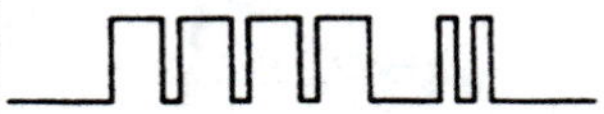	Short circuit in shift control solenoid valve A	Fail-safe item
43	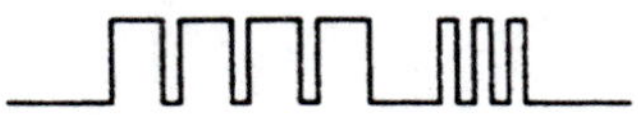	Open circuit in shift control solenoid valve B	Fail-safe item
44	 12A0105	Short circuit in shift control solenoid valve B	Fail-safe item

FIGURE 7–43 KM-176 fault code chart. (Courtesy of Chrysler)

Output code		Item	Fail-safe	Remarks (Relationship to the self diagnosis function)
No.	Display pattern			
11		Microprocessor failure	Locked in 3rd gear	When code No. 31 has occurred 4 or more times.
12		1st gear commanded when driving at high speed	Locked in 3rd (D) or 2nd (2, L) gear	When code No. 32 has occurred 4 or more times.
13		Open circuit in pulse generator B	Locked in 3rd (D) or 2nd (2, L) gear	When code No. 33 has occurred 4 or more times.
14		Open or short circuit in shift control solenoid valve A	Locked in 3rd gear	When code No. 41 or 42 has occurred 4 or more times.
15		Open or short circuit in shift control solenoid valve B	Locked in 3rd gear	When code No. 43 or 44 has occurred 4 or more times.
16		Open or short circuit in pressure control solenoid valve	Locked in 3rd (D) or 2nd (2, L) gear	When code No. 45 or 46 has occurred 4 or more times.
17		Gear shifting out of synchronization	Locked in 3rd (D) or 2nd (2, L) gear	When code No. 51, 52, 53 or 54 has occurred 4 or more times

FIGURE 7–44 KM-176 fail-safe code chart. (Courtesy of Chrysler)

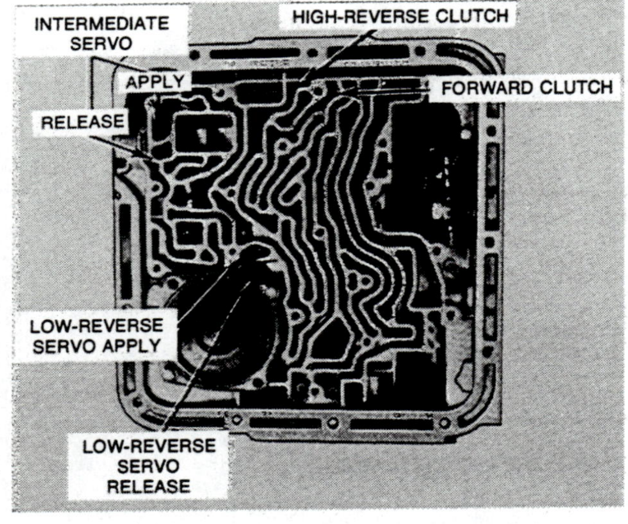

FIGURE 7–45 Air testing a transmission. (Courtesy of Ford)

Turning the compressed air on and off will cause the piston to cycle back and forth between application and release. By repeating a few of these cycles on each piston and servo, you will test the return spring action as well as the seals. Any loud hiss of air escaping while the air is applied indicates a hydraulic leak in that particular circuit.

1. Test Equipment

A number of different types of air nozzles can be used for air testing. The first type uses a piece of curved tubing with the end cut at a 45° angle. In Figure 7–46 you see two types of air nozzles, one with a cone-shaped rubber tip and the other type mentioned before. An air pressure regulator is also needed to control the maximum air pressure used for the tests (Figure 7–47).

Some transmissions require the use of an air *test plate,* which bolts to the transmission case in

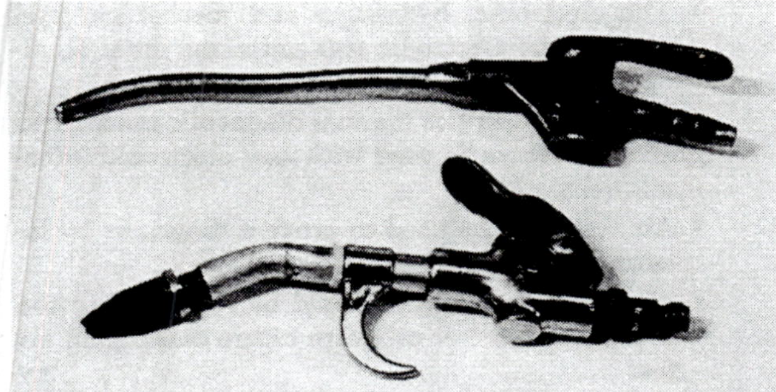

FIGURE 7–46 Two types of air test nozzles.

FIGURE 7–47 An air regulator is used to control the maximum air pressure used in air testing.

the same position as the valve body. This plate seals the hydraulic circuits in the case, which are exposed when the valve body is removed. An air test plate for a Ford AOD transmission is shown in Figure 7–48.

2. Test Procedures
The specific test procedures of the transmission being tested should always be looked up in the service manual first since the procedures can change for different transmissions. For most transmissions the air test procedures should include the following steps:

1. Read the specifications and procedures in the manual.
2. Support the vehicle on jack stands.
3. Remove the pan and valve body.
4. Install the air test plate if necessary.
5. Adjust the pressure regulator to the proper pressure.
6. Apply air pressure to the test point.
7. Listen for the "thud" of the piston.
8. Listen for the hissing noise of an air leak.
9. Cycle the air on and off a few times to test the return spring action.
10. Write down the test results.

FIGURE 7–48 Air test plate for Ford AOD transmission.

RESULTS/CONCLUSIONS

PASSAGE	TESTS OK IF	LEAKING IF
Reverse-and-High Clutch	Dull thud or you can feel piston movement at the clutch drum.	Hissing or no piston movement.
Forward Clutch	Dull thud or you can feel piston movement on the input shell.	Hissing or no piston movement.
Intermediate Servo Apply	Front band tightens.	Hissing or no application.
Intermediate Servo Release	Band releases while applying pressure to both passages 6 and 7.	Hissing or no band release.
Low-and-Reverse Servo Apply	Rear band tightens.	Hissing or no band apply.
Low-and-Reverse Servo Release	No sound of air escaping.	Hissing.
Governor Supply	Click, whistle, or buzz.	Hissing only.

3. *Test Results*

A good air test will apply the piston with a dull thud and there will be very little air loss with no loud hissing sounds. A servo will not make the same thud, but its operation can be watched as the band is applied. Any loud hissing sound indicates a leak in that particular hydraulic circuit. All the seals, sealing rings, and gaskets in that circuit must be inspected to locate the leak.

SUMMARY

The following summary points cover the most important ideas from each section of this chapter.

- To provide the best diagnosis of an automatic transmission problem, information should be gathered from four sources:
  1. Question the customer.
  2. Diagnose the fluid.
  3. Check the condition of the vehicle.
  4. Road test the vehicle.
- Use factory service manual diagnostic charts to make service recommendations.
- If more information is needed, perform additional tests before making service recommendations.
- The three types of tests used to diagnose leaks are: visual, powder, and dye.
- Hearing devices can be used to find transmission noise.
- Pressure tests provide a way to measure the performance of each hydraulic circuit.
- The stall test provides a dynamic test of the holding ability of the clutches and bands.
- Some manufacturers do not recommend use of the stall test.
- Throttle valve operation can be checked by measuring mainline pressure while the TV cable or vacuum modulator is operated to cause mainline boost.
- The governor pressure should be tested for proper pressure and for a sticking valve.
- The fluid cooler should be tested for volume and pressure.
- Converter clutch problems can be in the electronic control system as well as the hydraulic system.
- The most advanced electronic transmissions have a fail-safe system that locks the transmission in second or third gear after a critical fault code occurs for the fourth time.
- The electronic, hydraulic, and mechanical systems of the electronic transmissions must be diagnosed separately.
- The factory service manual diagnostic procedures should always be used with new electronic transmissions.
- Air tests can be used to prove a diagnosis by locating the leaking seal.
- Shop compressed air should be regulated to the recommended test pressure before making an air test.
- Always refer to the factory service manual for specific instructions about the vehicle being tested.

SELF-TEST

Before going on to the next chapter, complete the self-test according to your instructor's directions. Read carefully and choose the best answer.

1. Technician A says, "Since most customers don't know much about cars, you can't trust what they say about problems with the vehicle." Technician B says, "You can learn a lot about the problems of a vehicle by asking the owner questions." Who is right?

a. A only
b. B only
c. Both A and B
d. Neither A nor B

2. To reach the best diagnosis of a transmission malfunction, information about the problem should be gathered from ________________ areas.

a. One
b. Two
c. Three
d. Four

3. Technician A says, "The purpose of questioning the customer is to help pinpoint the type of malfunction." Technician B says, "You must pinpoint the type of transmission problem before choosing the diagnostic tests." Who is right?

a. A only
b. B only
c. Both A and B
d. Neither A nor B

4. Technician A says, "The fluid should always be diagnosed before doing any other tests." Technician B says, "Diagnosing the fluid and road testing are the only tests you need to make." Who is right?

a. A only
b. B only
c. Both A and B
d. Neither A nor B

5. Technician A says, "In some cases the information from the four testing areas is enough to base a diagnosis on." Technician B says, "In some cases the information from the four test areas is not enough and special tests must also be performed." Who is right?
   a. A only
   b. B only
   c. Both A and B
   d. Neither A nor B

6. Technician A says, "Most transmissions leak a little; it's nothing to worry about." Technician B says, "Any leak that isn't repaired can lead to a major failure." Who is right?
   a. A only
   b. B only
   c. Both A and B
   d. Neither A nor B

7. Technician A says, "The pitch or tone of a transmission noise can be used to help identify its source." Technician B says, "The driving conditions occurring while you are hearing the transmission noise can help identify the source of the problem." Who is right?
   a. A only
   b. B only
   c. Both A and B
   d. Neither A nor B

8. Technician A says, "Transmission pressure tests can be made at many different test points on the transmission case." Technician B says, "One good high-pressure gauge is all you need to make any transmission pressure test." Who is right?
   a. A only
   b. B only
   c. Both A and B
   d. Neither A nor B

9. Technician A says, "The stall test is a good way to test for slipping clutches." Technician B says, "Stall testing can damage a transmission and some manufacturers recommend not using it on their transmissions." Who is right?
   a. A only
   b. B only
   c. Both A and B
   d. Neither A nor B

10. Technician A says, "The throttle valve linkage is only used to make a 3–2 downshift." Technician B says, "If the throttle valve linkage is not adjusted properly, the main line pressure can be too high or too low." Who is right?
    a. A only
    b. B only
    c. Both A and B
    d. Neither A nor B

11. Technician A says, "If the governor pressure is below normal, the transmission will not upshift or downshift properly." Technician B says, "Governor pressure is not used in some transmissions." Who is right?
    a. A only
    b. B only
    c. Both A and B
    d. Neither A nor B

12. Technician A says, "When doing a cooler flow test you should check both flow and pressure." Technician B says, "If the fluid cooler becomes blocked, the bypass circuit will handle the fluid." Who is right?
    a. A only
    b. B only
    c. Both A and B
    d. Neither A nor B

13. Technician A says, "Some converter clutch control systems use electrical tests in their diagnosis." Technician B says, "Some transmissions use the cooler flow pressure to diagnose converter clutch operation." Who is right?
    a. A only
    b. B only
    c. Both A and B
    d. Neither A nor B

14. Technician A says, "Some electronic transmissions have a self-diagnosis feature." Technician B says, "The electronic sensors should be checked first." Who is right?
    a. A only
    b. B only
    c. Both A and B
    d. Neither A nor B

15. Technician A says, "Air testing is an excellent way to check clutch piston seals or servo seals." Technician B says, "Low air pressure should always be used to prevent seal damage." Who is right?
    a. A only
    b. B only
    c. Both A and B
    d. Neither A nor B

GLOSSARY

diagnostic chart chart found in the service manual that lists the problem, probable cause, and remedy.

diagnostic checksheet checksheet developed by manufacturers to provide a systematic approach to transmission diagnosis.

DVOM digital volt-ohmmeter.

high-pressure gauge pressure test gauge that will measure a maximum pressure of 350 to 400 psi.

leakage hydraulic fluid that gets past the seal in a hydraulic circuit.

no drive transmission condition in which the transmission will not engage in gear.

no shift transmission condition in which no upshifts will occur.

slippage condition that occurs when a clutch or band will not fully engage.

tee adapter that is used to splice a vacuum or pressure gauge into a line to take measurements.

test light electrical test tool that tests for electrical power in a circuit.

test plate (air test plate) adapter plate used to perform air tests on an automatic transmission.

throttle valve test pressure test designed to test the function of the throttle valve.

◀ Chapter 8 ▶

IN-CAR ADJUSTMENTS AND REPAIRS

INTRODUCTION

In this chapter you will study the minor in-car repairs and adjustments that can be performed without removing the transmission from the vehicle. Proper adjustment of the gear selector linkage is essential to operation of the transmission. Throttle valve linkage or cables must also be adjusted correctly or a major transmission failure may occur. Transmissions that require periodic band adjustments will display poor shift timing and engine flair or "buzz up" between gears when the bands are out of adjustment. Any time the adjustment of these devices is not within specification, the performance of the transmission is impaired, and in some cases, serious damage is the result.

In addition to the adjustments just mentioned, there are repair procedures that can be performed with the transmission still in the vehicle. Transmission problems that fall into the "not shifting" category can usually be repaired in the vehicle because the governor and throttle valve components, along with the valve body, are accessible on most transmissions without total disassembly. The amount and type of repairs that can be performed in-car varies greatly between transmissions. In this chapter we provide a general overview of in-car repair procedures.

8.1 PERFORMANCE OBJECTIVES

After studying this chapter, you should have fulfilled the following performance objectives by being able to:

1. Describe why gear selector linkage and throttle valve (TV) cables must be adjusted properly.
2. Describe how transmission bands are adjusted.
3. Explain what repairs can be performed on the governor.
4. Describe the repair procedures for the vacuum modulator and throttle valve.
5. Explain the service procedures used on the valve body.
6. Explain how to repair the transmission fluid cooler and lines.
7. Describe how to replace the output seal.
8. Complete all the competency objectives listed for this chapter.
9. Complete the self-test with at least the minimum score required by your instructor.

8.2 COMPETENCY OBJECTIVES

The competency objectives differ from the performance objectives in being more job related. The automotive terms must be well understood so that the theory will be clear. The terms are used to describe the service procedures outlined in Part II. The competency tasks are related to job skills needed to perform service and repair procedures and should be understood thoroughly.

8.2.1 Automotive Terms

The following list may include terms that are unfamiliar to you. Read the terms, then note their definitions as you study the chapter.

adjusting sleeve
adjusting slot
air pressure regulator
air test plate
Arkansas stone
cable linkage
column-mounte selector
compression union fitting
connecting pin

external adjustment screws
farrel
floor-mounted selector
drop-in governor
graduated rods
internal adjusting screws
locking nut
manual adjusting cable
modulator adjusting screw
neutral safety switch
reverse (back) flushing
rod linkage
scored valves
selector pawl
shaft-mounted governor

8.2.2 Competency Tasks

The competency tasks listed here are related directly to knowledge or skills needed to become a successful automatic transmission/transaxle technician. Be sure to complete all the tasks before going on to Chapter 9.

1. Adjust solid-type manual valve linkage on a vehicle with a steering-column-mounted gear selector.
2. Adjust cable-type manual valve linkage used with a floor- or column-mounted shifter.
3. Adjust rod-type throttle valve linkage.
4. Remove, inspect, repair, and adjust throttle valve cables on various makes of vehicles.
5. Adjust bands on various transmissions.
6. Remove, inspect, and repair the governor.
7. Remove, inspect, and repair the throttle valve.
8. Remove, inspect, test, and adjust different types of vacuum modulators.
9. Remove, disassemble, clean, reassemble, and install the valve body.
10. Flush fluid cooler and repair cooler lines.
11. Remove and replace the output shaft bushing and seal.

8.3 IN-CAR ADJUSTMENTS

For an automatic transmission to operate properly, all of the external control devices must be in good working order and adjusted to specification. It is clear that broken throttle valve cable will not move the throttle valve, and no TV pressure will be produced. However, if the throttle valve cable is working properly but is out of adjustment, the results can be as serious as a broken cable. If the cable breaks, the driver will notice a definite change in operation and will probably have it repaired, but with the cable out of adjustment, the driver will probably continue to drive the vehicle and could cause severe damage to the transmission. All transmission adjustments are important and should be checked according to the manufacturer's recommendations. Before making any adjustments, check the accelerator linkage for full opening of the throttle.

8.3.1 Manual Valve

The manual valve, which is located in the valve body, is the valve that controls which gear the transmission is in. The manual valve is moved through its different gear positions by either linkage rods or cables which are connected to the gear selector. The two types of gear selectors, column mounted and floor mounted, are designed with shift gates that act as selector stops to hold the shift lever in each gear position. Figure 8–1 shows how the pawl on the selector lever engages the stops on the shift gate. On the column shifter the gear selector lever must be pulled toward the driver first to release the pawl before moving the selector up or down to change the gear selection. All the parts of the gear selector mechanism should fit snugly together. If excess play is noted in the selector, the worn parts must be replaced to return the selector to its original condition (Figure 8–2). Before adjusting the manual valve linkage, always check the gear selector for proper operation and correct any faults before continuing the adjustment. All pivot points on rod-type linkage should also be checked for excess play. Replace bushings or linkage parts

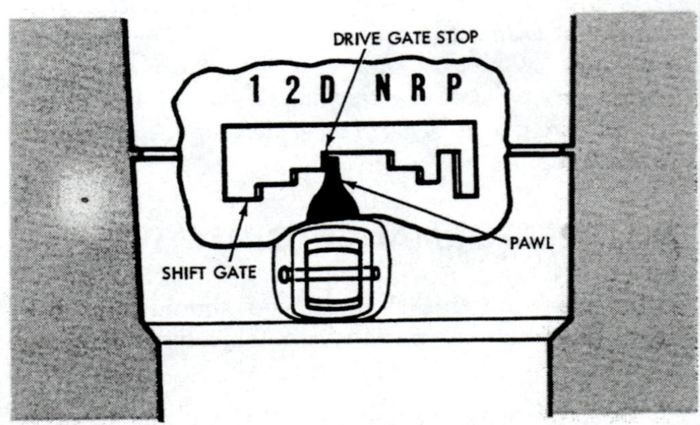

FIGURE 8–1 Selector pawl and selector gate. (Courtesy of Chrysler)

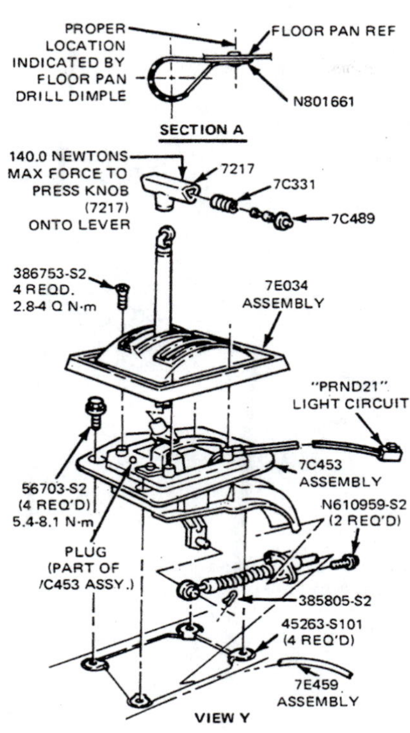

FIGURE 8–2 All gear selector parts should fit properly with minimum play. (Courtesy of Chrysler)

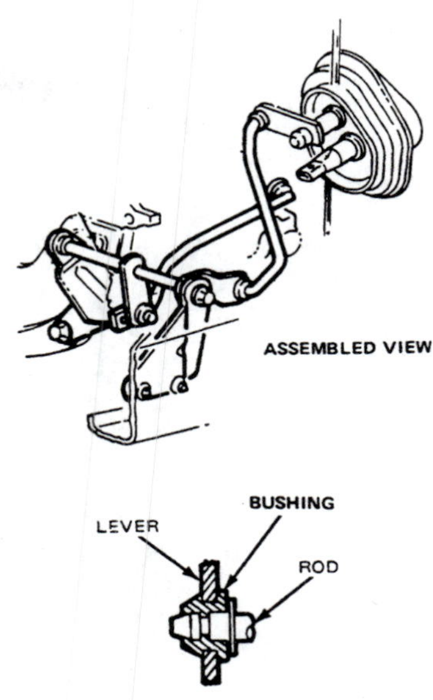

FIGURE 8–3 All linkage bushings should fit tightly or be replaced. (Courtesy of Ford)

as necessary to repair the linkage, as shown in Figure 8–3. On cable-equipped gear selectors, all cable mounting brackets must be firmly attached and the cables tightly secured to the brackets (Figure 8–4).

1. Adjusting Rod Linkage

The solid rod type of linkage used to connect the gear selector to the manual valve lever will always include some type of adjustment component to adjust the overall length of the linkage rod. There are two popular methods of making this adjustment. The first method, shown in Figure 8–5, uses a slot and clamping stud and nut. One end of a linkage rod is a flattened area with a long open slot down its center. A special stud, which is attached to another part of the linkage or the manual lever, sticks through the slot and uses the adjusting nut to clamp the rod to the stud. By loosening the adjusting nut, the stud can slide back and forth in the slot

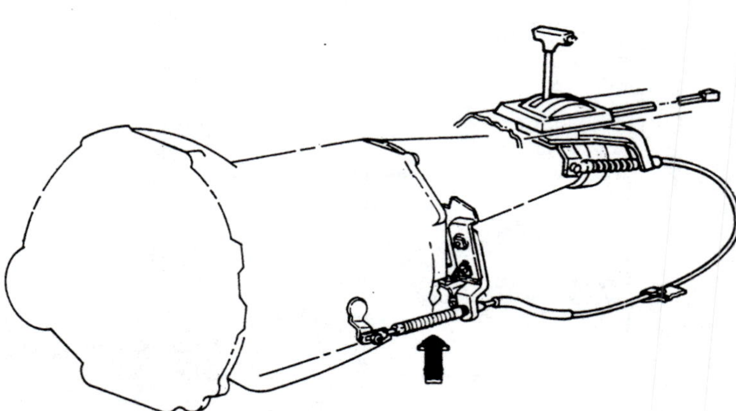

FIGURE 8–4 The mounting bracket and cable should be mounted securely. (Courtesy of Ford)

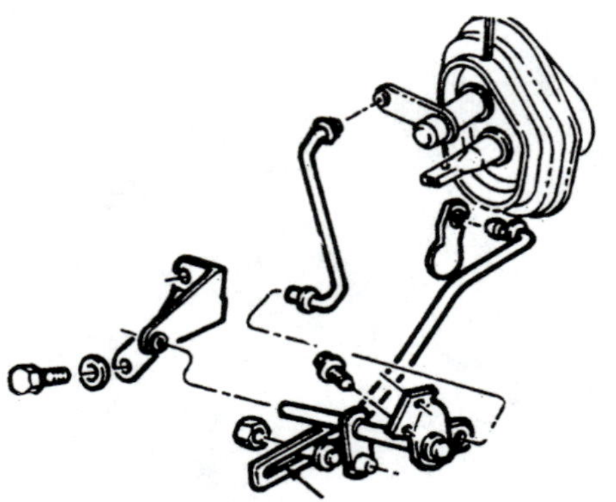

FIGURE 8–5 Linkage adjustment that uses a slotted rod with a clamping stud and nut. (Courtesy of Ford)

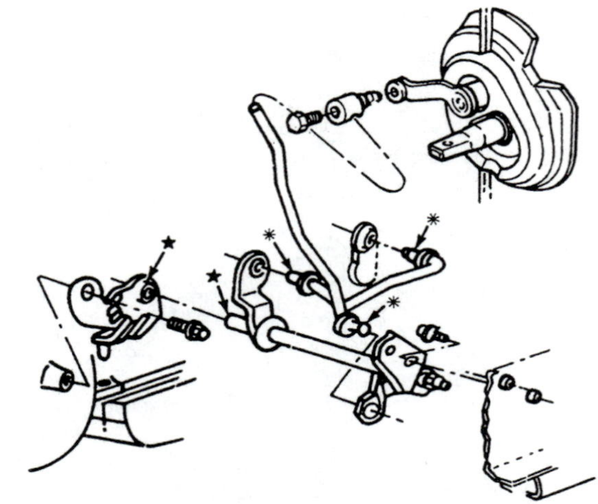

FIGURE 8–7 Adjustment sleeve adjuster. (Courtesy of Ford)

to adjust the length of the rod. Many floor-mounted gear selectors use this type of adjustment (Figure 8–6). Always use penetrating oil on the adjustment nut before trying to loosen it, to prevent twisting off the stud.

The other type of adjustment uses an adjustment sleeve, which can slide on the linkage rod and is clamped in place with a pinch bolt. This type of adjustment device is shown in Figure 8–7.

As always, the adjustment procedure for the vehicle being serviced should come from the service manual. Most adjustment procedures follow these basic steps.

1. Raise the vehicle if necessary.
2. Place the gear selector in drive (D).
3. Loosen the adjustment device on the linkage.
4. Move the manual lever to the end of its travel, then back up the proper number of detents until the transmission is in drive (D).
5. Check gear selector to make sure that it has not moved.
6. Tighten the adjusting device.
7. Test for proper operation.

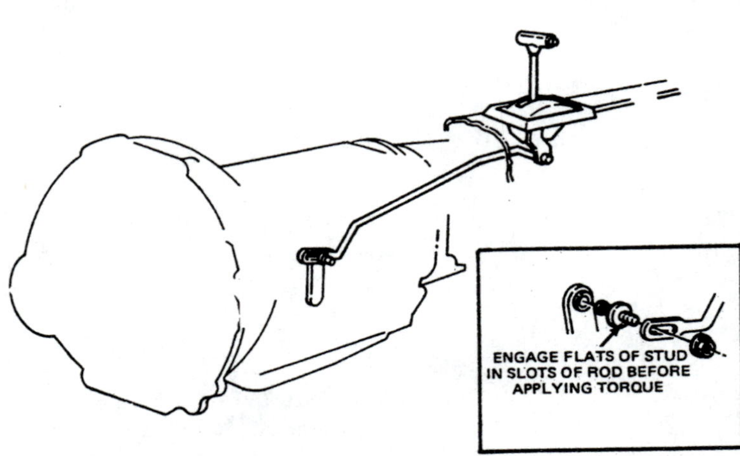

FIGURE 8–6 Floor shift control that uses a slotted rod adjustment. (Courtesy of Ford)

If the linkage does not perform properly, look for worn motor mounts, play in the gear selector, bent linkage rods, loose linkage pivot points, worn bushings, or defective manual valves detent spring.

2. Adjusting Cables

On many vehicles a selector cable has replaced the solid rod type of linkage. A cable has many advantages over other types of linkages, but it must be mounted securely or it will not operate properly. If the mounting brackets or cable housing connections are loose, the cable will not transfer movement as it is designed to do. Always tighten loose brackets and cable housing retaining nuts before trying to adjust the cable.

In this section we describe three types of cable adjustment devices that are representative of those used in the industry. The first type is the slotted cable end, which uses a stud and an adjustment nut. This is similar to the device used with rod linkage and is shown in Figure 8–8. The adjusting procedures for this device are the same as those used for rod linkage with *adjusting slots.*

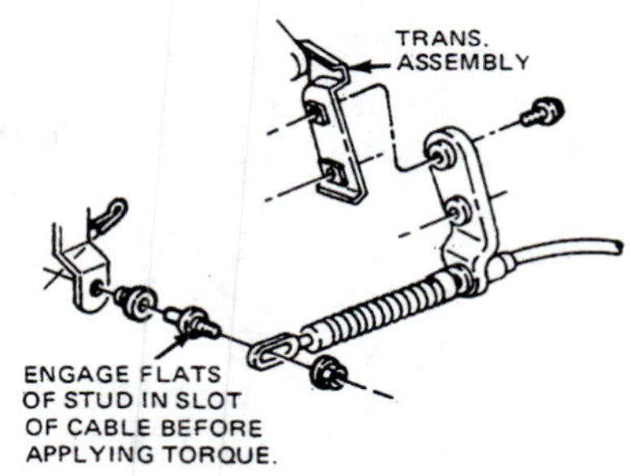

FIGURE 8–8 The slotted end of this cable is similar to the rod linkage described previously. (Courtesy of Ford)

The second type of cable adjustment uses an *adjusting sleeve* (Figure 8–9). The last few inches of the cable are threaded and the adjustment sleeve slides on over the threaded area. Two *locking nuts* are used, one on either side of the sleeve, to change the position of the sleeve, thereby adjusting its length.

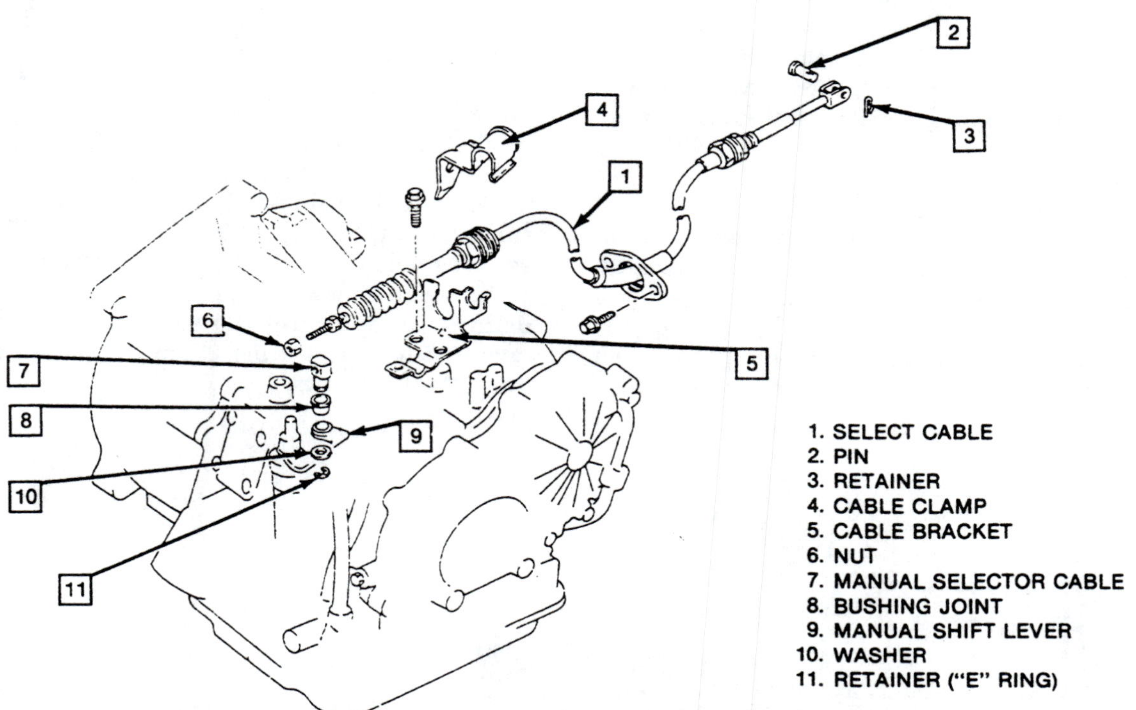

FIGURE 8–9 Sleeve adjuster that uses a locknut on each side of the sleeve to adjust its position on the cable. (Reprinted with permission of General Motors Corporation)

The third type of cable adjustment uses a self-adjusting device. This device has a locking clip that is released to adjust the cable housing length and then locked in to hold the cable adjustment. This type of adjustment is shown in Figure 8–10. There will be more information about this type of adjuster later in the unit.

The main purpose of all of these adjustment procedures is to make sure that the manual valve is positioned correctly in each gear. If the linkage keeps the detent from holding the manual valve in its proper position, problems will occur.

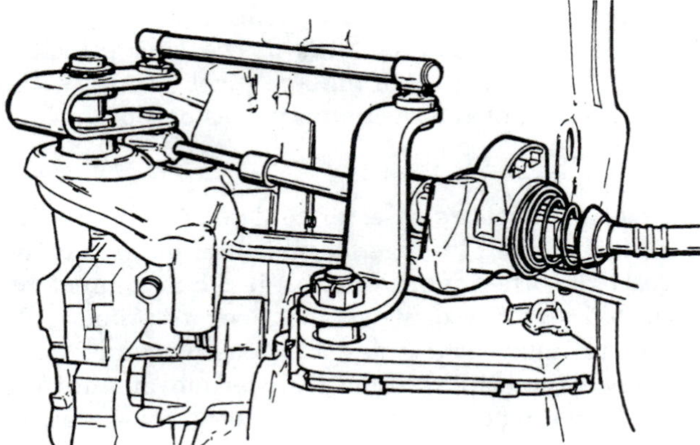

FIGURE 8–10 Cable adjuster with a self-adjustment feature. (Reprinted with permission of General Motors Corporation)

8.3.2 Throttle Valve

The throttle valve is used to modulate a control pressure that represents the engine load. Early automatic transmissions used a rod linkage to connect the carburetor throttle lever to the throttle valve in the transmission. With any change of throttle opening on the carburetor the throttle valve would respond accordingly. Later transmissions replaced the rod linkage with a vacuum modulator. Engine intake manifold vacuum is used to modulate the throttle valve to produce throttle pressure. Because the engine vacuum gives a better representation of engine load, transmission performance is improved.

Some of the latest automatic transmissions use a cable to operate the throttle valve. The general procedures for adjusting these three types of throttle valve operating devices are explained below.

1. Adjusting Rod Linkage

Throttle valve linkage rods have adjustment features similar to those used on manual valve linkage. On most vehicles equipped with this type of linkage, the adjustment is made by holding the throttle fully open (engine not running) and then adjusting the rod's length until the throttle valve is in the fully open position. Test the linkage for free movement and reinstall any return springs removed while making the adjustment. Refer to the service manual for the exact procedure before beginning the job.

2. Adjusting Vacuum Modulators

It might seem that there is nothing to adjust on a vacuum modulator, but that is not always the case. The vacuum modulator shown in Figure 8–11 has an adjustment screw located inside the modulator in the center of the diaphragm. By turning the screw in or out, the throttle pressure is adjusted up or down. This feature allows the technician to fine tune the shift timing of the transmission. Check the service manual to see which transmissions have the feature and follow the manufacturer's recommendations. In most cases the adjustments are made a quarter-turn at a time, then pressure-tested to evaluate the results.

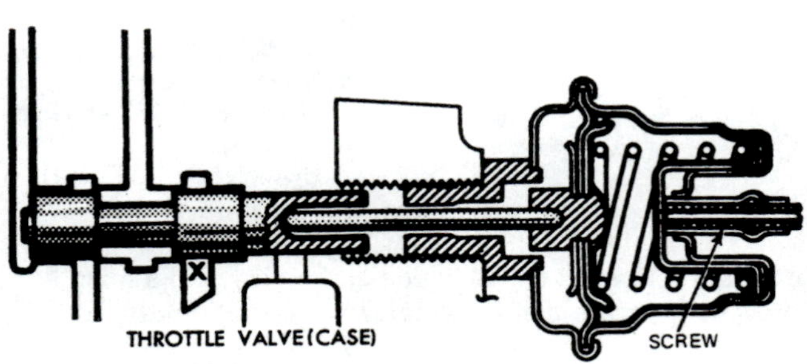

FIGURE 8–11 Vacuum modulator with internal adjustment of the throttle pressure. Follow service manual procedures in making adjustments.

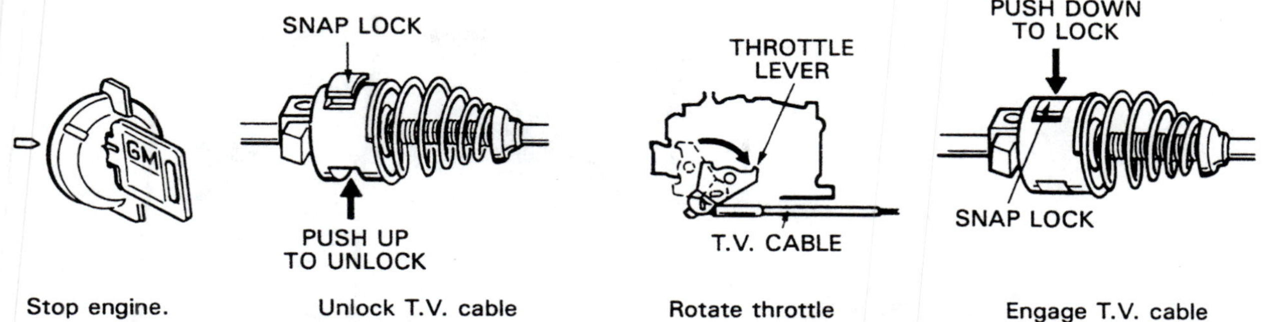

Stop engine.

Unlock T.V. cable "snap-lock" button.

Rotate throttle lever by hand to wide open throttle and hold open.

Engage T.V. cable "snap-lock" button.

FIGURE 8–12 Manual adjustment throttle cable. (Reprinted with permission of General Motors Corporation)

3. *Adjusting Cables*

Most throttle valve cables have an adjustment device built into the engine end of the cable housing. Some cables use a manual type of adjuster which must be unlocked by pushing up the snap lock. Once unlocked, the throttle is opened fully (engine not running), then the snap ring is relocked and the cable is adjusted (Figure 8–12).

A self-adjusting type of TV cable is used on most late-model vehicles. With this type of adjuster, a readjusting tab is depressed which releases the slider, which then returns to its original position. After the tab is released, the throttle is opened fully (engine not running), which pulls the cable into adjustment, as shown in Figure 8–13. Another type of self-adjuster uses an adapter and an inch-pound

Stop engine.

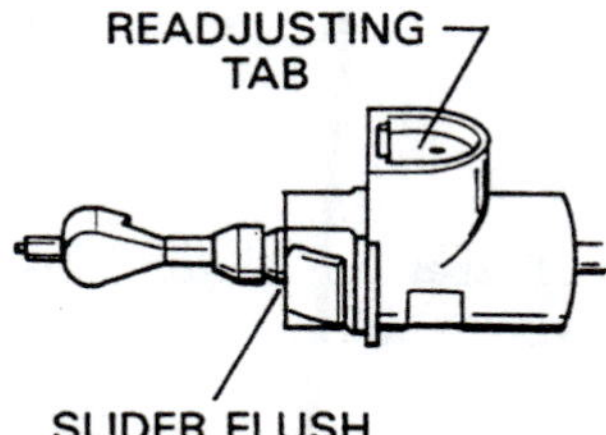

With engine off and throttle linkage at idle position, depress and hold the metal re-adjusting tab to release slider. Move slider in against base of the adjuster housing and release tab.

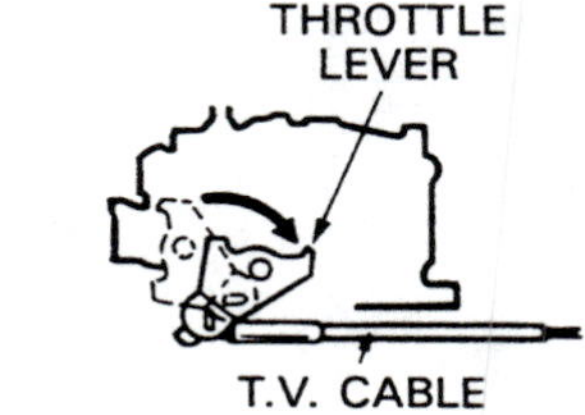

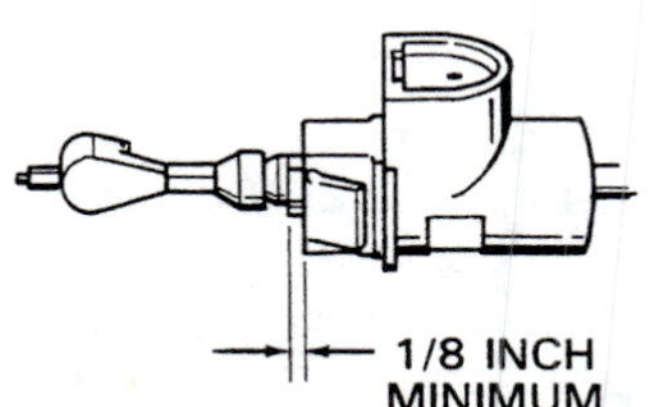

With engine off, rotate the throttle linkage to the wide open throttle position. The cable slider should adjust or ratchet out of the adjuster housing toward the throttle linkage. It must move at least three ratchet clicks or approximately one-eighth inch.

FIGURE 8–13 Self-adjusting throttle valve cable used on many vehicles. (Reprinted with permission of General Motors Corporation)

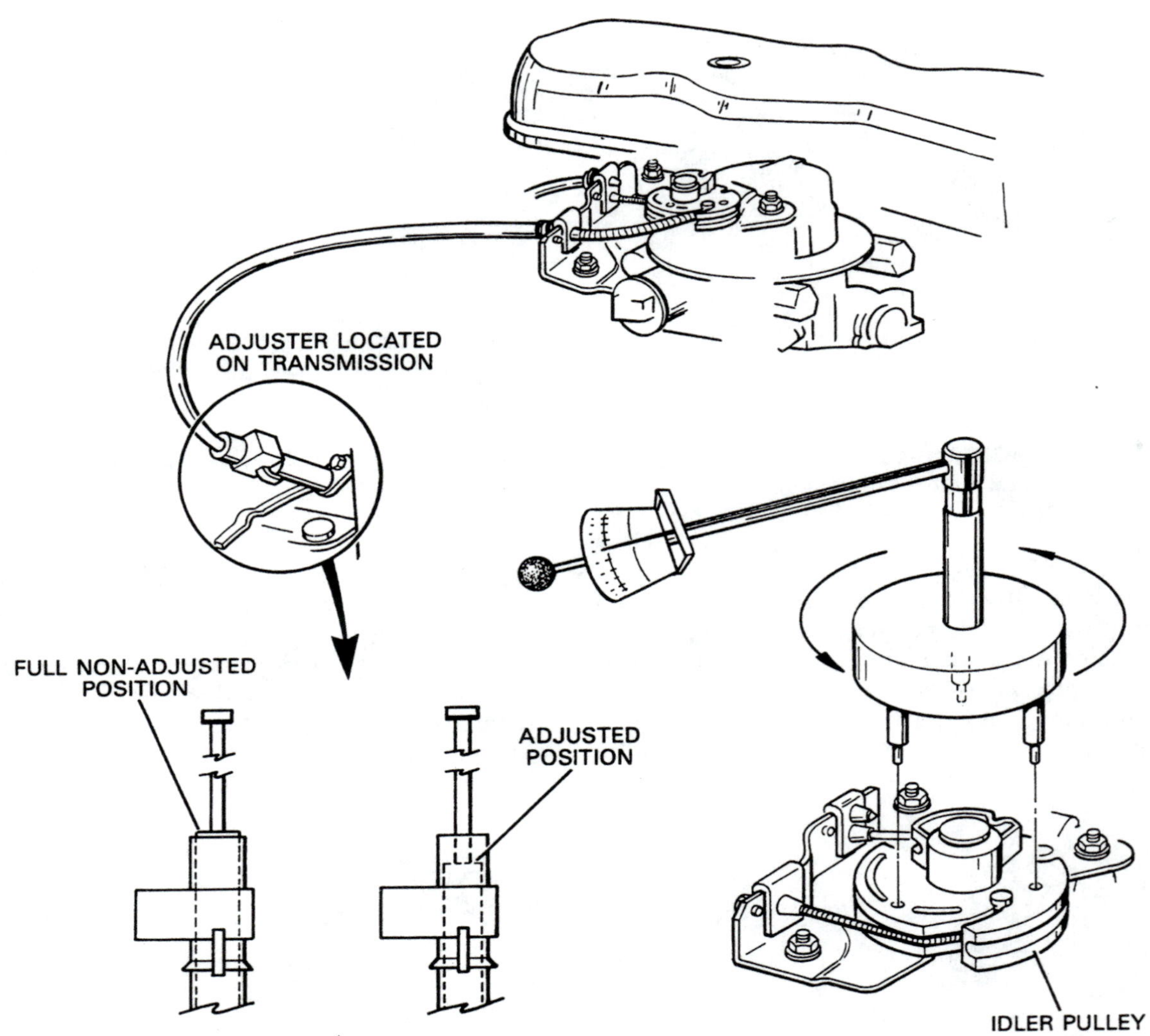

FIGURE 8–14 Throttle valve cable that uses an adapter and torque wrench to adjust the cable. (Reprinted with permission of General Motors Corporation)

torque wrench to turn the cable idler pulley, which sets the adjustment of the cable. This type of adjuster is shown in Figure 8–14. Always refer to the service manual for the exact procedures recommended for the vehicle on which you are working.

8.3.3 Downshift

Many transmissions use a separate downshift or detent valve in the valve body to control forced downshifts. This valve is connected by a linkage rod or cable to the throttle lever of the carburetor or fuel injector. Anytime that the operator of the vehicle uses a wide-open throttle, the linkage or cable activates the valve, which hydraulically causes a downshift. Exactly how this is done differs among various makes of transmissions. Studying each transmission in the manuals will explain the differences.

1. Adjusting Rod Linkage

The standard adjustment procedure for rod-type linkage is used in most cases. With the engine not running, the throttle lever is opened fully [wide-open throttle (WOT)], the linkage adjustment is checked for proper downshift valve operation. Some vehicles require a small clearance to be present in the linkage adjustment at WOT. Refer to the service manual for the exact procedure.

2. Adjusting Cables
The same types of cables are used for the detent or downshift valves as were used for manual and throttle valves. Both manual and self-adjusting types of cable adjusting devices are used. To provide the correct adjustment for each type of cable, always refer to the service manual for the correct adjustment procedure.

8.3.4 Bands

Band adjustments generally fall into two types, bands that are adjusted during transmission overhaul, and bands that require periodic adjustment during normal service. The adjustment procedure that is performed during overhaul is used for bands that use a graduated push rod for adjustment. This adjustment procedure is described in Chapter 9.

Bands that require periodic adjustment generally use the same type of adjusting device. This design uses an adjustment screw that can increase or decrease the clearance of the band around the drum. This type of *adjustment screw* is used both internally and externally (Figure 8–15), depending on the transmission design and how often the band needs adjustment. In many cases, bands that need more frequent adjustment have their adjustment screw located in the case, so external adjustments can be made.

1. External Adjustments
The procedures for making external band adjustments on most transmissions are very similar. The locking nut that is used to lock the adjustment screw to the case is loosened. Ford recommends replacing the locking nut with a new one to prevent an oil leak. The adjustment screw is then tightened to a specific torque setting with either a special torquing tool or a standard torque wrench (Figure 8–16). While torquing the screw the locknut should be held with a box end wrench to prevent interference during torquing. Once the proper torque setting is reached, the adjusting screw must be backed out a specific number of turns, which sets the proper band clearance. Now, holding the screw so that it cannot turn, tighten the locking nut to its torque setting. To learn the adjusting screw torque and the number of turns needed to back the screw out, a service manual must be used. Always check and follow the manual's specifications and procedures.

2. Internal Adjustments
Internal band adjustments are made using the same basic procedure as those used for external adjustments. The one obvious difference is that the transmission oil pan must be removed to gain access to the adjusting screw. This type of adjustment is usually used on a low-reverse or rear band, while the external adjustment is usually found on the intermediate or front band.

Band adjustment is not difficult, but it must be done accurately to provide the proper band clearance. If the band is adjusted improperly, it will directly affect the shift timing and could cause transmission lockup.

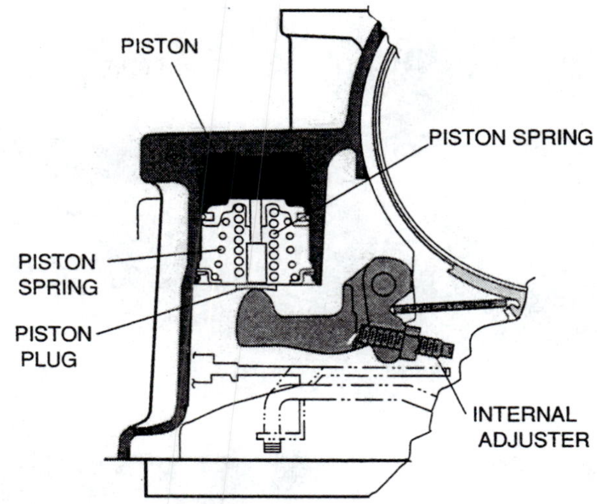

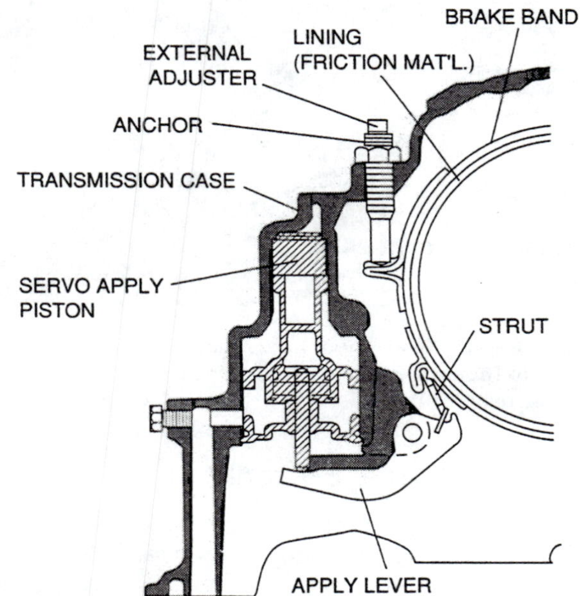

FIGURE 8–15 Band adjusting screws may be either internal or external. (Courtesy of Chrysler)

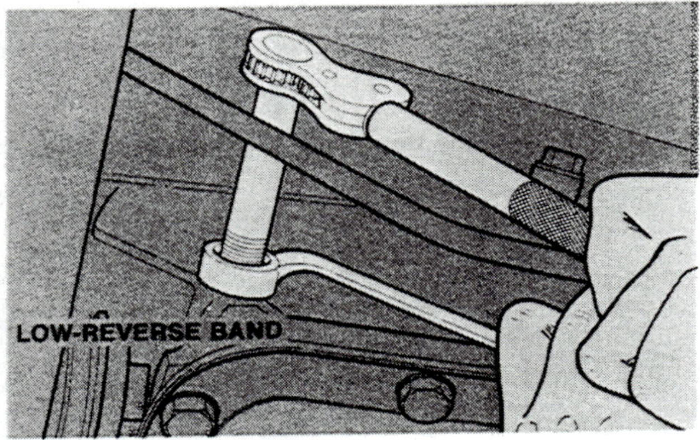

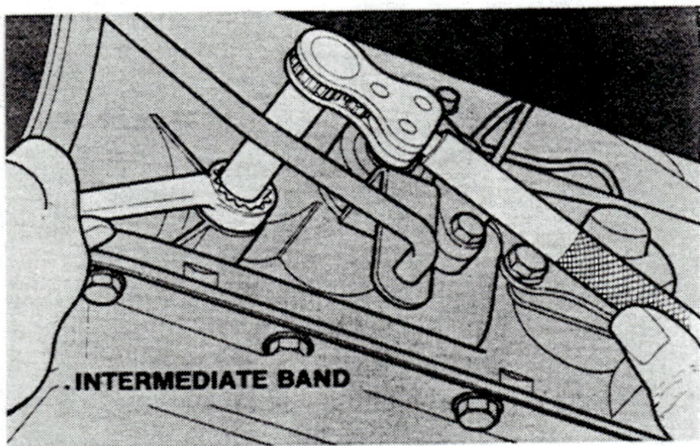

FIGURE 8–16 The band adjustment screw must be torqued to the proper setting before the band clearance is set. (Courtesy of Ford)

8.3.5 Electrical Switches

All vehicles equipped with an automatic transmission use some type of *neutral safety switch*. This device prevents the operator from starting the engine while the transmission is in gear. The safety switch allows starter operation in park (P) and neutral (N) only. If the switch moves out of position, the engine could start while in gear and serious damage could result. The safety switches are mounted either on the transmission or on the steering column and are adjustable. The adjustment procedures vary according to the design of the switch, so always refer to the service manual for the procedures that apply to the vehicle being serviced.

8.4 IN-CAR REPAIRS

Many automatic transmission repairs can be performed with the transmission still in the vehicle (Figure 8–17). Obviously, if the problem is a failed clutch pack, the transmission will be removed, disassembled, inspected, and rebuilt. But if the problem is erratic shifting being caused by a malfunction of the governor, throttle valve, or valve body, in most cases the repair can be completed without removing the transmission. Repairs to the fluid cooler and its lines, along with replacing the output seal and bushing, are considered in-car repairs and are explained in detail.

- GOVERNOR REPAIRS
- THROTTLE VALVE REPAIRS
- VALVE BODY REPAIRS
- REVERSE FLUSH COOLER
- COOLER LINE REPAIRS
- OUTPUT SEAL REPLACEMENT
- ELECTRICAL REPAIRS

FIGURE 8–17 In-car repairs.

8.4.1 Governor Repairs

There are two basic types of governors in wide use. The shaft-mounted type shown in Figure 8–18 bolts to a flange that is splined to the output shaft. The other type of governor is a drop-in design (Figure 8–19). This type of governor "drops in" to its mounting location from outside the case. The governor is held in place by a cover pan and a retainer spring. This type of governor is very easy to gain access to, while the other type requires removal of the extension housing and in some cases the transmission support cross member. To remove a shaft-mounted governor from some transaxles requires complete disassembly.

The first thing to check on a shaft-mounted governor is the governor valve movement. Use a short piece of wire to push on the valve to see if it is free to move. The mounting bolts should also be checked for proper torque since overtightened bolts

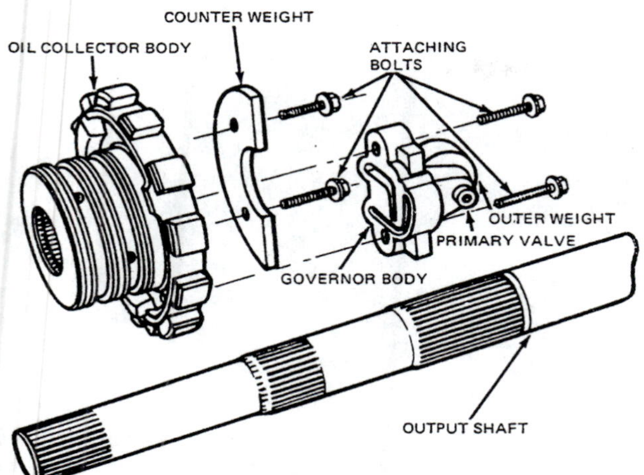

FIGURE 8–18 Shaft-mounted governor typical of those used in many RWD transmissions. (Courtesy of Ford)

can cause the governor valve to stick. If the governor valve is stuck, remove and disassemble the governor. If scouring is found on the valve, you may be able to remove it by following a basic valve smoothing procedure. This procedure can be used on any of the valve body's multiple land valves.

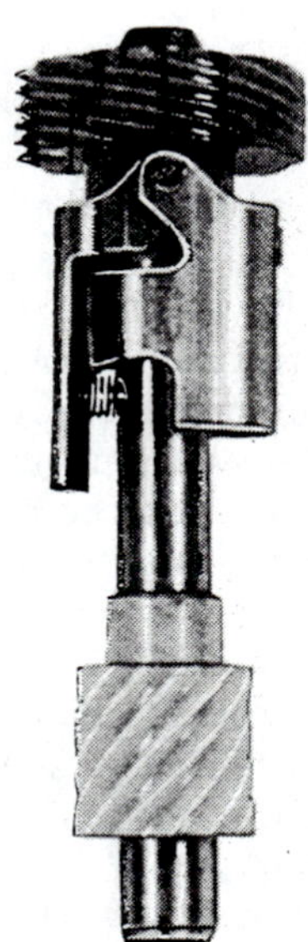

FIGURE 8–19 This type of governor is called "drop-in" because of its easy installment. (Reprinted with permission of General Motors Corporation)

1. Hold the valve flat against a smooth *Arkansas stone* (knife-sharpening stone).

2. Apply light pressure to the valve and slowly turn the valve against the stone.

3. Keep turning the valve until it looks and feels smooth.

4. Clean all governor parts with carburetor spray to remove varnish.

5. Oil the parts and reassemble.

6. Test for free movement. The valve should move in its bore with just the weight of the valve.

7. Retorque the mounting bolts as the governor is installed.

8. Using new gaskets and seals, replace the extension housing.

9. Finish reassembly and test governor operation.

By using this procedure to smooth a scored valve, the sharp edge of the valve land is preserved. This is important because if that edge is rounded off, the self-cleaning action of the valve is lost and it will be more likely to stick.

A drop-in governor is much easier to service than the shaft-mounted type. After removing the retainer spring and cover pan, the governor is simply lifted out of the case. The governor case clearance should be checked while removing the governor by moving it back and forth in its mounting hole. Excessive clearance must be repaired. There are two styles of *drop-in governors:* the valve style and the check ball style (Figure 8–20). The valve style can have a stuck valve, so check for free valve movement by turning the governor upside down, then right side up, while watching for movement of the valve through the fluid slots in its sides. If there is no movement or very sluggish movement, clean the valve with carburetor cleaner spray, blow it dry with shop air, then lubricate it with ATF and retest. If it still does not move freely, disassemble the governor and smooth the valve. Thoroughly clean all parts with carburetor spray, lubricate, and reassemble. If the valve does not operate freely, replace the governor. Always examine the governor drive gear for wear and replace the governor if wear is found (Figure 8–21). A new gasket or O-ring should be used to seal the cover pan once the governor is reinstalled in the transmission. Always check the transmission for leaks after the repair job is finished, then road test the vehicle to verify proper operation of the transmission.

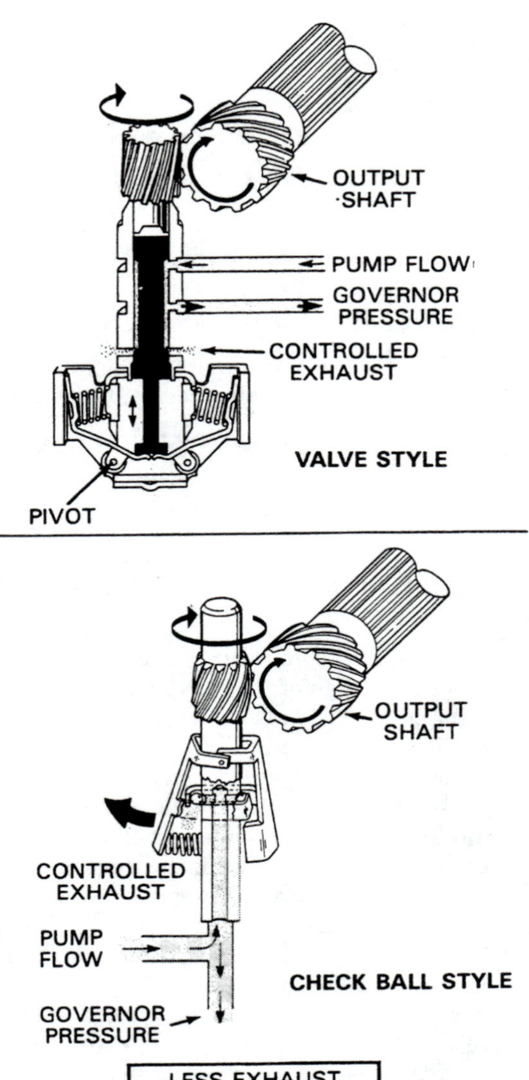

FIGURE 8–20 There are two designs for drop-in governors, one with a multiland valve and one with check balls. (Reprinted with permission of General Motors Corporation)

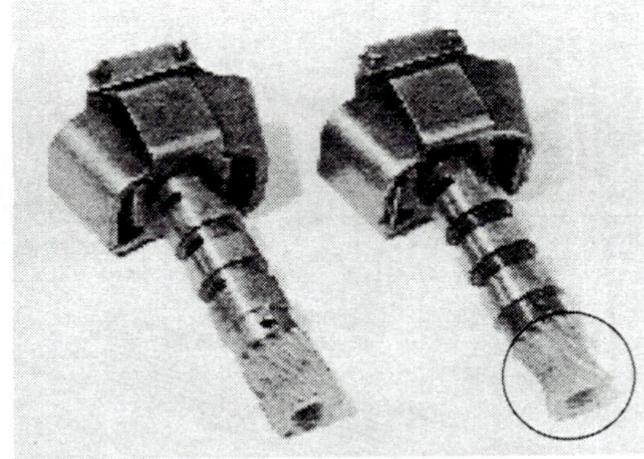

FIGURE 8–21 The drive gear of the governor can wear severely. (Reprinted with permission of General Motors Corporation)

8.4.2 Throttle Valve Repairs

The throttle valve itself has a very low rate of failure, with most of the system malfunctions occurring in the TV cable or vacuum modulator. The TV cable problems and adjustment have already been explained. The basic test procedure for a vacuum modulator has also been explained, so review that information if the procedures are unclear to you. In most cases, as a vacuum modulator fails, the normal shift speed will increase because of the higher-than-normal throttle pressure. In some cases, the failure is a hole through the diaphragm that allows ATF to be pulled up into the intake manifold and burned by the engine. The transmission will upshift only at its maximum speed in each gear and the vehicle will produce a huge amount of blue smoke. The fluid level of the automatic transmission will also be decreasing as fluid is sucked into the engine and burned.

If the problem involves a sticking throttle valve, the same procedure that is used to smooth and clean the governor valve can be used. In many cases, a thorough cleaning with carburetor cleaner spray will solve the problem. The throttle valve is located in either the case or the valve body. Check the service manual for removal procedures.

Replacing the vacuum modulator is a simple job. Always clean around the old modulator before removing it from the case to avoid getting dirt in the throttle valve. Remove all old seals, using new seals on the new modulator to prevent leaks, and replace any vacuum hose that is questionable. If a molded vacuum hose was used originally, do not replace it with a regular vacuum hose. Use only a molded replacement hose. If the modulator uses a *connecting pin* between the throttle valve and the diaphragm, be sure to reinstall it with the new modulator. Road test when finished and then check for leaks.

8.4.3 Valve Body Repairs

When the diagnosis of the transmission problem leads to the valve body, a thorough cleaning and inspection of the valve body is in order. Using the service manual procedures, the valve body is carefully removed, noting the position of any check balls or small valves that might be exposed during removal. Also note the length of the valve body mounting bolts as you remove them to prevent mixing the bolts during reinstallation. Many manuals list the size and position of mounting bolts along with their torque setting, as shown in Figure 8–22. With the valve body removed and on the bench, use a small screwdriver to try to move the valves in their bores. Be careful not to scratch or mar the valve lands. The valves are spring loaded and will resist movement, so moderate force is necessary to move the valves. It is easy to locate the sticking valve by watching the movements of each valve (Figure 8–23). Before disassembling the valve body, try cleaning the valves with carburetor spray. If this does not free the valves, carefully disassemble the valve body according to service manual procedures.

Use an exploded view of the valve body (Figure 8–24) to help keep the parts organized by laying them out on the bench or cookie sheet in the same order as they are shown in the illustration.

Clean and smooth the sticking valves until they are moving freely, then lubricate and reassemble the valve body. If the valves cannot be freed up, replace the valve body with a new or rebuilt unit. Be very careful to follow the service manual procedures and plan ahead so that you will have enough time to disassemble, inspect, clean, and reassemble the valve body in one setting. If you have to leave the valve body apart overnight, your chances of forgetting or misplacing something are much greater. Work smart and avoid problems before they happen.

8.4.4 Reverse Flush Cooler

If tests indicate that the cooler is blocked, it must be reverse or back-flushed to remove the debris. The purpose of reverse flushing is to flow a solvent through the cooler and lines in the reverse direction to normal flow to help dislodge the debris and wash

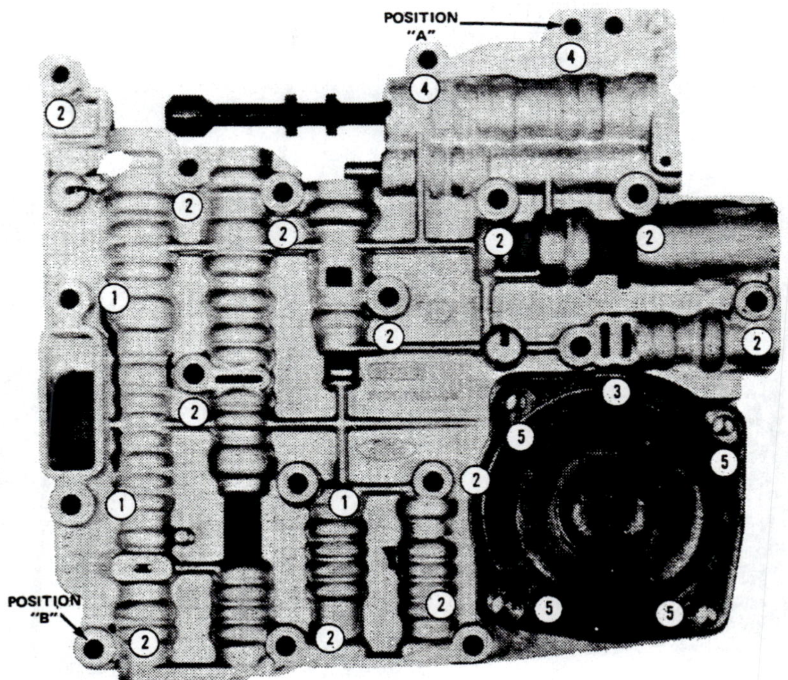

Position	Bolt Size Metric	Length in Millimeters	Length in Inches
1	M6 x 45	45mm	1.772
2	M6 x 40	40.1mm	1.578
3	M6 x 35	35mm	1.378
4	M6 x 30	29mm	1.141
5	M6 x 20	20mm	.787
Position	**Quantity**	**Torque N-m**	**Torque Lb-Ft**
1	3	8-11	6-8
2	12	8-11	6-8
3	1	8-11	6-8
4	2	8-11	6-8
5	4	9.5-13.5	7-10

FIGURE 8–22 The length and location of valve body bolts can be found in the shop manual. (Courtesy of Ford)

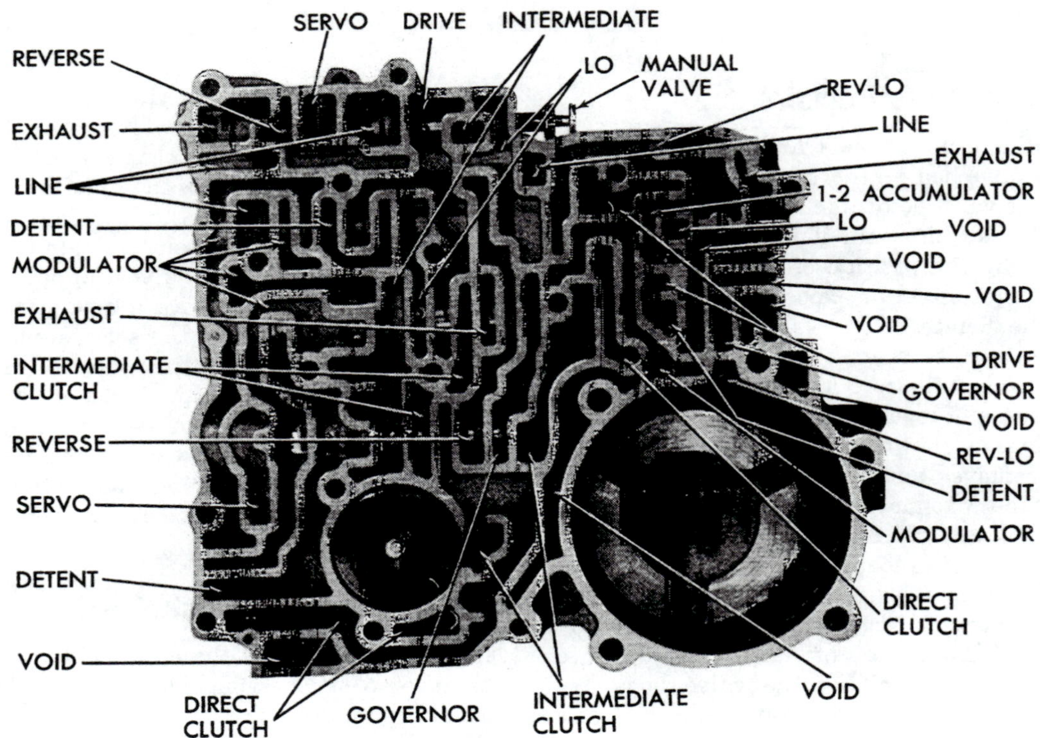

FIGURE 8–23 By using a small screwdriver to move each shift valve it is easy to locate a stuck valve. (Reprinted with permission of General Motors Corporation)

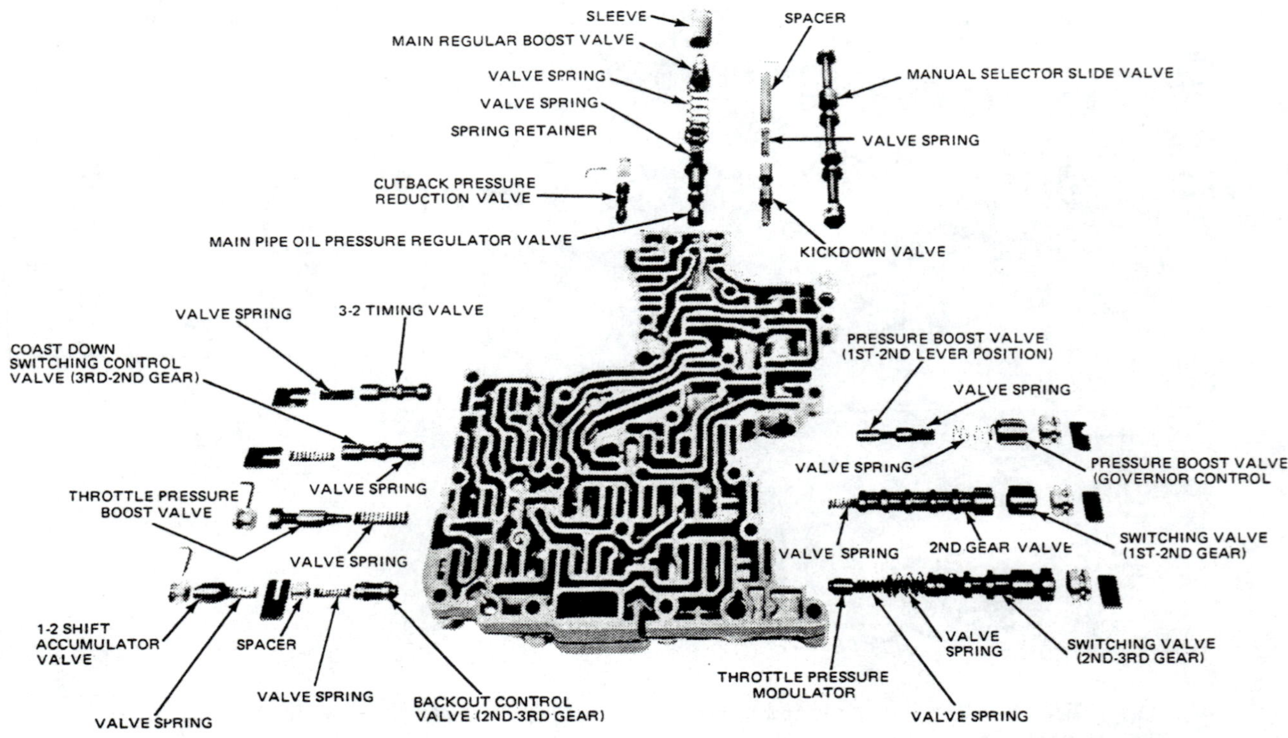

FIGURE 8–24 Exploded view of valve body. (Courtesy of Ford)

it out of the system. Both cooler lines are disconnected from the transmission and a length of hose long enough to reach the draw pan is placed on the cooler inlet line. Another piece of hose is slipped over the end of the outlet line and is brought up through the engine compartment (Figure 8–25). A funnel is placed in the hose and clean solvent is poured in the system. Occasionally, stop pouring the solvent and direct a few short blasts of low-pressure (25 psi) shop air into the hose. Repeat the process until you have used 3 to 4 quarts of solvent. During the last quart or two, watch the solvent coming out of the inlet line. If debris is still present in the solvent, continue to flush until the solvent is clear of debris. Once all of the debris is flushed out, blow all the solvent out of the system with low-pressure shop air, then pour 1 quart of fresh ATF into the line and blow it through the system to remove any solvent that is left. The cooler and lines should be clean now. Reconnect the cooler lines and add sufficient fluid to restore the proper fluid level.

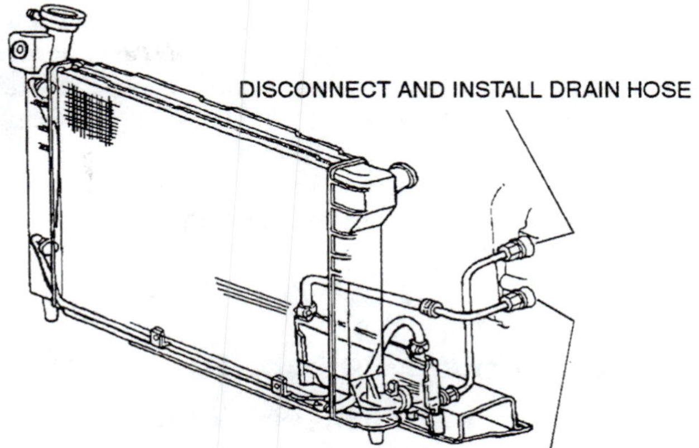

FIGURE 8–25 Any time the ATF is heavily contaminated, the cooler must be reverse flushed. (Courtesy of Ford)

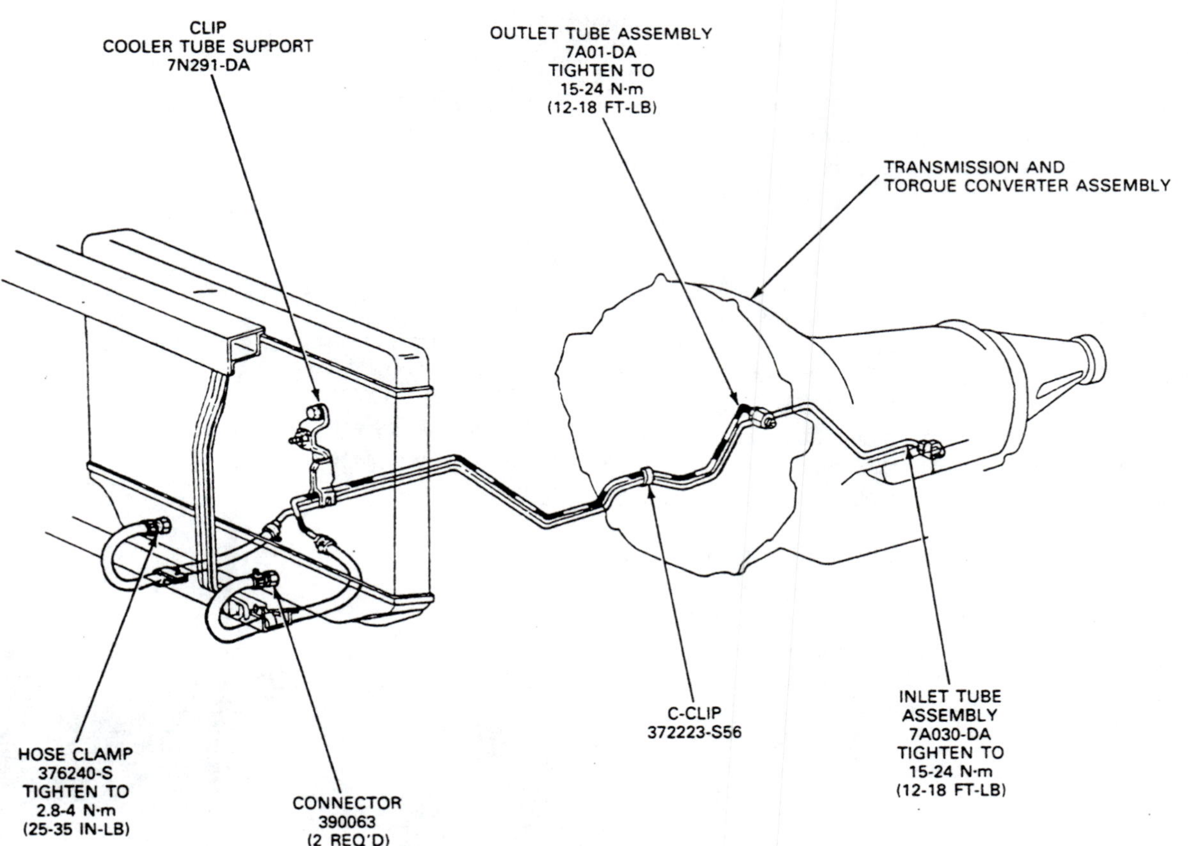

FIGURE 8–26 Fluid cooler that is not part of the radiator and uses air to cool the fluid. (Courtesy of Chrysler)

It is a good idea to retest the cooler flow and pressure to make sure that the restriction has been removed. If the restriction remains, check the lines and fittings for damage. If no restriction is found, remove the radiator and have a radiator shop repair or replace the fluid cooler. Some fluid coolers are separate from the radiator, so check the service manual for the exact information (Figure 8–26).

8.4.5 Cooler Line Repairs

When cooler lines develop leaks from vibration or rubbing, they must be replaced. The best method of repairing the cooler lines is to replace the faulty portion of the line with a bendable steel brake line of the proper diameter. A special minitubing cutter (Figure 8–27) is used to cut the line in areas with little clearance. The cut should be made about 1 in. from the leak on the longest side of the tubing (Figure 8–28). Be sure to thoroughly inspect the line for rubbed spots that could become leaks in the near future and replace that part of the line as well. Use the removed portion of tubing as a measuring and bending guide for the replacement tubing. The two pieces of tubing are joined together with a *compression union fitting.* This fitting uses *farrels,* which are compressed onto the outside of the tubing to provide a pressure seal. For the farrels to seal properly, the tubing must be clean, so sand the last few inches of each piece of tubing with 320-grit wet-or-dry sandpaper and wipe clean. Install the union by removing one compression nut and farrel from the fitting. Slide the compression nut on the tubing first, then the farrel, then place the fitting against the end of the tubing so that the tubing is fully inserted (Figure 8–29). Slide the farrel up next to the fitting, then start the compression nut. Lightly tighten the first side, then start the other side before fully tightening both sides. Be sure to check all fittings for leaks after the repair is finished. After the repair is completed, tie the cooler lines together with nylon wire ties to prevent rubbing or vibration damage. The union fitting, shown in Figure 8–30, provides a permanent repair for tubing which will not deteriorate with time. If the leak is in the center of the line, try removing only an inch of tubing with the leak in the center, then join the tubing with a union. Power-steering or air-conditioner hose can be used with a screw clamp to replace flexible line. A double flare on the tubing's end will improve the seal while not cutting the hose. Position the clamps next to the flares, not on them.

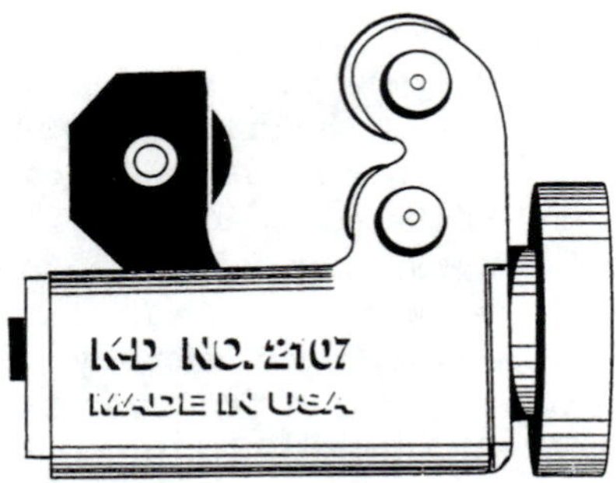

FIGURE 8–27 Minitubing cutter used to cut cooler lines in areas with limited space.

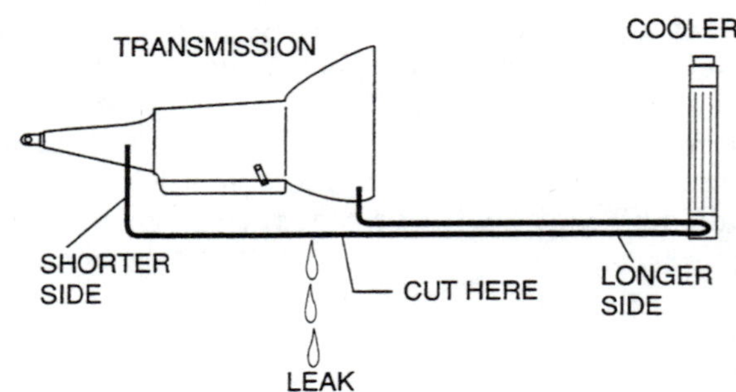

FIGURE 8–28 After examining the entire cooler line for leaks, cut the line 1 inch from the leak on the longer side of the line.

- CLEAN TUBING
- INSERT TUBING COMPLETELY
- SNUG FITTINGS
- TIGHTEN AFTER ALL PARTS ARE FULLY ASSEMBLED
- CHECK FOR LEAKS

FIGURE 8–29 Follow instructions closely when installing a compression union.

FIGURE 8–30 A compression union will permanently join two pieces of tubing.

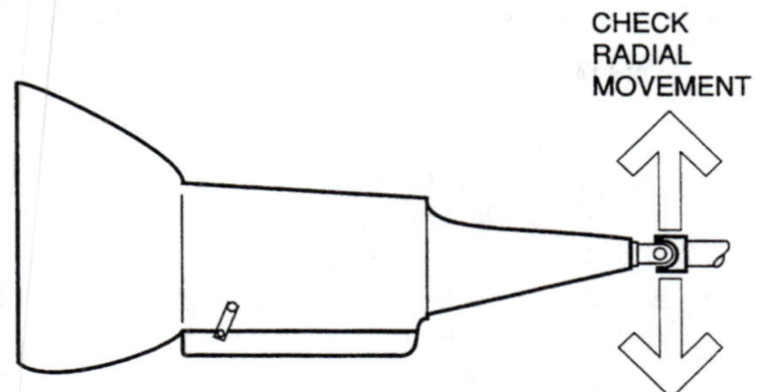

FIGURE 8–31 The drive shaft on RWD transmissions and drive axles on FWD transaxles should be checked for radial play when replacing the seals.

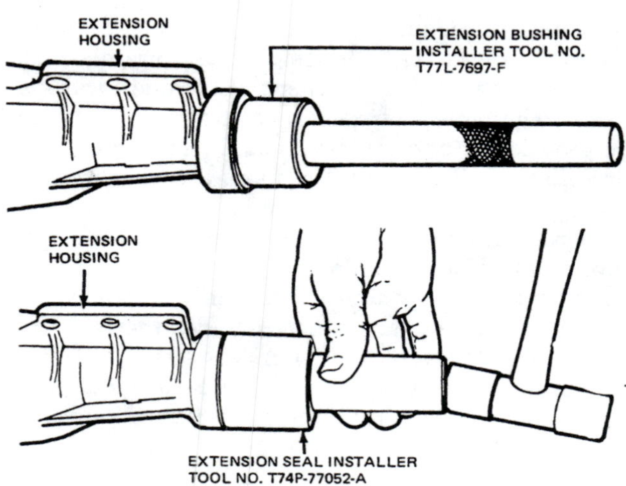

FIGURE 8–33 Using a bushing driver to install new bushings will prevent damage to the bushing.

8.4.6 Output Seal Replacement

The replacement of the output seal is a simple procedure. Check the service manual first for special procedures, then check the drive shaft slip yoke or inboard CV joints for radial play before removing the shaft (Figure 8–31). If the shaft has a significant amount of radial play, the bushing is worn. The drive shaft or axle shaft is removed according to the service manual procedure. A special tool is used to remove the seal and bushing (Figure 8–32). Some transaxles will not have bushing to support the axle shafts, so only the seals are removed. Wipe the surfaces clean, then install the new bushing first using the proper installing tool. The seal is installed next, using a seal installer (Figure 8–33). Do not forget to lubricate the seal before installing it; a dry seal can "burn" and lose its sealing ability. After reinstalling the drive shafts, road test the vehicle and check for leaks.

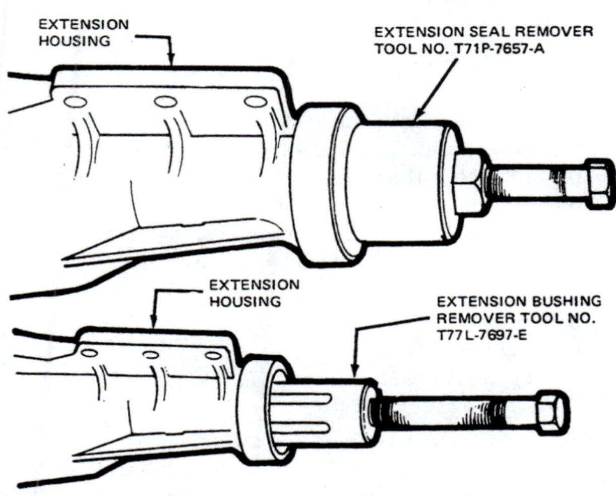

FIGURE 8–32 It is best to use a bushing driver to remove a worn bushing.

8.4.7 Electrical Repairs

The new electronically controlled transmissions include an electrical system with components that are usually accessible without removing and disas-

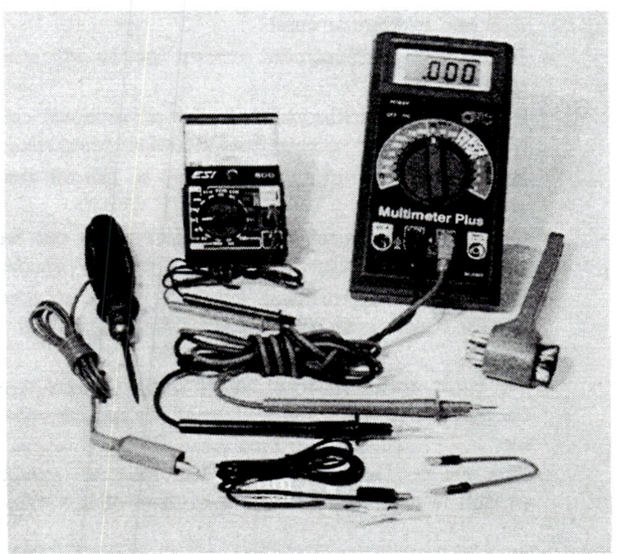

FIGURE 8–34 Basic electrical test equipment used to diagnose electrical problems.

sembling the transmission. Diagnostic procedures found in the factory service manuals are designed to isolate the failed component in the electrical system. Some general troubleshooting techniques can be used to find the problem, but the factory-written procedures will provide the most accurate diagnosis. Most of the electrical repairs consist of component replacement, wire replacement, and connector repair, which are standard repair techniques used on all electrical systems. Standard electrical test and repair equipment, which includes DVOM, analog multimeter, test light, jumper wires, and wire terminals and a crimping tool are used to diagnose and repair electrical malfunctions (Figure 8–34).

SUMMARY

The following ideas reflect the key points made in the various units of this chapter.

- The manual valve in the automatic transmission is moved by rod linkage or cables.
- The manual valve must be adjusted properly or transmission damage can occur.
- The throttle valve can be activated by rod linkage, cable, or vacuum modulator.
- An improperly adjusted throttle valve can damage a transmission by causing low mainline pressure.
- Some vacuum modulators have a throttle pressure adjustment screw inside the modulator.
- The downshift or detent valve is operated by either rod linkage or cable.
- Bands using adjustment screws can be adjusted at any time.
- Bands using *graduated rods* for adjustment can be adjusted only during transmission rebuilding.
- Bands must be adjusted properly to assure correct shift timing.
- On most transmissions, governor repairs can be performed with the transmission in the vehicle.
- On most transmissions, throttle valve repairs can be made with the transmission in the vehicle.
- On most transmissions, valve body repairs can be performed with the transmission in the vehicle.
- The correct adjustment of the neutral safety switch is essential to safe operation of the vehicle.
- Reverse flushing of the fluid cooler removes debris from the system.
- Use only air-conditioner or power-steering hose as replacements for hoses in cooler lines.
- Some cooler lines use special tools to disconnect the lines.
- It is best to make a permanent repair to the cooler lines whenever possible.
- Special tools, including seal and bushing removers and installers, are used to replace the output seal and bushing.
- Standard electrical repairs are used on transmission electrical systems.

SELF-TEST

Before going on to the next chapter, complete the self-test according to your instructor's directions. Read carefully and choose the best answer.

1. Technician A says, "If the manual valve is out of adjustment, it will effect the performance of the transmission." Technician B says, "If the manual valve is out of adjustment, the transmission will be damaged." Who is right?
   a. A only
   b. B only
   c. Both A and B
   d. Neither A nor B

2. Technician A says, "If the throttle valve is out of adjustment, the mainline pressure will always be lower than normal." Technician B says, "If the vacuum modulator is leaking, the throttle valve pressure will be higher than normal." Who is right?
   a. A only
   b. B only
   c. Both A and B
   d. Neither A nor B

3. A vehicle suddenly starts smoking badly; at the same time the automatic transmission begins to shift at higher speeds than usual. Technician A says, "An internal leak in the vacuum modulator is the problem." Technician B says, "The problem is caused by low mainline pressure." Who is right?
   a. A only
   b. B only
   c. Both A and B
   d. Neither A nor B

4. A vehicle with a three-speed automatic transmission has a poor 2–3 upshift, which lets the engine race before engaging third gear. Technician A says, "The problem is caused by the front band being out of ad-

justment." Technician B says, "The problem is caused by low mainline pressure." Who is right?

a. A only
b. B only
c. Both A and B
d. Neither A nor B

5. All transmission bands can be adjusted during normal periodic service.

a. True
b. False

6. An automatic transmission with a drop-in governor is not upshifting at all. Technician A says, "The drop-in governor is easy to remove and repair." Technician B says, "The transmission must be disassembled to remove the drop-in governor." Who is right?

a. A only
b. B only
c. Both A and B
d. Neither A nor B

7. On most automatic transmissions the valve bodies can be removed and repaired without removing the transmission.

a. True
b. False

8. A fluid cooler test showed restricted flow and low pressure. Technician A says, "The cooler should be reverse flushed and then retested." Technician B says, "The radiator and cooler should be taken to a radiator shop to be boiled out." Who is right?

a. A only
b. B only
c. Both A and B
d. Neither A nor B

9. Technician A says, "A blocked cooler is a sign of a torque converter failure." Technician B says, "After finding a blocked cooler, the transmission should be examined to find what caused the blockage." Who is right?

a. A only
b. B only
c. Both A and B
d. Neither A nor B

10. Technician A says, "Only certain kinds of hose can be used in cooling lines." Technician B says, "Fuel-line hose is a good replacement for cooler-line hose." Who is right?

a. A only
b. B only
c. Both A and B
d. Neither A nor B

11. A compression union fitting is used to make a temporary repair to a cooler line.

a. True
b. False

GLOSSARY

adjusting sleeve sleeve that is clamped to the linkage rod by a bolt.

adjusting slot elongated slot in the end of a rod or cable linkage to allow adjustment of the linkage.

air pressure regulator adjustable device used to regulate the maximum air pressure on a shop compressed air system.

air test plate (test plate) special tool adapter plate used to air test a transmission.

Arkansas stone type of knife-sharpening tool.

cable linkage linkage using a cable to transfer movement. Commonly used for throttle valve operation.

column-mounted selector gear shift selector that is mounted on the steering column.

compression union fitting fitting that is designed to join two pieces of tubing permanently.

drop-in governor governor that is extremely easy to remove and install, as it simply slides into the case and is held in place by its cover in most cases.

external adjustment screws band adjustment screws located on the outside of the transmission case.

farrel compression sleeve used in a compression union fitting.

floor-mounted selector a gear shift selector that is mounted on the floor of the vehicle.

graduated rods selective-fit servo rods used to adjust band clearance.

internal adjustment screws band adjustment screws located inside the oil pan of the transmission.

locking nut nut used to lock the band adjusting screw in place.

modulator adjusting screw internal adjustment found inside some vacuum modulators used to adjust the throttle pressure.

neutral safety switch electrical switch that prevents the vehicle from being started in gear. It allows starter action only in park (P) or neutral (N) position.

reverse (back) flushing procedure used to clean the fluid cooler while it is installed in the vehicle.

rod linkage linkage made of solid steel rods and bell cranks. Commonly used for manual valve linkage and for some throttle valve linkage.

scored valves multiland spool valve that has score marks on the land's surface.

selector pawl part of a gear selector that engages with the shift gate.

shaft-mounted governor type of governor that is mounted on the transmission output shaft. Also called a type 1 governor.

◀ Chapter 9 ▶

REBUILDING PROCEDURES AND TECHNIQUES

INTRODUCTION

In this chapter you will learn the basic rebuilding skills that will serve as the foundation for your career as an automatic transmission/transaxle technician. The chapter starts with the theme of organization that will be stressed throughout. The first section covers removal of the transmission and presents a plan that allows an orderly removal. The next section deals with the disassembly, the measurements and tests that should accompany the tear down. Proper cleaning techniques are also described in this section.

The next seven sections focus on subsystems of the automatic transmission/transaxle: torque converter, gear train, pump, clutches, bands, one-way clutches, and shift controls. In each section we cover the special inspection points and service techniques needed to rebuild the subsystem. The theory of basic repair procedures and techniques is explained in detail, providing the new technician with the knowledge and background for a full understanding of the individual rebuilding procedures detailed in the factory service manuals. In the next section we deal with assembly of the transmission after the subsystem components are reconditioned. The chapter ends with the summary and self-test.

9.1 PERFORMANCE OBJECTIVES

After studying this chapter, you should have fulfilled the following performance objectives by being able to:

1. Describe an organized plan to remove an automatic transmission/transaxle.
2. Explain what tests are performed during transmission disassembly.
3. Describe the inspection procedure used to check the torque converter.
4. Explain the gear train inspection checks.
5. Describe the pump measurements that are recommended.
6. Describe the steps in rebuilding a clutch pack.
7. Explain how to inspect a band.
8. Describe how to check a one-way clutch.
9. Explain what is done to shift control systems during rebuilding.
10. Complete all the competency objectives listed for this chapter.
11. Complete the self-test with at least the minimum score required by your instructor.

9.2 COMPETENCY OBJECTIVES

The competency objectives differ from the performance objectives in being more job related. The automotive terms must be well understood so that the theory will be clear. The terms are used to describe the service procedures outlined in Part II. The competency tasks are related to job skills needed to perform service and repair procedures and should be understood thoroughly.

9.2.1 Automotive Terms

The following list may include terms that are unfamiliar to you. Read the terms, then note their definitions as you study the chapter.

ballooning	cross member
bleed down	debris
body clearance	dial indicator
busing driver	end play
chain deflection	fire wall clearance
clutch pack clearance	fractional bolts

hiss
jack stand
lifting points
power washer
pump alignment tool
shoehorn
side clearance
thud
tip clearance
transmission jack
vernier caliper
visual inspection
water-based cleaning solution
yoke

9.2.2 Competency Tasks

The competency tasks listed here are related directly to knowledge or skills needed to become a successful automatic transmission/transaxle technician. Be sure to complete all the tasks before going on to Chapter 10. Since this chapter covers rebuilding procedures and techniques, the list of tasks will be long, but each task is very important, so take the time to learn them all.

1. List the major steps in an organized transmission removal.
2. Perform a transmission removal in an organized manner.
3. Measure the input shaft end play and explain why the measurement is needed.
4. Perform an air test during disassembly to find hydraulic leaks.
5. Thoroughly clean all transmission parts after disassembly.
6. Inspect and test the torque converter, finding all damage.
7. Flush the reusable torque converter to remove debris.
8. Measure chain deflection on a transaxle.
9. Inspect and measure for wear on the planet pinion gears.
10. Determine bushing wear.
11. Replace worn bushings and adjoining parts.
12. Inspect and measure thrust washers for wear.
13. Measure pump clearances and repair if necessary.
14. Rebuild the clutch pack.
15. Set the clutch pack clearance.
16. Inspect and replace faulty bands.
17. Renew the servo seals.
18. Adjust the band clearance according to the procedure recommended.
19. Inspect one-way clutches and replace faulty parts.
20. Test shift control devices for proper operation.
21. Recondition shift control devices that do not operate properly.
22. Follow the general transmission assembly procedures as they apply to your job.
23. Always use the service manual.

9.3 TRANSMISSION REMOVAL

In the following steps we provide you with an organized plan for transmission removal. Always remember that time is money when it comes to performing service operations on a vehicle. By using a plan of action, no time is wasted. So think the job through first, then make your plan and start to work. When removing any large unit such as an automatic transmission, remember the order in which you remove and disconnect things, since that list will be used in reverse order to reinstall the transmission.

9.3.1 Organize Tools

The first and most important tool is the service manual. Do not attempt to rebuild a transmission without a good-quality service manual. Even expert transmission technicians with many years of experience can find themselves in trouble without the use of a manual.

Determine if the vehicle uses metric or fractional bolts, then place the basic tools you will need in a tool tray so that they will be within reach under the vehicle to eliminate unnecessary trips to your toolbox. An organized method of storing the bolts that are removed will also save time and lost parts. Plastic oil containers make excellent bolt holders. A 1-quart plastic oil bottle with the top cut off makes a nice-sized bolt container. Now expand the idea by cutting a dozen bottles and storing them in the carton that the case of oil came in and you will have more than enough bolt storage. If you need to, you can label the containers as to where the bolts came from. Have clean bench space ready for the transmission once it is removed.

9.3.2 Check Fire Wall Clearance

The removal procedure for most RWD vehicles will involve lowering the rear end of the transmission after removing the cross member to gain access to the bell housing bolts. If the engine has the distributor mounted at the rear of the block, the distributor cap could hit the fire wall and break as the engine and transmission are lowered. Examine the rear of the engine to see if this problem will arise and remove any parts that might be damaged. While you are there, remove or disconnect the underhood items required before raising the vehicle. Remove the battery ground cable at this time.

9.3.3 Raise Vehicle

If you are using a frame contact hoist to raise the vehicle, make sure that the hoist arms are positioned properly to contact the vehicle's lift points. Refer to the service manual for the manufacturer's recommendations.

If a floor jack and jack stands are used, the vehicle must be raised high enough to provide ample work space and enough height to clear the transmission setting on a transmission jack. It is best to place the jack stands at the outer ends of the front control arms to provide as much working area as possible. After the weight of the vehicle is on the jack stands, test their stability. Have the jack within ½ in. on the chassis in case the stands fail; then try to shake the vehicle sideways. If the stands are stable, remove the jack and raise the rear of the vehicle. Transmission removal is easier if both ends of the vehicle are raised.

9.3.4 Drain Fluid

Various shops approach this step in different ways. Some shops would rather save the removal time and leave the fluid in the transmission. An extra driveshaft yoke is slipped onto the output shaft to prevent spillage, along with plugging the other openings or fittings with plastic plugs. By sealing the transmission this way, it is removed without making a mess in a shorter length of time. Shops that are under fewer time constraints, the pan is dropped and the fluid drained to minimize the fluid mess later.

9.3.5 Remove Linkage

Remove the manual valve linkage, downshift linkage or cable, throttle cable connections, cooler lines, speedometer cable, and wiring connections in a systematic manner by starting at one side of the transmission and removing all connections as you work around the transmission. On some vehicles the starter will also need to be removed. If any of the connections are hard to reach at this time, wait until the transmission is lowered to remove them. Mark the wiring connectors with number tape to prevent problems during reinstallation.

9.3.6 Remove Drive Shaft

On a RWD vehicle the driveshaft is removed by unbolting the rear universal joint after marking the universal joint cup and differential yoke for alignment during reinstallation. The universal joint caps should be taped onto the cross to prevent loss. Remove the bolts from the center support bearing, if any, slide the driveshaft out, and store it in a safe place. Place an extra driveshaft yoke on the output shaft to prevent leaks. Remove the bell housing cover and mark the torque converter and flywheel with a felt-tip permanent marker, then remove converter bolts and push the converter back away from the flywheel.

9.3.7 Transmission Jack

Position the transmission jack under the transmission and place the adjustable sides in contact with the transmission oil pan. If the jack has a retaining chain or cord, attach it around the transmission. Raise the jack enough to support the transmission so that the rear transmission mount can be removed.

9.3.8 Remove Cross Member

With the transmission jack supporting the weight of the transmission, remove the bolts that join the transmission and the transmission mount. Leave the mount attached to the cross member. Now remove the bolts that attach the cross member to the frame and slide the cross member back in the frame or remove it.

9.3.9 Lower Transmission

Once the cross member is removed, the transmission jack can be carefully lowered to allow the rear of the transmission to tilt down. This tilting of the transmission provides better access to the bell housing bolts, and in most cases the bolts can be reached with a long extension bar, so an air impact tool can be used. At this point, remove any connections to the transmission that were too difficult to reach before. The extra space around the transmission should be helpful. Now remove the dust cover from the torque converter and remove the bolts that attach the torque converter to the flywheel. Then pry the torque converter away from the flywheel. Remove all but two mounting bolts, one on each side, then place the jack under the transmission and raise until its weight is supported. Remove the last two bolts and gently move the tail housing of the transmission to the right and left to break it loose, then move the transmission away from the engine until the bell housing is clear of the flywheel. Be sure to hold the torque converter in place as the transmission is lowered.

On all FWD and some RWD vehicles, an engine support fixture must be used to hold the engine up. The manufacturer's service manual will describe proper use of the fixture.

9.3.10 Remove the Transmission

Once the bell housing is clear of the flywheel, start lowering the transmission slowly. Watch closely for any cables or wires still attached to the transmission as it is being lowered. Try to keep the transmission level as it is lowered to prevent it from falling off the jack. Now carefully roll the transmission out from under the vehicle and this portion of the job is finished. Make a special effort to remember the order in which items are removed because you will need to follow those steps in reverse to reinstall the transmission.

9.4 TRANSMISSION DISASSEMBLY

The step-by-step procedures for disassembling and reconditioning the transmission you are servicing can be found in the service manual. Read all the information in the manual before starting to disassemble the transmission. Then keep the manual handy to refer to as needed.

Most transmission shops use specially made workbenches that are designed to control and catch transmission fluid as the transmission is disassembled. Slide the torque converter off and carefully lay it aside for inspection. Then place the transmission on the workbench with the input shaft pointing toward you.

9.4.1 End Play

Before the transmission is disassembled, a measurement of gear train end play must be taken. End-play measurement techniques vary among different transmissions, so refer to the service manual for proper instructions. In the most common type of end-play measurement, a dial indicator is used. The indicator is mounted to the oil pump or to the front of the transmission so that it is positioned at the end of the turbine (input) shaft. The turbine

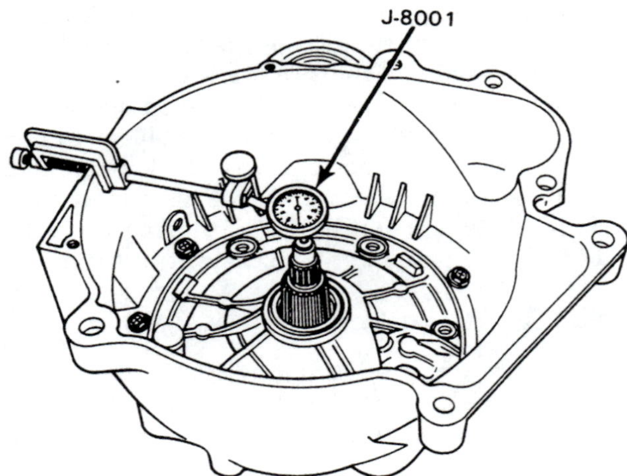

FIGURE 9–1 Dial indicator setup used to measure gear train end play. (Courtesy of Ford)

shaft on most transmissions will have a slight amount of axial clearance or end play. Before mounting the dial indicator, push the shaft in, then pull it out as far as it will move, then move the indicator into position. Once the indicator is in place, turn the dial until the zero is lined up with the needle. Now push in on the turbine shaft until it seats at the other end of the clearance. The dial indicator will now show the amount of end play present in the transmission. Record the measurement that will be used during the final assembly. A typical dial indicator installation is shown in Figure 9–1.

There are many different methods for measuring the axial end play of the gear train components. Always check the manual for the proper procedure.

9.4.2 Air Tests

If an air test was not part of the diagnosis procedure used to find the transmission malfunction, it is an excellent idea to perform an air test as you disassemble the transmission. Once the valve body is removed, most transmissions can be air tested. Always use low-pressure (25 to 30 psi) regulated shop air, not full-pressure shop air, which can damage components. Remember to listen for the thud of clutch piston application and for the hiss of air leakage (Figure 9–2). When you hear hissing you know that the circuit has a hydraulic leak that must be found and repaired. Some clutches can be air tested with the transmission fully disassembled. On many three-speed transmissions, the front and rear clutches can be placed on the pump and air tested through the passages in the pump (Figure

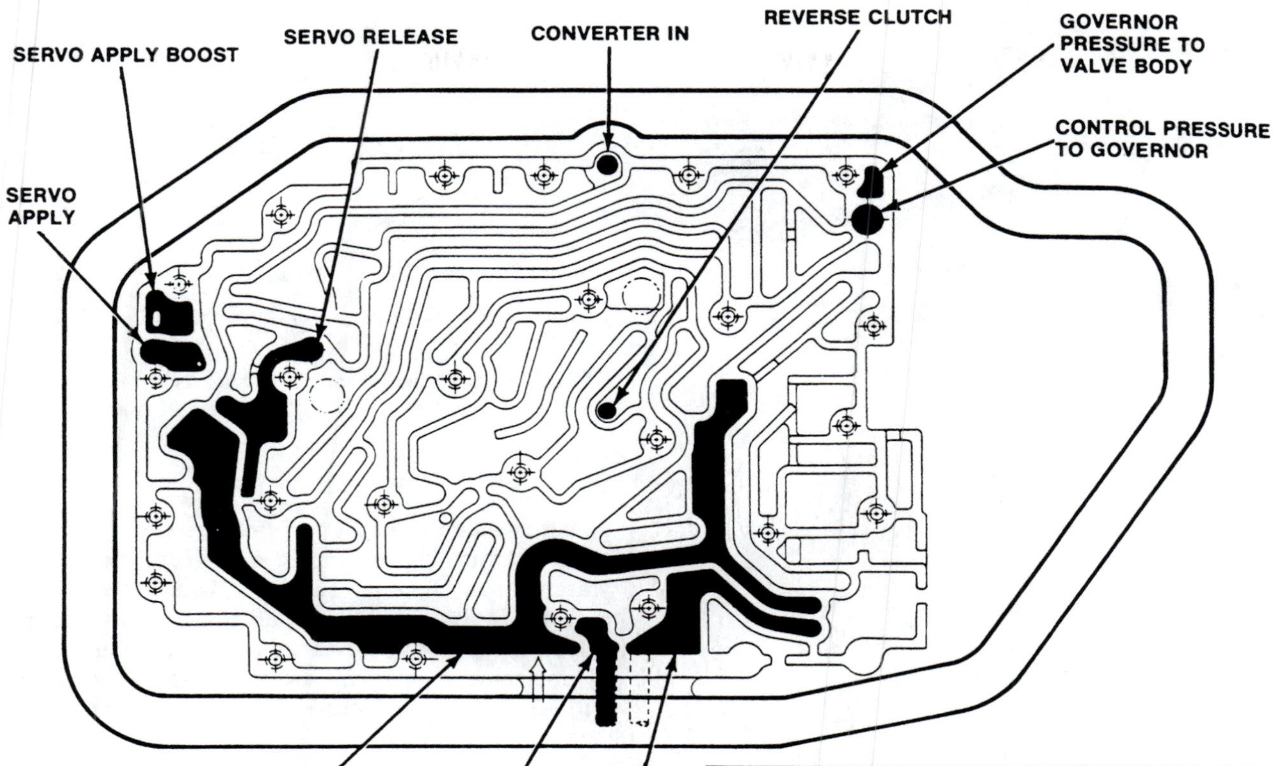

SERVO APPLY BOOST
SERVO RELEASE
CONVERTER IN
REVERSE CLUTCH
GOVERNOR PRESSURE TO VALVE BODY
CONTROL PRESSURE TO GOVERNOR
SERVO APPLY
PUMP IN
DIRECT CLUTCH
INTERMEDIATE CLUTCH

FIGURE 9–2 Clutches and servos should be air tested during disassembly. (Courtesy of Ford)

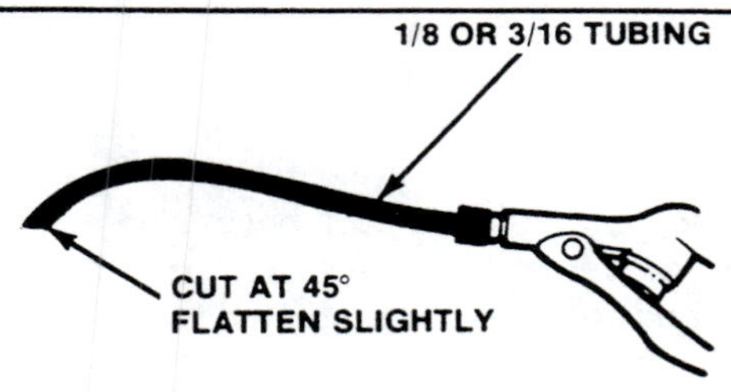

1/8 OR 3/16 TUBING
CUT AT 45°
FLATTEN SLIGHTLY

NOZZLE FOR AIR PRESSURE TESTS

9–3). This tests the clutch seals and the sealing rings.

9.4.3 Special Tools

Because of their complex design, many automatic transmissions use specially designed tools to make disassembly and assembly easier. Following is just a partial list of some of the major types of special tools:

- Special slide hammers
- Pump pullers
- Pump alignment tools
- Center support lifter
- Output shaft support

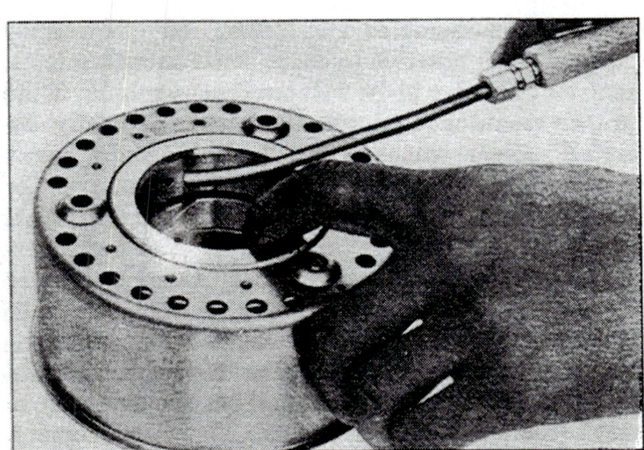

FIGURE 9–3 Some clutches may be air tested in this manner. (Courtesy of Ford)

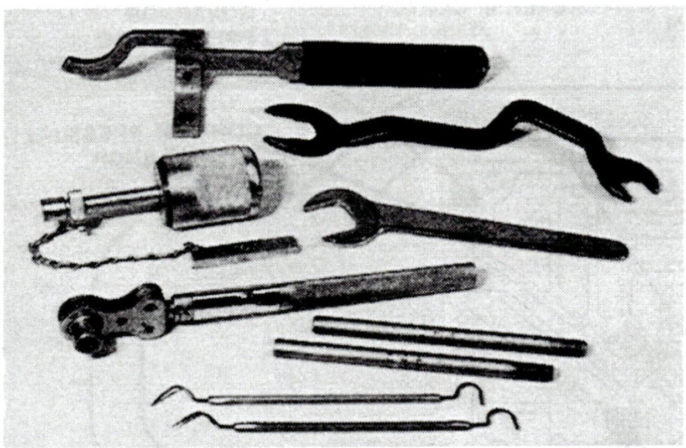

FIGURE 9–4 Special tools.

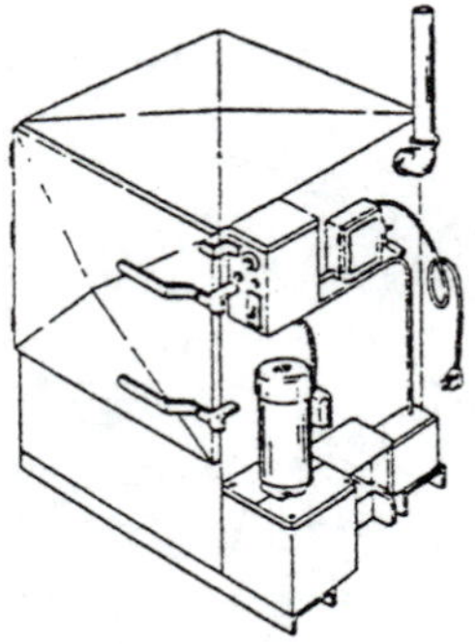

FIGURE 9–5 A power parts washer is the best way to clean parts efficiently.

- Clutch compressors
- Seal installers
- Air test plates
- Converter leak tester
- Converter test equipment

A few special tools are shown in Figure 9–4. The names and part numbers of special tools are given in the factory service manuals, and if the tools are available, they should always be used. Some jobs that require special tools can be done without the tool, but it makes the job much more difficult. Job experience and advice from a seasoned transmission technician, plus the manual, is the best method of learning the individual service needs of each transmission.

9.4.4 Cleaning

Once the automatic transmission has been completely disassembled, it must be thoroughly cleaned. It is possible to clean some subassemblies, such as the valve body, without disassembling if the proper cleaning equipment is used. Specially designed power washers are available from many sources. These power washers come in top- or front-loading models and feature turntables that rotate the parts as they are sprayed with high-pressure streams of heated cleaning solution (Figure 9–5). Most power washers are fully automatic, with wash, rinse, and dry cycles, and use a water-based cleaning solution which includes biodegradable detergents. Other specialized washers are available to clean just valve bodies or flush torque converters. In a transmission shop this type of equipment is a timesaver, freeing technicians to perform more important work. One note of warning about the use of power washers is that clutch friction discs and bands cannot be washed in a machine that uses a water-based cleaning solution. The water will attack the adhesive that bonds the friction material to the disc or band. If these parts are ever washed by mistake, they must be replaced because they will fail in the near future and cause a comeback.

9.5 TORQUE CONVERTER

The torque converter must be visually inspected to find possible damage or problems. Some rebuilders prefer to perform the inspection as the converter is removed. By inspecting first, no time will be lost in cleaning the converter that must be replaced. Some manufacturers use measurement procedures to evaluate the condition of the torque converter, whereas others simply state that if certain conditions are noticed, the torque converter is to be replaced. Inspection and evaluation of the torque converter are essential in preventing installation of a damaged converter on the rebuilt transmission.

9.5.1 Inspection

Visual inspection should start with the converter pilot. Examine the surface that comes in contact with the crankshaft pilot hole for wear and around the base of the pilot for cracks (Figure 9–6).

The area surrounding the pilot should be inspected next. If imprints of the flywheel bolts can be seen next to the pilot on the front surface of the torque converter, it has ballooned. Ballooning is a condition in which the torque converter is distorted, causing the flat front surface to be pushed forward into a convex shape until it contacts the flywheel and flywheel bolts. If the pressure and heat are

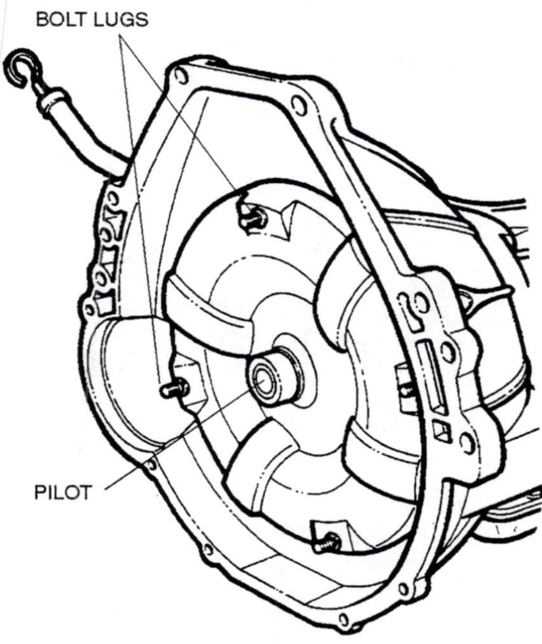

FIGURE 9–6 Examine the converter pilot and mounting lugs for cracks and wear. (Reprinted with permission of General Motors Corporation)

FIGURE 9–7 The flywheel bolt marks on this torque converter show that this converter has ballooned. It must be replaced.

great enough, an imprint of the flywheel bolts will be embedded in the front face of the converter (Figure 9–7). The internal clearance settings of the converter are destroyed when it balloons, so the converter must be replaced.

Next, look at the mounting lugs or studs. Inspect for thread damage and leaks around the lugs or studs. Also look at the bottom of the mounting lugs bolt holes to see if there has been bolt contact with the face of the converter. If the wrong-length bolts are used to secure the converter to the flywheel, the bolts will bottom against the face of the converter and dent the surface. The inside of the converter face is where the converter clutch makes contact, so any damage to that surface would affect converter clutch operation. Examine the bolt holes carefully.

Inspect all welds for signs of leakage or cracks starting. Also look for discolored metal, which could indicate extremely high temperatures in the converter. If any signs of cracks or leaks are found, leak tests should be performed. The leak tester shown in Figure 9–8 uses a rubber plug which seals the converter hub so that air pressure can be used to test for the leak. After the tester is installed, air pressure is applied and measured with a tire gauge. After a short time, measure the pressure again. If the pressure has dropped, there is a leak. A soap-and-water solution can be applied to the suspected leak areas to find the exact location of the leak. Any leaking or cracked converters must be replaced.

The pump drive hub is the last area to be examined. Look closely around the base of the hub for cracks in the weld and at the bottom of the pump drive slots for cracks. The surface of the hub should also be checked for seal or bushing wear. The best test of hub surface condition is performed by using your fingernail to "feel" the surface. If any roughness is felt as you slide your fingernail across the hub, the converter should be repaired or replaced. A slightly rough hub can be polished with 400- or

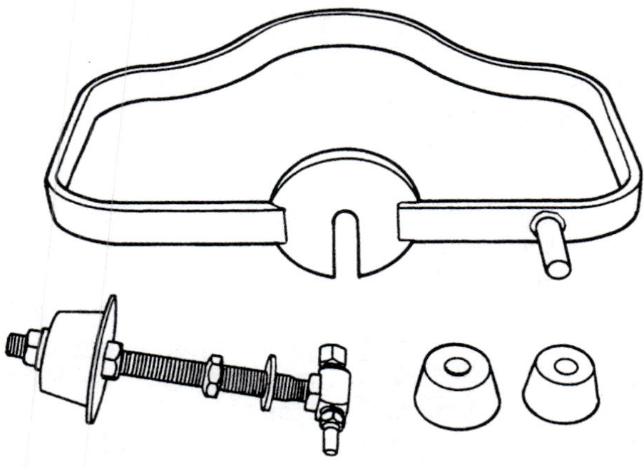

FIGURE 9–8 Converter leak tester. (Courtesy of Ford)

600-grit wet-and-dry automotive sandpaper. The sandpaper should be wetted in solvent and the sanding should be done around the hub. Many rebuilders start their inspection at the hub, since it is a high-wear area, then follow the reverse of the procedure just described. The order of the inspection is not important as long as a complete inspection is performed.

9.5.2 Measurement

Ford Motor Company recommends the following tests and measurements for evaluating the condition of the torque converter: end play check, one-way clutch check, stator-to-turbine interference check, and the stator-to-impeller interference check.

1. End-Play Check

Using the special holding tool shown in Figure 9–9 to grip the turbine, the amount of end play between the turbine and stator can be measured. After the holding tool is in place, a dial indicator is attached to the tool and is positioned so that it contacts the converter housing next to the hub. After zeroing the indicator, the holding tool is lifted up and the end play is read from the dial indicator (Figure 9–10). Compare the measurement with the factory specifications to determine if the unit is serviceable.

2. One-Way Clutch Check

To perform this test, a holding wire is placed inside the hub and inserted into a groove in the stator thrust washer (Figure 9–11). A torquing tool that engages the stator splines is installed next. While gripping the holding wire tightly, turn the torquing tool in both directions with a torque wrench. The one-way clutch should turn freely in a clockwise direction and should lock up and hold up to 10 lb-ft of torque in the counterclockwise direction, as shown in Figure 9–12. If the converter fails the test, it should be replaced.

3. Stator and Turbine Interference Check

Place the holding fixture in a vice, then place the converter on the fixture with the hub facing up. Insert the holding wire, then install the turning tool in the turbine splines. Next, slide the turning tool guide over the tool and into the hub. Now rotate the turbine with a torque wrench. It should turn both directions with less than 5 lb-ft of torque without loud, scraping sounds. Replace the converter if it fails this test.

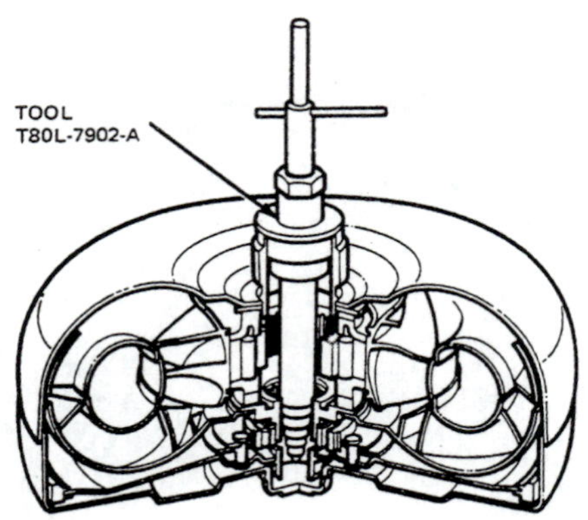

FIGURE 9–9 End-play check on a Ford torque converter using a special holding tool. (Courtesy of Ford)

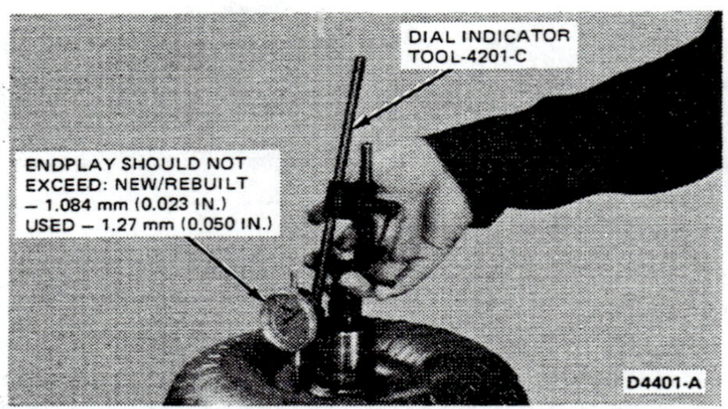

FIGURE 9–10 A dial indicator is used to measure end play. (Courtesy of Ford)

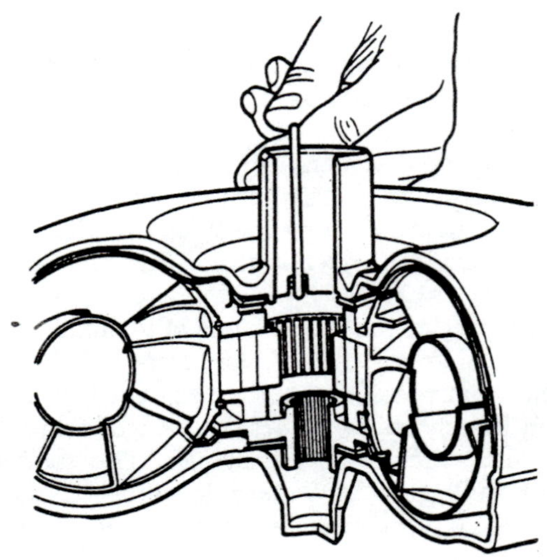

FIGURE 9–11 Installing the holding wire for a one-way clutch test. (Courtesy of Ford)

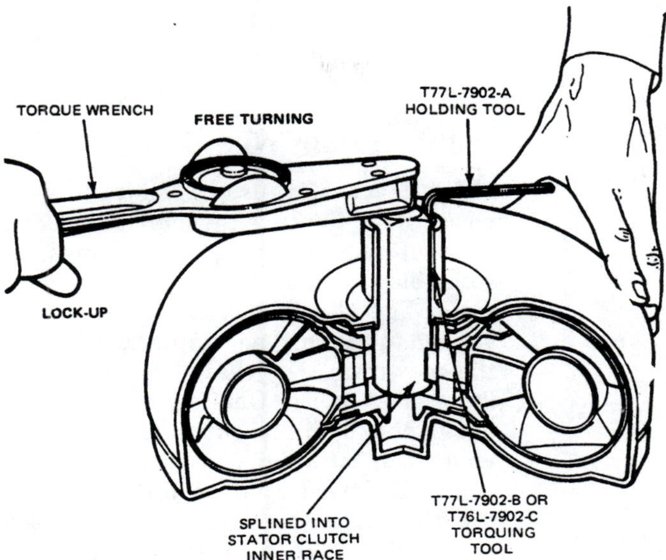

FIGURE 9–12 Check holding ability with a torque wrench. (Courtesy of Ford)

4. *Stator-to-Impeller Interference Check*
Place the assembled oil pump on the workbench with the stator support pointed up, then carefully lower the torque converter onto the support until it is fully engaged. Now rotate the converter while holding the pump stationary (Figure 9–13). Listen for a scraping sound as you turn the converter in both directions. If you hear a scraping noise, the converter should be replaced.

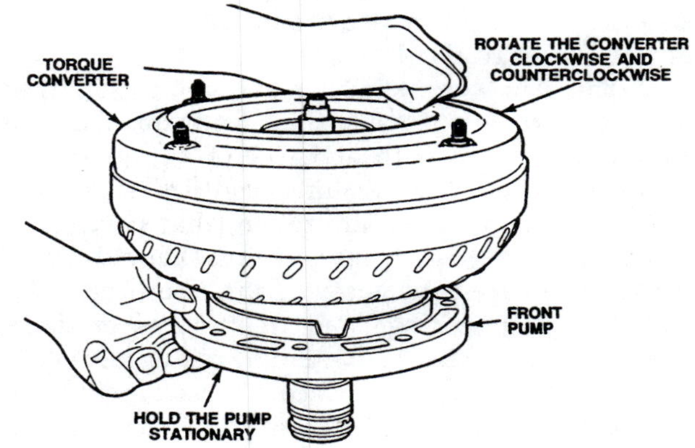

FIGURE 9–13 Listen for scraping sounds while making this impeller-to-stator interference check. (Courtesy of Ford)

9.5.3 Cleaning

All torque converters should be flushed and cleaned thoroughly before being reused in a rebuilt transmission. The specially designed torque converter washers use both converter movement and internal spray fixtures to remove and flush any debris from inside the converter. Without flushing the converter, the chances of contaminating the rebuilt transmission are excellent. Flushing the torque converter and fluid cooler should be done on every transmission rebuilt.

To lower the cost of replacement parts, many transmission shops are now rebuilding torque converters in their own shop. Torque converter rebuilding equipment designed for small shop use has become a popular growth area for transmission repair shops.

9.6 GEAR TRAIN

The gear train components covered in this section are the input shaft, chain and sprockets for transaxles, planetary gear sets, and output shafts. We describe the inspection process in general and the repair and replacement procedures for the major components.

9.6.1 Inspection

After the parts have been cleaned, a close visual inspection for signs of wear or stress is started. The first place to look on each part is where two parts are splined together. Normally, parts that are splined together have a small amount of play, or free movement, between parts. Through the stress of normal operation, the splines wear and the amount of play increases. Too much play allows the

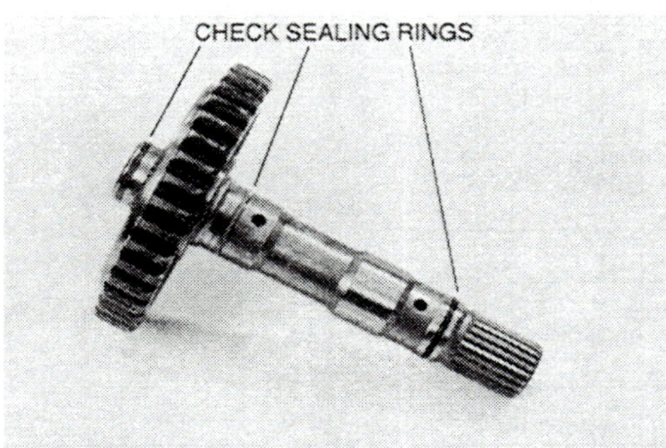

FIGURE 9–14 Examine the edges of the contact surface of sealing rings to determine wear.

parts to become noisy and misaligned. At this point, the parts must be replaced. Making the judgment about how much play is acceptable takes experience. If you doubt your decision, ask the advice of any seasoned transmission technician.

The next wear point is where a bushing in another part rides against a shaft or drum. This area should be very smooth and free of any grooves or depressions on the bushing contact surface. If grooves or depressions are found, that part should be replaced along with the bushing that rides on it. Bushing replacement is covered in another section.

The sealing rings and the sleeves or drums they seat in constitute the next area of inspection. Examine the sealing surface of the rings to see if the edges of the rings are sharp or rounded (Figure 9–14). Rounded edges on the sealing rings indicate wear on the rings. The bore the rings seal against must also be smooth, with no grooves or depressions. Inspect all parts for signs of wear and loose fit.

9.6.2 Chain Wear

Many transaxles use a chain drive to transfer power from the turbine shaft to the gear train because of their design. In many transaxles, the chain resembles a camshaft timing chain, only on a larger scale. The chain runs on a set of sprockets, one splined to the turbine shaft and the other splined to the gear train. The chain does wear, and as it does it becomes noisy. Chain wear is normally tested while the chain is installed by measuring the amount of total deflection on the slack side of the chain. The most common procedure calls for pushing the chain outward and marking where the outer edge of the chain extends on the case behind the chain. Then push the chain inward and measure from the mark to the edge of the chain (Figure 9–15). Although many aftermarket chain tensioners are available as a "quick fix," the recommended repair for a loose chain is to replace all worn parts.

9.6.3 Planet Pinion Wear

The planetary gear sets must be closely inspected to find any wear that has occurred. If the transmission operates quietly in each gear, chances are that there is little or no wear in the planetary gear sets. But if the transmission is noisy in any of the lower gears or overdrive, there is a wear problem and the worn parts must be identified and replaced.

The planet pinion gears receive the most wear because of their size. The teeth of the planet pinion

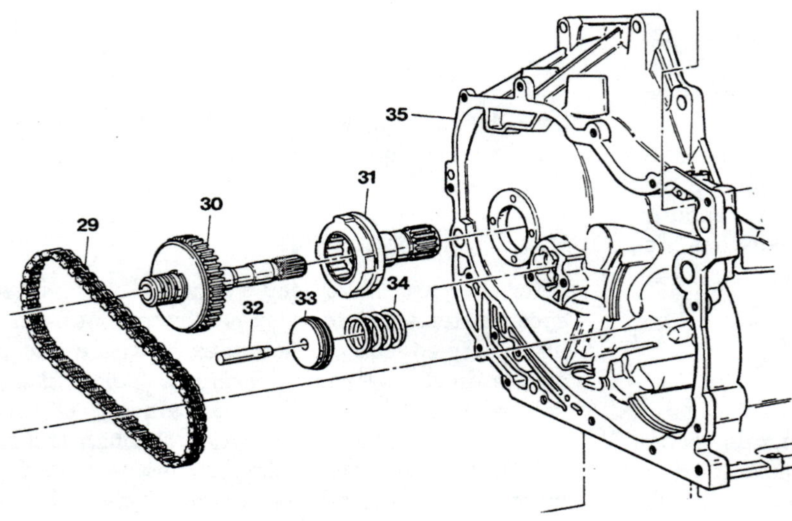

FIGURE 9–15 Drive chain wear should be measured. (Reprinted with permission of General Motors Corporation)

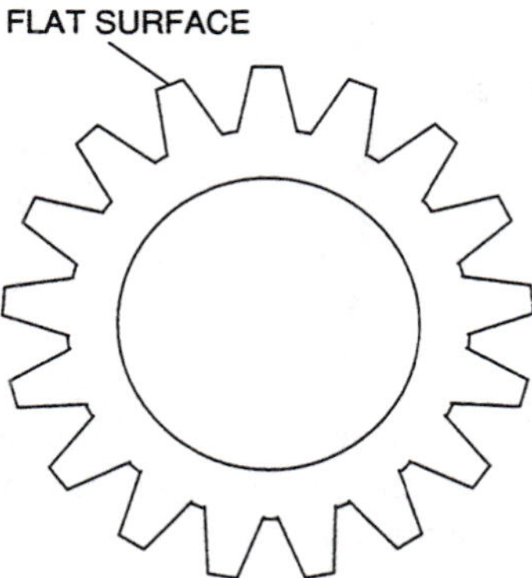

FIGURE 9–16 The edge of a new pinion gear has a flat surface.

FIGURE 9–17 A worn pinion gear can have a sharp edge.

gears should be examined to determine if they are wearing thin. A new pinion gear has a small flat area at the top edge of the tooth, as shown in Figure 9–16. As wear occurs on the tooth, the flat area becomes narrower until in cases of extreme wear, the edge of the tooth becomes sharp (Figure 9–17).

The thrust washers at each side of the pinion gears must also be checked for wear. Some transmissions have a tendency to wear out the pinion thrust washer, so planet pinion side play should always be checked. Specially designed aftermarket shims that lock to the planet carrier are available to reduce the pinion side clearance. If any roughness is felt in the pinions as they are turned, the planet carrier assembly should be rebuilt or replaced. Refer to the service manual for the exact procedure.

9.6.4 Bushing Wear

All the bushings in the transmission should be visually inspected for signs of wear. When a worn bushing is found, always check the bushing contact surface of the adjoining part for damage. Replacing worn bushings is a simple procedure but does require special tools. A bushing driver is used to remove and install bushings (Figure 9–18). The

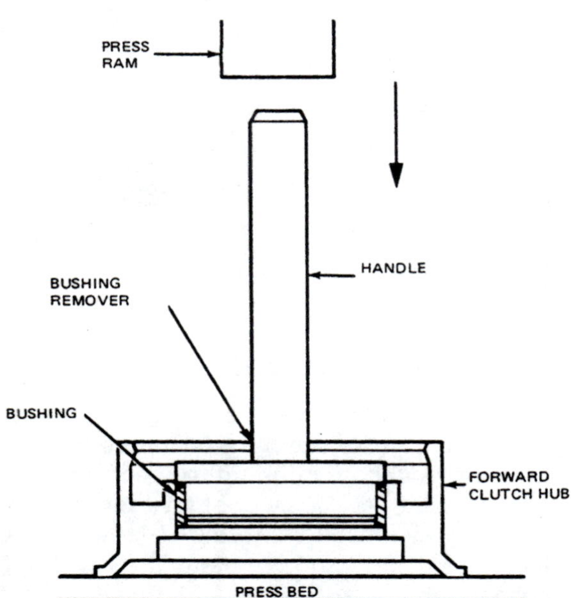

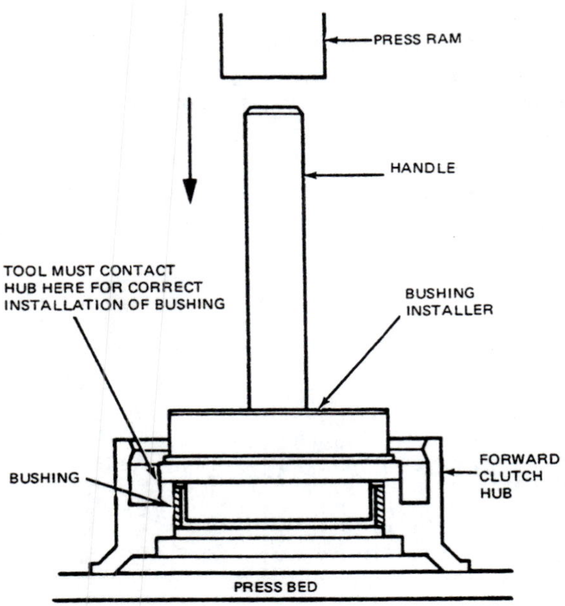

FIGURE 9–18 A bushing should always be removed and installed using a bushing driver. (Courtesy of Ford)

driver must match the size of the bushings or damage will occur during installation. The service manual lists the bushing drivers used for each specific transmission.

9.6.5 Thrust Washer Wear

The transmission thrust washers, both friction and antifriction types, should be inspected for wear. The plain thrust washer (friction type) should be inspected visually first. If the thrust surface shows wear, the thickness of the washer should be measured with a micrometer and the reading compared to the factory specifications (Figure 9–19). An early clue that there are worn thrust washers can come from an input shaft end play reading that is over-specifications.

The roller thrust bearings (antifriction type) are checked by pushing the races together and turning the bearing to feel for roughness. The bearing should be washed in solvent and lightly oiled before testing to remove any dirt that might cause roughness during the test. If any roughness if felt in a roller thrust bearing, it should be replaced. All the other roller thrust bearings and support bearings should be inspected closely to see if they have been contaminated with metal particles and damaged.

9.7 PUMP

The pump is the source of all hydraulic power for the automatic transmission. If the pump is unable to provide the proper flow of fluid to the hydraulic circuits, the transmission is doomed to fail. An early clue to pump wear problems can come from the mainline pressure test. A low-pressure reading indicates a worn pump or pressure regulator problem.

THICKNESS	IDENTIFICATION NUMBER AND/OR COLOR
2.90 - 3.01mm (0.114" - 0.119")	1 - ORANGE
3.08 - 3.19mm (0.121" - 0.126")	2 - WHITE
3.26 - 3.37mm (0.128" - 0.133")	3 - YELLOW
3.44 - 3.55mm (0.135" - 0.140")	4 - BLUE
3.62 - 3.73mm (0.143" - 0.147")	5 - RED
3.80 - 3.91mm (0.150" - 0.154")	6 - BROWN
3.98 - 4.09mm (0.157" - 0.161")	7 - GREEN
4.16 - 4.27mm (0.164" - 0.168")	8 - BLACK
4.34 - 4.45mm (0.171" - 0.175")	9 - PURPLE

FIGURE 9–19 The thickness of all thrust washers is listed in the service manual. (Reprinted with permission of General Motors Corporation)

9.7.1 Inspection

The pump should be fully disassembled and all parts inspected for wear. On a gear crescent and gerotor pump, the pump body should be closely inspected for signs of wear (Figure 9–20). The gears and gerotors should be inspected along with the pump cover. The trailing edge of the crescent should be closely inspected because extreme wear in this area indicates a badly worn pump that must be replaced. If the pump cover is deeply worn, it should be replaced. Inspect any valves located in the pump body and clean and polish the valves if necessary. Follow the service manual procedures.

Vane pumps require more attention than other pumps because of their complexity and because of the materials from which they are made. Most vane pumps have an aluminum body, which is softer than the cast iron used for other types of pumps. Study and follow the factory service manual procedures for checking and measuring a vane pump.

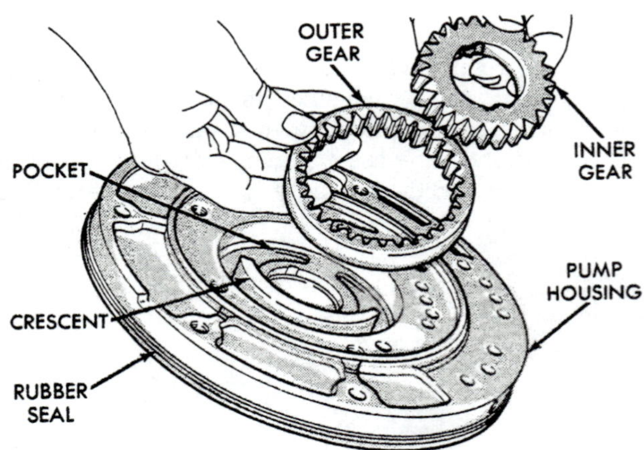

FIGURE 9–20 A pump body must be checked for wear. (Courtesy of Chrysler)

9.7.2 Measurement

Body, side, and tip clearance on gear crescent and gerotor pumps are the measurements to be taken. Not all manufacturers use all these measurements, so refer to the service manual for exact procedures.

Body clearance is measured between the driven (outside) gear and the pump body with a feeler gauge, as shown in Figure 9–21. If out of specifications, replace the driven gear.

Side clearance is measured across the side of the gears using a straightedge and feeler gauge, as

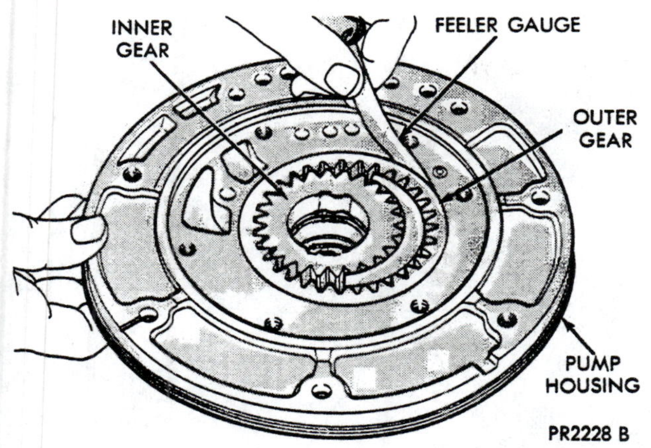

FIGURE 9–21 Measure gear-to-body clearance as shown. (Courtesy of Chrysler)

FIGURE 9–22 Side clearance is measured using a straightedge. (Reprinted with permission of General Motors Corporation)

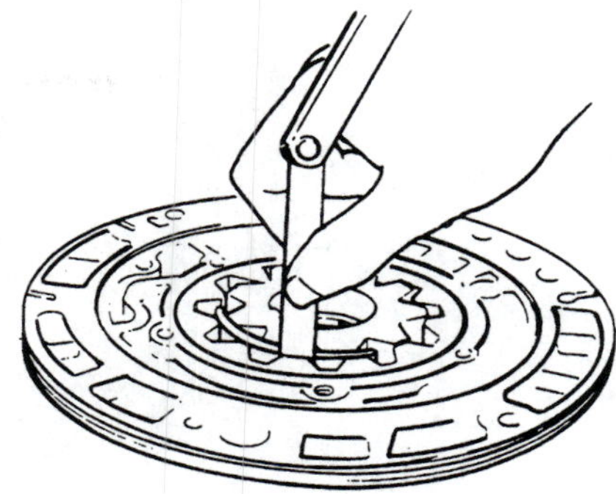

FIGURE 9–23 Measure tip clearance here. (Reprinted with permission of General Motors Corporation)

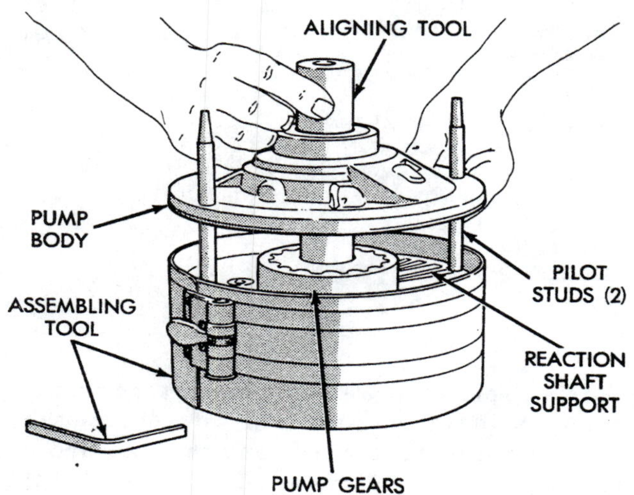

FIGURE 9–24 A pump alignment tool resembles a large hose clamp. (Courtesy of Chrysler)

seen in Figure 9–22. If out of specifications, replace both gears.

Tip clearance is measured between the tip of the driving (inner) and driven (outer) gears and the crescent is shown in Figure 9–23. If out of specifications, replace the worn gear.

While the pump is disassembled, replace the front seal and bushing. Always replace the converter hub bushing along with the front seal to assure long seal life.

Some manufacturers recommend the use of an alignment tool to assemble the pump (Figure 9–24). The tool holds the pump halves in alignment while the bolts are snugged down, and then the bolts should be torqued to specification following the proper tightening sequence. After assembling the pump, check for free gear movement by putting the pump and converter together and turning the pump. If the pump does not turn freely, repair or replace the pump as necessary.

9.8 CLUTCHES

The basic steps for clutch rebuilding are the same for all multidisc clutches. Those basic steps are explained in this section and will apply to most transmissions. The factory service manual should always be referred to first to assure that the proper procedures are being used. A typical clutch assembly is shown in Figure 9–25.

9.8.1 Disassembly

Start the clutch disassembly by removing the snap ring that retains the pressure plate, as shown in Figure 9–26. Next remove the pressure plate and

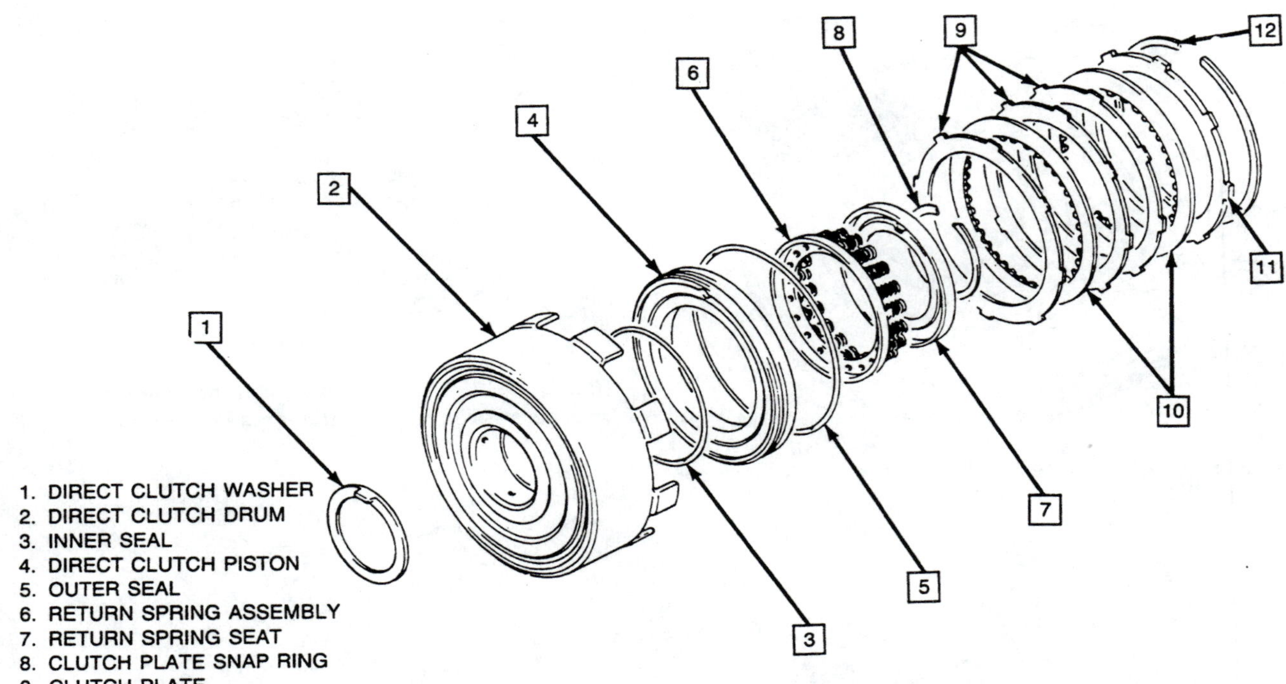

FIGURE 9–25 Typical multidisc clutch. (Reprinted with permission of General Motors Corporation)

the clutch discs (Figure 9–27). Inspect the pressure plate and discs for wear and save the reusable parts. Steels that are smooth and not discolored are reusable. Count the frictions and steels so that the correct number of discs are used during assembly.

FIGURE 9–26 Remove the snap ring with a screwdriver. (Courtesy of Chrysler)

The friction discs are always replaced when rebuilding a transmission. Now compress the piston return spring and remove the snap ring and retainer (Figure 9–28). If the clutch piston is hard to remove, shop air can be applied to the piston through the fluid inlet hole to blow the piston out (Figure 9–29). Inspect the seals on the piston and in the drum for signs of seal failure. If the clutch has failed and burned, you need to find the hydraulic leak that caused the failure. Inspect all the parts of the circuit until the cause of the failure is found.

9.8.2 Piston Seals

Next remove the old seals with a sharp-pointed pick. Rinse the piston in solvent and blow dry. Install the new seal with the lip pointing toward the fluid (Figure 9–30). Wash and dry the clutch drum, then coat the seal contact areas with clean ATF. To ease the job of installing the piston, lubricate the seals with Transjel assembly lube or petroleum jelly. The lube helps protect the seals from damage as they are installed. Place the piston in the clutch drum at a slight angle and rotate the pis-

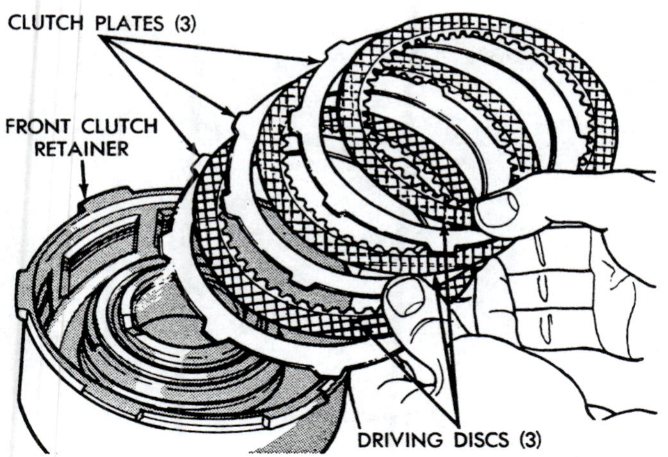

FIGURE 9–27 Remove the clutch discs and plates. (Courtesy of Chrysler)

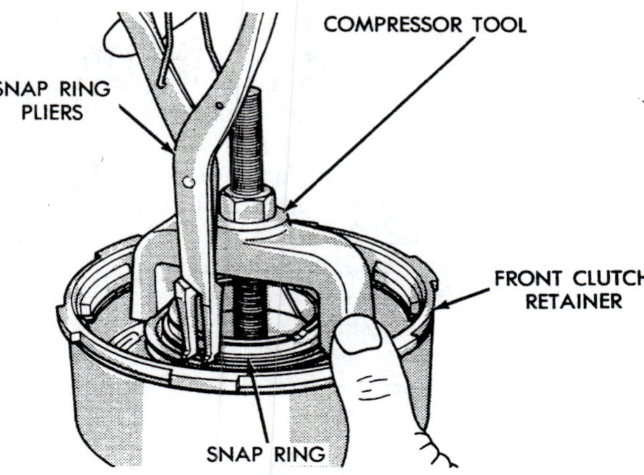

FIGURE 9–28 After compressing the piston return spring, remove the snap ring. (Courtesy of Chrysler)

ton as you press down lightly. If the seals hang up, a 0.006-in. feeler gauge can be used as a "shoehorn" to help the installation. Insert the feeler gauge between the piston and drum, then move the gauge around the piston to force the seal lip down. Repeat this process on the other seal. This must be done very carefully so as not to damage the seal. Some clutch pistons require special installing tools that compress the seal and "shoehorn" it into the piston bore. If the manual recommends such tools, trying to install the piston without the tool usually results in a torn seal. If it appears that the seal has been damaged, replace it with a new one. Work very carefully! After the piston is installed, replace the return spring or springs, and the retainer. Compress the spring and install the snap ring.

9.8.3 Clutch Discs

The friction discs must be soaked in clean ATF to prelubricate them so that they will not be damaged during the startup. Some manufacturers recom-

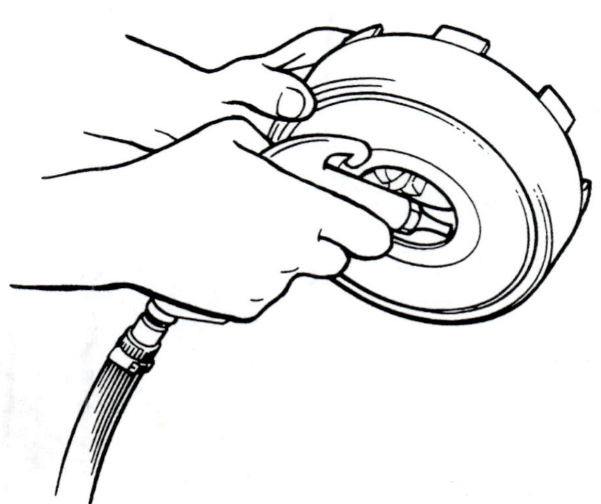

FIGURE 9–29 Compressed air can be used to force a piston out of the drum. (Reprinted with permission of General Motors Corporation)

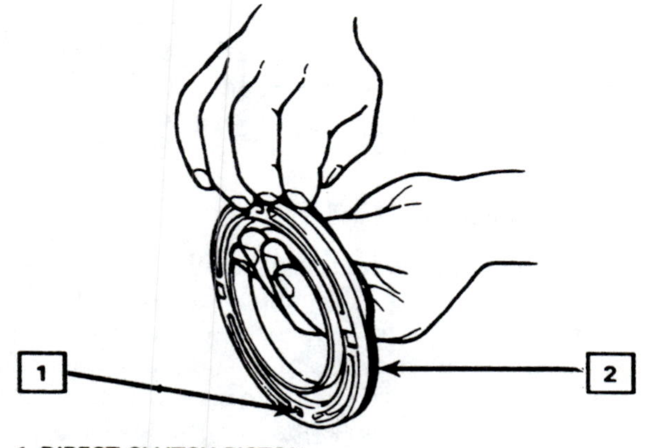

FIGURE 9–30 Install new seals with the lips pointing in the proper direction. (Reprinted with permission of General Motors Corporation)

mend soaking the discs a minimum of 2 hours, so allow ample time. If the clutch pack has a wave plate, it should be placed next to the piston, and if no wave plate is used, a steel plate is first. A friction disc is next, with the rest of the clutch pack alternating until the pressure plate is installed. Make sure that the same number of discs and plates are installed as were removed. The snap ring can now be installed and the clutch is rebuilt. If aftermarket clutch plate parts are used in the rebuilding job, you should know that they could be made with Dexron-compatible friction material. Check the instruction sheet to make sure of which type ATF to use after the rebuild.

9.8.4 Clutch Pack Clearance

For the clutch pack to have a long service life, the friction discs and steel plates must have the space to turn freely when the clutch is not applied. This space, called clutch pack clearance, must always be checked to assure proper clutch operation. Most manufacturers recommend checking the clearance with a feeler gauge placed in between the back side of the pressure plate and the snap ring (Figure 9–31). One manufacturer uses a vernier caliper to measure the distance between the top of the snap ring and the top of the pressure plate, as shown in Figure 9–32. The clearance is adjusted by using selective-fit pressure plates or snap rings. Refer to the factory service manual for the correct procedure.

9.9 BANDS

The transmission band is a holding device that is used to temporarily lock the planetary gear set's reaction member to the transmission case. The bands and their servos are removed during disassembly so that the parts are ready for inspection. A typical band and servo are shown in Figure 9–33.

9.9.1 Inspection

The bands' friction material should be checked for cracks and flaking. The thickness of the friction material should also be measured and compared to the thickness of a new band or the factory specification if one is given. The band contact surface on the clutch drum must also be inspected for surface damage (Figure 9–34). If the drum is rough, it must be replaced. If the drum surface is too smooth, it should be sanded with medium-grit sandpaper to provide the proper surface finish. Any bands that show cracking or flaking or are too thin must also be replaced.

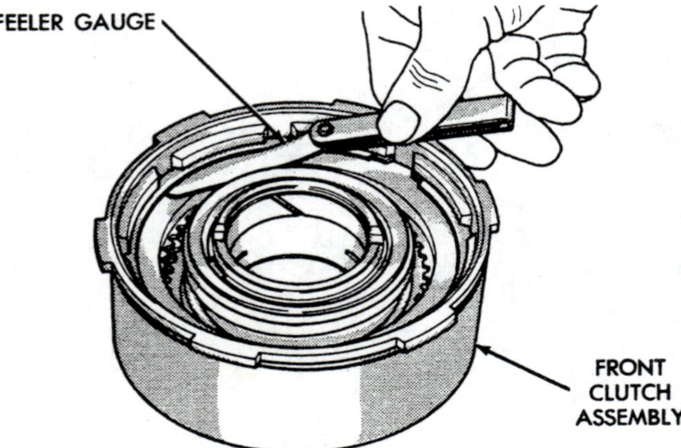

FIGURE 9–31 One method of measuring clutch pack clearance. (Courtesy of Chrysler)

9.9.2 Replacement

The bore of the servo in the transmission case should be inspected for wear along with the servo piston, push rod, return spring, and retainer. Any parts showing extreme wear must be replaced. Most servo pistons use a cast iron sealing ring similar to an engine compression ring. Care should be used in spreading the new sealing ring when installing it, as they are easily broken. Some servos use a neoprene lip seal that is bonded to the servo piston. If this seal is bad, the piston must be replaced. Other manufacturers use replaceable lip seals or O-rings to seal the servos. The service manual will provide the proper instructions for the particular transmission you are rebuilding. Always use the service manual.

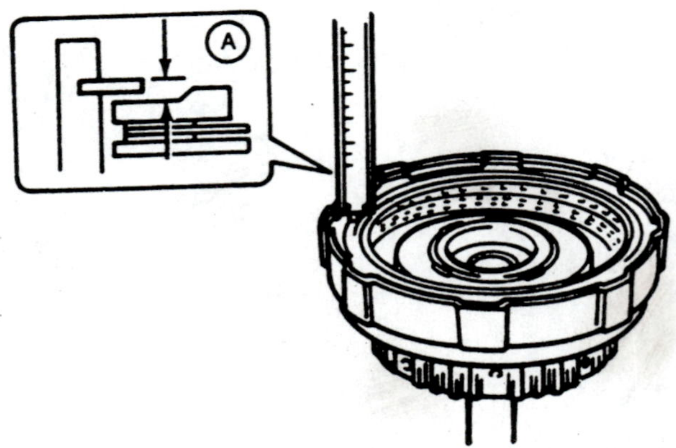

FIGURE 9–32 A vernier caliper is used by some manufacturers to measure clutch pack clearance. (Reprinted with permission of General Motors Corporation)

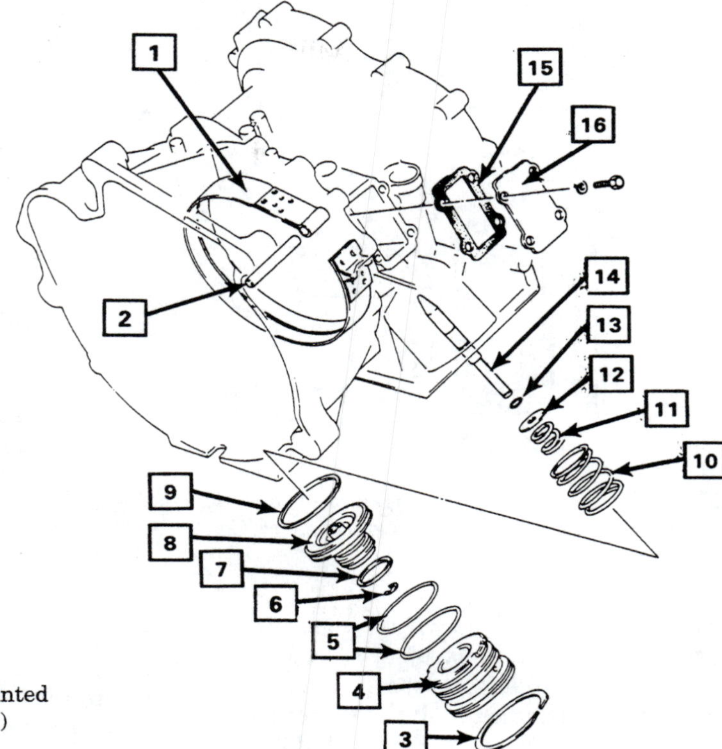

1. SECOND BRAKE BAND
2. PIN
3. PISTON COVER SNAP RING
4. PISTON COVER
5. COVER SEAL
6. RETAINER
7. SEAL RING
8. SECOND BRAKE PISTON
9. PISTON SEAL
10. PISTON SPRING
11. BRAKE ROD SPRING
12. WASHER
13. PISTON ROD SEAL
14. SECOND BRAKE PISTON ROD
15. COVER GASKET
16. COVER

FIGURE 9–33 Typical band and servo. (Reprinted with permission of General Motors Corporation)

9.9.3 Band Adjustments

Most transmissions require some type of band adjustment, although some bands need no adjustment because of the length of the servo travel. A servo that has a long travel can make up for wear on the band and does not need an adjustment. The procedures for adjusting internal and external screw adjusters were explained in Chapter 8.

Graduated push rods are another type of band adjustment that is widely used. This type of adjustment is made during transmission assembly. The

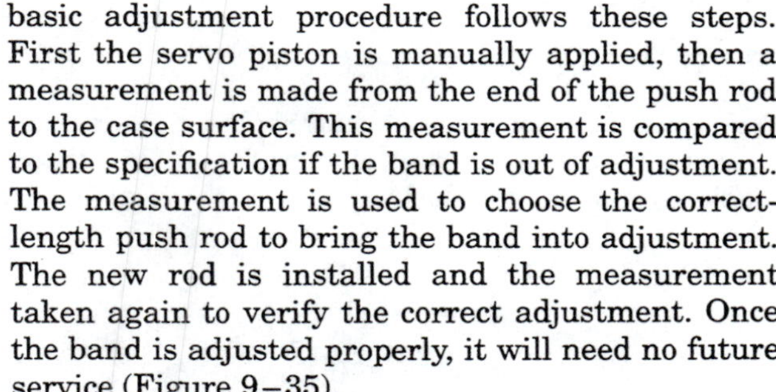

basic adjustment procedure follows these steps. First the servo piston is manually applied, then a measurement is made from the end of the push rod to the case surface. This measurement is compared to the specification if the band is out of adjustment. The measurement is used to choose the correct-length push rod to bring the band into adjustment. The new rod is installed and the measurement taken again to verify the correct adjustment. Once the band is adjusted properly, it will need no future service (Figure 9–35).

FIGURE 9–34 The band friction surface on drums should be inspected for surface damage.

9.10 ONE-WAY CLUTCHES

One-way clutches of both the roller and sprag types are used in two ways, as holding devices and also as coupling devices for power transfer.

9.10.1 Inspection

It is hard to hand test a one-way clutch and be sure that it will be able to hold the much greater engine torque. It is best to diagnose a possible slipping one-way clutch thoroughly during the road test to provide a positive identification of a slipping one-way clutch. Procedures for those tests are listed in the service manuals. One common cause of one-way clutch slippage is weak springs (Figure 9–36). In some cases the one-way will slip when the trans-

Piston rod length	Identification mark
121.3 mm (4.77 in)	Unmarked
122.7 mm (4.83 in)	Marked

FIGURE 9–35 Graduated push rods are used to adjust band clearance. (Reprinted with permission of General Motors Corporation)

mission is cold but will hold when at operating temperature. This condition is also caused by weak springs. The races, rollers, or sprags must all be inspected for surface damage. All the contact surfaces must be smooth. Replace any parts that are rough or show any type of surface damage.

9.10.2 Replacement

You must be very careful when replacing a one-way clutch because it is easy to install the new clutch backward so it will lock up and freewheel in the wrong directions. Always test all one-way clutches during disassembly and note the direction of lockup and the direction of freewheeling. Write the notes where they will not be lost and if a one-way clutch is replaced, use the notes to guarantee proper installation. Replacement procedures are explained clearly in the service manuals.

9.11 SHIFT CONTROLS

All shift control devices should be inspected and cleaned and their operation verified to prevent malfunctions and comebacks. The full-range operation of the shift controls should have been tested during the road test section of the diagnosis. Any problems that were spotted during the test should be corrected at this time.

9.11.1 Governor

The governor should be cleaned and oiled with ATF and tested to see if the weight of the governor valve alone will cause it to move from one end of its bore to the other. If the valve does not pass this test, disassemble the governor and polish the valve. The procedure for polishing hydraulic valves was described in Chapter 8. If the governor has two valves, as shown in Figure 9–37, both valves must be checked. If any spring loading is used on the valve, the spring must be removed to test the valve movement. All hydraulic valves must move freely with their own weight in order to work properly.

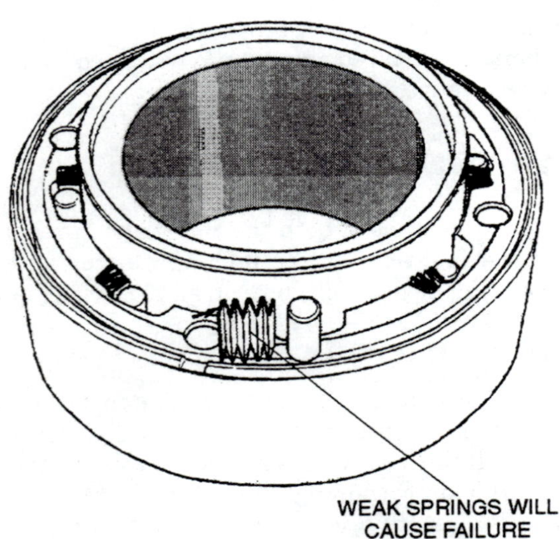

FIGURE 9–36 Weak springs in a one-way clutch can cause slippage. (Courtesy of Chrysler)

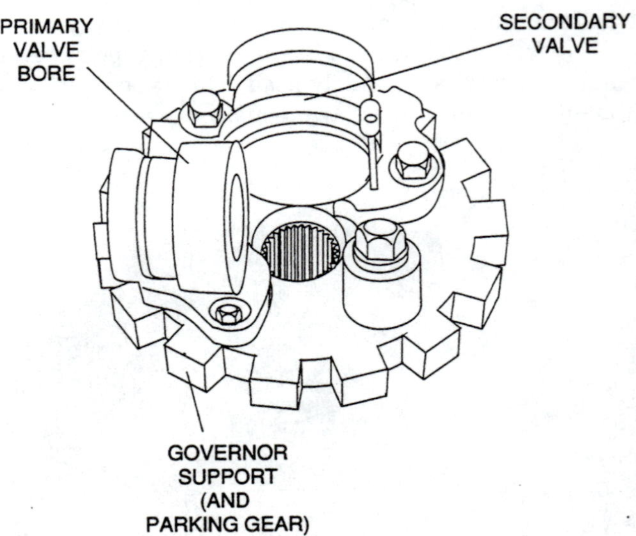

FIGURE 9–37 Both governor valves must be checked for free movement. (Courtesy of Chrysler)

9.11.2 Throttle Valve

The throttle valve must be able to move freely in its bore and should be tested for free movement. Some throttle valves are located in the transmission case, while others are housed in the valve body. The action of the vacuum modulator should have been tested during diagnosis, but if it was not, test the modulator for vacuum leaks at this time. It should hold a vacuum for at least 30 seconds with no bleed down (Figure 9–38). On transmissions that use throttle valve cables, free movement of the cable, linkage, and throttle valve must all be checked.

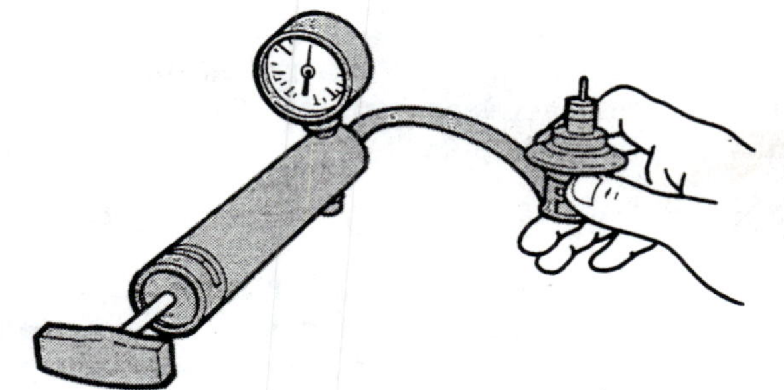

FIGURE 9–38 The vacuum modulator should be tested with a vacuum hand pump. (Courtesy of Ford)

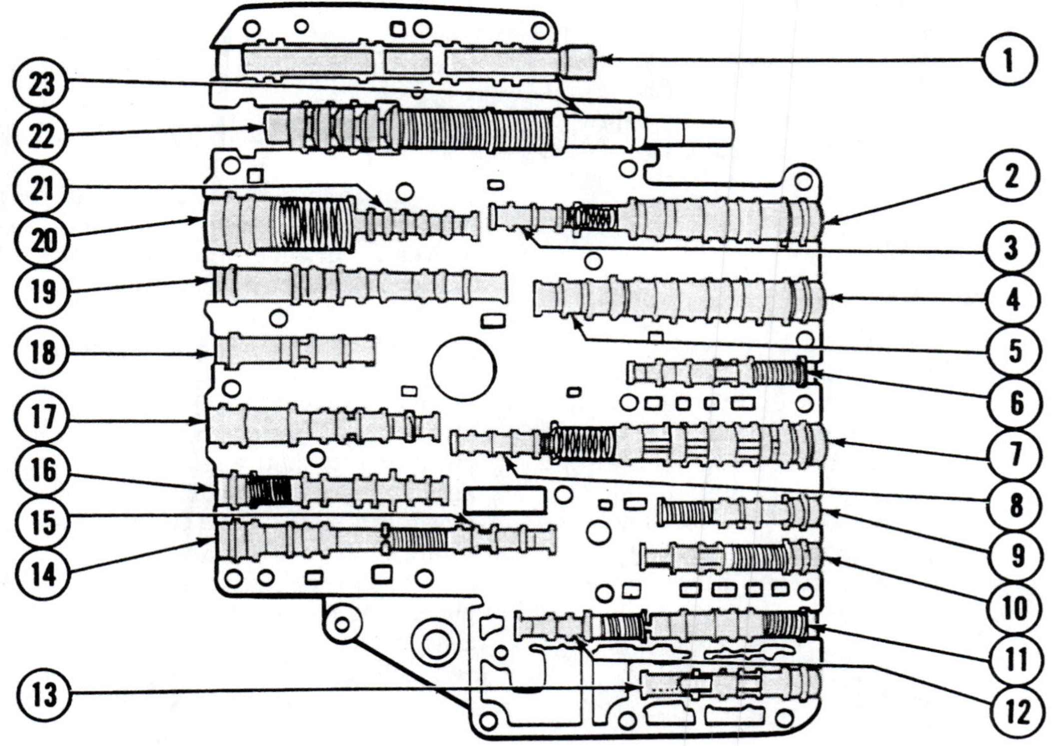

VALVE IDENTIFICATION

1. MANUAL VALVE
2. 2-3 SHIFT VALVE
3. 2-3 TV MODULATOR VALVE
4. 1-2 SHIFT VALVE
5. 1-2 THROTTLE DELAY VALVE
6. 2-1 SCHEDULING VALVE
7. 3-4 SHIFT VALVE
8. 3-4 TV MODULATOR VALVE
9. 2-4 INHIBIT VALVE
10. 3-2 CONTROL VALVE
11. TV LIMIT VALVE
12. N-D ENGAGEMENT VALVE
13. 2-3 SERVO REGULATOR VALVE
14. TV/LINE MODULATOR VALVE
15. 4-3 SCHEDULATING VALVE
16. BACKOUT VALVE
17. ACCUMULATOR REGULATOR VALVE
18. CONVERTER REGULATOR VALVE
19. CONVERTER CLUTCH CONTROL VALVE
20. MAIN REGULATOR BOOST VALVE
21. MAIN REGULATOR VALVE
22. THROTTLE VALVE (TV)
23. THROTTLE PLUNGER

FIGURE 9–39 Typical valve body. (Courtesy of Ford)

Adjustment of the throttle valve cable will be made after the transmission is reinstalled, but checking all the components for smooth, free operation at this time is a good plan.

9.11.3 Valve Body

The typical valve body, shown in Figure 9–39, has many different valves housed in a single casing. They all must work freely to operate properly, so they must be thoroughly cleaned during rebuilding. Specially designed power washers can wash, rinse, and dry the valve body without disassembling it. Spray carburetor cleaner or lacquer thinner also does an excellent job of cleaning a valve body. If a problem was diagnosed in the valve body, the valves involved should be removed, cleaned, polished, and tested for free movement. If the transmission is highly contaminated with debris, it should be totally disassembled and cleaned, polished, and tested or simply replaced with a rebuilt valve body. In most cases its best to disassemble the valve body totally for cleaning.

9.11.4 Accumulators

All accumulator seals should be checked for possible leaks because a leak past the accumulator piston will lower the pressure in the rest of that hydraulic system. The lower pressure can cause a clutch failure. If the transmission being rebuilt has a burned clutch, check the accumulator for that clutch carefully. Always reseal the accumulators during rebuilding. The accumulator spring should also be inspected and replaced if found faulty (Figure 9–40).

FIGURE 9–40 The accumulator spring and seals must be inspected. (Courtesy of Chrysler)

9.11.5 Shift Solenoids

Proper operation of the shift solenoids must be verified before they are reused. Operation of the solenoid is easily checked by using jumper wires and a 12-V power source. Connect one jumper from the body or ground wire of the solenoid to the negative terminal of the power source and the other jumper from the positive terminal of the source to the solenoid lead. Listen for a click in the solenoid, then disconnect the positive lead.

The ability of the valve portion of the shift solenoid to seal must also be checked. A vacuum hand pump and the proper-size hose to adapt to the valve end of the solenoid can be used to verify the valve's sealing ability. Compare tests on a new solenoid with the old if you are unsure of the results.

9.12 TRANSMISSION ASSEMBLY

As with earlier units, this is not a specific list of procedures. The service manuals are the best source for detailed procedures; this text will cover the general background information needed to fill in the gaps left by the manuals and provide an overview of transmission rebuilding.

Cleanliness is important in transmission rebuilding because the hydraulic system is hypersensitive to dirt. Care must be taken at every step of rebuilding to do the cleanest work possible. During assembly parts should be rinsed in solvent and blown dry if they have become dusty or dirty while awaiting assembly. Only lint-free cloth should ever be used to wipe parts since any lint left on the components is washed down by the fluid and ends up clogging the filter. All parts and seals must be properly lubricated to prevent the damage caused by dry startup. Special assembly lubricants are available in jelly form to be used to hold thrust washers in place during assembly and to provide startup lubrication. Dry startup will cause unwanted wear and damage to critical components and seals. During assembly, do not use extreme force in putting parts together. They are close fitting but will go together if they are assembled properly. If parts do not go together with ease, check your assembly procedure in the manual because something is probably installed incorrectly. Stop at that point and disassemble parts until the problem is found.

Aligning clutches to slide onto the splines of their adjoining part can be a hard task. A very light downward pressure while turning the parts will usually get the job done. Have patience and try to feel what is happening as the parts go together.

Make totally sure that all thrust washers are in the proper location and facing the right direction. Great damage is caused by a roller thrust bearing that is installed backwards. Follow the manual closely to avoid this problem. As a general rule, a gasket sealer is not used to seal gaskets in an automatic transmission, but a few manufacturers recommend the use of special sealers for specific problem areas in their transmissions. Follow the manufacturers' directions to the letter and do not use sealers anywhere other than as specified in the instructions.

When installing any component that is bolted on, install all the bolts before tightening, then snug all the bolts down, and finish by torquing the bolts in two steps. The first step should be half the torque specification, then the second step to the full torque setting. All bolts must be clean and lightly oiled to give true torque readings. Always follow the torque sequence chart if the manual shows one. If none is shown, start in the center of the part and move outward in gradually increasing circles. If the part is circular, use a crisscross pattern. After the pump is installed, take an end-play measurement on the input shaft. If the end play is too much or too little, disassemble the transmission to the selective thrust washer and change it to the proper size to bring the end play into specification. Then reassemble and measure the end gap again to verify the proper clearance. The main points to remember are to work cleanly and carefully while following the procedures listed in the manual.

SUMMARY

The individual points made in each section are too numerous to list in a summary. All of the items are of great importance and would be impossible to omit from a summary. Take the time to review the chapter to help reinforce what you have learned.

SELF-TEST

Before going on to the next chapter, complete the self-test according to your instructor's directions. Read carefully and choose the best answer.

1. A dial indicator is mounted to the front of an automatic transmission and positioned so that it is at the end of the input shaft. Technician A says, "The measurement being taken must be made before the transmission is disassembled." Technician B says, "The measurement being taken must be made after the transmission is reassembled." Who is right?
a. A only **c.** Both A and B
b. B only **d.** Neither A nor B

2. Once the transmission failure has been diagnosed, there is no need to perform another test.
a. True
b. False

3. The fluid cooler of an automatic transmission is found to be clogged with debris. Technician A says, "The failed part could be the torque converter." Technician B says, "If the converter passes all the tests, it must be thoroughly flushed and cleaned for reuse." Who is right?
a. A only
b. B only
c. Both A and B
d. Neither A nor B

4. There is no way to recondition planet pinions that have too much end play.
a. True
b. False

5. A bushing is badly worn with deep grooves on its surface. Technician A says, "You only need to replace the bushing; the other parts should be all right." Technician B says, "The adjoining part on which the bushing rides must be closely inspected." Who is right?
a. A only
b. B only
c. Both A and B
d. Neither A nor B

6. The gear crescent hydraulic pump should be measured for tip, side, and body clearance.
a. True
b. False

7. Before installing new friction discs in a clutch pack, the discs should be soaked in ATF for a few hours.
a. True
b. False

8. Technician A says, "All piston seals must be lubricated before installing a piston." Technician B says, "For some clutch pistons an installing tool must be used to protect the seals." Who is right?
a. A only
b. B only
c. Both A and B
d. Neither A nor B

9. Technician A says, "Clutch pack clearance is always measured with a feeler gauge." Technician B says, "Selective-fit steel plates are used to adjust the pack clearance." Who is right?
a. A only
b. B only
c. Both A and B
d. Neither A nor B

10. The friction surface of the band must be inspected for cracking and flaking.
a. True
b. False

11. A failed one-way clutch is easy to identify during disassembly.
    a. True
    b. False
12. A hydraulic valve is hard to move in its bore. Technician A says, "Clean it with carburetor cleaner spray, oil it, and test it." Technician B says, "The valve should move in the bore with only the weight of the valve." Who is right?
    a. A only
    b. B only
    c. Both A and B
    d. Neither A nor B
13. Keeping the transmission clean during assembly is of little importance.
    a. True
    b. False
14. A good service manual can answer your questions about procedures and reduce comebacks.
    a. True
    b. False

GLOSSARY

ballooning condition that can occur to a torque converter which has been overheated.

bleed down condition in which the fluid in a component leaks out slowly.

body clearance measurement between the oil pump body and outside of the outer pump gear.

bushing driver special tool used to remove and install bushing.

chain deflection amount of play on the slack side of the drive chain.

clutch pack clearance free play needed in a clutch pack to allow complete disengagement of the clutch.

cross member bolt-in support member that supports the rear of the transmission and can be removed to aid in transmission removal.

debris small particles of friction material (metal or plastic) caused by wear.

dial indicator measurement tool used to measure end play.

end play amount of axial play found in a gear train.

fire wall clearance amount of free or open space between the fire wall and the closest engine component.

fractional bolts fasteners measured using the English measurement system.

hiss sound of air escaping past a leaking seal during air testing.

jack stand safety stand used to support a vehicle once it is raised in the air.

lifting points points on the body or frame where a jack or lift should be placed to raise a vehicle off the ground.

power washer parts washing machine.

pump alignment tool special tool that holds the pump halves in place while they are bolted together.

shoehorn using a feeler gauge to help ease a lip seal into its bore.

side clearance measurement between the side of the oil pump gears and the pump cover.

thud sound a clutch piston makes when it is in proper operating condition and is being air tested.

tip clearance measurement between the tip of the oil pump gears and the crescent divider.

transmission jack jack that is specially designed for removing and installing transmissions.

vernier caliper type of measurement tool.

visual inspection thorough examination of a part, looking for any wear, deformation, or malfunction.

water-based cleaning solution type of cleaning solution used in power cleaning washer which is mixed with water.

yoke splined end of a drive shaft which slides over the transmission output shaft.

◀ Part 3 ▶

SPECIFIC APPLICATIONS

◀ Chapter 10 ▶

CHRYSLER CORPORATION

10.1 PERFORMANCE OBJECTIVES

After studying this chapter, you should have fulfilled the following performance objectives by being able to:

1. List the Chrysler transmissions/transaxles described in the chapter.
2. Describe the basic components of each transmission/transaxle.
3. Describe the power flow in each gear position, including which coupling and holding devices are applied for each transmission/transaxle.
4. Write a clutch and band chart for each transmission/transaxle listed in the chapter.
5. Complete the self-test with at least the minimum score required by your instructor.

10.2 OVERVIEW

The Torque Flite automatic transmission produced by the Chrysler Corporation was used first in 1956. The Torque Flite was the first automatic transmission to use a Simpson gear set, and although it has had many small changes in components, its basic design has remained the same. There are two basic models of the transmission, the A-904 for light-duty and the A-727 for heavy-duty applications. The design of the two transmissions is the same, with the A-727 being built with slightly larger components to enable it to handle higher torque loads. The A-904 model has three late-model versions: the A-904T, A-998, and A-999, which have slight changes but are basically the same design.

The A-500 transmission, an overdrive version of the A-999, was introduced in 1988. The three-speed gear train remains the same, with the overdrive unit being placed in the tail housing.

The A-404 transaxle, introduced in 1978, uses the same gear train design as that of other Torque Flite transmissions. Other versions of the A-404, which have varying bell housing designs, are the A-413, A-415, and A-470.

The A-604 four-speed electronically controlled transaxle is the first transaxle to use adaptive electronic controls. This means that the onboard computer is adjusting and adapting the hydraulic pressures and shift timing continuously based on data received from its sensors.

The recommended fluid for all these transmissions is Type 7176. In emergencies, Dexron II can be substituted.

A chart comparing generic names of parts to the manufacturer's name is shown in Figure 10–1.

GENERIC NAME	=	CHRYSLER'S NAME
FRONT CLUTCH	=	FRONT CLUTCH
REAR CLUTCH	=	REAR CLUTCH
FRONT RING GEAR	=	FRONT ANNULUS GEAR
FRONT PINION CARRIER	=	FRONT PLANET CARRIER
REAR RING GEAR	=	REAR ANNULUS GEAR
REAR PINION CARRIER	=	REAR PLANET CARRIER
FRONT BAND	=	KICKDOWN BAND
ROLLER CLUTCH	=	OVERRUNNING CLUTCH
MAIN LINE PRESSURE	=	LINE PRESSURE
THROTTLE PRESSURE	=	THROTTLE

FIGURE 10–1 General factory name list. (Courtesy of Chrysler)

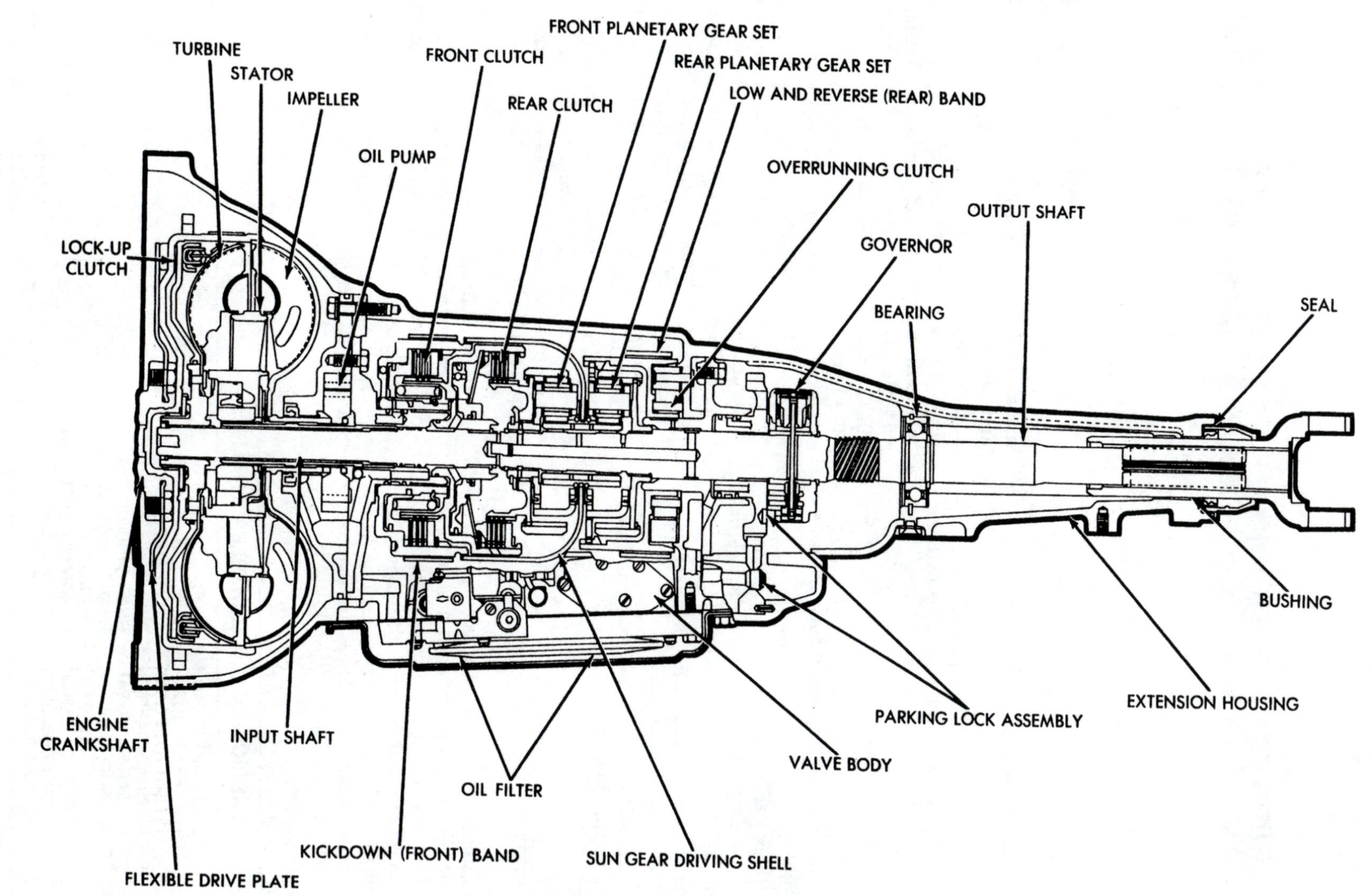

FIGURE 10–2 A-904 cross section. (Courtesy of Chrysler)

The A-904 Torque Flite transmission, also known as the Torque Flite "6," is widely used by the Chrysler Corporation in its RWD vehicles. The A-998 and A-999 are later-model versions of the A-904, with some minor modifications. The A-904 as used in a Jeep vehicle is shown in Figure 10–2.

10.3 A-904: RWD THREE-SPEED TRANSMISSION

10.3.1 Basic Description

The transmission description is divided into eight areas. All of the transmissions are described in this manner to make their comparison easier.

1. *Torque Converter*
A conventional three-element torque converter is used with a hydraulic converter clutch. The torque converter clutch is controlled hydraulically, with no electronic assistance.

2. *Gear Train*
The gear train uses a Simpson gear set with two ring gear, two pinion carriers, and a common sun gear.

3. *Coupling Devices*
The coupling devices are the front clutch, which drives the sun gear, and the rear clutch, which drives the front ring gear.

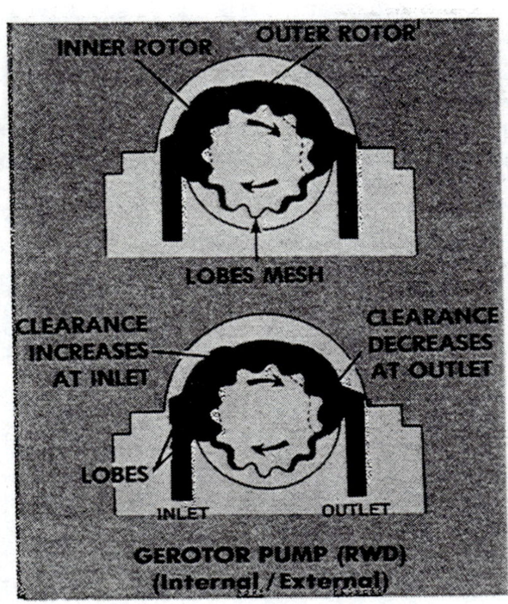

FIGURE 10–3 A-904 gerotor oil pump. (Courtesy of Chrysler)

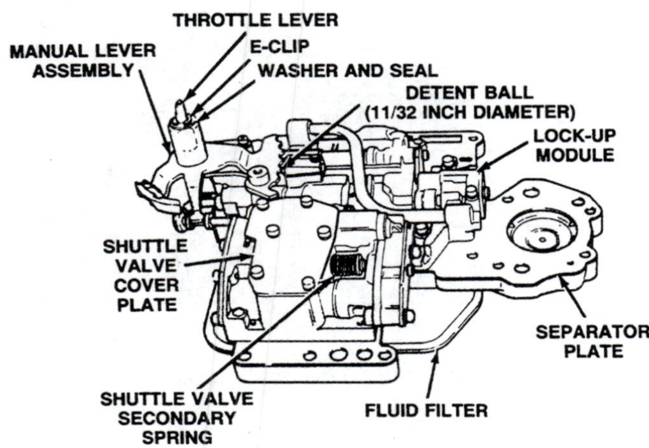

FIGURE 10–4 A-904 valve body controls. (Courtesy of Chrysler)

4. *Holding Devices*
The front band is used to hold the sun gear, while the rear band is used to hold the rear pinion carrier. The roller clutch (overrunning) is also used to hold the rear pinion carrier.

5. *Pump*
The oil pump is a gerotor design, which is a positive-displacement type. The pump is shown in an exploded view in Figure 10–3.

6. *Shift Control*
Shift control is fully hydraulic. The valve body controls are shown in Figure 10–4.

7. *Governor*
The governor is a shaft-mounted type which uses a primary and a secondary weight to create a two-stage governor pressure (Figure 10–5).

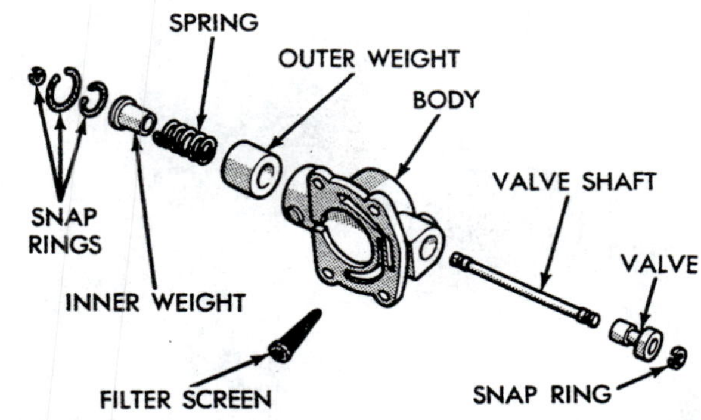

FIGURE 10–5 A-904 governor. (Courtesy of Chrysler)

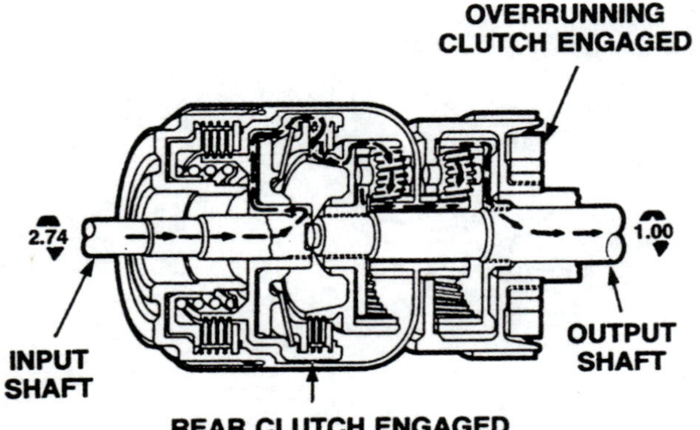

FIGURE 10–6 A-904 in first gear. (Courtesy of Chrysler)

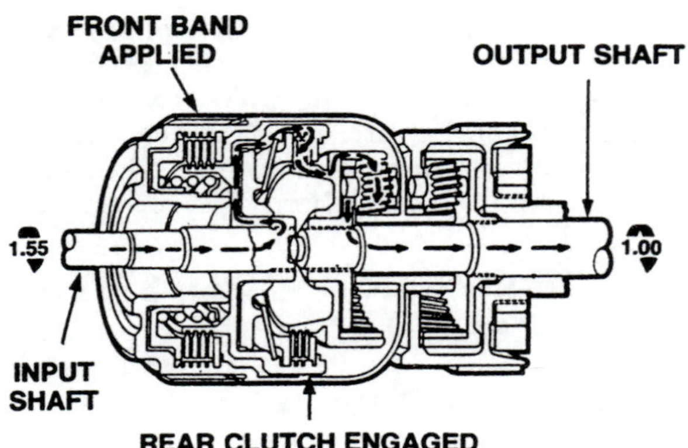

FIGURE 10–7 D2 A-904 in second gear. (Courtesy of Chrysler)

8. Throttle Valve
The throttle valve is connected to the accelerator linkage by rod linkage.

10.3.2 Power Flow

The power flow is described by stating the coupling and holding device action (applied, or holding) on the members of the planetary gear set (sun gear, planet pinion, and ring gear) in each gear range of the transmission.

1. Neutral
In neutral all of the coupling and holding devices are released. The rear clutch hub is turning with the turbine shaft, but the power flow stops there.

2. Drive First (D1)
In first gear the rear clutch is applied, which drives the front ring gear. The roller (overrunning) clutch is holding the rear pinion carrier, as shown in Figure 10–6. The first-gear ratio is 2.74:1. In manual first gear the rear band is also applied.

3. Drive Second (D2)
In second gear the rear clutch remains applied. The front (kickdown) band is applied, which holds the sun gear as the reaction member (Figure 10–7). The second-gear ratio is 1.55:1. The same devices are used in manual second gear.

4. Drive Third (D3)
The rear clutch is still applied driving the front ring gear. The front clutch is also applied, which drives the sun gear, causing a direct drive (Figure 10–8).

5. Reverse (R)
In reverse the front clutch is engaged, driving the sun gear. The rear band is also applied, which holds

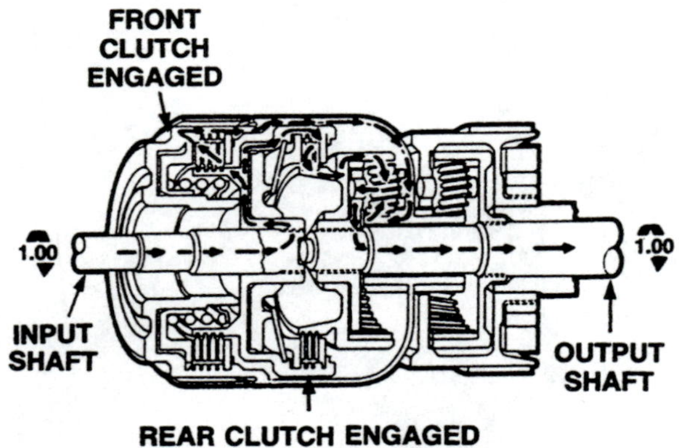

FIGURE 10–8 D3 A-904 in third gear. (Courtesy of Chrysler)

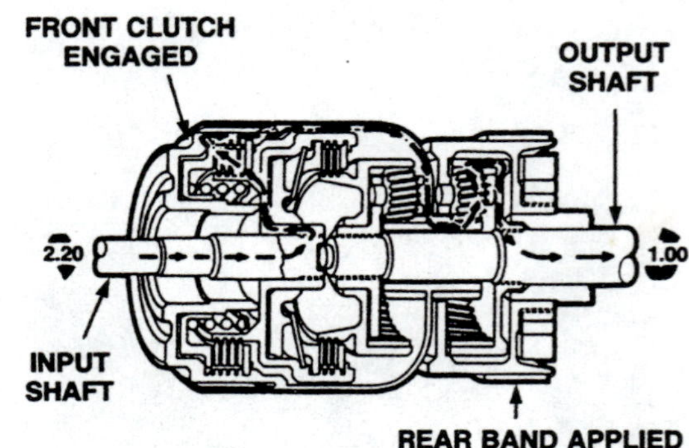

FIGURE 10–9 R A-904 in reverse gear. (Courtesy of Chrysler)

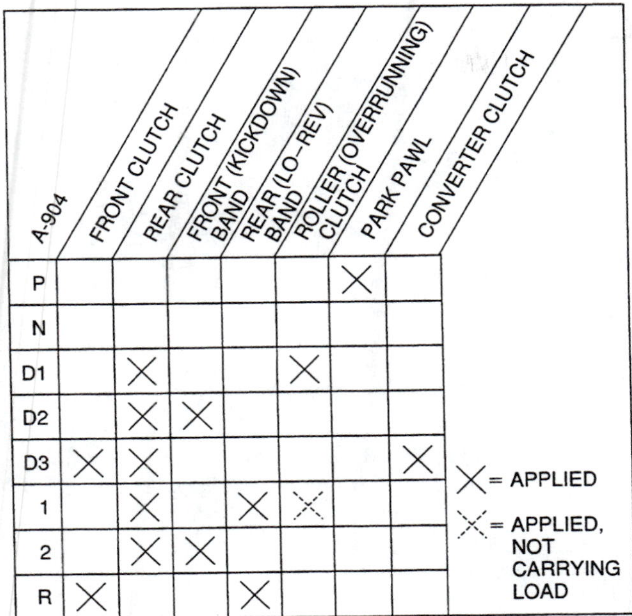

A-904	FRONT CLUTCH	REAR CLUTCH	FRONT (KICKDOWN) BAND	REAR (LO-REV) BAND	ROLLER (OVERRUNNING) CLUTCH	PARK PAWL	CONVERTER CLUTCH
P						X	
N							
D1		X			X		
D2		X	X				
D3	X	X					X
1		X		X	(X)		
2		X	X				
R	X			X			

X = APPLIED

(X) = APPLIED, NOT CARRYING LOAD

FIGURE 10–10 A-904 clutch and band chart, standardized version.

Drive Elements	Gearshift Lever Position: P	R	N	D: 1	D: 2	D: 3	2: 1	2: 2	1
Front Clutch		•				•			
Front Band					•			•	
Rear Clutch				•	•	•	•	•	•
Rear Band		•							•
Roller Clutch				•			•		•

FIGURE 10–11 A-904 clutch and band chart, factory version. (Courtesy of Chrysler)

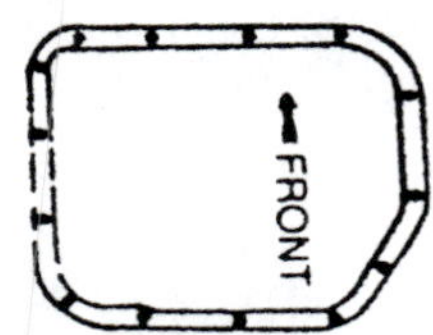

FIGURE 10–12 A-904 pan gasket identification.

the rear pinion carrier as the reaction member. The result is a reverse gear with a ratio of 2.74:1. Reverse gear is shown in Figure 10–9.

10.3.3 Clutch and Band Charts

In this section we provide two clutch and band charts. The first chart, the author's design, uses a standardized format for listing the coupling and holding devices to aid comparison between transmissions. This chart is shown in Figure 10–10. The second chart, the manufacturer's design, which is found in service manuals, is shown in Figure 10–11.

10.3.4 Identification

The shape of the transmission oil pan or its gasket is a quick means of identifying an automatic transmission. In Figure 10–12 you see the pan gasket shape and number of bolt holes for the A-904 transmission. The location of the factory identification tag and its code are shown in Figure 10–13.

10.3.5 Components

In this section exploded drawings of the A-904 transmission subassemblies are shown, along with lists of the part names. The manufacturer's part names are used to eliminate confusion about component names. The drawings to study are as follows:

Lockup converter, Figure 10–14
Oil pump, Figure 10–15
Front clutch, Figure 10–16
Clutch pack, Figure 10–17
Rear clutch, Figure 10–18
Valve body, Figure 10–19
Overrunning clutch, Figure 10–20
Planetary gear set, Figure 10–21
Kickdown band and servo, Figure 10–22
Thrust washer chart, Figure 10–23

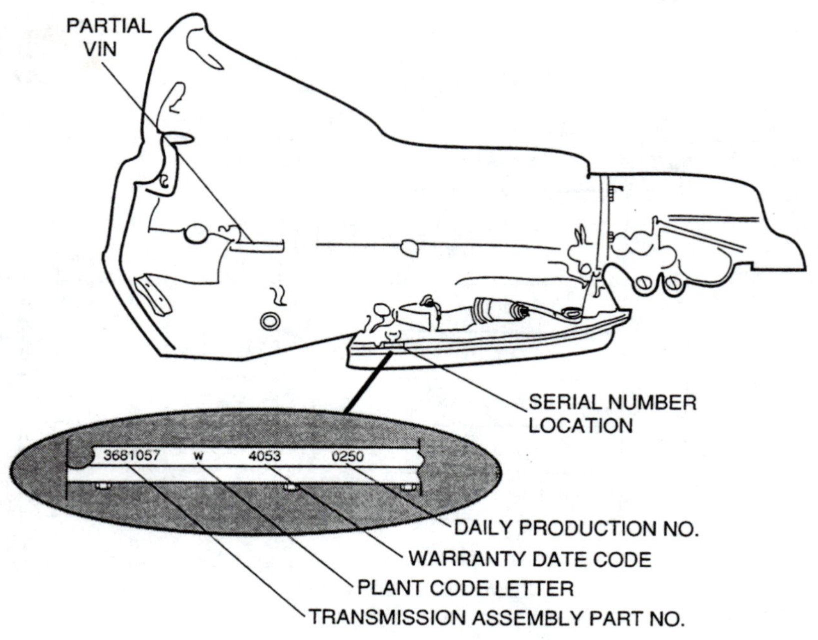

FIGURE 10–13 A-904 factory markings. (Courtesy of Chrysler)

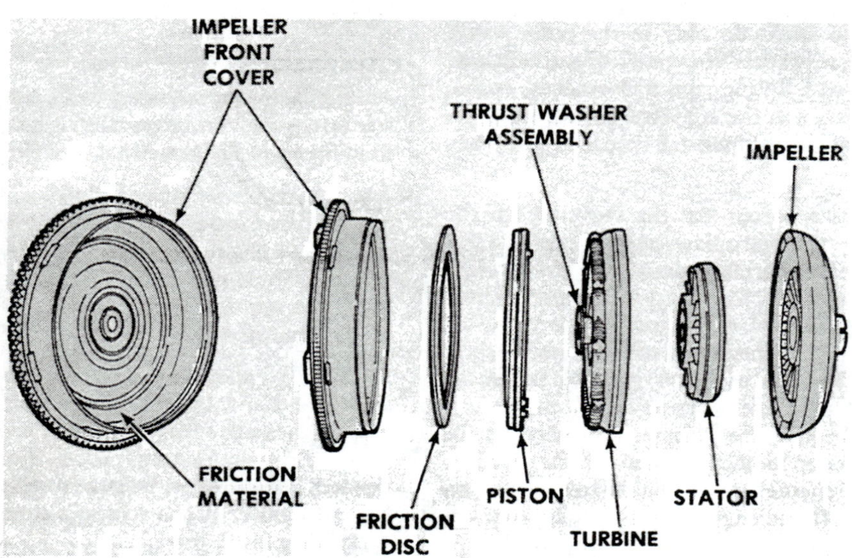

FIGURE 10–14 A-904 torque converter. (Courtesy of Chrysler)

FIGURE 10–15 A-904 oil pump. (Courtesy of Chrysler)

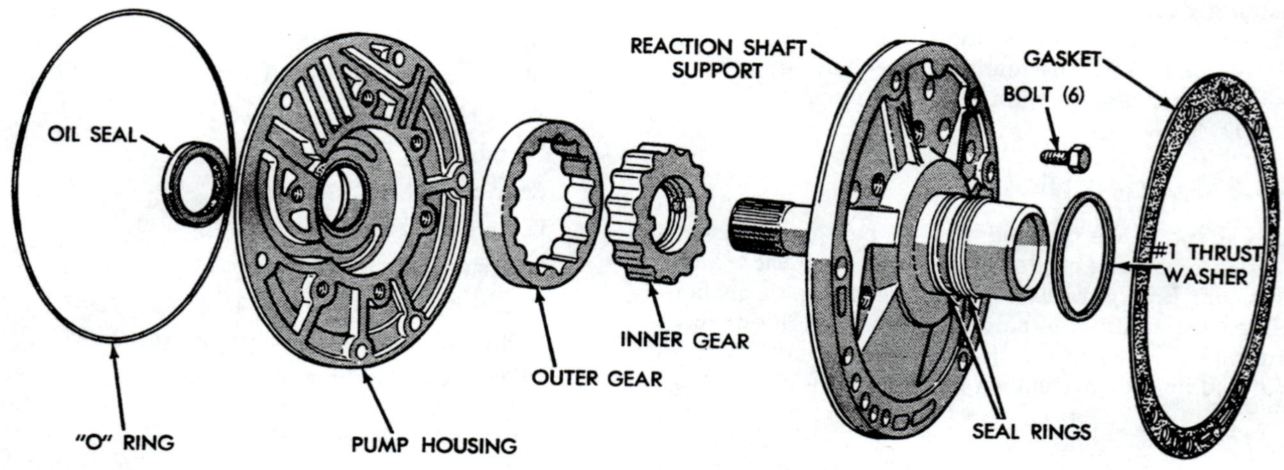

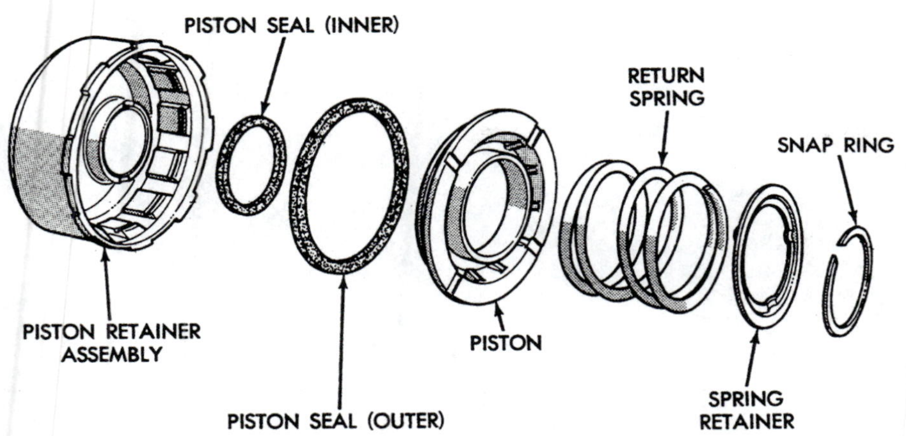

FIGURE 10–16 A-904 front clutch. (Courtesy of Chrysler)

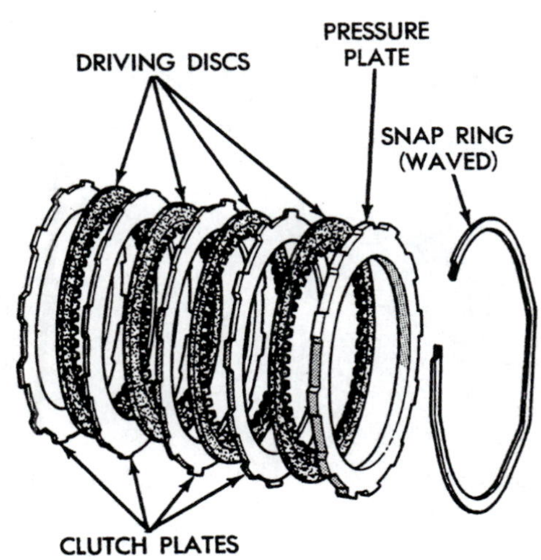

FIGURE 10–17 A-904 clutch pack. (Courtesy of Chrysler)

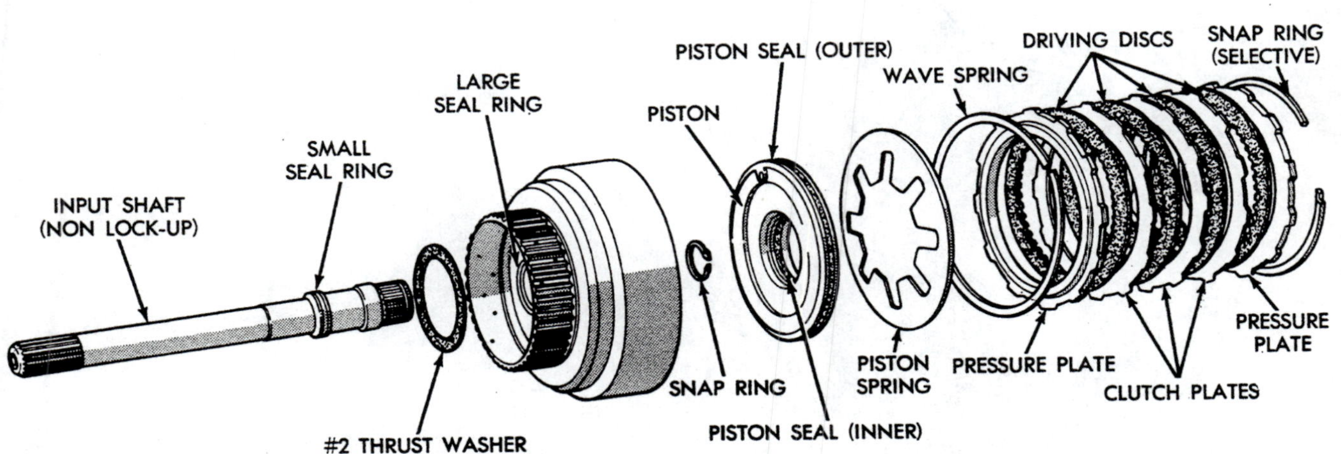

FIGURE 10–18 A-904 rear clutch. (Courtesy of Chrysler)

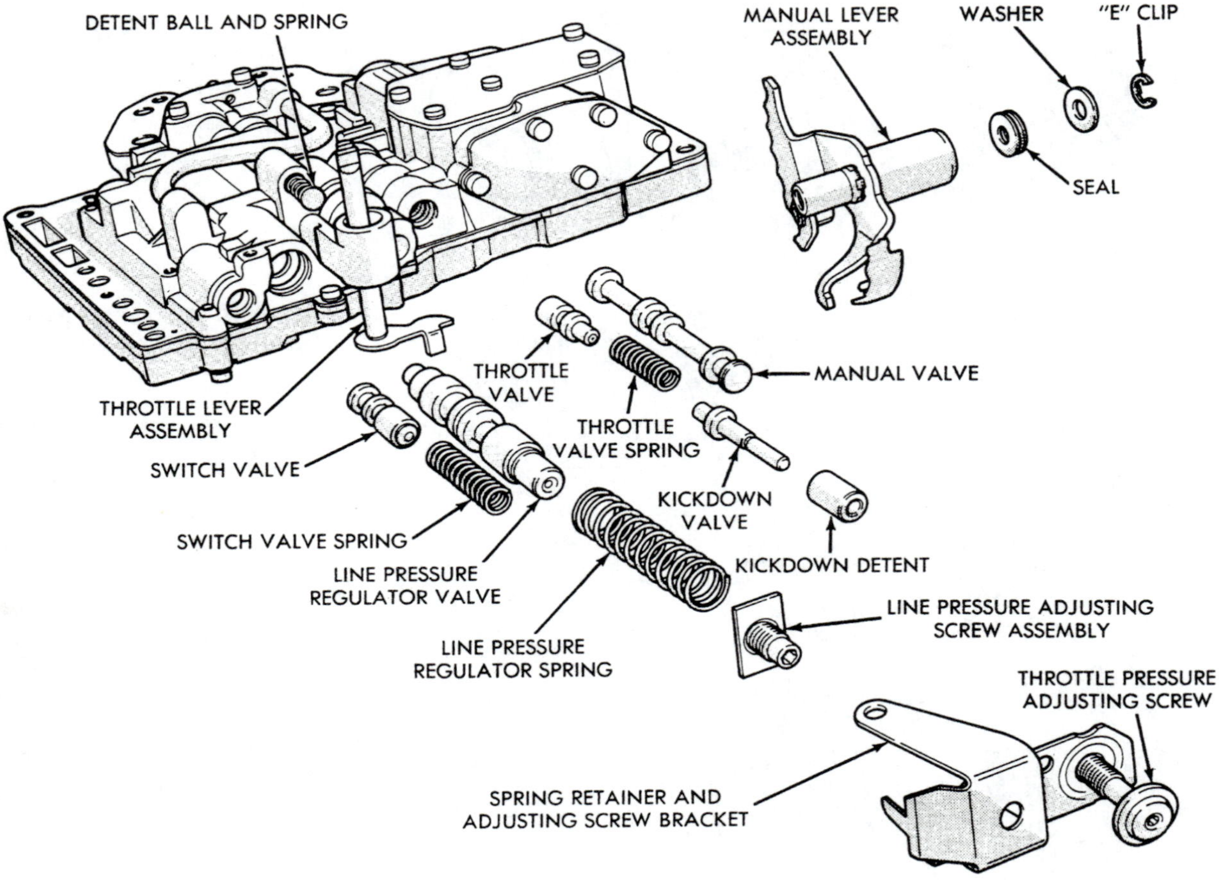

DETENT BALL AND SPRING
MANUAL LEVER ASSEMBLY
WASHER
"E" CLIP
SEAL
THROTTLE VALVE
MANUAL VALVE
THROTTLE LEVER ASSEMBLY
THROTTLE VALVE SPRING
SWITCH VALVE
KICKDOWN VALVE
SWITCH VALVE SPRING
KICKDOWN DETENT
LINE PRESSURE REGULATOR VALVE
LINE PRESSURE ADJUSTING SCREW ASSEMBLY
LINE PRESSURE REGULATOR SPRING
THROTTLE PRESSURE ADJUSTING SCREW
SPRING RETAINER AND ADJUSTING SCREW BRACKET

FIGURE 10–19 A-904 valve body. (Courtesy of Chrysler)

OUTER RACE (CAM)
ROLLER
SPRING
LOCKED
FREE-WHEELING
INNER RACE (HUB)
SPRING RETAINER

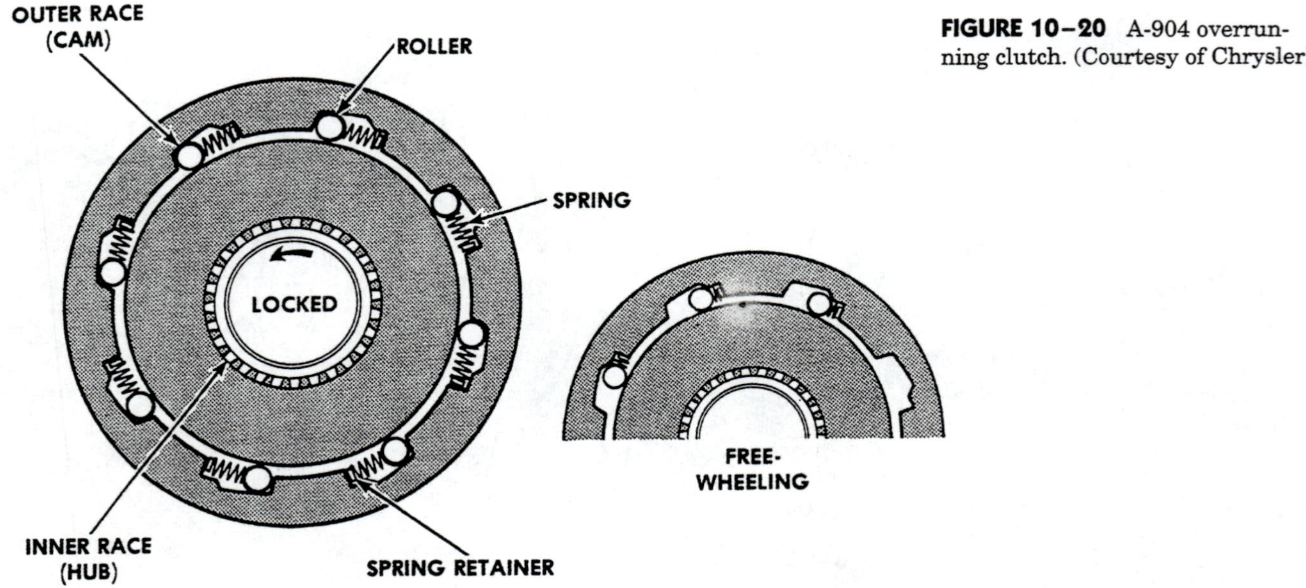

FIGURE 10–20 A-904 overrunning clutch. (Courtesy of Chrysler)

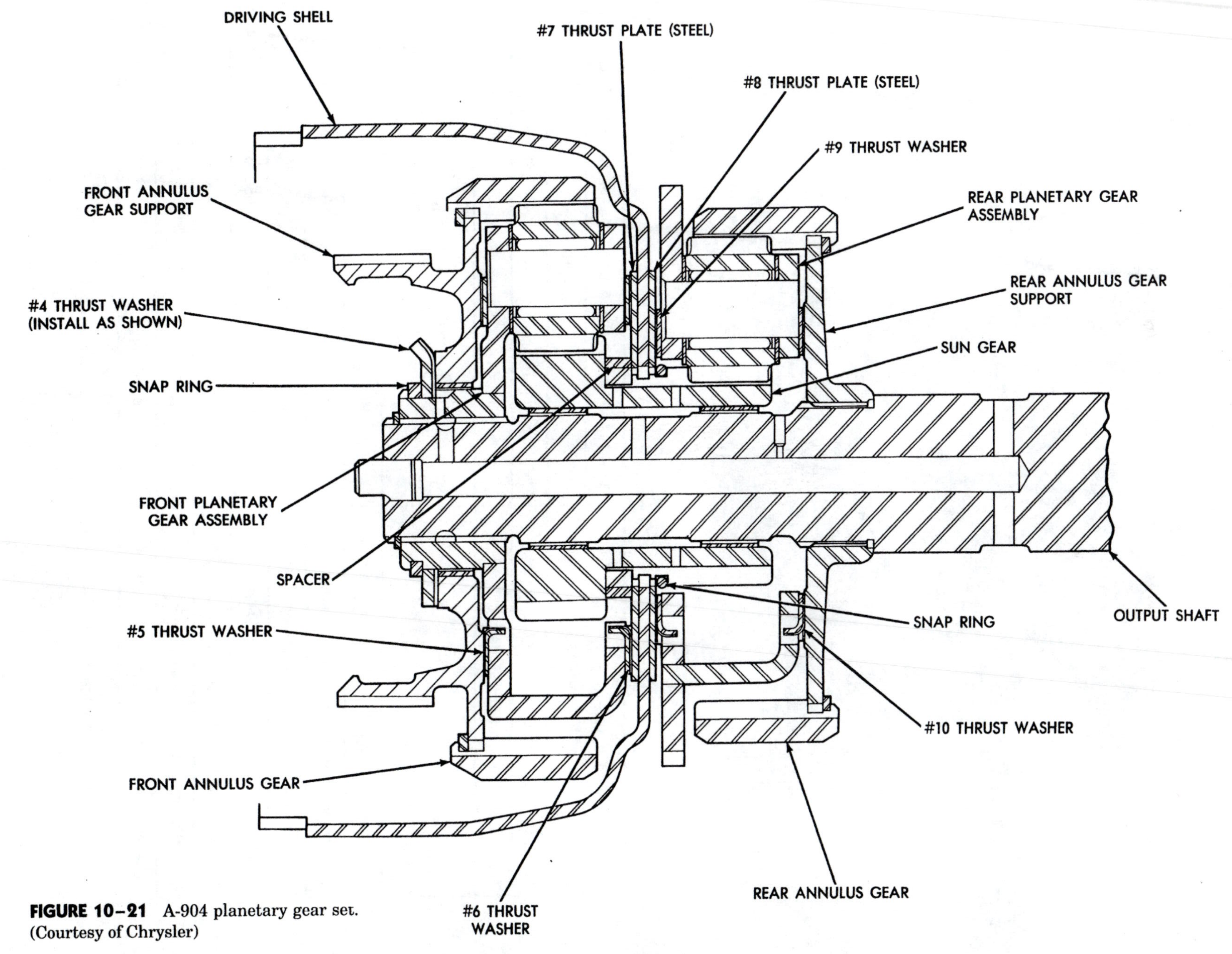

FIGURE 10–21 A-904 planetary gear set. (Courtesy of Chrysler)

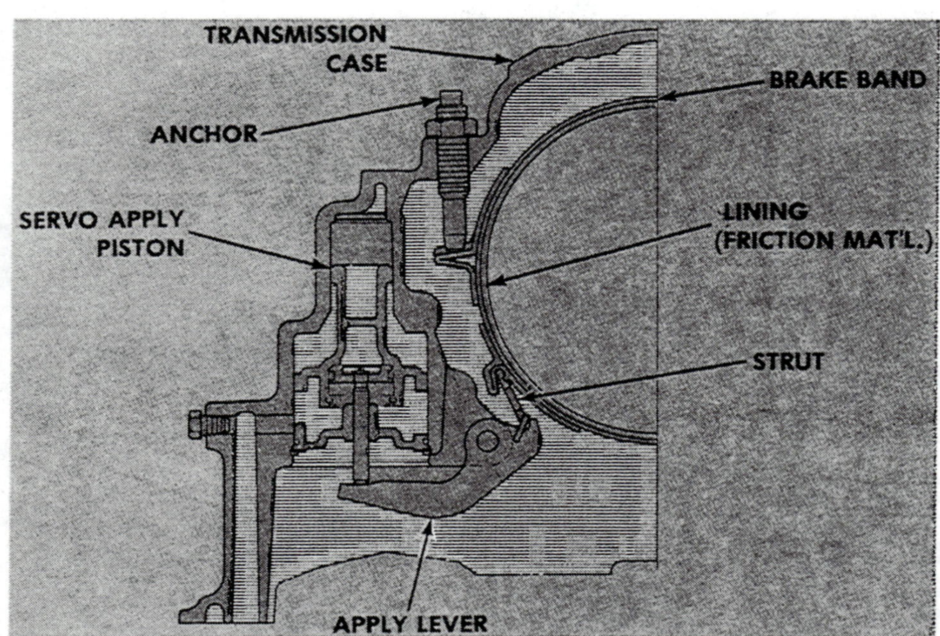

FIGURE 10–22 A-904 kick-down band and servo. (Courtesy of Chrysler)

THRUST WASHERS	THRUST WASHER NO. AND TRANSMISSION MODEL	
	904 HD	
Reaction Shaft Support to Front Clutch Retainer	No. 1	.061 to .063
Rear Clutch to Front Clutch Retainer	No. 2	.061 to .063
Output Shaft to Input Shaft	No. 3	Selective .052 to .054 – Tin .068 to .070 – Red .083 to .085 – Green
Front Annulus Support to Rear Clutch Retainer	No. 4	.121 to .125
Front Annulus Support to Front Planetary Gear	No. 5	.048 to .050
Front Planetary Gear to Driving Shell	No. 6	.048 to .050
Sun Gear and Driving Shell Front Thrust Plate	No. 7	.050 to .052
Sun Gear and Driving Shell Rear Thrust Plate	No. 8	.050 to .052
Rear Planetary Gear to Driving Shell	No. 9	.048 to .050
Rear Planetary Gear to Rear Annulus Support	No. 10	.048 to .050

FIGURE 10–23 A-904 thrust washer chart. (Courtesy of Chrysler)

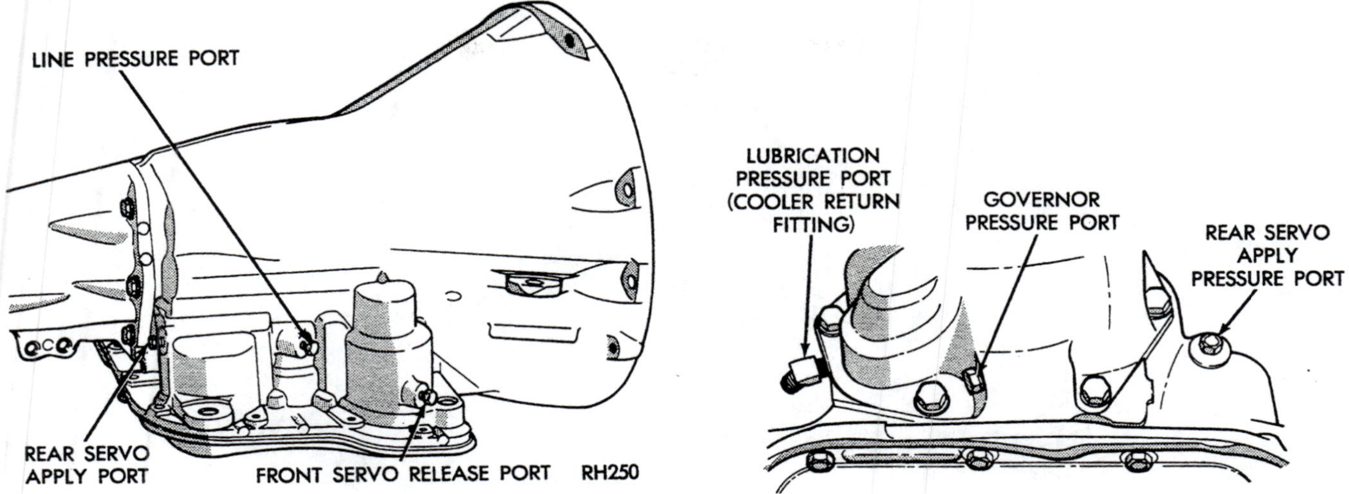

FIGURE 10–24 A-904 pressure test points. (Courtesy of Chrysler)

Lube Pressure	Closed throttle Full throttle	5-30 psi (34-207 kPa) 5-30 psi (34-207 kPa)
Line Pressure	Closed throttle Full throttle	54-60 psi (372-414 kPa) 94 psi (648 kPa)
Front Servo Release	Third gear only	No more than 3 psi (21 kPa) lower than line pressure.
Rear Servo Apply	1 Range R Range	No more than 3 psi (21 kPa) lower than line pressure. 160 psi (1103 kPa) at idle, builds to 270 psi (1862 kPa) at 1600 rpm,
Governor	D Range Closed throttle	Pressure should respond smoothly to changes in mph and return to 0 to 1½ psi (0-77 kPa) when stopped with transmission in D, 1, 2. Pressure above 1½ psi (7 kPa) at standstill will prevent transmission from downshifting.

FIGURE 10–25 A-904 pressure test chart. (Courtesy of Chrysler)

10.3.6 Pressure Test

One of the key tests in diagnosis is the hydraulic system pressure tests. The location of the test points of the A-904 transmission are shown in Figure 10–24. A pressure chart listing the pressure specification of this transmission is shown in Figure 10–25.

10.3.7 Air Test

Air testing is used during preliminary diagnosis of certain malfunctions and also during the disassembly process to verify component operation or failure. The technician must know which hydraulic circuit is being served by each passageway to be able to air test a transmission accurately. This information is presented in the drawing of air test passages in Figure 10–26.

10.3.8 Special Attention

In this section we show and explain various points of special interest about the A-904 transmission. The information presented about each item is included with each illustration.

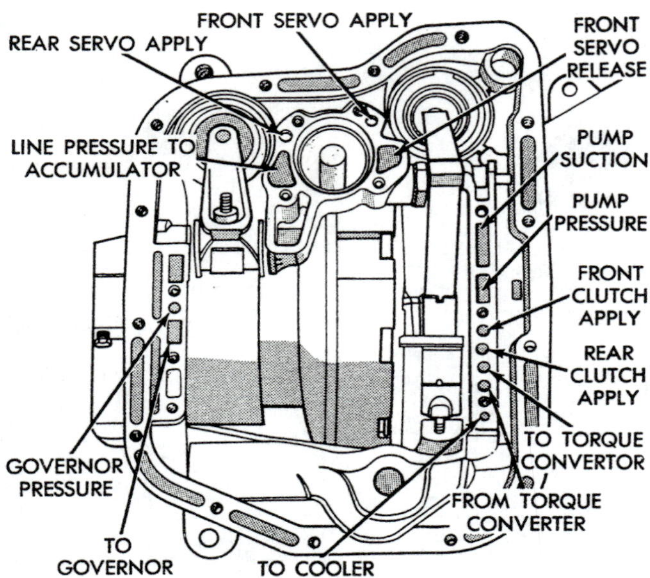

FIGURE 10–26 A-904 air test. (Courtesy of Chrysler)

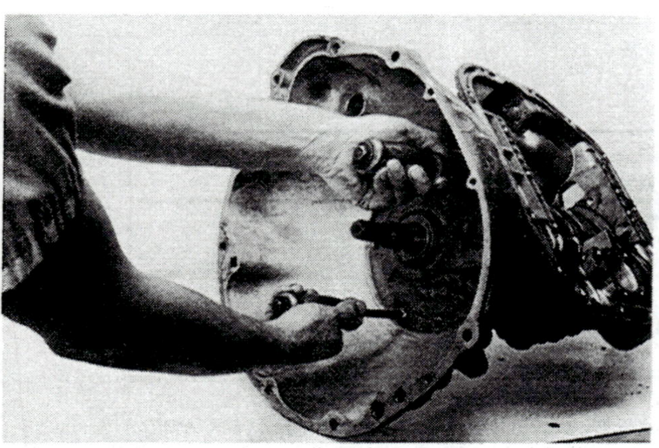

A904–1 A pair of slide hammers threaded into the oil pump are used to remove the pump.

A904–2 Gerotor pump gears should be measured to find wear.

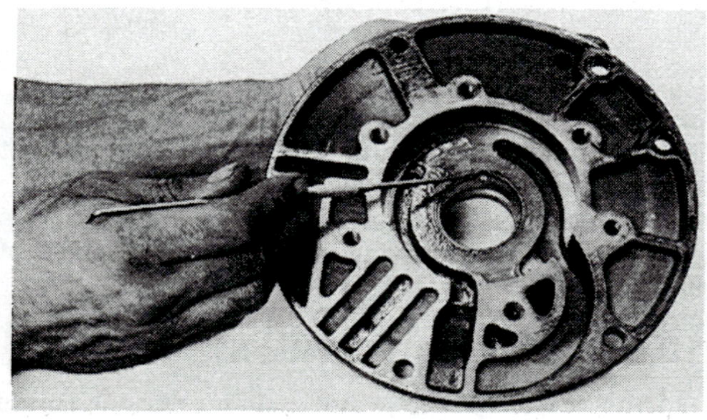

A904–3 The pump bushing should be checked for wear and replaced if necessary.

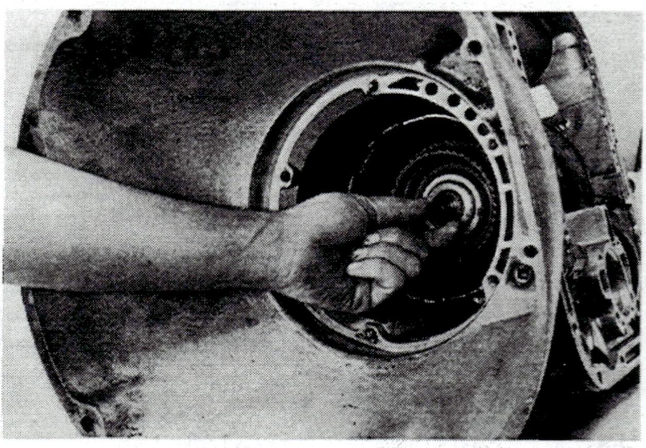

A904–4 The turbine shaft thrust washer should be measured to determine wear.

A904–5 The input ring gear snap ring must be removed to remove the gear train.

A904–6 The low roller clutch must be inspected for wear or damage.

A904–7 The rear pinion carrier bushing support should be examined for grooving.

A904–8 The speedometer gear retainer must be aligned with this reference mark. The numbers on the retainer refer to the number of teeth on the gear.

10.4 A-500: RWD FOUR-SPEED TRANSMISSION

10.4.1 Basic Description

The A-500 is an overdrive version of the A-904 transmission. The overdrive unit is mounted after the three-speed gear train in the extension housing.

The transmission description is divided into eight areas. All of the transmissions are described in this manner to make their comparison easier.

1. *Torque Converter*

The A-500 uses a conventional-type three-element torque converter with a hydraulic converter clutch.

2. *Gear Train*

The A-500 uses a Simpson gear set for the three-speed portion of the transmission and an additional simple planetary gear set in the overdrive unit.

3. *Coupling Devices*

The front clutch drives the sun gear and the rear clutch drives the front ring gear as input members. The overdrive unit uses an overrunning clutch to drive the output shaft during direct drive. The direct clutch is used to provide power flow during direct drive coast down and also in reverse gear. The direct clutch is spring applied.

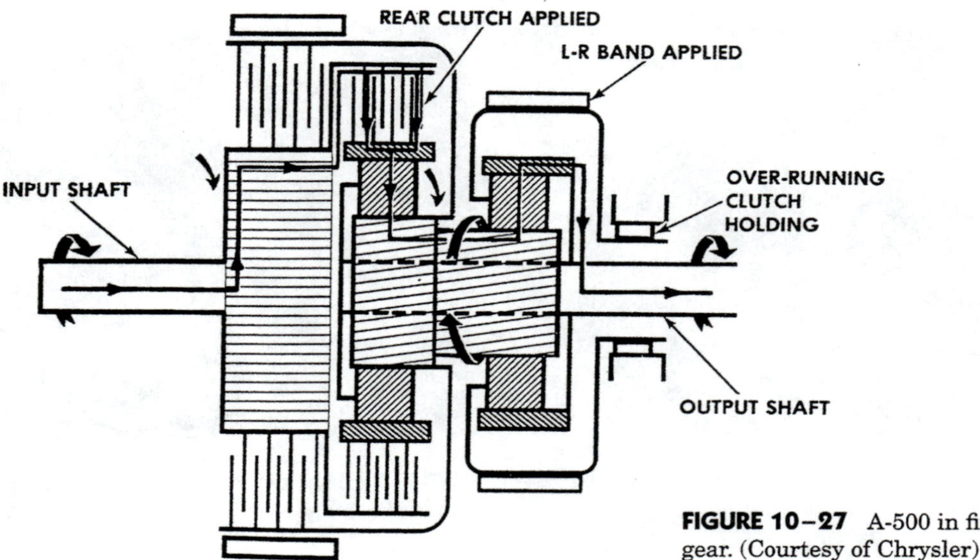

FIGURE 10–27 A-500 in first gear. (Courtesy of Chrysler)

4. Holding Devices
The front band is used to hold the sun gear, and the rear band holds the rear pinion carrier. An overrunning clutch is used to hold the rear pinion carrier. The overdrive clutch is used to hold the overdrive sun gear stationary.

5. Pump
The A-500 uses the standard gerotor pump used in all RWD Torque Flite transmissions.

6. Shift Control
The shift control combines hydraulic and electronic control systems. The three-speed portion of the transmission is hydraulically controlled, with the overdrive and converter clutch being electronically controlled.

7. Governor
The A-500 governor is shaft-mounted, with dual weights to provide the proper rate of pressure increase.

8. Throttle Valve
The throttle valve is controlled by rod linkage connected to the accelerator linkage of the fuel system.

10.4.2 Power Flow

1. Neutral (N)
The hydraulic devices are all released, so only the turbine shaft and rear clutch hub are rotating.

2. Drive First (D1)
The rear clutch is applied driving the front ring gear as input. The overrunning clutch is holding the rear pinion carrier as the reaction member (Figure 10–27). The output members, front pinion carrier, and rear ring gear, are splined to the intermediate shaft, which drives the output shaft through the overdrive overrunning clutch and the spring applied direct clutch (Figure 10–28). The first-gear ratio is 2.74:1. In manual low gear the rear band is also applied to hold the rear pinion carrier.

3. Drive Second (D2)
The rear clutch remains applied, driving the front ring gear. The front band is applied to hold the sun gear as the reaction member (Figure 10–29). The overdrive unit is still in direct drive. The second-gear ratio is 1.54:1. Manual second gear uses all of the same devices.

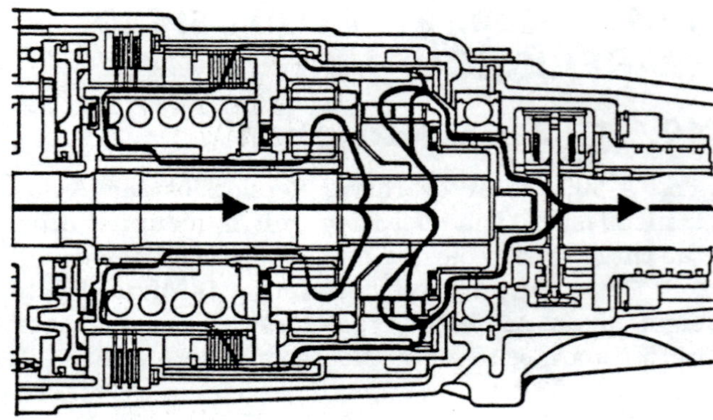

FIGURE 10–28 A-500 overdrive unit in direct drive. (Courtesy of Chrysler)

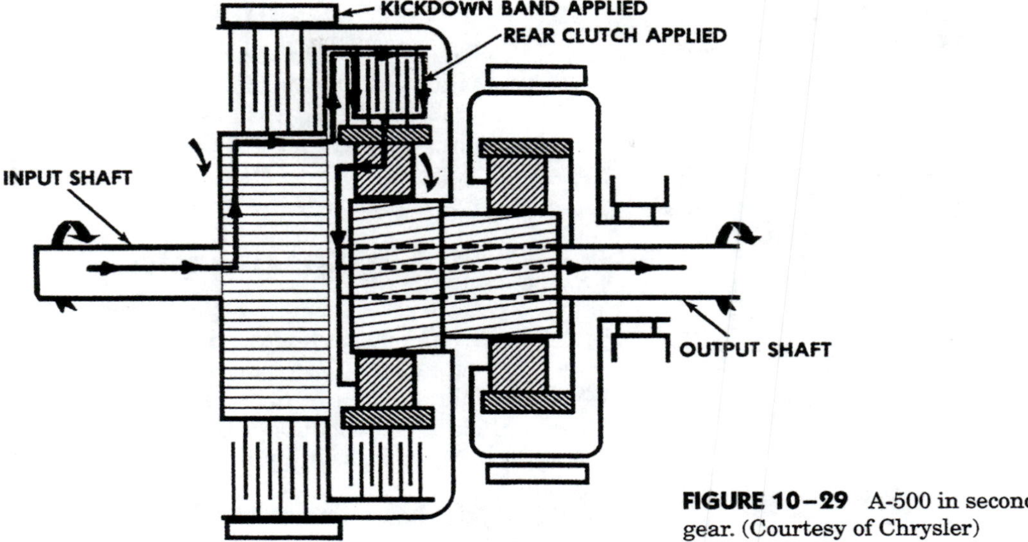

FIGURE 10–29 A-500 in second gear. (Courtesy of Chrysler)

4. *Drive Third (D3)*
In third gear the front clutch is driving the sun gear and the rear clutch is driving the front ring gear as inputs, which provide a direct drive (Figure 10–30). The overdrive unit is still in direct drive.

5. *Drive Fourth (D4)*
In fourth gear the front and rear clutches remain applied, keeping the Simpson gear set in direct drive. The overdrive clutch is applied, which releases the direct clutch at the same time. As the piston movement applies one clutch it releases the other. The overdrive clutch holds the sun gear as the reaction member while the pinion carrier, which is splined to the intermediate shaft, is the input (Figure 10–31), with the ring gear as output, with a ratio of 0.69:1.

6. *Reverse (R)*
In reverse gear the front clutch is driving the sun gear while the rear band holds the rear pinion carrier (Figure 10–32). The overdrive unit is in direct drive, but because of the reverse rotation of the output shaft, the direct clutch carries the torque load, not the overrunning clutch.

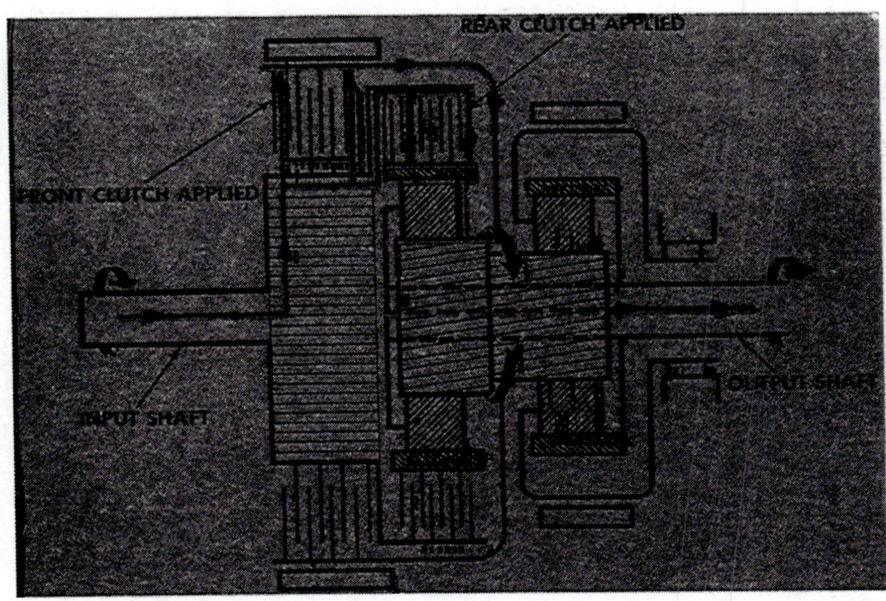

FIGURE 10–30 A-500 in third gear. (Courtesy of Chrysler)

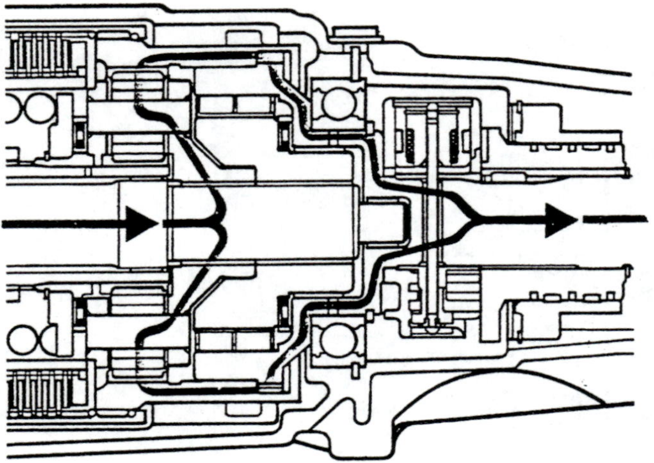

FIGURE 10–31 A-500 in fourth gear. (Courtesy of Chrysler)

10.4.3 Clutch and Band Charts

In this section we provide two clutch and band charts. The first chart, the author's design, uses a standardized format for listing the coupling and holding devices to aid comparison between transmissions. The chart is shown in Figure 10–33. The second chart, the manufacturer's design, which is found in service manuals, is shown in Figure 10–34.

10.4.4 Identification

The shape of the transmission oil pan or its gasket is a quick means of identifying an automatic transmission. In Figure 10–35 you see the pan gasket shape and number of bolt holes for the A-500 transmission. The location of the factory identification tag and its code are shown in Figure 10–36.

10.4.5 Components

In this section exploded drawings of the A-500 transmission subassemblies are shown, along with lists of the part names. The drawing to study is as follows the overdrive unit, Figure 10–37. The gear train components of the A-500 are similar to the A-904, so these drawings will not be duplicated.

10.4.6 Pressure Test

One of the key tests in diagnosis is the hydraulic system pressure test. The location of the test points of the A-500 transmission is shown in Figure 10–38.

10.4.7 Air Test

Air testing is used during preliminary diagnosis of certain malfunctions and also during the disassembly process to verify component operation or failure. The technician must know which hydraulic circuit is being served by each passageway to be able to air test a transmission accurately.

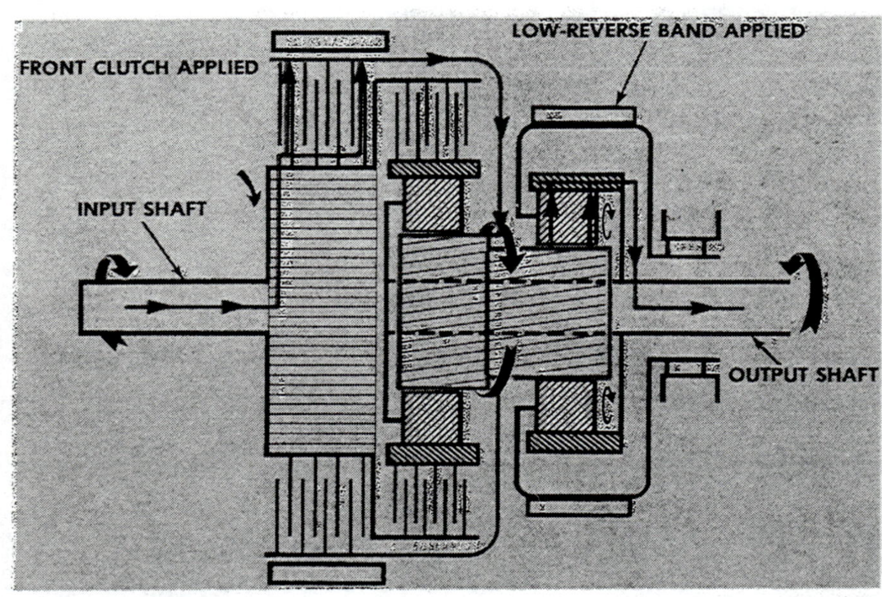

FIGURE 10–32 A-500 in reverse gear. (Courtesy of Chrysler)

A-500	FRONT CLUTCH	REAR CLUTCH	OVERDRIVE CLUTCH	DIRECT CLUTCH*	FRONT (KICKDOWN) BAND	REAR (LO-REV) BAND	LOW-OVERRUNNING CLUTCH	OVERDRIVE OVERRUNNING CLUTCH	PARK PAWL	CONVERTER CLUTCH
P				X					X	
N				X						
D1		X		X			X	X		
D2		X		X	X			X		
D3	X	X		X				X		
D4		X	X							X
1		X		X		X	X (dashed)	X		
2		X		X	X			X		
3	X	X		X				X		
R	X			X		X				

X = APPLIED

X (dashed) = APPLIED, NOT CARRYING LOAD

* = SPRING APPLIED

FIGURE 10–33 A-500 clutch and band chart, standardized version.

LEVER POSITION	A500 OVER-DRIVE	START SAFETY	PARKING SPRAG	TRANSMISSION CLUTCHES FRONT	REAR	O'RUNNING	LOCKUP	BANDS K/D FRONT	REVERSE/REAR	OVERDRIVE CLUTCHES O/D	O'RUNNING
P-Park		X	X								
R-Reverse	2.21			X					X		
O-Drive											
First	2.74				X	X					X
Second	1.54				X			X			X
Third	1.00			X	X		X*				X
O/D	0.69			X	X		X			X	
2-Second											
First	2.74				X	X					X
Second	1.54				X			X			X
1-Low	2.74				X	X			X		X

*3-speed only. No direct gear lockup on A-500.

FIGURE 10–34 A-500 clutch and band chart, factory version. (Courtesy of Chrysler)

10.4.8 Special Attention

In this section we show and explain various points of special interest about the A-500 transmission. The information presented about each item is included with each illustration.

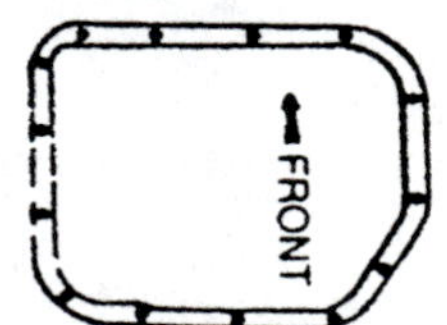

FIGURE 10–35 A-500 pan gasket identification.

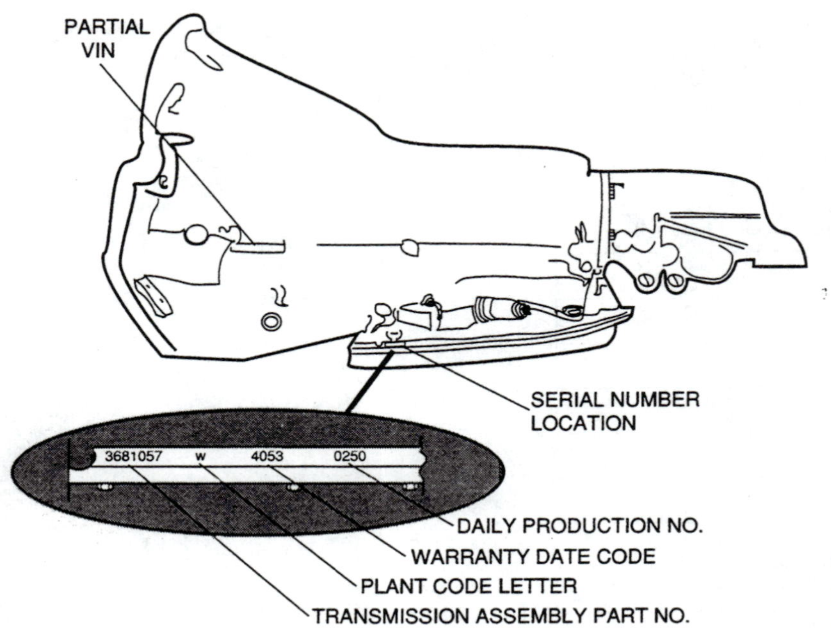

FIGURE 10–36 A-500 serial number identification. (Courtesy of Chrysler)

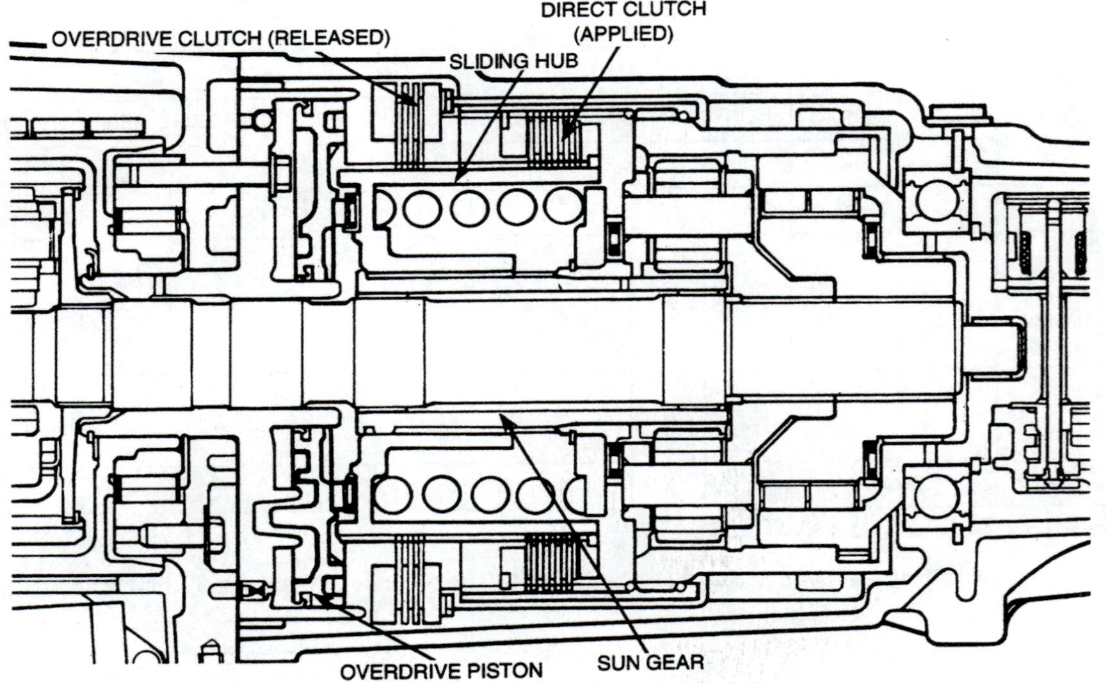

FIGURE 10–37 A-500 overdrive unit. (Courtesy of Chrysler)

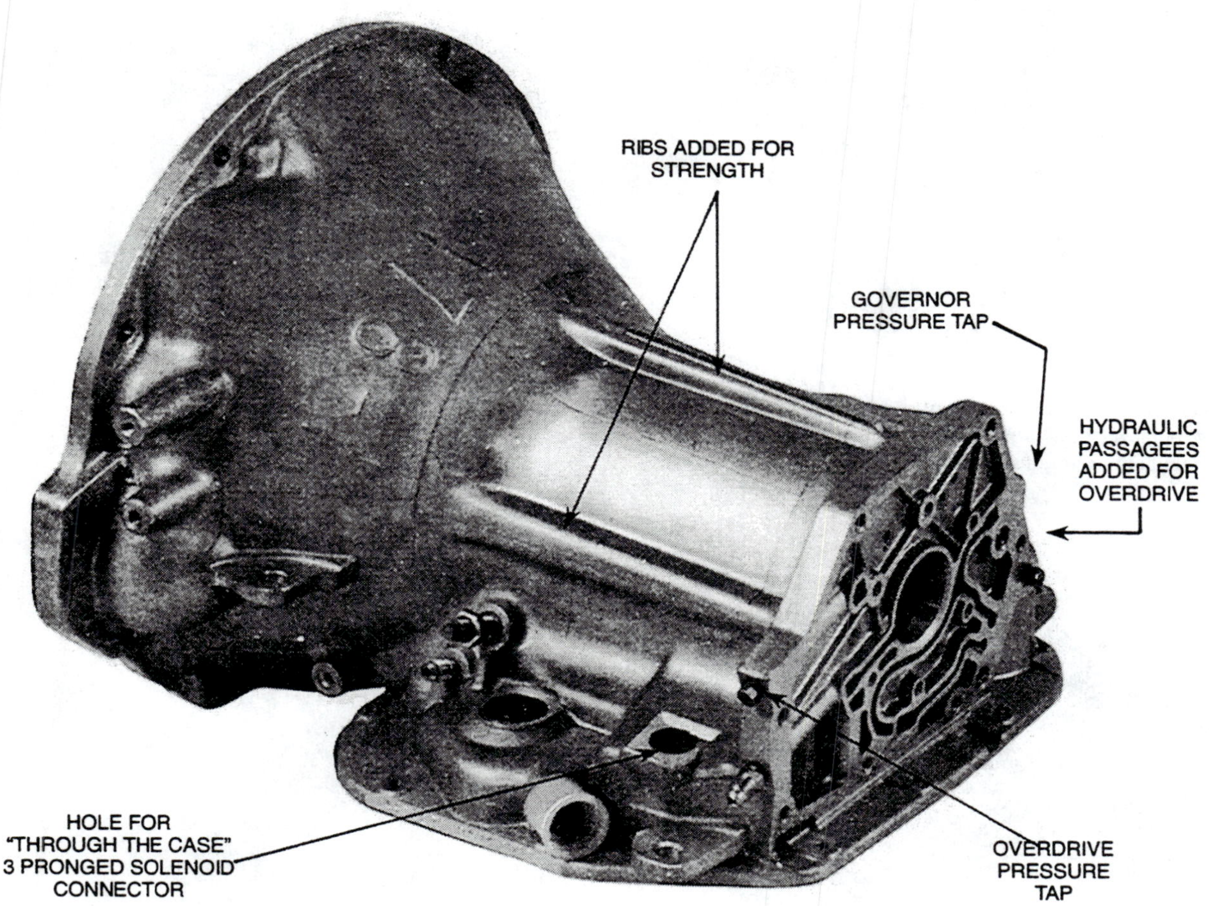

RIBS ADDED FOR STRENGTH

GOVERNOR PRESSURE TAP

HYDRAULIC PASSAGEES ADDED FOR OVERDRIVE

HOLE FOR "THROUGH THE CASE" 3 PRONGED SOLENOID CONNECTOR

OVERDRIVE PRESSURE TAP

FIGURE 10–38 A-500 pressure test points. (Courtesy of Chrysler)

A500–1 The lockup solenoid (left) and overdrive solenoid (right) provide control of those circuits.

A500–2 The plastic tower at the right front is the three-prong solenoid connector that sticks through the case.

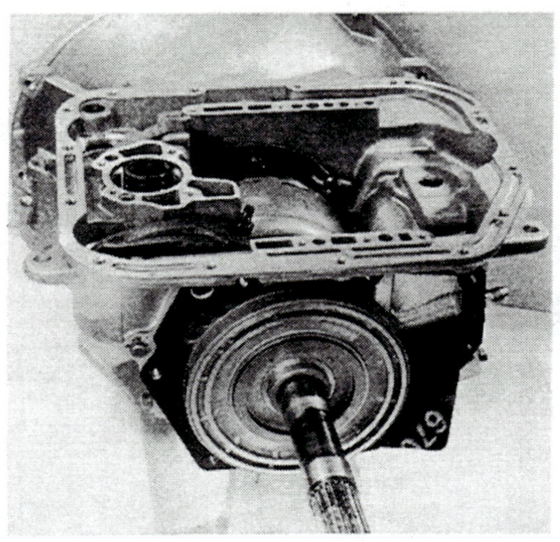

A500–3 With the overdrive case removed, the overdrive piston is visible. The three-speed portion of the transmission is basically a A-999.

A500–6 The tubing to carry governor oil is seen at the lower left.

A500–4 The open end of the overdrive unit shows the overdrive clutch pack and sliding hub in the middle.

A500–7 A double roller clutch is used for normal direct-drive use and should be closely inspected.

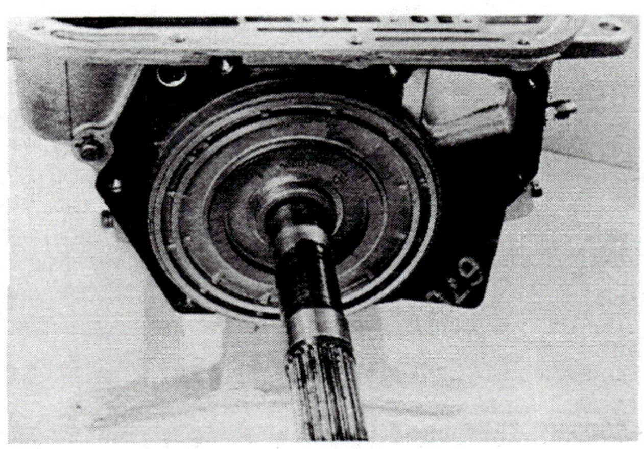

A500–5 The two holes at the upper left are for governor supply oil and governor pressure.

A500–8 The double one-way clutch, overdrive pinion carrier, and sun gear should be inspected for wear.

A500–9 The sliding hub (left) is splined to the sun gear. Inspect all parts for wear.

A500–11 Inside the sliding hub a 800-lb spring is mounted. Use extreme caution in disassembling. Follow the manufacturer's procedure exactly.

A500–10 Inside the direct clutch drum are the clutch plate grooves, next the ring gear, then the outer race for the double one-way clutch.

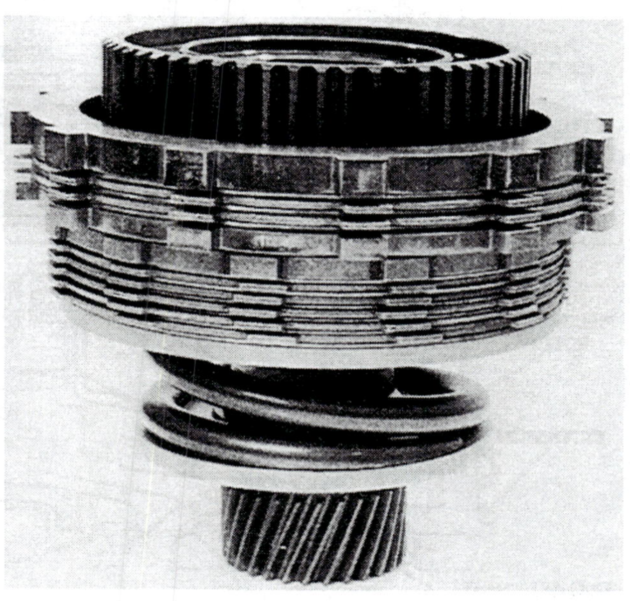

A500–12 The overdrive unit components from the bottom to the top are the OD sun gear, direct clutch spring, direct clutch pack, overdrive clutch pack, and sliding hub.

10.5 A-404: FWD THREE-SPEED TRANSAXLE

10.5.1 Basic Description

The A-404 Torque Flite transaxle was introduced in 1978 in front-wheel-drive vehicles. It is based on the traditional Torque Flite design used by Chrysler for many decades (Figure 10–39).

The transmission description is divided into eight areas. All the transmissions are described in this manner to make their comparison easier.

1. Torque Converter

The A-404 uses a conventional three-element torque converter. The later-model versions use a hydraulic converter clutch.

2. Gear Train

A Simpson gear set is used similar to the other Torque Flite transmissions. This gear train has been highly developed by Chrysler and is widely used.

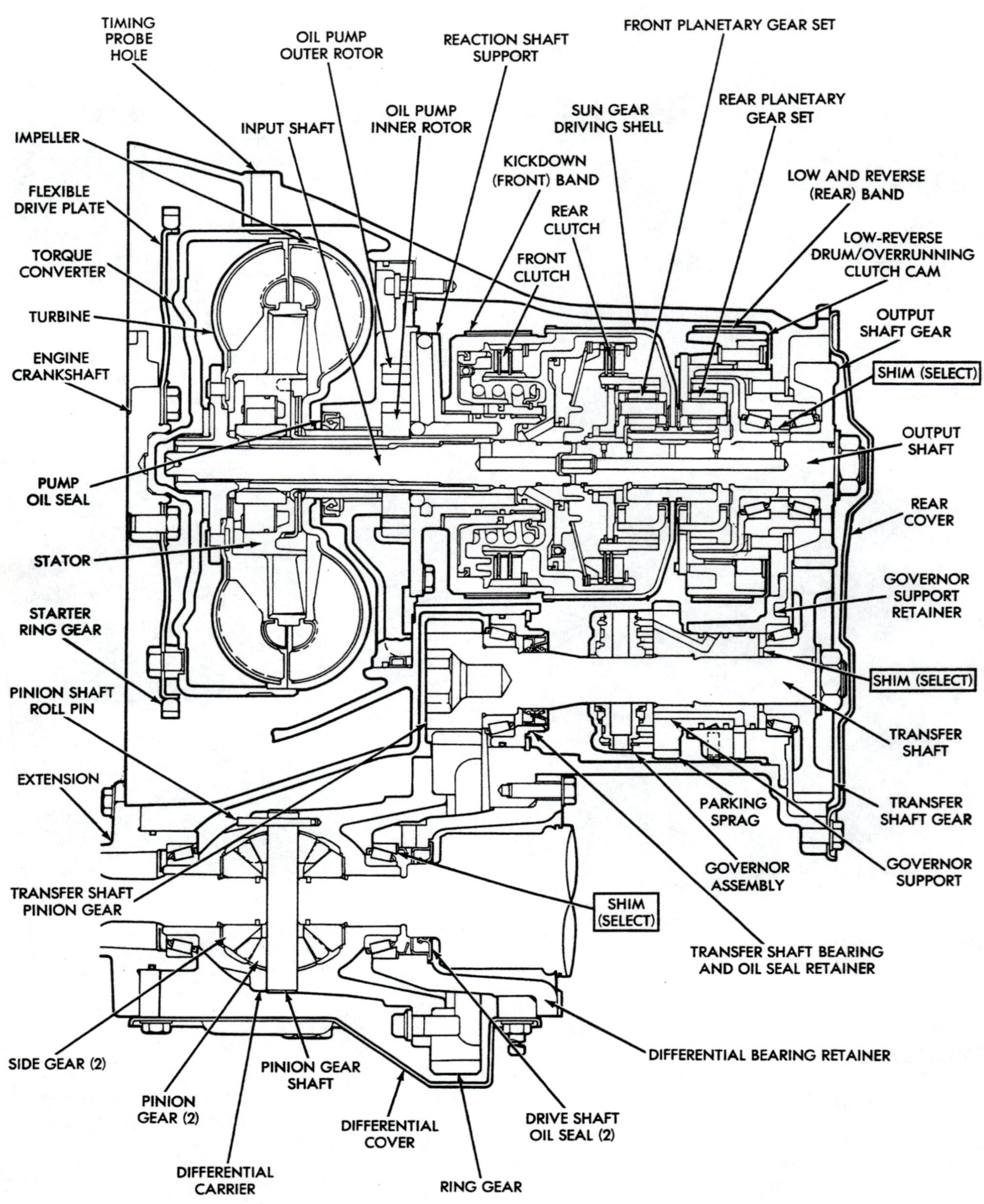

FIGURE 10–39 A-404 cutaway view. (Courtesy of Chrysler)

3. *Coupling Devices*
The front clutch is used to connect the input shaft to the sun gear. The rear clutch connects the input shaft to the front ring gear.

4. *Holding Devices*
The front (kickdown) band is used to hold the sun gear while the rear (low–reverse) band is used to hold the rear pinion carrier. An overrunning (roller) clutch is also used to hold the rear pinion carrier in D1.

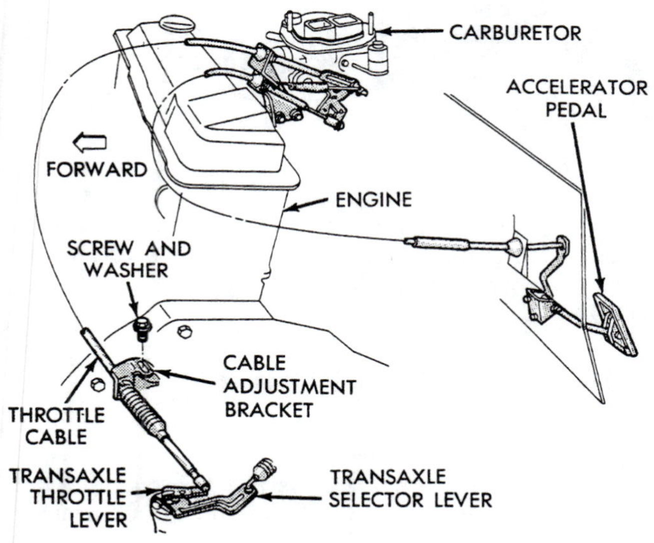

FIGURE 10–40 A-404 throttle valve cable. (Courtesy of Chrysler)

5. *Pump*
The A-404 uses a gear crescent oil pump, which should always be checked for proper gear clearance.

6. *Shift Control*
The shift control is hydraulic, with the converter clutch controlled electronically.

7. *Governor*
The governor is a two-stage shaft-mounted design that is located on the transfer shaft. The governor can be removed after the oil pan and valve body have been removed. Follow the manual procedures carefully.

8. *Throttle Valve*
The throttle valve is controlled by a throttle valve cable connecting the carburetor throttle linkage to the transaxle throttle shaft (Figure 10–40).

10.5.2 Power Flow

The power flow is described by stating the coupling and holding device action (applied, or holding) on the members of the planetary gear set (sun gear, pinion carrier, and ring gear) in each gear range of the transmission.

1. *Neutral (N)*
In neutral none of the hydraulic devices are applied. The turbine shaft is turning the rear clutch hub, but the power flow stops there.

2. *Drive First (D1)*
In first gear the rear clutch is applied, which drives the front ring gear as the input member. The over-

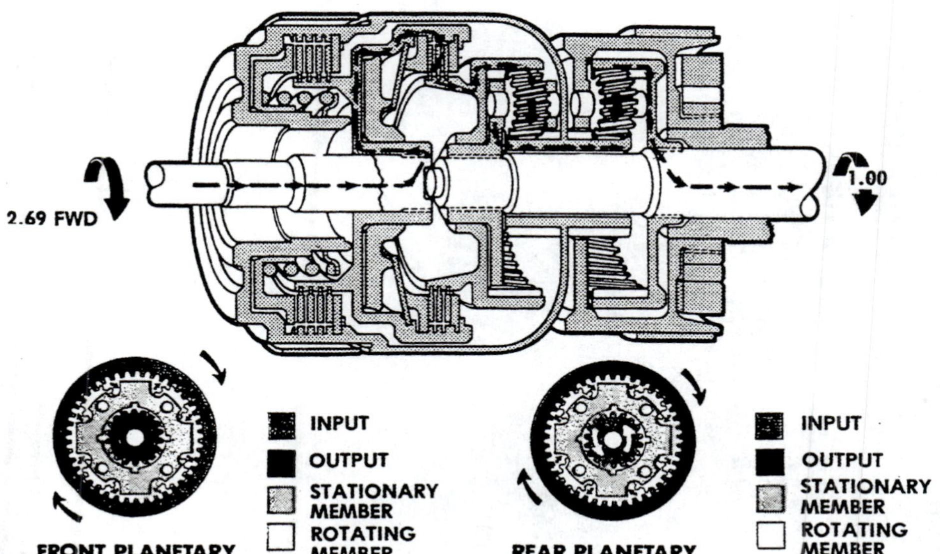

FIGURE 10–41 A-404 in first gear. (Courtesy of Chrysler)

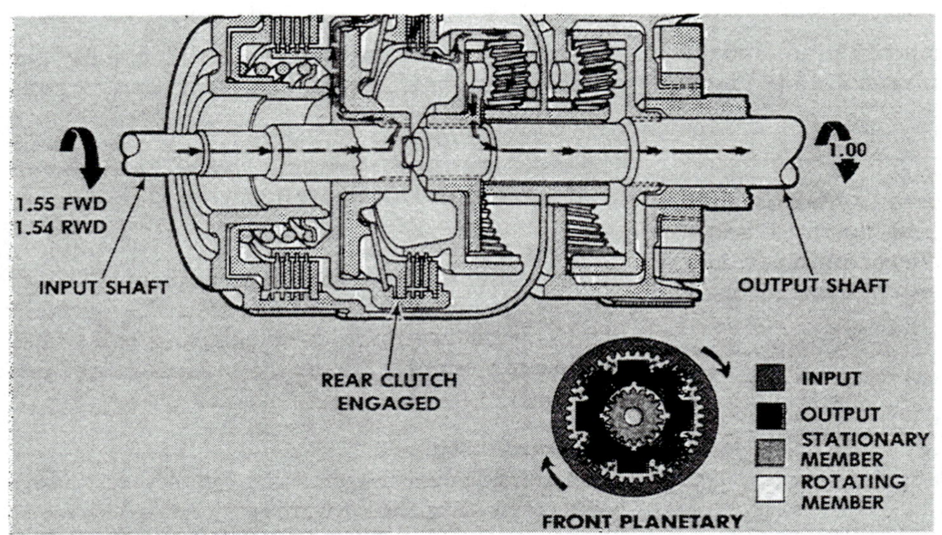

FIGURE 10–42 A-404 in second gear. (Courtesy of Chrysler)

running (roller) clutch is holding the rear pinion carrier stationary as the reaction member (Figure 10–41). The first-gear ratio is 2.69:1. In manual first gear the rear band is also applied.

3. *Drive Second (D2)*
For second gear the rear clutch still provides input and the front band is also applied, which holds the sun gear as the reaction (Figure 10–42). The second-gear ratio is 1.55:1. In manual second gear the same devices are applied.

4. *Drive Third (D3)*
In third gear the rear clutch remains applied, driving the front ring gear, and the front clutch is applied, which drives the sun gear to provide a direct-drive condition (Figure 10–43).

5. *Reverse (R)*
In reverse gear the front clutch remains applied, driving the sun gear as input. The low–reverse band is applied to hold the rear pinion carrier stationary, which leads to the reverse rotation (Figure 10–44).

10.5.3 Clutch and Band Charts

In this section we provide two clutch and band charts. The first chart, the author's design, uses a standardized format for listing the coupling and holding devices to aid comparison between transmissions. This chart is shown in Figure 10–45. The second chart, the manufacturer's design, which is found in service manuals, is shown in Figure 10–46.

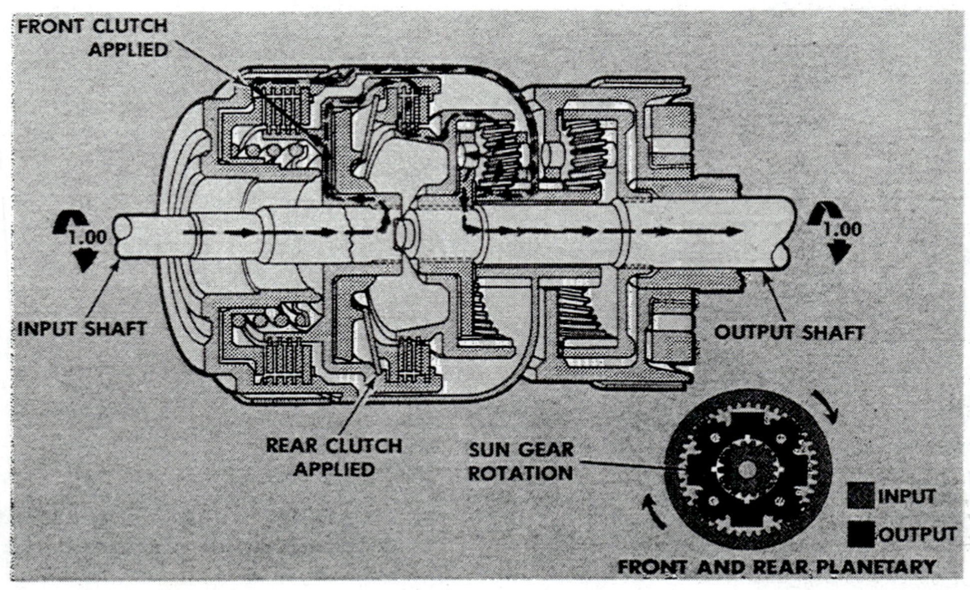

FIGURE 10–43 A-404 in third gear. (Courtesy of Chrysler)

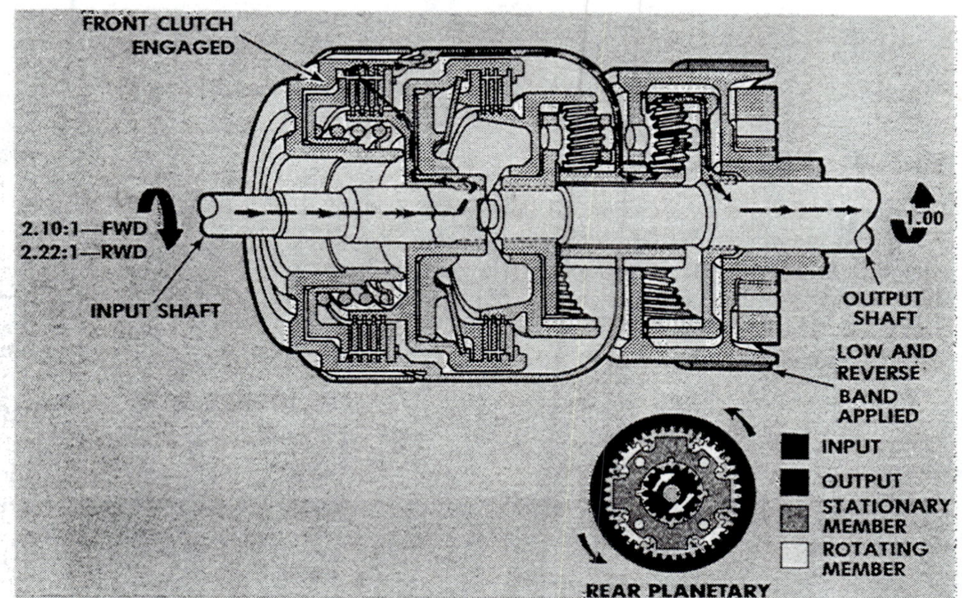

FIGURE 10–44 A-404 in reverse gear. (Courtesy of Chrysler)

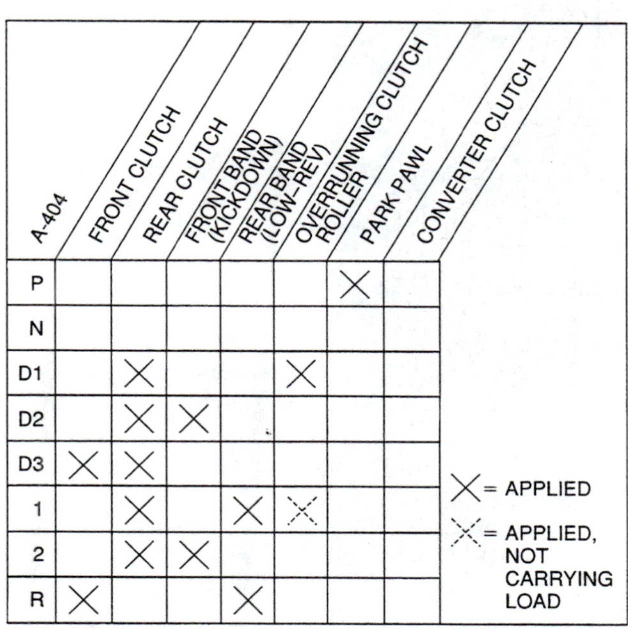

A-404	FRONT CLUTCH	REAR CLUTCH	FRONT BAND (KICKDOWN)	REAR BAND (LOW-REV)	OVERRUNNING CLUTCH ROLLER	PARK PAWL	CONVERTER CLUTCH
P						X	
N							
D1		X			X		
D2		X	X				
D3	X	X					
1		X		X	X (dashed)		
2		X	X				
R	X			X			

X = APPLIED

X (dashed) = APPLIED, NOT CARRYING LOAD

FIGURE 10–45 A-404 clutch and band chart, standardized version.

FIGURE 10–46 A-404 clutch and band chart, factory version. (Courtesy of Chrysler)

Lever Position	Gear Ratio	Start Safety	Parking Sprag	Clutches Front	Clutches Rear	Clutches Over-running	Bands (Kickdown) Front	Bands (Low-Rev.) Rear
P—PARK		X	X					
R—REVERSE	2.10			X				X
N—NEUTRAL		X						
D—DRIVE								
First	2.69				X	X		
Second	1.55				X		X	
Direct	1.00			X	X			
2—SECOND								
First	2.69				X	X		
Second	1.55				X		X	
1—LOW (First)	2.69				X			X

10.5.4 Identification

The shape of the transmission oil pan or its gasket is a quick means of identifying an automatic transmission. In Figure 10–47 you see the pan gasket shape and number of bolt holes for the A-404 transaxle. The location of the factory identification tag and its code are shown in Figure 10–48.

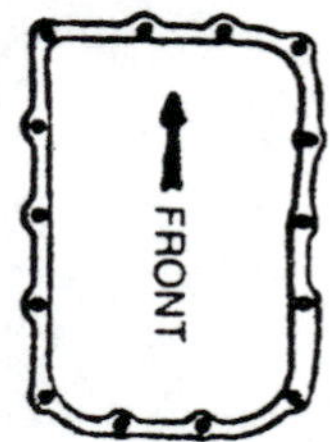

FIGURE 10–47 A-404 pan gasket identification.

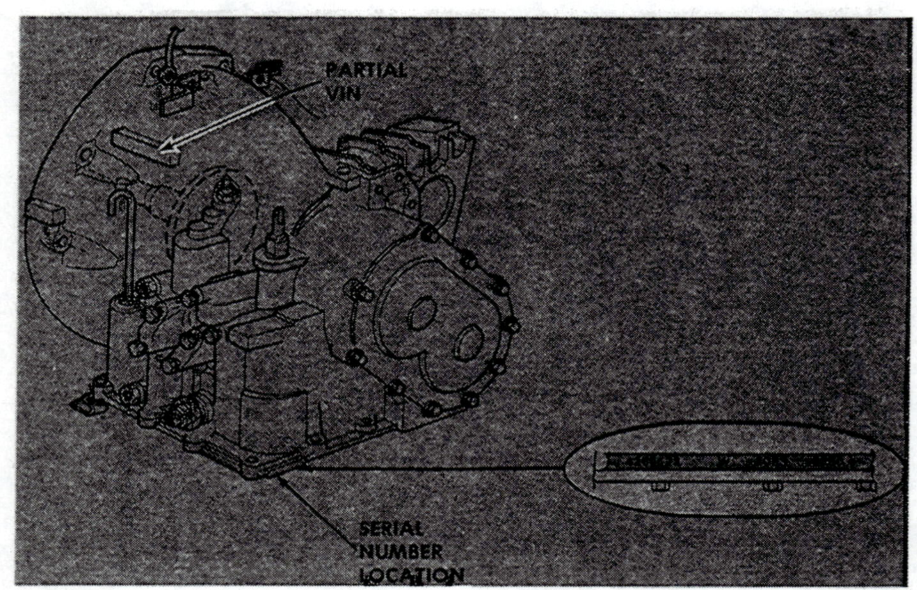

FIGURE 10–48 A-404 identification numbers. (Courtesy of Chrysler)

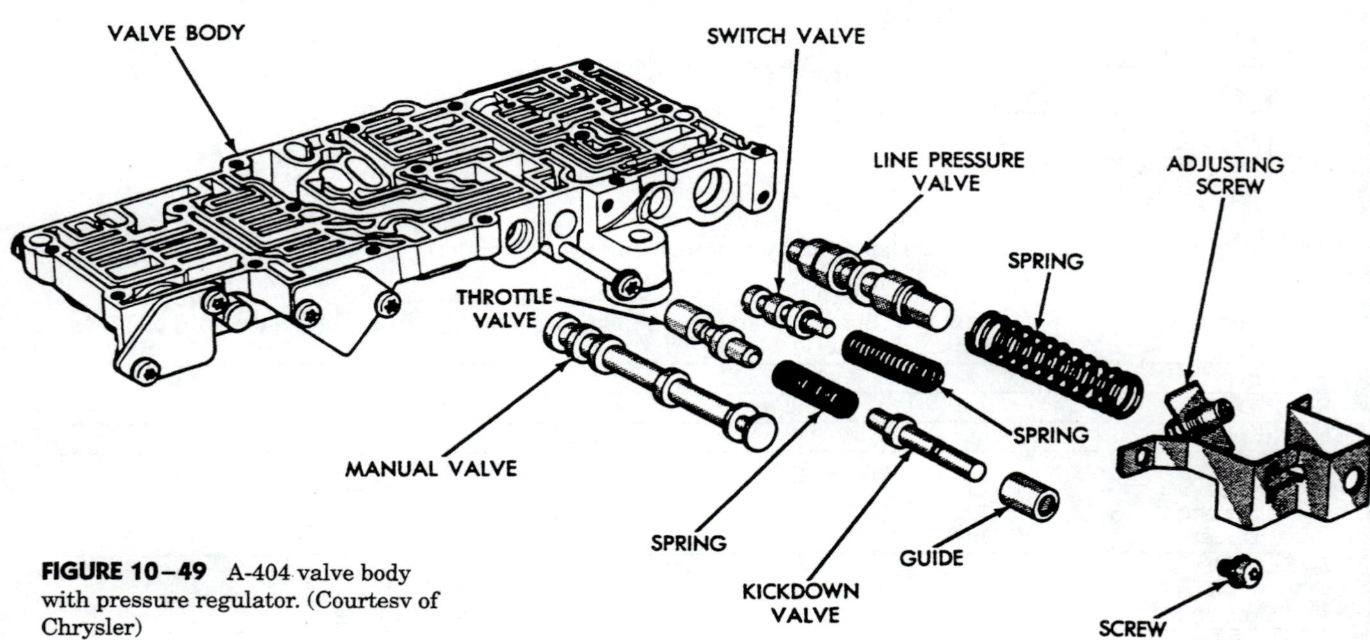

FIGURE 10–49 A-404 valve body with pressure regulator. (Courtesv of Chrysler)

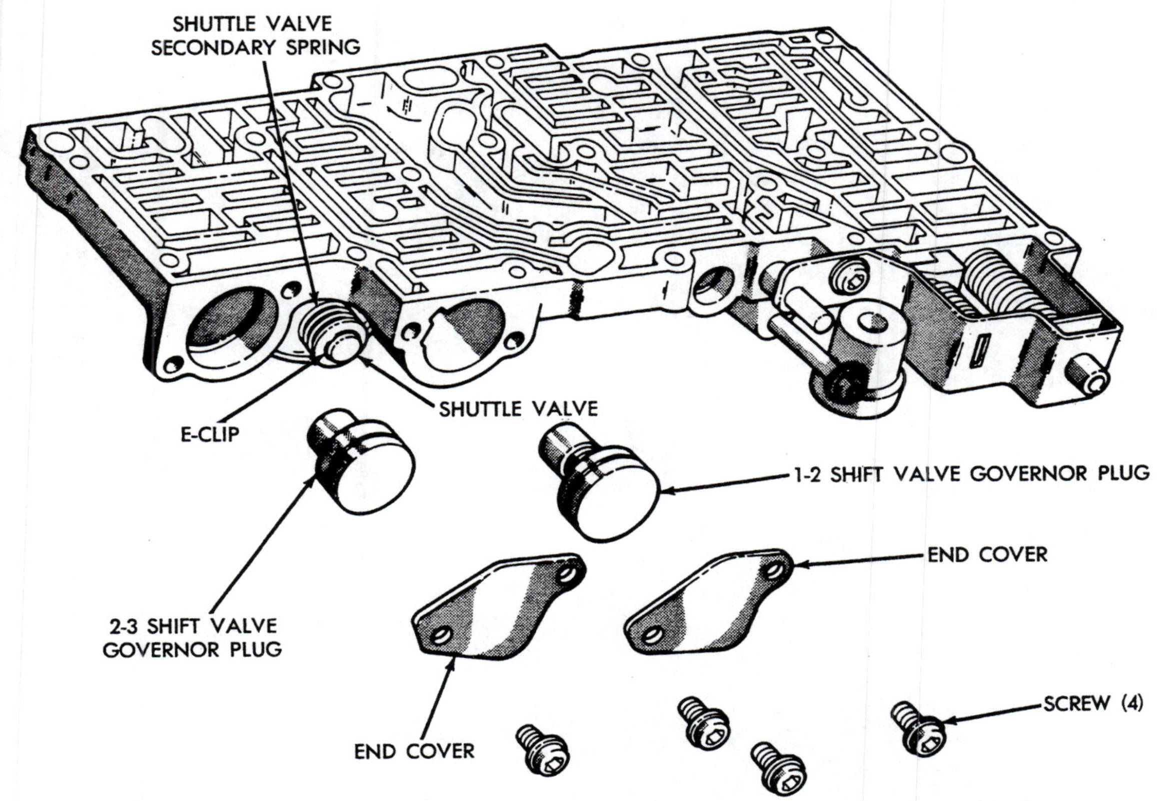

FIGURE 10–50 A-404 valve body: governor plugs. (Courtesy of Chrysler)

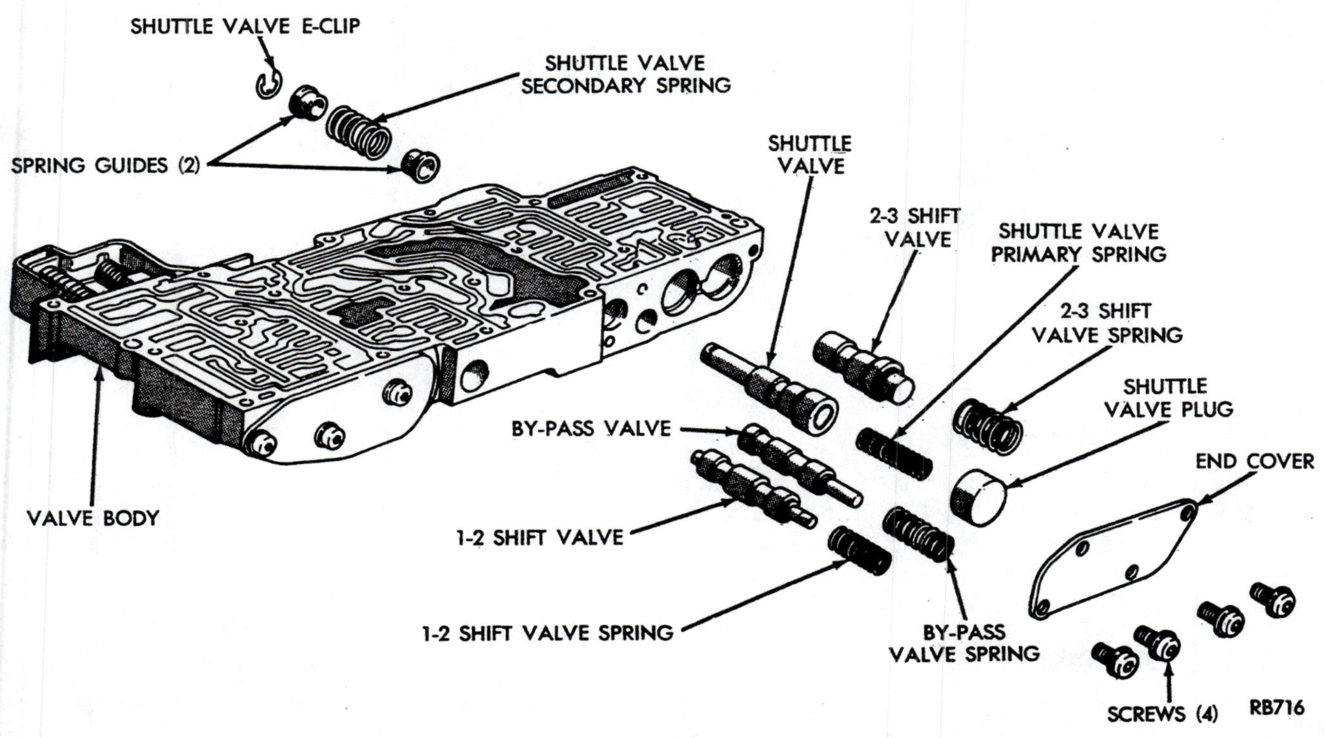

FIGURE 10–51 A-404 valve body: shift valves. (Courtesy of Chrysler)

10.5.5 Components

In this section exploded drawings of the A-404 transaxle subassemblies are shown, along with lists of the part names. The manufacturer's part names are used to eliminate confusion about component names. The drawings to study are as follows:

- Pressure regulator and manual valve, Figure 10–49
- Governor plugs, Figure 10–50
- Shift valves, Figure 10–51
- Oil pump, Figure 10–52
- Front clutch, Figure 10–53
- Rear clutch, Figure 10–54

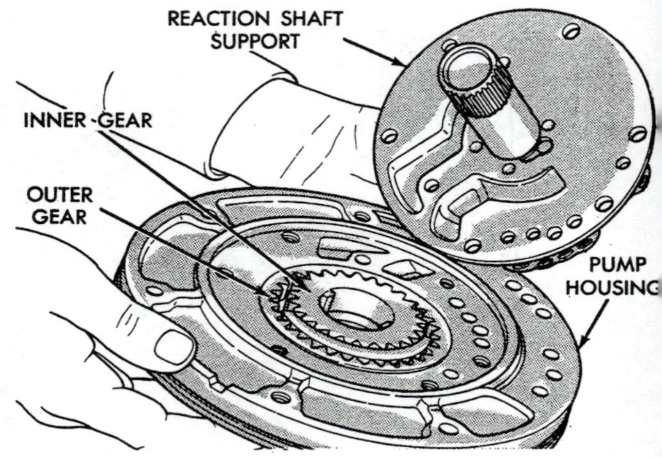

FIGURE 10–52 A-404 oil pump. (Courtesy of Chrysler)

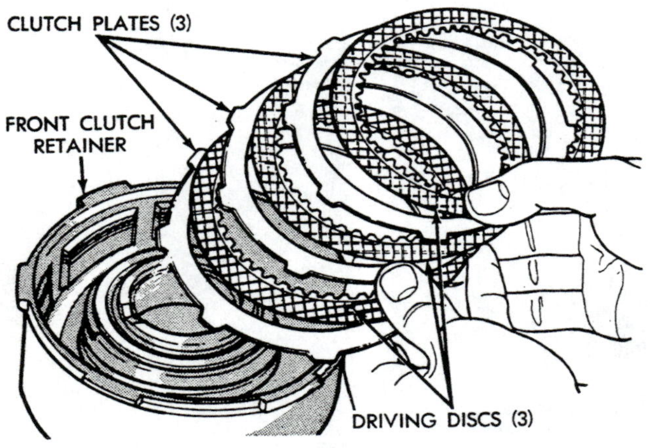

FIGURE 10–53 A-404 front clutch. (Courtesy of Chrysler)

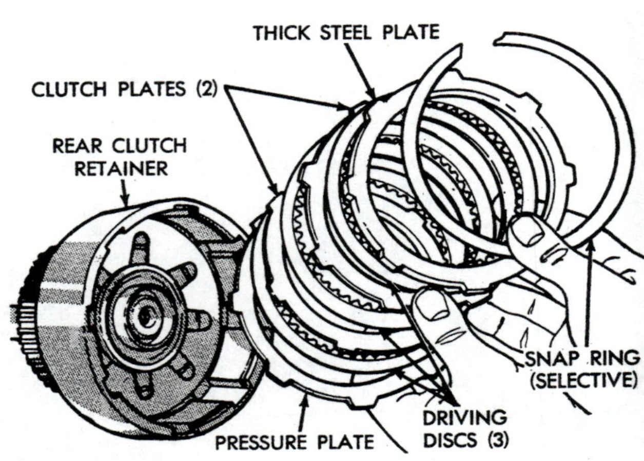

FIGURE 10–54 A-404 rear clutch. (Courtesy of Chrysler)

10.5.6 Pressure Test

One of the key tests in diagnosis is the hydraulic system pressure test. The location of the test points of the A-404 transaxle is shown in Figure 10–55. A pressure chart listing the pressure specification of this transaxle is shown in Figure 10–56.

10.5.7 Air Test

Air testing is used during preliminary diagnosis of certain malfunctions and during the disassembly process to verify component operation or failure. The technician must know which hydraulic circuit is being served by each passageway to be able to air test a transmission accurately. This information is presented in the illustration of air test passages, Figure 10–57.

10.5.8 Special Attention

In this section we show and explain various points of special interest about the A-404 transaxle. The information presented about each item is included with each illustration.

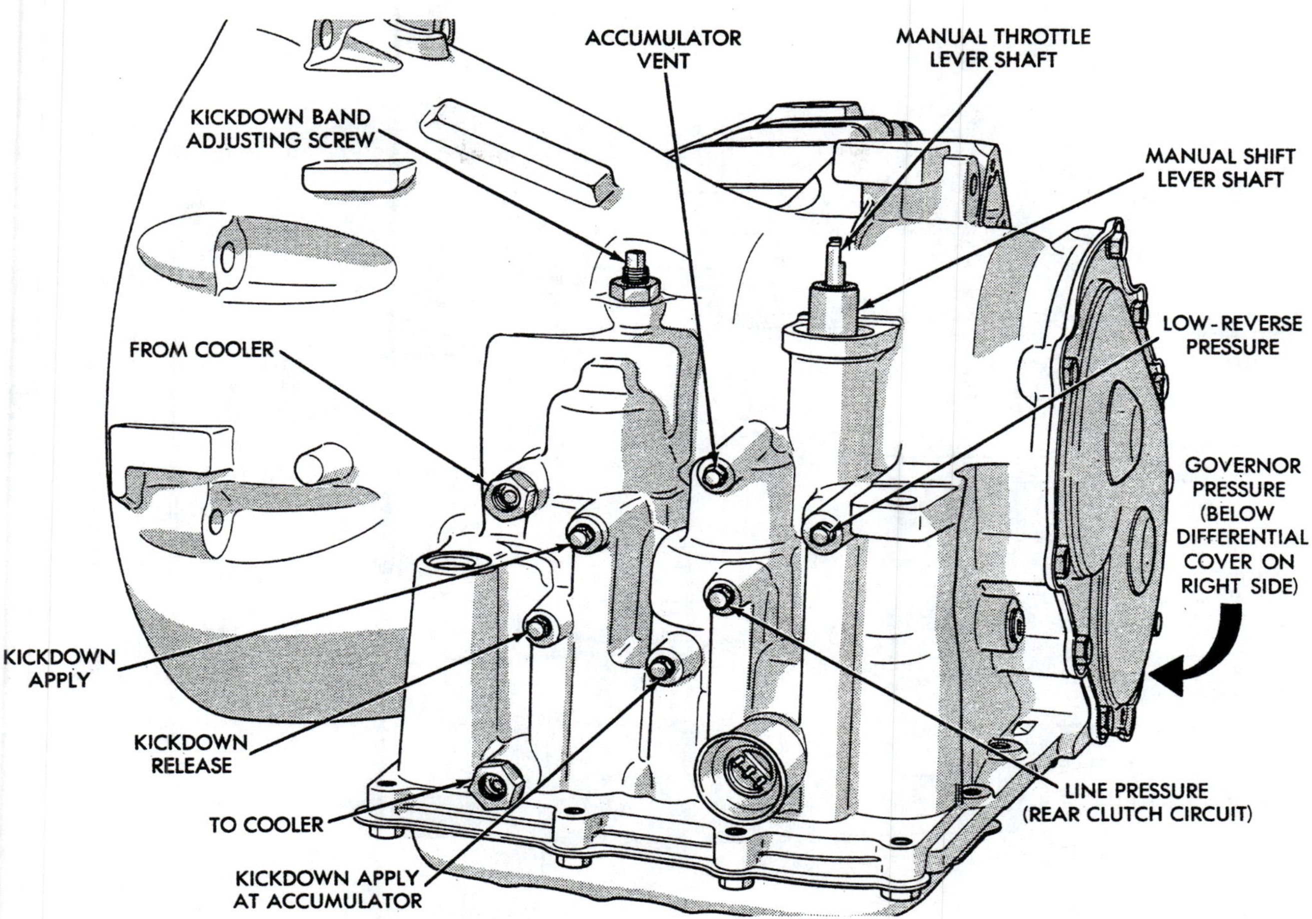

FIGURE 10–55 A-404 pressure test points. (Courtesy of Chrysler)

AUTOMATIC SHIFT SPEEDS AND GOVERNOR PRESSURE CHART (APPROXIMATE MILES AND KILOMETERS PER HOUR)

Vehicle	M and Z		M, Z, P, D, G, V		M, Z, P, D, C, V High Altitude	
Engine (Liter)	1.7L.		2.2 and 2.6L.		2.2L.	
Overall Top Gear Ratio	3.48		2.78		3.22	
Throttle Minimum	MPH	km/hr	MPH	km/hr	MPH	km/hr
1-2 Upshift	11-15	18-24	10-14	16-23	11-15	18-24
2-3 Upshift	16-21	26-34	15-20	24-32	16-22	26-35
3-1 Downshift	11-14	18-23	10-13	16-21	11-15	18-24
Throttle Wide Open						
1-2 Upshift	33-39	53-63	37-44	60-71	33-38	53-61
2-3 Upshift	55-64	89-103	61-71	98-114	62-73	100-117
Kickdown Limit						
3-2 WOT Downshift	51-60	82-97	57-66	92-106	56-66	90-106
3-2 Part Throttle Downshift	28-32	45-51	26-30	42-48	29-33	47-53
3-1 WOT Downshift	30-35	48-56	32-38	51-61	31-36	50-58
Governor Pressure*						
15 psi	23-26	37-42	22-24	35-39	24-27	39-43
50 psi	54-61	87-98	61-68	98-109	61-68	98-109

*Governor pressure should be from zero to 3 psi at stand still or downshift may not occur.
NOTE: Changes in tire size will cause shift points to occur at corresponding higher or lower vehicle speeds.
Km/hr. = Kilometers per hour.

FIGURE 10–56 A-404 pressure test charts. (Courtesy of Chrysler)

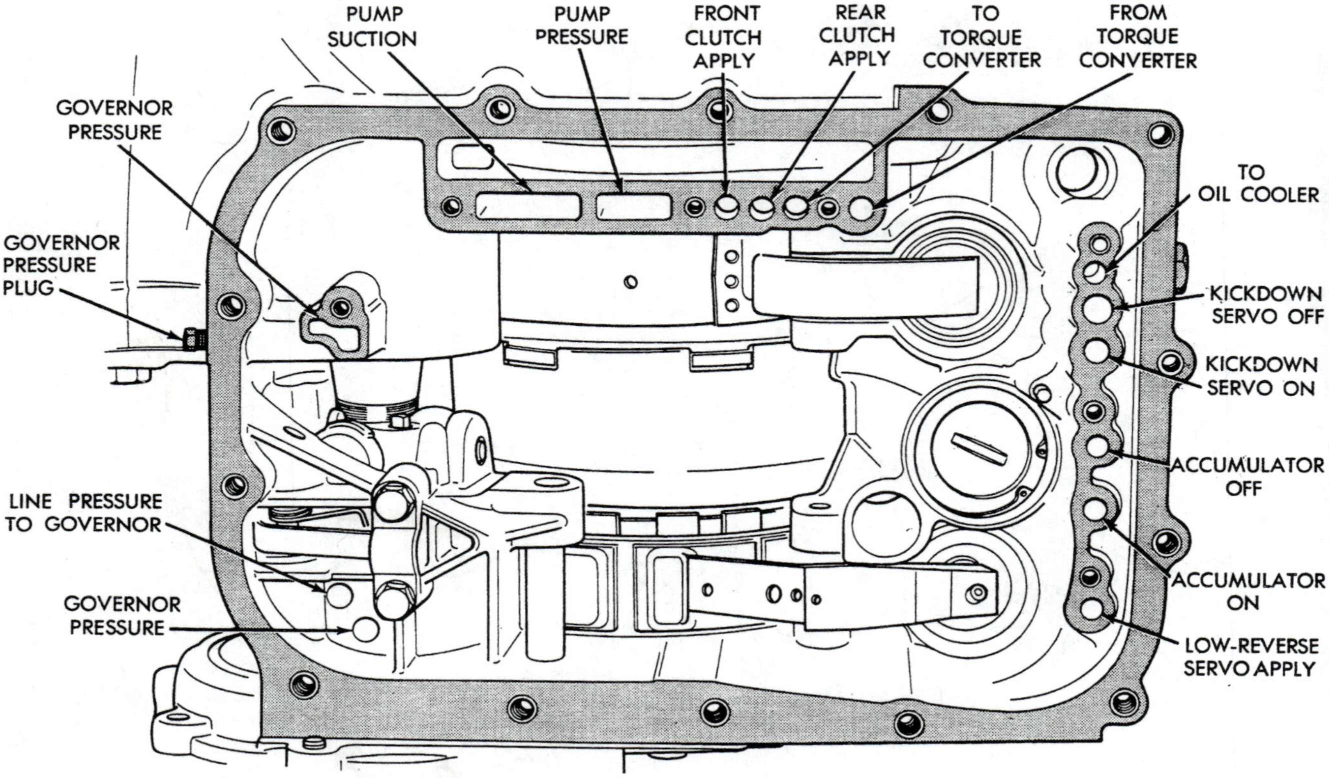

PUMP SUCTION
PUMP PRESSURE
FRONT CLUTCH APPLY
REAR CLUTCH APPLY
TO TORQUE CONVERTER
FROM TORQUE CONVERTER
GOVERNOR PRESSURE
TO OIL COOLER
GOVERNOR PRESSURE PLUG
KICKDOWN SERVO OFF
KICKDOWN SERVO ON
ACCUMULATOR OFF
LINE PRESSURE TO GOVERNOR
ACCUMULATOR ON
GOVERNOR PRESSURE
LOW-REVERSE SERVO APPLY

FIGURE 10–57 A-404 air test. (Courtesy of Chrysler)

A404–1 The pump body, cover, and gears must be measured to determine wear.

A404–2 All contact areas and splines on the front and rear clutches and kickdown band should be checked for wear.

A404–3 The input ring gear and front pinion carrier must be inspected.

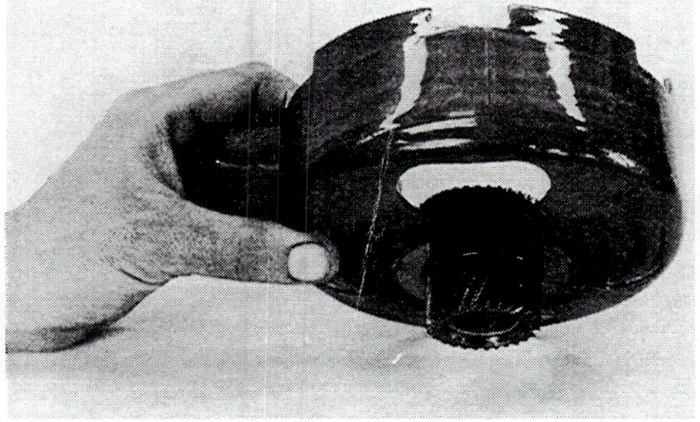

A404–4 Sun gear-to-drive shell wear must be checked.

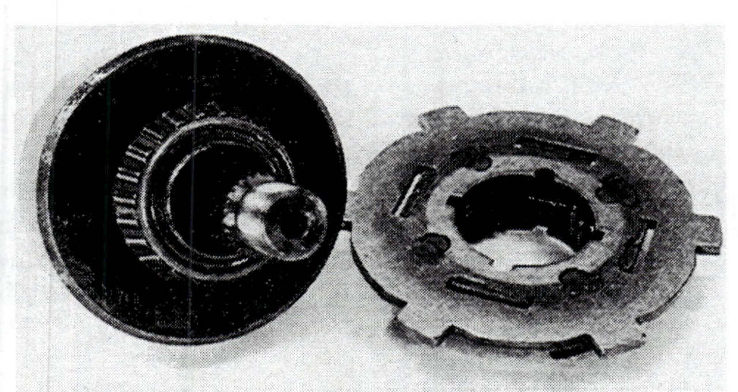

A404–5 The rear pinion carrier and output ring gear should be checked for wear or damage.

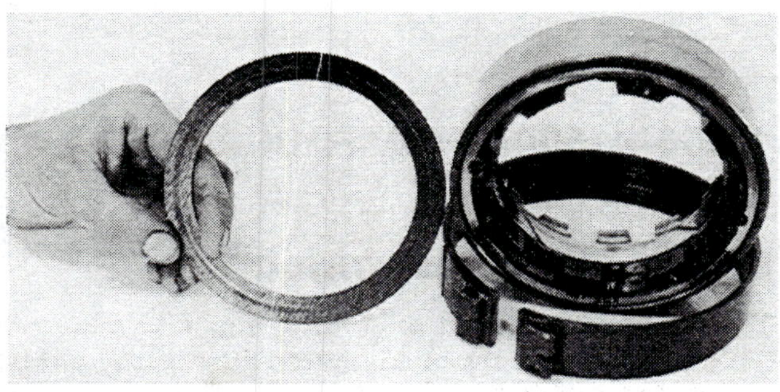

A404–6 The low–reverse drum/overrunning clutch cam (right), low reverse band, and number 11 thrust washer should be inspected and measured for wear.

A404–7 The output shaft and transfer shaft bearings must be inspected closely.

A404–8 The other transfer shaft bearing must also be inspected.

A404–9 The differential carrier bearing races must be inspected.

A404–10 All differential parts should be examined for damage from particle contamination.

10.6 A-604: FWD FOUR-SPEED TRANSAXLE

10.6.1 Basic Description

The A-604, introduced on 1989 model Chrysler vehicles, is the first transaxle to feature a fully adaptive electronic control system. The computer sensor feedback information is processed continuously by the on-board computer, and based on this input the transaxle controls are constantly being adapted to match vehicle operating conditions. Because of the continuous computer control, the gear train can be designed with fewer clutches and one-way clutches than would normally be used (Figure 10–58).

1. *Torque Converter*
The A-604 uses a conventional three-element torque converter with a hydraulic converter clutch that is computer controlled.

2. *Gear Train*
The A-604 uses a gear train that consists of two interconnected planetary gear sets. The front sun gear is either an input or a reaction member. The front pinion carrier and rear ring gear are connected as one unit and can both be input and reaction members. The front ring gear and rear pinion carrier are one piece also and serve as output members. The rear sun gear is an input member.

3. *Coupling Devices*
The A-604 has three input clutches: underdrive, overdrive, and reverse. The underdrive clutch drives the rear sun gear (Figure 10–59), the overdrive clutch drives the front pinion carrier/rear ring gear (Figure 10–60), and the reverse clutch drives the front sun gear (Figure 10–61). No one-way clutches are used as input coupling devices in this transaxle.

4. *Holding Devices*
Two holding clutches are used in the A-604. The 2–4 clutch holds the front sun gear (Figure 10–62). The low–reverse clutch holds the front planetary carrier/rear ring gear (Figure 10–63). Again no one-way clutches are used as holding devices in the gear train.

5. *Pump*
The A-604 uses a standard gear crescent type of oil pump with no special features.

6. *Shift Control*
The A-604 is the first fully computer-controlled transaxle to feature adaptive memory. The computer sensors are shown in Figure 10–64. Four solenoids, the low–reverse, the 2–4/low–reverse, the overdrive, and the underdrive, are used to control the gear changes. All the solenoids are contained in the solenoid assembly, which bolts to the front of the case (Figure 10–65).

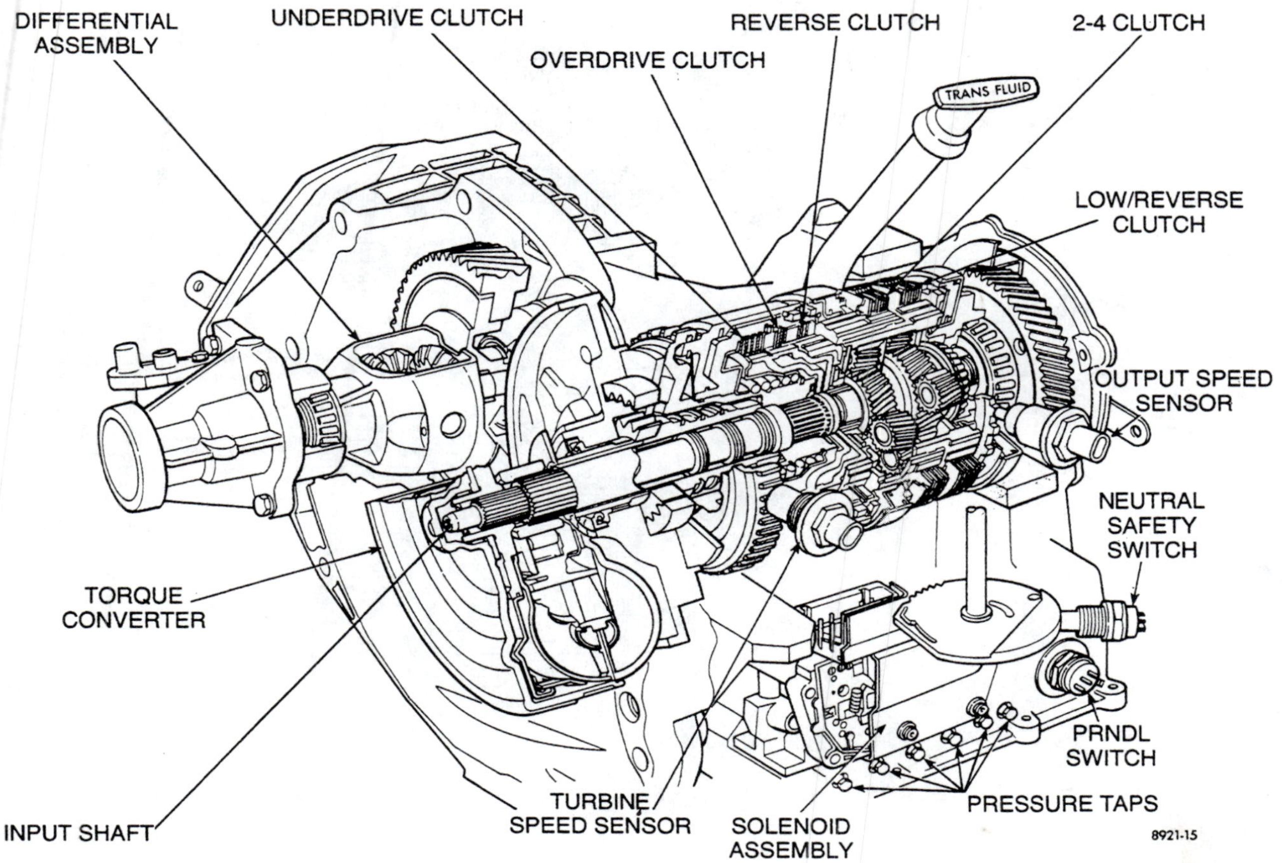

DIFFERENTIAL ASSEMBLY
UNDERDRIVE CLUTCH
REVERSE CLUTCH
2-4 CLUTCH
OVERDRIVE CLUTCH
TRANS FLUID
LOW/REVERSE CLUTCH
OUTPUT SPEED SENSOR
NEUTRAL SAFETY SWITCH
TORQUE CONVERTER
PRNDL SWITCH
PRESSURE TAPS
INPUT SHAFT
TURBINE SPEED SENSOR
SOLENOID ASSEMBLY
8921-15

FIGURE 10–58 A-604 cutaway view. (Courtesy of Chrysler)

UNDERDRIVE CLUTCH
REAR SUN GEAR
HUB
INPUT SHAFT
INPUT CLUTCH RETAINER
UNDERDRIVE CLUTCH HUB

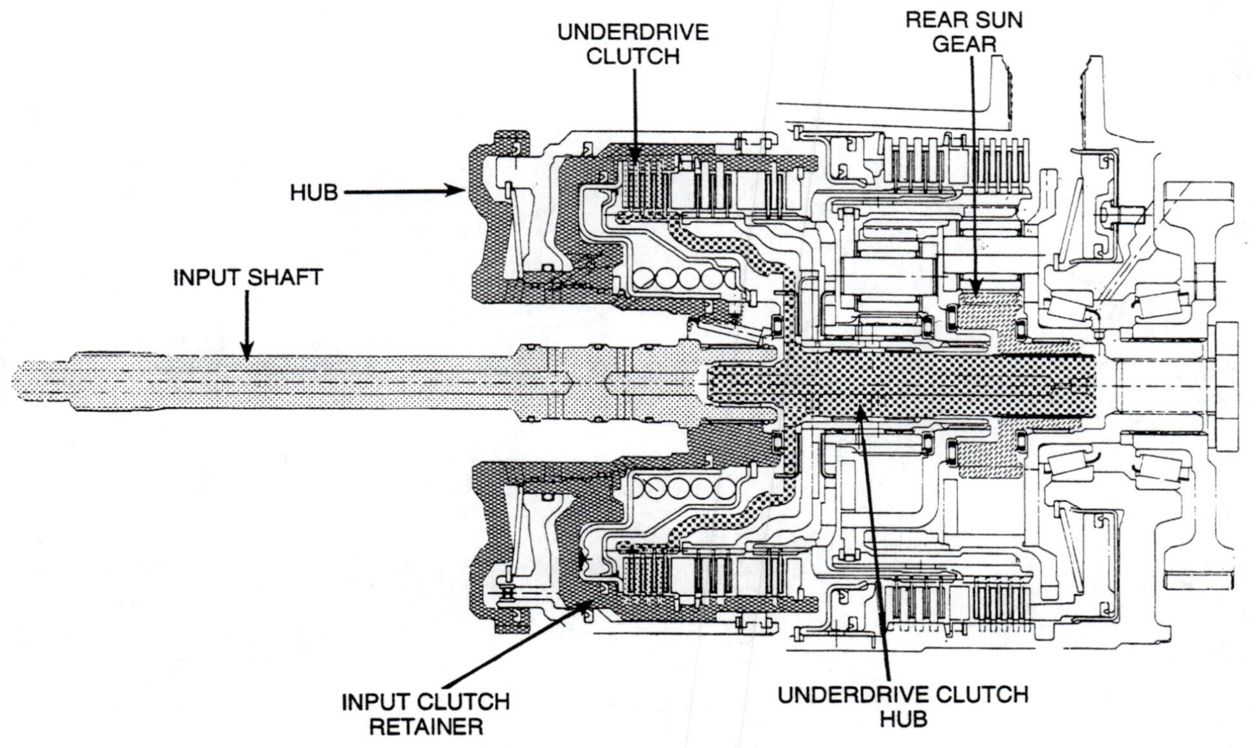

FIGURE 10–59 A-604 underdrive clutch. (Courtesy of Chrysler)

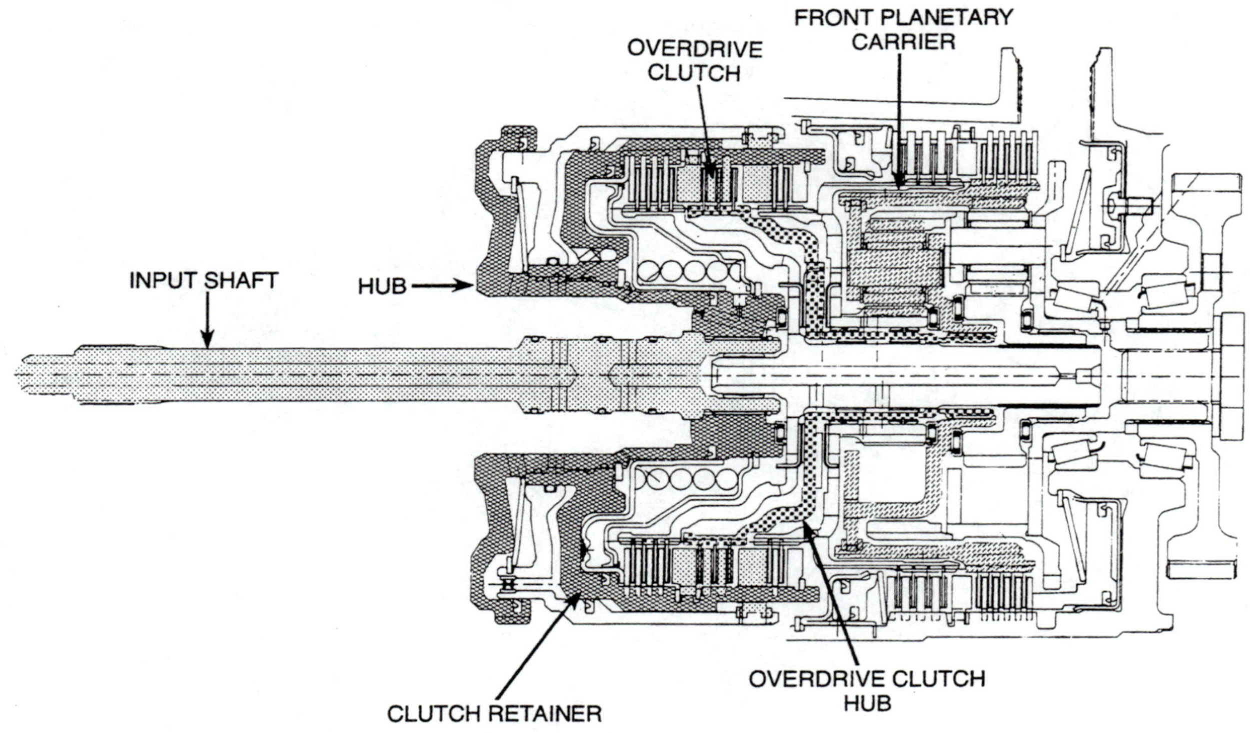

FIGURE 10–60 A-604 overdrive clutch. (Courtesy of Chrysler)

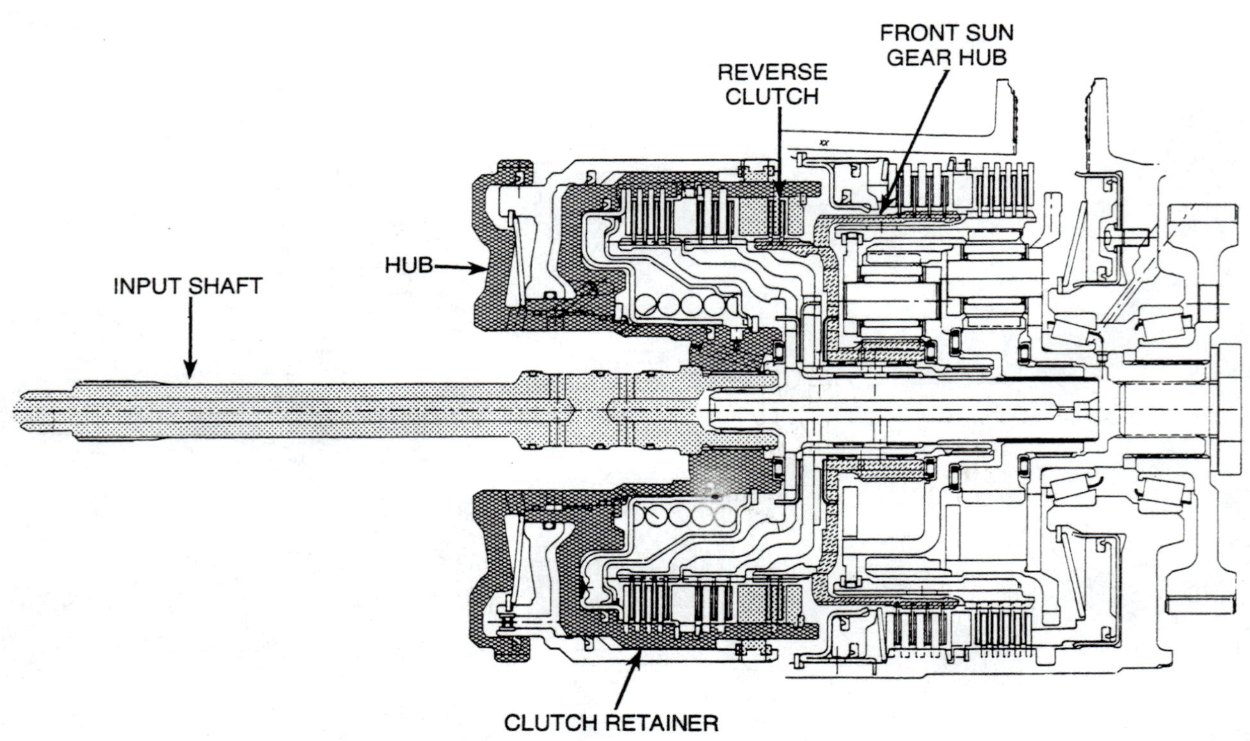

FIGURE 10–61 A-604 reverse clutch. (Courtesy of Chrysler)

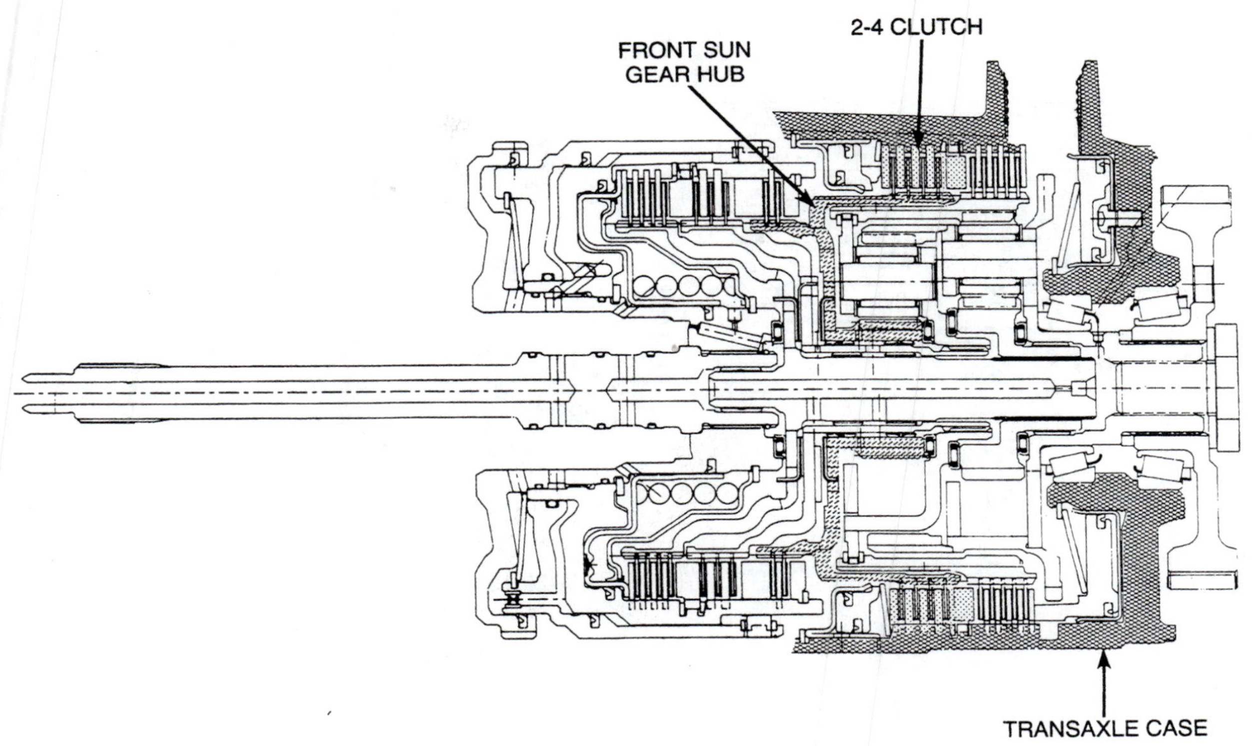

FIGURE 10–62 A-604 2–4 clutch. (Courtesy of Chrysler)

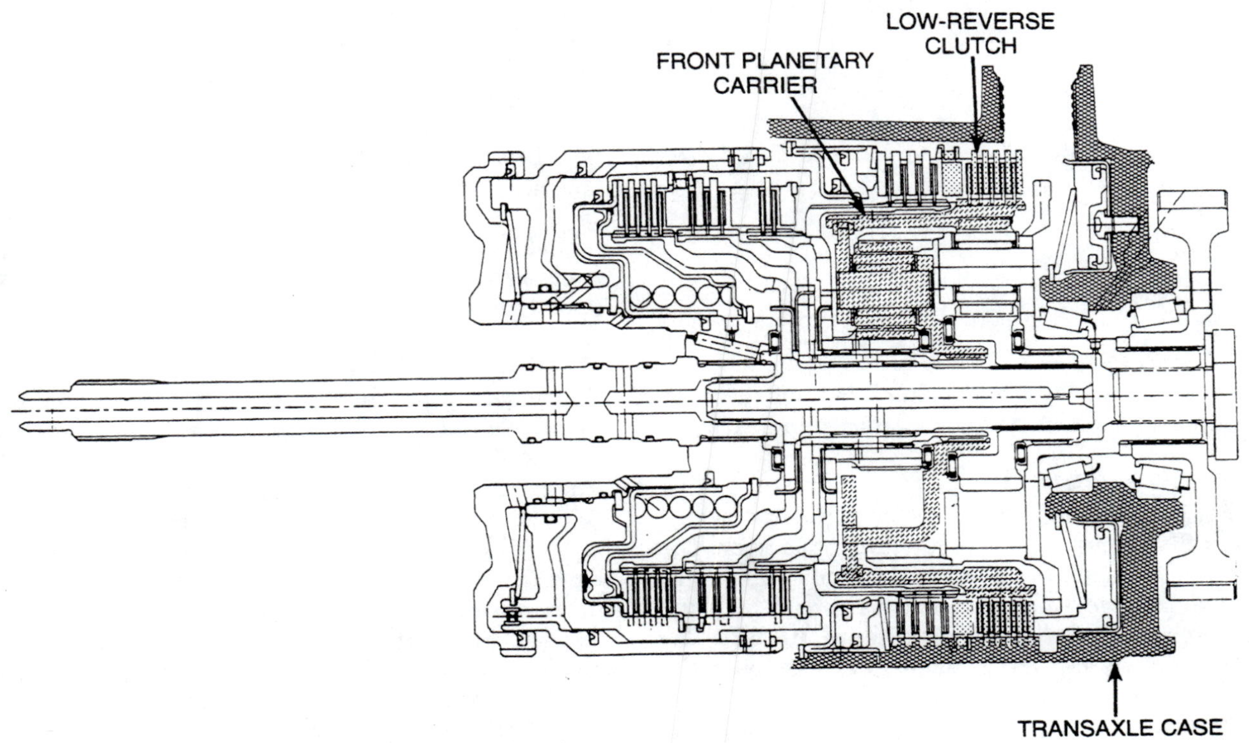

FIGURE 10–63 A-604 low–reverse clutch. (Courtesy of Chrysler)

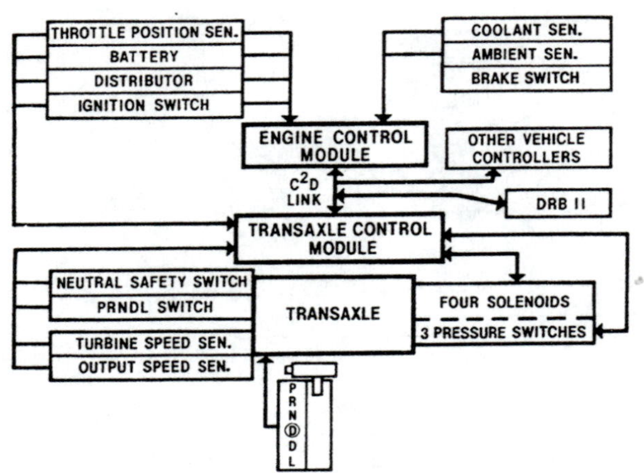

FIGURE 10–64 A-604 shift control solenoids. (Courtesy of Chrysler)

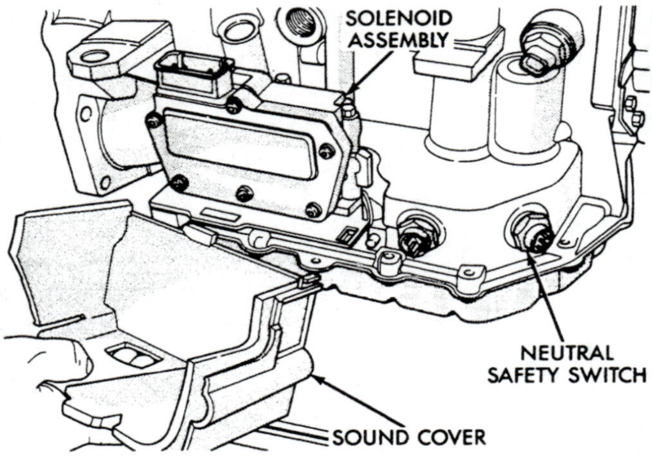

FIGURE 10–65 A-604 shift solenoid assembly. (Courtesy of Chrysler)

7. *Governor*

The A-604 does not use a governor system because the computer is receiving data continuously about the vehicle speed from the output speed sensor and the vehicle speed sensor.

8. *Throttle Valve*

No throttle valve system is used on the A-604 because of the ability of the computer to do a better job.

10.6.2 Power Flow

1. *Neutral (N)*

In neutral the low–reverse clutch is applied in anticipation of the transaxle being placed in gear.

2. *Drive First (D1)*

In first gear the underdrive clutch is applied, which drives the rear sun gear as the input member. The low–reverse clutch is holding the front pinion carrier/rear ring gear as the reaction member with the rear pinion carrier as output (Figure 10–66). The first-gear ratio is 2.84:1. In manual first gear the same devices are applied, but the upshift speed is increased.

3. *Drive Second (D2)*

In second gear the underdrive clutch remains applied, driving the rear sun gear. The 2–4 clutch is also applied, which holds the front sun gear (Figure 10–67). The second-gear ratio is 1.57:1. Manual second gear uses the same devices with higher upshift speeds.

4. *Drive Third (D3)*

In third gear the underdrive clutch remains applied, driving the rear sun gear. The overdrive clutch is also applied, which drives the front pinion carrier/rear ring gear as an input (Figure 10–68), which produces direct drive.

5. *Drive Fourth (D4)*

In fourth gear the overdrive clutch is applied, which drives the front pinion carrier/rear ring gear as the input member, while the 2–4 clutch holds the front sun gear as the reaction member (Figure 10–69). The fourth-gear ratio is 0.69:1.

6. *Reverse (R)*

In reverse the reverse clutch is applied, which drives the front sun gear as the input member, while the low–reverse clutch holds the front pinion carrier/rear ring gear and gives a reverse-gear ratio of 2.21:1 (Figure 10–70).

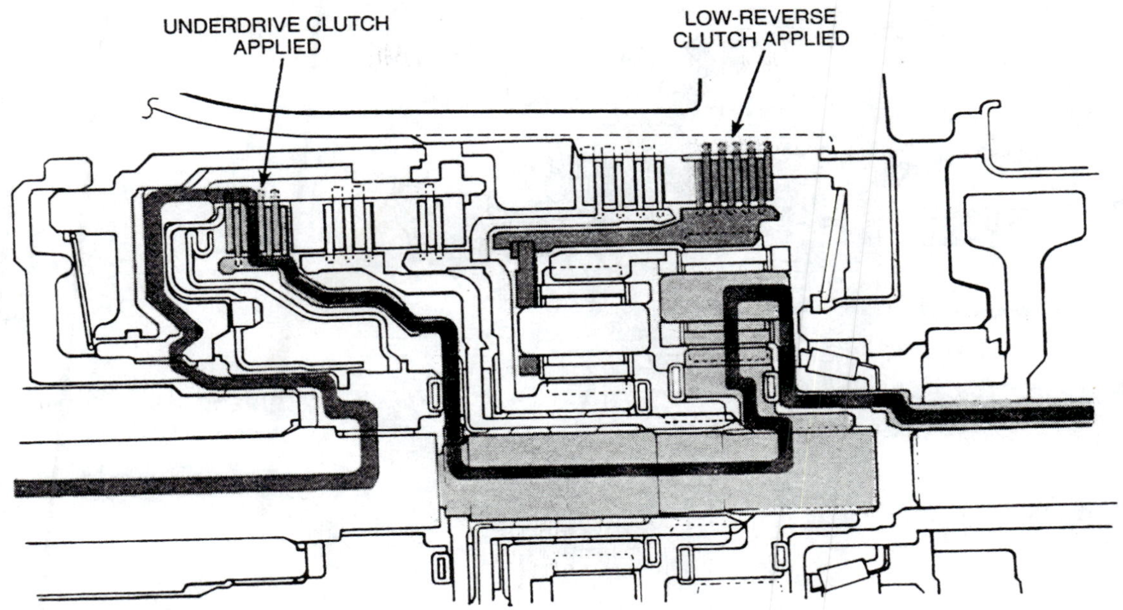

FIGURE 10–66 A-604 in first gear. (Courtesy of Chrysler)

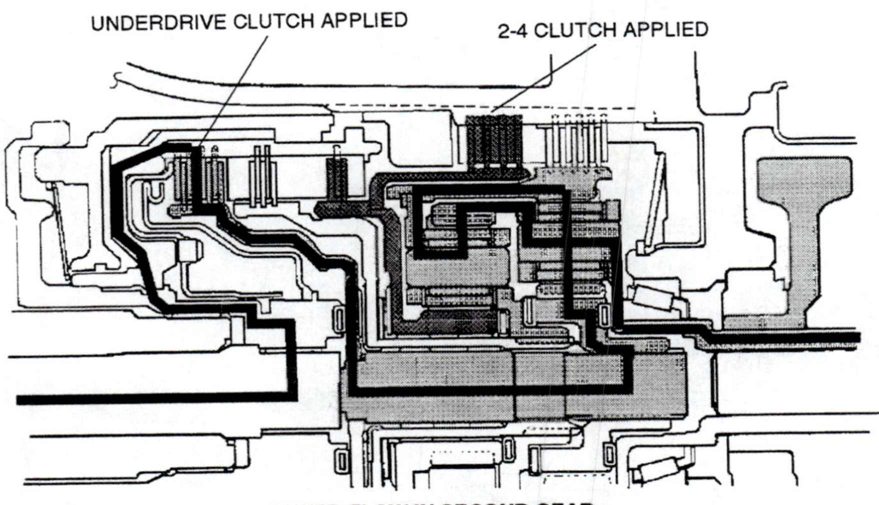

FIGURE 10–67 A-604 in second gear. (Courtesy of Chrysler)

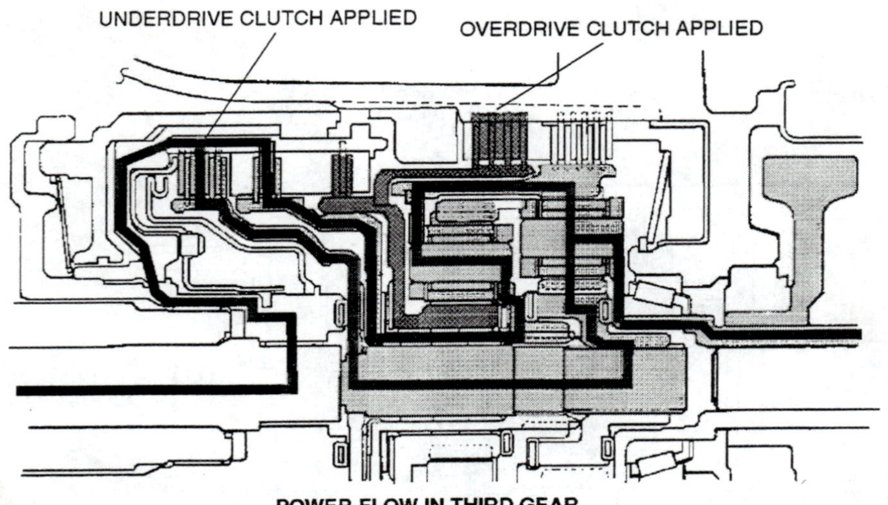

FIGURE 10–68 A-604 in third gear. (Courtesy of Chrysler)

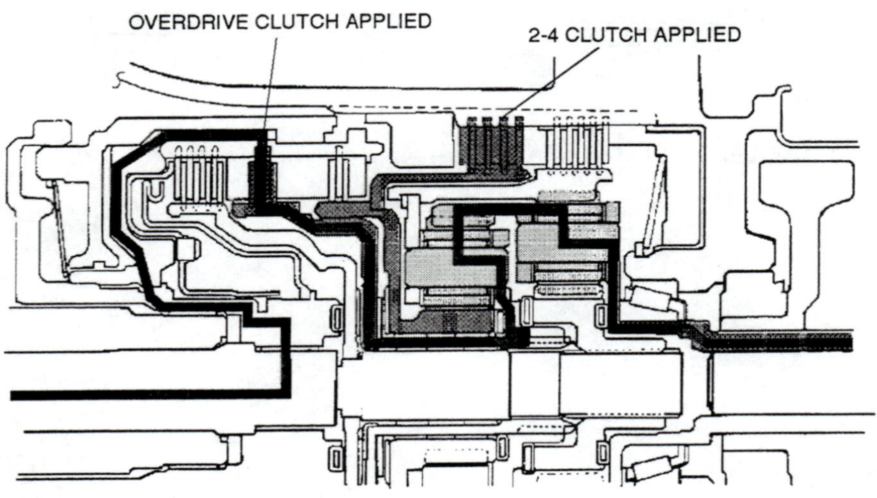

FIGURE 10–69 A-604 in fourth gear. (Courtesy of Chrysler)

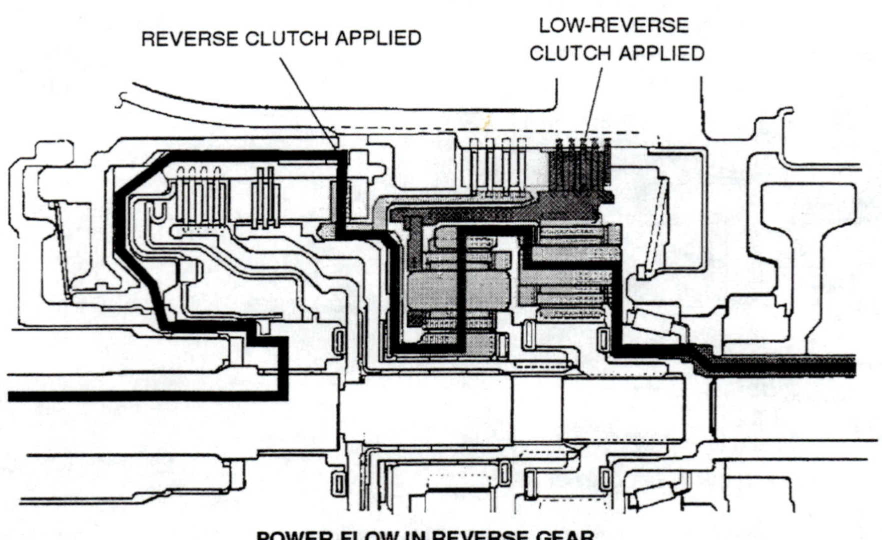

FIGURE 10–70 A-604 in reverse gear. (Courtesy of Chrysler)

10.6.3 Clutch and Band Charts

In this section we provide two clutch and band charts. The first chart, the author's design, uses a standardized format for listing the coupling and holding devices to aid comparison between transmissions. This chart is shown in Figure 10–71. The second chart, the manufacturer's design, which is found in service manuals, is shown in Figure 10–72.

10.6.4 Identification

In Figure 10–73 you see the pan gasket shape and number of bolt holes for the A-604 transaxle. The location of the factory identification tag and its code are shown in Figure 10–74.

10.6.5 Components

In this section exploded drawings of the A-604 transaxle subassemblies are shown, along with lists of the part names. The manufacturer's part names are used to eliminate confusion about component names. The illustrations to study are as follows:

Entire transaxle, Figure 10–75
Valves, Figure 10–76
Valve body, Figure 10–77

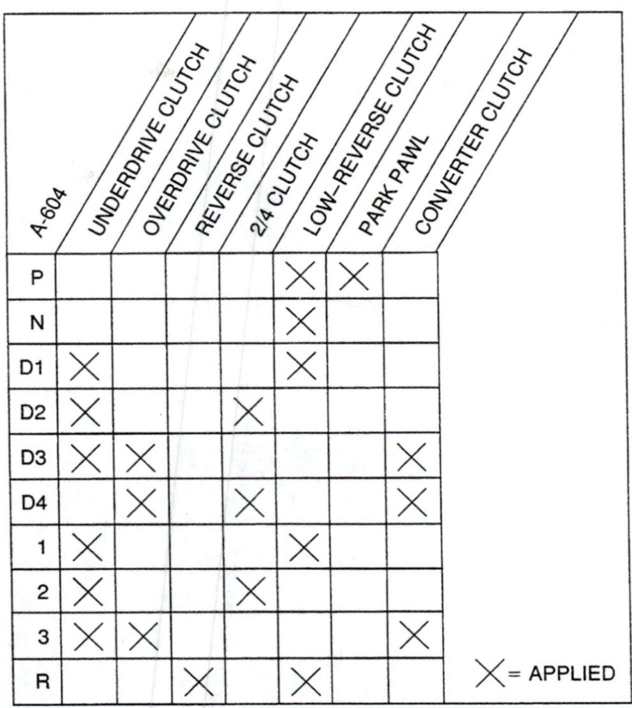

A-604	UNDERDRIVE CLUTCH	OVERDRIVE CLUTCH	REVERSE CLUTCH	2/4 CLUTCH	LOW-REVERSE CLUTCH	PARK PAWL	CONVERTER CLUTCH
P					X	X	
N					X		
D1	X				X		
D2	X			X			
D3	X	X					X
D4		X		X			X
1	X				X		
2	X			X			
3	X	X					X
R			X		X		

X = APPLIED

FIGURE 10–71 A-604 clutch and band chart, standardized version.

ELEMENTS IN USE AT EACH POSITION OF THE SELECTOR LEVER

Shift Lever Position	Start Safety	Park Sprag	CLUTCHES: Underdrive	Overdrive	Reverse	2/4	Low/ Reverse
P — PARK	X	X					X
R — REVERSE					X		X
N — NEUTRAL	X						X
OD — OVERDRIVE First			X				X
Second			X			X	
Direct			X	X			
Overdrive				X		X	
D — DRIVE* First			X				X
Second			X			X	
Direct			X	X			
L — LOW* First			X				X
Second			X			X	
Direct			X	X			

*Vehicle upshift and downshift speeds are increased when in these selector positions.

FIGURE 10–72 A-604 clutch and band chart, factory version. (Courtesy of Chrysler)

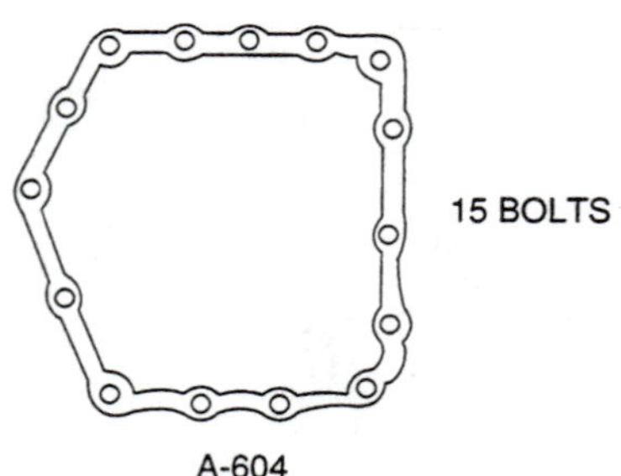

FIGURE 10–73 A-604 pan gasket identification.

Solenoid assembly, Figure 10–78
Oil pump, Figure 10–79
Input clutch assembly, Figure 10–80
Input hubs, Figure 10–81
2–4 clutch, Figure 10–82
Low–reverse clutch, Figure 10–83
Planetary gear set, Figure 10–84

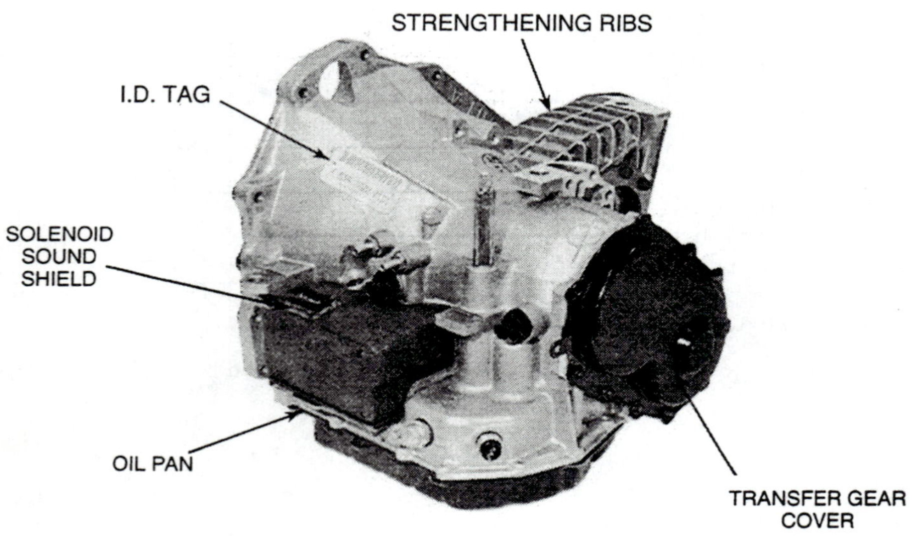

FIGURE 10–74 A-604 identification number location. (Courtesy of Chrysler)

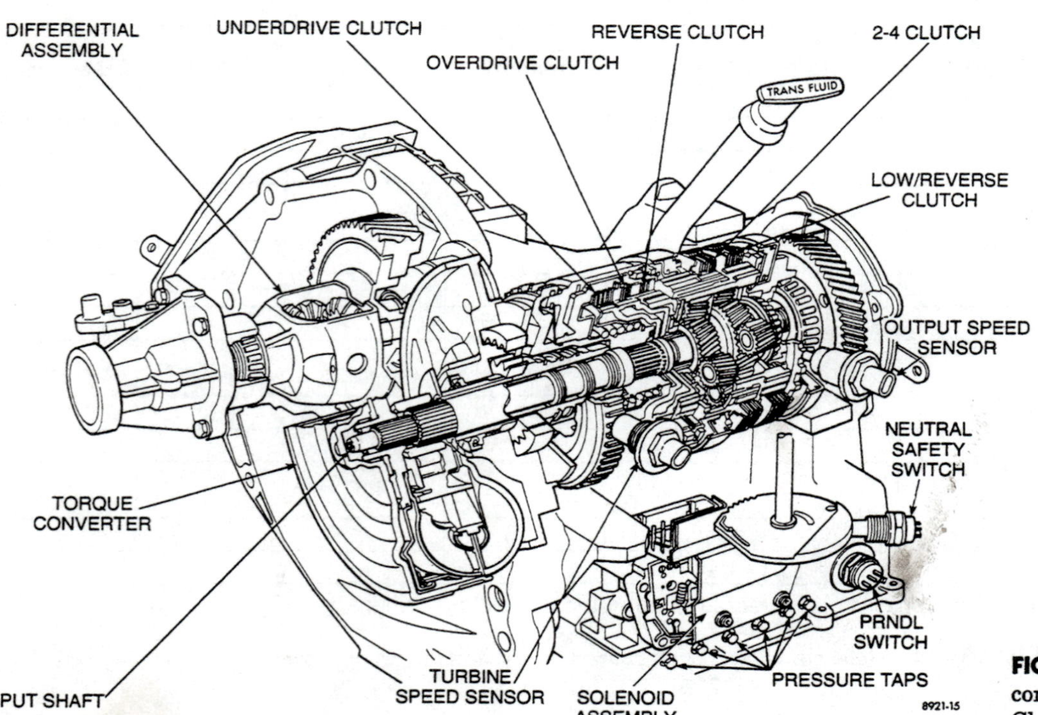

FIGURE 10–75 A-604 components. (Courtesy of Chrysler)

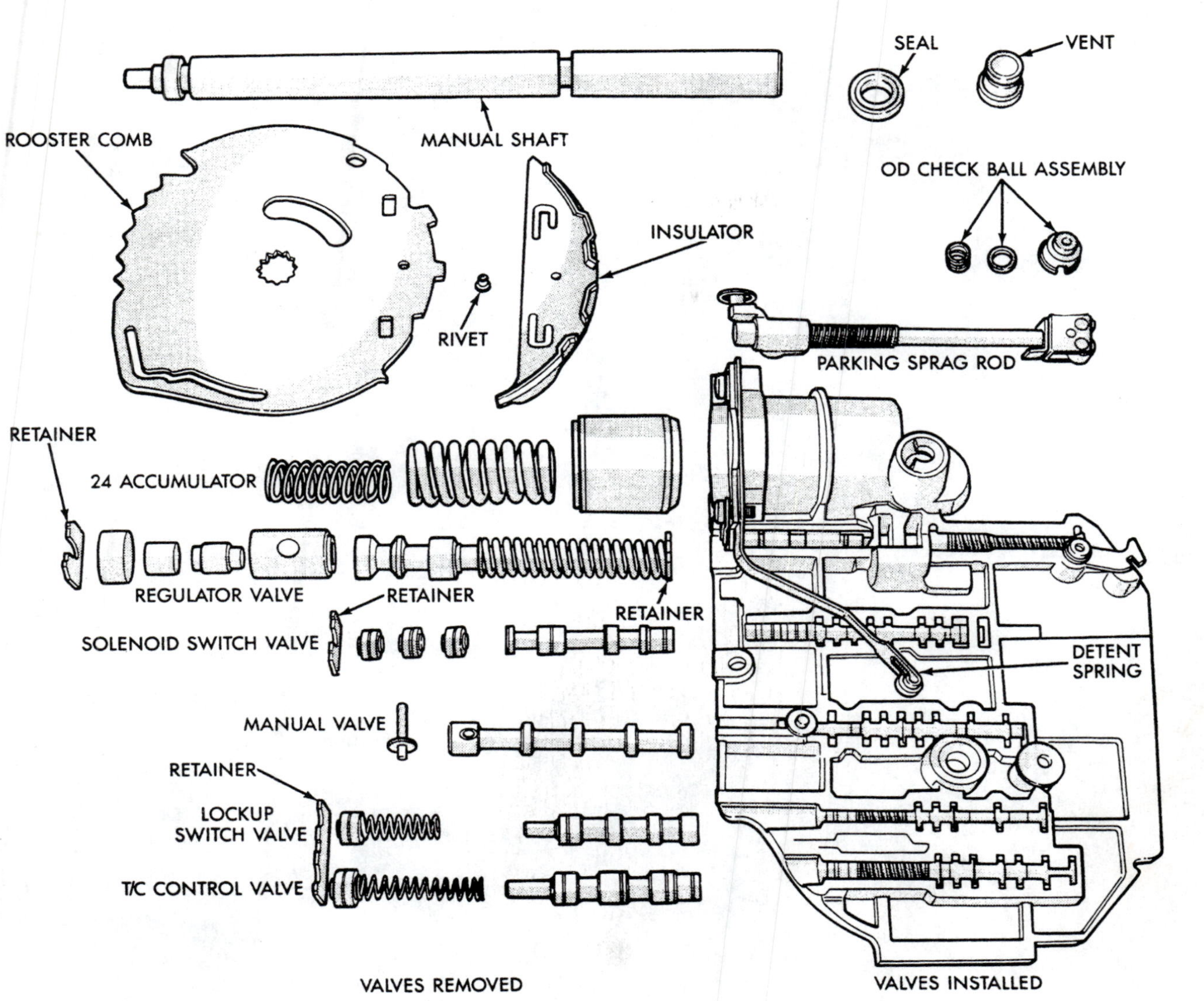

SEAL
VENT
ROOSTER COMB
MANUAL SHAFT
OD CHECK BALL ASSEMBLY
INSULATOR
RIVET
PARKING SPRAG ROD
RETAINER
24 ACCUMULATOR
REGULATOR VALVE
RETAINER
RETAINER
SOLENOID SWITCH VALVE
DETENT SPRING
MANUAL VALVE
RETAINER
LOCKUP SWITCH VALVE
T/C CONTROL VALVE
VALVES REMOVED
VALVES INSTALLED

FIGURE 10–76 A-604 valve body. (Courtesy of Chrysler)

VENT
SEAL
SELECTOR SHAFT
PARKING SPRAG ROD
ACCUMULATOR
FILTER

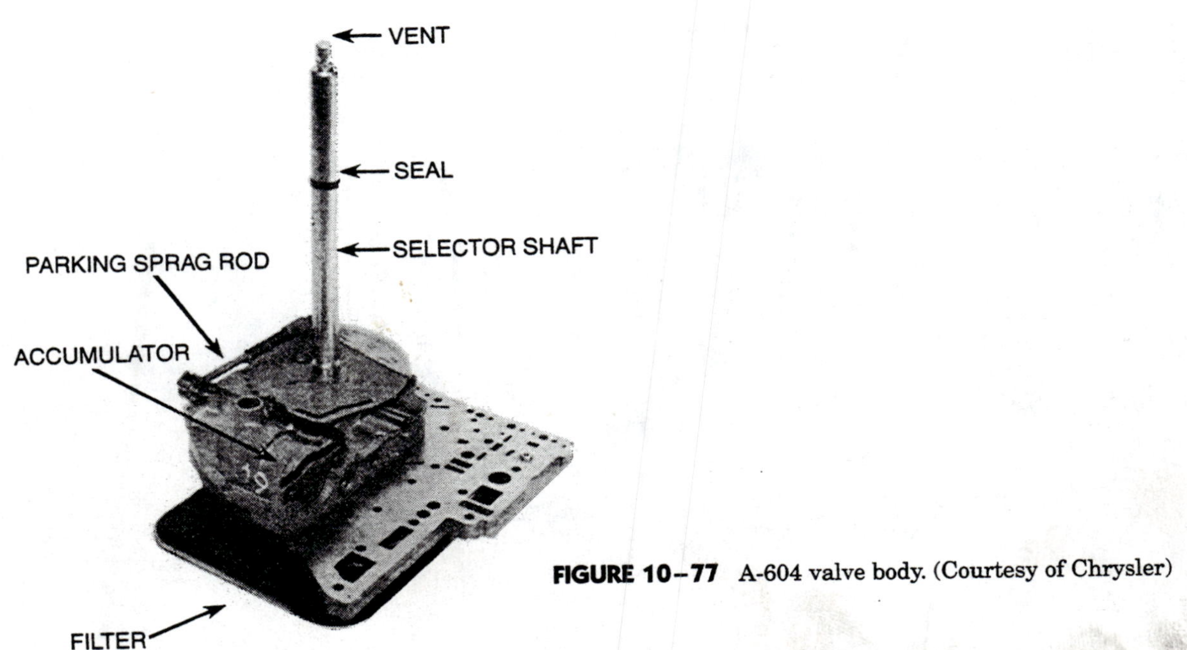

FIGURE 10–77 A-604 valve body. (Courtesy of Chrysler)

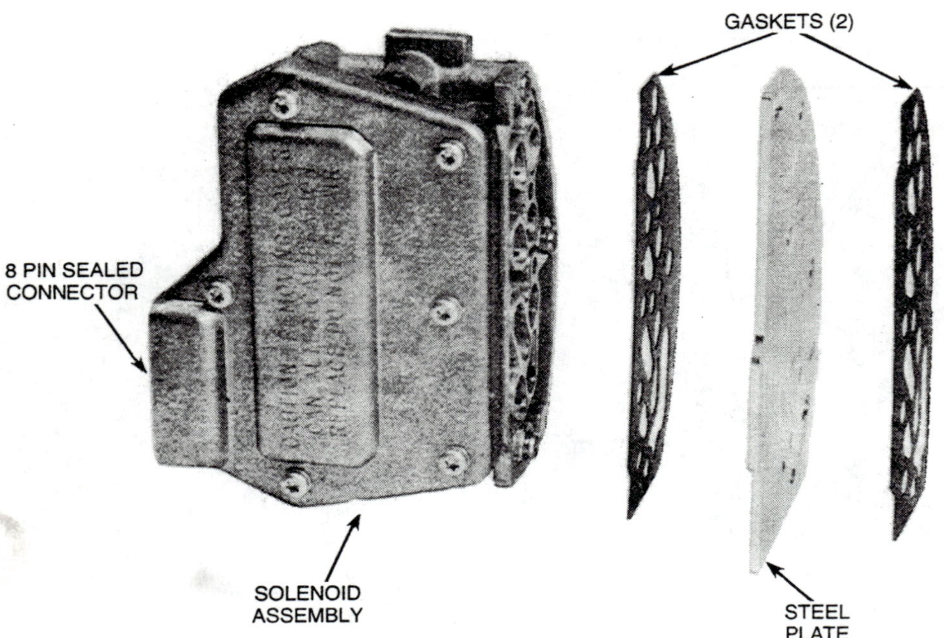

FIGURE 10–78 A-604 solenoid assembly. (Courtesy of Chrysler)

FIGURE 10–79 A-604 oil pump. (Courtesy of Chrysler)

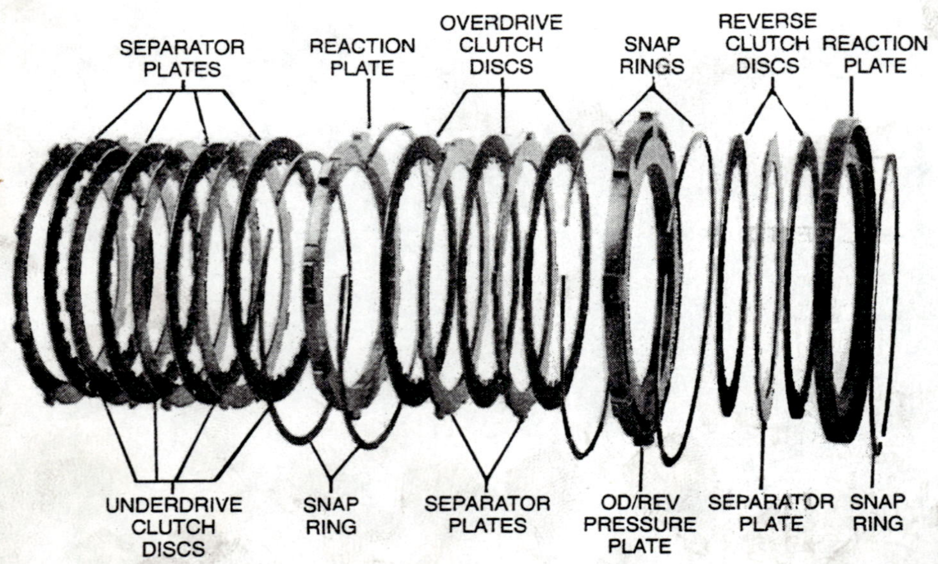

FIGURE 10–80 A-604 input clutches. (Courtesy of Chrysler)

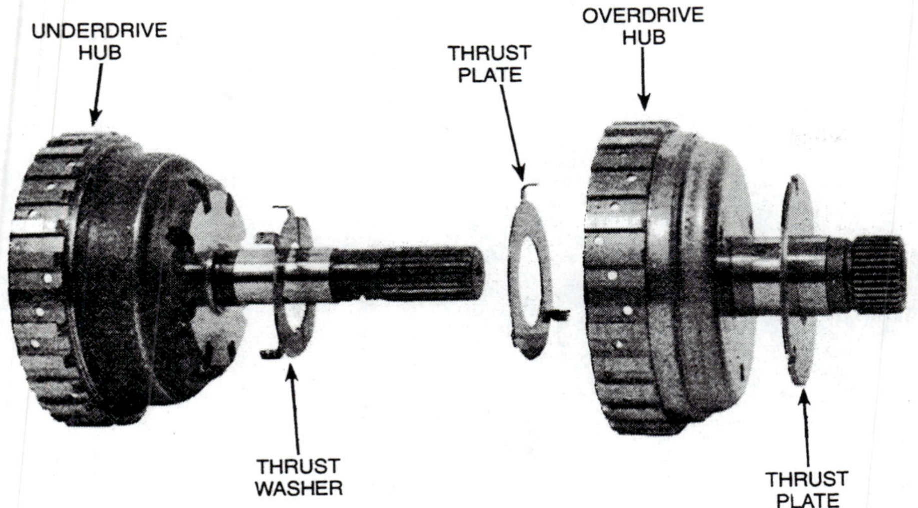

FIGURE 10–81 A-604 input hubs. (Courtesy of Chrysler)

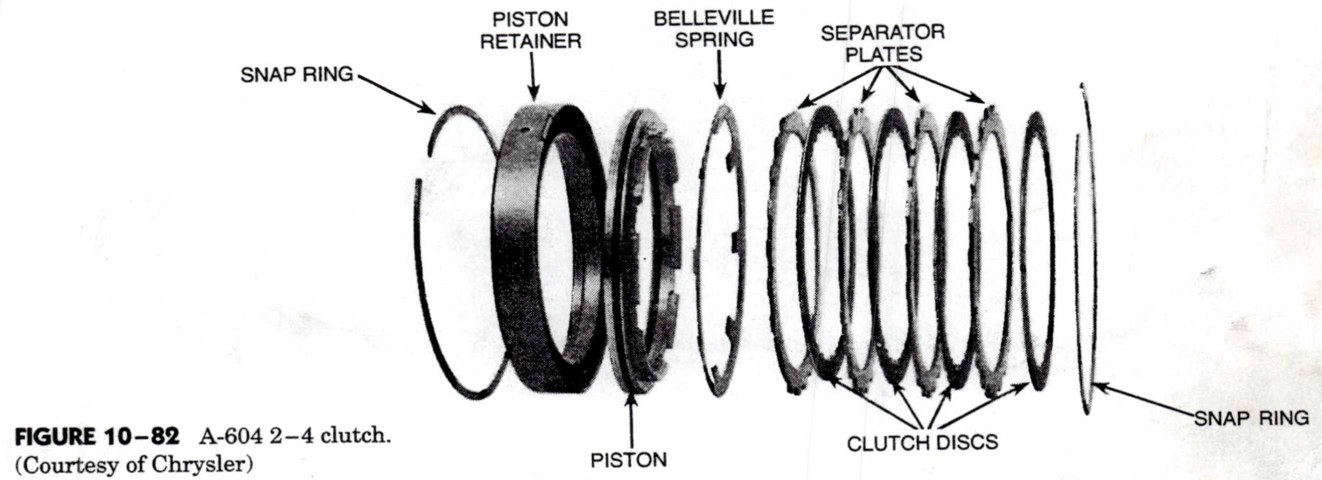

FIGURE 10–82 A-604 2–4 clutch. (Courtesy of Chrysler)

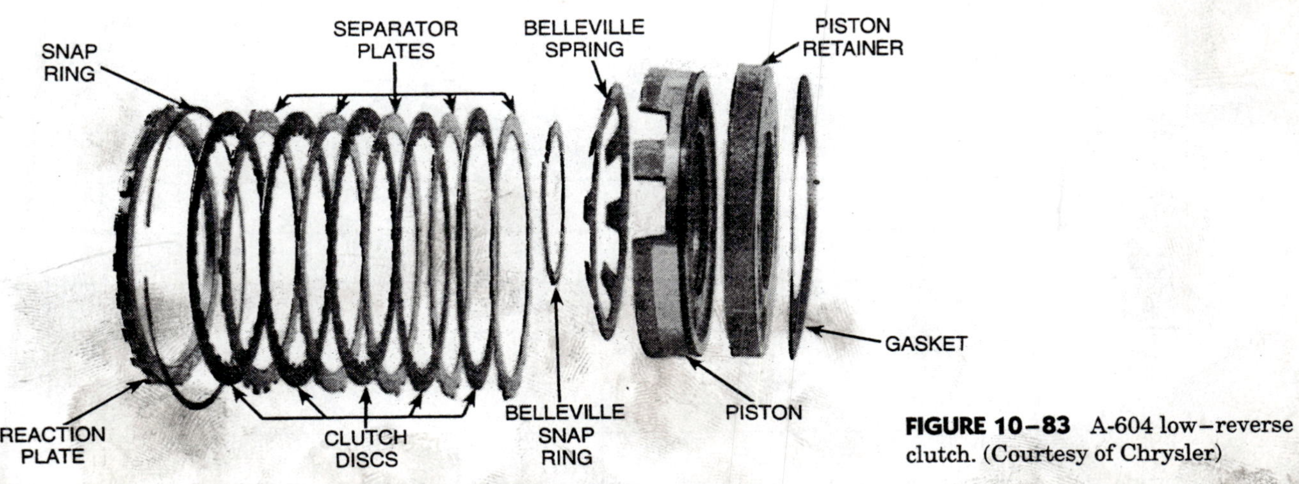

FIGURE 10–83 A-604 low–reverse clutch. (Courtesy of Chrysler)

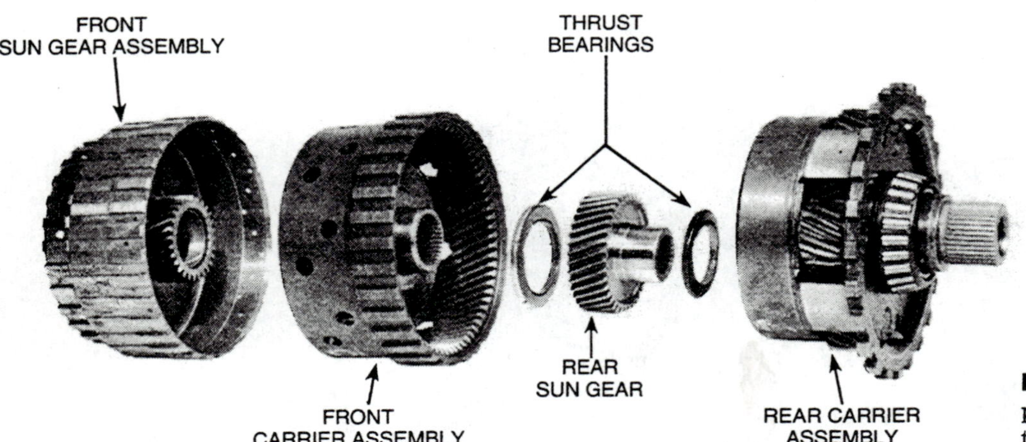

FIGURE 10–84 A-604 planetary gear set. (Courtesy of Chrysler)

10.6.6 Pressure Test

One of the key tests in diagnosis is the hydraulic system pressure test. The location of the test points of the A-604 transaxle is shown in Figure 10–85. A pressure chart listing the pressure specification of this transaxle is shown in Figure 10–86.

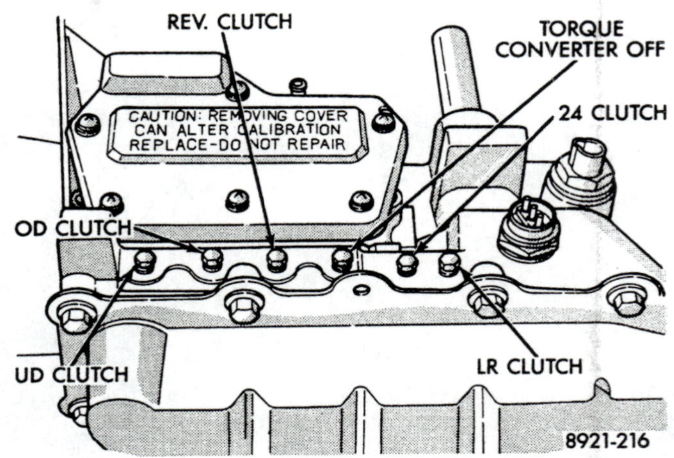

FIGURE 10–85 A-604 pressure test points. (Courtesy of Chrysler)

FIGURE 10–86 A-604 pressure test chart. (Courtesy of Chrysler)

(on hoist, with front wheels free to turn)
PRESSURE TAP ORDER ON CASE FROM BELLHOUSING TO END COVER
ALL PRESSURE SPECIFICATIONS ARE PSI

Gear Selector Position	Actual Gear	PRESSURE TAPS					
		Under-Drive Clutch	Over-Drive Clutch	Reverse Clutch	Lockup Off	2/4 Clutch	Low/ Reverse Clutch
PARK * 0 mph	PARK	0-2	0-5	0-2	60-110	0-2	115-145
REVERSE * 0 mph	REVERSE	0-2	0-7	165-235	50-100	0-2	165-235
NEUTRAL * 0 mph	NEUTRAL	0-2	0-5	0-2	60-110	0-2	115-145
L # 20 mph	FIRST	110-145	0-5	0-2	60-110	0-2	115-145
D # 30 mph	SECOND	110-145	0-5	0-2	60-110	115-145	0-2
D # 45 mph	DIRECT	75-95	75-95	0-2	60-90	0-2	0-2
OD # 30 mph	OVERDRIVE	0-2	75-95	0-2	60-90	75-95	0-2
OD # 50 mph	OVERDRIVE LOCKUP	0-2	75-95	0-2	0-5	75-95	0-2

***Engine speed at 1500 rpm**
#CAUTION: Both front wheels must be turning at same speed.

10.6.7 Air Test

Air testing is used during preliminary diagnosis of certain malfunctions and during the disassembly process to verify component operation or failure. The technician must know which hydraulic circuit is being served by each passageway to be able to air test a transmission accurately. This information is presented in the following drawings:

Air test plate, Figure 10–87

Air testing, Figure 10–88

The overdrive, reverse, and underdrive clutches are tested through the test plate. To test the 2–4 clutch, apply air to the feed hole in the clutch retainer and watch for the piston to be applied and released. For the low–reverse clutch, apply air to the feed hole at the rear of the case between two bolt holes, watching for application and release of the clutch.

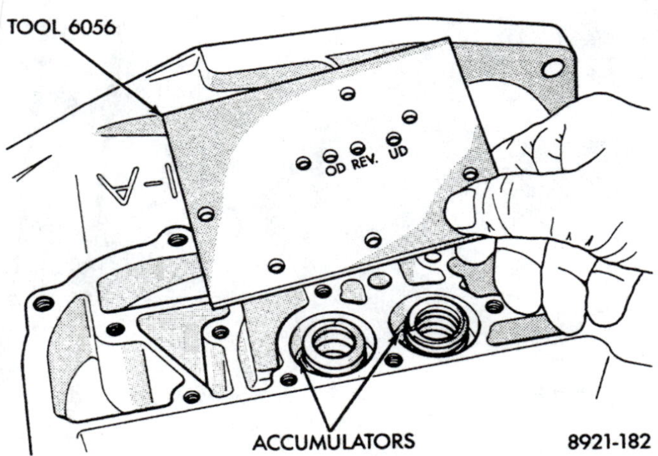

FIGURE 10–87 A-604 air test plate. (Courtesy of Chrysler)

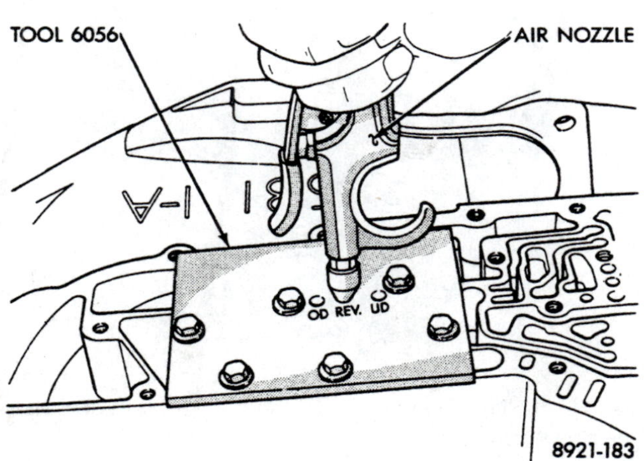

FIGURE 10–88 A-604 air testing. (Courtesy of Chrysler)

10.6.8 Special Attention

In this section we show and explain various points of special interest about the A-604 transaxle. The information presented about each item is included with each illustration.

A604–1 The gearlike teeth around the front of the input clutch assembly are for the turbine speed sensor.

A604–2 The overdrive–reverse piston (right) mounts between the clutch retainer and the input hub (speed sensor teeth). The piston moves in two directions to apply two different clutch packs.

A604–3 The underdrive piston not shown rides inside the clutch retainer.

A604–4 The three clutch packs are visible: first, the reverse clutch; second, the overdrive clutch; and third, the underdrive clutch.

A604–5 The driven hubs that ride inside the clutch packs are shown at the left.

A604–6 From right to left: the underdrive hub, the overdrive hub, and the front sun gear.

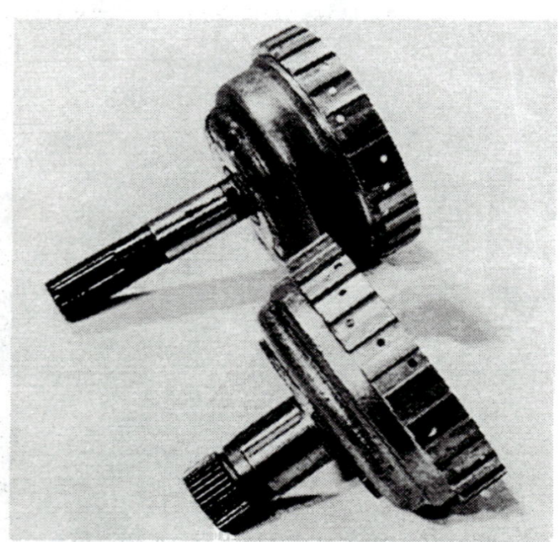

A604–7 Both driven hubs must be inspected for wear and damage.

A604–8 The front sun gear and hub splines should also be checked.

A604–9 The front carrier assembly and rear carrier assembly are shown here.

A604–10 The grooves on the outside of the front carrier hold the low–reverse clutch discs.

A604–11 The underdrive clutch hub is splined to the rear sun gear as input for gear reduction.

A604–12 A 3-lb coffee can with a hole in the bottom makes an excellent work stand.

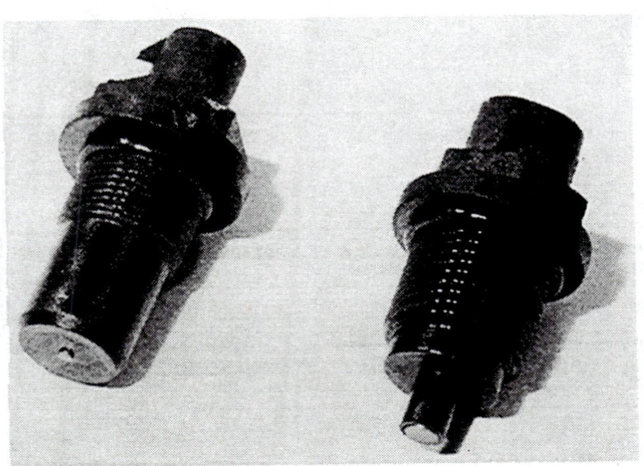

A604–13 The two speed sensors are shown here, turbine speed in the left and output speed in the right. Note the different threads to prevent improper installation.

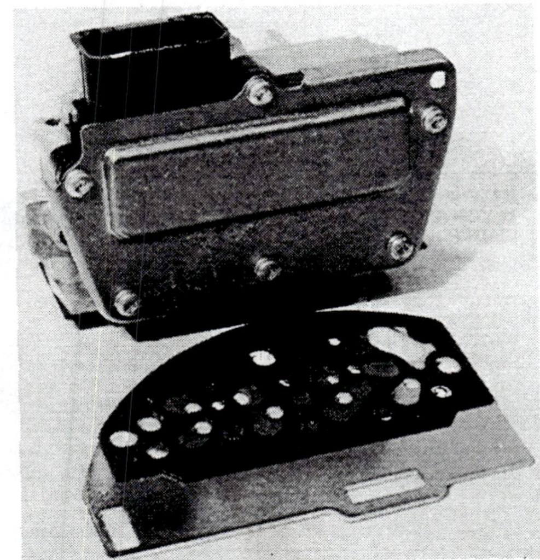

A604–14 Four solenoids and three pressure switches are contained in the solenoid assembly. The assembly must be replaced as a unit.

A604–15 The wiring connector for the solenoid assembly should be checked for broken or bent pins.

A604–16 The four accumulators are the same size but use two different springs.

A604–17 The detent has an extra notch to hold the park rod in place during removal.

A604–18 The filter is held in place by the O-ring seal.

FIGURE 10–89 Chrysler summary comparison chart.

CHRYSLER	TORQUE CONVERTER	GEAR TRAIN	COUPLING DEVICES	HOLDING DEVICES	PUMP	SHIFT CONTROL	GOVERNOR	THROTTLE VALVE
A-904	3-ELEMENT W/ CONVERTER CLUTCH	SIMPSON GEAR SET	FRONT CLUTCH REAR CLUTCH	KICKDOWN BAND ONE-WAY CLUTCH LO-REV BAND	GEROTOR	HYDRAULIC	SHAFT MOUNTED	ROD LINKAGE
A-500	3-ELEMENT W/ CONVERTER CLUTCH	SIMPSON & SIMPLE PLANETARY GEAR SET	FRONT CLUTCH REAR CLUTCH OVERDRIVE ONE-WAY CLUTCH DIRECT CLUTCH	KICKDOWN BAND ONE-WAY CLUTCH LO-REV BAND OVERDRIVE CLUTCH	GEROTOR	HYDRAULIC & ELECTRONIC	SHAFT MOUNTED	ROD LINKAGE
A-404	3-ELEMENT	SIMPSON GEAR SET	FRONT CLUTCH REAR CLUTCH	KICKDOWN BAND ONE-WAY CLUTCH LO-REV BAND	GEAR/CRESENT	HYDRAULIC	SHAFT MOUNTED	CABLE
A-604	3-ELEMENT W/CONVERTER CLUTCH	INTER-CONNECTED PLANETARY GEAR SET	UNDERDRIVE CLUTCH OVERDRIVE CLUTCH REVERSE CLUTCH	2/4 CLUTCH LOW-REV CLUTCH	GEAR/CRESENT	FULLY ELECTRONIC	NONE	NONE

SUMMARY

In this chapter, four Chrysler transmission/transaxles have been profiled. The electronic transaxle, A-604, is the most advanced automatic transaxle available. The performance of this transaxle is superior in every way, but they are also more complex and require a full understanding of computer functions as well as automatic transaxle knowledge. See Figure 10–89 for a quick comparison of all the transmissions/transaxles.

SELF-TEST

Before going on to the next chapter, complete the self-test according to your instructor's directions. Read carefully and choose the best answer.

1. Which of the following was the first transmission to use a Simpson gear set?
   a. A-404
   b. A-904
   c. Both a and b
   d. Neither a nor b
2. Which of the following is an overdrive version of an A-904 transmission?
   a. A-500
   b. A-404
   c. Both a and b
   d. Neither a nor b
3. Which of the following is not a transaxle?
   a. A-604
   b. A-404
   c. A-500
   d. None of the above
4. Which of the following is a three-speed transaxle?
   a. A-904
   b. A-404
   c. A-604
   d. None of the above
5. Which of the following has no one-way clutches?
   a. A-904
   b. A-404
   c. A-604
   d. A-500
6. Which of the following is electronically controlled?
   a. A-904
   b. A-404
   c. A-500
   d. A-604
7. Which transmission uses a large spring to apply its direct clutch?
   a. A-500
   b. A-904
   c. A-404
   d. A-604
8. Which of the following uses a gerotor pump?
   a. A-500
   b. A-404
   c. A-604
   d. None of the above
9. Which of the following is from a Chrysler import vehicle?
   a. A-604
   b. A-904
   c. A-500
   d. None of the above
10. Which of the following is the fully adaptive transaxle?
    a. A-404
    b. A-500
    c. A-904
    d. A-604

◀ Chapter 11 ▶

FORD MOTOR COMPANY

11.1 PERFORMANCE OBJECTIVES

After studying this chapter, you should have fulfilled the following performance objectives by being able to:

1. List the Ford transmissions/transaxles described in the chapter.
2. Describe the basic components of each transmission/transaxle.
3. Describe the power flow in each gear position, including which coupling and holding devices are applied, for each transmission/transaxle.
4. Write a clutch and band chart for each transmission/transaxle listed in the chapter.
5. Complete the self-test with at least the minimum score required by your instructor.

11.2 OVERVIEW

This chapter profiles four transmissions/transaxles produced by Ford Motor Company. The E4OD is a newer transmission, which is described as a C-6 overdrive with electronic shift control. The A4LD overdrive is a lighter-duty transmission than the AOD and is basically a C-3 with an overdrive gear set added. The ATX is Ford's first front-wheel-drive transaxle, while the AXOD is an automatic overdrive transaxle with the AXOD-E having electronic shift control. This selection of transmissions/transaxles provides a representative sample of Ford Motor Company's automatic transmissions. A comparison of generic names with Ford names is shown in Figure 11–1.

Ford uses a wide range of transmission fluids for its transmissions. The following chart lists the ATF recommendations for each transmission/transaxle.

C-3: Type F

C-6 (1976 and older): Type F

C-6 (1977 and newer): Type CJ

AOD: Type CJ

AOD-E: Mercon

A4LD: Type CJ

E4OD: Mercon

ATX (average climates): Type CJ

ATX (cold climates): Type MV

AXOD: CJ

AXOD-E: Mercon

4EAT: Mercon

Dexron II may be substituted for Type CJ or Mercon.

GENERIC NAME	=	FORD'S NAME
FRONT CLUTCH	=	REVERSE AND HIGH CLUTCH
REAR CLUTCH	=	FORWARD CLUTCH
FRONT RING GEAR	=	FORWARD RING GEAR
FRONT PINION CARRIER	=	FORWARD PINION CARRIER
REAR RING GEAR	=	LOW AND REVERSE RING GEAR
REAR PINION CARRIER	=	LOW AND REVERSE PINION CARRIER
FRONT BAND	=	INTERMEDIATE BAND
REAR BAND	=	LOW AND REVERSE BAND
ROLLER CLUTCH	=	ONE-WAY CLUTCH
MAIN LINE PRESSURE	=	CONTROL PRESSURE
THROTTLE PRESSURE	=	THROTTLE PRESSURE (T.V.)
CLUTCH DRUM	=	CLUTCH CYLINDER
VACUUM MODULATOR	=	VACUUM DIAPHRAGM

FIGURE 11–1 Generic names and Ford names. (Courtesy of Ford)

In profiling each transmission/transaxle the same format for presenting the information is used to facilitate understanding of the information given. The first section covers the following eight areas:

1. Torque converter
2. Gear train
3. Coupling devices
4. Holding devices
5. Pump
6. Shift control
7. Governor
8. Throttle valve

The power flow unit traces the power flow in each gear, while the clutch and band chart unit shows two types of charts.

11.3 A4LD: RWD FOUR-SPEED TRANSMISSION

11.3.1 Basic Description

The A4LD automatic overdrive transmission is based on the C-3 transmission. An overdrive planetary gear set is placed in front of the three-speed Simpson gear set in an elongated case. The A4LD is designed for medium-duty use with V6 power plants, see Figure 11–2.

The transmission description is divided into eight areas. All the transmissions are described in this manner to make their comparison easier.

1. Torque Converter
The A4LD uses a conventional three-element torque converter with a hydraulic converter clutch. The converter clutch is computer controlled through the override solenoid (Figure 11–3).

2. Gear Train
The A4LD overdrive unit uses the pinion carrier as the input member, the sun gear as reaction or input member, and the ring gear as the output member. A one-way clutch is used to couple the pinion carrier to the ring gear during direct drive. The overdrive clutch connects the pinion carrier and the sun gear for total lockup in direct drive (Figure 11–4). The three-speed portion of the gear train is a Simpson gear set similar to the C-3 transmission.

3. Coupling Devices
The overdrive unit coupling devices are the overdrive clutch and the overdrive one-way clutch. The other coupling devices are the same as those used in the C-3 transmission.

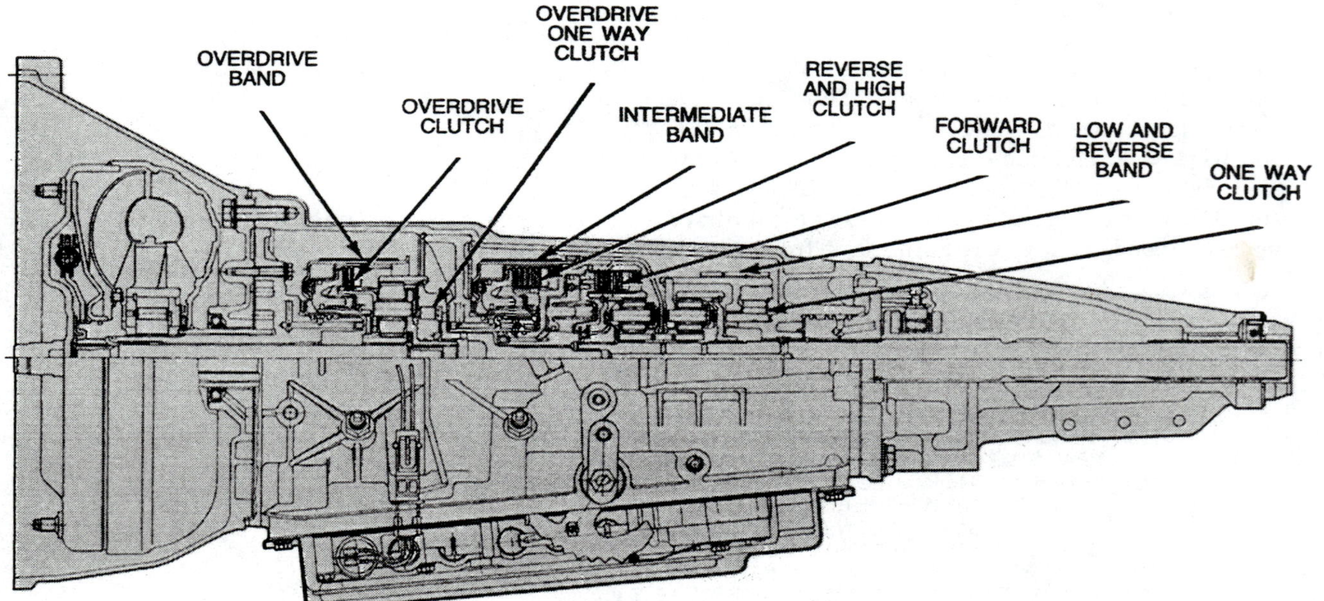

FIGURE 11–2 A4LD cutaway view. (Courtesy of Ford)

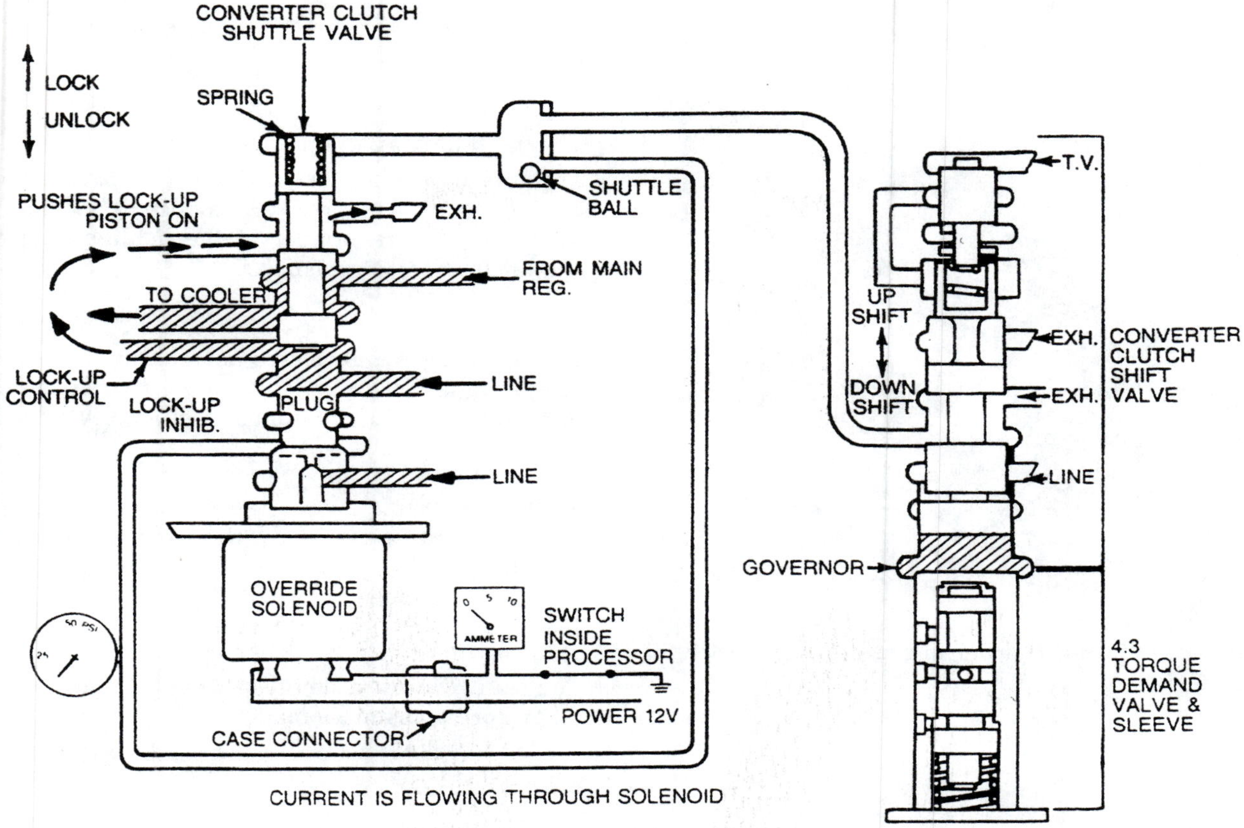

CONVERTER CLUTCH
SHUTTLE VALVE
LOCK
UNLOCK
SPRING
PUSHES LOCK-UP
PISTON ON
EXH.
SHUTTLE
BALL
T.V.
FROM MAIN
REG.
TO COOLER
LOCK-UP
CONTROL
LOCK-UP
INHIB.
PLUG
LINE
LINE
UP
SHIFT
DOWN
SHIFT
EXH.
EXH.
CONVERTER
CLUTCH
SHIFT
VALVE
LINE
GOVERNOR
OVERRIDE
SOLENOID
AMMETER
SWITCH
INSIDE
PROCESSOR
POWER 12V
CASE CONNECTOR
4.3
TORQUE
DEMAND
VALVE &
SLEEVE
CURRENT IS FLOWING THROUGH SOLENOID

FIGURE 11–3 A4LD converter clutch controls. (Courtesy of Ford)

TORQUE CONVERTER
TURBINE
IMPELLER
REACTOR
OVERDRIVE
CLUTCH
OVERDRIVE
ONE-WAY CLUTCH
FORWARD CLUTCH
REVERSE AND
HIGH CLUTCH
GOVERNOR
PARKING
GEAR
ONE-WAY
CLUTCH
VALVE BODY
LOW AND REVERSE BAND
INTERMEDIATE BAND
OIL PUMP
OVERDRIVE
BAND
INPUT
SHAFT
(HIDDEN
FROM VIEW)
PISTON PLATE CLUTCH
AND DAMPER ASSEMBLY
CONVERTER COVER

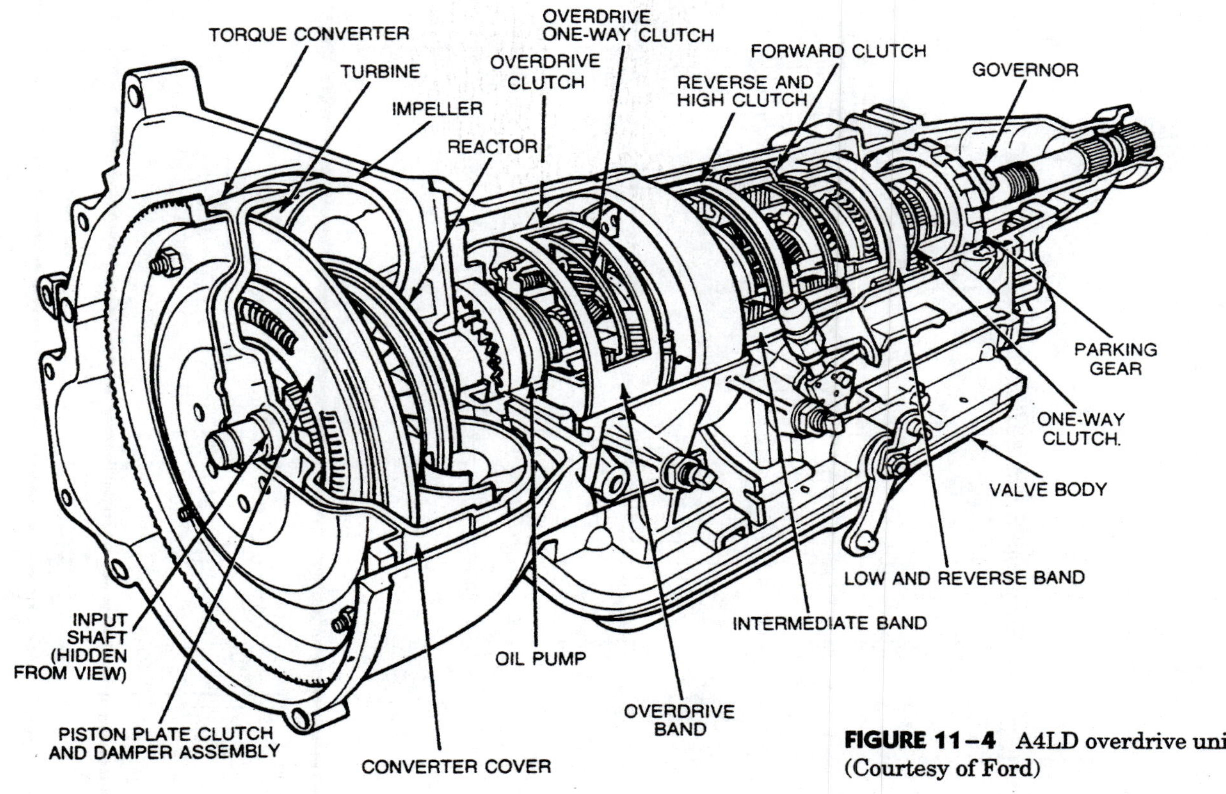

FIGURE 11–4 A4LD overdrive unit. (Courtesy of Ford)

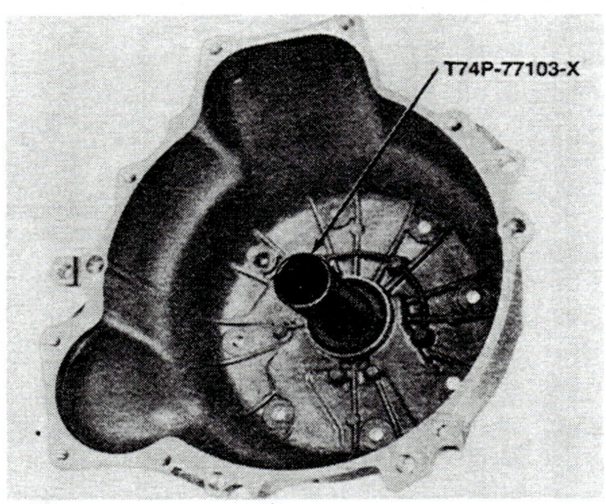

FIGURE 11–5 A4LD pump alignment tool. (Courtesy of Ford)

4. Holding Devices
The overdrive unit uses an overdrive band to hold the overdrive sun gear to produce the overdrive condition. The remainder of the holding device is similar to the C-3 transmission.

5. Pump
The A4LD uses a gear crescent design oil pump. If the pump is disassembled, it must be reassembled using a front pump alignment tool to prevent pump breakage (Figure 11–5).

6. Shift Control
The shift control system for the A4LD combines hydraulic and electronic controls to provide the best possible operation (Figure 11–6).

7. Governor
The A4LD uses a shaft-mounted governor, like other Ford transmissions.

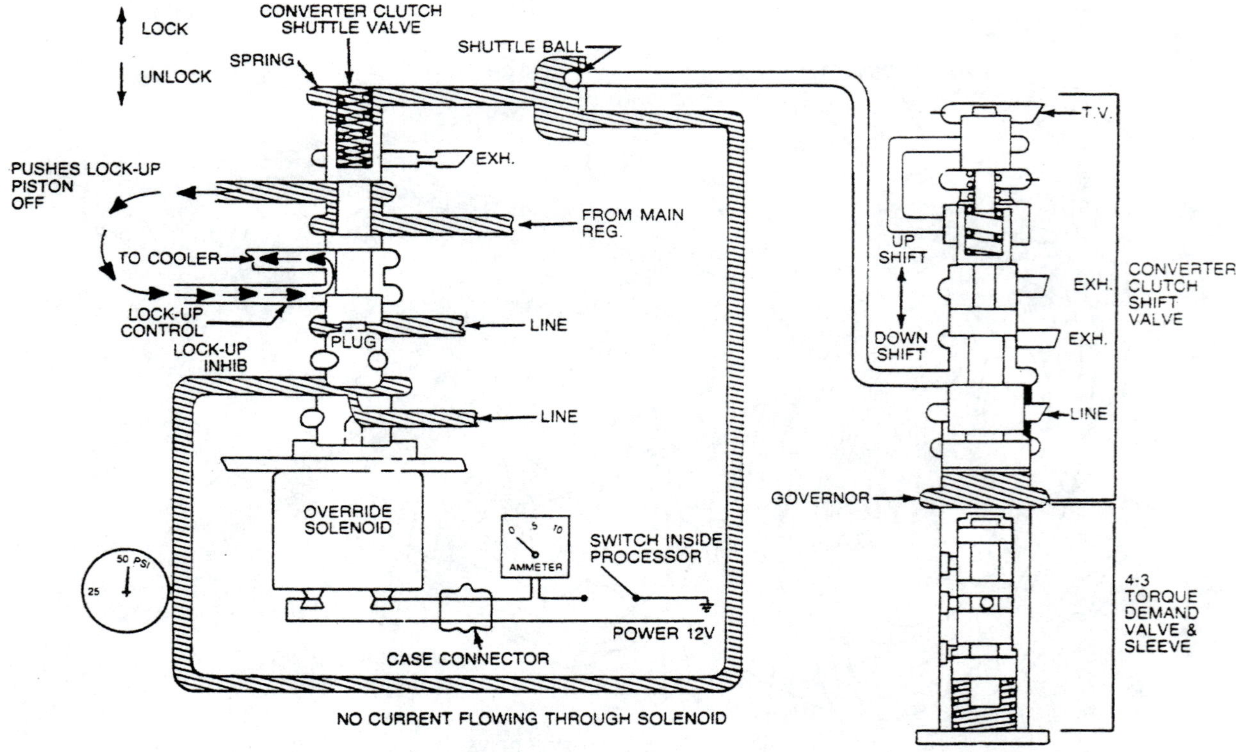

FIGURE 11–6 A4LD control solenoids. (Courtesy of Ford)

8. Throttle Valve
The throttle valve is operated by a vacuum modulator valve assembly which moves the throttle valve as engine intake manifold vacuum changes.

11.3.2 Power Flow

Since the power flow in the three-speed portion of the A4LD is the same as that of the C-3, that description will not be repeated. The operation of the overdrive unit is described for direct drive, used during first, second, third, and reverse gears, and for overdrive, which provides a fourth gear.

1. Direct Drive
The input pinion carrier drives the output ring gear through the overdrive one-way clutch under normal operating conditions. When engine braking is needed and the gear selector is placed in a lower range, the overdrive clutch is applied, which connects the pinion carrier to the sun gear to provide a total lockup of the planetary gear set.

2. Overdrive
In overdrive the overdrive band is applied, which holds the sun gear stationary, causing the planetary gear set to operate in overdrive mode. The rest of the three-speed gear train remains in direct drive. The overdrive ratio is 0.75:1.

11.3.3 Clutch and Band Charts

The first chart, the author's design, is shown in Figure 11–7. The second chart, the manufacturer's design, is shown in Figure 11–8.

11.3.4 Identification

The shape of the transmission oil pan or its gasket is a quick means of identifying an automatic transmission. In Figure 11–9 you see the pan gasket shape and number of bolt holes for the A4LD transmission. The location of the factory identification tag and its code are shown in Figure 11–10.

11.3.5 Components

In this section exploded drawings of the A4LD transmission subassemblies are shown along with lists of the part names. The manufacturers' part names are used to eliminate confusion about component names. The illustrations to study are as follows:

A4LD	OVERDRIVE CLUTCH	REVERSE AND HIGH CLUTCH	FORWARD CLUTCH	OVERDRIVE BAND	INTERMEDIATE BAND	LOW AND REVERSE BAND	OVERDRIVE ONE-WAY CLUTCH	LOW ONE-WAY CLUTCH	PARK PAWL	CONVERTER CLUTCH
P									X	
N										
D1			X				X	X		
D2			X		X		X			
D3		X	X				X			X
D4		X	X	X						X
1	X		X			X	(X)	(X)		
2	X		X				(X)			
3	X	X	X				(X)			X
R	X	X				X	(X)			

X = APPLIED
(X) [dotted X] = APPLIED, NOT CARRYING LOAD

FIGURE 11–7 A4LD clutch and band chart, author's version.

GEAR	OVER-DRIVE BAND A	OVER-DRIVE CLUTCH B	OVER-DRIVE ONE WAY CLUTCH C	INTERMEDIATE BAND D	REVERSE AND HIGH CLUTCH E	FORWARD CLUTCH F	LOW AND REVERSE BAND G	ONE WAY CLUTCH H	GEAR RATIO
1 — MANUAL FIRST GEAR (LOW)		APPLIED	HOLDING			APPLIED	APPLIED	HOLDING	2.47:1
2 — MANUAL SECOND GEAR		APPLIED	HOLDING	APPLIED		APPLIED			1.47:1
D — DRIVE AUTO. — 1ST. GEAR		APPLIED	HOLDING			APPLIED		HOLDING	2.47:1
Ⓓ— O/D AUTO. — 1ST. GEAR			HOLDING			APPLIED		HOLDING	2.47:1
D — DRIVE AUTO. — 2ND. GEAR		APPLIED	HOLDING	APPLIED		APPLIED			1.47:1
Ⓓ— O/D AUTO. — 2ND. GEAR			HOLDING	APPLIED		APPLIED			1.47:1
D — DRIVE AUTO. — 3RD. GEAR		APPLIED	HOLDING		APPLIED	APPLIED			1.0:1
Ⓓ— O/D AUTO. — 3RD. GEAR			HOLDING		APPLIED	APPLIED			1.0:1
Ⓓ— OVERDRIVE AUTOMATIC FOURTH GEAR	APPLIED				APPLIED	APPLIED			0.75:1
REVERSE		APPLIED	HOLDING		APPLIED		APPLIED		2.1:1

FIGURE 11–8 A4LD clutch and band chart, factory version. (Courtesy of Ford)

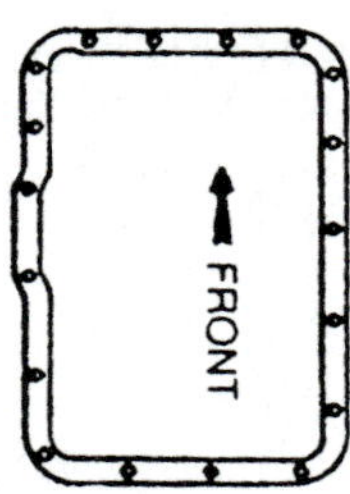

FIGURE 11–9 A4LD pan gasket identification.

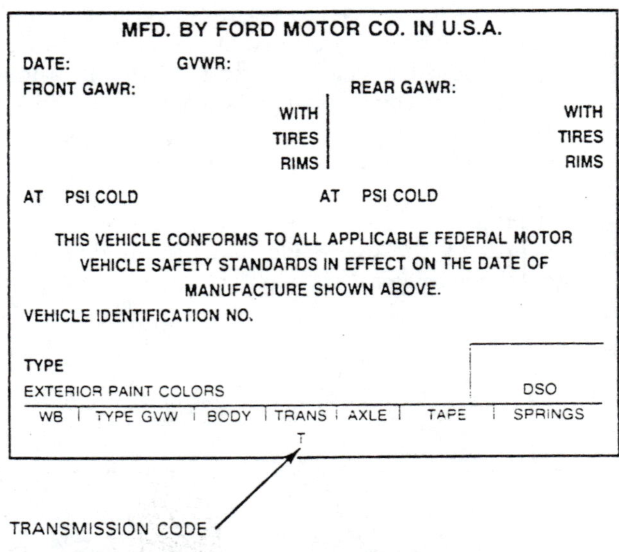

FIGURE 11–10 A4LD identification tags. (Courtesy of Ford)

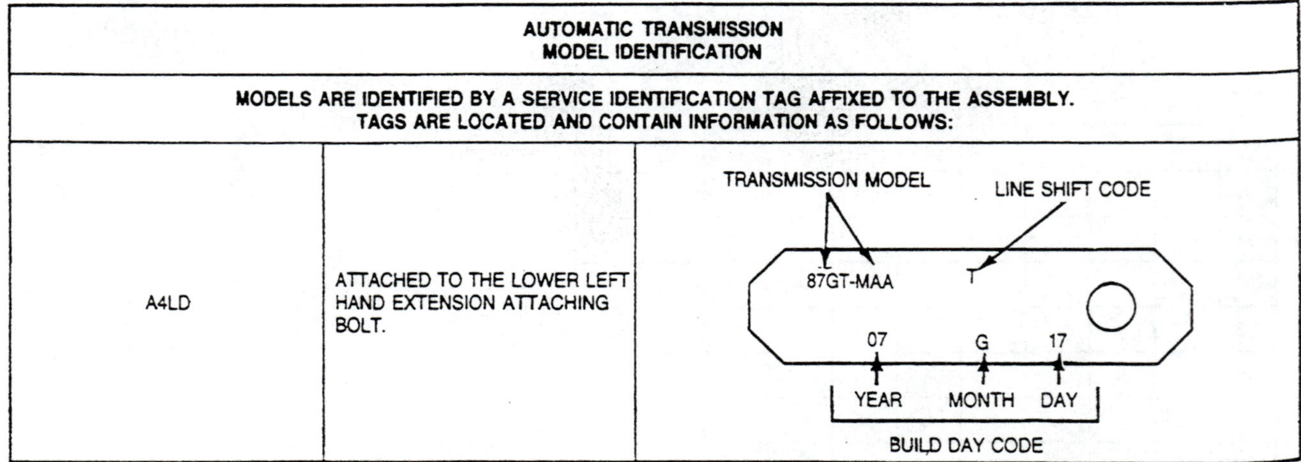

AUTOMATIC TRANSMISSION MODEL IDENTIFICATION

MODELS ARE IDENTIFIED BY A SERVICE IDENTIFICATION TAG AFFIXED TO THE ASSEMBLY. TAGS ARE LOCATED AND CONTAIN INFORMATION AS FOLLOWS:

A4LD	ATTACHED TO THE LOWER LEFT HAND EXTENSION ATTACHING BOLT.	TRANSMISSION MODEL / LINE SHIFT CODE / 87GT-MAA T / 07 G 17 / YEAR MONTH DAY / BUILD DAY CODE

Entire transmission, Figure 11–11

Thrust washer location, Figure 11–12

Electrical solenoids, Figure 11–13

Valve body, Figure 11–14

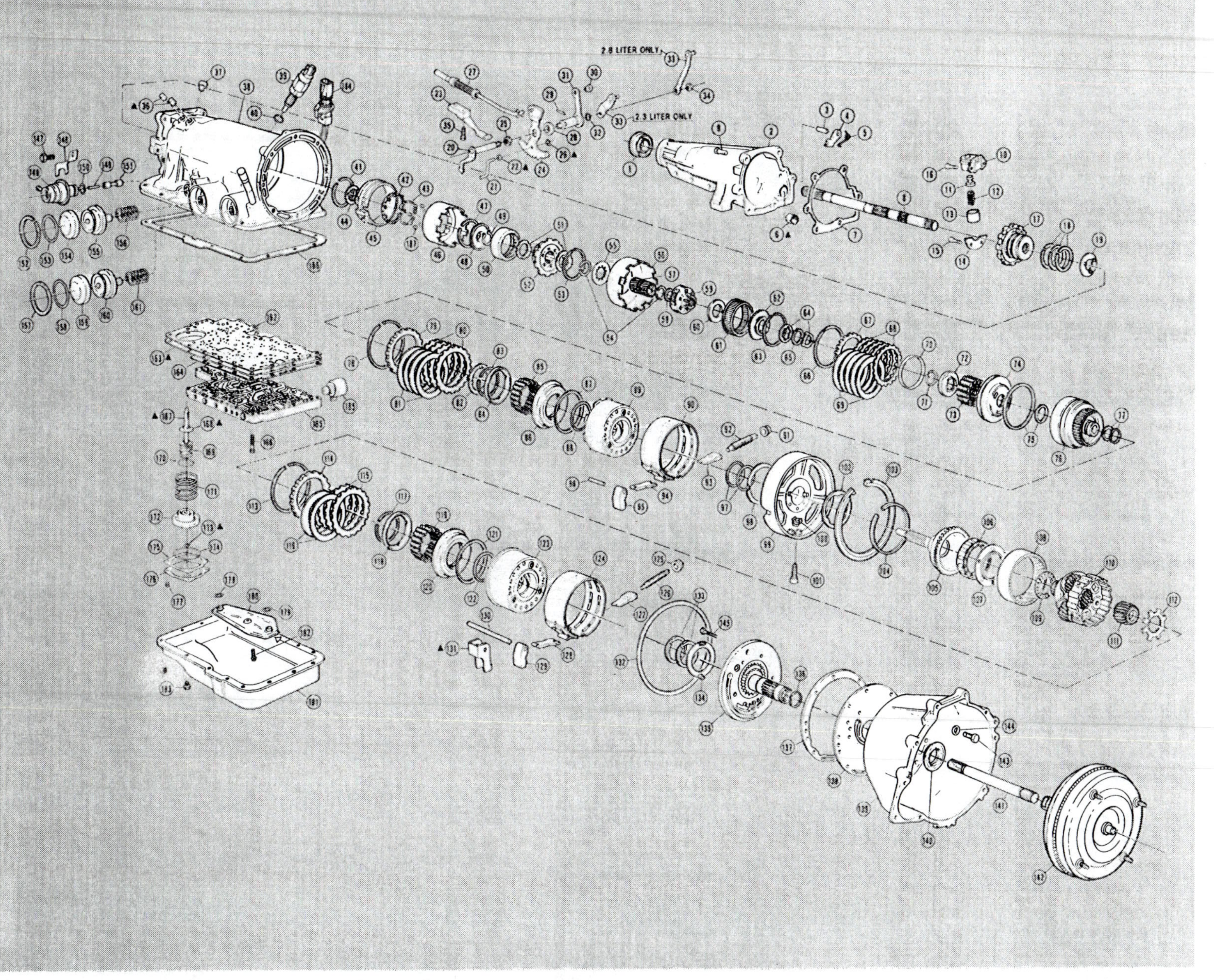

FIGURE 11–11 A4LD entire transmission. (Courtesy of Ford)

No.	Part No.	Description
1.	7052	SEAL ASSY (EXT. HSG.) OIL
2.	7A039	HOUSING (EXTN.)
3.	7D071	SHAFT (PARKING PAWL)
4.	7A441	PAWL (PARKING)
5.	7D070	SPRING (PARKING PAWL RETURN)
▲ 6.	7D419	CUP — PARKING ROD GUIDE
7.	7086	GASKET (EXTN. HSG.)
8.	7060	SHAFT ASSY (OUTPUT)
9.	E800152-S72	EXTENSION TO CASE
10.	7A300	BODY — GOV. VALVE
11.	7C054	VALVE (GOVERNOR PRIMARY)
12.	7A302	SPRING (GOVERNOR VALVE)
13.	7D324	WEIGHT — (GOVERNOR OUTER)
14.	7F124	COUNTERWEIGHT — GOVERNOR
15.	E602164-S72	BOLT (GOV. BODY TO COLLECTOR BODY) — (2 REQ'D)
16.	E800156-S	BOLT — M6 × 20 (GOV. BODY TO COLLECTOR BODY) — (2 REQ'D)
17.	7D220	BODY (GOV. OIL COLLECTOR)
18.	7D011	RING (GOV. HSG. SEAL) — (3 REQ'D)
19.	7B368	WASHER (OUTPUT SHAFT THRUST GR)
20.	7D261	LEVER ASSY — DWN/SHFT DET. — INNER
21.	7E333	PIN — MAN. VLV. DET. LEVER — INNER
▲ 22.	E630020-S	WASHER — FLAT STEEL
23.	7E332	SPRING ASSY — MAN. VLV. DETENT
24.	7C494	LEVER — MANUAL VALVE
25.	E820112-S	NUT (LEV. TO LEV. ASSY DWN/SHFT DET. INNER)
▲ 26.	E662312-S	CLIP — ROD RETAINING
27.	7D410	ROD ASSY — PARK PAWL ACTU.
28.	7B498	SEAL ASSY — MAIN CONTROL LVR. OIL
29.	E840125-S	PIN — SPRING ROLLER (RETAIN OUTER MAN. LVR. ASSY)
30.	7341	INSULATOR — GEAR SHIFT ARM
31.	7A256	LEVER ASSY — MANUAL CONTROL
32.	386078-S	O'RING — OUTER MAN. LVR. SHAFT OIL
33.	7A394	LEVER ASSY — DWN/SHFT CNTL — OUTER
34.	E820109-S72	NUT — HEX M8 × 1 (OUTER MAN. LVR. TO SHAFT)
35.	E800185-S72	SCREW M8 × 30 (VALVE BODY TO CASE)
▲ 36.	E840115-S	PIN — REV. BAND ANCHOR (2 REQ'D)
37.	7034	VENT ASSY — CASE
38.	7005	CASE ASSEMBLY
39.	7A247	SWITCH ASSY — GR. SHIFT NEUTRAL
40.	E853116-S	SEAL — O'RING
41.	E860120-S	RING — RETAINING
42.	7D191	RETAINER — OVERRUN CL. SPRING
43.	7D170	SPRING — OVERRUN CLUTCH
44.	7D422	WASHER (O.P. SHAFT HUB THRUST)
45.	7D095	BAND ASSY — REVERSE
46.	7C498	DRUM ASSY (REV. BRAKE)
47.	E860122-S	RING 87 MM RETAIN FORWARD RING GEAR TO HUB
48.	7D164	HUB — OUTPUT SHAFT — 57 EXT — 34 INT TEETH
49.	E861125-S	RETAINING RING 25 × 1.2
50.	7A153	GEAR — OUTPUT SHAFT RING
51.	7D423	WASHER — PLANET CARRIER THRUST — (2 REQ'D)
52.	7D006	PLANET ASSY (REV.)
53.	E860119-S	RING (PLANET TO DRUM)
54.	E860121-S	RING — 39 MM (INPUT SHELL TO SUN GR. ASSY) — (2 REQ'D)
55.	7D066	WASHER (INPUT SHELL THRUSTS)
56.	7D064	SHELL (INPUT)
57.	7D063	GEAR ASSY (SUN)
58.	7D235	BRG. THRUST — SUN GEAR RACE — RR
59.	7A398	PLANET ASSY (FWD)
60.	7F374	BRG. ASSY — CL. INT. DRUM THRUST
61.	7D392	GEAR (RING FWD) 72 EXT. 57 INT. TEETH
62.	7D393	HUB (FWD RING GEAR)
63.	E860122-S	RING — RET 87 MM (FWD. RING GR. TO HUB)
64.	7D090	WASHER (FWD. CYL. HUB THRUST)
65.	E661138-S	RING (RETAIN HUB) 38 × 1.75 MM
66.	E860115-S	RET RING (SEL FIT)
67.	7B066	PLATE (FWD CLUTCH PRESSURE)
68.	7B442	PLATE (CLUTCH) FORWARD
69.	7B164	PLATE ASSY — CLUTCH (FWD)
70.	7E457	SPRING — FORWARD CLUTCH CUSHION
71.	E860109-S	RING 34 MM (HUB TO FWD. RING GEAR)
72.	7D041	RET (FWD. CL. PISTON SPRING)
73.	7C151	SPRING — FWD. CL. PISTON (15 REQ'D)
74.	7A262	PISTON ASSY (FWD. CLUTCH)
75.	7A548	SEAL (CLUTCH PISTON OIL)
76.	7D424	CYL ASSY (FWD CLUTCH)
77.	7D019	SEAL (FWD CLUTCH CYL) — 2 REQ'D
78.	E860126-S	RET RING (SELECT FIT)
79.	7B066	PLATE (CLUTCH PRESS) REV.
80.	7B442	PLATE (CLUTCH) HIGH
81.	7B164	PLATE ASSY (CLUTCH) HIGH
82.	7D428	WASHER (INTM. BRAKE DRUM THRUST)
83.	E860125-S	RING 63 MM (HIGH CL. PST. IN INT. BRK. DRUM)
84.	7D041	RET (REV. CLUTCH PISTON SPRING) — 8 TABS
85.	7C151	SPRING (REV. CLUTCH PISTON) 20 REQ'D
86.	7A258	PISTON (REV. CLUTCH)
87.	7A548	SEAL (CLUTCH PISTON OIL)
88.	7D404	SEAL (HIGH CLUTCH PISTON INNER)
89.	7D044	DRUM ASSY (INTERM. BRAKE)
90.	7D034	BAND ASSY (INTERM. SERVO)
91.	388307-S100	NUT & SEAL — HEX
92.	7C492	SCREW (REV. BAND ADJ)
93.	7D430	STRUT (INTERM. BRK. BAND ANCHOR)
94.	7D029	STRUT (INTERM. BRK. BAND APPLY)
95.	7D396	LEVER (INTERM. BAND SERVO)
96.	7D433	SHAFT (INTERM. BAND ACT. LEVER)
97.	7D429	SEAL RING (HIGH CLUTCH) 2 REQ'D — VITON
98.	7D014	WASHER (FRT. PUMP INPUT THRUST) — SEL. FIT
99.	7G033	SUPPORT ASSY — CENTER O/D
100.	826160	NUT & CAGE ASSY S/L MTL. M6
101.	804371	SCREW CAP — HEX 8.8 M6 × 15
102.	7L326	WASHER (CENTER SUPPORT THRUST)
103.	E860366-S	RING RETAINING (RETAIN 7G033 IN CASE)
104.	E860119-S	RING — RET (110.1 MM × 1.6)
105.	7A658	SHAFT — CENTER ASSY — O/D
106.	7C109	CLUTCH ASSY — OVERRUN — O/D
107.	7L339	WASHER — OVER CLUTCH — O/D
108.	7653	GEAR — O/D RING
109.	7L495	BRG ASSY — O/D INNER RACE
110.	7B446	CARRIER ASSY — PLT. GEAR — O/D
111.	7D063	GEAR ASSY — SUN O/D
112.	7660	ADAPTER — O/D CLUTCH
113.	E860126-S	RING — RETAINING (SEL. FIT)
114.	7B066	PLATE — O/D CLUTCH PRESSURE
115.	7B442	PLATE — O/D CLUTCH
116.	7B164	PLATE ASSY — O/D CLUTCH INT. SPLINE
117.	E860125-S	RING — RET 63 MM (O/D CL. PST. TO O/D BRK. DRUM)
118.	7D041	RETAINER — O/D CL. PST. SPRING — 8 TABS
119.	7C151	SPRING — O/D CL. PISTON (20 REQ'D)
120.	7A258	PISTON — O/D CLUTCH
121.	7A548	SEAL — O/D CL. PISTON — OUTER
122.	7D404	SEAL — O/D CL. PISTON — INNER
123.	7L669	DRUM ASSY — O/D
124.	7D034	BAND ASSY — O/D
125.	388307-S100	NUT & SEAL — HEX
126.	7C492	SCREW — O/D BAND ADJ
127.	7D430	STRUT — O/D BRK. DRUM ANCHOR
128.	7D029	STRUT — O/D BRK. DRUM APPLY
129.	7D396	LEVER — O/D BAND SERVO
130.	7D433	SHAFT — O/D BAND ADJ. LEVER
▲131.	7A653	BRACKET — O/D
132.	7D441	SEAL (FRONT OIL PUMP)
133.	7D429	SEAL (INTERM. BRK. DRUM) — 2 REQ'D
134.	7D014	WASHER (FRT. PUMP INPUT THRUST) SEL. FIT
135.	7L201	SUPPORT & GEAR ASSY (FRT. PUMP)
136.	7L323	SEAL (FRONT PUMP SUPPORT)
137.	7A136	GASKET — OIL PUMP
138.	7B472	PLATE (OIL PUMP ADAPTOR)
139.	7975	HSG. ASSY — CONVERTER
140.	7A248	SEAL ASSY (FRT OIL PUMP)
141.	7017	INPUT SHAFT
142.	7902	CONVERTER ASSEMBLY
143.	E800152-S72	SCREW M10 × 30
144.	E830124-S	WASHER — FLAT — 10" DIA. (CONV. HSG. TO CASE) 8 REQ'D
145.	E800163-S	BOLT — FLG. HD. 8.8 × M6 × 35.0 (PUMP SUPT ASSY TO CONV. AS ASSY) 5 REQ'D
146.	7E458	CLAMP — TV CONTROL DIAPHRAGM
147.	E800341-S72	BOLT M6 × 12MM (VALVE CLAMP TO CASE)
148.	7A377	DIAPHRAGM ASSY — TV CONTROL
149.	7A380	ROD — TV CONTROL
150.	E853110-S	O'RING — THROTTLE VALVE
151.	7D080	VALVE — THROTTLE CONTROL
152.	E860343-S	RING — RET. 67 × 15 INTERMEDIATE
153.	7A114	SEAL — SERVO COVER TO CASE — INTERM.
154.	7D027	COVER — INTER. BAND SERVO
155.	7E221	PISTON & ROD ASSY — INTERMEDIATE
156.	7D028	SPRING INTERM. BAND SERVO PISTON
157.	E860343	RING — RET. 67 × 15 — O/D
158.	7A114	SEAL — SERVO COVER TO CASE — O/D
159.	7D027	COVER — O/D BAND SERVO
160.	7E221	PISTON & ROD ASSY — O/D
161.	7D028	SPRING — O/D BAND SERVO PISTON
162.	7D100	GASKET — CONT. VLV. BDY. SEP.
▲163.	7A008	PLATE — VLV. BDY. SEPARATING
164.	7D100	GASKET — CONT. VLV. BDY. SEPARATING
165.	7A100	CONTROL ASSY — MAIN
166.	E800153-S72	SCREW M6 × 40 (VALVE BODY TO CASE) 19 REQ'D
▲167.	7D190	ROD — REV. BAND SERVO PISTON
▲168.	E830138-S	RET — REV. SERVO CUSHION SPRING
169.	7E207	SPRING — REV. SERVO OCCUM.
170.	7423	SEAL — REV. BND. SERVO PST. OIL — SMALL
171.	7D031	SPRING — REV. SERVO PISTON
172.	7D030	PISTON & ROD ASSY — REV. SERVO
▲173.	E860167-S	RING RETAINER (RET. ROD TO PISTON)
174.	7423	SEAL — REV. BND. SERVO RET. OIL — LARGE
175.	7L173	GASKET — REV. SERVO SEP. PLATE COVER
176.	7D036	COVER — REV. BND. SERVO PISTON
177.	E800156-S72	BOLT M6 × 20 (REV. SERVO TO VLV. BDY.) 4 REQ'D
178.	E853137-S	O'RING — OIL SCREEN ASSY — SMALL
179.	E853132-S	O'RING — OIL SCREEN ASSY — LARGE
180.	7A098	SCREEN ASSY — OIL PAN
181.	7A264	OIL.PAN
182.	E800154-S72	SCREW — M6 × 45 (VLV. BDY. TO CASE) 5 REQ'D
183.	E800158-S72	SCREW — M8 × 14 (OIL PAN TO CASE) 18 REQ'D
184.	14488	CONNECTOR — CONV. CL. OVERRIDE
185.	6916	SOLENOID ASSY — O/D SHIFT
186.	7A191	GASKET — OIL PAN

▲NOT SERVICED

FIGURE 11–11 *(continued)*

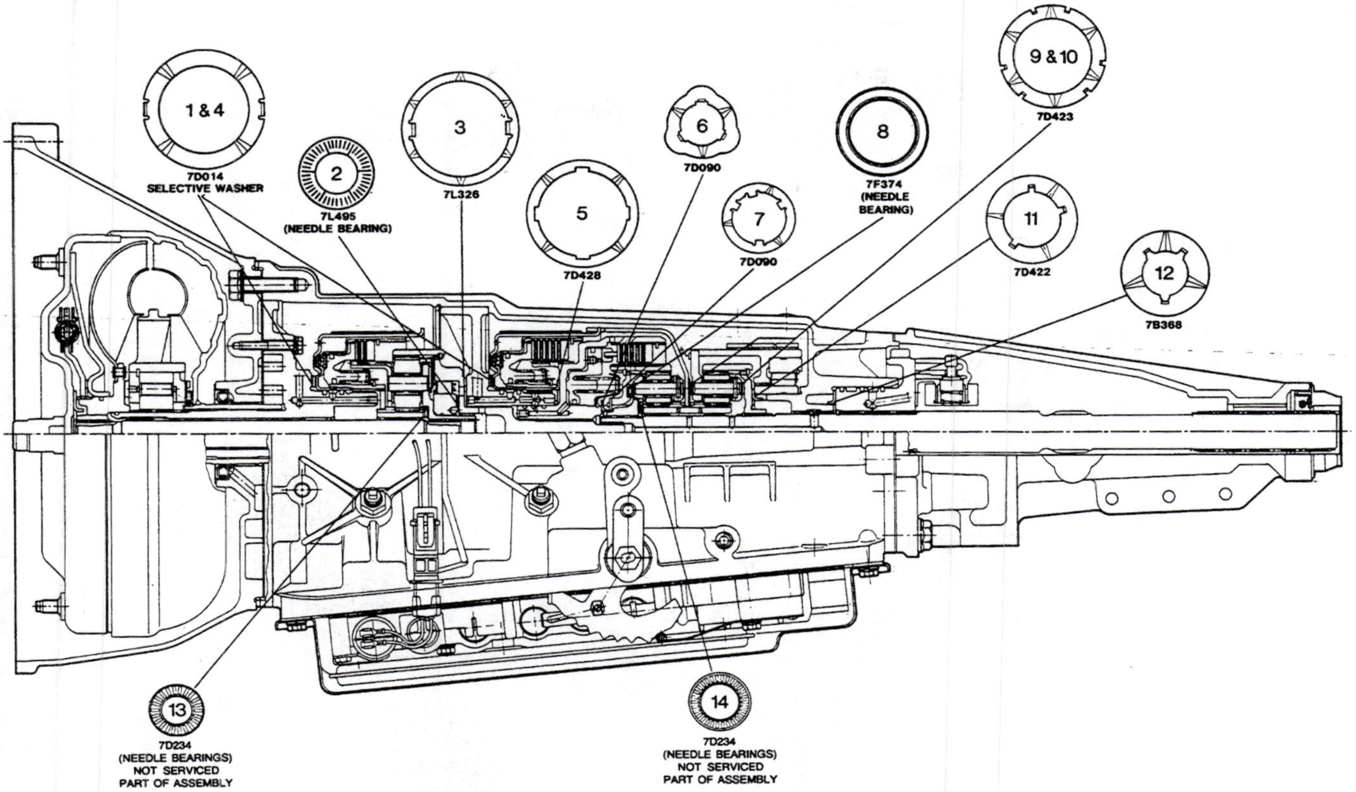

FIGURE 11–12 A4LD thrust washer location. (Courtesy of Ford)

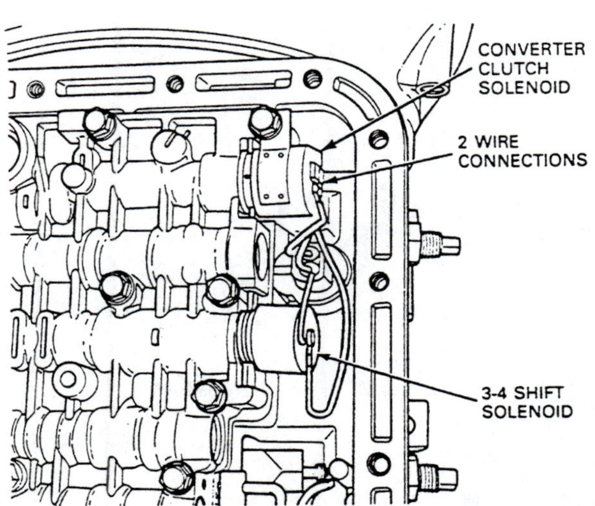

FIGURE 11–13 A4LD electrical solenoids. (Courtesy of Ford)

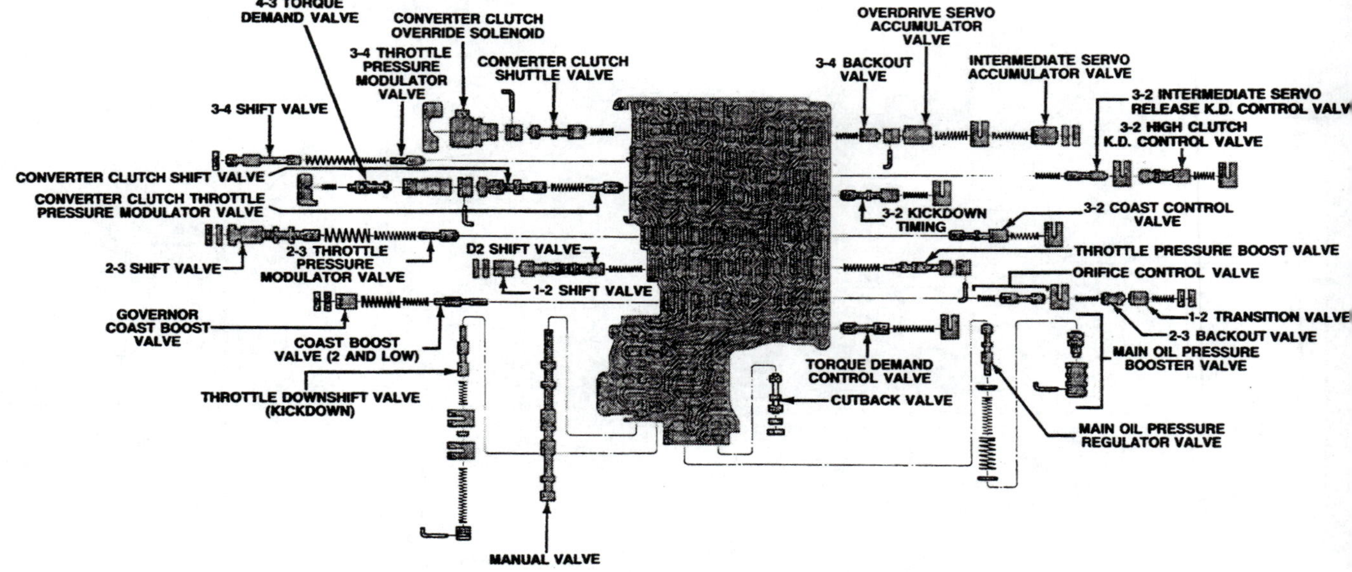

FIGURE 11–14 A4LD valve body. (Courtesy of Ford)

Torque converter, Figure 11–15
Valve body bolt location, Figure 11–16
Overdrive unit, Figure 11–17
Governor, Figure 11–18
Forward gear train, Figure 11–19
Rear end-play fixture, Figure 11–20

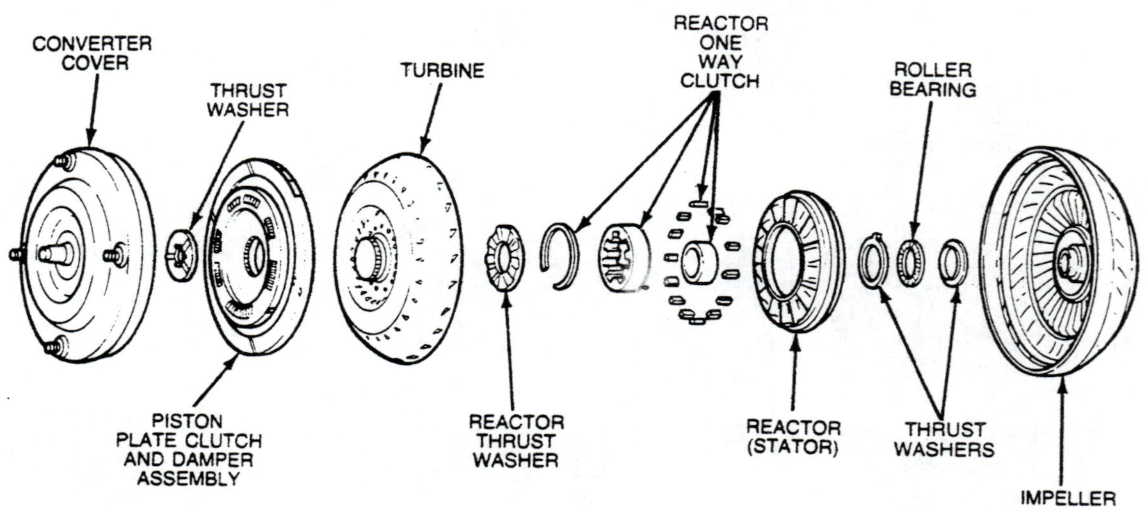

FIGURE 11–15 A4LD torque converter. (Courtesy of Ford)

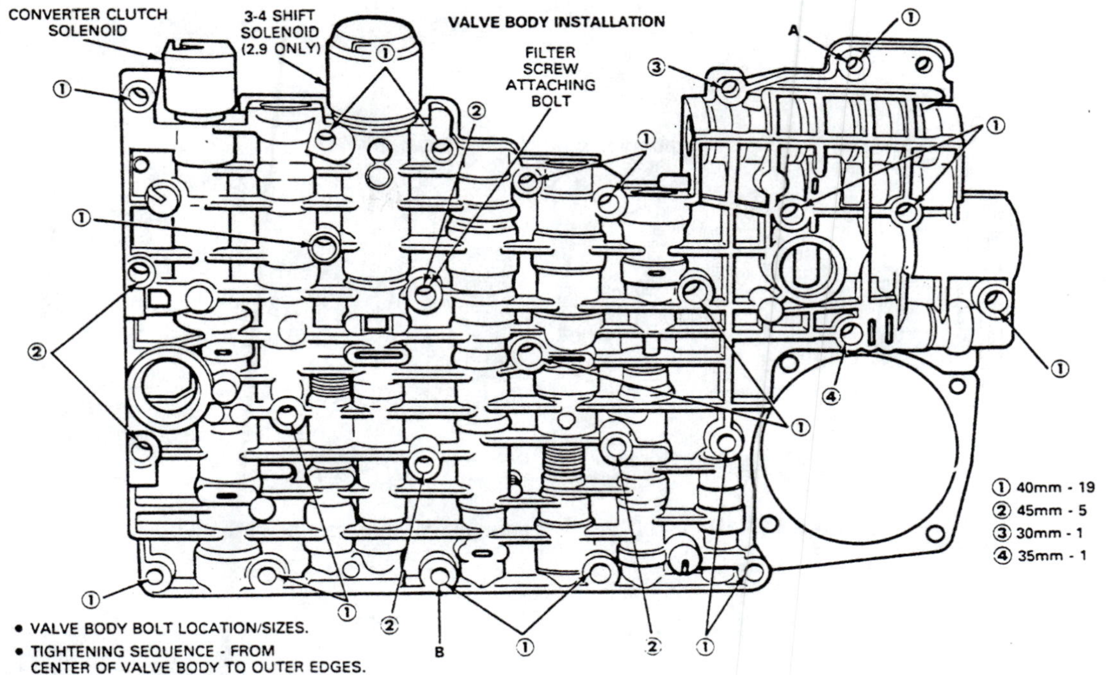

FIGURE 11–16 A4LD valve body bolt location. (Courtesy of Ford)

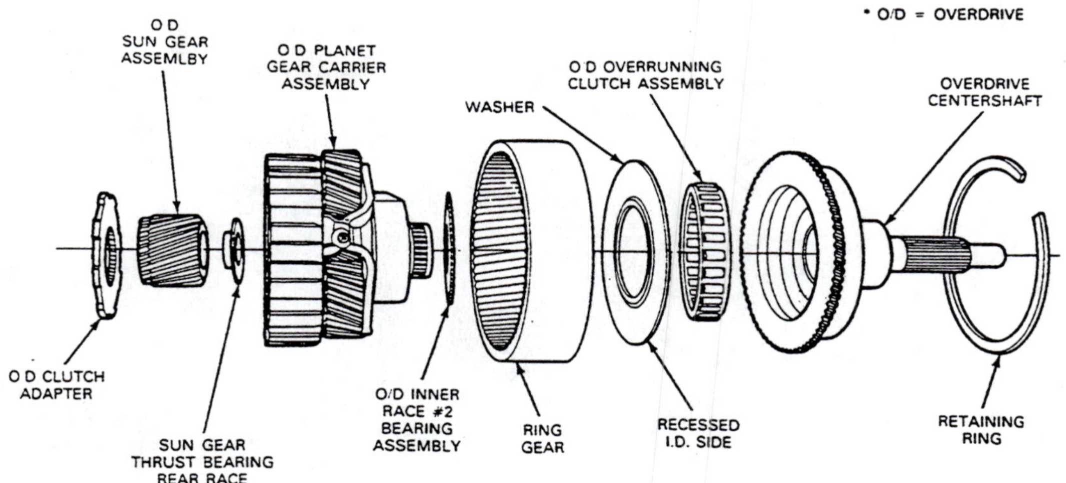

FIGURE 11–17 A4LD overdrive unit. (Courtesy of Ford)

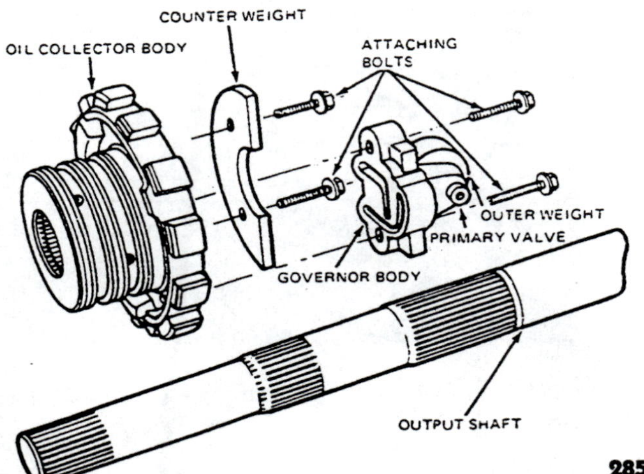

FIGURE 11–18 A4LD governor. (Courtesy of Ford)

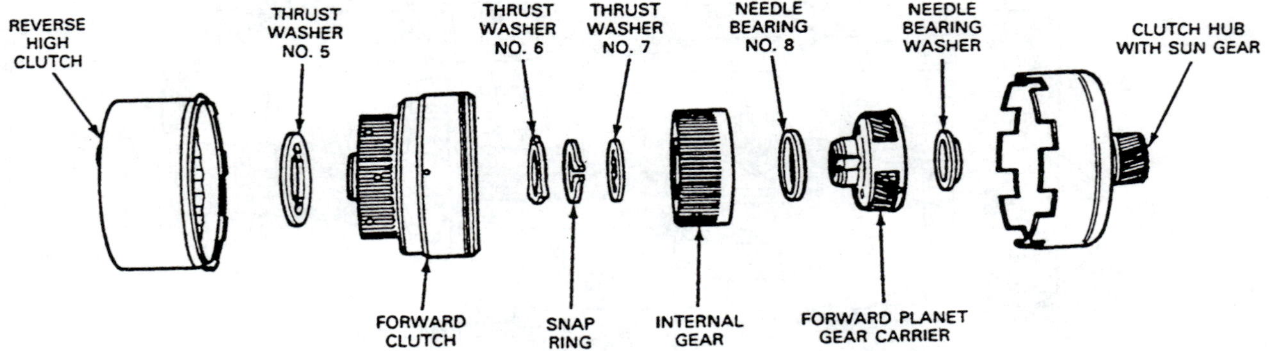

FIGURE 11–19 A4LD forward gear train. (Courtesy of Ford)

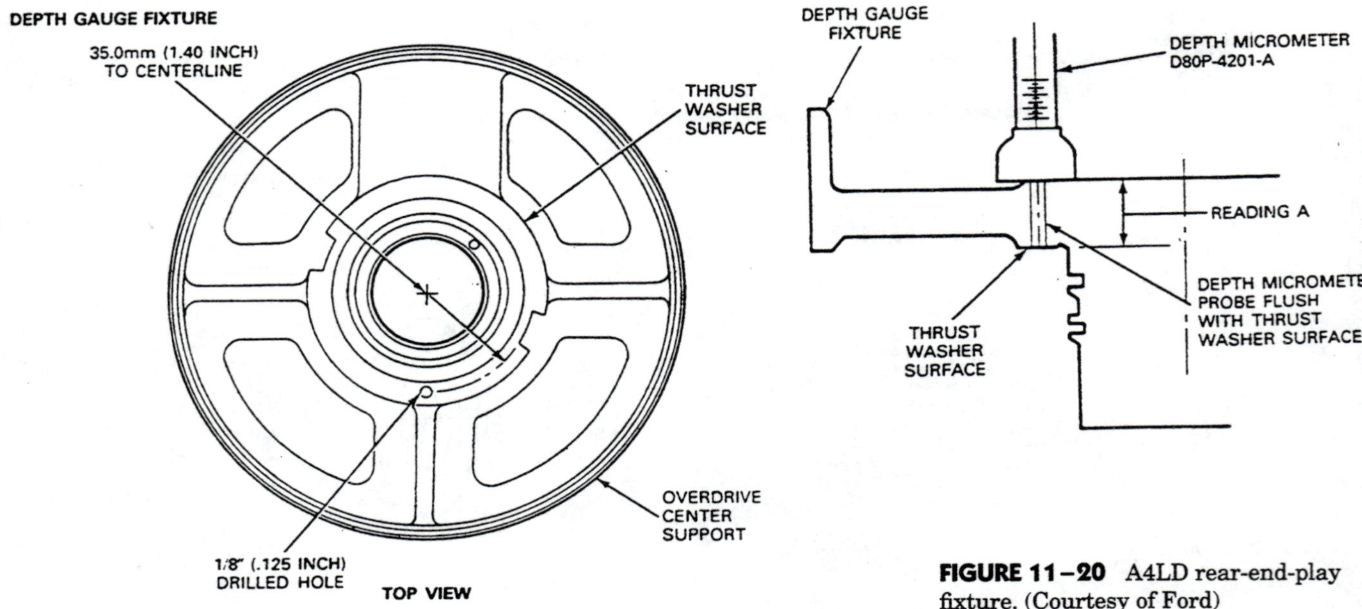

FIGURE 11–20 A4LD rear-end-play fixture. (Courtesy of Ford)

11.3.6 Pressure Test

One of the key tests in diagnosis is the hydraulic system pressure test. The location of the test points of the A4LD transmission are shown in Figure 11–21. A pressure chart listing the pressure specification of this transmission is shown in Figure 11–22.

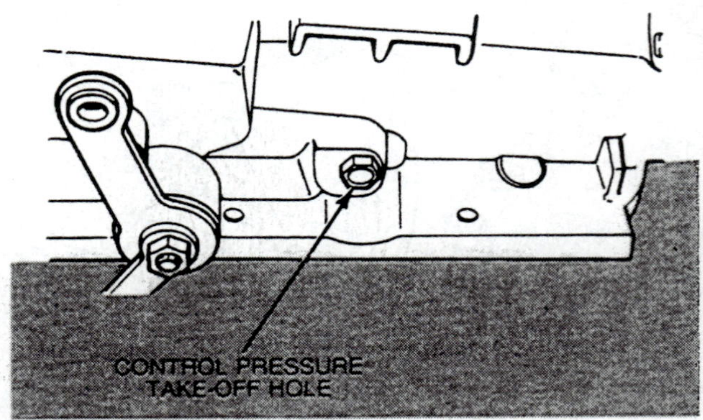

FIGURE 11–21 A4LD pressure test points. (Courtesy of Ford)

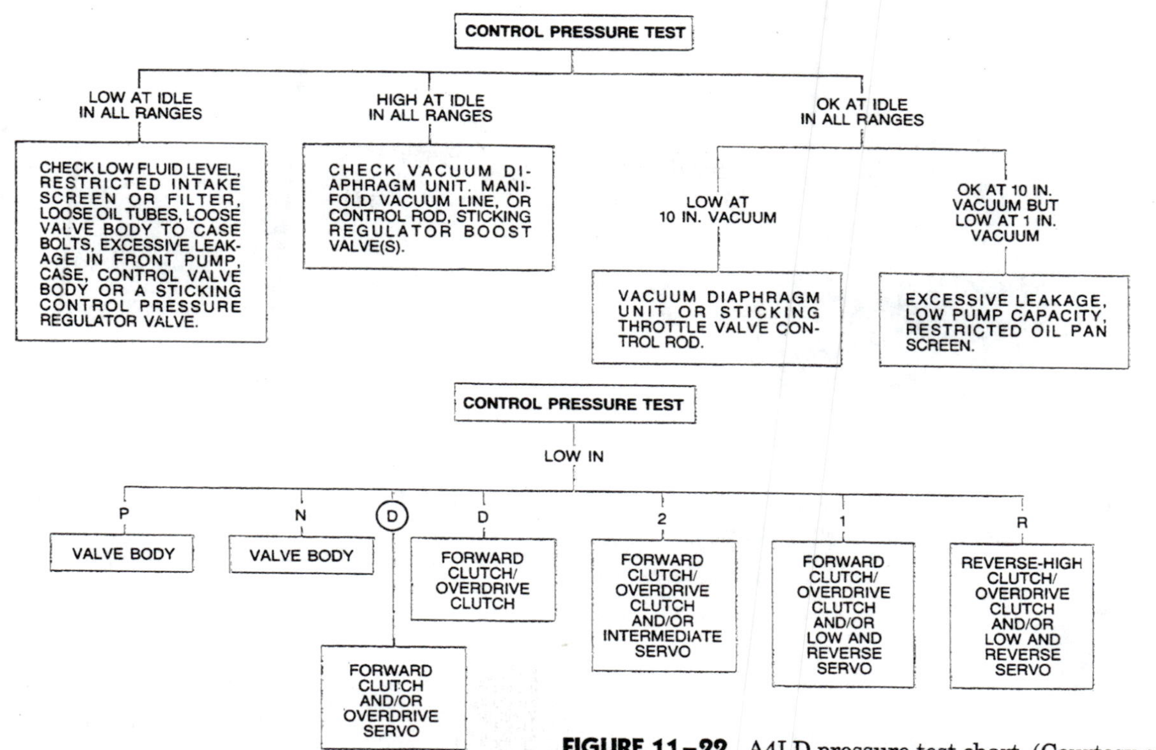

FIGURE 11–22 A4LD pressure test chart. (Courtesy of Ford)

FIGURE A4LD–1 The bell housing and pump cover are combined in one piece, as in the C-3 transmission.

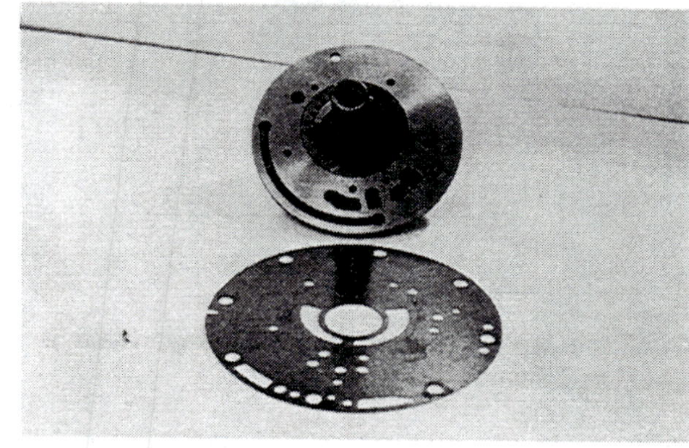

FIGURE A4LD–2 The oil pump body, gears, and adapter plate should be inspected closely.

FIGURE A4LD–3 Special alignment tool used to align the pump body and gears during installation.

FIGURE A4LD–4 The alignment tool slides over the stator support to center the pump gears (not shown).

FIGURE A4LD-5 The overdrive clutch, overdrive sun gear, and adapter must be examined carefully.

FIGURE A4LD-6 The overdrive pinion carrier has a one-way clutch inner race on its back side. The rest of the one-way clutch is mounted in the ring gear.

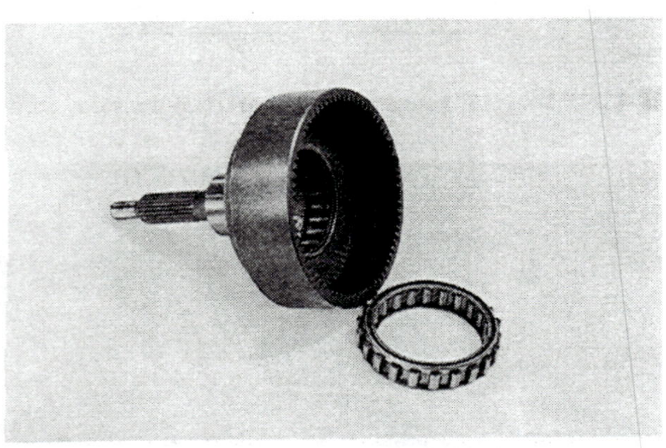

FIGURE A4LD-7 The overdrive one-way clutch is a sprag type. Examine it closely.

FIGURE A4LD-8 The center overdrive support on the right has two holes drilled in it to measure end play through. The support on the left is the stock.

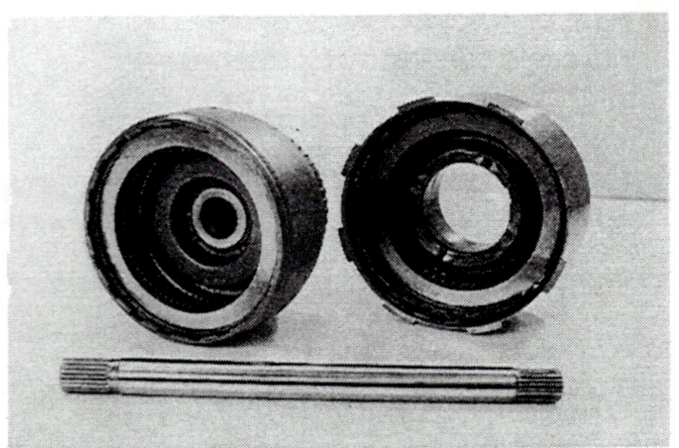

FIGURE A4LD-9 The forward clutch, high-reverse clutch, and the input shaft must all be inspected closely.

FIGURE A4LD-10 The rear pinion carrier, ring gear, and reverse brake drum should all be checked for wear.

FIGURE A4LD–11 The intermediate and overdrive servo piston are slightly different in size. Replace all seals.

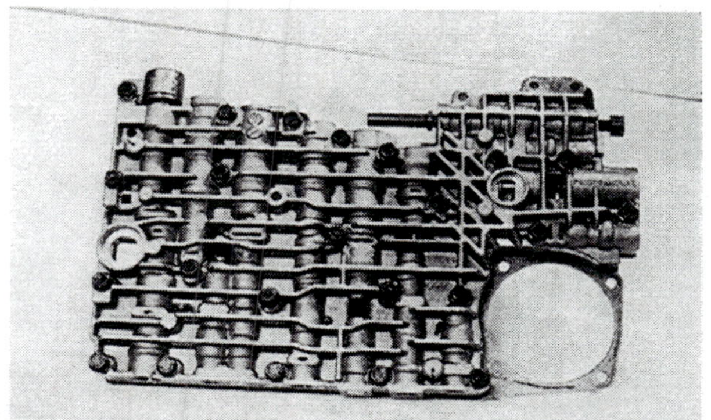

FIGURE A4LD–12 The converter clutch solenoid is located at the upper left corner of the valve body.

11.3.7 Air Test

Air testing is used during preliminary diagnosis of certain malfunctions and also during the disassembly process to verify component operation or failure. The technician must know which hydraulic circuit is being served by each passageway to be able to air test a transmission accurately.

11.3.8 Special Attention

In this section we show and explain various points of special interest about the A4LD transmission. The information presented about each item is included with each illustration.

11.4 E4OD: RWD FOUR-SPEED OVERDRIVE AUTOMATIC TRANSMISSION

11.4.1 Basic Description

The E4OD transmission is the latest step in the evolution of the C-6 transmission. With the addition of an overdrive gear set and electronic shift control, the proven strength of the C-6 is upgraded to meet the economic needs of today (Figure 11–23).

1. *Torque Converter*
The torque converter used by the E4OD is the standard three-component design with an electronically controlled converter clutch.

2. *Gear Train*
The E4OD has two gear sets, the overdrive and the main gear set. The overdrive gear set is a simple planetary set with the planetary carrier serving as the input, the sungear working as the reaction member, and the ring gear acting as the output. The main gear set is a Simpson design with the front ring gear and sun gear working as input members, the sun gear and rear carrier as reaction members, and the front planetary carrier and rear ring gear serving as output members (Figure 11–24).

3. *Coupling Devices*
The clutches used to connect the gear train components are the overdrive one-way, direct, forward, and coast.

4. *Holding Devices*
The clutches used as holding devices are the intermediate, intermediate one-way, reverse, band, and low–reverse one-way.

5. *Pump*
The E4OD uses a gerotor-type positive-displacement pump with the pump control valves built into the pump housing (Figure 11–25).

6. *Shift Control*
The shifting of the E4OD is controlled by the ECC-IV computer through four solenoids: solenoid 1, shift control; solenoid 2, shift control; solenoid 3, converter clutch control; solenoid 4, coast clutch control. The solenoid placement on the valve body is shown in Figure 11–26, while the solenoid application chart is shown in Figure 11–27.

7. *Governor*
Electronically controlled transmissions do not use governors.

8. *Throttle Valve*
As with the governors, most electronically controlled transmissions do not use a throttle valve system.

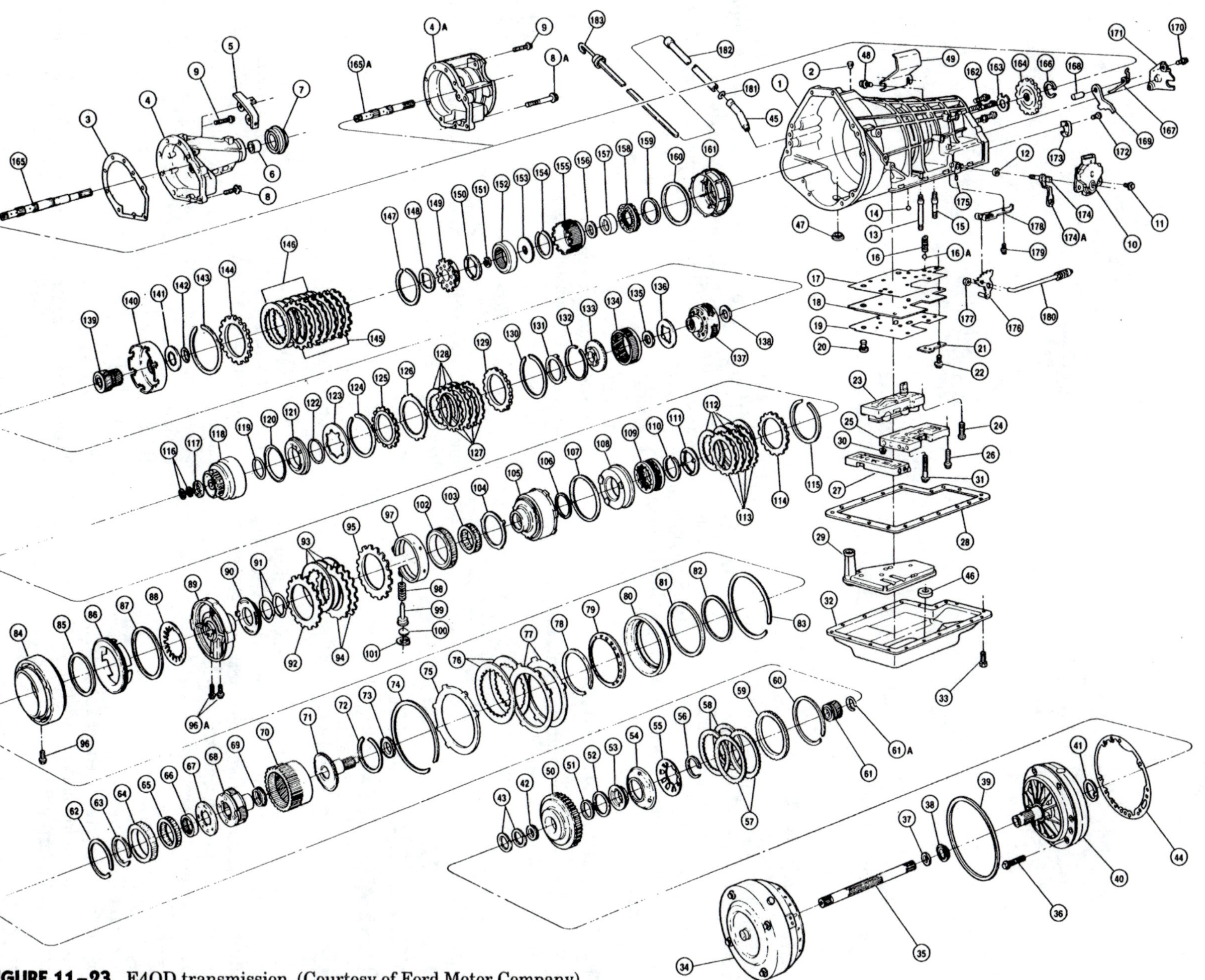

FIGURE 11–23 E4OD transmission. (Courtesy of Ford Motor Company)

E4OD EXPLODED VIEW LEGEND

No.	Part No.	Description
1.	7005	CASE ASSEMBLY
2.	7034	VENT ASSEMBLY
3.	7086	GASKET — EXTENSION HOUSING
4.	7A039-CB	EXTENSION ASSEMBLY (4X2)
#	7A041	— EXTENSION & BUSHING ASSY.
#	7A040	— EXTENSION
4A.	7A039-DA	EXTENSION ASSEMBLY (4X4)
	7A039-EA	EXTENSION ASSEMBLY (SUPERDUTY)
#5.	7H102	BRACKET — WIRING
6.	7A034	BUSHING — EXTENSION HOUSING (4X2)
7.	7052	SEAL — EXTENSION HOUSING (4X2)
8.	N605802-S36	BOLT — EXTENSION (4X2 BOTTOM) (2 PCS.) M10X1.5X35MM
8A.	N606569-S36	BOLT — EXTENSION (SUPERDUTY & 4X4 BOTTOM) (2 PCS.) M10X1.5X90MM
9.	N605803-S36	BOLT — EXTENSION (TOP) (7 PCS.) M10X1.5X40MM
10.	7F293	SENSOR — MANUAL LEVER POSITION
11.	N805312-S100	BOLT ASSEMBLY (2 PCS.) M6X1.0X30MM
12.	7B498	SEAL — MANUAL LEVER
13.	N805331-S	STUD — CASE TO SOLENOID BODY (1 PC.) M6X1.0X79MM
14.	7E195	BALL — RUBBER CHECK (10 PCS.) (2 IN MAIN CONTROL)
	379581-S	BALL — STEEL CHECK (1 PC.)
15.	N805330-S	STUD — CASE TO CONTROL ASSEMBLY (4 PCS.) M6X1.0X61.25MM
16.	7D017	EPC BLOW-OFF SPRING
16A.	353078-S	EPC BLOW-OFF BALL
17.	7D100	GASKET — SEPARATOR
#18.	7A008	PLATE — SEPARATOR
19.	7C155	GASKET — SEPARATOR
20.	7G308	SCREEN — SOLENOID
#21.	7F282	PLATE — SEPARATOR PLATE REINFORCING
22.	N605772-S	BOLT (3 PCS.) M6X1.0X16MM
23.	7G391	SOLENOID BODY ASSEMBLY
24.	N805329-S	BOLT — TORX HEAD (9 PCS.) M6X1.0X40MM
25.	7A100	MAIN CONTROL BODY ASSEMBLY
26.	N805326-S	BOLT (18 PCS.) M6X1.0X42.5MM
27.	7G422	ACCUMULATOR BODY ASSEMBLY
28.	7A191	GASKET — OIL PAN
29.	7G186-AA	FILTER AND SEAL ASSEMBLY (4X2)
	7G186-BA	FILTER AND SEAL ASSEMBLY (4X4)
30.	N805328-S	NUT (5 PCS.) M6X1.0
31.	N805327-S	BOLT (7 PCS.) M6X1.0X66MM
32.	7A264-FA	PAN — OIL (4X2)
	7A264-GA	PAN — OIL (4X4)
33.	N605902-S36	BOLT — OIL PAN (20 PCS.) M8X1.25X12MM
34.	7902	TORQUE CONVERTER ASSEMBLY
	87650-S2	— PLUG — CONVERTER DRAIN 1/8 IN-27
35.	7017	SHAFT — INPUT
36.	N805260-S	BOLT & WASHER ASSEMBLY — PUMP (9 PCS.) M8X1.25X65MM
	7G379	— WASHER — REPLACEMENT (9 PCS.)
37.	7L323	SEAL RING — TEFLON
38.	7A248	SEAL — CONVERTER HUB
39.	7D441	SEAL — SQUARE CUT O.D. PUMP
40.	7A103	PUMP ASSEMBLY
41.	7D014	WASHER — PUMP THRUST
42.	7E486	NEEDLE BEARING ASSEMBLY
43.	7G402	SEAL RING — TEFLON (2 PCS.)
44.	7A136	GASKET — PUMP
45.	7N463	STUB TUBE
46.	7L027	MAGNET — PAN
47.	7N171	PLUG — CONVERTER ACCESS
48.	N605770-S36	BOLT — HEAT SHIELD (2 PCS.)
49.	7A434	HEAT SHIELD — SOLENOID BODY CONNECTOR
50.	7G387	COAST CLUTCH CYLINDER ASSEMBLY
51.	7A548-JA	SEAL — INNER
52.	7A548-EA	SEAL — OUTER
53.	7G419	PISTON
54.	7N519	RING — PISTON APPLY
55.	7B070-EA	SPRING — PISTON RETURN
56.	N804949-S	RING — RETAINING
57.	7B442-CA	PLATE — COAST CLUTCH EXTERNAL SPLINE
58.	7B164-CA	PLATE — COAST CLUTCH INTERNAL SPLINE
59.	7B437-CA	PLATE — COAST CLUTCH PRESSURE
60.	N804950-S	RING — RETAINING (SELECTIVE FIT)
	N804951-S	RING — RETAINING
	N804952-S	RING — RETAINING
61.	7670	GEAR — OVERDRIVE SUN
61A.	377300-S	RING — RETAINING
62.	377155-S	RING — RETAINING (OUTER RACE TO OVERDRIVE RING GEAR)
63.	377135-S	RING — RETAINING (OVERDRIVE OWC TO OUTER RACE)
*64.	7G389	RACE — OVERDRIVE ONE WAY CLUTCH OUTER
*65.	7G381	CLUTCH ASSEMBLY — OVERDRIVE ONE WAY
*66.	7G388	RACE — OVERDRIVE ONE WAY CLUTCH INNER
67.	7G400	WASHER — THRUST
68.	7E031	CARRIER ASSEMBLY — OVERDRIVE PLANETARY
#	7L676	— CARRIER
#	7D008-CA	— PLANET GEARS (4 PCS.)
#	7A238-CA	— PLANET SHAFTS (4 PCS.)
#	7A242-AA	— THRUST WASHERS (8 PCS.)
#	7D037-BA	— NEEDLE BEARINGS (80 PCS.)
#	380225-S	— RETAINING PINS (4 PCS.)
#	7E486	— NEEDLE BEARING ASSEMBLY
69.	7G128	NEEDLE BEARING ASSEMBLY
70.	7653	GEAR — OVERDRIVE RING
71.	7G382	CENTER SHAFT
72.	7G375	RING — RETAINING (CENTER SHAFT TO OVERDRIVE RING GEAR)
73.	7G178	NEEDLE BEARING ASSEMBLY
74.	7B421	RING — OVERDRIVE RETAINING
75.	7B066-BB	PLATE — OVERDRIVE CLUTCH PRESSURE
76.	7B164-EA	PLATE — OVERDRIVE CLUTCH INTERNAL SPLINE
77.	7B442-DA	PLATE — OVERDRIVE CLUTCH EXTERNAL SPLINE
78.	N804948-S	RING — RETURN SPRING RETAINING
79.	7B070-CA	SPRING — OVERDRIVE RETURN
80.	7G418	PISTON — OVERDRIVE
81.	7A548	SEAL — OVERDRIVE OUTER
82.	7F225	SEAL — OVERDRIVE INNER (SAME AS INTERMEDIATE INNER)
83.	7B421	RING — INT./O.D. CYLINDER RETAINING
84.	7G385	CYLINDER — INTERMEDIATE/OVERDRIVE
85.	7F225	SEAL — INTERMEDIATE INNER
86.	7E005	PISTON — INTERMEDIATE
87.	7F224	SEAL — INTERMEDIATE OUTER
88.	7B070-DB	SPRING — INTERMEDIATE RETURN
89.	7G033	SUPPORT ASSEMBLY — CENTER
90.	7L326	WASHER — THRUST
91.	7D429-A	SEAL — DIRECT CLUTCH CAST IRON (2 PCS.)
92.	7B066-CA	PLATE — INTERMEDIATE CLUTCH APPLY
93.	7F219	PLATE — INTERMEDIATE CLUTCH INTERNAL SPLINE
94.	7B442	PLATE — INTERMEDIATE CLUTCH EXTERNAL SPLINE
95.	7B437	PLATE — INTERMEDIATE CLUTCH PRESSURE
96.	N805310-S101	BOLT — CYLINDER HYDRAULIC FEED (1 PC.) M10X1.5X24MM
96A.	N805311-S101	BOLT — CENTER SUPPORT HYDRAULIC FEED (2 PCS.) M12X1.75X31MM
97.	7D034	BAND ASSEMBLY
98.	7D028	SPRING — SERVO RETURN
99.	7E221	PISTON ASSEMBLY — SERVO

#NOT SERVICED
*SERVICED IN KITS ONLY

FIGURE 11–23 *(continued)*

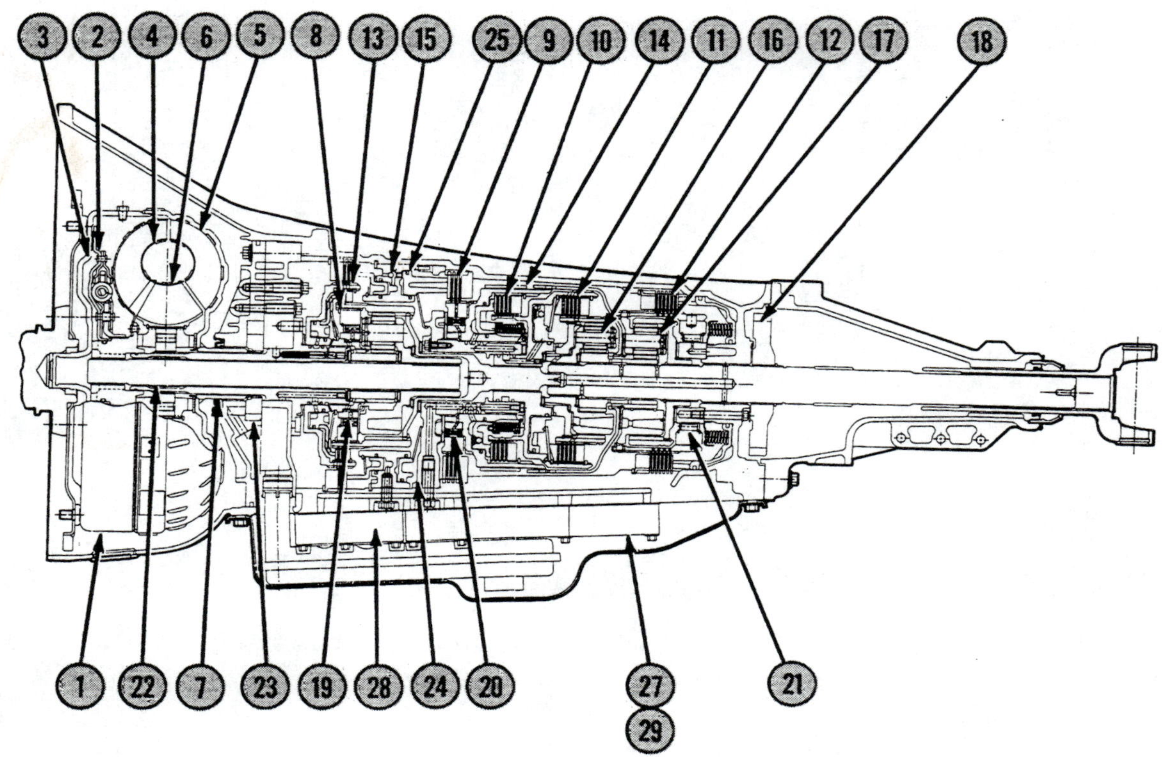

1. TORQUE CONVERTER
2. CONVERTER CLUTCH (PISTON PLATE CLUTCH AND DAMPER ASSEMBLY)
3. CONVERTER COVER
4. TURBINE
5. IMPELLER
6. REACTOR
7. IMPELLER HUB
8. COAST CLUTCH
9. INTERMEDIATE CLUTCH
10. DIRECT CLUTCH
11. FORWARD CLUTCH
12. REVERSE CLUTCH
13. OVERDRIVE CLUTCH
14. BAND
15. OVERDRIVE PLANETARY SYSTEM
16. FORWARD PLANETARY SYSTEM
17. REVERSE PLANETARY SYSTEM
18. PARKING GEAR
19. OVERDRIVE ONE-WAY SPRAG CLUTCH
20. INTERMEDIATE ONE-WAY SPRAG CLUTCH
21. LOW-REVERSE ONE-WAY ROLLER CLUTCH
22. INPUT SHAFT
23. PUMP
24. CENTER SUPPORT
25. INTERMEDIATE/OVERDRIVE CYLINDER
26. INTERMEDIATE SERVO
27. MAIN CONTROL BODY ASSEMBLY
28. ACCUMULATOR BODY ASSEMBLY
29. SOLENOID BODY ASSEMBLY

FIGURE 11–24 E4OD main gear set. (Courtesy of Ford Motor Company)

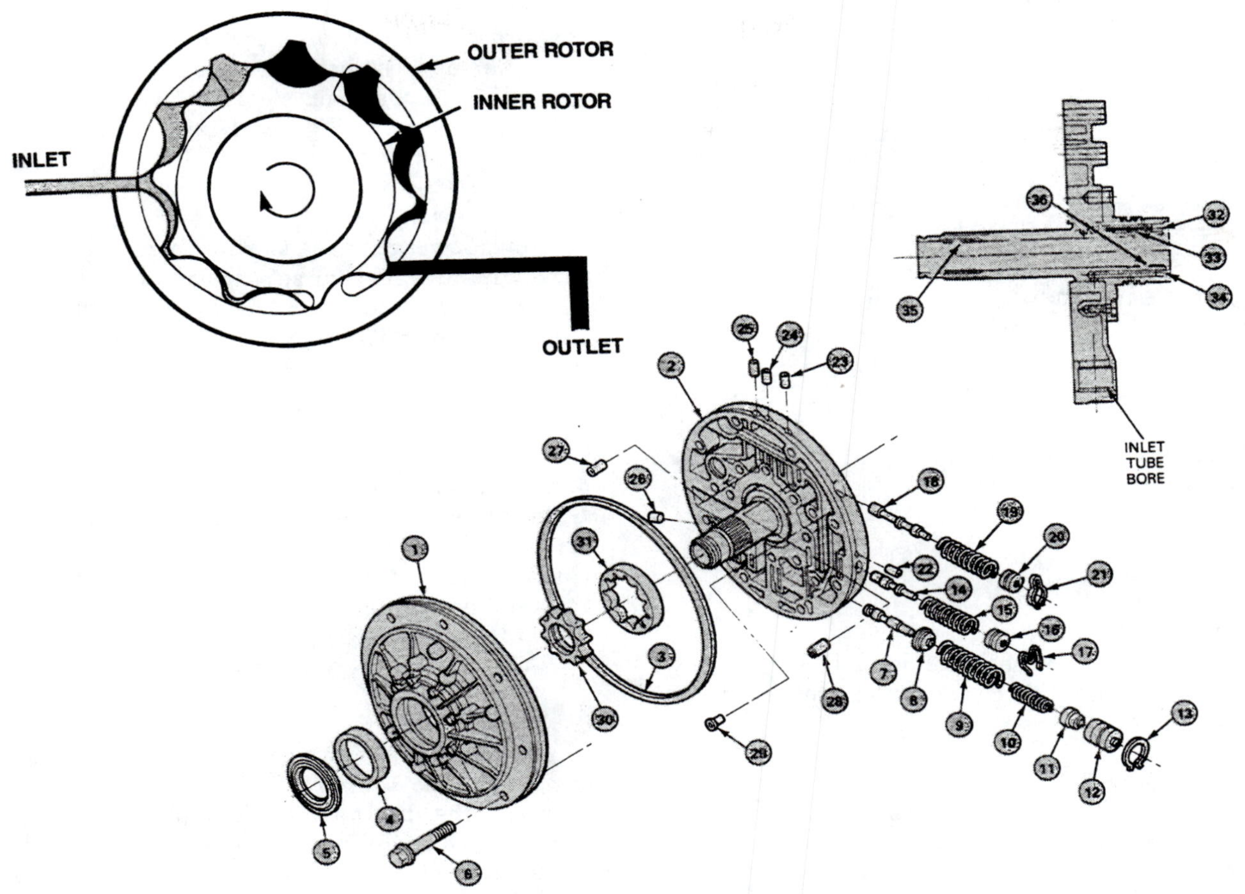

Description	Part Number	Description	Part Number
1. Pump Body	7A105	20. Plug	7F187
2. Control Body	7G406	21. Clip	7E335
3. Square Cut O.D. Pump Seal	7D441	22. Solid Cup Plug	N805212
4. Converter Hub Bushing	7B258	23. Solid Cup Plug	N805212
5. Seal	7A248	24. Solid Cup Plug	N805212
6. Bolt and Washer Assembly	N805260	25. Solid Cup Plug	N805212
7. Main Regulator Valve	7C338	26. Solid Cup Plug	N805212
8. Spring Retainer	7E337	27. Orificed Cup Plug (.077-.083 inch diameter orifice)	N805213
9. Outer Spring (Green)	7A270	28. Orificed Cup Plug (.049-.055 inch diameter orifice)	N805214
10. Inner Spring (Green)	7G498		
11. Main Regulator Booster Valve	7D003	29. Air Bleed Check Valve Assembly	7H000
12. Main Regulator Booster Sleeve	7D002	30. Inner Gerotor Gear	7C010
13. Retainer	N660225	31. Outer Gerotor Gear	7C011
14. Converter Regulator Valve	7G307	32. Orifice Cup Plug (.057-.062 inch diameter orifice)	N805802
15. Spring (White)	7G316		
16. Plug	7F187	33. Valve Assembly	7A250
17. Clip	7G007	34. Solid Cup Plug	N805175
18. Converter Clutch Control Valve	7L318	35. Front Input Shaft Bushing	7B261
19. Spring (Yellow)	7L490	36. Rear Input Shaft Bushing	7D018

FIGURE 11–25 E4OD gerotor pump. (Courtesy of Ford Motor Company)

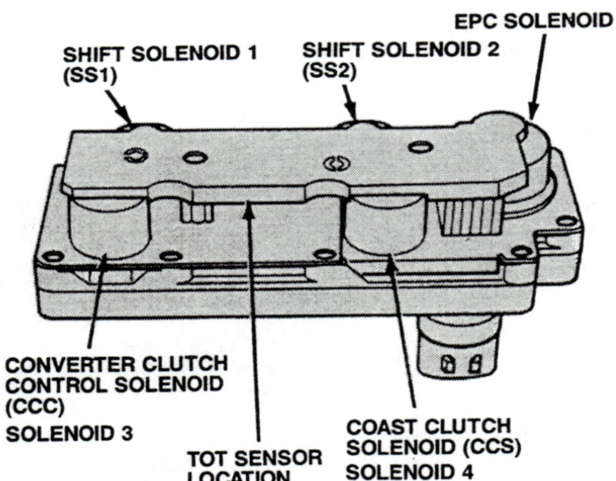

FIGURE 11–26 E4OD solenoids on valve body. (Courtesy of Ford Motor Company)

11.4.2 Power Flow

1. *Neutral (N)*
In neutral none of the coupling or holding devices are applied and the converter clutch is also released.

2. *First Gear (D1)*
In first, second, and third gears the overdrive gear set is in direct drive. This is accomplished by the action of the overdrive one-way clutch, which couples the planetary carrier and ring gear together to provide a direct drive.

The main gear set has the forward clutch and low–reverse one-way clutch applied, which provides a 2.71 to 1 gear ratio (Figure 11–28).

3. *Second Gear (D2)*
The overdrive gear set remains in direct drive. The forward clutch remains applied to drive the front ring gear and the band is applied to hold the sun gear. This combination causes a gear reduction of 1.54 : 1, as shown in Figure 11–29.

4. *Third Gear (D3)*
The overdrive gear set is still operating in direct drive. In the main gear set the band is released, but the forward clutch remains applied, driving the front ring gear. The direct clutch is applied, which drives the sun gear, causing direct drive, one-to-one operation (Figure 11–30).

5. *Fourth Gear (D4)*
In fourth gear the main gear set remains in direct drive, while in the overdrive gear set the overdrive clutch is applied, which holds the sun gear as the reaction member, causing an overdrive gear ratio of 0.71 : 1 (Figure 11–31).

6. *Reverse Gear (R)*
In reverse gear the overdrive gear set is in direct drive with the coast clutch applied. In the main gear set, the direct clutch is applied, driving the sun gear while the reverse clutch is applied, holding the rear planetary carrier as the reaction member, which provides the reverse rotation at a gear ratio of 2.18 : 1.

FIGURE 11–27 E4OD solenoid application chart. (Courtesy of Ford Motor Company)

Gear Selector Position	Gear	Shift Control		Converter Clutch Control Sol. 3	Coast Clutch Control Sol. 4
		Sol. 1	Sol. 2		
Ⓓ	4 3 2 1	OFF OFF ON ON	OFF ON ON OFF	ON/OFF Based on EEC-IV Strategy	OFF OFF OFF OFF
Ⓓ Overdrive Cancel Switch Pressed	3 2 1	OFF ON ON	ON ON OFF		ON ON ON
2	2	OFF	OFF		OFF
1	1	ON	OFF	OFF	OFF

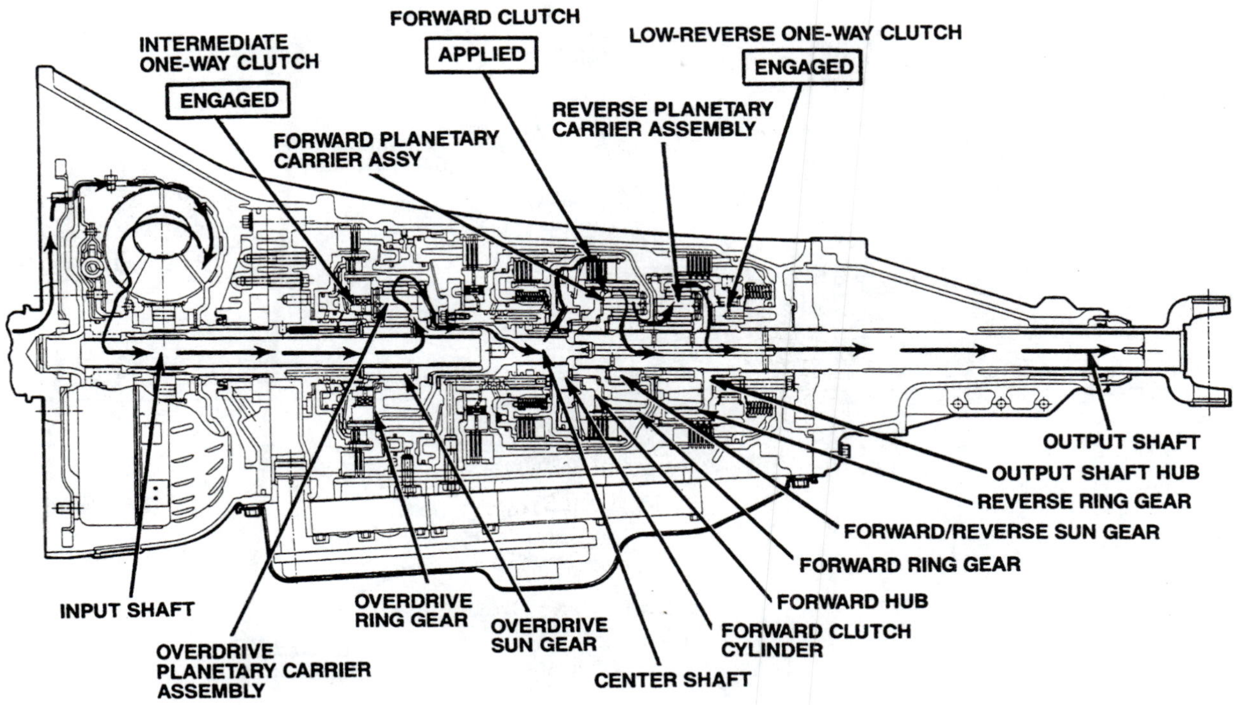

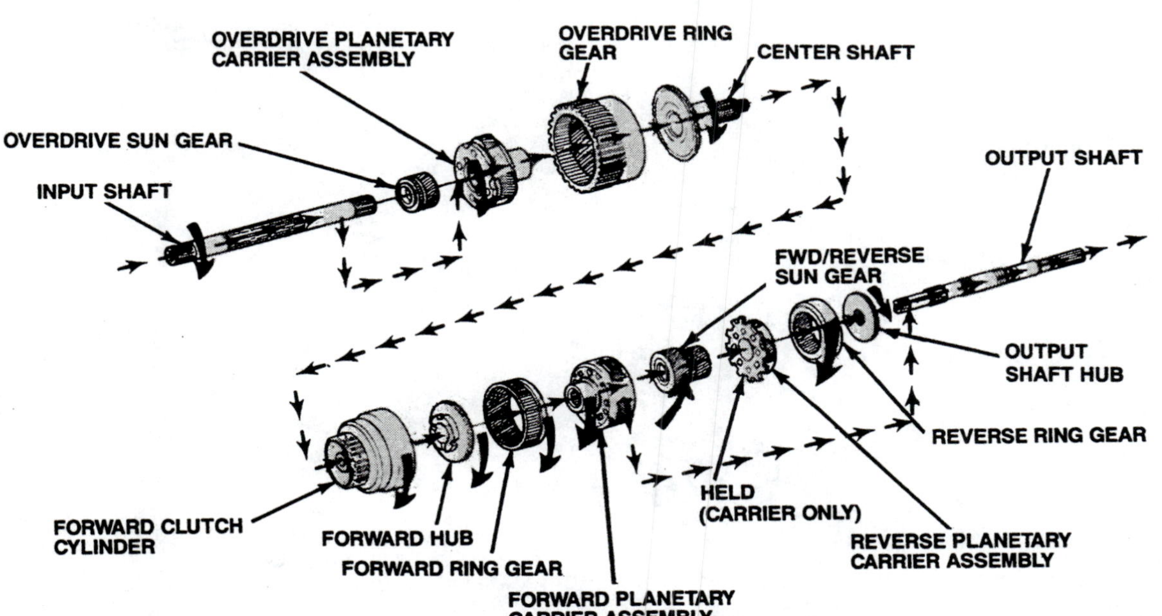

FIGURE 11–28 E4OD first gear. (Courtesy of Ford Motor Company)

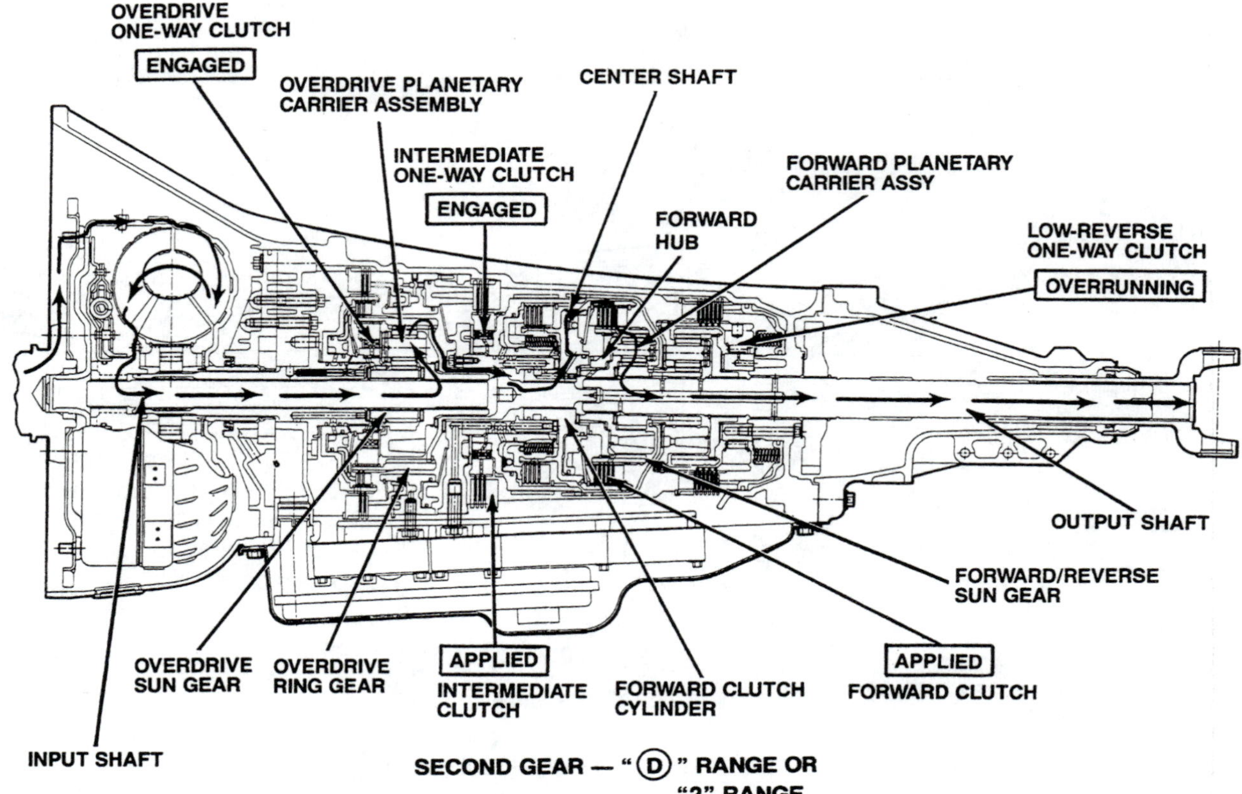

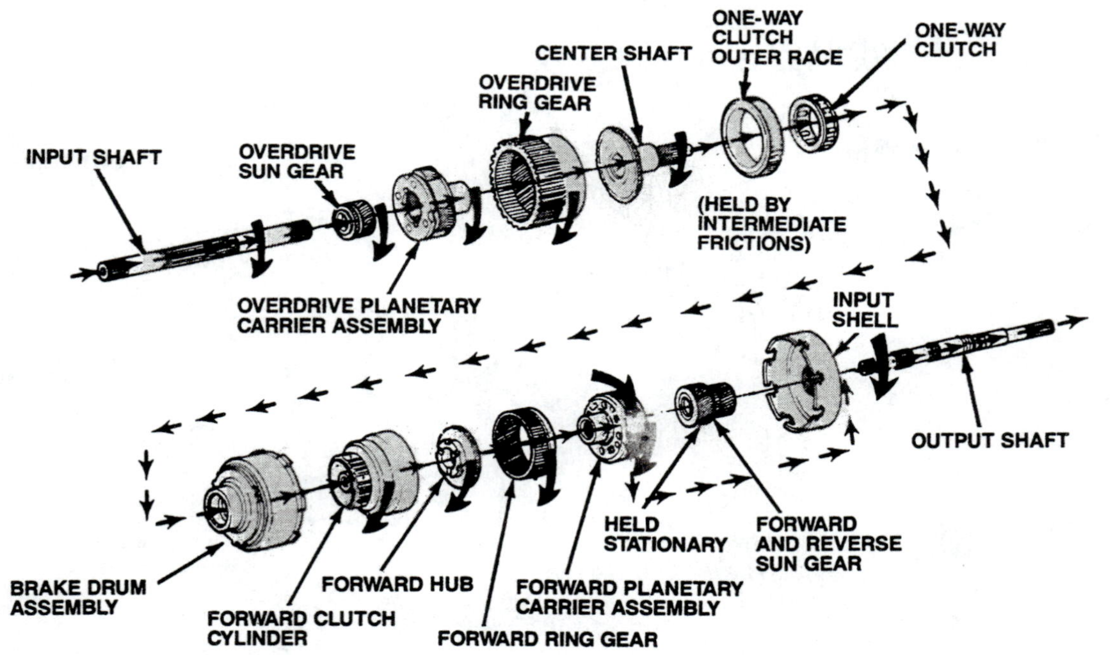

FIGURE 11–29 E4OD second gear. (Courtesy of Ford Motor Company)

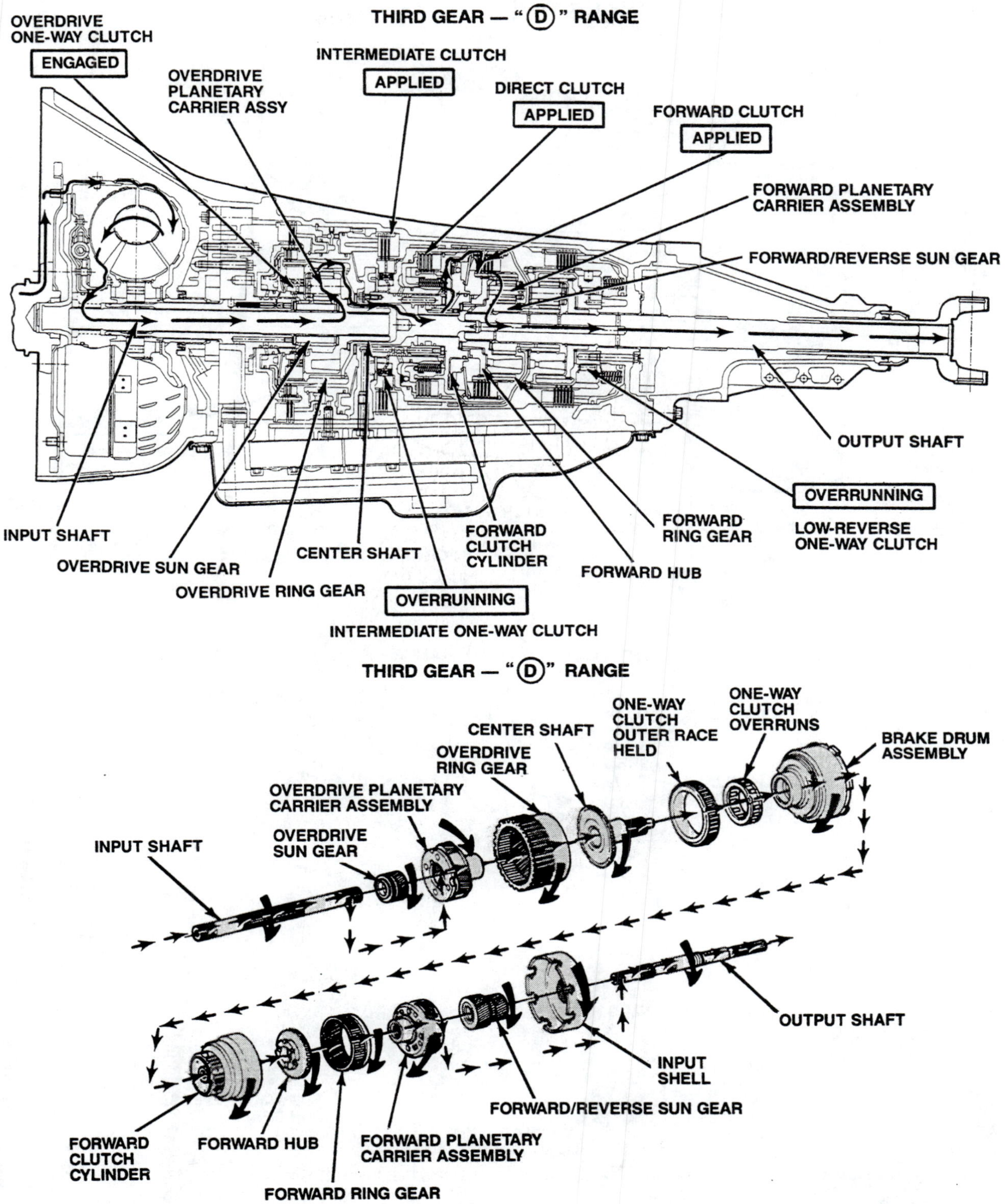

THIRD GEAR — "(D)" RANGE

OVERDRIVE ONE-WAY CLUTCH
ENGAGED
OVERDRIVE PLANETARY CARRIER ASSY
INTERMEDIATE CLUTCH
APPLIED
DIRECT CLUTCH
APPLIED
FORWARD CLUTCH
APPLIED
FORWARD PLANETARY CARRIER ASSEMBLY
FORWARD/REVERSE SUN GEAR
OUTPUT SHAFT
OVERRUNNING
LOW-REVERSE ONE-WAY CLUTCH
FORWARD RING GEAR
FORWARD HUB
FORWARD CLUTCH CYLINDER
CENTER SHAFT
INPUT SHAFT
OVERDRIVE SUN GEAR
OVERDRIVE RING GEAR
OVERRUNNING
INTERMEDIATE ONE-WAY CLUTCH

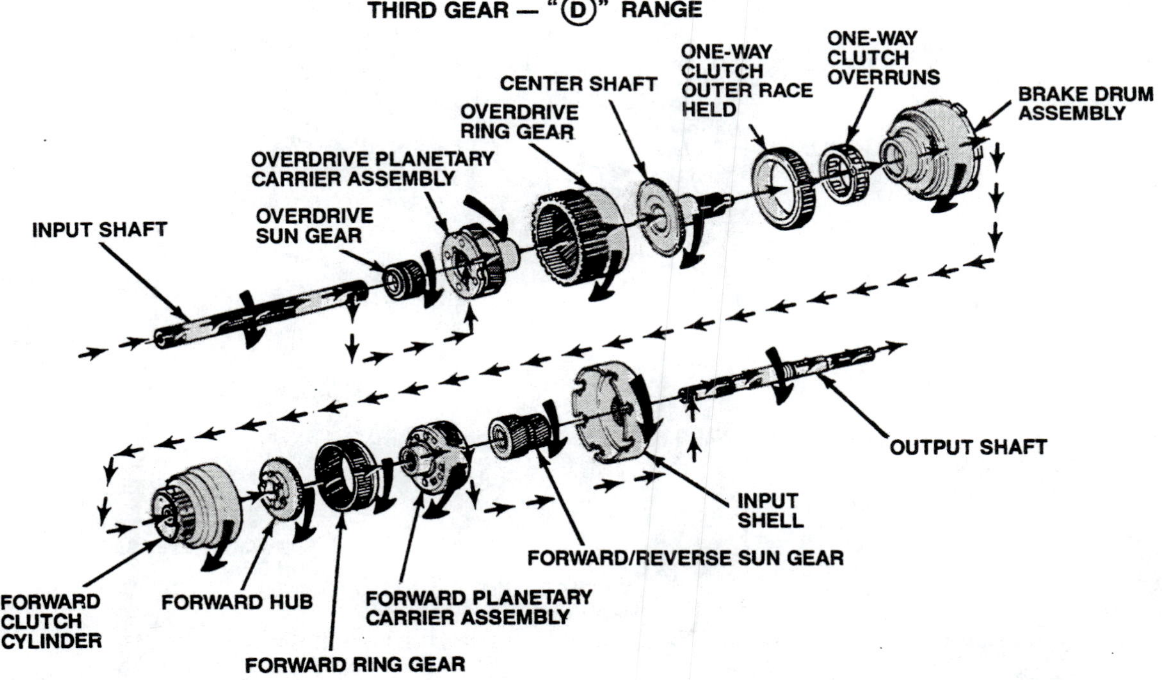

FIGURE 11–30 E4OD third gear. (Courtesy of Ford Motor Company)

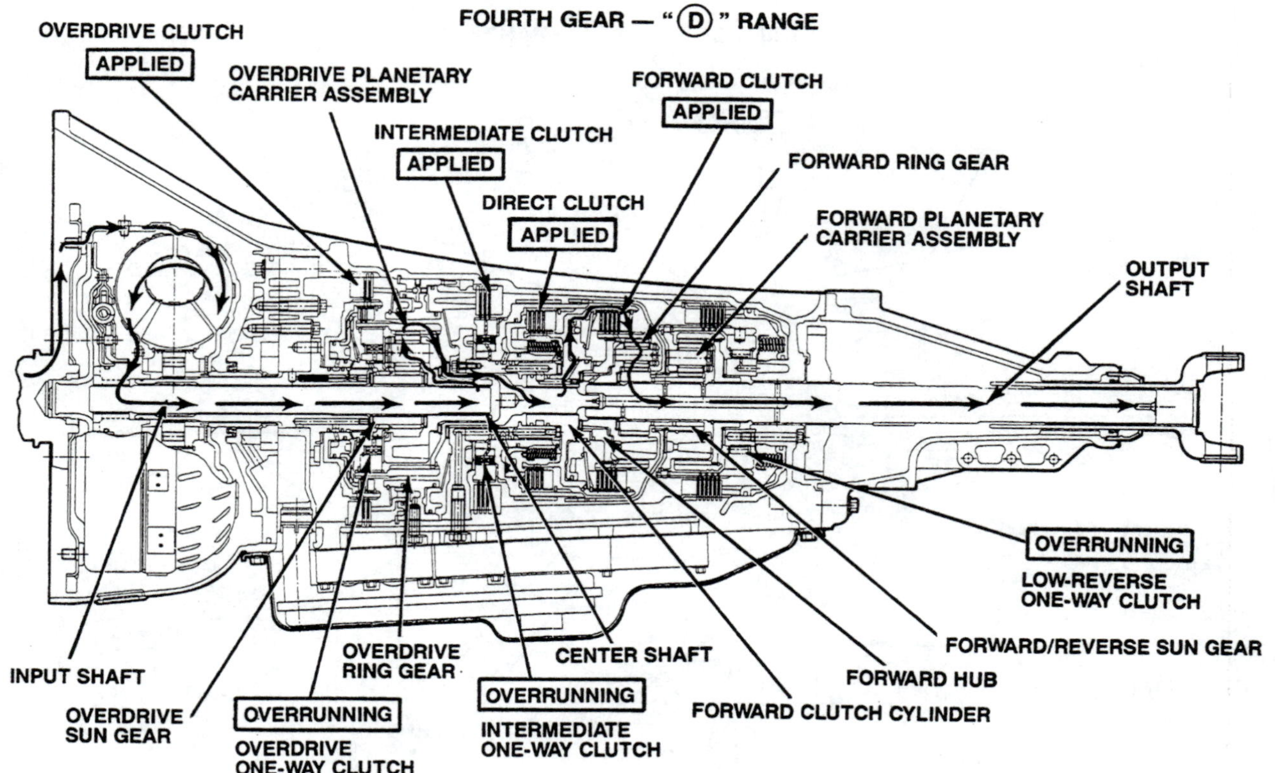

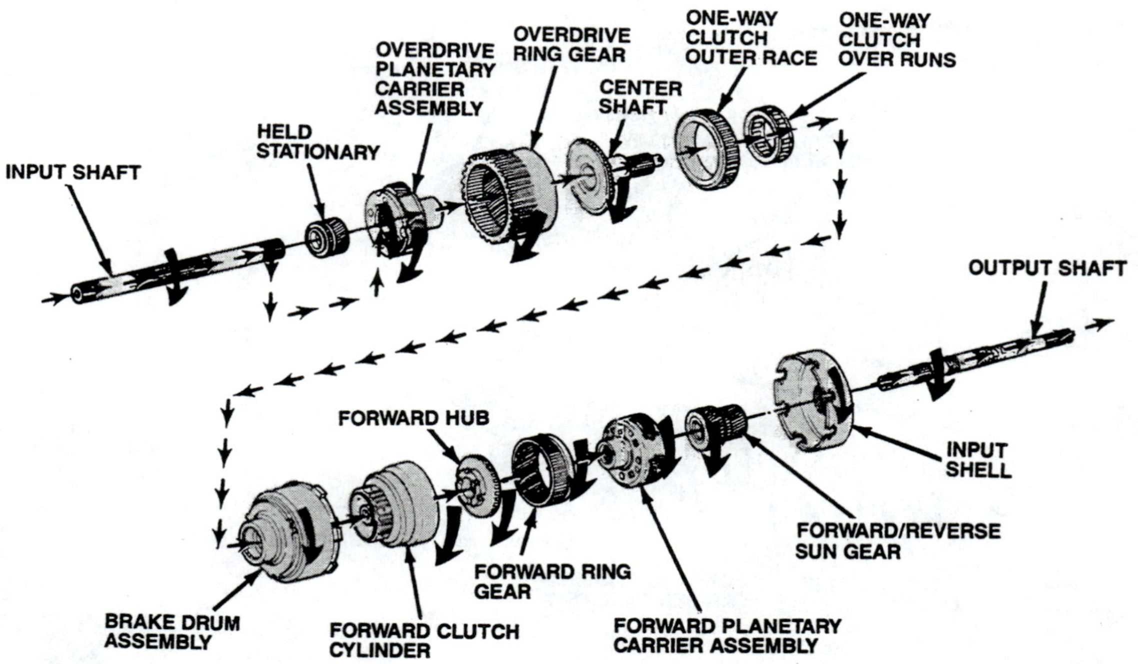

FIGURE 11–31 E4OD fourth gear. (Courtesy of Ford Motor Company)

11.4.3 Clutch and Band Charts

The clutch and band charts for the E4OD are shown in Figures 11–32 and 11–33.

11.4.4 Identification

The E4OD can be identified by the shape if the pan gasket (Figure 11–34) and by the manufacturer's code.

11.4.5 Components

Review the following illustrations to learn the features of the E40D.

Exploded view, Figure 11–35
Sensor location, Figure 11–36
ECA inputs and outputs, Figure 11–37
Clutch assemblies, Figure 11–38
Forward drive, Figure 11–39
Low–reverse drive, Figure 11–40

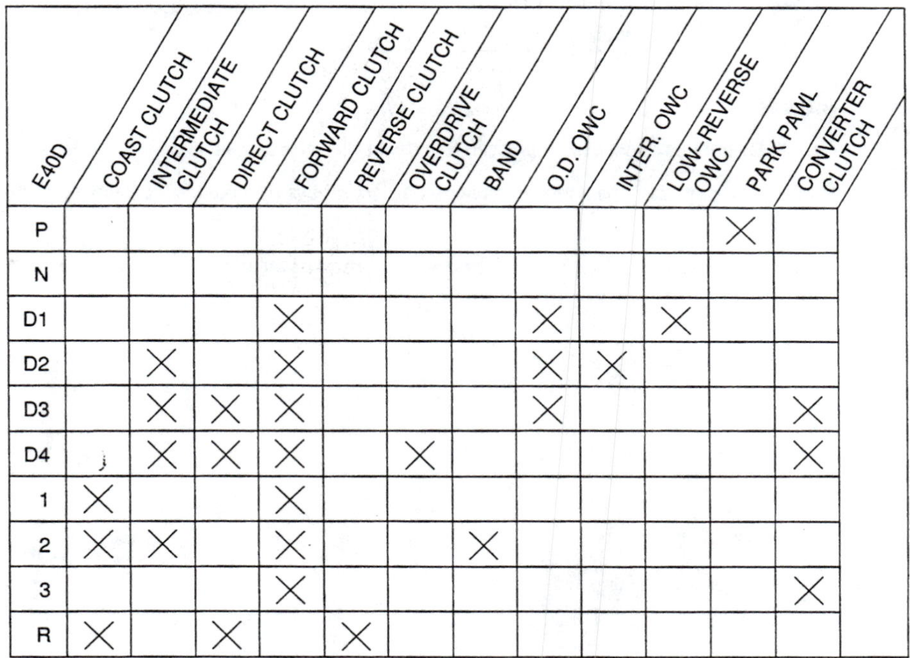

E40D	COAST CLUTCH	INTERMEDIATE CLUTCH	DIRECT CLUTCH	FORWARD CLUTCH	REVERSE CLUTCH	OVERDRIVE CLUTCH	BAND	O.D. OWC	INTER. OWC	LOW–REVERSE OWC	PARK PAWL	CONVERTER CLUTCH
P											X	
N												
D1				X				X		X		
D2		X		X				X	X			
D3		X	X	X				X				X
D4		X	X	X		X						X
1	X			X								
2	X	X		X			X					
3				X								X
R	X		X		X							

FIGURE 11–32 E4OD clutch and band chart, standardized version.

Gear	Friction Elements							One-Way Clutches Drive		
	Coast	Inter-mediate	Direct	Forward	Reverse	Over-Drive	Band	O/D OWC	Inter-mediate OWC	Low Reverse OWC
	1	2	3	4	5	6	7	8	9	10
Ⓓ first	*			apply				hold		hold
				D1 Coasting ⟶				OR*		OR
Ⓓ second	*	apply		apply				hold	hold	OR
				D2 Coasting ⟶				OR*	OR	OR
Ⓓ third	*	apply	apply	apply				hold	OR	OR
				D3 Coasting ⟶				OR*	OR	OR
Ⓓ fourth		apply	apply	apply		apply		OR	OR	OR
				D4 Coasting ⟶				OR	OR	OR
1	apply			apply	apply			INEFF		INEFF
2	apply	apply		apply			apply		INEFF'	OR
R	apply		apply		apply			INEFF		INEFF

OD — Overdrive
OWC — One-Way Clutch
OR — Overrunning
* — In D Range with Overdrive Cancel Switch pressed, the Coast Clutch is applied and the OD One-Way is by passed.
INEFF — Indicates that a related component renders the one-way inoperative (without load) unless the component slips.

FIGURE 11–33 E4OD clutch and band chart, manufacturer's version. (Courtesy of Ford Motor Company)

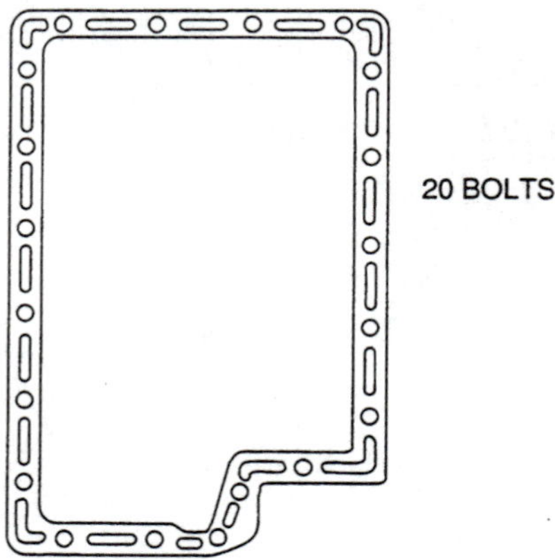

FIGURE 11–34 E4OD pan gasket shape. (Courtesy of Ford Motor Company)

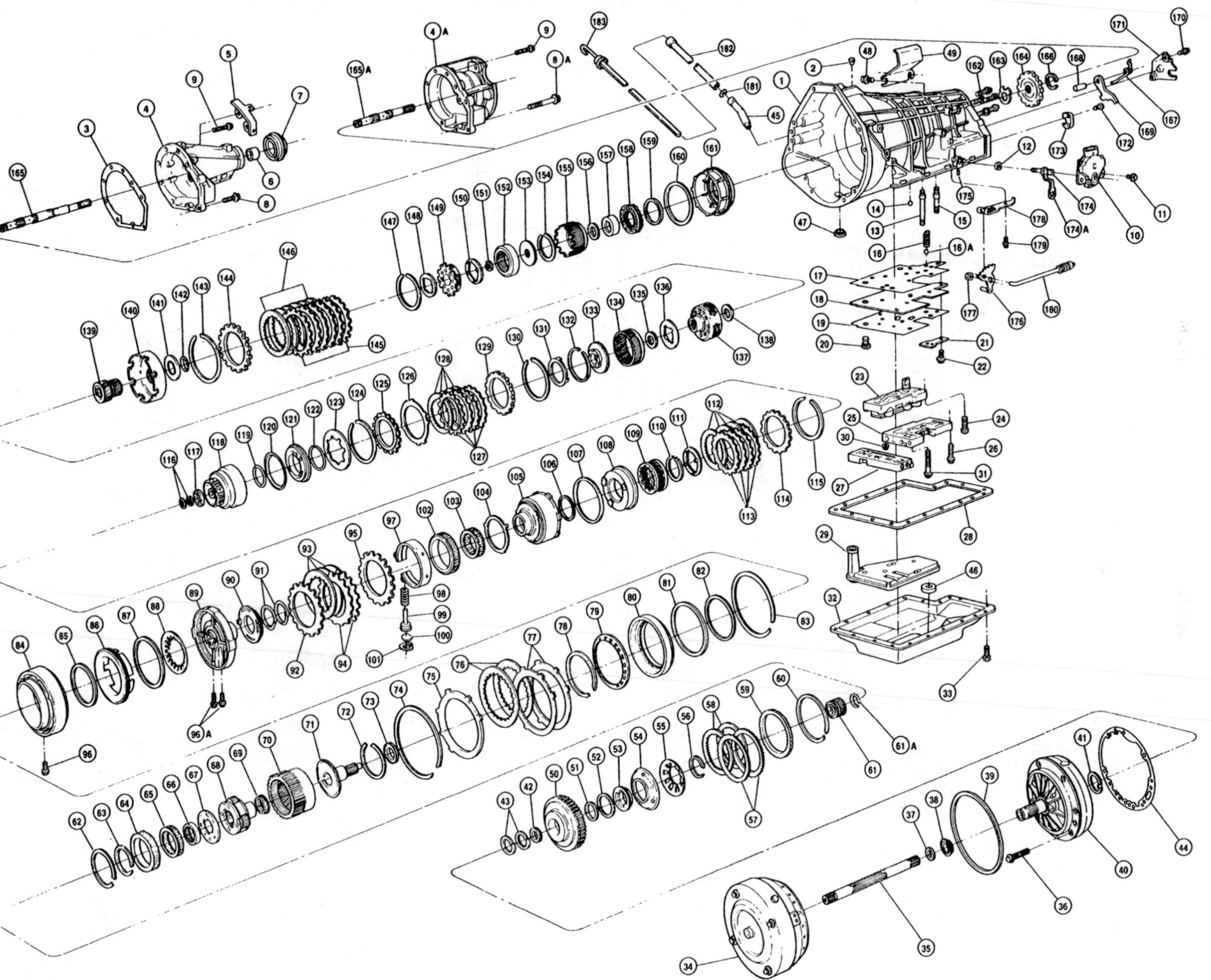

FIGURE 11–35 E4OD exploded view of transmission. (Courtesy of Ford Motor Company)

E4OD EXPLODED VIEW LEGEND

No.	Part No.	Description
1.	7005	CASE ASSEMBLY
2.	7034	VENT ASSEMBLY
3.	7086	GASKET — EXTENSION HOUSING
4.	7A039-CB	EXTENSION ASSEMBLY (4X2)
#	7A041	— EXTENSION & BUSHING ASSY.
#	7A040	— EXTENSION
4A.	7A039-DA	EXTENSION ASSEMBLY (4X4)
	7A039-EA	EXTENSION ASSEMBLY (SUPERDUTY)
#5.	7H102	BRACKET — WIRING
6.	7A034	BUSHING — EXTENSION HOUSING (4X2)
7.	7052	SEAL — EXTENSION HOUSING (4X2)
8.	N605802-S36	BOLT — EXTENSION (4X2 BOTTOM) (2 PCS.) M10X1.5X35MM
8A.	N606569-S36	BOLT — EXTENSION (SUPERDUTY & 4X4 BOTTOM) (2 PCS.) M10X1.5X90MM
9.	N605803-S36	BOLT — EXTENSION (TOP) (7 PCS.) M10X1.5X40MM
10.	7F293	SENSOR — MANUAL LEVER POSITION
11.	N805312-S100	BOLT ASSEMBLY (2 PCS.) M6X1.0X30MM
12.	7B498	SEAL — MANUAL LEVER
13.	N805331-S	STUD — CASE TO SOLENOID BODY (1 PC.) M6X1.0X79MM
14.	7E195	BALL — RUBBER CHECK (10 PCS.) (2 IN MAIN CONTROL)
	379581-S	BALL — STEEL CHECK (1 PC.)
15.	N805330-S	STUD — CASE TO CONTROL ASSEMBLY (4 PCS.) M6X1.0X61.25MM
16.	7D017	EPC BLOW-OFF SPRING
16A.	353078-S	EPC BLOW-OFF BALL
17.	7D100	GASKET — SEPARATOR
#18.	7A008	PLATE — SEPARATOR
19.	7C155	GASKET — SEPARATOR
20.	7G308	SCREEN — SOLENOID
#21.	7F282	PLATE — SEPARATOR PLATE REINFORCING
22.	N605772-S	BOLT (3 PCS.) M6X1.0X16MM
23.	7G391	SOLENOID BODY ASSEMBLY
24.	N805329-S	BOLT — TORX HEAD (9 PCS.) M6X1.0X40MM
25.	7A100	MAIN CONTROL BODY ASSEMBLY
26.	N805326-S	BOLT (18 PCS.) M6X1.0X42.5MM
27.	7G422	ACCUMULATOR BODY ASSEMBLY
28.	7A191	GASKET — OIL PAN
29.	7G186-AA	FILTER AND SEAL ASSEMBLY (4X2)
	7G186-BA	FILTER AND SEAL ASSEMBLY (4X4)
30.	N805328-S	NUT (5 PCS.) M6X1.0
31.	N805327-S	BOLT (7 PCS.) M6X1.0X66MM
32.	7A264-FA	PAN — OIL (4X2)
	7A264-GA	PAN — OIL (4X4)
33.	N605902-S36	BOLT — OIL PAN (20 PCS.) M8X1.25X12MM
34.	7902	TORQUE CONVERTER ASSEMBLY
	87650-S2	— PLUG — CONVERTER DRAIN 1/8 IN-27
35.	7017	SHAFT — INPUT
36.	N805260-S	BOLT & WASHER ASSEMBLY — PUMP (9 PCS.) M8X1.25X65MM
	7G379	— WASHER — REPLACEMENT (9 PCS.)
37.	7L323	SEAL RING — TEFLON
38.	7A248	SEAL — CONVERTER HUB
39.	7D441	SEAL — SQUARE CUT O.D. PUMP
40.	7A103	PUMP ASSEMBLY
41.	7D014	WASHER — PUMP THRUST
42.	7E486	NEEDLE BEARING ASSEMBLY
43.	7G402	SEAL RING — TEFLON (2 PCS.)
44.	7A136	GASKET — PUMP
45.	7N463	STUB TUBE
46.	7L027	MAGNET — PAN
47.	7N171	PLUG — CONVERTER ACCESS
48.	N605770-S36	BOLT — HEAT SHIELD (2 PCS.)
49.	7A434	HEAT SHIELD — SOLENOID BODY CONNECTOR
50.	7G387	COAST CLUTCH CYLINDER ASSEMBLY
51.	7A548-JA	SEAL — INNER
52.	7A548-EA	SEAL — OUTER
53.	7G419	PISTON
54.	7N519	RING — PISTON APPLY
55.	7B070-EA	SPRING — PISTON RETURN
56.	N804949-S	RING — RETAINING
57.	7B442-CA	PLATE — COAST CLUTCH EXTERNAL SPLINE
58.	7B164-CA	PLATE — COAST CLUTCH INTERNAL SPLINE
59.	7B437-CA	PLATE — COAST CLUTCH PRESSURE
60.	N804950-S	RING — RETAINING (SELECTIVE FIT)
	N804951-S	RING — RETAINING
	N804952-S	RING — RETAINING
61.	7670	GEAR — OVERDRIVE SUN
61A.	377300-S	RING — RETAINING
62.	377155-S	RING — RETAINING (OUTER RACE TO OVERDRIVE RING GEAR)
63.	377135-S	RING — RETAINING (OVERDRIVE OWC TO OUTER RACE)
*64.	7G389	RACE — OVERDRIVE ONE WAY CLUTCH OUTER
*65.	7G381	CLUTCH ASSEMBLY — OVERDRIVE ONE WAY
*66.	7G388	RACE — OVERDRIVE ONE WAY CLUTCH INNER
67.	7G400	WASHER — THRUST
68.	7E031	CARRIER ASSEMBLY — OVERDRIVE PLANETARY
#	7L676	— CARRIER
#	7D008-CA	— PLANET GEARS (4 PCS.)
#	7A238-CA	— PLANET SHAFTS (4 PCS.)
#	7A242-AA	— THRUST WASHERS (8 PCS.)
#	7D037-BA	— NEEDLE BEARINGS (80 PCS.)
#	380225-S	— RETAINING PINS (4 PCS.)
#	7E486	— NEEDLE BEARING ASSEMBLY
69.	7G128	NEEDLE BEARING ASSEMBLY
70.	7653	GEAR — OVERDRIVE RING
71	7G382	CENTER SHAFT
72.	7G375	RING — RETAINING (CENTER SHAFT TO OVERDRIVE RING GEAR)
73.	7G178	NEEDLE BEARING ASSEMBLY
74.	7B421	RING — OVERDRIVE RETAINING
75.	7B066-BB	PLATE — OVERDRIVE CLUTCH PRESSURE
76.	7B164-EA	PLATE — OVERDRIVE CLUTCH INTERNAL SPLINE
77.	7B442-DA	PLATE — OVERDRIVE CLUTCH EXTERNAL SPLINE
78.	N804948-S	RING — RETURN SPRING RETAINING
79.	7B070-CA	SPRING — OVERDRIVE RETURN
80.	7G418	PISTON — OVERDRIVE
81.	7A548	SEAL — OVERDRIVE OUTER
82.	7F225	SEAL — OVERDRIVE INNER (SAME AS INTERMEDIATE INNER)
83.	7B421	RING — INT./O.D. CYLINDER RETAINING
84.	7G385	CYLINDER — INTERMEDIATE/OVERDRIVE
85.	7F225	SEAL — INTERMEDIATE INNER
86.	7E005	PISTON — INTERMEDIATE
87.	7F224	SEAL — INTERMEDIATE OUTER
88.	7B070-DB	SPRING — INTERMEDIATE RETURN
89.	7G033	SUPPORT ASSEMBLY — CENTER
90.	7L326	WASHER — THRUST
91.	7D429-A	SEAL — DIRECT CLUTCH CAST IRON (2 PCS.)
92.	7B066-CA	PLATE — INTERMEDIATE CLUTCH APPLY
93.	7F219	PLATE — INTERMEDIATE CLUTCH INTERNAL SPLINE
94.	7B442	PLATE — INTERMEDIATE CLUTCH EXTERNAL SPLINE
95.	7B437	PLATE — INTERMEDIATE CLUTCH PRESSURE
96.	N805310-S101	BOLT — CYLINDER HYDRAULIC FEED (1 PC.) M10X1.5X24MM
96A.	N805311-S101	BOLT — CENTER SUPPORT HYDRAULIC FEED (2 PCS.) M12X1.75X31MM
97.	7D034	BAND ASSEMBLY
98.	7D028	SPRING — SERVO RETURN
99.	7E221	PISTON ASSEMBLY — SERVO

#NOT SERVICED
*SERVICED IN KITS ONLY

FIGURE 11–35 *(continued)*

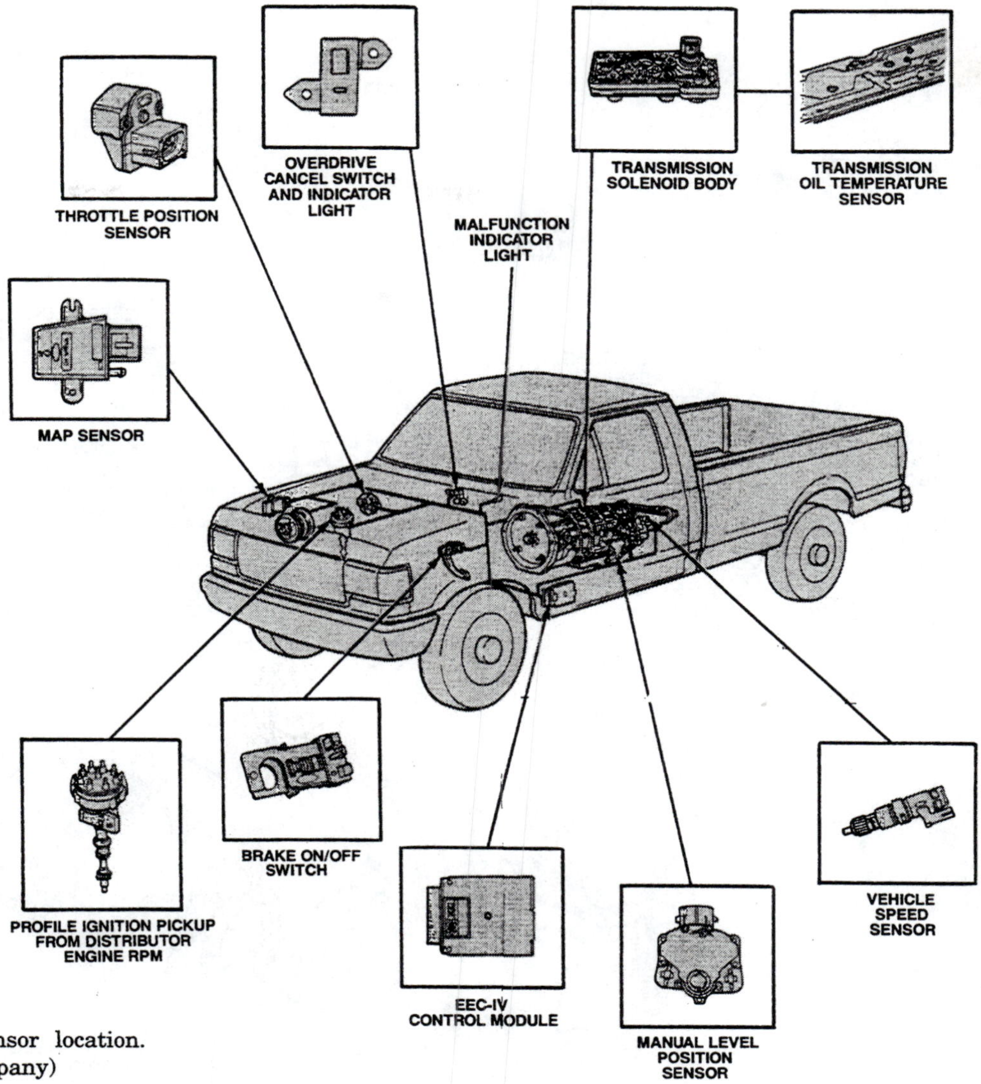

OVERDRIVE CANCEL SWITCH AND INDICATOR LIGHT
TRANSMISSION SOLENOID BODY
TRANSMISSION OIL TEMPERATURE SENSOR
THROTTLE POSITION SENSOR
MALFUNCTION INDICATOR LIGHT
MAP SENSOR
BRAKE ON/OFF SWITCH
PROFILE IGNITION PICKUP FROM DISTRIBUTOR ENGINE RPM
EEC-IV CONTROL MODULE
MANUAL LEVEL POSITION SENSOR
VEHICLE SPEED SENSOR

FIGURE 11–36 E4OD sensor location. (Courtesy of Ford Motor Company)

INPUTS
OUTPUTS
FIPL SENSOR
BP SENSOR
ENGINE RPM SENSOR
BOO SWITCH
MANUAL LEVER POSITION SENSOR
VSS
TOT SENSOR
OVERDRIVE CANCEL SWITCH
TRANSMISSION ECA
SOLENOID 1 (SHIFT CONTROL)
SOLENOID 2 (SHIFT CONTROL)
SOLENOID 3 (CONVERTER CLUTCH CONTROL)
SOLENOID 4 (COAST CLUTCH CONTROL)
VARIABLE FORCE SOLENOID (VFS) (LINE PRESSURE CONTROL)

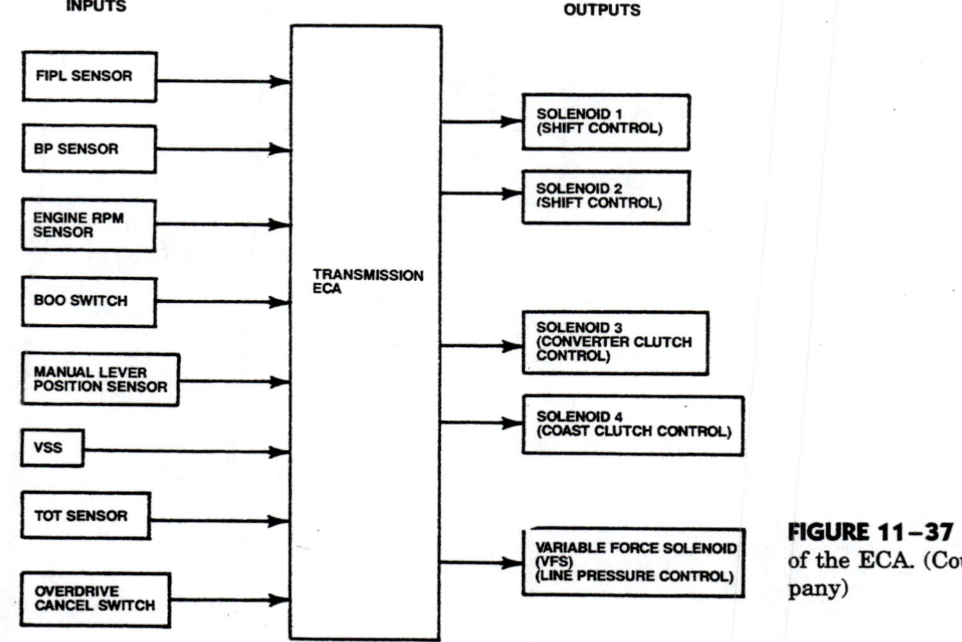

FIGURE 11–37 E4OD inputs and outputs of the ECA. (Courtesy of Ford Motor Company)

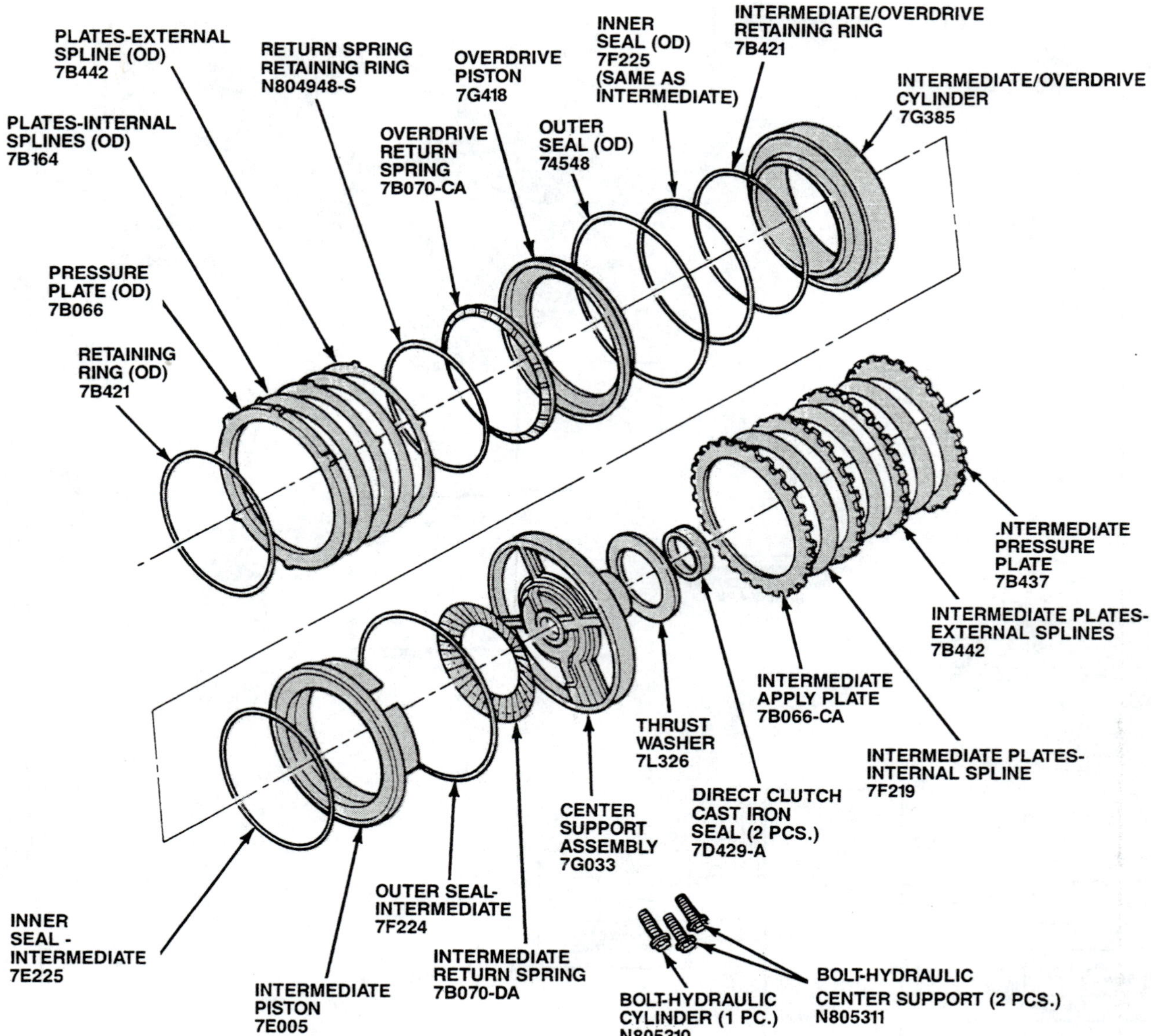

FIGURE 11–38 E4OD clutch assemblies. (Courtesy of Ford Motor Company)

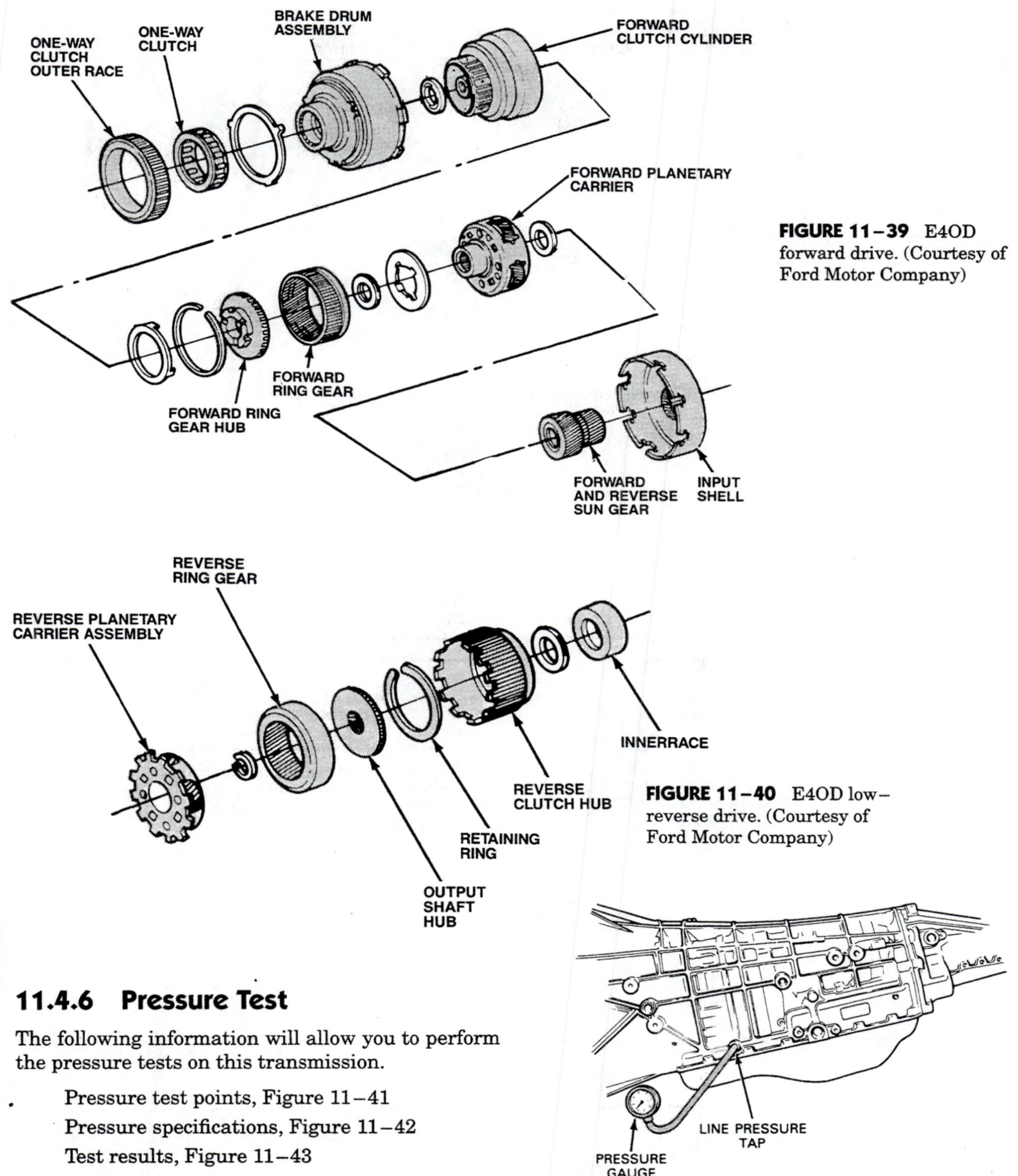

FIGURE 11–39 E4OD forward drive. (Courtesy of Ford Motor Company)

FIGURE 11–40 E4OD low–reverse drive. (Courtesy of Ford Motor Company)

FIGURE 11–41 E4OD pressure test points. (Courtesy of Ford Motor Company)

11.4.6 Pressure Test

The following information will allow you to perform the pressure tests on this transmission.

Pressure test points, Figure 11–41
Pressure specifications, Figure 11–42
Test results, Figure 11–43

11.4.7 Air Test

The air test locations are shown in the illustration showing air test passages, Figure 11–44.

Range	Idle		Stall	
	5.8L			
	KPA	PSI	KPA	PSI
P, N	379-448	55-65	—	—
R	510-682	74-99	1082-1255	157-182
Ⓓ, 2	379-448	55-65	1076-1200	156-174
1	510-682	74-99	1082-1255	157-182
	7.3L Diesel			
P, N	379-448	55-65	—	—
R	510-682	74-99	1110-1282	161-186
Ⓓ, 2	379-448	55-65	1076-1200	156-174
1	510-682	74-99	1110-1282	161-186
	7.5L			
P, N	379-448	55-65	—	—
R	510-682	74-99	1082-1255	157-182
Ⓓ, 2	379-448	55-65	1076-1200	156-174
1	510-682	74-99	1082-1255	157-182

FIGURE 11–42 E4OD pressure specifications. (Courtesy of Ford Motor Company)

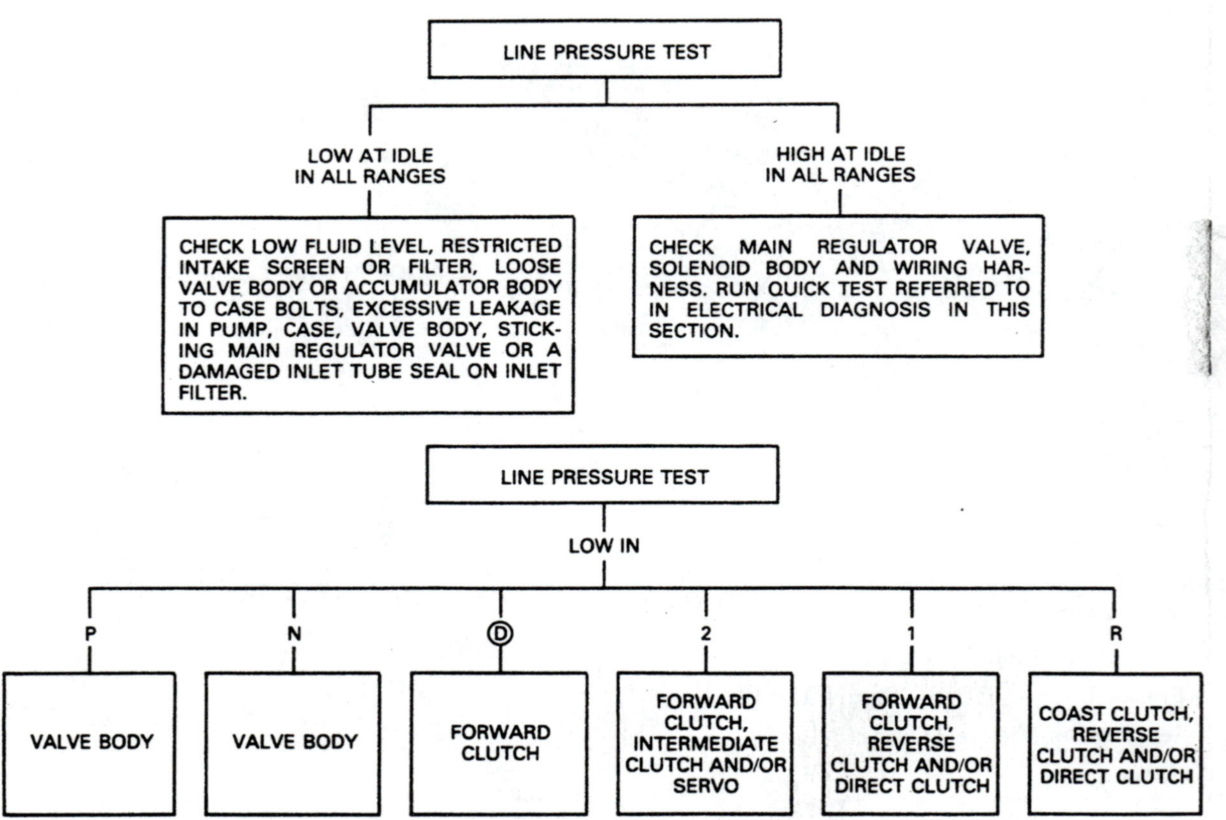

FIGURE 11–43 E4OD test results. (Courtesy of Ford Motor Company)

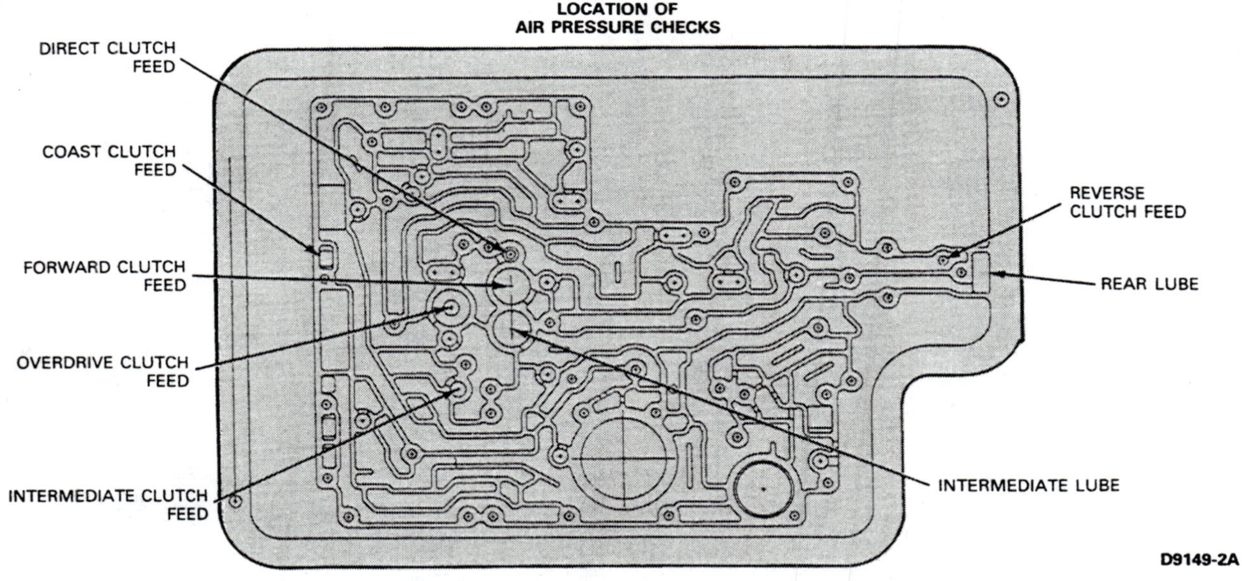

FIGURE 11–44 E4OD air test. (Courtesy of Ford Motor Company)

11.5 ATX: FWD THREE-SPEED TRANSAXLE

11.5.1 Basic Description

The ATX transaxle is a very compact unit that packages a three-speed automatic transmission and final drive assembly into a minimum amount of space (Figure 11–45).

The transaxle description is divided into eight areas. All of the transmissions/transaxles are described in this manner to make their comparison easier.

1. *Torque Converter*
The ATX uses a unique torque converter that has dual outputs feed through a planetary gear set (Figure 11–46). The output are the converter sun gear, which drives the turbine shaft, and the converter pinion carrier, which drives the intermediate shaft. By using various members of the converter planetary gear set as the output member, the power flow can switch from hydraulic to mechanical. This design of converter was used only a few years and then discontinued.

2. *Gear Train*
A Ravignaux gear set is used to provide a three-speed gear train. The front sun gear and rear sun gear act as reaction members, and the pinion carrier is the output member.

3. *Coupling Devices*
The direct clutch connects the intermediate shaft to the front sun gear. The intermediate clutch connects the intermediate shaft to the ring gear and the one-way clutch connects the turbine shaft to the front sun gear.

4. *Holding Devices*
The reverse clutch is used to hold the ring gear and the band is used to hold the rear sun gear.

5. *Pump*
A gear crescent oil pump is used in the ATX transaxle. The pump is driven by a long oil pump shaft, which splines into the torque converter (Figure 11–47).

6. *Shift Control*
The shift control system on the ATX transaxle is fully hydraulic and does not use electronic controls at this time.

7. *Governor*
The ATX transaxle is the first Ford transmission to use a drop-in governor (Figure 11–48).

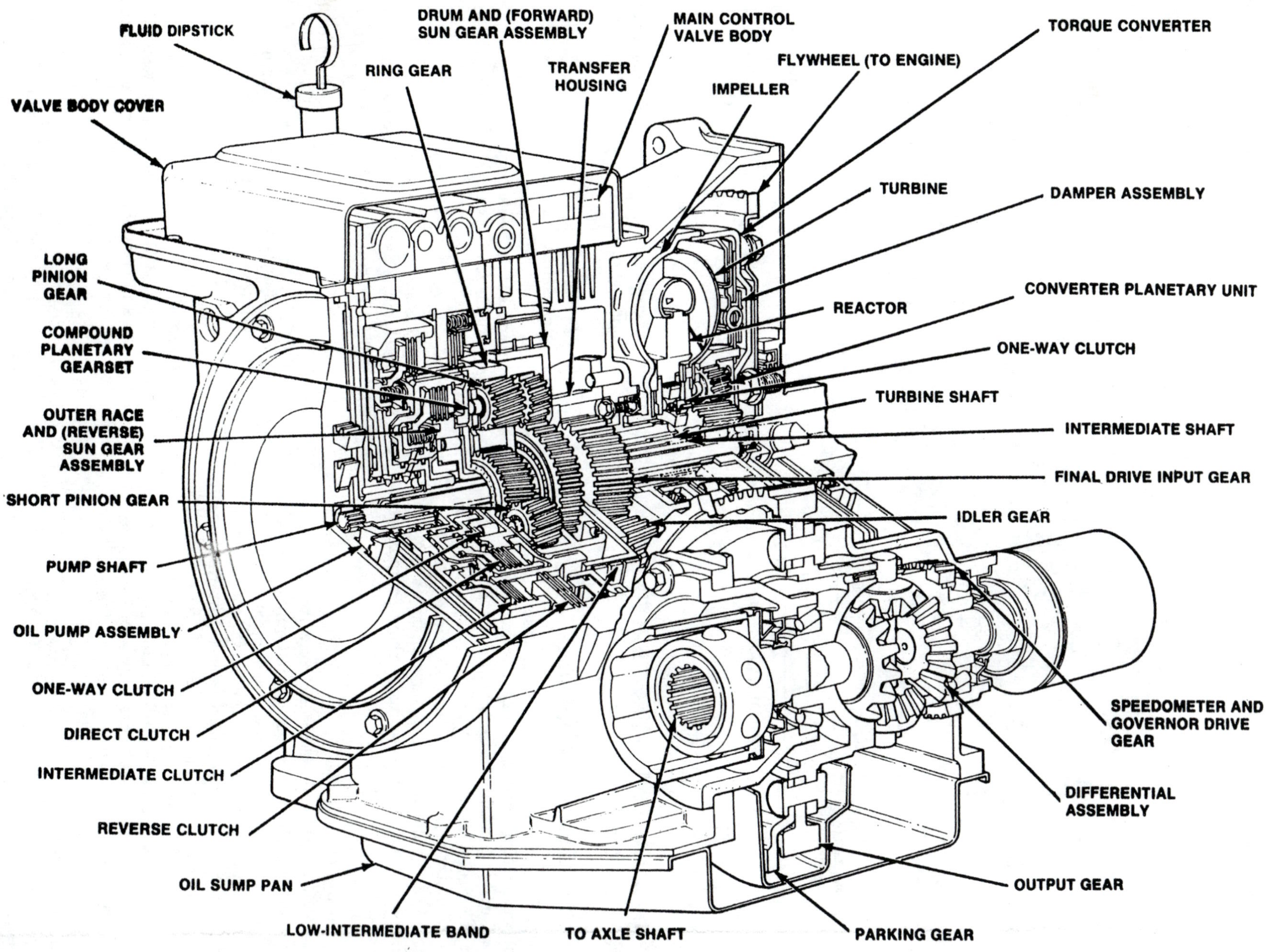

FIGURE 11–45 ATX cutaway view. (Courtesy of Ford)

FIGURE 11–46 ATX torque converter. (Courtesy of Ford)

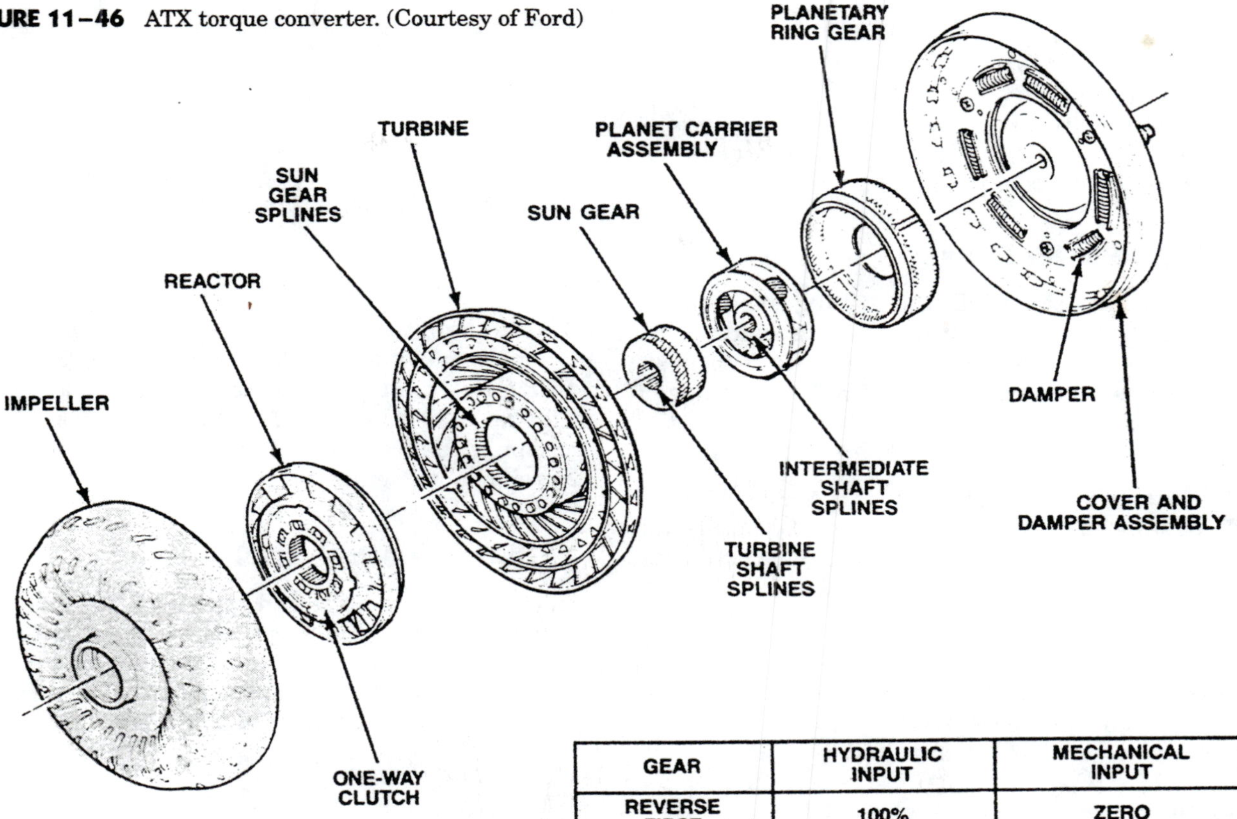

PLANETARY RING GEAR
TURBINE
PLANET CARRIER ASSEMBLY
SUN GEAR SPLINES
SUN GEAR
REACTOR
IMPELLER
DAMPER
INTERMEDIATE SHAFT SPLINES
COVER AND DAMPER ASSEMBLY
TURBINE SHAFT SPLINES
ONE-WAY CLUTCH

GEAR	HYDRAULIC INPUT	MECHANICAL INPUT
REVERSE FIRST	100%	ZERO
SECOND	38%	62%
HIGH	7%	93%

INLET CAVITY FROM SUMP
BODY
CRESCENT
DRIVEN GEAR
DRIVE GEAR
DRIVE GEAR INSERT
SEAL
OUTLET (PRESSURE)
TEFLON SEALS
DRIVE SHAFT
PUMP SUPPORT
CLUTCH SUPPORT SURFACE
GASKET

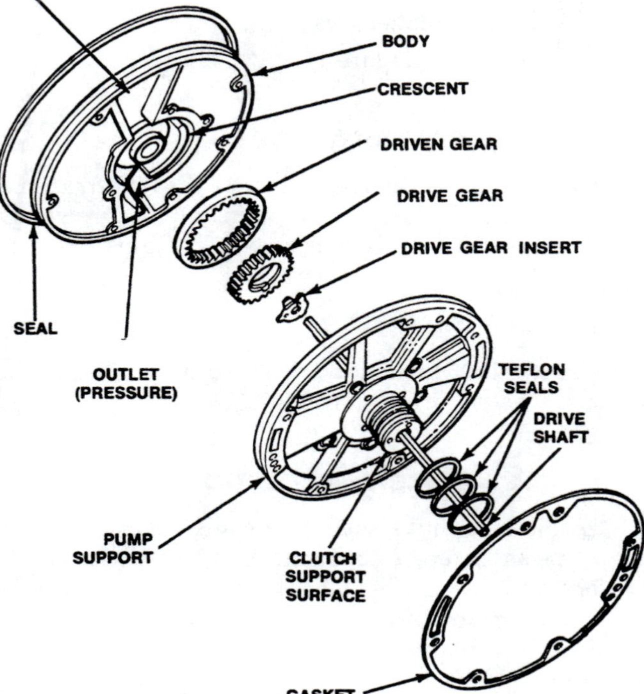

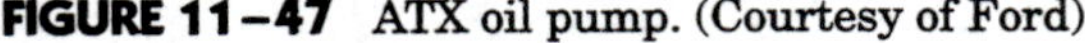

FIGURE 11–47 ATX oil pump. (Courtesy of Ford)

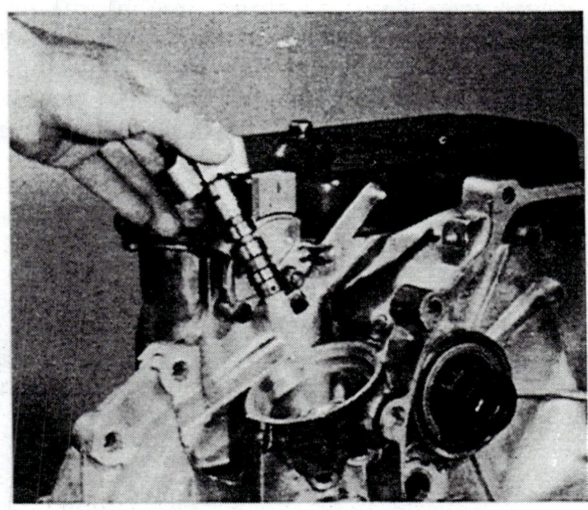

FIGURE 11–48 ATX governor. (Courtesy of Ford)

8. Throttle Valve
The throttle valve is located in the valve body and is operated by linkage connected to the accelerator linkage of the vehicle.

11.5.2 Power Flow

The power flow is described by stating the coupling and holding device action (applied, or holding) on the members of the planetary gear set (sun gear, pinion carrier, and ring gear) in each gear range of the transmission.

1. Neutral (N)
All coupling and holding devices are released, but the turbine shaft is turning the front sun gear through the one-way clutch (Figure 11–49).

2. First Gear (D1)
In first gear the turbine shaft drives the front sun gear through the one-way clutch. The band is applied to hold the rear sun gear and a first-gear ratio of 2.79:1 is produced (Figure 11–50). In manual first gear the direct clutch is also applied.

3. Second Gear (D2)
In second gear the intermediate shaft drives the ring gear through the applied intermediate clutch. The band is still applied, holding the rear sun gear as reaction member, which provides a second-gear ratio of 1.61:1 (Figure 11–51).

4. Third Gear (D3)
In third gear both the direct and intermediate clutches are applied, which drives the sun gear and ring gear at the same speed, producing a direct drive. By coupling the ring gear and front sun gear together, the turbine shaft and intermediate shaft are also coupled, which puts the converter planetary gear set into direct-drive mode and provides a mechanical power flow (Figure 11–52).

5. Reverse Gear (R)
In reverse gear the directed clutch is applied to drive the front sun gear. The reverse clutch is applied to hold the ring gear, so the output pinion carrier is driven in reverse at a ratio of 1.97:1.

11.5.3 Clutch and Band Charts

The first chart, the author's design, is shown in Figure 11–53. The second chart, the manufacturer's design, is shown in Figure 11–54.

11.5.4 Identification

The shape of the transaxle oil pan or its gasket is a quick means of identifying an automatic transaxle. In Figure 11–55 you see the pan gasket shape and number of bolt holes for the ATX transaxle. The location of the factory identification tag and its code are shown in Figure 11–56.

11.5.5 Components

In this section exploded drawings of the ATX transaxle subassemblies are shown along with lists of the part names. The manufacturer's part names are used to eliminate confusion about component names. The illustrations to study are as follows:

Exploded view, Figure 11–57
Valve body bolt tightening sequence, Figure 11–58
Torque converter, Figure 11–59
Band and servo, Figure 11–60
Thrust washer location, Figure 11–61
Oil pump, Figure 11–62

11.5.6 Pressure Test

The location of the test points of the ATX transaxle is shown in Figure 11–63 and the pressure specification of this transaxle is shown in Figure 11–64.

11.5.7 Air Test

The test information is presented in the illustration of air test points, Figure 11–65.

11.5.8 Special Attention

In this section we show and explain various points of special interest about the ATX transaxle. The information presented about each item is included with each illustration.

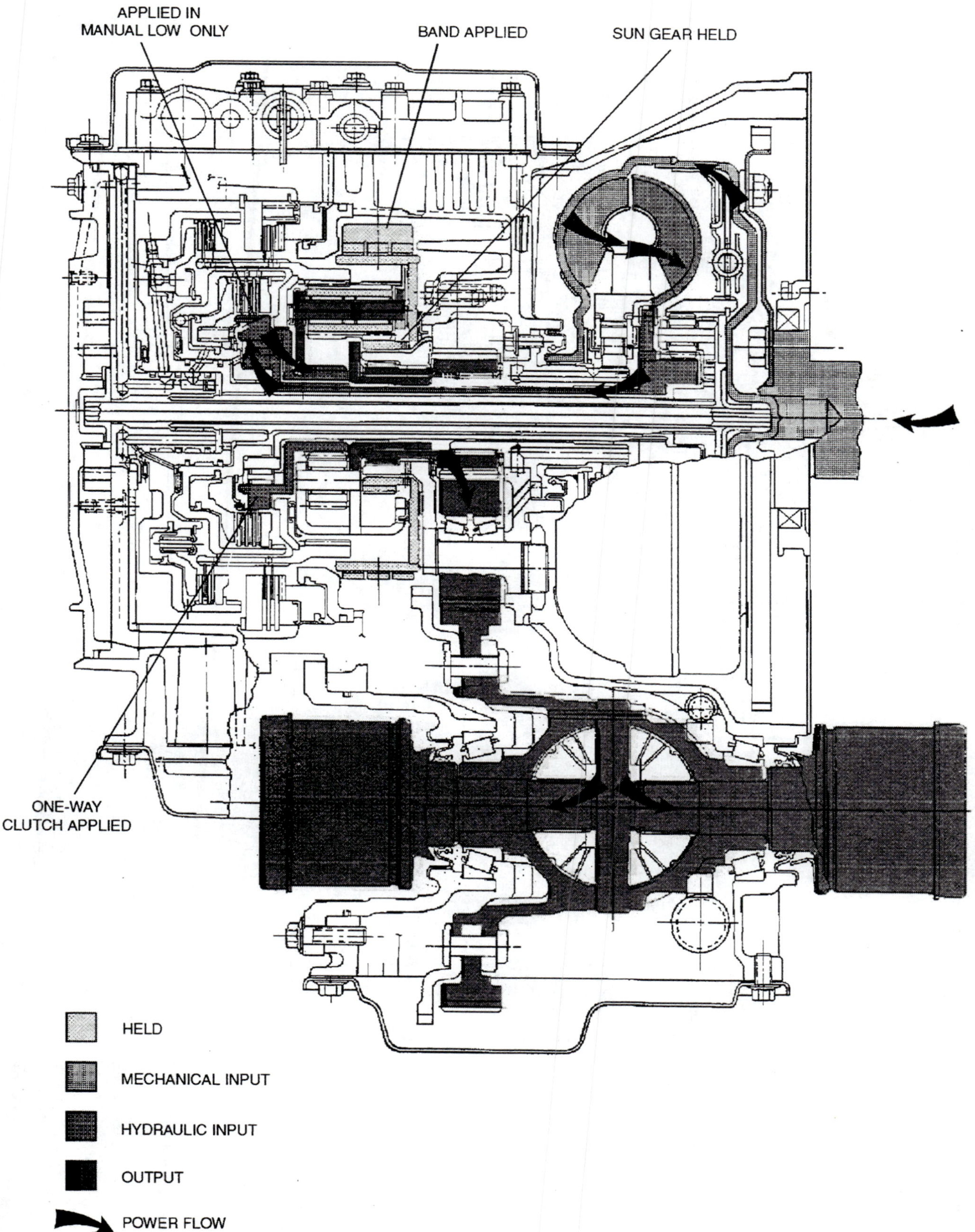

FIGURE 11–49 ATX in neutral. (Courtesy of Ford)

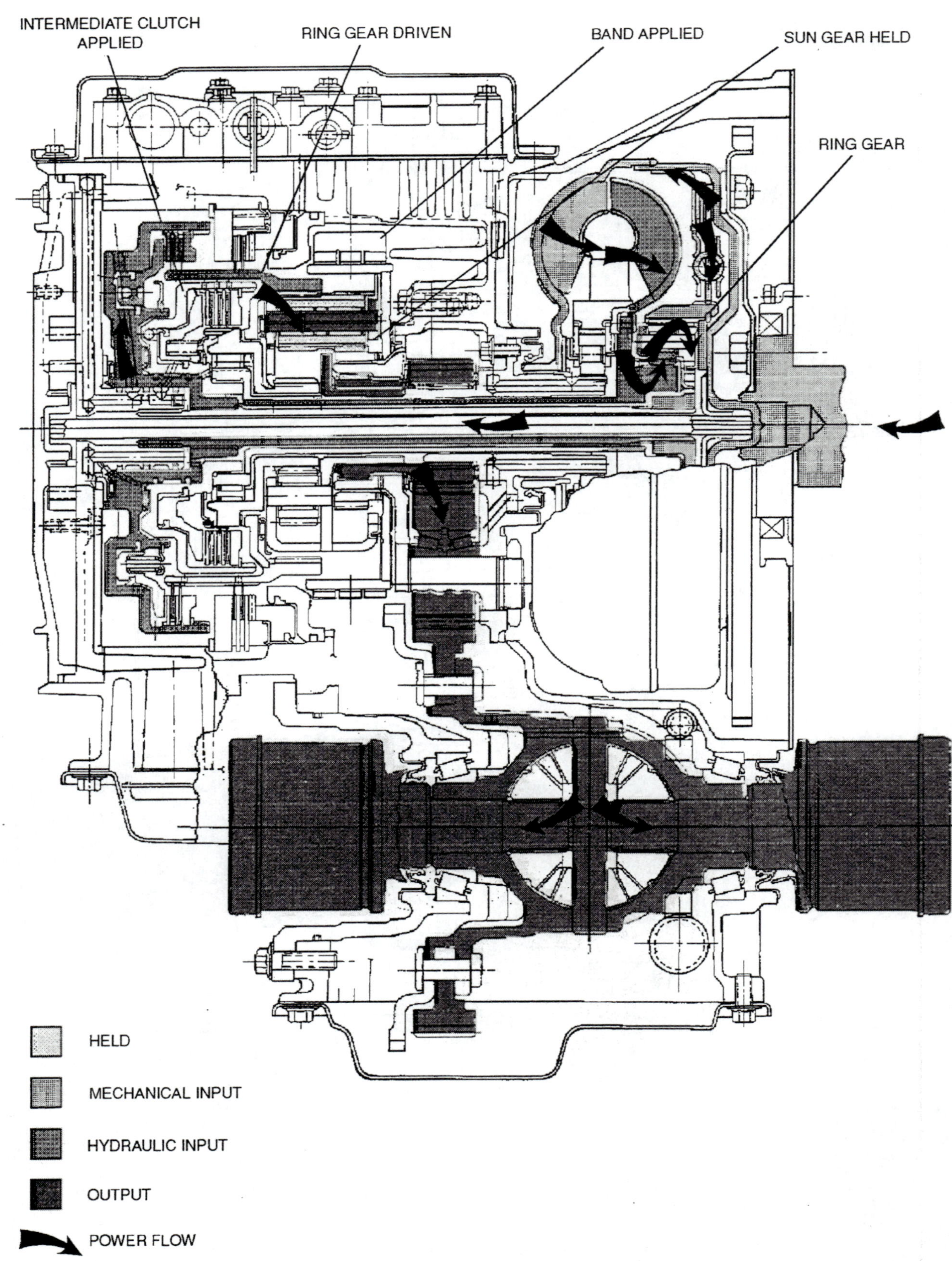

FIGURE 11–50 ATX in first gear. (Courtesy of Ford)

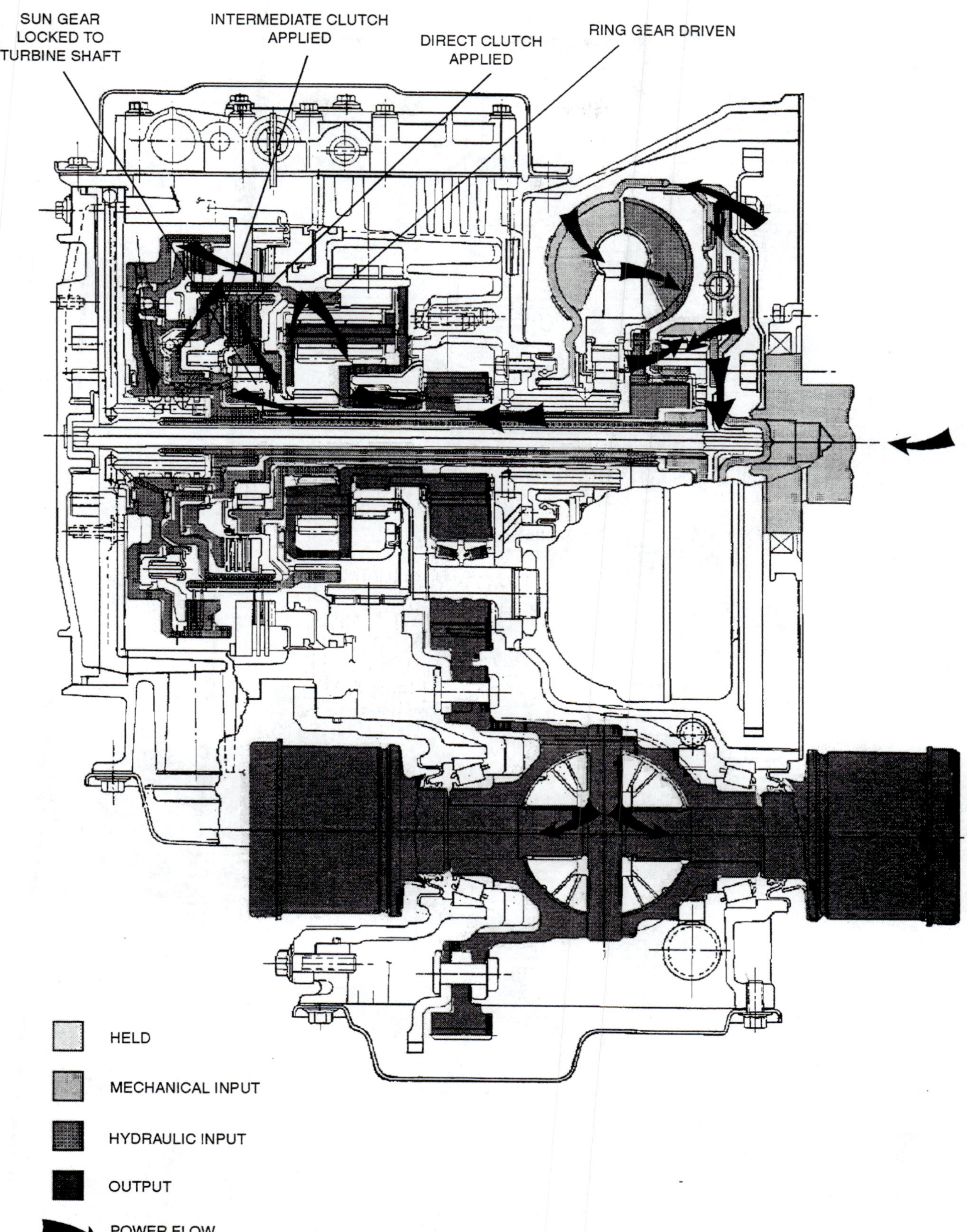

FIGURE 11–51 ATX in second gear. (Courtesy of Ford)

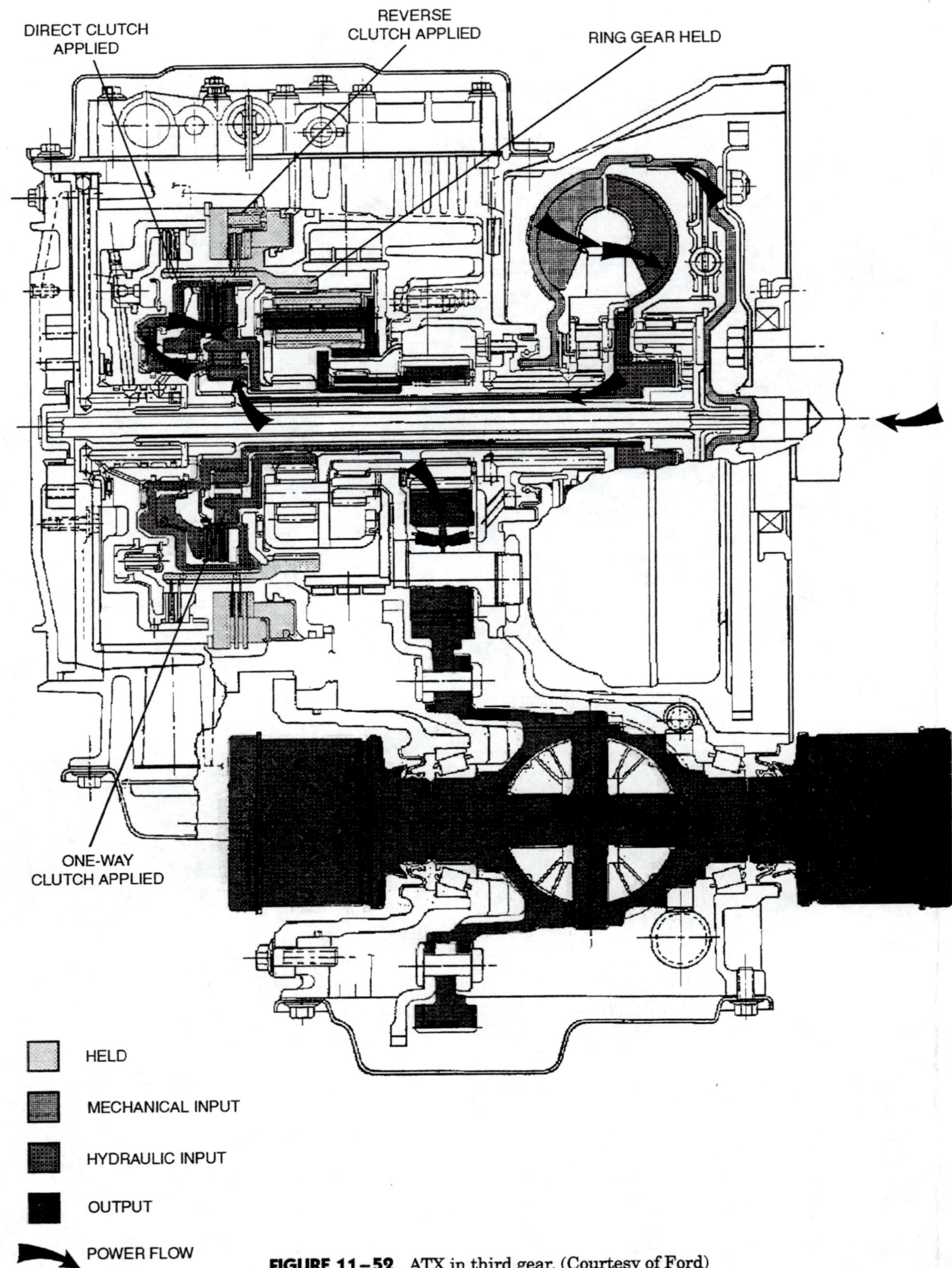

FIGURE 11–52 ATX in third gear. (Courtesy of Ford)

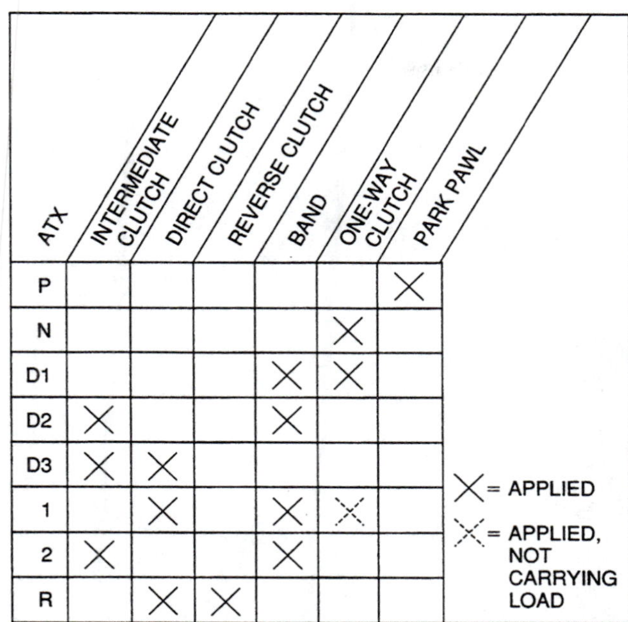

ATX	INTERMEDIATE CLUTCH	DIRECT CLUTCH	REVERSE CLUTCH	BAND	ONE-WAY CLUTCH	PARK PAWL
P						X
N					X	
D1				X	X	
D2	X			X		
D3	X	X				
1		X		X	(X)	
2	X			X		
R		X	X			

FIGURE 11–53 ATX clutch and band chart, standardized version.

Range and Gear		Band	Direct Clutch	Intermediate Clutch	Reverse Clutch	One-Way Clutch
Park						Applied
Reverse			Applied		Applied	Applied
Neutral						Applied
D	1st	Applied				Applied
	2nd	Applied		Applied		
	3rd		Applied	Applied		
2	1st	Applied				Applied
	2nd	Applied		Applied		
1	1st	Applied	Applied			Applied

FIGURE 11–54 ATX clutch and band chart, factory version. (Courtesy of Ford)

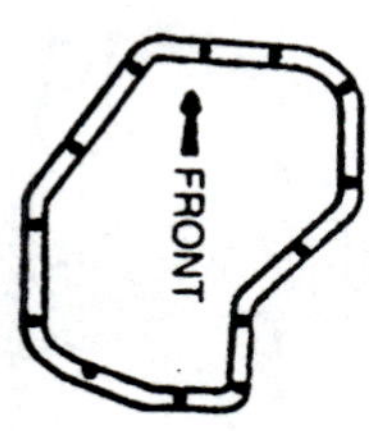

FIGURE 11–55 ATX pan gasket identification.

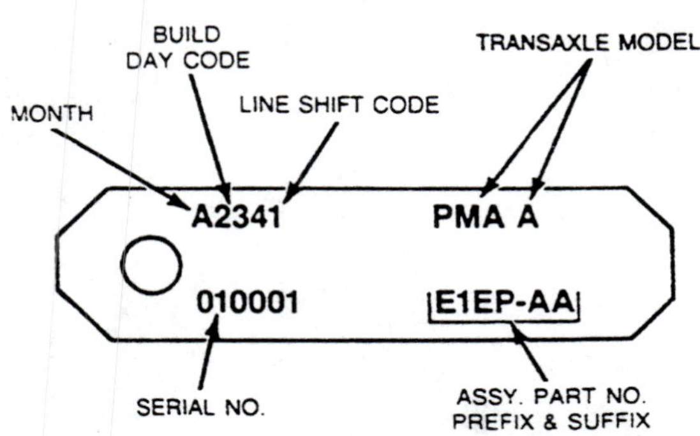

FIGURE 11–56 ATX identification tag. (Courtesy of Ford)

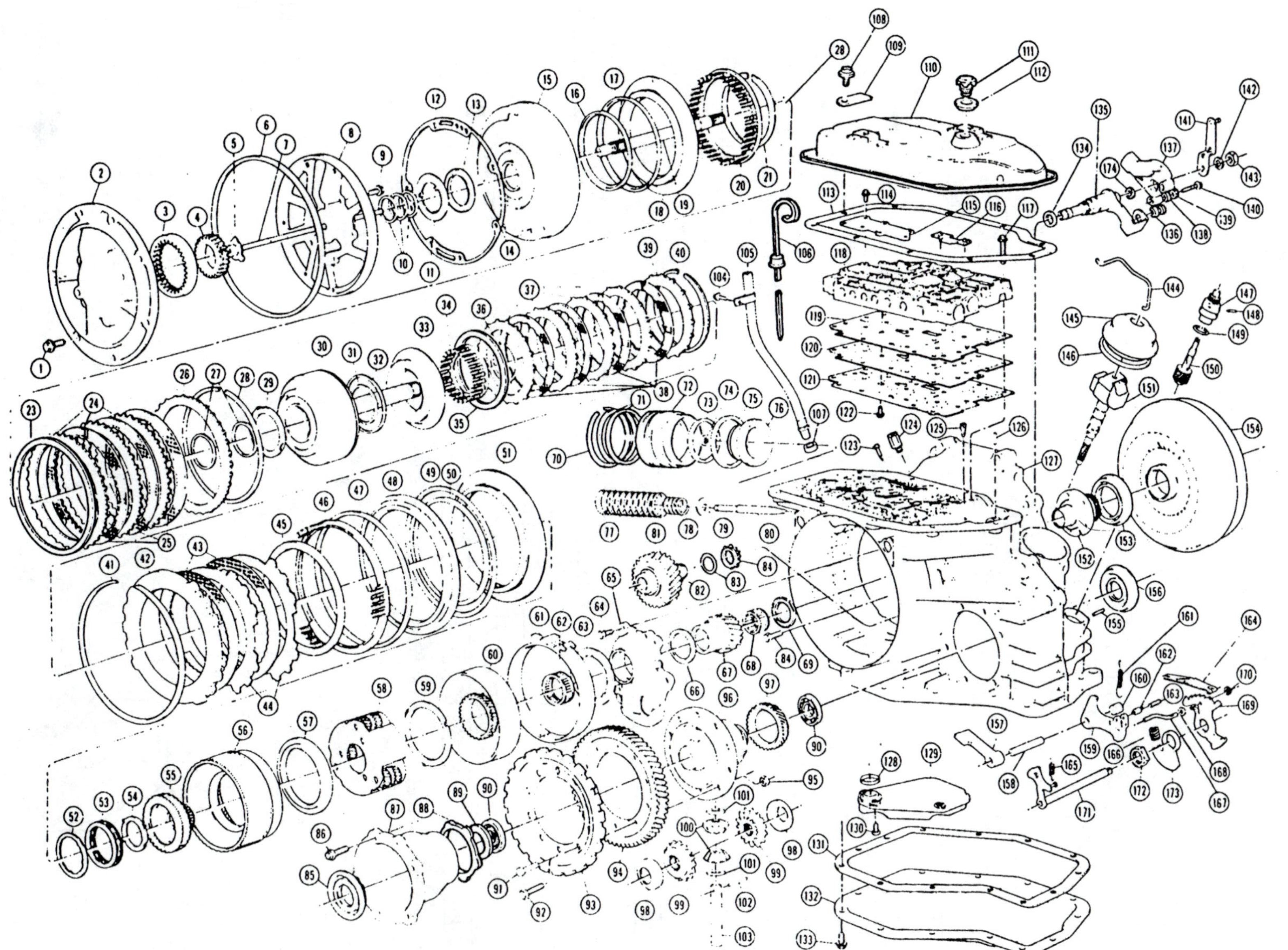

FIGURE 11–57 ATX exploded view. (Courtesy of Ford)

No.	Part Number	Description
1	N801003-S	BOLT & WSHR. ASSY. (7A103 TO 7005) M6-1 X 40 (7 REQ'D.)
2	7F370	BODY & SLEEVE ASSY. — OIL PUMP
3	7C011	GEAR — OIL PUMP DRIVEN
4	7C009	GEAR ASSY. — OIL PUMP DRIVE
5	7F402	INSERT — OIL PUMP DRIVE GEAR
6	7N265	SEAL — OIL PUMP
7	7B328	SHAFT — OIL PUMP DRIVE
8	7D043	SUPPORT & BSHG. ASSY. — OIL PUMP
9	N605772-S	BOLT (7A108 TO 7F370) M6-1 X 16MM LG. (5 REQ'D.)
10	7F425	SEAL — INTERM. CLUTCH — INNER (TEFLON)
11	7F387	OIL PUMP THRUST WASHER (SELECTIVE)
12	7A136	GASKET — OIL PUMP
13	7F374	BRG. ASSY. — INTERM. CLUTCH DRUM THRUST
14	N801098-S	RING — 17.0 RETAINING RD. WIRE EXTERNAL
15	7F389	CYLINDER — INTERM. CLUTCH
16	7F225	SEAL — INTERM. CLUTCH PISTON — INNER
17	7F224	SEAL — INTERM. CLUTCH PISTON — OUTER
18	7E005	PISTON — INTERM. CLUTCH
19	7F351	SHAFT — INTERM. CLUTCH
20	7F222	RET. & SPRING ASSY. — INTERM. CLUTCH
21	N800644-S	RING — 111.76MM RETAINING EXTERNAL
22		
23	7F154	SPRING — REV. CLUTCH CUSHION
24	7F220	PLATE — INTERM. CL. EXT. SPLINE
25	7E312	PLATE ASSY. — INTERM. CL. INT. SPLINE
26	7F226	PLATE — INTERM. CLUTCH PRESSURE
27	7F424	SEAL — INTERM. CLUTCH — OUTER (TEFLON)
28	N800650-1-2-S	RING — RETAINING INT. (SELECTIVE)
29	7F373	BRG. ASSY. — DIRECT & INTERM. CLUTCH
30	7F360	CYL. SHAFT & RACE ASSY. — DIRECT CLUTCH
31	7F234	SEAL — DIRECT CL. PISTON — INNER
32	7C000	SEAL — DIRECT CL. PISTON OIL — OUTER
33	7C117	PISTON — DIRECT CLUTCH
34	7F235	RET. & SPRING ASSY. — DIRECT CLUTCH
35	7B488	SPRING — DIRECT CLUTCH CUSHION
36	N800643-S	RING — 59.5MM RETAINING. EXTERNAL
37	7B442	PLATE — DIRECT CLUTCH EXT. SPLINE (AS REQ'D.)
38	7D239	PLATE ASSY. — DIRECT CL. INT. SPLINE (AS REQ'D.)
39	7B477	PLATE — DIRECT CLUTCH PRESSURE
40	N800646-7-8-S	RING — RETAINING INT. (SELECTIVE)
41	N800654-S	RING — RETAINING INT.
42	7D408	PLATE — REVERSE CLUTCH PRESSURE
43	7E312	PLATE ASSY. — REV. CL. INT. SPLINE
44	7E315	PLATE — REV. CLUTCH EXT. SPLINE
45	7F154	SPRING — REV. CLUTCH CUSHION
46	7F153	SPRING & RET. ASSY. — REV. CLUTCH
47	N800633-S	SEAL — 196.0MM
48	7D042	PISTON — REVERSE CLUTCH
49	7D403	SEAL — REV. CL. PISTON — OUTER
50	7D404	SEAL — REV. CL. PISTON — INNER
51	7F341	CYLINDER — REVERSE CLUTCH
52	7A623	BEARING — ONE-WAY CLUTCH
53	7F386	SPRING & ROLLER ASSY. — ONE-WAY CLUTCH
54	7F369	WASHER — DIRECT CL. CYL. THRUST
55	7N107	GEAR ASSY. — 1ST 3RD REVERSE SPEED
56	7F348	GEAR ASSY. — INTER. & REV. CL. RG.
57	7F473	RACE & BRG. ASSY. — PLANT THRUST REAR
58	7A398	PLANE ASSEMBLY
59	7D423	WASHER — PLANETARY THRUST — FRONT
60	7F362	DRUM & SUN GEAR ASSY. — LOW INTERM.
61	7D034	BAND ASSY. — LOW INTERM.
62	7F380	BEARING ASSY. — TRANSFER
63	7F368	WASHER — INTERM. SUN GR. THRUST
64	N605787-S100	BOLT — M8-1.25 X 25.0 HEX FLANGE HD. (5 REQ'D.)
65	7F334	HOUSING — FINAL DRIVE GEAR
66	7F405	BRG. ASSY. — FINAL DRIVE GEAR THRUST - REAR
67	7F342	GEAR — FINAL DRIVE INPUT
68	7F403	BRG. ASSY. — FINAL DRIVE INPUT GEAR
69	7F404	BRG. ASSY. — FINAL DRIVE GEAR THRUST — FRONT
70	N800645-S	RING — 103.5MM RET. FLAT INTERNAL
71	7F427	SEAL — LOW & INTERM. BAND SERVO PISTON COVER
72	7D027	COVER — LOW INTERM. BAND SERVO
73	7D025	SEAL — LOW INTERM. SERVO PISTON — SMALL
74	N663108-S	RING — 15.8MM RETAINING EXTERNAL
75	7D024	SEAL — LOW INTERM. SERVO PISTON — LARGE
76	7D022	PISTON — LOW & INTERM. SERVO
77	7D028	SPRING — LOW INTERM. SERVO PISTON
78	7F390	SPRING — SERVO PISTON CUSHION
79	N800640-S	WASHER — 9.7MM X 30 X 2.5 FLAT STEEL
80	7D023	ROD — LOW INTERM. SERVO PISTON NOT AVAILABLE
81	7F475	GEAR & BRG. ASSY. — IDLER GEAR
82	7F358	SHAFT — IDLER GEAR
83	N800679-S	SEAL — 22.8 X 1.6 O-RING
84	N801218-S2	NUT — M25 X 1-12 POINT
85	1177	SEAL ASSY. — TRANSAXLE — DIFF.
86	N605788-S100	BOLT — M8-1.25 X 30 HEX FLANGE HD. (6 REQ'D.)
87	7F114	RETAINER — DIFF. BEARING
88	76345	GASKET — DIFF. BEARING RETAINER
89	4A451	SHIM — DIFF. BEARING (SELECTIVE)
90	4020	BALL BEARING — DIFF.
91	N647416-S2	RIVET — M10 X 38 SOLID FLAT HD. (REF. ONLY — PRODUCTION)
92	N800746-S	BOLT — M10 X 1.5 X 40 HEX HD. (10 REQ'D) SERVICE ONLY
93	7A233	GEAR — OUTPUT SHAFT PARK
94	7F343	GEAR — FINAL DRIVE OUTPUT
95	N800380-S	NUT — M10 X 1.5 HEX PLT. — (10 REQ'D.) SERVICE ONLY
96	4026	DIFF. ASSY. — TRANSAXLE
97	17285	GEAR — SPEEDO DRIVE
98	4228	WASHER — TRANSAXLE DIFF. SIDE GR. THRUST
99	4236	GEAR — TRANSAXLE DIFF. SIDE
100	4215	PINION — TRANSAXLE DIFF.
101	4230	WASHER — TRANSAXLE DIFF. PINION THRUST
102	N800979-S2	PIN — 4.75MM X 38.1MM
103	4211	SHAFT — TRANSAXLE DIFF. PINION
104	N605770-S2	BOLT — M6-1 X 12 HEX FLANGE HD.
105	7A228	TUBE ASSY. — OIL FILTER
106	7A020	INDICATOR ASSY. — OIL LEVEL
107	7N243	GROMMET (SEAL FILLER TUBE TO CASE)
108	N605771-S2	BOLT — M6-1 X 14MM LG. (10 REQ'D.)
109	7B148	IDENTIFICATION TAG
110	7G004	COVER ASSY. — MAIN CONTROL
111	7034	VENT ASSY. — MAIN CONTROL COVER
112	7G005	GROMMET — MAIN CONTROL COVER
113	7F396	GASKET — MAIN CONTROL COVER
114	N800671-S51M	BOLT — M6-1.0 X 45 HEX FLANGE HD. (7 REQ'D.)
115	7F422	PLATE — MAIN OIL PRESS. REG. EXH.
116	7E170	PLATE — TRANS.
117	N800670-S	BOLT — M6-1.0 X 40 HEX FLANGE HD. (20 REQ'D.)
118	7A100	CONTROL ASSY. — MAIN
119	7D100	GASKET — MAIN CONTROL (BET. 7A092 & 7A008)
120	7A008	PLATE — CONTROL VALVE BODY SEP.
121	7D100	GASKET — MAIN CONTROL (BET. 7A008 & 7006)
122	N605770-S2	BOLT — M6-1 X 12 HEX FLANGE HD. (2 REQ'D.)
123	N802807	PIN — TIMING (2.3L ONLY)
124	N802684-S100	COMM. ASSY. PUSH-IN
125	7E242	SCREEN ASSY. — GOV. OIL
126	N800673-S	PIN — 3.2MM X 25.65 DOWEL HRDN.
127	7F333	CASE & HSG. ASSY.
128	7B304	GASKET — OIL FILTER
129	7B155	FILTER ASSY. — OIL
130	N605771-S2	BOLT — M6-1 X 14MM LG. (3 REQ'D.)
131	7A191	GASKET — OIL PAN
132	7A264	PAN — OIL
133	N605785-S2	BOLT — M8-1.25 X 16 HEX FLANGE (13 REQ'D.)
134	7F376	SEAL — MANUAL CONTROL LEVER
135	7A256	LEVER ASSY. — MANUAL CONTROL
136	7341	INSULATOR — GEAR SHIFT ARM
137	7A247	SWITCH ASSY. — NEUTRAL START
138	44717-S2	WASHER — #12 FLAT (2 REQ'D.)
139	N800723-S2	WASHER — 6.0MM HELICAL SPG. LK. (2 REQ'D.)
140	N800670-S2	BOLT — M6-1.0 X 40 HEX FLANGE HD. (2 REQ'D.)
141	7F291	LEVER ASSY. — THROTTLE VALVE — OUTER
142	N630173-S2	WASHER — 8MM LOCK
143	N620041-S2	NUT — M8 X 1.25 HEX
144	7F394	CLIP — GOV. COVER RETAINING
145	7A301	COVER — GOVERNOR
146	N801011-S	SEAL — 77.9MM X 3.40 RECT. SECT.
147	17292	RETAINER — SPEEDO DRIVEN GEAR
148	N800674-S	PIN — 3MM X 19.9 DOWEL HRDN.
149	N800635-S	SEAL — 25.06MM X 2.6 O-RING
150	17271	GEAR — SPEEDO DRIVEN
151	7C053	GOVERNOR ASSEMBLY
152	7F363	SUPPORT ASSY. — CONV. REACTOR
153	7F401	SEAL ASSY. — CONV. IMP. HUB
154	7902	CONVERTER ASSEMBLY
155	N646325-S	PIN — SPEEDO RETAINING
156	1177	SEAL ASSY. — TRANSAXLE — DIFF.
157	7D430	STRUT — LOW INTERM. BAND ANCHOR
158	7D071	SHAFT — PARKING PAWL
159	7A441	PAWL — PARKING BRAKE
160	N802384-S	PLUG — 12.0MM CUP
161	7D070	SPRING — PARK PAWL RETURN
162	7D339	PIN — PARKING PAWL ROLLER
163	7D169	ROLLER — PARKING BRAKE
164	7E332	SPRING ASSY. — MANUAL VALVE DETENT
165	7F292	SPRING — THROTTLE VALVE CONTROL LEVER
166	7A180	SPRING — PARK PAWL RATCHETING
167	7E333	ACTUATOR — MANUAL LEVER
168	N630065-S	WASHER
169	7C494	LEVER — MANUAL VALVE DETENT — INNER
170	W623451-S	NUT — STAMPED
171	7F448	SHAFT ASSY. — TV LEVER ACTUATING
172	N800630-S	NUT — M20 X 1.5 HEX
173	7A118	LEVER — PARK PAWL ACTUATING
174	7F337	SEAL — THROTTLE CONTROL LEVER SHAFT

FIGURE 11–57 *(continued)*

20
21
22
23
24
19
4
3
25
18
6
5
26
2
1
17
7
8
11
27
9
10
16
15
14
13
12

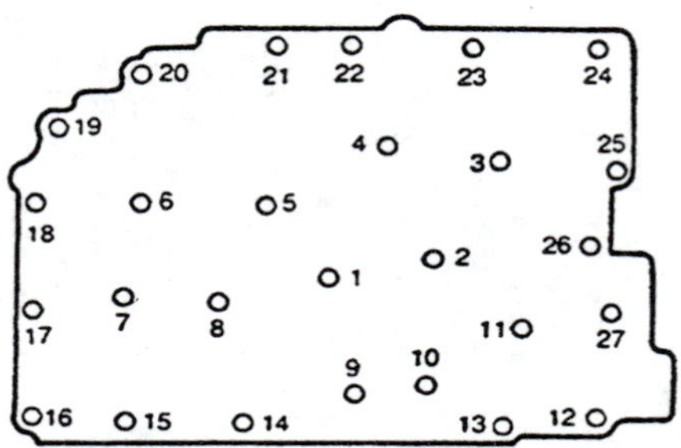

FIGURE 11–58 ATX valve body bolt-tightening sequence. (Courtesy of Ford)

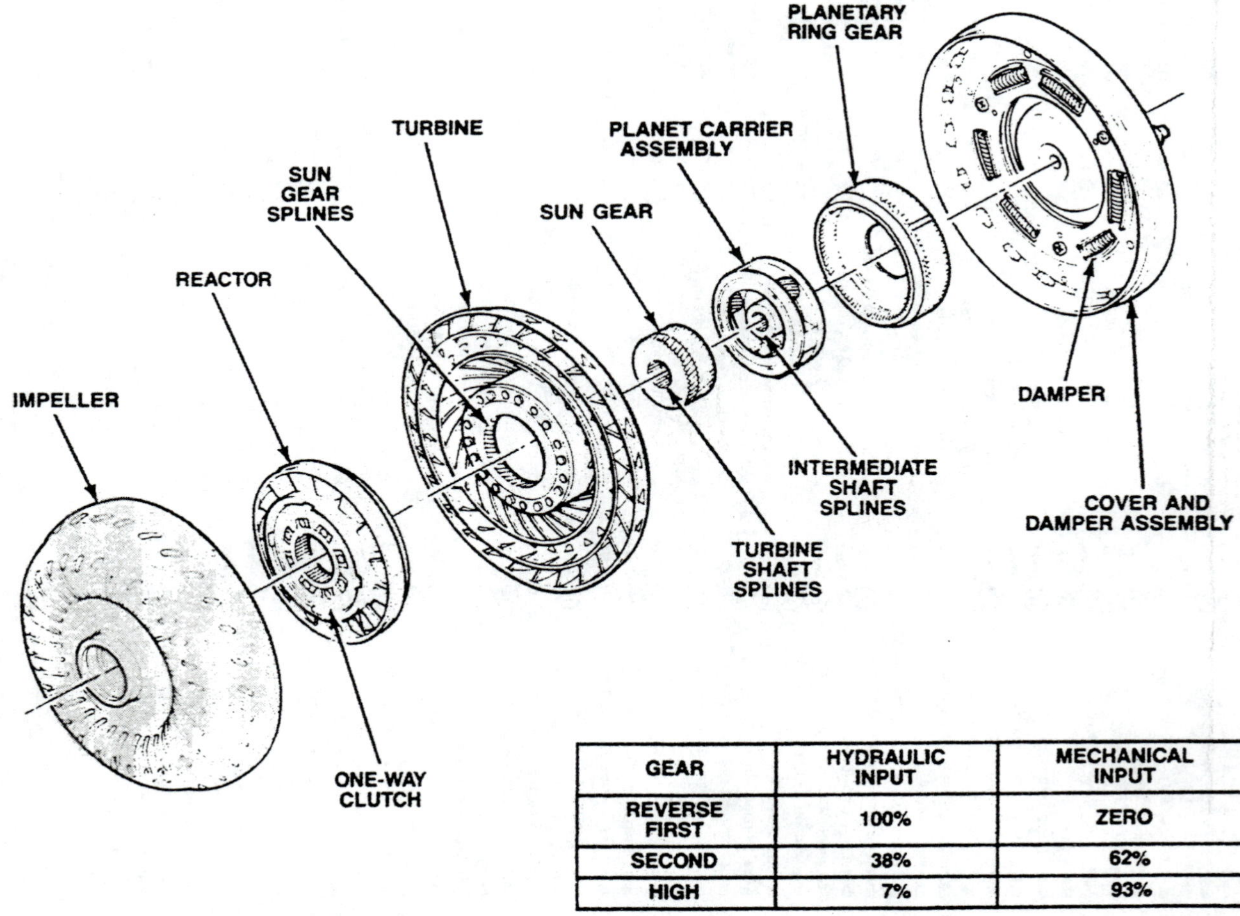

PLANETARY RING GEAR
TURBINE
PLANET CARRIER ASSEMBLY
SUN GEAR SPLINES
SUN GEAR
REACTOR
IMPELLER
DAMPER
INTERMEDIATE SHAFT SPLINES
COVER AND DAMPER ASSEMBLY
TURBINE SHAFT SPLINES
ONE-WAY CLUTCH

GEAR	HYDRAULIC INPUT	MECHANICAL INPUT
REVERSE FIRST	100%	ZERO
SECOND	38%	62%
HIGH	7%	93%

FIGURE 11–59 ATX torque converter. (Courtesy of Ford)

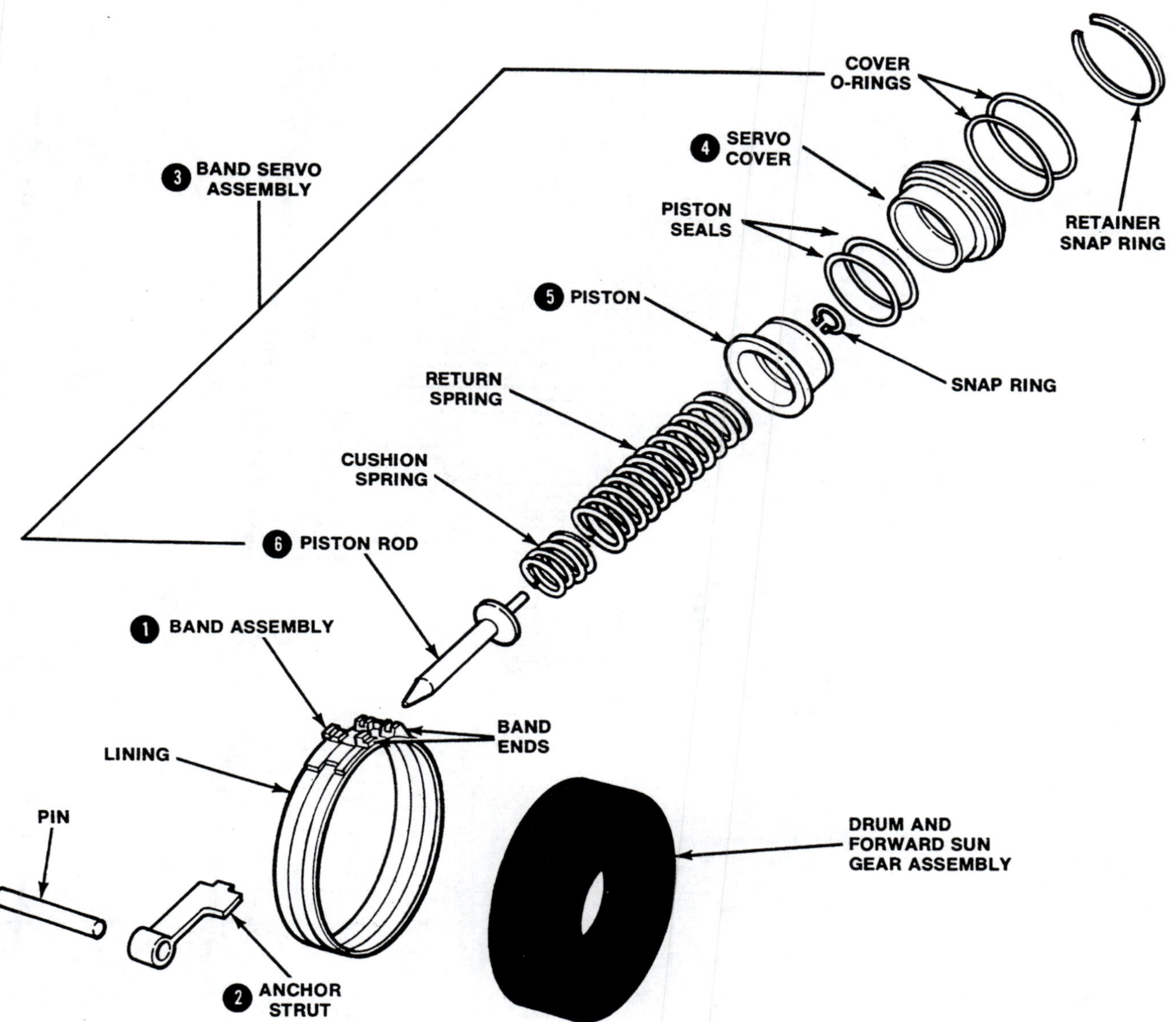

FIGURE 11–60 ATX band and servo. (Courtesy of Ford)

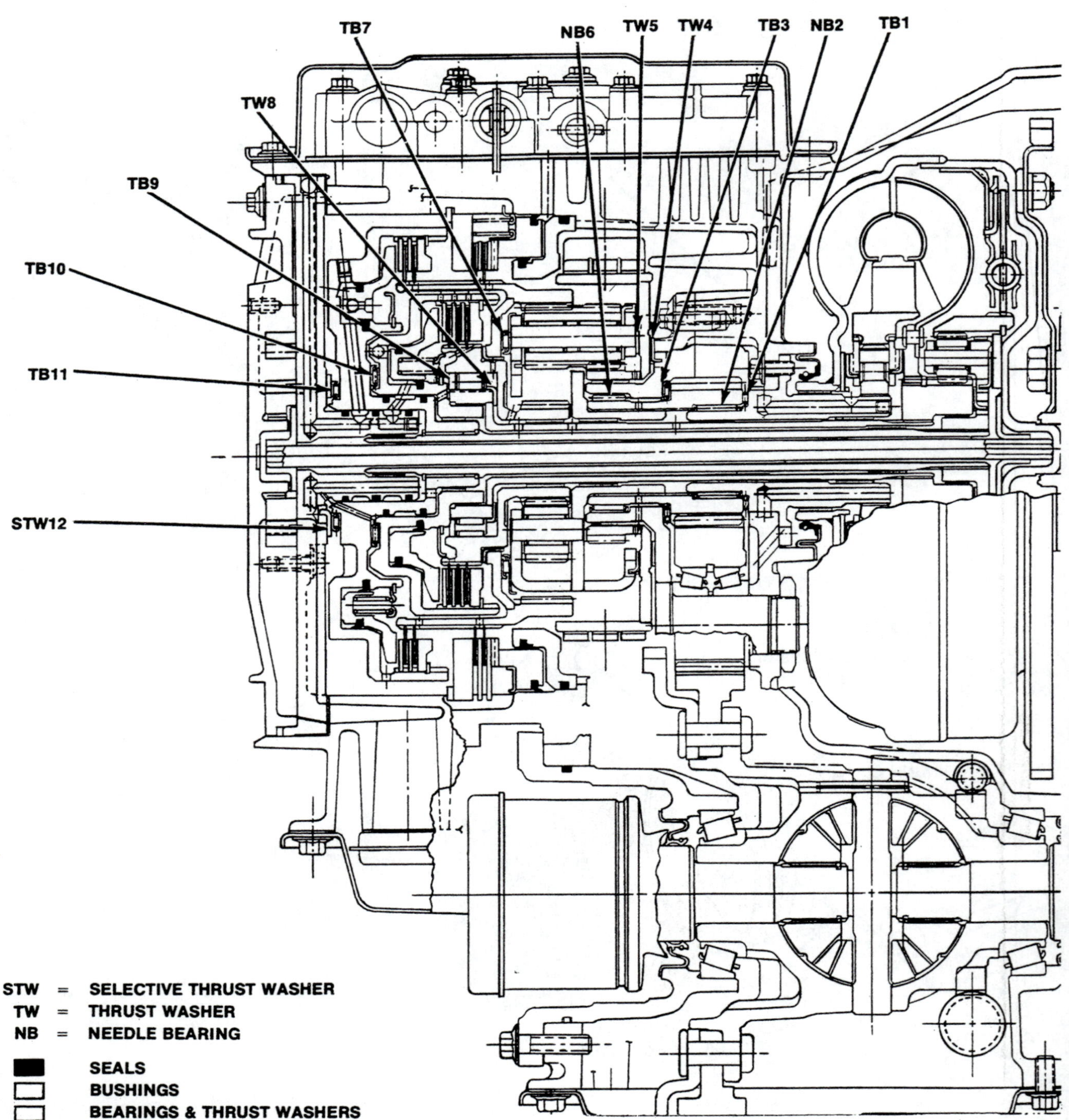

FIGURE 11–61 ATX thrust washer location. (Courtesy of Ford)

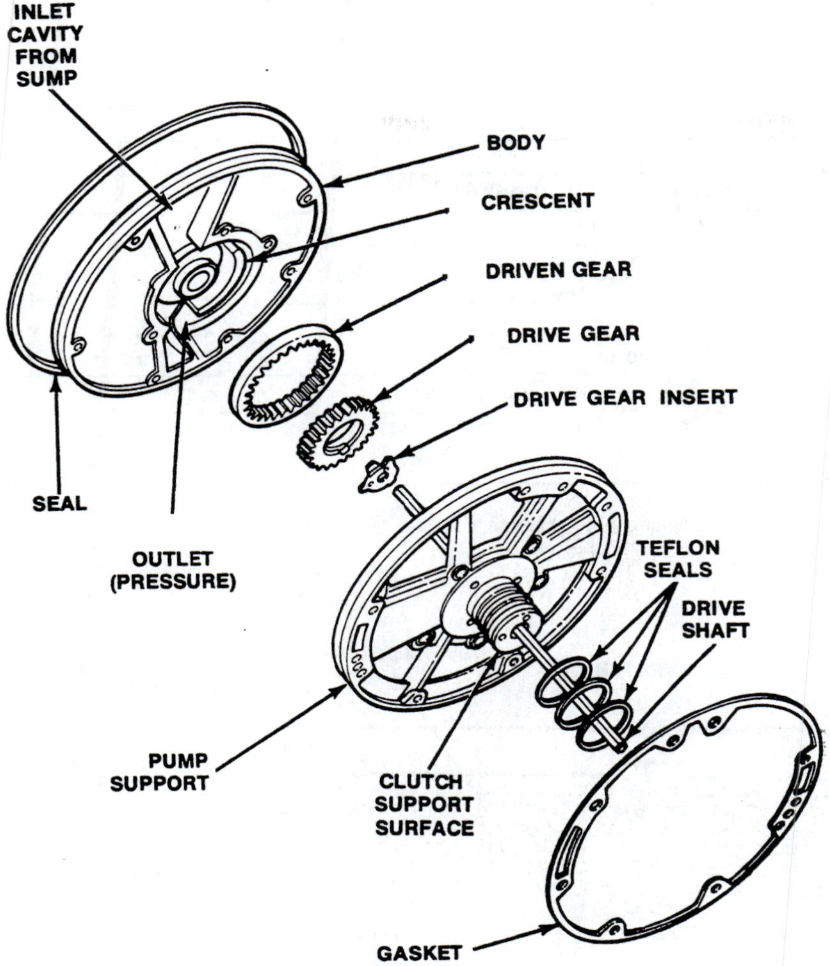

FIGURE 11–62 ATX oil pump. (Courtesy of Ford)

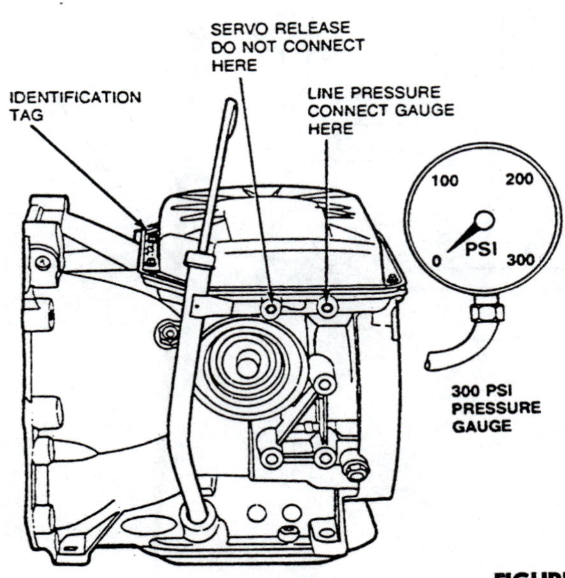

FIGURE 11–63 ATX pressure test points. (Courtesy of Ford)

CONTROL PRESSURE CONDITION	POSSIBLE CAUSE(S)
Low in P	Valve body
Low in R	Direct clutch, reverse clutch, valve body
Low in N	Valve body
Low in D	Servo, valve body
Low in 2	Servo, valve body
Low in 1	Servo, direct clutch, valve body
Low at idle in all ranges	Low fluid level, restricted inlet screen, loose valve body bolts, pump leakage, case leakage, valve body, excessively low engine idle, fluid too hot.
High at idle in all ranges	T.V. linkage, valve body
Okay at idle but low at W.O.T.	Internal leakage, pump leakage, restricted inlet screen, T.V. linkage, valve body (T.V. or T.V. limit valve sticking)

FIGURE 11–64 ATX pressure test charts. (Courtesy of Ford)

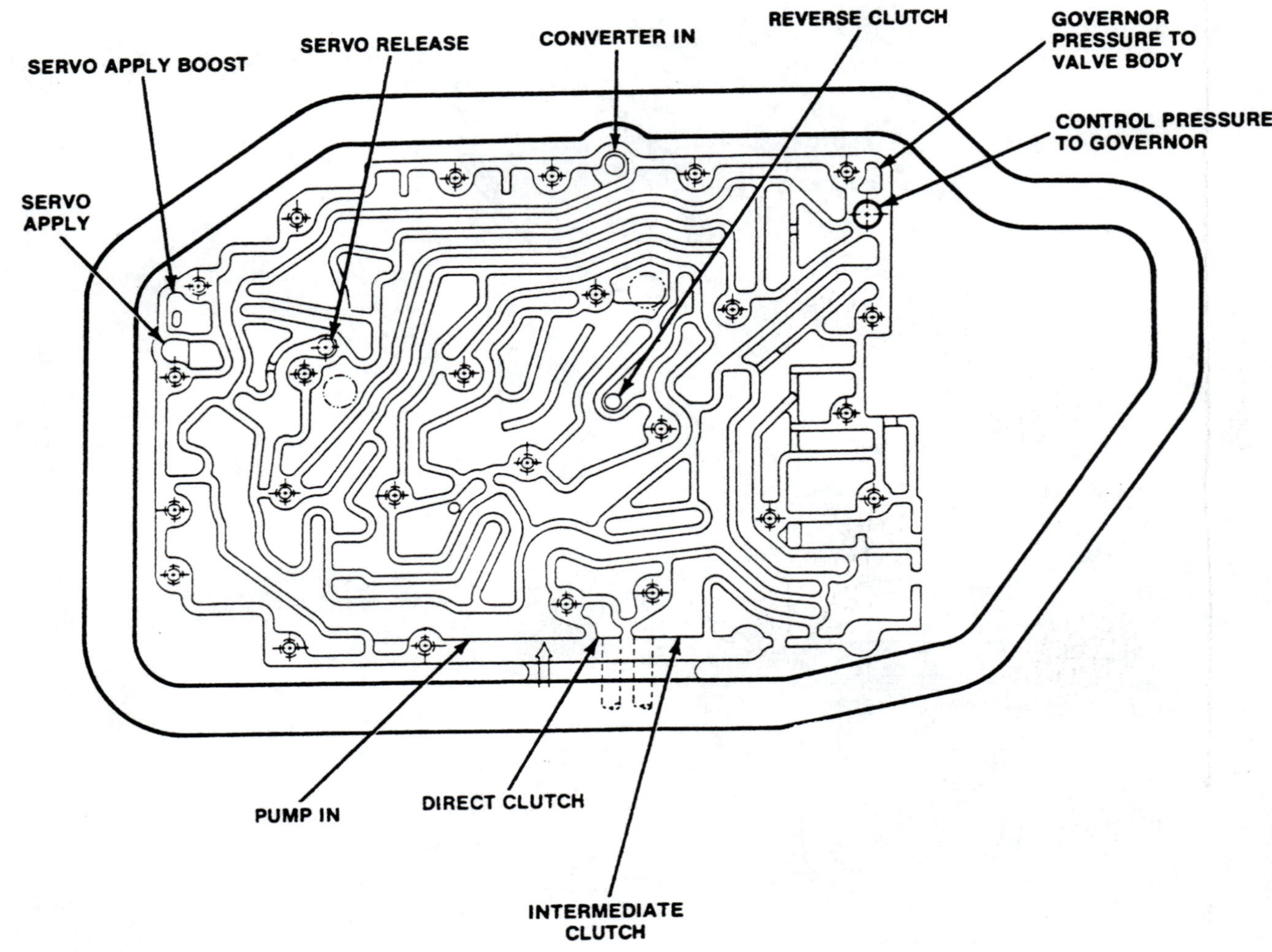

FIGURE 11–65 ATX air test points. (Courtesy of Ford)

FIGURE ATX-1 The oil pump is removed using two adapters and slide hammers.

FIGURE ATX-2 The oil pump gears, driveshaft, and drive adapter should be inspected closely.

FIGURE ATX-3 The intermediate clutch should be disassembled and inspected.

FIGURE ATX-4 The direct clutch and sun gear have a one-way clutch mounted in between. Inspect all parts.

FIGURE ATX-5 Check the pinion carrier for wear or damage.

FIGURE ATX-6 The drum and forward sun gear assembly should also be checked.

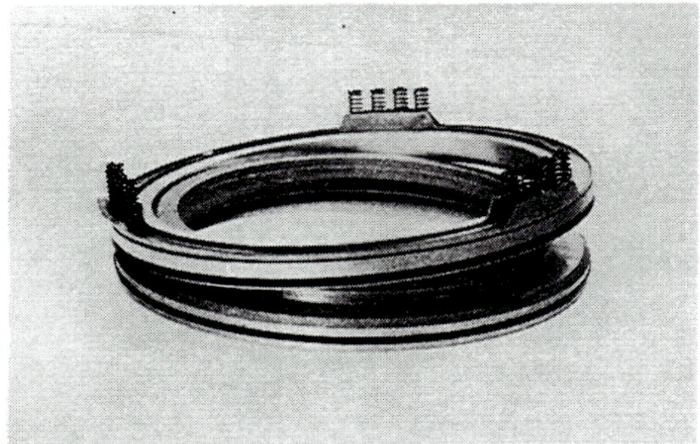

FIGURE ATX–7 The reverse clutch should be inspected and the seals replace.

FIGURE ATX–8 The final drive support and final drive input gear must be examined for wear.

FIGURE ATX–9 The final drive idler gear is located in the case.

FIGURE ATX–10 This unit bolts on in place of the oil pan to provide a power-takeoff point for a four-wheel-drive system.

11.6 AXOD: FWD FOUR-SPEED TRANSAXLE

11.6.1 Basic Description

The AXOD is an automatic overdrive transaxle used widely in midsized front-wheel-drive Ford vehicles (Figure 11–66). The transmission areas is divided into eight areas. All the transmissions are described in this manner to make their comparison easier.

1. Torque Converter
The AXOD uses a conventional three-element torque converter that is equipped with a hydraulic converter clutch. The converter clutch is controlled by the EEC-IV on-board computer.

2. Gear Train
The gear set used in the AXOD is similar to that used in the HM 4T60 transaxle. It has two planetary gear sets which are interconnected, with the front carrier and rear ring gear joined together and acting as input and reaction members. The front ring gear and rear carrier are also joined and are the output members. The front sun gear is an input member and the rear sun gear is a reaction member.

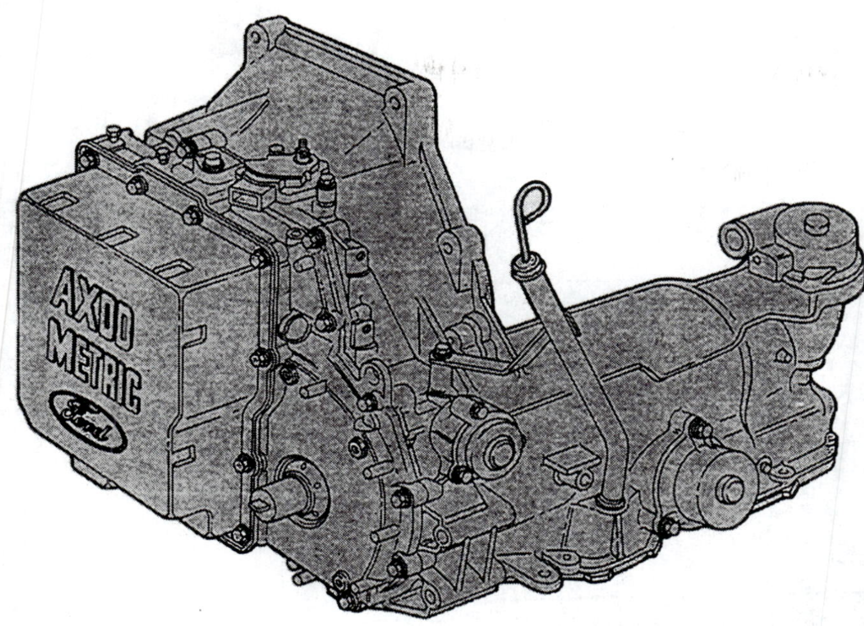

FIGURE 11–66 AXOD is a technically advanced automatic transaxle. (Courtesy of Ford)

3. *Coupling Devices*
The coupling devices used to provide input into the AXOD are the forward clutch, the direct clutch, the direct one-way clutch, and the intermediate clutch.

4. *Holding Devices*
The holding devices used to hold reaction members are the low one-way clutch, the overdrive band, the reverse clutch, and the low–intermediate band.

5. *Pump*
The AXOD uses a variable-displacement vane pump that is mounted on the outside of the valve body. The pump is driven by a driveshaft that extends through the valve body into the torque converter.

6. *Shift Control*
The shift control is hydraulic with computer control of the converter clutch through the bypass clutch solenoid. Three pressure switches are also used to provide the computer with operation data.

7. *Governor*
The AXOD uses a drop-in governor similar to that used in the ATX transaxle.

8. *Throttle Valve*
The throttle valve is operated by a cable that connects to the accelerator linkage. If the vehicle is operated with the TV cable out of adjustment, the transaxle can suffer serious damage.

11.6.2 Power Flow

The power flow is described by stating the coupling and holding device action (applied, or holding) on the members of the planetary gear set (sun gear, pinion carrier, and ring gear) in each gear range of the transmission.

1. *Neutral (N)*
In neutral all coupling and holding devices are released, so that the only rotation in the transaxle is the turbine shaft driving the sprockets and drive chain.

2. *First Gear (D1)*
In first gear the forward clutch is applied, which drives the front sun gear. The low one-way clutch is also driving the front sun gear. The low–intermediate band is applied, which holds the rear sun gear as the reaction member (Figure 11–67). The first-gear ratio is 2.77:1. In manual low gear the direct clutch is also applied.

3. *Second Gear (D2)*
In second gear the forward clutch and low intermediate band are still applied. The intermediate clutch is also applied, which drives the front pinion carrier/rear ring gear combination, which produces a gear ratio of 1.54:1 (Figure 11–68).

4. *Third Gear (D3)*
In third gear the forward and intermediate clutches remain applied and the direct clutch and direct

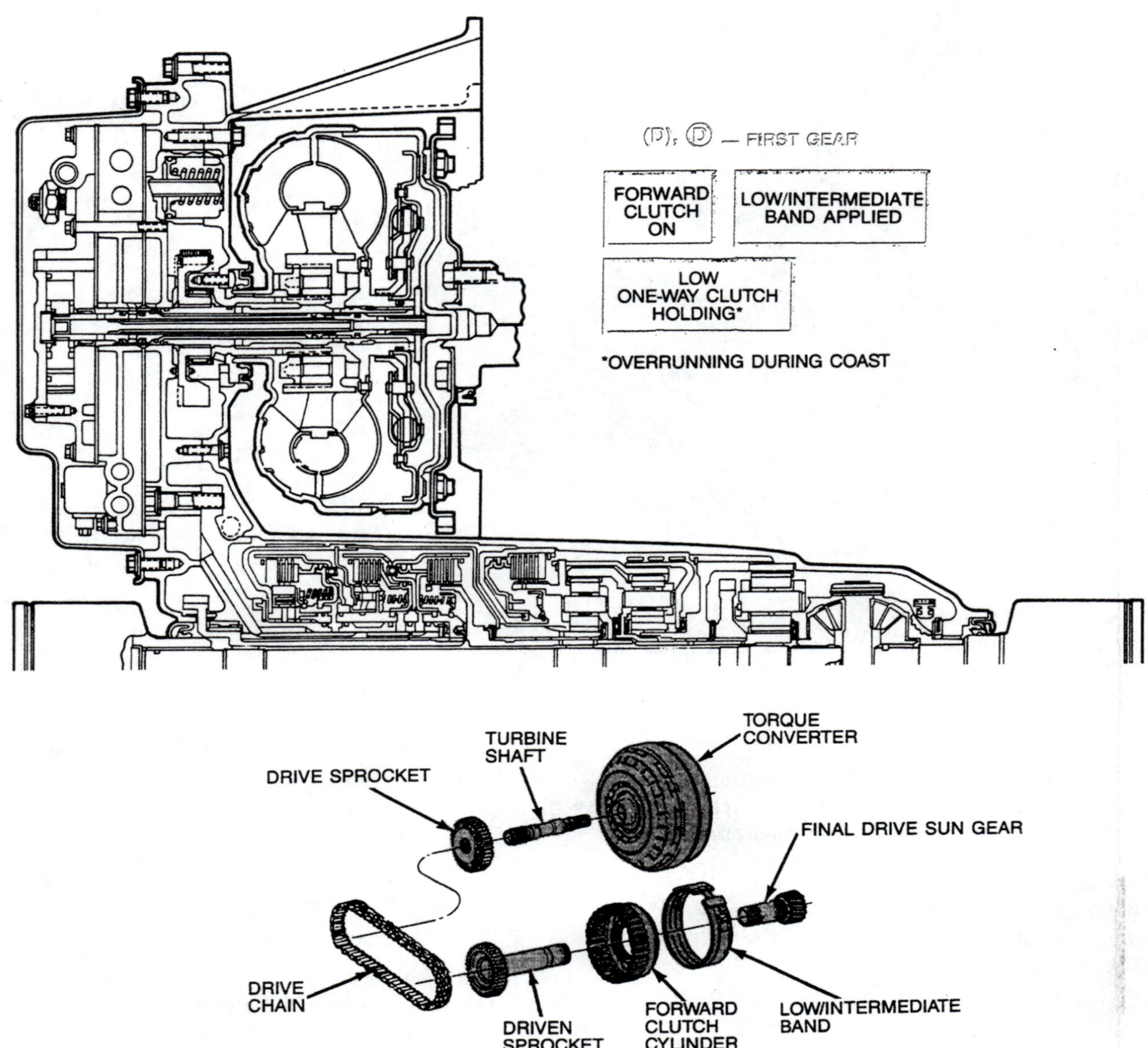

FIGURE 11–67 AXOD in first gear. (Courtesy of Ford)

one-way clutches are also applied, which connects all the input members together, causing a direct drive (Figure 11–69).

5. Fourth Gear (D4)
In fourth gear the intermediate clutch and direct clutch both remain applied to drive the front pinion carrier as an input member. The overdrive band is applied, which holds the front sun gear, producing an overdrive gear ratio of 0.69:1 (Figure 11–70).

6. Reverse Gear (R)
In reverse gear the forward clutch and low one-way clutch are applied to drive the front sun gear as the input member. The reverse clutch is holding the front pinion carrier as a reaction member, which causes a reverse gear ratio of 2.26:1 (Figure 11–71).

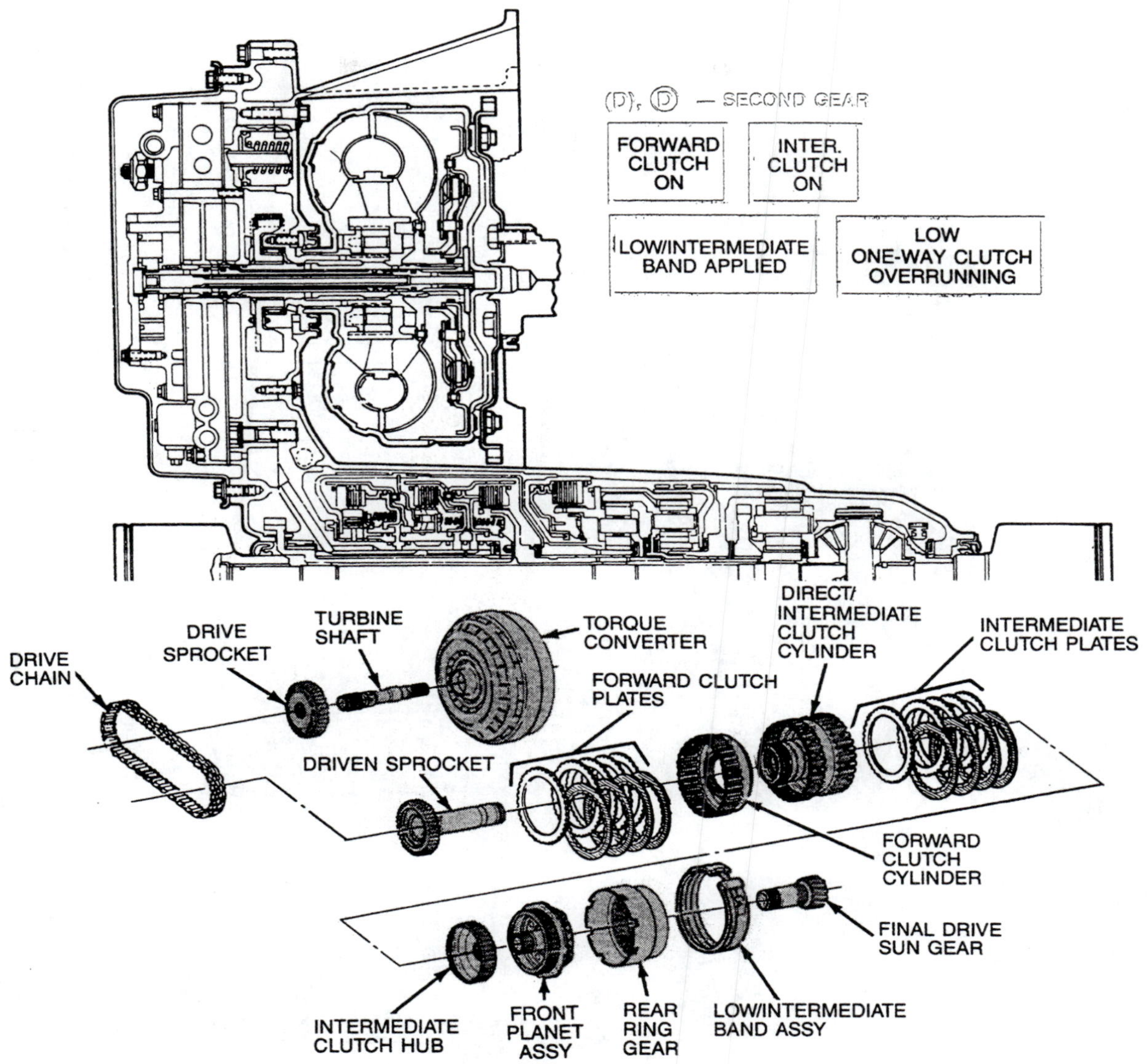

FIGURE 11–68 AXOD in second gear. (Courtesy of Ford)

11.6.3 Clutch and Band Charts

The first chart, the author's design, is shown in Figure 11–72. The second chart, the manufacturer's design, is shown in Figure 11–73.

11.6.4 Identification

The shape of the transmission oil pan or its gasket is a quick means of identifying an automatic transmission. In Figure 11–74 you see the pan gasket shape and number of bolt holes for the AXOD transaxle. The location of the factory identification tag and its code are shown in Figure 11–75.

11.6.5 Components

In this section exploded drawings of the AXOD transaxle subassemblies are shown along with lists of the part names. The manufacturer's part names are used to eliminate confusion about component names. The illustrations to study are as follows:

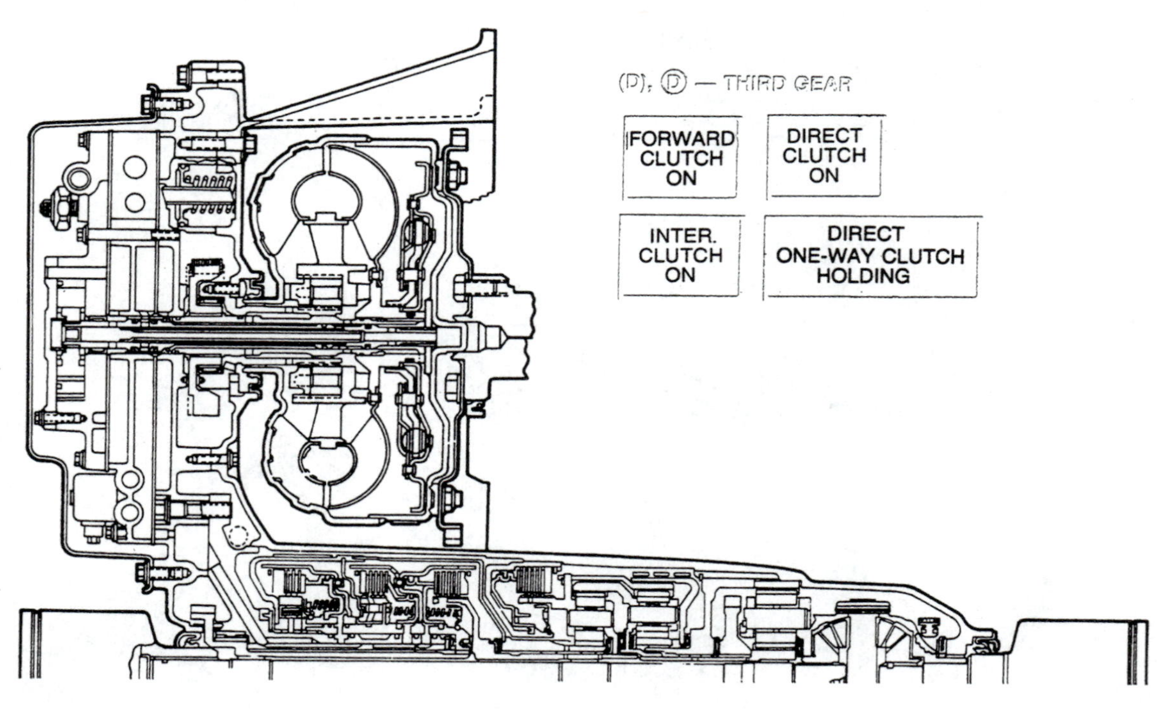

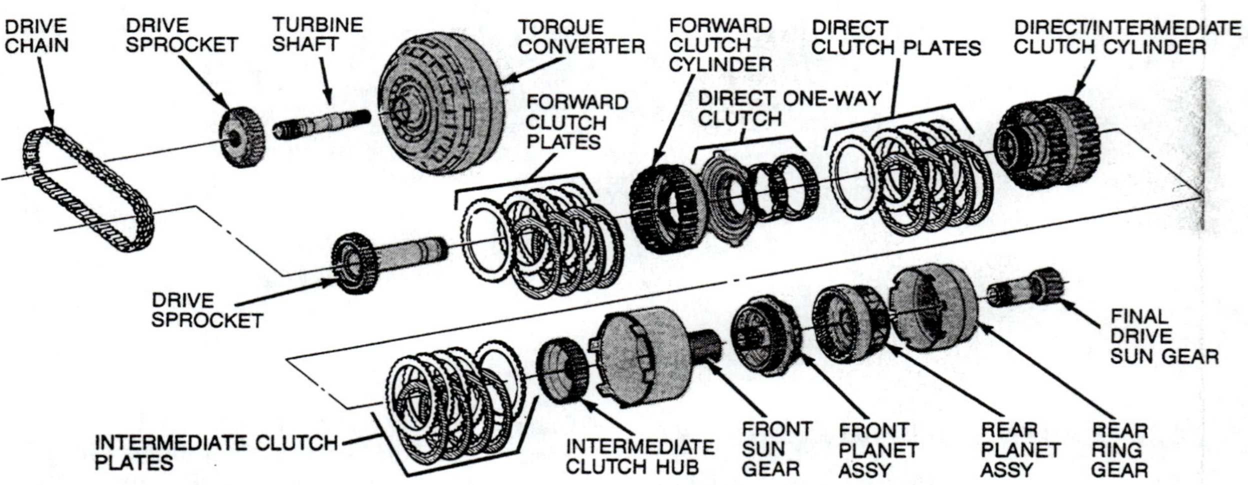

FIGURE 11–69 AXOD in third gear. (Courtesy of Ford)

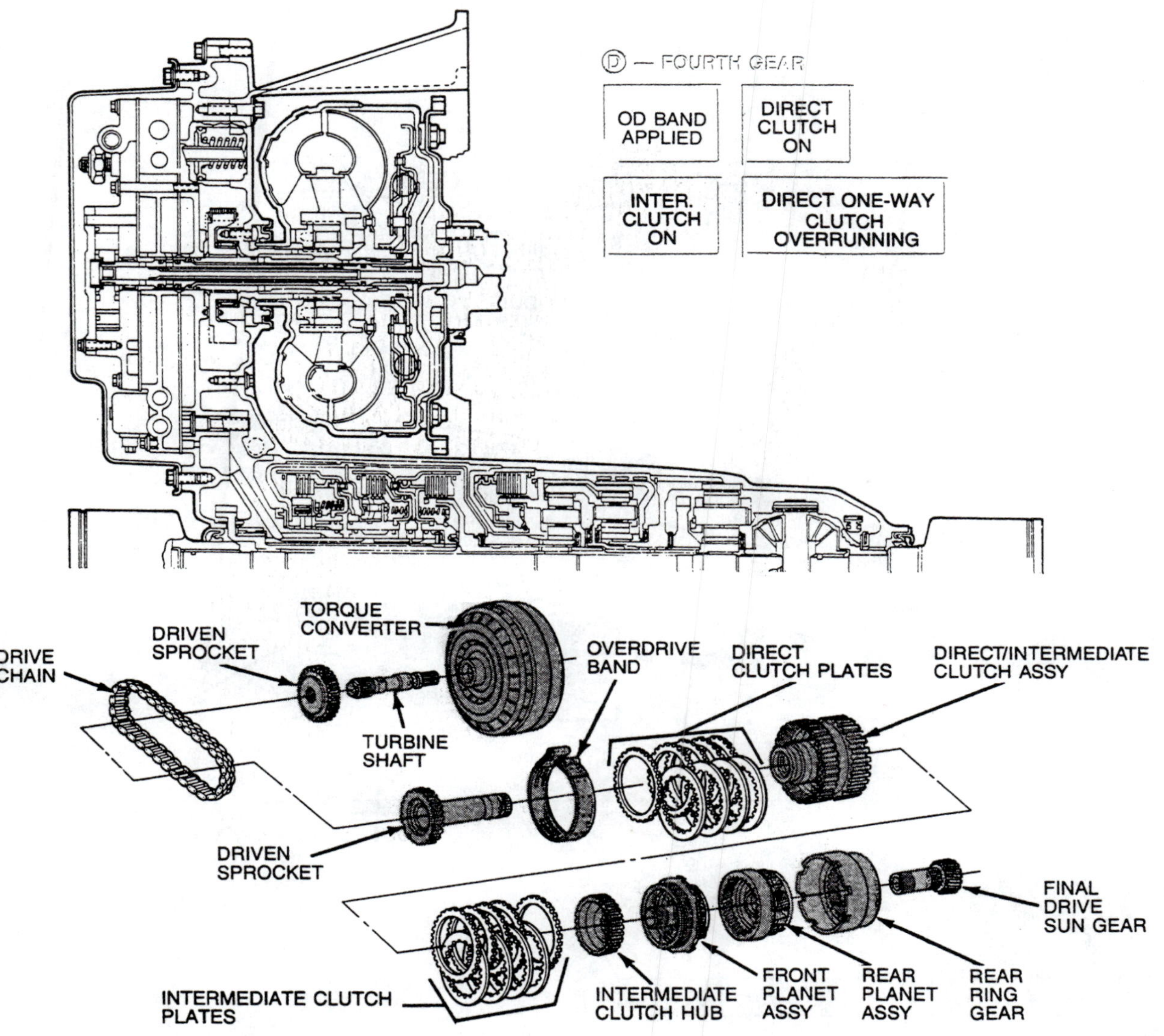

FIGURE 11–70 AXOD in fourth gear. (Courtesy of Ford)

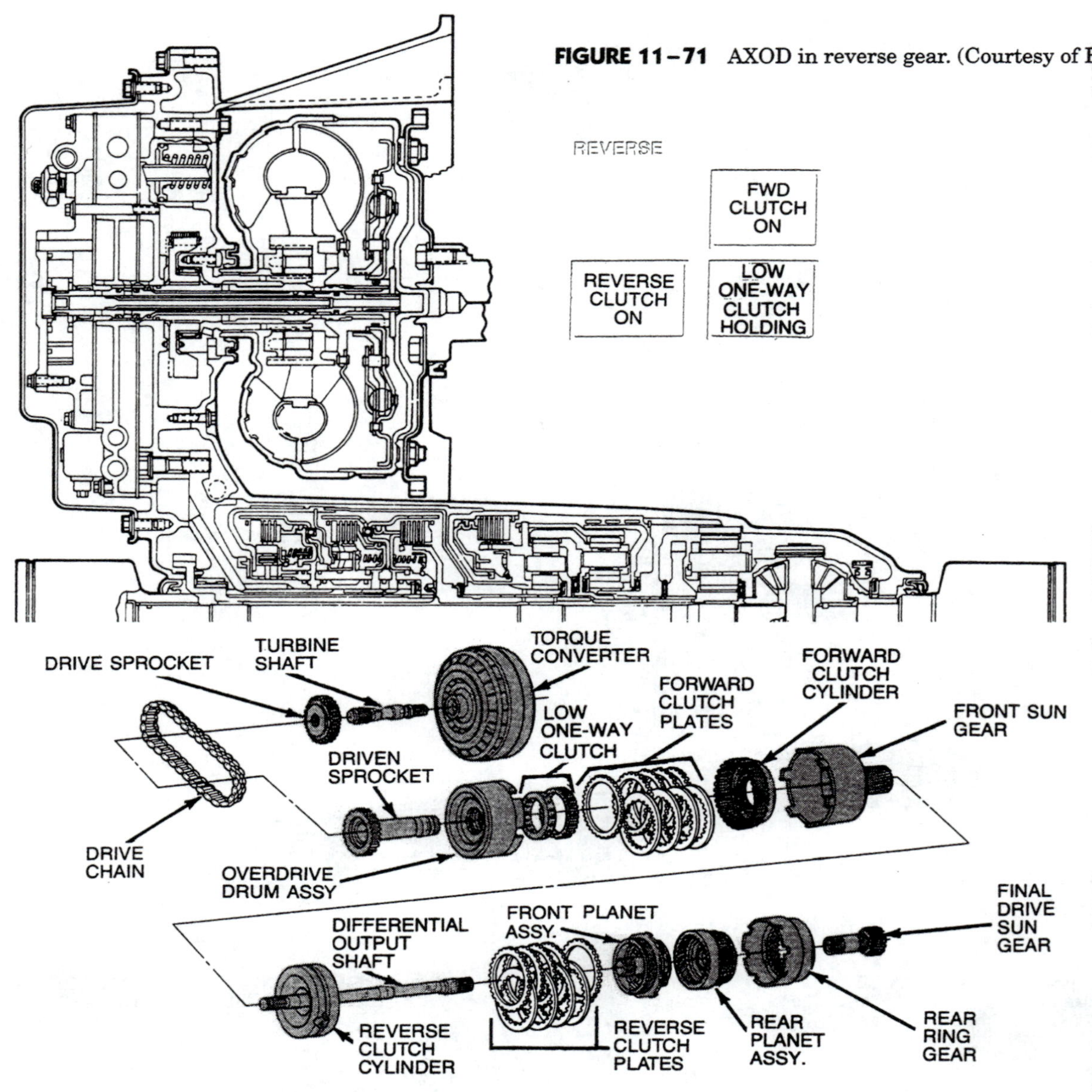

FIGURE 11–71 AXOD in reverse gear. (Courtesy of Ford)

	FORWARD CLUTCH	DIRECT CLUTCH	INTERMEDIATE CLUTCH	REVERSE CLUTCH	OVERDRIVE BAND	LOW–INTERMEDIATE BAND	LOW–ONE-WAY CLUTCH	DIRECT ONE-WAY CLUTCH	PARK PAWL	CONVERTER CLUTCH
P									X	
N										
D1	X					X	X			
D2	X		X			X				
D3	X	X	X					X		X
D4		X	X		X					X
1	X	X				X	X			
2	X		X			X				
3	X	X	X							X
R	X			X			X			

X = APPLIED

FIGURE 11–72 AXOD clutch and band chart, standardized version.

GEAR	OVER DRIVE BAND	FOR-WARD CLUTCH	LOW ONE-WAY CLUTCH	DIRECT CLUTCH	DIRECT ONE-WAY CLUTCH	INTER-MEDIATE CLUTCH	REV CLUTCH	LOW INTER. BAND	RATIO
MANUAL LOW		APPLIED	HOLD	APPLIED				APPLIED	2.77:1
• COASTING		APPLIED		APPLIED	HOLD			APPLIED	2.77:1
DRIVE 1st GEAR		APPLIED	HOLD					APPLIED	2.77:1
• COASTING		APPLIED	O/R					APPLIED	Freewheel
DRIVE 2nd GEAR		APPLIED	O/R			APPLIED		APPLIED	1.543:1
DRIVE 3rd GEAR		APPLIED		APPLIED	HOLD	APPLIED			1.000:1
• COASTING		APPLIED	HOLD	APPLIED					1.000:1
DRIVE 4th GEAR	APPLIED			APPLIED	O/R	APPLIED			.694:1
REVERSE		APPLIED	HOLD				APPLIED		2.263:1

FIGURE 11–73 AXOD clutch and band chart, factory version. (Courtesy of Ford)

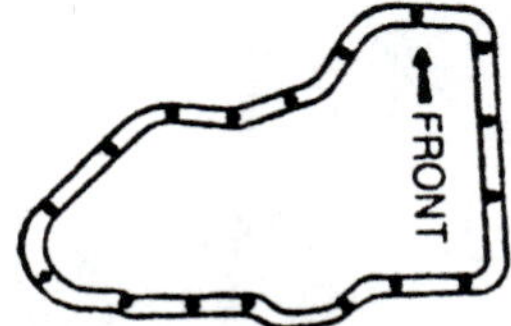

FIGURE 11–74 AXOD pan gasket identification.

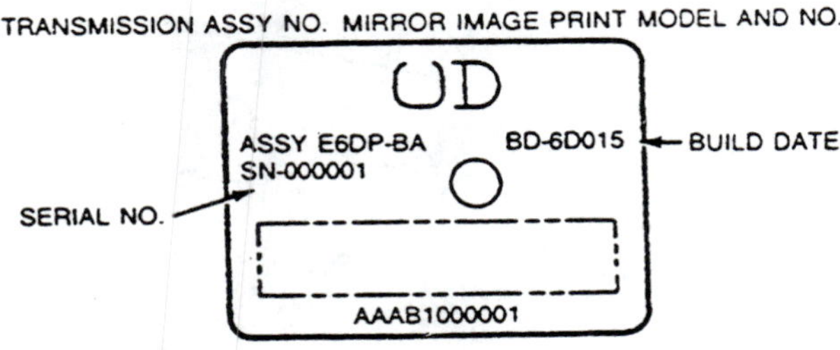

FIGURE 11–75 AXOD identification tag. (Courtesy of Ford)

Exploded view, Figure 11–76
Push connect fittings, Figure 11–77
Oil pump, Figure 11–78
Planetary gear set, Figure 11–79
Clutch assemblies, Figure 11–80
Thrust washer location, Figure 11–82
Oil tubes, Figure 11–81

11.6.6 Pressure Test

One of the key tests in diagnosis is the hydraulic system pressure test. The location of the test points of the AXOD transaxle is shown in Figure 11–83. A pressure chart listing the pressure specifications of this transaxle is shown in Figure 11–84.

11.6.7 Air Test

The technician must know which hydraulic circuit is being served by each passageway to be able to air test a transmission accurately. This information is presented in the illustration of the air test plate, Figure 11–85.

11.6.8 Special Attention

In this unit we show and explain various points of special interest about the AXOD transaxle. The information presented about each item is included with each illustration.

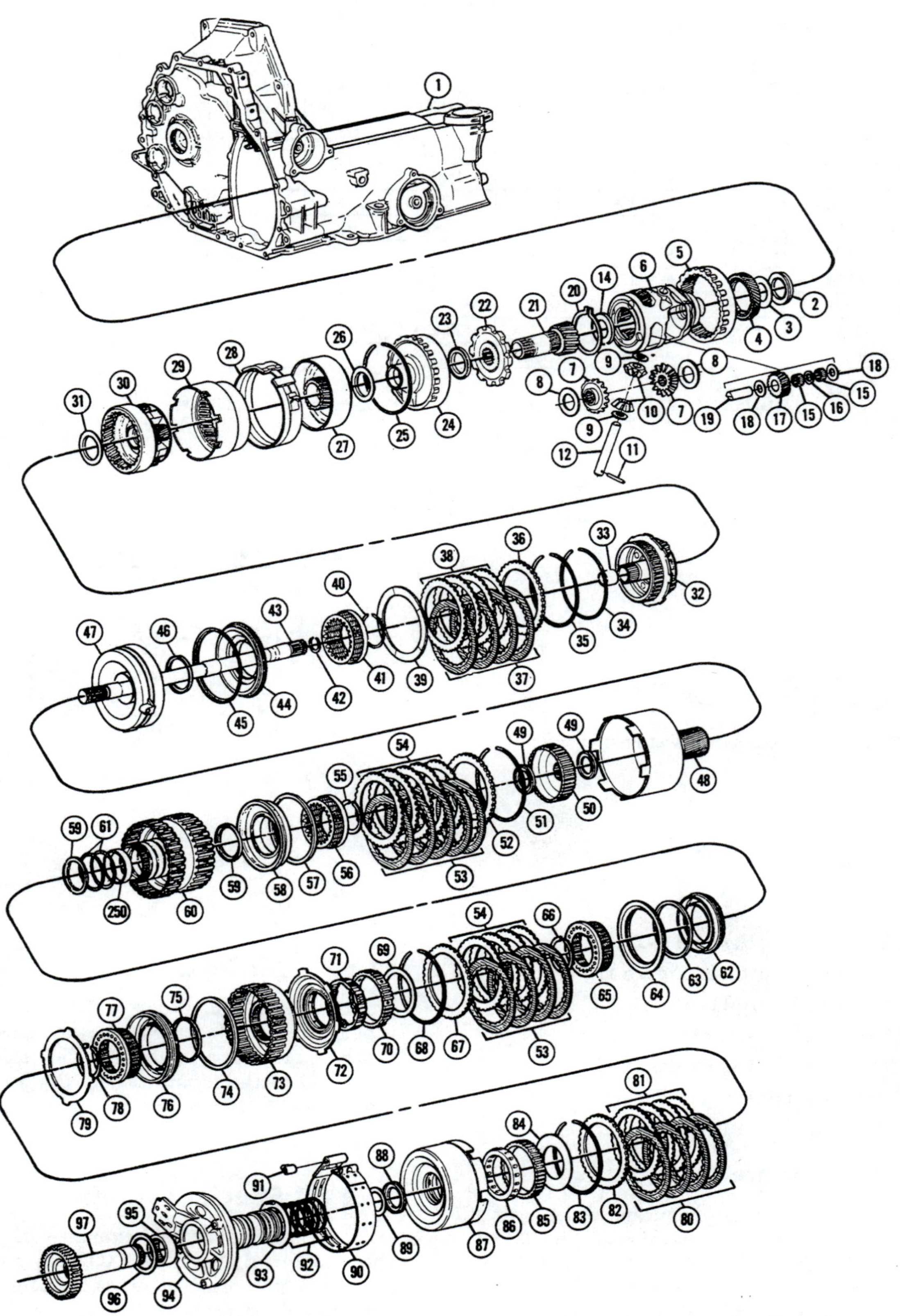

FIGURE 11–76 AXOD exploded view. (Courtesy of Ford)

No.	Part No.	Description
1.	7005	CASE ASSY
2.	7G112	BRG & RACE ASSY — DIFF CARRIER THRUST (#19)
3.	7G103	WASHER — DIFF CARRIER THRUST (#18 — SEL FIT
4.	7G237	GEAR — GOVERNOR DRIVE
5.	7G334	GEAR — FINAL DRIVE RING
6.	4205	CASE — TRANSAXLE DIFF GEAR
7.	4236	GEAR — DIFF SIDE (2 REQ'D)
8.	4228	WASHER — DIFF SIDE GEAR THRUST (2 REQ'D)
9.	4230	WASHER — RR AXLE DIFF PINION THRUST (2 REQ'D)
10.	4215	PINION — REAR AXLE DIFF (2 REQ'D)
11.	67638-S	PIN — COILED SPRING (RETAINS DIFF PINION SHAFT)
12.	4211	SHAFT — DIFF PINION
13.		
14.	7G107	BRG & RACE ASSY — FINAL DRIVE CARRIER (#17)
15.	7G216	BRG — FINAL DRIVE PLANET GEAR NEEDLE (168 REQ'D)
16.	7G217	SPACER — FINAL DRIVE PLANETARY GEAR (4 REQ'D)
17.	7G214	GEAR — FINAL DRIVE PLANET (4 REQ'D)
18.	7G215	WASHER — FINAL DRIVE PLANETARY GEAR THRUST (8 REQ'D)
19.	7G213	SHAFT — FINAL DRIVE PINION (4 REQ'D)
20.	N803202-S	RING — 77.3 RET EXT (RETAIN PINION SHAFTS INTO CARRIER)
21.	7G193	GEAR ASSY — FINAL DRIVE SUN
22.	7A233	GEAR — PARKING
23.	7G106	BRG & RACE ASSY — FINAL DRIVE GEAR THRUST (#16)
24.	7A130	SUPPORT ASSY — PLANET REAR
25.	N803197-S	RING — 150.7 RET INT (USED AS REAR SUPPORT RET RING)
26.	7G178	BRG & RACE ASSY — SUN GEAR THRUST — RR (#15)
27.	7B459	GEAR & DRUM ASSY — RR SUN
28.	7D034	BAND ASSY — LOW & INTERM
29.	7G211	GEAR — REAR RING
30.	7G224	GEAR ASSY — PLANET REAR
31.	7G177	BRG. & RACE ASSY — PLANET THRUST — CENTER (#13)
32.	7G218	PLANET ASSY — FRONT
33.	7G220	BUSHING — FRT PLT GR CARRIER
34.	7G290	RETAINING RING — SHELL — REAR
35.	N803049-52S	RING — 153.9 RET INT (RETAIN REV CL PRESS PLATE TO CYL) — SEL FIT
36.	7D408	PLATE — REV CLUTCH PRESSURE
37.	7E312	PLATE ASSY — REV CL INT SPLINE (FRICTION) 4 REQ'D
38.	7E315	PLATE — REV CL EXT SPLINE (STEEL) 4 REQ'D
39.	7F154	SPRING — REV CLUTCH CUSHION
40.	N803048-S	RING — 67.0 RET TYPE SU EXT (RET REV CL SPG & RET TO CYL)
41.	7G335	SUPT & SPRING ASSY — REV CLUTCH
42.	N803200-S	RING — 27.0MM RET EXT (RET DIFF CARRIER OUTPUT SHAFT)
43.	7G251	SHAFT — DIFF OUTPUT
44.	7D402	PISTON — REVERSE CLUTCH
45.	7D403	SEAL — REV CLUTCH PISTON — OUTER
46.	7D404	SEAL — REV CLUTCH PISTON — INNER
47.	7F341	CYLINDER — REV CLUTCH
48.	7G304	GEAR & SHELL ASSY — FRT SUN
49.	7G239	BRG & RACE ASSY — FRT SUN GR THRUST (#10 & #11) — 2 REQ'D
50.	7F221	HUB — INTERM CLUTCH
51.	7G346	RING P INTERM CLUTCH PLATE (SEL FIT)
52.	7B455	PLATE — CLUTCH PRESSURE (INTERM)
53.	7B164	PLATE ASSY — CL INT SPLINE (USED IN INTERM & DIRECT CLUTCH) AS REQ'D
54.	7E314	PLATE — CLUTCH EXT SPLINE (USED IN INTERM & DIRECT CLUTCH) AS REQ'D
55.	N803175-S	RING — 72.0 RET STYLE SU EXT (RET INTERM CL SPG & RET TO CYL)
56.	7G297	SUPT & SPRING ASSY — INTERM CLUTCH
57.	7G243	SEAL — INTERM CLUTCH — OUTER
58.	7E005	PISTON — INTERM CLUTCH
59.	7G240	SEAL — INTERM/DIR CL INNER (2 REQ'D)
60.	7G120	CYLINDER ASSY — DIR/INTERM CLUTCH
61.	7G102	SEAL — INTERM & DIR CL HUB 2 REQ'D
62.	7F254	PISTON ASSY — DIRECT CLUTCH
63.	7G241	SEAL — DIRECT CLUTCH — OUTER
64.	7G341	RING — DIRECT CLUTCH (PISTON)
65.	7G298	SUPT & SPRING ASSY — DIRECT CLUTCH
66.	N803176-S	RING — 77.0 RET STYLE SU EXT (RET DIR CL SPG & RET TO CYL)
67.	7B455	PLATE — CLUTCH PRESSURE (DIRECT)
68.	7G347	RING — DIR CL PLATE (SEL FIT)
	N803054-S	RING — 152.26 RET INT (RET DIR CL PRESS PLATE TO CYL)
69.	7G116	WASHER — DIR CLUTCH THRUST (#7)
70.	7G125	RACE — DIR ONE-WAY CL — OUTER
71.	7G158	CLUTCH ASSY — DIRECT ONE-WAY
72.	7G156	RACE & BSHG ASSY — DIR OWC — INNER
73.	7D424	CYLINDER ASSY — FWD CLUTCH
74.	7G243	SEAL — FWD CLUTCH — OUTER
75.	7G242	SEAL — FWD CLUTCH — INNER
76.	7L140	PISTON — FORWARD CLUTCH
77.	7G299	SUPT & SPRING ASSY — FWD CLUTCH
78.	N803053-S	RING — 85.0 RET TYPE SU EXT (RET FWD CL SPG & RET TO CYL)
79.	7G159	SPRING — FORWARD CLUTCH WAVE
80.	7E311	PLATE ASSY — FWD CL INT SPLINE (FRICTION) AS REQ'D
81.	7E314	PLATE — FWD CL EXT SPLINE (STEEL) AS REQ'D
82.	7B066	PLATE — FWD CL PRESSURE
83.	N803054-58S	RING — 152.26 RET INT (FWD) SEL FIT (RET FWD CL PRESS PLT)
84.	7D076	WASHER — FWD CLUTCH THRUST (#6)
85.	7G205	RACE — LOW OWC — OUTER
86.	7G206	CLUTCH ASSY — LOW ONE-WAY
87.	7G207	DRUM ASSY — OVERDRIVE
88.	7G128	BRG & RACE ASSY — DIR CL HUB (#9)
89.	7G273	WASHER — DRIVEN SPROCKET SUPT THRUST — RR (#8) SEL FIT
90.	7F196	BAND ASSY — OVERDRIVE
91.	7G343	RETAINER — 0/D BAND
92.	7D019	SEAL — FWD CLUTCH CYL (5 REQ'D)
93.	7D014	WASHER — SUPPORT THRUST — FRT (#5) SEL FIT
94.	7G166	SUPPORT ASSY — DRIVEN SPROCKET
95.	7G247	BRG ASSY — DRIVEN SPROCKET
96.	7G115	WASHER — DRIVEN SPROCKET THRUST (#4)
97.	7G132	SPROCKET ASSY — DRIVEN

FIGURE 11–76 *(continued)*

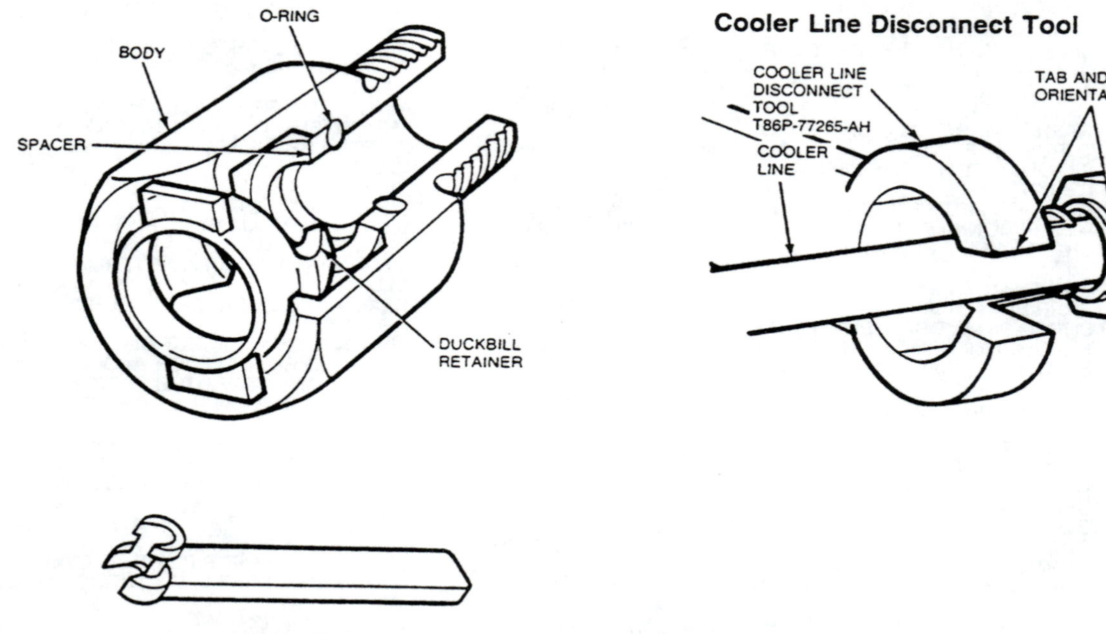

FIGURE 11–77 AXOD push connect fittings. (Courtesy of Ford)

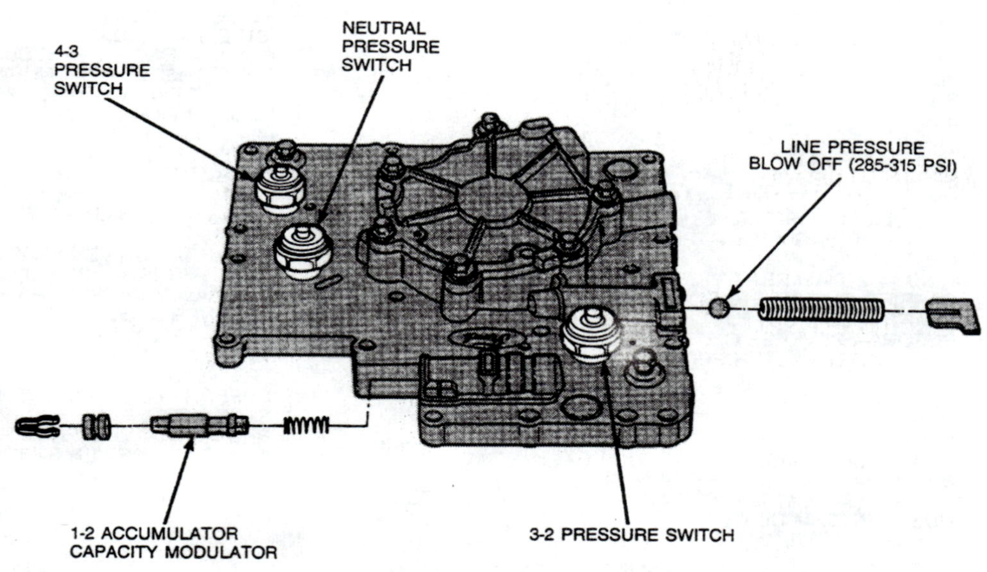

FIGURE 11–78 AXOD oil pump. (Courtesy of Ford)

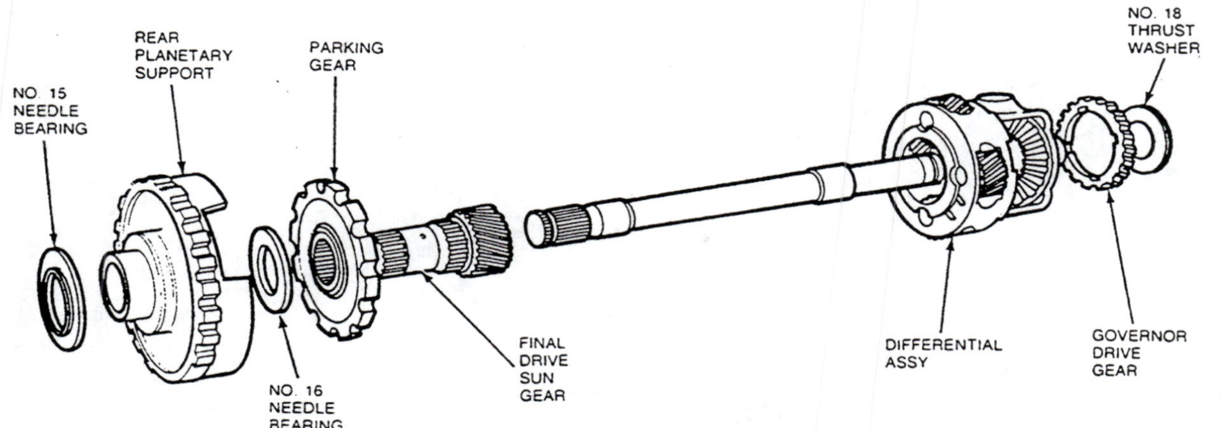

FIGURE 11–79 AXOD planetary gear set. (Courtesy of Ford)

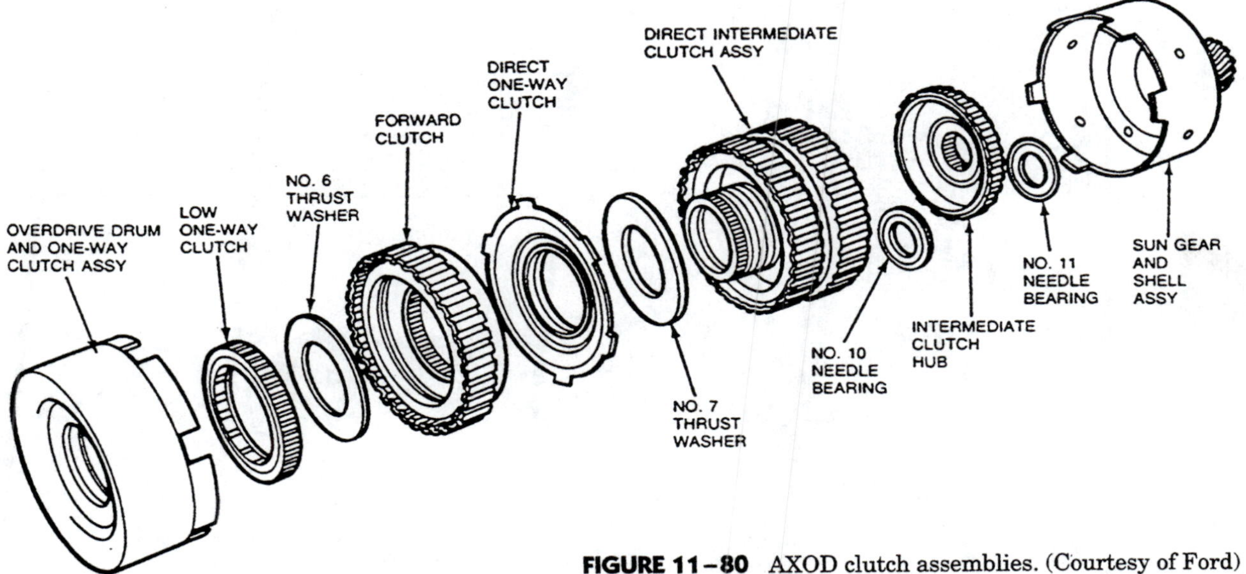

FIGURE 11–80 AXOD clutch assemblies. (Courtesy of Ford)

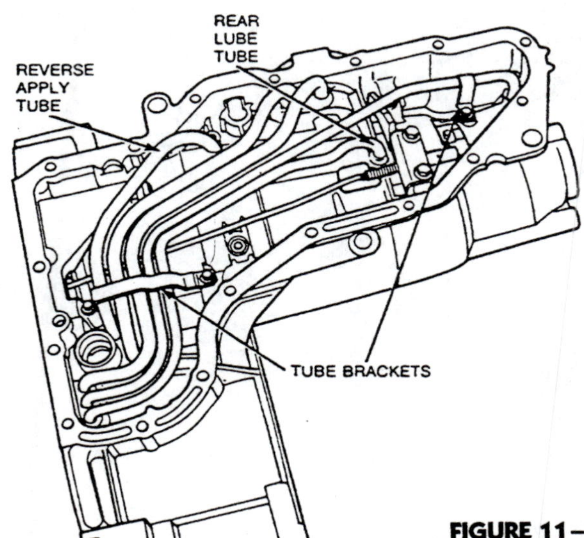

FIGURE 11–81 AXOD oil tubes. (Courtesy of Ford)

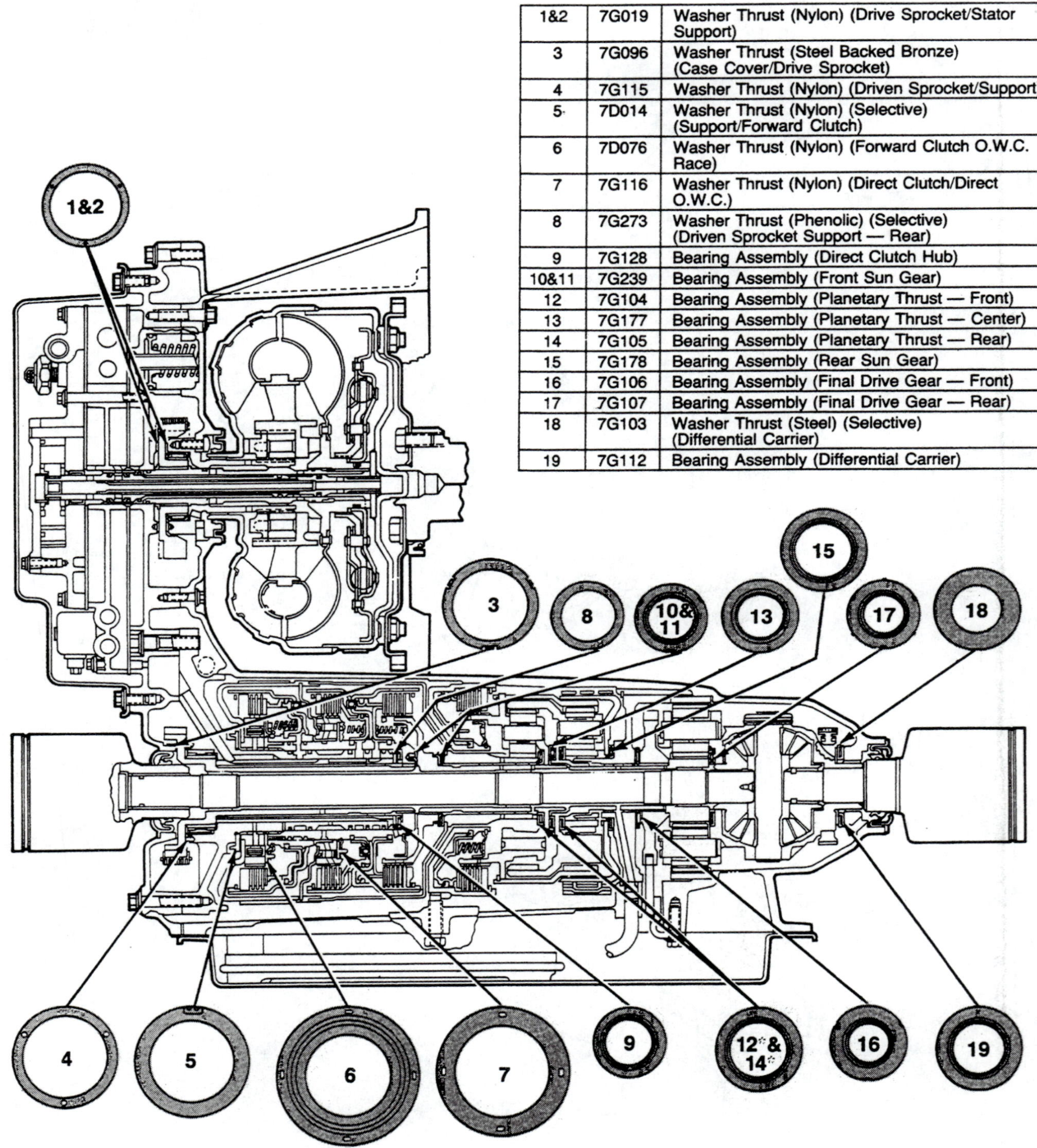

1&2	7G019	Washer Thrust (Nylon) (Drive Sprocket/Stator Support)
3	7G096	Washer Thrust (Steel Backed Bronze) (Case Cover/Drive Sprocket)
4	7G115	Washer Thrust (Nylon) (Driven Sprocket/Support)
5	7D014	Washer Thrust (Nylon) (Selective) (Support/Forward Clutch)
6	7D076	Washer Thrust (Nylon) (Forward Clutch O.W.C. Race)
7	7G116	Washer Thrust (Nylon) (Direct Clutch/Direct O.W.C.)
8	7G273	Washer Thrust (Phenolic) (Selective) (Driven Sprocket Support — Rear)
9	7G128	Bearing Assembly (Direct Clutch Hub)
10&11	7G239	Bearing Assembly (Front Sun Gear)
12	7G104	Bearing Assembly (Planetary Thrust — Front)
13	7G177	Bearing Assembly (Planetary Thrust — Center)
14	7G105	Bearing Assembly (Planetary Thrust — Rear)
15	7G178	Bearing Assembly (Rear Sun Gear)
16	7G106	Bearing Assembly (Final Drive Gear — Front)
17	7G107	Bearing Assembly (Final Drive Gear — Rear)
18	7G103	Washer Thrust (Steel) (Selective) (Differential Carrier)
19	7G112	Bearing Assembly (Differential Carrier)

FIGURE 11–82 AXOD thrust washer location. (Courtesy of Ford)

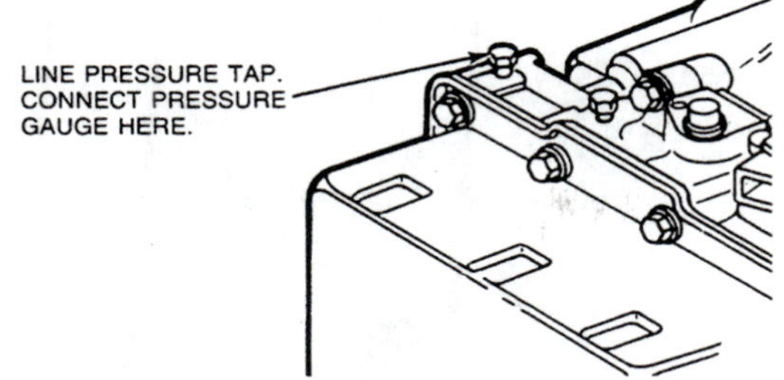

FIGURE 11–83 AXOD pressure test point. (Courtesy of Ford)

Range	Idle		WOT Stall	
	kPa	psi	kPa	psi
P, N	558-655	81-95	—	—
R	641-1048	93-152	1669-1924	242-279
(D), D, 1	558-655	81-95	1089-1262	158-183
L	772-1165	112-169	1089-1262	158-183

FIGURE 11–84 AXOD pressure test chart.

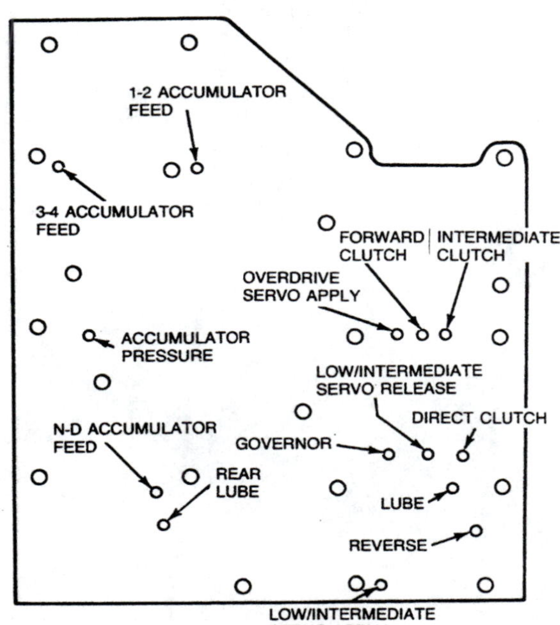

FIGURE 11–85 AXOD air test plate.

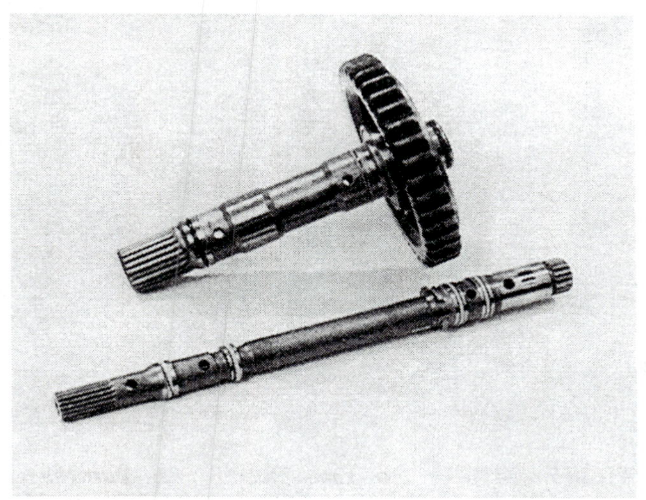

FIGURE AXOD–1 The oil pump drive shaft, turbine shaft, and drive sprocket must be inspected closely for wear. Replace all the seals.

FIGURE AXOD–2 The driven sprocket support should be examined and sealing ring replaced.

FIGURE AXOD–3 Inspect the forward clutch and its thrust washer for wear.

FIGURE AXOD–4 The three clutch drums shown here are, from left to right, the forward clutch and the combination direct/intermediate drum. Inspect closely.

FIGURE AXOD–5 The direct one-way clutch mounts in the front end of the direct clutch drum. Check for wear or damage.

FIGURE AXOD–6 The front sun gear and drive shell must be checked carefully.

FIGURE AXOD–7 The front sun gear rides around the output shaft when engaged in the planetary gear set.

FIGURE AXOD–8 The reverse clutch mounts just behind the front sun gear on splines on the front planet assembly.

FIGURE AXOD–9 The front planet assembly (left) must be checked for wear.

FIGURE AXOD–10 With the front planet assembly engaged in the rear assembly, the gear train forms a compact unit.

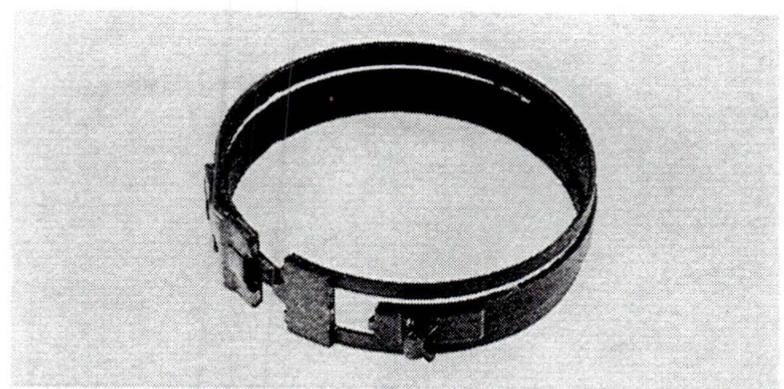

FIGURE AXOD–11 This double-wrap band is the low–intermediate band, which rides on the rear sun gear drum. Check it carefully.

FIGURE AXOD–12 The rear planet assembly (left) and rear ring gear (right) must be inspected for wear or damage.

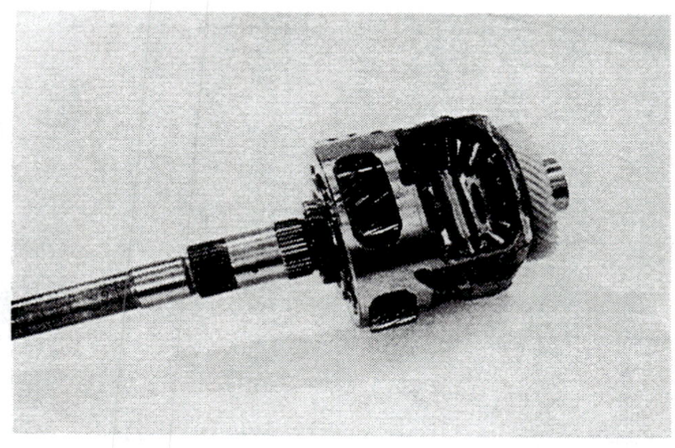

FIGURE AXOD–13 The final drive components must all be inspected for wear or damage.

FIGURE AXOD–14 The chain cover houses the shift accumulators and, in the lower center, the oil level thermostat valve. Check all parts carefully.

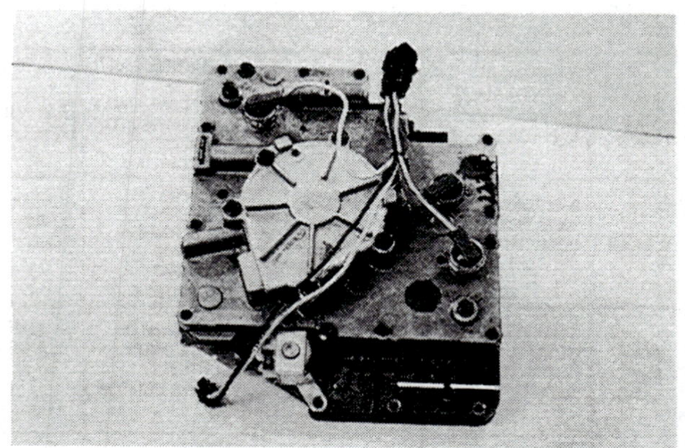

FIGURE AXOD–15 The valve body has three oil pressure switches and a converter clutch solenoid. Check them closely.

FIGURE AXOD -16 A variable-displacement oil pump is located in the valve body. Inspect for wear or damage.

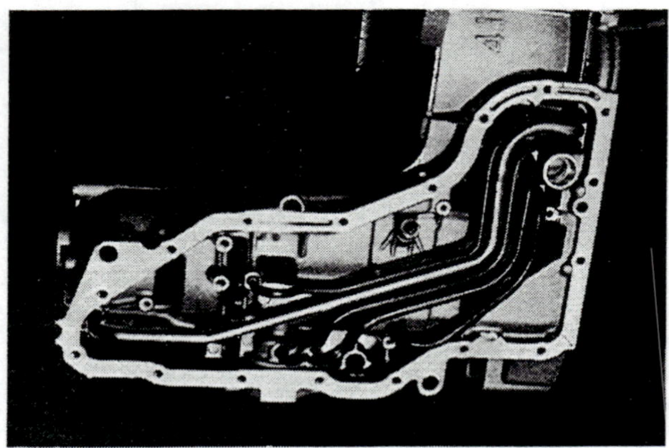

FIGURE AXOD–18 Five oil transfer tubes are used in the AXOD; check them carefully.

FIGURE AXOD–17 The drop-in governor is easy to inspect. Also check case wear.

SUMMARY

In this chapter we profiled five RWD transmissions and three FWD transaxles produced by Ford Motor Company for use in their vehicles. The transmissions showed great variety in their use of different types of gear set in the gear trains. Many other items are very similar in design and are used throughout the transmission line (Figure 11–86). Take time now to review any transmissions/transaxles that you do not completely understand.

FIGURE 11–86 Summary comparison chart.

FORD MOTOR COMPANY	TORQUE CONVERTER	GEAR TRAIN	COUPLING DEVICES	HOLDING DEVICES	PUMP	SHIFT CONTROL	GOVERNOR	THROTTLE VALVE
A4LD RWD, 4SPD	3-ELEMENT W/ HYDRAULIC CONVERTER CLUTCH	SIMPSON W/ OVERDRIVE UNIT	OVERDRIVE CLUTCH OVERDRIVE 1-WAY REV-HIGH CLUTCH FORWARD CLUTCH	OVERDRIVE BAND INTER-BAND LOW-REV BAND LOW 1-WAY	GEAR/CRESCENT	HYDRAULIC W/ ELECTRONIC CONVERTER CLUTCH	SHAFT-MOUNTED TYPE	VACUUM MODULATOR
E4OD	3-ELEMENT W/ ELECTRONIC CONVERTER CLUTCH	SIMPSON W/ OVERDRIVE UNIT	FORWARD COASTING INTERMEDIATE OD. OWC INTER OWC OVERDRIVE	REVERSE LO-REV OWC BAND	GEROTOR	ELECTRONIC CONTROL	NONE	NONE
ATX FWD, 3SPD	3-ELEMENT W/ DUAL OUTPUT PLANETARY GEARS	RAVIGNEAUX	DIRECT CLUTCH INTERMEDIATE CLUTCH REVERSE CLUTCH	BAND ONE-WAY CLUTCH	GEAR/CRESCENT	FULLY HYDRAULIC	DROP IN TYPE	ROD LINKAGE
AXOD AXOD/E FWD, 4SPD	3-ELEMENT W/ HYDRAULIC CONVERTER CLUTCH	INTER-CONNECTED PLANETARY SETS	FORWARD DIRECT INTERMEDIATE DIRECT ONE-WAY	LOW ONE-WAY REVERSE CLUTCH OVERDRIVE BAND LOW-INT BAND	VANE	HYDRAULIC W/ ELECTRONIC CONVERTER CLUTCH ELECTRONIC CONTROL	DROP IN TYPE	T.V. CABLE

SELF-TEST

Before going on to the next chapter, complete the self-test according to your instructor's directions. Read carefully and choose the best answer.

1. Which transmission uses a Ravigneaux gear set?
   - a. A4LD
   - b. E4OD
   - c. ATX
   - d. All of the above
   - e. None
2. Which transmission uses a drop-in governor?
   - a. E4OD
   - b. A4LD
   - c. ATX
   - d. All of the above
   - e. None
3. Which transmission uses a planetary gear set in the torque converter?
   - a. A4LD
   - b. E4OD
   - c. AXOD
   - d. ATX
   - e. None
4. Which transmission uses a dual-output torque converter?
   - a. ATX
   - b. E4OD
   - c. A4LD
   - d. AXOD
   - e. None
5. Which transmission is basically a C-3 with an overdrive unit added?
   - a. ATX
   - b. A4LD
   - c. E4OD
   - d. AXOD
   - e. None
6. Which transmission uses a vane pump?
   - a. AXOD
   - b. ATX
   - c. E4OD
   - d. A4LD
   - e. None
7. Which transmission uses a throttle valve cable to control the throttle valve?
   - a. AXOD
   - b. ATX
   - c. E4OD
   - d. A4LD
   - e. None
8. Which transmission uses a fully hydraulic shift control system?
   - a. AXOD
   - b. ATX
   - c. A4LD
   - d. All of the above
   - e. None
9. Which transmission uses two interconnecting planetary gear sets?
   - a. E4OD
   - b. A4LD
   - c. ATX
   - d. AXOD
10. Which transmission has a forward clutch?
    - a. E4OD
    - b. ATX
    - c. AXOD
    - d. All of the above
    - e. None
11. Which transmission has three bands?
    - a. A4LD
    - b. AXOD
    - c. E4OD
    - d. ATX
    - e. None
12. Which transmission uses a Simpson gear set?
    - a. AXOD
    - b. E4OD
    - c. A4LD
    - d. All of the above

Chapter 12

GENERAL MOTORS CORPORATION

12.1 PERFORMANCE OBJECTIVES

After studying this chapter, you should have fulfilled the following performance objectives by being able to:

1. List the General Motors transmissions/transaxles described in this chapter.
2. Describe the basic components of each transmission/transaxle.
3. Describe the power flow in each gear position, including which coupling and holding devices are applied, for each transmission/transaxle.
4. Write a clutch and band chart for each transmission/transaxle listed in the chapter.
5. Complete the self-test with at least the minimum score required by your instructor.

12.2 OVERVIEW

In this chapter the following General Motors Hydra-Matic transmission/transaxles are profiled: HM 4L60, HM 4L80E, HM 3T40, and HM 4T60/4T60E. The choice of the transmissions profiled in this chapter is based on the popularity of the transmission and the extent of its current use. Some transmissions were chosen because of their unique features to show as wide a variety of designs as possible. Two RWD transmissions are explained, along with two FWD transaxles. The HM 4T60E, and HM 4L80E transaxles are controlled electronically using shift solenoids to control the gear changes.

The terms used to describe the transmission parts are different from those used in Part I of the book. The component names used by General Motors are used in the descriptions to acquaint the student technician with the manufacturer's nomenclature. A chart comparing the generic terms and the General Motors terms is shown in Figure 12–1.

All General Motors Hydra-Matic transmissions/transaxles are designed to use Dexron II ATF or its equivalent.

12.3 HM 4L60: RWD FOUR-SPEED TRANSMISSION

12.3.1 Basic Description

The HM 4L60 is the medium-sized rear-wheel-drive transmission produced by Hydra-Matic. The design is based around two separate planetary gear set (Figure 12–2). The HM 4L60 offers a wider range of gear ratios, thereby providing increased vehicle performance.

GENERIC NAME	=	GENERAL MOTORS' NAME
FRONT CLUTCH	=	DIRECT CLUTCH
REAR CLUTCH	=	FORWARD CLUTCH
FRONT RING GEAR	=	INPUT RING GEAR
FRONT PINION CARRIER	=	OUTPUT CARRIER
REAR RING GEAR	=	OUTPUT RING GEAR
REAR PINION CARRIER	=	REACTION CARRIER
FRONT BAND	=	INTERMEDIATE BAND
REAR BAND	=	REAR BAND
ROLLER CLUTCH	=	ONE-WAY CLUTCH
MAIN LINE PRESSURE	=	DRIVE OIL
THROTTLE PRESSURE	=	MODULATOR PRESSURE
DOWNSHIFT VALVE	=	DETENT VALVE

FIGURE 12–1 General Motors nomenclature. (Reprinted with permission of General Motors Corporation)

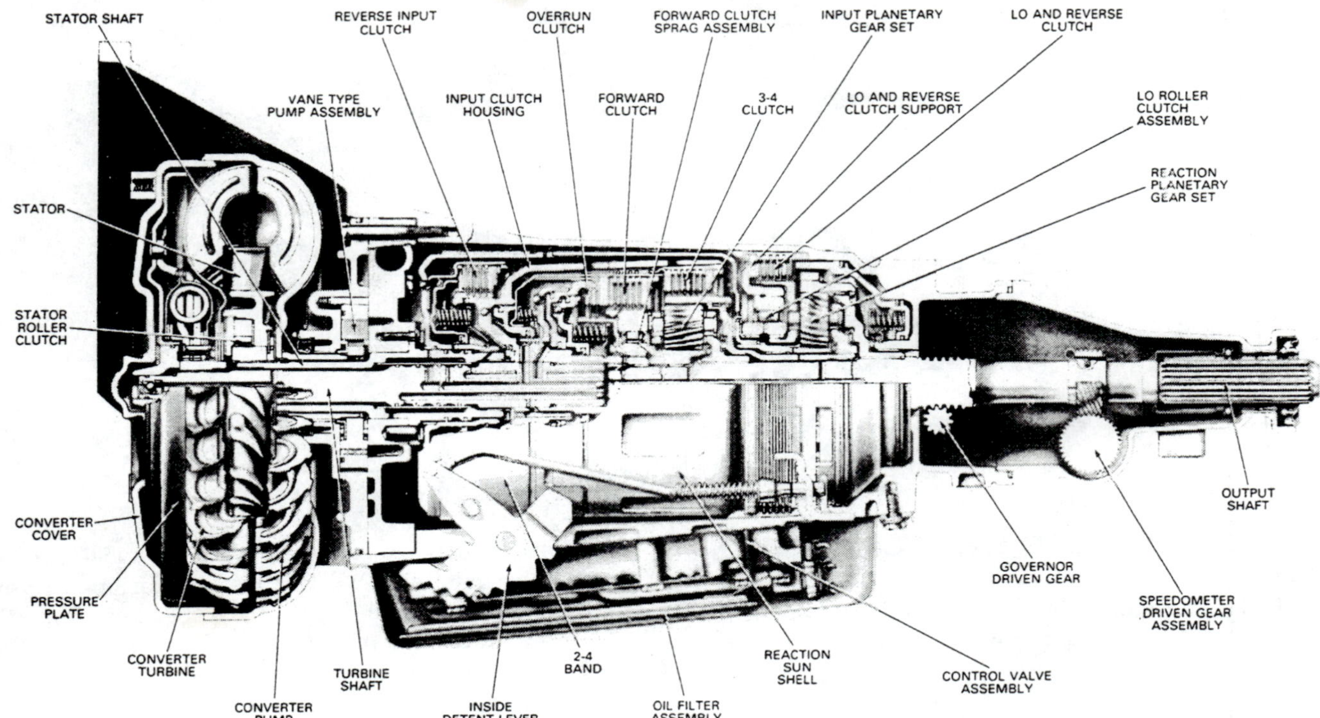

FIGURE 12–2 THM 4L60 cutaway view. (Reprinted with permission of General Motors Corporation)

FIGURE 12–3 THM 4L60 torque converter. (Reprinted with permission of General Motors Corporation)

CONVERTER CLUTCH RELEASED

CONVERTER HOUSING COVER ASSEMBLY

TURBINE THRUST SPACER

PRESSURE PLATE ASSEMBLY

PRESSURE PLATE SPRING

TURBINE ASSEMBLY

STATOR ASSEMBLY

THRUST BEARING ASSEMBLY

CONVERTER PUMP ASSEMBLY

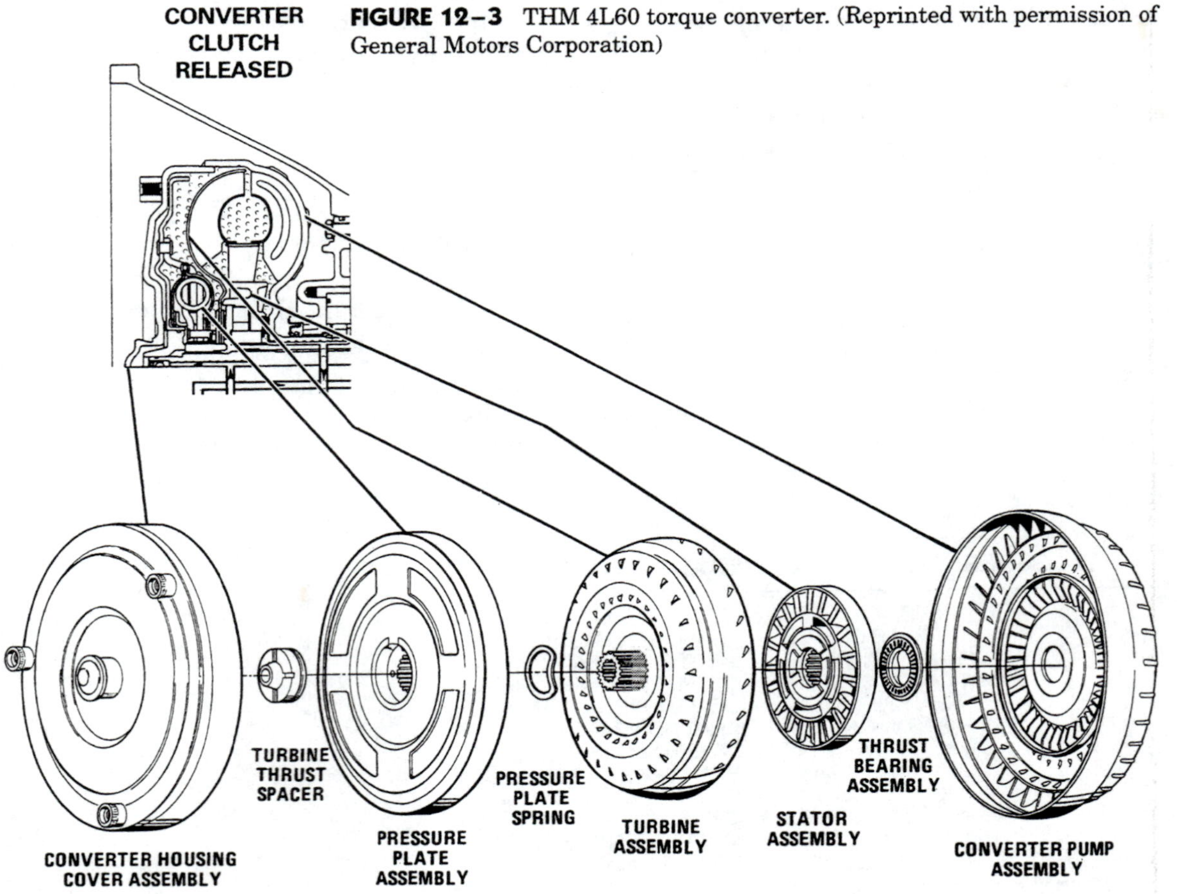

1. Torque Converter

A conventional three-element torque converter is used along with a hydraulic converter clutch. The converter clutch is controlled by either a vacuum-electrical system or by the on-board computer. The torque increase is approximately 2:1 (Figure 12–3).

2. Gear Train

The HM 4L60 gear train is unique in that it uses two separate planetary gear sets. In the front gear set the sun gear and ring gear are the input members, with the pinion carrier as the output member. The ring gear of the front gear set is attached to the pinion carrier of the rear gear set, making it an input member also. The rear sun gear is also a reaction member along with the rear pinion carrier. The rear ring gear is the output member and is splined to the output shaft (Figure 12–4).

3. Coupling Devices

The coupling devices include the following: the reverse input clutch, overrun clutch, forward clutch, 3–4 clutch, and forward sprag clutch (Figure 12–5).

4. Holding Devices

The holding devices are the 2–4 band, the low roller clutch, and the low–reverse clutch.

5. Pump

The HM 4L60 uses a variable-capacity vane pump housed in an aluminum pump body (Figure 12–6).

6. Shift Control

The shift control is fully hydraulic, with a cross-section view of the valve body shown in Figure 12–7.

7. Governor

A drop-in governor is used, as shown in Figure 12–8.

8. Throttle Valve

The throttle valve is controlled by a cable connected to the carburetor linkage (Figure 12–9).

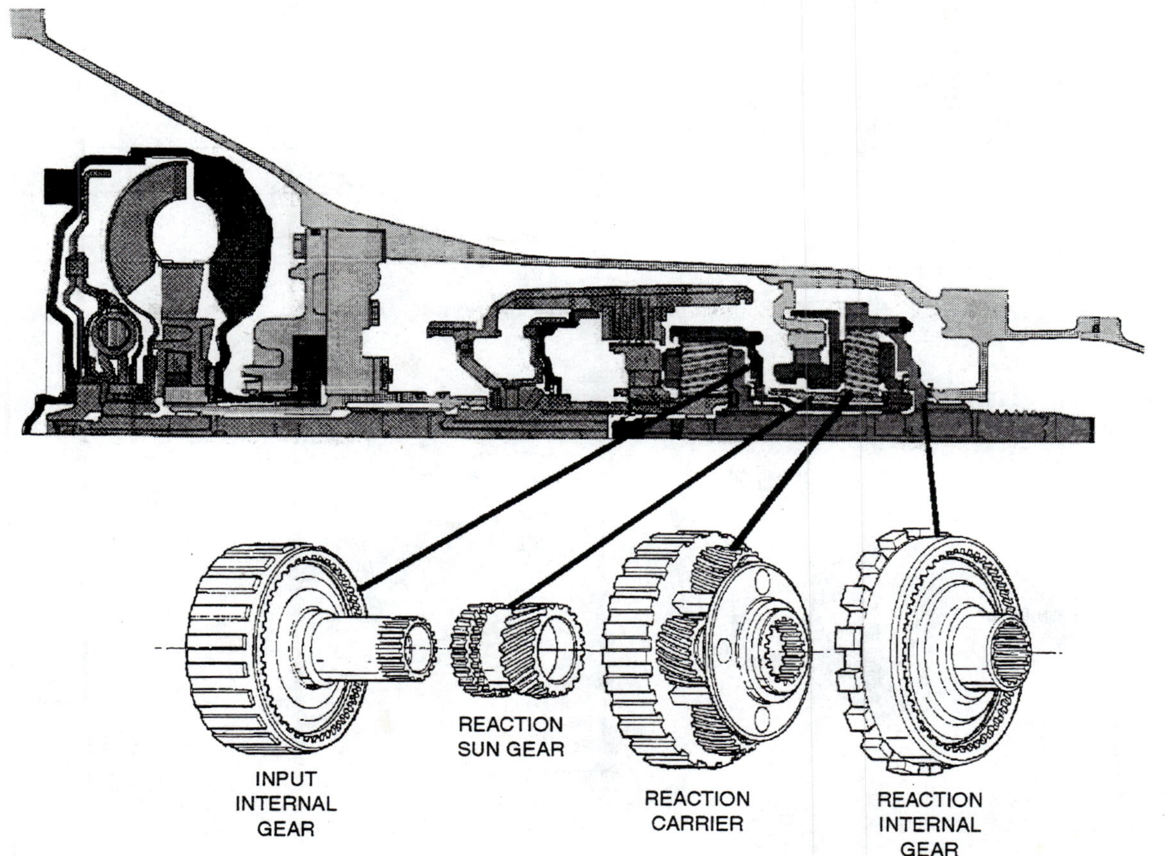

FIGURE 12–4 THM 4L60 gear train. (Reprinted with permission of General Motors Corporation)

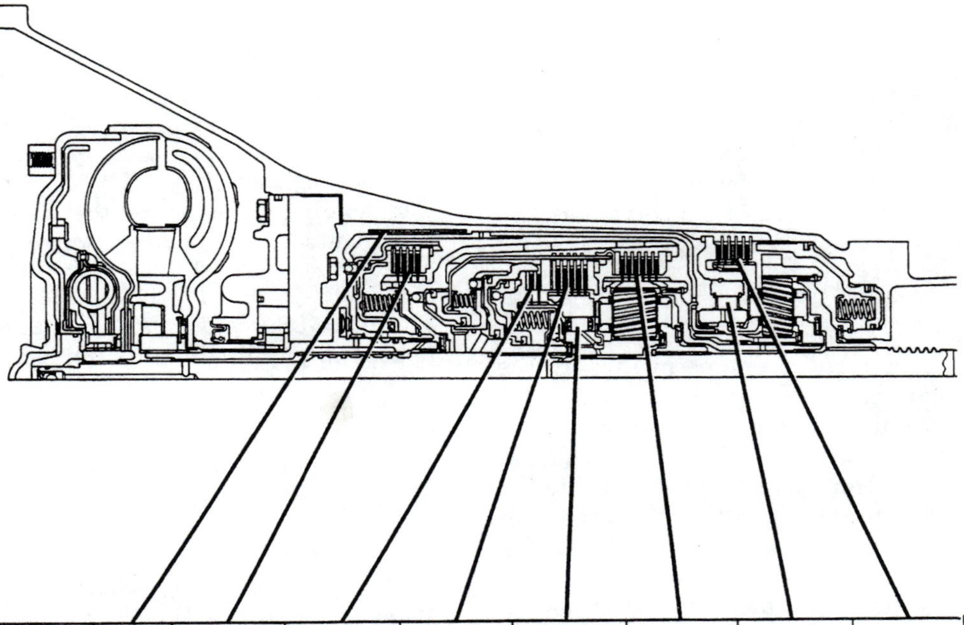

GEAR RANGE	2-4 BAND	REVERSE INPUT CLUTCH	OVERRUN CLUTCH	FORWARD CLUTCH	FORWARD SPRAG CL. ASSEMBLY	3-4 CLUTCH	LO ROLLER CLUTCH	LO-REV. CLUTCH
1ST DR4				ON	ON		ON	
2ND DR4	ON			ON	ON			
3RD DR4				ON	ON	ON		
4TH DR4	ON			ON		ON		
3RD DR3			ON	ON	ON	ON		
2ND DR2	ON		ON	ON	ON			
1ST LO			ON	ON	ON		ON	ON
REV.		ON						ON

FIGURE 12–5 THM 4L60 coupling and holding devices. (Reprinted with permission of General Motors Corporation)

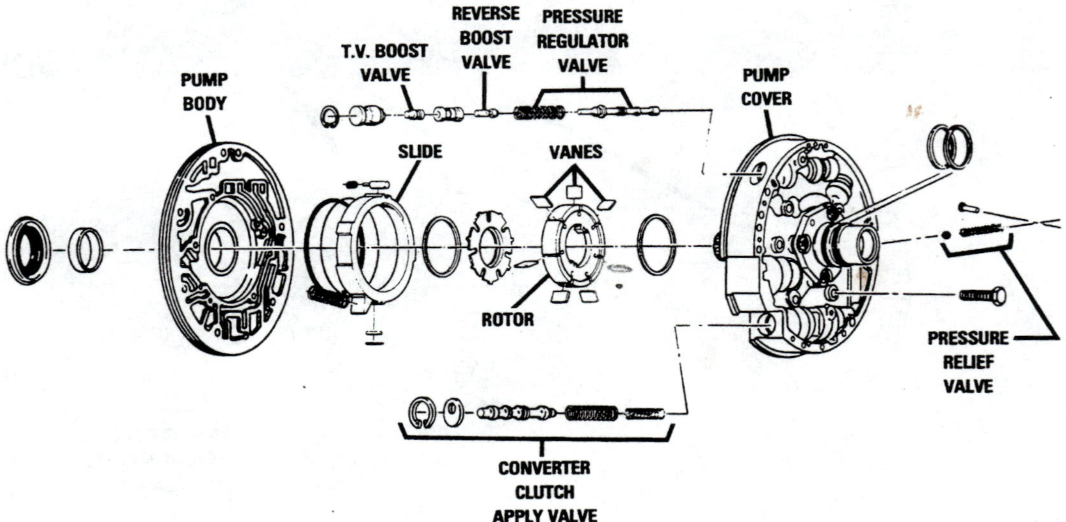

FIGURE 12–6 THM 4L60 oil pump. (Reprinted with permission of General Motors Corporation)

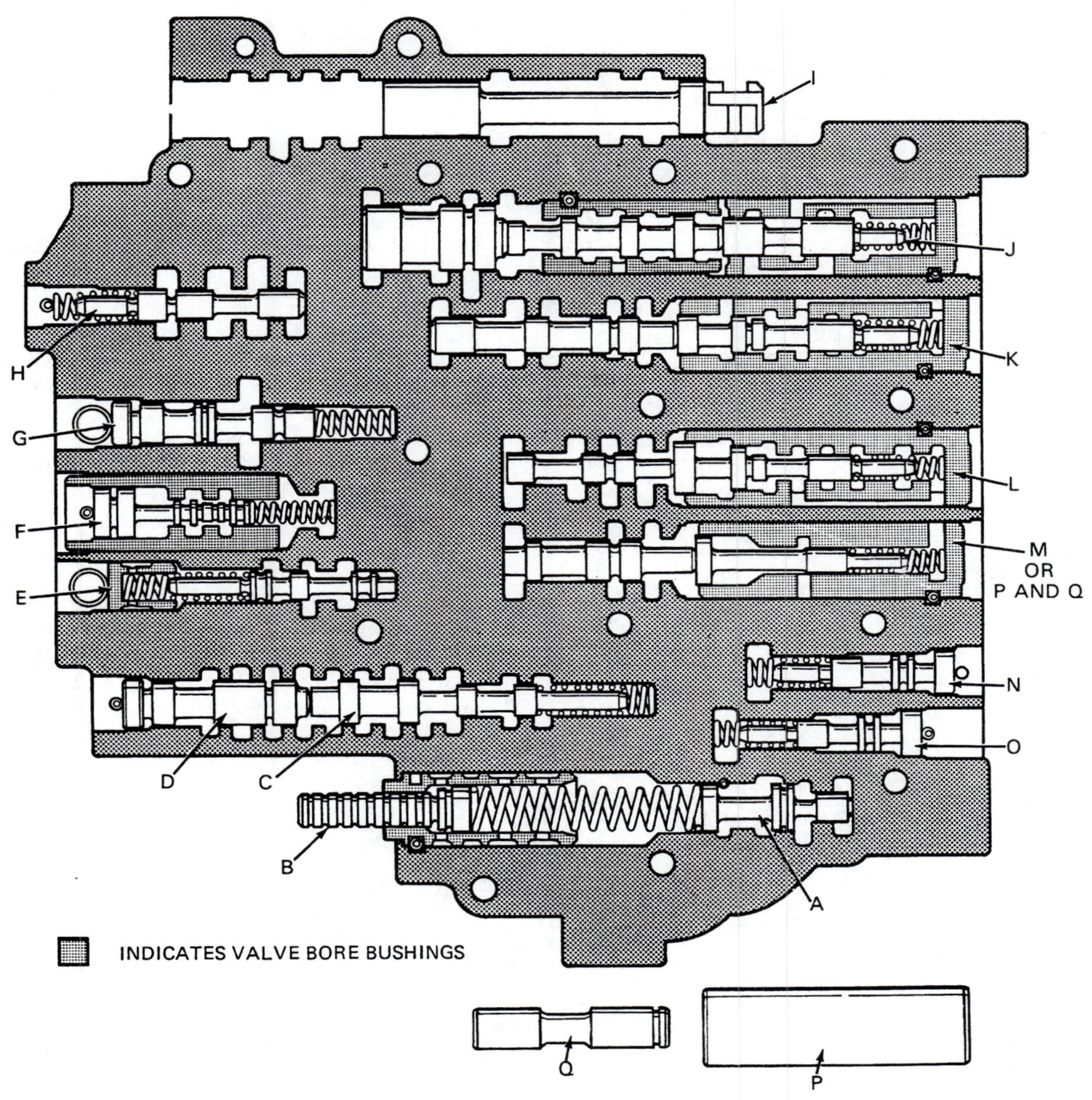

A THROTTLE VALVE
B T.V. PLUNGER & BUSHING
C 4-3 SEQUENCE VALVE
D 3-4 RELAY VALVE
E T.V. LIMIT VALVE TRAIN
F ACCUMULATOR VALVE TRAIN
G LINE BIAS VALVE TRAIN
H 3-2 CONTROL VALVE TRAIN
I MANUAL VALVE
J 1-2 SHIFT VALVE TRAIN
K 2-3 SHIFT VALVE TRAIN
L 3-4 SHIFT VALVE TRAIN
M CONVERTER CLUTCH SHIFT VALVE TRAIN
N M.T.V. UP VALVE TRAIN
O M.T.V. DOWN VALVE TRAIN
P CONVERTER CLUTCH T.V. BUSHING BORE PLUG (ECM CONTROLED VEHICLES)
Q CONVERTER CLUTCH SHIFT VALVE BORE PLUG (ECM CONTROLED VEHICLES)

FIGURE 12–7 THM 4L60 valve body. (Reprinted with permission of General Motors Corporation)

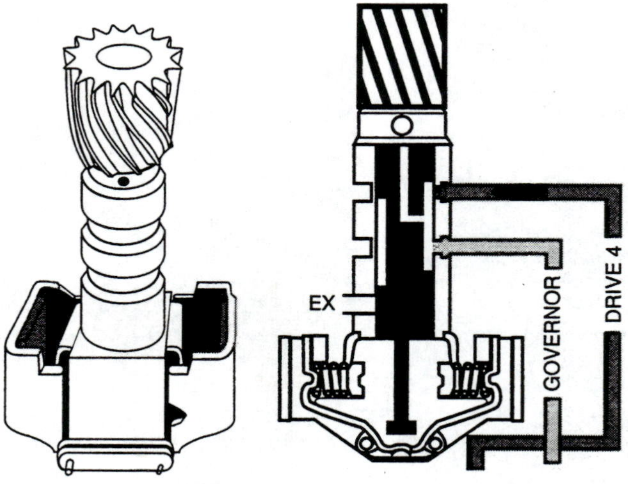

FIGURE 12-8 THM 4L60 governor. (Reprinted with permission of General Motors Corporation)

12.3.2 Power Flow

The power flow is described by stating the coupling and holding device action (applied, or holding) on the members of the planetary gear set (sun gear, pinion carrier, and ring gear) in each gear range of the transmission.

1. Neutral (N)
In neutral all the coupling and holding devices are released. Only the turbine shaft and clutch drum are rotating.

2. First Gear (D1)
In first gear the forward clutch is applied, which provides input to the forward sprag, which is holding and driving the front sun gear. The low roller clutch is holding the rear pinion carrier as a reaction member (Figure 12–10). The first-gear ratio is 3.06:1. In manual low the low–reverse clutch and the overrun clutch are also applied.

3. Second Gear (D2)
In second gear the forward clutch and sprag remain engaged and the 2–4 band is applied. The band holds the rear sun gear, which provides a second-gear ratio of 1.62:1 (Figure 12–11). In manual second gear the overrun clutch is also applied.

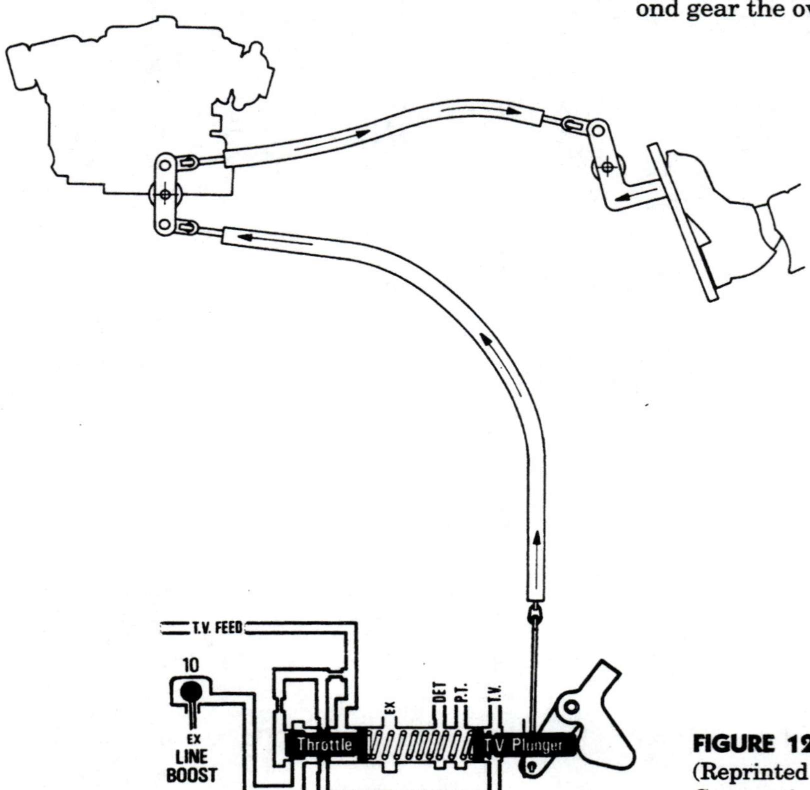

FIGURE 12-9 THM 4L60 throttle valve linkage. (Reprinted with permission of General Motors Corporation)

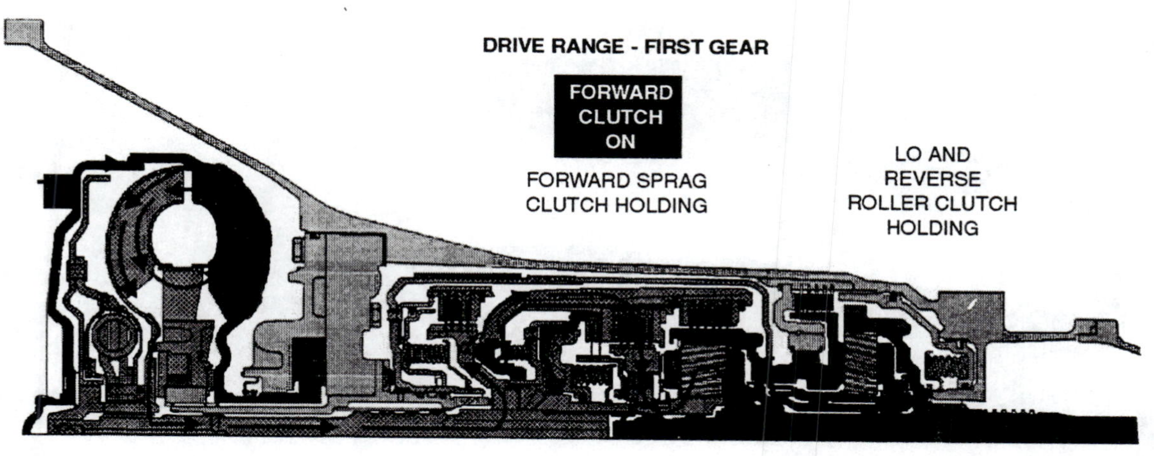

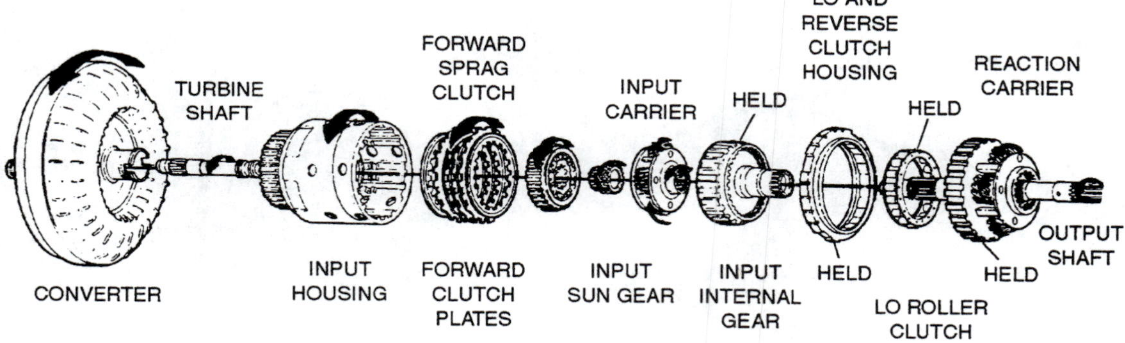

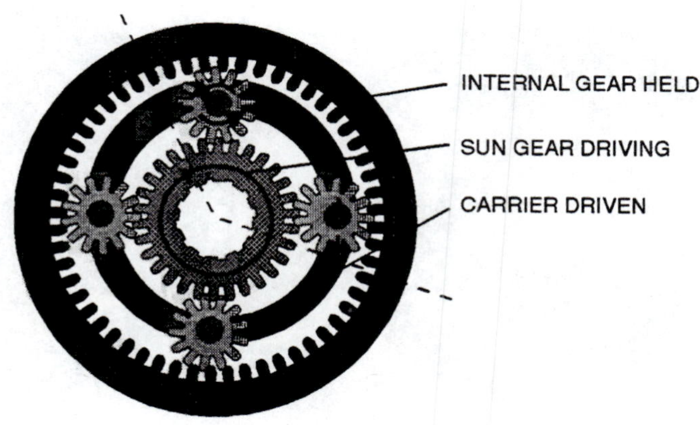

FIGURE 12–10 THM 4L60 in first gear. (Reprinted with permission of General Motors Corporation)

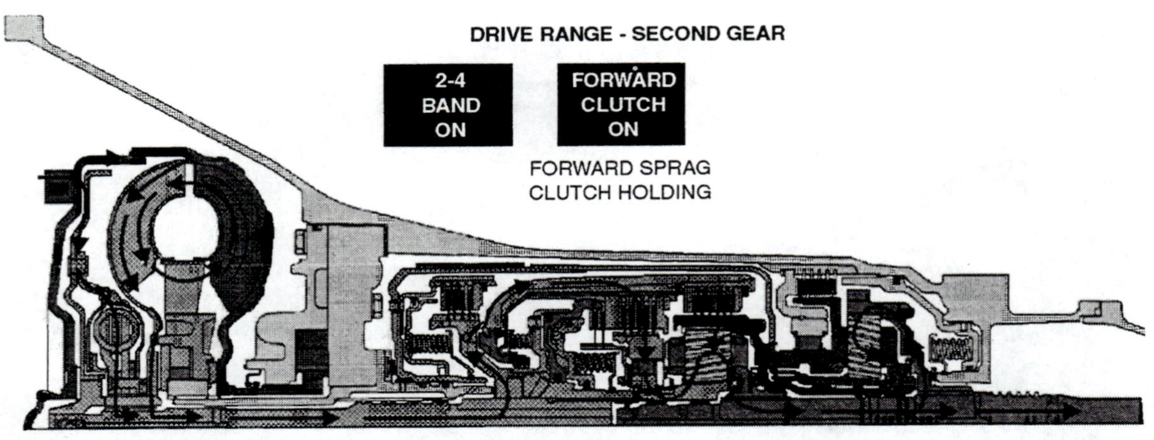

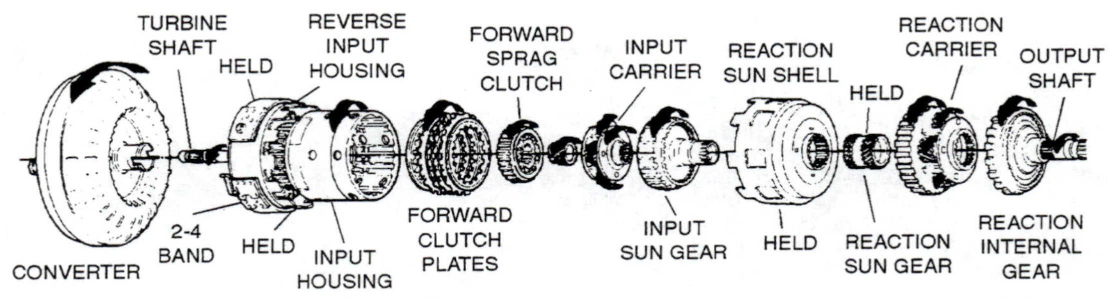

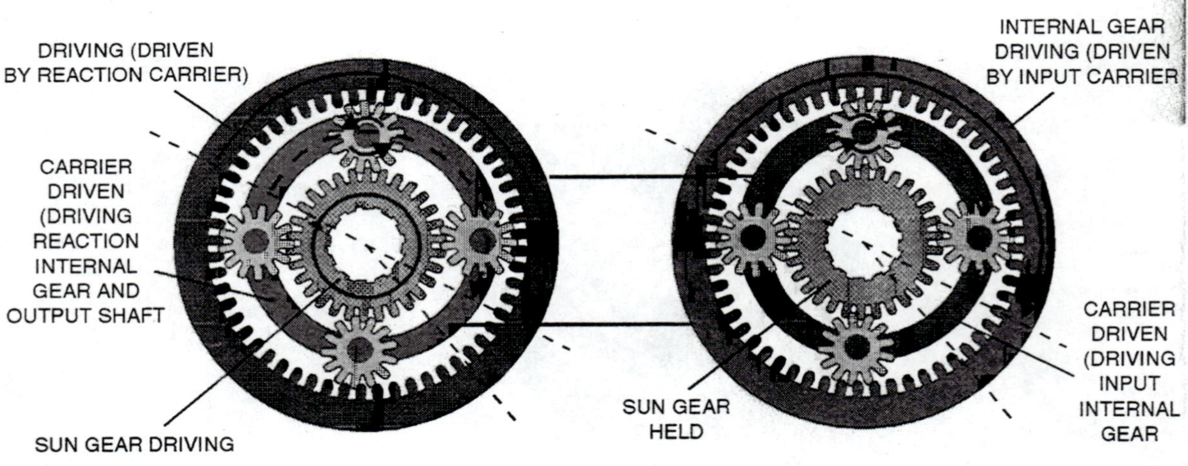

FIGURE 12–11 THM 4L60 in second gear. (Reprinted with permission of General Motors Corporation)

4. Third Gear (D3)

For third gear the forward clutch and sprag remain engaged and the 3–4 clutch is applied. The 3–4 clutch drives the front ring gear at the same speed that the forward clutch and sprag drive the front sun gear, which provides direct drive. In manual third gear, the overrun clutch is again applied, in addition to the other devices.

5. Fourth Gear (D4)

The forward clutch and 3–4 clutch are still applied, but the forward sprag is overrunning. The 2–4 band is applied, which holds the rear sun gear as a reaction member, while the 3–4 clutch provides input to the rear pinion carrier. This combination provides a 0.70:1 gear ratio for fourth gear (Figure 12–12).

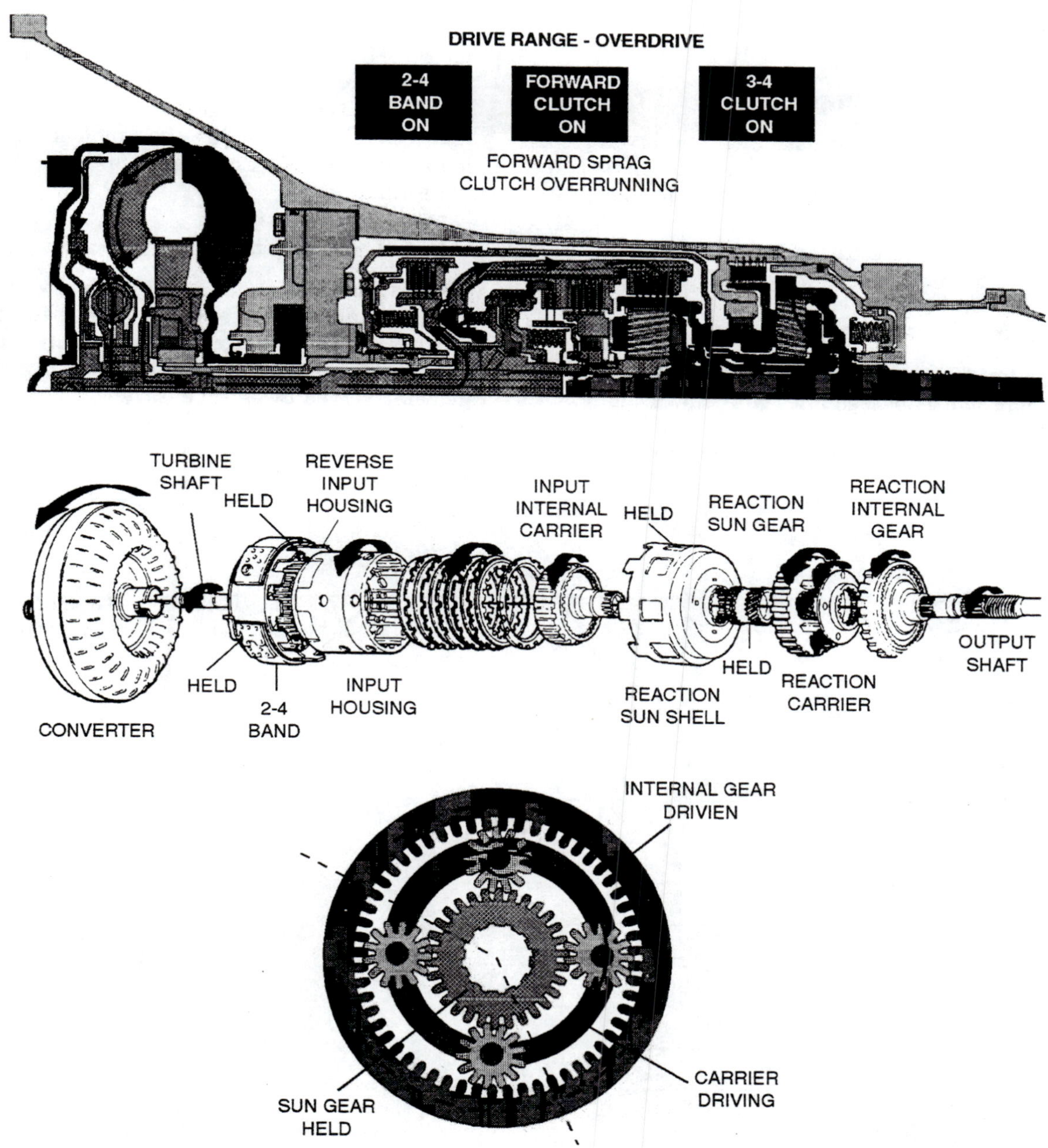

FIGURE 12–12 THM 4L60 in fourth gear. (Reprinted with permission of General Motors Corporation)

6. *Reverse Gear (R)*
In reverse gear the reverse input and low-reverse clutches are applied. The reverse input clutch drives the rear sun gear as input, while the low–reverse clutch holds the pinion carrier as the reaction member. The reverse-gear ratio is 2.29:1.

12.3.3 Clutch and Band Charts

The first chart, the author's design, is shown in Figure 12–13. The second chart, the manufacturer's design, is shown in Figure 12–14.

12.3.4 Identification

The shape of the transmission oil pan or its gasket is a quick means of identifying an automatic transmission. In Figure 12–15 you see the pan gasket shape and number of bolt holes for the HM 4L60 transmission. The location of the factory identification tag and its code are shown in Figure 12–16.

12.3.5 Components

In this section exploded drawings of the HM 4L60 transmission subassemblies are shown along with lists of the part names. The manufacturer's part names are used to eliminate confusion about component names. The illustrations to study are as follows:

Internal parts, Figure 12–17
Pump, Figure 12–18
Valve body, Figure 12–19

12.3.6 Pressure Test

One of the key tests in diagnosis is the hydraulic system pressure test. The location of the test points of the HM 4L60 transmission is shown in Figure 12–20. A pressure chart listing the pressure specification of this transmission is shown in Figure 12–21. To aid in finding the problem quickly, a diagnostic chart is also used in pressure testing this transmission.

12.3.7 Air Test

Air testing is used during preliminary diagnosis of certain malfunctions and also during the disassembly process to verify component operation or failure. The technician must know which hydraulic circuit is being served by each passageway to be able to air test a transmission accurately. This information is presented in the following illustrations:

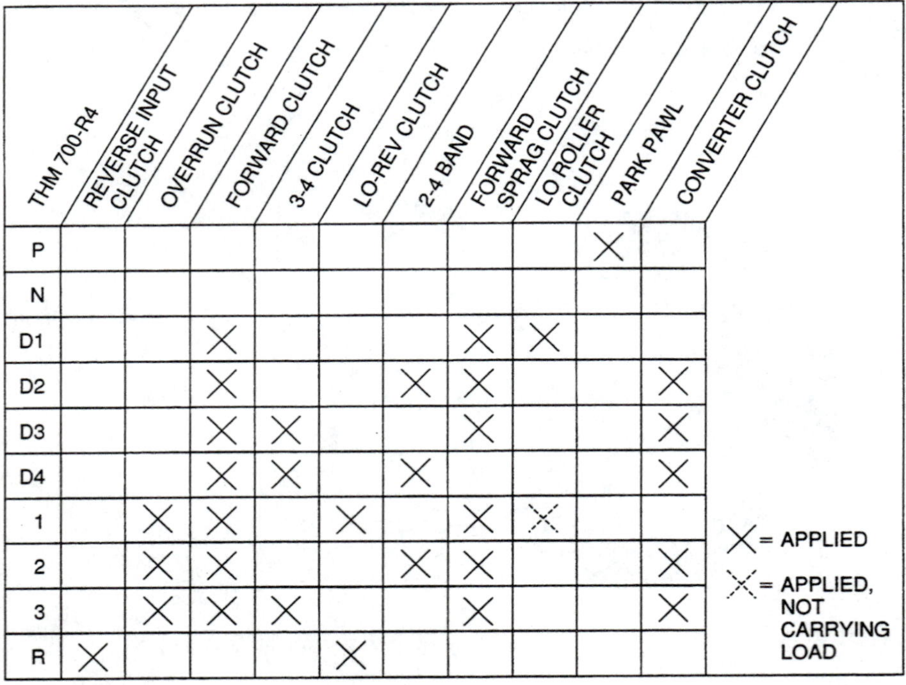

THM 700-R4	REVERSE INPUT CLUTCH	OVERRUN CLUTCH	FORWARD CLUTCH	3-4 CLUTCH	LO-REV CLUTCH	2-4 BAND	FORWARD SPRAG CLUTCH	LO ROLLER CLUTCH	PARK PAWL	CONVERTER CLUTCH
P									X	
N										
D1			X				X	X		
D2			X			X	X			X
D3			X	X			X			X
D4			X	X		X				X
1		X	X		X		X	X (dashed)		
2		X	X			X	X			X
3		X	X	X			X			X
R	X				X					

X = APPLIED
X (dashed) = APPLIED, NOT CARRYING LOAD

FIGURE 12–13 THM 4L60 clutch and band chart, standardized version.

GEAR RANGE	2-4 BAND	REVERSE INPUT CLUTCH	OVERRUN CLUTCH	FORWARD CLUTCH	FORWARD SPRAG CL. ASSEMBLY	3-4 CLUTCH	LO ROLLER CLUTCH	LO-REV. CLUTCH
1ST DR4				ON	ON		ON	
2ND DR4	ON			ON	ON			
3RD DR4				ON	ON	ON		
4TH DR4	ON			ON		ON		
3RD DR3			ON	ON	ON	ON		
2ND DR2	ON		ON	ON	ON			
1ST LO			ON	ON	ON		ON	ON
REV.		ON						ON

FIGURE 12–14 THM 4L60 clutch and band chart, factory version. (Reprinted with permission of General Motors Corporation)

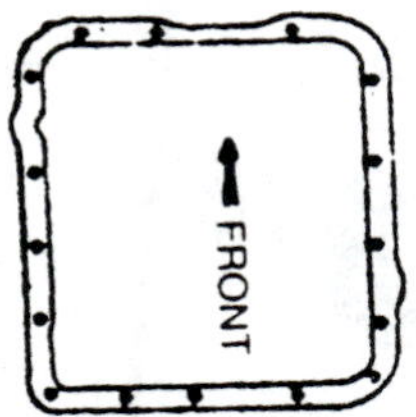

FIGURE 12–15 THM 4L60 pan gasket identification. (Reprinted with permission of General Motors Corporation)

Pump air test, Figure 12–22

Overrun and forward clutch, Figure 12–23

3–4 clutch, Figure 12–24

Reverse input, Figure 12–25

Low–reverse clutch, Figure 12–26

12.3.8 Special Attention

In this section we show and explain various points of special interest about the THM 700-R4 transmission. The information presented about each item is included with each illustration.

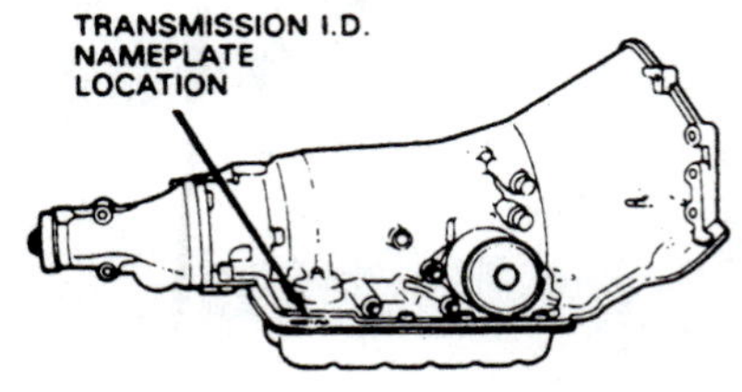

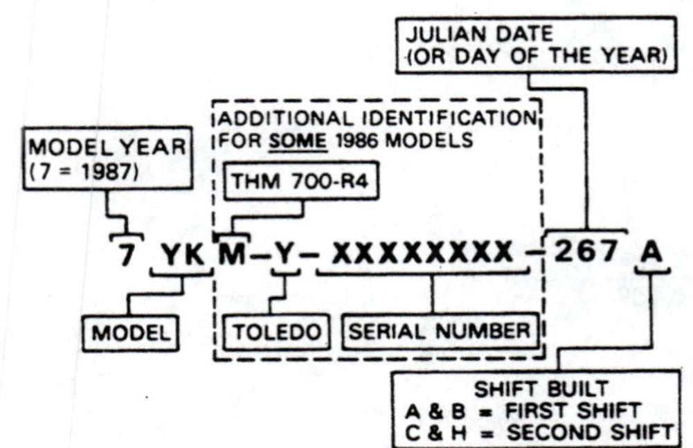

FIGURE 12–16 THM 4L60 identification tag location. (Reprinted with permission of General Motors Corporation)

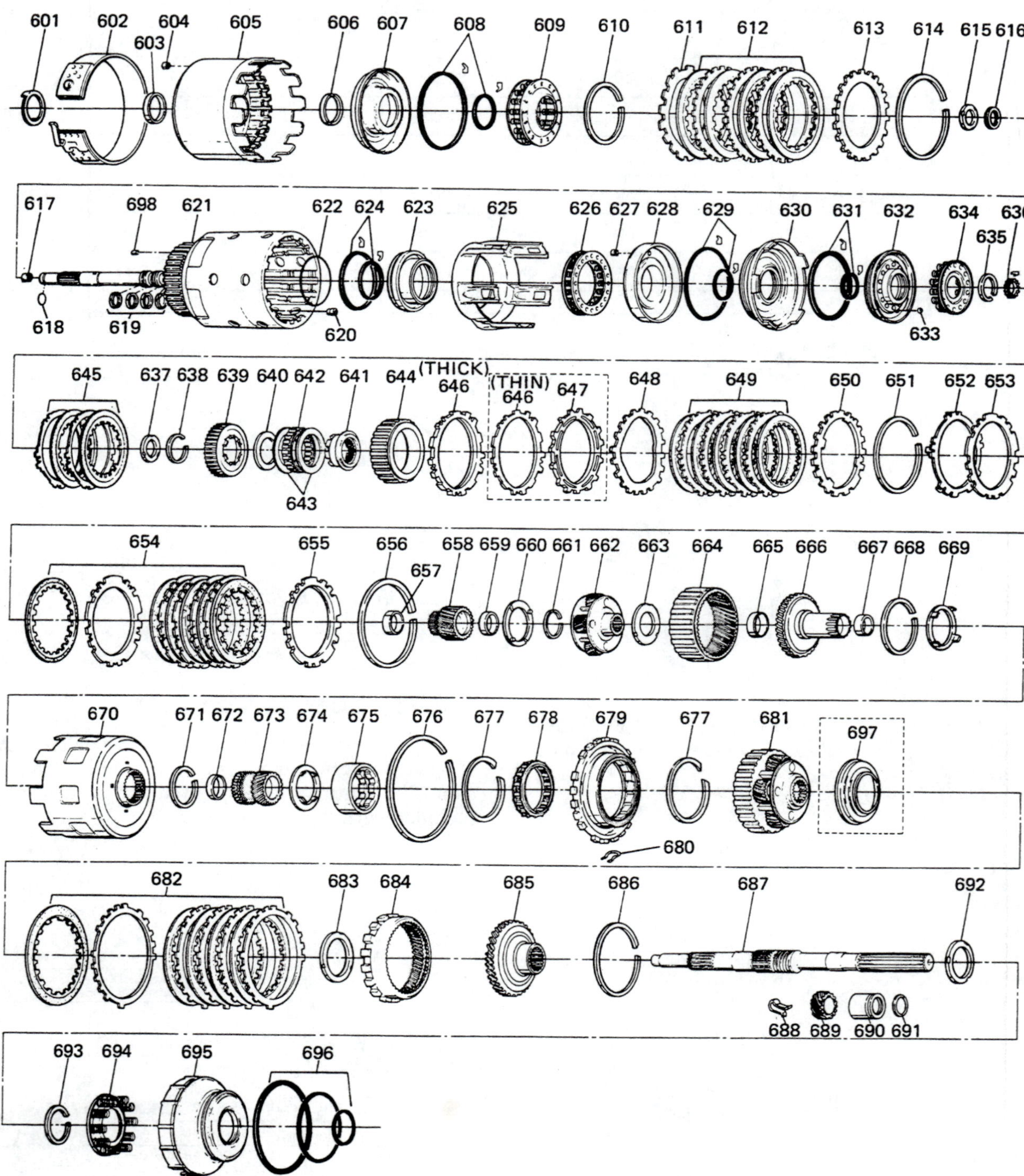

FIGURE 12–17 THM 4L60 internal parts. (Reprinted with permission of General Motors Corporation)

ILL. NO.	DESCRIPTION
601	WASHER, THRUST (PUMP TO DRUM)
602	BAND ASSEMBLY, 2-4
603	BUSHING, REVERSE INPUT CLUTCH – FRONT
604	RETAINER & BALL ASSEMBLY, CHECK VALVE
605	HOUSING & DRUM ASSEMBLY, REVERSE INPUT CLUTCH
606	BUSHING, REVERSE INPUT CLUTCH – REAR
607	PISTON ASSEMBLY, REVERSE INPUT CLUTCH
608	SEALS, REVERSE INPUT CLUTCH – INNER & OUTER
609	SPRING ASSEMBLY, REVERSE INPUT CLUTCH
610	RING, REVERSE INPUT CLUTCH SPRING RETAINER
611	PLATE, REVERSE INPUT CLUTCH (WAVED)
612	PLATE ASSEMBLY, REVERSE INPUT CLUTCH
613	PLATE, REVERSE INPUT CLUTCH BACKING
614	RING, REVERSE INPUT CLUTCH RETAINING
615	BEARING ASSEMBLY, STATOR SHAFT/ SELECTIVE WASHER
616	WASHER, THRUST (SELECTIVE)
617	RETAINER & BALL ASSEMBLY, CHECK VALVE
618	SEAL, "O" RING (TURBINE SHAFT/ SELECTIVE WASHER)
619	RING, OIL SEAL (TURBINE SHAFT)
620	RETAINER & CHECK BALL ASSEMBLY
621	HOUSING & SHAFT ASSEMBLY, INPUT
622	SEAL, "O" RING INPUT TO FORWARD HSG.
623	PISTON, 3RD & 4TH CLUTCH
624	SEAL, 3RD & 4TH CLUTCH – INNER & OUTER
625	RING, 3RD & 4TH CLUTCH APPLY
626	SPRING ASSEMBLY, 3RD & 4TH CLUTCH
627	RETAINER & BALL ASSEMBLY, FORWARD CLUTCH HOUSING
628	HOUSING, FORWARD CLUTCH
629	SEAL, FORWARD CLUTCH – INNER & OUTER
630	PISTON, FORWARD CLUTCH
631	SEAL, OVERRUN CLUTCH – INNER & OUTER
632	PISTON, OVERRUN CLUTCH
633	BALL, OVERRUN CLUTCH
634	SPRING ASSEMBLY, OVERRUN CLUTCH
635	SNAP RING, OVERRUN CLUTCH SPRING RETAINER
636	SEAL, INPUT HOUSING TO OUTPUT SHAFT
637	BEARING ASSEMBLY, INPUT SUN GEAR
638	SNAP RING, OVERRUN CL. HUB RETAINING
639	HUB, OVERRUN CLUTCH
640	WEAR PLATE, SPRAG ASSEMBLY
641	RETAINER & RACE ASSEMBLY, SPRAG
642	FORWARD SPRAG ASSEMBLY
643	RETAINER RINGS, SPRAG ASSEMBLY
644	RACE, FORWARD CLUTCH – OUTER
645	PLATE ASSEMBLY, OVERRUN CLUTCH
646	PLATE, FORWARD CLUTCH APPLY (V-8 MODELS THICK – L-4 & V-6 THIN)
647	PLATE, FORWARD CLUTCH SPACER (2.5L, L-4 & 2.8L V-6 ENGINES ONLY)
648	PLATE, FORWARD CLUTCH (WAVED)
649	PLATE ASSEMBLY, FORWARD CLUTCH
650	PLATE, FORWARD CLUTCH BACKING
651	RING, FORWARD CLUTCH BACKING PLATE RETAINER

ILL. NO.	DESCRIPTION
652	PLATE, 3RD & 4TH CLUTCH RING RETAINER
653	PLATE, 3RD & 4TH CLUTCH APPLY
654	PLATE ASSEMBLY, 3RD & 4TH CLUTCH
655	PLATE, 3RD & 4TH CLUTCH BACKING
656	RING, 3RD & 4TH CLUTCH BACKING PLATE RETAINER
657	BUSHING, INPUT SUN GEAR – FRONT
658	GEAR, INPUT SUN
659	BUSHING, INPUT SUN GEAR – REAR
660	WASHER, THRUST (INPUT CARRIER/RACE)
661	RET., OUTPUT SHAFT TO INPUT CARRIER
662	CARRIER ASSEMBLY, INPUT – COMPLETE
663	BEARING ASSEMBLY, THRUST (INPUT CARRIER TO REACTION SHAFT)
664	GEAR, INPUT INTERNAL
665	BUSHING, REACTION CARRIER SHAFT – FRONT
666	SHAFT, REACTION CARRIER
667	BUSHING, REACTION CARRIER SHAFT – REAR
668	RING, REACTION SHAFT/INTERNAL GEAR RETAINER
669	WASHER, THRUST (REACTION SHAFT/SHELL)
670	SHELL, REACTION SUN
671	RING, REACTION SUN GEAR RETAINER
672	BUSHING, REACTION SUN
673	GEAR, REACTION SUN
674	WASHER, THRUST (RACE/REACTION SHELL)
675	RACE, LO & REVERSE ROLLER CLUTCH
676	RING, LO & REVERSE SUPPORT TO CASE RETAINER
677	RING, LO & REVERSE RETAINER (ROLLER ASSEMBLY/CAM)
678	CLUTCH ASSEMBLY, LO & REVERSE ROLLER
679	SUPPORT ASSEMBLY, LO & REVERSE CLUTCH
680	SPRING, TRANSMISSION LO & REVERSE CLUTCH SUPPORT RETAINER
681	CARRIER ASSEMBLY, REACTION
682	PLATE ASSEMBLY, LO & REVERSE CLUTCH
683	BEARING ASSEMBLY, THRUST (REACTION CARRIER/SUPPORT)
684	GEAR, INTERNAL REACTION
685	SUPPORT, INTERNAL REACTION GEAR
686	RING, REACTION GEAR/SUPPORT RETAINER
687	SHAFT, OUTPUT
688	CLIP, SPEEDO DRIVE GEAR
689	GEAR, SPEEDO DRIVE
690	SLEEVE, OUTPUT SHAFT
691	SEAL, OUTPUT SHAFT
692	BRG., REACTION GEAR SUPPORT TO CASE
693	RING, LO & REVERSE CLUTCH RETAINER
694	SPRING ASSEMBLY, LO & REVERSE CLUTCH
695	PISTON, LO & REVERSE CLUTCH
696	SEAL, TRANSMISSION (LO & REVERSE CLUTCH – OUTER, CENTER – INNER)
697	DEFLECTOR, OIL (HIGH OUTPUT MODELS ONLY)
698	PLUG, ORIFICED CUP

FIGURE 12–17 *(continued)*

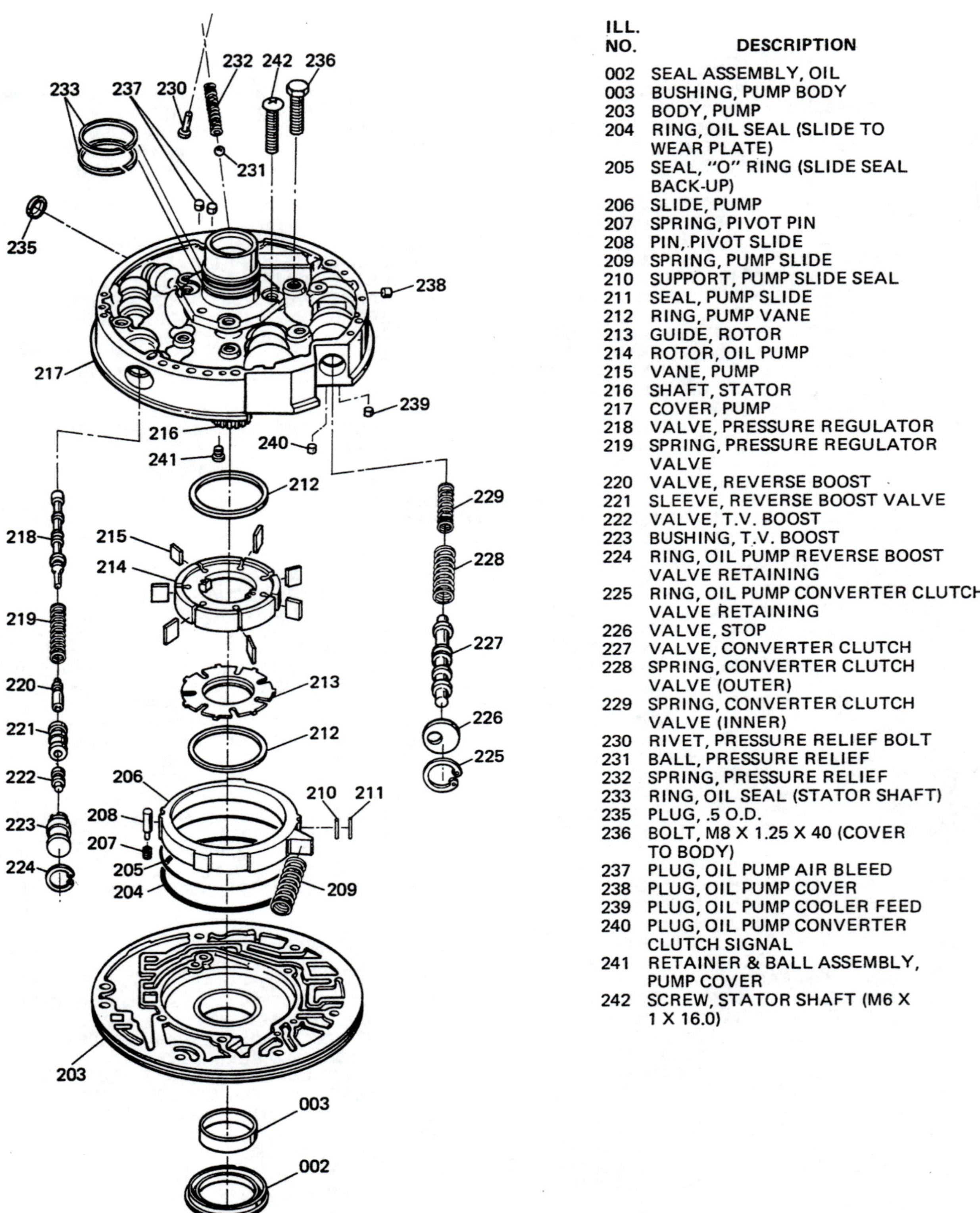

ILL. NO.	DESCRIPTION
002	SEAL ASSEMBLY, OIL
003	BUSHING, PUMP BODY
203	BODY, PUMP
204	RING, OIL SEAL (SLIDE TO WEAR PLATE)
205	SEAL, "O" RING (SLIDE SEAL BACK-UP)
206	SLIDE, PUMP
207	SPRING, PIVOT PIN
208	PIN, PIVOT SLIDE
209	SPRING, PUMP SLIDE
210	SUPPORT, PUMP SLIDE SEAL
211	SEAL, PUMP SLIDE
212	RING, PUMP VANE
213	GUIDE, ROTOR
214	ROTOR, OIL PUMP
215	VANE, PUMP
216	SHAFT, STATOR
217	COVER, PUMP
218	VALVE, PRESSURE REGULATOR
219	SPRING, PRESSURE REGULATOR VALVE
220	VALVE, REVERSE BOOST
221	SLEEVE, REVERSE BOOST VALVE
222	VALVE, T.V. BOOST
223	BUSHING, T.V. BOOST
224	RING, OIL PUMP REVERSE BOOST VALVE RETAINING
225	RING, OIL PUMP CONVERTER CLUTCH VALVE RETAINING
226	VALVE, STOP
227	VALVE, CONVERTER CLUTCH
228	SPRING, CONVERTER CLUTCH VALVE (OUTER)
229	SPRING, CONVERTER CLUTCH VALVE (INNER)
230	RIVET, PRESSURE RELIEF BOLT
231	BALL, PRESSURE RELIEF
232	SPRING, PRESSURE RELIEF
233	RING, OIL SEAL (STATOR SHAFT)
235	PLUG, .5 O.D.
236	BOLT, M8 X 1.25 X 40 (COVER TO BODY)
237	PLUG, OIL PUMP AIR BLEED
238	PLUG, OIL PUMP COVER
239	PLUG, OIL PUMP COOLER FEED
240	PLUG, OIL PUMP CONVERTER CLUTCH SIGNAL
241	RETAINER & BALL ASSEMBLY, PUMP COVER
242	SCREW, STATOR SHAFT (M6 X 1 X 16.0)

FIGURE 12–18 THM 4L60 oil pump. (Reprinted with permission of General Motors Corporation)

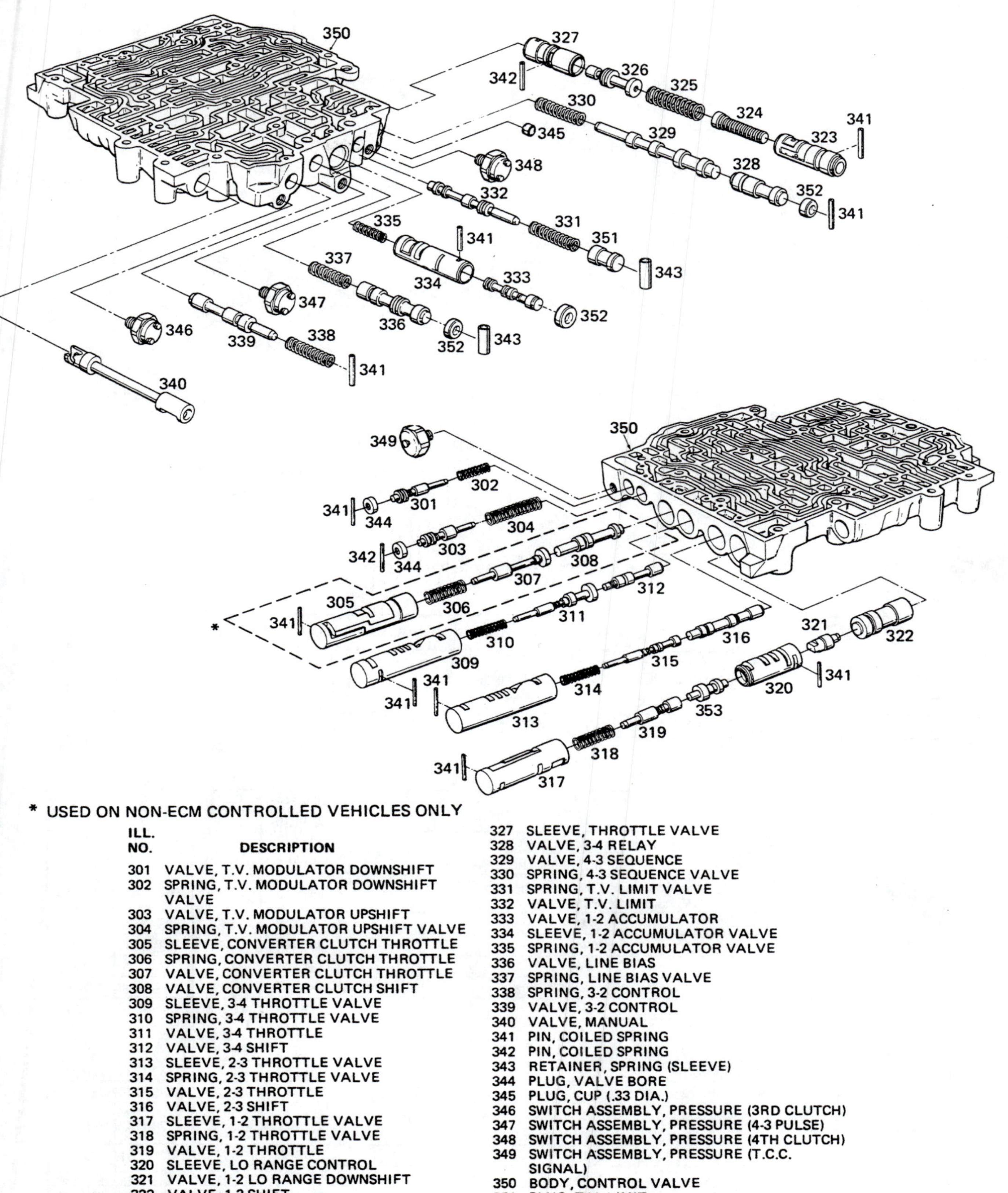

* USED ON NON-ECM CONTROLLED VEHICLES ONLY

ILL. NO.	DESCRIPTION
301	VALVE, T.V. MODULATOR DOWNSHIFT
302	SPRING, T.V. MODULATOR DOWNSHIFT VALVE
303	VALVE, T.V. MODULATOR UPSHIFT
304	SPRING, T.V. MODULATOR UPSHIFT VALVE
305	SLEEVE, CONVERTER CLUTCH THROTTLE
306	SPRING, CONVERTER CLUTCH THROTTLE
307	VALVE, CONVERTER CLUTCH THROTTLE
308	VALVE, CONVERTER CLUTCH SHIFT
309	SLEEVE, 3-4 THROTTLE VALVE
310	SPRING, 3-4 THROTTLE VALVE
311	VALVE, 3-4 THROTTLE
312	VALVE, 3-4 SHIFT
313	SLEEVE, 2-3 THROTTLE VALVE
314	SPRING, 2-3 THROTTLE VALVE
315	VALVE, 2-3 THROTTLE
316	VALVE, 2-3 SHIFT
317	SLEEVE, 1-2 THROTTLE VALVE
318	SPRING, 1-2 THROTTLE VALVE
319	VALVE, 1-2 THROTTLE
320	SLEEVE, LO RANGE CONTROL
321	VALVE, 1-2 LO RANGE DOWNSHIFT
322	VALVE, 1-2 SHIFT
323	SLEEVE, THROTTLE VALVE PLUNGER
324	PLUNGER, THROTTLE VALVE
325	SPRING, THROTTLE VALVE
326	VALVE, THROTTLE
327	SLEEVE, THROTTLE VALVE
328	VALVE, 3-4 RELAY
329	VALVE, 4-3 SEQUENCE
330	SPRING, 4-3 SEQUENCE VALVE
331	SPRING, T.V. LIMIT VALVE
332	VALVE, T.V. LIMIT
333	VALVE, 1-2 ACCUMULATOR
334	SLEEVE, 1-2 ACCUMULATOR VALVE
335	SPRING, 1-2 ACCUMULATOR VALVE
336	VALVE, LINE BIAS
337	SPRING, LINE BIAS VALVE
338	SPRING, 3-2 CONTROL
339	VALVE, 3-2 CONTROL
340	VALVE, MANUAL
341	PIN, COILED SPRING
342	PIN, COILED SPRING
343	RETAINER, SPRING (SLEEVE)
344	PLUG, VALVE BORE
345	PLUG, CUP (.33 DIA.)
346	SWITCH ASSEMBLY, PRESSURE (3RD CLUTCH)
347	SWITCH ASSEMBLY, PRESSURE (4-3 PULSE)
348	SWITCH ASSEMBLY, PRESSURE (4TH CLUTCH)
349	SWITCH ASSEMBLY, PRESSURE (T.C.C. SIGNAL)
350	BODY, CONTROL VALVE
351	PLUG, T.V. LIMIT
352	PLUG, VALVE BORE (12.5 - O.D.)
353	VALVE, 1-2 LO RANGE UPSHIFT

FIGURE 12–19 THM 4L60 valve body. (Reprinted with permission of General Motors Corporation)

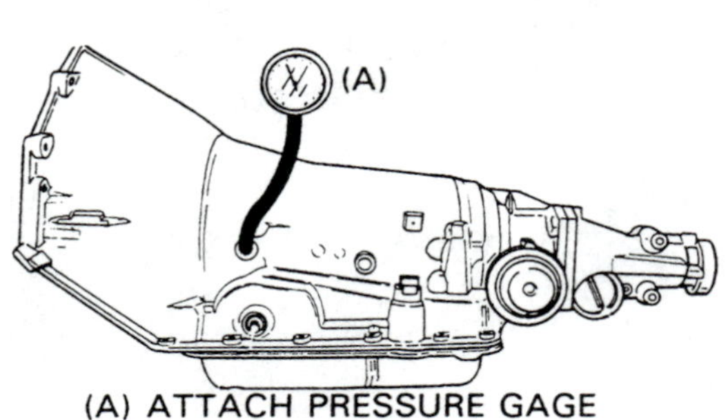

FIGURE 12–20 THM 4L60 pressure test points. (Reprinted with permission of General Motors Corporation)

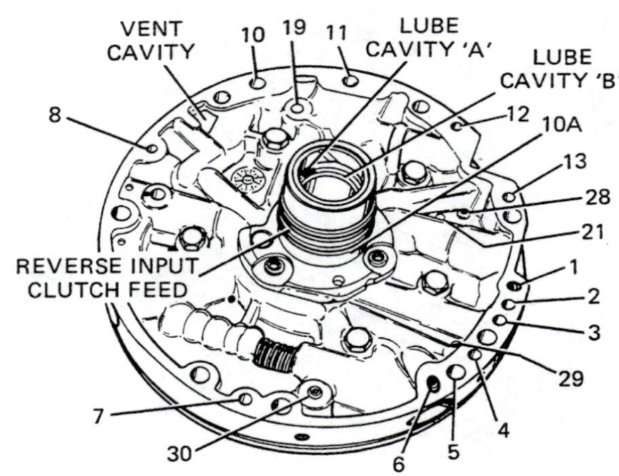

FIGURE 12–22 THM 4L60 oil pump passages for air testing. (Reprinted with permission of General Motors Corporation)

FIGURE 12–21 THM 4L60 pressure test chart. (Reprinted with permission of General Motors Corporation)

***NOTICE**	Total running time for this combination not to exceed 2 minutes.

CAUTION	Brakes must be applied at all times.

AUTOMATIC TRANSMISSION OIL PRESSURES

RANGE	MODEL	NORMAL OIL PRESSURE AT MINIMUM T.V.		NORMAL OIL PRESSURE AT FULL T.V.	
		kPa	PSI	kPa	PSI
PARK, NEUTRAL, OVERDRIVE & MANUAL 3RD @ 1000 RPM	YLM, YTM	384-444	56-64	818-1040	119-151
	YMM	451-515	65-75	1115-1430	162-207
	YXM	451-515	65-75	840-1053	122-153
	MCM, MHM, PAM, TAM, YFM, MTM, PRM, TNM, TRM, PBM, TBM	451-515	65-75	844-1068	122-155
	TJM, TKM, MWM, MZM, TUM, TXM, FAM, MDM, MPM, MAM, MSM, MMM, MRM, MXM, MKM, MUM	451-515	65-75	851-1063	123-154
	YPM	384-444	56-64	876-1333	127-193
	YKM	384-444	56-64	883-1129	128-164
	TSM	384-444	56-64	962-1237	139-179
	YAM, YCM, YWM, YZM, YDM	384-444	56-64	1049-1359	152-197
REVERSE @ 1000 RPM *@ 2000 RPM	YTM	632-729	92-106	*1345-1710	195-248
	YMM	742-846	108-123	*1834-2351	266-341
	YLM	632-729	92-106	*1380-1782	200-258
	YXM	742-847	108-123	*1381-1731	200-251
	MCM, MHM, PAM, TAM, YFM, MTM, PRM, TNM, TRM, PBM, TBM	742-847	108-123	*1388-1755	201-254
	TJM, TKM, MWM, MZM, TUM, TXM, FAM, MDM, MPM, MAM, MSM, MMM, MRM, MXM, MKM, MUM	742-847	108-123	*1399-1747	203-253
	YPM	632-730	92-106	*1441-2191	209-318
	YKM	632-730	92-106	*1452-1856	211-269
	TSM	632-730	92-106	*1581-2034	229-295
	YAM, YCM, YWM, YZM, YDM	632-730	92-106	*1724-2234	250-324
MANUAL 2ND & MANUAL LO @ 1000 RPM	TSM, YAM, YCM, YKM, YLM, YPM, YTM, YWM, YZM, YDM	1120-1293	162-187	1120-1293	162-187
	FAM,MCM,MDM,MHM,MPM,PAM,TAM,YFM,YMM,YXM,MAM,MSM,MMM,MRM,MXM, MTM,PRM,MKM,MUM,TJM,TKM,TNM,TRM,MWM,MZM,TUM,TXM,PBM,TBM	1127-1286	163-186	1127-1286	163-186

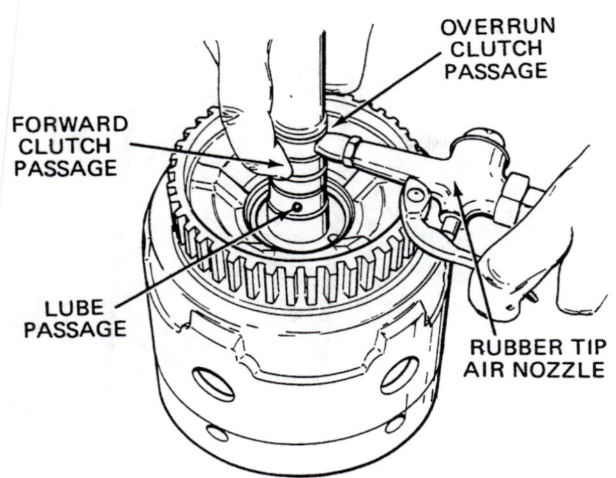

FIGURE 12–23 THM 4L60 overrun and forward clutch air test. (Reprinted with permission of General Motors Corporation)

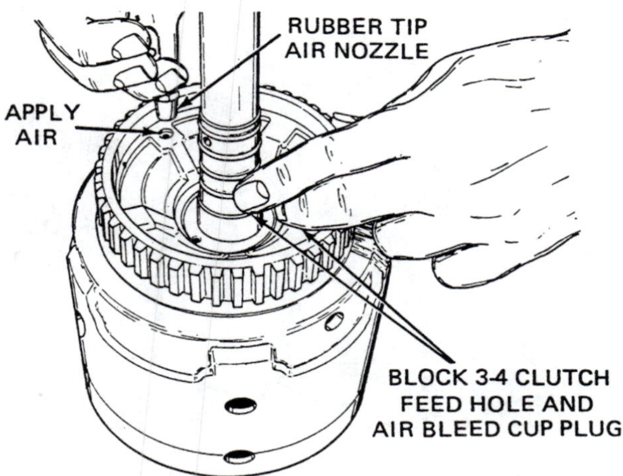

FIGURE 12–24 THM 4L60 3–4 clutch air test. (Reprinted with permission of General Motors Corporation)

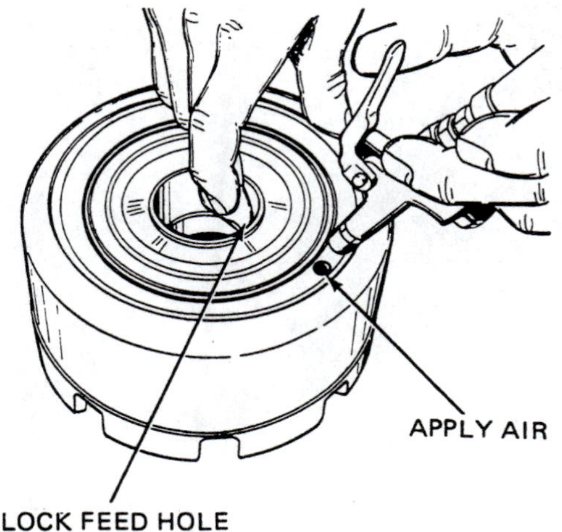

FIGURE 12–25 THM 4L60 reverse input clutch air test. (Reprinted with permission of General Motors Corporation)

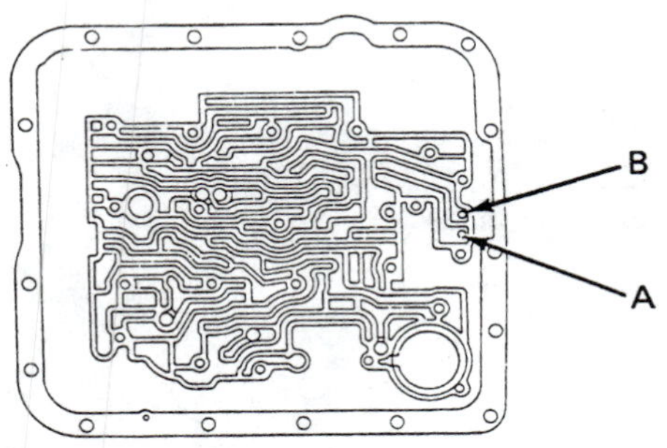

FIGURE 12–26 THM 4L60 low–reverse clutch air test. (Reprinted with permission of General Motors Corporation)

FIGURE 4L60–1 The governor should be inspected for free valve movement, gear wear, and governor-to-case fit.

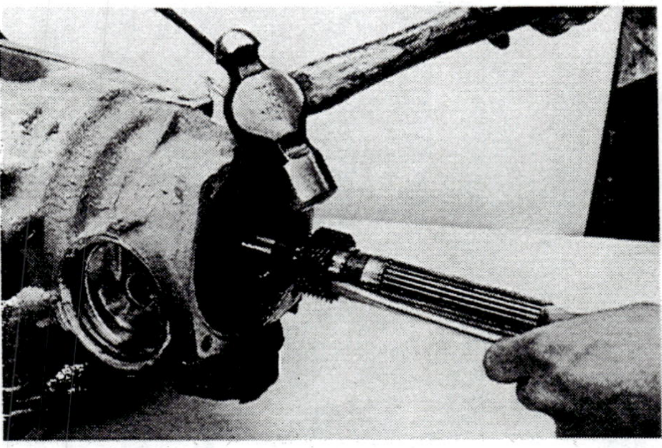

FIGURE 4L60–2 While holding the clip down with a screwdriver, the speedometer gear can be removed.

FIGURE 4L60–3 The filter is free to move and is held in place by the spring clip being pointed out.

FIGURE 4L60–4 Take careful note of wire routes and connections before removing any connectors.

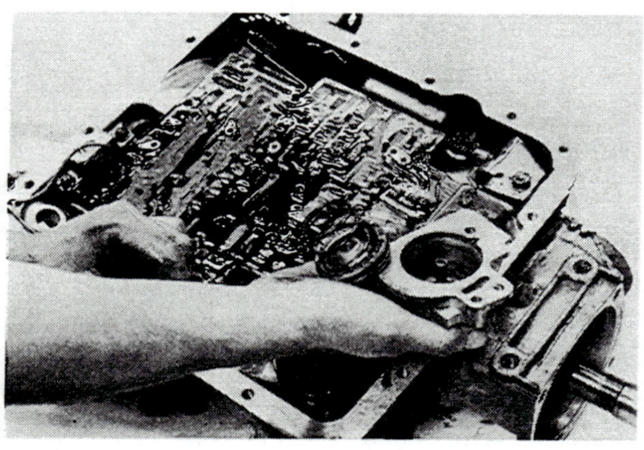

FIGURE 4L60–5 The accumulator seals and spring should be inspected.

FIGURE 4L60–6 A broken spring like this will cause hard shifts.

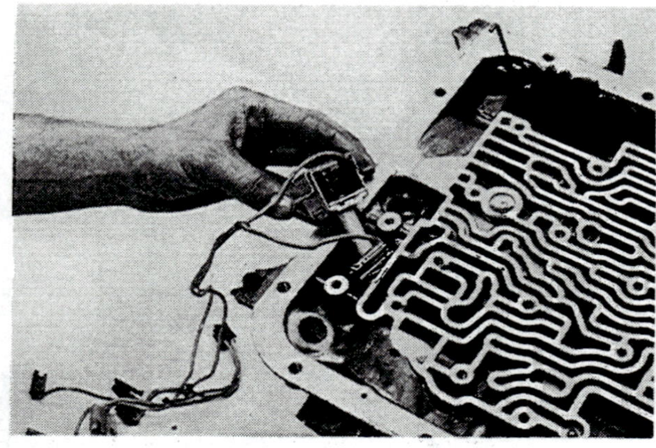

FIGURE 4L60–7 The converter clutch solenoid must be checked for proper operation and its seals replaced.

FIGURE 4L60–8 The oil pump is showing much wear on the cover. Badly worn parts must be replaced.

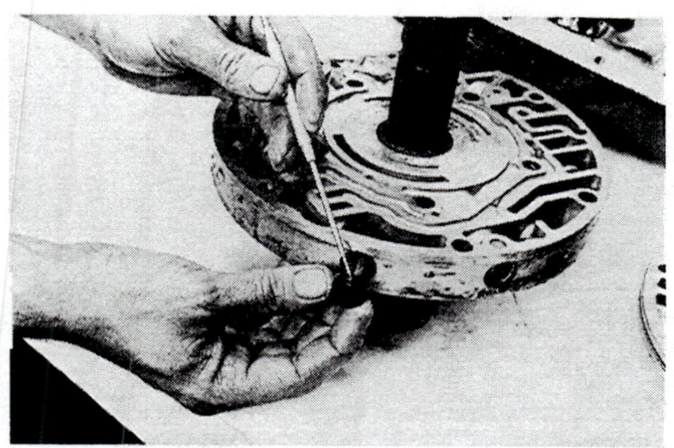

FIGURE 4L60–9 The pump filter seals must be replaced during rebuilding.

FIGURE 4L60–10 The outer pump ring seal must be replaced.

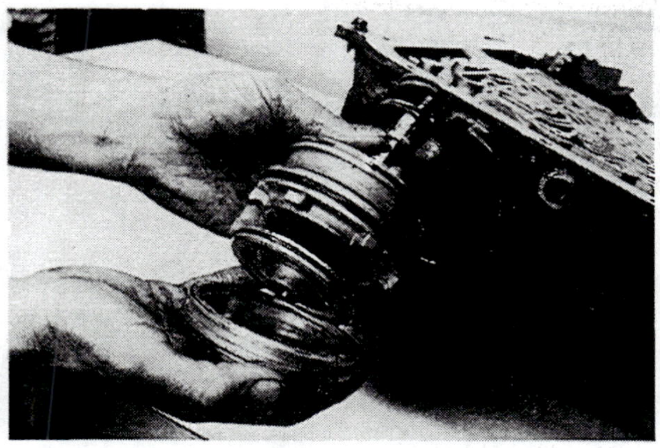

FIGURE 4L60–11 All the seals in the 2–4 servo should be replaced.

FIGURE 4L60–12 Removing the main gear train components.

FIGURE 4L60–13 The band anchor pin should be removed along with the band.

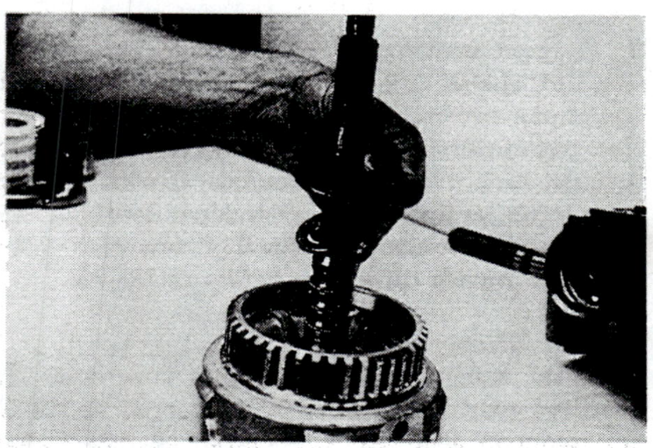

FIGURE 4L60–14 All thrust bearings and washers should be inspected.

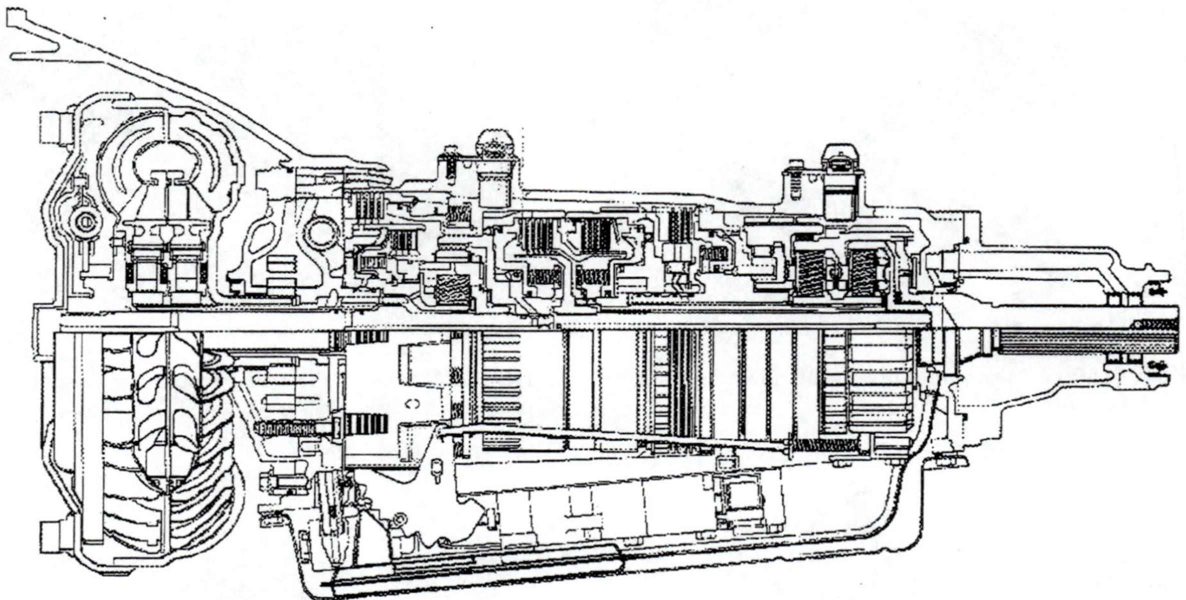

FIGURE 12–27 4L80E transmission. (Reprinted with permission of General Motors Corporation)

12.4 HM 4L80E: FWD FOUR-SPEED TRANSMISSION

12.4.1 Basic Description

The HM 4L80E is an electronically controlled, overdrive version of the HM 3L80, which was known previously as the THM-400. This transmission is designed to handle high torque loads for medium-sized trucks and is one of the heavier-duty Hydra-Matic transmissions (Figure 12–27).

1. Torque Converter
The HM 4L80E has a unique torque converter in that it has two stators, a primary and a secondary. This two-stator converter can increase the torque as much as 3.5:1. Each stator has its own overrunning clutch, so they can work independently of each other. An electronically controlled converter clutch is used to provide direct drive (Figure 12–28).

2. Gear Train
The gear train uses two planetary gear sets. The overdrive gear set uses the planet carrier as the input member and the ring gear as the output (Figure 12–29).

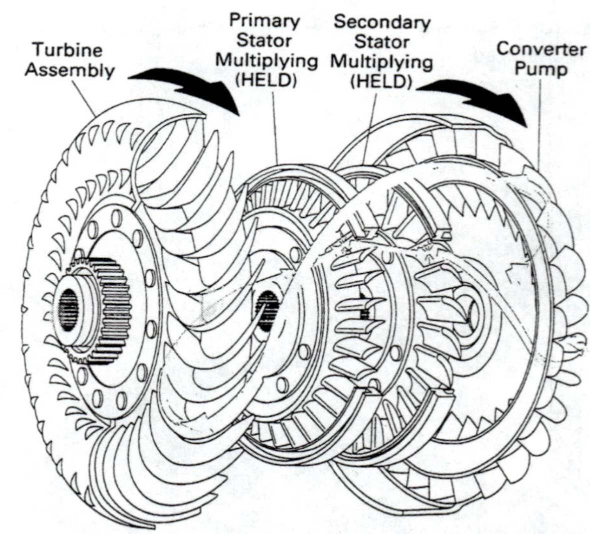

FIGURE 12–28 4L80E torque converter. (Reprinted with permission of General Motors Corporation)

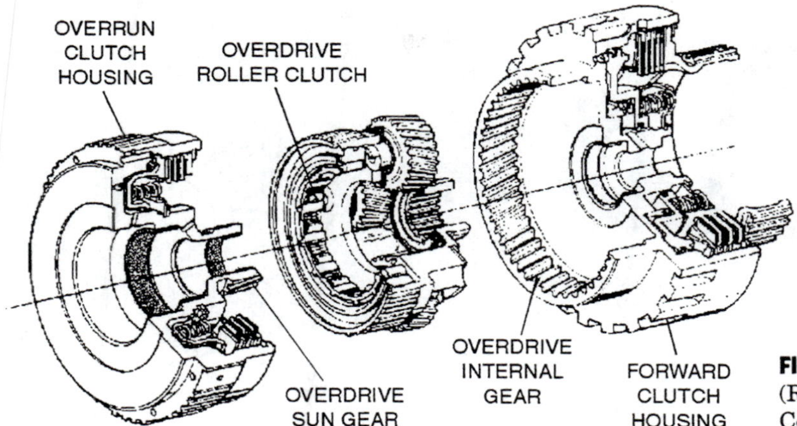

FIGURE 12–29 4L80E overdrive gear train. (Reprinted with permission of General Motors Corporation)

The main gear set is a modified Simpson design using the rear ring gear and sun gears as the input members. The sun gear and front carrier are reaction members, with the front ring gear/rear carrier serving as output (Figure 12–30).

3. Coupling Devices
The overrun clutch and overdrive roller clutch couple the planet carrier and the sun gear together in the overdrive planetary gear assembly. The forward clutch drives the rear ring gear of the main gear set, with the direct clutch driving the sun gear.

4. Holding Devices
The fourth clutch is used in the overdrive gear set to hold the sun gear to create an overdrive condition. The front band, intermediate sprag clutch, and intermediate clutch are used to hold the main sun gear, while the low roller clutch and the rear band are holding the front (reaction) planet carrier of the main gear set.

5. Pump
The HM 4L80E uses a positive-displacement gear crescent pump to provide dependable service. The pressure regulator and torque converter clutch spool valves are located in the pump housing (Figure 12–31).

6. Shift Control
The HM 4L80E is electronically controlled using the components shown in Figure 12–32. This system is similar to the ignition/fuel control systems used today, which have input sensors, an electronic control unit, and output activators. In operation the input data from the sensors are analyzed by the computer, which then energizes the activators, causing a shift to occur.

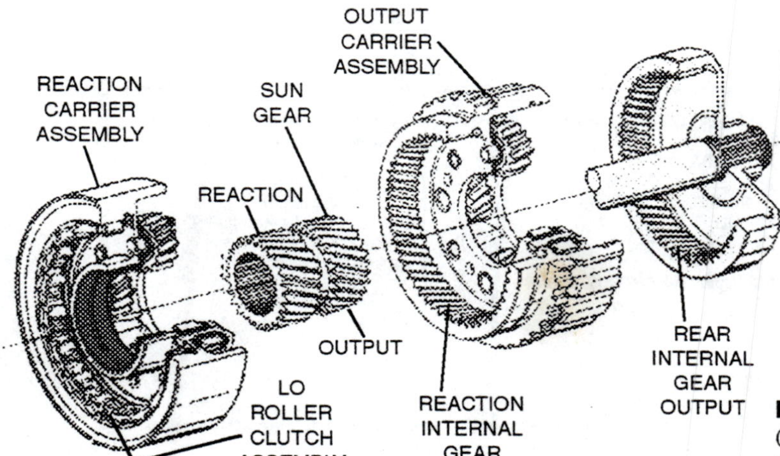

FIGURE 12–30 4L80E main gear train. (Reprinted with permission of General Motors Corporation)

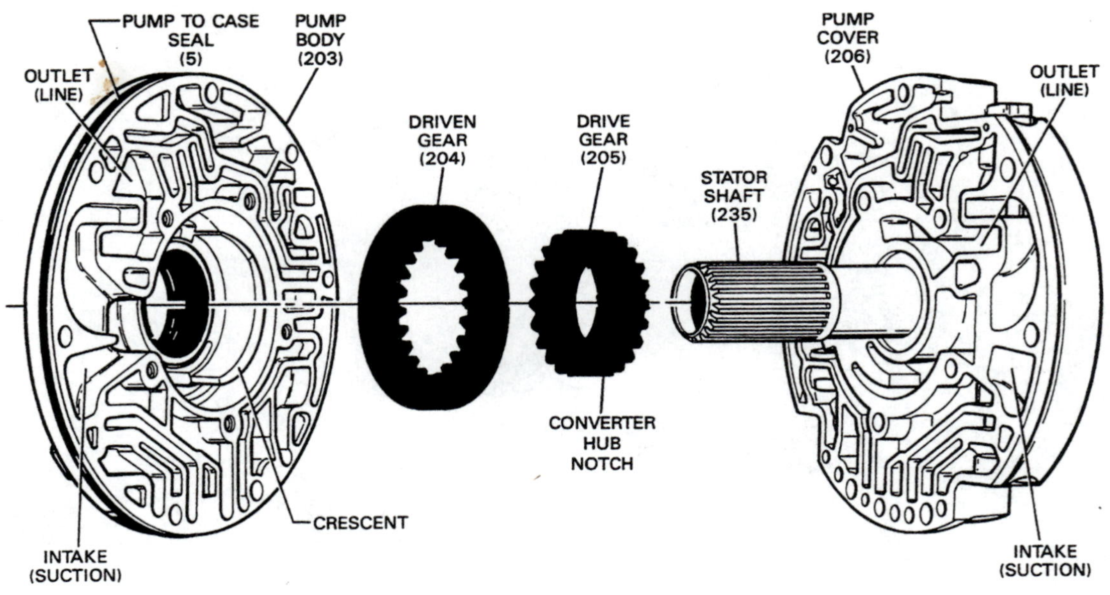

FIGURE 12–31 4L80E hydraulic pump. (Reprinted with permission of General Motors Corporation)

I F G ALDL PCM

E D 3 4 A B 2 1 C H

INPUTS **OUTPUTS**

INFORMATION SENSORS

A. PRESSURE SWITCH MANIFOLD (PSM)
B. TRANSMISSION INPUT SPEED SENSOR (TISS)
C. TRANSMISSION OUTPUT SPEED SENSOR (TOSS)
D. TRANSMISSION FLUID
E. ENGINE COOLANT TEMPERATURE SENSOR (CTS)
F. THROTTLE POSITION SENSOR (TPS)
G. ENGINE SPEED SENSOR
H. BRAKE SWITCH
I. A/C REQUEST SWITCH

⇨

ELECTRONIC CONTROLLERS

- POWERTRAIN CONTROL MODULE (PCM) OR TRANSMISSION CONTROL MODULE (TCM) (SEE NOTE BELOW)
- ASSEMBLY LINE DIAGNOSTIC LINK (ALDL)

⇨

ELECTRONICALLY CONTROLLED TRANSMISSION COMPONENTS

1. SHIFT SOLENOID "A"
2. SHIFT SOLENOID "B"
3. PULSE WIDTH MODULATED TCC SOLENOID (PWM)
4. VARIABLE FORCE MOTOR

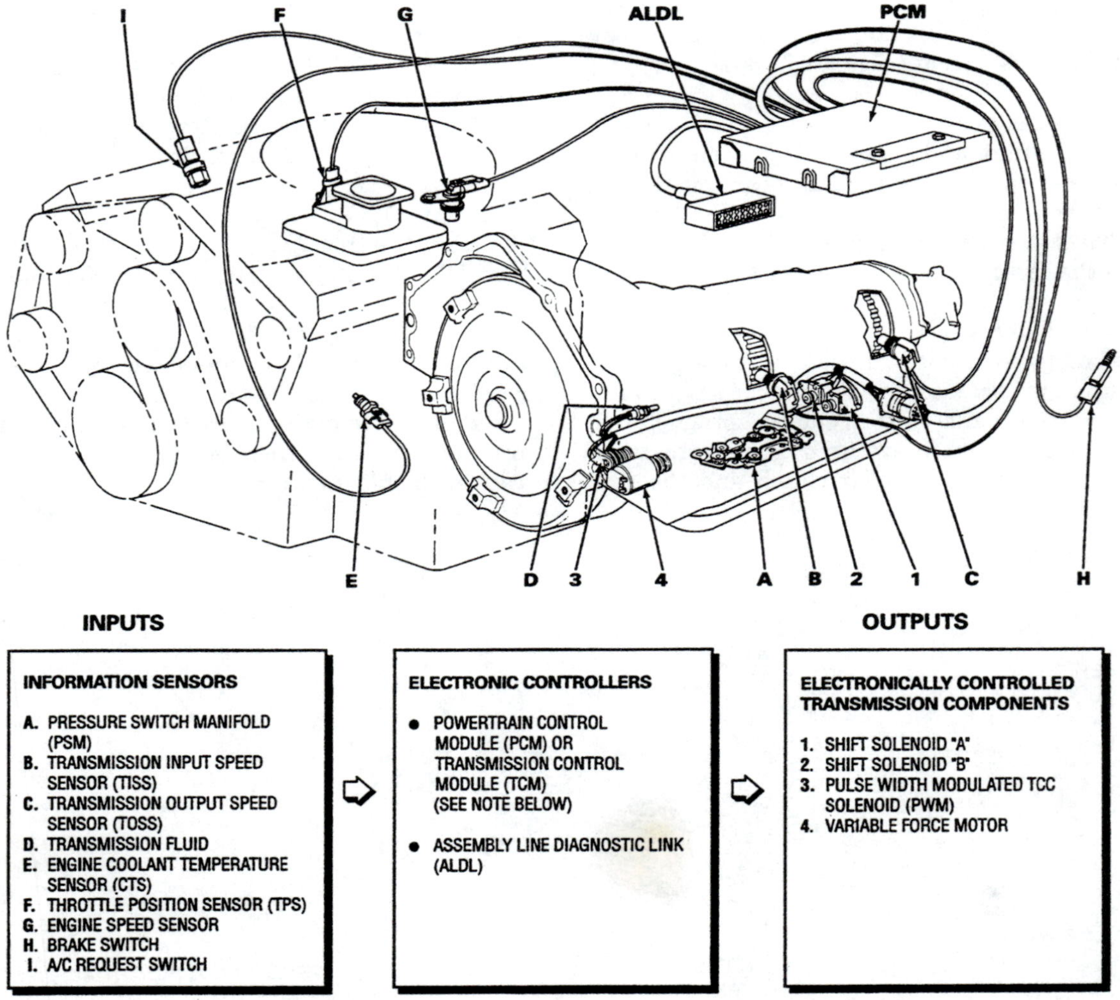

FIGURE 12–32 4L80E electronic components. (Reprinted with permission of General Motors Corporation)

7. Governor
This transmission has no need of a governor, as the vehicle speed information is now supplied by the input sensors to the computer.

8. Throttle Valve
The torque signal information normally provided by the throttle valve comes from the computer for this transmission. The computer then controls the force motor, which regulates the torque signal pressure.

12.4.2 Power Flow

1. Neutral (N)
The only coupling or holding device active in neutral is the overdrive roller clutch; all others are inactive.

2. First Gear (D1)
Because this transmission has two gear sets, overdrive and main, the description of the power flow in each gear will include both gear sets.

The overdrive roller clutch is holding, which causes the input planet carrier to drive the sun gear, creating a direct drive in the overdrive gear set. This is the operating mode of the overdrive gear set in all except fourth gear.

In the main gear set the forward clutch is applied, which drives the rear ring gear as input. The low roller clutch is holding the front planet carrier as the reaction member, which causes the output carrier to be driven at a 2.48:1 ratio (Figure 12–33). In manual gear the rear band also holds the reaction member to provide engine braking.

3. Second Gear (D2)
The overdrive gear set remains in direct drive, and the forward clutch is engaged, providing input. The intermediate clutch and sprag are applied, which holds the sun gear as the reaction member, giving a 1.48:1 gear ratio. In manual second gear the front band is also applied.

4. Third Gear (D3)
The overdrive gear set is still in direct drive. The forward clutch is also applied, providing input power to the rear ring gear and the direct clutch is applied to drive the sun gear as input, with the result of direct drive in the main gear set (Figure 12–34).

5. Fourth Gear (D4)
In fourth gear the main gear set remains the same, with the forward and direct clutches applied, giving a direct drive. The overdrive gear set's fourth clutch is applied, which holds the sun gear as the reaction member. This puts the gear set in overdrive mode with a gear ratio of 0.75:1 (Figure 12–35).

6. Reverse Gear (R)
In reverse the overdrive gear set is back to the direct drive mode, with the planet carrier and sun gear locked together by the overdrive roller clutch. In the main gear the direct clutch is applied, driving the sun gear while the rear band holds the front planetary carrier, which drives the ring gear output in a reverse direction, with a ratio of 2.08:1.

12.4.3 Clutch and Band Charts

For the author's standardized chart, see Figure 12–36, and for the manufacturer's chart, see Figure 12–37.

12.4.4 Identification

The shape of the transaxle oil pan or its gasket is a quick means of identifying an automatic transaxle. The pan gasket shape and number of bolt holes for the HM 4L80E transaxle and the location of the factory identification tag and its code are shown in Figure 12–39.

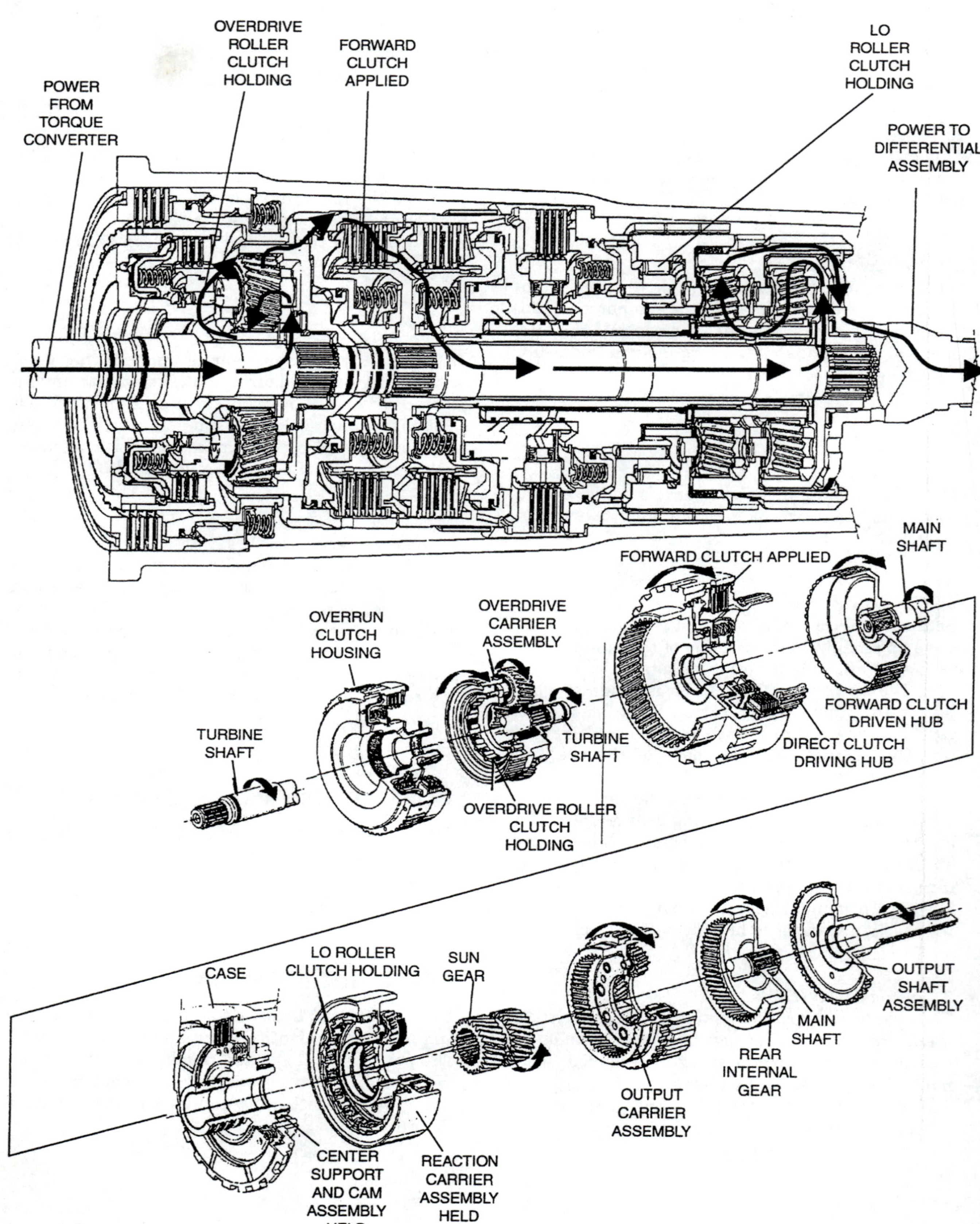

FIGURE 12–33 4L80E first gear. (Reprinted with permission of General Motors Corporation)

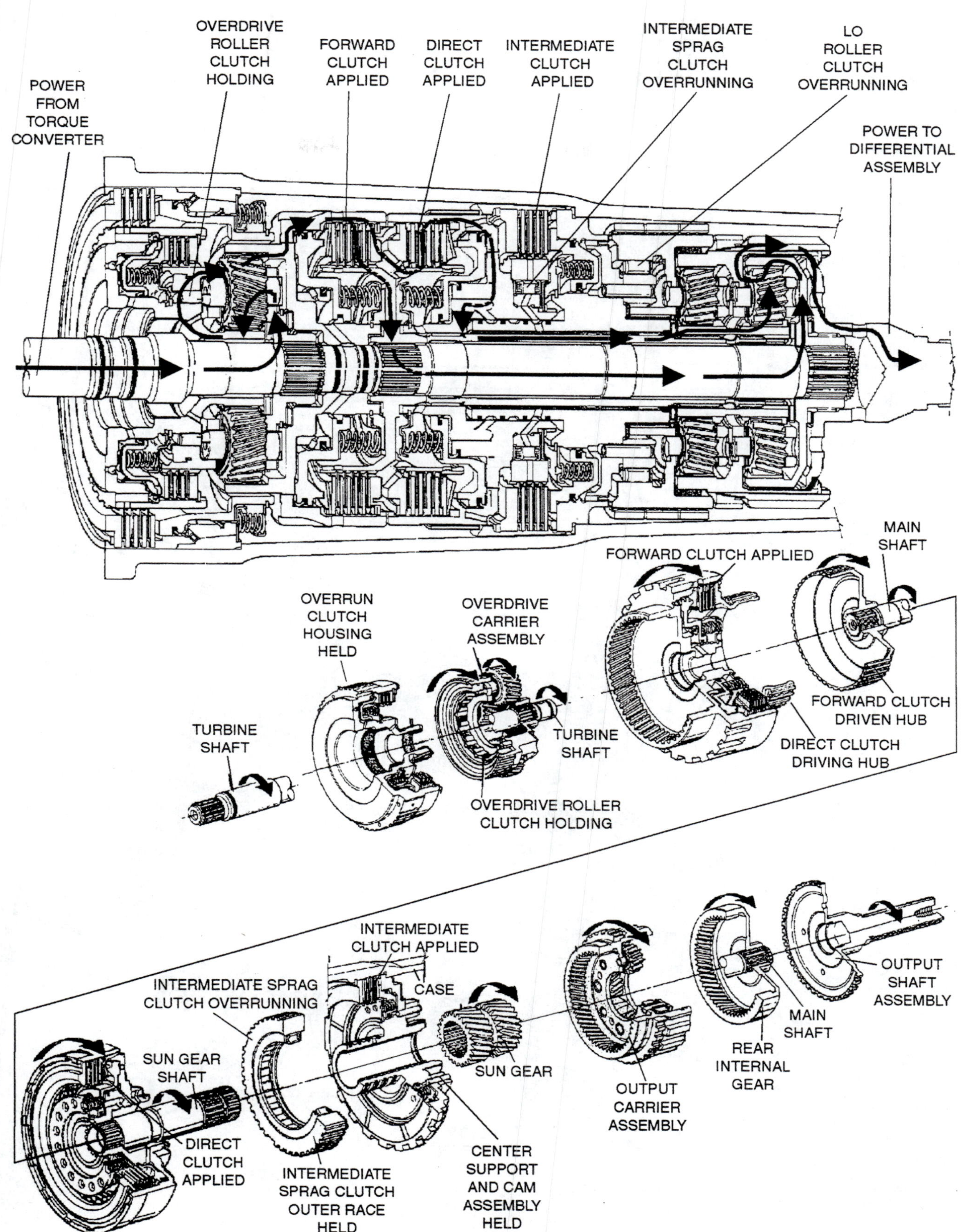

FIGURE 12–34 4L80E third gear. (Reprinted with permission of General Motors Corporation)

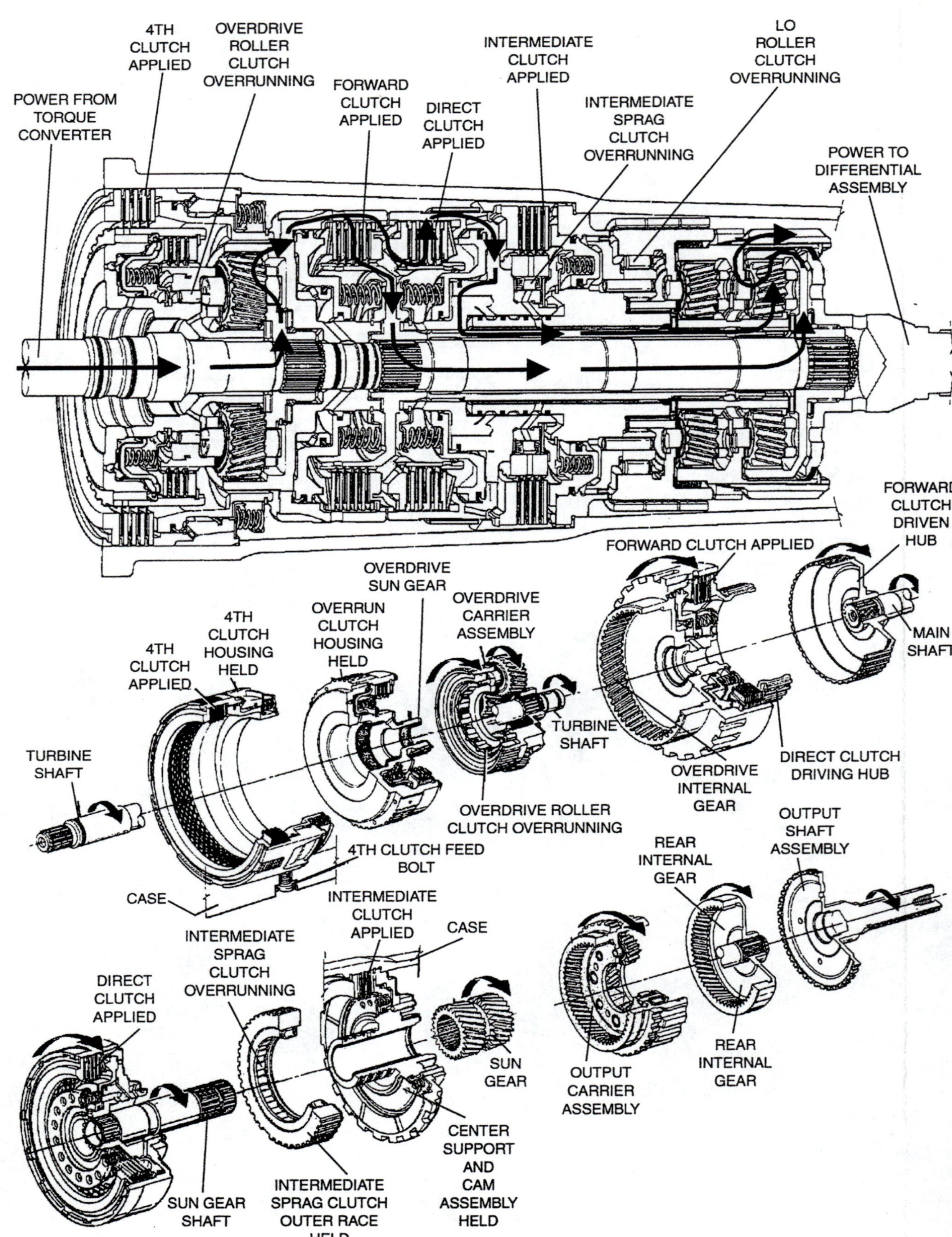

FIGURE 12–35 4L80E fourth gear. (Reprinted with permission of General Motors Corporation)

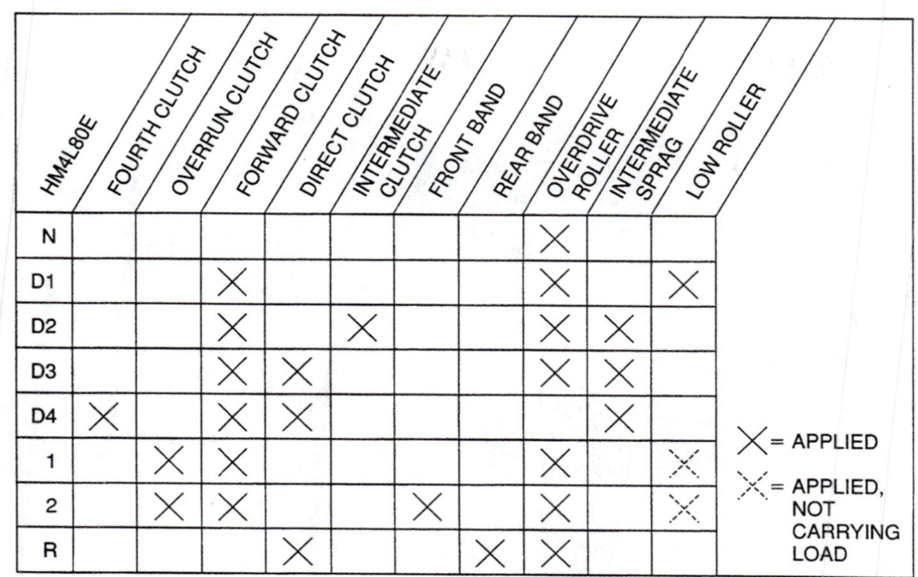

HM4L80E	FOURTH CLUTCH	OVERRUN CLUTCH	FORWARD CLUTCH	DIRECT CLUTCH	INTERMEDIATE CLUTCH	FRONT BAND	REAR BAND	OVERDRIVE ROLLER	INTERMEDIATE SPRAG	LOW ROLLER
N								X		
D1			X					X		X
D2			X		X			X	X	
D3			X	X				X	X	
D4	X		X	X					X	
1		X	X					X		X (dashed)
2		X	X			X		X		X (dashed)
R				X			X	X		

FIGURE 12–36 4L80E clutch and band chart, standardized version.

FIGURE 12–37 4L80E clutch and band chart, manufacturer's version. (Reprinted with permission of General Motors Corporation)

RANGE	GEAR	SOLENOID @A	SOLENOID @B	FOURTH CLUTCH	OVERRUN CLUTCH	OVERDRIVE ROLLER CLUTCH	FORWARD CLUTCH	DIRECT CLUTCH	FRONT BAND	INTERMEDIATE SPRAG CLUTCH	INTERMEDIATE CLUTCH	LO ROLLER CLUTCH	REAR BAND
P-N		ON	OFF			HOLDING							
R	REVERSE	ON	OFF			HOLDING		APPLIED					APPLIED
[D]	1st	ON	OFF			HOLDING	APPLIED			*		HOLDING	
	2nd	OFF	OFF			HOLDING	APPLIED			HOLDING	APPLIED	OVERRUNNING	
	3rd	OFF	ON			HOLDING	APPLIED	APPLIED		OVERRUNNING	APPLIED	OVERRUNNING	
	4th	ON	ON	APPLIED		OVERRUNNING	APPLIED	APPLIED		OVERRUNNING	APPLIED	OVERRUNNING	
D	1st	ON	OFF		APPLIED	HOLDING	APPLIED			*		HOLDING	
	2nd	OFF	OFF		APPLIED	HOLDING	APPLIED			HOLDING	APPLIED	OVERRUNNING	
	3rd	OFF	ON		APPLIED	HOLDING	APPLIED	APPLIED		OVERRUNNING	APPLIED	OVERRUNNING	
2	1st	ON	OFF		APPLIED	HOLDING	APPLIED			*		HOLDING	
	2nd	OFF	OFF		APPLIED	HOLDING	APPLIED		APPLIED	HOLDING	APPLIED	OVERRUNNING	
1	1st	ON	OFF		APPLIED	HOLDING	APPLIED			*		HOLDING	APPLIED
	2nd	OFF	OFF		APPLIED	HOLDING	APPLIED		APPLIED	HOLDING	APPLIED	OVERRUNNING	

*HOLDING BUT NOT EFFECTIVE

ON = SOLENOID ENERGIZED

OFF = SOLENOID DE-ENERGIZED

@ THE SOLENOID'S STATE FOLLOWS A SHIFT PATTERN WHICH DEPENDS UPON VEHICLE SPEED AND THROTTLE POSITION. IT DOES NOT DEPEND UPON THE SELECTED GEAR.

NOTE: DESCRIPTIONS ABOVE EXPLAIN COMPONENT FUNCTION DURING ACCELERATION.

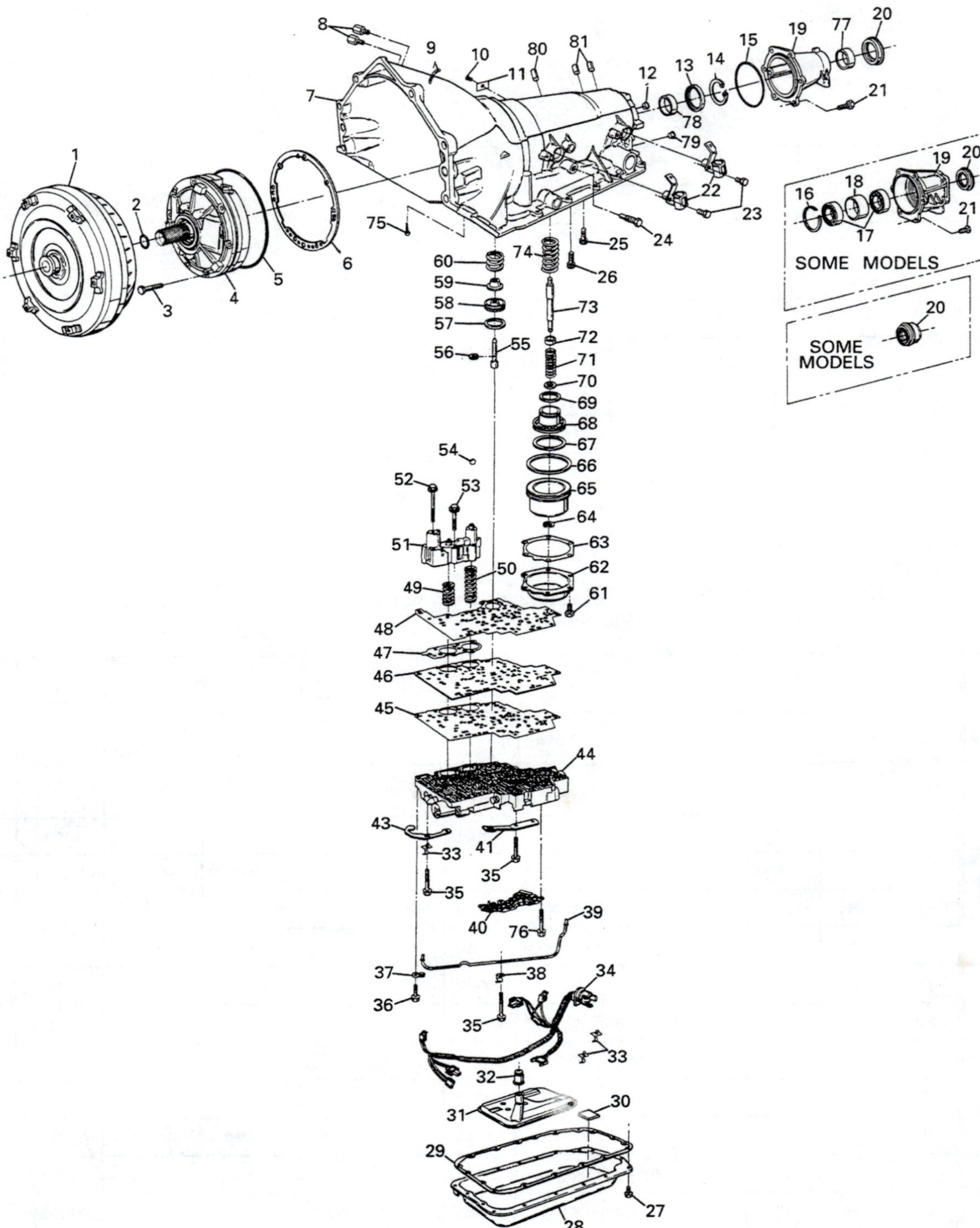

FIGURE 12–38 4L80E oil pan shape and identification tag location. (Reprinted with permission of General Motors Corporation)

1 TORQUE CONVERTER ASSEMBLY
2 SEAL, O-RING (TURBINE SHAFT/TURBINE HUB)
3 BOLT & SEAL ASSEMBLY, PUMP TO CASE
4 PUMP ASSEMBLY, COMPLETE
5 SEAL, OIL PUMP TO CASE
6 GASKET, PUMP COVER TO CASE
7 CASE ASSEMBLY, COMPLETE
8 CONNECTOR, INVERTED FLARED TUBE
9 PIPE, VENT
10 SCREW, NAMEPLATE
11 NAMEPLATE
12 CUP, ORIFICE W/SEAL/PLUG-REAR LUBE (4WD)
13 SEAL ASSEMBLY, REAR LUBE
14 RING, SNAP SEAL RETAINER
15 RING, SEAL EXTENSION TO CASE
16 RING, SNAP INTERNAL
17 BEARING ASSEMBLY, BALL
18 SPACER, BEARING
19 EXTENSION ASSEMBLY, CASE
20 HELIXSEAL ASSEMBLY, CASE EXTENSION
21 BOLT, HEX HD (M10 X 1.5 X 30.0)
22 SENSOR ASSEMBLY, SPEED INPUT & OUTPUT
23 BOLT, METRIC HEX
24 PLUG, OIL TEST HOLE (HEX HD 1/8 PIPE)
25 BOLT, CASE TO CENTER SUPPORT
26 BOLT, CASE (4TH CLUTCH)
27 BOLT, HEX FLANGE HD (PAN TO CASE)
28 PAN, TRANSMISSION OIL
29 SEAL, TRANS. OIL PAN
30 MAGNET, CHIP COLLECTOR
31 FILTER ASSEMBLY, TRANSMISSION OIL
32 SEAL ASSEMBLY, FILTER NECK
33 CLAMP, ELECTRICAL CABLE
34 HARNESS ASSEMBLY, ELECTRICAL WIRING
35 BOLT, HEX HD. (M6 X 1.0 X 55.0)
36 BOLT, M6 X 1.0 X 35.0 LG V/B TO C/P
37 RETAINER, LUBE PIPE
38 CLAMP, LUBE PIPE
39 PIPE, LUBE
40 MANIFOLD, PRESSURE SWITCH
41 SPRING ASSEMBLY, MANUAL DETENT
43 STOP, DIPSTICK (FLUID LEVEL INDICATOR)
44 BODY ASSEMBLY, CONTROL VALVE
45 GASKET, VALVE BODY TO SPACER PLATE
46 PLATE, VALVE BODY SPACER
47 GASKET, ACCUMULATOR HSG. TO SPACER PLATE
48 GASKET, SPACER PLATE TO CASE
49 SPRING, 4TH CLUTCH ACCUM. PISTON
50 SPRING, 3RD CLUTCH ACCUM. PISTON
51 HOUSING, ACCUMULATOR
52 BOLT, ACCUM. HOUSING TO VALVE BODY (LONG)
53 BOLT, ACCUM. HOUSING TO VALVE BODY (SHORT)
54 BALL, .25 DIAMETER
55 PIN, FRONT SERVO PISTON
56 RING, FRONT SERVO SPRING RETAINER
57 RING, OIL SEAL
58 PISTON, FRONT SERVO
59 RETAINER, FRONT SERVO SPRING
60 SPRING, FRONT SERVO PISTON
61 BOLT, REAR SERVO COVER
62 COVER, REAR SERVO
63 GASKET, REAR SERVO COVER
64 CLIP, RETAINING (BOTTOM)
65 PISTON, REAR SERVO
66 RING, OIL SEAL ACCUM. PISTON (OUTER)
67 RING, OIL SEAL ACCUM. PISTON (INNER)
68 PISTON, REAR ACCUMULATOR
69 SEAL, REVERSE SERVO PISTON
70 WASHER, SERVO PISTON
71 SPRING, REAR SERVO
72 RETAINER, REAR PISTON SPRING
73 PIN, REAR BAND APPLY (SELECTIVE)
74 SPRING, REAR ACCUMULATOR
75 SCREEN, PWM SOLENOID
76 BOLT, SPECIAL
77 BUSHING, CASE EXTENSION
78 BUSHING, TRANSMISSION CASE
79 PLUG, DIRECT OIL GAL (.25 DIA. CUP)
80 PIN, ANCHOR FRONT BAND
81 PIN, ANCHOR REAR BAND

FIGURE 12–38 *(continued)*

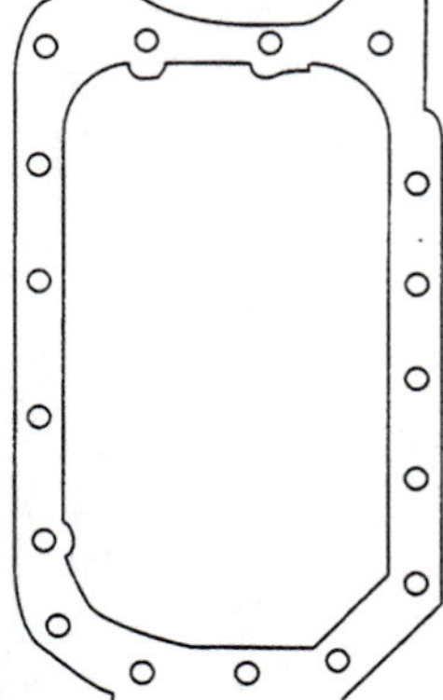

FIGURE 12–39 4L80E transmission case and internal parts. (Reprinted with permission of General Motors Corporation)

12.4.5 Components

In this section exploded drawings of the HM 4L80E automatic transaxle subassemblies are shown along with lists of the part names. The manufacturer's part names are used to eliminate confusion about component names. The illustrations to study are as follows:

Case and associated parts, Figure 12–38

Valve body, Figure 12–40

Internal parts, Figure 12–41

Washer and bushing location, Figure 12–42

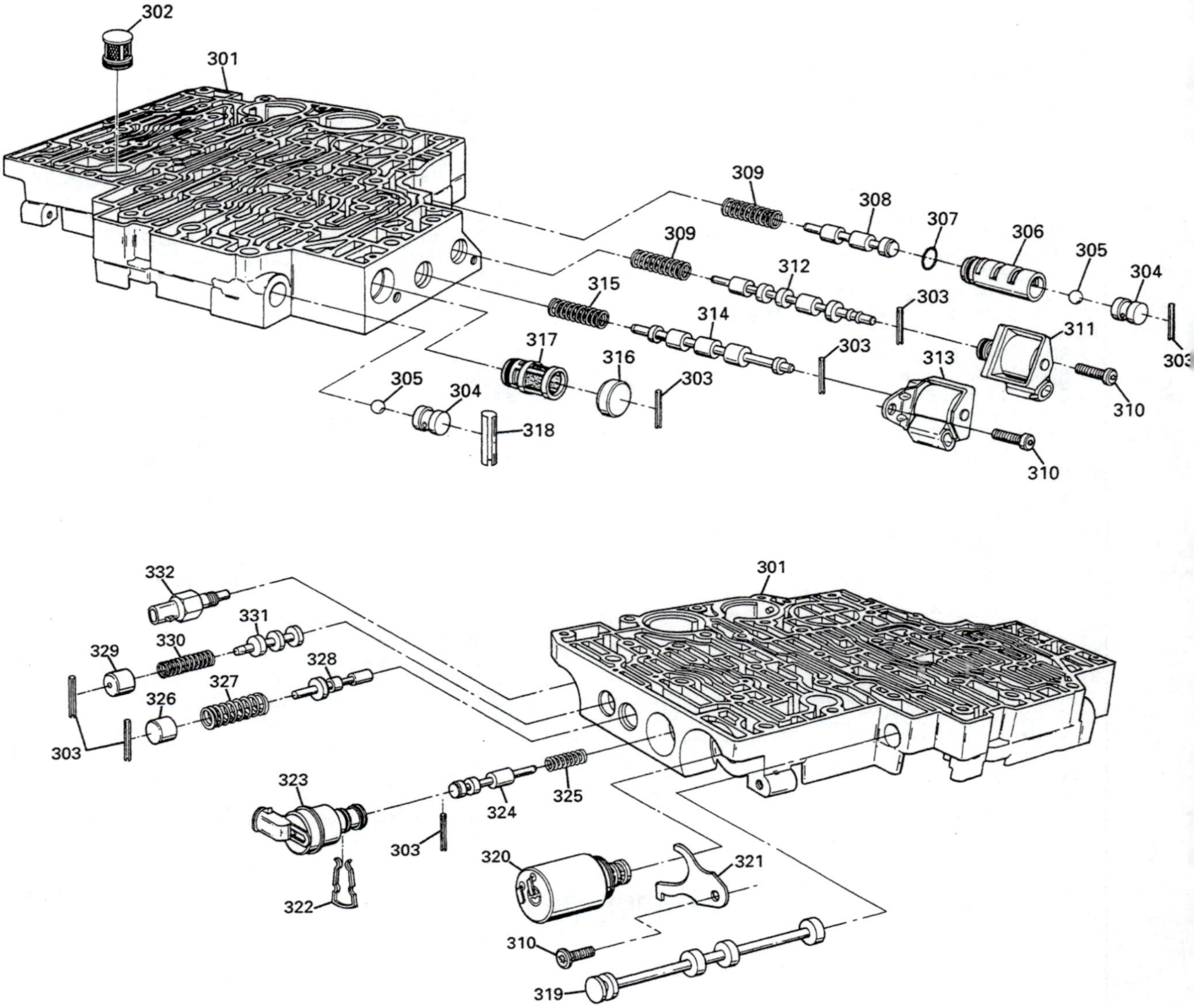

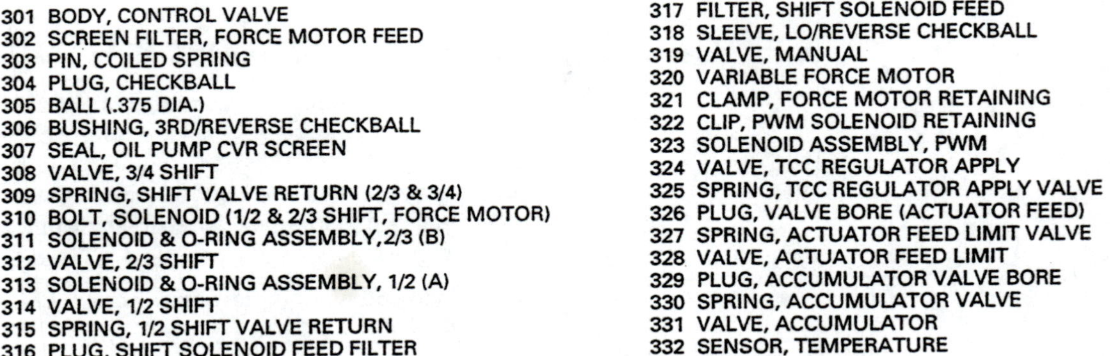

301 BODY, CONTROL VALVE
302 SCREEN FILTER, FORCE MOTOR FEED
303 PIN, COILED SPRING
304 PLUG, CHECKBALL
305 BALL (.375 DIA.)
306 BUSHING, 3RD/REVERSE CHECKBALL
307 SEAL, OIL PUMP CVR SCREEN
308 VALVE, 3/4 SHIFT
309 SPRING, SHIFT VALVE RETURN (2/3 & 3/4)
310 BOLT, SOLENOID (1/2 & 2/3 SHIFT, FORCE MOTOR)
311 SOLENOID & O-RING ASSEMBLY,2/3 (B)
312 VALVE, 2/3 SHIFT
313 SOLENOID & O-RING ASSEMBLY, 1/2 (A)
314 VALVE, 1/2 SHIFT
315 SPRING, 1/2 SHIFT VALVE RETURN
316 PLUG, SHIFT SOLENOID FEED FILTER
317 FILTER, SHIFT SOLENOID FEED
318 SLEEVE, LO/REVERSE CHECKBALL
319 VALVE, MANUAL
320 VARIABLE FORCE MOTOR
321 CLAMP, FORCE MOTOR RETAINING
322 CLIP, PWM SOLENOID RETAINING
323 SOLENOID ASSEMBLY, PWM
324 VALVE, TCC REGULATOR APPLY
325 SPRING, TCC REGULATOR APPLY VALVE
326 PLUG, VALVE BORE (ACTUATOR FEED)
327 SPRING, ACTUATOR FEED LIMIT VALVE
328 VALVE, ACTUATOR FEED LIMIT
329 PLUG, ACCUMULATOR VALVE BORE
330 SPRING, ACCUMULATOR VALVE
331 VALVE, ACCUMULATOR
332 SENSOR, TEMPERATURE

FIGURE 12–40 4L80E hydraulic valve body. (Reprinted with permission of General Motors Corporation)

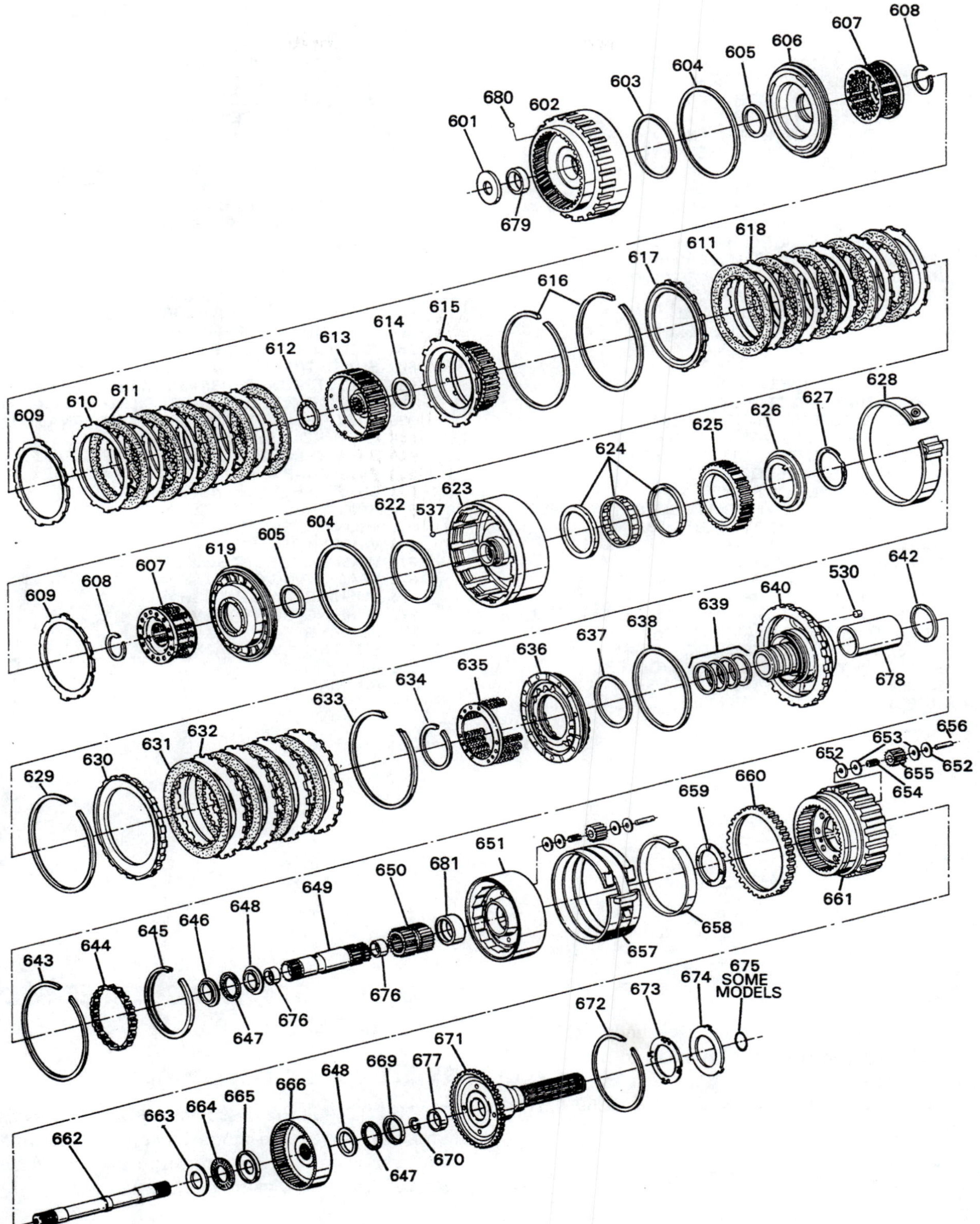

FIGURE 12–41 4L80E internal parts. (Reprinted with permission of General Motors Corporation)

530 PLUG, ORIFICE CENTER SUPPORT
537 BALL, CHECK
601 BEARING ASM., THRUST CARRIER/FORWARD CLUTCH
602 HOUSING ASSEMBLY, FORWARD CLUTCH
603 SEAL, CLUTCH (CENTER)
604 SEAL, CLUTCH (OUTER)
605 SEAL, CLUTCH (INNER)
606 PISTON, FORWARD CLUTCH
607 SPRING & RETAINER ASSEMBLY
608 RING, SNAP
609 PLATE, CLUTCH (.054 DISHED)
610 PLATE, CLUTCH (.0775 FLAT)
611 PLATE ASSEMBLY, CLUTCH
612 WASHER, THRUST CLUTCH HUB HOUSING
613 HUB, FORWARD CLUTCH DRIVEN
614 WASHER, THRUST FORWARD CLUTCH
615 HUB, DIRECT CLUTCH DRIVING
616 RING, SNAP (6.24 O.D. X .062)
617 PLATE, DIRECT CLUTCH BACKING
618 PLATE, CLUTCH (.0915 FLAT)
619 PISTON, DIRECT CLUTCH
622 SEAL, CLUTCH (CENTER)
623 HOUSING, DIRECT CLUTCH
624 SPRAG ASSEMBLY, INTERMEDIATE CLUTCH
625 RACE, INTERMEDIATE CLUTCH (OUTER)
626 RETAINER, INTERMEDIATE CLUTCH
627 RING, EXTERNAL LOCKING
628 BAND ASSEMBLY, FRONT
629 RING, SNAP (INTERMEDIATE CLUTCH RETAINER)
630 PLATE, INTERMEDIATE CLUTCH BACKING
631 PLATE ASSEMBLY, INTERMEDIATE CLUTCH
632 PLATE, INTERMEDIATE CLUTCH
633 RING, SNAP CENTER SUPPORT/CASE
634 RING, SNAP INTERMEDIATE CLUTCH
635 SPRING & RETAINER ASM., INTERMEDIATE CLUTCH
636 PISTON, INTERMEDIATE CLUTCH
637 SEAL, INTERMEDIATE CLUTCH (INNER)
638 SEAL, INTERMEDIATE CLUTCH (OUTER)
639 RING, OIL SEAL
640 SUPPORT & RACE ASSEMBLY, CENTER
642 WASHER, THRUST SUPPORT/REACTION DRUM
643 SPACER, SUPPORT TO CASE
644 ROLLER CLUTCH ASSEMBLY
645 RING, REACTION DRUM SPACER
646 RACE, THRUST BEARING TO CENTER SUPPORT
647 BEARING, NEEDLE THRUST
648 RACE, THRUST BEARING
649 SHAFT ASSEMBLY, SUN GEAR
650 GEAR, SUN
651 DRUM & CARRIER ASSEMBLY, REACTION
652 WASHER, PINION THRUST (BRONZE)
653 WASHER, PINION THRUST (STEEL)
654 ROLLER, NEEDLE BEARING
655 PINION, PLANET
656 PIN, PLANET PINION
657 BAND ASSEMBLY, REAR BRAKE
658 RING, FRONT INTERNAL GEAR
659 WASHER, FRONT INTERNAL/REACTION CARRIER
660 RING, OUTPUT SPEED SENSOR
661 CARRIER ASSEMBLY, OUTPUT
662 SHAFT, TRANSMISSION MAIN
663 RACE, THRUST BEARING TO SUN GEAR
664 BEARING, NEEDLE THRUST RR INTERNAL GEAR
665 RACE, THRUST BEARING TO RR INTERNAL GEAF
666 GEAR, REAR INTERNAL
669 RACE, THRUST BEARING TO OUTPUT SHAFT
670 RING, SNAP MAINSHAFT INTERNAL GEAR
671 SHAFT & BUSHING ASSEMBLY, OUTPUT
672 RING, SNAP (OUTPUT SHAFT/ FRONT INTERNAL GEAR)
673 WASHER, THRUST
674 WASHER, THRUST SELECTIVE
675 SEAL, O-RING OUTPUT SHAFT
676 BUSHING, SUN GEAR SHAFT
677 BUSHING, OUTPUT SHAFT
678 BUSHING
679 BUSHING, 1.536" DIA. X 3.52"
680 BALL, CHECK
681 BUSHING, REACTION DRUM

FIGURE 12–41 *(continued)*

12.4.6 Air Test

Due to the placement of the valve body, it is not practical to air test this transmission in the normal manner. It is recommended to air test the individual clutches as is done with the HM 4L60 (THM 700-R4) transmission.

12.4.7 Special Attention

In this section we show and explain various points of special interest about the HM 4L80E transmission. The information presented about each item is included with each illustration.

12.5 HM 3T40: FWD THREE-SPEED TRANSAXLE

12.5.1 Basic Description

The HM 3T40 is the first Hydra-Matic transaxle designed for a traverse-mounted engine. The unit is a true transaxle because it incorporates the differential and final drive gears (Figure 12–43).

1. Torque Converter
The HM 3T40 uses a conventional three-element torque converter with a hydraulic converter clutch.

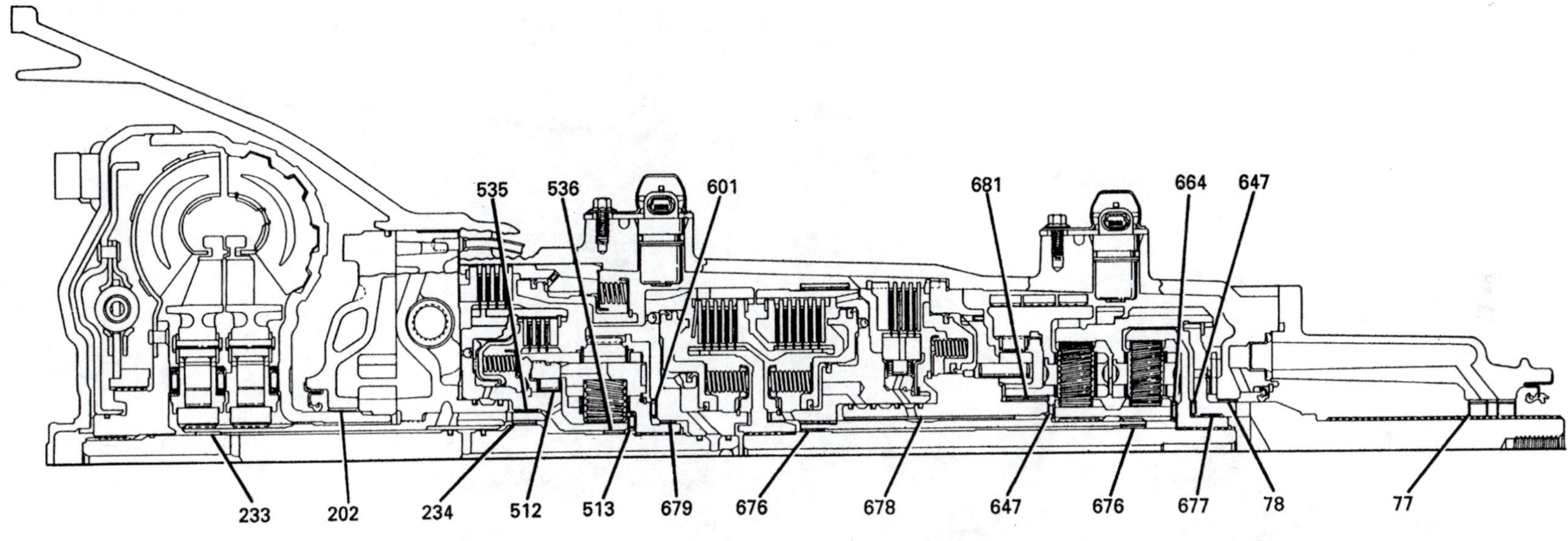

77 BUSHING, CASE EXTENSION
78 BUSHING, CASE TRANS
202 BUSHING, PUMP BODY
233 BUSHING, STATOR SHAFT (FRONT)
234 BUSHING, STATOR SHAFT (REAR)
512 ROLLER CLUTCH ASSEMBLY, OVERDRIVE
513 BEARING ASM., THRUST CARRIER/OVERRUN CLU.
535 BUSHING, OVERRUN CLU. HSG.
536 BUSHING, 1.12" O.D. X 0.50"
601 BEARING ASM., THRUST CARRIER/FORWARD CLU
647 BEARING, NEEDLE THRUST
664 BEARING, NEEDLE THRUST RR INTERNAL GEAR
676 BUSHING, SUN GEAR SHAFT
677 BUSHING, OUTPUT SHAFT
678 BUSHING
679 BUSHING, 1.536" DIA. X 3.52"
681 BUSHING, REACTION DRUM

FIGURE 12–42 4L80E thrust washer and bushing location. (Reprinted with permission of General Motors Corporation)

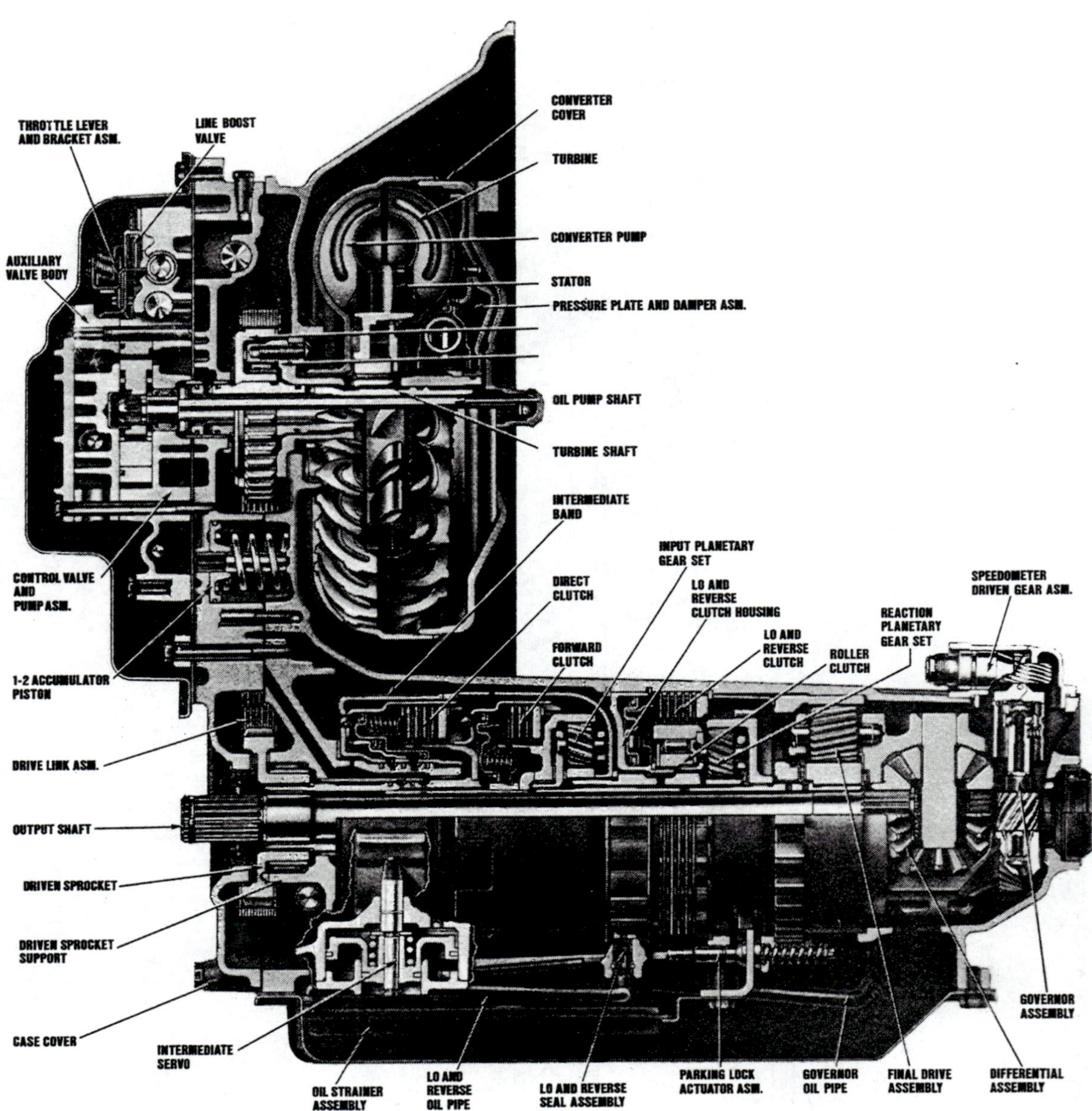

FIGURE 12–43 THM 3T40 cutaway view. (Reprinted with permission of General Motors Corporation)

The converter clutch is shown applied in Figure 12–44 and released in Figure 12–45.

2. Gear Train

The gear train uses a conventional Simpson gear set with the front ring gear and sun gear as input members, the sun gear and rear pinion carrier as reaction members, and the front pinion carrier and rear ring gear as output members. The final drive also uses planetary gears, with the sun gear as input, the ring gear as reaction and the pinion carrier as the output member.

3. Coupling Devices

The coupling devices are the direct clutch, which drives the sun gear, and the forward clutch, which drives the front ring gear (Figure 12–46).

4. Holding Devices

The holding devices are the intermediate band,

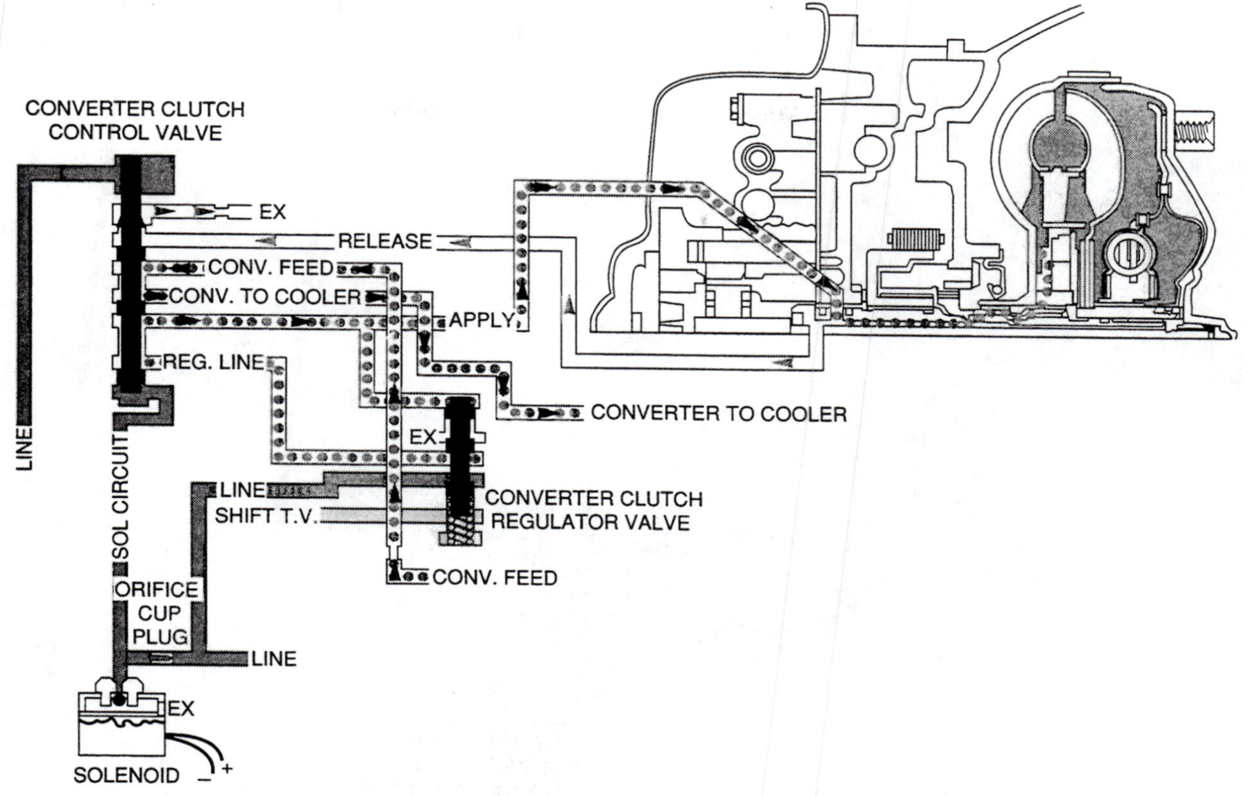

FIGURE 12–44 THM 3T40 converter clutch applied. (Reprinted with permission of General Motors Corporation)

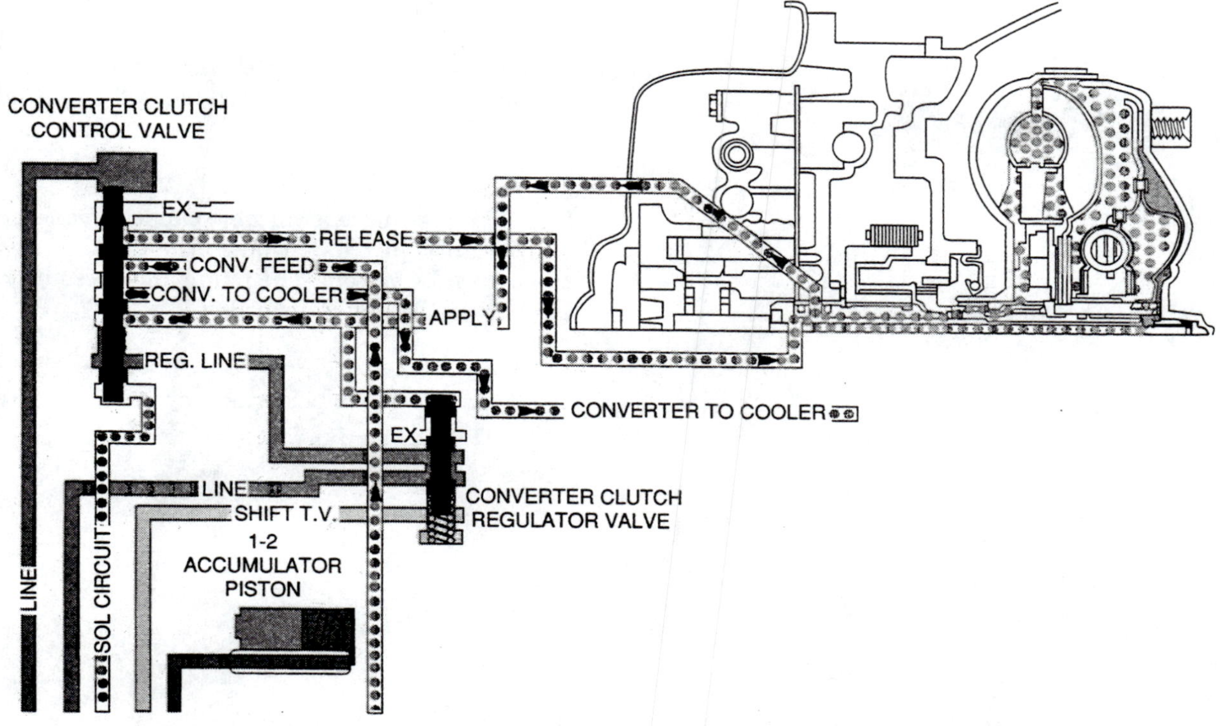

FIGURE 12–45 THM 3T40 converter clutch released. (Reprinted with permission of General Motors Corporation)

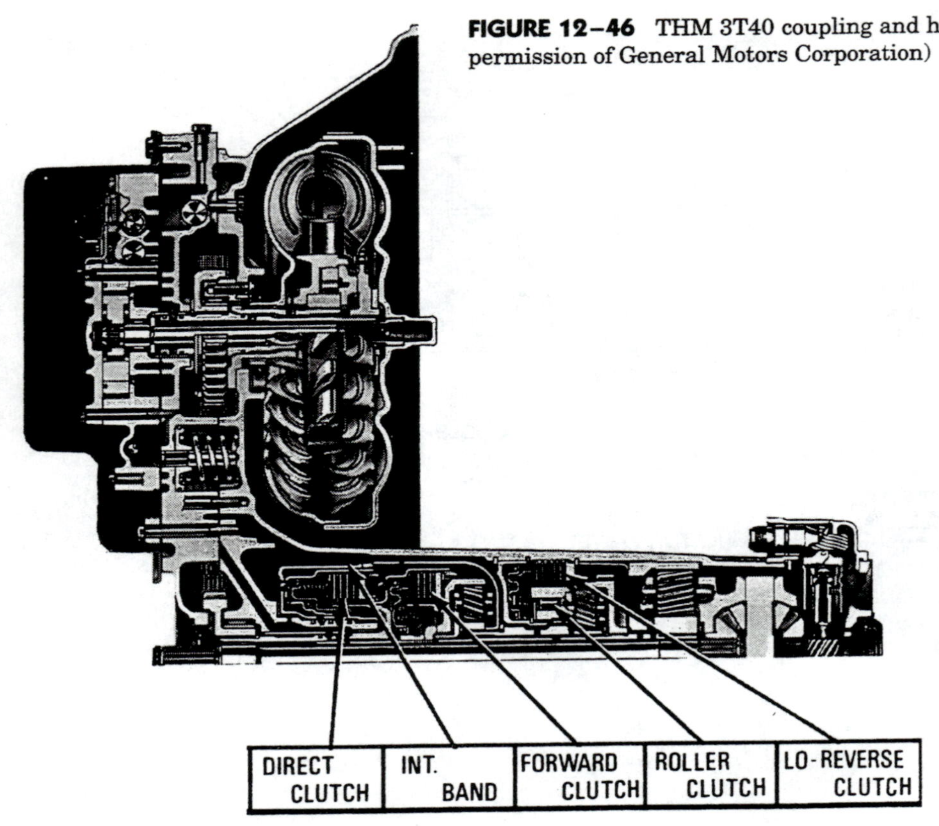

FIGURE 12–46 THM 3T40 coupling and holding devices. (Reprinted with permission of General Motors Corporation)

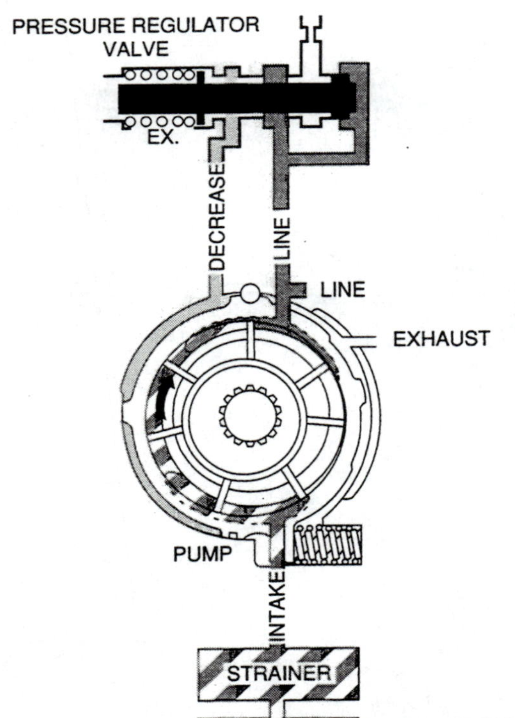

FIGURE 12–47 THM 3T40 oil pump. (Reprinted with permission of General Motors Corporation)

which holds the sun gear, the low roller clutch, and the low–reverse clutch, which holds the rear pinion carrier (Figure 12–46).

5. *Pump*
The HM 3T40 uses a variable-capacity vane pump, which can adjust its output to match the needs of the hydraulic system. The pump and pressure regulator are shown in Figure 12–47.

6. *Shift Control*
The shift control is performed by a fully hydraulic valve body.

7. *Governor*
A typical Hydra-Matic drop-in governor is used, as shown in Figure 12–48.

8. *Throttle Valve*
The throttle valve is operated by a cable connected to the carburetor throttle linkage (Figure 12–49).

12.5.2 Power Flow

1. *Neutral (N)*
All coupling and holding devices are released and not holding. The turbine shaft and forward clutch drum are turning with the converter.

2. *First Gear (D1)*
The forward clutch is applied, making the front ring gear input. The low roller clutch is holding the rear pinion carrier, causing a 2.74:1 gear reduction. In manual first (1), the low–reverse clutch is applied to hold the rear pinion carrier. With the low–reverse clutch applied there is engine braking in first gear.

3. *Second Gear (D2)*
The intermediate band is applied while the forward clutch remains applied. The band holds the sun gear, and a gear reduction of 1.57:1 is produced (Figure 12–50).

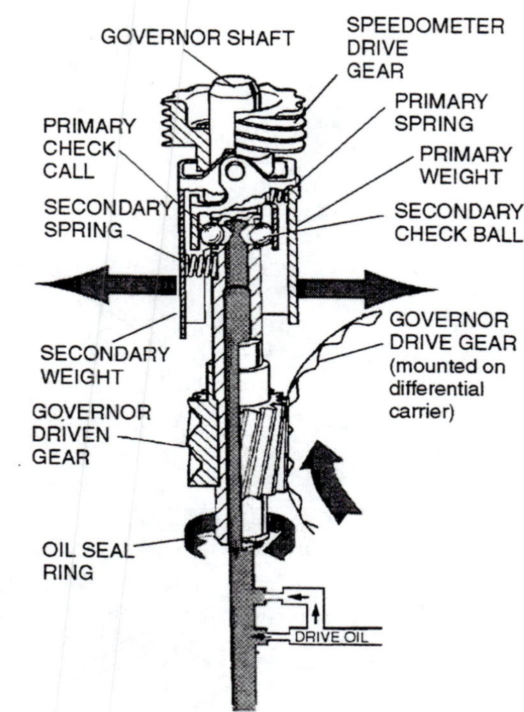

FIGURE 12–48 THM 3T40 governor. (Reprinted with permission of General Motors Corporation)

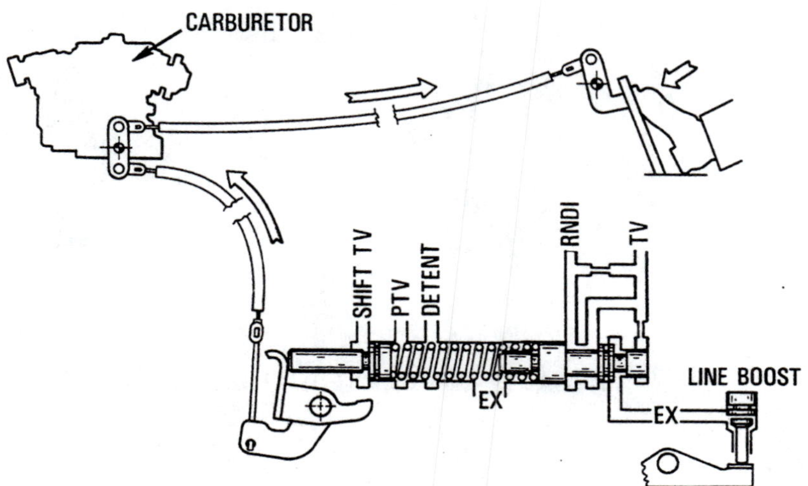

FIGURE 12–49 THM 3T40 throttle valve. (Reprinted with permission of General Motors Corporation)

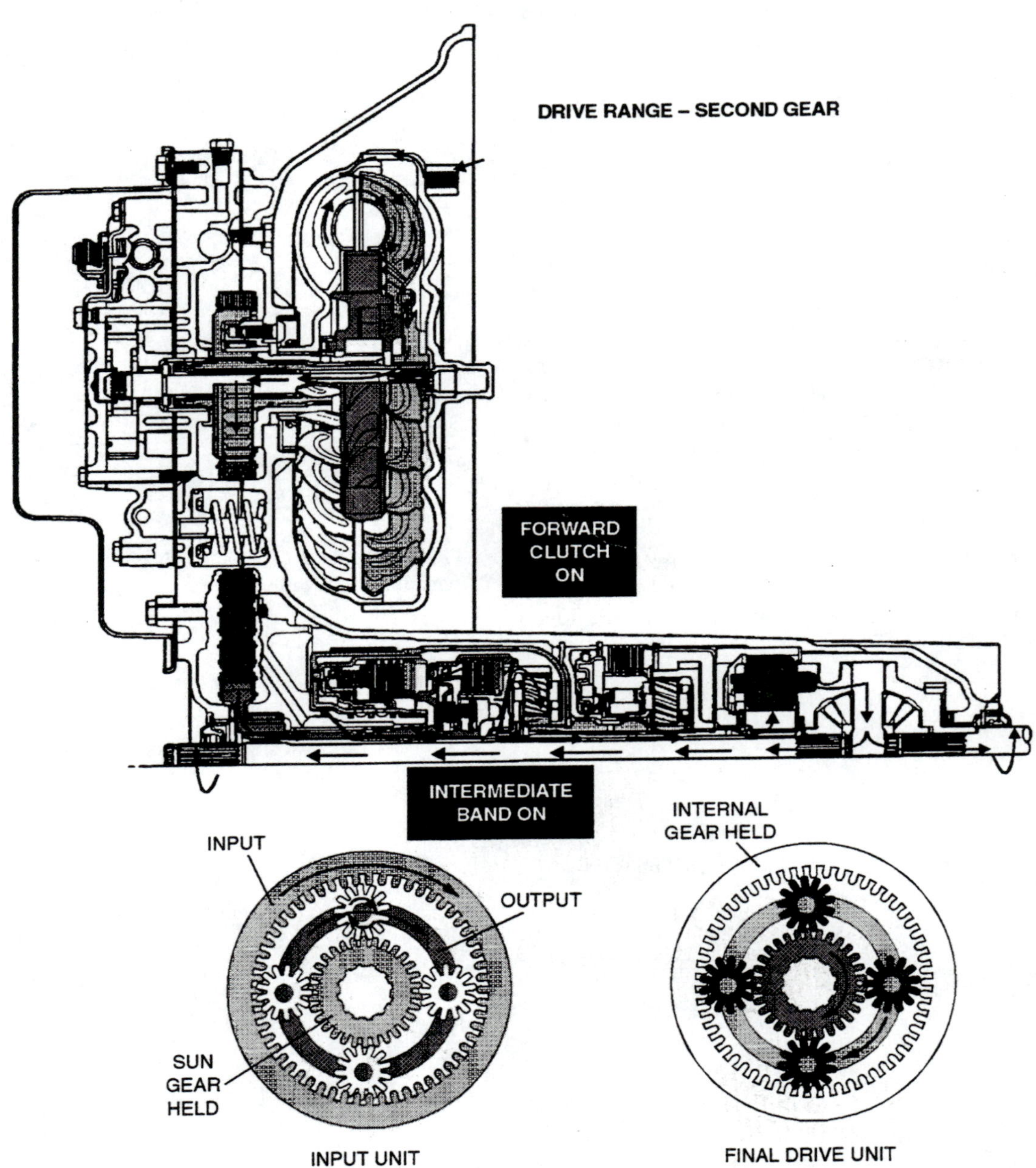

FIGURE 12–50 THM 3T40 in second gear.

4. Third Gear (D3)

The intermediate band is released and the direct clutch is applied. The forward clutch remains applied. The front ring gear and sun gear are now both input, so direct drive is achieved (Figure 12–51).

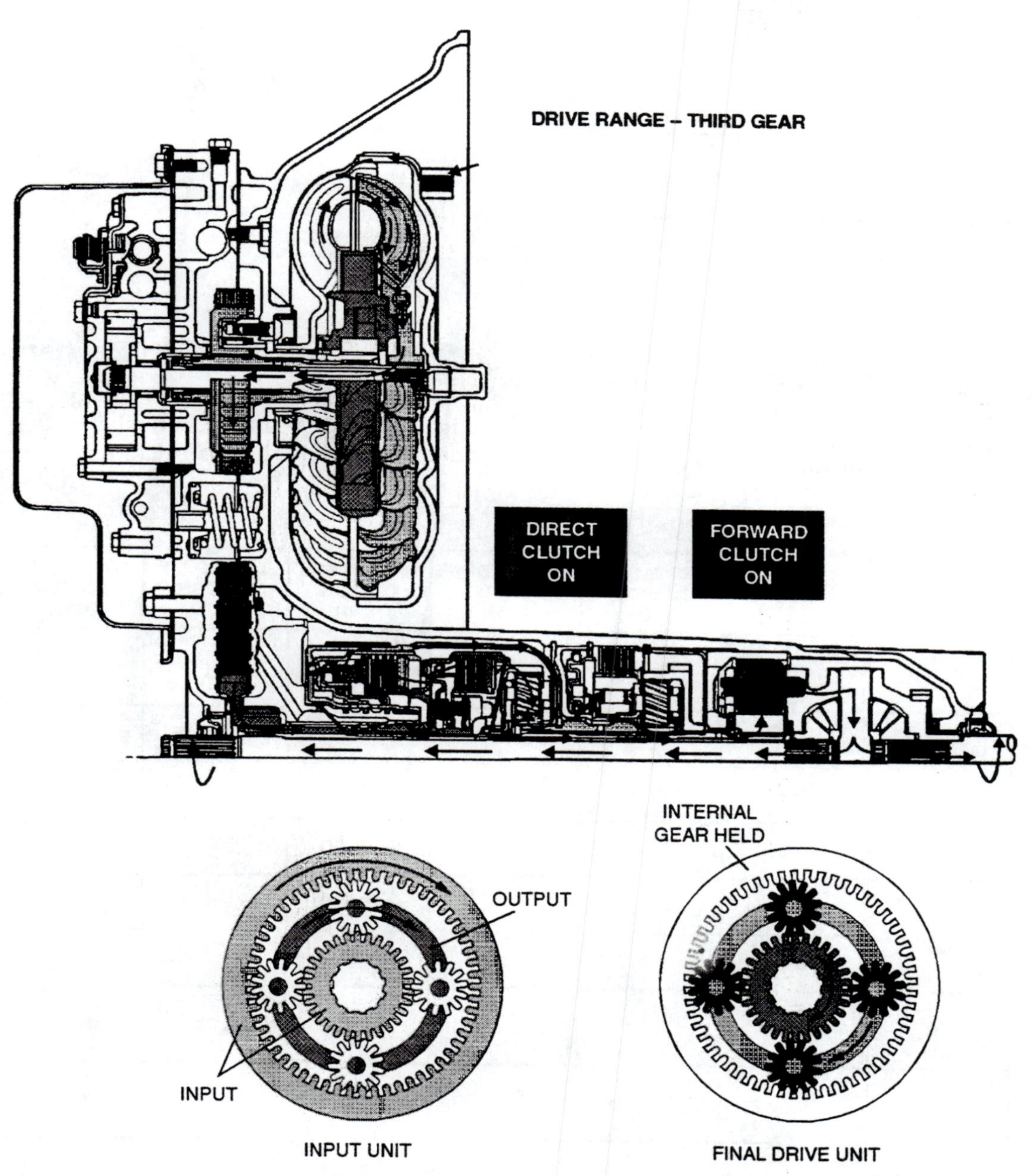

FIGURE 12–51 THM 3T40 in third gear.

THM12SC	DIRECT CLUTCH	FORWARD CLUTCH	LO-REV CLUTCH	INTERMEDIATE BAND	LO ROLLER CLUTCH	PARK PAWL	CONVERTER CLUTCH
P						X	
N							
D1		X			X		
D2		X		X			
D3	X	X					X
1		X	X		X (dashed)		
2		X		X			
R	X		X				

X = APPLIED

X (dashed) = APPLIED, NOT CARRYING LOAD

FIGURE 12–52 THM 3T40 clutch and band chart, standardized version.

5. *Reverse Gear (R)*

To provide reverse, the direct clutch is applied for input through the sun gear. The low–reverse clutch is applied to hold the rear pinion carrier, which gives a 2.07:1 gear reduction in reverse.

12.5.3 Clutch and Band Charts

The first chart, the author's design, is shown in Figure 12–52. The second chart, the manufacturer's design, is shown in Figure 12–53.

RANGE	GEAR	DIRECT CLUTCH (610)	INTERMEDIATE BAND (606)	FORWARD CLUTCH (624)	LO ROLLER CLUTCH (662)	LO-REVERSE CLUTCH (649)
P-N						
D	1st			APPLIED	HOLDING	
	2nd		APPLIED	APPLIED		
	3rd	APPLIED		APPLIED		
2	1st			APPLIED	HOLDING	
	2nd		APPLIED	APPLIED		
1	1st			APPLIED	HOLDING	APPLIED
R	REVERSE	APPLIED				APPLIED

FIGURE 12–53 THM 3T40 clutch and band chart, factory version. (Reprinted with permission of General Motors Corporation)

12.5.4 Identification

The shape of the transmission oil pan or its gasket is a quick means of identifying an automatic transmission. In Figure 12–54 you see the pan gasket shape and number of bolt holes for the HM 3T40 transaxle. The location of the factory identification tag and its code are shown in Figure 12–55.

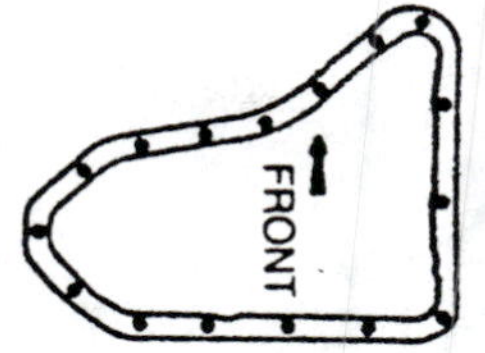

FIGURE 12–54 THM 3T40 pan gasket identification. (Reprinted with permission of General Motors Corporation)

12.5.5 Components

In this section exploded drawings of the HM 3T40 transmission subassemblies are shown along with lists of the part names. The drawings to study are as follows:

Case and associated parts, Figure 12–56

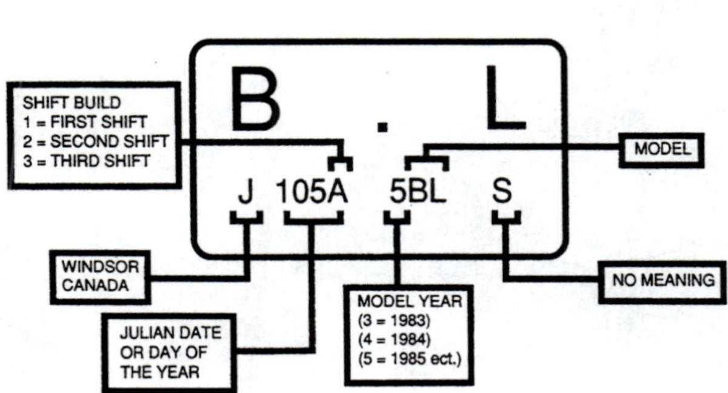

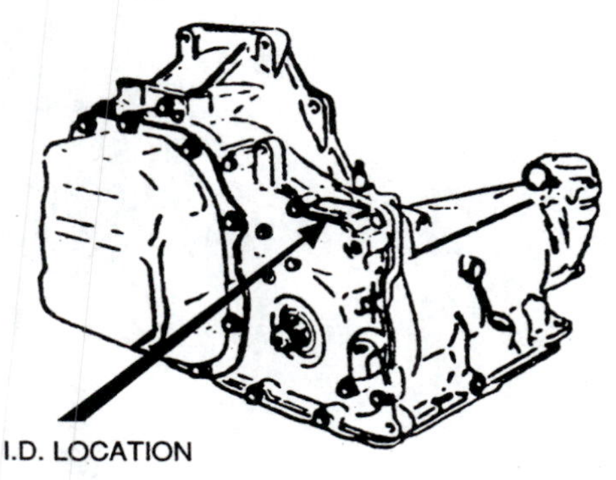

FIGURE 12–55 THM 3T40 identification tag location. (Reprinted with permission of General Motors Corporation)

ILLUSTRATION NO.	GROUP NO.	DESCRIPTION
1	4.115	Converter Assembly
2	4.115	Bushing, Converter Pump
3	4.256	Ring Oil Seal
4	4.256	Governor Assembly, Complete
5	4.343	Gear, Speedometer Drive
6	4.330	Washer, Speedo Gear Thrust
7	4.229	Seal, O-Ring
8	8.900	Screw Governor Cover to Case
9	4.256	Cover, Governor
10	4.337	Speedo Driven Gear
11	4.338	Seal, O-Ring
12	4.338	Sleeve Speedo Driven Gear
13	8.900	Bolt, Speedo Gear Retaining
14	4.338	Retainer, Speedo Gear
15	4.103	Case, Assembly
16	4.265	Ball (6.3 mm. dia.)
17	4.128	Connector, Cooler Fitting
18	4.226	Shaft, Oil Pump Drive
19	4.265	Gasket, Spacer Plate
20	4.265	Plate, Valve Body Spacer
21	4.224	Control Valve and Oil Pump Asm.
22	4.275	Link, Throttle Lever to Cable
23	4.275	Lever and Bracket Asm., Throttle
24	8.900	Bolt, Valve Body/Case
25	4.217	Gasket, Valve Body Cover
26	4.215	Cover, Valve Body
27	8.900	Screw, Valve Body Cover
28	4.176	Ring, Retaining - Axle Joint
29	4.175	Shaft, Output
30	4.172	Ring, Snap
31	4.318	Seal Asm., Axle Oil
32	4.197	Seal, O-Ring
33	4.197	Stainer Asm., Transmission Oil
34	4.196	Gasket, Transmission Oil Pan
35	4.195	Pan, Transmission Oil
36	4.217	Screw, Transmission Oil Pan

FIGURE 12–56 Parts list for THM 3T40 (page 384).

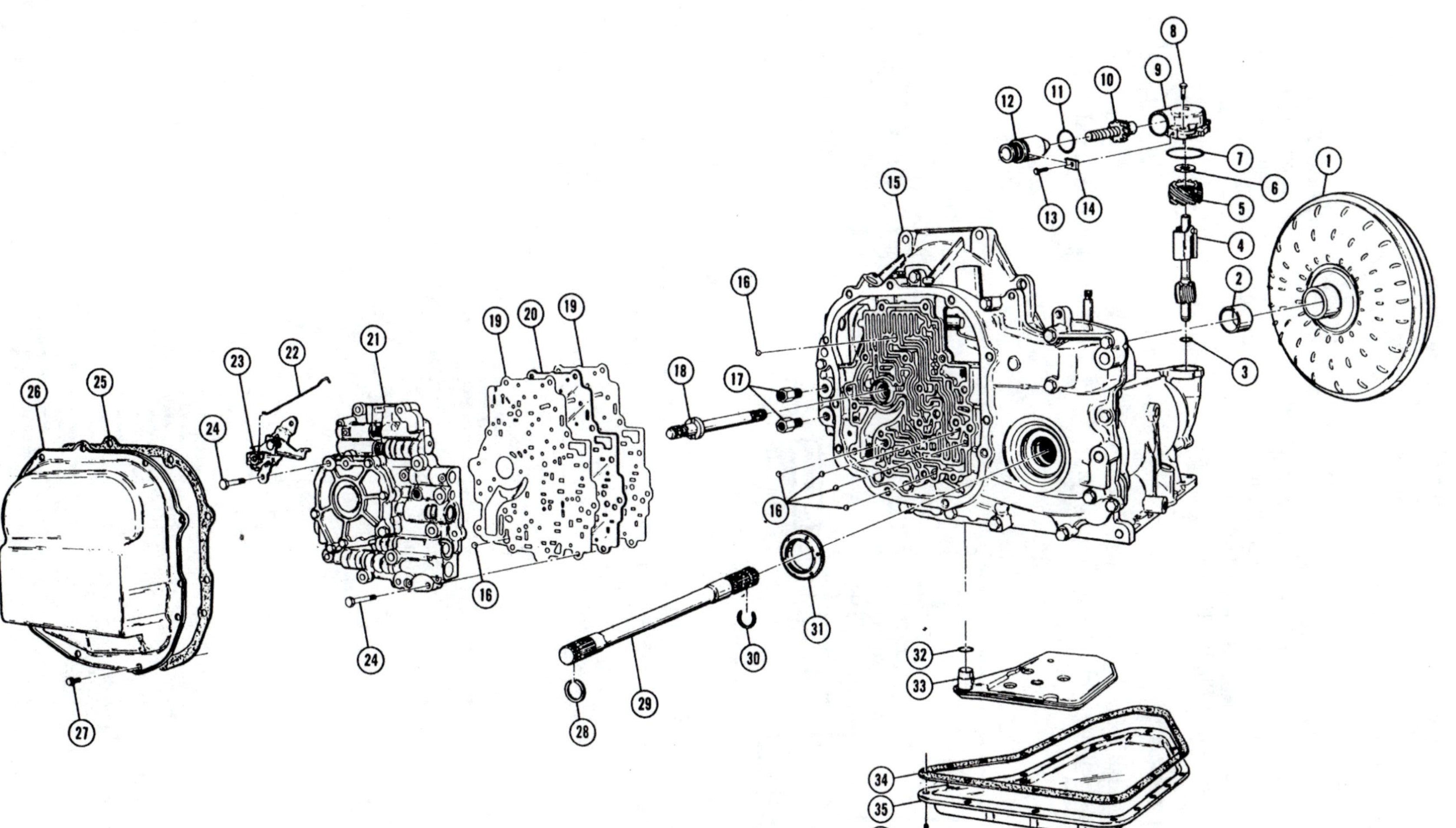

FIGURE 12–56 THM 3T40 case and parts. (Reprinted with permission of General Motors Corporation)

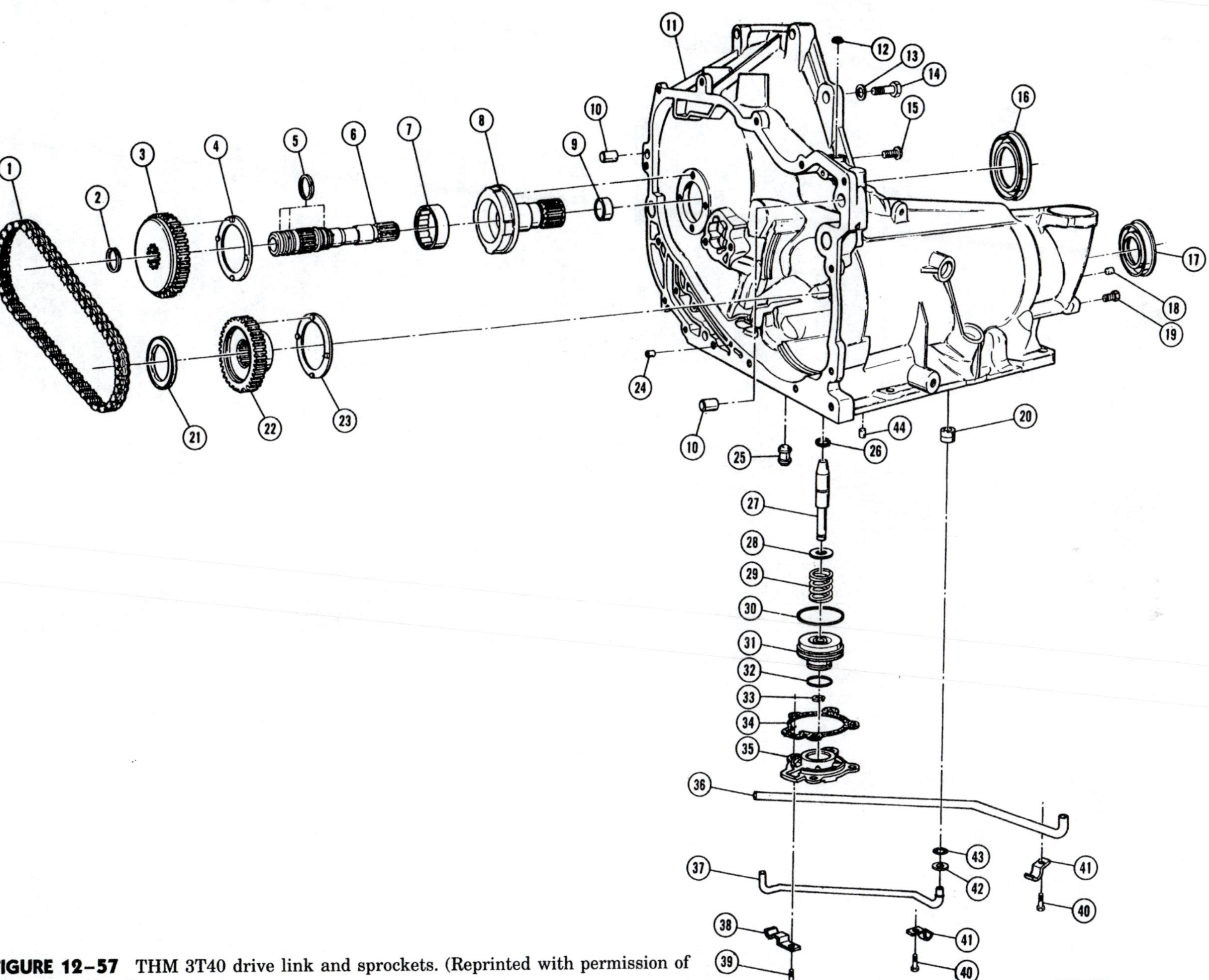

FIGURE 12–57 THM 3T40 drive link and sprockets. (Reprinted with permission of General Motors Corporation)

Drive link and sprockets, Figure 12–57
Internal parts, Figure 12–58
Washer and bushing location, Figure 12–59

ILLUSTRATION NO.	GROUP NO.	DESCRIPTION
1	4.131	Link Assembly, Drive
2	4.131	Ring, Snap
3	4.131	Sprocket Drive
4	4.131	Washer, Case Cover to Dr. Skt. Thrust
5	4.131	Ring, Oil Seal Turbine Shaft
6	4.131	Shaft, Turbine
7	4.131	Bearing Assembly
8	4.130	Support, Drive Sprocket
9	4.226	Bushing, Drive Sprocket Support
10	4.226	Pin, Dowel-Case Cover to Case
11	4.103	Case Transaxle
12	4.275	Seal Assembly, Manual Shaft
13	4.226	Washer
14	8.900	Bolt, Case to Case Cover
15	8.900	Screw - Socket Button Head
16	4.226	Seal Assembly, (Converter)
17	4.318	Seal Assembly, (Axle)
18	4.294	Plug, Cup (Parking Pawl Shaft)
19	8.971	Plug, (Gov. Pressure Pickup)
20	4.162	Reverse Oil Seal - Case to Housing
21	4.131	Bearing Assembly, Driven Sprocket Thrust
22	4.131	Sprocket, Driven
23	4.131	Washer, Driven Sprocket/Support Thrust
24	4.105	Plug, Cup (3rd Oil)
25	4.105	Check Valve, Accumulator Exhaust
26	4.228	Ring, Oil Seal Inter. Band App. Pin
27	4.228	Pin, Intermediate, Band Apply
28	4.228	Retainer, Inter., Servo Spring
29	4.233	Spring, Inter., Servo Cushion
30	4.228	Ring, Oil Seal Outer, Int. Servo
31	4.228	Piston, Intermediate Servo
32	4.228	Ring, Oil Seal - Inner Int. Servo
33	4.934	Ring, Snap
34	4.212	Gasket, Intermediate Servo Cover
35	4.228	Cover, Intermediate Servo
36	4.248	Pipe, Governor Oil
37	4.248	Pipe, Reverse Oil
38	4.248	Retainer, Reverse Oil Pipe
39	8.900	Bolt, Int. Servo Cover
40	8.900	Bolt, Pipe Ret/Case
41	4.256	Retainer, Governor and Reverse Oil Pipe
42	4.162	Ring - Seal Backup
43	4.248	Seal, O Reverse Pipe to Case
44	4.105	Plug, Orifice

FIGURE 12–57 *(continued)*

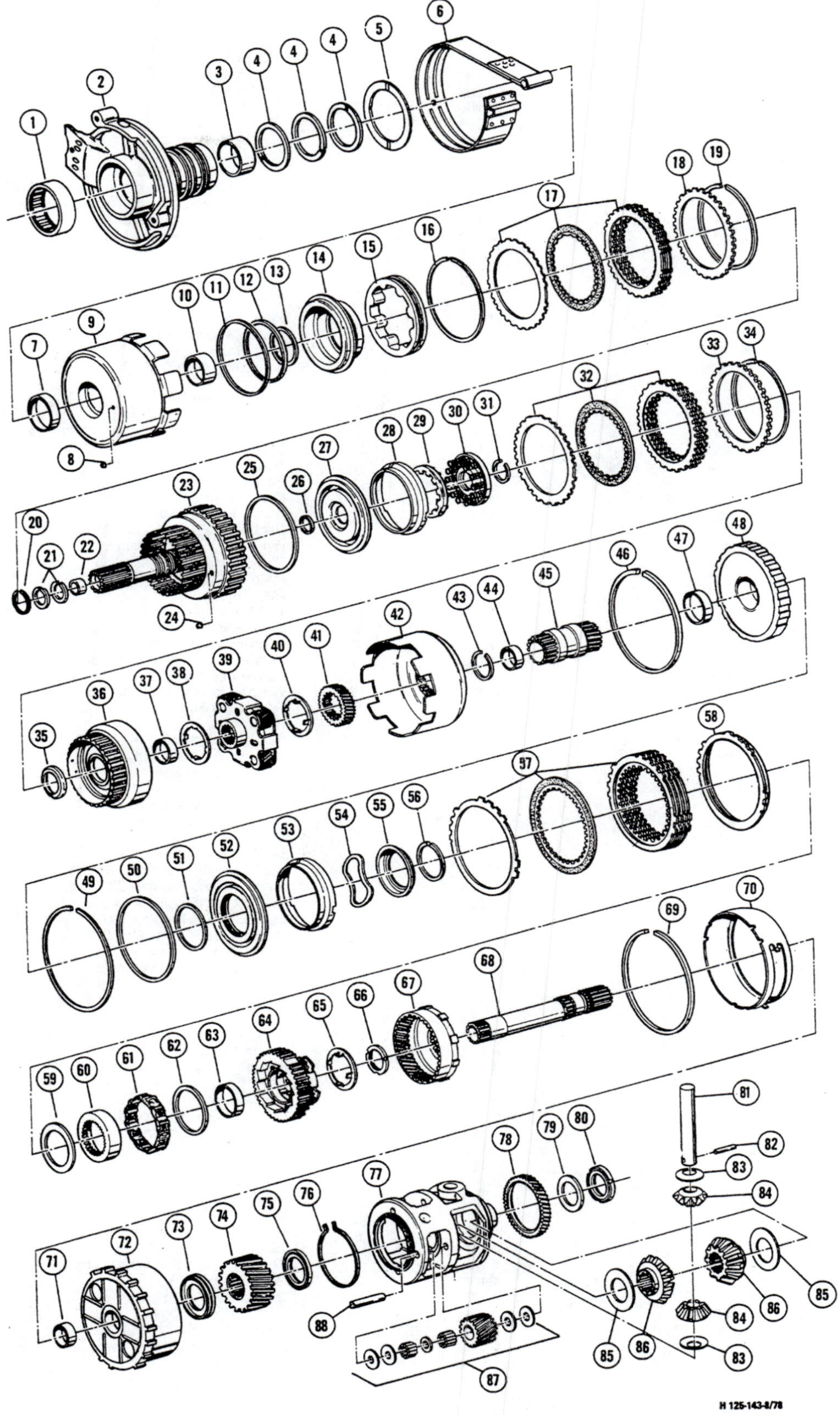

FIGURE 12–58 THM 3T40 internal parts. (Reprinted with permission of General Motors Corporation)

ILLUSTRATION NO.	GROUP NO.	DESCRIPTION
1	4.131	Bearing Assembly
2	4.130	Support Assembly, Driven Sprocket
3	4.226	Bushing, Driven Sprocket Support
4	4.130	Ring, Oil Seal
5	4.169	Washer, Thrust
6	4.251	Band Assembly, Intermediate
7	4.169	Bushing, Direct Clutch
8	4.169	Retainer and Ball Assembly, Check Valve
9	4.169	Housing and Drum Assembly, Direct Clutch
10	4.169	Bushing, Direct Clutch Drum
11	4.166	Seal, Direct Clutch Piston Outer
12	4.166	Seal, Direct Clutch Center
13	4.166	Seal, Direct Clutch Piston Inner
14	4.166	Piston, Direct Clutch
15	4.164	Apply Ring and Release Spring Assembly
16	4.164	Ring, Snap
17	4.163	Plate, Direct Clutch
18	4.163	Plate, Clutch Backing, Direct
19	4.163	Ring, Snap
20	4.169	Snap Ring, Selective
21	4.123	Ring, Oil Seal
22	4.158	Bushing, Input Shaft
23	4.169	Housing Assembly, Forward Clutch
24	4.169	Retainer and Ball Assembly, Check Valve
25	4.166	Seal, Forward Clutch Piston Outer
26	4.166	Seal, Forward Clutch Piston Inner
27	4.166	Piston, Forward Clutch
28	4.166	Ring, Forward Clutch Apply
29	4.163	Guide, Release Spring
30	4.163	Retainer & Spring Assembly, Fwd. Cl.
31	4.172	Ring, Snap Spring Retainer
32	4.163	Plate, Forward Clutch
33	4.163	Plate, Clutch Backing, Forward
34	4.164	Ring, Snap
35	4.158	Washer, Input Shaft Thrust
36	4.158	Gear, and Input Internal
37	4.158	Bushing, Input Internal Gear
38	4.159	Washer, Input Carr./Ip. Int. Gr. Thrust
39	4.175	Carrier Assembly, Input
40	4.159	Washer, Input Carr./Ip. Sun Gr. Thrust
41	4.159	Gear, Input Sun
42	4.175	Drum Input
43	4.216	Ring, Snap Selective
44	4.159	Bushing, Reaction Sun Gear
45	4.180	Gear, Reaction Sun
46	4.164	Ring Snap
47	4.159	Bushing, Lo and Reverse Clutch Housing
48	4.162	Housing, Lo and Reverse
49	4.162	Ring, Snap
50	4.166	Seal, Lo and Reverse Piston Outer
51	4.166	Seal, Lo and Reverse Piston Outer
52	4.166	Piston, Lo and Reverse Clutch
53	4.166	Ring, Lo and Reverse Clutch Apply
54	4.164	Spring, Lo and Reverse Clutch Release
55	4.164	Retainer, Lo and Reverse Clutch Spring
56	4.172	Ring, Snap
57	4.164	Plate, Lo and Reverse Clutch
58	4.164	Plate, Lo and Reverse Clutch Backing
59	4.180	Spacer, Rev. Housing/Lo Race Selective
60	4.180	Race, Lo Roller Clutch
61	4.180	Roller Assembly, Lo Clutch
62	4.180	Washer, Reaction Carr./Int. Gr. Thrust
63	4.159	Bushing, Reaction Carrier
64	4.175	Carrier Assembly, Reaction
65	4.180	Washer, Reaction Carr./Int. Gr. Thrust
66	4.159	Bearing, Reaction Sun/Int. Gr. Thrust
67	4.187	Gear, Reaction Internal
68	4.175	Shaft, Final Drive Sun Gear
69	4.164	Ring, Snap
70	4.167	Spacer, Final Drive Internal Gear
71	4.319	Bushing, Final Drive Internal Gear
72	4.175	Gear, Final Drive Internal
73	4.178	Bearing, Thrust Sun Gear/Int. Gr.
74	4.178	Gear, Final Drive Sun
75	4.159	Bearing, Thrust Sun Gear/Carrier
76	4.164	Ring, Snap
77	4.175	Differential, Carrier
78	4.256	Gear, Governor Drive
79	4.176	Washer, Diff. Carr./Case Sel. Thrust
80	4.176	Bearing Assembly, Diff. Carr./Case Thrust
81	4.175	Shaft, Differential Pinion
82	4.175	Pin, Diff. Pinion Shaft Retaining
83	4.175	Washer, Pinion Thrust
84	4.175	Pinion, Differential
85	4.175	Washer, Diff. Side Gear Thrust
86	4.175	Gear Differential Side
87	4.175	Pinion, Final Drive Planet - Pkg.
88	4.175	Pin, Planet Pinion

FIGURE 12–58 *(continued)*

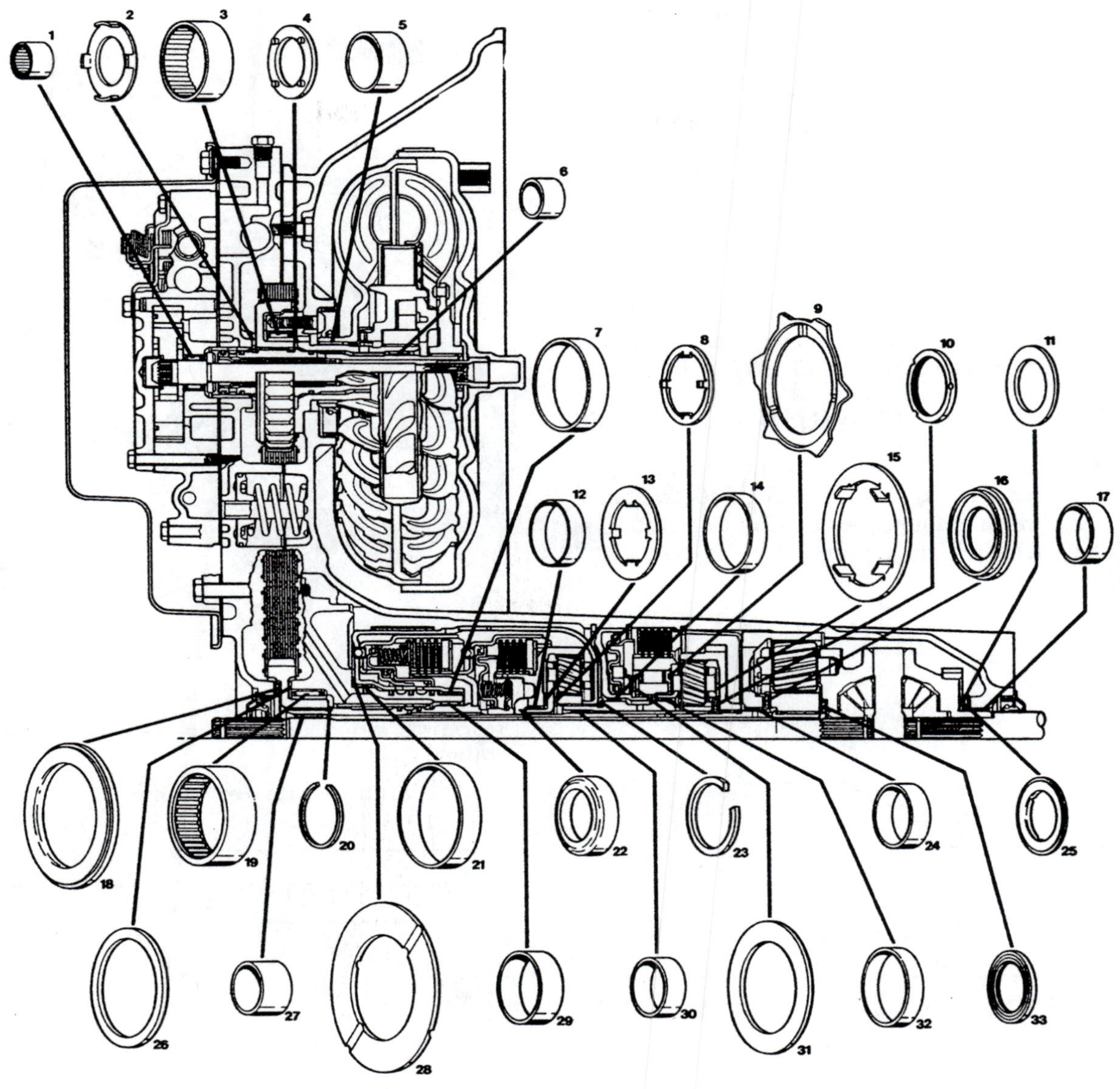

1. Pump Shaft Roller Bearing Assy. Group 4.226
2. Case Cover To Driven Sprocket Thrust Washer Group 4.131
3. Bearing Assembly Group 4.131
4. Case Cover To Drive Sprocket Thrust Washer Group 4.131
5. Converter Bushing Group 4.115
6. Drive Sprocket Support Bushing Group 4.226
7. Direct Clutch Drum Bushing Group 4.169
8. Input Carrier To Input Sun Gear Thrust Washer Group 4.159
9. Reaction Carrier to Lo Race Thrust Washer Group 4.180
10. Reaction Sun To Internal Gear Thrust Bearing Group 4.159
11. Differential Carrier To Case Selective Thrust Washer Group 4.176
12. Input Internal Gear Bushing Group 4.158
13. Input Carrier To Input Internal Gear Thrust Washer Group 4.159
14. Lo and Reverse Clutch Housing Bushing Group 4.159
15. Reaction Carrier To Internal Gear Thrust Washer Group 4.180
16. Sun Gear To Internal Gear Thrust Bearing Group 4.178
17. Case Bushing Group 4.319
18. Driven Sprocket Thrust Bearing Assembly Group 4.131
19. Bearing Assembly Group 4.131
20. Selective Snap Ring Group 4.169
21. Direct Clutch Bushing Group 4.169
22. Input Shaft Thrust Washer Group 4.158
23. Selective Snap Ring Group 4.216
24. Final Drive Internal Gear Bushing Group 4.319
25. Differential Carrier To Case Thrust Bearing Assembly Group 4.176
26. Driven Sprocket Support Thrust Washer Group 4.131
27. Input Shaft Bushing Group 4.158
28. Thrust Washer Group 4.169
29. Driven Sprocket Support Bushing Group 4.226
30. Reaction Sun Gear Bushing Group 4.159
31. Reverse Housing To Lo Race Selective Washer Group 4.180
32. Reaction Carrier Bushing Group 4.159
33. Sun Gear To Carrier Thrust Bearing Group 4.159

FIGURE 12–59 THM 3T40 thrust washer and bushing location. (Reprinted with permission of General Motors Corporation)

12.5.6 Pressure Test

The location of the test points of the HM 3T40 transaxle is shown in Figure 12–60. A pressure chart listing the pressure specifications of this transmission is shown in Figure 12–61.

12.5.7 Air Test

No air test recommendations are currently listed in the service manuals. Adapt the unit air test procedures shown for the HM 4L60 (THM 700-R4).

12.5.8 Special Attention

In this section we show and explain various points of special interest about the HM 3T40 transmission. The information presented about each item is included with each illustration.

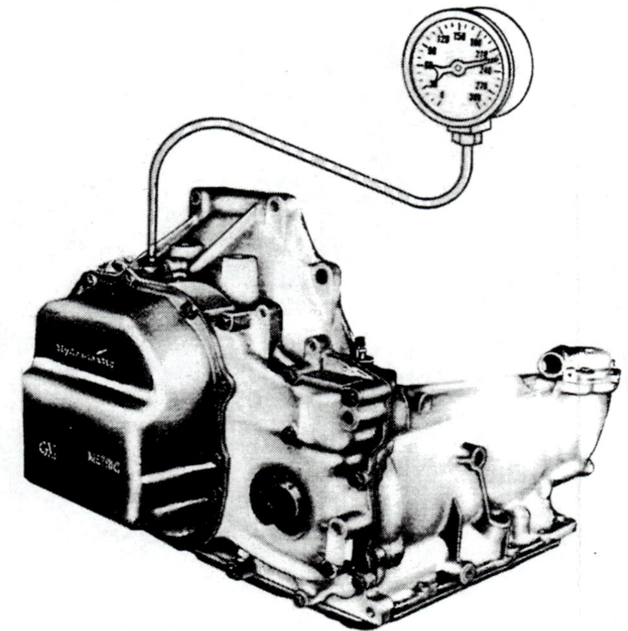

FIGURE 12–60 THM 3T40 pressure test points. (Reprinted with permission of General Motors Corporation)

FIGURE 12–61 THM 3T40 pressure test chart. (Reprinted with permission of General Motors Corporation)

NOTICE Total running time for this combination not to exceed 2 minutes.

CAUTION Brakes must be applied at all times.

MODEL	RANGE	NORMAL OIL PRESSURE AT MINIMUM T.V.		NORMAL OIL PRESSURE AT FULL T.V.	
		kPa	P.S.I.	kPa	P.S.I.
PZ, CV	Park at 1,000 RPM	480 - 620	70 - 90	No T.V. pressure in Park. Line pressure is the same as Park at minimum T.V.	
PZ CV	Reverse at 1,000 RPM	830 - 1100 830 - 1100	120 - 160 120 - 160	1480 - 1895 1725 - 2135	215 - 275 250 - 310
PZ CV	Neutral at 1,000 RPM	480 - 620 480 - 620	70 - 90 70 - 90	830 - 1100 965 - 1240	120 - 160 140 - 180
PZ CV	Drive at 1,000 RPM	Same as Neutral		Same as Neutral	
PZ, CV	Intermediate at 1,000 RPM	860 - 1070	125 - 155	860 - 1070	125 - 155
PZ, CV	Lo at 1,000 RPM	Same as Intermediate		No T.V. pressure in Lo Range. Line Pressure is the same as Intermediate at minimum T.V.	

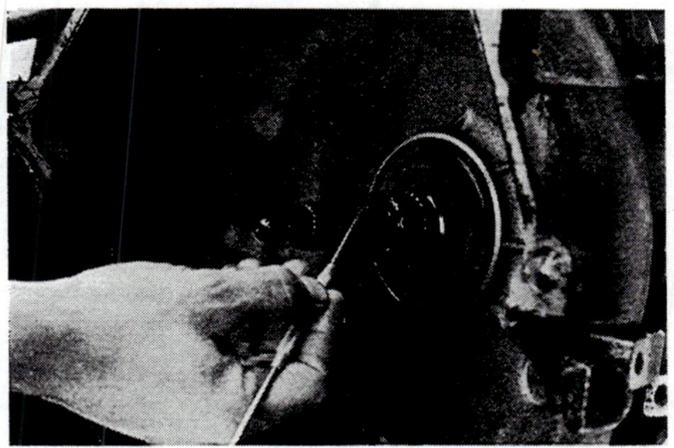

FIGURE 3T40–1 The converter clutch seal should be replaced.

FIGURE 3T40–2 Check contact surface on governor cover for wear.

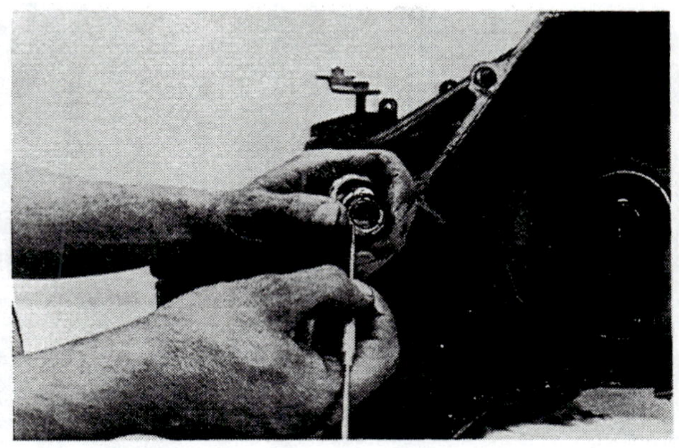

FIGURE 3T40–3 Inspect governor thrust washer for wear.

FIGURE 3T40–4 Inspect the oil pump drive shaft splines for damage.

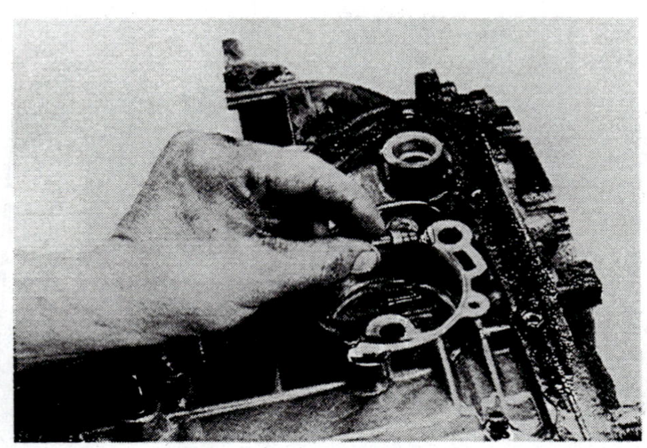

FIGURE 3T40–5 Be careful not to lose the direct clutch accumulator exhaust check valve.

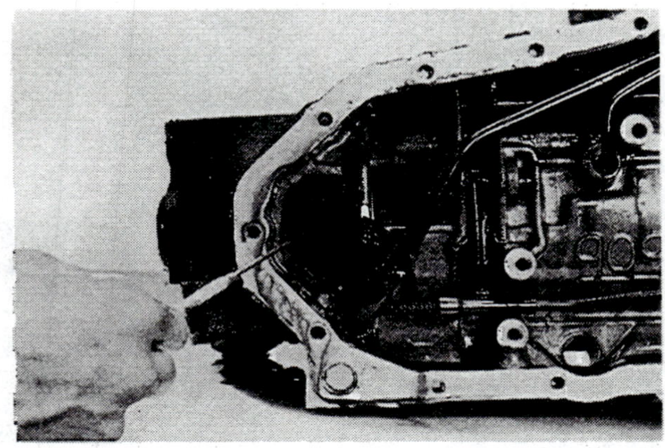

FIGURE 3T40–6 This plastic oil weir is used to control lube oil around the final drive.

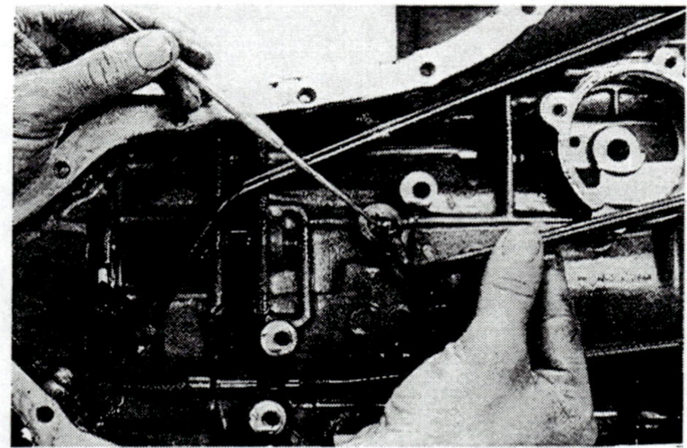

FIGURE 3T40–7 O-ring seals are used at the ends of the oil feed tubes.

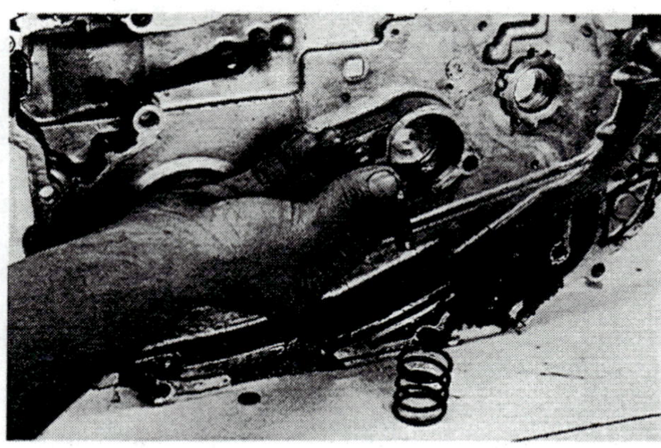

FIGURE 3T40–8 The accumulator seals and spring must be inspected.

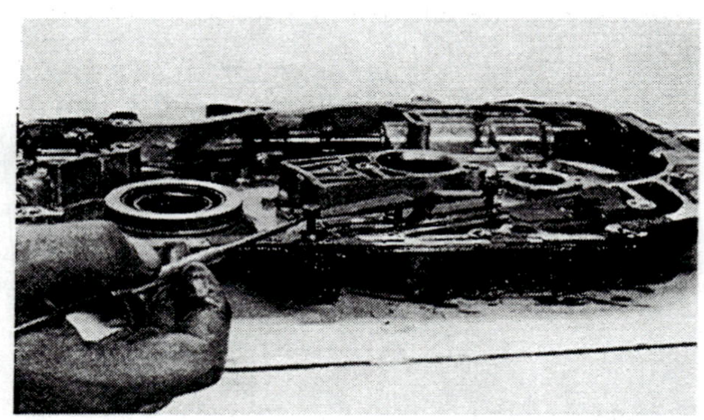

FIGURE 3T40–9 Thermostatic element that controls the fluid flow from the upper sump to the lower sump.

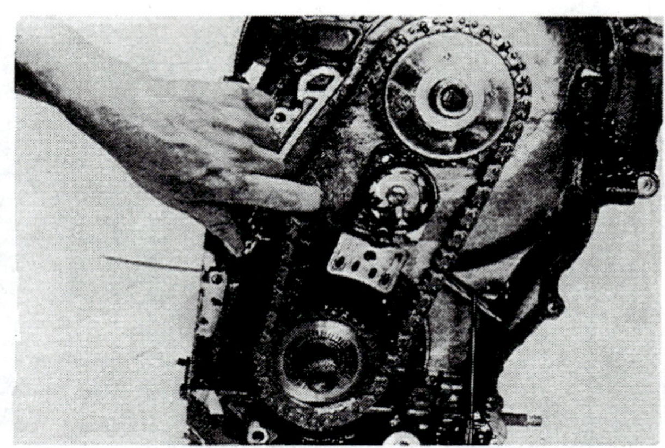

FIGURE 3T40–10 Drive chain wear should be checked by measuring the chain deflection.

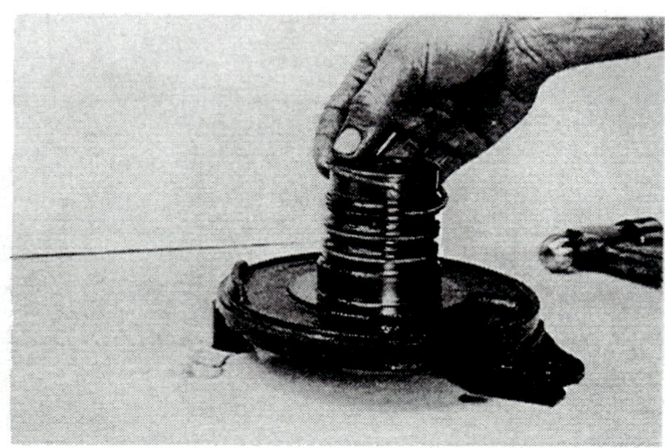

FIGURE 3T40–11 The Teflon sealing ring should always be replaced.

FIGURE 3T40–12 The band contact area on this clutch drum is badly burned.

12.6 HM 4T60/4T60E: FWD FOUR-SPEED TRANSAXLE

12.6.1 Basic Description

The HM 4T06/4T60-E is the most advanced transaxle produced by Hydra-Matic. The 4T60 is hydraulically controlled, while the 4T60-E is electronically controlled. Its compound planetary gear set is found only in this transaxle, so study its construction and operation closely. This transaxle is also more sensitive to operator input because the hydraulic version uses both a throttle valve cable and a vacuum modulator to control the transmission's throttle valve pressure. The 4T60-E uses the computer inputs from the vehicle speed sensor and the throttle position sensor to control shifting. A cutaway view of the HM 4T60 is shown in Figure 12–62.

1. *Torque Converter*
A typical three-element torque converter is used with a hydraulic converter clutch added to improve economy. Both the standard spring-dampened pressure plate and viscous clutch are used with this transaxle, depending on the vehicle application (Figures 12–63 and 12–64).

2. *Gear Train*
The converter turbine shaft torque is transferred through the drive link to the input shaft to the planetary input members. The input members are the front sun gear and the front pinion carrier/rear ring gear combo. The front pinion carrier and rear ring gear are built together in one piece, and the front ring gear and rear pinion carrier are also a single unit. The combination of these parts together is one of the features that makes this transaxle unique.

The reaction members are the front carrier/rear ring combo and the rear sun gear. The output members are the front ring/rear carrier combo (Figure 12–65).

3. *Coupling Devices*
The coupling devices are the second clutch, third clutch, third roller clutch, input sprag, and input clutch (Figure 12–66).

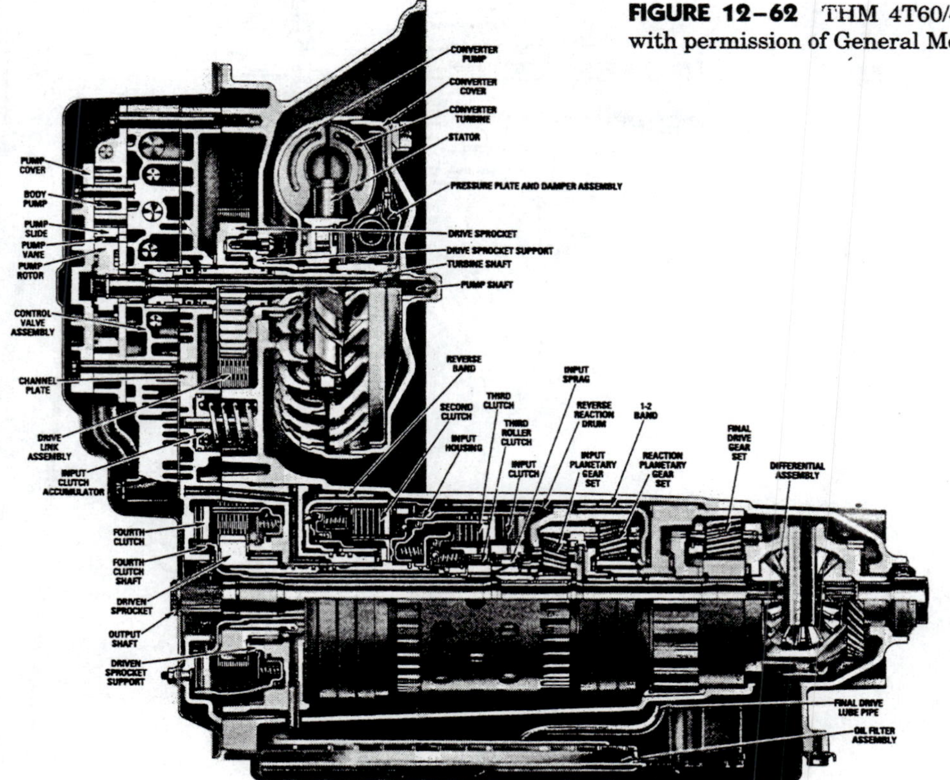

FIGURE 12–62 THM 4T60/4T60E cutaway view. (Reprinted with permission of General Motors Corporation)

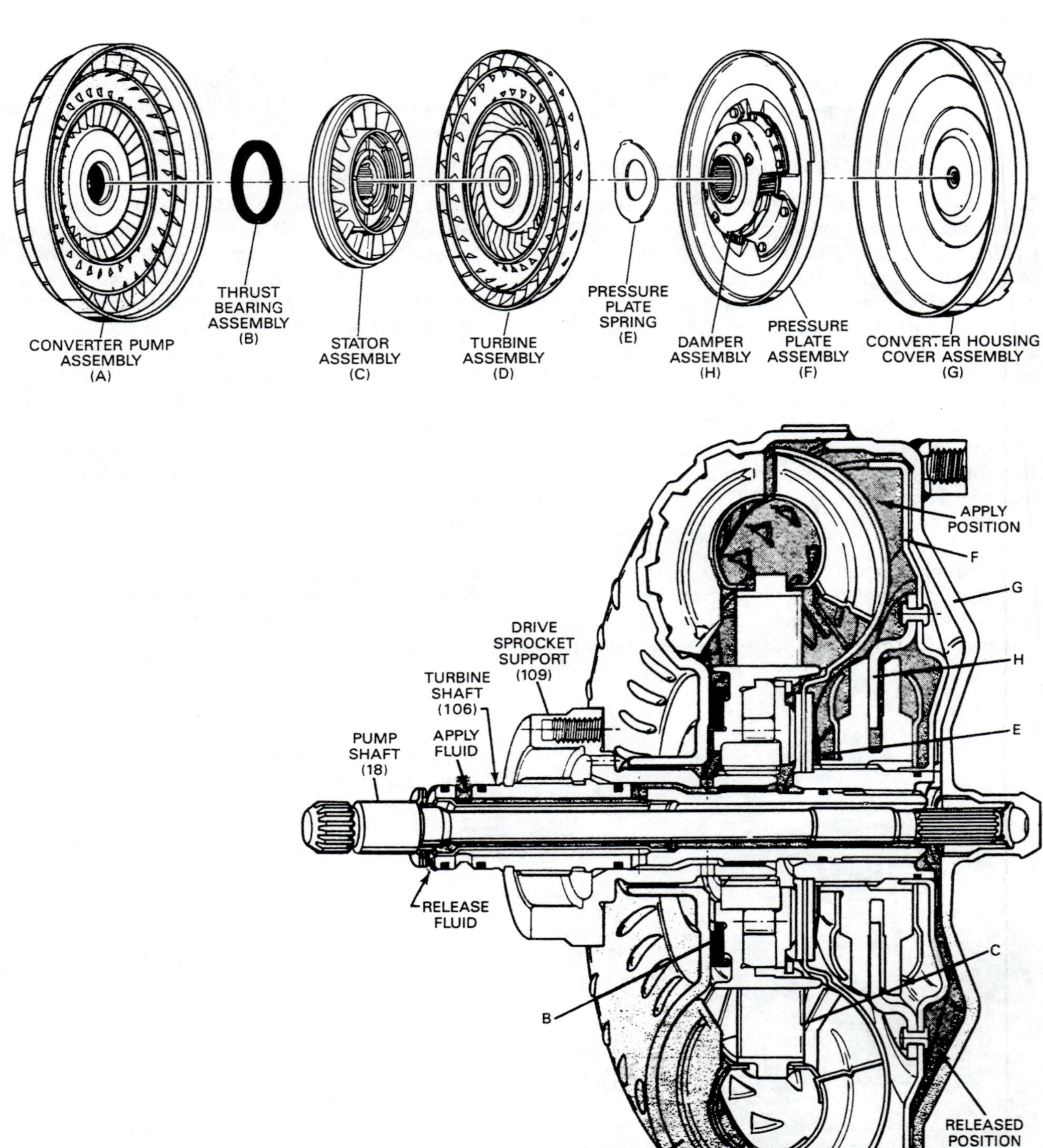

FIGURE 12–63 THM 4T60/4T60E torque converter. (Reprinted with permission of General Motors Corporation)

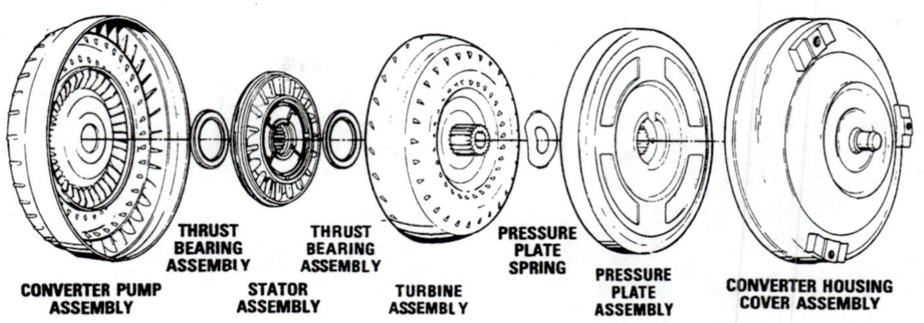

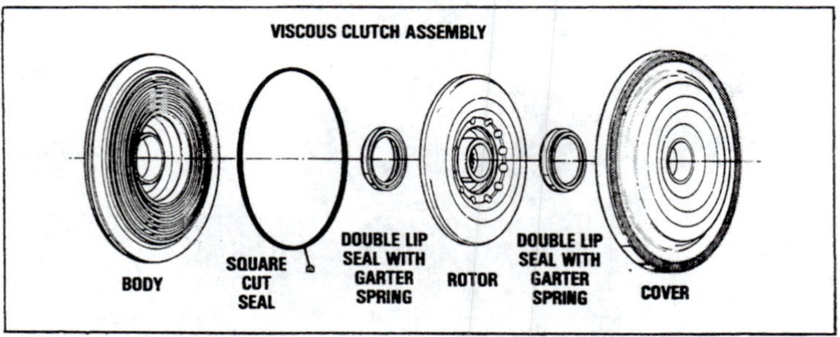

FIGURE 12–64 THM 4T60/4T60E viscous converter clutch. (Reprinted with permission of General Motors Corporation)

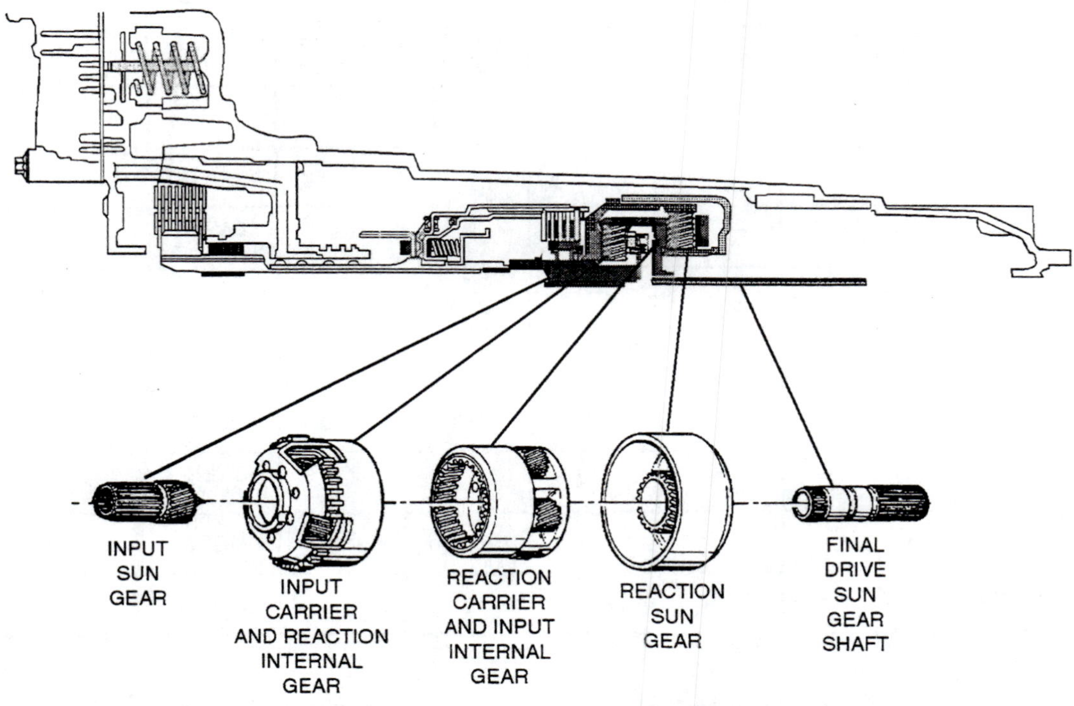

FIGURE 12–65 THM 4T60/4T60E planetary gear set. (Reprinted with permission of General Motors Corporation)

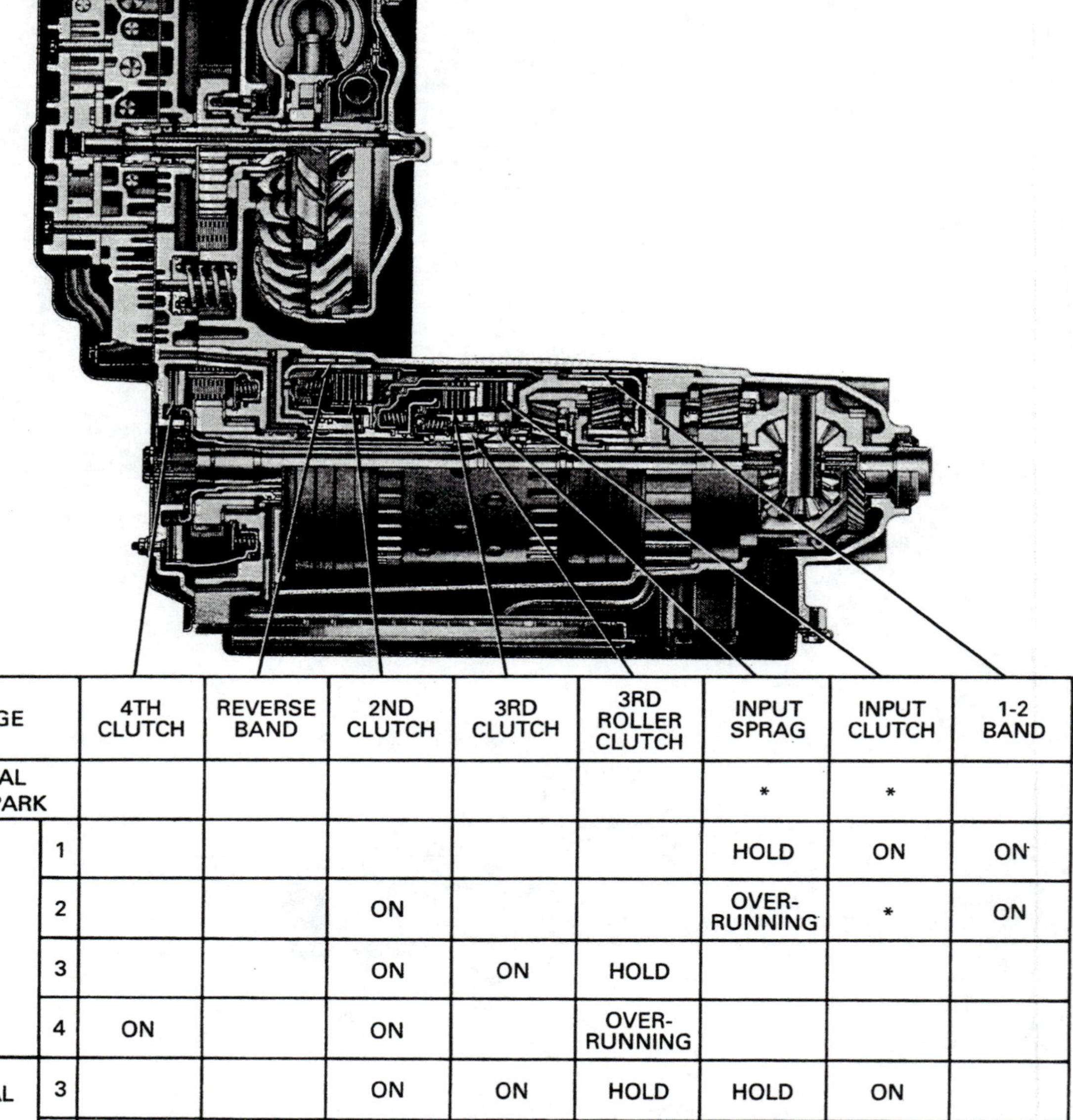

RANGE		4TH CLUTCH	REVERSE BAND	2ND CLUTCH	3RD CLUTCH	3RD ROLLER CLUTCH	INPUT SPRAG	INPUT CLUTCH	1-2 BAND
NEUTRAL PARK							*	*	
DRIVE	1						HOLD	ON	ON
	2			ON			OVER-RUNNING	*	ON
	3			ON	ON	HOLD			
	4	ON		ON		OVER-RUNNING			
MANUAL	3			ON	ON	HOLD	HOLD	ON	
	2			ON			OVER-RUNNING	*	ON
	1				ON	HOLD	HOLD	ON	ON
REVERSE			ON				HOLD	ON	

*APPLIED BUT NOT EFFECTIVE

FIGURE 12–66 THM 4T60/4T60E coupling and holding devices. (Reprinted with permission of General Motors Corporation)

4. Holding Device

The holding devices used in this transaxle are the fourth clutch, reverse band, and the 1–2 band (Figure 12–66).

5. Pump

The HM 4T60 uses a variable-capacity vane pump drive by the oil pump drive shaft, which splines to the converter housing. The pump is shown at maximum and minimum output in Figure 12–67.

6. Shift Control

The 4T60 uses a fully hydraulic valve body, including many specialized valves to improve the quality of shift performance. The 4T60-E uses solenoids to control valve movement in the valve body.

7. Governor

The HM 4T60 uses a drop-in governor, as shown in Figure 12–68. This governor design uses check balls and centrifugal weights to produce a variable restriction. The vehicle speed sensor information is used by the 4T60-E instead of a governor.

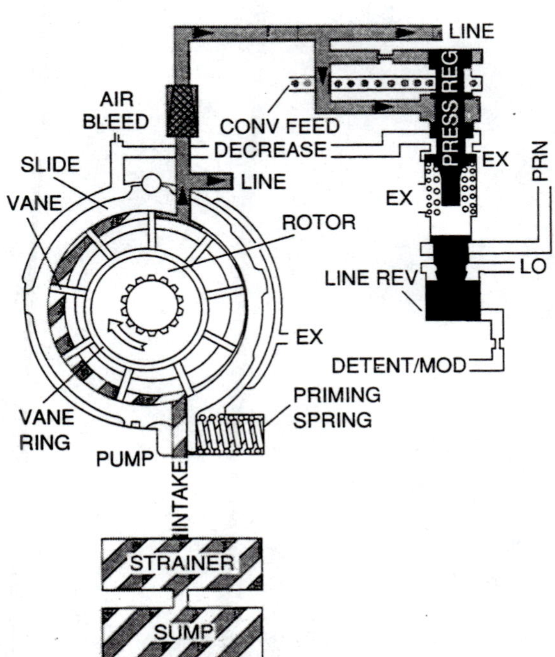

FIGURE 12–67 THM 4T60/4T60E oil pump. (Reprinted with permission of General Motors Corporation)

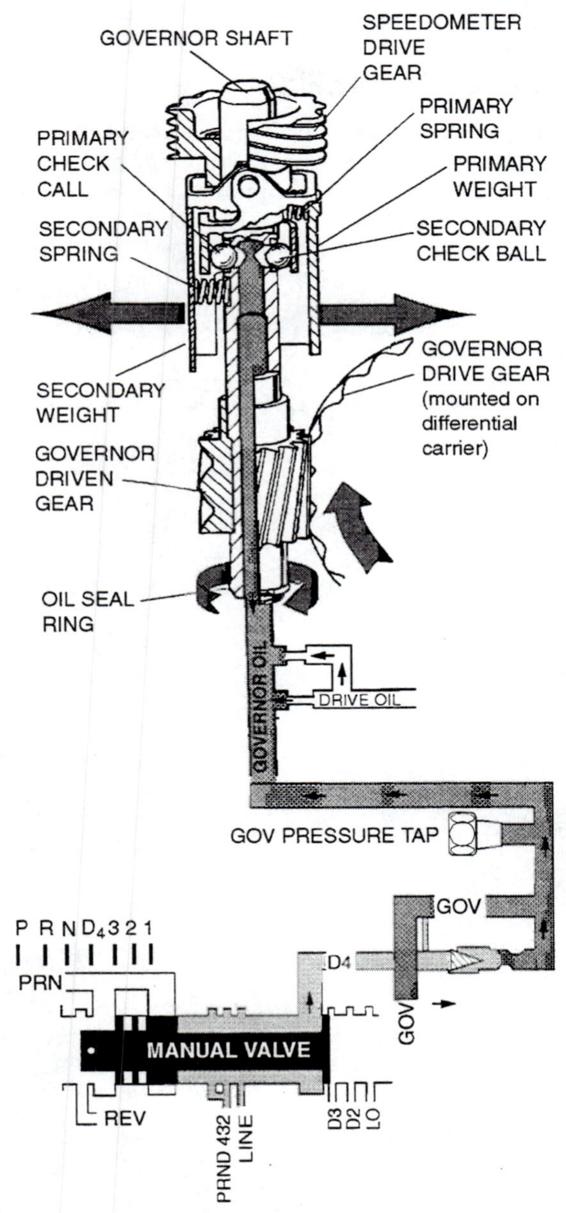

FIGURE 12–68 THM 4T60/4T60E governor. (Reprinted with permission of General Motors Corporation)

8. Throttle Valve
The throttle valve function is shared by two devices in the HM 4T60. The shift timing is controlled by the throttle valve pressure, which is controlled through the TV cable from the accelerator linkage (Figure 12–69). The shift feed is controlled by a vacuum modulator which changes the mainline pressure to provide the proper rate of clutch application to produce the smoothest shift possible (Figure 12–70). The 4T60-E uses the throttle position sensor to establish the engine load so that the ECM can provide the proper line pressure.

12.6.2 Power Flow

The power flow is described by stating the coupling and holding device action (applied, or holding) on the members of the planetary gear set (sun gear, pinion carrier, and ring gear) in each gear range of the transmission.

1. Neutral (N)
In neutral the only coupling devices working are the input clutch and input sprag, so the front sun gear is being driven.

2. First Gear (D1)
In drive first the input clutch and sprag are applied, which drives the front sun gear as input. The 1–2 band is applied, which drives the front sun gear as input. The 1–2 band is applied, which holds the rear sun gear, causing a 2.92:1 gear reduction (Figure 12–71). In manual low gear the third clutch and third roller clutch are also applied.

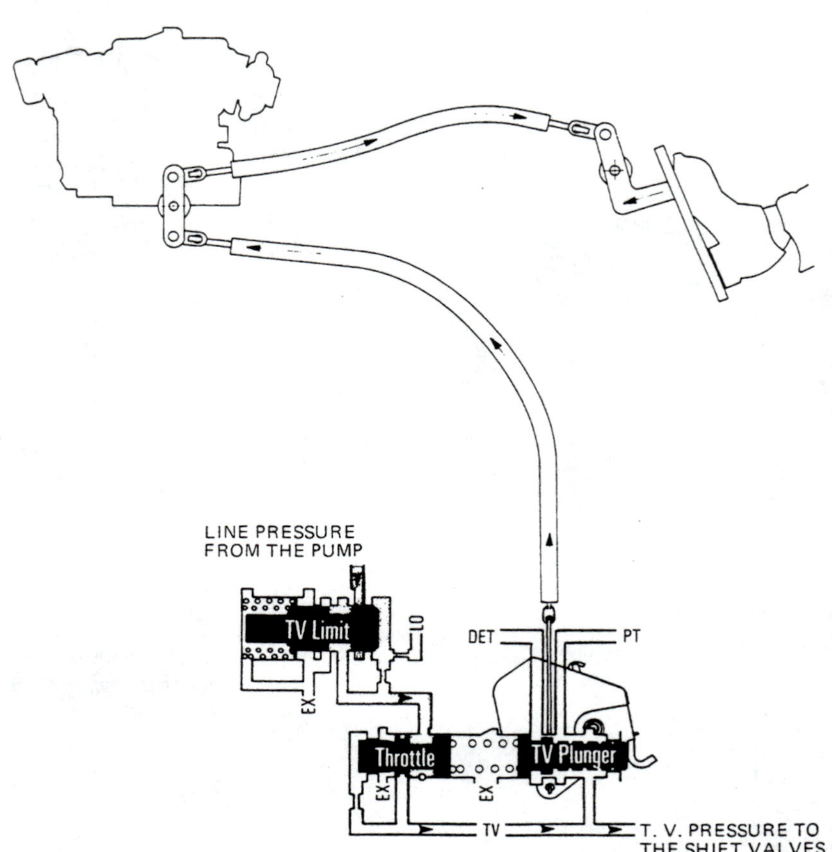

FIGURE 12–69 THM 4T60/4T60E throttle valve cable. (Reprinted with permission of General Motors Corporation)

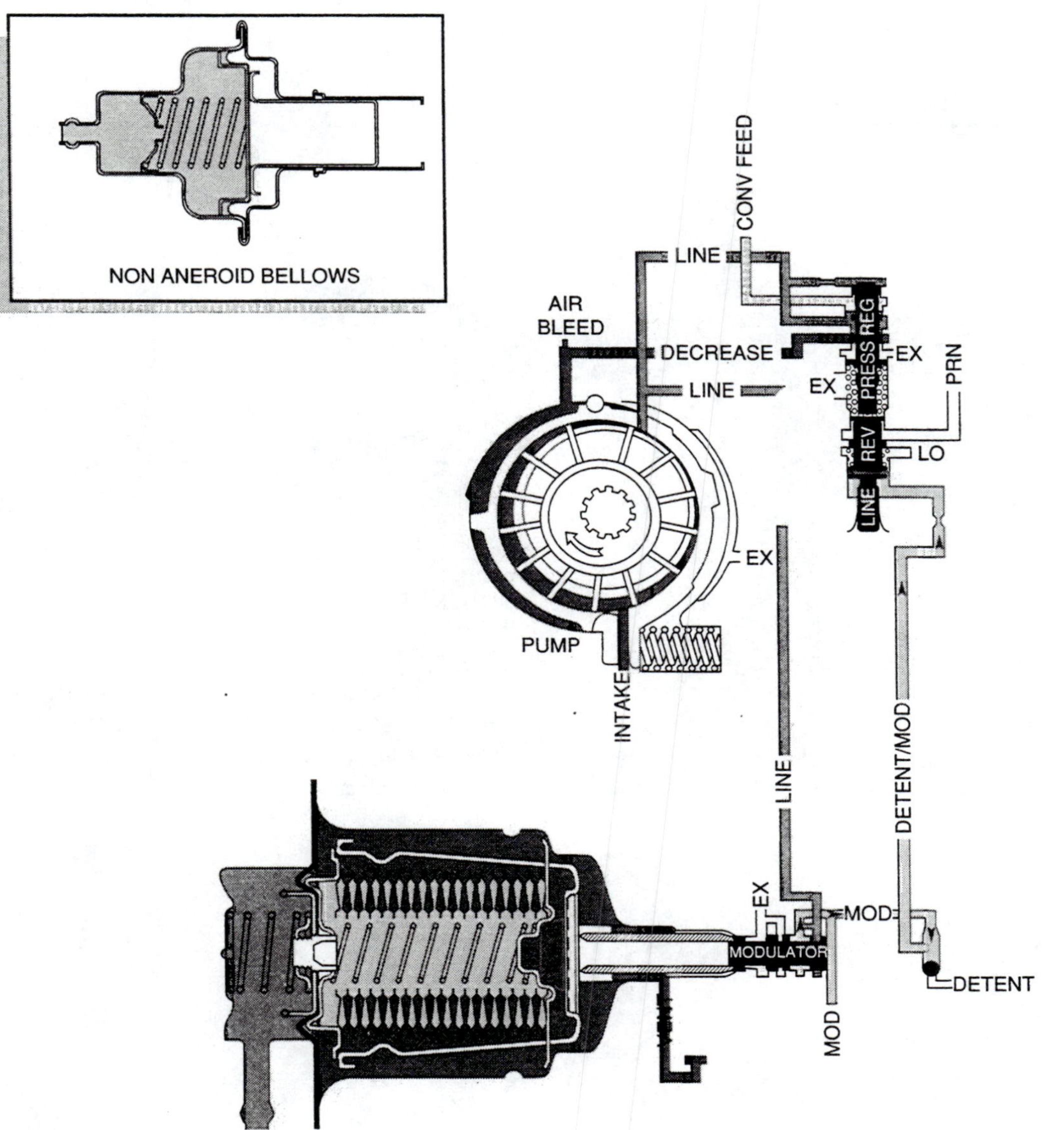

FIGURE 12–70 THM 4T60/4T60E vacuum modulator. (Reprinted with permission of General Motors Corporation)

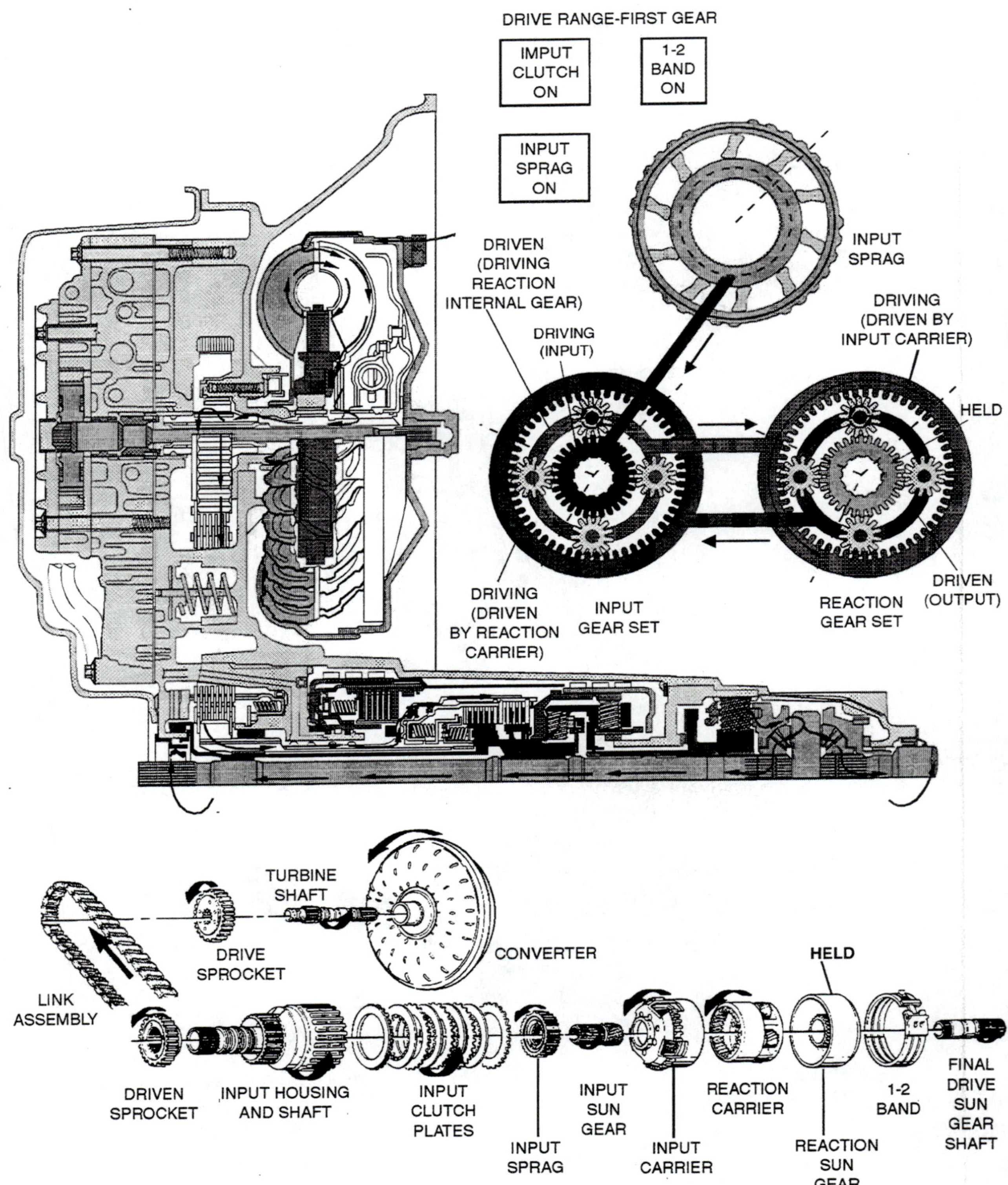

FIGURE 12–71 THM 4T60/4T60E in first gear. (Reprinted with permission of General Motors Corporation)

3. *Second Gear (D2)*

In second gear the input clutch and sprag are still applied, but not carrying a load, the sprag is overrunning. The second clutch is applied, which drives the front carrier/rear ring as input. The 1–2 band is still holding the rear sun gear as the reaction member (Figure 12–72). The second-gear ratio is 1.57:1. In manual second gear the same devices are applied.

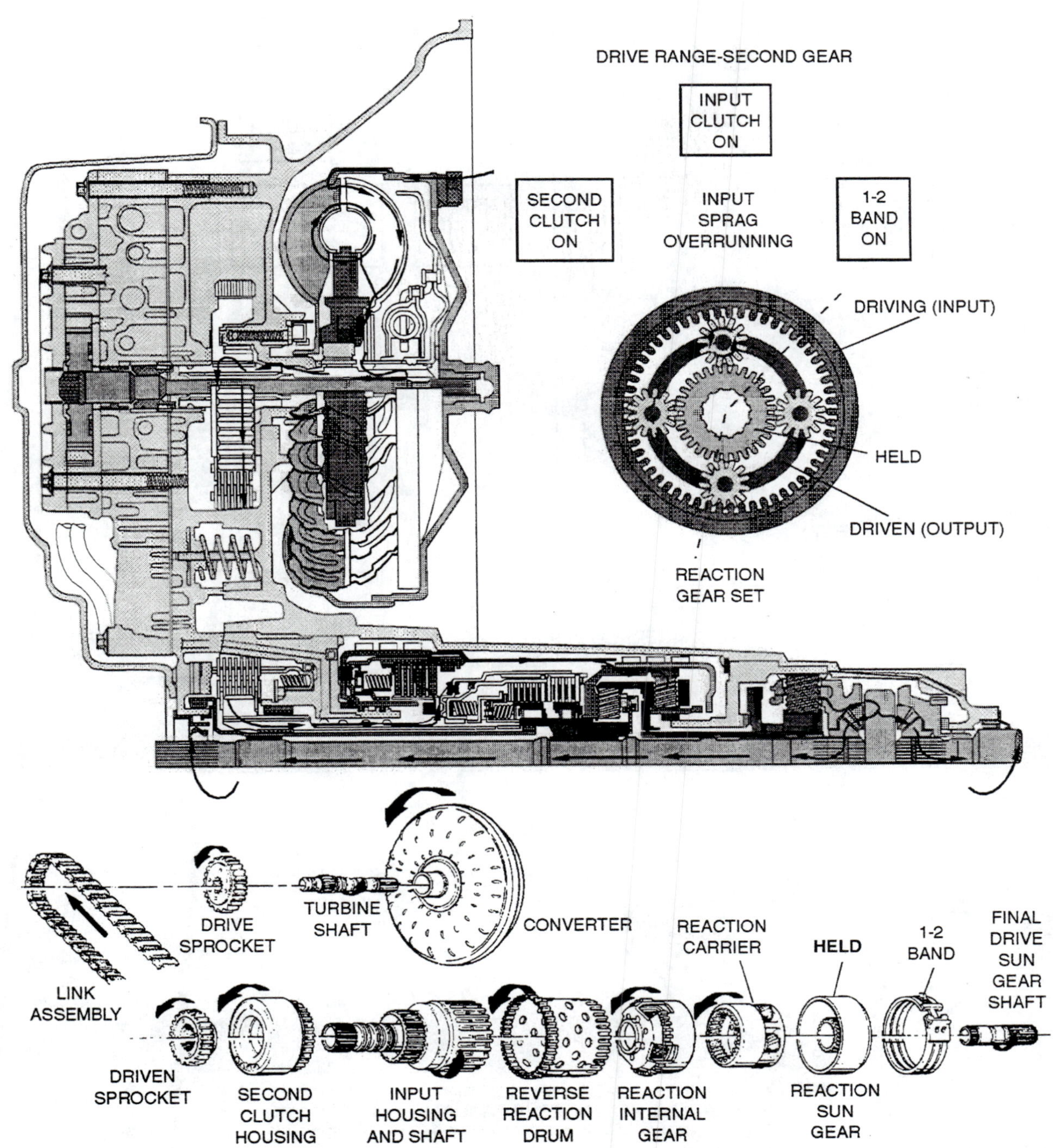

FIGURE 12–72 THM 4T60/4T60E in second gear. (Reprinted with permission of General Motors Corporation)

4. Third Gear (D3)

In third gear the second clutch remains applied and the third clutch and third roller clutch are applied, which causes a direct drive condition (Figure 12–73). For manual third gear the input sprag and clutch are also applied.

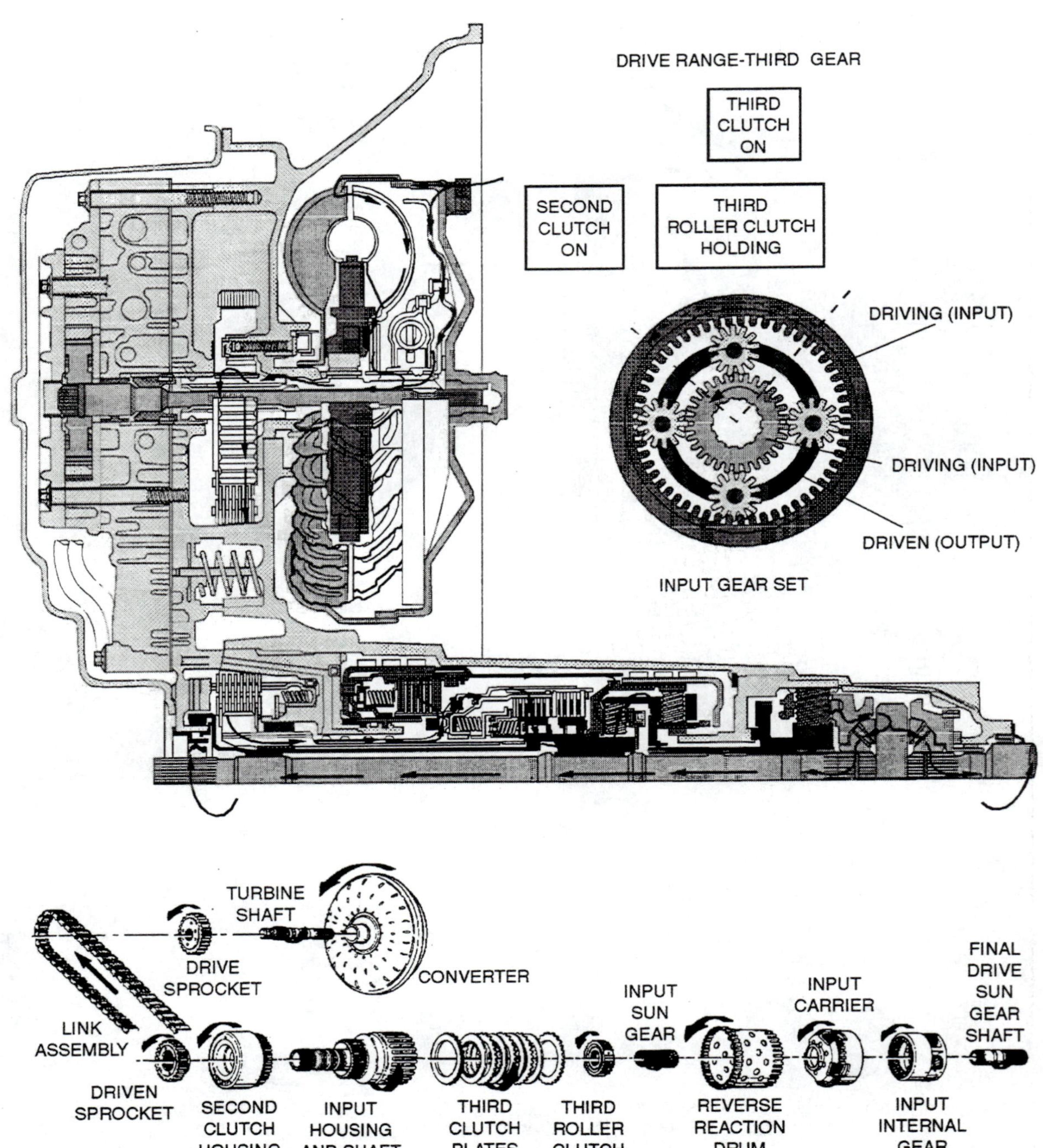

FIGURE 12–73 THM 4T60/4T60E in third gear. (Reprinted with permission of General Motors Corporation)

5. Fourth Gear (D4)

In fourth gear the second clutch is applied, which drives the front carrier/rear ring as input. The fourth clutch is applied, which holds the front sun gear as the reaction member and an overdrive ratio of 0.70:1 is created (Figure 12–74).

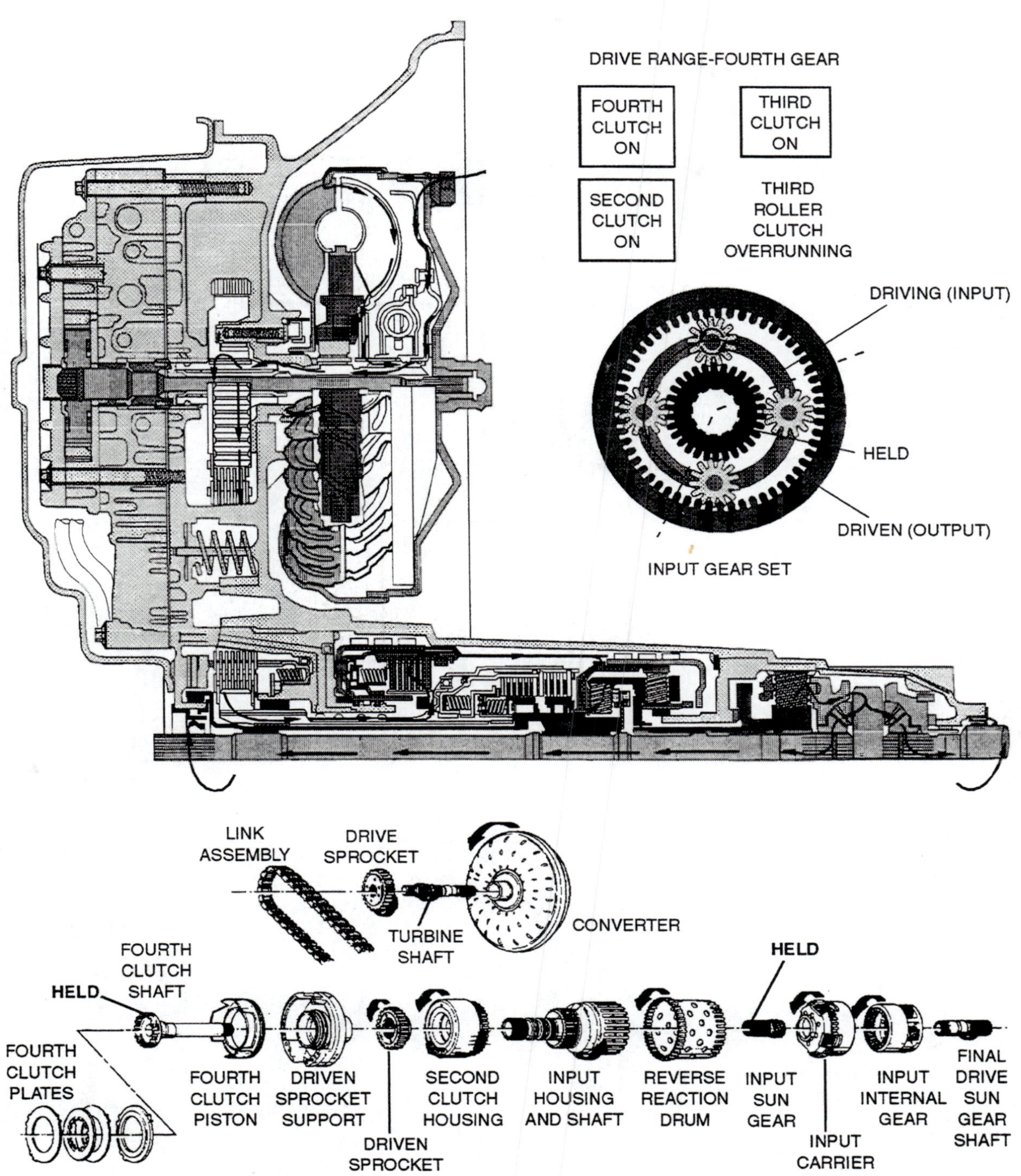

FIGURE 12–74 THM 4T60/4T60E in fourth gear. (Reprinted with permission of General Motors Corporation)

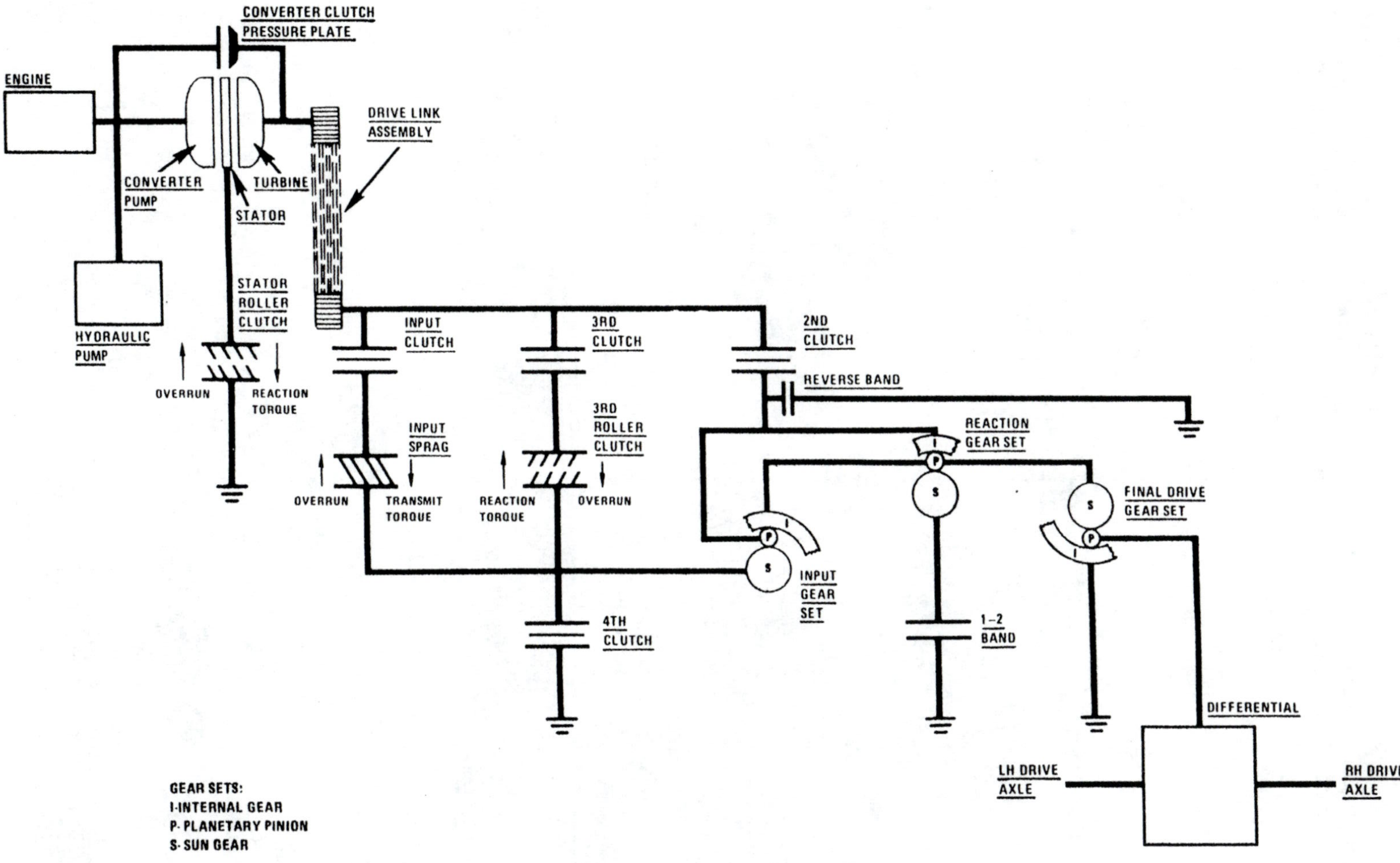

FIGURE 12–75 THM 4T60/4T60E schematic. (Reprinted with permission of General Motors Corporation)

6. *Reverse Gear (R)*
For reverse gear the input clutch and sprag drive the front sun gear as input. The reverse band holds the front carrier/rear ring as the reaction member and creates a 2.38:1 gear ratio.

The factory service manual uses a power flow schematic (Figure 12–75) to aid the technician in understanding this new approach to gear trains. Many of the newer transmissions/transaxles use schematics to help explain the gear train and hydraulic system functions.

12.6.3 Clutch and Band Charts

The first chart, the author's design, is shown in Figure 12–76. The second chart, the manufacturer's design, is shown in Figure 12–77.

12.6.4 Identification

In Figure 12–78 you see the pan gasket shape and number of bolt holes for the HM 4T60/4T60E transaxle. The location of the factory identification tag and its code are shown in Figure 12–79.

12.6.5 Components

In this section exploded drawings of the HM 4T60/4T60E transaxle subassemblies are shown along with lists of the part names. The drawings to study are as follows:

Case with drive link, Figure 12–80
Internal components, Figure 12–81
Internal linkage, Figure 12–82
Valve body, Figure 12–83
Valve body (4T60E), Figure 12–84
Washer and bushing location, Figure 12–85

12.6.6 Pressure Test

The location of the test points of the HM 4T60/4T60E transaxle are shown in Figure 12–86. A pressure chart listing the pressure specifications of this transaxle is shown in Figure 12–87.

4T60/4T60E	2ND CLUTCH	3RD CLUTCH	INPUT CLUTCH	4TH CLUTCH	REVERSE BAND	1-2 BAND	3RD ROLLER	INPUT SPRAG	PARK PAWL	CONVERTER CLUTCH
P			x					x	X	
N			x					x		
D1			X			X		X		
D2	X		x			X				
D3	X	X					X			
D4	X	x		X						
1		X	X			X	X	X		
2	X		x			X				
3	X	X	X				X	X		
R			X		X			X		

X = APPLIED
x (dotted X) = APPLIED, NOT CARRYING LOAD

FIGURE 12–76 THM 4T60/4T60E clutch and band chart, standardized version.

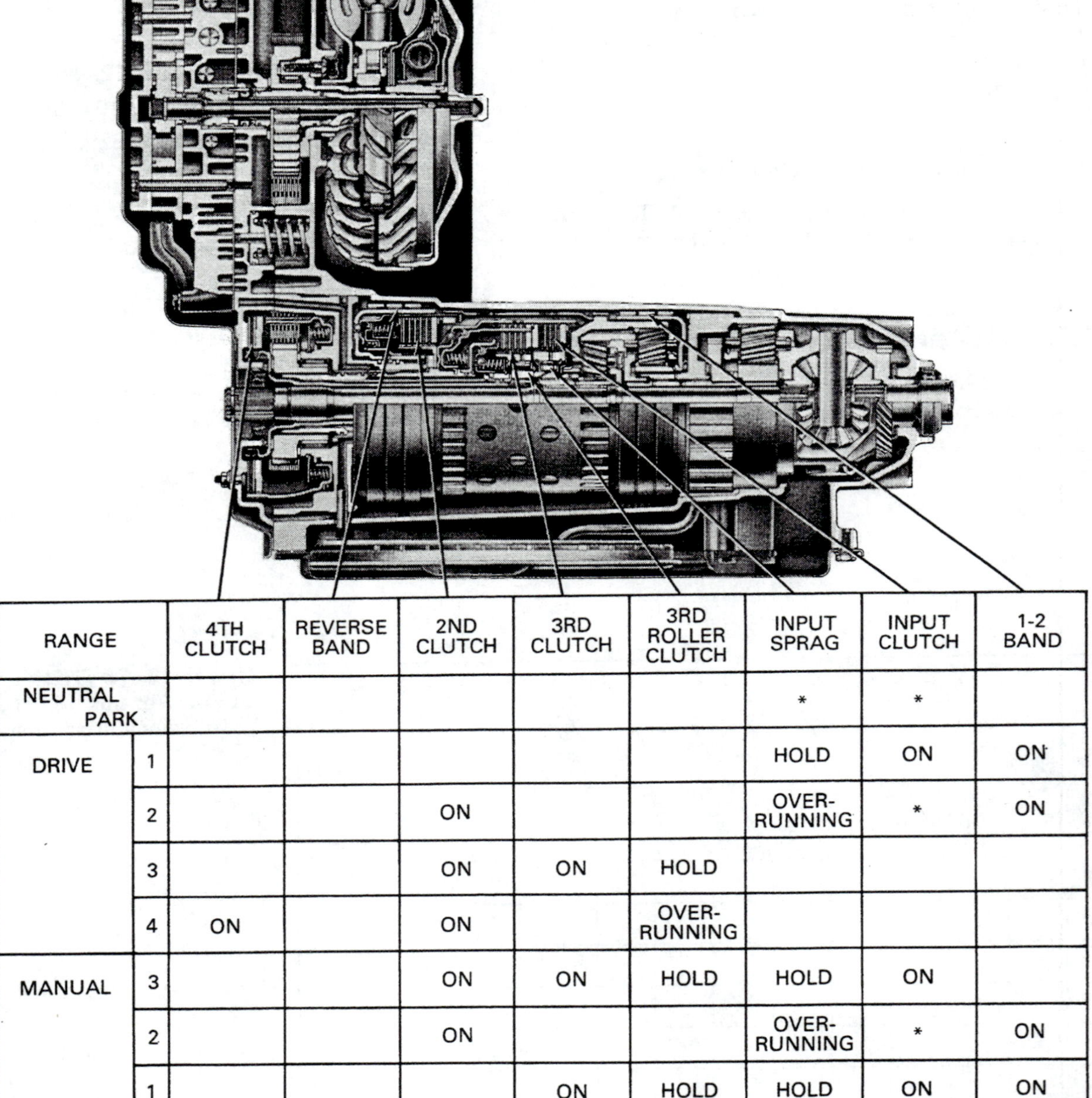

RANGE		4TH CLUTCH	REVERSE BAND	2ND CLUTCH	3RD CLUTCH	3RD ROLLER CLUTCH	INPUT SPRAG	INPUT CLUTCH	1-2 BAND
NEUTRAL PARK							*	*	
DRIVE	1						HOLD	ON	ON
	2			ON			OVER-RUNNING	*	ON
	3			ON	ON	HOLD			
	4	ON		ON		OVER-RUNNING			
MANUAL	3			ON	ON	HOLD	HOLD	ON	
	2			ON			OVER-RUNNING	*	ON
	1				ON	HOLD	HOLD	ON	ON
REVERSE			ON				HOLD	ON	

*APPLIED BUT NOT EFFECTIVE

FIGURE 12–77 THM 4T60/4T60E clutch and band chart, factory version. (Reprinted with permission of General Motors Corporation)

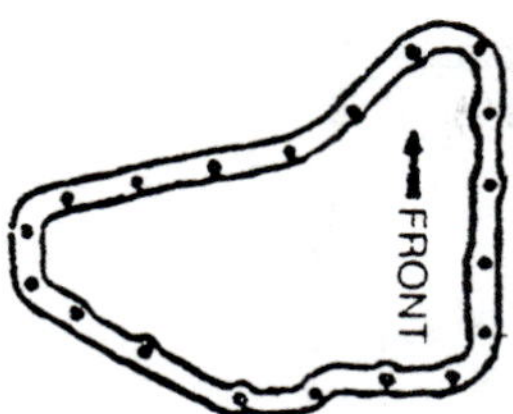

FIGURE 12–78 THM 4T60/4T60E pan gasket identification.

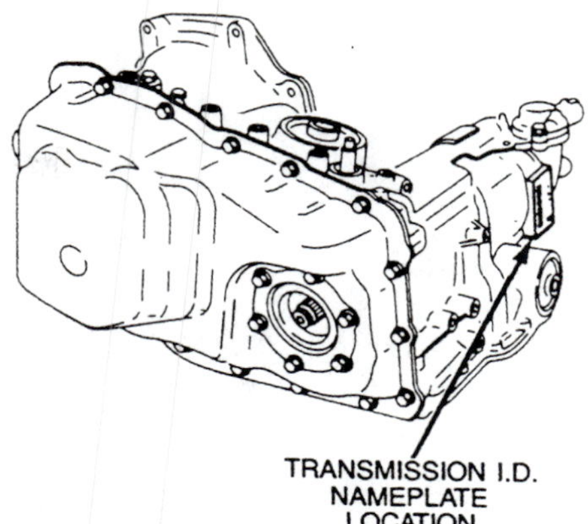

FIGURE 12–79 THM 4T60/4T60E identification tag location. (Reprinted with permission of General Motors Corporation)

ILL. NO.	DESCRIPTION
501	PLATE ASSEMBLY, 4TH CLUTCH
502	PLATE, 4TH CLUTCH APPLY
503	BEARING ASSEMBLY, 4TH CLUTCH HUB/ CHANNEL PLATE
504	BEARING ASSEMBLY, 4TH CLUTCH SHAFT
505	HUB & SHAFT ASSEMBLY, 4TH CLUTCH
506	WASHER, THRUST (4TH CLUTCH HUB/ DRIVEN SPROCKET)
507	RING, OIL SEAL (SHAFT/SLEEVE) (2)
508	WASHER, THRUST (DRIVE SPROCKET/ CHANNEL PLATE)
509	RING, SNAP (TURBINE SHAFT/DRIVE SPROCKET)
510	LINK ASSEMBLY, DRIVE
511	SPROCKET, DRIVE
512	WASHER, THRUST (DRIVE SPROCKET/ SPROCKET SUPPORT)
513	SHAFT, TURBINE
514	RING, OIL SEAL (TURBINE SHAFT/SUPPORT)
515	SEAL, "O" RING (TURBINE SHAFT/ TURBINE HUB)
516	BEARING ASSEMBLY, DRAWN CUP
517	SUPPORT, DRIVE SPROCKET
518	BUSHING, DRIVE SPROCKET SUPPORT
519	SPROCKET, DRIVEN
520	WASHER, THRUST (DRIVEN SPROCKET/ SPROCKET SUPPORT)
521	RING, SNAP (4TH CLUTCH RET. SPRING)
522	SPRING ASM., 4TH CLUTCH PISTON RETURN
523	PISTON, 4TH CLUTCH
524	SEALS, 4TH CLUTCH PISTON
525	CASE, TRANSMISSION
526	CONNECTOR, COOLER (1)
527	PIN, DOWEL
528	VENT ASSEMBLY
529	PLUG, PIPE (LINE PRESSURE)
532	PIN, ANCHOR (1-2 BAND) (2)
533	PIN, ANCHOR (REVERSE BAND) (2)
534	PLUG, CASE SERVO (ORIFICE)
535	PLUG, CUP (PARK LOCK-OUT)

ILL. NO.	DESCRIPTION
536	SCREW, NAMEPLATE
537	NAMEPLATE
538	PLUG, PIPE (GOVERNOR PRESSURE)
539	BUSHING, CASE
540	SEAL ASSEMBLY, AXLE OIL
541	HELIX SEAL ASSEMBLY, (CONVERTER OIL)
542	SCREW, BUTTON HEAD (4) (CASE/ DRUM SPROCKET)
543	RING, SERVO COVER RETAINING
544	COVER, SERVO (REVERSE)
545	SEAL, "O" RING (COVER TO CASE)
546	RING, SNAP (BAND APPLY PIN)
547	RING, OIL SEAL PISTON
548	PISTON, REVERSE SERVO
549	SPRING, REVERSE SERVO CUSHION
550	RETAINER, SERVO CUSHION SPRING
551	PIN, REVERSE APPLY
552	SPRING, SERVO RETURN
553	RING, SERVO COVER RETAINING
554	COVER, SERVO (1-2)
555	SEAL, "O" RING (COVER TO CASE)
556	RING, SNAP (BAND APPLY PIN)
557	RING, OIL SEAL PISTON
558	PISTON, 1-2 SERVO
559	SPRING, 1-2 SERVO CUSHION
560	RETAINER, SERVO CUSHION SPRING
561	PIN, 1-2 BAND APPLY
562	SPRING, SERVO RETURN
563	SPRING, REVERSE SERVO CURVED
564	RING, RETAINING (OUTPUT SHAFT)
565	SHAFT, OUTPUT
566	BEARING, INPUT SUN GEAR/OUTPUT SHAFT
567	RING, SNAP (OUTPUT SHAFT/DIFFERENTIAL)
568	RETAINER, SERVO SPRING
569	CONNECTOR, COOLER
570	BALL, CONNECTOR COOLER
571	SPRING, CONNECTOR COOLER
572	CONNECTOR, INVERTED FLARED

LEGEND
490130440-T4

FIGURE 12–80 THM 4T60/4T60E case and drive link parts list (see p. 408). (Reprinted with permission of General Motors Corporation)

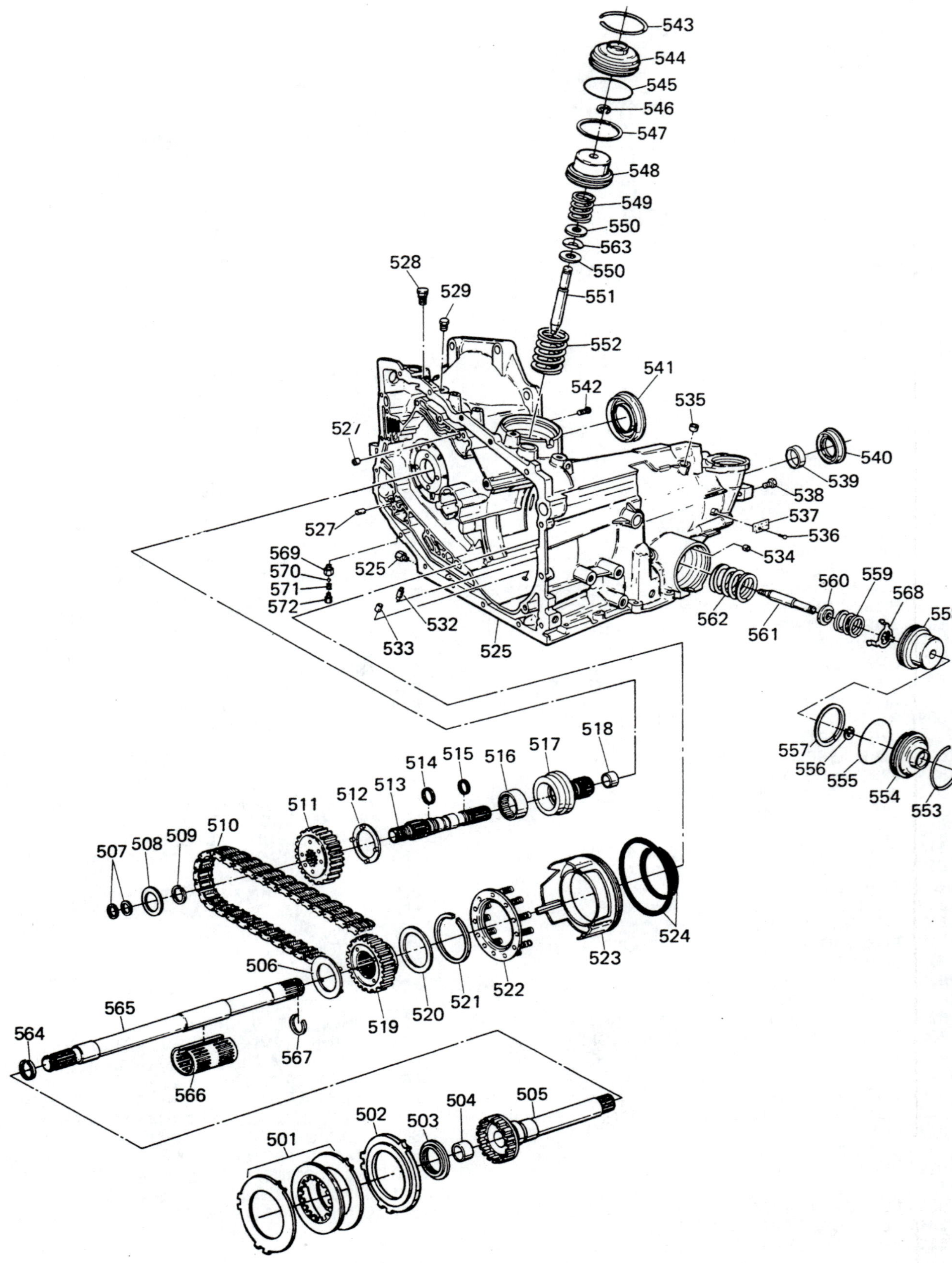

FIGURE 12–80 THM 4T60/4T60E case and drive link. (Reprinted with permission of General Motors Corporation)

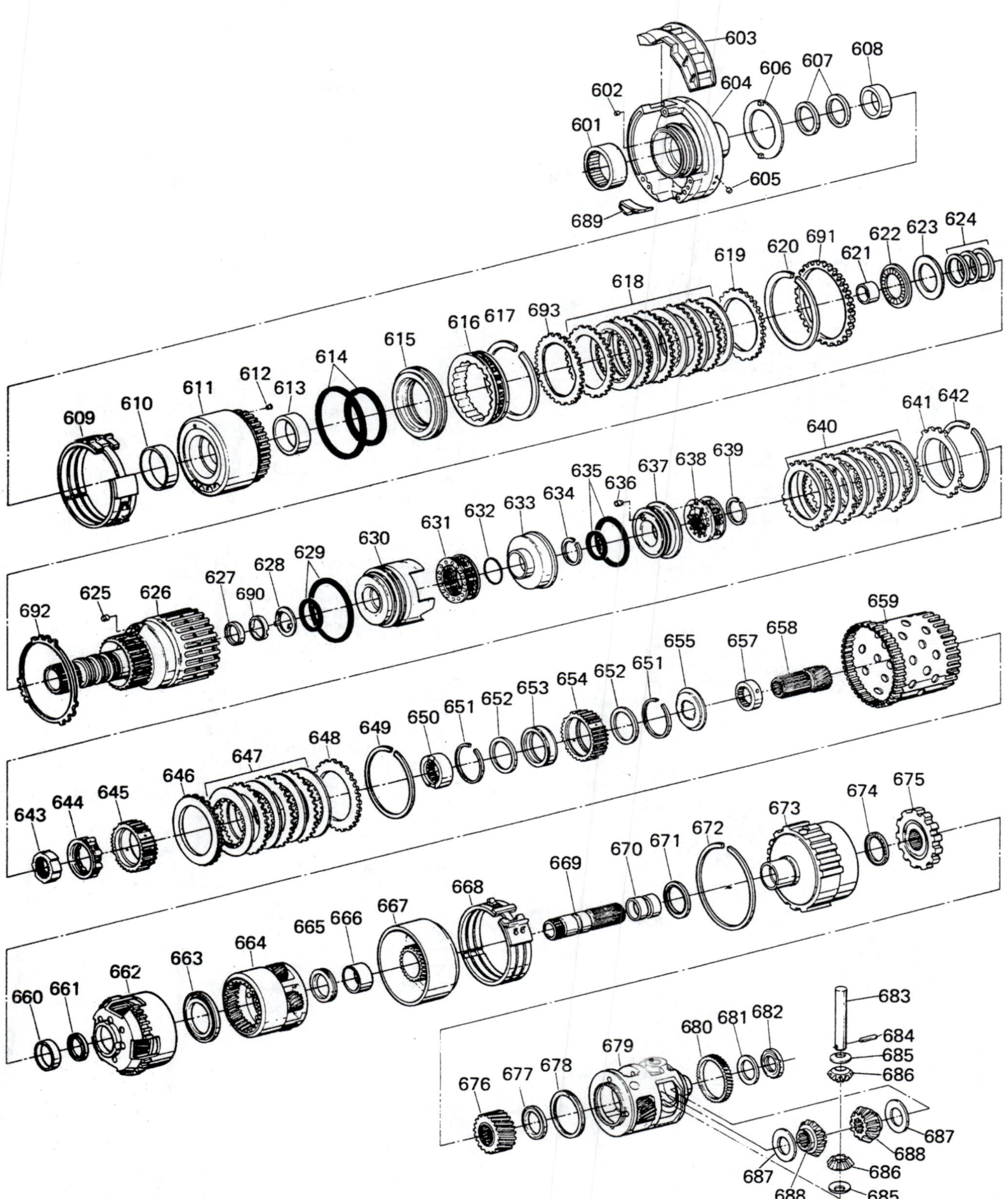

FIGURE 12–81 THM 4T60/4T60E internal parts. (Reprinted with permission of General Motors Corporation)

ILL. NO.	DESCRIPTION
601	BEARING ASSEMBLY, DRAWN CUP
602	PLUG, CUP (ORIFICED)
603	SCOOP, CHAIN SCAVENGING
604	SUPPORT, DRIVEN SPROCKET
605	PLUG, CUP (4)
606	WASHER, THRUST (SUPPORT/2ND CLUTCH)
607	SEAL, "O" RING (SUPPORT/2ND CLUTCH)
608	BUSHING, DRIVEN SPROCKET SUPPORT
609	BAND, REVERSE
610	BUSHING, 2ND CLUTCH FRONT
611	HOUSING, 2ND CLUTCH
612	RETAINER & BALL ASSEMBLY
613	BUSHING, 2ND CLUTCH REAR
614	SEALS, 2ND CLUTCH PISTON
615	PISTON, 2ND CLUTCH
616	APPLY RING & SPRING RETURN
617	RING, SNAP (2ND CLUTCH HUB)
618	PLATE ASSEMBLY, 2ND CLUTCH
619	PLATE, 2ND CLUTCH BACKING
620	RING, SNAP (2ND CLUTCH BACKING)
621	BUSHING, INPUT SHAFT
622	BEARING, THRUST (SUPPORT/SELECTIVE THRUST WASHER)
623	WASHER, THRUST (SELECTIVE)
624	RING, OIL SEAL (INPUT SHAFT)
625	RETAINER & BALL ASSEMBLY
626	HOUSING & SHAFT ASSEMBLY, INPUT
627	SEAL, INPUT SHAFT/4TH CLUTCH SHAFT
628	WASHER, THRUST (INPUT SHAFT/SUN)
629	SEALS, INPUT CLUTCH PISTON
630	PISTON, INPUT CLUTCH
631	SPRING & RETAINER ASSEMBLY, INPUT
632	SEAL, "O" RING (SHAFT/3RD CL. HOUSING)
633	HOUSING, 3RD CLUTCH PISTON
634	RING, SNAP (SHAFT/3RD CLUTCH HOUSING)
635	SEALS, 3RD CLUTCH PISTON
636	RETAINER & BALL ASSEMBLY
637	PISTON, 3RD CLUTCH
638	SPRING RETAINER & GUIDE ASM., 3RD CL.
639	RING, SNAP (SHAFT/3RD CL. SPRING RET.)
640	PLATE ASSEMBLY, 3RD CLUTCH
641	PLATE, 3RD CLUTCH BACKING
642	RING, SNAP (3RD CLUTCH BACKING PLATE)
643	CAM, 3RD ROLLER CLUTCH
644	ROLLER ASSEMBLY, 3RD CLUTCH
645	RACE, 3RD ROLLER CLUTCH
646	PLATE, INPUT CLUTCH APPLY
647	PLATE ASSEMBLY, INPUT CLUTCH
648	PLATE, INPUT CLUTCH BACKING
649	RING, SNAP (INPUT CLUTCH BACKING PLATE)

ILL. NO.	DESCRIPTION
650	RACE, INPUT SPRAG INNER
651	RING, SNAP (SPRAG)
652	WEAR PLATE, INPUT SPRAG
653	SPRAG ASSEMBLY, INPUT CLUTCH
654	RACE, INPUT SPRAG OUTER
655	RETAINER, INPUT SPRAG
657	SPACER, INPUT SUN GEAR
658	GEAR, INPUT SUN
659	DRUM, REVERSE REACTION
660	BUSHING, REACTION INTERNAL GEAR
661	BEARING ASSEMBLY, (INPUT SUN/CARRIER)
662	CARRIER ASSEMBLY, INPUT
663	BEARING ASM., (INPUT/REACTION CARRIER)
664	CARRIER ASSEMBLY, REACTION
665	BEARING ASSEMBLY, (REACTION CARRIER/ SUN GEAR)
666	BUSHING, REACTION SUN
667	GEAR & DRUM ASM., REACTION SUN
668	BAND, 1-2
669	SHAFT, FINAL DRIVE SUN GEAR
670	BUSHING, FINAL DRIVE INTERNAL
671	BEARING ASSEMBLY, REACTION SUN GEAR/ INTERNAL GEAR
672	RING, SNAP (INTERNAL GEAR/CASE)
673	GEAR, FINAL DRIVE INTERNAL
674	BEARING ASM., (INT. GEAR/PARK GEAR)
675	GEAR, PARKING
676	GEAR, FINAL DRIVE SUN
677	BEARING, THRUST (SUN GEAR/CARRIER)
678	RING, SNAP (FINAL DRIVE CARRIER)
679	CARRIER, FINAL DRIVE
680	GEAR, GOVERNOR DRIVE
681	WASHER, CARRIER/CASE SELECTIVE
682	BEARING ASM., (SELECTIVE WASHER/CASE)
683	SHAFT, DIFFERENTIAL PINION
684	PINION, DIFFERENTIAL PINION SHAFT RET.
685	WASHER, PINION THRUST
686	PINION, DIFFERENTIAL
687	WASHER, DIFFERENTIAL SIDE GEAR THRUST
688	GEAR, DIFFERENTIAL SIDE
689	WEIR, OIL RESERVOIR
690	SLEEVE, LOCK UP
691	SUPPORT, 2ND CLUTCH HOUSING
692	PLATE, REVERSE REACTION DRUM
693	PLATE, 2ND CLUTCH WAVED

FIGURE 12–81 *(continued)*

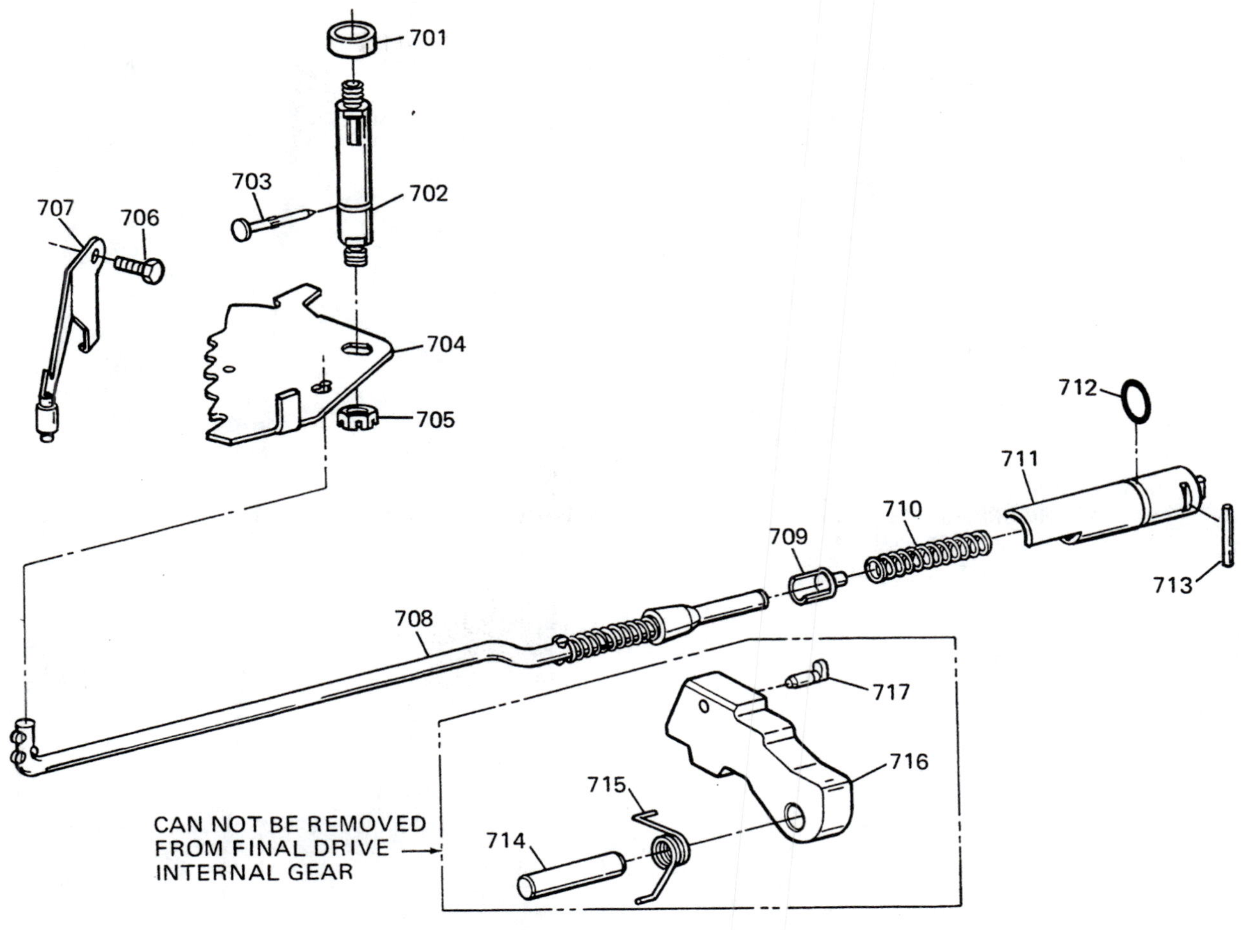

ILL. NO.	DESCRIPTION
701	SEAL, MANUAL SHAFT
702	SHAFT, MANUAL
703	PIN, MANUAL SHAFT TO CASE
704	LEVER & PILOT ASM., INSIDE DETENT
705	NUT, HEX
706	BOLT, M6X1X16 (MANUAL DETENT SPRING)
707	ROLLER & SPRING ASM., MANUAL DETENT
708	ACTUATOR ASSEMBLY, PARKING LOCK
709	PLUNGER ASSEMBLY, PAWL LOCK-OUT
710	SPRING, PAWL LOCK-OUT
711	GUIDE, ACTUATOR
712	SEAL, "O" RING (BUSHING/ACTUATOR GUIDE)
713	PIN, GUIDE RETAINING
714	SHAFT, PARKING LOCK PAWL
715	SPRING, PARKING PAWL RETURN
716	PAWL, PARKING LOCK
717	PIN, PARKING PAWL LOCK-OUT

FIGURE 12–82 THM 4T60/4T60E internal linkage. (Reprinted with permission of General Motors Corporation)

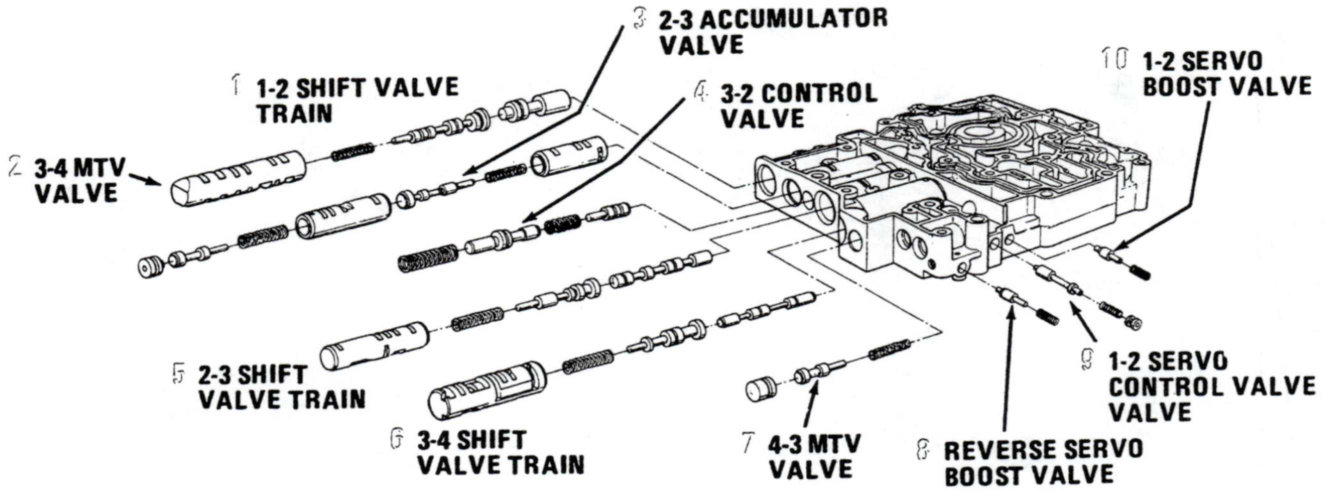

FIGURE 12–83 THM 4T60/4T60E valve body. (Reprinted with permission of General Motors Corporation)

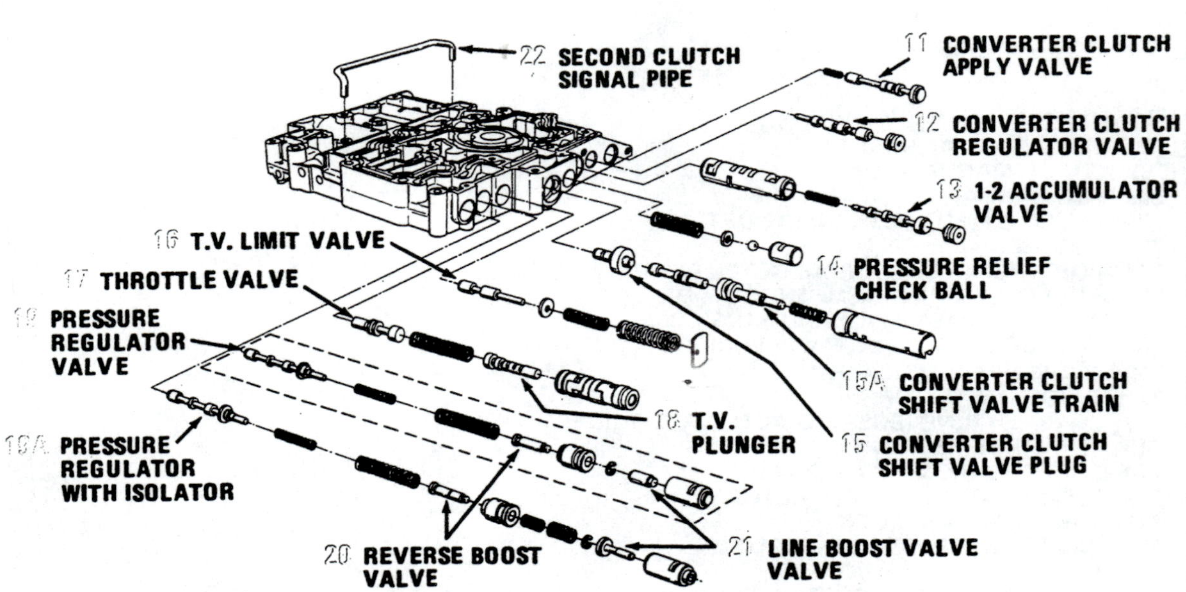

FIGURE 12–84 THM 4T60/4T60E valve body. (Reprinted with permission of General Motors Corporation)

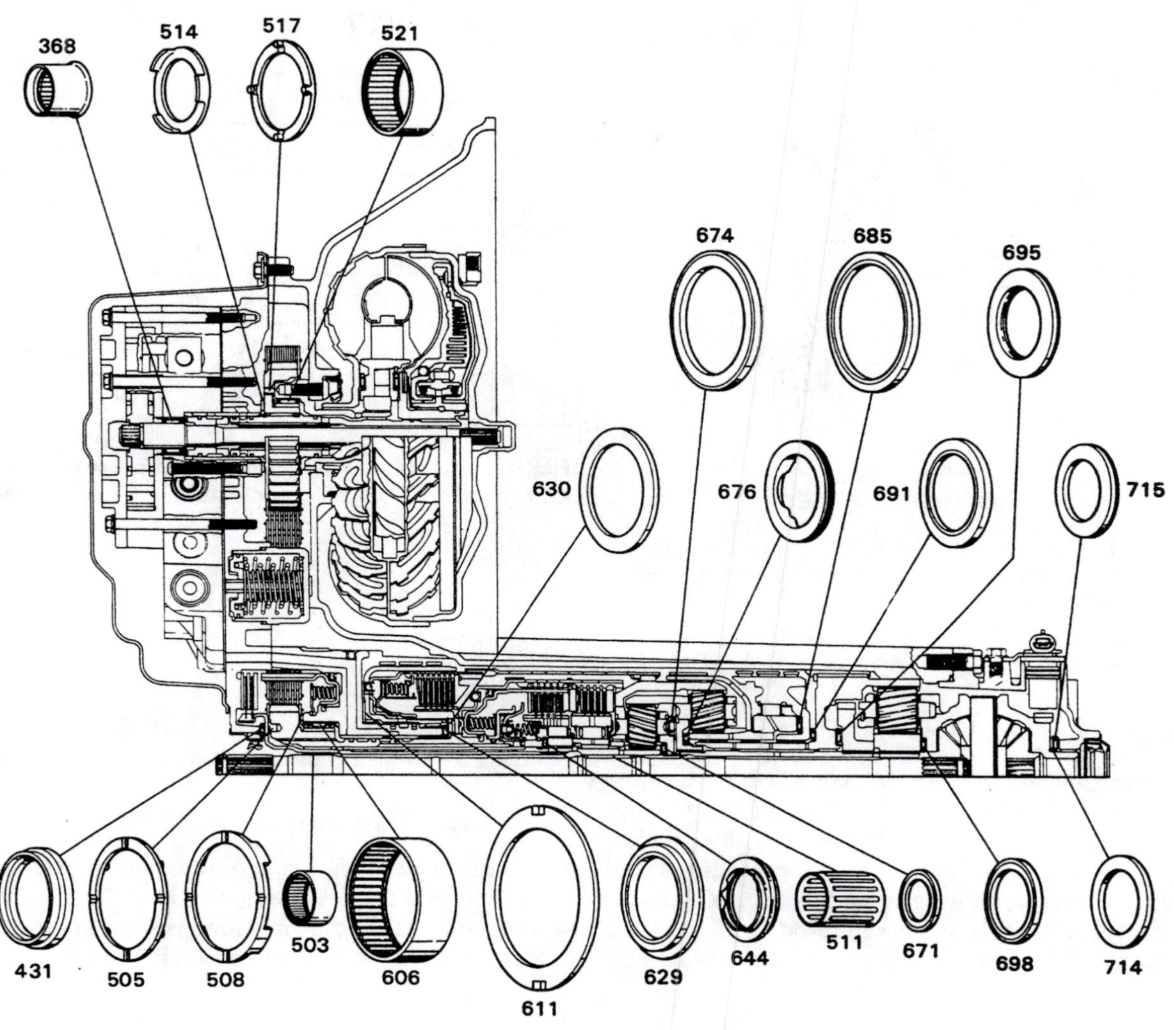

368 SLEEVE, OIL PUMP DRIVE
431 BEARING ASM., 4TH CHANNEL HUB/CHANNEL PLATE
503 BEARING ASSEMBLY, 4TH CLUTCH
505 WASHER, THRUST (4TH CLUTCH HUB/ DRIVEN SPROCKET)
508 WASHER, THRUST (DRIVEN & 2ND CLUTCH DRUM)
511 BEARING, INPUT SUN GEAR
514 WASHER, THRUST (DRIVE SPROCKET/CHANNEL PLATE)
517 WASHER, THRUST (DRIVE SPROCKET/SUPPORT)
521 BEARING ASSEMBLY, DRIVE SUPPORT/SPROCKET (DRAW CUP)
606 BEARING ASSEMBLY, DRAWN CUP
611 WASHER, THRUST (DRIVEN SPROCKET SUPPORT/ 2ND CLUTCH DRUM)
629 BEARING, THRUST (SUPPORT SPROCKET/ THRUST WASHER)
630 WASHER, THRUST (BEARING/INPUT CLUTCH HUB) (SELECTIVE)
644 BEARING ASSEMBLY, THRUST
671 BEARING ASSEMBLY, THRUST
674 BEARING ASSEMBLY, THRUST (INPUT/ REACTION CARRIER)
676 BEARING ASSEMBLY, THRUST (REACTION CARRIER/ SUN GEAR)
685 BEARING ASSEMBLY, THRUST ASSEMBLY/ LO RACE
691 BEARING ASSEMBLY, THRUST (1-2 SUPPORT/ INTERNAL GEAR)
695 BEARING ASSEMBLY, THRUST (INTERNAL GEAR/ PARKING GEAR)
698 BEARING ASSEMBLY, THRUST CARRIER/SUN GEAR
714 WASHER, DIFFERENTIAL CARRIER/CASE (THRUST)
715 BEARING ASSEMBLY, THRUST (DIFFERENTIAL CARRIER/CASE)

FIGURE 12–85 THM 4T60/4T60E thrust washer and bushing location. (Reprinted with permission of General Motors Corporation)

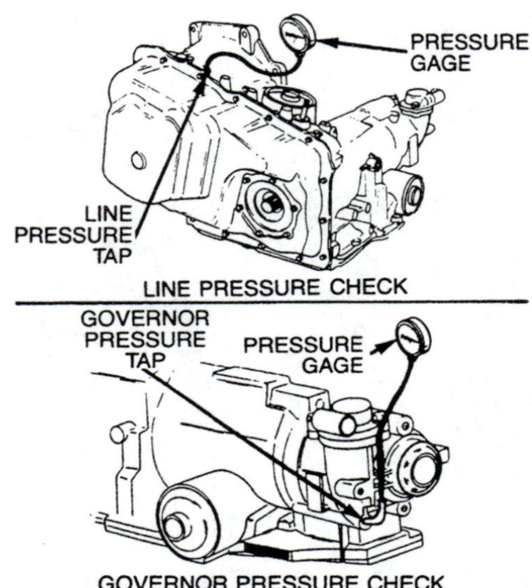

FIGURE 12–86 THM 4T60/4T60E pressure test points. (Reprinted with permission of General Motors Corporation)

MODEL			7ADH, 7AFH, 7AHH, 7ALH, 7ARH, 7CAH, 7CBH		7ACH, 7BBH, 7BCH, 7BJH, 7BKH, 7BNH, 7BRH, 7BSH, 7BTH, 7BUH, 7BZH, 7FBH, 7FCH, 7FJH, 7FKH, 7FLH, 7FNH, 7FRH, 7FSH, 7FTH, 7FUH, 7FZH, 7HAH, 7HCH	
		RANGE	kPa	PSI	kPa	PSI
TRANSMISSION LINE PRESSURE	MINIMUM LINE (1250 R.P.M.)	D4,D3,D2	422 - 475	61 - 69	422 - 475	61 - 69
		D1	946 - 1324	137 - 192	998 - 1276	145 - 185
		P,R,N	422 - 475	61 - 69	422 - 475	61 - 69
	FULL LINE (1250 R.P.M.)	D4,D3,D2	1030 - 1266	150 - 184	1152 - 1393	167 - 202
		D1	946 - 1324	137 - 192	998 - 1276	145 - 185
		P,R,N	1436 - 1764	209 - 257	1573 - 1901	228 - 276

FIGURE 12–87 THM 4T60/4T60E pressure test chart. (Reprinted with permission of General Motors Corporation)

12.6.7 Air Test

This transmission is another case in which nothing is mentioned in the current service manuals about air testing. For all cases such as this, it is recommended to apply the basic air test procedures and test each clutch individually as the transmission is disassembled. Use shop air regulated to 25 to 30 psi and have all clutch discs and pressure plates in place while testing. Apply air through the ball check valve while plugging other holes if necessary.

12.6.8 Special Attention

In this section we show and explain various points of special interest about the HM 4T60/4T60E transaxle. The information presented about each item is included with each illustration.

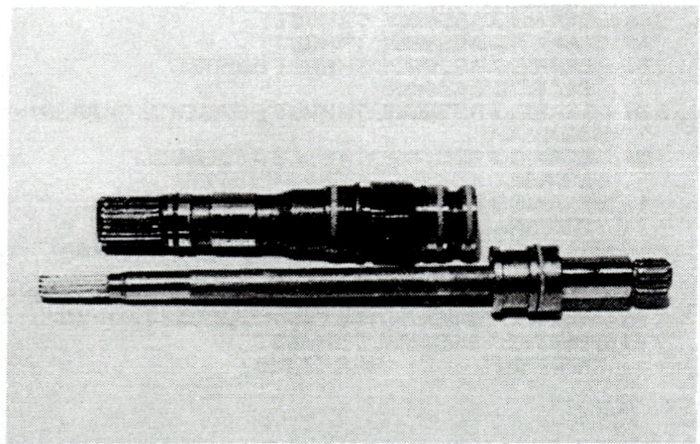

FIGURE 4T60/E–1 The splines and contact areas of the turbine shaft and oil pump drive shaft should be inspected. Replace all seals.

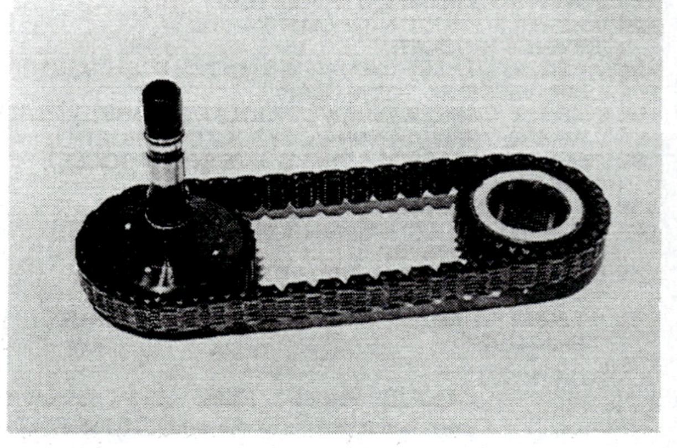

FIGURE 4T60/E–2 Inspect drive link and sprockets.

FIGURE 4T60/E–3 The driven sprocket and driven sprocket support should be inspected for wear and damage.

FIGURE 4T60/E–4 The other side of the driven sprocket support has a hub with sealing rings. Replace the seals.

FIGURE 4T60/E–5 The driven sprocket splines to the input housing. Inspect for wear and replace seals.

FIGURE 4T60/E–6 The reverse band rides around the second clutch housing, with the second clutch splined to the input housing. Inspect for wear.

FIGURE 4T60/E–7 The second clutch uses a special type of snap ring to retain its pressure plate.

FIGURE 4T60/E–8 The third clutch and input clutch packs are located in the input housing.

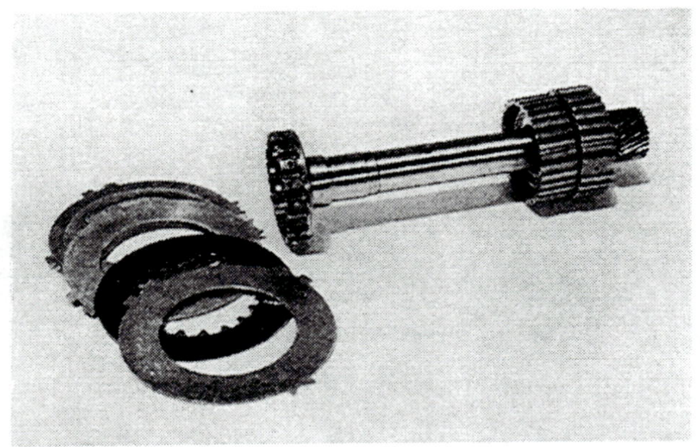

FIGURE 4T60/E–9 The fourth clutch pack and fourth clutch shaft must also be checked.

FIGURE 4T60/E–10 These gear train components are from right to left: the second clutch housing, the reverse reaction drum, and the input carrier/reaction ring gear. Inspect all parts.

FIGURE 4T60/E–11 At the right is the input carrier/reaction ring gear, and at the left is the reaction/carrier/input ring gear. Inspect carefully.

FIGURE 4T60/E–12 At the right both planetary components are combined with the output shaft and sun gear also in place. At the left, the reaction sun gear is shown.

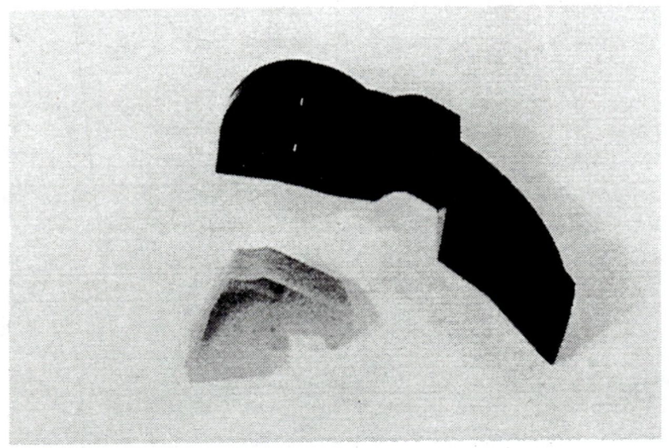

FIGURE 4T60/E–13 These oil weirs are used to control lubrication oil flow in critical areas. Check for cracks.

FIGURE 4T60/E–14 All parts of the governor should be inspected thoroughly.

FIGURE 4T60/E–15 The variable-displacement pump must be fully inspected and rebuilt if necessary.

FIGURE 4T60/E–16 The final drive parts include the final drive internal gear and the differential/final drive carrier. Inspect for wear or damage.

FIGURE 12–88 Summary chart of GM transmissions/transaxles.

GENERAL MOTORS	TORQUE CONVERTER	GEAR TRAIN	COUPLING DEVICES	HOLDING DEVICES	PUMP	SHIFT CONTROL	GOVERNOR	THROTTLE VALVE
4L60 (700-R4)	3-ELEMENT W/ CONVERTER CLUTCH	INTER-CONNECTED PLANETARY GEAR SETS	REVERSE INPUT CLUTCH OVERRUN CLUTCH FORWARD CLUTCH 3-4 CLUTCH FORWARD SPRAG CLUTCH	2-4 BAND LO-ROLLER CLUTCH LO-REV CLUTCH	VANE	HYDRAULIC	DROP IN	CABLE
4L80E	4-ELEMENT W/ CONVERTER CLUTCH DUAL STATOR	OVERDRIVE GEAR SET MODIFIED SIMPSON	OVERRUN CLUTCH OVERDRIVE OWC FORWARD CLUTCH DIRECT CLUTCH	FOURTH CLUTCH FRONT BAND INTERMEDIATE & LOW OWC REAR BAND	GEAR/CRESCENT	ELECTRONIC	NONE	NONE
3T40 (125C)	3-ELEMENT W/ CONVERTER CLUTCH	SIMPSON	DIRECT CLUTCH FORWARD CLUTCH	INTERMEDIATE BAND LO ROLLER CLUTCH LO-REV CLUTCH	VANE	HYDRAULIC	DROP IN	CABLE
4T60/E (440T4)	3-ELEMENT W/ CONVERTER CLUTCH	INTER-CONNECTED PLANETARY GEAR SETS	SECOND CLUTCH THIRD CLUTCH THIRD ROLLER CLUTCH INPUT SPRAG INPUT CLUTCH	FOURTH CLUTCH REVERSE BAND 1-2 BAND	VANE	HYDRAULIC ELECTRONIC	DROP IN NONE	CABLE & VACCUUM MODULATOR

SUMMARY

This chapter profiled four General Motors transmissions/transaxles that are widely used today. They are summarized in Figure 12–88. Each profile included a description of the basic components, an explanation of the power flow in each gear, and two clutch and band charts, one from the author and the other from the manufacturer. Reviewing any sections you did not understand fully is recommended.

SELF-TEST

Before going on to the next chapter, complete the self-test according to your instructor's directions. Read carefully and choose the best answer.

1. The ________________ transmission uses a converter clutch.
   a. 3T40
   b. HM 4L80E
   c. HM 4L60
   d. All of the above
   e. None of the above
2. The ________________ transmission uses a vane-type pump.
   a. 4L80E
   b. 3T40
   c. HM 4L60
   d. All of the above
   e. None of the above
3. The ________________ transaxle use a gear crescent pump.
   a. HM 3T40
   b. HM 4T60
   c. HM 4L80E
   d. All of the above
   e. None of the above
4. The ________________ transmission has three speeds.
   a. HM 4L60
   b. HM 4L80E
   c. HM 3T40
   d. All of the above
   e. None of the above
5. Which of the following are transaxles?
   a. HM 3T40
   b. HM 4T60
   c. HM 4T60E
   d. All of the above
   e. None of the above
6. Which of the following uses a Simpson gear set?
   a. HM 4L60
   b. HM 4T60
   c. HM 3T40
   d. All of the above
   e. None of the above
7. Which of the following uses a vacuum modulator to control the throttle valve?
   a. HM 4L80E
   b. HM 3T40
   c. HM 4L60
   d. All of the above
   e. None of the above
8. Which of the following uses both a throttle valve cable and vacuum modulator?
   a. HM 4T60
   b. HM 3T40
   c. HM 4L80E
   d. All of the above
   e. None of the above
9. Which transmission is basically the same as another three-speed model but with another planetary gear set added?
   a. HM 4T60
   b. HM 4L60
   c. Both a and b
   d. Neither a nor b
10. Which of the following uses electronic controls on the converter clutch?
    a. HM 4T60
    b. HM 4L60
    c. HM 3T40
    d. All of the above
    e. None of the above
11. Which of the following uses electronic shift controls?
    a. HM 3T40
    b. HM 4L60
    c. HM 4T60E
    d. All of the above
    e. None of the above
12. Which type of ATF is used in Hydra-Matic transmissions/transaxles?
    a. Mercon
    b. Type 7176
    c. Dexron II
    d. Type F

Chapter 13

ASIAN IMPORTS

13.1 PERFORMANCE OBJECTIVES

After studying this chapter, you should have fulfilled the following performance objectives by being able to:

1. List the Asian transmissions/transaxles.
2. Describe the basic components of each transmission/transaxle.
3. Describe the power flow in each gear position, including which coupling and holding devices are applied, for each transmission/transaxle.
4. Write a clutch and band chart for each transmission/transaxle listed in the chapter.
5. Complete the self-test with at least the minimum score required by your instructor.

13.2 OVERVIEW

In this chapter, two transaxles used in Asian imports are profiled. The Nissan RL4F02A is built by the Japanese Automatic Transmission Company (JATCO), which also produces transmissions for Ford import vehicles. The Toyota A-240-L is not an overdrive transmission, in that fourth gear is direct drive (1:1). Most of the other four-speed automatic transmissions have an overdrive fourth gear. The A-240-E is the same as the A-240-L except for fully computerized shift control. Both transaxles profiled use Dexron II.

13.3 NISSAN JATCO RL4F02A: FWD FOUR-SPEED TRANSAXLE

13.3.1 Basic Description

The Jatco RL4F02A (referred to hereafter as the RL4) is an automatic four-speed overdrive transaxle produced by the Japanese Automatic Transmission Company (Jatco). A cross-sectional view of the RL4 is shown in Figure 13–1.

The transmission description is divided into eight areas. All the transmissions are described in this manner to make their comparison easier.

1. Torque Converter
The RL4 uses a conventional three-element torque converter that has a hydraulic converter clutch (lockup) which is controlled electronically.

2. Gear Train
The RL4 uses two interconnected planetary gear sets to achieve a four-speed overdrive gear train (Figure 13–2).

3. Coupling Devices
The coupling devices used are the reverse, high, and low clutches (Figure 13–3).

4. Holding Devices
The holding devices used in the RL4 are the band brake, the low and reverse brake, and the one-way clutch.

5. Pump
The oil pump is a variable-displacement vane type, which is shown in Figure 13–4.

6. Shift Control
The RL4 shift control system is hydraulic and uses electronic devices to control fourth gear and the converter clutch.

7. Governor
The governor, of drop-in design, produces two-stage governor pressure.

8. Throttle Valve
The throttle valve is connected to the fuel system throttle linkage by the TV cable.

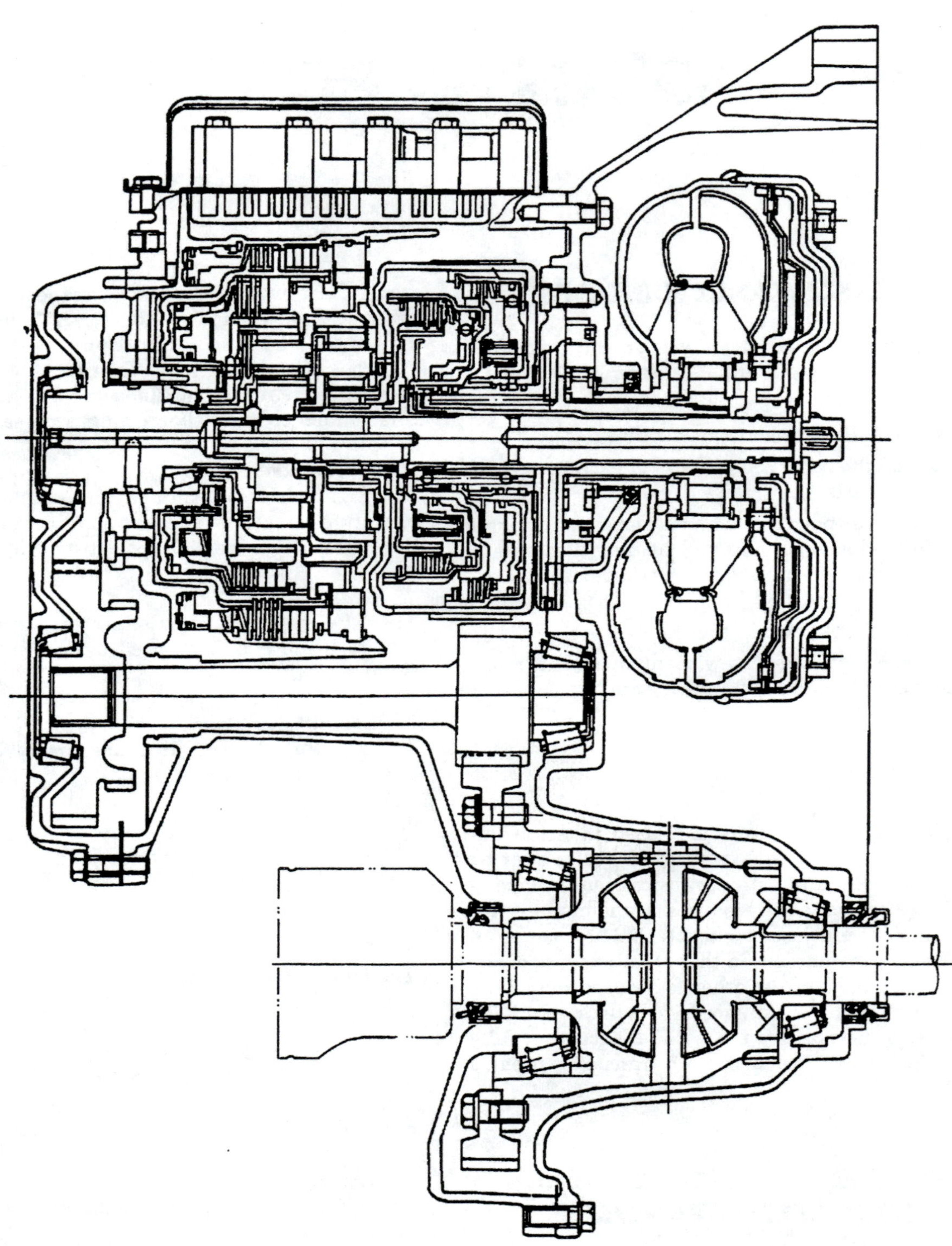

FIGURE 13–1 RL4 cross-sectional view. (Courtesy of Nissan)

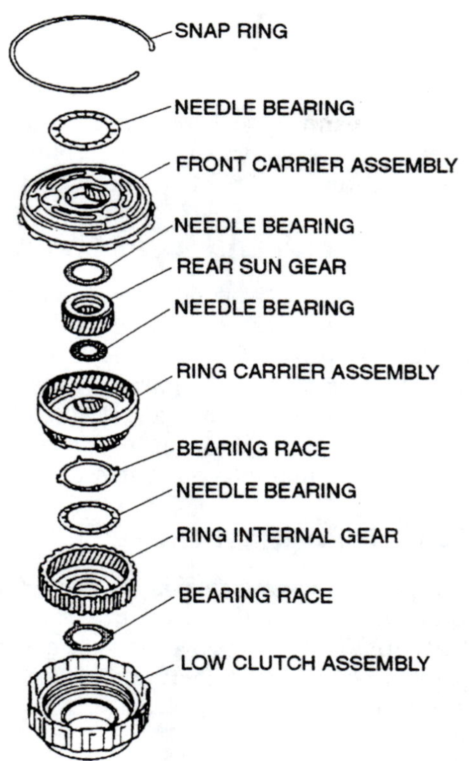

FIGURE 13–2 RL4 gear train. (Courtesy of Nissan)

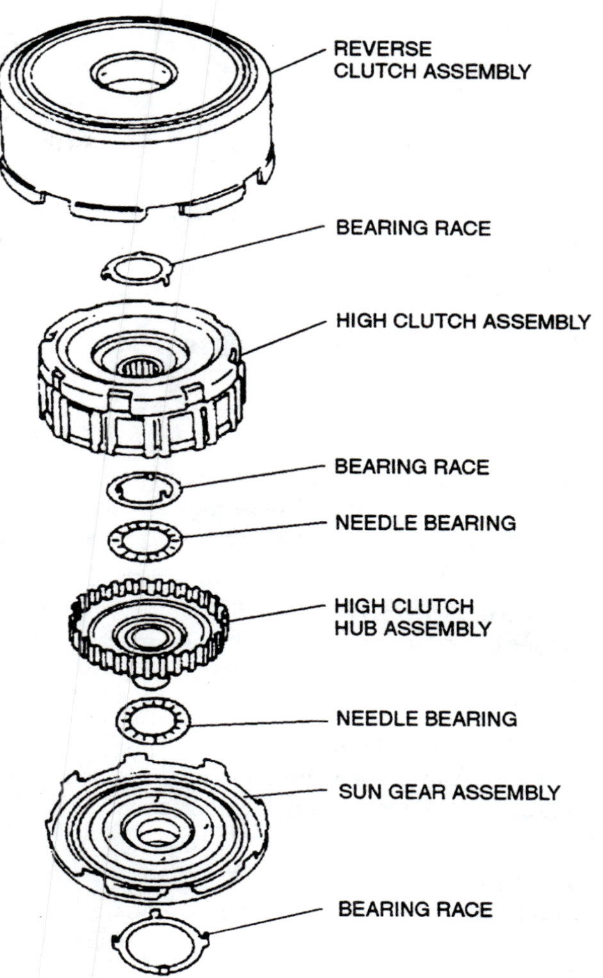

FIGURE 13–3 RL4 coupling devices. (Courtesy of Nissan)

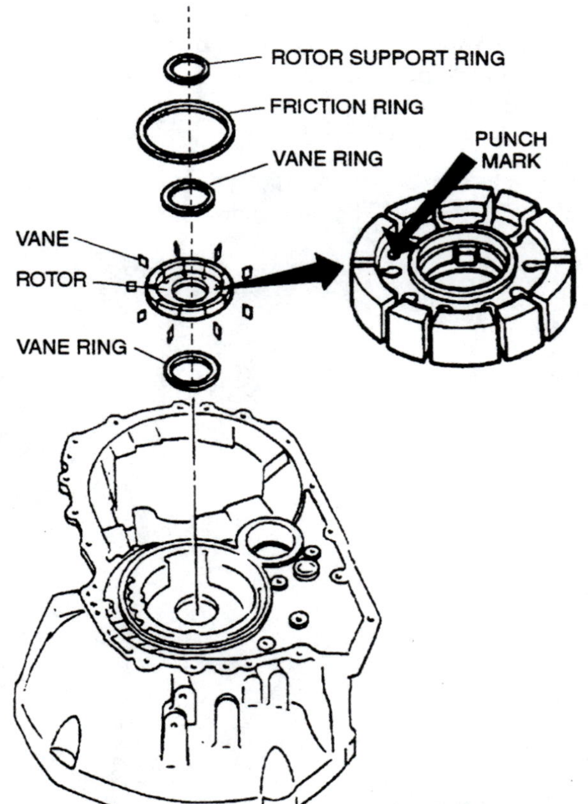

FIGURE 13–4 RL4 valve oil pump. (Courtesy of Nissan)

13.3.2 Power Flow

The power flow is described by stating the coupling and holding device action (applied, or holding) on the members of the planetary gear set (sun gear, pinion carrier, and ring gear) in each gear range of the transmission.

1. Neutral (N)
In neutral all of the coupling and holding devices are released, with only the turbine shaft and clutch hubs rotating.

2. First Gear (D1)
In first gear the low clutch is applied and the one-way clutch is holding. The first-gear ratio is 2.78:1. In manual first gear, the low and reverse brake is also applied.

3. Second Gear (D2)
In second gear the low clutch remains applied, and the band is also applied. A ratio of 1.54:1 is produced.

4. Third Gear (D3)
In third gear the low clutch is still applied and the high clutch is also applied. The gear set is in direct drive.

5. Fourth Gear (D4)
In fourth gear the high clutch remains applied and the band is also applied, causing an overdrive condition with a ratio of 0.69:1.

6. Reverse Gear (R)
In reverse gear the reverse clutch is applied and the low and reverse brake is also applied. The reverse-gear ratio is 2.27:1.

13.3.3 Clutch and Band Charts

In this section we provide two clutch and band charts. The first chart, the author's design, uses a standardized format for listing the coupling and holding devices to aid comparison between transmissions. This chart is shown in Figure 13–5. The second chart, the manufacturer's design, which is found in service manuals, is shown in Figure 13–6.

13.3.4 Identification

The shape of the transmission oil pan or its gasket is a quick means of identifying an automatic transmission. In Figure 13–7 you see the pan gasket shape and number of bolt holes for the RL4 transaxle.

13.3.5 Components

In this section exploded drawings of the RL4 automatic transaxle subassemblies are shown, along with lists of the part names. The manufacturer's parts names are used to eliminate confusion about component names. The drawings to study are as follows:

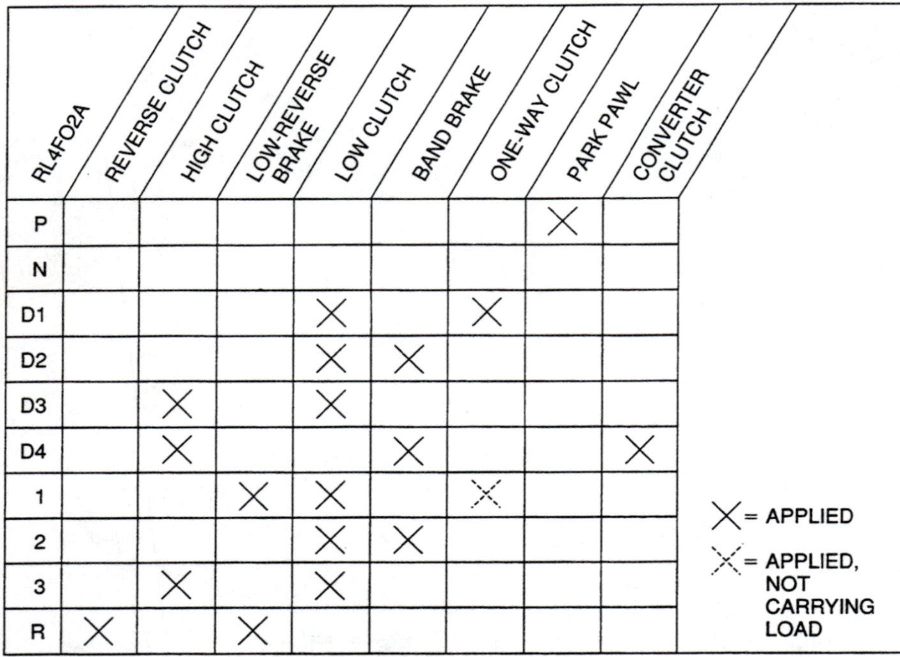

RL4FO2A	REVERSE CLUTCH	HIGH CLUTCH	LOW-REVERSE BRAKE	LOW CLUTCH	BAND BRAKE	ONE-WAY CLUTCH	PARK PAWL	CONVERTER CLUTCH
P							X	
N								
D1				X		X		
D2				X	X			
D3		X		X				
D4		X			X			X
1			X	X		X (dotted)		
2				X	X			
3		X		X				
R	X		X					

X = APPLIED
X (dotted) = APPLIED, NOT CARRYING LOAD

FIGURE 13–5 RL4 clutch and band chart, standardized version.

FIGURE 13–6 RL4 clutch and band chart, factory version. (Courtesy of Nissan)

Range		Gear ratio	Reverse clutch	High clutch	Low clutch	Band servo		Low & reverse brake	One-way clutch	Parking pawl	Lock-up
						Operation	Release				
Park		–								on	
Reverse		2.272	on					on			
Neutral		–									
Drive	D_1 Low	2.785			on				on		
	D_2 Second	1.545			on	on					
	D_3 Top (3rd)	1.000		on	on	(on)	on				
	D_4 O.D. (4th)	0.694		on		on					on
2	2_1 Low	2.785			on				on		
	2_2 Second	1.545			on	on					
1	1_1 Low	2.785			on			on	on		
	1_2 Second	1.545			on	on					

Cross section, Figure 13–8
Exploded view 1, Figure 13–9
Exploded view 2, Figure 13–10
Reverse clutch, Figure 13–11
High clutch, Figure 13–12
Low clutch, Figure 13–13
Low and reverse brake, Figure 13–14
Brake band servo, Figure 13–15
Oil pump, Figure 13–16
Valve body, Figure 13–17
Valve body cross section, Figure 13–18
Governor, Figure 13–19

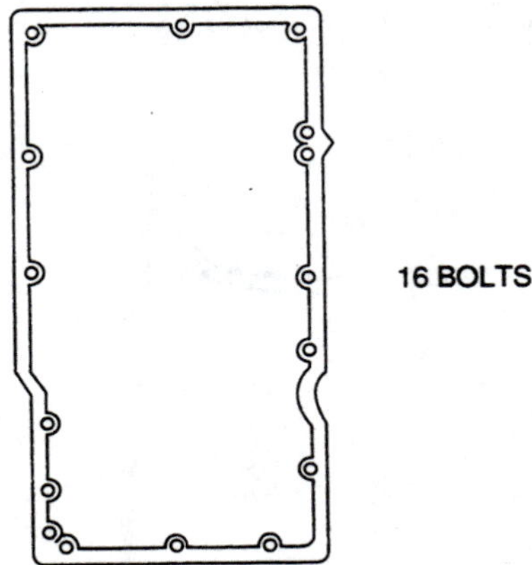

FIGURE 13–7 RL4 pan gasket identification.

13.3.6 Pressure Test

One of the key tests in diagnosis is the hydraulic system pressure test. The location of the test points of the RL4 transaxle is shown in Figure 13–20. A pressure chart listing the pressure specifications of this transaxle is shown in Figure 13–21.

13.3.7 Air Test

Air testing is used during preliminary diagnosis of certain malfunctions and during the disassembly process to verify component operation or failure. The technician must know which hydraulic circuit is being served by each passageway to be able to air test a transmission accurately. This information is presented in the following drawings:

Oil pump passages, Figure 13–22
Converter housing passages, Figure 13–23
Case passages, Figure 13–24

13.3.8 Special Attention

In this unit we show and explain various points of interest about the RL4 transaxle. The information presented about each item is included with each illustration.

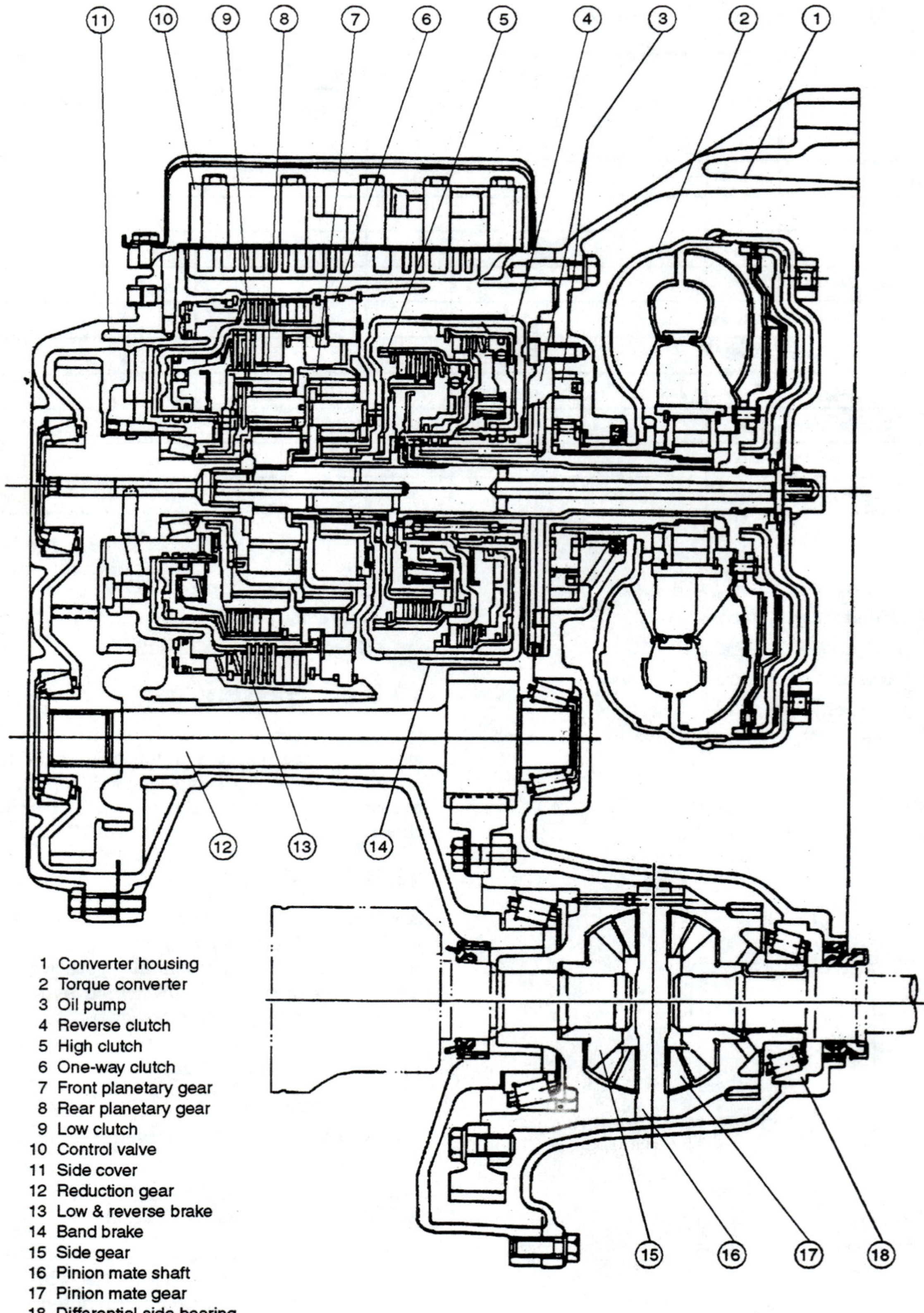

FIGURE 13–8 RL4 cross section. (Courtesy of Nissan)

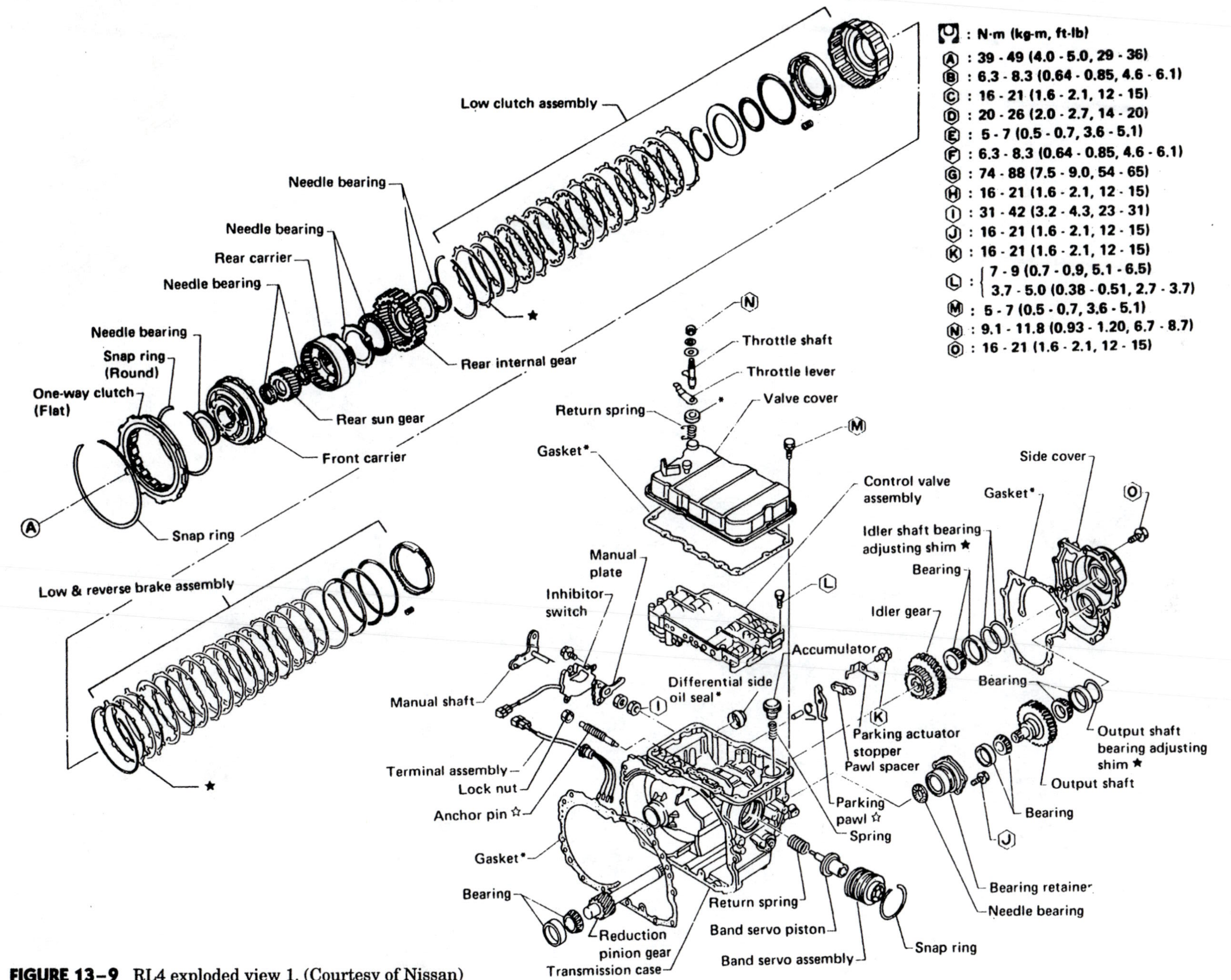

FIGURE 13–9 RL4 exploded view 1. (Courtesy of Nissan)

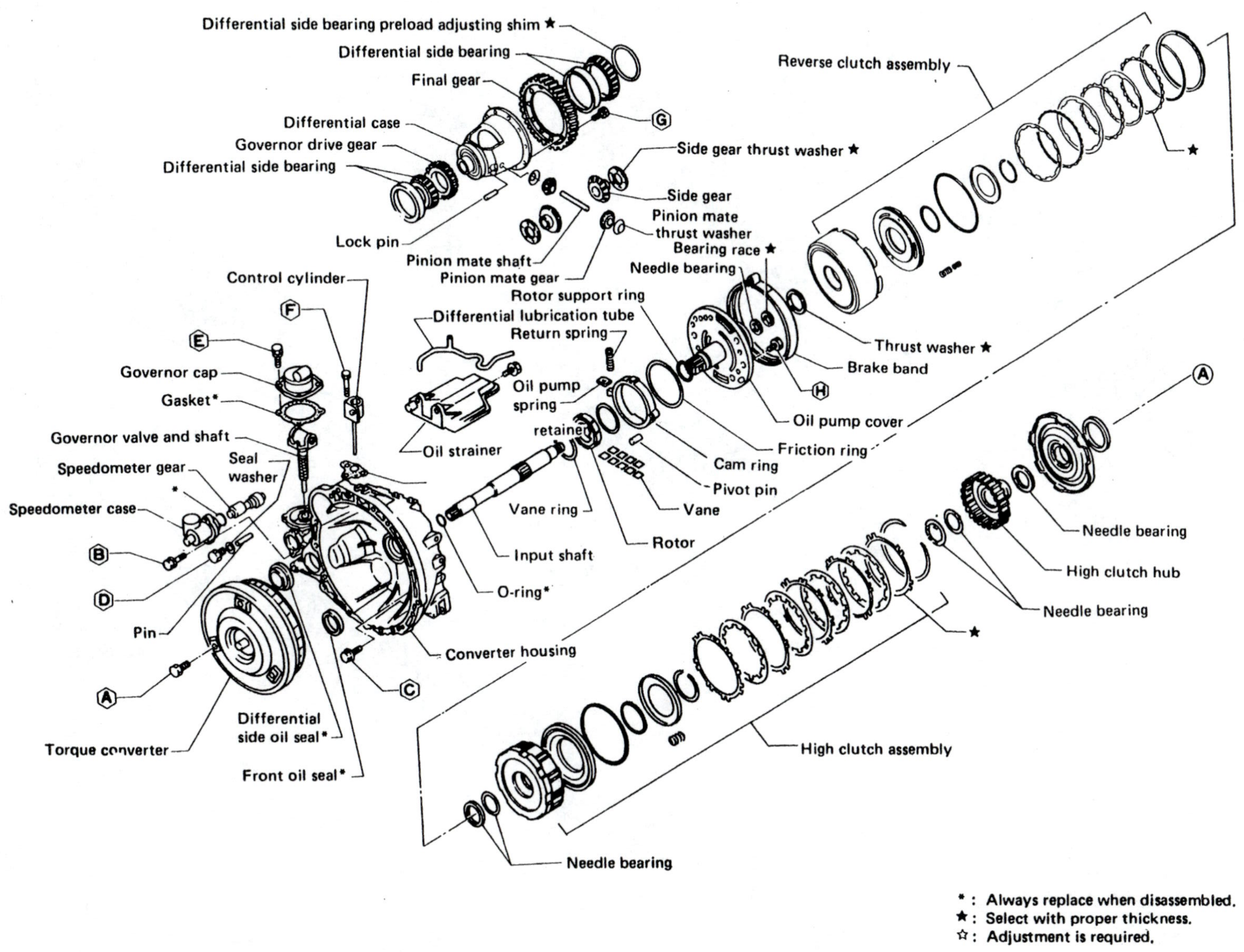

* : Always replace when disassembled.
★ : Select with proper thickness.
☆ : Adjustment is required.

FIGURE 13–10 RL4 exploded view 2. (Courtesy of Nissan)

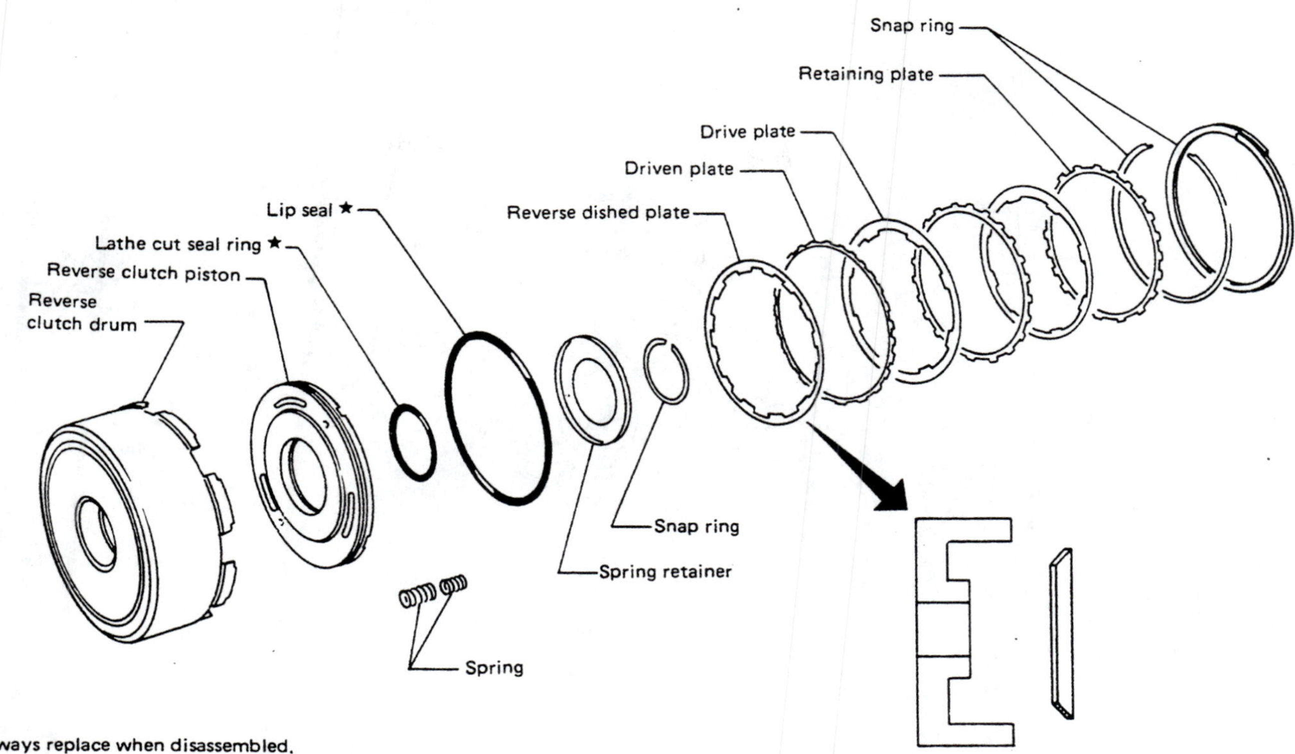

FIGURE 13–11 RL4 reverse clutch. (Courtesy of Nissan)

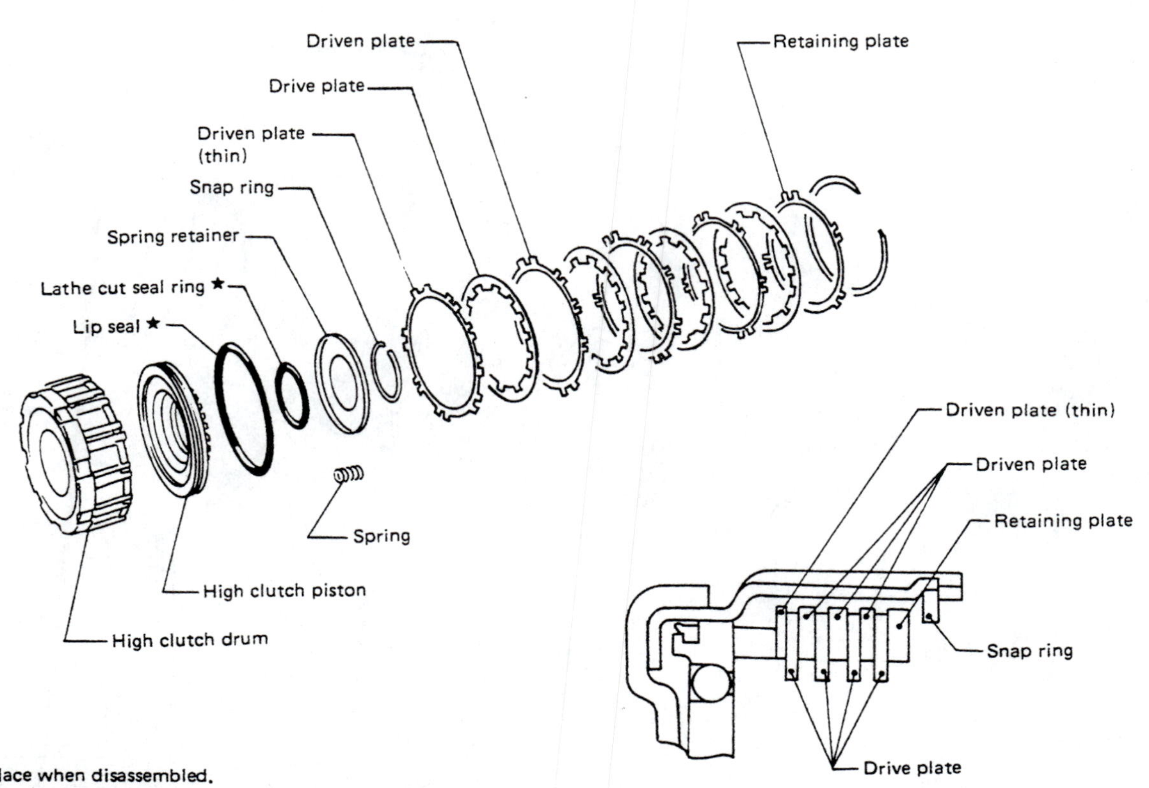

FIGURE 13–12 RL4 high clutch. (Courtesy of Nissan)

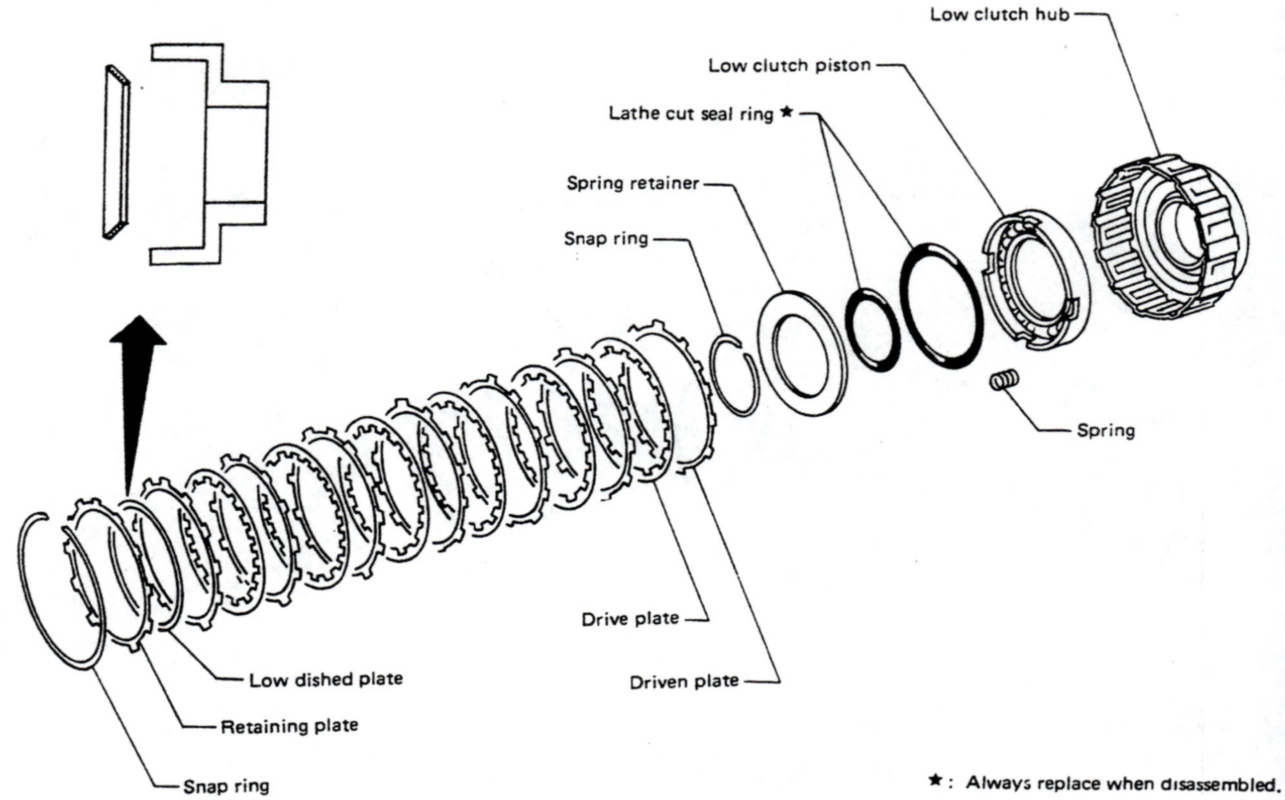

Low clutch hub
Low clutch piston
Lathe cut seal ring ★
Spring retainer
Snap ring
Spring
Drive plate
Driven plate
Low dished plate
Retaining plate
Snap ring
★: Always replace when disassembled.

FIGURE 13–13 RL4 low clutch. (Courtesy of Nissan)

Low & reverse clutch piston
Lathe cut seal ring ★
Snap ring
Dished plate
Driven plate
Drive plate
Spring
Spring retainer
Retaining plate
Snap ring
★ Always replace when disassembled.

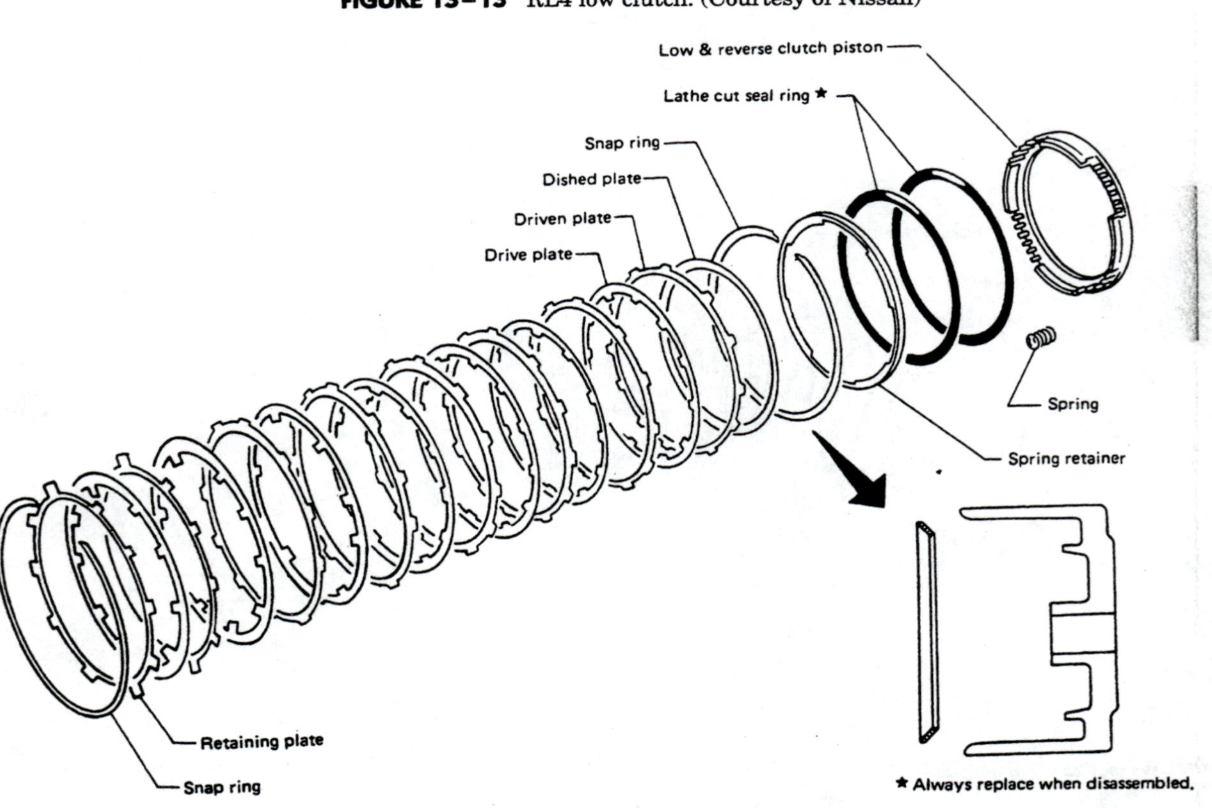

FIGURE 13–14 RL4 low and reverse brake. (Courtesy of Nissan)

FIGURE 13–15 RL4 brake band servo. (Courtesy of Nissan)

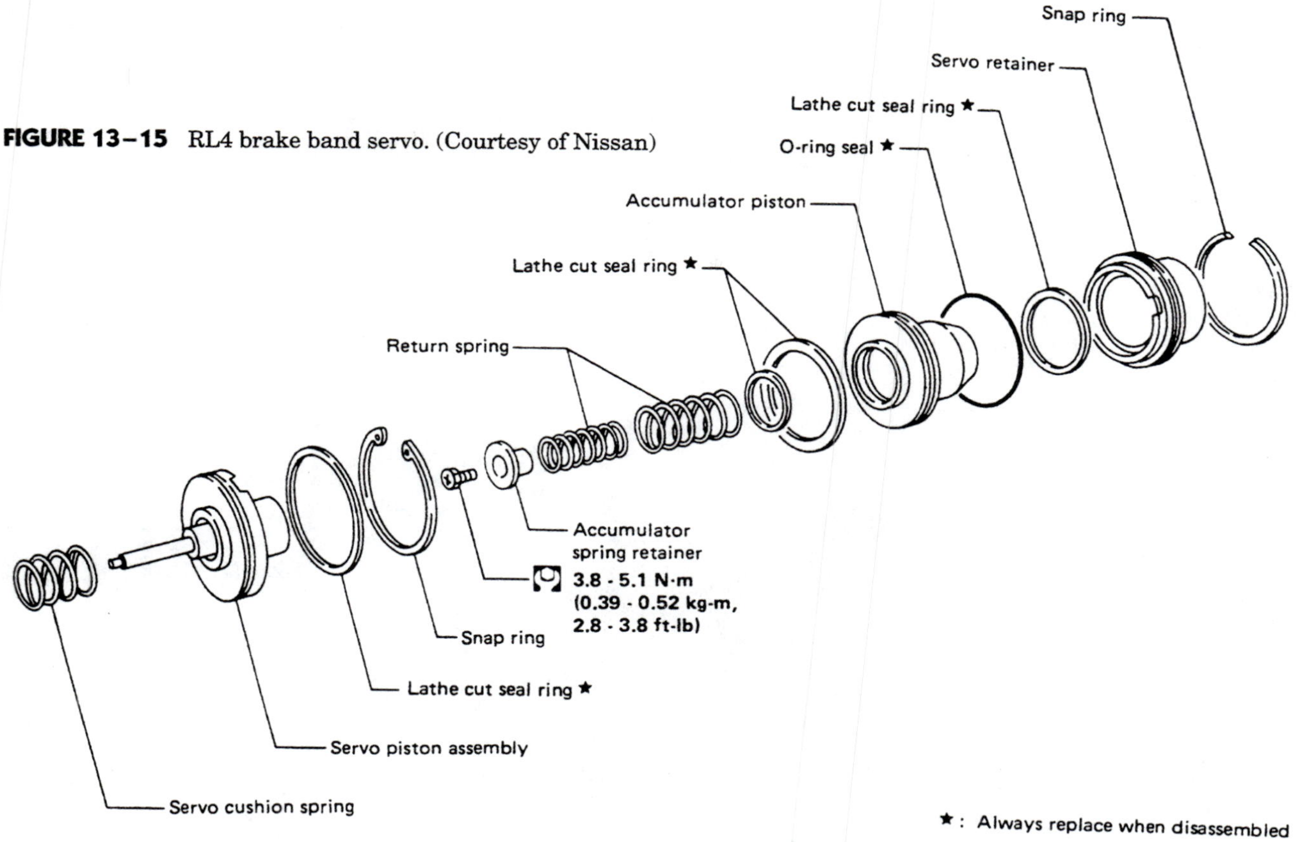

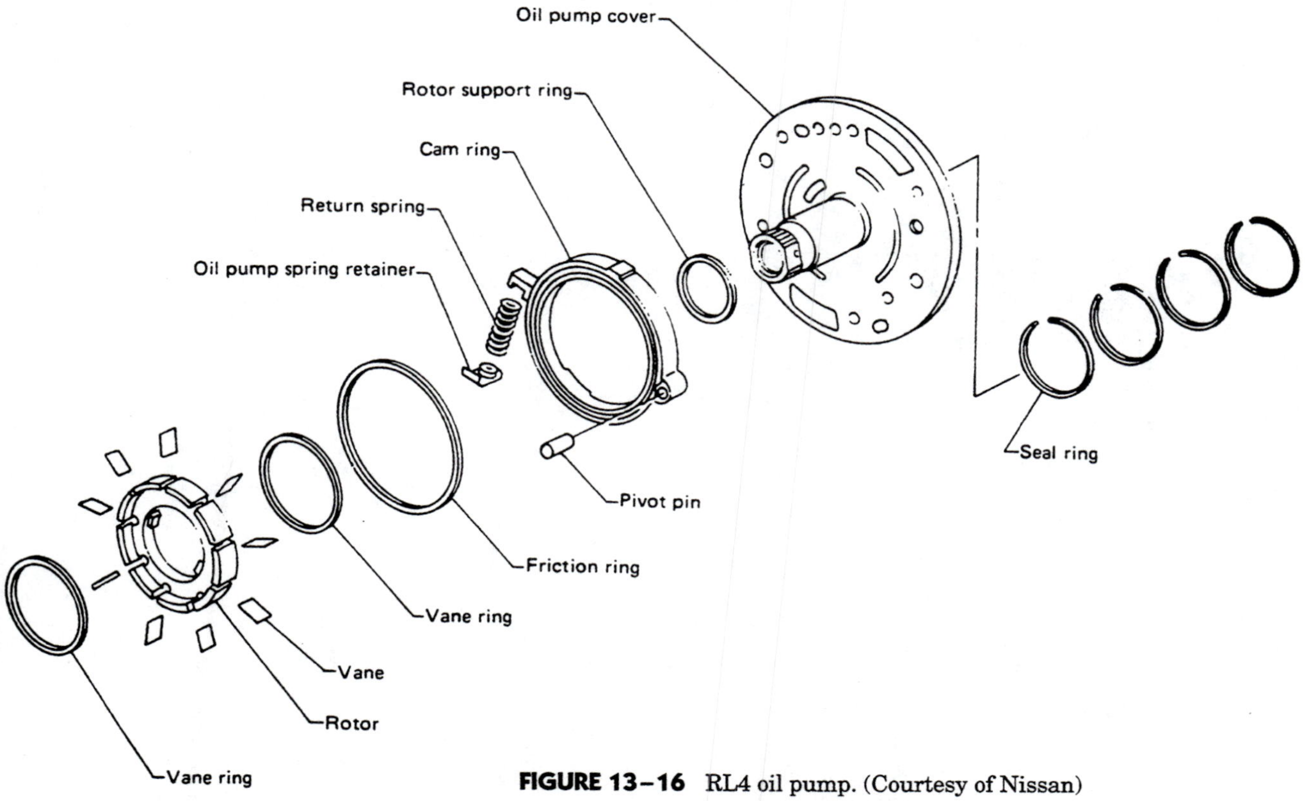

FIGURE 13–16 RL4 oil pump. (Courtesy of Nissan)

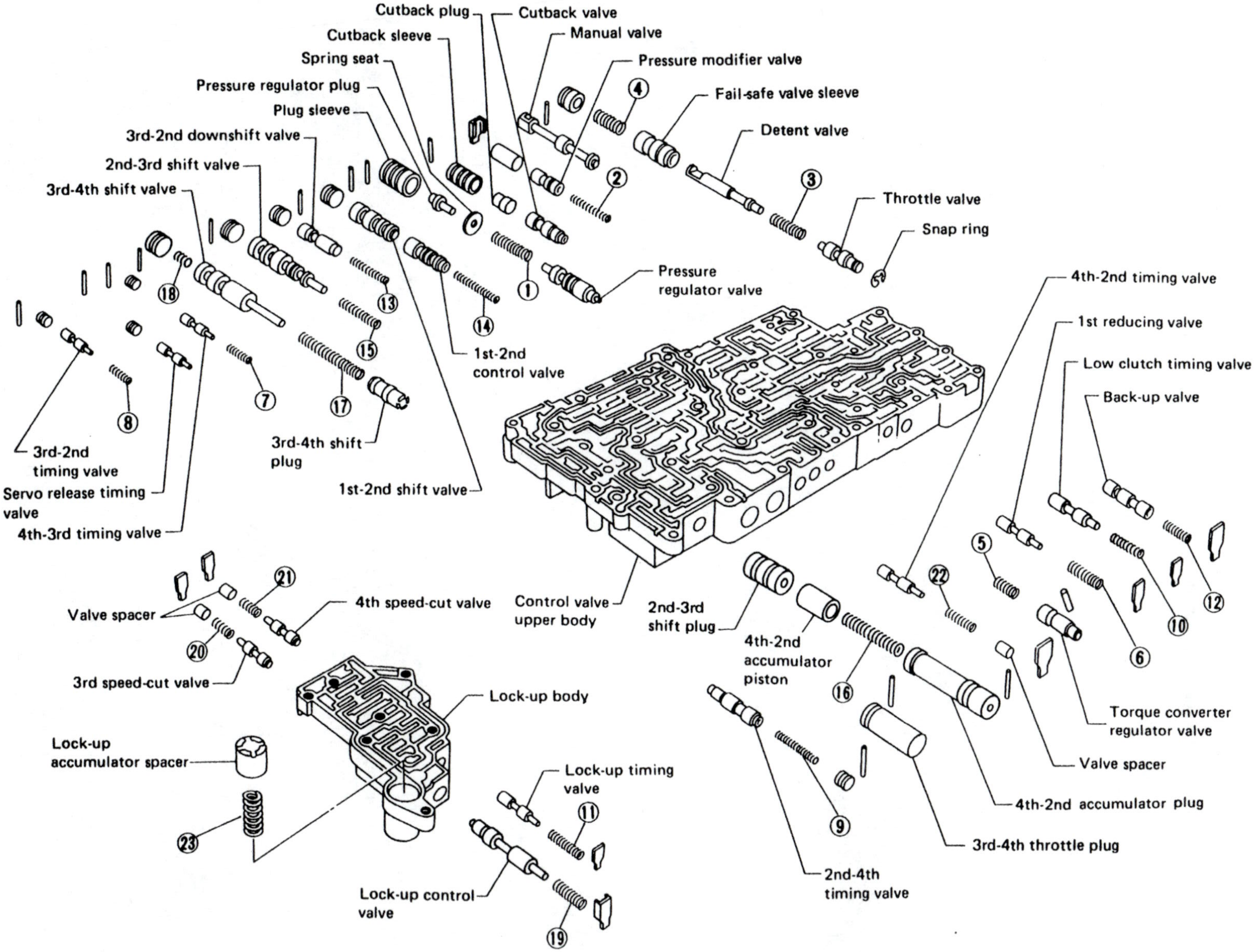

FIGURE 13–17 RL4 valve body. (Courtesy of Nissan)

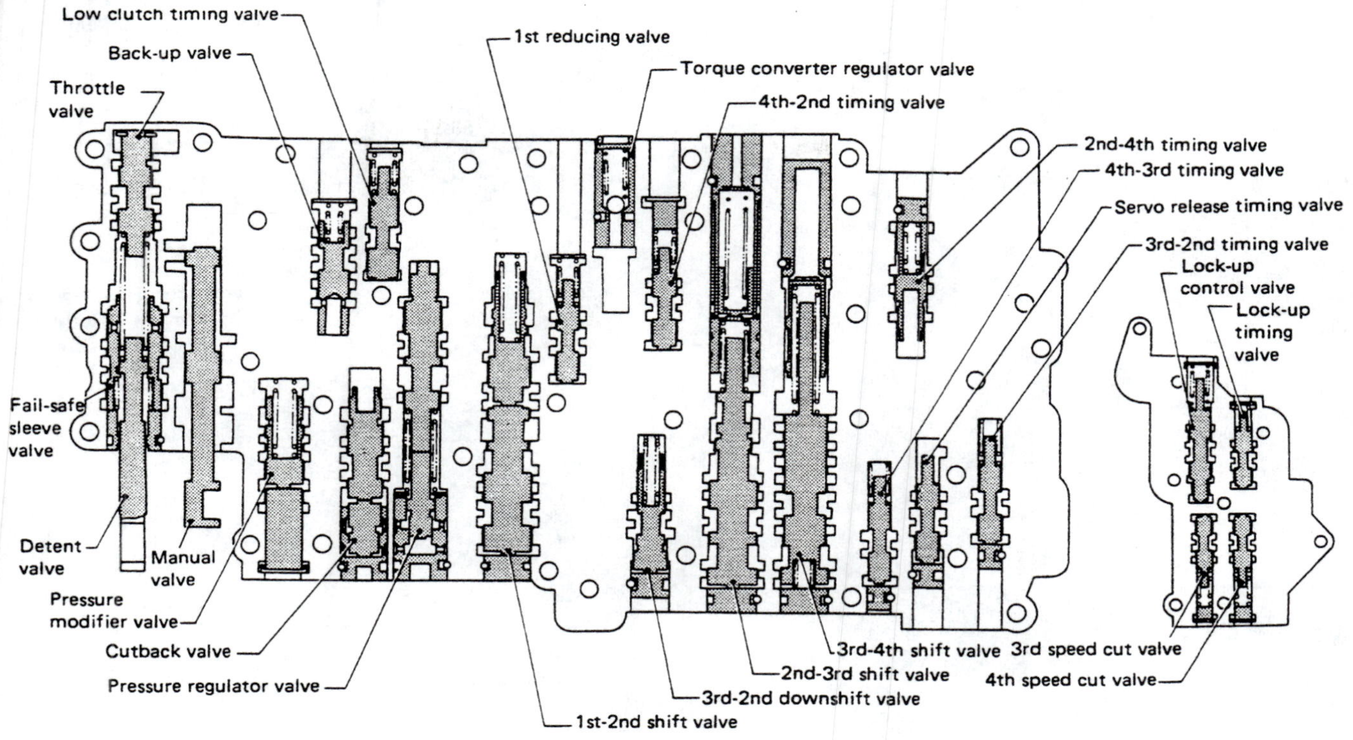

FIGURE 13–18 RL4 valve body, cross section. (Courtesy of Nissan)

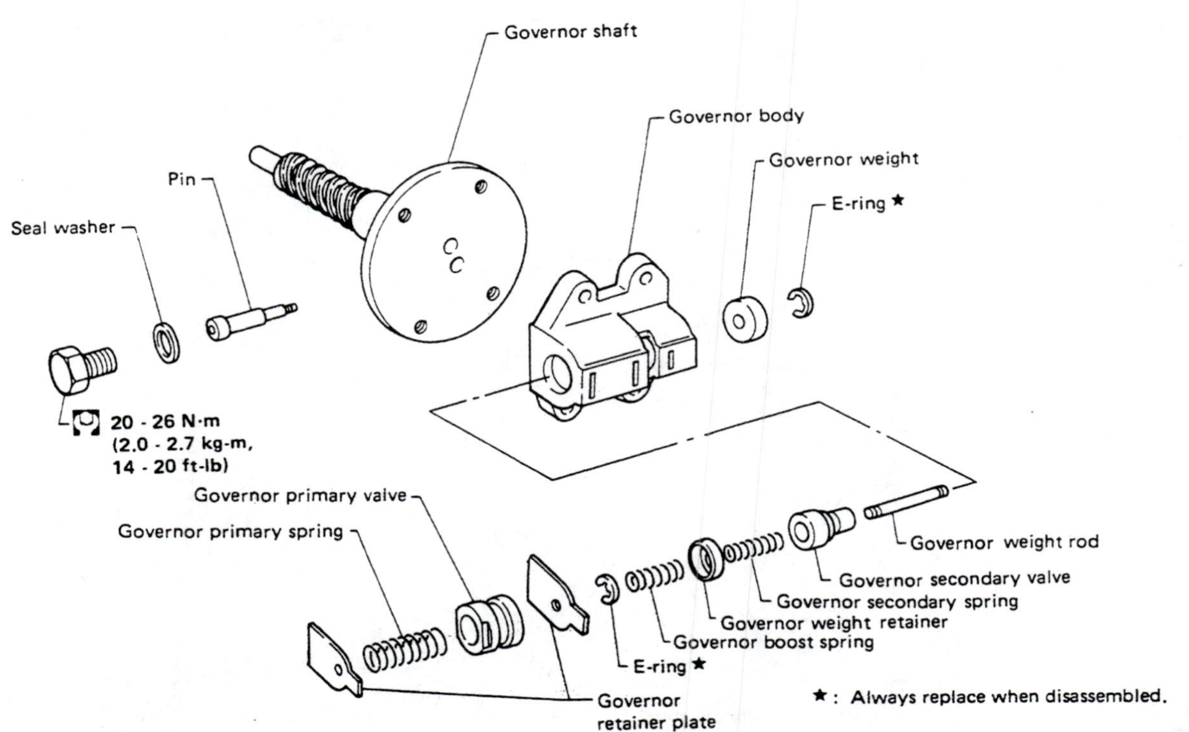

FIGURE 13–19 RL4 governor. (Courtesy of Nissan)

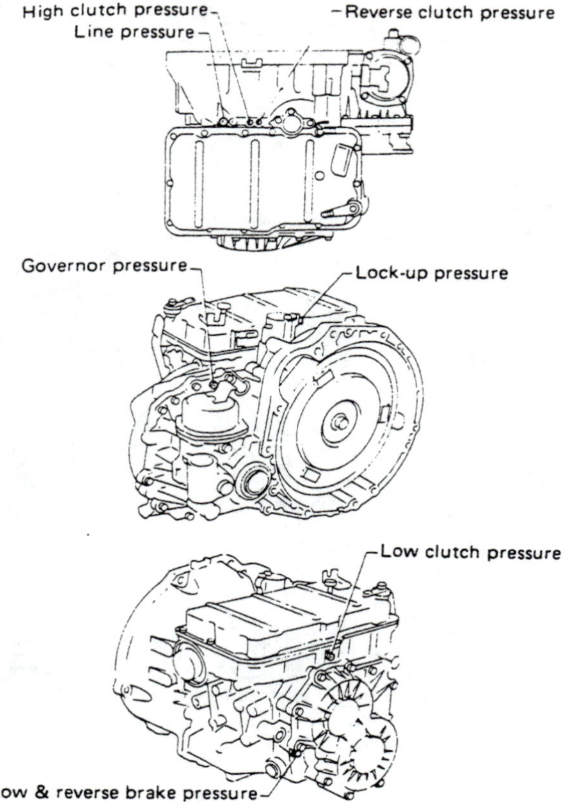

FIGURE 13–20 RL4 pressure test points. (Courtesy of Nissan)

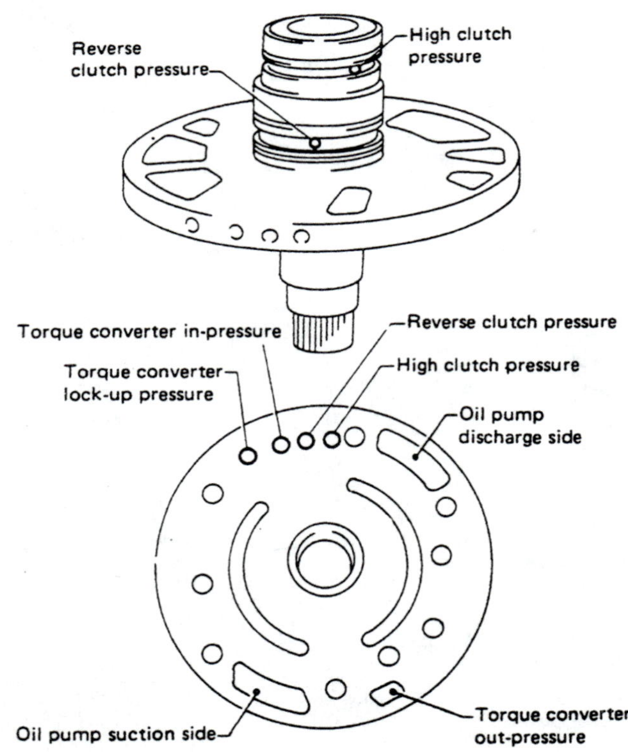

FIGURE 13–22 RL4 oil pump passages. (Courtesy of Nissan)

At Idle	
Range	**Line Pressure kPa (kg/cm², psi)**
R	
D	367.8 – 436.4
2	(3.75 – 4.45,
1	53.3 – 63.3)

At Stall	
Range	**Line Pressure kPa (kg/cm², psi)**
R	
D	1,206 – 1,363
2	(12.3 – 13.9,
1	175 – 198)

FIGURE 13–21 RL4 pressure charts. (Courtesy of Nissan)

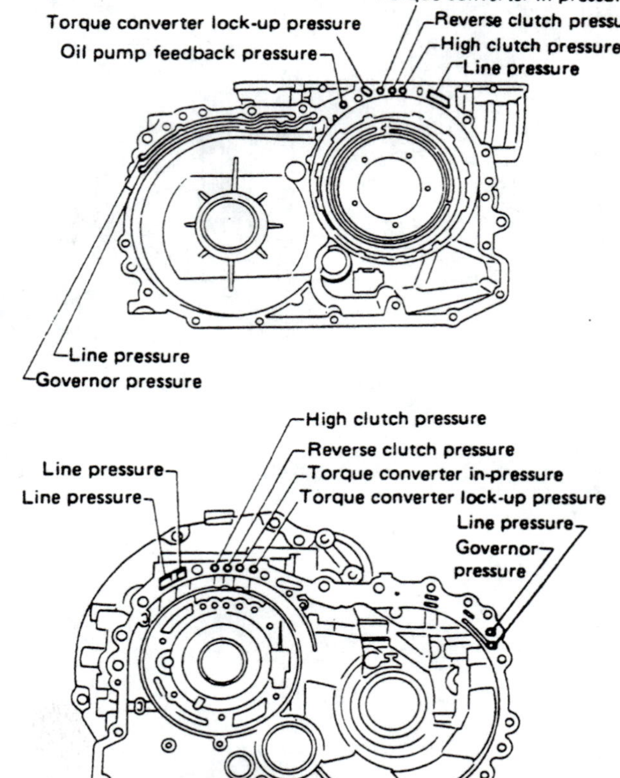

FIGURE 13–23 RL4 converter housing passages. (Courtesy of Nissan)

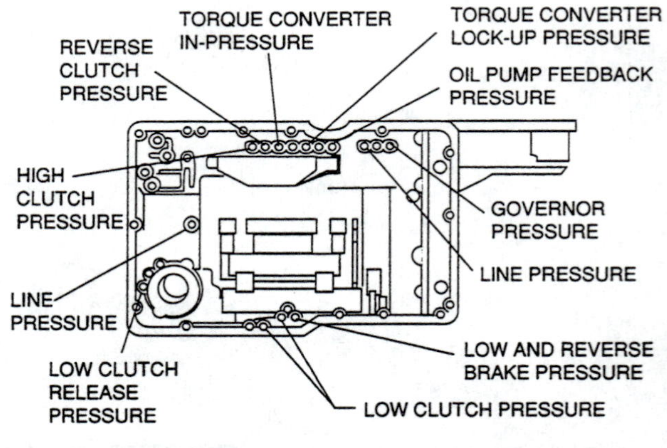

FIGURE 13–24 RL4 case passages. (Courtesy of Nissan)

FIGURE RL4–1 The valve body includes electrical shift solenoids.

FIGURE RL4–2 Drop-in governor that uses a spool valve to regulate the governor pressure.

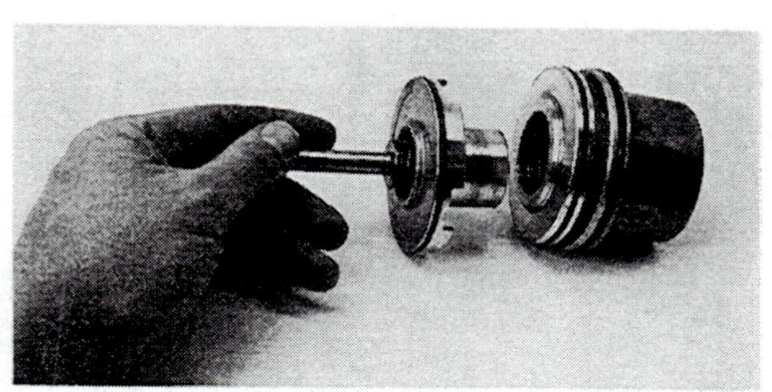

FIGURE RL4–3 The brake band servo has many seals to inspect and replace.

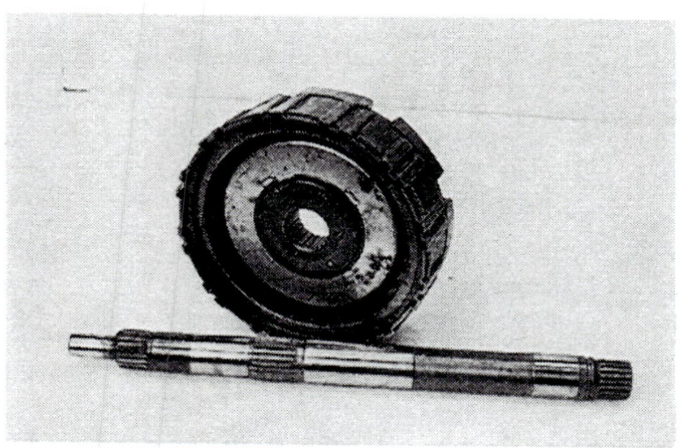

FIGURE RL4–4 The high clutch is splined to the turbine shaft.

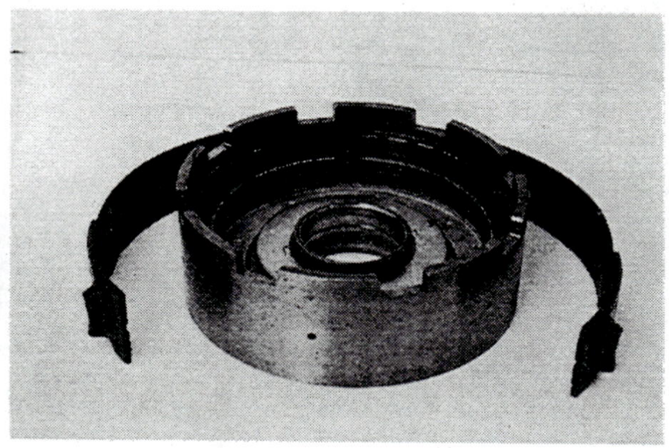

FIGURE RL4–5 The brake band applies around the reverse clutch drum.

FIGURE RL4–6 The high clutch hub passes through the front sun gear to spline into the front carrier.

FIGURE RL4-7 The high clutch hub drives the front carrier.

FIGURE RL4-8 The front carrier being removed from the gear train.

FIGURE RL4-9 The rear sun gear being removed.

FIGURE RL4-10 The rear carrier being removed.

FIGURE RL4-11 Low clutch assembly with the low-reverse brake discs around the outside.

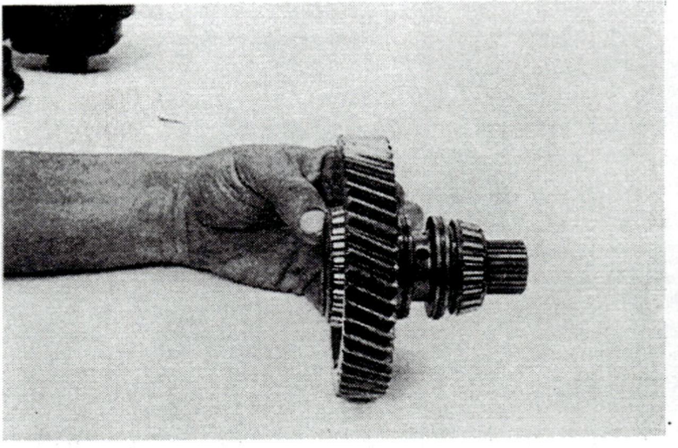

FIGURE RL4-12 The transaxle power output is transferred to the output shaft by this gear.

13.4 TOYOTA A240L: FWD FOUR-SPEED TRANSAXLE

13.4.1 Basic Description

The A240L transaxle is unique in the way that it achieves its final overdrive gearing (Figure 13–25). All of the four-speed transmissions studied up to now have used a direct-drive (1:1) third gear and an overdrive fourth gear. The A240L uses a direct-drive fourth gear combined with an overdrive ratio (0.89:1) on the counter gear to achieve the overdrive. An underdrive unit (fourth speed) is used to provide greater gear reduction in first, second, and third gears (Figure 13–26).

The transmission description is divided into eight areas. All the transmissions are described in this manner to make their comparison easier.

1. Torque Converter

The A240L uses a conventional three-element torque converter equipped with a hydraulic converter clutch. The converter clutch control system is fully hydraulic and applies the clutch only in fourth gear (Figure 13–27).

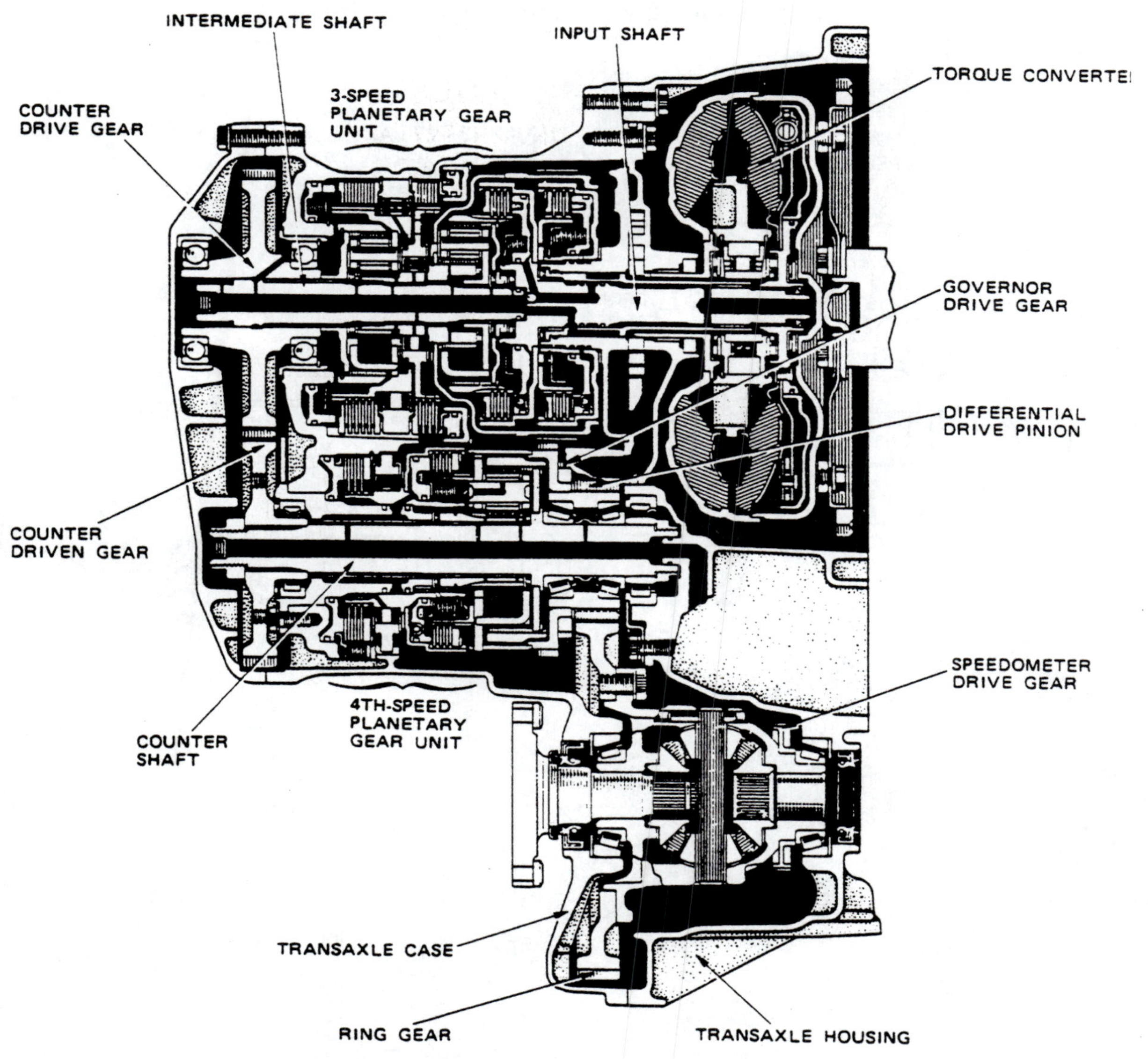

FIGURE 13–25 A240L cross-sectional view. (Courtesy of Toyota)

Counter drive gear overdrives counter driven gear
COUNTER DRIVE GEAR
Revolves as a unit
3-SPEED PLANETARY GEAR UNIT
INPUT SHAFT
DIFF. DRIVE PINIO
4TH-SPEED PLANETARY GEAR UNIT
Revolves as a unit
COUNTER DRIVEN GEAR
Drive pinion is overdriven
Counter drive gear overdrives counter driven gear
COUNTER DRIVE GEAR
Input speed is reduced
3-SPEED PLANETARY GEAR UNIT
INPUT SHAFT
DIFF. DRIVE PINION
4TH-SPEED PLANETARY GEAR UNIT
Input speed is again reduced
COUNTER DRIVEN GEAR
Drive pinion is underdriven

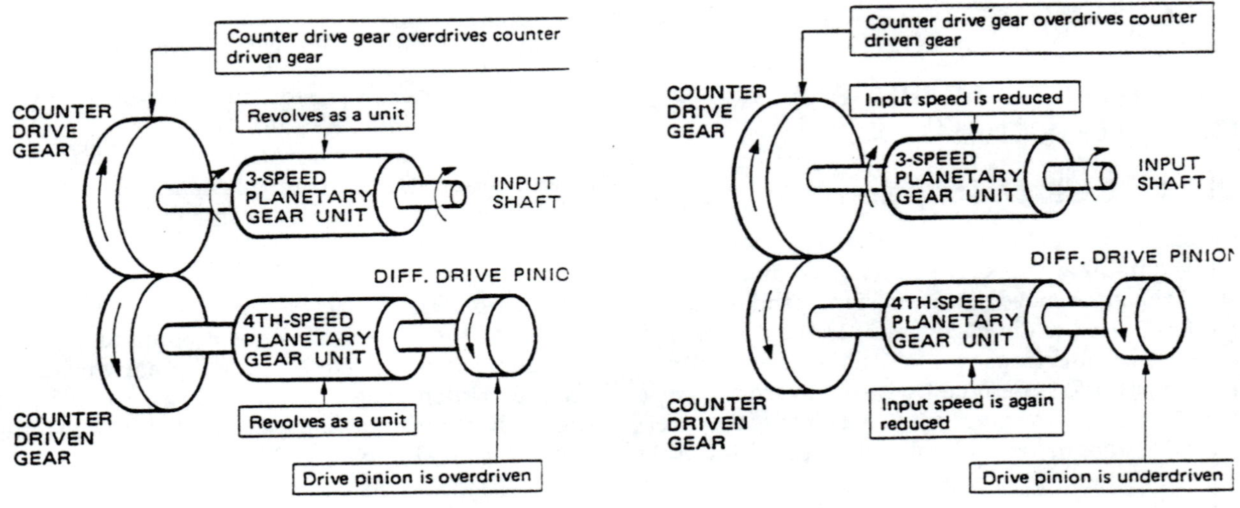

FIGURE 13–26 A240L gear ratios. (Courtesy of Toyota)

FIGURE 13–27 A240L converter clutch. (Courtesy of Toyota)

PUMP IMPELLER
TURBINE
LOCK-UP CLUTCH
FRONT COVER
LINE PRESSURE
CONVERTER PRESSURE
DRAIN
LINE PRESSURE (C3) (FRON 3-4 SHIFT VALVE)
GOVERNOR PRESSURE
TO COOLER
RELAY VALVE
SIGNAL VALVE
TURBINE
PUMP IMPELLER
FRONT COVER
LOCK-UP CLUTCH
STATOR
ONE-WAY CLUTCH
ENGINE
DRIVE PLATE
FRONT COVER
LOCK-UP CLUTCH
TURBINE HUB
INPUT SHAFT

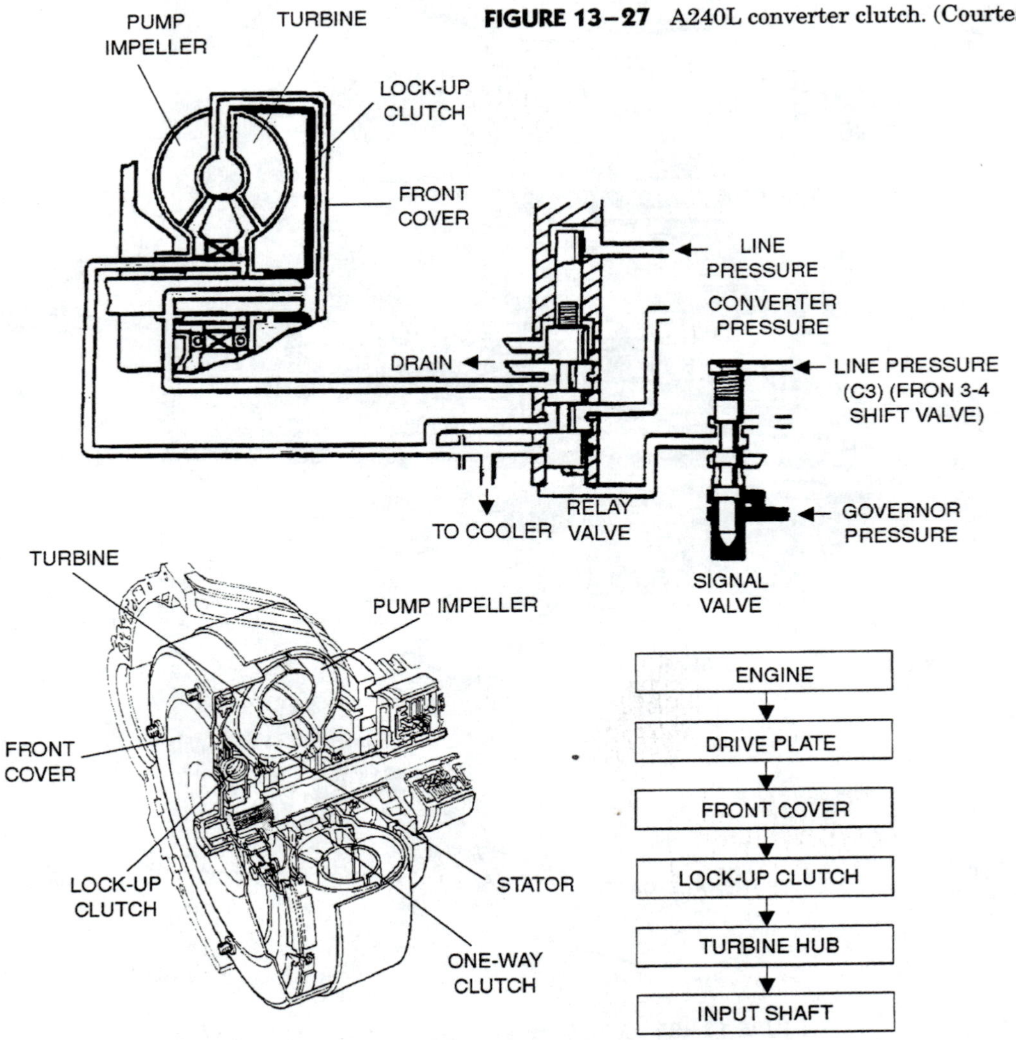

2. Gear Train

The three-speed portion of the transaxle is a Simpson gear set with the same input, reaction, and output members as all the other Simpson gear sets. The three-speed gear train is mounted on the transaxle intermediate shaft. The underdrive (fourth-speed) gear set is mounted on the counter shaft and includes the pinion carrier as the input member, the sun gear as a reaction and input member, and the ring gear as the output member.

3. Coupling Devices

The coupling devices used are the forward clutch (C1), the direct clutch (C2), and the UD direct clutch (C3) (Figure 13–28).

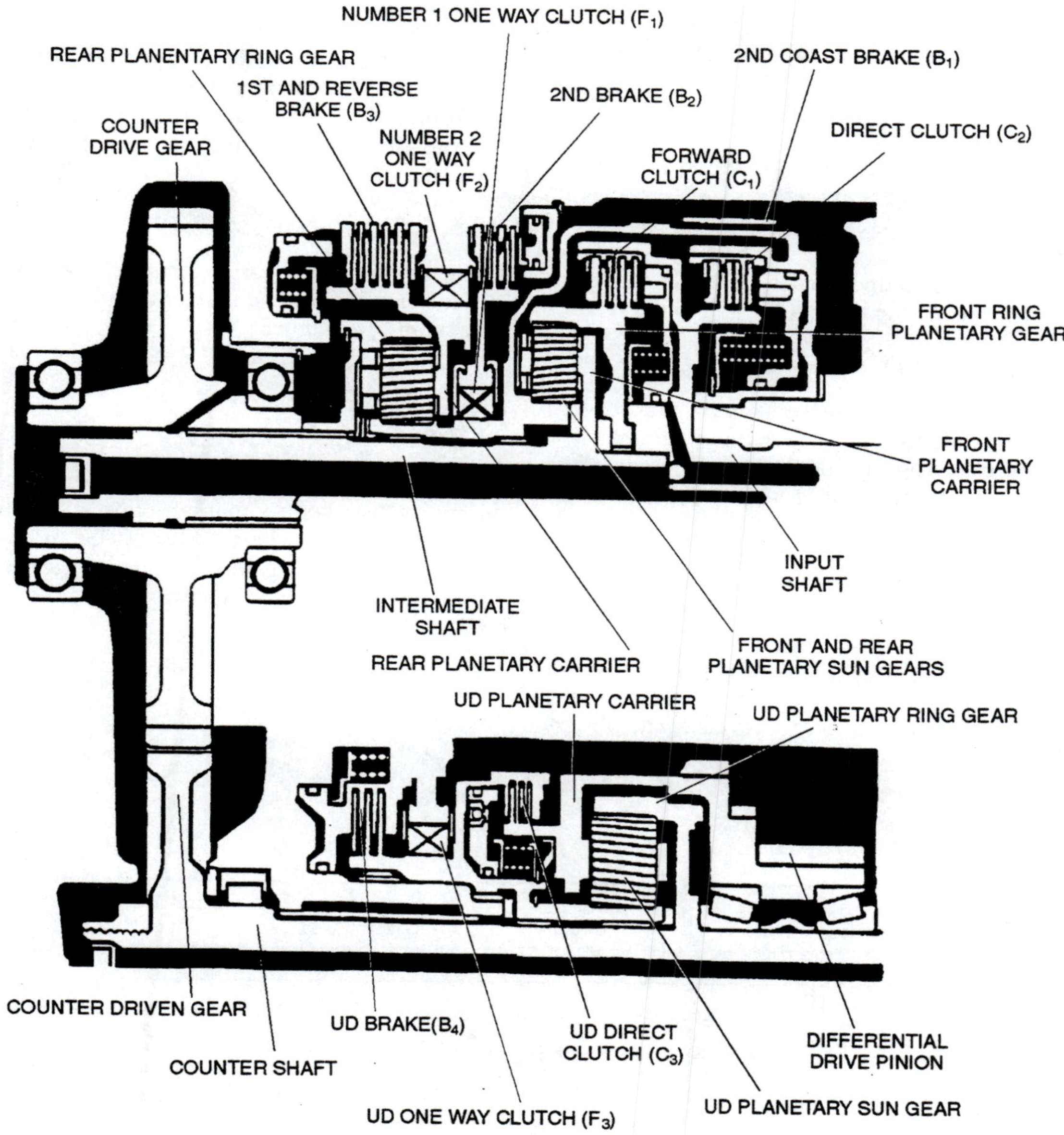

FIGURE 13–28 A240L coupling and holding devices. (Courtesy of Toyota)

4. *Holding Devices*
The holding devices used are the second coast brake (B1), the second brake (B2), the first and reverse brake (B3), the UD brake (B4), the first one-way clutch (F1), the second one-way clutch (F2), and the UD one-way clutch (F3).

5. *Pump*
The oil pump is a gear crescent design, which is mounted in the front of the case next to the torque converter.

6. *Shift Control*
The A-240L shift control system is hydraulic for the first three gears with electronic control of the fourth gear.

7. *Governor*
The governor is the drop in-type, which produces a two-stage governor pressure.

8. *Throttle Valve*
The throttle valve is operated by a cable that connects to the accelerator linkage.

13.4.2 Power Flow

The power flow for the first three gears and reverse is the same as that of any other Simpson gear set. The unique features of this transaxle occur after the Simpson gear set, so this is the area that will be described.

The output of the Simpson gear set drives a counter shaft through a set of counter gears. The counter gears have an overdrive ratio of 0.89:1, which drives the counter shaft faster than the Simpson gear set output. The fourth-speed (underdrive) gear set is mounted on the counter shaft. During the first three gears and reverse, the underdrive (UD) unit is in gear reduction. This is done by driving the pinion carrier as the input member, holding the sun gear as the reaction member with the UD brake (B4) and one-way clutch (F3), and using the ring gear as output. The UD gear set provides a 1.45:1 gear reduction to offset the counter gear overdrive. In fourth gear, the UD direct clutch (C3) is applied, which drives the sun gear as input also, causing a direct drive. The final gear ratios for each gear are shown in the far-right column of Figure 13–29.

13.4.3 Clutch and Band Charts

In this section we provide two clutch and band charts. The first chart, the author's design, uses a standardized format for listing the coupling and holding devices to aid comparison between transmissions. This chart is shown in Figure 13–30. The second chart, the manufacturer's design, which is found in service manuals, is shown in Figure 13–31.

13.4.4 Identification

The shape of the transmission oil pan or its gasket is a quick means of identifying an automatic transmission. In Figure 13–32 you see the pan gasket shape and number of bolt holes for the 240L transaxle.

13.4.5 Components

In this section exploded drawings of the A240L automatic transaxle subassemblies are shown, along with lists of the part names. The manufacturer's parts names are used to eliminate confusion about component names. The drawings to study are as follows:

Exploded view 1, Figure 13–33
Exploded view 2, Figure 13–34
Exploded view 3, Figure 13–35
Oil pump, Figure 13–36

	3-speed Planetary Gear	Counter Gears	4th-speed Planetary Gear	Total Transmission Gear Ratio
1st	2.810	0.892	1.452	3.643
2nd	1.549	↑	↑	2.008
3rd	1.000	↑	↑	1.296
4th	↑	↑	1.000	0.892
Rev.	2.296	↑	1.452	2.977

FIGURE 13–29 Gear ratio chart. (Courtesy of Toyota)

A-240L	DIRECT CLUTCH C2	FORWARD CLUTCH C1	2ND BRAKE B2	1ST & REV BRAKE B3	UD BRAKE B4	UD DIRECT CLUTCH C3	2ND COAST BRAKE B1	#1 ONE-WAY CLUTCH F1	#2 ONE-WAY CLUTCH F2	UD ONE-WAY CLUTCH F3	PARK PAWL	CONVERTER CLUTCH
P					X						X	
N					X							
D1		X			X				X	X		
D2		X	X		X			X		X		
D3	X	X			X					X		
D4	X	X				X						X
1		X		X	X				(X)	X		
2		X	X		X		X	(X)		X		
3	X	X			X					X		
R	X			X	X							

X = APPLIED

(X) = APPLIED, NOT CARRYING LOAD

FIGURE 13–30 A240L clutch and band chart, standardized version.

Shift lever position	Gear position	C_1	C_2	C_3	B_1	B_2	B_3	B_4	F_1	F_2	F_3
P	Parking							○			
R	Reverse		○				○	○			
N	Neutral							○			
D	1st	○						○		○	○
	2nd	○				○		○	○		○
	3rd	○	○			○		○			○
	OD	○	○	○		○					
2	1st	○						○		○	○
	2nd	○			○	○		○	○		○
L	1st	○					○	○		○	○

FIGURE 13–31 A240L clutch and band chart, factory version. (Courtesy of Toyota)

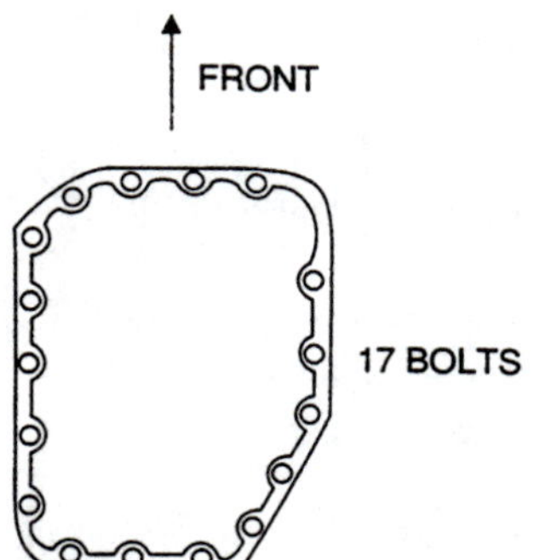

FIGURE 13–32 A240L pan gasket. (Courtesy of Toyota)

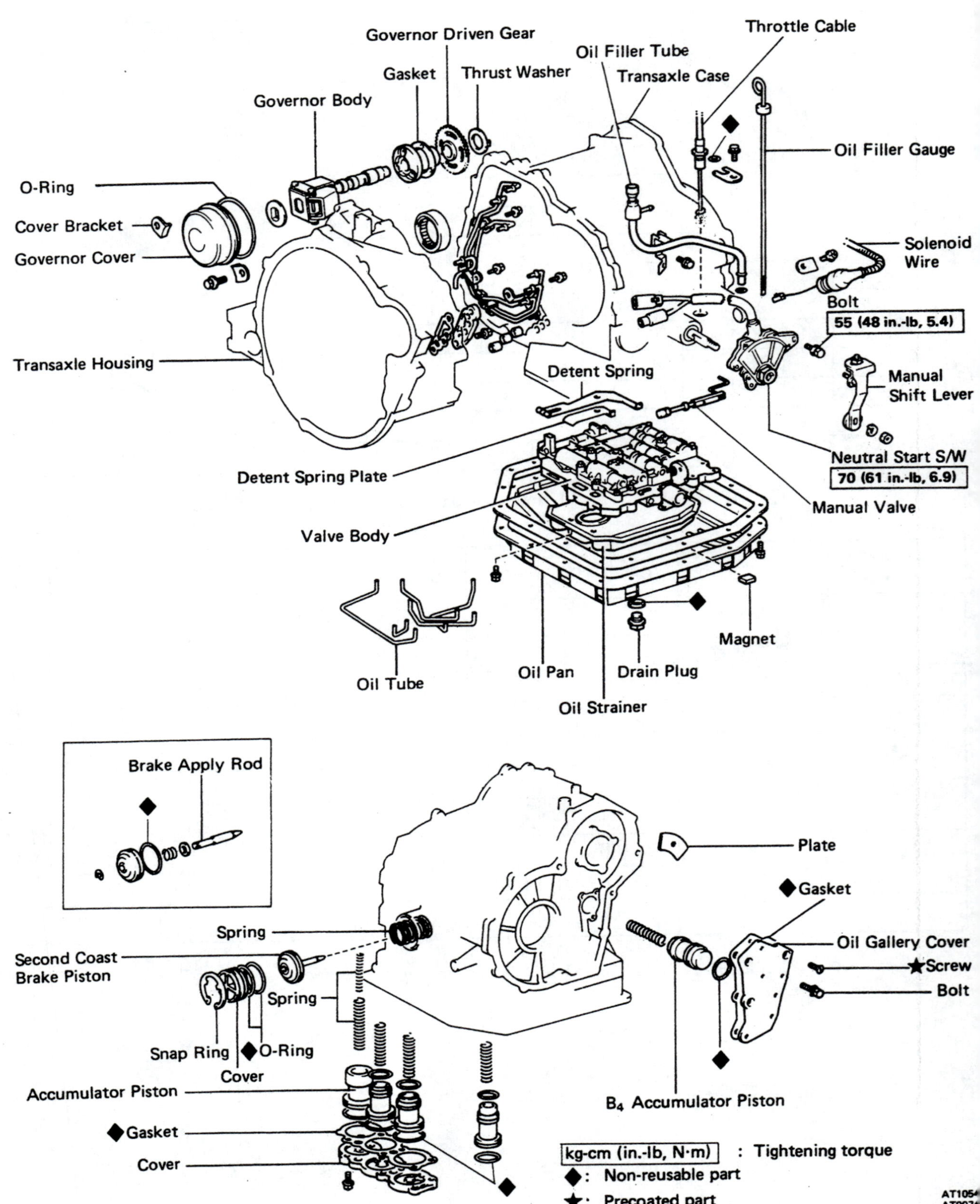

FIGURE 13–33 A240L exploded view 1. (Courtesy of Toyota)

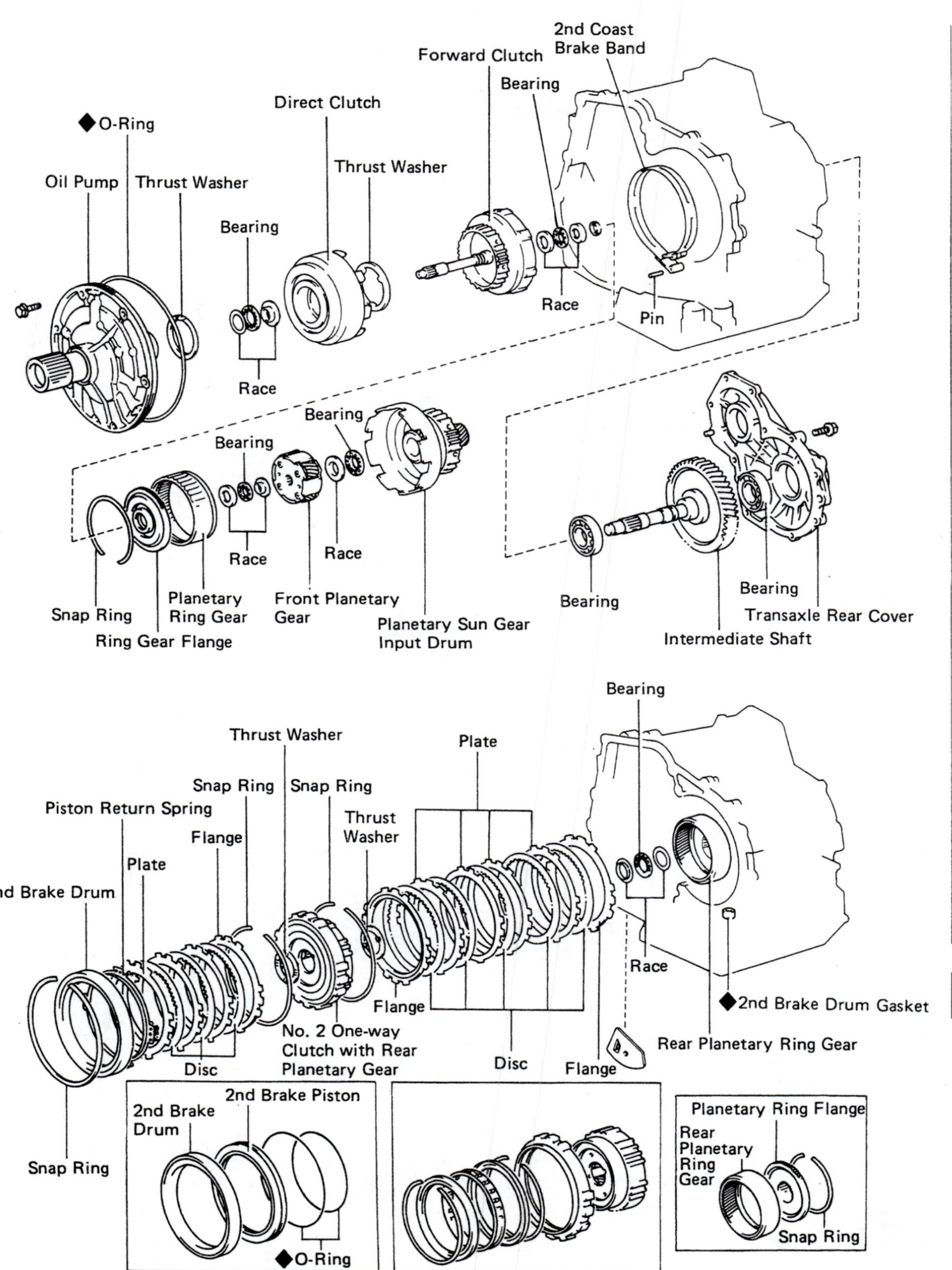

FIGURE 13–34 A240L exploded view 2. (Courtesy of Toyota)

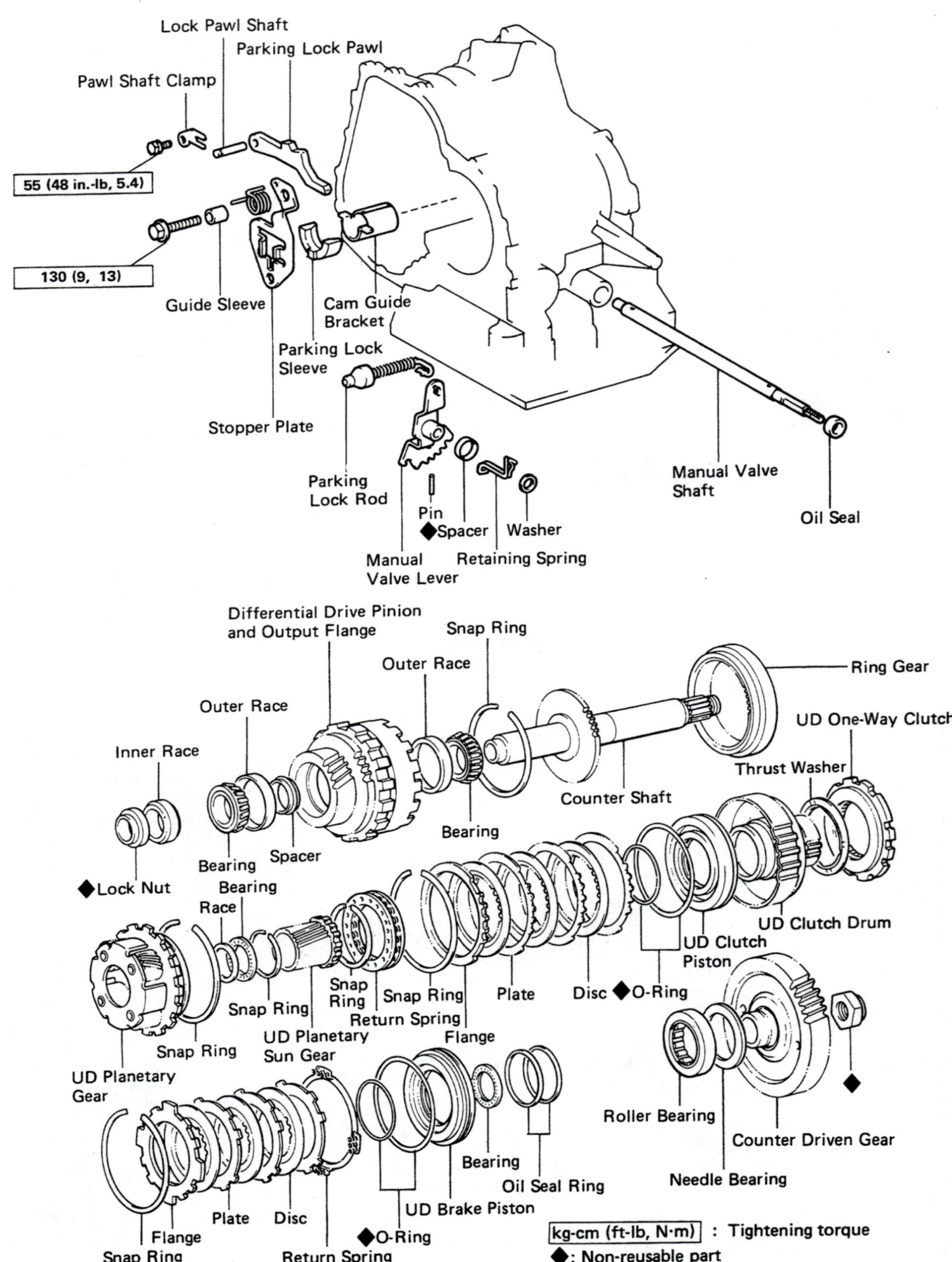

FIGURE 13–35 A240L exploded view 3. (Courtesy of Toyota)

Direct clutch, Figure 13–37
Forward clutch, Figure 13–38
Sun gear, Figure 13–39
Rear planetary gear, Figure 13–40
Underdrive unit, Figure 13–41
Upper valve body, Figure 13–42
Lower valve body, Figure 13–43
Thrust bearing location, Figure 13–44

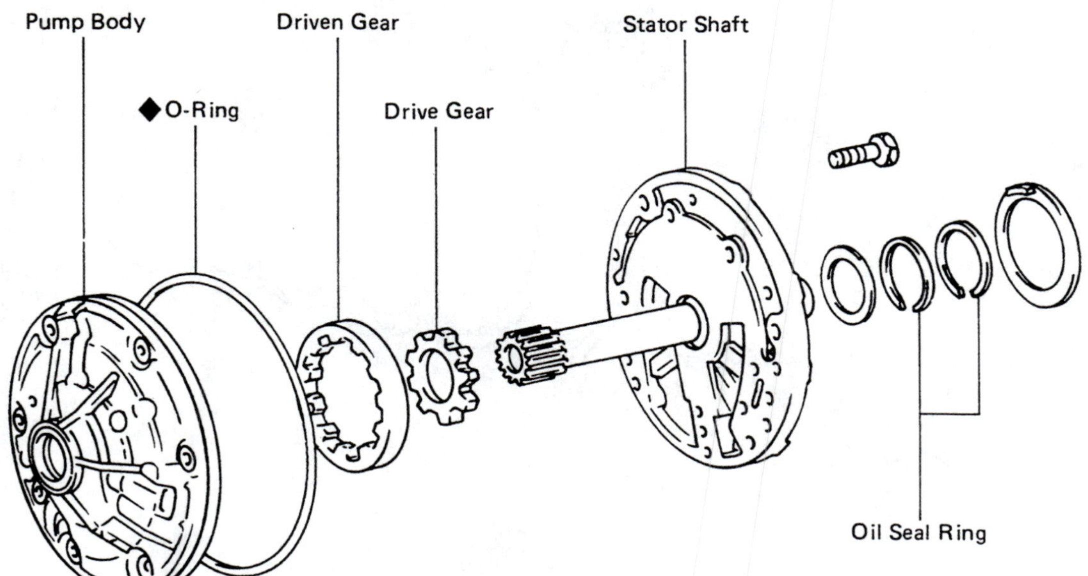

FIGURE 13–36 A240L oil pump. (Courtesy of Toyota)

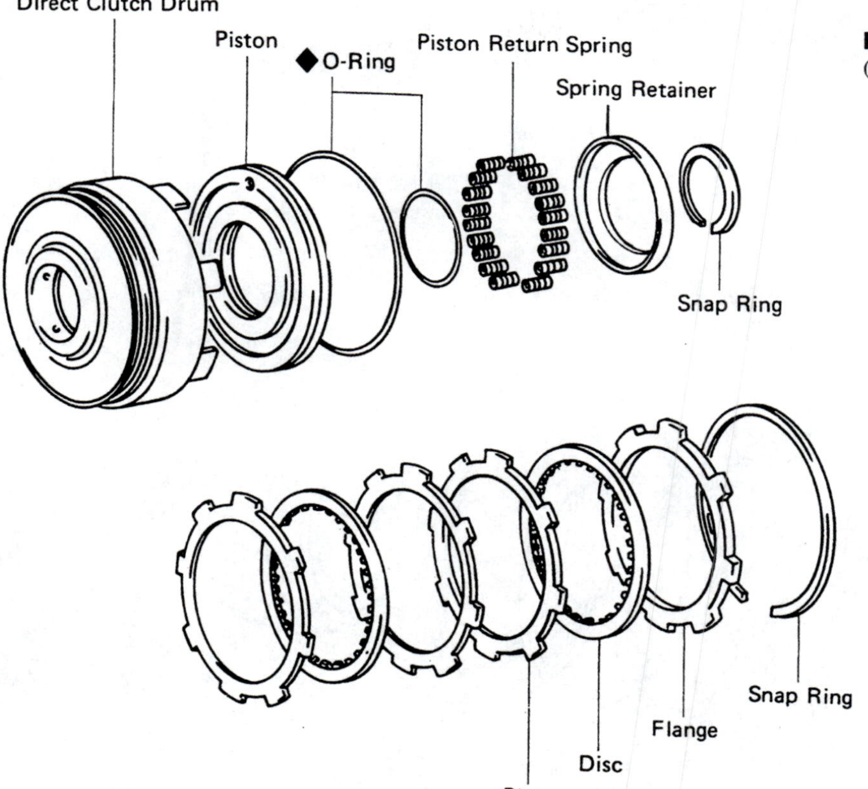

FIGURE 13–37 A240L direct clutch. (Courtesy of Toyota)

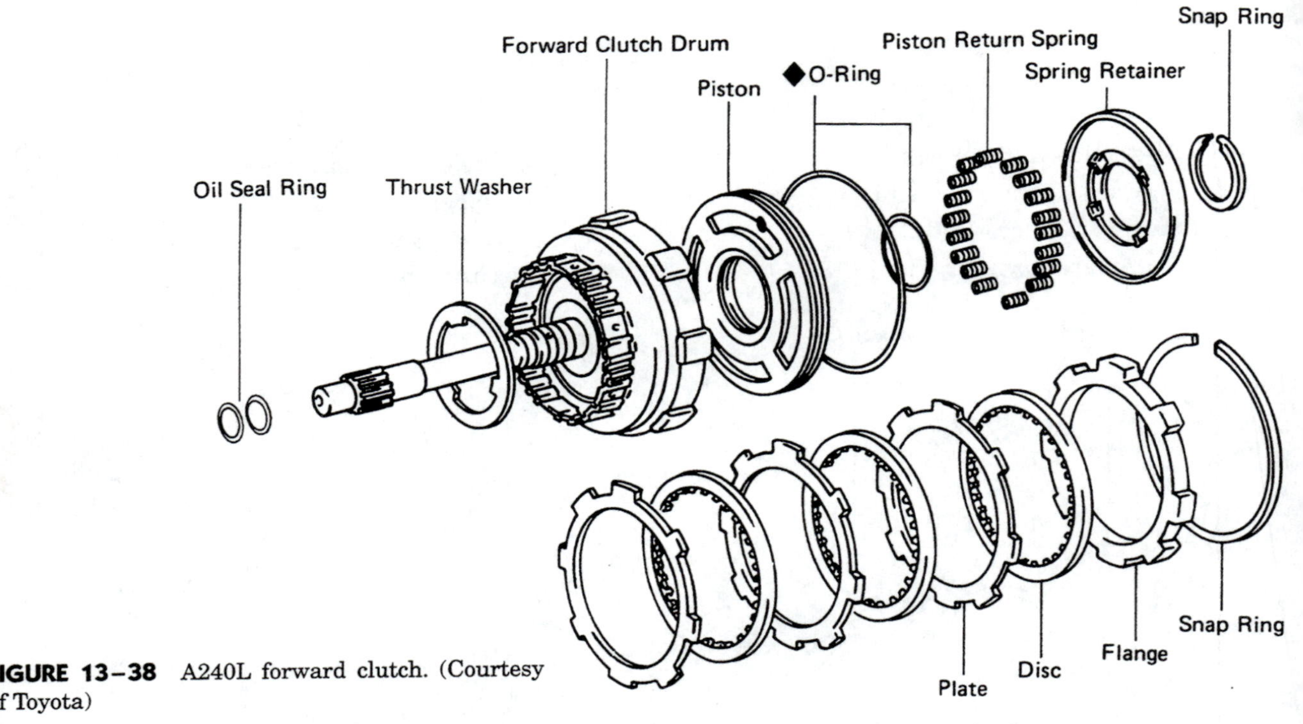

FIGURE 13–38 A240L forward clutch. (Courtesy of Toyota)

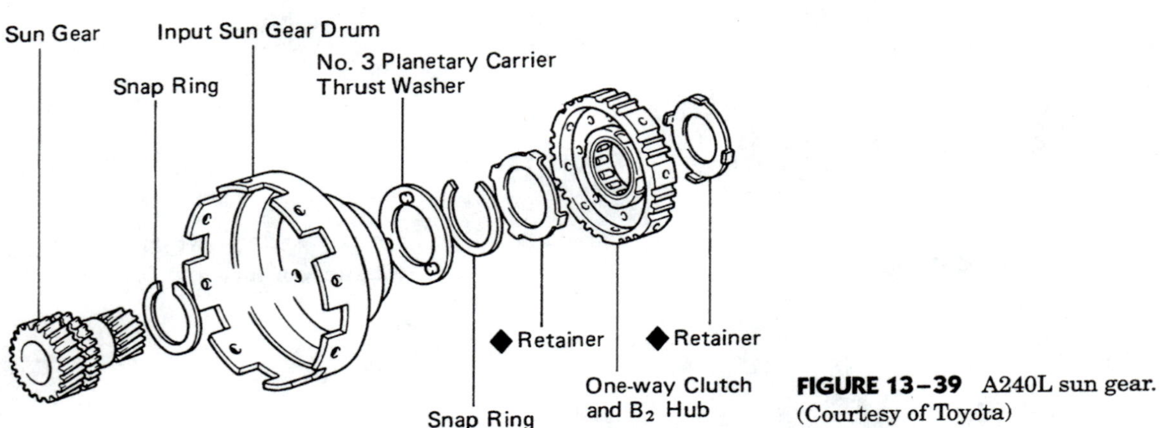

FIGURE 13–39 A240L sun gear. (Courtesy of Toyota)

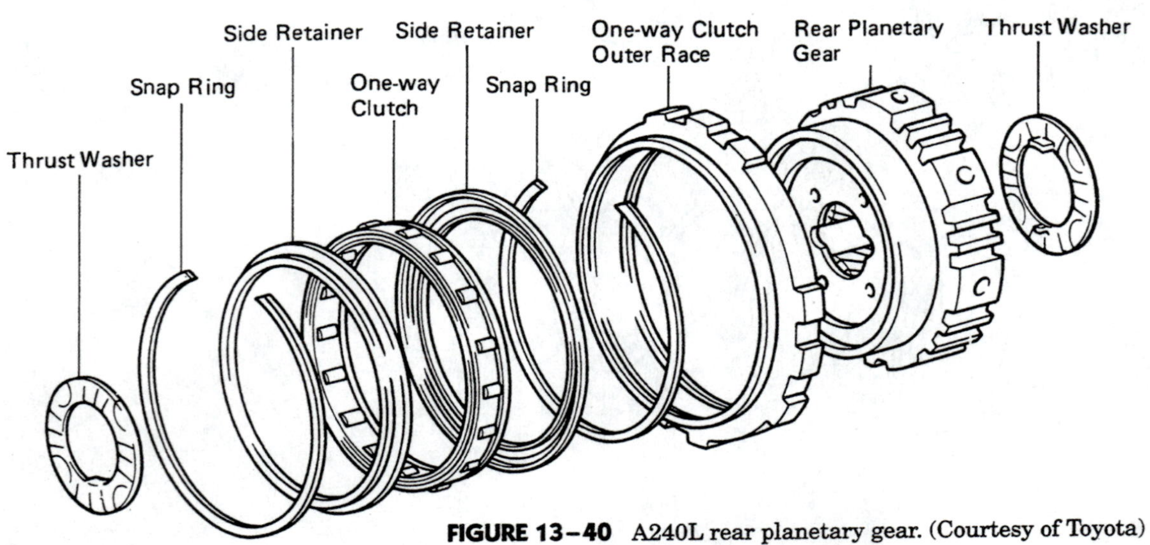

FIGURE 13–40 A240L rear planetary gear. (Courtesy of Toyota)

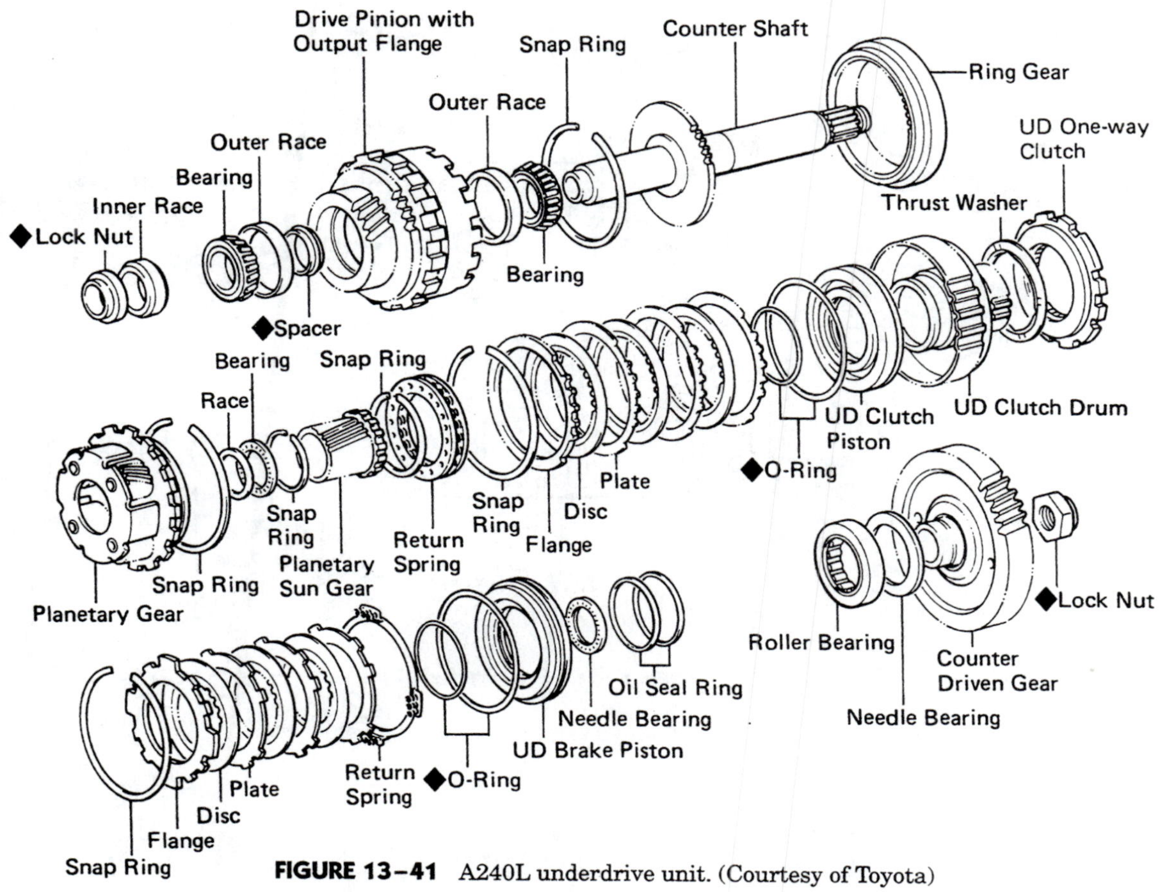

Drive Pinion with Output Flange
Snap Ring
Counter Shaft
Ring Gear
Outer Race
Outer Race
UD One-way Clutch
Bearing
Inner Race
◆Lock Nut
Thrust Washer
Bearing
◆Spacer
Bearing
Snap Ring
Race
UD Clutch Drum
UD Clutch Piston
◆O-Ring
Plate
Snap Ring
Disc
Snap Ring
Return Spring
Flange
Planetary Sun Gear
Snap Ring
Planetary Gear
◆Lock Nut
Roller Bearing
Counter Driven Gear
Oil Seal Ring
Needle Bearing
Needle Bearing
UD Brake Piston
Return Spring
◆O-Ring
Plate
Disc
Flange
Snap Ring

FIGURE 13–41 A240L underdrive unit. (Courtesy of Toyota)

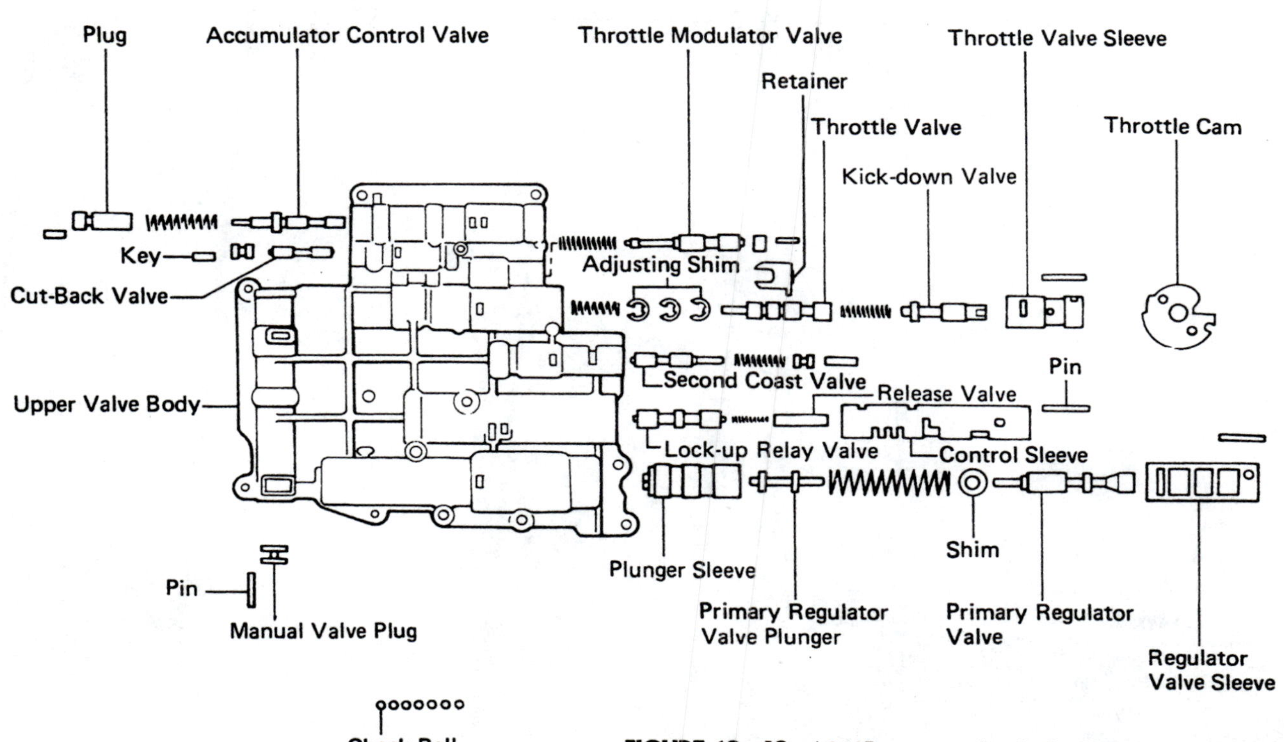

FIGURE 13–42 A240L upper valve body. (Courtesy of Toyota)

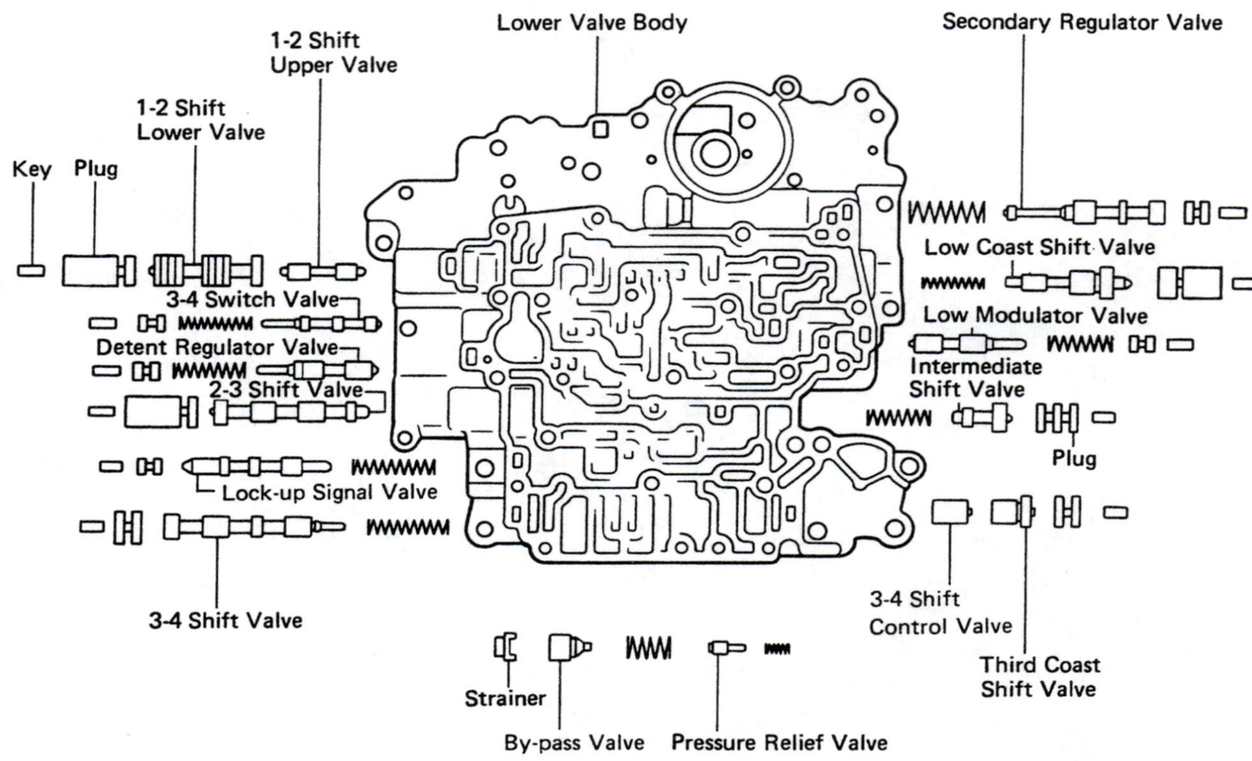

FIGURE 13–43 A240L lower valve body. (Courtesy of Toyota)

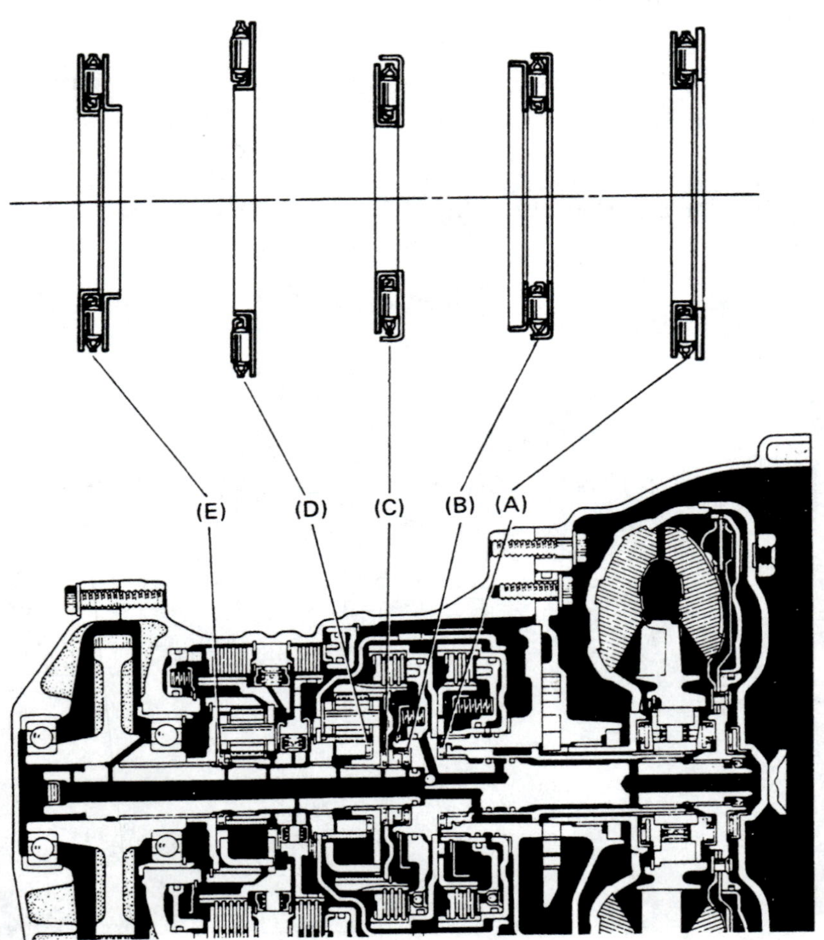

FIGURE 13–44 A240L thrust bearing location. (Courtesy of Toyota)

13.4.6 Pressure Test

One of the key tests in diagnosis is the hydraulic system pressure test. The location of the test points of the 240L transaxle are shown in Figure 13–45. A pressure chart listing the pressure specifications of this transaxle is shown in Figure 13–46.

13.4.7 Air Test

No procedures for air testing are described in the manufacturer's service manual, so each clutch pack should be tested individually as the transaxle is disassembled.

13.4.8 Special Attention

In this section we show and explain various points of special interest about the A240L transaxle. The information presented about each item is included with each illustration.

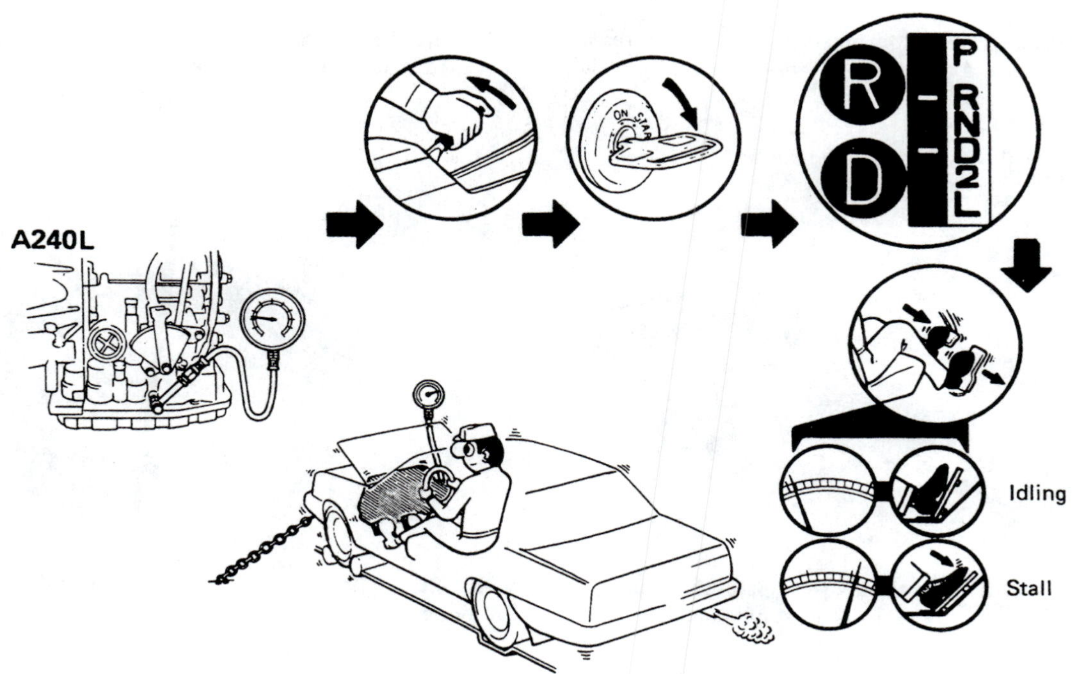

FIGURE 13–45 A240L pressure test. (Courtesy of Toyota)

ATM/ Engine	Line pressure		kg/cm² (psi, kPa)	
	"D" range		"R" range	
	Idling	Stall	Idling	Stall
A240L/4A-C	3.7 – 4.3 (53 – 61, 363 – 422)	9.2 – 10.7 (131 – 152, 902 – 1,049)	5.4 – 7.2 (77 – 102, 530 – 706)	14.4 – 16.8 (205 – 239, 1,412 – 1,648)
A131L/4A-C	3.7 – 4.3 (53 – 61, 363 – 422)	9.2 – 10.7 (131 – 152, 902 – 1,049)	5.4 – 7.2 (77 – 102, 530 – 706)	14.4 – 16.8 (205 – 239, 1,412 – 1,648)
A130L/1C	3.7 – 4.3 (53 – 61, 363 – 422)	8.5 – 10.0 (121 – 142, 834 – 981)	5.4 – 7.2 (77 – 102, 530 – 706)	13.2 – 15.6 (188 – 222, 1,294 – 1,530)

FIGURE 13–46 A240L pressure chart. (Courtesy of Toyota)

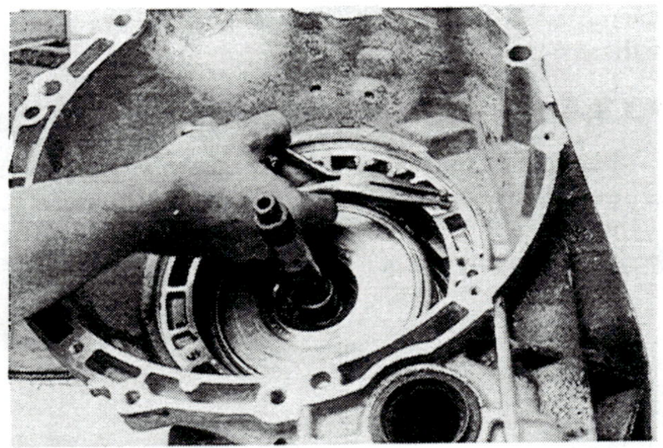

FIGURE A240L–1 This pin must be removed to release the second coast brake band.

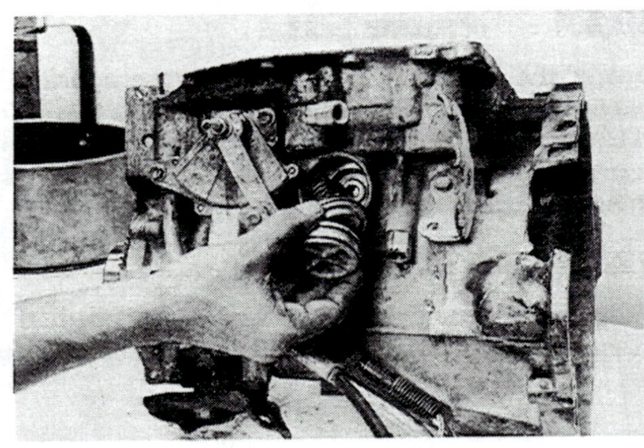

FIGURE A240L–2 All the seals and components of the second coast brake servo must be checked.

FIGURE A240L–3 The three-speed planetary sun gear, one-way clutch, and brake discs must be inspected.

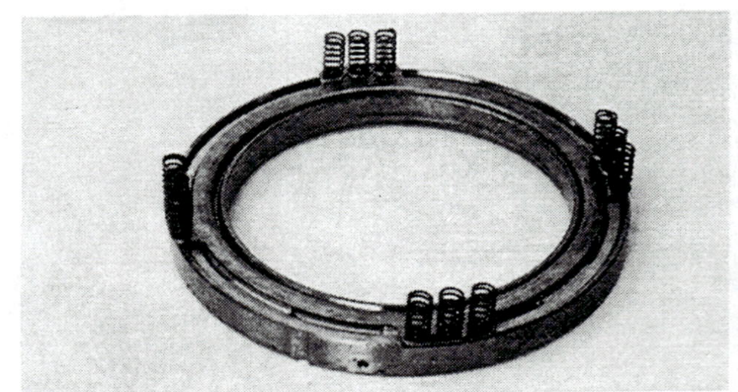

FIGURE A240L–4 The low–reverse brake piston has a unique design.

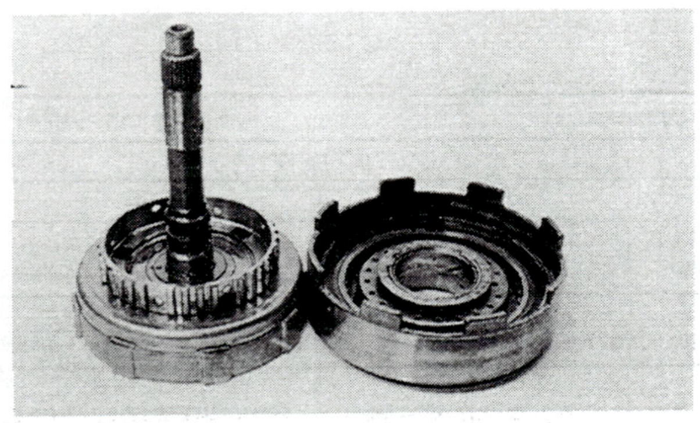

FIGURE A240L–5 All contact areas of the forward clutch and direct clutch should be inspected for wear.

FIGURE A240L–6 The oil pump body must be checked for wear.

FIGURE A240L–7 The oil pump gears have a unique design.

FIGURE A240L–8 The drop-in governor is easily removed.

FIGURE A240L–9 Retainer supporting the differential carrier.

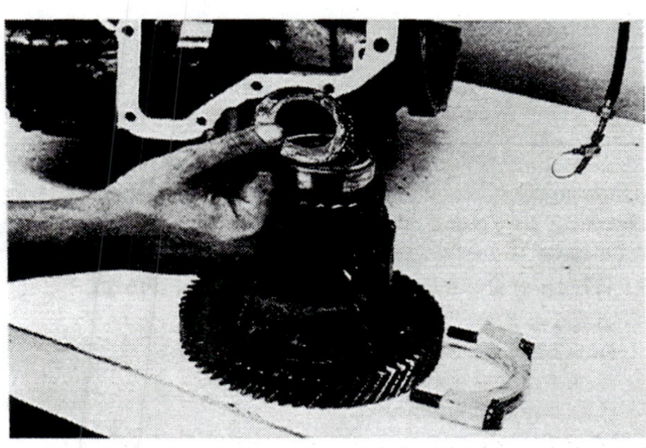

FIGURE A240L–10 Shims are used to preload the carrier bearings

FIGURE A240L–11 The gearing of the counter gears provides an overdrive ratio.

SUMMARY

The transmissions/transaxles profiled in this chapter are all produced by Japanese manufacturers and in many ways are similar in design to our domestic transmissions. The complex overdrive transaxles with electronic shift controls are equal to our best domestic products. The automatic transmissions/transaxles produced by the Asian manufacturers are unique in many ways and provide a challenge to the student technician. They are summarized in Figure 13–47.

ASIAN IMPORTS	TORQUE CONVERTER	GEAR TRAIN	COUPLING DEVICES	HOLDING DEVICES	PUMP	SHIFT CONTROL	GOVERNOR	THROTTLE VALVE
RL4 FWD, 3 SP.	3-ELEMENT HYDRAULIC CONVERTER CLUTCH	INTER-CONNECTED PLANETARIES	REVERSE CLUTCH HIGH CLUTCH LOW CLUTCH	BAND BRAKE LOW-REVERSE BRAKE LOW ONE-WAY CLUTCH	VANE	HYDRAULIC & ELECTRONIC	DROP IN	CABLE
A240L FWD 4 SP.	3-ELEMENT HYDRAULIC CONVERTER CLUTCH	SIMPSON GEAR SET PLUS SIMPLE PLANETARY GEAR SET	FORWARD CLUTCH DIRECT CLUTCH UD DIRECT CLUTCH	SECOND COAST BRAKE SECOND BRAKE FIRST & REV BRAKE UD BRAKE FIRST ONE-WAY CLUTCH SECOND ONE-WAY CLUTCH UD ONE-WAY CLUTCH	GEAR/CRESCENT	HYDRAULIC & ELECTRONIC	DROP IN	CABLE

FIGURE 13–47 Asian imports summary comparison chart.

SELF-TEST

Before going on to the next chapter, complete the self-test according to your instructor's directions. Read carefully and choose the best answer.

1. Which of the following uses a vane oil pump?
   - **a.** RL4
   - **b.** A240L
   - **c.** All of the above
   - **d.** None of the above
2. Which of the following uses a gear crescent pump?
   - **a.** RL4
   - **b.** A240L
   - **c.** All of the above
   - **d.** None of the above
3. Which transaxles use electronic shift controls?
   - **a.** RL4
   - **b.** A-240L
   - **c.** Both a and b
   - **d.** Neither a nor b
4. Which of the following uses a converter clutch?
   - **a.** A240L
   - **b.** RL4
   - **c.** Both a and b
   - **d.** Neither a nor b
5. Which transaxle uses an underdrive gear set?
   - **a.** RL4
   - **b.** A240L
   - **c.** All of the above
   - **d.** None of the above
6. Which of the following uses Dexron II ATF?
   - **a.** RL4
   - **b.** A240L
   - **c.** All of the above
   - **d.** None of the above
7. Which of the following uses a drop-in governor?
   - **a.** RL4
   - **b.** A240L
   - **c.** Both a and b
   - **d.** Neither a nor b
8. Which of the following uses a vacuum modulator?
   - **a.** A-240L
   - **b.** RL4
   - **c.** Both a and b
   - **d.** Neither a nor b

Chapter 14

EUROPEAN IMPORTS

14.1 PERFORMANCE OBJECTIVES

After studying this chapter, you should have fulfilled the following performance objectives by being able to:

1. List the European transmissions/transaxles described in this chapter.
2. Describe the basic components of each transmission/transaxle.
3. Describe the power flow in each gear position, including which coupling and holding devices are applied, for each transmission/transaxle.
4. Write a clutch and band chart for each transmission/transaxle listed in the chapter.
5. Complete the self-test with at least the minimum score required by your instructor.

14.2 OVERVIEW

The two automatic transaxles profiled in this chapter are the Volkswagen 087 and the Renault MB-1. Volkswagen is the largest European automobile manufacturer, so the 087 transaxle is profiled to provide an example of German engineering. The Renault MB-1 is produced in France and is one of the earliest electronically controlled transaxles to be produced. The European imports include many unique transmission designs that are used in limited-production vehicles. A general knowledge of these unique transmissions is not necessary for the student technician at this time. For this reason, the chapter is limited to the widely used Volkswagen and Renault transaxles. Many of the design features of these transaxles are similar to those of domestic transmissions, with both using a Simpson gear set. Both transaxles also use Dexron II ATF.

14.3 VOLKSWAGEN 087: FWD THREE-SPEED TRANSMISSION

14.3.1 Basic Description

The VW 087 is technically a transmission because the transmission section and the final drive section bolt together to form a transaxle. The VW 087 is an extremely compact transmission, being designed for use in a small vehicle (Figure 14–1).

The transmission description is divided into eight areas. All the transmissions are described in this manner to make their comparison easier.

1. Torque Converter

The VW 087 uses a conventional three-element torque converter with no converter clutch. The back side of the torque converter has air ducts that cause an airflow across the back of the housing to cool the converter and fluid (Figure 14–2).

2. Gear Train

The VW 087 uses a Simpson three-speed gear set. The gear train is arranged with the output gear next to the torque converter and the pump and input clutches at the other end of the gear train. A hollow turbine shaft drives the input clutch hub. As with any Simpson gear set, the front ring gear and sun gear are the input, the rear pinion carrier and sun gear are the reaction members, and the front pinion carrier and rear ring gear are the output.

3. Coupling Devices

The holding devices used in the VW 087 are the second-gear brake band, which holds the sun gear, the first/reverse brake (clutch), which holds the rear pinion carrier, and the first-gear one-way clutch, which also holds the rear pinion carrier.

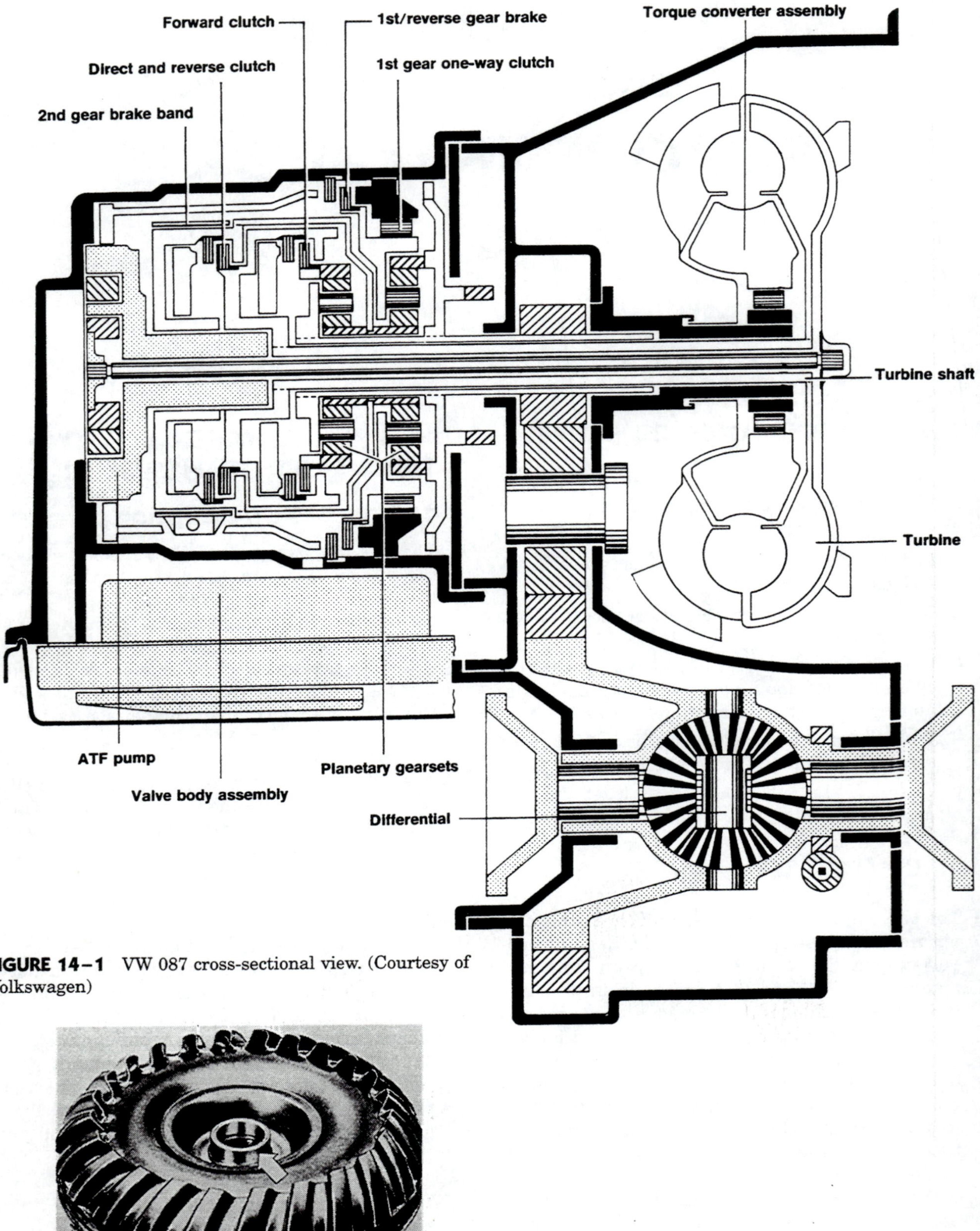

Forward clutch
1st/reverse gear brake
Torque converter assembly
Direct and reverse clutch
1st gear one-way clutch
2nd gear brake band
Turbine shaft
Turbine
ATF pump
Planetary gearsets
Valve body assembly
Differential

FIGURE 14–1 VW 087 cross-sectional view. (Courtesy of Volkswagen)

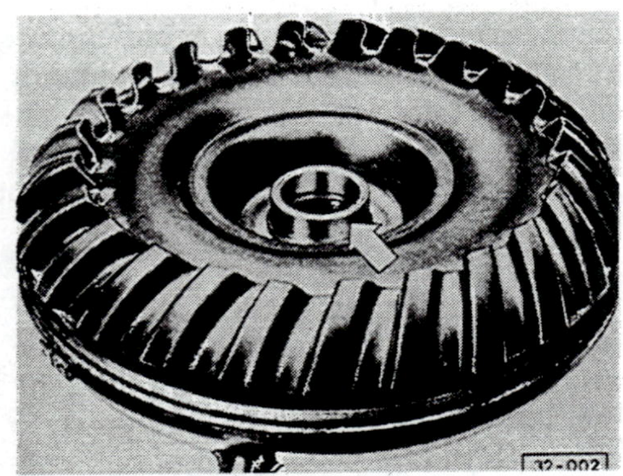

FIGURE 14–2 VW 087 torque converter with cooling ducts. (Courtesy of Volkswagen)

4. Pump

The oil pump, of gear crescent design, is mounted in the back end of the transmission. The pump is driven by a drive shaft that runs in the hollow turbine shaft and is splined to the converter housing at one end and the pump drive plate at the other.

5. Shift Control

The shift control system of the VW 087 is fully hydraulic with no electronic assistance.

6. Governor

The governor, of drop-in type, is mounted in the bell housing (Figure 14–3). The governor is a single-action design and is easily serviced.

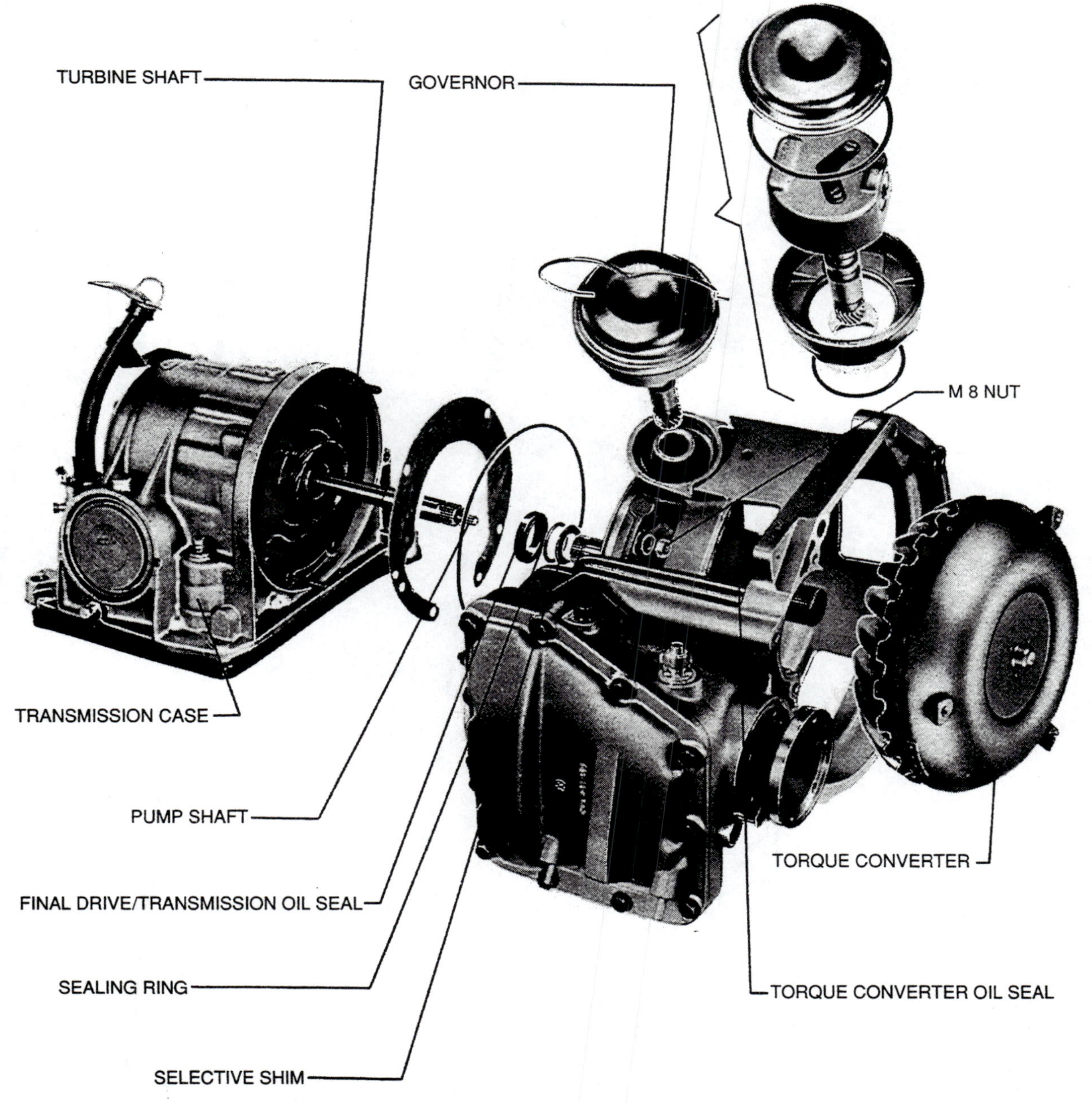

FIGURE 14–3 VW 087 governor. (Courtesy of Volkswagen)

7. *Throttle Valve*
The throttle valve is located in the valve body and is operated in a unique way. The accelerator pedal is connected by the accelerator cable directly to the throttle valve lever on the transmission. The throttle cable then connects the transmission lever to the carburetor (Figure 14–4).

14.3.2 Power Flow

The power flow is described by stating the coupling and holding device action (applied, or holding) on the members of the planetary gear set (sun gear, pinion carrier, and ring gear) in each gear range of the transmission.

1. *Neutral (N)*
In neutral all the coupling and holding devices are released and only the turbine shaft is turning, along with the input clutch hub (Figure 14–5).

2. *First Gear (D1)*
In first gear the forward clutch is applied, which drives the front ring gear. The rear pinion carrier is held by the one-way clutch, making it the reaction

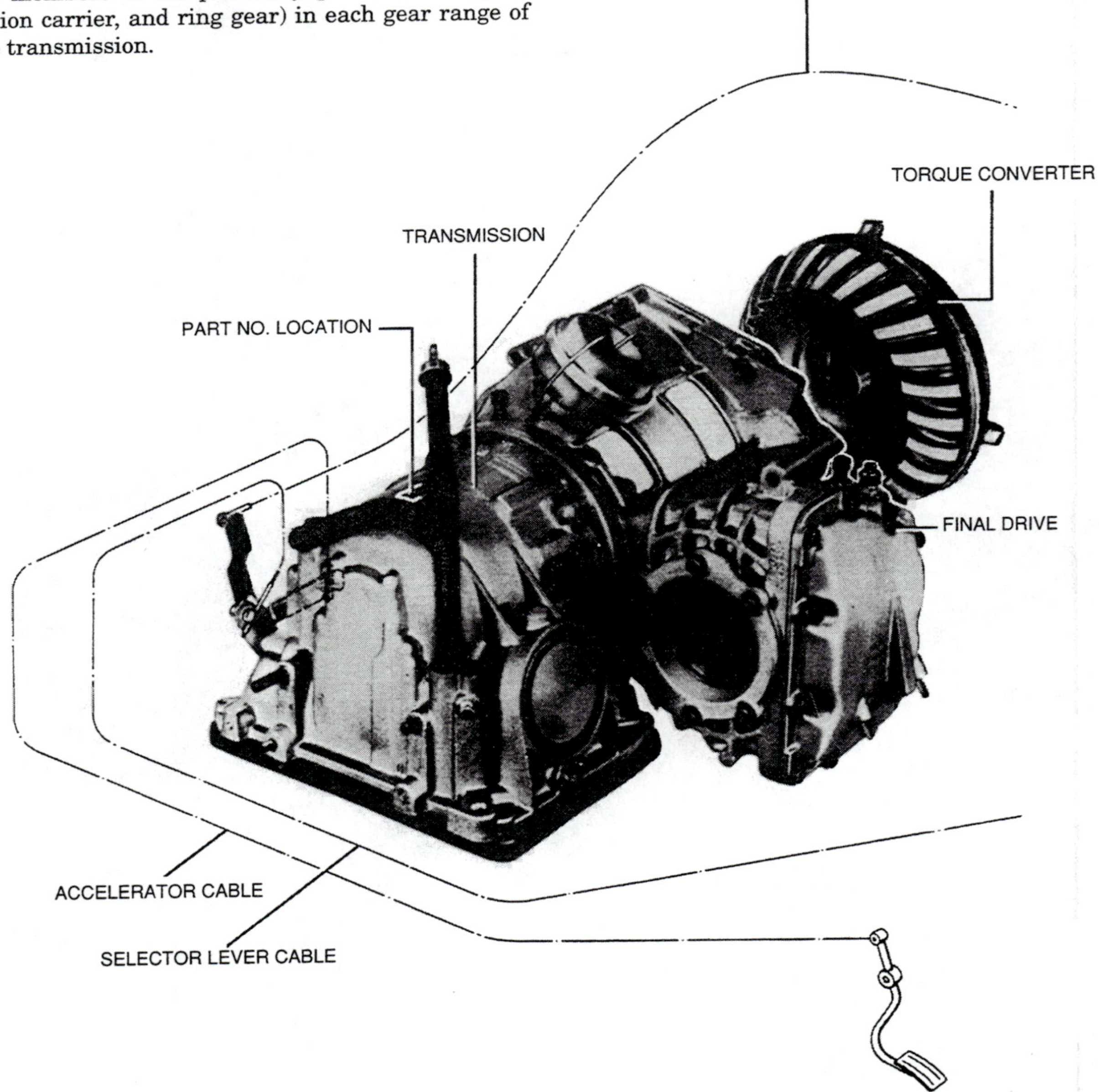

FIGURE 14–4 VW 087 throttle cables. (Courtesy of Volkswagen)

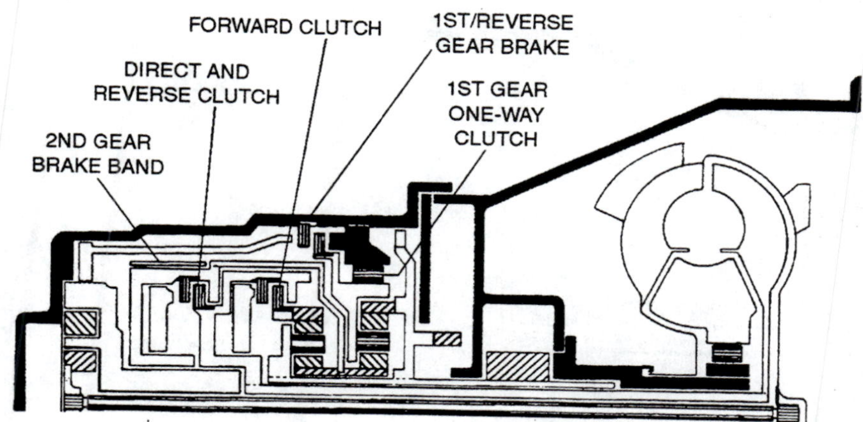

FIGURE 14–5 VW 087 in neutral gear. (Courtesy of Volkswagen)

member, and the rear ring gear is the output member (Figure 14–6). In manual first gear the first reverse brake (clutch) is also applied.

3. *Second Gear (D2)*
In second gear the forward clutch is still applied, driving the front ring gear. The second-gear brake band is also applied to hold the sun gear as the reaction member, and the front pinion carrier is the output member (Figure 14–7).

4. *Third Gear (D3)*
In third gear the forward clutch is still driving the front ring gear, and the direct and reverse clutch is also applied to drive the sun gear. With the sun gear and front ring gear driven at the same speed, the planetary gear set will produce a direct drive (Figure 14–8).

5. *Reverse Gear (R)*
In reverse gear the direct and reverse clutch is applied and driving the sun gear. The first/reverse brake is applied, which holds the rear pinion carrier as the reaction member, causing the rear ring gear to be driven in the reverse direction of input (Figure 14–9).

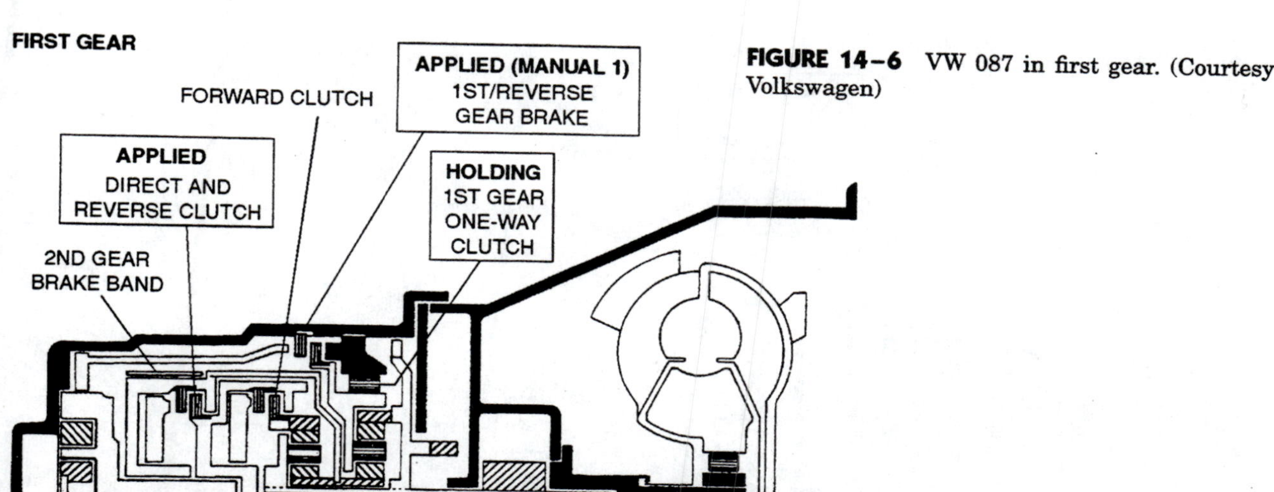

FIGURE 14–6 VW 087 in first gear. (Courtesy of Volkswagen)

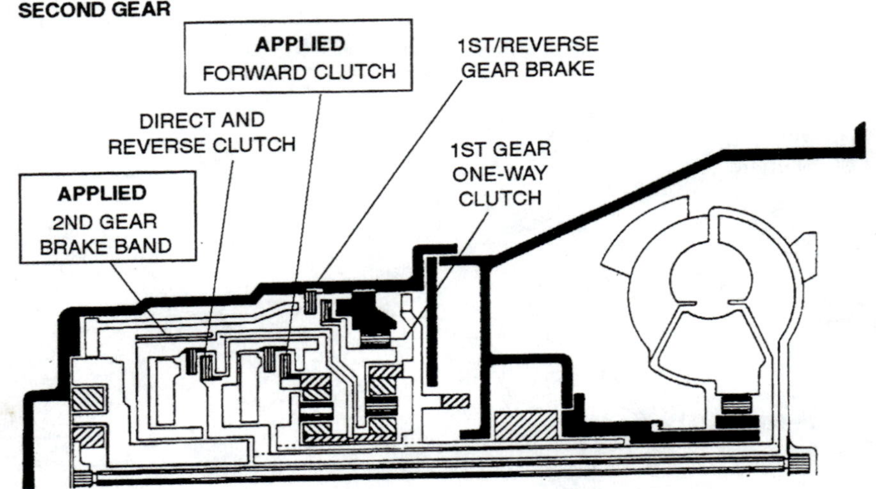

FIGURE 14–7 VW 087 in second gear. (Courtesy of Volkswagen)

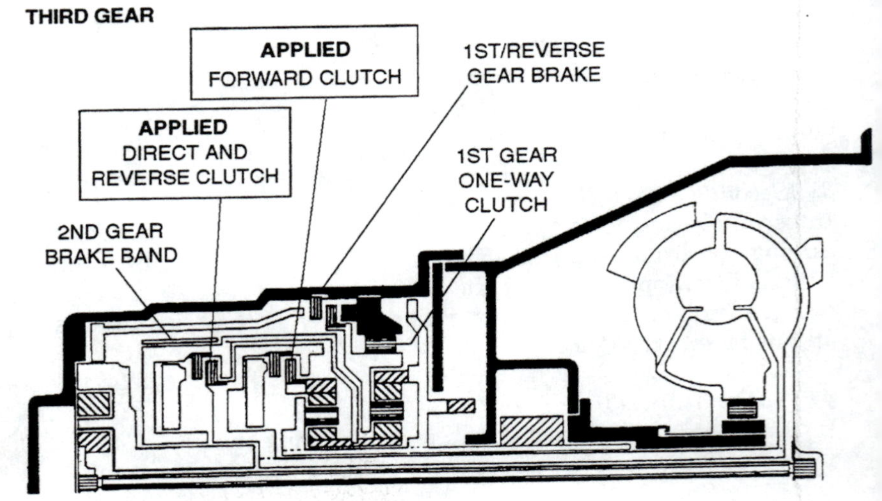

FIGURE 14–8 VW 087 in third gear. (Courtesy of Volkswagen)

FIGURE 14–9 VW 087 in reverse gear (Courtesy of Volkswagen)

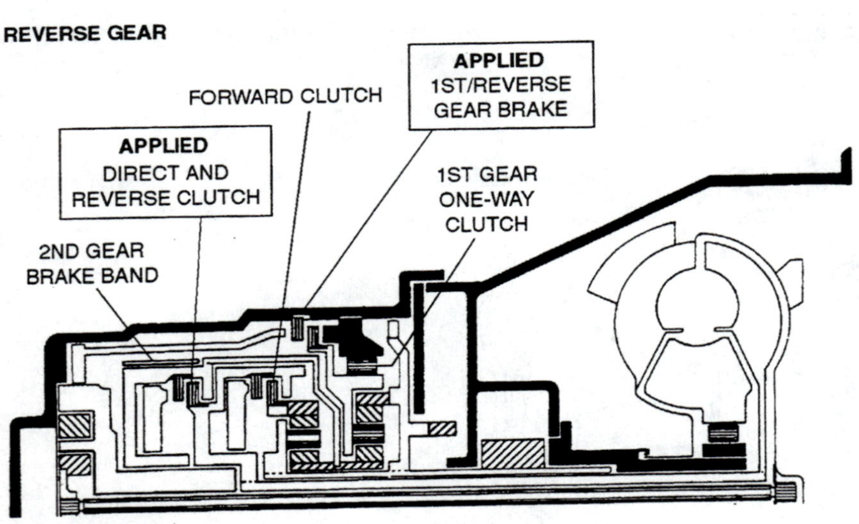

14.3.3 Clutch and Band Charts

In this section we provide two clutch and band charts. The first chart, the author's design, uses a standardized format for listing the coupling and holding devices, to aid comparison between transmissions. This chart is shown in Figure 14–10. The second chart, the manufacturer's design, which is found in service manuals, is shown in Figure 14–11.

14.3.4 Identification

The shape of the transmission oil pan or its gasket is a quick means of identifying an automatic transmission. In Figure 14–12 you see the pan gasket shape and number of bolt holes for the Volkswagen 087 transaxle.

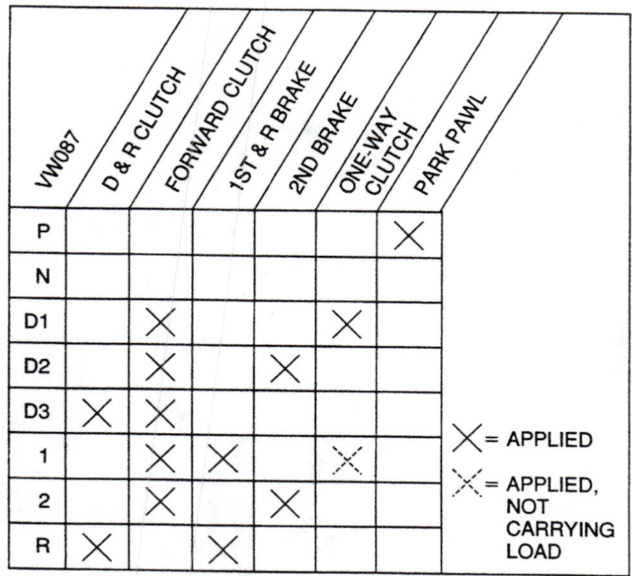

FIGURE 14–10 VW 087 clutch and band chart, standardized version.

Selector lever position	1	2 or D	2 or D	D	R
Gears	1st	1st	2nd	3rd	Reverse
Forward clutch	applied	applied	applied	applied	released
D + R clutch	released	released	released	applied	applied
1st + R gear brake plates	applied	released	released	released	applied
2nd gear brake band	released	released	applied	released	released
One-way clutch	inactive	holding	overrun	overrun	inactive

FIGURE 14–11 VW 087 clutch and band chart, factory version. (Courtesy of Volkswagen)

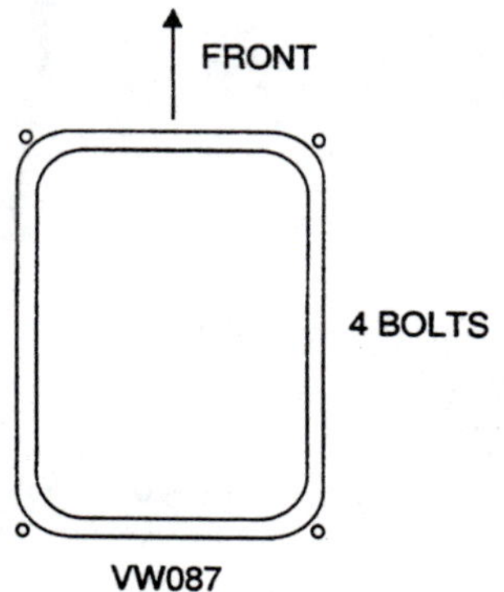

FIGURE 14–12 VW 087 pan gasket.

This pan gasket is unique in that it is a large O-ring which fits into a groove in the transmission case. Because of this gasket and the edge strength of the oil pan, only four bolts are used.

14.3.5 Components

In this section exploded drawings of the Volkswagen 087 transaxle subassemblies are shown, along with lists of the part names. The manufacturer's parts names are used to eliminate confusion about the component names. The drawings to study are as follows:

Transaxle parts, Figure 14–13

Exploded view, Figure 14–14

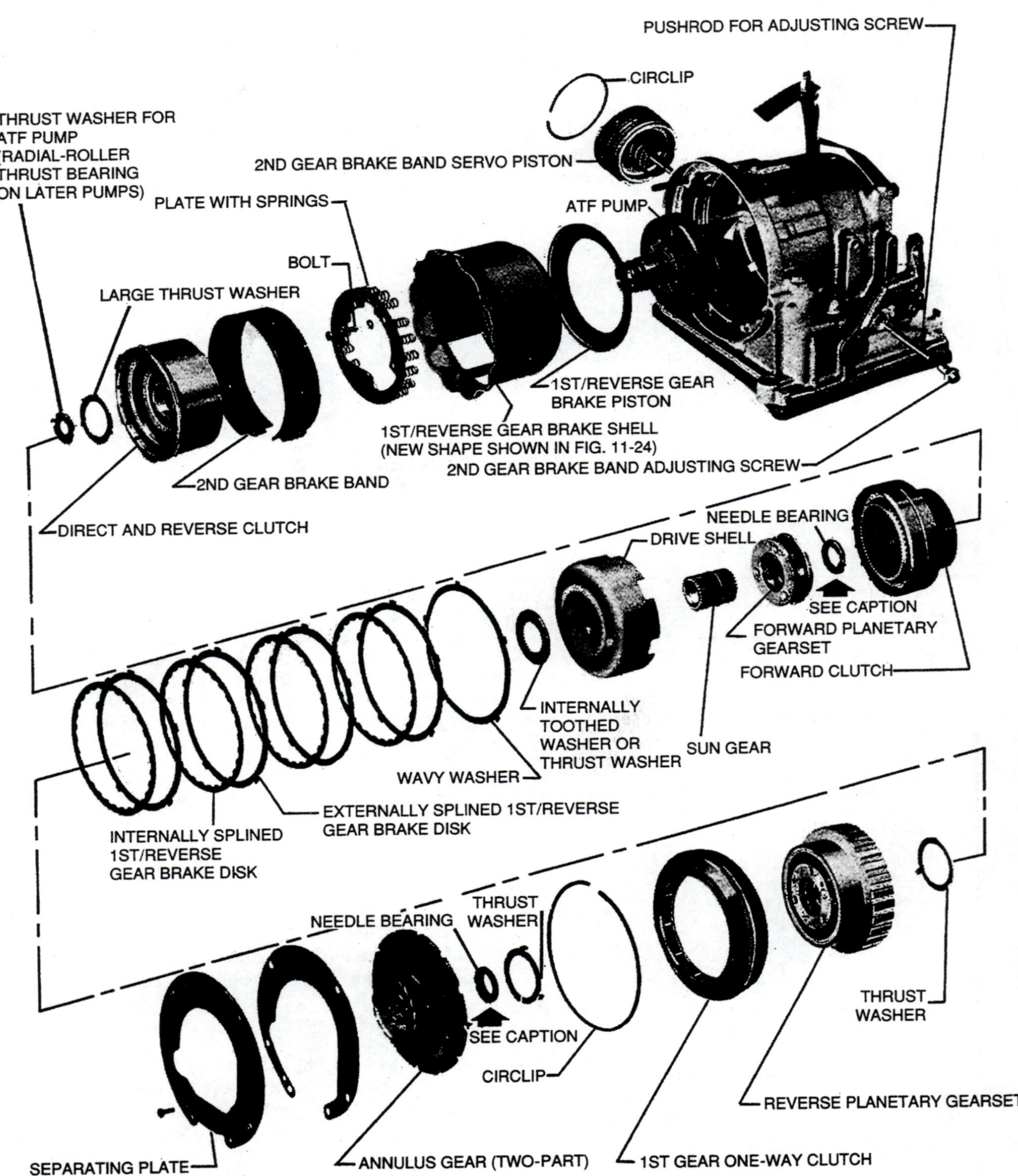

FIGURE 14–13 VW 087 transaxle parts. (Courtesy of Volkswagen)

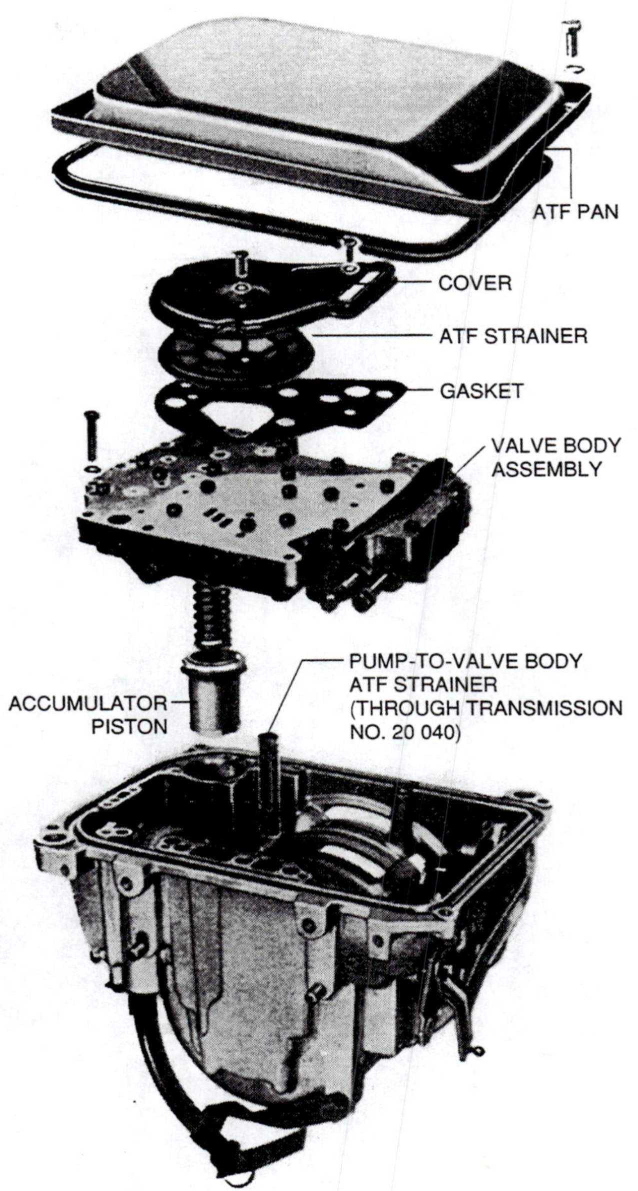

FIGURE 14–14 VW 087 exploded view. (Courtesy of Volkswagen)

Valve body assembly, Figure 14–15
Governor, Figure 14–16
Second-gear servo, Figure 14–17
Oil pump, Figure 14–18
Direct and reverse clutch, Figure 14–19
Forward clutch, Figure 14–20
First-gear one-way clutch, Figure 14–21
Internal linkage, Figure 14–22

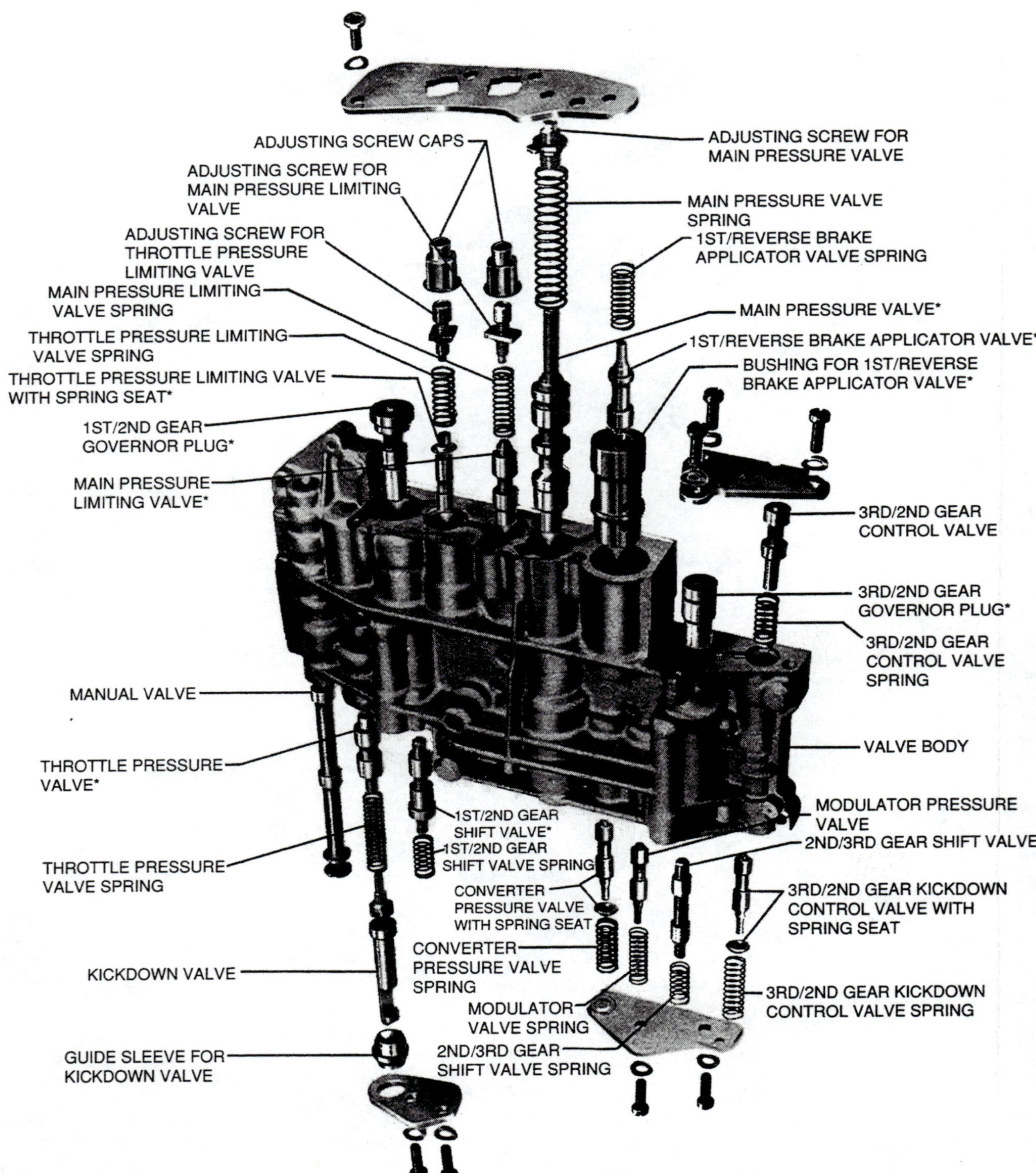

FIGURE 14–15 VW 087 valve body assembly. (Courtesy of Volkswagen)

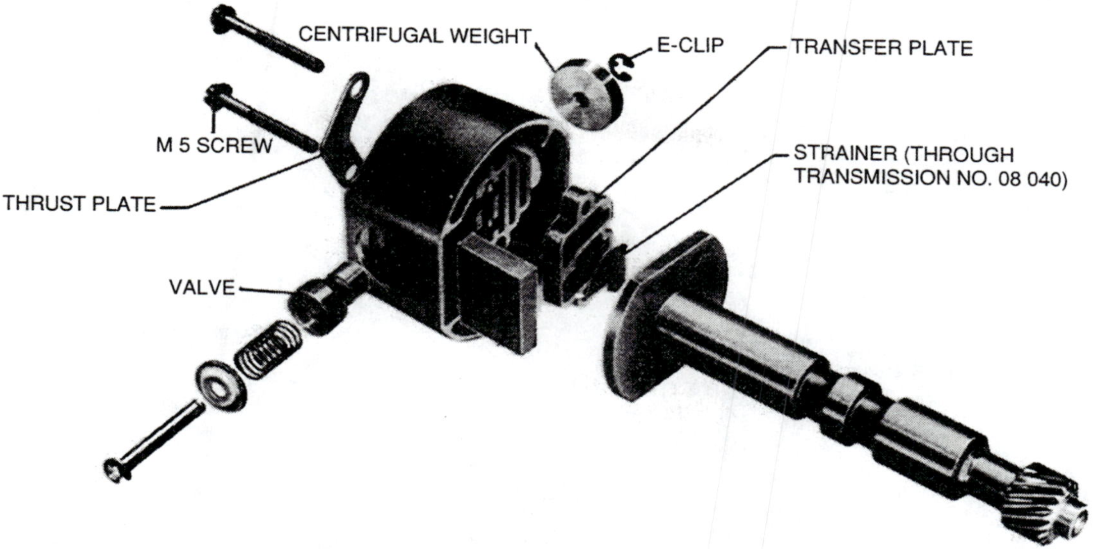

FIGURE 14–16 VW 087 governor. (Courtesy of Volkswagen)

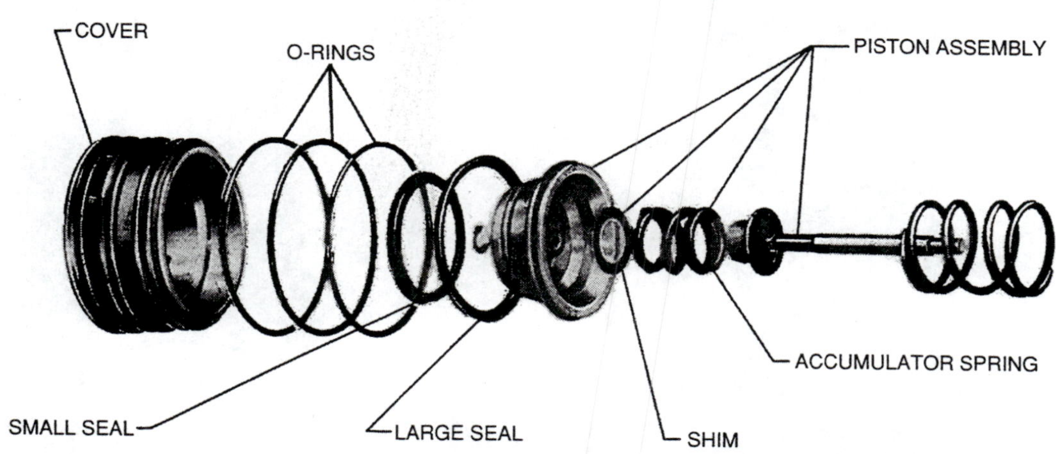

FIGURE 14–17 VW 087 second-gear servo. (Courtesy of Volkswagen)

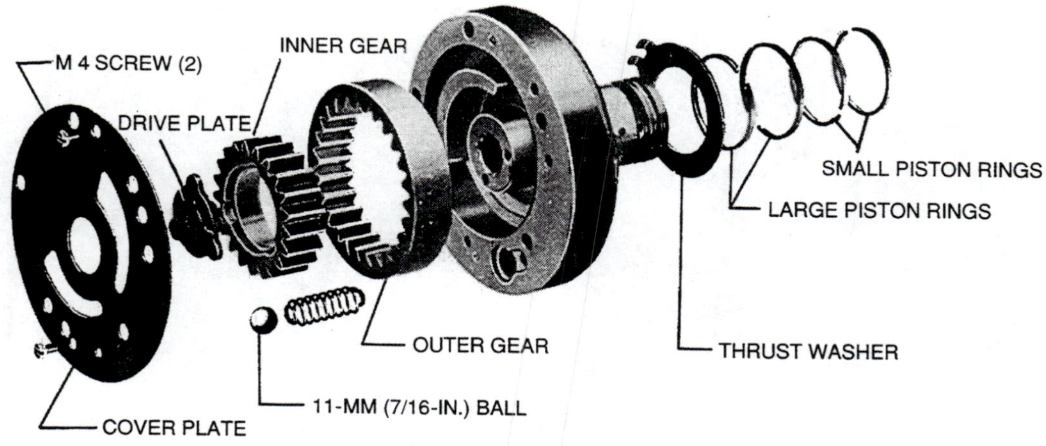

FIGURE 14–18 VW 087 oil pump. (Courtesy of Volkswagen)

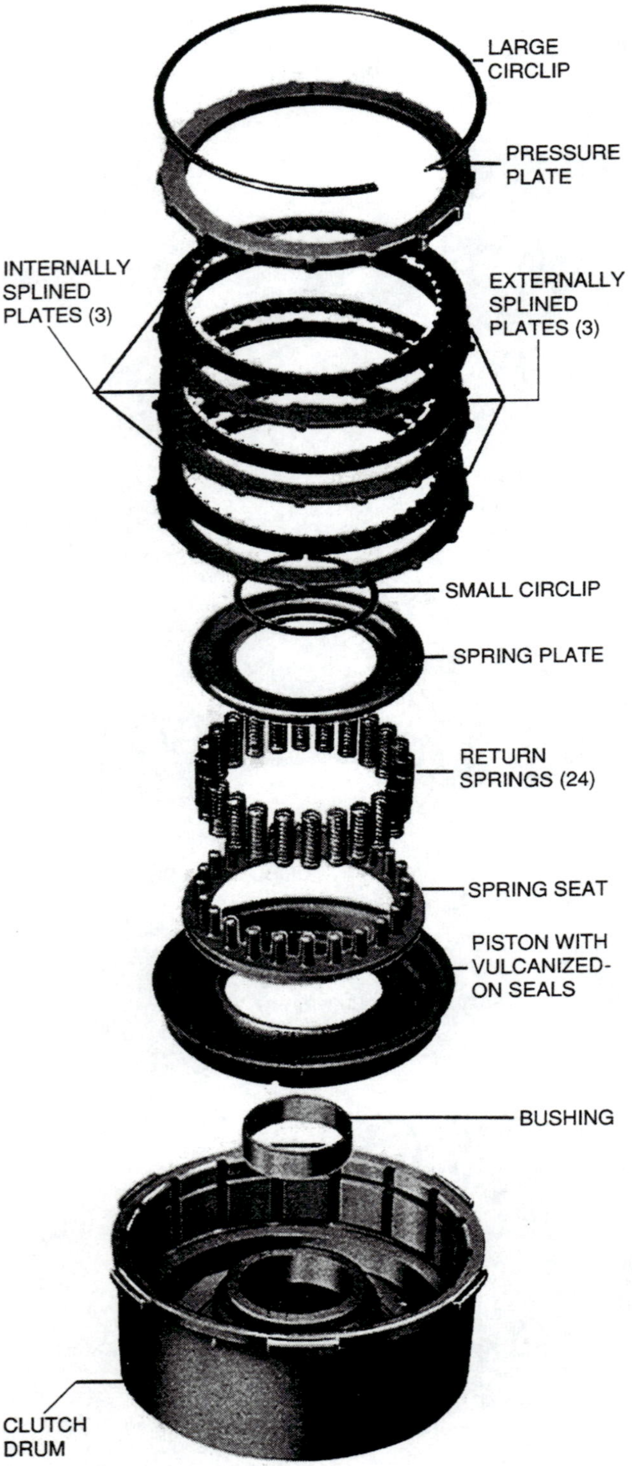

LARGE
CIRCLIP
PRESSURE
PLATE
INTERNALLY
SPLINED
PLATES (3)
EXTERNALLY
SPLINED
PLATES (3)
SMALL CIRCLIP
SPRING PLATE
RETURN
SPRINGS (24)
SPRING SEAT
PISTON WITH
VULCANIZED-
ON SEALS
BUSHING
CLUTCH
DRUM

FIGURE 14–19 VW 087 direct and reverse clutch. (Courtesy of Volkswagen)

CLUTCH
PLATE
CIRCLIP
PRESSURE
PLATE
EXTERNALLY
SPLINED
PLATES (2)
INTERNALLY
SPLINED
PLATES (3)
FORWARD
ANNULUS
GEAR
THRUST
GEAR
DIAPHRAGM
SPRING
CIRCLIP
DIAPHRAGM
SPRING
PISTON
CLUTCH
DRUM

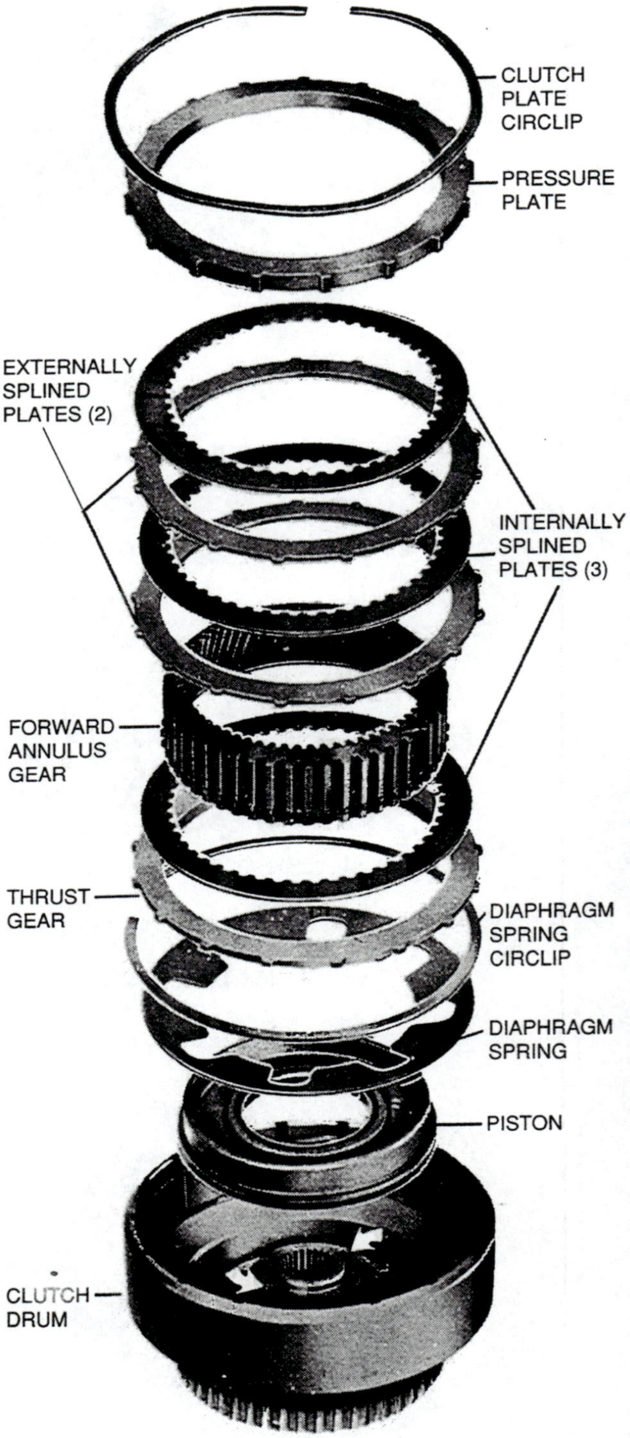

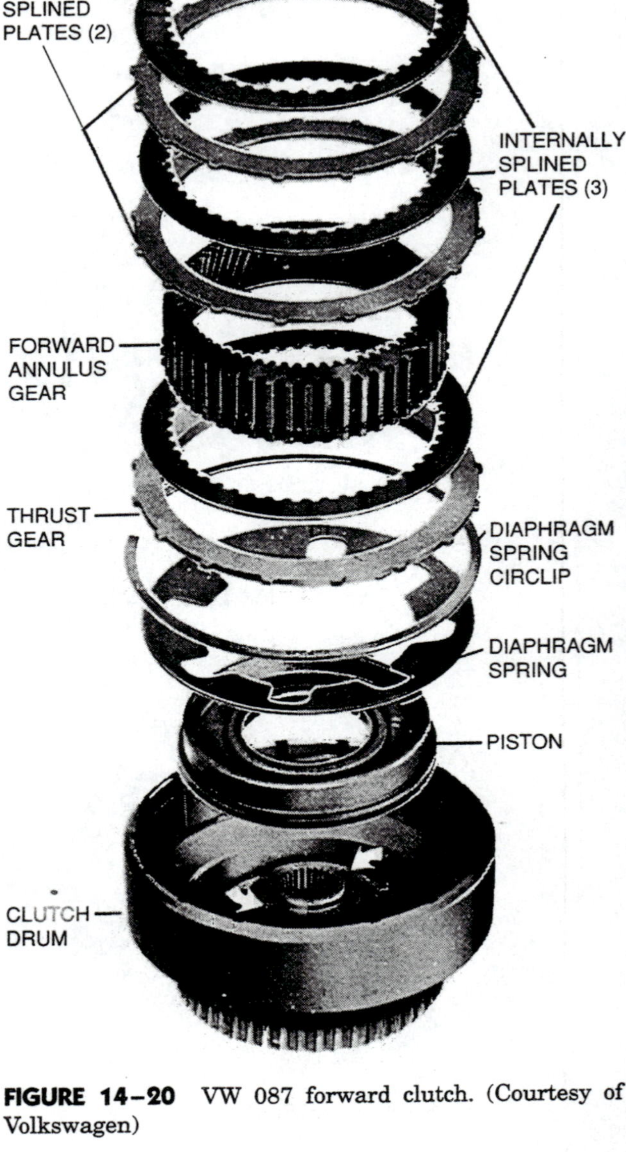

FIGURE 14–20 VW 087 forward clutch. (Courtesy of Volkswagen)

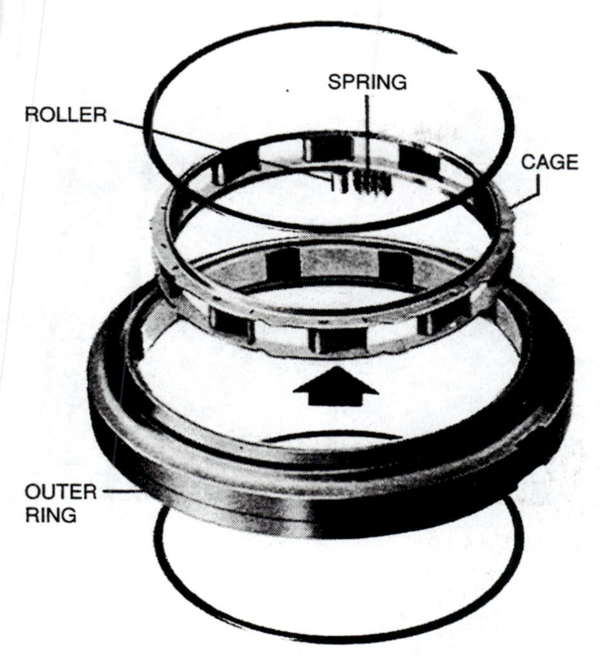

FIGURE 14–21 VW 087 first-gear one-way clutch. (Courtesy of Volkswagen)

FIGURE 14–22 VW 087 internal linkage. (Courtesy of Volkswagen)

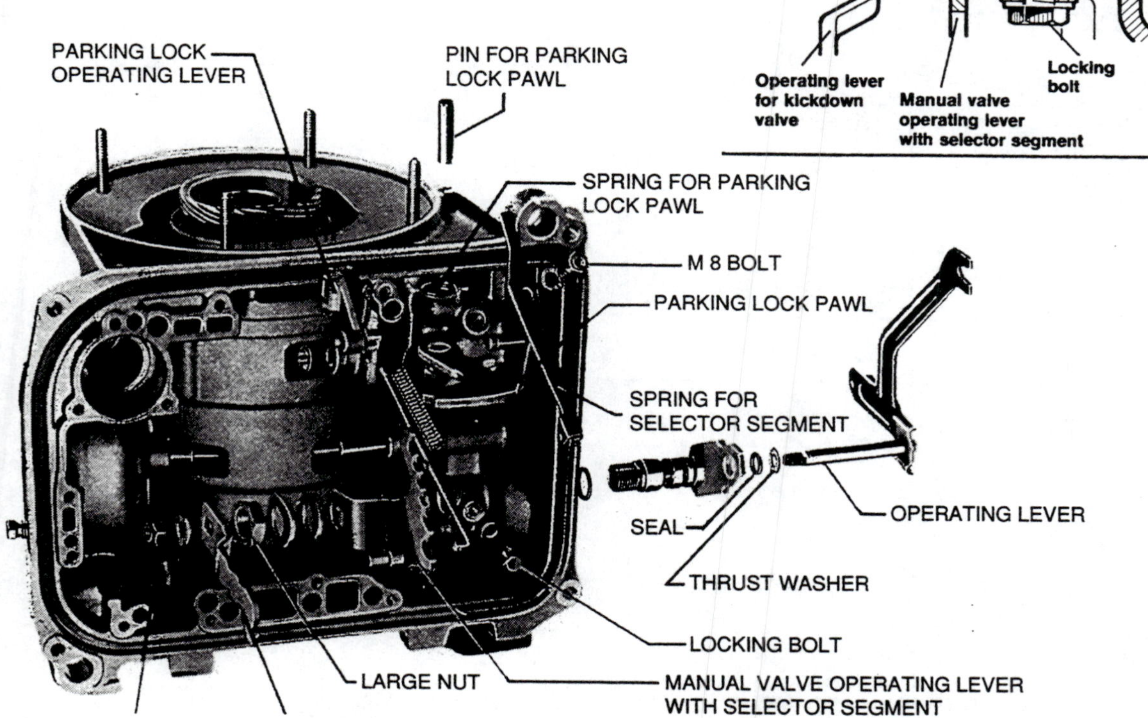

14.3.6 Pressure Test

One of the key tests in diagnosis is the hydraulic system pressure test. The location of the test points of the Volkswagen 087 transaxle are shown in Figure 14–23. A pressure chart listing the pressure specification of this transaxle is shown in Figure 14–24.

FIGURE 14–23 VW 087 pressure test point. (Courtesy of Volkswagen)

14.3.7 Air Test

Air testing is used during preliminary diagnosis of certain malfunctions and also during the disassembly process to verify component operation or failure. The technician must know which hydraulic circuit is being served by each passageway to be able to air test the transmission accurately.

14.3.8 Special Attention

In this unit we show and explain various points of special interest about the Volkswagen 087 transaxle. The information presented about each item is included with each illustration.

Selector lever position	Accelerator pedal position	Main pressure bar (psi)	Test conditions
D code letters: RM, RP, RY	idle speed	2.90-3.00 (42-44)	accelerate up to 50 km/h (31 mph), release gas pedal (idle speed) and check pressure on gauge*
D code letters: RM, RY	full throttle	5.65-5.75 (80-82)	*
D code letters: RP	full throttle	7.3-7.4 (106-107)	*
R code letters: RM, RP, RY up to 16 07 0	idle speed	7.62-8.22 (110-119)	vehicle stationary
R code letters: RP, RY from 17 07 0	idle speed	9.1-9.7 (129-138)	vehicle stationary

*These tests should be performed on dynamometer

FIGURE 14–24 VW 087 pressure chart. (Courtesy of Volkswagen)

FIGURE VW 087–1 The accumulator spring and seals should always be inspected.

FIGURE VW 087–2 The second-gear brake band piston is removed this way.

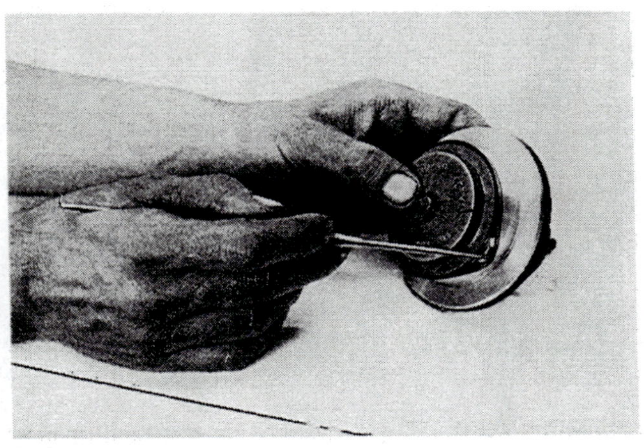

FIGURE VW 087–3 The piston seals must be examined and replaced.

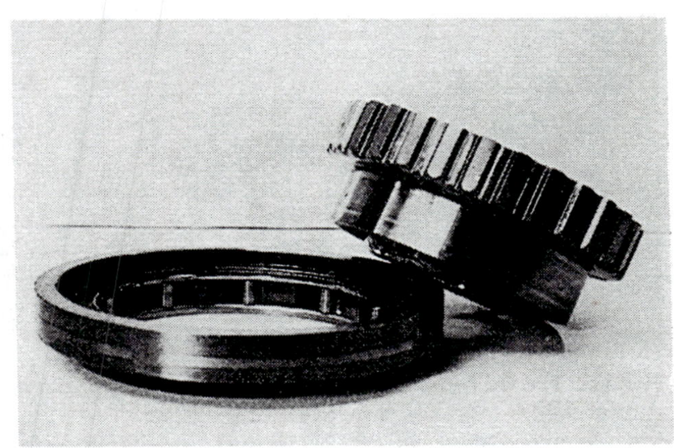

FIGURE VW 087–4 The one-way clutch must be checked for signs of wear.

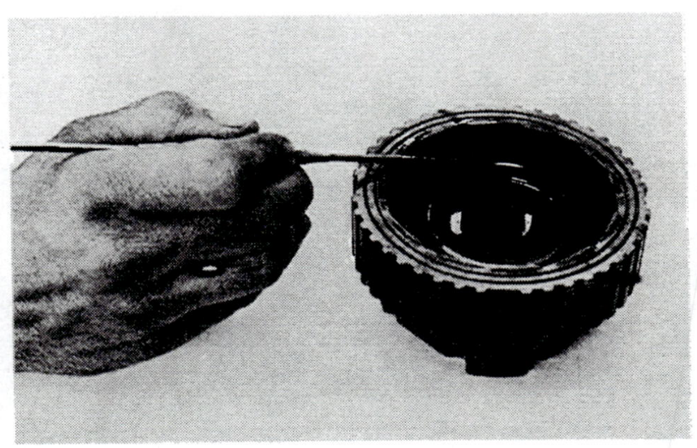

FIGURE VW 087–5 The reverse planetary gear set thrust washer must be checked for wear.

FIGURE VW 087–6 The reverse ring gear is removed, showing the reverse planet carrier.

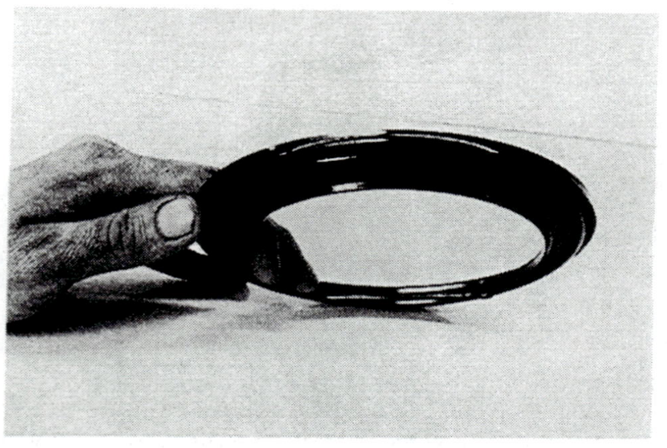

FIGURE VW 087–7 The seal on the first–reverse brake piston must be examined for failure.

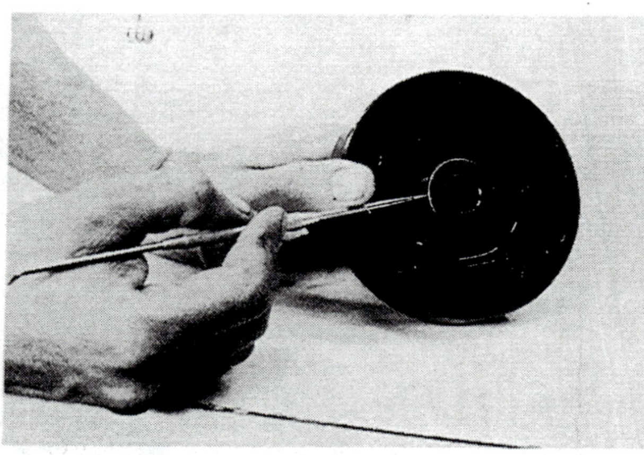

FIGURE VW 087–8 The center hub of the oil pump body should be examined for wear.

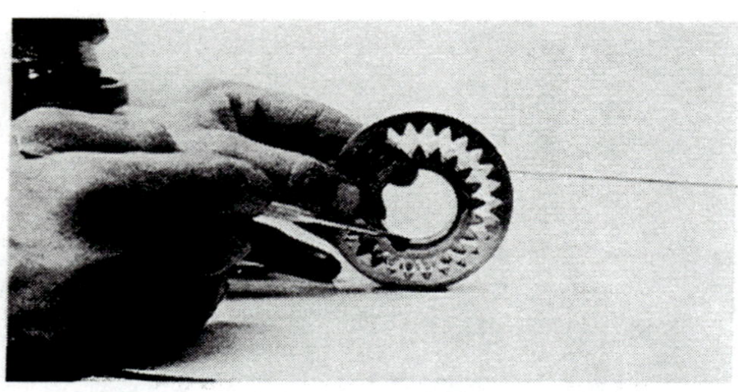

FIGURE VW 087–9 The inner surface of the oil pump gear should be checked for wear and grooving.

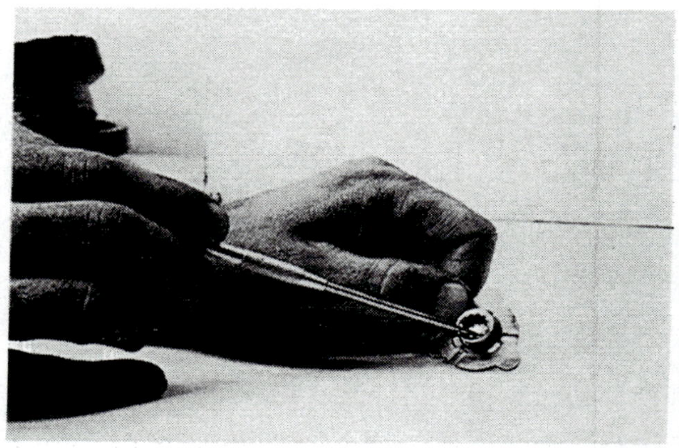

FIGURE VW 087–10 The pump drive plate splines must be checked for wear.

FIGURE VW 087–11 Some Volkswagen transmissions use a bolt on a fluid cooler like this.

FIGURE VW 087–12 The fluid cooler bolts to the indicated holes in the back of the transmission case.

FIGURE VW 087–13 O-rings seal the cooler to the case, while drilled bolts allow fluid to enter and leave the cooler.

14.4 RENAULT MB-1: FWD THREE-SPEED TRANSAXLE

14.4.1 Basic Description

The Renault MB-1 is similar in its basic design to the VW 087. A Simpson gear set is used, along with the same basic power flow as the Volkswagen transmission (Figure 14–25). The MB-1 does add the feature of electronic shift control.

The transmission description is divided into eight areas. All the transmissions are described in this manner to make their comparison easier.

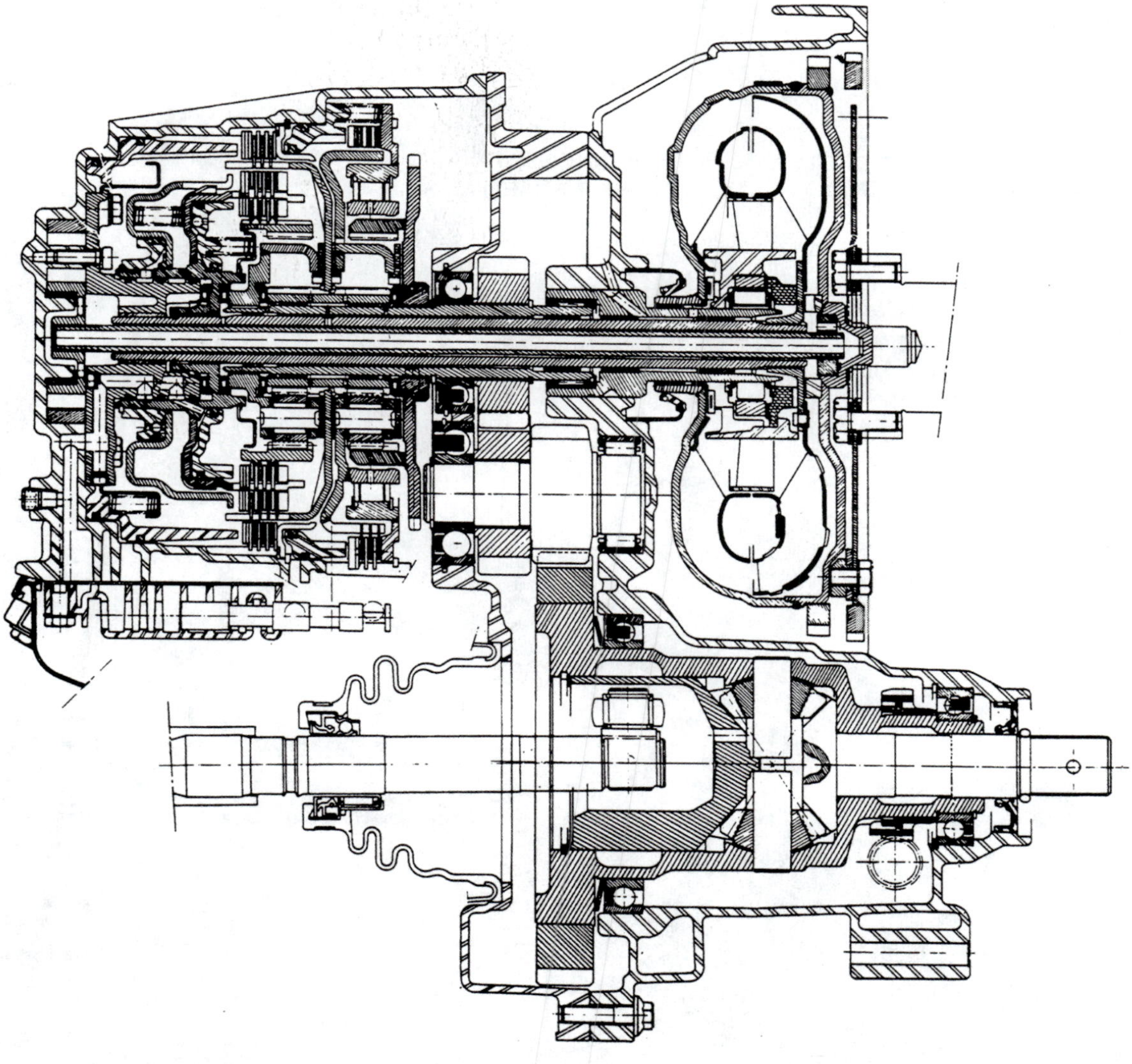

FIGURE 14–25 MB-1 cross-sectional view. (Courtesy of Chrysler)

1. Torque Converter
The torque converter used in the MB-1 is a conventional three-element design with no converter clutch.

2. Gear Train
As mentioned earlier, the MB-1 uses a Simpson gear set with the output end of the gear set next to the torque converter. Following traditional Simpson design, the front ring gear and sun gear are input. The rear pinion carrier and sun gear are the reaction members and the front pinion carrier and rear ring gear are the output members (Figure 14–26).

3. Coupling Devices
The input coupling devices are the E1 clutch (forward), which drives the front ring gear, and the E2 clutch (high and reverse clutch), which drives the sun gear.

4. Holding Devices
The holding devices are the F1 brake (clutch), which holds the rear pinion carrier, and the F2 brake clutch, which holds the sun gear. The RL roller clutch is also used to hold the rear pinion carrier.

5. Pump
The oil pump is mounted in the back end of the case and is a gear crescent design. The pump is driven by a drive shaft which runs through the hollow turbine shaft.

6. Shift Control
The shift control system used on the MB-1 is electronic. Two shift solenoids are controlled by an on-board computer which is constantly monitoring vehicle operating conditions through its sensors (Figure 14–27).

COMPONENT LEGEND

P = Sun Gear
S = Pinions (Gears)
PS1 = Forward Pinion Carrier
PS2 = Rear Pinion Carrier
C1 = Forward Internal Gear
C2 = Rear Internal Gear
F1 = F1 Brake
RL = Roller Clutch
F2 = F2 Brake
E1 = E1 Clutch
E2 = E2 Clutch

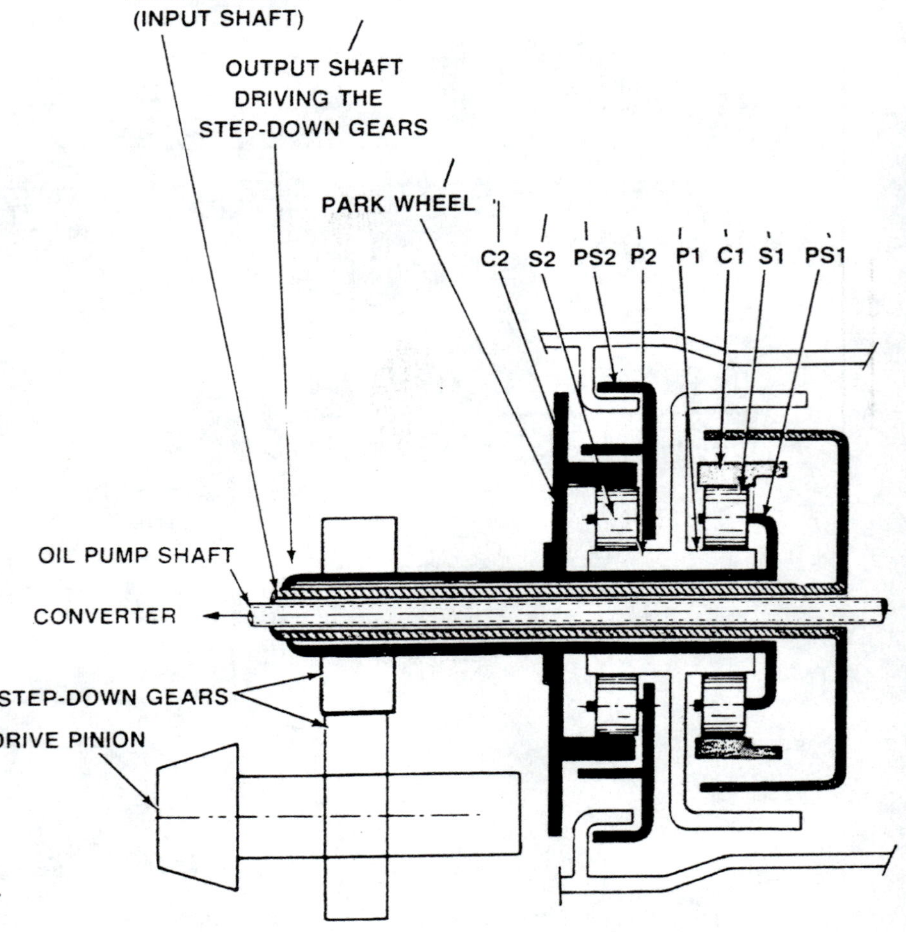

FIGURE 14–26 MB-1 gear train.
(Courtesy of Chrysler)

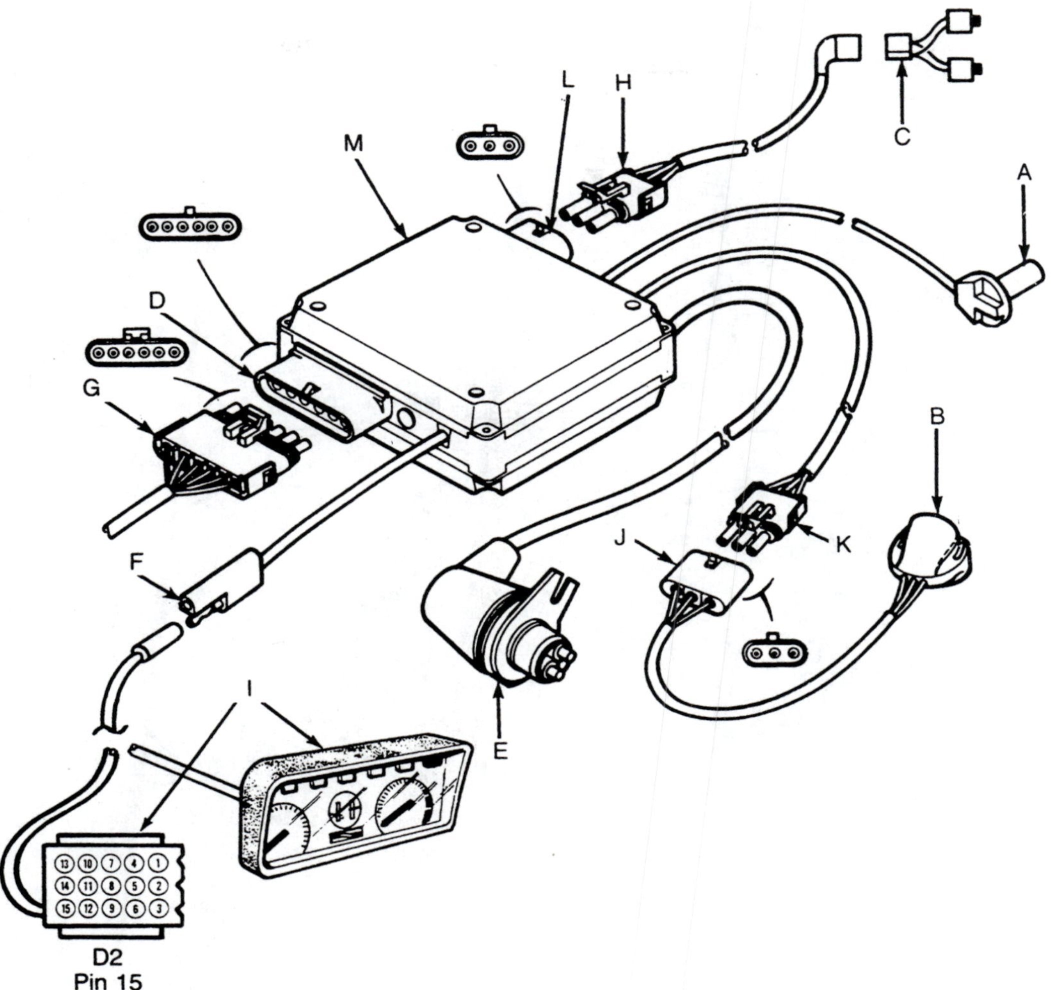

A. Road Speed Sensor
B. Throttle Position Sensor
C. Solenoid Ball Valves
D. Computer 6-Way Connector
E. Multifunction Switch
F. B.Vi. 958 Diagnostic Connector
G. 6-Way Connector
H. 3-Way Connector
I. MS. 1700 Diagnostic Connector or Warning Light (Early Models)
J. Potentiometer Connector
K. 3-Way Connector
L. Computer 3-Way Connector
M. Computer

FIGURE 14–27 MB-1 computer and sensors. (Courtesy of Chrysler)

7. *Governor*
No governor is used.

8. *Throttle Valve*
No throttle valve is used.

14.4.2 Power Flow

The power flow is described by stating the coupling and holding device action (applied, or holding) on the members of the planetary gear set (sun gear, pinion carrier, and ring gear) in each gear range of the transmission.

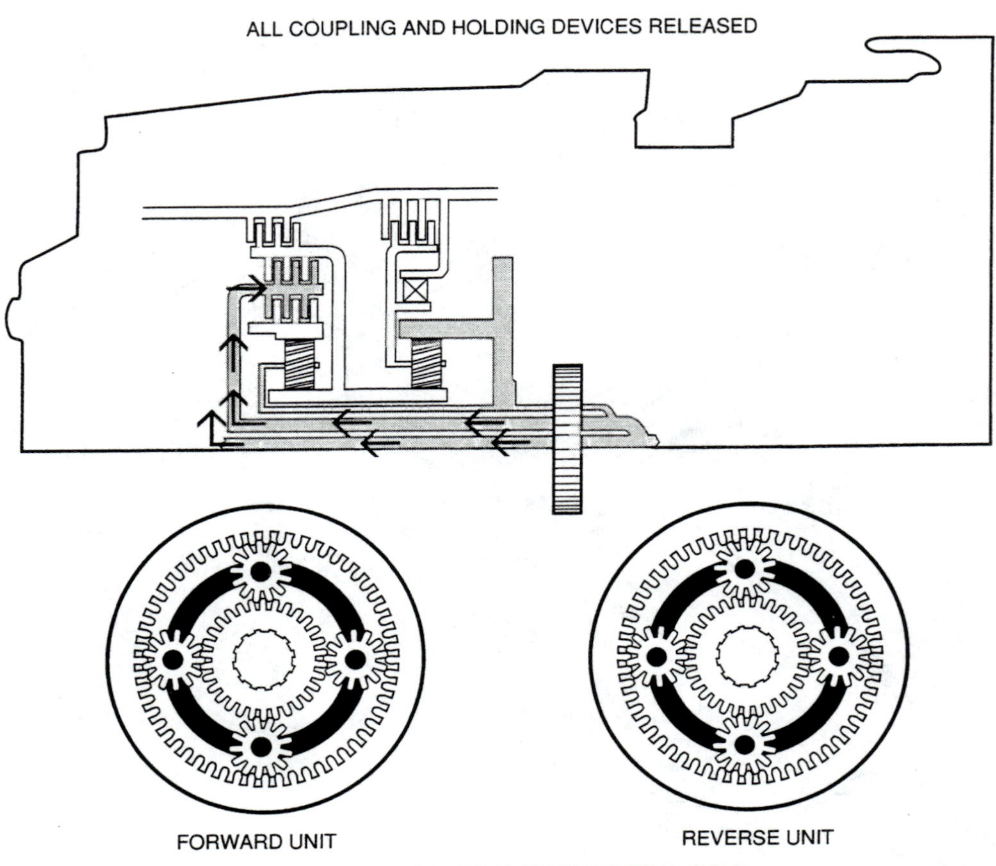

FIGURE 14–28 MB-1 in neutral gear. (Courtesy of Chrysler)

1. Neutral (N)
In neutral all coupling and holding devices are released. Only the turbine shaft and clutch hub are turning (Figure 14–28).

2. First Gear (D1)
In first gear the E1 (forward) clutch is applied, which drives the front ring gear. The RL roller clutch holds the rear pinion carrier as the reaction member, with the rear ring gear as the output (Figure 14–29). The first-gear ratio is 2.5:1. In manual first gear the F1 brake (low and reverse clutch) is also applied.

3. Second Gear (D2)
In second gear the E1 clutch remains applied, driving the front ring gear. The F2 brake (intermediate clutch) is applied to hold the sun gear. The front pinion carrier is the output member, producing a 1.5:1 gear ratio (Figure 14–30).

4. Third Gear (D3)
In third gear the E1 clutch remains applied, driving the front ring gear and the E2 (direct and reverse) clutch is also applied, driving the sun gear, which produces a direct drive (Figure 14–31).

5. Reverse Gear (R)
In reverse gear the E2 clutch is applied to drive the sun gear. The F1 brake is also applied to hold the rear pinion carrier. A reverse-gear ratio of 2:1 is achieved (Figure 14–32).

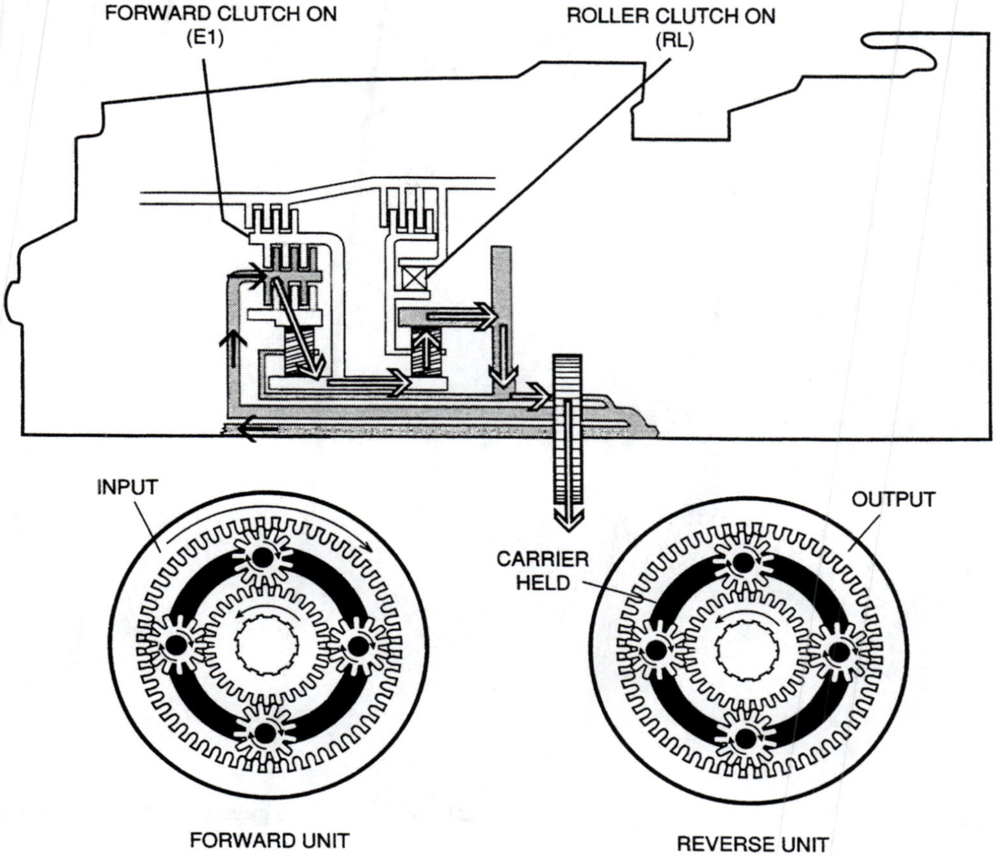

FIGURE 14–29 MB-1 in first gear. (Courtesy of Chrysler)

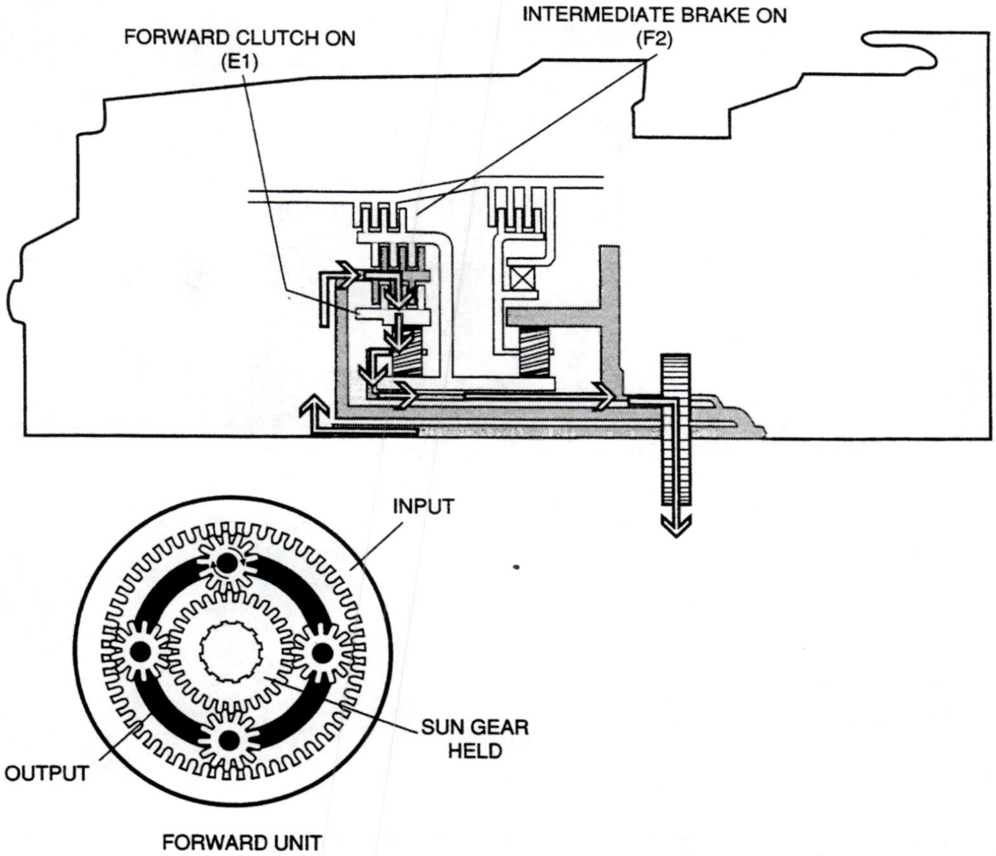

FIGURE 14–30 MB-1 in second gear. (Courtesy of Chrysler)

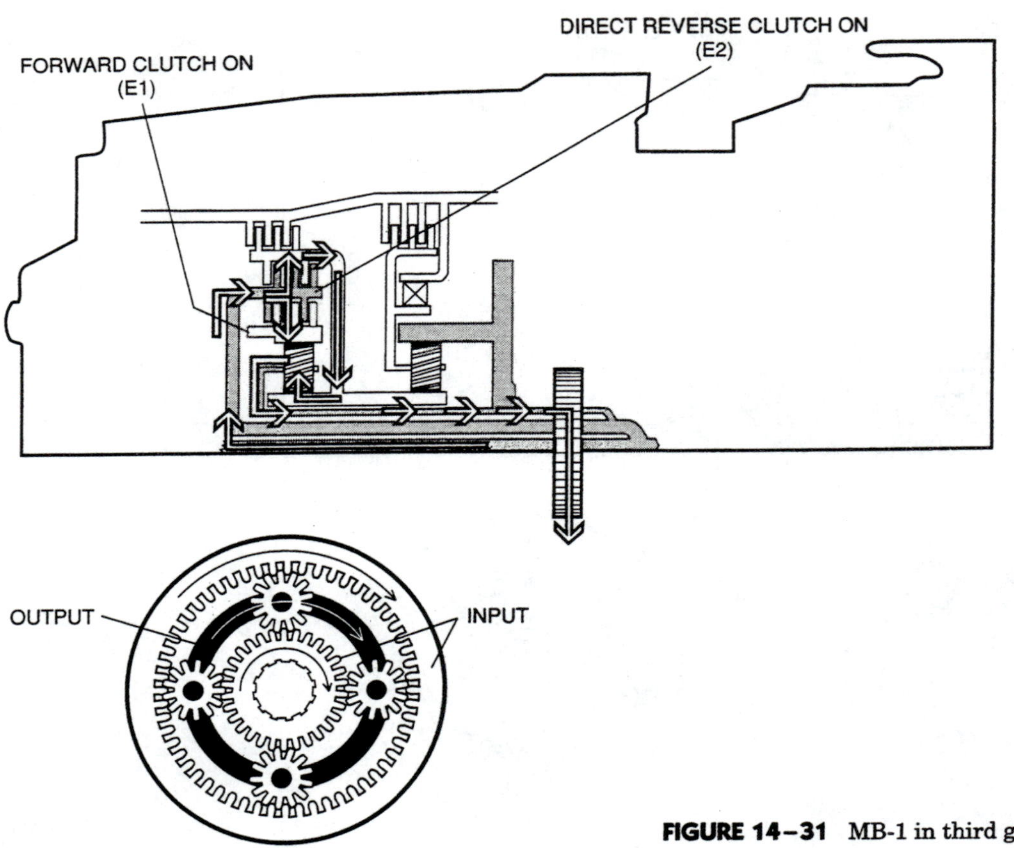

FIGURE 14–31 MB-1 in third gear. (Courtesy of Chrysler)

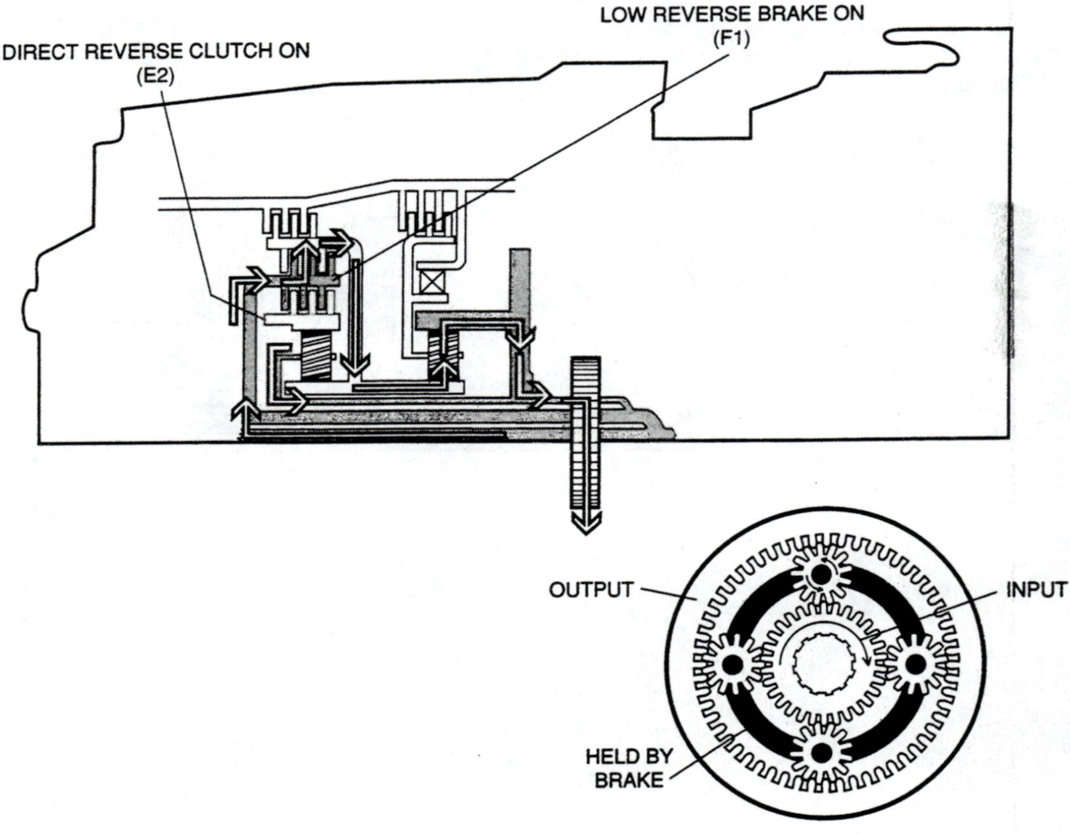

FIGURE 14–32 MB-1 reverse gear. (Courtesy of Chrysler)

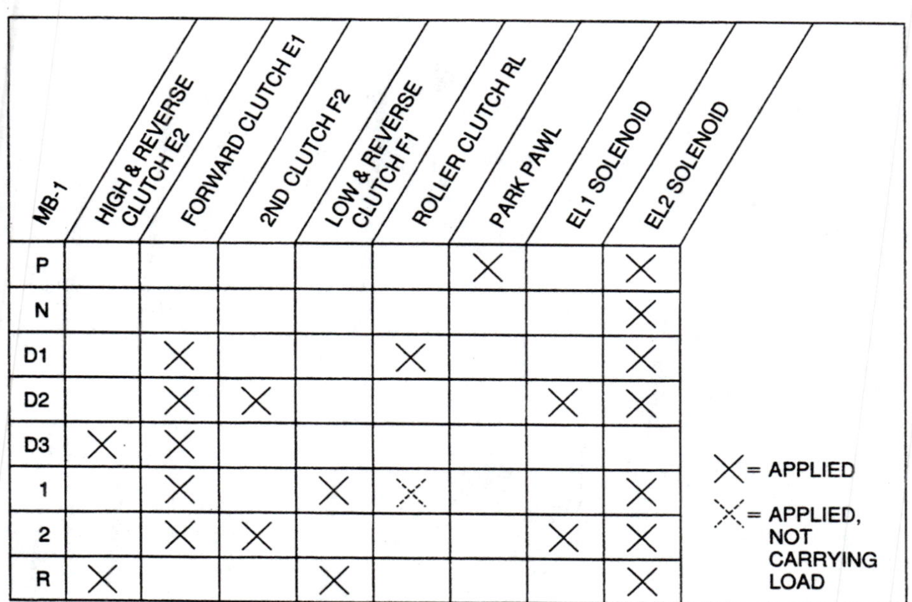

MB-1	HIGH & REVERSE CLUTCH E2	FORWARD CLUTCH E1	2ND CLUTCH F2	LOW & REVERSE CLUTCH F1	ROLLER CLUTCH RL	PARK PAWL	EL1 SOLENOID	EL2 SOLENOID
P						X		X
N								X
D1		X			X			X
D2		X	X				X	X
D3	X	X						
1		X		X	X (dotted)			X
2		X	X				X	X
R	X			X				X

X = APPLIED
X (dotted) = APPLIED, NOT CARRYING LOAD

FIGURE 14–33 MB-1 clutch and band chart, standardized version.

14.4.3 Clutch and Band Charts

In this section we provide two clutch and band charts. The first chart, the author's design, uses a standardized format for listing the coupling and holding devices to aid comparison between transmissions. This chart is shown in Figure 14–33. The second chart, the manufacturer's design, which is found in service manuals, is shown in Figure 14–34.

Selector lever position		RL	E1	E2	F1	F2	EL1	EL2
P								X
R				X	X			X
N								X
A	1	X	X					X
	2		X			X	X	X
	3		X	X				
2nd HOLD			X			X	X	X
1st HOLD			X		X			X

RL = Freewheel
E1 = Clutch 1
E2 = Clutch 2
F1 = Brake 1
F2 = Brake 2
EL1 = Solenoid valve 1
EL2 = Solenoid valve 2

FIGURE 14–34 MB-1 clutch and band chart, factory version. (Courtesy of Chrysler)

14.4.4 Identification

The shape of the transmission oil pan or its gasket is a quick means of identifying an automatic transmission. In Figure 14–35 you see the pan gasket shape and number of bolt holes for the Renault MB-1 transaxle. The location of the factory identification tag and its code is shown in Figure 14–36.

14.4.5 Components

In this section exploded drawings of the Renault MB-1 transaxle subassemblies are shown, along with lists of the part names. The manufacturer's parts names are used to eliminate confusion about component names. The drawings to study are:

Exploded view, Figure 14–37
Gear set, Figure 14–38
Clutch, Figure 14–39
Brake, Figure 14–40
Valve body, Figure 14–41
Electronic control, Figure 14–42

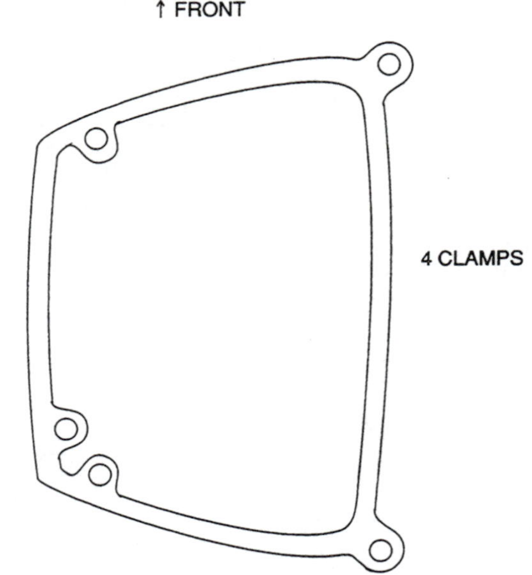

FIGURE 14–35 MB-1 pan gasket identification.

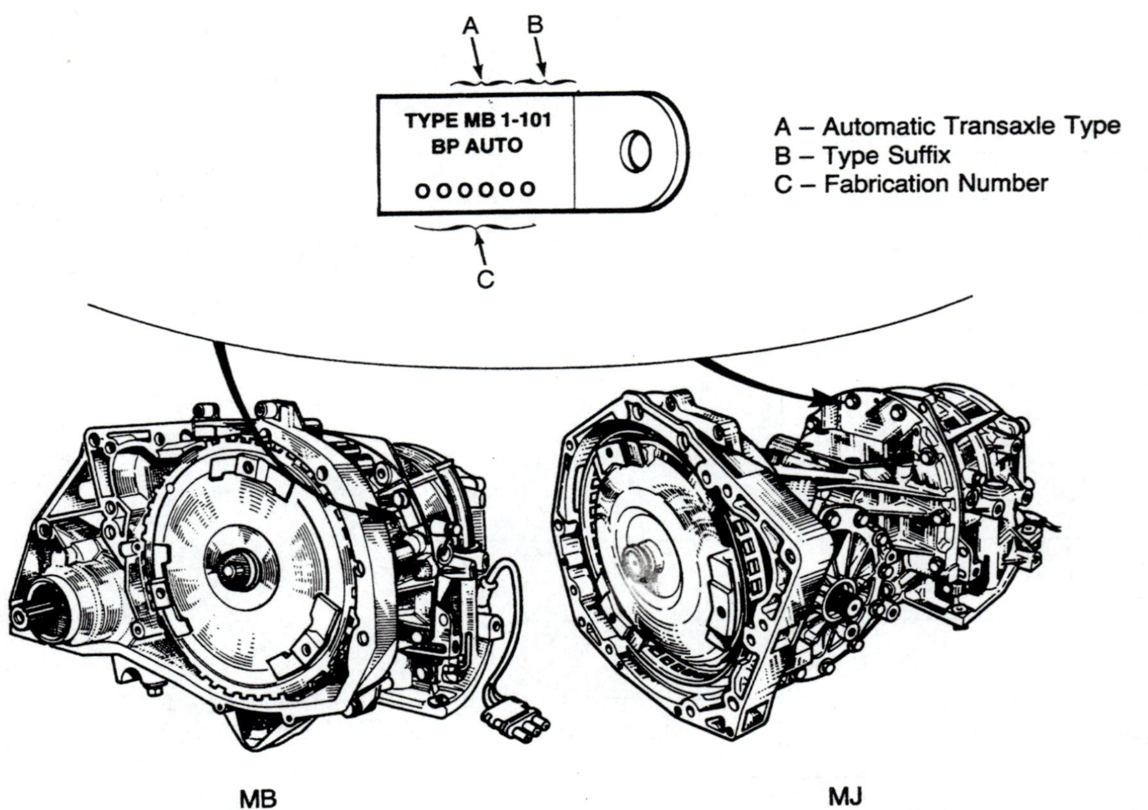

FIGURE 14–36 MB-1 identification tag. (Courtesy of Chrysler)

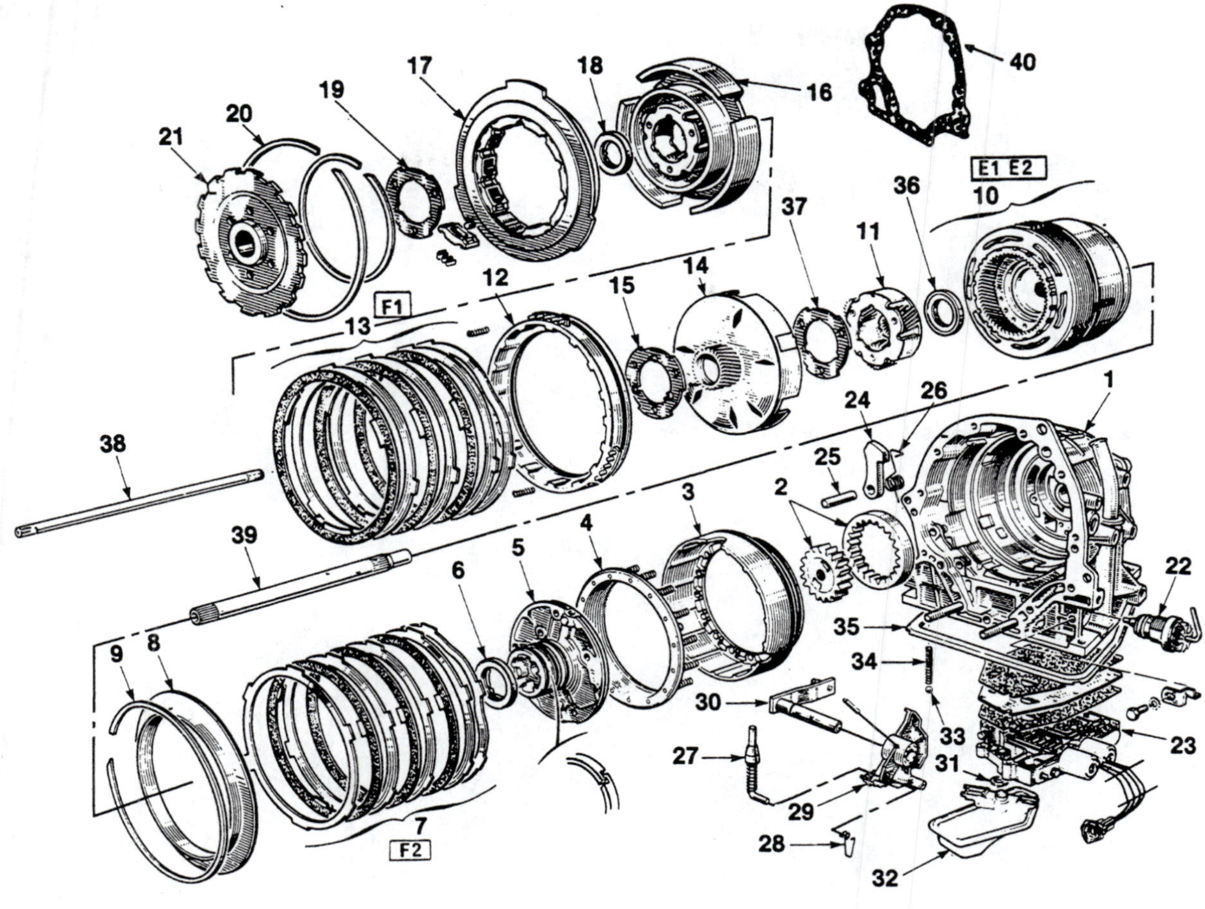

1 - Rear case
2 - Oil pump
3 - F2 piston
4 - F2 cup
5 - Feed hub
6 - Needle roller thrust bearing
7 - F2 disc stack
8 - F1 piston carrier
9 - Snap ring
10 - E1 - E2 clutches
11 - Forward drive train
12 - F1 piston
13 - F1 disc stack
14 - E2 bellhousing
15 - Friction washer (1.5 mm thick)
16 - Reverse drive train
17 - Freewheel
18 - Needle roller thrust bearing
19 - Nylon friction washer (thickness to be determined)
20 - Snap ring
21 - "Park" wheel
22 - Capsule
23 - Valve Body
24 - "Park" latch
25 - "Park" latch shaft
26 - "Park" latch spring
27 - "Park" linkage
28 - Safety clip
29 - Quadrant
30 - Input shaft
31 - Filter screen seal
32 - Filter screen
33 - Quadrant lock ball
34 - Quadrant spring
35 - Sump plate gasket
36 - Needle roller bearing
37 - Friction washer (1.5 mm thick)
38 - Pump shaft
39 - Turbine shaft
40 - Rear Case-to-Intermediary Case gasket

FIGURE 14–37 MB-1 exploded view. (Courtesy of Chrysler)

FIGURE 14–38 MB-1 gear set. (Courtesy of Chrysler)

FIGURE 14–39 MB-1 clutch. (Courtesy of Chrysler)

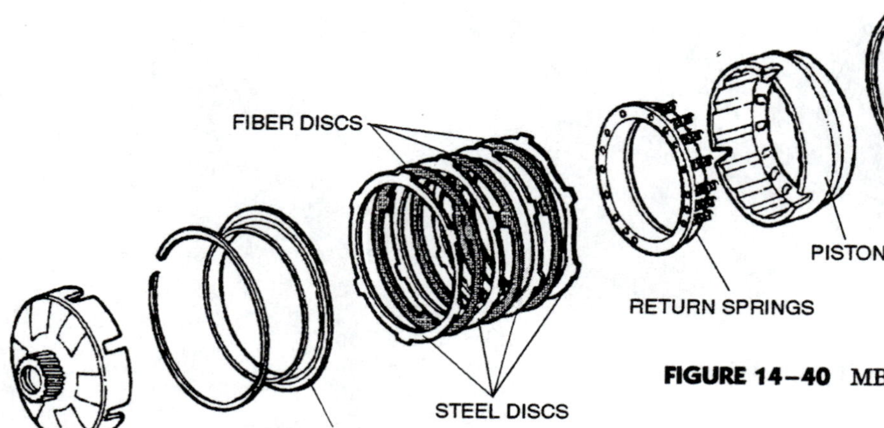

FIGURE 14–40 MB-1 brake. (Courtesy of Chrysler)

FIGURE 14–41 MB-1 valve body. (Courtesy of Chrysler)

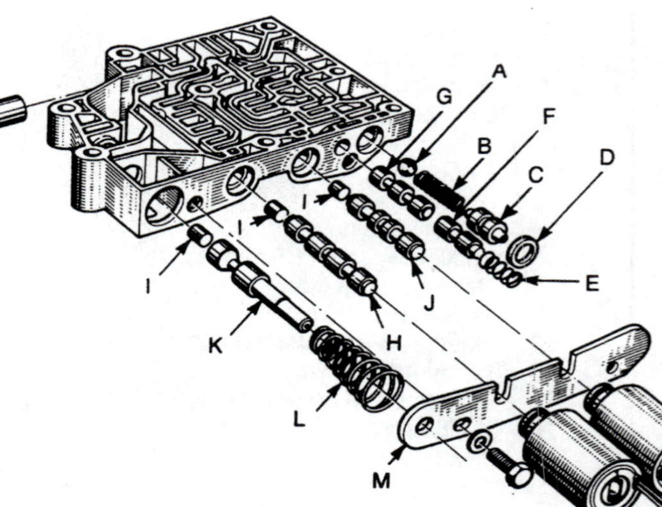

A. Pressure limiting valve (VLP) ball
B. Pressure limiting valve (VLP) medium spring
C. Pressure limiting valve (VLP)
D. Pressure limiting valve (VLP) seal
E. Sequence valve (VS) small spring
F. Sequence valve (VS)
G. Sequence valve (VS)
H. Pilot valve 1 (VP 1)
I. Plungers
J. Pilot valve 2 (VP2)
K. Pressure regulating valve (VRP)
L. Pressure regulating valve (VRP) spring
M. Closure plate
N. Manual valve (VM)

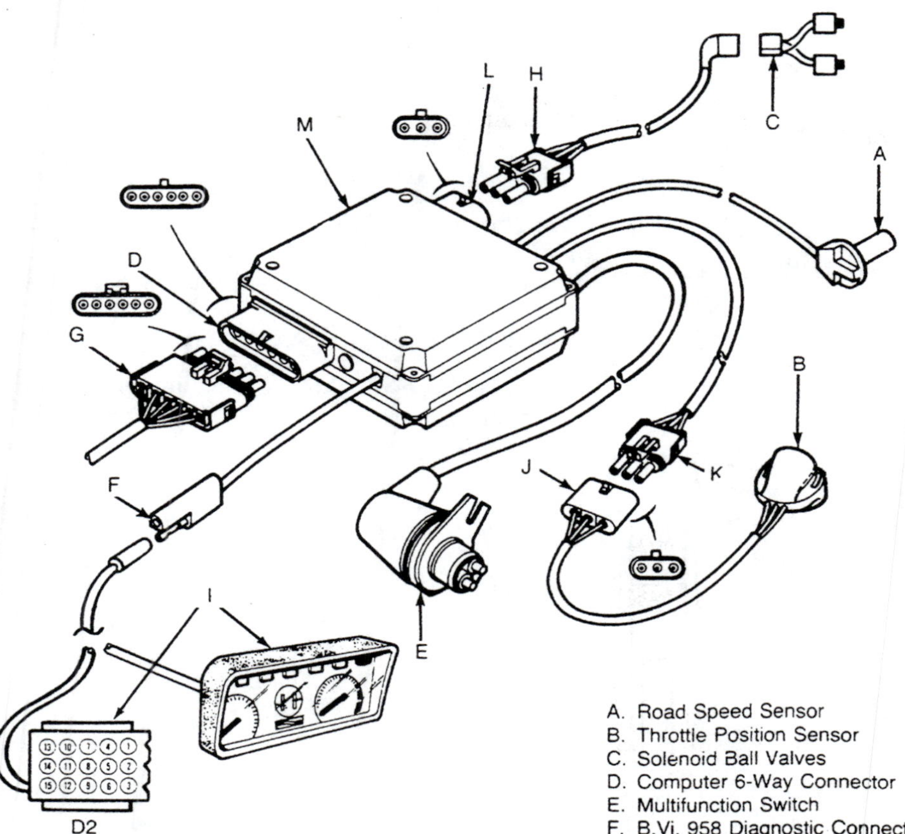

A. Road Speed Sensor
B. Throttle Position Sensor
C. Solenoid Ball Valves
D. Computer 6-Way Connector
E. Multifunction Switch
F. B.Vi. 958 Diagnostic Connector
G. 6-Way Connector
H. 3-Way Connector
I. MS. 1700 Diagnostic Connector or Warning Light (Early Models)
J. Potentiometer Connector
K. 3-Way Connector
L. Computer 3-Way Connector
M. Computer

FIGURE 14–42 MB-1 electronic control. (Courtesy of Chrysler)

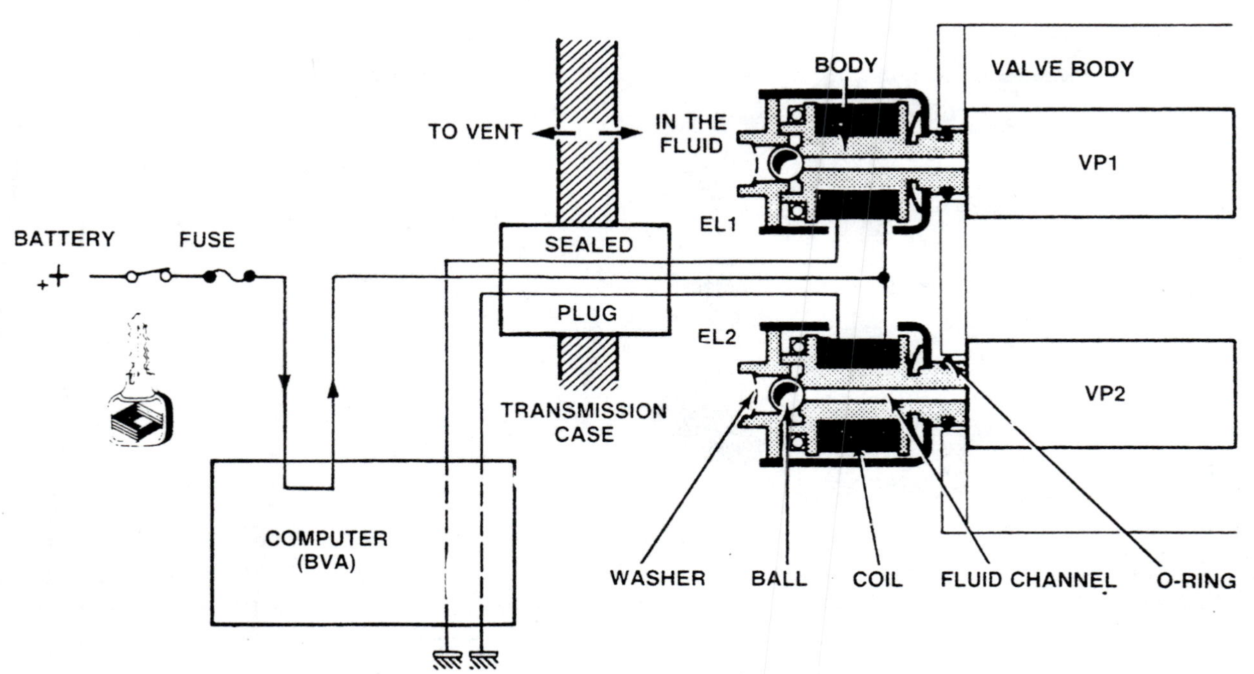

FIGURE 14–43 MB-1 solenoid valves. (Courtesy of Chrysler)

Solenoid valves, Figure 14–43
Speed sensor, Figure 14–44
Multifunction switch, Figure 14–45

14.4.6 Pressure Test

One of the key tests in diagnosis is the hydraulic system pressure test. The location of the test points of the MB-1 transaxle are shown in Figure 14–46.

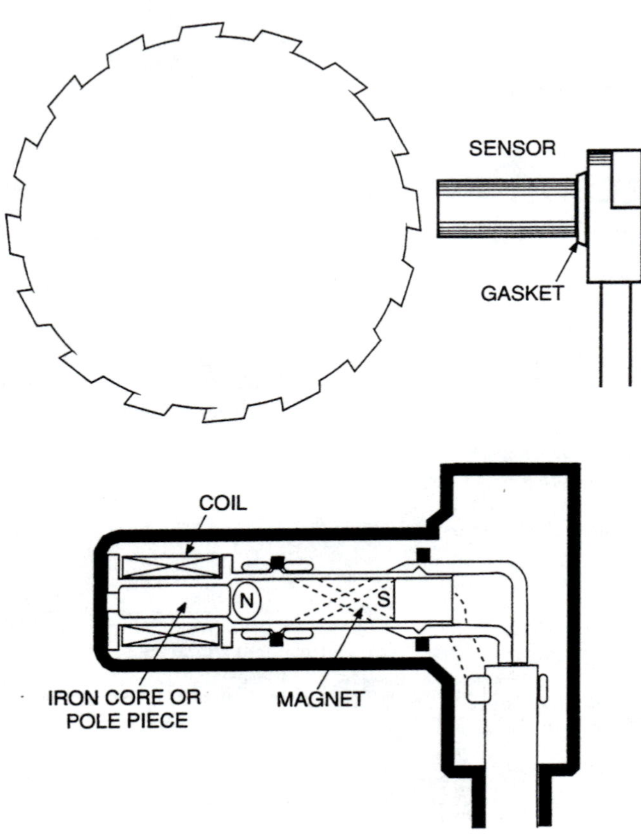

FIGURE 14–44 MB-1 speed sensor. (Courtesy of Chrysler)

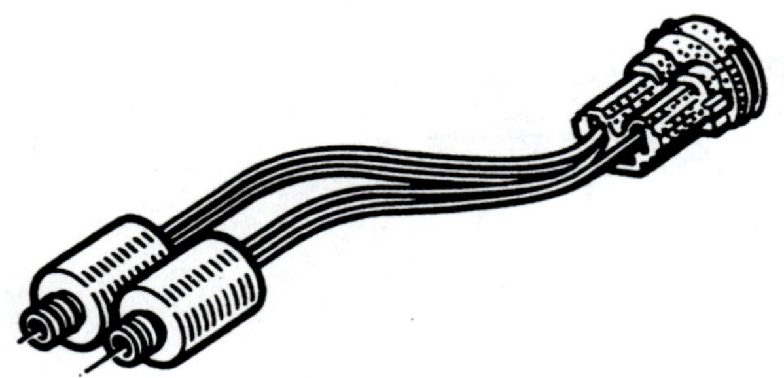

FIGURE 14–45 MB-1 multifunction switch. (Courtesy of Chrysler)

A pressure chart listing the pressure specifications of this transaxle is shown in Figure 14–47.

14.4.7 Air Test

The manufacturer's service manual does not include any procedures for air testing. Testing the clutches and brakes individually is recommended.

14.4.8 Special Attention

In this section we show and explain various points of special interest about the MB-1 transaxle. The information presented about each item is included with each illustration.

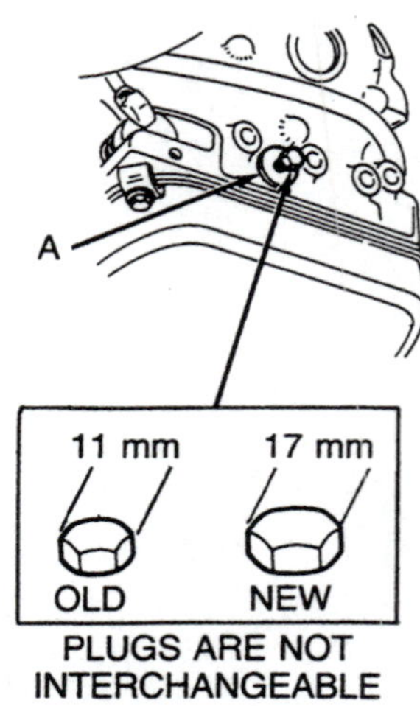

FIGURE 14–46 MB-1 pressure test point. (Courtesy of Chrysler)

CORRECT OIL PRESSURE	
MB1	4.4 BARS (64 PSI)
MB3	4.4 BARS (64 PSI)
MJ3	4.6 BARS (66.7 PSI)

FIGURE 14–47 MB-1 pressure chart. (Courtesy of Chrysler)

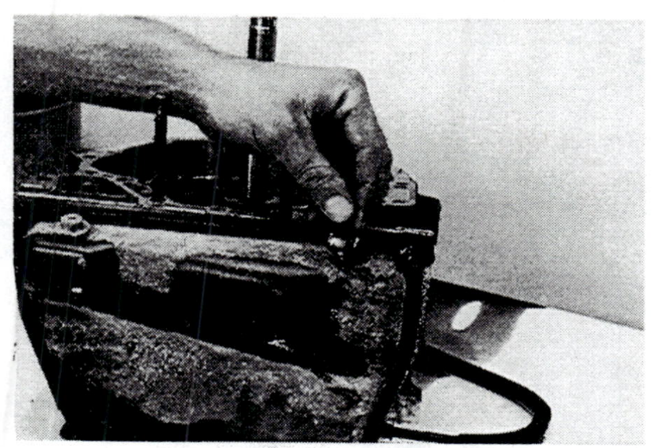

FIGURE MB-1–1 The oil pan is held in place by four clamps and bolts.

FIGURE MB-1–2 Access to the fluid filter and valve body is wide open on the MB-1.

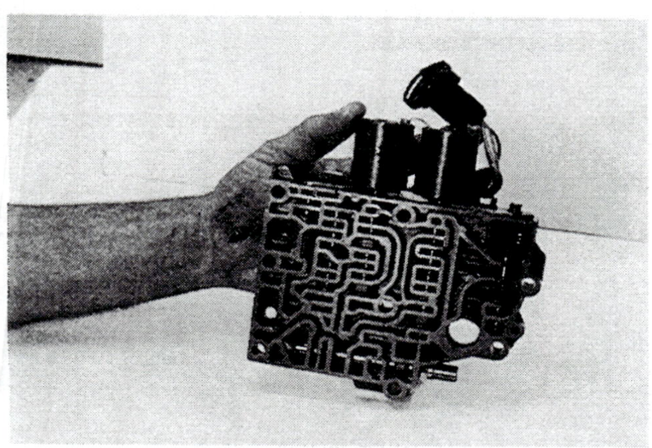

FIGURE MB-1–3 The valve body is extremely simple because of the electronic control.

FIGURE MB-1–4 The shift solenoids mount in the holes below each solenoid.

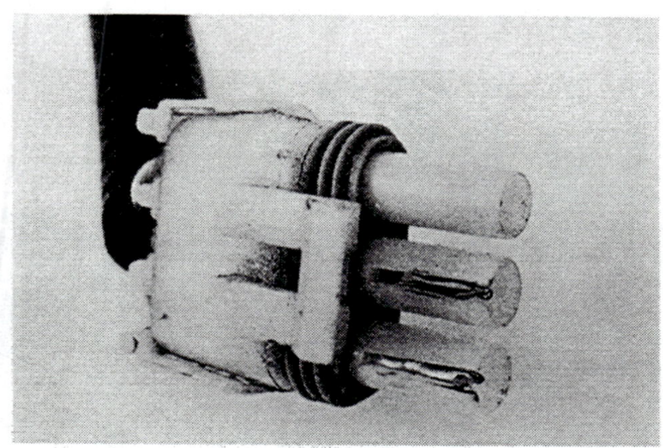

FIGURE MB-1–5 Weather-pack wiring connectors are used for shift solenoid wiring to minimize poor connections.

FIGURE MB-1–6 With the bell housing removed the park wheel and park pawl are visible.

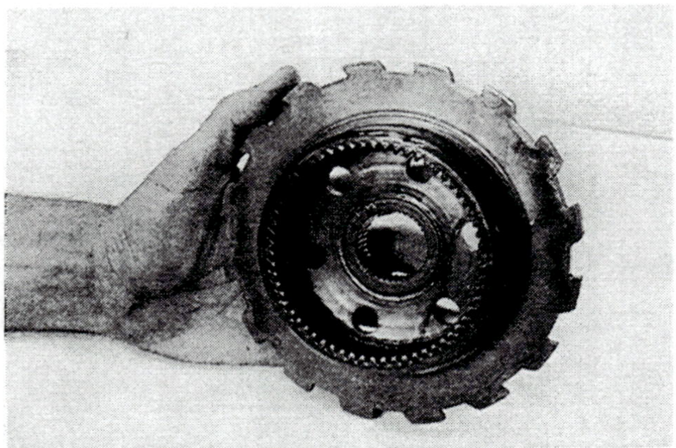

FIGURE MB-1–7 On the inside of the park wheel is the rear ring gear.

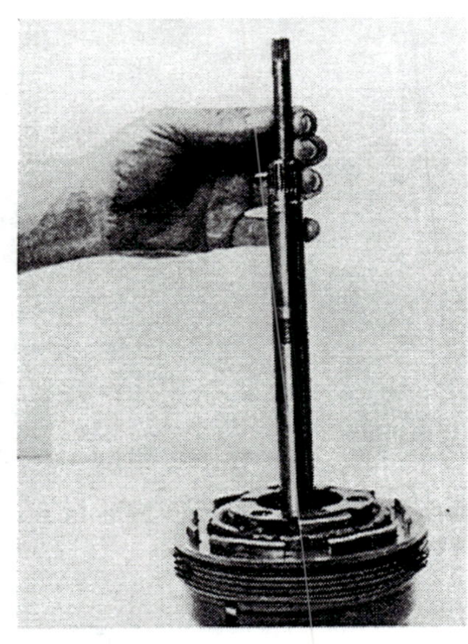

FIGURE MB-1–8 The oil pump drive shaft rides inside the hollow turbine shaft.

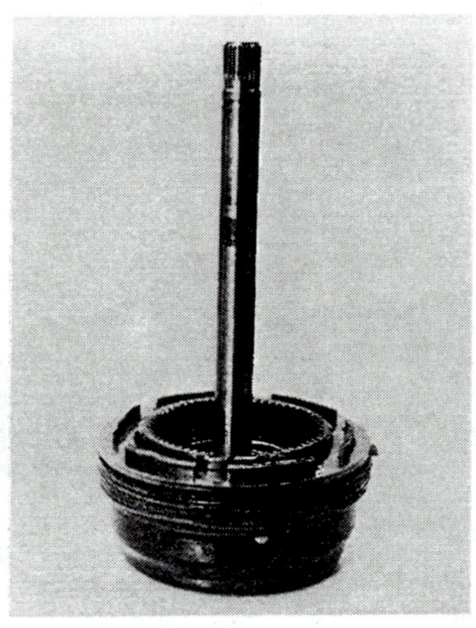

FIGURE MB-1–9 Assembly that contains the E1 and E2 clutches.

FIGURE MB-1–10 The inner rear hub surface must be checked for wear and grooving.

FIGURE MB-1–11 The roller clutch must be checked carefully for wear and signs of failure.

FIGURE MB-1–12 The gear train components are ready to be removed.

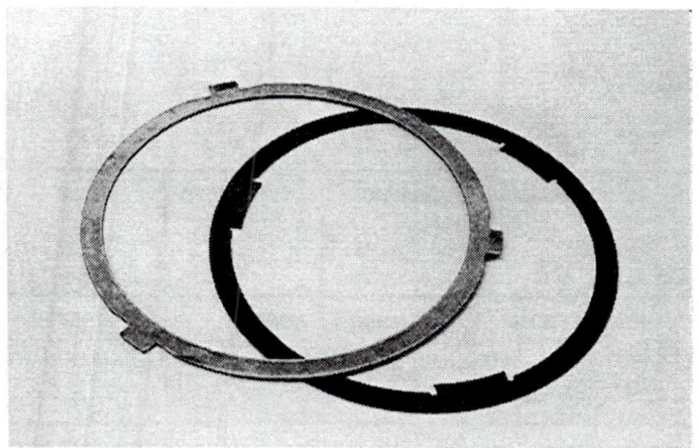

FIGURE MB-1–13 The disc and plates use only three tangs for attachment.

FIGURE MB-1–14 With the gear train removed, the oil pump is visible.

FIGURE MB-1–15 The oil pump cover must be checked for excessive wear.

FIGURE MB-1–16 The transmission power output gear at the right drives the idler gear.

FIGURE MB-1–17 The final drive gear is driven by the idler gear.

SUMMARY

The two transaxles profiled in this chapter are representative of the European imports currently available in the low- to mid-price range (Figure 14–48). Both transaxles use a Simpson three-speed gear set, which is common in many domestic transmissions. The electronics used to control the MB-1 seem simple compared to the latest domestic systems, but the MB-1 system has proved to be very reliable. The industry is steadily moving toward electronic control systems, so it is imperative for the student technician to fully understand this type of system.

EUROPEAN IMPORTS	TORQUE CONVERTER	GEAR TRAIN	COUPLING DEVICES	HOLDING DEVICES	PUMP	SHIFT CONTROL	GOVERNOR	THROTTLE VALVE
VW-087	3-ELEMENT	SIMPSON	FORWARD CLUTCH DIRECT & REVERSE CLUTCH	SECOND GEAR BRAKE FIRST/REV. BRAKE FIRST ONE-WAY CLUTCH	GEAR/CRESCENT	HYDRAULIC	DROP-IN TYPE	CABLE
MB-1	3-ELEMENT	SIMPSON	E1 CLUTCH E2 CLUTCH	F1 BRAKE F2 BRAKE RL ROLLER CLUTCH	GEAR/CRESCENT	ELECTRONIC	NONE	NONE

FIGURE 14–48 European imports summary comparison chart.

SELF-TEST

Complete the self-test according to your instructor's directions. Read carefully and choose the best answer.

1. Which of the following uses an electronic shift control system?
   a. VW 087
   b. MB-1
   c. Both a and b
   d. Neither a nor b
2. Which of the following uses a vane oil pump?
   a. VW 087
   b. MB-1
   c. Both a and b
   d. Neither a nor b
3. Which of the following uses a Simpson gear set?
   a. VW 087
   b. MB-1
   c. Both a and b
   d. Neither a nor b
4. Which of the following uses a drop-in governor?
   a. VW 087
   b. MB-1
   c. Both a and b
   d. Neither a nor b
5. Which of the following does not use a throttle valve?
   a. VW 087
   b. MB-1
   c. Both a and b
   d. Neither a nor b
6. Which of the following has its oil pump mounted in the back of the case?
   a. VW 087
   b. MB-1
   c. Both a and b
   d. Neither a nor b

◀ INDEX ▶